WHO'S WHO OF BRITISH MEMBERS OF PARLIAMENT

Volume
I
1832 – 1885

Who's Who
of British
Members of Parliament

VOLUME
I
1832–1885

A Biographical Dictionary
of the House of Commons

Based on annual volumes of
'Dod's Parliamentary Companion' and other sources

MICHAEL STENTON
Peterhouse, Cambridge

THE HARVESTER PRESS

HUMANITIES PRESS

First published in England in 1976 by
THE HARVESTER PRESS LIMITED
Publisher: John Spiers
2 Stanford Terrace,
Hassocks, Sussex, England
and in the USA by
Humanities Press Inc.,
Atlantic Highlands, NJ 07716

Who's Who of British Members of Parliament Volume 1
© 1976 The Harvester Press Limited

Harvester Press
British Library Cataloguing in Publication Data
Who's who of British members of parliament.
   Vol. 1: 1832–1885
   Index.
   ISBN 0–85527–219–8
   1. Stenton, Michael
   328.41'07'30922   JN503
   Great Britain – Parliament – House of Commons –
   Biography

Humanities Press
Library of Congress Cataloging in Publication Data
Stenton, Michael.
   Who's Who of British members of Parliament.

   Includes index.
   1. Great Britain. Parliament. House of Commons
– Biography.   I. Dod's Parliamentary companion.
II. Title.
JN672.S73   328.41'092'2 [B] 76-12565
ISBN 0-391-00613-4

Typeset by Input Typesetting Ltd, London
Printed in Great Britain by
Unwin Brothers Limited, Old Woking, Surrey

Contents

Preface by Michael Stenton

The principle of this book is to transform what is in fact a contemporary document – the annual editions of *Dod's Parliamentary Companion* – into a compilation of the fullest and most useful entries that Dod provides on each MP's parliamentary career. These little political 'biographies' have been rounded off with material that was no part of Dod's concern: the ostensible cause of a man's departure from the House of Commons, the leading features of his subsequent career, if any, and the date of his death. This book flaunts the vices of hindsight. Anyone seeking to trace a young Member of Parliament making some slight contribution to an unimportant debate will find here the *curriculum vitae* of the fully fledged politician, perhaps swathed in offices and titles, with attention drawn solely to his major attainments and characteristics.

An approach to history and the potentialities of men and periods which depends upon preserving a degree of constructive ignorance about what happens next might be somewhat hampered by this book. Every entry points inflexibly towards success or failure; high office or defeat at the polls. The advantages are as plain as the distortion.

Although the politics of one particular debate may be blurred by a hasty and unconsidered use of a historical work whose Whiggish inclination is always towards the successful aspects of completed careers, the pattern of advancement of two generations of MPs stands out more sharply in this light. Precisely because the book is a collection of the most substantial summaries of parliamentary 'lives', it becomes almost a broad view of 50 years of Parliamentary history, and in doing so acts as a corrective, in the hands of those reading *Hansard* or manuscript collections, to a tendency of the study of politics towards the merely incidental or even the merely biographical, as well as helping one to grasp these notorious nettles.

This is, however, not a fresh study of Parliament. Few attempts have been made to revise Dod's entries: they have simply been supplemented. This reformulation of *Dod* should prove a sound basis for any biographical search. The political descriptions were vouched for – in an advertising slip circulated by Dod with the 1879 edition – in the following terms: 'in all possible cases the *exact words of the member himself* has been preferred to any other indication of his political opinions; and much care has been taken in recording each member's *votes or opinions* on all important questions.' But if this is *Dod's* chief value, the other material Dod supplies can also be awkward to recover without a disproportionate expenditure of energy: family, education, constituency, non-parliamentary connections and the Member's London club.

*   *   *

Charles Roger Phipps Dod (1793–1855) was the son of a county Leitrim vicar whose family were of Shropshire origin. He entered the King's Inns, Dublin, in 1816, but soon abandoned his legal studies, became a journalist and gravitated to London. Like several others, he saw in the Great Reform Act a peg on which to hang a new political handbook and launched the *Parliamentary Pocket Companion* in 1833. He was in a strong position in doing this, for Dod was one of the small group of men who lifted *The Times* to its unique position in the history of journalism. During the editorial reigns, first of Thomas Barnes and then, after 1841, of the legendary Delane, Charles Dod served and then succeeded John Tyas as head of the Press Gallery staff at the time when *The Times* was establishing its tradition of comprehensive and reliable Parliamentary reporting. Such a tradition was long thwarted by over-crowding and poor acoustics in the Gallery: problems which Fleet Street overcame only when the place was burnt down in 1834; but the new Gallery contained nineteen press boxes (*The Times* was allotted three of the best, while *Hansard* made do with one) providing facilities for Dod to organise his team of scribes systematically. With his own pen, Dod produced the daily summaries which readers were reasonably expected to prefer to the prestigious and exhaustive but practically unreadable full reports. Charles Dod (or 'Dodd' before 1847) was also an obituary writer whose use of the columns of *The Times* was considered rather too free and pointed by his superiors. [1]

Dod also produced a *Peerage, Baronetage and Knightage* annually from 1841 and a volume of *Electoral Facts* in 1853. His son, Roger Phipps Dod, later a captain in the Shropshire yeomanry, took over most of the work of producing both the *Peerage* and the retitled *Parliamentary Companion* in 1843. This task he continued after his father's death in 1855 until his own, as a result of a shooting accident, ten years later. *Dod's Parliamentary Companion* then assumed the name under which it has flourished ever since.

There are other nineteenth century annual publications which supplement without supplanting *Dod* as a guide to Parliament. *Vacher's Parliamentary Companion* runs, like *Dod,* from 1833 to the present and provides lists of Members, constituencies, election results and office holders, but it lacks the element of political description. Debrett's *Illustrated House of Commons,* begun in 1867, offers a paragraph on each MP and every member of the judicial bench, but sadly its claim to distinction rests upon the heraldic shields it bestows wherever possible: there are no portraits. One of Charles Dod's most distinguished successors as head of *The Times's* parliamentary staff was Charles Ross, who edited *Ross's Parliamentary Record* from 1875: a periodical cast in the form of a dictionary of Parliamentary business –

1. Mowbray Morris to John Walter 1856, Vol. ii, *History of The Times* (1935–52), pp. 593–4.

bills, summaries of debates, major division lists, dates and names of resolutions – which reverted to its original name of the *Parliamentary Record* in 1880.

Dod's 'lives' and his *Parliamentary Companion* are not only invaluable, but the original volumes are hard to find. Editions from the first 20 years of publication are particularly rare: the British Union Catalogue of Periodicals records only one complete set which is no longer complete – if it ever was.

M.S.

Acknowledgements

The compilation of a volume of this nature is never easy and Charles Dod himself would have paid tribute to the manner in which Mavis Thomas and Brenda Fenn, together with Mollie Colewell and Brenda Harris, coped with the small print of the *Parliamentary Companion*. Our thanks go to Professor J. R. Vincent for his invaluable help and advice, to David Holland, formerly Librarian, House of Commons Library, to John Palmer, also of the House of Commons Library, to F. W. S. Craig of Political Reference Publications, to R. L. Arundale and G. Awdry of the National Liberal Club Library, and to the staff of Cambridge University Library. The Editor and all the others who have worked on this volume are much indebted to Mr Alastair Everitt of The Harvester Press without whose organising and beavering this book would not have been possible.

M.S.

Advice to Readers

This is the first volume of four, which taken together will supply biographies of every Member of Parliament to have sat in the House of Commons between 1832–1975. Volume I comprises more than 3050 lives for the years 1832–1885 inclusive. Volume II covers the years 1886–1918, Volumes III and IV will cover the period from 1919–1975.

The foundation of the whole set of reference works is the long run of *Dod's Parliamentary Companion*, published annually (sometimes twice a year) since 1832 and still continuing. The fullest and best entry for each MP has been taken from this source, and supplemented where possible with important additional information. Yet the personal and idiosyncratic style of Charles Dod's original entries has been maintained, with minor adjustment where events he mentions in the present tense have been rendered into the past. The biographies have then been organised into these new volumes, for ease of reference.

The following notes on the location of each biography in particular volumes, party labels, supplementary data which has been specially researched, changes of names and further guidance on supplementary sources will assist the user:

WHICH VOLUME IS AN MP IN?

The biography of an MP is printed in the volume whose dates cover the *end of his career in Parliament*, rather than his year of initial entry. This rule is followed rigidly, with a handful of exceptions for the giants and those who sat before 1885 but retired in 1886. Thus, the biography of W. E. Gladstone is printed both in Volume I (for 1832–85) and Volume II (for 1886–1918) since one could hardly omit from a handbook on mid-Victorian politicians such a major figure although he died in 1898, having left the House in 1895. The few exceptions to the date rule should not cause the reader difficulty, and the system of two-entries for this handful of major figures may be some extra help. The great majority of those who sat both before and after 1886 have been included in Volume II, and left out of Volume I.

WHICH VOLUME OF 'DOD' IS THE PRINCIPAL SOURCE FOR EACH LIFE?

In the majority of cases the very last entry has been used but there are a few exceptions when an earlier volume provides substantially more biographical material. For example, the 1836 entry for George Benvenuto Mathew is three times as large as the one which appeared in the 1841 volume, therefore this has been selected. After certain general elections Dod ran a second edition. Unless otherwise specified the first edition of Dod is the one which has been used. The year of Dod which has been used as the source has been clearly indicated in square brackets at the end of each entry.

PARTY LABELS

Those given by Charles Dod are used.

SUPPLEMENTARY DATA ADDED

Each entry essentially follows that of Dod but a number of consistent changes have been made to ensure that all the information appears in the same order. The publishing history of the *Parliamentary Companion* has been described above and it is not surprising that there were a variety of conventions and styles throughout its first 53 years. This becomes clear when the material is brought together in alphabetical sequence. Occasionally there are discrepancies in the spelling of place names, family names and the names of country houses, and in every case the variation has been retained unless we have been sure that the variation is an error rather than a difference in spelling which has developed over the years. Likewise, the address of a country house may change with alternative neighbouring towns or villages becoming the address. This is not an untypical feature of the English countryside – even today – and an extreme example is found in the entry of BLAKEMORE, Thomas William Booker-. Here his address is given as The Leys, Herefordshire, whereas the address of his mother's father is given as The Leys, Monmouthshire – the neighbouring county. Other variations used by Dod have also been retained; Brecknockshire and Breconshire are used interchangeably, as also are Salop and Shropshire.

The consistent order that we have followed is: name, address, clubs, birth, details of parentage, marriage, education, career prior to entering Parliament, political principles or affiliations, views on controversial or important questions, full Parliamentary career including every occasion when a person unsuccessfully contested a seat, reason for finally leaving Parliament, subsequent career when known, and the date of death when this can be traced. It was found that Dod was less concerned in giving full information about the occasions when MPs were unsuccessful candidates and a considerable amount of checking and adding of details has been necessary. Neither could Dod include any information about contested seats after an MP had finally left Parliament. This information has been researched and added to the relevant entries.

There were a number of successful candidates who entered and left Parliament between editions and no entries are to be found in Dod. In those cases we have provided all the information about the Parliamentary career, together with full details about any other seats contested either before or after they sat. We have added further information when this has been available. There are also a few entries of people who, while having been elected to Parliament, may not have actually sat in the house as they were unseated shortly after the election. As these are listed in such standard works as Dod's *Electoral Facts* and McCalmont's *Parliamentary Poll Book* entries for these have been composed from all available material and inserted.

CHANGES OF NAMES
Many individuals changed their family names during this period and there are sometimes discrepancies between the names recorded in standard works such as Dod's *Electoral Facts* and McCalmont's *Parliamentary Poll Book,* and those which appeared in *Dod's Parliamentary Companion.* As a general rule we have followed the *Parliamentary Companion* and where necessary cross references are given in the text and in the name index. The name index also clearly indicates with an asterisk those members who continued to sit after 1885 and who will appear in Volume II.

OTHER CONVENTIONS FOLLOWED
'Returned in 1852' etc., means elected at the general election in that year.
'Retired in 1859' etc., means that the sitting MP failed to contest his seat. There is no implication that the man took a sober decision to end his political career. Where the word is not used it is because there is something standing in the text constituting the formal cause of the MPs departure from the House of Commons: electoral defeat, a peerage, a government appointment, etc. To 'contest' a seat, or to be 'a candidate', is, by gentlemanly omission, not to be elected.

DOD AND THE PRE-1832 HOUSE
Dod treats the pre-1832 House of Commons with mild disfavour and rarely records the full details of any MP's career before that date. The reader will recognise the characteristically disdainful '*formerly* represented', etc.

SUPPLEMENTARY SOURCES
After the convenience of *Dod,* the way is hard. In this book attempts have been made, usually with success, to trace those MPs who left the House of Commons, inherited a title from some very distant relative and died in obscurity, or emigrated and changed their names. Peerages and Baronetages are very useful in tracing such people, and some even thornier problems have been solved by using L. G. Pine's *New Extinct Peerage, 1884–1971* (London, 1972). The *Dictionary of National Biography* is excellent for the prominent but is otherwise not a very rewarding place to hunt. The contemporary *Men of the Times* (London, 1852–1887) covers a larger number of MPs in varying detail. Best of all is the invaluable *Modern English Biography* by F. Boase (Reprinted, London, 1965) which is very often a valuable supplement to *Dod* and covers a good many Welsh, Scottish and Irish MPs despite its English bias. Boase confines his attention to persons dying after 1850. Before 1850 the researcher's task is much harder; *Who's Who* began in 1849, and obituaries in *The Times* and in the *Gentleman's Magazine* are probably the main source of biographical detail. Further electoral details are available in *McCalmont's Parliamentary Poll Book, British Election Results 1832–1918* 8th revised edition, J. Vincent and M. Stenton, eds., (Harvester Press, 1971) and H. J. Hanham's edition of Dod's *Electoral Facts 1832–1853* (Harvester Press, 1971) which has much constituency material. Unfortunately, McCalmont anachronistically denotes both Whigs and Radicals as 'Liberals'. The

original distinction survives, as a check on the label offered in this volume, in H. Stooks Smith, *The Parliaments of England* (Reprinted, Chichester, 1973) which covers elections up to 1848.

ABBREVIATIONS
The following abbreviations are used in this book:

B. means born; *Bart.* Baronet; *Bp.* Bishop; *bro.* brother; *Capt.* Captain; *Co.* county; *Col.* Colonel; *Coll.* College; *d.* daughter; *Dept.* Deputy; *educ.* educated; *E.I.C.* East India Company; *eld.* eldest; *Gen.* General; *Gov.* Governor; *Hon.* Honourable; *jun.* junior; *Lieut.* Lieutenant; *Maj.* Major; *m.* married; *Nr.* near; *PC.* Privy Councillor; *Pres.* President; *Rt.* Right; *Sec.* Secretary; *sen.* senior; *s.* son; *Visct.* Viscount.

Who's Who of British
Members of Parliament, 1832–1885

ABDY, Sir Thomas Neville, Bart. 19 Chapel Street, Grosvenor Square, London. Albyns, Essex. Reform. Only s. of Capt. Anthony Abdy, R.N., by the d. of Admiral Sir Thomas Rich. His grandfather assumed the name of Abdy in lieu of his patronymic, Rutherforth, on inheriting the estates of Sir John Abdy, of Albyns, whose baronetcy became extinct. B.1810; m.1841; Hariett, 2nd d. of Rowland Alston, Esq., of Pishiobury, Hertfordshire. Educ. at St. John's Coll., Cambridge, where he graduated B.A. 1833. A Liberal opposed to the endowment of the Roman Catholic Clergy. Was an unsuccessful candidate for Maldon in 1841. First returned for Lyme Regis 1847. Sat until he retired in 1852. Unsuccessfully contested Essex E. 28 Nov.1868. Sheriff of Essex 1875. Died 1877. [1852]

ABERCROMBY, Hon. George Ralph. Airthrey Castle, Stirlingshire. United Service. Eld. s. of Lord Abercromby, and nephew to Lord Dunfermline, and to Visct. Melville. B.1800; m. in 1832, d. of Lord Medwyn, one of the Scottish Judges. A Lieut.-Col. in the army. Lord Lieut. of Clackmannanshire. A Reformer. Unsuccessfully contested Stirlingshire 5 Aug. 1837, but the election was declared void and he was returned at the following election on 30 Apr. 1838. Returned for Clackmannan and Kinross July 1841. Accepted Chiltern Hundreds in 1842. Succeeded as 3rd Baron Abercromby 14 Feb. 1843. Died 25 June 1852. [1842]

ABERCROMBY, Rt. Hon. James. 7 Carlton Gardens, London. Stubbing Court, Derbyshire. 3rd s. of Sir Ralph Abercromby, who fell in Egypt, and bro. of Lord Abercromby; b.1776; m.1802, Mary Anne, d. of Egerton Leigh, Esq., of High Leigh, Co. of Chester. Lord Chief of the Court of Exchequer in Scotland before its suppression; which he recommended, the Court being useless. Was appointed Master of the Mint and a member of the Cabinet, on the formation of Visct. Melbourne's Administration in 1834; but went out of office on its dissolution, in the same year. Was chosen Speaker 19 Feb. 1835, by a majority of 316 over 306, who voted for Sir Charles Manners Sutton, the Conservative Ministerial Candidate. Wished to give the Reform Act a fair trial; friendly to a shorter duration of Parliament; and said he would support election by ballot, if it should be found that the elective franchise could not otherwise be fairly exercised. Sat for Calne in four Parliaments; had a pension of £2,000 per annum for the loss of his judicial office; was previously Land-Steward to the Duke of Devonshire. Sat for Edinburgh from 1832. Sat until created Lord Dunfirmaline 1839; subsequently connected with the United Industrial School for ragged children in Edinburgh. Died 1858. [1838]

ACHESON, Visct. 59 Lower Grosvenor Street, London. Gosford Castle, Co. Armagh. Reform. Eld. s. of the Earl of Gosford. B.1806; m. 1832, d. of 10th Earl of Meath. Col. of the Armagh Militia. A moderate Reformer, against the tithe system, but also against a repeal of the Union. Sat for Armagh County from 1830 until he retired 1847. Created Baron Acheson of Clancairney 18 Sept. 1847. Succeeded as 3rd Earl of Gosford 27 Mar. 1849. Died 1864. [1847]

ACKERS, B. St. J. A conservative. Candidate for Gloucester in the gen. election of 1880. Returned for Gloucestershire W. 10 Mar. 1885. Defeated 4 Dec. 1885. High Sheriff of Co. of Gloucester 1904. Died 1915.

ACKERS, James. 2 Blandford Square, London. Heath House, Shropshire. Oxford & Cambridge, and University. B. 1811; m. 1833, d. of B. Williams, Esq. Was a first class man in Civil Law at Cambridge. A Magistrate of Herefordshire. A Conservative, voted for agricultural protection 1846. First returned for Ludlow in 1841. Sat until he retired 1847. Purchased estate of Prinknash, Gloucestershire in 1847. Died 1868.   [1847]

ACLAND, Sir C.T. Dyke. Continued in House after 1885: full entry in Volume II.

ACLAND, Rt. Hon. Sir Thomas Dyke, Bart., D.C.L. sen. 85 Jermyn Street, London. Killerton, Devon. Minehead, Somerset. Athenaeum, Travellers', and University. S. of Sir T.D. Acland, by the d. of Sir Richard Hoare, Bart. B. in London 1787; m. 1808, Lydia, d. of Henry Hoare, Esq., of Mitcham Grove, Surrey (she died 1856). Educ. at Christ Church, Oxford, where he graduated M.A. 1814, D.C.L. 1831. Patron of 7 livings. 'Generally and decidedly a Conservative', favourable to the endowment of the Roman Catholic Clergy. Sat for the county of Devon from 1812-1818 and from 1820-1831. Sat for Devon N. from 1837 until he retired 1857. Died 22 July 1871.   [1857]

ACLAND, Sir Thomas Dyke, Bart., jun. Killerton, Exeter. Holnicote, Minehead, Somerset. Athenaeum. B. at Killerton, Devon 1809, the eld. s. of Sir Thomas Dyke Acland, Bart., M.P. for Devon for many years, by Lydia Elizabeth, d. of Henry Hoare, Esq., of Mitcham, Surrey. M. 1st 1841, Mary, eld. d. of Sir Charles Mordaunt, Bart. (she died 1851); 2ndly 1856, Mary, d. of John Erskine. Educ. at Harrow and at Christ Church, Oxford, and became a fellow of All Souls. Was 1st class in classics and mathematics 1831, graduated M.A. 1835. A D.C.L. at Oxford and a Privy Councillor, and one of the Delegates for the Oxford Local Examinations. A Major Royal 1st Devon Yeomanry Cavalry, and Hon. Col. 3rd Battalion Devon Rifle Volunteers. Was 2nd Church Estates Commissioner Jan. 1869-Feb. 1874. A Liberal and hearty supporter of Gladstone. Sat for W. Somerset July 1837-July 1847. Unsuccessfully contested Birmingham Apr. 1859. Sat for N. Devon 1865-85, and briefly for Wellington div., Somerset 1885-86. Sat until he retired 1886. Died 1898.   [1886]

A'COURT, Charles Henry Wyndham. 34 St.

James's Place, London. Amington Hall, Tamworth, Staffordshire. Travellers'. B. at Heytesbury, Wiltshire, the s. of Lieut.-Gen. Charles A'Court (who was bro. to the first Lord Heytesbury), by Mary Elizabeth Catherine, only d. of Abraham Gibbs, Esq. Bro.-in-law to the Rt. Hon. Sidney Herbert. M. 1854, Emily, eld. d. of Henry Currie, Esq., of West Horsley Place, Surrey. Educ. at Eton and at St. John's Coll., Cambridge, where he graduated B.A. 1841. Was Private Sec. to Lord Eliot (Chief Sec. in Ireland) from 1841-4, Private Sec. to Lord Heytesbury (Lord Lieut. of Ireland) from 1844-46. A 'Liberal Conservative', who favoured a continuance of the Maynooth Grant. Voted against the ballot 1853. Sat for Wilton from July 1852 until he was appointed Income Tax Inspector in Ireland 1855. Subsequently became Assistant Controller at the National Debt office. Died 1903.   [1855]

A'COURT, Capt. Edward Henry. 41 St. James's Place, London. Carlton. Next bro. of Lord Heytesbury. A Capt. in the Navy. A Conservative, but in favour of free trade. Sat for Heytesbury from 1820-1832. Sat for Tamworth from 1837 until he retired 1847.   [1847]

ACTON, Sir John Emerich Edwart Dalberg-, Bart. Aldenham, Bridgnorth, Shropshire. Athenaeum, and Brooks's. S. of Sir Ferdinand Richard Edward Acton, by Marie Louise, only d. of the Duke of Dalberg. B. at Naples, 1834. Appointed a Dept.-Lieut. of Shropshire 1855. Patron of 1 living. A Liberal, in favour of the ballot, and of education being based on religion; considered that 'every day of Tory rule is a calamity for the Irish nation, and for the Catholic religion.' First elected for Carlow, May 1859. Returned for Bridgnorth in 1865 but unseated on petition. Defeated in same constituency in 1868. Professor of Modern History, Cambridge 1895; created Baron Acton 1897. Died 1902.   [1864]

ACTON, Joseph. Wigan. B. at Wigan 1803. Unmarried. A Solicitor, but retired from practice 1838. Appointed a Magistrate for Lancashire Feb. 1840, elected Mayor of Wigan Nov. 1839 and again Nov. 1853. A Liberal, in favour of Parliamentary Reform, and vote by ballot, opposed to 'the infliction of civil disabilities on the ground of religious opinions, and therefore disposed to favour the admission of Jews to Parliament,' in favour of a wide extension of general education, Church reform etc. First elected for Wigan Oct. 1854, and sat until he retired 1857. Died 8 Dec. 1862.   [1857]

ACTON, Col. William. 36 Jermyn Street, London. West Aston, Co. Wicklow. Carlton. Eld.

s. of Thomas Acton, Esq., of West Aston, by the d. of Joshua Davies, Esq. B. 1789, m. in 1817, d. of Thomas Walker, Esq., a Master in Chancery; was Sheriff of Wicklow in 1820. Lieut.-Col. of the Wicklow Militia. A Conservative, voted for agricalutural protection, 1846; first returned for Wicklow in 1841, having been an unsuccessful candidate at the general elections in 1832 and 1837. Sat until he accepted Chiltern Hundreds 27 Apr. 1848. Died 10 Apr. 1854.   [1847 2nd ed.]

ADAIR, Sir Hugh Edward. 2 Upper Hyde Park Street, London. Flixton Hall, Bungay, Norfolk. Aldborough, Saxmundham, Suffolk. Ballymena, Co. Antrim. United University and Travellers'. B. 1815, the 2nd s. of Sir Robert Shafto Adair, Bart., of Flixton Hall, by the d. of the Rev. James Strode, of Berkhampstead, Hertfordshire. M. 1856, Harriet Camilla, eld. d. of Alexander Adair, Esq., of Heatherton Park, Somerset. Was a Gentleman-Commoner of St. John's Coll., Oxford where he graduated M.A. 1843. A Liberal, and voted for the disestablishment of the Irish Church 1869. Favoured the total abolition of Church rates. Sat for Ipswich from 1847 until his defeat in 1874. Died 1902.   [1873]

ADAIR, Sir Robert Alexander Shafto. Flixton Hall, Harleston, Norfolk. Aldborough, Suffolk. 7 Audley Square, London. Reform. Eld. s. of Sir Robert Shafto, Bart. of Flixton Hall, by Elizabeth Maria, d. of the Rev. James Strode, of Berkhampstead, Hertfordshire. B.1811; m. 1836, Theodosia, d. of Gen. the Hon. Robert Meade and grand-d. of the 1st Earl of Clanwilliam. Appointed Lieu.-Col. East Suffolk Artillery 1853. A Liberal, desired to promote concessions for effecting educational objects. Contested Suffolk E. unsuccessfully in 1841 and 1843. Sat for Cambridge from July 1847 till July 1852, when he was an unsuccessful candidate; re-elected Aug. 1854. Defeated Mar. 1857. Contested Canterbury July 1865 and Antrim Aug. 1869. Died 1869. [1856]

ADAM, Sir Charles, K.C.B. 14 Berkeley Square, London. Barnes, Clackmannanshire. Reform. Eld. s. and heir apparent of the Rt. Hon. William Adam, Lord Chief Commissioner of the Jury Court of Scotland, by the Hon. Eleanora Elphinstone, sister of Visct. Keith; m. sister of the Countess of Minto, d. of Patrick Byrsone, Esq. and grand-d. of Principal William Robertson, His Majesty's Historiographer. Vice-Admiral of the Blue. A Lord of the Admiralty, from April 1835 (salary £1,000). First sat for Clackmannan and Kinross counties in 1831. Sat until he retired in 1841. First Sea Lord 1846-47. Died 16 Sept. 1853.   [1838]

ADAM, Rt. Hon. Sir William Patrick. 65 Eaton Square, London. Blair Adam House, Blair Adam, Kinross-shire.   Brooks's,   Athenaeum,   and Reform. S. of Admiral Sir Charles Adam, K.C.B., Governor of Greenwich Hospital, by Elizabeth, d. of Patrick Brydone, Esq. B. 1823; m. 1856, Emily, d. of Gen. Sir William Wyllie, G.C.B. Educ. at Rubgy, and at Trinity Coll., Cambridge. Called to the bar at the Inner Temple, May 1849. Was private sec. to Lord Elphinstone (Governor of Bombay) from Dec. 1853-Sept. 1858, a Lord of Treasury from Apr. 1865-July 1866; and from Dec. 1868-Aug. 1873. Was Chief Commissioner of Works and Buildings and Paymaster Gen. from the last date to Feb. 1874; re-appointed to the last-named office Apr. 1880 (salary £2,000). A Dept.-Lieut. for the Cos. of Kinross and Fife. Author of *Thought on the Policy of Retaliation, and its probable effect on the consumer producer, and shipowner.* A Liberal. Unsuccessfully contested Clackmannanshire May 1851; first elected May 1859 and sat until 1880 when he was appointed Governor of Madras. Died 24 May 1881.   [1880 2nd ed.]

ADAMS, Edward Hamlyn. Middleton Hall. Entertained Whig principles, in favour of the ballot and the immediate abolition of slavery. Sat for Carmarthenshire from 1832 until he retired in 1835.   [1833]

ADAMS, William Henry. 3 Plowden Buildings, Temple, London. Boston, Lincolnshire. National. S. of Thomas Adams, Esq., of Normancross, Huntingdonshire, by Anna Maria, d. of William Farr, Esq., of Romsey, Hampshire. B. at Normancross 1809; m. 1832, Ann, d. of Thomas Watford, Esq. Called to the bar at the Middle Temple 1843, and joined the Northern Circuit. A Magistrate for Boston, of which town he was twice Mayor, and for several years Chairman of the Board of Guardians of the Boston Union. A 'Liberal-Conservative'; opposed to the war with China; favourable to the 're-adjustment' of the Income-tax, so as to relieve trades and professions, the reduction of the duty on tea, the wide extension of education, and a 'thorough revision' of the national expenditure. Unsuccessfully contested Boston, July 1852; first elected Apr. 1857, without opposition. Sat until appointed Attorney-General for Colony of Hong Kong, Apr. 1859; Chief Justice for the Colony, 5 July 1860. Died 29 Aug. 1865.   [1858]

ADARE, Visct. See DUNRAVEN, Earl of.

ADDERLEY, Rt. Hon. Sir Charles Bowyer, K.C.M.G. 35 Eaton Place, London. Hams Hall, Minworth,   Birmingham.   Norton,   Stoke-on-Trent. Carlton. Eld. s. of Charles Cle-

3

ment Adderley, Esq., by d. of Sir E.E. Hantopp, Bart. Was descended from an old Staffordshire family, having estates also in Warwickshire. B. 1814; m. 1842 Hon. Julia Anne Eliza, d. of 1st Lord Leigh. Educ. at Christ Church, Oxford, where he graduated B.A. 1838. Was Pres. of the Board of Health, and Vice-Pres. of the Board of Educ. from Mar. 1858-June 1859; Under-Sec. for the Colonies from July 1866-Dec. 1868. Appointed Pres. of the Board of Trade Feb. 1874 (salary £2,000). Patron of 3 livings. A Conservative. First returned for Staffordshire N. 1841. Sat until created Baron Norton Apr. 1878. Died 28 Mar. 1905. [1878]

ADDINGTON, Hon. William Wells. Up-Ottery Manor, Honiton, Devon. Army & Navy. Eld. surviving s. of 2nd Visct. Sidmouth, by Mary, eld. d. of Rev. John Young, of Thorpe, Northamptonshire. B. at Scotsbridge, near Rickmansworth 1824; m. 1848, Georgiana Susan, eld. d. of the Hon and Very Rev. George Pellew, D.D., Dean of Norwich. Entered the navy 1837; became a Lieut. R.N. 1846; retired Feb. 1848, after having served in the Mediterranean, South America, and the East Indies. Appointed a Dept.-Lieut, of Devon 1852. Capt. 3rd Devon Mounted Volunteer Rifles 1860. A Magistrate for Devon. A Conservative and a supporter of Lord Derby, but would offer no factious opposition to Lord Palmerston. Unsuccessfully contested Plymouth Oct. 1861. First elected for Devizes Feb. 1863. Sat until he succeeded to the Peerage (Visct. Sidmouth) 1864. Died 28 Oct. 1913. [1864]

ADEANE, Henry John. 8 Seamore Place, Curzon Street, London. Babraham, Cambridge. Arthur's, and Boodle's. B. at Babraham 1833, the 2nd s. of Henry John Adeane, Esq., M.P. of Babraham, Cambridgeshire, by his 2nd wife, Hon. Matilda Abigail, d. of 1st Lord Stanley of Alderley. M. 1860, Lady Elizabeth Philippa, eld. d. of 4th Earl of Hardwicke. Educ. at Harrow. Entered the army in 1851 but retired. Appointed Capt. Cambridgeshire Militia Jan. 1858. Custos Rot. of the Isle of Ely 1861. A Liberal, and supported any government in securing a powerful navy for England. Favoured the abolition of Church rates and considered that 'popular education should be founded on the Bible.' First returned for Cambridgeshire Apr. 1857 and sat until his retirement in 1865. Died 17 Feb. 1870. [1865]

AGG-GARDNER, J.T. Continued in House after 1885: full entry in Volume II.

AGLIONBY, Major Francis. The Nunnery, Ainstable, Cumberland. Cousin to Member for Cockermouth. A radical Reformer. Contested Cumberland W. unsuccessfully at the election of 1835, but was returned for Cumberland E. at the general election 10 Aug. 1837. MP from 1837 until his death in 1840. [1840]

AGLIONBY, Henry Aglionby. 5 Brick Court, Temple, London. Manor House, Caterham, Nr. Croydon. Nunnery, Penrith, Cumberland. Reform. B. 1790, the s. of the Rev. Samuel Bateman of Newbiggen Hall, Rector of Farthingstone. Assumed the name of Aglionby, in compliance with the testamentary injunction of one of his Aunts. Graduated at St. John's Coll., Cambridge, B.A. 1813, M.A. 1816. Called to the bar at Lincoln's Inn 1816, and joined the Northern circuit. A Liberal; in favour of the ballot, triennial Parliaments and free trade. Opposed to unrestricted paper currency, to the Bishops being in the House of Lords and having large revenues, to the taxes on malt, soap, insurances and the assessed taxes. Sat for Cockermouth from 1832 until his death on 31 July 1854. [1854]

AGNEW, Sir Andrew, Bart., sen. 7 Manchester Buildings, London. Lochnaw Castle, Wigtonshire. S. of the previous Bart. by Hon. Martha De Courcy, d. of John, 26th Lord Kingsale. B. 1793; m. 1816, Madalene, d. of Sir David Carnegie, Bart., of Southesk. Vice-Lieut. of Wigtonshire. Of Whig principles, inclining to Conservatism. Supported the Reform Act; was the mover of the Sabbath Observance Committee of 1832. Was first elected for Wigtonshire in 1830. Sat until he retired 1837. Died 12 Apr. 1849. [1837]

AGNEW, Sir Andrew, Bart., jun. 17 Prince's Gate, London. Lochnaw Castle, Stranraer, Wigtonshire. Brooks's, and Army & Navy. Eld. s. of Sir Andrew Agnew (7th Bart., MP), by Madeline, d. of Sir David Carnegie, Bart., MP, of Southesk. B. in Edinburgh 1818; m. 1846, Lady Louisa, d. of the 1st Earl of Gainsborough. Educ. at Harrow. Entered the army in 1835, and served with the 93rd Highlanders during the rebellion in Canada in 1838; afterwards became a Capt. 4th Light Dragoons. Appointed Dept.-Lieut. of Wigton, 1843, and Vice-Lieut. 1852. A Liberal, in favour of the extension of the suffrage, of the exemption of Dissenters from church-rates, and of a comprehensive measure of education; opposed to the ballot and to the Maynooth grant. Unsuccessfully contested Wigton district 29 July 1837. First elected for Wigtonshire, Feb. 1856. Sat until defeated in 1868. Died 25 Mar. 1892. [1867]

AGNEW, R. Vans-. See VANS-AGNEW, Robert.

AGNEW, William. 11 Great Stanhope Street, Mayfair. Summer Hill, Pendleton, Manchester. Reform, and Devonshire. Eld. s. of Thomas Agnew, Esq., of Manchester, who was Mayor of Salford in 1851, by Jane, 2nd d. of William Lockett, Esq., of Salford and of Lytham. B. at Manchester 1825; m. Mary, eldest d. of George Pixton Kenworthy, Esq., of Manchester and of Peel Hall, Astley, Manchester. A well-known Publisher, head of the firm of Messrs. Thomas Agnew and Sons, London, Liverpool and Manchester, also partner in the firm of Messrs. Bradbury, Agnew, and Co., Whitefriars, London. A Magistrate for Lancashire, also for Manchester and for Salford. A Liberal, in favour of the equalisation of the whole franchise of the country, the reform of the Land Laws, the abolition of the system of primogeniture, reform of the licensing system, etc. Sat for South-East Lancashire from April 1880. Defeated in 1886 contesting the Stretford division of Manchester; contested Prestwich in 1892. Created baronet 1885. Died 31 Oct. 1910.   [1885]

AINSWORTH, David. Continued in House after 1885: full entry in Volume II.

AINSWORTH, Peter. Smithills Hall, Lancashire. Union. Eld. s. of Richard Ainsworth, Esq., by the d. of James Noble, Esq., of Lancaster. B. 1790; m. 1815, Elizabeth, d. of Ashton Byrom, Esq., Fair View, Liverpool. Dept.-Lieut. for Lancashire. A Reformer, in favour of the ballot, and shortening the duration of Parliaments. At his first election for Bolton in 1835, succeeded against Col. Torrens, who was also a Reformer, but without the local connections of the Hon. Member. Sat until he retired 1847. Contested same seat in 1852. Died 18 Jan. 1870.   [1847]

AKERS-DOUGLAS, A. Continued in House after 1885: full entry in Volume II.

AKROYD, Col. Edward. 40 Lowndes Street, London. Bank Field, Halifax. Brooks's, and Reform. Eld. s. of Jonathan Akroyd, Esq., of Woodside, Halifax, Worsted Manufacturer, by Sarah, d. of David Wright, Esq., of Bradshaw. B. at Ovenden, Nr. Halifax 1810; m. 1838, Elizabeth, d. of the late John Fearby, Esq., of Poppleton Lodge, Nr. York. A Worsted Manufacturer under the old firm of James Akroyd and Son. A Magistrate and Dept.-Lieut. for the West Riding of Yorkshire. Chairman of the Halifax Chamber of Commerce. Lieut.-Col. Commandant 4th West York Volunteers. Patron of 1 living. A Liberal. Sat for Huddersfield from Apr. 1857-Apr. 1859, and for Halifax from July 1865

until he retired 1874. Died 19 Nov. 1887. [1873]

ALCOCK, Thomas. 28 Chesham Place, Belgrave Square, London. Kingswood-Warren, Epsom, Surrey, Brooks's, and Union. B. 1801, the s. of Joseph Alcock, Esq., of Roehampton, Surrey. M. 1831. d. of Rear-Admiral Henry Stuart. Educ. at Harrow. A Magistrate for Surrey. Patron of 2 livings. A Liberal, and favoured all national grants being given impartially to all denominations. In favour also of a large extension of the franchise. Voted against the Maynooth Grant 1851, in favour of the ballot 1853 and for the abolition of Church rates 1855. Sat for Newton, Lancashire 1826-30. Contested Ludlow unsuccessfully in 1837, but returned for that borough in 1839 (unseated on petition). Contested Surrey E. unsuccessfully in Feb. 1841, and returned for that Co. July 1847. Sat until 1865, when he retired. Died 22 Aug. 1866. [1865]

ALDAM, William. Warmsworth, Yorkshire. Reform. B. 1813. A Barrister. A Liberal, first returned for Leeds in 1841; was the 4th wrangler at Cambridge 1836. Retired 1847. Chairman of Quarter Sessions, West Riding of Yorkshire 1877 until his death 27 July 1890. [1847]

ALDRIDGE, Maj. J. First elected for Horsham 18 Nov. 1868, when he polled the same number of votes as his opponent but in May 1869 he declined to defend his seat and R.H. Hurst, Esq., was returned unopposed. Contested Horsham again 17 Dec. 1875.

ALEXANDER, Gen. Claud. 11 Great Queen Street, London. Ballochmyle, Mauchline, Ayrshire. Guards, United Service, and Army & Navy. Eld. s. of Boyd Alexander, Esq., of Ballochmyle, by Sophia Elizabeth, 3rd d. of Sir Benjamin Hobhouse, Bart., and sister of Lord Broughton, G.C.B. B. in London 1831; m. 1863, Eliza, only d. of Alexander Speirs, Esq., MP. Was educ. at Eton and at Christ Church, Oxford. Entered the Grenadier Guards as Ensign and Lieut. May, 1849; became Capt. and Lieut.-Col. Aug. 1860, Col. July 1875, and Hon. Major-Gen. 1883; served in the Crimean War, and received the 5th class of the Medjidie, the Crimean medal with a clasp for Sebastopol, also the Turkish medal. A Magistrate and Dept.-Lieut. for the counties of Ayr and Renfrew. A Conservative, not opposed to the assimilation of the county to the borough franchise. Unsuccessfully contested in Nov. 1868 South Ayrshire for which he sat from Feb. 1874. Sat until defeated in 1885. Created baronet 22 Jan. 1886. Died 23 May 1888. [1885]

ALEXANDER, John. 26 Inverness Terrace,

Kensington, London. Milford House, near Carlow. Carlton, Kildare Street Club, Dublin. Eld. s. of John Alexander, Esq., by Christian, d. of Lorenzo Nickson, Esq., of Chapel Izod House, Co. Kilkenny. This family is the same with the well-known claimants of the Earldom of Stirling. B. at Milford, Co. Carlow, 1802; m. 1848, eld. d. of Matthew Brinkley, Esq., of Parsonstown, Co. Meath, and grandd. of Bishop (Brinkley) of Cloyne. Educ. at Trinity Coll., Dublin, where he graduated M.A. Was High Sheriff of Carlow. A Conservative, in favour of the extinction of the income tax in 1860, and general retrenchment. First returned for Carlow bor. Jan. 1853, and sat until defeated in 1859. Died Oct. 1885.   [1858]

ALEXANDER, Nathaniel. 4 Charles Street, Berkeley Square, London. The Hall, Portglenone, Co. Antrim. Carlton. S. of Rev. Robert Alexander, and grands. of Bp. (Alexander) of Meath; b. 1815; m. 1842, Florinda, 2nd d. of R. Bagley, Esq., and niece of Lord Castlemaine. A Conservative, voted for agricultural protection, 1846. First elected for Antrim in 1841, on the accession of Gen. O'Neill to a Peerage. MP until his death 5th Jan. 1853.   [1852]

ALEXANDER, Visct. 5 Carlton Terrace, London. Caledon, Co. Tyrone. Carlton, Guards', Travellers', and White's. Only s. of the Earl of Caledon. B. 27 July 1812. A Lieut. in the 1st batt. of the Coldstream Guards. A Conservative. Was elected for Tyrone Co. without opposition in the room of Lord Claud Hamilton, who declined to come forward after the dissolution of Parliament in 1837. Succeeded Father as 3rd Earl of Caledon in 1837. Irish representative Peer 1841, until his death 30 Jan. 1855.   [1838]

ALFORD, Visct. 23 Belgrave Square, London. Belton House, Lincolnshire. Carlton. Eld. s. of Earl Brownlow. B. 1812; m. 1841, d. of 2nd Marq. of Northampton. Lieut.-Col. of the S. Lincoln Militia. The Earl of Bridgewater bequeathed a large fortune to his grand-nephew, Lord Alford, on condition that he obtained a Marquisate or Dukedom of Bridgewater. In the event of the Crown's not conferring the honour, the Egertons, of Tatton, inherited the estates. A Conservative, voted for agricultural protection 1846. Sat for Befordshire from 1835, retired 1847. Died 3 Jan. 1851.   [1847]

ALLCROFT, John Derby. 108 Lancaster Gate, London. Harlington, Middlesex. Stokesay Castle, Ludlow, Shropshire. S. of J. M. Allcroft, Esq., by Hannah, d. of Thomas Derby, Esq. B. at Worcester 1822; m. 1864, Mary Jewell, d. of John Blundell, Esq., of Timsbury Manor, Hampshire.

Was head of the firm of Messrs. Dent, Allcroft and Company, London. Appointed Treasurer of Christ's Hospital, London 1873. Patron of 5 livings. A Conservative. Unsuccessfully contested Worcester Feb. 1874; first elected for that city Mar. 1878. Sat until he retired 1880. Died 29 July 1893.   [1880]

ALLEN, Henry George., Q.C. 66 St. James's Street, London. Paskeston, Pembrokeshire. Arthur's, and Oxford & Cambridge. 2nd s. of John Hensleigh Allen, Esq., of Cresselly, Pembrokeshire (who sat for Pembroke district 1818-26), by Gertrude, 3rd d. of Lord Robert Seymour, MP for Carmarthenshire. B. in Portland Place, London 1815. Educ. at Rugby and at Christ Church, Oxford. Was called to the bar at Lincoln's Inn May 1841 and joined the South Wales Circuit. Was Recorder of Andover 1857-1872, when he resigned. For 16 years Chairman of Pembrokeshire Quarter Sessions. A Liberal. Sat for Pembroke district from Apr. 1880 to 1886, when he retired. Died 20 Nov. 1908.   [1886]

ALLEN, Maj. Ralph Shuttleworth. 9 Suffolk Street, London. Hempton Manor, Nr. Bath. Carlton, and United Service. S. of Henry Edmund Allen, Esq., and Fanny, his wife. B. at Toms in France 1817; m. 1st Anne Elizabeth, d. of Sir S. Cunard, Bart; 2ndly Ethel, only d. of J. B. Allen, Esq., of Lingford, Nr. Taunton. Educ. at Woolwich Military Academy. Appointed Maj. Royal Artillery, Oct. 1858. A Magistrate and Dept.-Lieut. for Somerset. A Conservative; voted against the disestablishment of the Irish Church. Sat for E. Somersetshire from Dec. 1868 until he accepted Chiltern Hundreds March 1879. Died 6 Feb. 1887.   [1879]

ALLEN, William Shepherd. 22 Montagu Place, Bedford Square, London. Woodhead Hall, Cheadle, Staffordshire. Reform, and United University. B. in Manchester 1831, s. of William Allen, Esq., a Magistrate for Staffordshire, by Maria, d. of William Shepherd, Esq. M. 1869, Elizabeth Penelope, only d. of John Candlish, Esq. MP. Educ. at Wadham Coll., Oxford, where he graduated B.A. 1854, M.A.1857, taking a 2nd class in law and history. A Magistrate and D.L. for Staffordshire. A Liberal. Sat for Newcastle-under-Lyme from 1865 to 1886, when he retired. Contested Stoke-on-Trent 1890. Died 15 Jan. 1915.   [1886]

ALLIX, John Peter. Swaffham House, Cambridgeshire. S. of J.P. Allix, Esq. B. 1785; m. 1816, d. of John Pardoe, Esq., of Leyton, Essex; was Sheriff of Cambridgeshire in 1828. A

Magistrate of Cambridgeshire. A Conservative, voted for agricultural protection 1846. First returned for Cambridgeshire in 1841. Sat until he retired 1847. [1847]

ALLMAN, Richard Lane. Woodlands, Bandon, Ireland. S. of James Clugstone Allman, Esq., of Bandon, by Sarah, d. of Richard Lane, Esq., of Cork. B. at Cork 1813; M. 1861, Frances Vernon, d. of James Splaine, Esq., of Garrane, Co. Cork. Educ. at Belfast Coll. A Magistrate for the Co. of Cork. A Liberal, and a supporter of Mr. Gladstone's ministry. Sat for Bandon from June 1880, which he contested unsuccessfully the previous April, until he retired in 1885. [1885]

ALLSOPP, Sir Henry. 83 Eaton Square, London. Hindlip Hall, Worcester. Carlton, and Windham. S. of Samuel Allsopp, Esq., of Burton- -on-Trent, by Frances, d. and heir of Charles Fowler, Esq., of Shrewsbury. B. at Burton- -on-Trent 1811; m. 1839, Elizabeth, 2nd. d. of William Tongue, Esq., of Comberford Hall, Tamworth. A Brewer. A Dept.-Lieut. for Stafford and a Magistrate for the Cos. of Stafford, Derby and Worcester. Patron of 1 living. A Conservative, in favour of the re-adjustment of local taxation. Sat for E. Worcestershire from Feb. 1874. Defeated 1880. Created Baronet May 1880. Created 1st Baron Hindlip Feb. 1886. Died 3rd Apr. 1887. [1880]

ALLSOPP, S.C. Continued in House after 1885: full entry in Volume II.

ALSAGER, Richard. 1 Derby Street, Westminster. Tooting. Carlton. Formerly a Capt. in the East India Company Merchant-service. A Conservative. MP for Surrey E. from 1835 until his death in 1841. [1840]

ALSTON, Rowland. 48 Harley Street, London. Pishiobury, Hertfordshire. Reform. Of Whig principles. Contested Hertfordshire at the general election after the passing of the Reform Bill, but was defeated by his Conservative opponent, Visct. Grimston. Sat for Herefordshire from 1835, until he was defeated in 1841. Died 21 Nov. 1865. [1840]

ALTHORP, Visct. (I). 12 Downing Street, London. Wimbledon Park, Surrey. Eld. s. of Earl Spencer. B. 1782; m. in 1814 Esther, d. of Rd. Acklom, Esq., of Wiseton Hall, Co. of Nottingham, who died childless, in 1818. Chancellor of the Exchequer, a Lord of the Treasury, and leader of the Ministerial party in the House of Commons. Sat for Northamptonshire S. from 1812, previously for Okehampton. Sat until he succeeded as 3rd Earl Spencer 10 Nov. 1834 and therefore obliged to relinquish Exchequer. Died 1 Oct. 1845. [1833]

ALTHORP, Visct. (II). 27 St. James's Place, London. Althorp Park, Northamptonshire. Brooks's. B. at Spencer House 1835, only s. of 4th Earl Spencer, by his 1st wife, Elizabeth Georgiana, 2nd d. of William Stephen Poyntz, Esq., of Cowdray House, Sussex. Nephew of 3rd Earl Spencer, who was long known, when Chancellor of the Exchequer, as Lord Althorp. Educ. at Harrow and at Trinity Coll., Cambridge. Appointed a Dept.-Lieut. of Northamptonshire 1857. A Liberal and a supporter of Lord Palmerston's Foreign Policy. Favoured the Maynooth Grant, a moderate extension of the suffrage, but opposed to 'a total obolition' of Church Rates, although in favour of an 'equitable adjustment' of the question. Insisted upon 'the extinction of the income tax in 1860.' Sat for Northamptonshire S. Apr.-Dec. 1857 when he succeeded as 5th Earl in Dec. 1857, and became Lord Lieut. of Ireland 1868-74 and 1882-85, Lord President of the Council 1880-83, and 1886. First Lord of the Admiralty 1892-95. Died 13 Aug. 1910.

[1857 2nd ed.]

AMBERLEY, Visct. 37 Chesham Place, London. Eld. s. of Earl Russell, by his 2nd wife, Lady Frances Anne Maria, 2nd d. of the 2nd Earl of Minto. B. in Chesham Place, 1842; m. 1864, Hon. Katherine Louisa, d. of the 2nd Lord Stanley of Alderley. A Liberal. Was an unsuccessful candidate at Leeds July 1865, and Devon S. 30 Nov. 1868. First elected for Nottingham May 1866. Sat until he retired in 1868. Died 9 Jan. 1876. [1867]

AMCOTTS, Lieut.-Col. Weston Cracroft. 30 Eaton Square, London. Hackthorn, Lincolnshire. Service, and Junior United Service. Eld. s. of Robert Amcotts, Esq., of Hackthorn, Lincolnshire, a Magistrate and Dept.-Lieut. for that Co., by Augusta, 2nd d. of Sir John Ingilby, Bart., of Ripley, Yorkshire. B. 1815; m. 1844, Williama Emma, 2nd d. of William George Cherry, Esq., of Buckland, Herefordshire. Educ. at Eton. Was formerly Cornet Royal Dragoons, also Maj. N. Lincolnshire Militia. Lieut.-Col. 1st Battalion Lincolnshire Volunteers. A Liberal, in favour of the establishment of county financial boards and of the repeal or reduction of the malt tax. Sat for Mid-Lincolnshire from Dec. 1868 until he retired 1874. Died 14 July 1883. [1873]

AMHURST-TYSSEN, W.A. See TYSSEN- AMHURST, W.A. Continued in House after 1885: full entry in Volume II.

AMORY, Sir John Heathcoat Heathcoat-,

Bart. 8 Hill Street, London. Knightshayes Court, Tiverton. Bolkham, Tiverton, Devon. Devonshire, and Reform. S. of Samuel Amory, Esq., of Portland Place, London, by Anne, d. of John Heathcote, Esq., who sat for Tiverton from 1832 to 1859. M. 1863, Henrietta Mary, d. of William Unwin, Esq. Educ. at University Coll., London. A Lace Manufacturer at Tiverton, a Partner in the firm of Messrs. Heathcote and Co. in that town. A Liberal. Sat for Tiverton from Dec. 1868 until he retired in 1885. Died 26 May, 1914.   [1885]

AMPHLETT, Rt. Hon. Sir Richard Paul. 32 Wimpole Street, London. Wychbold Hall, Droitwich. Carlton, and Oxford & Cambridge. Eld. s. of the Rev. Richard Holmden Amphlett, Rector of Hadzor, Worcestershire, by his 1st wife Sarah, d. of Nathaniel Paul, Esq. B. in Shropshire 1809; m. 1840, Frances, only d. and heir of Edward Ferrand, Esq., of St. Ives, Yorkshire. Educ. at Brewood School, Staffordshire and at St. Peter's Coll., Cambridge, where he gained a Fellowship. Was called to the bar at Lincoln's Inn 1834, and appointed a Queen's Counsel 1858. A Liberal-Conservative; voted against the disestablishment of the Irish Church 1869. Unsuccessful candidate for Lewes 29 Apr. 1859. Sat for Worcestershire E. from Dec. 1868. Sat until appointed a Baron of Exchequer 24 Jan. 1874. Was Knighted 27 Jan. 1874. Judge of Court of Appeal 1876-77. Struck with paralysis 3 Apr. 1877. Died 7 Dec. 1883.   [1873]

ANDERSON, Arthur. Oriental House, 122 Leadenhall Street, London. Norwood Grove, Surrey. Vaila, Shetland. B. in Shetland 1792; m. 1822, Mary Anne, eld. d. of C. Hill, Esq., of Scarborough. An active promoter of improvement in the fisheries, postal communications, etc. of the Orkney and Shetland Islands. Was a member of the Anti-Corn-Law League, and author of various pamphlets on the Corn Laws, Free Trade, etc. Managing Director, and one of the founders, of the Peninsular and Oriental Steam Navigation Company. Chairman of the Association of Proprietors of Steam Shipping. An East India proprietor. A Liberal, opposed to the application of State funds to religious endowments, but favourable to 'a national unsectarian system of education'; favourable to an extensive revision of our financial system, with a view to the more equitable apportionment of public burdens on the different classes of the community. First returned for Orkney and Shetland in 1847, defeating the family interest of the Earl of Zetland. Sat until he retired in 1852. Died 28 Feb. 1868.   [1852]

ANDERSON, George. Reform. Western Club, Glasgow. S. of George Anderson, Esq., of Luscar,

Fifeshire, by his marriage with Miss Rachel Inglis. B. at Liverpool 1819; m. 1877, Mary Brown, eld. d. of Thomas Clavering, Esq. Educ. at Edinburgh High School and at St. Andrew's University. For many years a merchant in Glasgow, but retired; published pamphlets on *Arrestment of Wages*, on *National Education*, *The Currency*, etc. An 'advanced' Liberal, in favour of the abolition of the laws of entail etc. Sat for Glasgow from Dec. 1868 until he accepted Chiltern Hundreds March 1885, on appointment as deputy Master of Melbourne Mint; retired 30 April 1895. Died 4 Nov. 1896.   [1885]

ANDERSON, Sir James. 48 Pall Mall, London. Blythswood Square, Glasgow. Reform. S. of John Anderson, Esq., of Stirling, Merchant. B. at Stirling, 1800; m. 1831, Janet, only d. of Robert Hood, Esq., of Glasgow. A Manufacturer at Glasgow. Elected Lord Provost of that city Nov. 1848. Knighted on the Queen's visit to Glasgow, Aug. 1849. A Liberal, in favour of 'a large extension of the suffrage, triennial parliaments, vote by ballot, and equal electoral districts'; opposed to all religious endowments; would support a national system of education 'on an unsectarian basis.' Contested Falkirk 14 July 1852. First returned for Stirling district in July 1852. Sat until he retired in 1859. Died 8 May 1864.   [1858]

ANDOVER, Visct. (I). Charlton, Wiltshire. Eld. s. of the Earl of Suffolk. B. 1804; m. in 1829, Isabella, 2nd d. of Lord Henry Howard. Of Whig principles. Sat for Malmesbury from 1832 until he retired in 1841. Succeeded as 17th Earl of Suffolk, Dec. 1851. Died 14 Aug. 1876.   [1838]

ANDOVER, Visct. (II). Charlton Park, Malmesbury, Wiltshire. Eld. s. of the Earl of Suffolk, by Isabella, 2nd d. of Lord Henry Howard, and niece of 12th Duke of Norfolk. B. 1833. Appointed Capt. North Gloucester Militia, May 1860. A Liberal, and was 'prepared to support a measure which shall make more efficient the representation of the people, and which shall include an extension of the borough franchise'; voted against Lord Russell's Reform Bill, 1866. First elected for Malmesbury, May 1859. Sat until defeated in 1868. Succeeded as 18th Earl Aug. 1876. Died 31 Mar. 1898.   [1867]

ANGERSTEIN, John. 23 St. James's Square, London. Weeting Hall, Norfolk. Woodlands, Kent. Athenaeum. S. of the celebrated Underwriter and founder of the Angerstein Gallery. Patron of 2 livings. A moderate Reformer. In favour of admitting Dissenters to the Universities, but not of exempting them from Church Rates. Opposed to pluralities in the

Church. Stated at his nomination that he had once sat for a nomination bor. for which the full equivalent had been paid, but it was with feelings of pain he did so, as he objected to such a system of representation. Unsuccessfully contested Greenwich in 1832. Sat for Greenwich from Jan. 1835 until he retired 1837. Contested Surrey E. 3 Aug. 1837. Died 10 Apr. 1858. [1837]

ANGERSTEIN, William. 15 Stratton Street, Piccadilly, London. Woodlands, Blackheath, London. Travellers'. B. 1811, s. of John Angerstein, Esq. (MP for Greenwich 1835-37), by Amelia, d. of William Locke, Esq., of Norbury Park, Surrey. Grands. of the well-known Underwriter and founder of the Angerstein Gallery. M. 1842 Mary Ann, only d. of William Nettleship, Esq. Educ. at Harrow and at Christ Church, Oxford. Appointed a Dept.-Lieut. of Kent 1860. A Liberal, favoured a large extension of the suffrage and a more equitable distribution of Parliamentary seats. Unsuccessfully contested Greenwich Feb. 1859, but elected the following May. Sat until defeated standing for W.Kent 1865 and contested the same seat 1868. High Sheriff for Norfolk 1872. Contested Greenwich 4 Aug. 1873. Died 31 May 1897. [1865]

ANNESLEY, Earl. 63 St. James's Street, London. Castle Wellan, Co. Down. Carlton, White's, and Coventry. An Irish Peer. S. of the 3rd Earl by his 2nd wife the 2nd d. of Hugh Moore, Esq., of Eglantine, Co. Down. B. in Rutland Square, Dublin 1830. Unmarried. Educ. at Cambridge. A Conservative, favouring 'a re-adjustment of taxation.' First returned for Great Grimsby July 1852. Sat until 1867. Died 10 Aug. 1874. [1857]

ANNESLEY, Hon. Hugh. 25 Norfolk Street, London. Castlewellan, Co. Down, Ireland. White's, Carlton, and Guards'. Sackville Street Club, Dublin. 2nd s. of 3rd Earl Annesley, by his 2nd wife Priscilla Cecelia, 2nd d. of Hugh Moore, Esq. of Eglantine House, Co. Down. B. in Rutland Square, Dublin 1831. Educ. at Eton and at Trinity Coll., Dublin. Entered the army in 1851, appointed Capt. and Lieut.-Col. Scots Fusilier Guards 1860. Was severely wounded at the battle of the Alma. A moderate Conservative. First elected for Cavan Apr. 1857. Sat until he retired 1874. Succeeded brother as 5th Earl 10 Aug. 1874. Irish representative Peer. Died 15 Dec. 1908. [1873]

ANSON, Hon. Augustus Henry Archibald. Shugborough, Tamworth. Army & Navy. 2nd s. of 1st Earl of Lichfield, by Louisa, youngest d. of Nathaniel Phillips, Esq., of Slebeck Hall, Pem-

brokeshire. B. at Shugborough, Staffordshire 1835; m. 1863, Amelia Mary, eld. d. of Rev. T. L. Claughton, Vicar of Kidderminster. Entered the army 1853, appointed Capt. in the Rifle Brigade 1855, exchanged to 84th Foot in 1856, to the 10th Dragoons, and then to the 7th Dragoons in 1858. Served in India and was wounded before Delhi in 1857, made a Maj. in the army 1859. Received the Victoria Cross for conspicuous bravery at Lucknow, etc. A Liberal, voted against Lord Russell's Reform Bill 1866. Sat for Lichfield from May 1859-Nov.1868, when he was an unsuccessful candidate there. Was an unsuccessful candidate for Bewdley Mar. 1869, but obtained his seat on petition, after scrutiny Apr. 1869. Sat until he retired 1874. Died 17 Nov. 1877. [1873]

ANSON, Gen. Sir George, G.C.B. 5 Bulstrode Street, London. Senior United Service, and Boodle's. Uncle of the Earl of Lichfield; b. 1769; m. in 1800 Frances, grandd. of Sir Robert Hamilton, Colonel of the 4th Dragoon Guards. Was Equerry to the Duke of Kent. Of Whig principles. Received the thanks of the House of Commons on 8 Mar. 1810, and 11 Nov. 1813, for services in the Peninsular War. First sat for Lichfield in 1806. Sat until he accepted Chiltern Hundreds, Aug. 1841. Died 4 Nov. 1849. [1841]

ANSON, Hon. George. 25 Hill Street, London. Shugborough Park, Staffordshire. Reform. S. of 1st Visct. Anson and bro. of 1st Earl of Lichfield. B. 1797; m. Hon. Isabella, 3rd d. of 1st Lord Forester. Became Col. in the army in 1838 and a Maj.-Gen. 1851. Was Aide-de-Camp to the Commander-in-Chief, was at Waterloo and was Clerk of the Ordnance from July 1846 to Mar. 1852. Commanded a division in Bengal in 1853 and was made Commander-in-Chief in India on 20 Nov. 1855. A Liberal, who said he would have 'resisted every attempt to impose a duty upon corn, whether for the purpose of protection or revenue.' Sat for Great Yarmouth from 1818-Jan. 1835, and unsuccessfully contested South Staffordshire in the May following. Sat for Stoke-upon-Trent from Feb. 1836-1837. Sat for Staffordshire S. from 1837 until he accepted Chiltern Hundreds in 1853. Died at Karhal, during the Mutiny on 22 May 1857. [1853]

ANSON, Visct. 11a Albany, London. Shugborough, Staffordshire. Brooks's. B. at Shugborough, Staffordshire 1825, the eld. s. of the Earl of Lichfield. Unmarried. Was précis writer to Lord Palmerston when Sec. of State for Foreign Affairs. Appointed Capt. of Staffordshire Yeomanry Cavalry 1845. A Liberal, voted against the ballot in 1853. Sat for Lichfield from 1847-Mar. 1854, when he succeeded as 2nd Earl.

Was Lord-Lieut. of Staffordshire 1863-71. Died 7 Jan. 1892. [1854]

ANSTEY, Thomas Chisholm. 3 Essex Street, Strand, London. 2nd s. of Thomas Anstey, Esq., of Anstey-Barton, Van Diemen's Land. B. in London 1816; m. 1839, Harriet, 2nd d. of J.E. Strickland, Esq., of Longhglyn House, Co. Roscommon. Educ. at Wellington, Somersetshire, and at University Coll., London. Called to the bar at the Middle Temple in 1839. Professor of Law and Jurisprudence at the Colleges of St. Peter and St. Paul, Bath. Author of *British Catholics and the New Parliament* (1841); *A Guide to the Laws affecting Roman Catholics*; *A Letter to Lord Cottenham on Petitions of Right*; *A Letter to W.H. Watson, Esq., M.P. on Legal Fees on Petitions of Right*; *Guide to the History of the Laws and Constitution of England, in Six Lectures*; together with numerous miscellaneous papers in the *Portfolio, Dublin Review, Law Magazine*, etc. A Liberal, opposed to 'centralisation'; in favour of the repeal of the Union both with Ireland and Scotland; thought 'that the abolition of excise duties, the reduction of customs, and the repeal of all currency laws are the only methods of insuring protection to all.' First returned for Youghal in 1847. Defeated contesting Bedford in 1852. Attorney General at Hong Kong Oct. 1855 to 30 Jan. 1859; acting Judge to High Court of Bombay in 1865. Died in Bombay 12 Aug. 1873. [1852]

ANSTRUTHER, Sir Robert, Bart. 1 Eccleston Square, London. Balcaskie, Pittenweem, Fifeshire. Bramore, Caithness. Eld. s. of Sir Ralph Abercrombie Anstruther (4th Bart.) by Jane, eld. d. of Major-Gen. Sir Henry Torrens, K.C.B. B. in Edinburgh 1834; m. 1857, Louisa, eld. d. of the Rev. William Knox Marshall, B.D., Rector of Wragby, and Canon of Hereford. Educ. at Harrow. Served in the Grenadier Guards from 1853-62, and received the rank of Capt. and Lieut.-Col. May 1861. A Dept.-Lieut. of Caithness and Lord-Lieut. of the Co. of Fife. Patron of 1 living. A Liberal. First elected for Fifeshire, Apr.1864. Sat until he retired in 1880. Elected for St. Andrew's district in 1885 and sat until his death 21 July 1886. [1880]

ANSTRUTHER, Sir Windham Charles James Carmichael-, Bart. 44 St. James's Place, London. Carmichael House, Thankerton, Lanarkshire. Carlton, and Arthur's. Only s. of Sir Windham Carmichael-Anstruther, (4th) Bart., by his 1st wife, Meredith Maria, 2nd d. of Charles Wetherell, Esq. B. 1824; m. 1872 Janetta, only d. of Robert Barbour, Esq., of Bolesworth Castle, Cheshire. Was Heritable Carver of the Royal Household in Scotland. A Dept.-Lieut. and

Magistrate for Lanarkshire. A Liberal-Conservative. Sat for S. Lanarkshire from Feb. 1874. Defeated 1880. Vice-Lieut. of Lanarkshire 1890-95. Died 26 Jan. 1898. [1880]

ANTROBUS, Sir Edmund, Bart. 11 Grosvenor Crescent, London. Amesbury, Salisbury. Carlton, and United University. Eld. s. of Sir Edmund Antrobus, of Amesbury Abbey, Wiltshire, by Anne, only d. of the Hon. Hugh Lindsay, and niece of 6th Earl of Balcarres. B. in the Parish of St. George's, Hanover Sq., 1818; m. 1847, Marianne Georgiana, eld. d. of Sir George Bashwood, Bart. Educ. at St. John's Coll., Cambridge. A Dept.-Lieut. of Wiltshire. Appointed Capt. Wiltshire Yeomanry Cavalry, 1851. A Liberal-Conservative, voted for the disestablishment of the Irish Church. 1869. Sat for Surrey E. from 1841-41. First elected for Wilton, Mar. 1855. Sat until he accepted Chiltern Hundreds Feb. 1877; Sheriff of Wiltshire 1880. Died 1 Apr. 1899. [1876]

APSLEY, Visct. 16 Arlington Street, London. Eld. s. of the Earl Bathurst. B. 1790. Unmarried. A Conservative. Was a Commissioner for the affairs of India, and a Clerk to the Teller of the Exchequer. Sat for Cirencester from 1812. Sat until he succeeded father as 4th Earl July 1834. Died 26 May 1866. [1833]

ARBUTHNOT, Col. George. 5 Upper Eccleston Street, London. United Service, Army & Navy, Carlton, and Athenaeum. 2nd s. of John Alves Arbuthnot, Esq., of Cowarth Park, Berkshire (who was High Sheriff of Berkshire 1873), by Mary, d. of George Arbuthnot, Esq., of Elderslie House, Surrey. B. at Madras 1836; m. 1870, Caroline Emma Nepean, younger d. of Capt. Andrew Nepean Aitcheson, H.E.I.C.S. Was educ. at Eton and at Trinity Coll., Cambridge. Entered the Royal Artillery as Lieut. Sept. 1855, became Capt. 1864, Major 1868, Brevet Lieut.-Col. 1877, and retired on half pay the same year. Served during the Indian Mutiny and subsequently in Abyssinia. Author of a work entitled *Herzegovina, or Omar Pasha and the Christian Rebels*. A Conservative. Unsuccessfully contested Hereford Dec. 1868 and Mar. 1869. Sat for Hereford from Feb. 1871-Feb.1874, when he was unsuccessful; re-elected Mar. 1878. Defeated 1880. [1880]

ARBUTHNOTT, Hon. Sir Hugh, K.C.B. 5H Albany, London. Hulton-Bervie, Kincardineshire. Carlton, and Athenaeum. 2nd s. of 7th Visct. Arbuthnott, by the 2nd d. of William Graham, Esq., of Morphie, Kincardineshire. Entered the army 1796 and became a General 1854. Was Col. of the 38th Foot from 1843-62 when he was appointed Col. of the 79th. Received a gold medal for Busaco, and also served at the siege of Copenhagen and at Corunna, Fuentes d'onor, etc. A Dept.-Lieut. of Kincardineshire. Of Conservative principles. Voted for inquiry into Maynooth 1853. Sat for Kincardineshire from 1826 until his retirement in 1865. Died 11 July 1868. [1856]

ARCHBOLD, Robert. 55 Jermyn Street, London. Davidstown, Nr. Castle Dermo, Kildare. S. of James Archbold, Esq., of Davidstown; m. Miss Copeland (she died 1842). A Dept.-Lieut. and Magistrate for Co. Kildare. A radical Reformer, voted for agricultural protection 1846. First elected for Kildare 11 Aug. 1837, defeating Edward Ruthven, Esq., one of the previous members. Sat until he retired in 1847. [1847]

ARCHDALL, Maj.-Gen. Mervyn. 16 Waterloo Place, London. Castle Archdall, Enniskillen. Lieut.-Governor of the Isle of Wight, and Governor of Fermanagh Co. Of Conservative principles. Sat for Fermanagh almost uninterruptedly from the Union until he retired in 1835. [1833]

ARCHDALL, Mervyn Edward. Castle Archdall, Fermanagh. Trillie, Tyrone. Carlton, and Army & Navy. Sackville Street Club, Dublin. Eld. s. of Edward Archdall, Esq., of Riversdale and Castle Archdall, Co. Fermanagh, by the 2nd d. of William Humphreys, Esq., of Ballyhaise, Co. Cavan. Nephew of Gen. Archdall, who sat for Fermanagh in eleven Parliaments. B. 1812. Capt. in the Enniskillen Dragoons, exchanged to half--pay unattached in 1847. A Conservative, in favour of 'safe and progressive' improvement and of sound 'economy but not unwise retrenchment.' Sat for Fermanagh from the retirement of his uncle in 1834 until he retired 1874. [1873]

ARCHDALL, William Humphrys. Riversdale, Enniskillen, Ireland. Carlton. S. of Edward Archdall, Esq., by Matilda, d. of William Humphrys, Esq., of Baillyhaise, Co. Cavan. Bro. of Mervyn E. Archdall, Esq., who sat for Fermanagh from 1834 to 1874. B. in Dublin, 1813; m. 1845, Emily Mary, d. of the Hon. and Rev. John Charles Maude, and grand-d. of 1st Visct. Hawarden. Fermanagh was represented continuously by members of Mr. Archdall's family for more than 150 years. Educ. at Tamworth School, and at Exeter Coll., Oxford. A Conservative. Sat for Fermanagh from Feb. 1874 until he retired in 1885. [1885]

ARKWRIGHT, Augustus Peter. 3 Spring Gardens, London. Willersley, Matlock. United Service. S. of Peter Arkwright, Esq., by his marriage with Miss Mary Ann Hurt. B. at Wirksworth, Derbyshire 1821. Unmarried. Educ. at the Naval Coll., Portsmouth, became a Commander R.N. 1859, Capt. June 1877, on the retired list. A Conservative, voted against the disestablishment of the Irish Church 1869, gave Lord Beaconsfield's Party a general support. Sat for N. Derbyshire from Dec. 1868 until defeated 1880. Died 6 Oct. 1887. [1880]

ARKWRIGHT, Francis. Coton House, Rugby. Junior Carlton. Eld. s. of Rev. Godfrey Harry Arkwright, of Sutton Scarsdale, by his 1st wife, Frances Rafela, d. of Sir Henry Fitz-Herbert, Bart., of Tissington Hall, Derbyshire. B. 1846; m. 1st, 1868, Louisa, d. of Henry Milbank, Esq. and Lady Margaret Milbank (she died 1873), 2ndly, 1875, Hon. Evelyn, d. of the 3rd Visct. Sidmouth. Educ. at Eton. Once in the 100th Regiment. Patron of 1 living. A Conservative. Sat for E. Derbyshire from Feb. 1874 until defeated 1880. Later a member of New Zealand Legislative Council. Died Mar. 1915. [1880]

ARKWRIGHT, George. 2D Albany, London. Sutton, Derbyshire. Carlton, Arthur's, and Oxford & Cambridge. B. 1807, the s. of Robert Arkwright, Esq., of Sutton, Nr. Chesterfield, Derbyshire, by the d. of Stephen George Kemble, Esq., of Durham. Great-grands. of Sir Richard Arkwright. Graduated at Trinity Coll., Cambridge, M.A. 1833, and called to the bar at Lincoln's Inn in the same year. A Conservative; voted for agricultural protection 1846 and for inquiry into Maynooth 1853. Unsuccessfully contested Derbyshire N. 1837. Sat for Leominster from Feb. 1842 until his death 5 Feb. 1856. [1855]

ARKWRIGHT, Richard. 8 Cadogan Place, London. Carlton, and White's. 2nd s. of John Arkwright, Esq., of Hampton Court, Herefordshire, by Sarah, eld. d. of Sir Hungerford Hoskyns, Bart., of Harewood, Herefordshire. B. at Hampton Court, Herefordshire 1835; m. 1862, Lady Mary Caroline, 2nd d. of the 2nd Earl of Stratford. Educ. at Harrow and at Trinity Coll., Cambridge, where he graduated 1857. Was called to the bar at Lincoln's Inn 1859, but had ceased to practise. A Dept.-Lieut. of Herefordshire. A Conservative. Sat for Leominster from Feb. 1866 until he accepted Chiltern Hundreds. Died 14 Nov. 1918. [1874]

ARMITAGE, Benjamin. 39 Devonshire Place, London. Chomlea Bank, Pendleton, Lancashire. Devonshire. B. in Salford 1823, s. of Sir Elkanah Armitage, of Hope Hall, Pendleton, Lancashire (Mayor of Manchester 1848), by his 1st wife Miss Mary Bowers. M. 1st. 1845, d. of John Smith of

Bingley, Yorkshire; 2ndly 1856, d. of George Southam of Manchester. Educ. at Barton Hall School, Patricroft, near Manchester. A manufacturer at Manchester. Elected Resident of the Manchester Chamber of Commerce 1878-9, 1879-80 and 1880-81; then became one of the directors. A Trustee of the Manchester Grammar School. A Liberal. Sat for Salford W. from Apr. 1880 to 1886, when he was defeated, standing as a Gladstonian Liberal. Contested the same seat 1892. Died 4 Dec. 1899.   [1886]

ARMITSTEAD, George. 4 Cleveland Square, London. Kinloch Laggan, Kingussie, Scotland. New Liberal Club, Edinburgh. Eastern Club, Dundee. Reform. 2nd s. of George Armitstead, Esq., of Easingwold, Yorkshire, for many years settled as a Merchant at Riga. B. at Riga 1824; m. 1848, Jane Elizabeth, eld. d. of Edward Baxter, Esq., of Kincaldrum, Forfarshire. Educ. at Wiesbaden and Heidelberg. A Merchant and Senior Partner of the firm of Messrs. Armitstead in London and Messrs. George Armitstead and Co., Dundee. A Magistrate for Perthshire and Forfarshire, and a Dept.-Lieut. for the latter. A Liberal, in favour of the pressure of business in Parliament being lightened by a well-organised system of county government; also of shorter Parliaments, etc. Unsuccessfully contested Dundee April 1859; sat for that town from Dec. 1868 to Aug. 1873. Re-elected Apr. 1880. Retired at 1885 gen.-election. Created 1st Baron Armitstead in 1906. Died, without heir, 7 Dec. 1915.   [1885]

ARMSTRONG, Sir Andrew, Bart. Gallen Priory, King's County. University, and Reform. S. of E. Armstrong, Esq., of Gallen, by the 3rd d. of Frederick Trench, Esq., and sister of Lord Ashtown; b. 1786; m. 1835, d. of G.A. Fullerton, Esq. Was High Sheriff of King's Co. in 1811, and 1836. A Dept.-Lieut. of the Co. Was Receiver-General of Stamps in Ireland, and obtained a pension on the abolition of that office, but resigned it previous to his election. A Liberal, first returned for King's County in 1841. Sat until he retired in 1852. Died 27 Jan. 1862.   [1852]

ARMSTRONG, Richard. 32 Stephen's Green North, Dublin. Greenfield, Sutton, Co.Dublin. S. of William Armstrong, Esq., of Roxboro, Co. Armagh, and Elizabeth his wife. B. in Dublin 1815; m. 1847, Elizabeth, d. of Edward Meurant, Esq. Educ. at the Feinaiglian Institution, Luxanbourg, Dublin, and at Trinity Coll., Dublin. Was called to the bar in Ireland 1839. Appointed a Queen's Counsel 1854; made a Queen's serjeant and a bencher of King's Inns, Dublin 1861. A Liberal, and was in favour of a measure for securing

tenant-right in Ireland. First elected for Sligo bor., July 1865. Sat until he retired in 1868. Died, in Dublin, 26 Aug. 1880.   [1867]

ARMSTRONG, Robert Baynes. 29 Chester Square, Pimlico, London. 2 Cloisters, Temple, London. United University, and Reform. Eld. s. of John Armstrong, Esq., of Lancaster, by Deborah Anne, 4th d. of Robert Baynes, Esq., of Cockermouth. B. at Lancaster, 1785; m. 1842 Frances, youngest d. of Richmond Blamine, Esq., of Thackwood, Cumberland. Educ. at Clitheroe and Sedbergh Schools; formerly Fellow of St. John's Coll., Cambridge. Called to the bar at the Inner Temple 1814 and engaged on the Northern Circuit. Appointed a Queen's Counsel and elected a bencher of the Inner Temple 1840. Appointed Recorder of Hull 1836 but resigned 1837, on being made Recorder of Leeds. Recorder of Manchester and Recorder of Bolton from May 1848. A Reformer; in favour of vote by ballot, extension of the suffrage, and short Parliaments. Sat for Lancaster from Mar. 1848 until unseated at a by-election, 12 Apr. 1853. Died 15 Jan. 1869.
                                          [1852 2nd ed.]

ARNOLD, A. Continued in House after 1885: full entry in Volume II.

ARNOTT, Sir John. Cork, Ireland. Monkstown, Co. Cork. S. of John Arnott, Esq., of Auchtermuchty, Fifeshire, Scotland, by Elizabeth, d. of — Paton, Esq. B. at Auchtermuchty 1846, m. Margaretta, d. of John James McKinlay, Esq., of Stirling. Writer to the Signet. Educ. at Auchtermuchty School. A Merchant at Cork, Belfast, Dublin, Limerick, Glasgow and Newcastle. A Magistrate and Alderman of Cork; Mayor of Cork, 1859 and 1860. A Liberal. First returned for Kinsale, May 1859. Accepted Chiltern Hundreds May 1863. Purchased the *Belfast Northern Whig* in 1874; Chairman of Bristol Steam Navigation Co. 1877–96; Created Bart. 1 Feb. 1896; purchased Duke of Devonshire's Bandon estate in Co. Cork in 1896. Died 28 Mar. 1898.   [1863]

ARUNDEL AND SURREY, Earl of. 11 Carlton House Terrace, London. Littlehampton, Sussex. White's, and Brooks's. Eld. s. of the Duke of Norfolk. B. Nov. 7 1815; m. in 1839, d. of Sir Edmond Lyons, Bart. Of moderate Whig principles, in favour of free trade. Was a Cornet in the Royal Horse Guards. Sat for Arundel from 1837 till Aug. 1851, when he returned without opposition for Limerick city. Retired in 1852. Succeeded as 14th Duke Feb. 1856. Died 25 Nov. 1860. [1852]

ASHBURY, James Lloyd. 66 Grosvenor Street, London. 6 Eastern Terrace, Brighton. Carlton, and Junior Carlton. S. of John Ashbury, Esq., of Manchester. B. at Manchester 1834. Unmarried. A builder of Railway Rolling Stock. Chairman of the Denbigh, Ruthin and Corwen Railway, and other railways. A member of the Thames Yacht and 19 other boating clubs. A Liberal-Conservative, resisted all measures calculated to weaken the Church of England and favoured 'all causes of conflict between capital and labour' being removed. Sat from Feb. 1874 for Brighton, which he had contested unsuccessfully Dec. 1868. Sat until defeated 1880. Died 3 Sept. 1895.   [1880]

ASHER, A., Q.C. Continued in House after 1885: full entry in Volume II.

ASHLEY, Hon. Anthony Evelyn Melbourne. 61 Cadogan Place, London. Brooks's. 2nd surviving s. of the 7th Earl of Shaftesbury, by Lady Emily, eld. d. of the 5th Earl Cowper. B. 1836; m. 1866, Sybella Charlotte, 2nd d. of Sir Walter Rockliffe Farquhar (3rd) Bart., of Poulsden Park, Leatherhead. Educ. at Harrow and Trinity Coll., Cambridge, where he graduated M.A. 1858. Called to the bar at Lincoln's Inn 1863, and joined the Oxford circuit. Was for some time secretary to Lord Palmerston; was a Magistrate for Dorset and Treasurer of county courts of Dorset from 1863 to 1874. 2nd Church Estates Commissioner. Was Parliamentary Sec. to the Board of Trade from Apr. 1880 to May 1882, when he was appointed Under-Secretary for the Colonies (salary £1500). Author of *Life of Henry John Temple, Visct. Palmerston.* A Liberal. Was an unsuccessful candidate for the Isle of Wight, Feb. 1874; sat for Poole from May 1874 to Apr. 1880; sat for the Isle of Wight from 1880 until defeated in 1885. Died 16 Nov. 1907.   [1885]

ASHLEY, Lord D.C.L., sen. 49 Upper Brook Street. St. Giles House, London. Woodgates, Dorset. Carlton, Athenaeum. Born in 1801, the eld. s. of the Earl of Shaftesbury. M. 1830, Lady Emily, the eld. d. of the 5th Earl Cowper. Grad. at Christ Church, Oxford, where he was first class in classics 1822. Was Commissioner of the Board of Control from 1828-30 and Lord of the Admiralty from Dec. 1834-Apr. 1835, and one of the Ecclesiastical Commissioners from 1841-1847. A Conservative, but in favour of free trade and willing to repeal the window tax. A leading member of many charitable associations and well known for his exertions in favour of persons employed in mines, collieries and factories. Sat for Woodstock from 1826-30, for Dorchester in 1830 and 1831 and for Dorsetshire from Oct. 1831-Apr. 1846 when he accepted Chiltern Hundreds on the free trade question. Sat for Bath from 1847 until he succeeded his father as 7th Earl on 2 June 1851.

Was an active member of the House of Lords, and made Lord Lieut. of Dorset on 24 June 1856. Died 1 Oct. 1885.   [1851]

ASHLEY, Lord, jun. B. in Upper Brook Street, London 1831, the eld. s. of 7th Earl of Shaftesbury, by the eld. d. of 5th Earl Cowper. M. 1857, Lady Harriet, only d. of 3rd Marq. of Donegal. Educ. at Rugby. Entered the navy in 1848 and served in the Black Sea and the Baltic during the Russian War. A Lieut.-Col. Dorset Militia and appointed Dept.-Lieut. of Dorsetshire, 1857. A Liberal, and a 'staunch supporter of Protestantism' and of Lord Palmerston. Sat for Hull Apr. 1857-May 1859, when he was returned for Cricklade. Sat until he retired 1865. Succeeded as 8th Earl Oct. 1885. Died 13 Apr. 1886.   [1865]

ASHMEAD-BARTLETT, Sir E. Continued in House after 1885: full entry in Volume II.

ASPINALL, J.T.W. Only s. of John Aspinall, Esq., of Standen Hall, Nr. Clitheroe. McCalmont classed him as Liberal-Conservative. First contested Clitheroe in 1852; returned at by-election 28 May 1853; election declared void 28 July 1853. Died 12 Nov. 1865.

ASSHETON, Ralph. 11 Queen's Gate Place, London. Downham Hall, Clitheroe. Carlton, and United University. S. of William Assheton, Esq., of Downham, Lancashire, by Frances Annabella, d. of the Hon. William Cockayne. B. 1830; m. 1854, Emily Augusta, d. of Joseph Feilden, Esq., of Witton Park, Lancashire. Educ. at Eton and Trinity Coll., Cambridge, graduated B.A. 1852. A Magistrate for Lancashire and the W. Riding of Yorkshire, and one time Capt. Lancashire Militia. A Conservative. Sat for Clitheroe from July 1868 until defeated 1880. Died 22 June 1907.   [1880]

ASTELL, John Harvey. Woodbury Hall, St. Neots, Cambridgeshire. Carlton, and Union. 2nd s. of William Astell, Esq. (who represented Bedfordshire for some years), by Sarah, only d. of John Harvey, Esq., of Ickwell Bury, Bedfordshire. B. in London 1806; m. 1853, Annie Emelia, d. of Robert Parry Nisbet, Esq. Educ. at Putney, and at Haileybury Coll. Was engaged in the service of the East India Company in China from 1825-1834, and was afterwards Superintendent of British trade there under the Crown; an East India Director. A Magistrate for Cambridgeshire, and a Dept.-Lieut. for Bedfordshire. A Conservative, and gave a general support to Lord Derby; opposed to the Maynooth Grant. Sat for Cambridge bor. from July 1852-Mar. 1853. First elected for Ashburton May 1859. Sat until he retired 1865. Died 17 Jan. 1887. [1865]

ASTELL, William. 51 Old Broad Street. Everton House, Hampshire. Carlton. B. in 1774, the s. of Godfrey Thornton, Esq. M. in 1800. the only d. of John Harvey, Esq. Assumed the name of Astell in 1807. A Lieut.-Col. of the Bedfordshire Militia. A Director of the East India Company. Governor of the Russian Company. A Dept.-Lieut. of Bedfordshire. A Conservative and represented Bridgewater in Parliament from 1807-32. Voted against the Roman Catholic Relief Bill and the Reform Bill. Sat for Bedfordshire from 1841 until his death in 1846. [1845]

ASTLEY, Sir Jacob, Bart., D.C.L. 7 Cavendish Square, London. Melton Constable, Norfolk. B. 1797; m. 1819, Georgiana, d. of Sir Henry Watkin Dashwood, Bart., sister to the Marchioness of Ely (dead). Patron of 2 livings. A Trustee of the Norwich Union Fire Insurance Company. Of Whig principles. His father and grandfather both sat for Norfolk W. He sat for Norfolk W. from 1832 until defeated in 1837. [1837]

ASTLEY, Sir John Dugdale, Bart.(I). 10 Langham Place, London. Everleigh House, Nr. Pewsey, Wiltshire. B. in 1778; m. in 1803, Sarah, d. of William Page, Esq., of Gosport. Father--in-law of Lord Visct. Torrington. A Reformer. Sat for Wiltshire N. from 1820 until his retirement in 1835. Died 19 Jan. 1842. [1833]

ASTLEY, Sir John Dugdale, (II). 4 Lowndes Square, London. Elsham Hall, Brigg, Lincolnshire. Everley House, Ludgershall, Wiltshire. Guards'. Eld. s. of Sir Francis Dugdale Astley (2nd) Bart., by Emma Dorothea, 4th d. of Sir Thomas B. Lethbridge, Bart. B. at Rome 1828; m. 1858, only d. of Thomas George Corbett, Esq., of Elsham Hall, Brigg, Lincolnshire. Educ. at Eton and at Christ Church, Oxford. Entered the Scots Fusilier Guards Mar. 1848, became Lieut. and Capt. 1851, Capt. and Lieut.-Col. 1860. Served in the Crimean War, received 3 medals, and was wounded at the Alma. Patron of 3 livings. A Conservative, in favour of the re-adjustment of local taxation. Sat for N. Lincolnshire from Feb. 1874 until defeated 1880. Died 10 Oct. 1895. [1880]

ATHERLEY, Arthur. Parade, St. James's Park, London. Arundel, Sussex. A country gentleman, bro. to a Banker in the town; m. in 1793, Louisa, youngest d. of William, 5th Marq. of Lothian. A Whig, was a friend and supporter of Charles J. Fox. Sat in the Parliaments of 1802, 1806, 1812; and uninterruptedly for Southampton from 1831 until he retired in 1835. Died 21 Oct. 1844. [1833]

ATHERTON, Sir William. 13 Westbourne Terrace, London. 1 Paper Buildings, Temple, London. Reform. S. of the Rev. William Atherton, Wesleyan Minister by Margaret, d. of the Rev. Walter Morison, Minister of the Established Church in Scotland. B. in Glasgow, 1806; m. 1843, Agnes Mary, 2nd d. of Thomas James Hall, Esq., Chief Magistrate at Bow Street. Was called to the bar at the Inner Temple in 1839 (having practised as a special pleader from 1832 till that date), and joined the northern circuit. A Queen's Counsel and a bencher of the Inner Temple. Was Judge Advocate of the Fleet and Counsel to the Admiralty from 1855 till Dec. 1859, Solicitor-General from the latter date till June 1861, when he was appointed Attorney-General. A Liberal, opposed to the repeal of the Maynooth Grant; in favour of the ballot, a large reform in the law, and the removal of all religious disabilities. First returned for Durham in July 1852 and sat until his death 22 Jan. 1864. [1863]

ATKINSON, H.J. See FALMER-ATKINSON, H.J. Continued in House after 1885; full entry in Volume II.

ATTWOOD, John. 25 Park Lane, London. Hylands, Essex. S. of Jas. Attwood, Esq. Was one of the parties in the well-known cause of Small v. Attwood. Chairman of the Harwich Railway. A Conservative, but in favour of free trade. First returned for Harwich in 1841. Unseated on petition in 1849. [1847 2nd ed.]

ATTWOOD, Matthias. 27 Gracechurch Street, London. Muswell Hill, Middlesex. The Leasowes, Shropshire. Carlton. A Banker. A Director of the Pelican Assurance Company. A Dept.-Lieut. of Surrey. A Conservative, voted for agricultural protection 1846, entertained strong opinions of the necessity of enlarging the currency. Sat for Callington in the Parliaments of 1820 and 1826, and for Boroughbridge in those of 1830 and 1831. Sat for Whitehaven from 1832 until he retired 1847. Died 11 Nov. 1851. [1847]

ATTWOOD, Matthias Wolverley. 69 Lombard Street, London. Carlton, Union, and Windham. S. of Matthias Attwood, Esq., MP for Whitehaven. A Conservative. Contested Greenwich in 1835 and was first elected there 27 July 1837. Defeated in 1841 contesting City of London, Kinsale and Sunderland. Died 17 Sept. 1865. [1841]

ATTWOOD, Thomas. Bro. of the Member for Whitehaven in 1838. A Banker and Manufacturer at Birmingham and in London, and the head of the Political Union at the former place. An advocate of free trade, the ballot, annual Parliaments, universal suffrage, and of general reform. Opposed to the corn laws, to the monetary system, to monopolies, and to all unnecessary expenditure. Said he would resign his seat whenever a majority of his constituents were dissatisfied with his general parliamentary conduct. Sat for Birmingham from 1832 until he accepted Chiltern Hundreds Jan. 1840. Retired to St. Heliers to restore his health; requested by a Birmingham petition to re-enter political life in 1843. Died 5 Mar. 1856. [1838]

AUSTEN, Col. Thomas. Kippington, Kent. A Magistrate and Dept.-Lieut. of Kent. A Conservative. Said he would 'not only maintain the present insufficient protection to agriculture, but will use his best endeavours to extend it to honest and just limits.'; believed 'the grant to Maynooth to have been begun in error, and thinks that it ought to be suspended.' President of the W. Kent Agricultural Protection Society. First returned for W. Kent in Apr. 1845 without opposition and sat until he was defeated in Aug. 1847. Died 23 July 1859. [1846]

AYLMER, John Evans Freke-. Palace Chambers, Westminster, London. Aylmersfield, Streatham, Surrey. St. Stephen's. 2nd s. of Arthur Percy Aylmer, Esq., (2nd s. of Sir Fenton Aylmer, Bart., of Donadea Castle, Kildare), by Martha, d. of Richard Reynell, Esq., of Killynon, Co. Westmeath. B. 1838; m. 1861, Frances Margaretta, youngest d. of James Thomson, Esq., Hanseatic Consul to Gibraltar. Educ. at Trinity Coll., Dublin. Entered the Army July 1855; retired in 1871 as Captain 54th Foot. Served in Malta with the Crimean Light Division, and in India with the 33rd Foot. Served on the Staff in India and at home, and was a member of the Government Small Arms Committee. A Conservative, and a supporter of the policy of Lord Beaconsfield. Sat for Maidstone from April 1880 until he retired in 1885. Died 14 Oct. 1907. [1885]

AYRTON, Rt. Hon. Acton Smee. 11 Bolton Street, London. 3 Essex Court, Middle Temple, London. Reform. S. of Frederick Ayrton, Esq., formerly of Gray's Inn and of Bombay, by Julia, only child of Lieut.-Col. Nugent. B. at Kew 1816. Called to the bar in the Middle Temple 1853. Was Parliamentary Sec. to the Treasury from Dec. 1868-Nov. 1869, when he was appointed Chief Commissioner of Works and Buildings (salary £2,000). A 'Radical', in favour of more economic organisation of the army, navy, etc.; also in favour of short Parliaments, opposed to State religious endowments and to all systems of 'centralisation'. Unsuccessfully contested Tower Hamlets July 1852; first elected there July 1857. Sat until defeated 1874. Contested Mile End division of Tower Hamlets 1885. Died 30 Nov. 1886. [1873]

AYTOUN, Roger Sinclair. Upper Brook Street, London. Inchdairnie, Kirkcaldy, Fife. Brooks's. S. of John Aytoun, Esq., of Inchdairnie, Fife, by Margaret Anne, d. of J. Jeffray, Esq., M.D. B. in Edinburgh 1823. Educ. at Trinity Coll., Cambridge. A Liberal, and supported the disestablishment of the Irish Church 'as a measure of justice to Ireland.' First elected for Kirkcaldy July 1862. Sat until he retired 1874. [1873]

BACKHOUSE, Edmund. 49 Grosvenor Street, London. Middleton Lodge, Richmond, Yorkshire. S. of Edmund Backhouse, Esq., of Darlington, Banker, by Hannah Chapman, d. of Joseph Gurney, Esq., of Norfolk. B. at Darlington 1824; m. 1848, Juliet Mary, d. of Charles Fox, Esq., of Falmouth. Educ. at 'The Friends' School', Tottenham, London. A Banker at Darlington. A Liberal. Sat for Darlington from Dec. 1868 until he retired 1880. Died 7 June 1906. [1880]

BAGGALLAY, Sir Richard. 55 Queen's Gate, London. 10 Old Square, Lincoln's Inn, London. Kenyon House, Clapham, Surrey. Carlton. Eld. s. of Richard Baggallay, Esq. of Kingthorpe House, Upper Tooting, Surrey, by Anne, d. of Owen Marden, Esq. B. at Stockwell, Surrey, 1816; m. 1847 Marianne, youngest d. of Henry Charles Lacy, Esq. of Withdeane Hall, Sussex, MP for Bodmin. Educ. at Caius College, Cambridge where he graduated 14th Wrangler, B.A. 1839, M.A. 1842 and gained a Fellowship. Called to the bar at Lincoln's Inn 1843, made a Queen's Counsel 1861; Solicitor General from Sept.-Dec. 1868; and from Feb. 1874-Apr. following, when he became Attorney General. A bencher of Lincoln's Inn, and Counsel to the University of Cambridge, and a Magistrate for Surrey. A Conservative. Sat for Hereford from July 1865- Nov. 1868, when he was an unsuccessful candidate; MP for Mid-Surrey from Oct. 1870. Sat until he was appointed Lord Justice of Court of Appeal; Lord Justice of Appeal, 1876-1885. Died 13 Nov. 1888. [1875]

BAGGE, Sir William, Bart. 2 Albert Square, Victoria Square, London. Stradsett Hall, Market Downham, Norfolk. Carlton. Eld. s. of Sir Thomas Philip Bagge, Esq., of Stradsett Hall, Norfolk (whose family, originally Swedish, had held lands in that county since 1560), by Grace,

15

d. of Richard Salisbury, Esq., of Castle Park, Lancaster. B. at Stradsett Hall 1810; m. 1833 Frances, 4th d. of the late Sir Thomas Preston of Beeston Hall, Bart. Educ. at the Charterhouse and Balliol Coll., Oxford. A Magistrate and Dept.-Lieut. for Norfolk. Patron of 1 living. A Conservative; supported 'the Church of these realms as established at the Reformation'; voted for agricultural protection 1846, and in the minority of 53 who censured free trade, Nov. 1852. Unsuccessfully contested Norfolk Jan. 1835; sat for it from Aug. 1837-July 1857; re-elected July 1865. MP until his death 12 Feb. 1880. [1879]

BAGNALL, Charles. Sneaton Castle, Nr. Whitby. Conservative. S. of Thomas Bagnall, Esq., of Newberries Park, near Watford (who was High Sheriff of Staffordshire in 1863), by Mary, only d. of John North, Esq., of West Bromwich, Staffordshire. B. at West Bromwich, 1827; m. 1860, Harriet Curtis, 2nd d. of John Chapman, Esq., of Whitby. Educ. at King's Coll., London. An Ironmaster. A Magistrate for Staffordshire and for the North Riding of Yorkshire. A Conservative. Contested Walsall Apr. 1859. First elected for Whitby July 1865. Retired 1868. Contested seat again in Feb. 1874. Died 25 Feb. 1884. [1868]

BAGOT, Hon. William. 15 Dover Street, London. Pool Park, Denbighshire. Carlton. Eld. s. of Lord Bagot; b. at Blithfield House, Staffordshire 1811; m. 1851 Hon. Lucia, eld. d. of Baron Dover, and sister to 3rd Visct. Clifden. Appointed Lieut.-Col. of the Staffordshire Yeomanry Cavalry 1851. A Conservative, voted for agricultural protection, 1846, but against a repeal of the malt tax 1835. Sat for Denbighshire from 1835 until defeated in 1852. Col. commanding Staffordshire Yeomanry Cavalry 1854-74; succeeded father as 3rd Baron 12 Feb. 1856. Lord in Waiting 1866-68 and 1874-1880. Died 19 Jan. 1887. [1852]

BAGSHAW, John. 47 York Street, Portman Square, London. Cliff House, Dovercourt, Essex. Brooks's, and Reform. Eld. s. of John Bagshaw, Esq., a Banker of Coventry, by the d. of George Salmon, Esq., of Harbury, Warwickshire. B. 1784; m. Mary Anne, d. of John Henley, Esq., of London. Was educ. at Rugby. Formerly an East India Merchant, a Banker, and Head of the firm of Bagshaw and Co., of Calcutta, where he resided for many years. Was High-Steward of Harwich, a Magistrate for that bor., and for Essex; Director of the Northern and Eastern, and Eastern Counties Railways; Chairman of the Calcutta and Diamond Harbour Docks and Railway Company. A Liberal, in favour of the

ballot. Unsuccessfully contested Kidderminster in 1837, Harwich in 1841, Sudbury in 1832 and 1834. Sat for Sudbury from Jan. 1835 till July 1837; again unsuccessfully contested it, Mar. 1839; sat for Harwich from July 1847 till July 1852, when he was an unsuccessful candiate; re-elected June 1853, and sat until he retired in 1859. Died 20 Dec. 1861. [1858]

BAGSHAW, Robert John. The Terrace, Dovercourt New Town, Essex. Reform. Only s. of John Bagshaw, Esq., also member for Harwich, by Mary Ann, d. of John Henley, Esq., of London. B. 1803; m. Georgina, youngest d. of Richard Baker, Esq., of Barham House, Elstree, Hertfordshire. A retired East India Merchant. A Magistrate for Harwich, and a Dept.-Lieut. for Essex. Provincial Grand Master of Freemasons of Essex. A Liberal, in favour of an extension of the franchise, and the abolition of church-rates, and of vote by ballot; opposed to religious endowments by the state. Unsuccessfully contested Yarmouth July 1848. First elected for Harwich Dec. 1857. Sat until he retired in 1859. Sheriff of Essex 1873. Died 11 Aug. 1873. [1858]

BAGWELL, John. Marlfield, Clonmell, Tipperary. Eastgrove, Queenstown, Co. Cork. Reform. Kildare Street Club, Dublin. Eld. s. of Richard Bagwell, Esq., by Margaret, eld. d. of Richard Croker, Esq., of Ballinaguard. Nephew of Rt. Hon. Col. William Bagwell, MP. Muster-Master Gen. for Ireland. B. at Clogher, Co. Tyrone 1811; m. 1838 Hon. Elizabeth Frances, youngest d. of Hon. Francis Prittie, and sister of 3rd Lord Dunolley. Educ. at Winchester. A Magistrate and Dept.-Lieut. of Tipperary, High Sheriff for that Co. 1834. Lord of the Treasury from June 1859-July 1861. A Liberal. First returned for Clonmell Feb. 1857. Sat until defeated 1874. Died 2 Mar. 1883. [1873]

BAILEY, Crawshay. 16 New Street, Spring Gardens, London. Abaraman, near Pontyprydd, Glamorganshire. Nantyglo, Newport, Monmouthshire. Carlton, and Conservative. S. of John Bailey, Esq., who was descended from a family long settled in Yorkshire; uncle of Sir Joseph Bailey, Bart. B. at Wenham, Suffolk; m. Anne, d. of Joseph Moore, Esq., of Mitcham, Surrey (she died 1865). An Ironmaster in South Wales; a Dept.-Lieut. and Magistrate for Glamorganshire, and a Magistrate for Brecknockshire and Monmouthshire, of which last two he was Sheriff, in 1837 and 1850. Patron of 1 living. A Conservative, said he would 'uphold the Church and State, but at the same time with perfect freedom to civil and religious liberty'; would 'strenuously support the repeal of the malt and hop duties'; in favour of the

16

extension of the county franchise; voted against the ballot 1853. First elected for Monmouth district Apr. 1852. Sat until he retired in 1868. Died 9 Jan. 1872.   [1867]

BAILEY, Sir Joseph. 26 Belgrave Square, London. Glan Usk Park, Crickhowell. Langoed Castle, Brecknockshire. Carlton, Conservative, and Boodle's. S. of John Bailey, Esq., who was descended from a family long settled in Yorkshire. B. at Great Wenham Priory, Suffolk, 1783; m. 1st, 1810, d. of Joseph Latham, Esq., of Llangattock, Co. Brecon; 2ndly, 1830, d. of John Hopper, Esq., of Witton Castle, Durham. An Ironmaster of Brecknockshire and Monmouthshire. Was High Sheriff of Monmouthshire 1823; was a Magistrate for the Cos. of Brecon, Monmouth, Glamorgan, and Hereford, and a Dept.-Lieut. of Brecknockshire and Monmouthshire; Chairman of the Birkenhead Docks, and Vice-chairman of the Birkenhead Dock Company. Patron of 8 livings. A Conservative. Sat for Worcester from 1835 to 1847, when he was returned for Breconshire. MP until his death 20 Nov. 1858.   [1858]

BAILEY, Joseph. 26 Belgrave Square, London. Pen Myarth, Breconshire. Easton Court, Herefordshire. Carlton. S. of the member for Breconshire. B. 1812; m. in 1839, d. of W.C. Russell, Esq. A Dept.-Lieut. of Breconshire. Chairman of the Birkenhead, Lancashire and Cheshire Railway. Unsuccessfully contested the borough of Monmouth at the general elections in 1835 and 1837. Was shortly afterwards chosen for Sudbury in room of Sir James John Hamilton, Bart., who accepted the Chiltern Hundreds. A Conservative, noted for agricultural protection, 1846. First returned for Herefordshire 1837 and MP until his death in August 1850.   [1850]

BAILEY, Sir J.R. Continued in House after 1885: full entry in Volume II.

BAILLIE, Charles. A Conservative. First returned for Linlithgowshire 5 Feb. 1859 but shortly afterwards appointed Judge of the Court of Session in Scotland with courtesy title of Lord Jerviswood. Died 23 July 1879.

BAILLIE, Rt. Hon. Henry James. Elsenham Hall, Bishop's Stortford. Redcastle, Killearnan, Inverness-shire. Carlton, and Travellers'. Only s. of Col. Hugh Baillie, of Redcastle and Tarradale, Ross-shire, by the d. of the Rev. Henry Reynett, D.D. B. 1804; m. 1st, 1840, Hon. Philippa, d. of 6th Visct. Strangford (she died 1854); 2ndly, 1857, Clarissa, eld. d. of George Rush, Esq., of Elsenham Hall, Essex, and Farthinghoe Lodge,

Northamptonshire. Was one of the joint secretaries to the Board of Control, from Mar. till Dec. 1852. A Conservative, in favour of a moderate Parliamentary Reform. Was first elected for Inverness-shire, 1840. Sat until he retired in 1868. Died 16 Dec. 1885.   [1867]

BAILLIE, Col. Hugh Duncan. 34 Mortimer Street, London. Tarradale, Ross-shire. Carlton, and Athenaeum. S. of a former member for Bristol, and bro. of former members for Inverness and Bristol. B. 1777; m. 1st, d. of Rev. Reynett, D.D., 2ndly 1821, d. of Thomas Smith, Esq., of Castleton. A Col. in the army, Lord-Lieut. and Sheriff Principal of Ross-shire. A Liberal-Conservative, and 'has been so throughout.' Gave no pledge but 'to do his duty honestly.' Voted for free trade. Sat for Rye in the Parliament of 1830, and for Honiton from 1834 until he retired 1847. Died 21 June 1866.   [1847]

BAILLIE, Lieut.-Col. J. A Conservative. Sat for Inverness from Dec. 1832 until his death 17 May 1833.   [1833]

BAILLIE, James Evan. 1 Seymore Place, Curzon Street, London. A Banker at Bristol, and a West India Proprietor. Of Whig principles. Voted for the Reform Bill, was a supporter of the principle of free trade, a friend to the colonial interest, and opposed to all restrictions on the importation of corn. Sat for Bristol from 1830 until defeated Jan. 1835. Died 28 June 1835.   [1833]

BAILLIE,   William.   Polkemmet, Linlithgowshire. Carlton. New Club, Edinburgh. Eld. s. of Sir William Baillie, Bart., of Polkemmet, Linlithgowshire, by the d. of James Dennistoun, Esq. B. at Edinburgh 1816; educ. at Eton, and Christ Church, Oxford. A Conservative, voted for agricultural protection 1846. First returned for Linlithgowshire Aug. 1845, without opposition. Retired at 1847 general election. Capt. Royal Midlothian Yeoman Cavalry 1852-72. Succeeded as 2nd Bart. in 1854. Died 21 July 1890. [1847]

BAINBRIDGE, Edward Thomas. 10 Park Place, St. James's, London. A Banker in London, having connections more extensive than any other gentleman with Irish commercial and banking houses. A Dept.-Lieut. of Somerset. An East-India Proprietor. A Reformer, in favour of the ballot. First sat for Taunton in 1830. Sat until he accepted Chiltern Hundreds, Feb. 1842. Died 30 Sept. 1872.   [1841]

BAINE, Walter. 45 Pall Mall, London. Greenock. Reform. S. of Robert Baine, Esq., of Greenock. B. at Greenock 1781. Unmarried. A

Merchant. A Liberal. 'A supporter of Free Trade, and opposed to the present Corn and Game Laws.' A member of the Free Trade Club. First elected for Greenock 1845, when he was returned in opposition to Mr. Dunlop, who was against the increased grant to Maynooth. Retired 1847.
[1847]

BAINES, Edward, sen. 2 Tanfield Court, Temple, London. Reform. B. 1774. Editor and Proprietor of the *Leeds Mercury* from 1801. Has written a *History of Lancashire* and other works. A Reformer; in favour of the ballot, shorter parliaments, free-trade, the repeal of the corn laws, an equality of civil rights for dissenters and their exemption from Church Rates. Sat for Leeds from Feb. 1834, when he was elected in the place of J.B. Macaulay, Esq., appointed a member of the Council of India. Sat until he retired 1841 through ill health. Died 3 Aug. 1848. [1838]

BAINES, Edward, jun. 6 Belgrave Mansions, Grosvenor Gardens, London. Headingley Lodge, Leeds. Reform. 2nd s. of Edward Baines, Esq., who represented Leeds for many years, by Charlotte, d. of Matthew Talbot, Esq., author of *Analysis of the Bible*. B. at Leeds 1800; m. 1829, d. of Thomas Blackburn, Esq., of Liverpool. Educ. at the Protestant Dissenters' Grammar School, Manchester. Was 40 years proprietor of the *Leeds Mercury* (at first in conjunction with his father). For 33 years was President of the Yorkshire Union of Mechanics Institutes. A Magistrate and Dept.-Lieut. for the West Riding of Yorkshire. Author of *The History of the Cotton Manufacturer, Life of Edward Baines, Visit to the Vaudois of Piedmont, The Woollen Manufacture of England*, etc. A Liberal, in favour of the policy of non-intervention in Continental Wars. First elected for Leeds, Apr. 1859. Sat until defeated 1874. Knighted 16 Dec. 1880. Died 2 Mar. 1890. [1873]

BAINES, Right Hon. Matthew Talbot. 13 Queen Square, St. James's Park, London. Dalton Square, Lancaster. Reform and Brooks's. Eld. s. of Edward Baines, Esq., former MP for Leeds, by the d. of Matthew Talbot, Esq. B. at Leeds 1799; m. 1833, Anne, only d. of L. Threlfall, Esq., of Lancaster. Educ. at Richmond School, Yorkshire, and at Cambridge; was Senior Optime in 1820, Scholar of Trinity College, Cambridge, Dr. Hooper's Declamation Prizeman, and King William III's Declamation Prizeman. Called to the bar in 1825, at the Inner Temple, of which he was a bencher; made a Queen's Counsel in 1841. Was Recorder of Hull from 1837 till 1847. Was President of the Poor Law Board from Jan. 1849, to Mar. 1852, and from Dec. 1852 till Aug. 1855. Appointed Chancellor of the Duchy of Lancaster

Dec. 1855, salary £2000. Was a Magistrate for Lancashire and for the West Riding of Yorkshire, a Dept.-Lieut. for the latter, and Chairman of the General Annual Quarter Sessions for Lancashire. A Liberal, in favour of extension of the suffrage, short parliaments, and Church reform; voted against the ballot 1853. Sat for Hull from 1847 till 1852, when he was elected for Leeds. Sat until he retired in 1859. Died 22 Jan. 1860. [1858]

BAIRD, James. Gartsherrie House, Lanarkshire. Carlton. S. of Alexander Baird, Esq., of Lockwood, and bro. of William Baird, Esq., who sat for Falkirk from 1841-1846. B. at Old Monkland, Lanarkshire 1803; m. 1st, 1852, Charlotte, d. of Robert Lockhard, Esq., of Castlehill, Edinburgh; 2ndly, 1859, Isabella Agnes, d. of Admiral James Hay. An Ironmaster at the Gartsherrie Works, Nr. Airdrie. Founded Baird Trust in connection with the Church of Scotland at a cost of nearly £500,000 in 1873. A Moderate Conservative, in favour of a revision of the excise laws. First returned for Falkirk dist. Jan. 1851, and sat until he retired in 1857. Died 20 June 1876. [1857]

BAIRD, William. B. 1796, the s. of Alex. Baird, Esq., of Lockwood. M.1840. Was an Iron-Master. A Conservative. Sat for the district of Falkirk from 1841 until he accepted Chiltern Hundreds in 1846. Died 8 Mar. 1864. [1845]

BAKER, Edward. Old Cavendish Street, The Alfred, Salisbury. Boodle's, Crockford's, Travellers' and Arthur's. Lieut.-Col. in the Royal Wiltshire Yeomanry and Aide-de-Camp to the Queen. A Conservative. Sat for Wilton 6 Jan. 1823-1830, and from 1837 until he retired 1841. Died 24 Feb. 1862. [1838]

BAKER, Richard Baker Wingfield. 2 Lowndes Square, London. Orsett Hall, Romford, Essex. Boodle's and University. B. in London 1801, the 3rd s. of William Wingfield-Baker, Esq., Q.C., MP for Bodmin 1813, and Master in Chancery, by his 1st wife, Lady Charlotte Mary, d. of Henry, 1st Earl Digby. M. 1837, Margaret Maria, d. of Col. Thomas Hanmer and sister of Sir John Hanmer, Bart. Educ. at Rugby and at Christ Church, Oxford where he graduated B.A. 1827. Assumed in 1859 the additional name Baker, which his father had likewise assumed. Was Sec. to Lord Chancellor Cottenham. A Magistrate and Dept.-Lieut. for Essex. Patron of 1 living. A Liberal, who favoured the repeal of reduction of the malt tax, and 'direct taxation generally, but not the income tax.' Voted for the disestablishment of the Irish Church 1869. Sat for S. Essex (as Mr. Wingfield) Apr. 1857-Apr. 1859, and from Dec.1868-1874, when he was defeated. Died 15 Mar. 1880. [1873]

BALDOCK, Edward Holmes. 31 Grosvenor Place, London. Conservative, and Carlton. B.1812; m. 1852, Elizabeth Mary, eld. d. of Sir Andrew Vincent Corbet (2nd Bart.), of Acton Reynald, Shropshire. Appointed a Dept.-Lieut. of Middlesex 1852. A Conservative, opposed to the grant to Maynooth, and in favour of a revision of the Income Tax. First returned for Shrewsbury in 1847. Sat until he retired 1857. Died 15 Aug. 1875. [1857]

BALDWIN, Charles Barry. Bovine, King's Co. Guerston and Rockview, Devon. Carlton and Union. Eld. s. of Charles Baldwin, Esq., Lieut.-Col. of the King's Co. Militia; descended from Provost Baldwin, Trinity Coll., Dublin; m.d. of W. Boyd, Esq., formerly MP for Lymington. A Barrister; was Secretary, and afterwards sole Commissioner, to the French Claim Commission; resigned 1830. A Conservative. Was elected for Totnes in two Parliaments before the Reform Act; sat for it from 1839 until defeated in 1852. Died 13 Apr. 1859. [1852]

BALDWIN, Enoch. Grosvenor Hotel, Pimlico. The Mount, Stourport. S. of Enoch Baldwin, Ironfounder of Bewdley. B. at Stourport 1822; m. 1st, 1849, Elizabeth Langford, d. of H. Tildesley, of Willenhall, Staffordshire; 2ndly, 1876, Emily Lydia, d. of Rev. G. F. Driver, Wesleyan Minister, of Stourport. In 1839 became a member of the firm of Messrs. Baldwin, Son & Co., Iron-founders, Stourport. A Liberal, and in favour of still further relief being afforded to the agricultural interest, also of the assimilation of the borough and county franchise. Sat for Bewdley from July 1880 until he retired 1885. [1885]

BALDWIN, Herbert, M.D. Camden Place, Cork. Clarence. Dr. Baldwin was for many years a practising Physician in Cork; was first cousin to Mr. O'Connell, but possessed much influence amongst his fellow citizens independently of any extraneous support. M. 1st, Miss Dunne; 2ndly Miss Herrick. A Repealer, voted for the abolition of tithes, triennial Parliaments, vote by ballot, an extension of the franchise, and the removal of the taxes on knowledge. Sat for Cork from 1832. Was not returned in 1835, but succeeded in regaining his seat on petition. Retired 1837. [1837]

BALFOUR, Rt. Hon. A.J. Continued in House after 1885: full entry in Volume II.

BALFOUR, Sir G. Continued in House after 1885: full entry in Volume II.

BALFOUR, James. 3 Grosvenor Square, London. Whittingham House, Dunbar. M. in 1815, Eleanor d. of the Earl of Lauderdale. An East India Proprietor, and formerly Civil Servant to the Company at Madras, and Agent. Of Conservative principles. Sat for the Pittenween Crail, etc. district of burghs in the Parliaments of 1826 and 1830; from 1832 he sat for Haddingtonshire until he retired in 1835. Died 19 Apr. 1845. [1833]

BALFOUR, Rt. Hon. J.B. Continued in House after 1885: full entry in Volume II.

BALFOUR, James Maitland. Whittingham, Haddingtonshire. S. of James Balfour, Esq., and grandson maternally of the 8th Earl of Lauderdale. B. 1820; m. 1843, Lady Blanche, d. of 2nd Marq. of Salisbury. Appointed a Dept.-Lieut. of Haddington 1846. A Conservative, voted for agricultural protection 1846. First returned for the Haddington district in 1841. Sat until he retired 1847. Died 23 Feb. 1856. [1847]

BALFOUR, J.S. Continued in House after 1885: full entry in Volume II.

BALFOUR, Thomas F.R.S. 18 Curzon Street, Mayfair, London. 9 Doune Terrace, Edinburgh, Cliffdale, Orkney. S. of Capt. Balfour, R.N. of Elwick, Orkney. B. 1810. A Scotch Advocate. Director of the Highland Society. A Conservative. Sat for Orkney and Shetland from Feb. 1835 until he retired in Aug. 1837. [1836]

BALL, Edward. 41 South Audley Street, London. Burwell, near Newmarket. S. of Richard Ball Esq. by Elizabeth, d. of — Thwaites, Esq. B. at Hastings, 1793; m. d. of Salisbury Dunn, Esq. Educ. at Bromley. Appointed Dept.-Lieut. of Cambridge 1852. A Conservative opposed to the Maynooth grant; 'An earnest supporter of education based upon the Word of God'; voted for the abolition of church-rates, 1857. First returned for Cambridgeshire in July 1852. Accepted Chiltern Hundreds Jan. 1863. Died 9 Nov. 1865. [1862]

BALL, John. 13 Gate Street, Lincoln's Inn Fields, London. 85 St. Stephen's Green, Dublin. Oxford & Cambridge, and Stafford St. S. of the Rt. Hon. Nicholas Ball, Justice of the Court of Common Pleas in Ireland, by the d. of Thomas Sherlock Esq., of Butlers Town, Co. Killkenny. B. in Dublin 1818; m. 1856, Elize, d. of Count Parolini, of Bassano, in Venetian Lombardy. Educ. at Oscott Coll., and at Christ's Coll., Cambridge. Was called to the bar in Ireland 1843, but did not practise; held the office of a Commissioner of Poor Laws for some years, but resigned previous to his election for Carlow. Appointed Under Secretary of State for the Colonies Feb. 1855, salary £1,500. Author of various essays on mathematics and natural history, and of a political pamphlet entitled *What is to be done for Ireland*. A Liberal, in favour of vote by ballot and of 'complete equality for all religious denominations.' Was an unsuccessful candidate for Sligo bor. in July 1848; first returned for Carlow Co. in July 1852. Retired 1857. Contested Sligo Co. Apt. 1857 and Limerick Feb. 1858. Author of *The Alpine Guide* (1863-68); F.R.S. 1868. Died 21 Oct. 1889. [1857]

BALL, Rt. Hon. John Thomas, Q.C. 3 Merrion Square South, Dublin. Merton St. Doulough's, Nr. Dublin. Carlton. Eld. s. of Maj. Benjamin Marcus Ball, formerly of the 40th Foot. B. in Dublin 1815; m. Catherine, d. of the Rev. Charles R. Elrington, Fellow of, and Professor of Divinity in the University of Dublin. Educ. at Trinity Coll., Dublin, of which he was LL.D., created honorary D.C.L. at Oxford 1870. Was called to the bar in Ireland, 1840. Appointed a Queen's Counsel there 1854, and made Queen's Advocate 1865. Had been Judge of the Consistorial Court in Ireland. A Bencher of King's Inns, Dublin, also Vicar Gen. of the Province of Armagh. Was successively Solicitor Gen. and Attorney Gen. for Ireland for a few weeks in Nov. and Dec. 1868; re-appointed Attorney Gen. for Ireland Feb. 1874. A Liberal-Conservative and opposed to the 'Severance of Church from State.' Unsuccessfully contested the University of Dublin July 1865; first elected Dec. 1868. Sat until appointed Lord Chancellor of Ireland 1 Jan. 1875 to 1880. Died 17 Mar. 1898. [1874]

BALL, Nicholas, 85 Stephens Green, Dublin, Reform. A Sergeant-at-Law in Ireland. A Whig. Returned for Clonmel 20 Feb. 1836 on the death of Dominich Ronayne, Esq. Appointed Attorney-General for Ireland June? 1838. Sat until he retired in 1839 on appointment to Irish Bench. Died 19 Jan. 1865. [1838]

BANKES, Rt. Hon. George. 5 Old Palace Yard, London. Studland Manor, Wareham, Dorset. East Sheen, Surrey. Carlton, and United University. 2nd. s. of Henry Bankes, Esq., of Kingston Hall, Dorset, (MP for nearly 50 years), by the d. of William Woodley, Esq., Governor of the Leeward Islands. M. Georgina Charlotte, d. and heir of Sir Charles E. Nugent, Admiral of the Fleet. Called to the bar at Lincoln's Inn 1813. Was appointed a Commissioner of Bankrupts in 1822 and afterwards Cursitor-Baron of the Exchequer. Chairman of the Dorsetshire Sessions and Recorder of Weymouth. Was Sec. to the Board of Control from May 1829-Feb. 1830, and Judge Advocate General from Mar.-Dec. 1852. A Conservative; voted for inquiry into Maynooth 1853. Sat for Corfe Castle from 1816-32 and unsuccessfully contested University of Cambridge in 1829, and Weymouth Dec. 1832. Sat for Dorsetshire from 1841 until his death 6 July 1856. [1856]

BANKES, William John. 5 Old Palace Yard, London. Soughton Hall, near Northop, Flintshire. S. of Henry Bankes, Esq., Patron of the disfranchised borough of Corfe Castle, bro. of G. Bankes, Esq. the Cursitor-Baron of the Exchequer, grands. of the Earl of Eldon, and cousin of Lord Encombe. A Conservative, sat for Marlborough from 1829 to 1831, when he was not returned; also for the University of Cambridge for a few years of the Parliament of 1826. Sat for Dorsetshire from 1832 until he retired in 1834. Died 15 Apr. 1855. [1833]

BANNERMAN, Alex. 4 Berkeley Street, London. Reform. S. of T. Bannerman, Esq. B. 1783; m. Miss Guthrie. A Merchant, Shipowner, and Banker in Aberdeen. Of Whig principles. Sat for Aberdeen from 1832 until he retired in 1847. Unsuccessfully contested Elgin 6 Aug. 1847. A Commissioner of Greenwich Hospital. Knighted 1851, on appointment as Governor of Prince of Wales Island. Transferred in 1854 to Bahamas as Governor and Commander-in-Cihief. Held Chief Command of the colony of Newfoundland 1857-63. Died 1864. [1847]

BANNERMAN, Rt. Hon. H. Campbell. See CAMPBELL-BANNERMAN, Rt. Hon. H. Continued in House after 1885: full entry in Volume II.

BARBOUR, J. Doherty. A Liberal. returned for Lisburn 23 Feb. 1863, but unseated on petition.

BARCLAY, Alexander Charles. 25 Bolton Street, London. Brooks's, Boodle's, and Oxford & Cambridge. S. of David Barclay, Esq., of Eastwick Park, Leatherhead (formerly MP for Falmouth and Sunderland), by Maria Dorothea, d. of Sir Hedworth Williamson, Bart. B. at Long Ditton, Surrey, 1823. Educ. at Harrow and at Trinity Coll., Cambridge. A Liberal. Unsuccessfully contested Taunton Aug. 1859: first elected there July 1865. Sat until he retired 1880. Died 10 Jan. 1893. [1880]

BARCLAY, Charles. 43 Grosvenor Place, London. Bury Hill, Surrey, Henstrad House, Norfolk. A Brewer. Formerly belonged to the Society of Quakers. A Conservative. Was willing to substitute a property tax for the malt duty. Sat for Southwark from 1815 to 1818, and for Dundalk from 1826 to 1830. First sat for Surrey W. in 1835. Retired 1837. [1836]

BARCLAY, David. 8 Belgrave Square, London. Eastwich Park, Surrey. B. 1784, s. of Robert Barclay, Esq., of Bury Hill. M. 1818, Maria Dorothea, eld. sister of Sir Hedworth Williamson, Bart. (she died 1846). A Merchant and a Liberal. Sat for Penryn 1826. Unsuccessfully contested Sunderland in 1832 and 1833, but was returned in Jan. 1835; defeated July/Aug. 1837. Re-elected June 1841 and sat until he accepted Chiltern Hundreds Dec. 1847. Died 1 July 1861. [1847 2nd ed.]

BARCLAY, J.W. Continued in House after 1885: full entry in Volume II.

BARHAM, John. 26 Queen Anne Street, London. Stockbridge House, Hampshire. Appleby Castle, Westmoreland. S. of Joseph Foster Barham, Esq., and Charlotte, d. of Charles 9th Earl of Thanet; m. 1834, Catherine, eld. d. of the Earl of Verulam. Of Whig principles, in favour of shorter Parliaments. Unsuccessfully contested Westmoreland in 1832. Sat for Stockbridge in 1831, and for Kendal from the death of James Brougham, Esq., in 1834. Retired 1837. [1837]

BARING, Rt. Hon. Alex. The Grange, Hampshire. Shoreham, Sevenoaks, Kent. 82 Piccadilly, London. Bro. of Sir Thomas Baring, Bart; m. Anne, eld. d. of William Bingham, Esq., of Philadelphia. An East India Proprietor; formerly a Merchant. Patron of 7 livings; a Trustee of the British Museum. President of the Board of Trade from Dec. 1834. Sat for Taunton from 1812-1820; for his own (before it was disenfranchised) borough of Callington from 1820-31; in the Parliament of 1831, he sat for Thetford of which he was a patron. Sat for Essex N. from 1832 to Apr. 1835 when created Baron Ashburton. Died 12 May 1848. [1835]

BARING, Hon. Alexander Hugh, 58 Lowndes Square, London. Buckenham, Brandon, Norfolk. B. in London 1835, the eld. s. of Lord Ashburton, by the d. of the Duke of Bassano (in France). M. 1863, Hon. Leonora Caroline, 2nd d. of 9th Lord Digby. Educ. at Harrow and at Christ Church, Oxford and graduated B.A. 1857. A Liberal-Conservative. First elected for Thetford in Dec. 1857, on the resignation of his father. Sat until he accepted Chiltern Hundreds in Nov. 1867. Succeeded as 4th Baron Ashburton in Sept. 1868. Died 18 July 1899. [1867]

BARING, Hon. Francis, 15 Pall Mall, London. Carlton, and Travellers'. 2nd s. of 1st Lord Ashburton by the eld. d. of William Bingham, Esq., of Philadelphia. B. 1800; m. 1833, Madlle Claire Hortense, d. of the Duke of Bassano (in France). A Liberal-Conservative; gave frequent support to Lord Palmerston's government. Voted against the repeal of the malt tax in 1835. Represented Thetford from 1832-1841; again elected without opposition Aug. 1848. Sat until he accepted Chiltern Hundreds Nov. 1857. Succeeded bro. as 3rd Baron Ashburton Mar. 1864. Died 6 Sept. 1868. [1857 2nd ed.]

BARING, Rt. Hon. Sir Francis Thornhill, Bart. 5 Belgrave Square, London. Manor House, Lee, Kent. Athenaeum, Brooks's, United University, and Reform. S. of Sir Thomas Baring (2nd Bart.), by the d. of Charles Sealy, Esq., of Calcutta. B. 1796; m. 1st, 1825, d. of Sir G. Grey, Bart, 2ndly 1841, d. of 1st Earl of Effingham. Educ. at Eton, and at Christ Church, Oxford, where he obtained a double first class 1817, and graduated M.A. 1821. Called to the bar at Lincoln's Inn 1823. Was a Lord of the Treasury from 1830-June 1834; one of the joint secretaries of the Treasury from June-Nov. 1834, and from Apr. 1835-1839; was Chancellor of the Exchequer from 1839-1841, and 1st Lord of the Admiralty from Jan. 1849-Mar. 1852. A Liberal, voted against the ballot 1853. Sat for Portsmouth from 1826 until he retired in 1865. Created Baron Northbrook Jan. 1866. Died 6 Sept. 1866. [1865]

BARING, Henry Bingham. 36 Wilton Place, London. Travellers', Brooks's, and Athenaeum. Eld. s. of Henry Baring, Esq., by his wife, 2nd d. of William Bingham, Esq., of Philadelphia. B. 1804; m. 1st, 1827, Lady Augusta, 5th d. of the 6th Earl of Cardigan (she died Jan. 1853); 2ndly, 1854, Mademoiselle Marie de Martinoff. Educ. at Christ Church, Oxford, graduated B.A. 1825. Was a Lord of the Treasury from Sept. 1841 till July 1846. A Liberal-Conservative, voted against Lord Russell's Reform Bill, 1866. Sat for Callington in the Parliament of 1831. Sat for Marlborough from 1832 until he retired in 1868. Died 26 Apr. 1869. [1867]

BARING, Thomas. 41 Upper Grosvenor Street, London. Norman Court, Winchester, Hampshire. Carlton, and Travellers'. 2nd. s. of Sir Thomas Baring (2nd Bart.), and nephew of 1st Lord Ashburton. B. 1800. A Dept.-Lieut. of London. A Conservative, 'paired' against the disestablishment and disendowment of the Irish Church 1869. Returned for Yarmouth Jan. 1835; defeated at the 1837 gen. election. Contested Yarmouth again in Aug. 1838 and 1841. Contested London

21

in 1843. Sat for Huntingdon from Apr. 1844. MP until his death 18 Nov. 1873.   [1873]

BARING, T.C. Continued in House after 1885: full entry in Volume II.

BARING, Hon. Thomas George. B. 1826, the eld. s. of Rt. Hon. Sir Francis Thornhill Baring, Bart., by his 1st wife, Jane, youngest d. of Sir George Grey, Bart. M. 1848, Elizabeth Harriet, 3rd d. of Henry Charles Sturt, Esq., of Critchell, Dorset. Educ. at Christ Church, Oxford, where he was 2nd class in classics 1846. Appointed Capt. Hampshire Yeomanry Cavalry 1854. Private Sec. to Mr. Labouchere at the Board of Trade, to Sir George Grey at the Home Office, to Sir Charles Wood at the India Board, and at the Admiralty. A Lord of the Admiralty May 1857-Mar.1858, Parliamentary Under-Sec. of State for India June 1859-Jan. 1861 and Aug. 1861-Apr. 1864. Under-Sec. of State for War Jan. 1861-July 1861 and 1868-72, and Under-Sec. for the Home Department, Salary £1,500. First Lord of the Admiralty 1880-5. A Liberal, favoured an extension of the suffrage. Unsuccessful at Penryn July 1852, but returned there in Apr. 1857, until he succeeded as 2nd Baron Northbrook 1866. Viceroy of India 1872-76. Advanced to Earldom June 1876. Died 15 Nov. 1904.   [1865 2nd ed.]

BARING, Visct. Continued in House after 1885: full entry in Volume II.

BARING, Rt. Hon. William Bingham. 12 Stanhope Street, London. Carlton, and Athenaeum. Eld. s. of Lord Ashburton, and a nephew of Sir Thomas Baring, Bart. B. 1799; m. in 1823, Harriet, d. of the 6th Earl of Sandwich. A Merchant. Was Paymaster-general of the Forces from Feb. 1845 till July 1846. Was one of the Secretaries to the Board of Controul. A Conservative, voted for the admission of Dissenters to the Universities, and also for free trade; in 1832, displaced Mr. Buller East, a Conservative; sat for Thetford in the Parliament of 1826, for Callington in that of 1830, for Winchester in 1832 and 1835, and for Staffordshire N. from 1837 till 1841, when he was again returned for Thetford. Sat until he succeeded father as 2nd Baron in May 1848. Died 23 Mar. 1864.   [1847 2nd ed.]

BARKLY, Henry. 50 Eaton Place, London. Sparrows Herne, Hertfordshire, Wyndham, and Carlton. Only s. of Aeneas Barkly Esq., (of Monteagle, Ross-shire) an eminent West India Merchant in London. Descended from a junior branch of the ancient family of Berkeley of Mathers. B. in London 1815; m. in 1840 Elizabeth Helen, 2nd. d. of J.F. Trinnis, Esq., of Hiefield House, Hertfordshire. A West India proprietor. Of 'Liberal-Conservative' principles, and 'a supporter of Sir R. Peel's commercial policy.' First elected for Leominster in 1845, when he was returned without a contest. Sat until appointed Governor of British Guiana 12 Dec. 1848; K.C.B. 1853; Governor of Jamaica, Mauritius and Cape of Good Hope in subsequent career; F.R.S. 1864. Died 20 Oct. 1895. [1847 2nd ed.]

BARNARD, Edward George. Deptford Green, London. Gosfield Hall, Essex. Reform. A Shipbuilder and patron of 1 living. In favour of the ballot, triennial Parliaments and repeal of the assessed taxes, etc. Sat for Greenwich from 1832 until his death on 14 June 1851.   [1851]

BARNARD, Thomas. Bedford. Cople, Nr. Bedford. S. of Thomas Barnard, Esq., of Bedford, Banker. B. at Bedford 1830. Unmarried. Educ. at the Bedford Grammar School. A Banker at Bedford. A Liberal, in favour of Lord Palmerston's foreign policy, 'extension of the franchise, total abolition of church-rates, a large and liberal scheme of education and a comprehensive plan of legal reform.' First returned for Bedford bor. Mar. 1857. Defeated in 1859.   [1858]

BARNE, Lieut.-Col. Frederick St. John Newdigate. Sotterley Park, Wangford, Suffolk. Arthur's, Guards', and Carlton. Eld. s. of Frederick Barne, Esq., of Sotterley Park, Suffolk (who sat for Dunwich from 1829 to 1832), by Mary Anne Elizabeth, eld d. of Sir John Courtenay Honywood, Bart. B. at Sotterley 1841; m. 1871, Lady Constance Adelaide, 5th d. of the 5th Marq. of Hertford. Was educ. at Eton. Entered the army as Ensign and Lieut. Scots Fusilier Guards 1859, and retired as Lieut.-Col. 1872. A Conservative. Sat for East Suffolk from Feb. 1876 until he retired in 1885. Sheriff of Suffolk 1892. Died 25 Jan. 1898.   [1885]

BARNEBY, John. 34 Portman Square, London. Brockhampton House, Herefordshire. Carlton, United Univ., Boodle's and Arthur's. B. Nov. 1799; m. 1838 eld. d. of Henry Elwes, Esq., of Colesborne, Gloucestershire. Chairman of the Herefordshire Quarter Sessions. A Conservative and sat for Droitwich in 1835. Patron of 1 living. Sat for Worcestershire. E. from 1837 until his death in Dec. 1846.   [1845]

BARNES, A. Continued in House after 1885: full entry in Volume II.

BARNES, Lieut.-Gen. Sir Edward. A Tory. Returned for Sudbury 25 July 1834. Defeated in

22

1835. Re-elected July 1837. MP until his death Feb.? 1839. [1837]

BARNES, Thomas. The Quinta, near Chirk. Limefields, Nr. Bolton. S. of James Rothwell Barnes, Esq., a Magistrate for Lancashire. B. at Farnworth, near Bolton, 1813; married. A Merchant and Manufacturer of cotton fabrics. A Dept.-Lieut. of Lancashire. A Liberal, in favour of vote by ballot, and triennial parliaments; opposed to all grants of public money to religious bodies. Sat for Bolton from July 1852 till Apr. 1857, when he was an unsuccessful candidate; re-elected Feb. 1861, and sat until defeated in 1868. Contested Bury 30 Apr. 1859. [1867]

BARNETT, Charles James. 4 Dorset Square, London. A Banker of London. He voted for the Reform Act; was an advocate of Church reform, of the repeal of the septennial Act, of vote by ballot, and of the immediate abolition of slavery. Superseded Mr. Alderman Winchester, who had voted against the Reform Bill. First sat for Maidstone in 1831, and sat until defeated in 1835. Died 31 Dec. 1882. [1833]

BARNETT, E.W. A Conservative. Returned for Dover at a by-election 23 Sept. 1873. Retired in 1874.

BARNETT, Henry. 15 Halkin Street, London. Beckett House, Faringdon, Berkshire. Travellers'. S. of George Henry Barnett, Esq., of Glympton Park, by Elizabeth, only sister of Visct. Stratford de Redcliffe. B. in London 1815; m. 1838, d. of John Stratton, Esq., of Chesterton, Oxfordshire. Educ. at Eton and at Christ Church, Oxford. A Banker in London. A Magistrate and Dept. Lieut. for Oxfordshire. A Maj. Oxfordshire Yeomanry Cavalry. A moderate Conservative. First elected for Woodstock July 1865. Sat until he retired 1874. Died 5 May 1896. [1873]

BARRAN, J. Continued in House after 1885: full entry in Volume II.

BARRINGTON, Hon. Capt. George. Greathan, Durham. 2nd. s. of Viscount Barrington, an Irish peer, and Prebendary of Durham and Rector of Sedgefield. Captain Barrington was b. in 1794, and m. in 1827 Caroline, 3rd d. of Earl Grey. A Lord of the Admiralty, and as such a Member of the Government. Returned for Sunderland in 1832. Accepted Chiltern Hundreds 1833. [1833]

BARRINGTON, Visct., sen. 20 Cavendish Square, London. Beckett, Berkshire. Travellers'. A Peer of Ireland. B. 1793; m. 1823, the Hon. Jane Elizabeth, 4th d. of 1st Lord Ravensworth

(she was for some years a lady of the bedchamber to the Queen Dowager). Educ. at Christ Church, Oxford, graduated B.A. 1814. A Conservative, voted for inquiry into Maynooth Coll. 1853. Sat for Berkshire from 1837. Retired 1857. Died 9 Feb. 1867. [1857]

BARRINGTON, Rt. Hon Visct., jun. 19 Hertford Street, London. Beckett House, Shrivenham, Berkshire. Carlton and Travellers'. An Irish Peer. Eld. s. of the 6th Visct. Barrington, by the Hon. Jane Elizabeth, 4th d. of 1st Lord Ravensworh. B. in Lower Brook Street, London 1824; m. 1846, only d. of John Morritt, Esq., of Rokeby Park. Appointed Vice-Chamberlain of the Queen's Household Feb. 1874. Became Lieut. Wiltshire Yeomanry Cavalry 1844. A Dept.-Lieut. of Berkshire 1852. Was some time Private Sec. to the Earl of Derby. A Conservative, in favour of the eventual repeal of the malt tax. Unsuccessfully contested Buckingham May 1859 and Durham N. 1865: first elected for Eye July 1866. Sat until he retired 1880. Created Baron Shute of Beckett 17 Apr. 1880. Died 6 Nov. 1886. [1880]

BARRON, Sir Henry Winston, Bart. 2 Halkin Street, Belgrave Square, London. Barroncourt, Waterford. Glenanna, Dungarvan, Co. Waterford. S. of Pierce Barron, Esq., of Ballyneil, Co. Waterford, by the only d. of Henry Winston, Esq., of Fethard. B. at Ballymil, Co. Waterford, 1795; m. 1st, 1822, Anna Leigh Guy, only d. of Sir Gregory Page Turner, Bart. (she died 1852); 2ndly, 1863, Augusta Anne, youngest d. of Lord Charles Somerset. A Magistrate and Dept.-Lieut. for the city and Co. of Waterford. Author of *Notes on Education in Holland and Germany*, and works on Italy. A Liberal. Sat for Waterford city from 1832 till 1841, when he was an unsuccessful candidate, but was seated on petition; lost his seat at the gen. election in 1847; again sat from Feb. 1848 till July 1852; re-elected July 1865. Defeated in 1868; returned for same seat at 1869 by-election but the result was declared void. Died 19 Apr. 1872. [1867]

BARROW William Hodgson. 35 Westbourne Terrace, London. Southwell, Nottinghamshire. Carlton. 2nd s. of Rev. Richard Barrow, by the d. of George Hodgkinson, Esq., and nephew of Dr. Barrow, Archdeacon of Nottingham. B. at Southwell, Nottinghamshire 1784. Practised as an Attorney from 1806-33. A Magistrate for Nottinghamshire from 1837 and Dept.-Lieut. from 1854. A Conservative. First returned for Nottinghamshire S. Feb. 1851. Sat until he retired 1874. Died 29 Jan. 1876. [1873]

BARRY, Arthur Hugh Smith-. Fota Island, Co. Cork. Eld. s. of James Hugh Smith-Barry, Esq., of Fota Island, Co. Cork, and Marbury Hall, Cheshire, who was High Sheriff of Cheshire 1846, by Eliza, eld. d. of Shallcross Jacson, Esq., of Newton Bank, Co. Chester. B. 1843; m. 1868, Lady Mary Frances, d. of the 3rd Earl of Dunraven. A Liberal. Sat for Cork Co. from Feb. 1867 until he retired 1874. [1873]

BARRY, Charles Robert. 3 Fitzwilliam Square East, Dublin. Reform. S. of James Barry, Esq., of Limerick, Solicitor, by Ellen, d. of John Purcell, Esq. B. at Limerick, 1824; m. 1855, Kate, 3rd d. of John Fitzgerald, Esq., of Dublin. Educ. at Dalton's School, Limerick, Middleton Foundation School, Co. Cork, and Trinity Coll., Dublin. Called to the bar in Ireland 1845, joined the Munster circuit 1848, made a Queen's Counsel in 1859, and was first Crown Prosecutor for Dublin from 1859 till 1865, when he was appointed law adviser to the Crown. A Liberal, and supporter of Lord Palmerston's government. Elected for Dungarvan in 1865. Defeated in 1868. Solicitor Gen. for Ireland 21 Dec. 1868 to Jan. 1870; drafted Irish Land Act 1870; Judge of Queen's bench, Ireland, 1872-1883; Lord Justice of Appeal for Ireland 1883, until his death on 15 May 1897. [1867]

BARRY, Garrett Standish, Lemlara House, Co. Cork. Was called to the Irish Bar; Dept.-Lieut. of the county. A Reformer. An advocate for the total extinction of tithes, the popular election of the Magistracy, shortening the duration of Parliaments, and the vote by ballot. Did not vote on Mr. O'Connell's motion for a repeal of the Union. Sat for Cork Co. from 1832. Sat until he retired in 1841. Died 26 Dec. 1864. [1840]

BARRY, George Richard. 7 Pembridge Square, Bayswater, London. Lota Lodge, Glanmire, Co. Cork. S. of John Richard Barry, Esq., by Eliza Mary, d. of James Haly, Esq., of Cork. B. at Cork 1825; m. Marie Teresa, d. of François Beguinot, Esq., of Bellevue, Mauritius. Educ. at the Royal Coll., Mauritius. A Merchant from 1850 in Bengal, and a large landed proprietor in the East Indies. A Liberal, and as a member of the Roman Catholic religion was in favour of complete civil and religious liberty and of 'Denominational education.' In favour also of a measure of 'tenant--right' by which due compensation should be secured to the tenant for his improvements. First elected for the Co. Cork July 1865. MP until his death 31 Jan. 1867. [1865]

BARRY, J. Continued in House after 1885: full entry in Volume II.

BARTLETT, E. Ashmead. See ASHMEAD-BARTLETT, E. Continued in House after 1885: full entry in Volume II.

BARTTELOT, Sir W.B. Continued in House after 1885: full entry in Volume II.

BASKERVILLE, Thomas Baskerville Mynors, B.C.L. 3 Suffolk Street, London. Clyro Court, Radnorshire. Carlton, and University. 2nd s. of P.R. Mynors, Esq., of Tieago, Herefordshire. In 1817, assumed the name of Baskerville. B. 1790; m. 1837, d. of Rev. P.C. Guise. A Dept.-Lieut. of Wiltshire and of Radnorshire. Was High Sheriff of Wiltshire 1827. A Conservative, voted for agricultural protection 1846. First returned for Herefordshire in 1841. Sat until he retired 1847. [1847]

BASS, H.A. Continued in House after 1885: full entry in Volume II.

BASS, Sir Michael Arthur, Bart., Chesterfield House, Mayfair, London. Rangemore, Burton-on-Trent. Reform, Brooks's, Devonshire, and Oxford & Cambridge. B. at Burton-on-Trent 1837, the eld. s. of Michael Thomas Bass, Esq., MP for Derby 1848-83 (died 1884), by Eliza Jane, eld. d. of Major Samuel Arden of Longholt Hall, Staffordshire. M. 1869, Harriet Georgina, 4th d. of Edward Thornewill, Esq., of Dove Cliff. Educ. at Harrow and at Trinity Coll., Cambridge, where he graduated M.A. 1863. A Partner in the firm Messrs. Bass and Co., Burton-on-Trent. A Magistrate and Dept.-Lieut. of Staffordshire. A Liberal; sat for Stafford July 1865-Dec.1868, and for East Staffordshire 1868-85. Returned again in 1886 as a Gladstonian Liberal, and sat until created Baron Burton Aug. 1886. Died 1 Feb. 1909. [1886]

BASS, Michael Thomas. 101 Eaton Square, London. Rangemore, Burton-on-Trent. Devonshire and Reform. S. of Michael Thomas Bass, Esq., of Burton-on-Trent, and grand-s. of William Bass, Esq., both of whom carried on extensive brewing establishments. B. at Burton--on-Trent 1799; m. 1835, eld. d. of Maj. Samuel Arden, of Longcroft Hall, Staffs. Educ. at Burton--on-Trent Grammar School and at Nottingham. A Brewer and Merchant. Appointed Dept.-Lieut. of Staffordshire 1852. A Liberal. Sat for Derby from Aug. 1848. MP until his death 29 Apr. 1884. [1883]

BASSETT, Francis. The Heath, Leighton Buzzard, Bedfordshire. S. of John Dollin Bassett, Esq. B. at Leighton Buzzard, Bedfordshire, 1820; m. 1842, Ellen, d. of Edward Harris, Esq. of Stoke

Newington, London. Educated at Grove House, Tottenham. A Banker; Magistrate for Bedfordshire since June 1872. Sat until he accepted Chiltern Hundreds Apr. 1875. Sheriff of Bedfordshire 1882. D. 9 June 1899.   [1875]

BASSETT, John. A Conservative. Returned for Helston 12 Mar. 1840. Retired in 1841.

BATEMAN, John. Fladonys Hotel, Oxford Street, London. Oak Park, Dineen, Co. Kerry, Carlton. M. 1824, d. of N. Bland, Esq., of Reindall's Park, Leatherhead. A Conservative. Returned for Tralee in 1837 and unseated in 1838. Died 1863.   [1838]

BATES, Sir E. Continued in House after 1885: full entry in Volume II.

BATESON, Sir Robert, Bart., sen. Belvoir Park, Antrim. Magherafelt, Co. Derry. Carlton, Union. B. 1782; m. 1811, Catherine, youngest d. of Samuel Dickson, Esq., of Ballynaguile. Dept.-Lieut. for Co. Down. A Conservative. First sat for Londonderry in 1830, when he ousted George Dawson, Esq., the bro.-in-law of Sir Robert Peel. Sat until he accepted Chiltern Hundreds May 1842. Died 21 Apr. 1863.   [1842]

BATESON, Sir Robert, jun. Belvoir Park, Antrim. Magherafelt, Co. Derry. Carlton, Union. Eld. s. of Sir Robert Bateson, Bart. B. 1816. A Conservative, supporting the time-honoured institutions of the country, as well as the agricultural interests; believed the pledging of MPs to be irrational as it implied pledging a juryman before trial to a particular decision. First returned for Londonderry Co. in 1842, on the retirement of his father, and remained MP until his death on 23 Dec. 1843.   [1843]

BATESON, Sir Thomas, Bart. 12 Grosvenor Place, London. Sackville Street Club, Dublin. Belvoir Park, Belfast. Carlton, Junior Carlton, Travellers', and White's. Eld. s. of Sir Robert Bateson (1st Bart.) who sat for Londonderry from 1830 till 1842, by Catherine, youngest d. of Samuel Dickson, Esq. B. 1819; m. 1849, Hon. Caroline Elizabeth Anne, 2nd. d. of 4th Lord Dynevor. Formerly a Capt. in the 13th Light Dragoons. A Dept.-Lieut. of Down and Londonderry. A Lord of the Treasury from March till Dec. 1852. A Conservative, and endeavoured 'to maintain inviolate the connexion between Church and State.' Sat for Londonderry from 1844 till 1857, when he accepted Chiltern Hundreds. Elected for Devizes April 1864. Sat until he retired in 1885. Created Baron Deramore Nov. 1885. Died 1st Dec. 1890.   [1885]

BATHURST, Allen Alexander, 20 Grosvenor Gardens, London. Hyams, Bagshot, Surrey. Carlton, White's, and Travellers'. Eld. s. of Hon. Lieut.-Col. Seymour Thomas Bathurst, by Julia, only d. of John Peter Hankey, Esq. Was nephew and heir-pres. to Earl Bathurst. B. 1832; m. 1st 1862, Hon. Muriel Leicester, d. of 2nd Lord de Tablay (she died 1872); 2ndly 1874, Evelyn, only d. of George Barnard Hankey, Esq. of Felcham Park, Surrey. Educ. at Eton and at Trinity Coll., Cambridge. A Conservative. First elected for Cirencester Mar. 1857. Sat until he succeeded Uncle as 6th Earl Bathurst Feb. 1878. Died 1 Aug. 1892.   [1877]

BATHURST, Col. Sir Frederick Thomas Arthur Hervey-. 34a Charles Street, Berkeley Square, London. Clarendon Park, Salisbury, Wiltshire. White's, Guards', and Carlton. Eld. s. of Sir Frederick Hutchinson Hervey-Bathurst, by his 1st wife, Louisa Mary, eld. d. of Walter Smythe, Esq., of Brambridge, Hampshire. B. in London 1833. Educ. at Eton. Appointed Lieut. and Capt. Grenadier Guards 1854, served in the Eastern Campaign of 1854-5; made Lieut.-Col. 1861. A Conservative, in favour of a readjustment of Church rates, but not of their total abolition. First elected for Wiltshire S. Feb. 1861 and sat until defeated 1865. Succeeded as 4th Bart. in 1881. Died 20 May 1900.   [1865]

BAXTER, Right Hon. William Edward. Kincaldrum, Forfar. Reform, and Devonshire. Eld. s. of Edward Baxter, Esq., of Kincaldrum, a Merchant at Dundee, by Euphemia, d. of William Wilson, Esq., of Dundee. B. at Dundee, 1825; m. 1847 Jessie, eld d. of Mr. J. Home Scott, of Dundee. Educ. at the Dundee Public Seminaries, and at the University of Edinburgh A Dept.-Lieut. for Forfar. Was Secretary to the Admiralty from Dec. 1868 to Mar. 1871, and joint-secretary to the Treasury from the latter date to Feb. 1873. Author of *Impressions of Central and Southern Europe, The Tagus and the Tiber, America and the Americans*, etc. A Liberal. First returned for Montrose, March 1855. Sat until he retired at 1885 gen. election. Died 10 August 1890. [1885]

BAYNTUN, Samuel Adlam. Browfort House, Wiltshire. United Service. A Lieutenant in the 1st Life Guards. A Reformer, in favour of the ballot, of the immediate abolition of slavery, a fixed duty on foreign corn, the repeal of the taxes of industry and knowledge, the substitution of a graduated property tax for the assessed taxes and taxes on the industrious classes, and the abolition of the monopoly of the East India Company. Opposed to the General Registry Bill, and flogging in the Army; sat first for York in 1830, and continued until his death in Oct.? 1833.   [1833]

BAZLEY, Sir Thomas, Bart. 1c, King Street, St. James's , London. Eyford, Bourton--on-the-Water, Gloucestershire. Reform, and Brooks's. Union Club, Manchester. S. of Thomas Bazley, Esq., Merchant, by Anne, d. of C. Hilton, Esq. B. at Gilnow, Nr. Bolton 1797; m. 1828 Mary, 2nd d. of Sebastian Nash, Esq. Educ. at the Grammar School, Bolton. A Cotton-Spinner and Merchant at Manchester. A Magistrate and Dept.-Lieut. for Lancashire. President of the Chamber of Commerce at Manchester for 14 years, was a member of the Royal Commission of 1851, and a member of the Royal Commission for the amalgamation of the commercial laws of the United Kingdom. A 'staunch Liberal.' First elected for Manchester Nov. 1858. Sat until he retired 1880. Died 18 Mar. 1885.   [1880]

BEACH, Sir M.E. Hicks-. See HICKS-BEACH, Sir M.E. Continued in House after 1885: full entry in Volume II.

BEACH, Sir Michael Hicks Hicks-. Williamstrip Park, Gloucestershire. B. at Netheravon House, Wiltshire, 1809, the eld. s. of Michael Beach Hicks-Beach, Esq., by Caroline Jane, eld. d. of William Mount, Esq., of Wasing Place, Berkshire. M. 1832, Harriet Vittoria, d. of John Stratton, Esq. of Farthinghoe Lodge, Northamptonshire. A Dept.-Lieut. of Gloucestershire and patron of 1 living. Appointed Lieut.-Col. of North Gloucester Militia 1844. A Conservative, sincerely attached to 'our constitution', specially its 'Protestant Institutions', but gave his aid to 'all such practical Reforms as can be safely adopted', and was anxious to advance the 'proper education' of the people. Sat for Gloucestershire E. from Jan 1854 until his death 29 Nov. 1854.   [1854]

BEACH, W.W.B. Continued in House after 1885: full entry in Volume II.

BEALE, Samuel. 10 Park Street, Westminster, London. Warfield Grove, Bracknell, Berkshire. Reform. S. of William Beale, Esq., of Camp Hill, Birmingham, a Magistrate for Warwickshire. B. at Birmingham 1803; m. 1st, 1823, Emma, d. of the Rev. Edmund Butcher, of Sidmouth, Devon; 2ndly, 1856, Mary, d. of John Johnson, Esq., of Field House, Nr. Chester. An Iron Master. A Magistrate for Warwickshire, Chairman of the Midland Railway. Of decidedly 'Liberal' opinions. First returned for Derby Apr. 1857. Sat until defeated 1865. Died 11 Sept. 1874. [1865]

BEAMISH, Francis Bernard. Grenville House, Cork, Ireland. Reform. S. of William Beamish, Esq., of Beaumont, near Cork, a Porter-brewer on an extensive scale in Cork. B. at Beaumont, near Cork, 1802; m. 1827, Hon. Katherine, sister of the 28th Baron Kingsale. Educ. at Rugby. A Liberal, in favour of 'an adjustment' of tenant-right in Ireland. Sat for Cork city from July 1837 till July 1841; re-elected Aug. 1853. Sat until he retired in 1859. Died 1 Feb. 1868.   [1858]

BEAUCLERK, Maj. Aubrey William. 12 Chester Street, Grosvenor Place, London. St. Leonard's House, Sussex. Ardglass Castle, Co. Down. B. 1801; eld. s. of Charles Beauclerk, Esq., by Emily, d. of William Ogilvie, Esq., and the Dowager Duchess of Leinster. M. 1834, Ida, 3rd sister of H.D. Goring, Esq., MP. A cousin of the Duke of St. Albans. A Major in the army. A radical Reformer, an opposer of the assessed and other partial taxes; in favour of the ballot, the shorter duration of Parliaments, cheap government, a reform of the Church, relieving Dissenters from Church rates, the abolition of tithes, a small fixed duty on corn, and the repeal of the taxes on knowledge. Sat for Surrey E. from 1832 until he retired 1837. Died 1 Feb. 1854.   [1837]

BEAUMONT, Frederick Edward Blackett. 7 Grosvenor Mansions, London. Junior United Service. S. of Edward Blackett Beaumont, Esq., and Jane his wife. B. 1833. Unmarried. Educ. at Harrow and at the Royal Military Academy, Woolwich. Entered the Royal Engineers Aug. 1852, became Capt. Apr. 1859, Major July 1872, retired upon a pension Oct. 1877. Served with the local rank of Capt. in the Turkish Contingent Engineers in 1855-6, and received a Turkish medal; served also on the staff of the Royal Engineers during the Indian Mutiny, and received a medal with one clasp for Lucknow. A Liberal, voted for the disestablishment of the Irish Church 1869. Sat for S. Durham from Dec. 1868 until he retired 1880. Died 20 Aug. 1899. [1880]

BEAUMONT, H.F. Continued in House after 1885: full entry in Volume II.

BEAUMONT, Somerset Archibald. 23 Park Street, London. Travellers'. 3rd. s. of Sir Thomas Wentworth Beaumont, by Henrietta Jane Emma, d. of J. Atkinson, Esq., of Maple Hayes, Staffordshire. B. 1835. Bro. to the member for Northumberland S. Educ. at Harrow and Trinity Coll., Cambridge. Appointed Dept.-Lieut. of Northumberland 1863. A Liberal, voted for the disendowment of the Irish Church 1869. In favour of a further redistribution of Parliamentary seats, and of the assimilation of the borough and county franchise. Sat for Newcastle-on-Tyne from Dec.

1860-July 1865, when he was an unsuccessful candidate. Sat for Wakefield from Dec. 1868 until he retired 1874. Died 8 Dec. 1921. [1873]

BEAUMONT, Thomas Wentworth. 24 St. James's Place, London. Bretton Hall, Yorkshire. Hexham Abbey and Bywell Hall, Northumberland. S. of Col. T.R. Beaumont, who represented Northumberland S. in seven Parliaments. B. 1792; m. d. of J. Atkinson, Esq., of Maple Hayes, Staffordshire and sister of Lady Ingilby. Patron of 9 livings, and reputed one of the wealthiest commoners in England. Of Whig principles. Sat for Northumberland S. from 1818, with the exception of the Parliament of 1826, when he lost his election, and was returned for Stafford. Sat until he retired 1837. [1837]

BEAUMONT, W.B. Continued in House after 1885: full entry in Volume II.

BEAUVOIR, Sir John Edmund de. 6 Connaught Place, London. Clewer House, Windsor. 11 Holles Street, Dublin. Eld. s. of J.E. Browne, Esq., Bart. a relative of the Marq. of Sligo. Changed his name to de Beauvoir in 1825, having m. the niece of Benyon de Beauvoir of Culford Hall, and Englefield House, Berkshire, and being the eld. s. of a Bart., he claimed knighthood, which was conferred. Was for a short time in the 26th regt. or Cameronians. A Reformer, in favour of the ballot and triennial Parliaments. In 1832 he declared himself in favour of such a reform of the church establishment as would leave no curate with less than 250/- per annum, no pastor with more than 600/-, no bishop more than 1,000/-, and no archbishop more than 5,000/-. He was unsuccessful in his contest for Windsor in 1832, being beaten by a majority of 25 votes; in 1835 he was returned by a majority of 9 votes, but he was unseated on petition and in Apr. 1835 the seat was assigned to Sir J. Elley. Again contested Windsor in July 1837 and June 1841. [1835]

BECKETT, Rt. Hon. Sir John. 11 Stratford Place, London. Gledhow, Yorkshire. Somerley Park, Lincolnshire. Athenaeum. Eld. s. of Sir John Beckett, Bart., a Banker at Leeds. B. 1776; m. 1817, Anne, 3rd surviving d. of the Earl of Lonsdale. A Banker; was educ. for the bar. Was Judge Advocate from 1828-1830; resumed that office in Dec. 1834, but resigned in Apr. 1835. A Conservative. Sat for Lord Lonsdale's disfranchised bor. of Haslemere in several Parliaments. Contested E. Retford unsuccessfully in 1832, and Leeds in 1834. Sat for Leeds from 9 Jan. 1835. Defeated in 1837. [1837]

BECKETT, William. 18 Upper Brook Street, London. Kirstall Grange, Yorkshire. Carlton, and Union. S. of Sir John Beckett, 1st. Bart., by the d. of Bishop (Wilson) of Bristol. B. at Leeds 1784; m. sister of H.C.M. Ingram, Esq. A Banker, a Magistrate of the West Riding, and a Lieut.-Col. of the Yorkshire Hussars. A Conservative. Sat for Leeds from 1841-July 1852, when he was elected for Ripon. Sat until he retired 1857. Died 26 Jan. 1863. [1857]

BECTIVE, Earl of. (I). 24 Grafton Street, Bond Street, London. Underly Hall, Kirkby, Lonsdale, Westmoreland. The Lodge, Virginia, Co. Cavan. Carlton, and White's, Sackville Street, Dublin. Eld. s. of Marq. of Headfort. B. in Cadogan Place, 1822; m. 1842, only d. and heir of William Thompson, Esq., an Alderman of London, who sat in Parliament from 1826 till his death in 1854, (she died 1864). Appointed State Steward to the Lord Lieut. of Ireland 1852. Was High Sheriff of Meath 1844, and of Cavan 1855. Col. of the Cavan Militia. A Conservative, voted against disestablishment of the Irish Church 1869 considering it as 'the first step towards the subversion and the overthrow of the Church of England'. First elected for Westmoreland, Apr. 1854. Sat until he succeeded as 3rd Marq. Dec. 1870. Died 22 July 1894. [1840]

BECTIVE, Earl of. (II). Continued in House after 1885: full entry in Volume II.

BEECROFT, George Skirrow. 4 Gloucester Terrace, Regent's Park, London. The Abbey House, Kirkstall, near Leeds. Carlton. Eld. s. of George Beecroft, Esq., of Kirkstall, near Leeds, by Mary, d. of John Audus, Esq., of Selby. B. at Outwood House, Horsforth, 1809; m. 1842, Mary Isabelle, only d. of George Beaumont, Esq., of Halifax. Was formerly an Ironmaster, at Kirkstall. A Magistrate and Dept.-Lieut. for the West Riding of Yorkshire. A moderate Conservative, in favour of extension of the franchise, so as to include 'the educated and intelligent classes'; though 'sincerely attached' to the Church of England, would accord the 'utmost freedom' to all other classes of religion; thought education should 'at least be assisted' by the state. First elected for Leeds June 1857. Sat until he retired in 1868. Died 18 Mar. 1869. [1867]

BELFAST, Earl of. 23 Arlington Street, Cowes, Isle of Wight. Eld s. of the Marq. of Donegal. B. 1797; m. Harriet, sister of the Earl of Glengall. Vice Chamberlain of the Household, to which office he was appointed by the Duke of Wellington. A moderate reformer, inclining to Conservatism, but voted for the Reform Bill;

adverse to the Repeal of the Union. Sat for Belfast in the Parliaments of 1820 and 1826 and first for Co. Antrim in 1830. Sat for Co. Antrim until the general election July/Aug. 1837 when he was elected for Belfast. Unseated on petition in 1838. Lord Lieut. of Co. Antrim Apr. 1841, until his death. Created Peer of the United Kingdom Aug. 1841; succeeded father as 3rd Marq. of Donegall 5 Oct. 1844. Died 20 Oct. 1883.   [1833]

BELL, Charles. 57½ Old Broad Street, London. Terrace House, Richmond, Surrey. Carlton, and Conservative. S. of Thomas Bell, Esq., a Merchant of London. B. in London, 1805. Un-married. A Merchant and Banker in London, a partner in the firm of Messrs. J. Thomson, Bonar & Company. Was a Commissioner of Lieutenan-cy for London from 1865. A Conservative, op-posed to the disestablishment of the Irish Church as 'a mere factious party manoeuvre,' and con-sidered that if carried it would only be 'the first step to indiscriminate spoliation,' in favour of an alteration in the bankrupt laws, so as more effec-tually to preserve the property of creditors, etc. Unsuccessfully contested Banbury 12 July 1865. Sat for London from Dec. 1868. MP until his death 9 Feb. 1869.   [1868]

BELL, Jacob. 15 Langham Place, London. West Hill, Wandsworth, Surrey. Eld. s. of John Bell, Esq., of Oxford Street, Chemist, and of Wandsworth. B. in London 1810. A Chemist in Oxford Street and Editor of the *'Pharmaceutical Journal'*. A Liberal, but opposed to extreme measures, in favour of free trade, and a supporter generally of Lord J. Russell's administration; op-posed to the endowment of the Roman Catholic Clergy. First returned for St. Albans Dec. 1850, but on 3 May 1852 the borough was disfranchised (for bribery and corruption) by Act of Parlia-ment. Died 12 June 1859.   [1852]

BELL, James. 1 Devonshire Place, Portland Place, London. Younger s. of John Bell, Esq., of 388 Oxford Street, Chemist, and of Wandsworth, Surrey. Bro. of Jacob Bell, Esq., whose election for St. Alban's in Dec. 1850 led to the dis-franchisement of that borough by Act of Parlia-ment in 1852. B. 1818. Educ. as an Architect. A Liberal, in favour of an extension of the suffrage, and vote by ballot; opposed to all religious en-dowments by the State, but against singling out the grant to Maynooth for special attack, while other endowments were left untouched. First returned for Guildford July 1852. Defeated Mar. 1857. Died 2 Feb. 1872.   [1856]

BELL, John. Thirsk, Reform. Only s. of John Bell, Esq., of Thirsk, by the d. of C. Charlton,

Esq. B. 1809. A Reformer, noted for agricultural protection, 1846. First returned for Thirsk in 1841. In July 1849, a Commission of Lunacy declared him to be of unsound mind. He remain-ed MP until his death 5 March 1851.   [1850]

BELL, Sir Isaac Lowthian. 11 Upper Wimpole Street, London. Rownton Grange, Northallerton. Reform. S. of Thomas Bell, Esq., Alderman of Newcastle-on-Tyne, Ironmaster, by Catherine, d. of Isaac Lowthian, Esq. B. at Newcastle-on-Tyne 1816; m. 1842, Margaret, d. of Hugh Lee Pattin-son, Esq., F.R.S. Educ. at Newcastle-on-Tyne, the University of Edinburgh and Sorbonne in Paris. An Ironmaster and Coal-Owner. A Magistrate and Dept.-Lieut. for the Co. of Durham and an Alderman and Magistrate for Newcastle-on-Tyne. Sheriff and twice (1854, 1863) Mayor of Newcastle-on-Tyne. Elected a Fellow of the Royal Society 1875. Was Pres. of the Iron and Steel Institute 1873 and 1874. Author of *Chemical Phenomena of Iron smelting,* and various scientific contributions to the Royal Society, the Institution of Civil Engineers, etc. A Liberal. Un-successfully contested Dec. 1868, N. Durham, for which he sat from Feb.-June 1874, when he was unseated on petition; and again contested it, but failed to regain his seat. Sat for Hartlepool from July 1875 until defeated 1880. Created 1st Baronet 1885. Died 20 Dec. 1904.   [1880]

BELL, Matthew. Woolsington, North-umberland. Carlton. Eld. s. of Matthew Bell, Esq., of Woolsington, by the d. of C.J. Brandling, Esq., of Gosforth House, Northumberland. B. 1793; m. in 1816, Elizabeth Anne, only d. of Henry Uttrick Reay, Esq., of Killingworth House, Northumberland. Was High Sheriff of Northumberland in 1816. A Conser-vative, voted for agricultural protection, 1846. In favour of the total extinction of tithes. Was elected for Northumberland S. in 1826 and 1830, but lost his seat in 1831. Sat for it from 1832. Sat until he retired in 1852. Died 28 Oct. 1871.   [1852]

BELLEW, Sir Patrick, Bart. Barmeath, Co. Louth, 61 Eccles Street, Dublin. B. 1798; m. 1829, Anna Fermina, d. of Don José de Mendoza y Rios. Lord-Lieut. of the Co. of Louth, and the Co. and town of Drogheda. A Reformer, opposed to the tithe system in Ireland. First sat for Louth in 1831, but retired in favour of his bro. R.M. Bellew, Esq., in the following year. In 1835 he was induced again to stand for Louth on the Reform interest and succeeded. Retired in 1837. Created Baron Bellew of Barmeath, Co. Louth 17 July 1848. Died 10 Dec. 1866.   [1837]

BELLEW, Richard Montequieu. Barmeath,

Louth. Reform, Brooks's and Wyndham. Second s. of Sir Edward Bellew, 6th Bart., and bro. of 1st Lord Bellew. B. 1803; m. 1828, d. of John Lalor, Esq., of Crana, (dead). Appointed a Lord of the Treasury, Aug. 1847, salary £1,200. Dept.-Lieut. for the co. Louth. A Reformer, said he would vote for the abolition of tithes in every shape, and for the appropriation of a large portion of the Church property to purposes of national utility. In favour of shortening the duration of Parliaments, admitting Dissenters to graduate at the Universities, and the vote by ballot. Sat for Louth from 1832 until he retired in 1852. Died 8 Jan. 1880. [1852]

BELLEW, Thomas A. Mount Bellew, Duleck, Co. Galway. 2nd. s. of Sir Michael Dillon Bellew, Bart., by Helena, d. of Thomas Dillon, Esq., of Dublin. A Liberal, said he would 'oppose any government that will not bring forward, as a cabinet measure, the appropriation of the Church temporalities to their primitive purposes.' First returned for Galway Co. in July 1852. Sat until defeated 1857. Died 24 July 1863. [1857]

BELLINGHAM, Alan Henry. Exton Park, Oakham, Rutlandshire. Castle Bellingham, R.S.O., Louth. United University. Eld. s. of Sir Alan Edward Bellingham, Bart., of Castle Bellingham, Co. Louth, by Elizabeth, only d. of Henry Clarke, Esq., of West Skirbeck House, Co. Lincoln. B. at Castle Bellingham 1846; m. 1874, Lady Constance, 2nd. d. of the 2nd Earl of Gainsborough. Was educ. at Harrow, and at Exeter Coll., Oxford, where he graduated B.A. 1869, M.A. 1872. Was called to the bar at Lincoln's Inn 1875. Private Chamberlain to Pope Leo XIII., and filled the same office to Pius IX. Capt. Louth Rifle Militia. Published *The Social Aspects of Catholicism and Protestantism,* a translation and adaptation of the French. A Conservative, in favour of Home Rule for Ireland, but entirely opposed to the separation of Great Britain and Ireland. Sat for Louth from May 1880. Retired in 1885. Succeeded to baronetcy April 1889. Died 9 June 1921. [1885]

BENBOW, John. 26 Mecklenburgh Square, London. Carlton and Conservative. M. Eliza, d. of —, who died Nov. 1825. Was a Solicitor. A Trustee and Auditor of Lord Ward etc. Director of the North Western, and the Shrewsbury and Birmingham Railways. A Conservative, at one time in favour of free trade, but voted for a return to agricultural protection 1850. Would not, however, advocate the reimposition of a duty on corn. Against the endowment of the Roman Catholic Clergy. Unsuccessfully contested Wolverhampton 26 July 1837. Sat for Dudley from 1844 (upon the retirement of Mr. Hawkes)

until his death 24 Feb. 1855. [1854]

BENETT, John. Norton Bavant and Pyt House, Wiltshire. Athenaeum. Eld. surviving s. of Thomas Benett, Esq., of Pyt House. B. 1773; m. 1801 Lucy, d. of Edmund Lambert, Esq., of Boyton House. Co. Wiltshire, dead. Patron of 1 living. A tithe owner. A Conservative, voted for agricultural protection, 1846; in favour of an increased property tax in lieu of the malt tax. Sat for Wiltshire S. from 1819 until he retired in 1852. [1852]

BENETT-STANFORD, Vere Fane. See STANFORD, Vere Fane Benett-.

BENNET, Philip. 39 Lowndes Street, London. Rougham Hall, Bury St. Edmund's, Suffolk. Tollesbury Lodge, Essex. Carlton, and National. S. of Philip Bennet, Esq., of Rougham-Old-Hall, Suffolk, and Tollesbury, Essex, by the d. and sole heir of the Rev. R. Kedington (a member of one of the oldest families in Suffolk). B. 1795 at Widcomb, near Bath (which place his grandfather represented in Parliament.) M. in 1822 d. and co-heir of Sir Thos. Pilkington, Bart., of Chevet, Yorkshire. Was educ. at Bury St. Edmund's, and Emmanuel Coll., Cambridge, where in 1822 he took the degree of M.A. having gained the classical prizes of his College two years in succession. Was Capt. of the West Suffolk Yeomanry from 1831; a Magistrate, and Dept.-Lieut. of the county of Suffolk. Patron of 1 living. Of Conservative principles, 'particularly attached to the Church.' Contested Bury St. Edmund's at the general election in 1832, but was defeated by one vote. First returned for Suffolk W. in 1845 without opposition. Sat until defeated in 1859. Died 17 Aug. 1866. [1858]

BENTALL, Edward Hammond. Heybridge, Maldon, Essex. S. of William Bentall, Esq., by his marriage with Miss Mary Hammond. B. at Goldhanger, Essex. 1814; m. 1846 Susannah Julia d. of George Woodgate, Esq., late of Broomfield Hall. An Engineer and Manufacturer of Agricultural Machines, his firm having been established since 1808. Capt.-Commandant of 1st Essex Engineer Volunteers. A Liberal. Sat for Maldon from Dec. 1868 until he retired 1874. Died 7 Aug. 1898. [1873]

BENTINCK, G.F. Cavendish. Continued in House after 1885: full entry in Volume II.

BENTINCK, George William Pierrepont. 48 Davies Street, Berkeley Square, London. Terrington, Lynn, Norfolk. White's, Travellers', and Carlton. Eld. s. of Vice-Admiral William

Bentinck (representative of a junior branch of the Duke of Portland's family), by Lady Frances, only d. of 1st Earl Manvers (subsequently wife to Henry William Stephens Esq.) B. in Portman Sq., 1803. 'A Tory', and when first in Parliament was not opposed to a moderate measure of reform. Was an unsuccessful candidate for Kendal Feb. 1843. Sat for W. Norfolk from July 1852–Dec. 1868, when he retired on account of ill-health; re-elected Feb. 1871. Sat until he accepted Chiltern Hundreds Feb. 1884. Died 20 Feb. 1886.   [1883]

BENTINCK, Lord Henry William Scott. 19 Cavendish Square, London. Welbeck Abbey, Nottinghamshire. S. of the 4th Duke of Portland, by the eld. d. and co-heir of Maj.-Gen. John Scott, of Balcomie, Fifeshire. B. 1804. Educ. at Christ Church, Oxford, when he was 2nd class in classics in 1826. A Conservative. First elected for North Nottinghamshire Mar. 1846. Sat until he retired 1857. Died 31 Dec. 1870.   [1857]

BENTINCK, Lord William George Frederick Scott. Harcourt House, Cavendish Square, London. Orange Farm, Norfolk. 2nd. s. of the Duke of Portland. B. 1802. A Major in the army. A Conservative, and leader of the Protectionist Party. Voted in favour of the principle of the Reform Act, but opposed Ministers on several of the details in Committee. Was first elected for Lynn Regis in 1828, when he replaced his uncle, Lord William Bentinck, and sat for it uninterruptedly until his death 21 Sept. 1848.   [1847]

BENTINCK, Rt. Hon. Lord William Henry Cavendish. G.C.B., G.C.H. 19 Cavendish Square, London. Welbeck Abbey, Nottinghamshire. Reform. Bro. to the Duke of Portland and uncle to the Member for Lynn. B. 1774; m. Lady Mary Atcheson, d. of the Earl of Gosford. A Gen. in the army, and Col. of the 11th Dragoons. Patron of 1 living. Was Governor-Gen. of India. A Whig. MP for Glasgow from 17 Feb. 1836 until his death 17 June 1839.   [1838]

BENYON, Richard. 34 Grosvenor Square, London. Englefield House, Reading. Carlton, Conservative and Boodle's. 2nd surviving s. of W.H. Fellowes, Esq. of Ramsey Abbey, Huntingdonshire, (formerly MP for that county), by Ennora, d. of Richard Benyon, Esq. of Englefield House, Berkshire; is therefore bro. to the Member for Huntingdonshire. B. 1811; m. 1858, Elizabeth Mary, 2nd d. of Robert Clutterbuck, Esq. of Watford House, Hertfordshire. Assumed the name Benyon, in lieu of his patronymic, on succeeding in 1854 to the estates of his maternal uncle, Richard Benyon de Beauvoir, Esq. of Englefield

House, Berkshire. Educ. at Charter House and St. John's Coll., Cambridge. Called to the bar at Lincoln's Inn 1836. High Steward of Reading from May 1870. Patron of 4 livings. A Conservative; voted against the disestablishment of the Irish Church, 1869. First elected for Berkshire, Apr. 1860. Sat until he accepted Chiltern Hundreds Feb. 1876. Died 26 July 1897.   [1875]

BERESFORD, Lord C.W. Continued in House 1885: full entry in Volume II.

BERESFORD, Denis William Pack. 30 Upper Harley Street, London. Fenagh Lodge, Leighlin Bridge, Co. Carlow. Carlton, and Army & Navy. S. of Sir Denis Pack, K.C.B., by Lady Elizabeth Louisa, 4th d. of the 1st Marq. of Waterford. B. in London 1818; m. 1863, Annette Caroline, only d. of R. Clayton Browne, Esq., of Browne's Hill, Co. Carlow. Educ. at the Royal Military Academy, Woolwich. Entered the Royal Artillery, June 1836. Assumed the name of Beresford. A Conservative, and desired to 'uphold intact the constitution we now enjoy'; in favour of civil and religious liberty. First elected for Carlow Co. July 1862. Sat until he retired in 1868. Died 28 Dec. 1881. [1867]

BERESFORD, George de la Poer, (I). 54 Harley Street, London. White's, and Travellers'. Eld. s. of Sir John Beresford, Bart. B. 1811. A Capt. in the army. A Conservative, first returned for Athlone in 1841. His election in 1841 was declared void on 13 June 1842. Succeeded as 2nd Bart. 2 Oct. 1844. Died 11 Feb. 1873.
        [1841 2nd ed.]

BERESFORD, George de la Poer, (II). Aubawn, Killeshandra, Co. Cavan. The Palace, Armagh. Kildare Street Club, Dublin. Carlton. Eld. s. of the Most Rev. Dr. Marcus Gervais Beresford, Archbishop of Armagh, by his 1st wife, Mary, d. of Col. Henry Peisley L'Estrange, of Moystoun, King's Co. B. at Clonervy, Co. Cavan 1831; m. 1860 Mary Annabella, d. of Rev. William Vernon Harcourt, rector of Bolton Percy, and canon of York. Educ. at Eton and at University Coll., Oxford. A Magistrate and Dept.-Lieut. for Cavan, of which Co. he was High Sheriff in 1867. A Conservative. Sat for Armagh city from Oct. 1875 until he retired in 1885. High Sheriff of Co. Armagh 1887. Died 3 Aug. 1906.   [1885]

BERESFORD, Vice-Admiral Sir John Poo, Bart., G.C.B. and K.I.C. The Hall, Yorkshire. Bagnall, Co. Waterford. Carlton. Natural s. of the first Marq. of Waterford, and bro. of Visct. Beresford. B. 1769; m. 1st, Mary, d. of Capt. Molloy, R.N. (dead); 2ndly, 1815, Henrietta, youngest d. of Henry Peirse, Esq., of Bedale, Yorkshire, by Charlotte, d. of 2nd Lord Monson.

Vice-Adm. of the White. Was a Lord of the Admiralty. Sat for Coleraine in several Parliaments previous to 1822, for Northallerton in those of 1826, 1830 and 1831. In 1832 he was returned, by a majority of one, for Coleraine, but was ousted, on petition, by Mr. Ald. Copeland. Sat for Chatham from 1835. Retired in 1837. Died 2 Oct. 1844. [1836]

BERESFORD, Lieut.-Col. Marcus. Hollanden, Melbury Road, Kensington, London. Carlton. 4th s. of Rev. Gilbert Beresford, of Aylestone, Leicestershire (formerly Rector of St. Andrew's Holborn), by Anne, only d. of Rev. H. Browne, Rector of Hoby, Leicestershire. Descended from the ancient family of Beresford, seated at Beresford, Alstonfield, Co. Stafford in 1087, and of which the Marq. of Waterford is a branch. B. at Aylestone, Leicestershire 1818; m. 1848, Elizabeth, eld. d. of William Green, Esq., M.D. of Durham (she died 1878). Educ. at King's Coll., London. Entered the N. American Militia in 1836, and served for 8 years. Was Commandant of the 7th Surrey Rifles and had the rank of Col. A Magistrate for Surrey from 1859. A Conservative, in favour of the equalization of poor-rates in the metropolis. Sat for Southwark from Feb. 1870 until he retired 1880. [1880]

BERESFORD, Rt. Hon. William. 3 King Street, St. James's, London. Elsfield, Oxford. Carlton, and Travellers'. Only s. of Marcus Beresford, Esq., by the d. of 1st Earl of Milltown, was therefore cousin to the Marq. of Waterford. B. 1798; m. 1834, d. of G.R. Heneage, Esq., of Hainton Hall, Lincolnshire. Educ. at St. Mary's Hall, Oxford, where he was second class; graduated B.A. 1819, M.A. 1824. Formerly a Maj. in the army and served 11 years in the 9th and in the 12th Lancers. Was War Sec. from Mar.-Dec. 1852. A Conservative. Contested Hythe unsuccessfully in 1837; sat for Harwich from 1841-1847, when he was returned for Essex N. Sat until defeated 1865. Died 6 Oct 1883. [1865]

BERESFORD-HOPE, Rt. Hon. Alexander James Beresford. Arklow House, 1 Connaught Place, Hyde Park, London. Bedgebury Park, Cranbrook, Kent. Beresford Hall, Ashbourne, Staffordshire. Carlton, Athenaeum, and the University. Youngest s. of Thomas Hope, Esq., of Deepdene, Surrey, author of *Anastasius*, by the Hon. Louisa, youngest d. of the 1st Lord Decies, Archbishop of Tuam (she m. 2ndly Visct. Beresford). B. in London 1820; m. 1842, the Lady Mildred Cecil, eld d. of 8th Marq. of Salisbury (she died 1881). Gained a scholarship and several prizes at Harrow; in 1840, the English and Latin declamation prizes at Trinity Coll., Cambridge,

and in 1841 the Members' B.A. prize for a Latin Essay; made LL.D. propter merita at Cambridge, hon D.C.L. at Oxford, hon LL.D. at Dublin. Assumed the name of Beresford by royal licence in 1854. President of the Institute of British Architects, also a Trustee of the British Museum. Patron of 2 livings. A Liberal-Conservative, and in favour of the maintenance of the Established Church, 'both as a devine institution, and as an estate of the realm'. Sat for Maidstone from June 1841-July 1852; and from Mar. 1857-Apr. 1859. Unsuccessfully contested Stoke in 1862, but sat for Stoke from July 1865-Feb. 1868, from which date he sat for Cambridge University. MP until his death 20 Oct. 1887. [1887]

BERKELEY, Charles Lennox Grenville. 7 Wilton Crescent, London. Travellers'. B. in London 1806, the 2nd s. of Admiral, the Hon. Sir George Berkeley, G.C.B. by the d. of Lord George Lennox. M. 1827, Augusta Elizabeth, d. of J.H. Leigh, Esq., of Stoneleigh Abbey, and sister to 1st Lord Leigh. One time Capt. in 52nd Light Infantry. Appointed Sec. to the Poor Law Board Dec. 1852 and Commissioner of Customs 1856-1886. A Liberal; favoured vote by ballot, opposed to the endowment of the Roman Catholic Clergy. Unsuccessfully contested Gloucestershire W. at the general election of 1847. Sat for Cheltenham from Aug. 1848-July 1852, and again from July 1855 until he accepted Chiltern Hundreds in Apr. 1856. Represented Evesham from 1852-55. Died 25 Sept. 1896. [1856]

BERKELEY, Hon. Charles Paget Fitz-Hardinge. 39 Hill Street, Berkeley Square, London. Old Park, Chichester, Sussex. Brooks's. 2nd s. of 1st Lord Fitz-Hardinge, by Lady Charlotte, d. of 4th Duke of Richmond. B. at Queenstown 1830; m. 1856, Louisa Elizabeth, only d. of Henry Lindow Lindow, Esq. Educ. at Rugby. A Dept.-Lieut. of Gloucestershire. A Liberal, and a supporter generally of Lord Palmerston; voted in favour of the abolition of Church rates, May 1862. First elected for Gloucester Feb. 1862. Retired 1865. Unsuccessfully contested Gloucestershire W. 1867 and 1874. Succeeded bro. as 3rd Baron Fitz-Hardinge in 1896. Died 3 Dec. 1916. [1865]

BERKELEY, Hon Craven Fitz-Hardinge. 33 St. James's Place, London. Brooks's. B. 1805, the youngest s. of 5th Earl of Berkeley, and bro. of Earl Fitz-Hardinge. M. 1st 1839, the Hon. Mrs. Talbot (dead) and then in 1845, Charlotte, 4th d. of the late Gen. Denzil Onslow, of Staughton House, Huntingdonshire, and widow of George Newton, Esq., of Croxton Park, Cambridgeshire. A Reformer, and favoured an extension of the suffrage, short Parliaments and the ballot. Opposed to the Maynooth Grant. Sat for Cheltenham from 1832-July 1847 and then re-elected in June 1848, but unseated on petition in the following Aug. Again returned in July 1852 and sat until his death 1 July 1855. [1855]

BERKELEY, Francis Henry Fitz-Hardinge. 1Victoria Square, Pimlico, London. 4th s. of 5th Earl Berkeley. B. 7th Dec. 1794. A Liberal, well known for his continued exertions in favour of vote by ballot: considered the existence of the Irish Church 'detrimental to the true interests of the Church of England.' Sat for Bristol from 1837. MP until his death 10 Mar. 1870. [1870]

BERKELEY, Hon. Francis William Fitz-Hardinge. Berkeley Lodge, Fishbourne, Chichester. Boodle's. Eld. s. of Lord Fitz-Hardinge, by his 1st wife, Lady Charlotte, 6th d. of the 4th Duke of Richmond. B. 1826; m. 1857, Georgina, only d. of Col. Holme Sumner, of Hatchlands, Surrey. Educ. at Rugby. Appointed Capt. Royal Horse Guards Sept. 1853, retired Dec. 1857, when he became honorary Col. of the S. Gloucester Militia; appointed Lieut.-Col. Commandant of the same regiment 1860. A Liberal, in favour of the extension of the suffrage to £5 householders and vote by ballot; the abolition of Church rates, and the general, but not compulsory education of the people; opposed to disturbing the present grant to Maynooth. First elected for Cheltenham May 1856. Sat until defeated 1865. Succeeded as 2nd Baron Fitz-Hardinge Oct. 1867. Died 29th Jan. 1896. [1865]

BERKELEY, Hon. George Charles Grantley Fitz-Hardinge. A younger s. of Earl Berkeley, and bro. of Earl Fitz-Hardinge. B. 1800; m. in 1824 Caroline, youngest d. of Paul Benfield, Esq., A Lieut. in the army. Author of a novel called *Berkeley Castle.* Brought forward a motion in support of agricultural protection 1850; a supporter of the game laws; in favour of the ballot. Sat for Gloucestershire W. from 1832. Was returned originally through the influence of Earl FitzHardinge, but was elected in 1847 in opposition to the Earl's candidate, Mr. Grenville Berkeley. Sat until defeated in 1852. Died 23 Feb. 1881. [1852]

BERKELEY, Sir George Henry Frederick, K.C.B. 22 Queen Street, Mayfair, London. Eld. s. of Admiral the Hon. Sir George Cranfield Berkeley, G.C.B. (next bro. to the 5th Earl Berkeley), by the d. of Lord George Lennox. B. 1785; m. 1815, Lucy, eld. d. and co-heir of Sir Thomas Sutton, Bart. Entered the army as Cornet Royal Horse Guards Blue 1802, served subsequently in Sicily and Egypt with the 35th

Foot, received a cross and 8 clasps for his services as Assistant Adjutant General at Busaco, Fuentes d'Onor, Badajos, Salamanca, Vittoria, St. Sebastian and Nive, was at Waterloo and received several foreign Orders of Knighthood, together with the Order of K.C.B. for his conduct there, became Col. of the 35th Foot in 1845. Gen. in the army 1854. Was Surveyor-Gen. of the Ordnance from June-Dec.1852. A Conservative. First returned for Devonport July 1852. MP until his death 25 Sept. 1857. [1857]

BERKELEY, Rt. Hon. Sir Maurice Frederick Fitz-Hardinge, K.C.B. Berkeley Lodge, Fishbourne, Chichester. Admiralty. Reform. 2nd. s. of the 5th Earl Berkeley, and next bro. to Earl Fitz-Hardinge. B. 1788; m. 1st, 1823, Lady Charlotte, 6th d. of the 4th Duke of Richmond (dead); 2ndly, 1834, Lady Charlotte, 3rd d. of 1st Earl of Ducie. Became Rear-Admiral of the Red, May 1854. Commanded the *Thunderer* at the capture of St. Jean d'Acre. Was a Lord of the Admiralty from Apr. 1833-Dec. 1834, and from July 1846-Mar. 1852, re-appointed Dec. following, salary £1,000. A Dept.-Lieut. for Sussex. A Liberal. Sat for Gloucester from Dec. 1832-Apr.1833, re-elected 1835. Was an unsuccessful candidate at the election in 1837, again returned in 1841. Sat until defeated 1857. Created 1st Baron Fitz-Hardinge Aug. 1861. Died 17 Oct. 1867. [1857]

BERNAL, Ralph. 75 Eaton Square, London. Athenaeum, and Reform. M. d. of — White, Esq., M.D., a Surgeon in the navy, of Chatham Dock Yard. A Barrister and West India Proprietor. Wrote various articles for the Annuals. Was, during the Grey and Melbourne ministries, Chairman of Committees of the whole House on Government measures. Of Whig principles. Declared himself in 1837 'a reluctant Convert' to the system of Election by Ballot. Sat for Rochester from 1820-1841, before which he sat a short time for Lincoln. Was not returned for Weymouth in 1841, but succeeded on petition. Sat until he retired 1847. Died 26 Aug. 1854. [1847]

BERNAL, Ralph, jun. See OSBORNE, Ralph Bernal-.

BERNAL-OSBORNE, R. See OSBORNE, Ralph Bernal-.

BERNARD, Hon. Henry Boyle. Coolmain Castle, Co. Cork. Carlton. 3rd. s. of 2nd Earl of Bandon, by Mary Susan Albinia, sister of 6th Visct. Midleton. B. in London 1812; m. 1848, Matilda Sophia, youngest d. of Lieut.-Gen. Turner, of Sutton, Middlesex. Educ. at Eton and at Oxford. Col. South Cork Light Infantry Militia. A Conservative. First elected for Bandon Feb. 1863. Sat until defeated in 1868. Died 14 Mar. 1895. [1868]

BERNARD, Percy Broderick. B.1844, the eld. s. of Hon. and Rt. Rev. Charles Broderick Bernard, D.D., Bishop of Tuam (2nd. s. of 2nd Earl of Bandon), by Hon. Jane Grace, d. of Percy Evans-Freke, and sister of 7th Lord Carberry. M. 1st, 1872, Isabel Emma Beatrice, d. of John Newton Lane, Esq., of King's Bromley, Co. Stafford (she died 1876): 2ndly, 1880, Mary Lissey, only d. of Denis Kirwan, Esq., of Castle Hacket, Co. Galway. A Magistrate for the Co. of Cork, and a Capt. of the S. Cork Militia, of which he was appointed Hon. Col. in July 1876. Was Private Sec. to the Duke of Marlborough while Lord Lieut. of Ireland from 1876-1880. A Conservative. Sat for Bandon from Apr.-May 1880 when he accepted Chiltern Hundreds. Died 18 July 1912.
[1880 2nd. ed.]

BERNARD, Thomas Tyringham. 23 Ovington Square, Brompton, London. Winchendon Priory, Thame. Union. 2nd surviving s. of Sir Scrope Bernard Morland, 4th Bart. (who assumed the name of Morland), by Harriett, only child of William Morland, Esq., of Lee, Kent. B. in Bolton Street, London 1791; m. 1st, 1819, Sophia Charlotte, only d. and heir of Sir David Williams (she died 1837); 2ndly, 1840, Martha Louisa, d. of William Minshull, Esq. (dead); 3rdly, 1864, Ellen, relict of Henry Elwes, Esq., of Marcham Park, Berkshire. Educ. at Eton and at Christ Church, Oxford. Patron of 1 living. A Liberal-Conservative, opposed Lord Palmerston on the vote of censure 1864, was against the ballot, the Maynooth Grant, and the abolition of Church rates without an equivalent; but supported a measure for the equalization of poor rates. First elected for Aylesbury Apr. 1857. Sat until he retired 1865. Succeeded as 5th Bart. 22 Jan. 1876. Died 8 May 1883. [1865]

BERNARD, Visct. 40 Lowndes Square, London. Bernard Castle, Co. Cork. Carlton. Eld. s. of the Earl of Bandon. B. Grosvenor Street 1810; m. 1832 eld. d. of Thomas Whitmore, Esq. of Apley, Shropshire. Graduated at Oriel Coll. Oxford. A Conservative and Protectionist. First returned for Bandon in Feb. 1842. Sat until he succeeded father as 3rd Earl of Bandon 1856. Representative peer of Ireland 21 Aug. 1858. Lord Lieutenant of Cork 2 Nov. 1874. Died 17 Feb. 1877.
[1852 2nd. ed.]

BERNARD, Hon. William Smyth. The Farm, Nr. Bandon. Harbour View, Kilbrittain, Co.

Cork. 4th s. of the 1st Earl of Bandon, by Lady Catherine Henrietta, only d. of 2nd Earl of Shannon. B. at Castle Bernard 1792; m. 1831, Elizabeth, only d. of Lieut. Col. Edward Gilliman, of Clan Coole, Co. Cork. Educ. at Bennycastle's Military Academy, Charlton, Kent. Entered the army in 1809, became Capt. in the 1st Dragoon Guards 1815; retired as Lieut. Col. 17th Light Dragoons 1857; served in the Peninsula with the 67th regiment at the siege of Cadiz and the battle of Barrossa for which he received a medal and one clasp; served also with the 4th Dragoons in the retreat from Burgos. A Magistrate for the county of Cork; High Sheriff in 1820. A Conservative. Sat for Bandon, from Dec. 1832 till Jan. 1835; re-elected Feb. 1857. MP until his death 6 Feb. 1863. [1862]

BEST, John. Hall Staircase, Inner Temple, London. Blakebrook House, Kidderminster. S. of W.B. Best, Esq., of Blakebrook House, near Kidderminster. B. at Kidderminster, 1821; m. 1848, eld d. of W. Trow, Esq., of Isinere House, Educ. at Shrewsbury School, and at St. Peter's Coll., Cambridge, where he graduated B.A. 1844. Was called to the bar at the Inner Temple Nov. 1846, and went the Oxford circuit. Was counsel in the Palace Court from Apr. 1847, till its suppression, 1849. A Conservative and Protectionist, 'thoroughly opposed to the extension of free trade, except on principles of reciprocity'; was opposed to the endowment of the Roman Catholic clergy. First returned for Kidderminster Aug. 1849. Defeated in 1852. Died 18 June 1865. [1852]

BETHELL, Richard. 7 Richmond Terrace, London. Rise and Walton Abbey, Yorkshire. Carlton. Br. of the Bishop of Bangor; b. 1772; m. 1800, Mary, 2nd. d. of William Welbach, Esq. of the City of London and Ravensworth, Cowton, Yorkshire. Patron of 1 living. A Conservative; voted against the Reform Bills; an advocate of the Corn Laws, but was not unfriendly to an efficient protecting fixed duty. Sat for Yorkshire E. from 1830 with the exception of 1831 until he retired 1841. Chairman of East Riding Quarter Sessions. Died 25 Dec. 1864. [1838]

BETHELL, Sir Richard. 25 Gloucester Square, Hyde Park, London. 3 Stone Buildings, Lincoln's Inn, London. Brooks's. S. of Richard Bethell, Esq., M.D., and descended from the old Welsh family of Ap Itheil. B. 1800; m. 1825, Ellinor Mary, d. of Robert Abraham, Esq. Was a Fellow of Wadham Coll., Oxford, where he was first class in classics, and second class in mathematics, 1818 (having graduated B.A. before the age of eighteen); created D.C.L. 1860. Was called to the bar at the Middle Temple Nov. 1823; made a

Queen's Counsel 1840; was Solicitor-Gen. from Dec. 1852 till Nov. 1856, and Attorney-Gen. from the last date till Mar. 1858; re-appointed Attorney-Gen June 1859. Was Vice-Chancellor of the County Palatine of Lancaster. Counsel to the University of Oxford. A Liberal, in favour of the ballot, the abolition of church-rates etc. Contested Shaftesbury 31 July 1847. Sat for Aylesbury from Apr. 1851 till May 1859, when he was elected for Wolverhampton. Sat until appointed Lord Chancellor (Lord Westbury) in 1861. [1861]

BEVAN, T. A Liberal. First elected for Gravesend Apr. 1880, but the election was declared void and he did not stand at the subsequent election of 1 July 1880. Sheriff of London and Middlesex 1878-79; Chairman of Magistrates Bench of Dartford Division of Kent to 1906. Died 1 Mar. 1907.

BEWES, Thomas Beaumont. Beaumont, Devon. Reform. M. 1st. d. of J. Culure, Esq., of Tothill House, Devon; 2ndly, d. of — Davis, Esq., of Greenwich. High Sheriff of Devon. A radical Reformer. In favour of removing the Bishops from the House of Lords. Sat for Plymouth from 1832 until he retired 1841. Died 18 Nov. 1857. [1838]

BIDDELL, William. The Hall, Lavenham, Suffolk. S. of Mr. Arthur Biddell, of Playford, Suffolk, by Jane, d. of Mr. Robert Ransome, of Ipswich. B. at Playford 1825; m. 1st, 1857, Ellen, d. of Mr. Arthur Bencome; 2ndly, 1868, Mary Anne, d. of Mr. Robert Howard, of Lavenham, Suffolk. A Land-agent, Auctioneer and Surveyor; and Director of the Suffolk branch of the Alliance Fire Office Co. An 'independent member, with Conservative proclivities.' Approved of the union of Church and State. Considered that elementary (but not denominational) religion should be taught in all parish schools. Was elected for Suffolk W. April 1880. Sat until he retired in 1885. Died 25 Oct. 1900. [1885]

BIDDULPH, M. Continued in House after 1885: full entry in Volume II.

BIDDULPH, Robert. 44 Charing Cross, London. Ledbury, Herefordshire. Eld. s. of John Biddulph, Esq. of Ledbury. Dept.-Lieut. of Herefordshire. A Director of the Economic Life Assurance Company; also of the Canada Company. A London Banker. Of Whig principles, in favour of the ballot. Sat for Hereford from 1832 until defeated in 1837. Sheriff of Hereford 1857. Died 28 Feb. 1864. [1837]

BIDDULPH, Col. Robert Myddelton-. 35

Grosvenor Place, London. Chirk Castle, Chirk, Denbighshire. Burg-Hill House, Hereford. Brooks's, and Arthur's. Eld. s. of Robert Biddulph, Esq. of Ledbury, Herefordshire, and Cofton Hall, Worcestershire (who assumed the name of Myddelton), by Charlotte, eld. d. of Richard Myddelton, Esq., of Chirk Castle, Denbighshire. B. in Manchester Square 1805; m. 1832, Fanny, 2nd d. of William Mostyn Owen Esq., of Woodhouse, Shropshire. Educ. at Eton and at Christ Church, Oxford. Lord-Lieut. and Costos Rot. of Denbighshire. Col. of the Denbighshire Militia. Patron of 1 living. A Liberal, voted for the ballot 1853; in favour of 'gradual reforms in Church and State'. Sat for Denbigh bor. in 1830 and 1831, and for Denbighshire from 1832 to 1835; was an unsuccessful candidate for that County in Jan. 1835, and July, 1841, but regained his seat in July, 1852. Sat until defeated in 1868. Died 21 Mar. 1872. [1867]

BIGGS, John. Stonygate, Knighton, Leicestershire. Reform. B. at Leicester, 1801. Unmarried. A Manufacturer at Leicester for which town he was a Magistrate from 1836. Elected Mayor there for 1840-41, for 1847-48, and a third time for 1855-56. A 'decided Liberal', in favour of such reform as would give 'the intelligence of the country more controul', in favour also of short Parliaments and the ballot, the abolition of church-rates etc. First elected for Leicester, June, 1856. Accepted Chiltern Hundreds 1862. Died 4 June 1871. [1861]

BIGGS, William. Highfild House, Leicester. B. at Leicester 1805. M. 1837, the youngest d. of John Worthington, Esq. A Magistrate, Town Councillor and Alderman of Leicester, and was Mayor of that town in 1842-3 and 1848-9. A Radical Reformer, opposed to all grants from the State for ecclesiastical purposes. Voted for the ballot 1853. Sat for Newport, Isle of Wight from 1852 until he accepted Chiltern Hundreds 21 Mar. 1857. Died 3 Oct. 1881. [1856]

BIGNOLD, Sir Samuel. 6 Crescent, New Bridge Street, Blackfriars, London. Surrey Street, Norwich. 3rd. s. of Thomas Bignold, Esq., of Norwich. B. in Norwich, 1791; m. 1815 only child of William Atkins, Esq., of Ridlington, Co. Norfolk. Was elected Sec. of the Norwich Union Insurance Company, 1814, and in the same capacity to the Norwich Life Assurance Company 1818. Was Sheriff of Norwich for 1830, elected Mayor in 1833, 1848 and 1853. A Magistrate for that city from 1830, a Magistrate and Dept.-Lieut. for the Co. of Norfolk from 1832. Patron of 2 livings. A Conservative, would have preferred the introduction of free trade by gradual means. First elected for Norwich Dec. 1854. Defeated 1857. Contested

34

same seat twice in 1859. Died 2 Jan. 1875. [1857]

BINGHAM, Lord. 7 Portland Place, London. White's, and United Services. B. in St. James's Parish, Westminster 1830, the eld. s. of the Earl of Lucan, by Lady Anne, 7th d. of 6th Earl of Cardigan. M. 1859, Lady Cecilia Catherine, youngest d. of 5th Duke of Richmond. Educ. at Rugby. Entered the army in 1848 and became Capt. and Lieut.-Col., Coldstream Guards 1859. Retired 1860. Appointed Aide-de-Camp to his father in the Crimean Campaign, 1854, and Brevet-Maj. 1855. A Liberal-Conservative and sat for Mayo from July 1865 until his retirement in 1874. In Nov. 1888 he succeeded as 4th Earl Lucan. Died 5th June 1914. [1873]

BIRCH, Sir Thomas Bernard, Bart. The Hasles, Prescot, Lancashire. Brooks's, Arthur's, University, and Reform. Only s. of Sir Joseph Birch, Bart., of the Hasles, Lancashire, (MP for Ludgershall, and subsequently for Nottingham), by the 3rd d. of Benjamin Heywood, Esq. of Liverpool. B. 1791. Educ. at Rugby, and at Jesus Coll., Cambridge, where he graduated M.A. 1816; called to the bar, at Lincoln's Inn, 1817, but never practised. Was private secretary to Lord Melbourne, when his lordship was Chief Secretary in Ireland. A Magistrate and Deputy-Lieut. of Lancashire, of which county he was Sheriff in 1841. A Whig, opposed to the taxes on tea, tobacco, etc., and pledged to support a property tax as a substitute. First returned for Liverpool in 1847. Retired in 1852. Died 3 Mar. 1880. [1852]

BIRBECK, Edward. Continued in House after 1885: full entry in Volume II.

BIRLEY, Hugh. 10 Upper Brook Street, London. Horstead Hall, Norwich. Carlton, and White's. S. of Joseph Birley, Esq., of Manchester, Cotton-Spinner and Manufacturer, by Jane d. of Thomas Hornby, Esq., of Kirkham. B. at Blackburn 1817; m. 1842, Marbella, d. of Joseph Baxendale, Esq. Educ. at Winchester. A well-known Manufacturer at Manchester. A Conservative who said he would give general support to Lord Beaconsfield's party. Sat for Manchester from Nov. 1868. MP until his death 9 Sept. 1883. [1883]

BISH, Thomas. 2 St. James's Square, London. Westminster, and Garrick. B. 1779; m. 1801, Mary, 2nd d. of John Collier, Esq., of Newport, Shropshire (dead). A Stock Broker and a Lottery Contractor. A Reformer, voted against the corn laws, in favour of the ballot, shortening the duration of Parliaments and the repeal of the assessed taxes. Entertained strong opinions on the necessity of the Bank affording the Country a better protection against forgery than their present notes, and thought that the Court and Parliament ought occasionally to be held in Dublin; was, however, opposed to a repeal of the Union. Was elected for Leominster in 1826, in opposition to Rowland Stephenson, Esq., the Banker; but was unseated on the ground of being a Lottery Contractor. Sat for it uninterruptedly from 1832, until he retired in 1837. Author of a pamphlet entitled *A Plea for Ireland.* [1837]

BISSET, Mordaunt Fenwick. Bagborough House, Taunton. Lessendrum House, Huntly, Scotland. Army & Navy, and Carlton. Only s. of Van Maurice George Fenwick-Bisset, formerly Archdeacon of Raphoe, Ireland, by Jane Harriet, d. of the late Maurice George Bisset, Esq. of Bath. B. at Raphoe, Ireland 1825; m. 1851, Susan only d. and heir of Francis Popham, Esq., of Bagborough, Somerset. Was educ. successively at Blackheath Proprietary School and the Royal School, Enniskillen, and Trinity Coll., Cambridge. Served in the 1st Dragoon Guards from 1844-49. A Magistrate for Somerset, and was High Sheriff of that Co. 1872. A Conservative. Sat for W. Somerset from Apr. 1880. Accepted Chiltern Hundreds 1883. [1883]

BLACK, Adam. 38 Drummond Place, Edinburgh. Reform. S. of Charles Black, Esq., of Edinburgh, Builder. B. in Edinburgh 1784; m. 1817, Isabella, only d. of James Tait, Esq., Architect. Educ. at the High School and University of Edinburgh. Was well known as a Bookseller in Edinburgh, Publisher of Sir Walter Scott's works, the *Encyclopaedia Britannica*, etc. and was author of several articles in the latter. Was Lord Provost of Edinburgh from 1843-1848. A Liberal, and would vote for any measure which would 'provide education for every child in the kingdom'; was in favour of Parliamentary Reform to a moderate extent, and vote by ballot; opposed to all religious endowments. First elected for Edinburgh Feb. 1856. Sat until defeated 1865. Died 24 Jan. 1874. [1865]

BLACKALL, Maj. Samuel Wensley. Colamber, Edgeworthstown, Longford. Junior United Service, and Sackville Street, Dublin. S. of Major Blackall, of the E.I.C.s. Service. B. 1809; m. 1833, Georgiana, d. of Henry Rowles, Esq., of Stratton Street, Piccadilly. Was educ. at Trinity Coll., Dublin. Entered the army as Ensign 85th foot in 1827, and eventually became a Major. Author of two pamphlets on Irish affairs. A Liberal, 'favoured the consideration of the repeal question'; in favour of the extension of the franchise and the tenant right bill. First returned for Longford in 1847. Sat until appointed Governor of Dominica Apr. 1851-57; Governor of Sierra Leone 1862; and Governor of Queensland from 1868 until his death 21 Jan. 1871. [1850]

BLACKBURN, Peter. 10 Prince's Gardens, London. Killearn, Glasgow. Carlton. S. of John Blackburn, Esq. a Jamaica Proprietor. B. at Levenside, Dumbartonshire 1811; m. 1838, d. of James Wedderburn, Esq., some years Solicitor-Gen. for Scotland. Educ. at Eton. Entered the army as Cornet 2nd Life Guards 1829, retired 1836. Was Chairman of the Edinburgh and Glasgow Railway from Sept. 1846. Was a Lord of the Treasury from Mar.-June 1859. A Liberal-Conservative. Unsuccessfully contested Edinburgh City July 1847, and Glasgow 1852. First elected for Stirlingshire Feb. 1855. Sat until defeated 1865. Died 20 May 1870. [1865]

BLACKBURNE, John. Churchyard Court, Temple, London. A native of Huddersfield. A King's Counsel, and Bencher of the Middle Temple. Chief Commissioner of the Corporation Inquiry. A Reformer, in favour of the ballot, triennial Parliaments, and the abolition of the Corn Laws. Sat for Huddersfield from 1833, when he was elected on the death of Capt. Fenton. MP until his death Apr. 1837. [1836]

BLACKBURNE, John Ireland, sen. 2 Park Street, Westminster, London. Hale, Lancashire. Boodle's, Carlton, and Crockford's. S. of John Blackburne, Esq., of Hale, who represented Lancashire for 47 years. B. May 1783; m. 1809, Anne, d. of William Bamford, Esq. Patron of 1 living. A Conservative, voted for agricultural protection 1846. Sat for Newton eleven years, from 1807-1808; and for Warrington from 1834, having unsuccessfully contested the bor. with Mr. Hornby in 1832. Sat until he retired 1847. Died 27 Jan. 1874. [1874]

BLACKBURNE, John Ireland, jun. Hale Hall, Liverpool. Carlton, and United Service. Eldest s. of John Ireland Blackburne, Esq. of Hale Hall, and Orford Hall, Lancashire (who sat for Newton for eleven years, and for Warrington for thirteen years), by Anne, d. of William Bamford, Esq., of Bamford in the same county. B. at Hale Hall, 1817; m. 1st, 1846, Mary, d. of Sir Henry Bold Hoghton, Bart., of Bold Hoghton Tower, Lancashire (she died 1855); 2ndly, 1857, Emma Jemima, widow of the 15th Visct. Hereford (she died 1870). Educ. at Eton. Was Capt. of 5th Dragoon Guards, which he entered in 1835, Col.-Commandant 4th Lancashire Militia from

1853. A Magistrate and Dept.-Lieut. for Lancashire. Patron of 1 living. A Liberal-Conservative, in favour of maintaining our institution in Church and State; also of the revision of the system of local taxation. Sat for South-West Lancashire from Nov. 1875 until he retired in 1885. Died 5 Sept. 1893. [1885]

BLACKETT, Christopher. Wylam, Northumberland. Brooks's and Travellers'. M. Aug. 15, 1818, Elizabeth, d. and co-heiress of Montague Burgoyne, Esq. Was formerly a Capt. in the 18th Hussars. Unsuccessfully contested the borough of Newcastle-upon-Tyne, on the death of Sir M.W. Ridley, Bart. in July 1836. Of Whig principles, but adverse to the ballot. Sat for Beeralston, Devon in the 1st parliament of William IV. Elected for Northumberland S. after the dissolution in 1837. Sat until he retired 1841. Died 1847. [1838]

BLACKETT, John Fenwick Burgoyne. 10 Eaton Place, London. Mylam Hall, Nr. Newcastle-on-Tyne. Brooks's, Athenaeum, and Alfred. B. in London 1821, the eld. s. of Christopher Blackett, Esq. of Wylam Hall, Northumberland (who was MP for the Southern division of that Co. from 1837-41), by Elizabeth, youngest d. and co-heir of Montagu Burgoyne, Esq., of Marle Hall, Essex. Unmarried. Educ. at Harrow and Christ Church, Oxford, where he was 2nd class in classics 1841, and was elected Fellow of Merton. Author of some articles in the *Edinburgh Review*. A Liberal, and favoured a 'vigorous measure of Parliamentary reform', an extension of the suffrage, short Parliaments and vote by ballot. Did not pledge himself to vote against the Maynooth Grant. Sat for Newcastle-upon-Tyne from July 1852 until he accepted Chiltern Hundreds in Jan. 1856. Died 25 Apr. 1856. [1855]

BLACKSTONE, William Seymour. Howbery, Oxfordshire. Castle Priory, Berkshire. Carlton. Grands. of the great lawyer whose name he bears. B. 1809. His family had the patronage of the living of Wallingford. Dept.-Lieut. for Berkshire. A Conservative, voted for agricultural protection, 1846. Sat for Wallingford from 1832 until he retired in 1852. Died 6 Jan. 1881. [1852]

BLACKNEY, Walter. 8 Manchester Buildings, London. A Repealer; popularly called Dr. Doyle's member. First sat for Carlow in the Parliament of 1831. Retired in 1835. [1833]

BLAIR, James. 3 Portman Square, London. Penninghame, Wigtonshire. Of an old Perthshire family. M. 27th Dec. 1815, Elizabeth Cutherim, youngest d. of the Hon. Edward Stopford, uncle of Earl of Courtown. A Conservative. Formerly sat, at various periods, for Aldborough, Minehead and Saltash. First contested Wigtonshire in 1835; first returned in 1837. Sat until defeated in 1841. Died 9 Dec. 1841.   [1840]

BLAIR, Col. James Hunter. 3 St. James's Place, London. Blairquhain Park, Athenry. White's, Guards' and Coventry. B. at Milton, Ayrshire 1817, the eld s. of Sir David Hunter Blair, Bart., by his 1st wife, Dorothea, 2nd. d. of Edward Hay Mackenzie, Esq., of Newhall and Cromartie. Unmarried. Educ. at Eton. Entered the Scots Fusilier Guards 1835, became a Lieut.-Col. in 1848. Appointed a Dept.-Lieut. of Ayrshire 1845. A Conservative; opposed to unreciprocated free trade, to the Maynooth Grant and to any extension of the franchise. Sat for Ayrshire from July 1852 until his death in 1854.   [1854]

BLAIR, Stephen. Mill Hill House, Bolton, Lancashire. National. Eld. s. of George Blair, Esq., of Mill Hill House, Bolton. B. at Bolton 1804; unm. A Merchant and Bleacher at Bolton. A Magistrate for Bolton, of which place he had been Mayor. A Conservative, voted for a return to agricultural protection 1850. First returned for Bolton Sept. 1848, without opposition. Defeated in 1852. Died 5 July 1870.   [1852]

BLAKE, Sir Francis, Bart. Tilmouth Park, Northumberland. M. Miss Neale, (dead). Of Whig principles. Had an estate in Domingo, but no slaves. Sat for Berwick-upon-Tweed from 1826. Sat until defeated Jan. 1835.   [1834]

BLAKE, John Aloysius. 44 Westland Row, Dublin. Stephen's Green, Dublin. Devonshire. S. of Andrew Blake, Esq., of Waterford (descended from the Blakes of Renvyle, Co. Galway), by Mary, d. of Patrick Galway, Esq. of Waterford. B. at Waterford 1826; m. 1874, Adelaide Mary, youngest d. of Nicholas Mahon Power, Esq., of Faithlegg, Co. Waterford. A Dept.-Lieut. and for some years MP of that county. Educ. at St. John's Coll., Waterford and the Government Coll., Pan Basses, in the Pyrenees, France. A Magistrate for the City of Waterford, of which he was also Mayor for 3 years, 1855-57. Chairman of a Select Committee on Fisheries 1868, and Chairman of a Royal Commission on Sea and Oyster Fisheries 1869; appointed Chairman of the Commission for Selecting Fishery Harbours in Ireland 1883. Author of several works, including *Defects of the Moral Treatment of Insanity in Public Asylums, The Sea and Inland Fisheries of Ireland,* etc. A Liberal; in favour of a native Parliament and of the system called 'Home Rule' for Ireland, also of

denominational education, the Permissive Bill, a peasant proprietary etc. Sat for Waterford City from Apr. 1857-Nov.1869; sat for the Co. of Waterford from Apr. 1880. Accepted Chiltern Hundreds Aug. 1884. Died 22 May 1887. [1884]

BLAKE, Mark. Balinafad, Co. Mayo. Reform. Was first returned for Mayo on the death of Sir William Brabazon in 1840. A Repealer and pledged to support Irish Manufacturers in and out of Parliament. Accepted Chiltern Hundreds in Feb. 1846. Died 27 June 1886.   [1845]

BLAKE, Martin Joseph. Ballyglunin Park, Athenry. Reform. Was representative of the Blakes of Ballyglunin, from which also sprang the Blakes, Baronets, of Langham, Suffolk. A Repealer, in favour of vote by ballot and of removing the Bishops from the House of Lords. Was an unsuccessful candidate for Galway at the general election in 1832, but on petition superseded Mr. M'Lachlan in 1833, from which period he continued to represent Galway. Sat until he retired 1857. Died Mar. 1861.   [1857]

BLAKE, Thomas. Lenanon, Ross, Herefordshire. Reform. S. of Wm. Blake of Ross, Herefordshire. B. 1825; m. 1st 1844, 2ndly 1874. An Accountant and Estate Agent in Ross. Chairman of the Ross School Board. A Liberal, in favour of household suffrage in counties. Contested Herefordshire Dec 1868; sat for Leominster from Feb. 1876 until defeated 1880. Sat for Forest of Dean div., Gloucestershire from Dec. 1885 until Chiltern Hundreds July 1887.   [1880]

BLAKE, Sir Valentine, Bart. The Castle, Co. Galway. B. 1780, the s. of the 11th Bart. M. 1st in 1803, the d. of Joseph Donnellan, Esq., and 2ndly in 1843, the d. of Robert MacDonnell, Esq., M.D. A Liberal. Sir Valentine represented Galway in the Parliaments before the Reform Act, after which he did not contest the seat again until a by-election in 1838 at which he was unsuccessful. Returned in 1841 and remained an MP until his death in Jan. 1847.   [1845]

BLAKE, William John. 62 Portland Place, London. Danesbury, Hertfordshire. Brooks's, Reform, and Athenaeum. Eld. s. of William Blake, Esq., of Danesbury, Hertfordshire. B. 1805, A Reformer, favourable to the ballot and to triennial parliaments. Was a First Class Man in classics and mathematics and obtained the prize for the Latin Essay at Oxford in 1827. Returned in 1837 for Newport. Defeated in 1841; contested seat again in 1847. Died 15 Sept. 1875. [1838]

BLAKEMORE, Richard. 15 Regent Street,

London. Leys, Herefordshire. Union. Eld. s. of Thomas Blakemore, Esq., of Littleton Hall, by the d. of John Partridge, Esq., of Ross, Herefordshire. B. 1775. Was High Sheriff of Glamorganshire in 1826, and of Herefordshire in 1830. A proprietor of tin works in Glamorganshire. A Dept.-Lieut. of Hereford and Monmouth. A Conservative, voted for agricultural protection, 1846. Contested Hereford in 1826, 1832, and 1835. First elected for Wells at the general election in 1837. Sat until he retired in 1852. [1852]

BLAKEMORE, Thomas William Booker-. 13 Cockspur Street, London. Velindra House, Glamorganshire. The Leys, Herefordshire. Carlton, and Parthenon. Eld. s. of the Rev. Luke Booker, LL.D., by the d. of Thomas Blakemore, Esq., of The Leys, Monmouthshire. B. 1801; m. 1824, Jane, only d. of John Coghlan, Esq., Educ. at Hartlebury, Worcestershire. Was High Sheriff of Glamorganshire in 1848. A Dept.-Lieut. for Glamorgan and Herefordshire. Author of a *Treatise on the Mineral Basin of South Wales.* Assumed by royal licence the name of Blakemore in addition to his patronymic, in accordance with the will of his uncle, Richard Blakemore, Esq., Sept. 1855. A Conservative, opposed the repeal of the Corn Laws; in favour of a moderate extension of the franchise; thought the State should supply 'a sound religious education to all denominations of Christians; opposed to the Maynooth Grant and the admission of Jews to Parliament.' First returned for Herefordshire Sept. 1850. MP until his death 7 Nov. 1858. [1858]

BLAMIRE, William. 11 Devonshire Place, London. The Oaks, and Thackwood, Cumberland. Wyndham. B. 1790, nephew of J.C. Curwen, Esq., MP for Cumberland. M. 1834, Dora, youngest d. of John Taubman, Esq., Nunnery, Isle of Man, and relict of Col. Wilks, Governor of St. Helena. An extensive farmer and grazier. A Reformer, in favour of a fixed duty upon corn, the removal of the taxes on knowledge, shortening the duration of Parliaments, the removal of all monopolies, and such a Church reform, as among other objects, would prevent the clergy engaging in any secular pursuits. First sat for Cumberland East in 1831. Sat until appointed Chief Tithe Commissioner in Aug. 1836, continuing until the Commission finished its work in Aug. 1851. Died 12 Jan. 1862. [1836]

BLAND, Loftus Henry. 33 Merrion Square North, Dublin. Blandsfort, Queen's Co. Oxford & Cambridge. S. of John Bland, Esq. (descended from General Humphrey Bland, who was governor of Gibraltar and commander-in-chief in Scotland, temp. Anne and George I), by Elizabeth, d. of Robert Birch, Esq., MP for Belturbet in the Irish House of Commons. B. at Blandsfort, Queen's Co., 1805; m. 1st, 1840, Charlotte Elizabeth, 2nd d. of General the Hon. Arthur Grove Annesley (she died 1842); 2ndly, Annie, d. of John P. Hackett, Esq., of Stratford Place, London. Educ. at Trinity Coll., Cambridge, where he graduated B.A. 1825, M.A. 1828. Was called to the bar in Ireland, 1831, and made a Queen's Counsel there, 1854. A Magistrate for King's and Queen's Cos. A Liberal, 'a friend of progressive legislation, reform of the representative system, a modified tenant right, civil liberty and religious equality'; voted for the ballot 1853. First returned for King's Co. in July 1852. Sat until defeated in 1859. Died 21 Jan. 1862. [1858]

BLANDFORD, George, Marq. of (I). 5 Grosvenor Gate, London. Eld. s. of the Duke of Marlborough. B. in 1793; m. 1819, his cousin, Jane, eld. d. of the Earl of Galloway. A Reformer, in favour of the ballot. Sat for Woodstock in the Parliaments of 1826 and 1830, but in that of 1831 gave way to Lord Stormont. Regained his seat in 1832 until he retired in 1835. Returned again 11 May 1838 and sat until succeeded as 6th Duke of Marlborough, Mar. 1840. Died 1 July 1857. [1839]

BLANDFORD, J.W. Marq. of (II). 36 Lower Brook Street, London. Blenheim House, Oxfordshire. Carlton. Eld. s. of the Duke of Marlborough. B. at Garboldisham Hall 1822; m. 1843, Lady Frances Anne Emily, eld d. of the 3rd Marq. of Londonderry. Educ. at Oriel Coll., Oxford. A Dept.-Lieut. of Oxfordshire, appointed Lieut. of the 1st Yeomanry Cavalry in that Co. 1843. A Conservative. First elected for Woodstock Apr. 1844, took the Chiltern Hundreds Apr. 1845, in consequence of having supported Sir R. Peel's free trade measures without the concurrence of the Duke of Marlborough, whose influence at Woodstock was paramount. Was again returned for that borough, however, without opposition in 1847. Stood an unsuccessful contest for Middlesex July 1852, but took his seat for Woodstock. Sat until he succeeded as 7th Duke July 1857. Lord President of the Council 1868, Lord-Lieut. of Ireland Dec. 1876-Apr.1880. Died 5 July 1883. [1857]

BLAYNEY, Hon. Cadwallader Davis. Cocoa Tree, St. James's Street. Castle Blayney, Co. Monaghan. Eld. s. of Lord Blayney, B. in 1803. A Conservative. Sat for Monaghan from 1830 until he succeeded to the Peerage (Lord Blayney) 8 Apr. 1834; Irish representative Peer from 1841. Died 18 Jan. 1874. [1834]

BLENCOWE, John George. Bineham, Lewes. Oxford & Cambridge. Eld. s. of Robert Willis Blencowe, Esq., of the Hooke, Nr. Lewes, by Charlotte Elizabeth, d. of the Rev. Sir Henry Poole, Bart. B. in London 1818; m. Frances, eld. d. of W.J. Campien, Esq., of Danny, Nr. Hurstpierpoint, Sussex. Educ. at Eton and at Christ Church, Oxford. A Liberal, and a supporter generally of Lord Palmerston; in favour of the total abolition of Church rates. First elected for Lewes Jan 1860. Retired 1865. Died 28 Apr. 1900. [1865]

BLENNERHASSETT, Arthur. Ballyseedy, Nr. Tralee. M. d. of A.D. Grady, Esq. Of a distinguished English family, settled in Ireland since the reign of Queen Elizabeth, different members of which have repeatedly represented the county in Parliament. Of Conservative principles. Contested Kerry, defeating Mr. Mullins, the late member (who was a radical Reformer) at the general election in 1837. Defeated 1841. [1838]

BLENNERHASSETT, Sir Rowland, Bart. 19 Bolton Street, London. Church-town, Beaufort, Co. Kerry. Only s. of Sir Arthur Blennerhassett, 3rd Bart., by his marriage with Miss Sarah Mahoney. B. 1839; m. 1870 Countess Charlotte De Leyden, only d. of Count De Leyden. A moderate Liberal. Sat for Galway bor. from July 1865 to June 1874; sat for Kerry from April 1880. Retired in 1885. H.M.'s Inspector of Reformatory and Industrial Schools in Ireland 1890-97; President of Queen's Coll., Cork 1897-1904. Died 22 March 1909. [1885]

BLENNERHASSETT, Rowland Ponsonby. 52 Hans Place, London. Kells, Cahirciveen, Co. Kerry. Reform. Only s. of Richard K. Blennerhassett, Esq., of Kells, by Honoria, d. of William Corrigal Ponsonby, Esq., of Crotto. B. at Kells, Co. Kerry, 1850; m. 1876, Mary Beatrice, 3rd d. of Walter Armstrong, Esq., Was educ. at Trinity Coll., Dublin, where he obtained first honours; also at Christ Church, Oxford. Was called to the bar at the Inner Temple, May 1878. A Magistrate for Kerry. A Liberal, in favour of the 'Home-Rule' movement. Sat for Kerry from Feb. 1872 until defeated in 1885 contesting N.E Manchester. Q.C. 1894; died 7 April 1913. [1885]

BLEWITT, Reginald James. Llanfarnam Abbey, Monmouthshire. Reform. B. 1799, the 2nd s. of Maj. Edward Blewitt, of Llanfarnam Abbey, Monmouthshire. His greatgrandfather was Sir Samuel Blewitt, High Sheriff of London, Master of Skinner's Company and s. of a Northamptonshire gentleman. Descended on the female side from Sir Edward Morgan, of Llanfarnam Abbey, Bart. Educ. at Rugby. Practised for some years as a Solicitor but retired in 1827. Kept his terms at Lincoln's Inn but was not called to the bar. In 1829 established and edited the *Monmouthshire Merlin*, a Liberal paper which he relinquished in 1832. A Reformer, a Magistrate and a Dept.-Lieut. for the Co. of Monmouth., acting occasionally as Chairman at the Quarter Sessions. Sat for Monmouth district from 1837 until he accepted Chiltern Hundreds in Mar. 1852. Died 11 Sept. 1878. [1851]

BLUNT, Sir Charles Richard, Bart. 35 Mortimer Street, Cavendish Square, London. Heathfield Park, Sussex. B. 1775; m. 1824, Sophia, d. of Richard Barker, Esq., and relict of Richard A'hmuty, formerly of Bengal, where Sir Charles was Judge of the Zillah of Beerbhoom. Of Whig principles; in favour of short Parliaments and the ballot. Sat first for Lewes in 1831, when he displaced Sir John Shelley, who had opposed the first Reform Bill. MP until his death 29 Feb. 1840. [1838]

BODKIN, John James. 41 Piccadilly, London. Kilcloony, Co. Galway. S. of John Bodkin, Esq., formerly Mayor of Galway. A Reformer, in favour of the ballot. Sat for the town of Galway in 1831, and represented Co. Galway from 1835 until he retired 1847. Died Jan. 1882. [1847]

BODKIN, William Henry. 8 Mansfield Street, London. Church Court, Temple, London. Hampstead Heath, Middlesex. Carlton. Only s. of Peter Bodkin, Esq., of Northampton Square, London, who was descended from an old family in Ireland. B. 1791; m. 1813, d. of P.R. Poland, Esq. A Barrister, Recorder of Dover, and Chairman of the Society of Arts in London. Wrote pamphlets on the Poor Laws. A Conservative, but in favour of free trade. First returned for Rochester in 1841. Sat until defeated 1847. Recorder of Dover until 1874. Knighted 3 Aug. 1867. Died 26 Mar. 1874. [1847]

BÖLCKOW, Henry William Ferdinand. 33 Princes Gate, London. Maston Hall, Middlesborough. Reform. S. of Heinrich Bölckow, a native of Germany, by Caroline his wife. B. in Mecklenburg-Schwerin, 1804; m. 1st 1840 Miriam, widow of C. Hay, Esq., 2ndly, 1851, Harriet, only d. of James Fauch, Esq. of Halifax. An Iron-Master in Yorkshire, and contributed greatly to the development and extension of the town of Middlesborough, and in partnership with Mr. Vaughan established iron works and conducted mining operations in the vicinity; the firm being afterwards constituted a

Limited Company under the title of Bölckow Vaughan & Co. Ltd. Made a gift of 'The Albert Park' to the people of Middlesborough at a cost of more than £20,000, and was instrumental in establishing schools, an infirmary, the exchange etc. in the town. In 1841 became a nationalised British subject by Act of Parliament, and in 1868, by a further Act received the full privileges of a British subject to sit in Parliament etc. Was the 1st Mayor of Middlesborough on its incorporation, 1853. A Magistrate and Dept.-Lieut. for the N. Riding of Yorkshire. A Magistrate for the Co. of Durham and for Middlesborough. A Liberal; voted for the disestablishment of the Irish Church 1869; was in favour of the 'total' abolition of Church rates and alteration of the rate paying clauses in the Reform Act. Sat for Middlesborough from Dec. 1868. MP until his death 18 June 1878. [1878]

BOLDERO, Col. Henry George. 11 Great Rider St., London. Hurst Grove, Maidenhead, Berkshire. Carlton. S. of Rev. J. Boldero, of Ampton, Suffolk, who was of an old family in the county. M. Mary, d. of J. Neeld, Esq., of Gloucester Place, London. Entered the Royal Engineers as Lieut. 1814; became a Capt. 1827; retired from the army as Lieut.-Col. 1851. Was clerk of the Ordnance from 1841 till 1846. Was presented with a silver cup by his constituents for his successful exertions in 1832 to preserve two members to Chippenham; made active exertions in relation to corporal punishment in the army, the comforts of assistant-surgeons in the navy, the claims of the Royal Marines, etc. A Conservative; in favour of a reduction in the public expenditure and promised to 'offer a steady resistance to the encroachments of Popery.' Sat for Chippenham in 1831 and from 1835 until he resigned at 1859 general election. Unsuccessfully contested Norwich 28 June 1859, but the election was declared void and he did not stand at the following election. Died 9 Apr. 1873. [1858]

BOLLING, William. Darcy Lever Hall, Nr. Bolton-le-Moors. 3rd s. of Edward Bolling, Esq., of Bolton, who was descended from the Bowlings, of Bowling Hall, Yorkshire. B. at Bolton 1785; m. 1824, d. of Rev. James Slade, vicar of Bolton. Educ. at the Bolton Grammar School. A Merchant and Manufacturer. A Conservative, but in favour of free trade; opposed to the endowment of the Roman Catholic clergy. Sat for Bolton-le-Moors from 1832 to 1841; at which last election he was an unsuccessful candidate; again returned in 1847. MP until his death in 1848. [1847 2nd ed.]

BOLTON, J.C. Continued in House after 1885: full entry in Volume II.

BOND, Joshua Walter McGeough. The Argory, Moy. Drumsill House, Armagh. Carlton, and Army & Navy. Eld. s. of Walter McGeough Bond, Esq., of the Argory, Co. Armagh, by Anne, 2nd. d. of Ralph Smyth, Esq., of Gaybrook, Co. Westmeath. B. in Dublin 1831; m. 1856, Albertine Louise, d. of Frederick Shanahan, Esq., Barrister-at-Law. Educ. at Cheltenham Coll. and Sandhurst. Formerly Lieut. 49th regiment. A Magistrate for the Co. of Armagh. A Conservative. First returned for Armagh City Dec. 1855; was an unsuccessful candidate in Apr. 1857, but regained his seat in May 1859. Sat until defeated 1865. Died 29 Aug. 1905. [1865]

BONHAM, Francis Robert. Brighton. Athenaeum. Appointed Store-keeper of the Ordnance under the Conservative administration in Nov. 1834; resigned in Apr. following. Sat for Rye in the Parliament of 1830; but was ousted by Col. de Lacy Evans, in 1831. Sat for Harwich from Jan. 1835. Defeated 1837. [1837]

BOOKER, Thomas William. See BLAKEMORE, Thomas William Booker-.

BOORD, Sir T.W. Continued in House after 1885: full entry in Volume II.

BOOTH, G. Sclater-. See SCLATER-BOOTH, G. Continued in House after 1885: full entry in Volume II.

BOOTH, Sir Robert Gore, Bart. 7 Buckingham Gate, London. Lissadell, Co. Sligo. Earlsfield, Co. Sligo. Carlton. Eld. s. of Sir Robert Newcomer Gore Booth, 3rd Bart. (who assumed the name of Booth) by the d. of Henry Irvine, Esq., of Streamstown, Sligo. B. at Bath, 1805; m. 1st, 1827, Hon. Caroline, 2nd d. of 1st Visct. Norton (she died 1828); 2ndly, 1830, Caroline, 2nd d. of Thomas Goold, Esq., Master in Chancery (Ireland), (she died 1855). Educ. at Westminster and Queen's Coll., Cambridge, where he graduated, M.A. 1826; was subsequently transferred *ad eundem* at Dublin. A Magistrate for Sligo; appointed a Dept.-Lieut. of Sligo 1841. Patron of 2 livings. A Conservative. First returned for the county of Sligo, March 1850. MP until his death 21 Dec. 1876. [1876]

BORLASE, W.C. Continued in House after 1885: full entry in Volume II.

BORTHWICK, Peter. 22 Queen Street, Mayfair, London. B. 1805. Delivered lectures and held disputations in the principal provincial towns, in favour of the gradual emancipation of the slaves in the West Indies, as contra--

distinguished from immediate freedom, and received the thanks of the West India Proprietors, accompanied by a service of plate and a public dinner. Was formerly a Fellow-Commoner of Downing Coll., Cambridge. A Conservative, voted for agricultural protection 1846. Unsuccessfully contested Evesham in 1832, sat for it from 1834 until the dissolution in 1837, when he was again returned, but unseated on petition, and he then remained out of Parliament until 1841 when he was again elected though absent from England. Sat until he retired 1847. Unsuccessfully contested St. Ives and Penryn July 1847. Editor of *Morning Post* 1850 until his death 18 Dec. 1852.
[1847]

BOSCAWEN-ROSE, Lord. St. James's Square, London. Newbury, Berkshire. Tregothnan, Cornwall. Carlton. Eld. s. of the Earl of Falmouth. B. 1811. A Conservative. First elected for Cornwall W. in July 1841. Sat until he succeeded father as 2nd Earl 29 Dec. 1841. Died 28 Aug. 1852.
[1842]

BOSS, Capt. John George, R.N. 26 Craven Street, London. Otterington Hall, Yorkshire. A Commander in the Navy. M. the 3rd d. of Sir James Pennyman, Bart. and niece of the 1st Earl Grey. A Reformer. Sat for Northallerton from 1832. Retired in 1835.
[1833]

BOTFIELD, Beriah, F.R.S., F.S.A. 5 Grosvenor Square, London. Norton Hall, Daventry, Northamptonshire. Deckar Hill, Shiffnal, Hopton Court, Ludlow. Carlton, Athenaeum, Conservative, United University, and Oriental. Eld. s. of Beriah Botfield, Esq., of Norton Hall, Northamptonshire, by Charlotte, d. of William Withering, Esq., M.D., of Edgbaston Hall, near Birmingham. B. at Earl's Ditton, Shropshire 1807; m. 1858, Isabella, 2nd d. of Sir Baldwin Leighton, Bart., of Loton Park, Shropshire. Educ. at Harrow and at Christ Church, Oxford, where he graduated B.A. 1828, M.A. 1847. Was High Sheriff of Northamptonshire in 1831, appointed a Dept.-Lieut. of that Co. in 1841, and of Shropshire in 1855. Served in the South Shropshire Yeomanry Cavalry as Cornet 1841, and Lieut. in 1848. Patron of 2 livings. Author of a *Tour in Scotland,* privately printed in 1829, and *Notes on the Cathedral Libraries of England,* published in 1849. Chevalier of the Order of Albert the Brave of Saxony, and Knight of the Order of Leopold of Belgium. A Liberal-Conservative, who wanted to promote 'the greatest happiness of the greatest number.' First returned for Ludlow in May 1840 and sat till the general election in 1847, when he was defeated; again elected for Ludlow in 1857 and was MP until his death 7 Aug. 1863.
[1863]

BOURKE, Rt. Hon. Robert. 18 Montagu Street, London. Coalstown, Haddington, Scotland. Carlton. B. at Hayes, Co. Meath 1827, 3rd s. of 5th Earl of Mayo, by Anne Charlotte, only d. and heir of the Hon. John Jocelyn of Fair Hill, Co. Louth, and grand-d. of 1st Earl of Roden. M. 1863, Lady Susan Georgiana, eld. d. of the Marq. Dalhousie, the distinguished Gov.-Gen. of India. Educ. at Enniskillen School, Hall Place, Kent and Trinity Coll., Dublin. Was called to the bar at the Inner Temple Nov. 1852. Was Under-Sec. of State for Foreign Affairs Feb. 1874-Apr. 1880. Became Lieut. South Middlesex Volunteers 1860. Author of *Parliamentary Precedents,* etc. A Conservative. Sat for King's Lynn from Dec. 1868-1886, when he was appointed Governor of Madras (until 1890). Created Baron Connemara, May 1887. Died 3 Sept. 1902.
[1886]

BOURKE, Hon. R.S. See NAAS, Rt. Hon. Lord.

BOURNE, Col. Sir James. 33 Onslow Square, London. Heathfield, Liverpool. Carlton, and Conservative. Eld. surviving s. of Peter Bourne, Esq., of Hackinsall, Lancashire and of Liverpool, by Margaret, only d. of James Drinkwater, Esq. B. 1812; m. 1841, Sarah Harriet, d. of Thomas Fournis Dyson, Esq., of Willow Hall, Yorkshire and Everton, Liverpool. Educ. at Shrewsbury School. A Magistrate and Dept.-Lieut. of the Co. Palatine of Lancaster, Lieut.-Col.-Commandant Lancashire Militia Artillery, and Col. 4th Brigade Lancashire Artillery Volunteers. A Conservative, in favour of a reduction of the Malt Tax. Unsuccessfully contested Wexford bor. July 1841; sat for Evesham from Apr. 1865 until he retired 1880. Created Baronet 10 May 1880. Companion of the Bath May 1881. Died 14 Mar. 1882.
[1880]

BOUSFIELD, Nathaniel George Philips. Tilson Hall, Windermere. Parkside, Kendal. Holy Wath, Coniston. Carlton, and Junior Carlton. S. of John Bousfield, Esq., of London, by Catherine, d. of W. Butler, Esq., of Wigan. B. at Dublin 1829; m. 1872, Catherine, d. of John Barrett, Esq., of Holy Wath, Coniston. Educ. at Liverpool Coll. A Maj. 1st Lancashire Rifle Volunteers at Liverpool. A Magistrate for Westmoreland. A Conservative, who would maintain the constitution in Church and State. Sat for Bath from Feb. 1874, until he retired 1880.
[1880]

BOUVERIE, Hon. D.P. A Whig. Returned for Salisbury 6 May 1833. Retired in 1835. Died 5 Nov. 1850.

BOUVERIE, Rt. Hon. Edward Pleydell. 44 Wilton Crescent, London. Reform and Brooks's. B.1818, the 2nd s. of 3rd Earl of Radnor, by 3rd d.

of Sir Henry P. St. John Mildmay, Bart. M. 1842, Elizabeth, youngest d. of Gen. Balfour of Balbernie, Fife. Educ. at Harrow and at Trinity Coll., Cambridge. Was Under-Sec. for the Home Department July 1850-Mar. 1852; held the joint offices of Vice-Pres. of the Board of Trade, Paymaster General of the Forces and Treasurer of the Navy, from Feb.-Aug.1855. Was President of the Poor Law Board Aug. 1855-Mar. 1858, Chairman of Committees of the whole House Apr. 1853-Mar. 1855, 2nd Church Estates Commissioner from Aug. 1859-Nov. 1865, and appointed an Ecclesiastical Commissioner for England in July 1869. Member of the Corporation of Foreign Landholders in 1877, and Chairman 1878. A Liberal, and favoured the disestablishment of the Irish Church 1869, and the assimilation of the burgh and county franchise in Scotland. Unsuccessfully contested Salisbury May and Nov. 1843. Sat for Kilmarnock from 1844 until his defeat in 1874. During this time he contested Berkshire July 1865. He later contested Liskeard Apr. 1880. Died 16 Dec. 1889. [1873]

BOUVERIE, Hon. Philip Pleydell–. 16 Hill Street, London. Brymore, Bridgewater, Somerset. Athenaeum. 5th s. of the 2nd Earl of Radnor, by the Hon. Anne Duncombe, 2nd d. and co-heir of Anthony Lord Feversham. B. 1788; m. 1811, Maria, the 3rd d. of Sir William Pierce Ashe A'Court, Bart., and sister to Lord Heytesbury (she died 1862). Educ. at Harrow. A Banker in London. A Dept.-Lieut. of Somerset, of which Co. he was Sheriff in 1843. A Commissioner of the Lieutenancy for London. A Liberal, in favour of the 'voluntary system' and the abolition of Church rates; would support education on a religious basis, and recommend government aid for all denominations, but was opposed to a compulsory rate; in favour of extension of the suffrage; regarded the grant to Maynooth as 'a compact,' and supported its continuance. Was an unsuccessful candidate for Devizes in Jan. 1835, and for Somerset W. in July 1847. First returned for Berkshire Apr. 1857. Sat until defeated 1865. Died 27 May 1872. [1865]

BOVILL, Sir William. 103 Victoria Street, Pimlico, London. 1 Brick Court, Temple, London. Worplesdon Lodge, Guildford, Surrey. Carlton, and Athenaeum. 2nd surviving s. of B. Bovill, Esq., of Durnsford Lodge, Wimbledon. B. 1814; m. 1844, Maria, eld. d. of J.H. Bolton, Esq., of Lee Park, Blackheath. Called to the bar at the Middle Temple 1841, and joined the Home Circuit, made a Queen's Counsel 1855. A Bencher of the Middle Temple. A Magistrate for Surrey. A Conservative, but disposed to give a 'general support' to Lord Palmerston; voted however against

Ministers on the vote of censure 1864. First returned for Guildford Mar. 1857. Sat until appointed Lord Chief Justice of the Common Pleas 29 Nov. 1866., until his death 1 Nov. 1873. [1865]

BOWEN, James Bevan. Llwyngwair, Newport, Pembrokeshire. United University. S. of George Bowen, Esq., of Llwyngwair, by Sarah, d. of John Thomas, Esq., of Long House, Pembrokeshire. B. at Llwyngwair 1828; m. 1857, Harriette, youngest d. of Rev. John Standley, of Southoe Rectory, Huntingdonshire. Educ. at King's Coll., London, and at Worcester Coll., Oxford, graduated M.A. 1851. Called to the bar at the Inner Temple 1856 and practised as an equity draughtsman and conveyancer. A Magistrate for Cardiganshire and a Magistrate and Dept.-Lieut. for Carmarthenshire and Pembrokeshire, was High Sheriff of the last in 1862. A moderate Conservative, not in favour of 'any interference' in the laws governing the sale of intoxicating liquors. Sat for Pembrokeshire from Nov. 1866-Nov. 1868; re-elected June 1876. Retired 1880. Died 14 Nov. 1905. [1880]

BOWES, John. 54 Conduit Street, London. Streatlam Castle and Hilton Abbey, Co. Durham. Reform. B. 1811. Patron of 1 living. A Reformer, in favour of triennial Parliaments and removing the Bishops from the House of Lords. Sat for Durham S. from 1832 until he retired 1847. Sheriff of Durham 1854. Became the oldest member of the Jockey Club. Died 9 Oct. 1885. [1847]

BOWLES, Admiral William. 8 Hill Street, London. Carlton. A Rear-Admiral and Companion of the Order of the Bath. Commanded the Zebra bomb-ship at the siege of Copenhagen in 1807; served as Commodore on the South American station, and was for 20 years Comptroller-General of the Coast-Guard Service. Also held the office of naval Aide-de-camp to her Majesty. Was a Lord of the Admiralty, and elected MP for Launceston, on the appointment of Sir Henry Hardinge as Governor-General of India. A Conservative, but in favour of free trade. Sat for Launceston from May 1844 until he retired in 1852. Admiral Nov. 1857; Admiral of the fleet 15 Jan. 1869. K.C.B. 10 Nov. 1862. Died 2 July 1869. [1852]

BOWMONT, Marq. of. Floors Castle, Kelso, Roxburghshire. Brook's, Arthur's, and White's. B. at Floors Castle 1839, the eld. s. of the Duke of Roxburghe, by Susanna Stephania, only d. of Sir James Charles Dalbiac, K.C.B. Educ. at Eton and at Christ Church, Oxford. A Magistrate for Roxburghshire and one of the Queen's

Body-Guard for Scotland. A Liberal. Sat for Roxburghshire from Feb. 1870 until he was defeated at the general election of 1874. Succeeded as 7th Duke of Roxburghe on 23 Apr. 1879. Died 23 Oct. 1892. [1873]

BOWRING, Edgar Alfred, C.B. 69 Westbourne Terrace, Hyde Park, London. Athenaeum, and Reform. S. of Sir John Bowring, who sat for Kilmarnock from 1835-1837, and afterwards for Bolton, at one time Plenipotentiary to China, by his 1st wife, Maria, d. of Samuel Lewin, Esq., of Hackney. The family of Bowring had long been settled in Devon. B. in London 1826; m. 1st, 1853, Sophia, d. of Thomas Cubitt, Esq., of Denbies, Dorking; 2ndly, 1858, Ellen, d. of Lewis Cubitt, Esq., of London and Brighton. Educ. at University Coll. School, and afterwards at University Coll., London. Was Private Sec. to the Earl of Clarendon 1846-7; to Earl Granville from 1848-1852; to Lord Stanley of Alderley 1852-3; Précis Writer and Registrar to the Board of Trade from 1849-1864; and was Sec. to the Royal Commission for the 1851 Exhibition from 1850-1868. Author of Translations of the poems of Schiller, Goethe, and Heine, *The Book of Psalms in English Verse,* etc. A Liberal, voted for the disestablishment of the Irish Church 1869; and in favour of the reduction of the public expenditure. Sat for Exeter from Dec. 1868 until defeated 1874. Died 8 Aug. 1911. [1873]

BOWRING, John, LL.D. 1 Queen Square, Westminster, London. Reform, Athenaeum, and Free Trade. Eld. s. of Charles Bowring, Esq., of Exeter, whose family was for many generations connected with the woollen trade of Devonshire. B. 1792; m. in 1816, Maria, d. of Samuel Lewin, Esq., of Hackney. Had honorary diplomas from the Universities of Holland and Italy; a Fellow of the Linnaean Societies of London and Paris, of the Historical Institute of the Scandinavian and Icelandic Societies, of the Royal Institute of the Netherlands, of the Royal Societies of Hungary and Copenhagen, of the Frisian, Athenian, and various other Societies; was for many years editor of the *Westminster Review;* published a number of works on foreign languages and literature, on politics and political economy, and translations from several languages. Dr. Bowring was employed by Earl Grey's Government, with Sir Henry Parnell, in the investigation of public accounts; and served with Mr. Villiers, as Commercial Commissioner in France, to arrange the bases of a treaty of commerce with that country. Made several Reports on Free Trade and Public Accountancy. A radical Reformer. Unsuccessfully contested Blackburn in 1832 and 1835, but in the latter year was returned for Kilmarnock; had no

seat in Parliament from 1837 till 1841, when he sat for Bolton. Unsuccessfully contested Kirkcaldy 27 Jan. 1841. Accepted the Chiltern Hundreds in 1849 on appointment as Consul-General at Canton; Governor of Hong Kong 1854-59; knighted 16 Feb. 1854. [1847 2nd ed.]

BOWYER, Sir George, Bart. 13 King's Bench Walk, Temple, London. Radley Park, Abingdon, Berkshire. Reform, and Oriental. Eld. s. of Sir George Bowyer, Bart., of Radley Park, Berkshire, by Anne Hammond, d. of Capt. Sir Andrew Snape Douglas. B. at Radley Park 1811. Received the honorary degree of M.A. at Oxford in 1839 and that of D.C.L. 1843. Called to the bar at the Middle Temple 1839, and appointed to the office of Reader there in 1850. A Magistrate and Dept.-Lieut. of Berkshire. A Knight of Malta and Honorary Pres. of the Assembly of the Maltese nobility. Author of *A Dissertation on the Statutes of the Italian Cities, Commentaries on the Constitutional Law of England, Commentaries on the Modern Civil Law, The Archbishop of Westminster and the New Hierarchy,* etc. A Liberal, in favour of the principle of the 'Ulster tenant-right'; voted for Lord Derby's Reform Bill, Mar. 1859, and for Lord Russell's Reform Bill, 1866. In favour of the system called 'Home Rule' for Ireland and a local Irish national Parliament, also of denominational and religious education. Was an unsuccessful candidate for Reading in July 1849. Sat for Dundalk from July 1852-Dec. 1868; sat for Wexford from Feb. 1874 until he retired 1880. Died 7 June 1883. [1880]

BOYD, John. Dunduan House, Coleraine. Carlton. S. of John Boyd, Esq., of Belle Isle, Co. Antrim, by Elizabeth, d. of — McCormack, Esq., B. at Roseyard, Co. Antrim, 1789; m. 1820, Anna Arabella, eld. d. of the Rev. Robert Hezlet. Educ. at Edinburgh. A Magistrate and Dept.-Lieut. for Londonderry. Of 'high Conservative principles', but voted for the repeal of the Corn Laws; voted for Lord Derby's Reform Bill, Mar 1859. Sat for Coleraine from 1842 till Mar. 1852; re-elected Apr. 1857. MP until his death 2 Jan 1862. [1861]

BOYLE, Hon. G.F. A Conservative, Returned for Buteshire at a by-election 6 Feb. 1865. Defeated at the gen. election that year. Succeeded his half-bro. as 6th Earl Glasgow Mar 1869. Died 23 Apr. 1890.

BOYLE, Hon. Robert Edward. 3 Hamilton Place, Roehampton. Brooks's, Guards', and Travellers'. B. in London 1809, the 2nd surviving s. of 8th Earl of Cork and Orrery. M. 1844, youngest d. of Abraham Wildey Robarts, Esq. Entered the army as Ensign 1826. Became Capt.

43

and Lieut.-Col. Coldstream Guards 1847, and Maj. in the army 1846. Appointed Sec. to the Master Gen. of the Ordnance, Dec. 1853. Was Sec. to the Order of St. Patrick from 1837. State Steward to the Lord-Lieut. of Ireland, Groom in Waiting to the Queen 1846-Mar. 1852, and Mar. 1853. A Liberal, in favour of free trade, extension of the franchise and the ballot. Opposed to any fresh endowments of any Church from public funds, but 'not opposed to the grant to Maynooth, though ready to vote for inquiry into its management.' Sat for Frome from 1847 until his death 3 Sept. 1854 at Varna. [1854]

BOYLE, Hon. William George. 10 Chesham Street, London. Marston House, Somersetshire. Guards', and Army & Navy. 2nd. s. of Charles Visct. Dungarvan (by Lady Catherine , 5th d. of the 2nd Earl of Howth) and bro. to 9th Earl of Cork and Orrery. Nephew to the Hon. R.E. Boyle, who sat for Frome from 1847 until his death in 1854. B. in Dublin 1830. Educ. at Eton. Entered the army 1849, appointed Lieut. and Capt. Coldstream Guards 1855. Brevet-Major 1854. A Liberal, in favour of Parliamentary reform. First elected for Frome July 1856. Defeated 1857. Died 24 Mar. 1908. [1857]

BRABAZON, Lord. 16 Regent Street, London. Kilruddery House, Bray, Wicklow. Eld. s. of the Earl of Meath and Bro. of the Lady of Visct. Acheson. Also styled 'Lord Ardee'. B. Oct. 1803; m. 1837, d. of Sir Rd. Brooke, Bart. Of Whig opinions. Sat for Dublin Co. 1830-32 and from 1837 until defeated in 1841. Sheriff of Wicklow in 1848. Lord Lieut. 1869 until his death. Built Town Hall of Bray at own expense. Succeeded as 11th Earl in Mar. 1851. Died 26 May 1887. [1840]

BRABAZON, Sir William, Bart. Brabazon Park, Co. Mayo. Westminster. A Reformer, in favour of the repeal of the Union, and of the 'total and unqualified abolition of tithes'. Unsuccessfully contested Mayo in 1832. First returned for Mayo Jan. 1835 and sat until his death in 1840. [1837]

BRACKLEY, Visct. 15a Hill Street, London. Worsley Hall, Manchester. Carlton, and Conservative. Eld. s. of the Earl of Ellesmere. B. in London 1823; m. 1846, youngest d. of the 1st Earl Cawdon. A Conservative, who said he would 'give free-trade a fair trial'. Opposed to the endowment of the Roman Catholic clergy. Unsuccessfully contested Newcastle-Under-Lyme 28 July 1847. First returned for Staffordshire N. in 1847. Accepted the Chiltern Hundreds in Jan. 1851. Succeeded as 2nd Earl of Ellesmere Feb. 1857. Died 19 Sept. 1862. [1850]

BRADLAUGH, C. Continued in House after 1885: full entry in Volume II.

BRADSHAW, James. 28 South Street, Park Lane. Carlton. S. of the Lady of Sir Harry Peyton, Bart., by her 1st husband. M. Miss Tree, a celebrated actress. A Conservative. Sat for Brackley from 1823-32 and for Berwick in 1835. Sat for Canterbury from 1837 until his death in 1847. [1845]

BRADY, Denis Caulfield. Westminster. Nephew of Denis Caulfield, Esq., an eminent Merchant of Newry. A Reformer, in favour of the ballot and of the abolition of tithes. Sat for Newry from Jan. 1835. Defeated in 1837. Died 30 Nov. 1886. [1837]

BRADY, John. Ely, Cambridgeshire. S. of Tobias Brady, Esq., by Margaret, d. of John Brady, Esq., of Cavan. B. in Cavan, 1812; m. 1847, Sarah, d. of John Rayner, Esq., of Ely (she died 1860). Educ. at Clones Grammar School; admitted a licentiate of the Apothecaries' Society of England in 1838, and a member of the College of Surgeons of England in 1840; elected honorary Fellow of the College of Surgeons in Ireland 1870. A Magistrate and Dept.-Lieut. of Leitrim. Appointed a Dept.-Lieut. of Cambridgeshire 1869. A Liberal, voted against the suspension of the Habeas Corpus Act in Ireland Feb. 1866; and for the system called 'Home Rule' for Ireland 1874. Sat for Leitrim from July 1852 until he retired 1880. [1876]

BRAMSTON, Thomas William. 15 Jermyn Street, London. Skreens, Essex. Carlton, and Travellers'. Eld. s. of Thomas Gardiner Bramston, Esq., of Skreens, Essex, by the d. of William Blaauw, Esq., of Queen Anne Street, London. B. 1796; m. 1830, Eliza, 5th d. and co-heir of Admiral Sir Eliab Harvey, G.C.B., of Rolls Park, Essex, who represented that Co. for nearly thirty years. Educ. at All Souls' Coll., Oxford, where he graduated B.A. 1819, M.A. 1823. A Dept.-Lieut. of Essex. Patron of 2 livings. A Liberal-Conservative, gave his support 'on several occasions in critical times' to Lord Palmerston's government, but voted against the Chinese war, and against Lord Palmerston on the Danish question 1864; generally gave his support to Lord Derby. Opposed to the appointment of Bishops by the Crown and to the sale of livings. Sat for Essex S. from 1835 until he retired 1865. Died 21 May 1871. [1865]

BRAND, Rt. Hon. Sir Henry Bouverie William, G.C.B. Speakers House, Palace Yard, Westminster, London. Glynde Place, Lewes,

Sussex. Reform, and Brooks's. 2nd s. of the 21st Baron Dacre, by the 2nd d. of the Hon. and Very Rev. Maurice Crosbie, Dean of Limerick. Was brother and heir presumptive of Baron Dacre. B. 1814; m. 1838, Eliza, d. of Gen. Robert Ellice. Was Private Sec. to Sir George Grey and was Keeper of the Privy Seal to the Prince of Wales for a few weeks in Feb. 1858. Lord of the Treasury from Apr. 1855-Mar. 1858, and Parliamentary Sec. to the Treasury from June 1859-July 1866. Was chosen Speaker of the House without opposition Feb. 1872, re-elected unanimously Mar. 1874, and a third time unanimously Apr. 1880 (salary £5,000). Became Dept.-Lieut. of Sussex 1852. A Liberal, in favour of a thorough reform of the land laws and believed 'that a comprehensive system of county government on a representative basis is urgently called for.' Sat for Lewes from July 1852-Dec. 1868 and from 1868 for Cambridgeshire. Sat until created Visc. Hampden 1884. Lord-Lieut. of Sussex 1886. Succeeded bro. as 23rd Baron Dacre, 1890. Died 14 Mar. 1892. [1884]

BRAND, Hon. Henry Robert, Temple Dinsley, Hitchin, Hertfordshire. Brooks's, and Travellers'. B. at Devonport 1841, the eld. s. of Rt. Hon. Visct. Hampden G.C.B., former Speaker of the House of Commons, by Eliza, d. of Gen Robert Ellice. M. 1st, 1864 Victoria, eld. d. of His Excellency M. van-der-Weyer (she died 1865); 2nd-ly, 1868, Susan, d. of Lord George Cavendish. Educ. at Rugby, and entered the army Dec. 1858. Became Lieut. and Capt. Coldstream Guards May 1863, retired October 1865. Appointed Surveyor General of the Ordnance, Jan. 1883. A Liberal. Sat for Hertfordshire Dec. 1868-Feb. 1874, when he was unsuccessful. Sat for Stroud July-Dec. 1874, when he was unseated on petition. Was also unsuccessful there May 1874. Sat for Stroud from 1880 until he retired in 1886. Succeeded as 2nd Visct. Hampden, March 1892. Died 22 Nov. 1906. [1886]

BRAND, Hon. T. See TREVOR, Hon. T.

BRASSEY, Henry Arthur. 6 Cromwell House, London. Brooks's, Devonshire, and Oxford & Cambridge. S. of Thomas Brassey, Esq., the well-known railway contractor. B. at Fareham, Hampshire 1840; m. 1866, Anna Harriet, d. of Major Stevenson, of Hawkhurst, Kent. Educ. at Harrow, and University Coll., Oxford. A Liberal. Sat for Sandwich from Dec. 1868 until he retired in 1885. Sheriff of Kent 1890. Died 13 May 1891. [1885]

BRASSEY, Sir Thomas, K.C.B. 24 Park Lane, London. Normanhurst Court, Battle, Sussex. The

Grange, Bulkely, Cheshire. Devonshire, United University, and Reform. Eld. s. of Thomas Brassey, Esq., of Great George Street, Westminster, and Lowndes Square, the well-known Railway Contractor. B. at Stafford 1836; m. 1860 Anna, d. of John Allnutt, Esq. Educ. at Rugby, and at University Coll., Oxford. Was called to the bar at Lincoln's Inn 1864. Appointed a (civil) Lord of the Admiralty Apr. 1880, and Secretary to the Admiralty 1884. A Magistrate for Sussex. Author of pamphlets *On Trades Unions, Our Naval Reserves,* and *Admiralty Administration.* A Liberal, in favour of our colonial empire being maintained by 'the timely and generous concession of self-government', and considered that 'the law of marine insurance urgently demanded reform'. Unsuccessfully contested Birkenhead Dec. 1861; Devonport July 1863; and Sandwich May 1866. Sat for Devonport for a few months in 1865, previous to the general election, when he was unsuccessful; sat for Hastings from Dec. 1868 until he retired in 1886. Contested Liverpool, Abercromby division 2 July 1886. Also contested St. Andrew's District 12 July 1886. Created 1st Baron Brassey 1886; Governor of Victoria 1895-1900; created 1st Earl Brassey 1911. Died 23 Feb. 1918. [1885]

BRECKNOCK, Earl of. A Liberal. Returned for Brecknock unopposed at a by-election 27 Feb. 1866. Sat until he succeeded as 3rd Marq. of Camden 6 Aug. 1866. Died 4 May 1872.

BREMRIDGE, Richard. 2 Cleveland Row, St. James's, London. Barnstaple. Carlton. Only s. of Samuel Bremridge, Esq., of Barnstaple, by Honor, d. of — Oxenham, Esq. B. at Barnstaple 1803; m. 1824, Caroline, youngest d. of John Toller, Esq., of Barnstaple. Educ. at Tiverton School. Admitted a Solicitor 1825. Coroner for Devonshire, to which office he was unanimously elected by the Freeholders of the Co. in 1841. A Conservative, and a supporter of Lord Derby; opposed to the ballot and the repeal of Church rates. Sat for Barnstaple from Aug. 1847-Apr. 1853, when he was unseated on petition; was an unsuccessful candidate there Oct. 1863, but obtained his seat on petition Apr. following. Retired 1865. Died 15 June 1878. [1865]

BRETT, Reginald Balliol. 1 Tilney Street, London. Devonshire, and Brooks's. Eld. s. of Right Hon. Sir William Balliol Brett, a Lord Justice of Appeal (who represented Helston from 1866 to 1868), by Eugenie, d. of Louis Mayer, Esq., B. in London 1852; m. 1879, Eleanor, youngest d. of M. Sylvain Van de Weyer, of New Lodge, Windsor (formerly Belgian Minister in London). Educ. at Eton and at Trinity Coll.,

Cambridge. A Liberal. Sat for Penryn from April 1880 to 1885. Contested Plymouth 24 Nov. 1885. Secretary to Office of Works 1895–1902; member of Committee of Imperial Defence 1905–1918. Died 22 Jan. 1930. [1885]

BRETT, William Balliol. 19 Princes Terrace, Hyde Park. London. Athenaeum, and Carlton. S. of the Rev. S.G. Brett, of Ranelagh, Chelsea, by Dora, 2nd d. of George Best, Esq., of Chilston Park, Kent. B. 1817; m. 1850, Eugenie Mayer, d. of Capt. Gurwood. Educ. at Westminster, and at Caius Coll., Cambridge, where he graduated M.A. 1842. Was called to the bar at Lincoln's Inn, Jan. 1846; made a Queen's Counsel, Mar. 1860, and a bencher of Lincoln's Inn same time. A Conservative, a general supporter of Lord Derby; in favour of a 'large but safe' extension of the franchise, and a 'fair settlement' of the church-rate question. Unsuccessfully contested Rochdale 15 Apr. 1865. Stood for Helston, May, 1866, when he polled equal numbers with the other candidate, and obtained the seat on petition, July following. Sat until appointed Judge July (?) 1868; Lord Justice of Appeal 1876; Master of the Rolls 1882; created Baron Esher July 1885; advanced to a Viscountcy Nov. 1897; Master of the Rolls 1882-97. Died 24 May 1899. [1867]

BREWER, William. 21 George Street, Hanover Square, London. S. of John Sherren Brewer, Esq., of Eaton, Norfolk, by his marriage with Miss Elizabeth Kitton. M. 1st. Janet, d. of John Dunkald, Esq., 2ndly, Emma, d. of William Rose, Esq. Educ. at Edinburgh, of which University he was M.D. Became Licentiate of the College of Surgeons, Edinburgh 1834, a member of the Coll. of Physicians, London, 1841. Chairman of the Metropolitan Asylums Board. Author of *The Army and Navy Reference Book*. A Liberal, and gave 'an unflinching support' to Mr. Gladstone; in favour of the immediate reduction of the national expenditure, and the repeal of the rate-paying clauses of the Reform Act. Unsuccessfully contested Colchester Feb 1867; first elected Dec. 1868. Defeated 1874. Died 3 Nov. 1881. [1873]

BREWSTER, Robert Abraham Brewster French-. Merrion Square, Dublin. Only s. of Henry French, Esq., by his 2nd wife, Elizabeth Mary, d. of the Right Hon. Abraham Brewster, Lord Chancellor of Ireland. Assumed in 1874 the additional name and arms of Brewster on succeeding to the estates of his maternal grandfather. A Conservative. Sat for Portarlington from March 1883. Retired in 1885. [1885]

BRIDGES, Sir Brook William, Bart. 120 Park Street, Grosvenor Square, London. Goodneston Park, Wingham, Kent. National. S. of Sir Brook Bridges 4th Bart. by his 1st wife, eld. d. of John Foote, Esq., a London Banker. B. at Goodneston Park, 1801; m. 1834, eld d. of Lewis Cage, Esq., of Milgate, Kent. Educ. at Winchester School and Oriel Coll., Oxford, where he graduated B.A. 1822, M.A. 1827. A Dept.-Lieut. of Kent. Was Capt. in the East Kent Yeomanry Cavalry from 1830 till 1853, when he resigned. Patron of 5 livings. A Conservative. Unsuccessfully contested Sandwich July 1837. Sat for Kent E. from Feb. till July 1852, when he was an unsuccessful candidate; re-elected Apr. 1857. Sat until created Lord Fitzwalter 17 Apr. 1868. Died 6 Dec. 1875. [1867]

BRIDGMAN, Hewitt. M. sister of Sir M. O'Loughlen, Bart. A Reformer, voted against the Corn Laws. Unsuccessfully contested Ennis in 1832, against Lieut. Macnamara, but returned unopposed in 1835. Sat until he retired 1847. [1847]

BRIGGS, Rawdon. 18 Manchester Buildings, London. S. of Mr. Briggs, the Banker, at Halifax. A Reformer, in favour of free-trade, the abolition of monopolies, the gradual abolition of the tax on corn, a property tax, and the abolition of Church rates. Sat for Halifax from 1832. Retired in 1835. [1833]

BRIGGS, William Edward. 53 Gloucester Road, London. Reform, and National Liberal. 2nd s. of Edward Briggs. Esq., of The Grange, Blackburn. B. at Blackburn 1847. Educ. at Rugby and Worcester Coll., Oxford. A Cotton Spinner and Manufacturer at Blackburn. A Liberal. Sat for Blackburn from Feb. 1874 until defeated in 1885. Contested Clitheroe in 1892 when he stood as a Liberal Unionist. [1885]

BRIGHT, Sir Charles Tilston. 69 Lancaster Gate, London. Victoria Street, Westminster, London. S. of Brailsford Bright, Esq., by the d. of Edward Tilston, Esq., B. at West Ham, Essex. 1832; m. 1853, d. of John Taylor, Esq., A Civil Engineer. Was Capt. 7th Surrey Volunteers 1860 and 1861. A Liberal, and in favour of 'such an extension of the franchise as would call into exercise more of the enlightened intelligence of the country', but against the ballot; in favour of the exemption of Dissenters from church-rates. First elected for Greenwich, July 1865. Retired in 1868. Died 3 May, 1888. [1867]

BRIGHT, Jacob. Continued in House after 1885: full entry in Volume II.

BRIGHT, Rt. Hon. John. One Ash, Rochdale. Reform, and Athenaeum. S. of Jacob Bright, Esq., of Greenbank, Nr. Rochdale. B. 1811, m. 1st 1839, Elizabeth, eld. d. of Jonathan Priestman, Esq., of Newcastle-on-Tyne (she died 1841); 2ndly 1847, Margaret Elizabeth, eld. d. of William Leatham, Esq., of Wakefield, Yorkshire (she died 1878). A Cotton-Spinner and Manufacturer, being a partner in the firm of John Bright and Brothers, of Rochdale. Was Pres. of the Board of Trade from Dec. 1868-Dec. 1870, and Chancellor of the Duchy of Lancaster from Oct. 1873-Feb.1874, and from Apr. 1880-July 1882. Elected Lord Rector of Glasgow University Nov. 1880; made D.L.C. of Oxford 1886. Previous to his return to Parliament was chiefly known as an active member of the anti-corn-law league. Unsuccessfully contested Durham City Apr. 1843. Again stood for Durham July 1843, when he was returned and continued to sit for that city until July 1847. Sat for Manchester from July 1847-Apr. 1857, when he was an unsuccessful candidate there; sat for Birmingham from Aug. 1857. A Liberal, opposed to Mr. Gladstone's Home Rule Scheme. MP until his death 27 Mar. 1888. [1888]

BRIGHT, Richard. Stocke House, Near Tring, Hertfordshire. Carlton, and Athenaeum. S. of Robert Bright, Esq., of Abbot's Leigh, a Merchant at Bristol (who was a younger bro. of Henry Bright, Esq., who represented Bristol from 1820-30), by Caroline, d. of T. Tyndall, Esq., of The Fort, Bristol. B. at Abbot's Leigh 1822; m. 1855, Emma Katherine, d. of Admiral Thomas Wolley, and relict of James Adam Gordon, Esq. Educ. at Rugby and at Christ Church, Oxford. Was called to the bar at the Inner Temple 1851. A Conservative, and in 'favour of a constitutional government in Church and State'. Sat for E. Somersetshire from Dec. 1868. MP until his death 28 Feb. 1878. [1877]

BRIGSTOCKE, William Papwell. 12 Suffolk Street, Combe Hay. A Reformer, in favour of the ballot, and the immediate abolition of slavery. Returned for Somersetshire E. in 1832 and remained an MP until his death in Jan. 1834. [1833]

BRINCKMAN, Col. Theodore Henry. 56 Park Street, Grosvenor Square, London. Eld. s. of Sir Theodore Henry Lavington Brinckman, Bart., by his 1st wife, Charlotte, only d. of 1st Lord Godolphin. B. at Tunbridge Wells 1830; m. 1861, Lady Cecilia Augusta, youngest d. of the 2nd Marq. of Conyingham. Was appointed Ensign 17th Foot 1849; became Capt. 1855, retired. Dept.-Lieut. of the Tower Hamlets from 1863. A

Liberal, and strongly in favour of Mr. Gladstone's policy. Voted for the disestablishment of the Irish Church 1869. Sat for Canterbury from Dec. 1868 until defeated 1874. Succeeded father as 2nd Baronet 1880. Died 7 May 1905. [1873]

BRINTON, John. Moor Hall, Stourport, Worcestershire. 52 Cornwall Gardens, London. Reform. B. at Kidderminster 1827, 3rd s. of Henry Brinton, a Magistrate at Kidderminster. M. 1st Anne, d. of S. Oldham of Rathminster, W. Dublin; 2ndly Mary, eld d. of Col. John Clayton R.E., of Durham. Head of the firm of John Brinton and Co., carpet manufacturers, and worsted spinners, Kidderminster, which he joined as a partner in 1848. A Magistrate for Worcestershire and Kidderminster, Chairman of the Kidderminster Board of Guardians, the Kidderminster School Board, and the local School of Art. A Liberal, was in favour of extension in Local Government and Reform of the Land Laws. Sat for Kidderminster from April 1880 until 1886, when he retired. [1886]

BRISCO, Musgrave. 38 Devonshire Place, London. Coghurst Hall, Hastings. United University. B. 1791, the eld. s. of Capt. Wastel Brisco of Coghurst, Sussex, by the d. of — Goulburn. M. 1828, d. of Henry Woodgate, Esq., of Spring Grove, Pembury, Kent. and niece of 6th Visct. Boyne. Educ. at Sidney Sussex Coll., Cambridge, where he graduated M.A. 1816. A Magistrate and Dept.-Lieut. for the Cos. of Sussex and Yorkshire. A Conservative, voted for agricultural protection, 1846, but did not favour the reimposition of the duty on corn, and opposed to 'any grant of public money for re-endowing any Roman Catholic establishment.' Sat for Hastings from 1844 until May 1854, when he accepted Chiltern Hundreds. Died 9 May 1854. [1854]

BRISCOE, John Ivatt. 60 Eaton Place, London. Fox Hills, Chertsey, Surrey. S. of John Briscoe, Esq., of Cross Deep, Twickenham, by Mary, d. of Stephen Winthrop, Esq., of the City of London, Merchant. B. at Twickenham 1791; m. 1819, Anne Maria, d. and sole surviving d. and heir of Sir Joseph Mawbay, Bart. Educ. at University Coll., Oxford, where he graduated B.A. in 1812 (2nd class in classics), M.A. 1815. Entered as a student of Lincoln's Inn, but was not called to the bar. A Magistrate for Surrey and Middlesex and a Dept.-Lieut. for Surrey. Author of a pamphlet on prison discipline. A Liberal, said he would 'promote the education of all classes of people.' Sat for Surrey W. from 1830-2, and for Surrey E. from the latter date to Jan. 1835, when he was an unsuccessful candidate. Sat for Westbury from

July 1837-June 1841. First elected for Surrey W. April 1857. MP until his death 16 Aug. 1870. [1870]

BRISE, Col. Samuel Brise Ruggles, C.B. 1 St. James's Place, London. Spain's Hall, Braintree, Essex. Carlton. Only s. of John Ruggles, Esq., who assumed the additional name of Brise and was High Sheriff of Suffolk in 1832, by Catherine, d. of J.A. Harrison, Esq., of Copford Hall, Essex. B. 1825; m. 1847, Marianne Weyland, 4th d. of Sir Edward Bowyer Smijth, Bart., of Hill Hall, Essex. Educ. at Eton and at Magdalen Coll., Cambridge. Entered the Army as Cornet, 1st Dragoon Guards 1844. Lieut.-Col. Commandant West Essex Militia from 1852. A Magistrate and Dept.-Lieut. of Essex and Suffolk. A Conservative, voted against the disestablishment of the Irish Church 1869. Sat for E. Essex from Dec. 1868 until he accepted Chiltern Hundreds 1883. K.C.B. 1897. Died 28 May 1899. [1883]

BRISTOW, Alfred Rhodes. Walbrook, London. Greenwich, London. Bushey Green House, Lewisham, Kent. Reform. S. of Isaac Bristow, Esq., of Greenwich, Kent, formerly a Government Contractor, by Henrietta Catherine, d. of the Baron Razehorm, of The Hague. B. at Greenwich, Kent, 1820; m. 1842, Margaret, eld. d. of John Oswald, Esq. of The Palace, Croydon, Surrey. Educ. at King's Coll., London. Admitted a Solicitor, 1842. A Member of the Metropolitan Board of Works from 1855, when he was chosen to represent Greenwich, Deptford, and Hatcham. A Dept.-Lieut. of Kent from 1861. An 'independent Liberal'. First elected for Kidderminster, Apr. 1859. Accepted Chiltern Hundreds 1862. Died 5 Apr. 1875. [1862]

BRISTOWE, Samuel Boteler. 2 Paper Buildings, Temple, London. Oxford & Cambridge. Eld. s. of Samuel Ellis Bristowe, Esq., of Beesthorpe, Newark, by his 1st wife, Mary Anne, d. of Samuel Fox, Esq., of Osmaston Hall, Co. Derby. B. at Beesthorpe 1822; m. 1856, Albertine Eugénie, d. of M. John J. Lavit of Paris. Educ. at Trinity Hall, Cambridge, where he obtained a Fellowship, graduated B.A. 1845, M.A. 1848. Called to the bar at the Inner Temple 1848. Appointed Recorder of Newark 1869, and resigned to become a candidate to represent Newark in Parliament. Published an edition (the 30th) of *Burns' Justice*. A Liberal. Sat for Newark from Apr. 1870 until defeated 1880. Unsuccessfully contested Nottinghamshire S. Apr. 1880. Judge of County Courts 1880-97. Died 5 Mar. 1897. [1880]

BROADHURST, H. Continued in House after 1885: full entry in Volume II.

BROADLEY, Henry. 3 Charles Street, St. James's, London. Beverley, Yorkshire. United University. B. 1793, the s. of H. Broadley, Esq. Was a Dept.-Lieut. of Yorkshire and Chairman of the Hull and Selby Railway from 1836-43. A Conservative, and voted for agricultural protection 1846. First returned for the county of Yorkshire (E. Riding) at the general election in 1837 and sat until he died on 8 Aug. 1851. [1851]

BROADLEY, William Henry Harrison-. Welton, Nr. Brough, Beverley. Carlton, and Senior University. S. of William Henry Harrison, Esq., of Ripon, by Mary, 2nd d. of Henry Broadley, Esq., R.N., whose eldest son settled at Kirkella, near Hull. B. at Hob-Green, near Ripon, 1820. Unmarried. Educ. at Rugby and at Brasenose Coll., Oxford. Assumed the name of Broadley in addition to his patronymic. A Magistrate and Dept.-Lieut. for the East Riding of Yorkshire, High Sheriff in 1867; and Hon. Col. Yorkshire Hussars. Patron of 3 livings. A Conservative. Sat for the East Riding of Yorkshire from Dec. 1868 until he retired in 1885. [1885]

BROADWOOD, Henry. Carlton, and Union. B. Aug. 8, 1795; m. d. of 2nd Earl of Lonsdale. Was of Emmanuel Coll., Cambridge. A Conservative, voted for agricultural protection, 1846. Contested Bridgewater unsuccessfully in 1834; was returned, in opposition to Mr. B. Sheridan, on Mr. Leader's vacating his seat to stand for Westminster in 1837. At the general election in the same year was again returned, as also in 1841 and 1847. Retired in 1852. [1852]

BROCKLEHURST, John. 33 Milk Street, London. Hurdsfield House, Macclesfield, Cheshire. Reform. 2nd s. of John Brocklehurst, Esq., of Jordan Gate, Macclesfield; m. in 1812, the 2nd d. of — Coare, Esq., of Islington (she died 1848). A Silk Manufacturer and Banker, in partnership with his bros., at Macclesfield. A Liberal, in favour of protection for the silk trade, and of a revenue being raised from foreign articles of luxury; in favour of short Parliaments and vote by ballot; voted in favour of Lord Derby's Reform Bill, Mar. 1859. First elected for Macclesfield in 1832. Sat until he retired in 1868. Died 13 Aug. 1870. [1867]

BROCKLEHURST, William Coare. Butley Hall, Prestbury, Macclesfield. B. 1818, the eld. s. of John Brocklehurst, Esq., of Hurdsfield, MP for Macclesfield 1832-68. M. 1840, Mary, d. of William Worthington, Esq., of Brocklehurst Hall, Cheshire. Engaged in the Silk Trade. President of the Macclesfield Chamber of Commerce. A Magistrate for Cheshire, and formerly Captain in the Earl of Chester's Yeomanry Cavalry. Succeeded his father as MP for Macclesfield in 1868, but in 1880 he was unseated on petition and the borough of Macclesfield was disfranchised. A Liberal. Defeated in 1886, standing as a Gladstonian Liberal. Died 3 June 1900.   [1886]

BROCKMAN, Edward Drake. The Paddock, Hythe. Beachborough, Kent. Reform. 5th s. of James Drake-Brockman, Esq., of Beachborough, Kent, by the d. of the Rev. William Tatton, D.D., Prebendary of Canterbury. Called to the bar at the Inner Temple 1819. Recorder of Folkestone. A Liberal, voted for the ballot 1853. First returned in 1847 for Hythe, in the neighbourhood of which his family had long been resident. Sat until he retired 1857. Died 7 Nov. 1858.   [1857]

BRODERICK, Hon. St. J.W. Continued in House after 1885: full entry in Volume II.

BRODERICK, Hon. William. 20 Beaufort Gardens, London. Peper Harrow, Godalming, Surrey. Eld. s. of 7th Visct. Midleton, by his 2nd wife, Hon. Harriet, 4th d. of 4th Visct. Midleton. B. 1830; m. 1853, Augusta Mary, 3rd d. of Rt. Hon. Sir Thomas Fremantle, Bart. Educ. at Balliol Coll., Oxford, where he graduated B.A. 1851; M.A. 1861. Called to the bar at Lincoln's Inn 1855. A Magistrate and Dept.-Lieut. of Surrey. A Conservative; a 'firm supporter of our constitution, and staunch adherer to the Protestant Church', opposed to the disestablishment of the Irish Church 1869, as being 'fatal to the future of Ireland.' Unsuccessfully contested E. Surrey, July 1865. Sat for the Surrey mid. division from Dec. 1868 until he succeeded as 8th Visct. Aug. 1870. Died 18 Apr. 1907.   [1870]

BRODIE, William Bird. 3 Sackville Street, London. The Close, Wiltshire. Reform. 2nd s. of the Rev. P.B. Brodie, of Winterstow, Wiltshire. B. 1780; m. 1st, 1810, Louisa, 2nd d. of Thomas Hussey, Esq. of Salisbury; 2ndly, 1829, Frances, youngest d. of the Rev. Rd. Huntley of Boxwell Court, Gloucestershire. Lieut.-Col. of the Salisbury Volunteer Infantry. A Banker in the same town. A Magistrate of the county of Wiltshire. Of Whig principles. First sat for Salisbury in 1832 and remained an MP until he accepted the Chiltern Hundreds in Apr. 1843. Died 24 Oct. 1863.   [1843]

BROGDEN, Alexander. 9 Victoria Chambers, London. Woodheads, Grange-over-Sands, Lancashire. Reform. S. of John Brogden, Esq., and Sarah Hannah, his wife. B. at Manchester 1825; m. 1848 Anne, d. of James Garstang, Esq., of Manchester. Educ. at King's Coll., London. An Ironmaster. A Liberal. Unsuccessfully contested Yarmouth July 1865; sat for Wednesbury from Dec. 1868 until he retired in 1885. Died 26 Nov. 1892.   [1885]

BROMLEY, Robert. Stoke Hall, Nottingham. Eld. s. of Sir Robert Howe Bromley, Bart., of Stoke Hall, Nottingham by the 2nd d. of Daniel Wilson, Esq. grands. of Sir George Smith, Bart., who in 1778 assumed by sign manuel, the name Bromley in lieu of his patronymic. B. 1815. Unmarried. A Conservative and in favour of protection to agriculture. Supported measures 'tending to reduce the taxation of the country.' First returned for Nottinghamshire South Apr. 1849, without opposition, on the retirement of Colonel Rolleston. Remained MP until his death in Jan. 1851.   [1850]

BROOKE, Sir Arthur Brinsley, Bart. 9 Little Ryder Street, London. Colebrook, Co. Fermanagh. Carlton. B. 1797, the s. of Sir Henry Brooke, 1st Bart., by the d. of the Hon. John Butler. M. 1841, youngest d. of Sir George Anson, G.C.B. A Conservative, voted for agricultural protection 1846, and for inquiry into Maynooth 1853. Sat for Fermanagh from 1840 until he died 20 Nov. 1854.   [1854]

BROOKE, Lord. (I). 7 Carlton Gardens, London. Warwick Castle, Warwickshire. Travellers', and Carlton. B. in Charles Street, Berkeley Square in 1818, the eld. s. of the Earl of Warwick. M. 1852, Hon. Anne, eld. d. of Lord Elcho and grand-d. of 7th Earl of Wemyss. Graduated at St. John's Coll., Oxford. Appointed Lieut.-Col. Commandant of the Warwickshire Yeomanry Cavalry 1848. A Conservative, and voted for the minority of 53 who censured free trade Nov. 1852. Opposed to the endowment of the Roman Catholic Church. First returned for Warwickshire S. without opposition in 1845 and sat until he succeeded his father as 4th Earl in Aug. 1853. Died 2 Dec. 1893.   [1853]

BROOKE, Lord. (II). Continued in House after 1885: full entry in Volume II.

BROOKS, Maurice. 7 Paddington Green, London. 47 Merion Square, Dublin. Devonshire. St. Stephen's Green, Dublin. Eld. s. of Thomas Brooks, of Abbey Street, Dublin. B. 1823; m. 1st, 1847, Hannah Maria, d. of Mr. James Rose, of Burford, Worcestershire (she died Jan. 1873); 2ndly, 1875, Jane, youngest d. of Robert McDowell, Esq., of Belfast. A Merchant in Dublin and London. A Magistrate and Dept. Lieut. for Dublin. Elected Lord Mayor of Dublin 1873-4. A Liberal, and a supporter of the system called 'Home Rule' for Ireland. Sat for the city of Dublin from Feb. 1874 until he retired in 1885. [1885]

BROOKS, Robert, W. Woodcote Park, Epsom, Surrey. Conservative. S. of William Brooks, Esq., of Laceby House, Lincolnshire. M. Hannah, d. of Joshua Penny, Esq. A Merchant and Ship-Owner. A Magistrate for Surrey. A Conservative. First elected for Weymouth, Apr. 1859. Sat until he retired in 1868. Died 5 June 1882. [1867]

BROOKS, W. Cunliffe. Continued in House after 1885: full entry in Volume II.

BROMLEY, W. Davenport. See DAVENPORT, W. Bromley-.

BROTHERTON, Joseph. 7 Manchester Buildings, London. Rose Hill, Pendleton, Salford. Reform. A retired Cotton and Silk Manufacturer. A Liberal, voted for the ballot 1853. Sat for the borough of Salford from 1832 until his death 7 Jan. 1857. [1856]

BROUGHAM, James. 48 Berkeley Square, London. 13 Quality Court, Chancery Lane, London. A bro. of Lord Henry Brougham, 1st Baron Brougham and Vaux; a Barrister. A Reformer, in favour of exempting Dissenters from the payment of Church rates; of excluding the Clergy from secular pursuits; of expelling the Bishops from the House of Lords; of throwing open the China trade; of doing away with all monopolies, and of a fixed duty on foreign corn. Sat for Tregorny in 1826, for Downton in 1830, and for Winchelsea in 1831. Sat for Kendal in 1833 and until his death in January 1834. [1833]

BROUGHAM, William. 25 Southampton Buildings, Chancery Lane, London. Bro. of Lord Brougham; a Master in Chancery. A Reformer, in favour of a fixed duty on corn, the repeal of the assessed taxes, the ballot, if found absolutely necessary; the abolition of the taxes on knowledge, and of doing away with the practice of the Peers voting by proxy, and flogging in the army. First sat for Southwark in 1831. Defeated in 1835 contesting Leeds. Succeeded bro. as 2nd. baron. Died 3 Jan. 1886. [1833]

BROWN, A.H. Continued in House after 1885: full entry in Volume II.

BROWN, Humphrey. 2 Little Smith Street, Westminster, London. Tewkesbury. S. of Humphrey Brown, Esq., of Tewkesbury, a Merchant and extensive Carrier. B. at Tewkesbury 1803; m. 1834, d. of Charles Edward

Chandler, Esq., of Tewkesbury. Was formerly a Merchant and Carrier at Tewkesbury, was an active promoter of the Birmingham and Gloucester Railway. Was well known as a Railway statist and traffic taker. A Liberal, and a supporter of 'free trade principles in the fullest sense', opposed to all religious endowments. First returned for Tewkesbury 1857, without opposition and sat until defeated 1857. Imprisoned for fraud Feb.–June 1858. Died 6 June 1860. [1857]

BROWN, James. Rossington, Bawtry. Harehills Grove, Leeds. Brooks's. A Liberal. Unsuccessfully contested Hull 29 July 1847. First returned for Malton, Mar. 1857. Sat until he retired in 1868 when Malton lost one of its members. Died 14 July 1877. [1867]

BROWN, James Clifton. Holmbush, Horsham. Reform. 2nd s. of Alexander Brown, Esq., of Beilby Grange, Yorkshire, by Sarah Benedict, d. of James Brown, Esq., of New York. B. at Beilby Grange, Wetherby, Yorkshire 1841; m. 1866, Amelia, d. of Charles Bowe, Esq., Merchant of Liverpool. Educ. at Trinity Hall, Cambridge, graduated M.A. 1867. A Magistrate for Sussex. A Liberal, but not in favour of disestablishment. Contested Sussex S. in 1886. Sat for Horsham from Feb. 1876. Defeated 1880. [1880]

BROWN, William. Fenton's Hotel, St. James's Street, London. Richmond Hill, Liverpool. S. of Alex. Brown of Baltimore, United States. B. at Ballymena, Co. Antrim 1784; m. 1810, d. of Andrew Gihon, Esq., of Ballymena. Educ. at Caterick, Yorkshire. Senior partner in the firm of Messrs. Brown, Shipley and Company. A Magistrate for Liverpool, a Dept.-Lieut. and Magistrate for Lancashire. A Liberal, voted for the ballot 1853. Author of *Letters advocating Commercial Freedom.* Unsuccessfully contested Lancashire S. 1844. First returned without opposition 1846. Sat until he retired 1857. Public benefactor in Liverpool, created Baronet 24 Jan. 1863. Sheriff of Lancashire 1863. Died 3 Mar. 1864. [1857]

BROWNE, Rt. Hon. Dominick. Castlemacgarrett, Co. Mayo. Brook's. S. of D.G. Browne, Esq., Governor of Co. Mayo. B. 1787; m. 1811, Catherine, d. and co-heiress of Henry Mouck, Esq., niece of the Earl of Arran, and sister to the wife of Sir Charles Paget. Uncle of Visct. Dillon, and maternally connected with the Marq. of Sligo, but of a distinct family. Dept.-Lieut. of Co. Mayo. Of Whig principles. In favour of the ballot, a partial reduction of the Church of Ireland, a Roman Catholic establishment in that country, and a plan of extensive emigration. Sat for Mayo in every Parliament from 1813, with the exception of that elected in 1826. Sat until created Baron Oranmore May 1836. Died 30 Jan. 1860. [1836]

BROWNE, George Ekins. 42 Palace Square, Norwood, London. Brownestown, Ballinrobe, Co. Mayo. Eld. s. of John Browne, Esq., of Brownestown, Mayo, a Magistrate for that Co., by Maria, d. of Walter Ekins, Esq., of Richmond House, Co. Wexford. B. 1837; m. 1858, Julia, d. of Maurice Blake, Esq., of Ballinafad, Co. Mayo (she died 1876). A Magistrate for Mayo. A Liberal, and demanded 'his country's inalienable birthright – a national Parliament.' Sat for Mayo from May 1870 until defeated 1880, largely due to C.S. Parnell's candidacy. [1880]

BROWNE, John. 31 Duke Street, St. James's, London. Mount Browne, Mayo. A relation of the Marq. of Sligo. Of Whig principles. Sat for Mayo Co. from 1830 until his defeat in 1835. [1833]

BROWNE, Lord John Thomas. 16 Mansfield Street, London. Westport House, Westport, Co. Mayo. 3rd. s. of 2nd Marq. of Sligo, by Lady Hester, eld. d. of 13th Earl of Clanricarde. B. at Westport, Co. Mayo, 1824. Unmarried. Served continuously in the navy from Dec. 1837 till Dec. 1850; became a Lieut. in 1846. A Liberal. First elected for Mayo Dec. 1857. Sat until he retired in 1868. Succeeded bro. as 4th Marq. Dec. 1896. Died 30 Dec. 1903. [1867]

BROWNE, Robert Dillon. Glencorrils, Co. Mayo, Ireland. Reform. Descended from the Kilmaine family; s. of Arthur Browne, Esq., of Glencorrils, Co. Mayo. First elected for Mayo in 1836, *vice* the Rt. Hon. Dominick Browne, created Lord Dranmore. A Repealer. MP until his death in 1850. [1849]

BROWNE, Hon. Valentine. See CASTLE-ROSSE, Rt. Hon. Visct.

BROWNE, Hon. William. 89 Jermyn Street, London. Woodlawn, Co. Kerry. S. of 1st Earl of Kenmare. B. 1791; m. 1826, d. of T. Segrave, Esq. A Dept.-Lieut. of Co. Kerry. A Liberal. First returned for Co. Kerry in 1841. Sat until he retired 1847. Died 4 Aug. 1876. [1847]

BROWNRIGG, John Studholme. Carlton. S. of John Studholme Brownrigg, Esq. B. 1786; m. 1812, Elizabeth, eld. d. of James Henry Cassamayor, Esq. A Merchant of London, and partner in the firm of Sir Charles Cockerell and Company. Dept.-Gov. of the Australian Agricultural Company, and Director of the Royal

Bank of Australasia. A Conservative, voted for agricultural protection 1846. Unsuccessfully contested Boston in 1832 but returned in 1835 and sat until retired 1847. Died 21 Sept. 1853. [1847]

BRUCE, Charles Lennox Cumming. Dunphail, Forres, Morayshire. Kinnaird House, Falkirk, Stirlingshire. Carlton, and United Service. 2nd. s. of Sir A.P. Gordon Cumming (1st Bart.) by the d. of Sir James Grant, of Grant. B. 1790; m. in 1820 grandd. of James Bruce, the Abyssinian traveller. A Dept.-Lieut. of Elginshire. Was one of the joint secretaries to the Board of Controul from Mar. till Dec. 1852. A Conservative, voted for inquiry into Maynooth 1853, and in favour of national education on a religious basis. Sat for Inverness district for several years before the Reform Act, and from 1833 till 1837. First returned for Elginshire in 1840 and sat until he retired in 1868. Died 1 Jan. 1875. [1867]

BRUCE, Rt. Hon. Lord Charles William Brudenell-. 77 Pall Mall, London. Youngest s. of the 1st Marq. of Ailesbury by his 2nd wife, Mary Elizabeth, youngest d. of the Hon. Charles Tollemache. B. 1834; m. 1860, Augusta Georgiana, 3rd d. of Frederick Charles William Seymour, Esq., Appointed Capt. of the 1st Life Guards 1859; Capt. Wiltshire Yeomanry 1861. Appointed Vice-Chamberlain of the Queen's Household Apr. 1880. A Magistrate for Wiltshire and Middlesex. A Liberal. Sat for North Wiltshire from Mar. 1865 to Feb. 1874, when he was an unsuccessful candidate there. Sat for Marlborough from Jan. 1878 until he retired in 1885. Died 16 April 1897. [1885]

BRUCE, Rt. Hon. Lord Ernest Augustus Charles Brudenell. 6 St. George's Place, London. Villa Marbella, Biarritz, France. Athenaeum, White's, and Travellers'. 2nd s. of the 1st Marq. of Ailesbury. B. at Warren's Hotel, St. James's Square, 1811; m. 1834, Hon. Louisa, 2nd d. of Lord Decies. Educ. at Eton and Trinity Coll., Cambridge, where he graduated M.A. 1831. Was Lord of the Bedchamber to William IV from Dec. 1834-Apr. 1835; Vice-Chamberlain to the Queen from Sept. 1841-July 1846, and from Dec. 1852-Mar. 1858. Appointed Maj. in the Wilts, Yeomanry Cavalry 1861; a Dept.-Lieut. of Wiltshire 1852 and a Magistrate for Wiltshire, Middlesex and Westminster, Nov. 1853. A Liberal, but was formerly ranked as Conservative; voted against Lord Russell's Reform Bill 1866, and in favour of Lord Derby's Reform Bill 1867, 'because it saved one seat for Marlborough', which he represented for 46 years. Voted for the total disendowment of the Irish Church, 1869. Sat for Marlborough from 1832 until he succeeded brother as 3rd Marq. Jan 1878. Died 18 Oct. 1886. [1877]

BRUCE, Rt. Hon. Henry Austin. 1 Queen's Gate, London. Duffryn, Aberdare, Glamorganshire. Athenaeum. 2nd. s. of John Bruce-Pryce, Esq., of Duffryn St. Nicholas, Glamorganshire (who assumed in 1805 the name of Bruce in lieu of his patronymic Knight, and that of Pryce in 1837), by Sarah, 2nd d. of Rev. Hugh W. Austin, Rector of St. Peter's in Barbados. B. at Duffryn, Aberdare, Glamorganshire 1815; m. 1st 1846, Annabella, only d. of Richard Beadon, Esq., of Clifton (she died July 1852); 2ndly 1854, Norah, youngest d. of Lieut.-Gen. Sir William Napier, K.C.B. Called to the bar at Lincoln's Inn 1837, but withdrew from practice in 1843. Was Under Secretary for the Home Department from Nov. 1862-Apr. 1864, 4th Church Estates' Commissioner from Nov. 1865-Aug. 1866; President of the Board of Health, and Vice-President of the Education Board of the Privy Council, from the last date till July 1866. Appointed Sec. of State for the Home Department, a Member of the Committee of Council on Education Dec. 1868, and an Ecclesiastical Commissioner for England Jan. 1869. Dept.-chairman of Quarter Sessions, Glamorganshire; Capt. Glamorganshire Rifle Volunteers; a Dept.-Lieut. of Glamorganshire. A Liberal, opposed to vote by ballot. Sat for Merthyr Tydvil from Dec. 1852-Nov.1868 when he lost his seat. Sat for Renfrewshire from Jan. 1869 until created Baron Aberdare of Duffryn, Glamorganshire 23 Aug. 1873. Lord President of the Council 1873-74; President University Coll., Wales from 1875. [1872]

BRUCE, Sir Henry Hervey, Bart. 7 Portman Square, London. Devon Hill, Coleraine, Ireland. Eld. s. of Sir James Robertson Bruce (2nd Bart), by Ellen, younger d. of Robert Hesketh Bamford-Hesketh, Esq., of Gwyrch Castle, Denbighshire. B. at Down Hill, near Coleraine, 1820; m. 1842 Mary Anne Margaret, only d. of Sir Juckes G.J. Clifton, Bart., of Clifton Hall. Educ. at Trinity Coll., Cambridge. Entered the 1st Life Guards as Cornet, May 1840, and served till Sept. 1841. A Magistrate of Londonderry, was Lieut. and Custos Rotulorum of that Co. from 1877, and served the office of High Sheriff 1845. A Conservative. Unsuccessfully contested Londonderry Co. March 1857; sat for Coleraine from Feb. 1862 to Feb. 1874, when he stood unsuccessfully; re-elected April 1880. Retired in 1885. Died 8 Dec. 1907. [1885]

BRUCE, Lord. Broom Hall, Fifeshire. Carlton. Eld. s. of the Earl of Elgin. B. 1811. A Conservative. First elected for Southampton in 1841, but unseated when result was declared void. Colonial Administrator. Created Baron Elgin (U.K. Peerage) Nov. 1849. Postmaster General June 1859. Viceroy of India Jan. 1862, until his death 20 Nov. 1863. [1842]

BRUCE, Hon. R.P. Continued in House after 1885: full entry in Volume II.

BRUCE, Hon. Thomas Charles. 42 Hill Street, Berkeley Square, London. Carlton, and Athenaeum. Youngest s. of the 7th Earl of Elgin, by his 2nd wife Elizabeth, youngest d. of Right Hon. James Townshend Oswald, of Dunnikier, Co. Fife. B. at Broomhall, Fife, 1825, m. 1863, Sarah Caroline, eld. d. of Thomas Thornhill, Esq., of Riddlesworth Hall, Norfolk. Educ. at Jesus Coll., Cambridge (Wrangler 1850), called to the bar at the Inner Temple 1854. Appointed Capt. Commandant 32nd Middlesex Rifle Volunteers 1860. A Director of the London and North Western Railway, and Chairman of the Imperial Ottoman Bank. A Conservative. Unsuccessfully contested Edinburgh July 1852; also Helston Nov. 1868. Was an unsuccessful candidate in May 1859, and again July 1865 for Portsmouth, for which he sat from Feb. 1874 until defeated in 1885. Chairman of Highland Railway Co. 1886. Died 23 Nov. 1890. [1885]

BRUDENELL, Lord. 17 Carlton House Terrace, London. Deanpark, Northamptonshire. Carlton. Eld. s. of the Earl of Cardigan. B. 1797; m. 1826, Elizabeth, eld. d. of Admiral Tollemache, whose marriage with Maj. Johnston was dissolved in 1826. Lieut.-Col. of the 11th Dragoons. A Conservative. Sat for Fowey in 1830 and 1831, and from then for Northamptonshire N. Sat until he retired in 1837. Summoned to Lords in 1838. Succeeded father as 2nd Marq. Jan. 1856. Died 6 Jan. 1878. [1837]

BRUEN, Francis. Avondale, Co. of Wexford. Bro. to the member for Carlow County. M. 1823, Lady Catherine Nugent, d. of the Marq. of Westmeath. A Dept.-Lieut. of Wexford. A Conservative. Was unsuccessful in contesting Carlow bor. in 1832. Sat for the bor. from 1835. Defeated in 1837; though he was returned in Feb. 1839 the poll was amended in July giving the seat to his opponent. Died 15 Dec. 1867. [1836]

BRUEN, Col. Rt. Hon. Henry. Oak Park, Co. Carlow, Ireland. Carlton. M. d. of T. Kavanagh, Esq., of Borris. Was Col. of the Carlow Militia. A Conservative and voted for agricultural protection 1846. Sat for the County of Carlow in the Parliaments of 1830 and 1831, but lost his seat in

1832. Was petitioned against in Feb. 1835, and the election declared void. On the new writ being issued Messrs. Vigors and Raphael were returned at the head of the poll, but unseated on petition by Col. Bruen and Mr. Kavanagh. In 1840, on the death of Mr. Vigors, he was again returned for the County of Carlow, and sat until his death in 1853. [1851]

BRUEN, Henry, Oak Park, Carlow. Carlton. Sackville Street, Dublin. Only s. of Col. Henry Bruen, of Oak Park, Carlow (who was for many years MP for that Co.), by Anne, d. of Thomas Kavanagh, Esq., of Borris House, Co. Carlow. B. 1828, m. 1854, Mary Margaret, the 3rd d. of Col. Conolly, of Castletown, Co. Kildare. A Conservative, believed it was the interest and the duty of the State to support religion. First returned for Carlow Co. Apr. 1857 and sat until defeated 1880. Died 8 Mar. 1912. [1880]

BRUGES, William Heald Ludlow. Seend, Nr. Melksham, Wiltshire. United University, and Conservative. Eld. and only surviving s. of Benjamin Pennell Ludlow, Esq. of Melksham, Wiltshire, by the d. of William Bruges, Esq., of Semington, Wiltshire. The family of Ludlow was of long standing in Wiltshire, and numbered amongst its members the republican general, Edmund Ludlow, whose estates were forfeited at the Restoration. B. at Melksham in 1796; m. 1st, 1827, Augusta, youngest d. of Samuel Heathcote, Esq., of Shawhill House, Wiltshire; 2ndly, 1834, Agnes, 3rd d. of Charles Penruddocke, Esq., of Winkton, near Christchurch, Hampshire. Assumed the additional name of Bruges in 1835, in compliance with the will of Thomas Bruges, Esq., of Seend. Was educ. at Queen's Coll., Oxford; called to the Bar in 1820, and practised in Chancery; but retired from the profession in 1826. A Magistrate, and Dept.-Lieut. for Wiltshire; Chairman of the Quarter Sessions for the northern division of that county; and many years Recorder of Devizes, which latter office he resigned on becoming a candidate for that bor. A Conservative, not pledged; 'a member of the Established Church, supporting its connexion with the State'; voted for agricultural protection, 1846. Represented Bath from 1837 to 1841; at the general election in Sept. 1841, he was an unsuccessful candidate. First returned for Devizes in 1844, when Mr. Sotheron accepted the Chiltern Hundreds. Accepted Chiltern Hundreds Jan.? 1848. [1847 2nd ed.]

BRYAN, Maj. George. Jenkinstown, Co. of Kilkenny. S. of George Bryan, Esq., of Jenkinstown, by Catherine Xaveria, only child of Henry Byrne, Esq., one of the Cabinteely family

and maternal grandson of Randle, Lord Glane. Had a son m. to a sister of the Countess of Shrewsbury. Of Liberal politics. Elected for Kilkenny Co. in 1837. Remained an MP until his death in 1843. [1843]

BRYAN, George Leopold. 43 Dover Street, London. Jenkinstown Park, Kilkenny, Ireland. Reform. Only s. of Lieut.-Col. George Bryan, of Jenkinstown, Co. Kilkenny, by Margaret, d. of Matthew Talbot, Esq., of Castle Talbot, Co. Wexford. B. at Ballyduff House 1828; m. 1849, Lady Elizabeth Georgiana, d. of 2nd Marq. of Conyngham. Educ. at Oscott Coll. A Magistrate and Dept.-Lieut. of Kilkenny, of which he was High Sheriff in 1852. An 'advanced Liberal', in favour of the system called 'Home Rule' for Ireland. Sat for the Co. of Kilkenny from July 1865 until he retired 1880. Died 29 June 1880. [1880]

BRYCE, Prof. James. Continued in House after 1885: full entry in Volume II.

BRYMER, W.E. Continued in House after 1885: full entry in Volume II.

BUCHANAN, T.R. Continued in House after 1885: full entry in Volume II.

BUCHANAN, Walter. 6 Brandon Street, Glasgow. Shandon, Dumbartonshire. Reform. S. of Andrew Buchanan, Esq., of Glasgow, by Margaret, d. of — Cockburn, Esq., of Edinburgh. B. at Glasgow 1797; m. 1st, 1824, Mary, d. of John Hamilton, Esq., of Middleton; 2ndly, 1851, Christina Louisa, d. of James Smith, Esq., of Jordanshill. Educ. at the University of Glasgow. A Merchant in Glasgow. A Magistrate for Lanarkshire and Dumbartonshire. A Liberal, in favour of extension of the franchise in accordance with the progress of education, and in favour of 'vote by ballot in those districts where it is needed'; in favour of Forbes Mackenzie's Act being modified, but not repealed. First returned for Glasgow Mar. 1857. Sat until he retired 1865. Died 1877. [1865]

BUCK, George Stucley. See STUCLEY, Sir George Stucley, Bart.

BUCK, Lewis William. 12 Norfolk Street, Park Lane, London. Moreton, Bideford, Devon. Carlton. Eld. surviving s. of George Stucley Buck, Esq., by Martha, d. of the Rev. Richard Keats. M. Anne, d. of Thomas Robins, Esq. A Dept.-Lieut. of Devon. A Conservative, opposed to the endowment of the Roman Catholic Clergy.

Sat for Exeter from 1826-1832; first elected for N. Devon Mar. 1839. Sat until he retired 1857. Died 25 Apr. 1858.   [1857]

BUCKINGHAM, James Silk. Was the proprietor and editor of a popular journal in India; was banished thence for contravening the Government regulations with respect to the press, and after his departure the journal was suppressed by the authorities. (In 1835 Mr. Tulk introduced a bill to compensate him, which was subsequently withdrawn owing to strong opposition on the part of the ministry.) On his arrival in this country he established the *Oriental Herald*. The *Athenaeum* was also projected by him. Author of Travels in Palestine, Syria, Arabia, Mesopotamia and India. A Reformer, advocating an extension of the suffrage, triennial Parliaments, vote by ballot, repeal of the corn laws, reduction of expenditure, a property tax in lieu of all other imposts, and free trade with all nations. Sat for Sheffield from 1832, until he retired in 1837. Travelled in America 1837-41. President of Temperance League 1851. Civil list pension 1851. Died 30 June 1855.   [1837]

BUCKLEY, Edmund. Higher Ardwick, Lancaster. Carlton. S. of John Buckley, Esq. of Stalybridge. An Iron-master and Proprietor of Coal-works at Manchester. A Director of several canal and railway companies connected with Manchester. A Conservative, but in favour of free trade. First returned for Newcastle-under-Lyme in 1841. Sat until he retired 1847.   [1847]

BUCKLEY, Sir Edmund, Bart. Carlton, and Union. A near relative of Edmund Buckley, Esq. of Ardwick, Nr. Manchester, who represented Newcastle-under-Lyme from 1841-47. B. in Manchester 1834; m. 1860, Sarah, eld. d. of William Rees, Esq. of Jonn Llandovery, Carmarthenshire. A Magistrate and Dept.-Lieut. for Merionethshire. A Conservative, was in favour of 'efficiently maintaining the army and navy.' Sat for Newcastle-under-Lyme from July 1865 until he accepted Chiltern Hundreds in 1878. Died 21 Mar. 1910.   [1878]

BUCKLEY, Lieut.-Gen. Edward Pery. 12 South Audley Street, London. New Hall, Salisbury, Wiltshire. Boodle's, Brooks's, and Senior United Service. S. of Edward Pery Buckley, Esq., of Minesteed Lodge, Hampshire (many years groom of the bedchamber to George III), by Lady Georgiana, eld. d. of 2nd Earl De La Warr. B. in Audley Square, London 1796; m. 1828, Lady Katherine, only d. of 3rd Earl of Radnor. Educ. at Harrow School and at the Royal Military Coll. Entered the Grenadier Guards

June 1812; became a Lieut.-Gen. in the army, Oct. 1858, served in the Peninsula and at Waterloo. Equerry to the Queen. A Magistrate and Dept.-Lieut. of Hampshire. A Liberal, in favour of progress generally, and of Parliamentary Reform; voted against Church rates 1855. First elected for Salisbury Nov. 1853. Sat until he retired 1865. Col. 1865. Died 28 May 1873.   [1865]

BUCKLEY, Nathaniel. Rycroft, Ashton-under-Lyne, Alderdale, Droylsden, Manchester. Reform. Edl. s. of Abel Buckley, Esq. B. at Ashton-under-Lyne 1821. Unmarried. A Cotton Manufacturer at Ashton. Dept.-Lieut. for Lancashire, also Magistrate for Lancashire and Cheshire. A Liberal. Sat from Sept. 1871 for Stalybridge (which he contested unsuccessfully Dec. 1868). Defeated 1874. Died 23 Mar. 1892.   [1873]

BULKELEY, Sir Richard Bulkeley Williams-, Bart. Baron Hill, Beaumaris. Reform, Arthur's, and Boodle's. S. of Sir Robert Williams (9th Bart). B. in the parish of Marylebone, London, 1801; m. 1st, 1828, d. of 1st Lord Dinorben; 2nd-ly, 1832, d. of Sir T.S.M. Stanley, Bart.; assumed the name of Bulkeley in 1827. A Dept.-Lieut. of Anglesea; appointed Lord Lieut. of Carnarvonshire, 1851; patron of 4 livings. A Liberal, voted against Lord Russell's Reform Bill 1866; in favour of the abolition of church-rates and a substitution of 'the voluntary principle'; favourable to the extension of education by 'denominational grants.' Sat for Beaumaris from 1830 till 1832, for Anglesea from 1832 till 1837, for Flint district from 1841 to 1847, when he was once more elected for Anglesea. Sat until he retired in 1868. High Sheriff of Anglesea 1870. Died 28 Aug. 1875.   [1867]

BULLER, Sir Arthur William. 43 Queen's Gate Terrace, South Kensington, London. Athenaeum. 2nd s. of Charles Buller, Esq. (formerly in the civil service of the E.I.C. in Bengal, and afterwards member for West Looe), by the d. of General Kirkpatrick. B. at Calcutta 1808. M. 1842, d. of Francis Templer, Esq., Treasurer of the island of Ceylon. Educ. at Edinburgh and at Trinity Coll., Cambridge, where he graduated M.A. 1834. Called to the bar at Lincoln's Inn 1834 and joined the Western Circuit. Was Queen's Advocate in Ceylon from 1840-July 1848, when he was appointed Judge of the supreme court of Calcutta. Retired in 1858. A Liberal and in favour of the 'independence and self-government of our Colonies.' In favour also of vote by ballot and opposed to all religious endowment. Sat for Devonport from Aug. 1859-June 1865, just previous to the general election when he was returned for Liskeard. Sat until his death on 30 Apr. 1869. [1869]

BULLER, Rt. Hon. Charles. 2 Chester Place, Chester Square, London. Athenaeum. B. at Calcutta, Aug. 1806. His father was in the civil service of the East India Company at Bengal. Was educ. at Harrow, at the University of Edinburgh, and at Trinity Coll., Cambridge; was called to the bar in 1831. Appointed Judge Advocate-General, June 1846; a Queen's Counsel, Nov. 1846. Was a contributor to several Reviews, and was an East India Proprietor. Was Secretary to the Board of Controul. A radical Reformer. Was chief secretary to Lord Durham when in Canada. Sat for West Loo in 1830. Sat for Liskeard from 1832 until his death in 1848. [1847 2nd ed.]

BULLER, Edward. 23 Hertford Street, London. Dilhorne Hall, Staffordshire. Brooks's, and Travellers'. Bro. of member for S. Devon. B. 1800; m. 1824, Mary-Anne, d. of Gen. Coote Manningham. Of moderate Whig principles. Represented N. Staffordshire from 1832, but did not contest the seat in 1841 and was returned for Stafford instead. Defeated in 1847 vainly contesting his old county seat. And again defeated in 1857 contesting Staffordshire N. [1847]

BULLER, Sir Edward Manningham-, Bart. 5 Old Palace Yard, Westminster, London. Dilhorn Hall, Cheadle, Staffordshire. Sheen Elms, Surrey. Brooks's, Travellers', and United University. 2nd s. of Sir Francis Buller Yarde-Buller, of Lupton, Devon, by Eliza Lydia, only d. and heir of John Holliday, Esq., of Dilhorn Hall, Staffordshire. B. at Churston Ferrers, Devonshire 1800; m. 1st, 1824, Mary Anne, d. and heir of Maj.-Gen. Coote Manningham (she died 1860); 2ndly, 1863, Georgina Charlotte, only d. of Admiral Sir Charles Edward Nugent, G.C.H., and relict of the Rt. Hon. George Bankes, MP. Educ. at Oriel Coll., Oxford, where he was 2nd class in classics. A Magistrate and Dept.-Lieut. of Staffordshire, of which he was High Sheriff 1853. A Liberal, in favour of the reduction of the Malt tax, and 'for adequate provision being made for the maintenance of the national churches' on the abolition of church rates. Sat for Staffordshire N. from July 1837-July 1841; was an unsuccessful candidate there, July 1847. Sat for the bor. of Stafford from July 1841-July 1847; re-elected for Staffordshire July 1865, and sat until he retired in 1874. [1873]

BULLER, James Wentworth. 109 Jermyn Street, London. Downes, Crediton, Devon. Athenaeum, and Brooks's. Eld. s. of James Buller,

Esq., of Downes and Shillingham (who sat for Exeter for more than twenty years), by Anne, d. of Bishop (Buller) of Exeter. B. at Downes 1798; m. 1831, Charlotte Juliana Jane, 3rd d. of Lord Henry Molyneux Howard, and niece of 15th Duke of Norfolk (she died 1855). Educ. at Harrow and at Oriel Coll., Oxford, where he was 1st class in classics 1819, and was subsequently Fellow of All Souls. A Magistrate and Dept.-Lieut. for Devon, and Lieut.-Col. Commandant of the 1st Devon Yeomanry Cavalry. Patron of 2 livings. Chairman of the Bristol and Exeter Railway. A Liberal. Sat for Exeter from 1830-Jan. 1835, when he was an unsuccessful candidate; unsuccessfully contested Devon N. Mar. 1839, first elected for Devon N. Apr. 1857. MP until his death 13 Mar. 1865. [1865]

BULLER, Sir John Buller Yarde-, Bart., 39 Belgrave Square, London. Lupton, Devon. Carlton, and United University. S. of Sir Francis Yarde-Buller, by the only d. and heir of John Holliday, Esq., of Lincoln's Inn, grands. of Mr. Justice Buller. B. at Dilhorne, 1799; m. 1823, Elizabeth, d. of Thomas Wilson Patten, Esq. Graduated at Oriel Coll., Oxford, where he was 2nd class in classics 1819, and received the hon. degree of D.C.L. 1853. A Dept.-Lieut. of Devon. Appointed one of the Special Dept.-Wardens of the Stannaries 1852. Patron of 2 livings. Lieut.-Col. of S. Devon Militia. A Conservative, opposed to the endowment of the Roman Catholic Clergy. Contested Devonshire S. unsuccessfully in 1832, but was elected in 1835, without opposition. Sat until he accepted Chiltern Hundreds in 1858. [1857]

BULTEEL, John Crocker. 4 Parliament Street, London. Fleet House, Devon. M. in 1826, Elizabeth, 2nd d. of Earl Grey. Of Whig principles, not unfavourable to a revision of the corn laws, and in favour of 'preliminary steps to the abolition of slavery, in the way of education being immediately entered upon.' Sat for Devon S. from 1832. Retired in 1835. [1833]

BULWER, Rt. Hon. Sir Edward George Earle Lytton. See LYTTON, Rt. Hon. Sir Edward George Earle Lytton Bulwer-.

BULWER, Rt. Hon. Sir Henry Lytton Earle, G.C.B. 53 Upper Brook Street, London. Eld. s. of Gen. William Earle Bulwer, of Woodalling and Heydon Hall, Norfolk, by the only d. and heir of Richard Warburton Lytton, Esq. of Knibworth, Hertfordshire. Elder bro. of the 1st Baron Lytton. B. 1804; m. 1848, Hon Georgiana, youngest d. of 1st Lord Cowley. Appointed Dept.-Lieut. of Hertfordshire 1849. Attached to the Mission at Berlin

Aug. 1827, to the embassy at Vienna 1829, at the Hague Apr 1830; was attached to the embassy at Paris 1832; appointed Sec. of legation at Brussels, Nov. 1835; Sec. of embassy at Constantinople, Oct. 1837; Sec. of embassy at Paris June 1839; envoy extraordinary and minister plenipotentiary Madrid Nov. 1843, and negotiated the peace between Spain and Morocco in 1844; appointed in the same capacity to Washington Apr. 1849; transferred to Tuscany 1852; made Ambassador at Constantinople May 1858 and returned to England 1865. A Liberal. Sat for Coventry from 8 Dec. 1832. From 9 Jan. 1835 he sat for Marylebone. Sat for Tamworth from Dec. 1868 until created Baron Dalling and Bulwer 21 Mar. 1871. Died 23 May 1872.   [1870]

BULWER, James Redfoord, Q.C. Temple Gardens, London. Carlton, and University. Eldest s. of the Rev. James Bulwer, rector of Hanworth-cum-Stody, Norfolk, by Eliza, only d. of Archibald Redfoord, Esq., of the Irish bar. B. 1820. Unmarried. Educ. at Trinity Coll., Cambridge; graduated B.A. 1842, M.A. 1846. Was called to the bar Jan. 1847 at the Inner Temple, of which he became a bencher 1865, and was appointed a Queen's Counsel the same year. A member of the South-Eastern Circuit. Was Recorder of Ipswich from June 1861 to Dec. 1866, when he was appointed Recorder of Cambridge. Lieut.-Col. of Inns of Court Volunteers. Editor of the Common Law Series of the Law Reports. A Conservative, in favour of the readjustment of taxation, also of increased facilities for the sale and transfer of property, and that every tenant should have full security for his capital. Sat for Ipswich from Feb. 1874 till Apr. 1880, when he again contested Ipswich but was unsuccessful. Sat for Cambridgeshire from Sept. 1881. Retired in 1885. Master in Lunacy 1886. Died 4 Mar. 1899. [1885]

BUNBURY, Edward Herbert. 15 Jermyn Street, London. Athenaeum, and Oxford & Cambridge. 2nd. s. of Sir Henry Bunbury, Bart., of Great Barton, Suffolk, by the d. of the Hon. Henry Edward Fox. B. 1811. Unmarried. Educ. at Trinity Coll., Cambridge, where he was senior medallist in 1833. Was called to the Bar at the Inner Temple in 1841. A Liberal, though unfavourable to the endowment of the Roman Catholic Clergy, refused to pledge himself. First returned for Bury St. Edmund's in 1847. Defeated in 1852. Contested same seat in 1868. Succeeded bro. as 9th Baronet 18 June 1886. Author of *A History of Ancient Geography* (1879). Died 5 Mar. 1895.   [1852]

BUNBURY, Thomas. St. James's Hotel, Jermyn Street, London. Moyle, Co. Carlow. University. A Conservative, Unsuccessfully contested the coun-

ty of Carlow in 1837. Was returned for it in 1841 and sat until his death in 1846.   [1845]

BUNBURY, William Bunbury McClintock-. Sussex Square, Hyde Park, London. Lisnavagh, Rathvilly, Co. Carlow, Ireland. Carlton. Kildare Street Club, Dublin. 2nd s. of John McClintock, Esq., of Drumcar, sometime MP for Louth, by his 1st wife, d. of William Bunbury, Esq., and sister of Thomas Bunbury, Esq. MP. Assumed the name of Bunbury in addition to his patronymic on the death of the latter, 1846. B. 1800; m. Pauline Caroline Diana Mary, d. of Sir James M. Stronge, Bart., of Tynan Abbey, Co. Armagh. Became a Capt. R.N. in 1856. A Magistrate for the counties of Carlow and Fermanagh. A Conservative, in favour of civil and religious liberty. Sat for Carlow county from July 1846 till July 1852, when he was an unsuccessful candidate; re-elected Apr. 1853, without opposition. Sat until he accepted Chiltern Hundreds 1862. Died 2 June 1866.   [1862]

BURDETT, Sr Francis, Bart. 25 St. James's Place, London. Foremark, Derbyshire. Ramsbury Manor, Wiltshire. Carlton, and Athenaeum. B. 1770; m. 1793, Sophia, youngest d. of Thomas Coutts, Esq., the Banker. Patron of 6 livings. Entered Parliament in 1796 as the representative of Boroughbridge, for which he continued to sit until elected for Westminster in 1807. In the intervening period, he thrice contested Middlesex unsuccessfully. Sir Francis's early advocacy of Reform, his confinement in the Tower and King's Bench Prison, his condemnation to pay a fine of £1,000, by the Court of King's Bench, for the course he took in advocating that Reform, are well known. He was a strong supporter of the Whig Government, and declared himself without confidence in that of Sir Robert Peel. Successfully contested Westminster 12 Dec. 1832 and again in 1835, but later he resigned his seat and recaptured it at a by-election 12 May 1837, standing as a Conservative. After his return for Wiltshire N. in July 1837 he generally voted with the Conservative Party. MP until his death in 1844. [1843]

BURDON, William Wharton. Hartford House, Northumberland. Clarence. S. of William Burdon, Esq., author of *Materials for Thinking*, (who m. d. of Gen Dickson); and through his grandmother connected with the Whartons of Westmoreland in which family the Dukedom of Wharton was supposed to be in abeyance. Coal-owner. LL.B. of Emmanuel Coll., Cambridge. Unmarried. A Reformer. In favour of 'liberty of action – liberty of conscience – liberty of speech – so long as they are within the pale of the law, and are not injurious to a neighbour; the encouragement of free trade, as far as may be consistent with the finances of the country; and the abolition of all monopolies, public and private.' Unsuccessfully contested Weymouth in 1832, with Sir Frederick Johnstone, Bart., losing the election by a majority of one. Sat for Weymouth from Jan. 1835. Retired in 1837. [1837]

BURGHLEY, Lord. (I). Brookfield House, Ryde, Isle of Wight. Carlton, and Junior Carlton. Eld. s. of the Marq. of Exeter. B. in Connaught Place 1825; m. 1848, Lady Georgiana Sophia, 2nd d. of the 2nd Earl of Longford. Educ. at St. John's Coll., Cambridge. Appointed a Dept.-Lieut. of Northamptonshire 1854, and was Lieut.-Col. of that Co. Militia from 1846. A Conservative, would uphold Church rates unless a good substitute be found for them; opposed to the 'secular system' in education. Sat for Lincolnshire S. from July 1847-Apr. 1857, when he was elected for Northamptonshire N. Sat until he succeeded as 3rd Marq. Jan. 1867. Died 14 July 1895. [1865]

BURGHLEY, Lord. (II). Continued in House after 1885: full entry in Volume II.

BURKE, Edmund Haviland-. 13 Arlington Street, Piccadilly, London. 13 Old Square, Lincoln's Inn, London. Union, and Reform. S. of Thomas William Aston Haviland-Burke, Esq., of Beaconsfield, Buckinghamshire (who assumed in 1816 the name of Burke, in addition to Haviland, on becoming sole representative of his great-uncle, the celebrated Edmund Burke), by Harriet Elizabeth, 3rd d. of William Munshull, Esq., of Aston Clinton, BuckinghamshirA Liberal, voted for the disestablishment of the Irish Church 1869. Unsuccessfully contested Christchurch July 1865; sat for that borough from Dec. 1868 until he retired 1874. [1873]

BURKE, Sir Thomas John, Bart. 112 Jermyn Street, London. Marble Hill, Loughrea, Co. Galway. Arthur's, and Junior United Service. Eld. s. of Sir John Burke, Bart., of Marble Hill, Co. Galway, by the d. of the Rt. Hon. John Calcraft. B. 1813, m. d. of A. Nugent, Esq. Was formerly a Capt. in the 1st Dragoons. A Whig, voted with Lord Palmerston on the vote of censure 1864. First returned for the Co. of Galway Apr. 1847, without opposition. Sat until he retired 1865. Died 9 Dec. 1875. [1865]

BURKE, Visct. 17 Stratton Street, London. Portumna Castle, Galway. Younger s. of the Marq. of Clanricarde, by the Hon. Harriet, only d. of the Rt. Hon. George Canning, and Viscountess Canning. B. 1832. Appointed attaché at Turin, Apr. 1852; 2nd Sec. there 1862. A

Liberal. Elected for Galway Co. Sept. 1867. Accepted Chiltern Hundreds Feb. 1871. Succeeded as 2nd Marq. of Clanricarde Apr. 1874. Died 12 Apr. 1916. [1870]

BURNABY, Gen. Edwyn Sherard. Palace Chambers, London. Baggrave Hall, Leicester. Only s. of Edwyn Burnaby, Esq. of Baggrave Hall, Leicestershire, by Annie Caroline, d. of Thomas Salisbury, Esq., of Oaksey Park, Wiltshire. B. 1830; m. 1864, Louisa Julia Mary, d. of Sir Wolston Dixie, Bart., of Bosworth Park, Leicestershire (she died 1881). Was educ. at Eton. Entered the Grenadier Guards as Ensign and Lieut. Nov. 1846; became Col. Commandant Oct. 1877; served in the Crimean Campaign 1854-55; at the battle of Inkerman and the siege of Sebastopol, where he received the brevet of Maj. and a medal and clasp; and was Brig. Gen. of the British Italian Legion 1855-57. Received Royal permission to accept the 2nd class order of the Medjidie 1881. A Magistrate for Leicester, Vice-Pres. of the Leicestershire Chamber of Commerce. Author of various works. A Conservative, but reserved to himself 'the right of giving an independent vote', said lapse of years may require', and would maintain 'our great institutions in Church and State'. Sat for Leicestershire. N. from Apr. 1880. MP until his death 31 May 1883. [1883]

BURR, Daniel Higford Davall. 16 Portland Place, London. Gayton Ross, Herefordshire. Windham. S. of Lieut.-Gen. Burr, of the Hon. E.I. Co's. Service who m. Miss Davies, co-heiress of the Dowager Duchess of Norfolk and of John Higford, Esq. of Dixton, Gloucestershire. B. 24 Mar. 1811. A Conservative. Educ. at Eton and afterwards at Christ Church, Oxford. Returned for Hereford in 1837. Defeated 1841. Contested Salisbury and Abingdon 1852. Sheriff of Berkshire 1851. Died 29 Nov. 1885. [1838]

BURRELL, Sir Charles Merrik, Bart. 5 Richmond Terrace, London. Knepp Castle, Sussex. Carlton, Arthur's, and United University. S. of Sir Wm. Burrell (2nd Bart) by Sophia, d. and co-heir of Sir Charles Raymond, Bart., of Valentine House, Essex. B. in Golden Square, 1774; m. Frances, d. of the 3rd Earl of Egremont (she died 1848). An East India Proprietor. A Dept.-Lieut. of Sussex. A Conservative, voted for inquiry into Maynooth 1853. First elected for Shoreham in 1806. MP until his death 4 Jan. 1862. [1861]

BURRELL, Sir Percy, Bart. 44 Berkeley Square, London. West Grinstead Castle, Horsham, Sussex. Carlton. 2nd. s. of Sir Charles Merrik Burrell, Bart., (who sat for Shoreham from 1806

till his death in 1862), by the d. of the 3rd Earl of Egremont. B. in Grosvenor Place 1812; m. 1856, eld. d. and co-heir of Vice-Admiral Sir George R. Brooke-Pechell, Bart. Appointed Captain 18th Sussex Rifle Volunteers 1861. A Dept.-Lieut. of Sussex. A moderate Conservative; voted against the abolition of church-rates, May 1862. First e

BURRELL, Sir Walter Wyndham, Bart. 9 King Street, St. James's, London. Ockendon House, Cuckfield, Sussex. Carlton. 3rd s. of Sir Charles Merrik Burrell, 3rd Bart. (who sat for Shoreham from 1806 till his death in 1862), by the d. of the 3rd Earl of Egremont. Bro. to Sir Percy Burrell, who sat for Shoreham from 1862 till his death in 1876. B. 1814; m. 1847, Dorothea, d. of Rev. John A. Jones, Rector of Burleigh-on-the-Hill, Rutlandshire. A Conservative. Unsuccessfully contested Sussex E. 19 July 1865. Sat for Shoreham from Aug. 1876. Sat until he retired in 1885. Died 23 Jan. 1886. [1885]

BURROUGHES, Henry Negus. 28 Bury Street, London. Burlingham Hall, Norfolk. Eld. s. of J. Burkin Burroughes, Esq., of Burlingham Hall, by Christabel, d. and heiress of Henry Negus, Esq., of Hoveton Hall. B. 1791, m. 1st, 1818, Jane Sarah, d. of Rev. Dixon Hoste, (she died 1851); 2ndly, 1854, Augusta Susanna, only surviving d. of Lieut.-Gen. Proctor, C.B. of Aberavesp Hall, Montgomeryshire. Was High Sheriff of Norfolk in 1817. Patron of 2 livings. A Conservative. Sat for Norfolk E. from 1837 until he retired 1857. Died 22 Mar. 1872. [1857]

BURROWES, Robert. Stradone House, Co. Cavan. Carlton. Eld. s. of Thomas Burrowes, Esq. of Stradone House, by Susan, d. of Rev. Henry Seward, of Badsey, Worcestershire. B. at Dublin 1810; m. 1838, Anne Frances, only d. of John Carden, Esq., of Barnane, Co. Tipperary. Educ. at Harrow and at Magdalene Coll., Cambridge. A Dept.-Lieut. of Cavan, of which he was High Sheriff 1838. A Conservative, in favour of 'an equitable settlement of the Tenant-right question.' First returned for Cavan Apr. 1855. Retired 1857. Died 30 Nov. 1881. [1857]

BURT, Thomas. Continued in House after 1885: full entry in Volume II.

BURTON, Henry. 1 Upper Brook Street, London. Hotham Hall, Yorkshire. B. 1792, m. 1st, 1814, Caroline, d. of John Campbell, Esq., of Liston Hall, Suffolk; 2ndly, 1819, Sarah, d. of Gen Christie Burton. A Reformer, in favour of short Parliaments. Patron of 1 living. Sat for Beverley from 1830 until he retired in 1837. [1837]

BURY, Rt. Hon. Visct., K.C.M.G. Quiddenham Hall, Thetford. 48, Rutland Gate, Knightsbridge, London. Brooks's, and Guards'. Only s. of 6th Earl of Albermarle, by Susan, d. of Sir Coutts Trotter, Bart. B. in London 1832; m. 1855, Sophia Mary, 2nd d. of Sir Aldan Napier McNab, Bart., of Dundurn Castle, Upper Canada. Educ. at Eton. Appointed Ensign and Lieut. Scots Fusilier Guards 1849. Retired 1854 (after having served in India as Aide-de-Camp to Lord Frederic Fitz-Clarence). Was Private Sec. to Earl (then Lord John) Russell in 1850-1. Lieut.-Col. Service Volunteer Rifles. Appointed Civil Sec. and Superintendent of Indian Affairs for the Province of Canada Dec. 1854. Was Treasurer of the Queen's Household from June 1859-May 1866. A Liberal, and a general supporter of Mr. Gladstone; voted for the disestablishment of the Irish Church 1869 and in favour of 'the application of its revenues to purposes of national utility in Ireland.' Sat for Norwich from Apr. 1857-July 1859, when he was unseated on petition, and for Wick from Oct. 1860-July 1865. Unsuccessfully contested Dover 12 July 1865. Sat for Berwick-on-Tweed from Dec. 1868. Retired 1874. Contested Stroud 22 Feb. 1875. Called to the House of Lords in his father's Barony Sept. 1876. Under-Sec. for War 1878-80. Succeeded his father as 7th Earl Albermarle Feb. 1891. Died 28 Aug. 1894. [1873]

BUSFIELD, William. Upwood, Yorkshire. Born at Myrtle Grove in 1773, the eld. s. of J.A. Busfield, Esq., of Myrtle Grove and Ryshworth Hall. A Magistrate and Registrar of the West Riding of Yorkshire. M. in 1800, Caroline, the eld. d. of Capt. Charles Wood, R.N., of Bowling Hall, niece to Sir Francis Wood, Bart. Educ. at Queen's Coll., Cambridge. Was for many years a Major in the 1st W. Yorkshire Militia, and a Dept.-Lieut. for the W. Riding of Yorkshire. Was 'a staunch Whig and Reformer.' Represented the borough of Bradfield from 1837-July 1841, when he was an unsuccessful candidate at the general election. He was again returned on the death of W.C. Lister, Esq., in the Sept. following and was re-elected in 1847 after which he sat until his death in 1851. [1851]

BUSZARD, Marston Clarke. 29 Porchester Terrace, London. 5 Crown Office Row, London. Lutterworth, Leicestershire. Reform. Eld. s. of Marston Buszard, Esq., M.D. of Lutterworth, Leicestershire, by Sarah Catherine, eld. d. of John Clarke, Esq. of Peatling Hall, Leicestershire (who was High Sheriff of Leicestershire 1820). B. at Lutterworth 1837; m. 1864, Louisa, d. of John Mayor Threlfall, Esq., of Singleton House, Higher Broughton, Manchester. Was educ. at

Rugby and at Trinity Coll., Cambridge; graduated B.A. 12th senior optime, 3rd class in classics and 1st class in Law tripos 1860; proceeded to the degrees of M.A. and LL.M. 1863, when he was also Chancellor's medallist for legal studies. Was called to the bar in 1862 at the Inner Temple of which he was elected a Bencher Apr. 1880. Appointed a Queen's Counsel 1877. A Liberal, and in favour of lowering the county franchise. Sat for Stamford from April 1880 which he had unsuccessfully contested Feb. 1874. Defeated in 1885 standing for Rutland. Contested Warwick South-East in 1886 as a Liberal Unionist. Recorder of Derby 1890-99. Died 11 Sept. 1921. [1885]

BUTLER, Charles Salisbury. Cazenoves, Upper Clapton, Middlesex. Reform, and City. S. of John Butler, Esq., who took an active part in Reform questions in Middlesex. M. Elizabeth, d. of Edward Kingstone, Esq. A Magistrate for Middlesex, the city of Westminster, and Chairman of the County Divisional Bench; a Magistrate also for the royalty of the Tower, and Chairman of Quarter Sessions there; a Dept.-Lieut. of the last place. Patron of 1 living. A Liberal, in favour of 'reform and retrenchments', and an extension of the suffrange; voted for the ballot 1853. First returned for the Tower Hamlets in July 1852. Sat until he retired in 1868. Contested Hackney 18 Nov. 1868. Chairman of Tower Hamlets' Quarter Sessions until his death on 11 Nov. 1870. [1867]

BUTLER, Hon. Pierce. Ballyconra, Co. Kilkenny. Reform. B. 1774, the bro. of the Earl of Kilkenny. M. 1800, Anne, the d. of Thomas Marsh, Esq. A Lieut.-Col. in the army. A Repealer; voted against the corn laws. Sat for the county of Kilkenny from 1832 until his death in 1846. [1845]

BUTLER, Pierce Somerset. 3 Victoria Square, Pimlico, London. Lodge Park, Co. Kilkenny. Eld. s. of Col. the Hon. Pierce Butler, grands. of Lord Mount-Garrett, and nephew of the 1st Earl of Kilkenny. B. 1801; m. in 1835, Jessy Anne, relict of P.A. Warren, Esq., of Lodge Park, Co. Kilkenny. Was called to the bar; a Capt. in the Kilkenny Militia. Was a candidate for the representation of the city of Kilkenny before the passing of the Reform Act, and petitioned, without success, against the return of Mr. (afterwards Chief Justice) Doherty. Opposed to the tithe system in Ireland, and supported a repeal of the Union. Was educ. at Trinity Coll., Dublin and obtained the highest classical honours there. Was returned for the county of Kilkenny, on the death of Major Bryan in 1843, without opposition. Sat until he

retired in 1852. Died 28 July 1865. [1852]

BUTLER-JOHNSTONE, Hon. Henry. 24 Park Street, Grosvenor Square, London. Auchen Castle and Corehead, Moffat, N.B. Carlton, and Conservative. 3rd. s. of the 13th Lord Dunboyne, by his 1st wife, Ellen, d. of David O'Connell, Esq. B. in Dublin 1809; m. 1843, Isabella Margaret Munro-Johnstone, only d. of Sir Alexander Munro, of Novar, Ross-shire; niece and heir of General Johnstone, of Corehead, Dumfries. Assumed the name of Johnstone after his marriage. A Dept.-Lieut. of Dumfries; appointed Major of that county Militia in 1846. An 'independent Conservative', in favour of preserving the right of voting to free-men; opposed to the Maynooth grant. First returned for Canterbury in July 1852, and sat till Feb. 1853, when the election was declared void, and the new writ suspended for bribery, etc., again elected in Mar. 1857. Accepted Chiltern Hundreds 1862. [1861]

BUTLER-JOHNSTONE, Henry Alexander Munro. 5 Hamilton Place, London. Culcairn, Ross-shire. Anchor Castle, Moffat, Dumfries-shire. Carlton. Only s. of Hon. Henry Butler-Johnstone (3rd son of 13th Lord Dunboyne), by Isabella, only d. of Sir Alexander Munro, and niece and heir of Gen. Johnstone, of Corehead, Dumfries, was therefore grands. to the 13th Lord Dunboyne. B. in Edinburgh 1837; m. 1877, Masie, Irmer Countess de Soyres. Educ. at Eton, and at Christ Church, Oxford, where he took a first class in honours at the final classical examination; graduated B.A. 1861, M.A. 1862. A Dept.-Lieut. for Ross-shire and a Magistrate for Dumfries-Shire. Author of *The Fair of Nijni Novgorod, The Eastern Question*, etc. A Conservative; voted for Mr. Gladstone's resolutions on the Irish Church in 1868, and therefore declared himself independent of a party leader. Sat for Canterbury from Feb. 1862 until he accepted Chiltern Hundreds in 1878. Contested Canterbury again in Apr. 1880. Died 17 Oct. 1902. [1878]

BUTT, Charles Parker, Q.C. 29 Cadogan Place, London. 4 Crown Office Row, Temple, London. Reform. Was called to the bar at Lincoln's Inn Nov. 1854, and joined the Northern circuit. Appointed Queen's Counsel 1868, a special pleader and practiced in the Admiralty Court and at the Common Law Bar. A Liberal. Unsuccessfully contested Tamworth, Feb. 1874. Sat for Southampton from Apr. 1880. Sat until appointed Judge 1883. Knighted Apr. 1883. Died 25 May 1892. [1883]

BUTT, George Medd. 17 Eaton Square, London. Carlton. S. of John Butt, Esq., of Sherborne, Dorset. B. at Sherborne; m. Frances Jane, eld. d. of Thomas Ffooks, Esq., of Sherborne. After having been a pupil of John George, Esq., of the Northern Circuit, practised for some years as a special pleader, was called to the bar at the Inner Temple in 1830, and joined the Western Circuit. Was made a Queen's Counsel in 1845 (during Lord Lyndhurst's Chancellorship) and was also a Bencher of the Inner Temple. A Conservative, voted for inquiry respecting Maynooth 1853, favoured the removal of all serious blots and anomalies in the representative system. Was an unsuccessful candidate for Weymouth July 1847, losing only by three votes; first returned at the head of the poll for Weymouth in July 1852. Sat until defeated 1857. Died 11 Nov. 1860. [1857]

BUTT, Isaac. LL.D. 60 Eccles Street, London. Carlton, and University, Dublin. Only s. of the Rev. Robert Butt, incumbent of Stranorlar, Co. Donegal. Related maternally to the celebrated Bishop (Berkeley) of Cloyne. B. at Glenfia, Co. Donegal, 1813; m. 1837, d. of H. Swanzy, Esq., of Rockfield, Co. Managhan. Educ. at the Royal School of Raphoe and at Trinity Coll., Dublin, where he obtained a scholarship in 1832, and took honours in both classics and mathematics; graduated in 1835, and was elected to the Whately Professorship of Political Economy May 1836. Called to the Irish bar Nov. 1844. A Liberal and in favour of complete 'Home Rule' for Ireland. Unsuccessfully contested Mayo July 1850. Sat for Harwich from May-July 1852 and for Youghal from the last date to July 1865; was unsuccessful at Monaghan July 1871; sat for Limerick from Sept. 1871. MP until his death 5 May 1879. [1879]

BUXTON, Charles. 7 Grosvenor Crescent, Belgrave Square, London. Foxwarren, Cobham, Surrey. Brooks's. 3rd s. of Sir Thos. Fowell Buxton, Bart., of Bellfield, Dorset, and Colne House, Norfolk, by Hannah, d. of the late John Gurney, Esq. of Earlham Hall, Norfolk. B. at Cromer Hall, 1823; m. 1850, Emily Mary, d. of Sir Henry Holland, Bart. M.D. Educ. at Trinity Coll., Cambridge where he gained a scholarship and prizes and took classical and mathematical honours. A Partner in the firm of Truman, Hanbury and Co., Brewers. Lieut.-Col. 1st Battalion of the Tower Hamlets Rifle Volunteers. A Magistrate for Surrey and Norfolk. Author of *Life of Sir Fowell Buxton*, etc. A Liberal. Sat for Newport from Apr. 1857-May 1859; then for Maidstone till July 1865, and for E. Surrey from the last date. MP until his death 10 Aug. 1871. [1871]

BUXTON, Sir Edward North, Bart. 10 Upper Grosvenor Street, London. Colne House, near Cromer, Norfolk. Brooks's. Eld. s. of Sir Thos. Fowell Buxton, Bart., by Hannah, 5th d. of John Gurney, Esq., of Earlham, Norfolk. B. at Earlham 1812; m. 1836, Catherine 2nd. d. of Samuel Gurney, Esq., of Ham House, Essex. Educ. at Cambridge. Declared himself 'a moderate Liberal, a Churchman, but closely connected with Dissenters, and heartily in favour of all measures of gradual reform.' Sat for Essex S. from 1847 to 1852. First returned for Norfolk E. (during his absence at Nice) Apr. 1857. MP until his death 11 June 1858. [1858]

BUXTON, Francis William. 42 Grosvenor Gardens, London. Brooks's. Youngest s. of Sir Edward North Buxton, Bart., of Colne Hall, Norfolk (who sat for South Essex from 1847 to 1852 and for North Norfolk from 1852 to 1857), by Catherine, 2nd d. of Samuel Gurney, Esq., of Upton, Essex. B. at St. James's Place, London 1847; m. 1872, Hon. Mary Emma, 4th d. of the 1st Lord Lawrence, of the Punjab. Was educ. at Trinity Coll., Cambridge, graduated B.A. 1868, M.A. 1872. Called to the bar at Lincoln's Inn Jan. 1872. Fellow of the Royal Institution; F.R.G.S., and a member of the Political Economy Club. A Banker in London, a Partner in the firm of Messrs. Prescot, Cave and Co., Threadneedle Street. A Liberal. Sat for Andover from Apr. 1880. Defeated in 1885. Member of London School Board for City Division 1899-1904. Died 14 Nov. 1911. [1885]

BUXTON, Sir Robert Jacob, Bart. 77 Harley Street, London. Shadwell Lodge, Thetford, Norfolk. Tockenham House, Wiltshire. Carlton, and St. Stephen's. Eld. s. of Sir John Jacob Buxton, 2nd Bart. (who represented Great Bedwin in Parliament), by Elizabeth, eld. d. of Sir Montagu Cholmeley, Bart. B. in London 1829; m. 1865, Mary Augusta Harriet, d. of Lieut.-Col. Johnstone. Appointed Lieut. 1st Suffolk Yeomanry Cavalry and a Dept.-Lieut. of Norfolk 1852. Capt. 20th Norfolk Rifle Volunteers 1860. Was High Sheriff of Norfolk for 1870. Patron of 4 livings. A Conservative. Unsuccessfully contested Bury St. Edmunds Apr. 1859; sat for South Norfolk from Apr. 1871 until defeated in 1885, contesting Southern division after redivision of county. Died 20 Jan. 1888. [1885]

BUXTON, Sydney Charles. Continued in House after 1885: full entry in Volume II

BUXTON, Thomas Fowell. 54 Devonshire Street, London. Northrepps Hall, Norfolk. Athenaeum. B. 1786; m. 1807, Hannah, d. of John Gurney, Esq., of Norwich. A Brewer in Lon-

don, a Director of the Alliance Assurance Company, treasurer to the Society for the Improvement of Prison Discipline, and to the Spital-fields' Sunday Schools. Was long distinguished as the leading advocate for the abolition of slavery. Of Whig principles, opposed to the Corn Laws, and published an *Inquiry into Prison Discipline*. Sat for Weymouth from 1818 until defeated in 1837. Created Bart. July 1840. Died 19 Feb. 1845.
[1837]

BUXTON, Sir Thomas Fowell, Bart. Colne Hall, near Cromer, Norfolk. Warlies, Essex. Brooks's. Eld. s. of Sir Edward North Buxton (2nd Bart.), by Catherine, 2nd d. of Samuel Gurney, Esq., of Ham House, Essex. B. 1837; m. 1862, Lady Victoria, d. of 1st Earl of Gainsborough. Educ. at Harrow and at Trinity Coll., Cambridge. A Partner in the Brewery of Truman, Hanbury, and Co. A Dept.-Lieut. of Norfolk and of Essex. Capt. Commandant 3rd Tower Hamlets Volunteers. A Liberal. First elected for Lynn Regis July 1865. Defeated in 1868. Unsuccessfully contested Westminster 7 Feb. 1874; Norfolk N. 24 Apr. 1876; and Essex W. Apr. 1880. Died 28 Oct. 1915. [1867]

BYNG, George. 5 St. James's Square, London. Wrotham Park, Middlesex. B. 1764, great grands. of Adm. Lord Byng and of Visct. Torrington, bro. to Lord Strafford. M. Harriet, the 8th d. of Sir William Montgomery, Bart. (she died 1845). Of Whig principles. Opposed to short Parliaments. Sat for Middlesex from 1790 until his death in Jan. 1847. [1846]

BYNG, Hon. G.H.C. See ENFIELD, Visct.

BYNG, George Stevens. See ENFIELD, Rt. Hon. Visct.

BYNG, Rt. Hon. Lieut.-Gen. Sir John, G.C.B., G.C.H. 6 Portman Square, London. Great grands. of Admiral Lord Byng and Visct. Torrington, and grand-nephew of the unfortunate Admiral Byng, executed in 1757, under the sentence of Court Martial. Bro. to the member for Middlesex, m. 1st, Mary, eld. d. of Peter Mackenzie; 2ndly, Marianne, 2nd d. of Sir Walter James, Bart. A Lieut.-Gen. in the army, Colonel of the 29th Foot, and Governor of Londonderry and Culmore. From 1832, the pay attached to this office was discontinued. He distinguished himself in the Peninsular War, as also at the Battle of Waterloo. Of Whig principles. Sat first for Poole in 1831, and sat until created Lord Strafford May 1835. Advanced to an Earldom Sept. 1847. Died 3 June 1860. [1835]

BYRNE, Garrett Michael. Continued in House after 1885: full entry in Volume II

CABBELL, Benjamin Bond. 52 Portland Place, London. 1 Brick Court, Temple, London. Cromer Hall, Norfolk. United University. Was called to the bar by the Society of the Middle Temple in 1816. Appointed Dept.-Lieut. of Middlesex 1852, Sheriff of Norfolk 1854. A Conservative, opposed to the grant to Maynooth, and was anxious to promote the improvement of the social, moral and mental condition of the industrious classes. Sat for St. Alban's from Aug. 1846 to July 1847; was an unsuccessful candidate for that city in 1837 and in Feb. 1841, as also for Marylebone in Aug. 1841. Sat for Boston from 1847 until he retired 1857. Died 9 Dec. 1874. [1857]

CADOGAN, Hon. Frederick William. 104 Piccadilly, London. Wembley Cottage, Sudbury. Youngest s. of 3rd Earl Cadogan, by Louisa Honoria, 5th d. of the late Joseph Blake, Esq., and sister of 1st Lord Wallscourt. B. 1821; m. 1851 Lady Adelaide, 8th d. of 1st Marq. of Anglesey. Educ. at Oriel Coll., Oxford. Called to the bar at the Inner Temple 1847. A Magistrate and Dept.-Lieut. of Middlesex. A Liberal; voted for the disestablishment of the Irish Church 1869; in favour of the establishment of county financial boards for local taxation, and supported 'all measures of retrenchment consistent with the dignity of the country.' Contested Bridgnorth 8 July 1852 and Stafford 28 Mar. 1857. Sat for Cricklade from Dec. 1868 until defeated 1874. Died 30 Nov. 1904. [1873]

CAINE, W.S. Continued in House after 1885: full entry in Volume II.

CAIRD, Sir James. 6 Serjeants Inn, Temple, London. Langley Park, Beckenham, Kent. Baldoon, Wigton. S. of James Caird, Esq., of Stranraer, Wigtonshire. B. 1816; m. 1843 Margaret, d. of Capt. Henryson, of the Royal Engineers (she died Mar. 1863). Educ. at the High School and Coll. of Edinburgh. Author of *High Farming, West of Ireland, English Agriculture*, etc. Declared himself 'a steady Liberal', giving a 'general support to Lord Palmerston,' strongly in favour of the policy of 'non-intervention' in Continental wars, and in favour of 'retrenchment to be effected by employing the ablest and most efficient public services.' Was an unsuccessful candidate for the Wigton district in July 1852; sat for Dartmouth from Apr. 1857-May 1859, when he was elected for Stirling. Retired 1865 general election. Senior Commissioner for enclosures 1865. Indian famine Commissioner 1878. President of the Statistical Society 1880-82. F.R.S.

1875, K.C.B. 1882. Director of Land Dept. of Board of Agriculture 1889-91. Died 9 Feb. 1892. [1865]

CAIRNS, Sir Hugh Mac-Calmont. 79 Eaton Place, London. 5 New Square, Lincoln's Inn, London. Carlton. 2nd s. of Williams Cairns, Esq., of Cultra, Co. Down. B. 1819; m. 1856, Mary Harriet, d. of John McNeile, Esq., of Parkmount, Co. Antrim. Educ. at Trinity Coll., Dublin, where he was first class in classics, and obtained other honours, received the honorary degree of D.C.L. at Oxford 1863. Called to the bar at the Middle Temple Jan 1844; made a Queen's Counsel and Bencher of Lincoln's Inn 1856. Was Solicitor Gen. from Mar. 1858-June 1859. A Conservative, in favour of 'a strict and undeviating neutrality' as to foreign politics; voted, however, against Lord Palmerston's policy on the Danish question 1864; would not reduce the franchise in boroughs so low as £5. First returned for Belfast in July 1852. Attorney-Gen. 10 July-29 Oct. 1866. Sat until he accepted Chiltern Hundreds on appointment as Lord Justice of Appeal Oct. 1866-Feb. 1868. Created Baron Cairns of Garmoyle, Antrim 26 Feb. 1867. Visct. Garmoyle and Earl Cairns (U.K. Peerage) 27 Sept. 1878. Lord Chancellor 1868 and 1874-80. Died Bournemouth 2 Apr. 1885. [1865]

CALCRAFT, John Hales. Rempstone, Wareham, Dorset. Eld. s. of the Rt. Hon. John Calcraft, Paymaster of the Forces, by Elizabeth, the 3rd d. and co-heir of Sir Thos. Pym Hales, Bart., of Beaksbourne. B. at Rempstone, Dorset, 1796; m. 1828, Lady Caroline Katherine, 5th d. of the 5th Duke of Manchester. Patron of 2 livings. A 'moderate Liberal', and a supporter generally of Lord Palmerston's policy, but when formerly in Parliament was ranked as a Conservative. Sat for Wareham from Dec. 1832 to July 1841, when he was defeated; was again elected in Apr. 1857 and sat until he retired in 1859. Sheriff of Dorset 1867. Died 13 Mar. 1880. [1858]

CALCRAFT, John Hales Montagu. Rempstone House, Wareham, Dorset. Arthur's. S. of John Hales Calcraft, Esq., a Magistrate, and Dept.-Lieut. of Dorset (who represented Wareham for many years), by Lady Caroline Katherine, d. of 5th Duke of Manchester. B. 1831. Entered the navy 1844; served during the Crimean War, and was put on the list of retired commanders, R.N., Oct. 1852, on account of ill-health. A Liberal. First elected for Wareham, July 1865. Returned at 1868 gen. election and sat until he died 1 Dec. 1868. [1867]

CALCUTT, Francis Macnamara. St. Catharine's, Ennislimon, Co. Clare. S. of William Calcutt, Esq., of Spring Gardens, Queen's Co., formerly in the 3rd Dragoon Guards, by Dora Catherine, d. of Francis Macnamara, Esq., of Doolin, Co. Clare, and sister of Major Macnamara, who represented Clare for many years. B. in Limerick, 1819; m. 1842, Georgina, d. of Capt. Martyn, of Curraghmore, Co. Mayo. Educ. at Trinity Coll., Dublin. A Liberal, in favour of the ballot and the abolition of Church temporalities in Ireland. Sat for Clare from Apr. 1857 till Apr. 1859, when he was an unsuccessful candidate; re-elected Mar. 1860. MP until his death in 1863. [1863]

CALLAGHAN, Daniel. B. in 1786, the s. of an eminent Merchant in Cork, whose ancestors had considerable possessions in Munster, of which they were deprived by Cromwell. Was a Distiller and Merchant at Cork. In 1830, it was understood that he was not a repealer, but before 1832 he declared in favour of a repeal of the Union. Favoured further reform and an extension of the suffrage. Also supported free trade principles, and voted generally with the Whigs, except on Irish Coercion Bills. Sat for Cork City from 1829 until his death in 1849; although he was not returned in 1835, he regained his seat on petition. [1847 2nd ed.]

CALLAN, Philip. 52 Claverton Street, St. George's Road, London. Irishtownlodge, Ardee, Ireland. S. of Owen Callan, Esq., of Cookstown House, Ardee, Ireland, by Elizabeth eld. d. of Patrick O'Carroll, Esq. B. at Cookstown House, Co. Louth, 1837; m. 1867, Jane Frances, eld. d. of Philip MacDonnell, Esq., of Ardee. Educ. at Clongowes Wood Coll., Ireland. Was called to the bar at the Inner Temple, May 1864, called to the bar in Ireland Jan. 1865. An 'Irish Nationalist'. Sat for Dundalk from Dec. 1868 to Feb. 1874, when he was returned both for Dundalk and the Co. of Louth, and elected to sit for the former, which he represented till Apr. 1880, when he was defeated, but was immediately returned for Louth. Defeated in 1885 contesting the Northern div. of the Co. Defeated also contesting the Northern div. of Louth in 1892 and the Southern div. in 1896. [1885]

CALLANDER, James Henry. 9 Pall Mall, London. Ardkinlas, Argyllshire. Craigforth House, Stirlingshire. The head of that family in Argyllshire; nephew of the Earl of Buchan. M. 1st, 29 Aug. 1837, Hon. Jane Erskine, youngest d. of Lord Erskine; 2ndly, 1 July 1847, Charlotte, only d. of J.G. Campbell, Esq., of the Islay family. A Reformer. Sat for Argyllshire from 1832 until he retired in 1835. Died 31 Jan. 1851. [1833]

62

CALLENDER, William Romaine. Mouldeth Hall, Manchester. Carlton, and Conservative. S. of William Romaine Callender, Esq., of Manchester, by Hannah, d. of Samuel Pope, Esq., of Exeter. B. at Manchester 1825; m. 1845, Hannah, only d. of John Mayson, Esq., of Manchester. A Cotton-Spinner and Merchant at Manchester and Bolton. A Magistrate and Dept.-Lieut. for the Co. Palatine of Lancaster. Published various pamphlets on commercial and educational subjects. A Conservative, was in favour of the union of Church and State, religious education, and also of a nine hours' bill for women and children. Sat for Manchester from Feb. 1874. MP until his death 22 Jan. 1876.
[1874]

CALLEY, Thomas. Salthorpe House, Wiltshire. Descended from the regicide of that name. Of Whig principles. First sat for Cricklade in 1831. Retired in 1834. [1833]

CALTHORPE, Hon. Frederick Henry William Gough. 33 Grosvenor Square, London. White's, Travellers', Brooks's, and Boodle's. Eld. s. of Lord Calthorpe, by Lady Charlotte Sophia, eld. d. of 6th Duke of Beaufort. B. in Grosvenor Square, London 1826. Educ. at Eton and at Trinity Coll., Cambridge. Appointed a Dept.-Lieut. of Warwickshire, 1852, and of Staffordshire 1859; Lieut. Gloucestershire Yeomanry Cavalry, 1853. Patron of 1 living. A Liberal, in favour of the entire abolition of church-rates, but not in favour of the ballot. Sat for Worcestershire E. from Feb. 1859 until he succeeded father as 5th Baron 2 May 1868. Died 25 June 1893. [1867]

CALVERT, Frederick. 8 Lincoln's Inn, New Square, London. 9 St. James's Place, London. Travellers', and Athenaeum. B. 1806, the 2nd s. of Gen. Sir Harry Calvert, Bart., by the 2nd d. of Thomas Hammerslay, Esq., of Pall Mall, and therefore bro. to Sir Harry Verney (who assumed the latter name in lieu of Calvert). Educ. at Harrow and at Christ Church, Oxford and elected fellow of Merton College and took the degree of M.A. Was called to the bar at the Inner Temple in 1831. Author of *Parties to Suits in Equity* and pamphlets on Joint Stock companies, Poor Law etc. A Liberal and general supporter of Lord Russell's Government. Sat for Aylesbury from Dec. 1850-1851, when he was unseated. Died 6 June 1891. [1851]

CALVERT, Nicholson. 89 Jermyn Street, London. Hunsden House, Hertfordshire. Bro. to Mr. Charles Calvert, the Brewer, many years member for Southwark. M. in 1789, Frances, youngest d. of Visct. Pery, and cousin of the Earl of Limerick. Of Whig principles. Sat for Hertford in the Parliaments of 1818 and 1826, when he was elected for Hertordshire, which he represented from that date. Sat until he retired in 1835. [1833]

CAMERON, Charles. Continued in House after 1885: full entry in Volume II.

CAMERON, (of Lochiel), Donald. Achnacarry, Fort William, Inverness-shire. White's, and Carlton. Eld. s. of Donald Cameron, Esq., of Lochiel, by Lady Vere Catherine Louisa, sister of the 5th Earl of Buckinghamshire. B. 1835; m. 1875, Lady Margaret Elizabeth, d. of the 5th Duke of Buccleuch. Educ. at Harrow. Entered the diplomatic service 1852 as attaché at Berne; was attaché to the Earl of Elgin's special mission to China from April 1857 to Aug. 1858. Appointed paid attaché to Stockholm Feb. 1858; 1st paid attaché at Berlin same year, and resigned June 1859. Was a Groom in Waiting to the Queen from Feb. 1874 to Apr. 1880. Of Conservative principles. Unsuccessfully contested Wycombe 18 Mar. 1862. Sat for Inverness-shire from Dec. 1868 until he retired in 1885. Died 30 Nov. 1905.
[1885]

CAMPBELL, Alexander. Monzie Castle, Perthshire. Inveran, Argyleshire. S. of Gen. Campbell. B. 1814. A Conservative; first returned for Argyleshire in 1841. Accepted Chiltern Hundreds in Sept. 1843. Unsuccessfully contested Edinburgh 14 July 1852 and Inverness 1 Apr. 1857 and again 4 May 1859. Assumed the additional surname of Cameron on his marriage 29 May 1844 to Christina, only child of Sir. D. Cameron of Fassifern. Died 5 Jan. 1869. [1843]

CAMPBELL, Alexander Henry. 43 Prince's Gate, London. Littlegrove, East Barnet, Hertfordshire. Werrington Park, Launceston, Cornwall. Conservative. S. of Colin Campbell, Esq., of Colgrain, Dumbartonshire, a Magistrate and Dept.-Lieut. for that county, by Janet Miller, d. of John Hamilton, Esq., of North Park, Scotland. B. at Possil House, Lanarkshire, 1822; m. 1858, Agnes, eld. d. of John Campbell Douglas, Esq., of Mains, Dumbartonshire. Educ. in Edinburgh, and in Paris. A Partner in the firm of Finlay, Campbell and Co., East India Merchants, London. Patron of 2 livings. A Conservative, in favour of all sects and denominations having the most complete freedom of worship, and of the army and navy being always kept in the highest state of efficiency. First elected for Launceston, July 1865. Accepted Chiltern Hundreds Mar. 1868. [1867]

CAMPBELL, Sir Archibald C. Continued in House after 1885: full entry in Volume II.

CAMPBELL, Sir Archibald Islay, Bart. 34 Eaton Street, London. Succoth, Dumbartonshire. Only s. of John Campbell, Esq. (who represented Dumbartonshire from 1826-1830), by the d. of F. Sitwell, Esq., of Barmoor. B. at Garscube, Dumbartonshire 1825. Educ. at Eton and at Christ Church, Oxford, where he was second class in classics 1847. Appointed Capt. of the Glasgow Yeomanry 1849. A Conservative, voted for inquiry into Maynooth 1853. First returned for Argyleshire June 1851. Retired in 1857. Lieut.-Col. of 1st Lanarkshire Rifle Corps 1860. Died 11 Sept. 1866. [1857]

CAMPBELL, Lord Colin. Argyll Lodge, Kensington, London. Inverary Castle, Inverary, Scotland. Youngest s. of the 8th Duke of Argyll, by Elizabeth Georgiana, eld. d. of the 2nd Duke of Sutherland. B. 1853. A Liberal. Sat for Argyllshire from Aug. 1878 until he retired 1885. Called to the bar May 1886. Practised in Bombay from 1888 until he died 18 June 1895. [1885]

CAMPBELL, Colin Minton. Woodseat, Ashbourne. National, and Conservative. S. of John Campbell, Esq., of Liverpool, by Mary, d. of Thomas Minton, Esq., of Stoke-on-Trent. B. at Liverpool 1827; m. 1853, Louisa Wilmot, d. of Rev. William A. Cave-Browne-Cave, of Stretton--in-le-field. Was the principal Partner in the firm of Messrs. Minton. A Magistrate for the Cos. of Stafford and Derby, and a Dept.-Lieut. for Stafford, for which Co. he served the office of High Sheriff 1869. Was Major 1st Battalion Staffordshire Rifle Volunteers. Capt. 20th Staffordshire Yeomanry Cavalry. Patron of 2 livings. A Conservative. Unsuccessfully contested Stoke-upon-Trent 20 Feb. 1868. Sat for Staffordshire N. from Feb. 1874 until he retired 1880. Died 7 Feb. 1885. [1880]

CAMPBELL, Sir G. Continued in House after 1885: full entry in Volume II.

CAMPBELL, H. See CAMPBELL-BANNERMAN, H. Continued in House after 1885: full entry in Volume II.

CAMPBELL, Sir Hugh Purves Hume-, Bart. 72 Portland Place, London. Purves Hall, and Marchmont House, Berwickshire. Carlton. B. 1812; m. 1st, 1834, Margaret Penelope, youngest d. of John Spottiswoode, Esq., of Spottiswoode; 2ndly, 1841, only d. of Sir Joseph Fuller, G.C.H. His father changed his name from Purves to Hume-Campbell, upon succeeding to the estates of his maternal ancestors, the Earls of Marchmont. A Conservative, voted for agricultural protection 1846. Was first elected for Berwickshire in Jan. 1834, on the death of Charles Marjoribanks, Esq. Sat until he retired in 1847. Died 30 Jan. 1894. [1847]

CAMPBELL, Sir John. 9 New Street, Spring Gardens, London. 14 Paper Buildings, Temple, London. Reform. S. of Dr. Campbell, Minister of Cupar, in Fife; m. d. of 1st Lord Abinger, who was created, 19th Jan. 1836, Baroness Stratheden in her own right. Was appointed Solicitor-Gen. on the elevation of Sir Wm. Horne to the Attorney-Generalship; succeeded him as Attorney-General, but lost his office on the dissolution of the Whig ministry, in Nov. 1834; resumed it in Apr. 1835. While a student of the Inner Temple, of which he was later a Bencher, he was connected with the *Morning Chronicle* newspaper, and otherwise with the periodical press. Sat for Stafford in the Parliaments of 1830 and 1831. Was elected for Dudley in 1832; but on taking office in 1834, lost his seat, and was out of Parliament for some months. Sat for Edinburgh from June 1834 until he retired in 1841. Created Baron Campbell of St. Andrews, Fife, 30 June 1841; Lord Chancellor of Ireland 1841; Chancellor of Duchy of Lancaster 1846; Chief Justice Queen's Bench 1850; Lord Chancellor 1859. Died 23 June, 1861. [1840]

CAMPBELL, J.A. Continued in House after 1885: full entry in Volume II.

CAMPBELL, John Henry. Exton, Bishop's Waltham, Hampshire. Conservative, and Arthur's Only s. of John Campbell, Esq., of Dunoon, Argyllshire, and nephew of Wadham Wyndham, Esq., previous member for Salisbury. M. 1839 Maria Kington, only d. of Lieut.-Col. Kington and Dowager Marchioness of Clanricarde. A Conservative. On the death of Mr. Wyndham in 1843 he came in for Salisbury, defeating Mr. Bouverie. Sat until he retired 1847. [1846]

CAMPBELL, Richard Frederick Fothringham. 17 Cavendish Square, London. Craigie House, Ayr, Scotland. Devonshire, Brooks's, and Junior United Service. Eld. surviving s. of James Campbell, Esq., of Craigie, by his 2nd wife, Grace Elizabeth, d. of the late Gen. Hay. Born at Edinburgh 1831; m. 1869, Arabella Jane, d. of Archibald Argyll Hay, Esq. and widow of Charles Tennent, Esq. Educ. at Rugby. Was formerly Capt. 8th Madras Cavalry, and served on the Staff during the Indian Mutiny. A Magistrate and Vice-Lieut. of Ayrshire, Lt.-Col. Ayrshire Yeomanry Cavalry. A Liberal Unionist, in favour of the principle of local control in licensing laws. MP for Ayr district from Apr. 1880 until his death in 1888. [1887]

CAMPBELL, Robert. A Liberal. Unsuccessfully contested Knaresborough 27 Mar. 1857. First elected for Helston 1 May 1866, recording the same number of votes as his opponent William B. Brett, Esq. The Mayor gave the casting vote to Mr. Campbell, and returned him, but on petition the return was erased and Mr. Campbell did not stand at the next election.

CAMPBELL, Robert James Roy. 62 Moorgate Street, London. Woodvale, Norwood, Surrey. Oriental. S. of Rupert Campbell, of Reay Bank, Morayshire (a Magistrate for that Co.), by Anne, his wife. B. at Fort George, Scotland 1813; m. 1836, Anne, d. of Charles Ewler, Esq., of Bengal. Educ. at Kilkenny and in Dublin. A Merchant in Bengal from 1838, and in London from 1849. Author of works on Banking and Exchange. A Liberal, in favour of Lord Palmerston's foreign policy; said he would support the 'full development of civil and religious liberty.' First elected for Weymouth, Apr. 1857. Defeated in 1859. Died 7 June 1862. [1858]

CAMPBELL, Walter Frederick. Islay Isle, Argyllshire. Woodhall, Co. Lanark. Brooks's, and Reform. S. of Col. John Campbell of Islay and Shawfield and of Lady Charlotte Maria Campbell, d. of John, the 5th Duke of Argyll, who, after the death of her 1st husband, married the Rev. Edward John Bury, and has since become celebrated as a novelist. B. 1799; m. 1831, Elinor, eld. d. of Francis Earl of Wemyss and March; 2ndly, 1837, Catherine Isabella, d. of S.T. Cole, Esq., by Lady Elizabeth Henrietta, sister of the Earl of Derby. Lords Tullamore and Uxbridge have married sisters of the hon. member. Voted for Catholic Emancipation, the Reform Bill and the Repeal of the Test and Corporation Acts. Proposed to give up Church Patronage to heads of families in communion with the Church. A Reformer. Sat for Argyllshire in 4 Parliaments previous to 1832, when, from family affliction, he did not offer himself. Was re-elected in 1835. Sat for Argyllshire 14 Mar. 1822 to 1832 and from 1835 until he retired 1841. Died 8 Feb. 1855. [1838]

CAMPBELL, Hon. William Frederick. Stratheden House, Knightsbridge, London. Hartrigge House, Jedburgh, Scotland. Reform, Brooks's, Windham, and Oxford & Cambridge. Eld. s. of Lord Campbell and Lady Stratheden. B. in London 1824. Unmarried. Educ. at Eton and at Trinity Coll., Cambridge, where he obtained the prize for English Essay 1844, and graduated M.A. 1846. Published in 1856 *Letters on the Repeal of the Oath of Abjuration*, and other pamphlets. A Liberal, in favour of the ballot; against the en-dowment of the Roman Catholic clergy. Sat for the bor. of Cambridge from July 1847 to July 1852. Unsuccessfully contested Cambridge 1854, Taunton Mar. 1857, and Harwich Mar. 1859. Elected May 1859 for Harwich and sat until he succeeded to the Peerage (Lord Stratheden) in 1860. [1860]

CAMPBELL-BANNERMAN, H. Continued in House after 1885: full entry in Volume II.

CANDLISH, John. Park Place, Sunderland. S. of John Candlish, Esq., of Seaham Harbour, Co. Durham. B. at Bellingham, Northumberland 1816; m. 1845, his cousin Miss Elizabeth Candlish. Educ. at a Private School at Bishopwearmouth. A Ship-owner and a Glass Bottle Manufacturer at Sunderland, of which borough he was an Alderman and twice filled the office of Mayor. Commissioner of the River Wear, etc. A Liberal, in favour of a stricter economy being enforced in public expenditure, and the removal of all burdens on shipping. An unsuccessful candidate for Sunderland July 1865. First elected for Sunderland Feb. 1866. Sat until he retired 1873. Died Mar. 1874. [1873]

CANNING, Hon. C.J. A Conservative. Contested Warwick at a by-election 23 Aug. 1836 and came top of the poll. Sat until he succeeded bro. as Visct. 15 Mar. 1837. Under-Sec. of State for Foreign Affairs 1841-46. Postmaster General 1853-55; Governor General of India 1855-62; 1st Viceroy of India 2 Aug. 1858. Created Earl Canning 21 May 1859. Died 17 June 1862.

CANNING, Rt. Hon. Sir Stratford, G.C.B. 29 Grosvenor Square, London. Athenaeum. S. of Stratford Canning, Esq., a London Merchant, and 1st cousin of Lord Gartagh and of the Rt. Hon. George Canning; m. 1st, d. of Thomas Raikes, Esq.; 2ndly in 1825, Eliza Charlotte, eld. d. of James Alexander, Esq., of Summer Hill, Tunbridge, late MP, nephew of the first Earl of Caledon. Had been Ambassador at several foreign courts. A Conservative. Sat 1831-32 for Stockbridge, and for King's Lynn from 1832 until appointed Ambassador to Constantinople 1841 to May 1858. Created Viscount Stratford de Redcliffe. Died 14 Aug. 1880. [1841]

CANTILUPE, Visct. 17 Upper Grosvenor Street, London. Buckhurst Park, Sussex. White's, Carlton, Travellers', and Crockford's. Eld. s. of the Earl of Delawarr. B. 25 Apr. 1814. A Lieut. in the Grenadier Guards. A Conservative. Returned for Helston in 1837. Accepted Chiltern Hundreds Feb. 1840. Sat for Lewes from 9 Mar. 1840 but was defeated 30 June 1841. Died 25 June 1850. [1838]

CAPPER, Charles. 9 Mincing Lane, London. Upton, Essex. Junior Athenaeum. B. 1822; m. 1845, Mary Jane, d. of James Dowey, Esq., of Stockport, Lancashire. A Merchant and Ship--owner, a Commissioner of Lieutenancy for London; Lieut.-Col. of 2nd administrative battalion of Essex Rifle volunteers. Author of a work entitled *The Port and Trade of London*. Chairman of the Southampton Dock Company, and of several public companies. A Conservative, friendly to a 'sound measure of reform.' First elected for Sandwich, May 1866. Retired in 1868. Died 21 Mar. 1869. [1867]

CARBUTT, Edward Homer. 19 Hyde Park Gardens, London. Llanwern House, Newport, Monmouthshire. Reform. B. 1838, the youngest s. of Francis Carbutt, Esq., a Magistrate for Leeds, many years a Director of the Midland Railway, and Chairman of the West Riding of Yorkshire Liberal Association. M. 1874, Mary, only d. of John Rhodes, Esq., of Potternewton, Leeds. Was a Manufacturing Engineer at Bradford, Partner in the firm of Messrs. Thwaites and Carbutt. Became a member of the Town Council of Leeds 1877, and elected Mayor the following year. An 'ardent Liberal', in favour of the formation of 'County Boards elected on a broad and popular basis', and reform of the Land Laws. Sat for Monmouth district from Apr. 1880 until defeated in 1886, when he stood as a Gladstonian Liberal. [1886]

CARDEN, Sir Robert Walter. 64 Wimpole Street, London. Mole Lodge, West Moulsey, Surrey. Youngest s. of James Carden, Esq., of Bedford Square, London, and Richmond, Surrey, by Mary, eld. d. of John Walter, Esq., of Teddington Grove, Middlesex, and Printing House Square, Blackfriars. B. in London 1801; m. 1827, Pamela Elizabeth Edith, d. of Dr. Andrews, of the 19th Foot (she died 1874). Was gazetted an officer of the 82nd Foot, but subsequently became a Stock and Sharebroker. Was an Alderman of London from 1849, and served the office of Sheriff in 1851. Appointed a Commissioner for Lieutenancy for London 1849. Elected Lord Mayor for 1857-8. A conservative, a supporter of the institutions of Church and State. Was an unsuccessful candidate for St. Alban's, Dec. 1850, and for Reading Nov. 1868. Sat for Gloucester from April 1857 to May 1859, when he was an unsussessful candidate there. Was also unsuccessful at Marylebone Apr. 1861. Stood for Barnstaple Feb. 1880; elected Apr. 1880. Retired in 1885. Created baronet 14 June 1886. Died 17 Jan. 1888. [1885]

CARDWELL, Rt. Hon. Edward. 74 Eaton Square, London. Ellerbeck, Chorley, Lancashire. Carlton, and Oxford & Cambridge. S. of John Cardwell, Esq., of Liverpool, Merchant. B. 1813; m. 1838, youngest child of Charles Stewart Parker, Esq., of Fairlie, Ayrshire. Educ. at Balliol Coll., Oxford, of which he became a Fellow, took a double first class degree in 1835, and was made an honorary D.C.L. 1863. Called to the bar at the Inner Temple 1838. Was Sec. to the Treasury from Feb. 1845-July 1846. Pres. of the Board of Trade from Dec. 1852-Feb. 1855. Chief Sec. for Ireland from June 1859-July 1861, Chancellor of the Duchy of Lancaster from the last date-Apr. 1864, when he became Sec. of State for the Colonies until July 1866. Appointed Sec. of State for War Dec. 1868. A Liberal-Conservative, voted against the ballot 1853. Sat for Clitheroe from 1842 (when he was seated on petition) until July 1847; sat for Liverpool from the last date until July 1852, when he was an unsuccessful candidate for that town and for Ayrshire; sat for Oxford City from Jan. 1853-Apr. 1857, when he was an unsuccessful candidate there; again returned for Oxford July 1857. Sat until created 1st Visct. Cardwell of Ellerbeach 6 Mar. 1874. Ecclesiastical Commissioner until Nov. 1882. Died 15 Feb. 1886. [1873]

CAREW, Robert Shapland, sen. 118 Pall Mall, London. Castleboros, Co. Wexford. Of Whig principles. Sat for Wexford Co. in the Parliaments of 1820, 1826, and 1832, and sat until created 1st Baron Carew of Castleborough, Co. Wexford 13 June 1834. U.K. Peerage 1838. Died 2 June 1856. [1833]

CAREW, Hon. Robert Shapland, jun. 28 Belgrave Square, London. Castleborough and Woodstown, Co. Waterford. Reform. Eld. s. of Lord Carew. B. 1818. A Whig. First elected for Waterford Co. in 1840. Retired 1847. Unsuccessfully contested Wexford Co. 26 July 1852. Succeeded father as 2nd Baron 2 June 1856. Lord-Lieut. of Wexford 1856, until his death 8 Sept. 1881. [1847]

CAREW, William Henry Pole. 77 Eaton Place, London. East Anthony, Cornwall. 2nd surviving s. of the Rt. Hon. Reginald Pole Carew by the d. of the 1st Lord Lyttleton. The name of this family was originally Pole, but the Right Hon. Reginald Pole assumed the name of Carew on succeeding to the estates of Sir Coventry Carew, of East Anthony. M. 2nd d. of John Buller, Esq., of Morval, Cornwall. A Conservative, voted for agricultural protection 1846. Thought 'a modified income tax the best of all taxes.' A Magistrate, and Dept.Lieut. of Cornwall. First returned for East Cornwall in 1845, without opposition.

Defeated in 1852. Unsuccessfully contested Liskeard 29 Apr. 1859.   [1852]

CARGILL, William Walter. 4 Connaught Place West, London. Carlton, and Conservative. S. of William Cargill, Esq., formerly a Capt. in the army, and 1st Superintendent of Otago, by Mary Anne, only d. of Thomas Yates, Esq., R.N. B. at Bilboa 1813; m. 1847, Helen, d. of Henry Fisher, Esq. Educ. at Edinburgh. Called to the bar at Lincoln's Inn, but never practised. A Capt. Perth Highland Rifle Volunteers. A Conservative. First elected for Berwick-upon-Tweed Jun 1863. Defeated 1865. Contested Taunton Apr. 1880. Died 23 May 1894.   [1865]

CARINGTON, Hon. Charles Robert. 8 Whitehall Yard, London. Wycombe Abbey, Buckinghamshire. White's, and Garrick. B. at Whitehall 1843, the eld. s. of Lord Carington, by his 2nd wife, d. of 19th Lord Willoughby De Eresby. Educ. at Eton and at Trinity Coll., Cambridge, where he graduated B.A. 1861. Entered the Royal Horse Guards 1865. Appointed Lieut. Buckinghamshire Militia 1863. Governor of New South Wales 1885-90, President of the Board of Agriculture 1905-11, Lord Privy Seal 1911-12. A Liberal, but voted against Earl Russell's Reform Bill 1866. Sat for Wycombe from July 1865 until he succeeded his father as 3rd Baron in Mar. 1868. Created Marq. of Lincolnshire in Feb. 1912. Died 13 June 1928.   [1867]

CARINGTON, Hon. Rupert Clement George. 8 Whitehall, London. Wycombe Abbey, High Wycombe, Bucks. Youngest s. of the 2nd Baron Carington, by his 2nd wife Hon. Charlotte Augusta Annabella, 3rd d. and co-heir of 20th Baron Willoughby de Eresby. B. 1852. Was a Lieut. in the Grenadier Guards, which he entered in 1871. Served with the 24th Foot in the Zulu campaign of 1879. Unsuccessfully contested Buckinghamshire in 1876. A Liberal, in favour of the lowering of the county franchise, and the reform of the Land laws. Sat for Buckinghamshire from Apr. 1880. Retired in 1885. Served in Boer War. Succeeded as 4th Baron Carington June 1928. Died 11 Nov. 1929.   [1885]

CARINGTON, Hon. William Henry Peregrine. 4 Royal Court, House of Lords, London. 2nd s. of 2nd Baron Carington, by his 2nd wife, d. of 19th Lord Willoughby De Eresby. B. 1845; m. 1871, Juliet, only d. of Francis Warden, Esq., of Paris. Appointed Groom-in-Waiting to the Queen Apr. 1880; Lieut. and Capt. Grenadier Guards 1867; Capt. and Lieut.-Col, Dec. 1872. Sec. to the (acting) Lord Great Chamberlain from 1871. A Liberal. Sat for Wycombe from Apr. 1868

until he accepted Chiltern Hundreds Feb. 1883. Treasurer to Prince of Wales 1901-10; Keeper of H.M. Privy Purse 1910-14. Died 7 Oct. 1914.   [1882]

CARNAC, Sir James Rivett, Bart. 21 Upper Harley Street, London. Senior United Service, and Oriental. Eld. s. of James Rivett Carnac, Esq., formerly acting Gov. of Bombay, who was 2nd s. of Thomas Rivett, Esq., of Derby, MP for that borough. B. 11 Nov. 1784; m. 3 June 1815, Maria, eld. d. of William Richards, Esq., of Ponglaise, Cardiganshire. Was formerly a Major on the Madras Establishment of the Hon. E.I. Co. Chairman of the E. India Co. A 'Constitutional Reformer', and a supporter of Lord Melbourne's government; but he gave no pledges. Returned in 1837 for Sandwich and sat until appointed Governor of Bombay 1838, retired through ill health 1841. Died Jan 1846.   [1838]

CARNAC, Sir John Rivett, Bart. 32 Jermyn Street, London. Warborne, Lymington, Hampshire. Conservative. S. of Sir James R. Carnac. (who was Governor of Bombay), by Anna Maria, the eld. d. of William Richards, Esq., of Penglais, Cardiganshire. B. at Baroda, in the East Indies 1818; m. 1840, Anne Jane, only child of Samuel Sproule, Esq., M.D. of the E.I.C.S. Was formerly Lieut. in the 21st Foot. Appointed Dept.-Lieut. of Hampshire 1852. A Conservative, 'decidedly opposed to any grant of public money for the maintenance of the Roman Catholic religion in these realms'; voted for well-digested measures of Parliamentary and law reform. First returned for Lymington in July 1852. Sat until he accepted Chiltern Hundreds 1860. Died 4 Aug. 1883.   [1857]

CARNEGIE, Hon. Charles. Kinnaird Castle, Brechin. Army & Navy. S. of Sir James Carnegie, by the d. of the Rev. D. Lysons, of Hempstead Court, Gloucester. Was therefore br. to the 6th Earl of Southesk. B. at Kinnaird Castle 1833, a Lieut. and afterwards in the 27th Enniskillens; retired 1855. A Liberal. First elected for Forfarshire Jan. 1860. Sat until appointed Inspector of Constabulary in Scotland 1872. Succeeded as 9th Earl Dec. 1878. Died 9 Sept. 1891.   [1872]

CARNEGIE, Hon. Swynfen Thomas. 37 Clarges Street, London. Spot, Staffordshire. Longwood, Hampshire. Carlton. S. of the 7th Earl of Northesk. B. 1813. A Capt. R.N. A Conservative, but supported free trade. Was a Lord of the Treasury. First returned for Stafford in 1841. Sat until defeated 1847. A Lord of Admiralty 9 Mar. 1859. Died 29 Nov. 1879. [1847]

67

CARRUTHERS, David. 5 Cornwall Terrace, London. A Conservative. Unsuccessfully contested Hull in 1832, but was returned at the top of the poll in the election of 8 Jan. 1835 and was MP until his death circa May 1835.   [1835]

CARTER, John Bonham, sen. 16 Duke Street, Westminster, London. Ditcham Park, Hampshire. Athenaeum. A Barrister; a native and Alderman of Portsmouth; distinguished himself at Cambridge. Of Whig principles. Sat for Portsmouth from 1818. MP until his death in 1838.   [1837]

CARTER, John Bonham, jun. Adhurst St. Mary, Petersfield, Hampshire. 29 Ashley Place, Victoria Street, London. Athenaeum, and Brooks's. S. of John Bonham Carter, Esq., MP for Portsmouth from 1818 until his death 1838. B. at Portsmouth 1817; m. 1st, 1848 Laura Maria youngest d. of George Thomas Nicholson, Esq., of Waverley Abbey, Surrey (she died Jan. 1862); 2ndly, 1864, Hon. Mary, eld. d. of 1st Baron Northbrook. Educ. at Trinity Coll., Cambridge. A Magistrate for Hampshire. Appointed Dept.-Lieut. for Hampshire 1848. Was a Lord of the Treasury for a few weeks June 1866. Became Chairman of Committees for the Whole House Apr. 1872. A Liberal. First returned for Winchester 1847. Sat until defeated 1874. Died 26 Nov. 1884.   [1873]

CARTER, Robert Meek. Hope Well House, Leeds. Eld. s. of John Carter, Esq., of Bridlington, Yorkshire, by Anne, d. of R. Meek, Esq., of Fraisthorp. B. at Skeffling, Holderness, E. Riding of Yorkshire 1814. A Coal Merchant, and carried on the business of a Cloth Finisher at Leeds, of which town he was an Alderman of 'thoroughly radical' opinions, was in favour of complete severance of Church from State; of trade societies being afforded legal protection for their funds etc. Sat for Leeds from Dec. 1868 until he accepted Chiltern Hundreds Aug. 1876. Died 9 Aug. 1882.   [1876]

CARTER, Samuel. 3 Church Court, Temple, London. Rockview House, Tavistock. S. of John Carter, Esq., of Tavistock. B. at Tavistock 1814. Unmarried. Entered as a student at the Middle Temple 1844; called to the bar, Nov. 1847. Author of a work called *Midnight Effusions,* also *The Avenger, a metrical tale.* Professed 'Democratic' opinions, and, 'if so instructed by his constituents, would give the Charter his cordial support; but, in the absence of that authority, would vote for an extension of the suffrage, the ballot, and triennial Parliaments.' A Chartist. Unsuccessfully contested Tavistock in July 1847, but was returned at a by-election in Apr. 1852 at the top of the poll. Also successful in the general election in July 1852, but was unseated on petition after being unable to prove his qualification. He later sat as a Liberal but was an unsuccessful candidate at Tavistock at the general elections of 1857 and 1865. Successfully contested Coventry in 1868 but was defeated later in the same year and again in 1874. Died 3 Jan. 1878.   [1852 2nd ed.]

CARTWRIGHT, Fairfax William. 7 New Burlington Street, London. Flore House, Weedon. Arthur's, Boodle's, Carlton, and Garrick. Eld. and only surviving s. of Lieut.-Gen. William Cartwright, Inspector of Constabulary, by Mary Anne, only d. and heir of Henry Jones, Esq. B. in London 1823. Educ. at Christ Church Coll., Oxford, and became Fellow of All Souls. Was formerly in the Austrian army; afterwards became Maj. 2nd Hussars, and served in the British German Legion. A Magistrate and Dept.Lieut. for Northamptonshire. A Conservative, and especially 'attached to the Union of Church and State.' Sat for Northamptonshire S. from Dec. 1868 until his death 2 Feb. 1881. [1880]

CARTWRIGHT, Col. Henry. 1 Tilney Street, Park Lane, London. Eydon Hall, Banbury. Carlton, and Travellers'. S. of William Ralph Cartwright, Esq., of Aynhoe, Northamptonshire (who represented that county from 1797 till 1846), by Julia Frances, only d. of Richard Aubrey, Esq. B. at Aynhoe, 1814; m. 1853, Jane, d. of W. Holbech, Esq., of Farnborough, Warwickshire. Educ. at Eton. Entered the army as Ensign and Lieut. Grenadier Guards, 1832, became Capt. and Lieut.-Col. 1846, and retired with the rank of Col. A Conservative, and though not opposed to any 'necessary reforms', would 'support all the institutions of the country in Church and State.' First elected for Northamptonshire S. Feb. 1858. Sat until he retired in 1868. Died 26 July 1890.   [1867]

CARTWRIGHT, William Cornwallis. 56 Eaton Place, London. Aynhoe Park, Banbury. Brooks's, and Athenaeum. Eld. s. of Sir Thomas Cartwright (Minister Plenipotentiary to the Diet of Frankfurt), by Elizabeth Augusta, Comtesse de Sandizell, d. of Comte de Sandizell, of Bavaria. B. in Munich 1826; m. Clementine Gaul, a German lady. Author of *History of Papal Conclaves.* Patron of 2 livings. A Liberal. Sat for Oxfordshire from Dec. 1868 until he retired in 1885. Contested Northamptonshire, Mid division, 14 July 1886. Died 8 Nov. 1915.   [1885]

CARTWRIGHT, William Ralph, D.C.L. 30 Albermarle Street, London. Aynhoe, Northamptonshire. Carlton. Uncle of 6th Visct. Chetwynd. B. 1771. M. 1st, 1794, Emma. d. of the 1st Visct. Hawarden; 2ndly, 1810, Julia Frances, d. of Col. Richard Aubrey. Patron of 2 livings. A Conservative and supporter of the Corn Laws. Sat for Northamptonshire S. from 1798 until he accepted Chiltern Hundreds in 1846, interrupted only by the Parliament of 1831, when he was obliged in consequence of his opposition to the first Reform Bill to give way to Lord Milton, later Earl Fitzwilliam. Died 1847.   [1844]

CASTLEREAGH, Rt. Hon. Visct. 25 Chesham Place, London. Carlton. Eld. s. of the Marq. of Londonderry. B. in South Street, Grosvenor Square, London 1805; m. 1846 the Dowager Viscountess Powerscourt, eld. d. of the 3rd Earl of Roden. Lord-Lieut. for Co. Down. Was a Lord of the Admiralty in 1828. Was appointed Vice-Chamberlain of the Household Dec. 1834, but resigned in Apr. following. Became Col. of the North Down Militia 1837, Lord-Lieut. of Down 1845. A Conservative, voted for agricultural protection, 1846. Sat for Co. Down from 1826 until he retired in 1852. Succeeded as 4th Marq. in Mar. 1854. Died Nov. 1872.   [1852]

CASTLEREAGH, Visct. 76 Eaton Place, London. Londonderry House, Park Lane, London. Eld. s. of the Marq. of Londonderry, by Mary Cornelia, only d. and heir of Sir John Edwards, Bart. B. in Park Lane, London 1852; m. 1875, Lady Theresa Susie Helen, d. of 19th Earl of Shrewsbury. A Conservative, not pledged as to 'Home Rule' question. Unsuccessfully contested Durham S. Feb. 1874, and Montgomery district May 1877. Sat for the Co. of Down from May 1878 until he succeeded as 6th Marq. Nov. 1884. Died 8 Feb. 1915.   [1884]

CASTLEROSSE, Rt. Hon. Visct. 11 Belgrave Square, London. Killarney House, Killarney, Co. Kerry. White's, Brooks's, and Travellers'. Only s. of 3rd Earl of Kenmare, by Catherine, d. and co-heir of Edmund O'Callaghan, Esq., of Kilgorey, Co. Clare. B. 1825; m. 1858, Gertrude Harriet, only d. of the Rev. Lord Charles Thynne. Lord-Lieut. and Magistrate of Kerry and High Sheriff of that Co. 1850-51. Controller of the Household from July 1856-Mar. 1858, and Vice-Chamberlain of the Household from June 1859-July 1866; reappointed to the latter office Dec. 1868. Of Whig principles; voted in favour of Mr. Gladstone's resolutions to disestablish the Irish Church 1869, as he was 'convinced that its existence was incompatible with the welfare of Ireland.' First returned for Kerry July 1852. Sat until he succeeded as 4th Earl Dec. 1871. Lord--in-Waiting 1872-74; Lord Chamberlain 1880-86. Died 9 Feb. 1905.   [1871]

CAULFEILD, James, C.B. Prince's Gate, Hyde Park, London. Copsewood, Co. Limerick. Senior United Service, Oriental, and Brooks's. 7th s. of Venerable John Caulfeild, Archdeacon of Kilmore (who was descended from a younger s. of the 5th Lord Charlemont), by Elizabeth, d. of — Gordon, Esq., of Kenmure, Dumfries. B. 1785; m. 1st, d. of Gen. Stafford; 2ndly, d. of Maj. Blake. Entered the military service of the East India Company in 1799, and became a Lieut.-Gen. Filled several political appointments in India, and was elected a Director of the E.I.C. in 1848. Author of a work *On the Government of India, Letters on the Affghan War*, etc. A Whig; voted for inquiry respecting Maynooth, but would maintain full civil and religious liberty; supported Parliamentary reform in cases 'where it was required.' Was an unsuccessful candidate for Abingdon in July 1845, and July 1847. First returned for Abingdon in July 1852 and sat until his death 4 Nov. 1852.   [1852]

CAULFEILD, James Molyneux. 7 St. James Street, London. Hockley, Armagh. Brooks's, Travellers', and Reform. Eld. s. of the Hon. Henry Caulfeild (who was heir presumptive to the Earldom of Charlemont), by Elizabeth Margaret, 2nd d. of Dodwell Browne, Esq., of Ralines, Co. Mayo. B. 1820. Served the office of High Sheriff of Armagh in 1842, and was Lieut.-Col. of the Tyrone Militia. Lord-Lieut. of Armagh. A Liberal, in favour of extension of the suffrage, vote by ballot, and a general revision of taxation. First returned in 1847 for Co. Armagh, which his father had represented for many years. Sat until he retired 1857. Succeeded uncle as 3rd Earl of Charlemont Dec. 1863. Died 12 Jan. 1892. [1857]

CAUSTON, R.K. Continued in House after 1885: full entry in Volume II.

CAVE, Hon. Robert Otway. Castle Otway, Co. Tipperary. Athenaeum, and Reform. Eld. s. of Henry Otway, Esq., of Castle Otway, who m. Sarah, only d. of Sir Thomas Cave, later Lady Braye, a Peeress in her own right. Assumed the surname Cave in 1818, upon succeeding to the Lincolnshire estates of the Cave family. M. 1833, Sophia, eld. d. of Sir F. Burdett, Bart., MP. A Reformer; in favour of the ballot, abolishing the 'name and reality' of tithes and making the ecclesiastical revenues available for national purposes. Sat for Leicester in the Parliament of 1826. MP for Tipperary until his death 30 Nov. 1844.   [1844]

CAVE, Rt. Hon. Sir Stephen. 35 Wilton Place, London. Cleve Hill, Bristol. Athenaeum, Carlton, and United Service. Eld. s. of Daniel Cave, Esq.,

69

of Cleve Hill, Bristol and Sidbury Manor, Devon, by Frances, d. of Henry Locock, Esq., M.D., of Northampton and sister to Sir Charles Locock, Bart. B. at Clifton 1820; m. 1852, Emma Jane, d. of Rev. William Smyth, Prebendary of Lincoln, of Elkington Hall, Louth, Lincolnshire. Educ. at Harrow and at Balliol Coll., Oxford, where he was 2nd class in classics, and graduated M.A. 1846. Called to the bar at the Inner Temple 1846 and joined the Western Circuit for a short time. Held the joint offices of Paymaster-Gen. and Vice-Pres. of the Board of Trade from July 1866-Dec.1868. Also Judge-Advocate-Gen. and Paymaster-Gen. from Feb. 1874-Dec. 1875, when he resigned the former office to proceed on a special mission to Egypt. Chairman of the West India Committee and a Director of the Bank of England. A Magistrate and Dept.-Lieut. for the Co. of Gloucester. A Magistrate for Sussex and a Commissioner of Lieutenancy for London. Appointed Chief Commissioner for negotiating a Fishery Convention in Paris 1866. A Conservative. First returned for Shoreham May 1859. Sat until he retired 1880. Died 6 June 1880. [1880]

CAVE, Thomas. Queensberry House, Richmond, Surrey. City Liberal. S. of George Cave, Esq., of Boddicote, by Harriet, d. of J. Gould, Esq. B. at Boddicote 1825; m. 1849, Elizabeth, d. of J. Shallcress, Esq. Was a Merchant in London. Sheriff of London and Middlesex 1863-4. A Liberal, in favour of the 'repeal of that source of irritation, the income-tax.' First elected for Barnstaple July 1865. Sat until he retired 1880. Died 2 Nov. 1894. [1880]

CAVENDISH, Hon. Charles Compton. Compton Place, Sussex. Brooks's, and Boodle's. Youngest s. of the 1st Earl of Burlington, (by Lady Elizabeth, d. of 7th Earl of Northampton), and cousin to the Duke of Devonshire. B. 1793; m. in 1814, Lady Catherine, eld. d. of 9th Marq. of Huntly. A Dept.-Lieut. of Buckinghamshire. Of Whig principles, supported 'the modification', if not 'the repeal' of the malt duties; 'would always lend his cordial assistance in resisting any attack on our Protestant institutions'; opposed to the ballot. Sat for Newton, Hampshire, from 1820-1830; for Yarmouth in 1831; for E. Sussex from 1832-1841; for Youghal from July 1841-July 1847, when he was first returned for Buckinghamshire and sat until he accepted Chiltern Hundreds in 1857. Created 1st Baron Chesham Jan. 1858. Died 10 Nov. 1863. [1857]

CAVENDISH, Lord. (I). 10 Belgrave Square, London. Compton Place, Sussex. Latimers, Buckinghamshire. Grands. of the Earl of Burlington, and of the first Lord Lismore, s. of William Cavendish, killed by a fall from his horse in 1812, and nephew of Members for Derby and Sussex. B. in 1808; m. in 1829, Blanche, 4th d. of the Earl of Carlisle. Of Whig principles, in favour of the immediate abolition of slavery. Sat for the University of Cambridge in 1829 and 1830, then ousted, and sat for Malton in 1831. Sat for Derbyshire N. from 1832 until he succeeded father as 2nd Earl of Burlington in 1834. [1833]

CAVENDISH, Lord. (II). See HARTINGTON, Marq. of. Continued in House after 1885: full entry in Volume II.

CAVENDISH, Lord. E. Continued in House after 1885: full entry in Volume II.

CAVENDISH, Lord Frederick Charles. 21 Carlton House Terrace, London. Devonshire, and Brooks's. 2nd surviving s. of 7th Duke of Devonshire, by Lady Blanche, 4th d. of 6th Earl of Carlisle. B.-at Compton Place, Eastbourne 1836; m. 1864, Hon. Lucy Caroline, 2nd d. of 4th Baron Lyttleton. Educ. at Trinity Coll., Cambridge. Was Private Sec. to Lord Granville from 1859-1864, and Private Sec. to Mr. Gladstone from July 1872-Aug. 1873. A Lord of the Treasury from Aug. 1873-Feb. 1874. Appointed Financial Sec. to the Treasury Apr. 1880 (salary £2,000). A Liberal; in favour of the 'total' abolition of Church rates and complete religious liberty. Sat for the N.W. Riding of Yorkshire from July 1865. MP until assassinated in Dublin 6 May 1882. [1882]

CAVENDISH, Lord George Henry. 3 Upper Eccleston Street, London. Ashford Hall, Bakewell, Derbyshire. Travellers'. 2nd s. of the Hon. William Cavendish, by Hon. Louisa, eld. d. of 1st Lord Lismore. Bro. of the 7th Duke of Devonshire. Was raised to the rank of a Duke's son by letters patent in 1858. B. 1810; m. 1835, Lady Louisa, youngest d. of the 2nd Earl of Harewood. Appointed Capt. 2nd Derbyshire Militia 1855, and Capt. 9th Derbyshire Rifle Volunteers 1860. Of Whig principles. Sat for Derbyshire N. from 1834 until he retired 1880. Died 23 Sept. 1880. [1880]

CAVENDISH, Hon. Col. Henry Frederick Compton. Burlington Gardens, London. Sutton House, Chiswick. Lieut.-Col. in the 1st Life Guards. S. of the Earl of Burlington, and cousin of the Duke of Devonshire. B. in 1789; m. 1st, 1811, Sarah, youngest d. of W. Augustus Fawkener, Esq., clerk of the Privy Council; 2ndly, 1819, Frances, sister of the Earl of Durham, d. of Wm. H. Lambton, Esq., and widow of the Hon. Fred.

Howard, killed at Waterloo. Extra Equerry to his Majesty, an office bringing no emolument. Of Whig principles. Sat for Derby from 1818 until he retired in 1835. Died 5 Apr. 1873.   [1833]

CAVENDISH, Hon. William George. Latimer, Chesham, Buckinghamshire. Eld. s. of the 1st Lord Chesham, by Lady Catherine, eld. d. of 9th Marq. of Huntly. B. 1815; m. 1849 Henrietta Frances, d. of the Rt. Hon. W.S. Lascelles. Of Whig principles. Gave Lord Palmerston 'an energetic but independent support.' In favour of an extension of the borough franchise. First elected for Buckinghamshire Dec. 1857. Sat until he succeeded to the Peerage (Lord Chesham) Nov. 1863. Died 26 June 1882.   [1863]

CAWLEY, Charles Edward. The Heath, Kensal, Manchester. National Club, Conservative Club, Manchester. S. of Samuel Cawley, Esq., of Gooden House, Heywood, Manchester, by Mary, his wife. B. at Gooden House 1812; m. 1843 Harriet, 3rd d. of George Motley, Esq., of Shuton House, Nottinghamshire. A Civil Engineer, became member of the Institution of Civil Engineers 1846. Was an Alderman of Salford from 1859. A Liberal-Conservative; 'paired' against the disestablishment of the Irish Church 1869; supported the maintenance of our Protestant constitution in Church and State, 'reforming abuses and correcting defects'. Sat for Salford from Dec. 1868. MP until his death 2 or 9 Apr. 1877.   [1876]

CAYLEY, Edward Stillingfleet. 11 Dean's Yard, Westminster, London. Wydale House, East Riding, Yorkshire. Only s. of John Cayley, Esq., of Low Hall, by Elizabeth, great-grand-d. of Bishop Stillingfleet. B. 1802; m. in 1823 his cousin, Emma, 3rd d. of Sir George Cayley, Bart., late MP for Scarborough (she died July 1848). Educ. at Rugby. Author of a work on commercial economy, and several political tracts. Declared himself 'not a Whig, but a Reformer'; opposed to the ballot and short Parliaments; in favour of a repeal of the malt tax; will give 'a general support' to Lord Palmerston. Sat for the North Riding of Yorkshire from 1832. MP until his death 25 Feb. 1862.   [1861]

CAYLEY, Sir George, Bart., F.R.S. 22 Downing Street, London. Brompton, Yorkshire. B. in 1773; m. 1795, Sarah, d. of the Rev. George Walker, of Notthingham. President of Philosophical Society at Manchester. Father-in-law of Mr. Cayley, Member for the North Riding of Yorkshire. A Reformer. Sat for Scarborough from 1832. Defeated in 1835. Chairman of the Polytechnic Institution, Regent Street, 1838. Died 15 Dec. 1857.   [1833]

CECIL, Lord Eustace Henry Brownlow Gascoyne. 82 Eccleston Square, London. Lytchett Heath, Poole. Carlton, and Athenaeum. 2nd surviving s. of 2nd Marq. of Salisbury by his 1st wife, Frances Mary, only d. and heir of Bamber Gascoyne, Esq. B. in Grafton Street, London 1834; m. 1860, Lady Gertrude Louisa, 4th d. of 2nd Earl of Eldon. Educ. at Harrow and at the Royal Military Coll., Sandhurst. Entered the army as Ensign 43rd Light Infantry 1851, retired as Capt. and Lieut.-Col. Coldstream Guards 1863. Was Surveyor-General of the Ordnance from Feb. 1874 to Apr. 1880. Author of *Impressions of Life at Home and Abroad*. A Conservative, and in favour of the reduction of local taxation. Sat for South Essex from July 1865 to Dec. 1868, when he sat for West Essex. Sat until he retired in 1885. Chairman of several companies. Died 3 July 1921.   [1885]

CECIL, Lord Robert T.G. See CRANBORNE, Visct.

CHADWICK, David. The Poplars, Herne Hill, London. 2 Moorgate Street, London. 64 Cross Street, Manchester. City Liberal. Youngest s. of John Chadwick, Esq., formerly of Macclesfield and afterwards of Manchester, Accountant, by Rebecca, his wife. B. at Macclesfield 1821; m. 1st, 1844, Louisa, youngest d. of William Bow, Esq., of Broughton, Nr. Manchester (she died 1877); 2ndly, 1878, Ursula, eld. d. of Thomas Sopwith, Esq., F.R.S., of Victoria Street, London. Commenced business as an Accountant 1843, was Treasurer to the Corporation and Magistrates, also to the Gas and Waterworks of Salford from 1844-1860. Head of the firm of Messrs. Chadwick, Adamson, Collier and Company, Accountants and Money Agents of London and Manchester. An Associate of the Institute of Civil Engineers and was Pres. of the Manchester Statistical Society. Author of *Poor-Rates and Principle of Rating, The Rate of Wages in 200 Trades for 20 Years, Suggestions for an Equitable Redistribution of Parliamentary Seats*, and other works. A Liberal, voted for the disestablishment of the Irish Church 1869, in favour of the reduction of the national expenditure, etc. Unsuccessfully contested Macclesfield July 1865; first elected for Macclesfield Dec. 1868. Sat until 1880 when the election was declared void. Died 19 Sept. 1895.   [1880]

CHAINE, James. Ballycraigie and Cairn Castle, Antrim, Ireland. Carlton, and Conservative. Kildare Street Club, Dublin. S. of James Chaine, Esq., (s. of William Chaine, Esq.) of Ballycraigie, Co. Antrim, by Maria Augusta, d. of P. Whittle, Esq., of Co. Antrim. B. at Ballycraigie 1841; m. 1863, Henrietta, d. of C.A. Creery, Esq., of Newcastle, Co. Down. Éduc. at Blackheath Proprietary School. A Magistrate for the Co. Antrim. A Conservative. Sat for the Co. Antrim from Feb. 1874 until he died on 4 May 1885. [1885]

CHALLIS, Thomas. 32 Wilson Street, Finsbury, London. Enfield, Middlesex. S. of Thomas Challis, Esq., of Islington, Co. Middlesex. B. in London 1795. Unmarried. A Skin Broker in Finsbury, a Hide and Skin Salesman in Leadenhall and Bermondsey markets. Elected an Alderman of London for Cripplegate ward in 1843; served the office of Sheriff of London in 1846. Elected Lord Mayor of London for 1852-3. A Director of the General Life and Fire Insurance Company. A Liberal, in favour of a wide extension of the franchise, equal electoral districts, vote by ballot, and short Parliaments. Opposed to all religious endowments, and considered the Maynooth Grant 'unjust and dangerous.' First returned for Finsbury July 1852. Sat until he retired 1857. Died 20 Aug. 1874. [1857]

CHALMERS, Patrick. Auldbara Castle, Forfarshire. Junior United Service, Clarence, and Reform. S. of Patrick Chalmers, Esq., of Auldbar, a Merchant in London, and of Frances, d. of John Inglis, Esq., an East India Director, and of the firm of Inglis, Ellice and Company. Mr. Chalmer's family was a branch of the Chalmers of Balnacraig, Aberdeenshire. B. 1802; m. 1839, relict of T.T. Vernon, Esq. Was a Capt. in the 3rd Dragoon Guards, but sold out in 1827. A Dept.-Lieut. of Forfarshire. A radical Reformer, in favour of free trade, the repeal of the Septennial Act, and was willing to vote for the ballot. Unsuccessfully contested Montrose district in 1832; was returned there in 1835. Accepted Chiltern Hundreds Apr. 1842. Died 23 June 1854. [1842]

CHAMBERLAIN, J. Continued in House after 1885: full entry in Volume II.

CHAMBERS, Montague. 2 & 3 Child's Place, Temple Bar, London. Union, Junior United Service, and Garrick. Youngest s. of George Chambers, Esq. (only s. of Sir William Chambers, Architect), by the eld. d. of the celebrated Lord Rodney. B. at Hartford, Huntingdonshire. Unmarried. Educ. at Sandhurst Military Coll., and at Christ's Coll., Cambridge. Was formerly in the Grenadier Guards. Called to the bar at Lincoln's Inn 1828, became a Queen's Counsel 1845 and joined the Home Circuit. A Liberal; in favour of economy in the public expenditure, but for the preservation of peace by an efficient maintenance of the Military and Naval establishments. Unsuccessfully contested Greenwich 11 Feb. 1852, but succeeded at the

following election 8 July 1852. He again contested the same seat 27 Mar. 1857 and 2 May 1859 but was defeated on both occasions. Unsuccessfully contested Beford July 1865; elected for Devonport May 1866. Sat until he retired 1874. Died 18 Sept. 1885. [1873]

CHAMBERS, Sir Thomas. 3 Pump Court, Temple, London. 63 Gloucester Place, Portman Square, London. Reform, and City Liberal. S. of Thomas Chambers, Esq., by Sarah his wife. B. at Hertford, 1814; m. 1851, Miss Diana White, niece and adopted d. of John Green,Esq., of Hertford (she died 1877). Educ. at Clare Coll., Cambridge. Called to the bar at the Middle Temple, 1840; made a Queen's Counsel 1861, Common Serjeant of London Jan. 1857; elected Recorder of London, Mar. 1878 (salary (£3000). A Commissioner of Lieutenancy for London. A Liberal, opposed to the principle of 'centralisation'. Sat for Hertford from July 1852 till July 1857, when he was unsuccessful. Elected for Marylebone July 1865. Sat until he retired in 1885. Died 24 Dec. 1891. [1885]

CHANDOS, Marq. of. (I). 91 Pall Mall, London. Wooton House, Buckinghamshire. Carlton, Athenaeum. Only s. of the Duke of Buckingham; b. 1797; m. 1819, Mary, youngest d. of the Marq. of Breadalbane. Chairman of the body of W. India Proprietors and Merchants, and High Steward of Winchester. Patron of 1 living. A Conservative; voted against the principle of the Reform Act, and introduced into it the tenant--at-will clause. Sat for Buckinghamshire from 1826. In favour of the Corn Laws and of the repeal of the Malt Tax. Sat for Buckinghamshire as 'Earl Temple' from 1818 until his father was created Duke of Buckingham 4 Feb. 1822. Thereafter sat as Marquis of Chandos. Sat until he succeeded his father as 2nd Duke of Buckingham 17 Jan. 1839. Author of several historical works. Died 29 July 1861. [1838]

CHANDOS, Marq. of. (II). 12 Grosvenor Square, London. Only s. of the Duke of Buckingham and Chandos. B. 1823; m. 1851, Caroline, only d. of Robert Harvey, Esq., of Langley Park, Buckinghamshire. Graduated at Christ Church, Oxford. Capt. of the Buckinghamshire Yeomanry Cavalry. Chairman of the London and North-Western Railway Company. Was a Lord of the Treasury from Mar.-Dec. 1852. Was privy seal to the Prince of Wales from Mar. 1852-Feb. 1853, a Dept.-Lieut. of Buckinghamshire and Northamptonshire from 1845, and a special Dept.-Warden of the Stannaries from Oct. 1852. A Conservative, and endeavoured 'to preserve unimpaired the Protestant religion.' First returned for Buckingham Feb.

1846, without a contest. Sat until he retired 1857. Contested Oxford University 1 July 1859. Succeeded Father as 3rd Duke of Buckingham. Died 26 Mar. 1889. [1857]

CHAPLIN, Edward. 25 Charles Street, Mayfair, London. Blankney, Sleaford, Lincolnshire. 3rd s. of the Rev. Henry Chaplin, by Caroline Horatia, d. of William Ellice, Esq. B. at Ryhall, Rutland 1842; m. 1877, Lady Gwendolen, 2nd d. of the 19th Earl of Shrewsbury and Talbot. Educ. at Harrow. Entered the Coldstream Guards as Lieut. and Capt. Mar. 1860, became Capt. and Lieut.-Col. Mar. 1871. A Conservative. Sat for Lincoln from Feb. 1874 until defeated 1880. Died 23 Dec. 1883. [1880]

CHAPLIN, Rt. Hon. H. Continued in House after 1885: full entry in Volume II.

CHAPLIN, Lieut.-Col. Thomas. 52 Welbeck Street, London. Blankney, Lincolnshire. S. of C. Chaplin, Esq., formerly MP for Lincolnshire. B. 1794; m. 1828, Millicent Mary, d. of William Reeve, Esq., of Leadenham, Lincolnshire. A Lieut.-Col. in the army and Capt. in the Coldstream Guards. Served in Spain, the Netherlands and France, was severely wounded at St. Sebastian on 31 Aug. 1813, for which he received a pension of £50. A Conservative, but was in favour of the repeal of the Assessed Taxes and the substitution of a Property Tax. Sat for Stamford in the Parliaments of 1826 and 1830; was ousted in a contest by Mr. Tennyson D'Eyncourt, later member for Lambeth, in 1831, but regained his seat in 1832. Sat until he accepted Chiltern Hundreds Apr. 1838. Died 10 May 1863. [1838]

CHAPLIN, William James. 2 Hyde Park Gardens, London. Ewhurst Park, Basingstoke, Hampshire. S. of William Chaplin, Esq., of Rochester. B. at Rochester 1787; m. 1816, Elizabeth, d. of William Alston, Esq. Educ. at Bromley. Chairman of the South-Western Railway, Director of the Paris and Rouen, Rouen and Havre, and Rhenish Railways. Was Sheriff of London and Middlesex 1845-6. A Dept.-Lieut. of Hampshire. A Liberal, considered a modification of the income tax imperatively necessary, voted for the ballot 1853. Sat for Salisbury from Jan 1847 until he retired 1857. Died 24 Apr. 1859. [1857]

CHAPMAN, Aaron. 2 Leadenhall Street, London. Highbury Park, Middlesex. Stakesby, Yorkshire. 9th s. of John Chapman, Esq., of Whitby. B. 1771; m. 1796, Elizabeth, d. of Joseph Barker, Esq., of Whitby. An eld. bro. of the Trini-

ty House, an East India Proprietor, a Director of the London Fire Assurance, the London Docks, and the Hudson's Bay Companies; had contracts from Government. A Conservative, voted for agricultural protection 1846. In favour of the repeal of the Assessed Taxes, and of a Property Tax in lieu of such as pressed upon industry. Objected to that system of free trade which gave to the foreign shipowner in entering the ports of this Country, advantages not enjoyed by the British. Sat for Whitby from 1832 until he retired 1847. [1847]

CHAPMAN, Benjamin James. 81 Jermyn Street, London. Killna Castle, Co. Westmeath. Reform. S. of Sir Thomas Chapman. B. 1810. A 'Radical'. first returned for Co. Westmeath in 1841. Sat until he retired 1847. Succeeded bro. as 4th Bart., 17 May 1851. Lord-Lieut. of Westmeath 1883. Died 3 Nov. 1888. [1847]

CHAPMAN, John. Hill-End, Mottram, Cheshire. Carlecote's, Dunford Bridge, Yorkshire. Carlton, and Conservative. S. of John Chapman, Esq., of Ashton, Lancashire, by Mary, d. of John Sidebottom, Esq., of Mottram, Cheshire. B. at Ashton 1810; m. 1836, his cousin Annie, d. of George Sidebottom, Esq., of Mottram, Cheshire. Was educ. at St. Mary Hall, Oxford. Graduated M.A. 1838. A Magistrate for Cheshire, Derbyshire, Lacashire and the West Riding of Yorkshire. A Dept.-Lieut. of Cheshire, of which he was High Sheriff in 1855. Was for some time Chairman of the Manchester, Sheffield and Lincolnshire Railway. Patron of 1 living. A Conservative; opposed to the exclusion of religious reading from schools; was not prepared to vote for the permissive Bill. Unsuccessfully contested Salisbury 30 Apr. 1859 and again 13 July 1865. Contested Whitby 23 Nov. 1859. Sat for Great Grimsby from Feb. 1862-June1865; re-elected Feb. 1874. MP until his death 18 July 1877. [1877]

CHAPMAN, Sir Montague Lowther. Kilna Castle, Westmeath. University, and Reform. Eld. s. of Sir Thomas Chapman, Bart. of St. Lucy's, Co. Westmeath. B. 1808; of Whig principles. In favour of the ballot and short Parliaments. Sat for the Co. of Westmeath from 1830 until he retired in 1841. Sheriff of Westmeath 1844. Died at sea between Melbourne and Sydney, May 1852. [1838]

CHARLESWORTH, John Charlesworth Dodgson-. 14 Clarges Street, London. Hatfield Hall and Chapelthorpe Hall, Wakefield, Yorkshire. Conservative. S. of John Dodgson-Charlesworth, Esq. B. at Chapelthorpe

Hall, near Wakefield; m. Sarah, 2nd d. of Walter Featherstonhaugh, Esq., of the Hermitage, Co. Durham. Educ. at St. John's Coll., Cambridge. A Magistrate and Dept.-Lieut. for the West Riding of York. A Conservative. First elected for Wakefield Mar. 1857. Defeated in 1859. Died 21 Mar. 1880. [1858]

CHARLEY, Sir William Thomas. 5 Crown Office Row, Temple, London. 4 Temple Chambers, St. James's Square, Manchester. National, Conservative, and Carlton. S. of Matthew Charley, Esq., of Finaghy House and Woodbourne, Co. Antrim, by Mary Ann, d. of John Roberts, Esq., of Collin House, Co. Antrim. B. at Woodbourne, Co. Antrim 1833. Unmarried. Educ. at private schools and afterwards proceeded to St. John's Coll., Oxford, where he graduated B.A. 1856, B.C.L. and D.C.L. (by accumulation) 1868. Called to the bar at the Inner Temple 1865, in which year he obtained the exhibition of the Council of Legal Education. A special pleader and conveyancer. Major 20th Middlesex Rifle Volunteers, and Vice-Pres. of numerous Conservative Associations. Appointed Common Serjeant of London Apr. 1878. Author of works entitled *Treatises on the Judicature Acts 1873, 1875, 1876 and 1877, The Real Property Acts 1874, 1875, 1876, and 1877*. A Conservative, and a firm supporter of 'the Union of Church and State'. Sat for Salford from Dec. 1868. Sat until defeated 1880. Unsuccessfully contested Ipswich 12 Dec. 1883 and 25 Nov. 1885. Also contested the East division of Belfast 9 Mar. 1892. Died 8 June 1904. [1880]

CHARLTON, Edmund Lechmere. Ludford Park, Herefordshire. Whitton Court, Shropshire. Hanley Castle, Worcestershire. S. of Nicholas Lechmere, Esq., of Manley Castle, who succeeded to the Charlton estates upon the demise of his uncle, Sir Francis Charlton, Bart., in 1784, and assumed that additional surname. B. 1789. A Barrister. Patron of 1 living. A moderate Reformer. Sat for Ludlow from Jan. 1835. Retired 1837. [1837]

CHATERIS, Hon. F. See ELCHO, Lord F.

CHATTERTON, Rt. Hon. Hedges E. A Conservative. Returned unopposed for Dublin University 12 Feb. 1867. Appointed Attorney-Gen. for Ireland and returned again 30 Mar. 1867. Sat until appointed Vice-Chancellor of Ireland July? 1867.

CHATTERTON, Col. James Charles, K.H. 26 Argyll Street, Regent Street, London. Castle Mahon, Co. Cork. United Service. 2nd s. of Sir James Chatterton (1st Bart.), of Castle Mahon, Cork, by the d. of Abraham Lane, Esq., of Cork. Heir presumptive to his bro. Sir William Abraham Chatterton, Bart. B. 1794; m. 1829, Annette, youngest d. of James Atkinson, Esq., of Lindall, Yorkshire. A Col. in the army, and Lieut.-Col. of the 4th Royal Irish Dragoon Guards; served for many years in Portugal, Spain, France, and Flanders; was at Waterloo, and at the capture of Paris, and wore a Peninsular medal and 7 clasps. One of the gentlemen of the Privy Chamber. A Magistrate and Dept.-Lieut. for the county of Cork; Provincial Grand Master of Munster; High Sheriff for Cork, 1851. A Conservative, and strongly in favour of agricultural protection. Was returned for the city of Cork in Feb. 1835, but unseated on petition in May of the same year; was an unsuccessful candidate for the same place in 1837, and again in 1841; was returned a second time for Cork Nov. 1849. Defeated in 1852. Contested same seat at by-election 20 Aug. 1853. Succeeded bro. as 3rd Bart. 7 Aug. 1855. General 1866. Died 5 Jan. 1874. [1852]

CHAYTOR, William Richard Carter. 5 Old Square, Lincoln's Inn, London. Witton Castle, Durham. S. of Sir William Chaytor, Member for Sunderland. Of Whig principles. Sat for Durham first in 1831. Retired in 1835. Succeeded as 2nd Bart. 1847. Died 9 Feb. 1871. [1833]

CHAYTOR, Sir William R.C., Bart. 3 Manchester Buildings, London. Croft Hall, Yorkshire. Witton Castle, Durham. B. 1777; m. 1803, d. of J. Carter, Esq., of Richmond. Sir William had considerable property in and near Sunderland. Of Whig principles. Sat for Sunderland from 1832. Defeated in 1835. Unsuccessfully contested Durham N. 10 Aug. 1837. Died 28 Jan. 1847. [1833]

CHEETHAM, John. Eastwood, Staleybridge, Cheshire. Reform. S. of George Cheetham, Esq. B. at Staleybridge, 1802; m. 1831, Emma, d. of Thomas Reyner, Esq., of Ashton-under-Lyne. A Merchant and Manufacturer. A Magistrate for Lancashire and Cheshire from 1836. A Liberal, in favour of an extension of the suffrage, a re-distribution of seats, and vote by ballot; opposed to all religious endowments. Was an unsuccessful candidate for Huddersfield in July 1847; sat for South Lancashire from July 1852 till Apr. 1859, when he was an unsuccessful candidate. Sat for Salford from Feb. 1865. Defeated in 1868. Died 18 May 1886. [1867]

CHEETHAM, John Frederic. Continued in House after 1885: full entry in Volume II.

CHELSEA, Visct. sen. 28 Lowndes Street, London. Carlton, White's, and Travellers'. Eld. s. of the Earl of Cadogan. B. in South Audley Street, London 1812; m. 1836, Mary, 3rd d. of the Hon. and Rev. Gerald Valerian Wellesley, D.D. Educ. at Oriel Coll., Oxford, where he graduated B.A. 1832. Appointed Col. of the Royal Westminster Middlesex Militia 1841. A Conservative, voted for the increase in the Maynooth Grant in 1845, but felt 'that the time is come for inquiry.' Sat for Reading from 1841-1847. Was an unsuccessful candidate in July 1847. First returned for Dover July 1852. Retired 1857. Unsuccessfully contested Middlesex 29 Apr. 1857. Succeeded as 4th Earl Sept. 1864. Died 8 June 1873.   [1857]

CHELSEA, Visct. jun. A Conservative. Unsuccessfully contested Bury 18 Nov. 1868. Returned for Bath 7 May 1873. Retired in 1874. Succeeded father as 5th Earl Cadogan in 1873. Under-Secretary for War 1875; for Colonies 1878-80; Lord Privy Seal 1886-92; Lord Lieut. of Ireland 1895-1902; 1st Mayor of Chelsea 1900. Died 6 Mar. 1915.   [1872]

CHESTER, Henry. Cartown, Co. Louth. Reform. Dept.-Lieut. of Co. Louth. A Liberal. Elected for Louth in 1837, in the room of Sir Patrick Bellew, Bart., who declined to come forward again for the county. Accepted Chiltern Hundreds in 1840.   [1840]

CHETWODE, Sir John, Bart. 47 Montagu Street, London. Oakley, Staffordshire. Chetwode, Buckinghamshire. S. of the 3rd Bart. B. 1764; m. 1st, 1785, d. of 5th Earl of Stamford, 2ndly, 1827, d. of John Bristow, Esq. A Conservative. Sat for Buckingham from 1841 until he died in 1845.   [1844]

CHETWYND, Capt. William Fawkener. Brocton Hall, Staffordshire. Arthur's, and The Union. Br. of Sir George Chetwynd, Bart. (who also represented Stafford, as well as his ancestors), and cousin of Visct. Chetwynd. B. 1788. Capt. in the 1st Life Guards. Of Whig principles. Voted against the admission of Dissenters to the Universities. Sat for Stafford from 1832 until he retired 1841. Died 25 Apr. 1873.   [1838]

CHICHESTER, Arthur. Walford House, Somerset. A Conservative, sat for Milbourne Port in the Parliament of 1826. Sat for Honiton from Jan. 1835. Retired in 1837.   [1837]

CHICHESTER, Lord Arthur. 23 Arlington Street, London. Ormeau, Co. Down. 3rd s. of the Marq. of Donegal. Capt. in the 87th Foot, and a native of Belfast. B. 1808. Of Whig principles, in

favour of the abolition of all monopolies. Sat for Belfast from 1832. Retired in 1835. Died 25 Jan. 1840.   [1833]

CHICHESTER, Lord John Ludford. 8 St. George's Place, Hyde Park Corner, London. S. of 2nd Marq. of Donegal. B. 1811; m. 1844, Caroline Mary, d. of Henry Bevan, Esq. Appointed Capt. 87th Foot in 1843, but retired from the army in 1844. A Conservative, voted in favour of free trade 1846. Voted 'for the repeal of the grant to Maynooth Coll.' First returned for Belfast Aug. 1845, without opposition. Sat until he retired in 1852. Died 22 Apr. 1873.   [1852]

CHICHESTER, Sir John Palmer Bruce. Arlington, Devon. A Lieut. in the navy. Of Whig principles, in favour of the ballot. Patron of 6 livings. Was first elected for Banstaple in 1831. Sat until he was defeated in 1841. Created Baronet 7 Sept. 1840. Died 10 Dec. 1851. [1840]

CHILD, Sir Smith, Bart. Rownall Hall, Cheadle, Staffordshire. Newfield and Stallington, Staffordshire. Duncosset, Islay, Argyllshire. Carlton, and National. S. of George Child, Esq., by Elizabeth, d. of T. Parsons, Esq., of Massachusetts, U.S.A., and grands. of Admiral Child, of Newfield, Staffordshire. B. at Newfield 1808; m. 1835, Sarah, d. and heir of Richard Clarke Hill, Esq., of Stallington, Staffordshire. Educ. at St. John's Coll., Oxford, graduated M.A. 1834. A Magistrate for Staffordshire. A Conservative, in favour of the constituency of counties being still further extended, and of county financial boards being established to regulate taxation; voted against the disestablishment of the Irish Church 1869. Sat for North Staffordshire from Feb. 1851-May 1859. Represented Staffordshire W. from Dec. 1868 until he retired 1874. Died 27 Mar. 1896.   [1873]

CHILDERS, Rt.Hon. H.C.E. Continued in House after 1885: full entry in Volume II.

CHILDERS, John Walbanke. 16 Eaton Square, London. Cantley Hall, Doncaster, Yorkshire. Reform, and United University. Eld. s. of Col. John Walbanke Childers, of Cantley, Yorkshire, by the 3rd d. and co-heir of Sampson, Lord Eardley. B. 1798; m. 1824, Anne, only d. of Sir Francis Lindley Wood, Bart. Educ. at Christ Church, Oxford. Patron of 1 living. A Magistrate for the West Riding of Yorkshire. A Whig. Sat for Cambridgeshire from 1832 to 1835; was unsuccessful at the general election in that year. First returned for Malton, Feb. 1836; sat till Apr. 1846, when he accepted the Chiltern Hundreds. Was again elected for Malton in 1847. Retired in 1852. Died 8 Feb. 1886.   [1852]

75

CHISHOLM, Alexander William. Erchless Castle, Inverness-shire. University, and Carlton. Commonly called 'The Chisholm'. A Conservative. Sat for Inverness-shire from May 1835 on Mr. Grant (later Lord Glenelf) being raised to the peerage, defeating a relative of that Noble Lord. Accepted Chiltern Hundreds June 1838. Died 8 Sept. 1838. [1838]

CHITTY, Joseph William. 33 Queen's Gate Gardens, London. 3 New Square, Lincoln's Inn, London. Devonshire, and Oxford & Cambridge. 2nd and only surviving s. of Thomas Chitty, Esq., of the Inner Temple. B. in London 1828; m. 1858, Clara Jessie, d. of Lord Chief Baron Sir Frederick Pollock. Was educ. at Eton and at Balliol Coll., Oxford, where he graduated B.A. 1851, 1st class in the honour school in classics; afterwards elected a Fellow of Exeter Coll., and Vineries scholar; subsequently graduated M.A. Called to the bar at Lincoln's Inn Apr. 1856. Appointed a Queen's Counsel 1874, and became a Bencher of Lincoln's Inn the same year. A Liberal. Sat for Oxford city from Apr. 1880 until appointed Judge Sept. 1881. Knighted 7 Dec. 1881. Lord Justice of Appeal Jan. 1897 until he died 15 Feb. 1899. [1881]

CHOLMELEY, Sir Hugh Arthur Henry, Bart. 10 Upper Belgrave Street, London. Eastonhall, Grantham. Norton Place, Market Rasen. Eld. s. of Sir Montagu John Cholmeley, (2nd) Bart., of Easton Hall, Grantham, by Lady Georgina, 5th d. of the 8th Duke of St. Albans. B. at Easton Hall 1839; m. 1874, Edith Sophia, d. of Sir Charles H. Rowley, Bart. Educ. at Harrow. Was once in the Grenadier Guards. A Liberal. Sat for Grantham from Dec. 1868 until he retired 1880. Died 14 Feb. 1904. [1880]

CHOLMELEY, Sir Montagu John, Bart. 10 Upper Belgrave Street, London. Easton Hall, Grantham. Norton Place, Market Rasen. Reform, and United University. S. of Sir Montagu Cholmeley, Bart., by the d. of John Harrison, Esq., of Norton Place, Lincolnshire. B. at Grantham 1802; m. 1829 Lady Georgina, 5th d. of 8th Duke of St. Albans. A Dept.-Lieut. of Lincolnshire. A Liberal, promised to uphold 'all the Protestant Institutions of the Country'; was at one time in favour of protection to agriculture. Sat for Grantham 1826. Unsuccessfully contested that borough 1830 and 1832. First elected for Lincolnshire Jan. 1847. Was an unsuccessful candidate there in July 1852, but regained his seat in Mar. 1857. MP until his death 18 Jan. 1874. [1873]

CHOLMONDELEY, Hon. Hugh. 2 Hamilton Place, London. Vale Royal, Cheshire. Carlton, and Crockford's. Eld. s. of Lord Delamere. B. 1812; an officer in the Guards; Col. of Cheshire Militia. A Conservative, voted for agricultural protection 1846. Sat for Denbighshire from 1840-1841, when he was first elected for Montgomery. Polled the same number of votes as Maj. Pugh in 1847, and therefore could not vote until after the report of a committee. He declined to defend his seat and therefore Mr. Pugh was declared elected. Succeeded father as 2nd Baron Delamere 30 Sept. 1855. Died 1 Aug. 1887. [1847 2nd ed.]

CHOLMONDELEY, Lord William Henry Hugh. 32 Chapel Street, Grosvenor Place, London. Cholmondeley Castle, Nantwich, Cheshire. 2nd s. of the 1st Marq. Cholmondeley, by Lady Georgina Charlotte, 2nd d. of 3rd Duke of Ancaster. B. in Piccadilly 1800; m. 1825, Marcia Emma, d. of the Rt. Hon. Charles Arbuthnot. Appointed a Dept.-Lieut. of Hampshire 1846. A Conservative, but did 'not consider it the duty of a Conservative to refuse attention to claims for necessary reforms.' First elected for Hampshire S. July 1852, without opposition. Sat until he retired 1857. Succeeded as 3rd Marq. 8 May 1870. Died 16 Dec. 1884. [1857]

CHRISTIE, Samuel. See CHRISTIE-MILLER, Samuel.

CHRISTIE, William Dougal. 5 King's Bench Walk, Temple, London. Hayes Park, Middlesex. Reform, and Oxford & Cambridge. Eld. s. of Dougal Christie, Esq., who was for many years a physician in Bombay. B. 1816. A barrister, and joined the Western Circuit. Was Private Sec. to the Earl of Minto, when his Lordship was First Lord of the Admiralty. A Liberal. A member of the Free Trade Club. Wrote pamphlets on the Ballot and on the Copyright question. Was not returned for Weymouth at the general election in 1841, but succeeded on petition. Sat until he accepted Chiltern Hundreds 1847. Sec. of legation at Berne 1851. Chargé D'Affaires in Argentine Republic in 1854. Envoy extraordinary to Emperor of Brazil 1859-1863. Unsuccessfully contested Cambridge 12 July 1865 and Greenock 18 Nov. 1868. Author of several works. Died 27 July 1874. [1847]

CHRISTIE, William Langham. 117 Eaton Square, London. Glyndebourne, Lewes. Carlton, and Oxford & Cambridge. Only s. of Langham Christie, Esq., of Preston Deanery, Northamptonshire, by Margaret Elizabeth, d. of W. Gosling, Esq., of Hassobury, Essex. B. 1830; m. 1855, Agnes Hamilton, d. of Col. Cleveland, of Tapley

Park, North Devon. Educ. at Eton, and at Trinity Coll., Cambridge. Was Capt. Northamptonshire Militia, retired 1856. A Magistrate for Sussex and Northamptonshire, and a Deputy-Lieut. for Sussex. Patron of 2 livings. A Conservative. Sat from Feb. 1874 for Lewes, which he had contested unsuccessfully Dec. 1868. Sat until he retired in 1885. Died 28 Nov. 1913.   [1885]

CHRISTIE-MILLER, Samuel. 2 Park Street, Westminster, London. Poynton Hall, Stockport, Cheshire. Carlton. 2nd s. of Thomas Christy, Esq., of Brooklands, Broomfield, Essex, by Rebecca, d. of Samuel Hewling, Esq., of Reading, Berkshire. Nephew to John Christy, Esq., of Apuldrefield, and Hatcham Manor House, New Cross. M. 1842, Mary, 3rd d. of Thomas Hardcastle, Esq., of Firwood, Banker at Bolton, Lancashire. A Dept.-Lieut. of London. A Conservative, voted against the Chinese war. First elected for Newcastle-under-Lyme in 1847, which had formerly been represented by his relative Wm. H. Miller, Esq., of Britwell House, Buckinghamshire. Accepted Chiltern Hundreds 1847. Again elected for Newcastle-under-Lyme in July 1852. Retired in 1859.   [1858]

CHRISTMAS, William. 10 Dover Street, London. Tramore. Mr. Christmas and his colleagues were elected in opposition to Mr. Wyse (whose property was chiefly in Waterford and its neighbourhood), and another candidate, a Repealer. Mr. Wyse stated that his opinion was in favour of repeal, but he declined to pledge himself to vote for any measure, having that object in view, which Mr. O'Connell might bring forward. This divided the Repeal party, and Mr. Christmas was elected for Waterford in 1832. A Conservative. Defeated in 1835.   [1833]

CHRISTOPHER, Rt. Hon. Robert Adam. See NISBET, Rt. Hon. Robert Adam Hamilton-.

CHRISTY, Samuel. See CHRISTIE-MILLER, Samuel.

CHURCHILL, Lord Alfred Spencer-. 16 Rutland Gate, London. Carlton, and Travellers'. 2nd s. of the 5th Duke of Marlborough, by his 1st wife, Lady Jane, d. of 8th Earl of Galloway. B. 1824. Appointed Lieut. 83rd Foot 1847, retired 1848; became Lieut.-Col. Oxfordshire Yeomanry Cavalry 1860. A moderate Conservative, voted with Lord Palmerston on the vote of censure 1864; would not oppose an extension of franchise commensurate with the increase of 'intelligence and education'; in favour of government grants for education being extended, as preferable to a rate; in favour also of the 'equitable adjustment of the Church rate question, but not total abolition.' Sat for Woodstock from Dec. 1845-July 1847; re-elected July 1857 and sat until he retired 1865. Contested Brecknock 4 Oct. 1866. Chairman of Council of Society of Arts 1875-6 and 1878-80. Died 21 Sept. 1893.   [1865]

CHURCHILL, Lord Charles, F.L.S. 14 Wyndham Place, London. Rookwood, Surrey. 2nd s. of the Duke of Marlborough. B. 1794; m. 1827, Etheldrep Catherine, 2nd d. of John Benett, Esq., MP for Wiltshire, of Pyt House in that county. Entered the army in 1811, and having served in Spain and France, sold out in 1832, as Lieut.-col. A Conservative. Sat for St. Albans in 1817; for Woodstock in 1830 and 1831; was not in the Parliament of 1832. Succeeded his bro. the Marq. of Blandford in the representation of Woodstock in Jan. 1835. Defeated in 1837. Died 28 Apr. 1840.   [1837]

CHURCHILL, Rt. Hon. Lord R. S. Continued in House after 1885: full entry in Volume II.

CHUTE, William Lyde Wiggett. The Vine, Hampshire. Pickenham Hall, Norfolk. Athenaeum. 2nd s. of the Rev. Jas. Wiggett, Rector of Crudwell and Hankerton, Wiltshire. B. 16 Jan. 1800; m. 1837, Martha, d. of T.R. Buckworth, Esq., of Cockly Clay, Norfolk. Was a second class man at Oxford. Assumed the name and arms of the ancient family of Chute in 1827, by royal licence, on succeeding to the estates of that family on the death of the Rev. Thomas Vere Chute. A Magistrate for the Cos. of Hampshire and Norfolk, and a Dept.-Lieut. for the latter, of which he was High Sheriff in 1832. A Conservative, voted for agricultural protection 1846. Sat for Norfolk W. from 1837 until he retired 1847. Died 6 July 1879.   [1847]

CLARK, James Johnston. Largantocher House, Maghera, Co. Londonderry. Only surviving s. of Alexander Clark, Esq., of Maghera, by Margaret, d. of James Johnston, Esq. B. at Maghera, 1809; m. 1837, Frances, d. of Robert Hall, Esq., of Merton Hall, Co. Tipperary. Educ. at Raphoe and Belfast. A 'moderate Conservative'; a supporter generally of Lord Derby's policy. A Magistrate for the Co. of Londonderry, and High Sheriff there in 1849. First returned for Londonderry Co. in Mar. 1857, on the occurrence of a vacancy; re-chosen at the general election in Apr. following. Retired in 1859. Died June 1891.   [1858]

CLARK, Stewart. Bailey's Hotel, London. Kilnside, Paisley. The Cliff, Wenges Bay, N.B. Cairnearth, Co. Antrim. Reform, and National Liberal. S. of John Clark, J.P. for Renfrewshire,

Manufacturer, by marriage with Elizabeth, d. of Geo. Aitken, of Arklestone, Paisley. B. at Paisley, 1830; educ. at the Grammar School, Paisley, and University of Glasgow. Studied for the legal profession, but was a Manufacturer. M. 1860, Annie, d. of John Smiley, of Larne, Co. Antrim. A Liberal. Sat for Paisley from 15 Feb. 1884 until he retired in 1885.   [1885]

CLARKE, Sir E. Continued in House after 1885: full entry in Volume II.

CLARKE, John Creemer. Wayste Court, Abingdon. Reform, National, and City Liberal. Eld. s. of Mr. Robert Clarke, of St. Giles's in the Wood, Devon, by Graciana, d. of John Creemer of Exbourne, Devon. Born at Exbourne, Devon, 1821; m. 1st, Anna Maria, d. of John Avis of Muirhead, Somerset (she died 1848); 2ndly, 1849, d. of Mr. John Joyce of Timberscombe, Somerset. A Merchant and Manufacturer. A Magistrate for Buckinghamshire and also for Abingdon, of which town he was chosen Mayor in 1870. A Liberal. Sat for Abingdon from Feb. 1874 until he retired in 1885. Died 11 Feb. 1895. [1885]

CLAY, James. 25 Montagu Square, London. Reform, and Oxford & Cambridge. S. of James Clay, Esq., a London Merchant, by the eld. d. of John Emes, Esq., formerly of Elvetham Park, Hampshire. Cousin to Sir William Clay, Bart. B. in London; m. Eliza Camilla, eld. d. of Joseph Allen Woolrych, Esq., formerly of Weobley, Herefordshire, a descendent of the ancient Shropshire family of that name. Educ. at Winchester and at Balliol Coll., Oxford, where he took honours. A 'thorough-going Reformer', in favour of triennial Parliaments. An unsuccessful candidate for Beverley 1837 and for Hull 1841. First returned for Hull in 1847; again returned in 1852, but on petition the election was declared void for bribery, Mar. 1853; regained the seat 1857. MP until his death 26 Sept. 1873. [1873]

CLAY, Sir William, Bart. 17 Hertford Street, London. Fulwell Lodge, Twickenham, Middlesex. Athenaeum, Union, and Reform. Only surviving s. of George Clay, Esq., (a Merchant and Shipowner in London), by the d. of Robert Monsom, Esq., of Scarborough. Was in partnership with his father, in the firm of George Clay and Son. B. in London 1791; m. 1822, Harriet, d. and co-heir of Thomas Dickason, Esq., of Fulwell Lodge, Middlesex. Was Sec. to the Board of Controul from 1839-1841. Author of a work on Joint-Stock Banking, pamphlets on the Currency, Banks of Issue etc. A Liberal, in favour of extension of the suffrage, the ballot, and Triennial Parliaments, voted for the abolition of

Church Rates. Sat for Tower Hamlets from 1832 until defeated 1857. Died 13 Mar. 1869. [1857]

CLAYTON, Richard Rice. 17 Hertford Street, London. Fulwell Lodge, Twickenham, Middlesex. Alfred, Union, and Reform. 4th s. of Sir Wm. Clayton, Bart. B. 1798; m. 1832, d. of Sir George Nugent. A Dept.-Lieut. of Buckinghamshire. High Sheriff of Buckinghamshire in 1838. A Conservative, voted for agricultural protection 1846. First elected for Aylesbury in 1841. Sat until defeated in July 1847. Died 4 May 1879. [1847]

CLAYTON, Sir William Robert, Bart. 79 Gloucester Place, London. Harleyford, Nr. Marlow. Marden Park, Surrey. White Hall, Norfolk. 'The Cottage', Marlow. Llandilo, Carmarthenshire. Brooks's, Reform, Junior United Service, and Wyndham. Eld. s. of Sir William Clayton, Bart. of Marden Park, Surrey. B.1786; m. 1817, Alice, d. and heiress of Col. O'Donel, and grand-d. of Sir Neil O'Donel, Bart. A Lieut.-Col. in the army, a Magistrate and Dept.-Lieut. of Buckinghamshire. Was at the battles of Vittoria, Pyrenees, Genappe, Quatre Bras, Waterloo, etc. Had Church patronage. A Reformer, voted for the Reform Bill in all its stages. Sat for Marlow from 1831. Had previously twice contested Marlow unsuccessfully. Sat until unseated on petition in 1842. Contested seat again in 1847. Sheriff of Buckinghamshire 1846. General 1865. Died 19 Sept. 1866.   [1842]

CLEMENT, William James. The Council House, Shrewsbury, Shropshire. Eld. s. of William Clement, Esq., who was a medical practitioner in Shrewsbury for upwards of 60 years. B. in Shrewsbury; m. 1845 Tuythesa, 2nd d. of W.P. Freme, Esq., of Wepre Hall, Flintshire. Educ. at Shrewsbury School and at the Univ. of Edinburgh. A Surgeon. An Honorary Fellow of the Royal College of Surgeons, Fellow of the Society of Apothecaries, London; Surgeon to the 1st Batt. Shropshire Volunteers. Magistrate for Shrewsbury, of which town he was Mayor 1863 and 1864. A Magistrate and Dept.-Lieut. of Merionethshire. Author of *Observations in Surgery and Pathology*, and many contributions to the medical journals. Patron of 1 living. A Liberal. First elected for Shrewsbury July 1865. MP until his death 29 Aug. 1870.   [1870]

CLEMENTS, Hon. Charles Skeffington. 2 Grosvenor Square, London. Killadoon, Celbridge, Ireland. Travellers', and Reform. 2nd surviving s. of the 3rd Earl of Leitrim, by the eld. d. and co-heir of William Bermingham, Esq., of Ross Hill, Co. Galway. Bro. to Visct. Clements who had previously represented Leitrim. B. in Dublin 1807. Educ. at Harrow. Entered the army in 1825, became a Capt. and retired in 1838. Was one of the Assistant Poor Law Commissioners in Ireland from 1838-1846. A Whig. First returned for Leitrim in 1847. Defeated in 1852. Died 29 Sept. 1877. [1847 2nd ed.]

CLEMENTS, Henry John. Ashfield, Co. Cavan. Carlton. Cousin to the Earl of Leitrim. M. d. of James Stewart, Esq., of Killymoon. Col. of Leitrim Militia. A Conservative. Represented the Co. of Leitrim from 1805-1818. First sat for Cavan Aug. 1840. MP until his death in 1843. [1842]

CLEMENTS, Lord. 19A Davies Street, Berkeley Square, London. Rynne, Co. Leitrim. Eld. surviving s. of the Earl of Leitrim. Appointed in 1843 Col. of Leitrim Militia. A Whig. First returned for Leitrim on the death of his bro. in 1839. Sat until he retired Aug. 1847. Succeeded as 3rd Earl 31 Dec. 1854. Died (murdered) 2 Apr. 1878. [1847]

CLEMENTS, Visct. 2 Grosvenor Square, London. Rynne, Co. Leitrim. Eld. s. of the Earl of Leitrim. B. 1805. Capt. in the Prince of Wales's Militia, Donegal. Of Whig principles. He sat for Leitrim in the Parliaments of 1826 and 1830 but lost his seat in 1831. He recovered it in 1832 and sat until his death 24 Jan. 1839. [1838]

CLERK, Rt. Hon. Sir George, Bart. 8 Park Street, Westminster, London. Pennycuick, Edinburgh. Carlton. B. 1787; m. in 1810, Maria Anne, d. of Ewan Law, Esq., and niece of the first Lord Ellenborough. Was a Lord of the Admiralty from 1819 to 1830, except for a short interval; Secretary to the Treasury in the Peel administration of 1834-35; was reappointed in 1841 to that office, which he continued to hold till Feb. 1845, when he was appointed Vice-President of the Board of Trade and Master of the Mint; resigned the latter offices, July 1846. An Advocate at the Scottish bar. A Conservative, but in favour of free trade. Sat for Edinburgh before 1832, but had no seat from that time till 1835, when he was again returned for Edinburgh; unsuccessfully contested it in 1837, and was returned for Stamford in 1838. Sat for Dover from 1847. Defeated in 1852. Contested same seat in 1857. Died 23 Dec. 1867. [1852]

CLIFFORD, Charles Cavendish. 6 St. James's Place, London. Westfield House, Ryde, Isle of Wight. Brooks's. 3rd s. of Admiral Sir Augustus William James Clifford, 1st Bart., by Lady Elizabeth Frances, sister of the 4th Marq. Townshend. B. 1821. Educ. at the Charterhouse School and Christ Church, Oxford, where he

graduated B.A. 1842; elected a Fellow of All Souls' 1843, and graduated B.C.L. 1846. Called to the bar 1847; was a private secretary to Lord Palmerston, both at the Home Office and the Treasury. A Liberal, in favour of 'progressive reform,' etc. Sat for the Isle of Wight from Apr. 1857 to Aug. 1865; sat for Newport 1870 until he retired 1885. Succeeded bro. as 4th Baronet 6 Jan 1892. Died 22 Nov. 1895. [1885]

CLIFFORD, Henry Morgan-. Llantilio Crossennsy, Monmouthshire. Brooks's, and Oxford & Cambridge. Only s. of Morgan Morgan-Clifford, Esq., of Perristone, Herefordshire, by the 2nd d. of Jonathan Willington, Esq., of Rapla, Co. Tipperary. His grandfather assumed the name of Clifford in 1760. B. 1806; m. 1834, Catherine, only d. of Joseph Yorke, Esq., of Forthampton Court, Gloucestershire, grand-d. of the Bishop (Yorke) of Ely. Educ. at Eton, and at Christ Church, Oxford, but did not graduate; studied the law for some time, but was not called to the bar. Chairman of the Herefordshire Quarter Sessions from 1845, and a Dept.-Lieut. of that Co. and of Monmouthshire. Appointed Col. of the Monmouthshire Militia Mar. 1858, a Commissioner of Lunacy 1853. 'A member of the advanced section of the Liberal Party'; in favour of extension of the franchise, the ballot, retrenchment, removal of Church rates, abolition of capital punishment, etc. First returned for Hereford July 1847. Sat until defeated 1865. Died 12 Feb. 1884. [1865]

CLIFTON, John Talbot. Lytham Hall, Lancashire. White's, Travellers', and Crockford's. Eld. s. of Thomas Clifton, Esq., of Clifton and Lytham Hall, Lancashire, whose ancestor, William De Clifton, held land in that Co. in 1257. B. in London 1819; m. 1844, the eld. d. of the Hon. Henry Cecil Lowther, MP, and grand-d. of the 5th Earl of Harborough. (She was born 1822). Entered the army as Cornet and Sub-Lieut. in the 1st Life Guards in 1839. A Conservative, voted for agricultural protection 1846. First returned for Lancashire N. 1844, when Lord Stanley accepted the Chiltern Hundreds, and was shortly afterwards summoned to the House of Peers. Sat until he unsuccessfully contested Peterborough 7 July 1852. Contested Preston 30 Apr. 1859. Col. of Militia 1852-70. Died Algiers 16 Apr. 1882. [1847]

CLIFTON, Sir Robert Juckes, Bart. Clifton Hall, Nottingham. B. 1826, the eld. s. of Sir Juckes Granville Clifton, 8th Bart., of Clifton Hall, by his 2nd wife, Marianne, d. of John Swinfen, Esq., of Swinfen, Staffordshire. Married. Of very Liberal opinions, and in favour of improving the conditions of Ireland, but did not consider the removal of the Established Church would effect that purpose. In favour also of giving legal protection to the funds of trade societies, of the adoption of household suffrage in the counties, of vote by ballot etc. Sat for Nottingham from Dec. 1861-Apr. 1866, when he was unseated on petition. Regained his seat in Dec. 1868 and sat until his death 30 May 1869.   [1869]

CLIFTON, Thomas Henry. Ashton Park, Preston, Lancashire. Carlton. Only s. of John Talbot Clifton, Esq., of Lytham Hall, Lancashire, by Lady Eleanor Cecily, eld. d. of the Hon. Col. Henry Cecil Lowther and sister of the 3rd Earl of Lonsdale. B. 1815; m. 1867, Madeline Diana Elizabeth, eld. d. of Sir Andrew Agnew, Bart., of Lochnaw Castle, Scotland. Educ. at Eton. Served in the 1st Life Guards. A Magistrate for Lancashire. A Conservative, and supporter of Lord Beaconsfield's government, in favour of the maintenance of the union of Church and State. Sat for N. Lancashire from Mar. 1874 until he retired 1880.   [1880]

CLINTON, Lord Arthur Pelham. 7 Lower Brook Street, London. Clumber Park, Worksop, Nottinghamshire. 3rd s. of 5th Duke of Newcastle, by Lady Susan, d. of 10th Duke of Hamilton. B. in London 1840. Unmarried. Educ. at Eton, and previously at Woodcote School, near Reading. Entered the navy 1854, made Lieut. 1861; served in Capt. Peel's naval brigade in India, and received two medals. A Liberal, but voted against Lord Russell's Reform Bill 1866; opposed to the ballot, and to the total abolition of church-rates. First elected for Newark, July 1865. Retired in 1868. Died 18 June 1870.   [1867]

CLINTON, Lord Charles Pelham Pelham-. 37 Lowndes Square, London. Carlton. 2nd s. of the 4th Duke of Newcastle, by Georgiana Elizabeth, d. of Edward Miller Mundy, Esq., of Shipley, Derbyshire. B. in London 1813; m. 1848, Elizabeth, only surviving child of William Grant, Esq., of Congalton. Educ. at Eton and at Christ Church, Oxford, where he graduated B.A. 1834. Was a Capt. 1st Life Guards, in which he served 18 years; retired from the army May 1851. A Conservative, opposed to the Maynooth Grant. Unsuccessfully contested Retford E. 14 Jan. 1835. Was an unsuccessful candidate for Sandwich July 1847. First returned for Sandwich May 1852. Retired 1857. Died 15 Dec. 1894.   [1857]

CLINTON, Lord Edward William Pelham-. Clumber, Worksop. Ollerton, Newark, Nottinghamshire. Army & Navy. 2nd s. of 5th Duke of Newcastle, by Lady Susan, only d. of 10th

Duke of Hamilton. B. in Park Lane, London 1836. m. 1865, d. of Sir William Hartopp, Bart. Educ. at Eton. Entered the Rifle Brigade 1854, became Capt. 1857. A Liberal, and said he would give an 'independent support' to a Liberal government. First elected for Nottingham N. July 1865. Retired in 1868. Lt.-Col. 1878-80. Groom-in-Waiting to the Queen 1881-94. Master of H.M. Household 1894-1901. Died 9 July 1907.   [1867]

CLINTON, Lord Robert Renebald Pelham-. Clumber Park, Worksop, Nottinghamshire. 6th s. of the 4th Duke of Newcastle, by Georgiana Elizabeth d. of Edward Miller Mundy, Esq., of Shipley, Derbyshire. B. 1820. Unmarried. Appointed 1st Lieut. Sherwood Rangers 1853. A Liberal-Conservative, was an 'unflinching friend to our Protestant institutions,' but would 'not flinch from the great principles of civil and religious liberty'; in favour of extension of the suffrage; always voted against the ballot; considered 'voluntary aids not sufficient' for educational purposes. First elected for N. Nottinghamshire July 1852. Sat until he retired 1865.   [1864]

CLIVE, Edward Bolton. 18 Grafton Street, London. Witfield, Herefordshire. Athenaeum, and Reform. A Cousin of the Earl of Powis. Was a Lieut.-Col. in the army, and a Capt. in the Grenadier Guards. Was at Waterloo. Was patron of 3 livings. A Reformer, who voted against the Corn Laws, and was opposed to the ballot and short Parliaments. Sat for Hereford City from 1826 until his death in June 1845.   [1844]

CLIVE, Col. Edward Henry. 78 Chester Street, London. Perrystone, Ross, Herefordshire. Guard's, Travellers', and Brooks's. Eld. s. of George Clive, Esq., of Perrystone Court, (who represented Hereford from Feb. 1857-Mar. 1869), by Anne Sybella, d. of Sir Thomas Farquhar, Bart. B. at Llwynwormwood, Glamorgan 1837; m. 1867, Isabella, eld. d. of Daniel Hale Webb, Esq., of Wykeham Park, Oxfordshire. Educ. at Harrow. Entered the army as Ensign, Rifle Brigade Aug. 1854; was transferred to the Grenadier Guards Dec. following; became Lieut. July 1856; Capt. May 1864. A Liberal, and in favour of the ballot. Sat for Hereford from Mar. 1869. Accepted Chiltern Hundreds in 1871. Lieut.-Col. commanding Grenadier Guards 1880-85; Governor of Sandhurst 1888-93. Retired 1898. Died 1 Mar. 1916.   [1870]

CLIVE, George. 13 Mansfield Street, Portland Place, London. Perrystone Court, Ross, Herefordshire. Ballacroy, Ballina, Co. Mayo. Travellers', and Oxford & Cambridge. 3rd s. of

Edward Bolton Clive, Esq., of Whitfield, Herefordshire (who was MP for the city of Hereford from 1826-1845), by the Hon. Harriet, 4th d. and co-heir of Andrew, Baron Archer, of Umberslade. B. at Verdun, in France 1806; m. 1835, Anne-Sybella Martha, d. of Sir Thomas Farquhar, Bart. Educ. at Harrow and at Brasenose Coll., Oxford, where he graduated B.A. 1826; M.A. 1829. Called to the bar at Lincoln's Inn 1830. Author of an edition of *Steer's Parish Law*. Was Under-Sec. for the Home Dept. from June 1859-Nov. 1862. Appointed a Poor Law Commissioner in 1836, a Police Magistrate in 1839, Judge of the County Court of Southwark 1847. Chairman of Quarter Sessions of Herefordshire. A Liberal, in favour of simplifying the title to land and of shortening entails. Sat for Hereford from Feb. 1857-Mar. 1869; re-elected Feb. 1874. Sat until he retired Mar. 1880. Died 8 June 1880. [1880]

CLIVE, Hon. George Herbert Windsor Windsor-. 12 Stratford Place, London. Oakley Park, Bromfield, Shropshire. Carlton. 2nd s. of the Hon. Robert Henry Clive and the Baroness Windsor. B. 1835; m. 1876, Hon. Gertrude Albertina, d. of the 19th Baron Clinton (she died 1878). Appointed Capt. 52nd Foot, 1859; exchanged to the Coldstream Guards 1860, became Capt. 1868, and retired 1870. A Conservative, and a supporter of 'constitutional principles.' Sat for Ludlow from Sept. 1860 until he retired in 1885. Died 28 Apr. 1918. [1885]

CLIVE, Henry Bayley. Styche, Market Drayton, Shropshire. Carlton, and Oxford & Cambridge. S. of William Clive, Esq., who was bro. to the celebrated Lord Clive, and uncle to the 1st Earl of Powis. B. at Styche, Shropshire, 1800. Educ. at Eton, and St. John's Coll., Cambridge. A Magistrate for Shropshire. A proprietor of East India Stock. A Conservative and Protectionist, opposed to the endowment of the Roman Catholic Clergy. First returned for Ludlow in 1847. Retired in 1852. Died 26 Feb. 1870. [1852]

CLIVE, Hon. Robert Henry. B. in 1789, the 2nd s. of 1st Earl of Powis. M. in 1819 Lady Harriet, d. of 5th Earl of Plymouth. Graduated LL.D. at St. John's Coll., Cambridge. An East India Proprietor. Was a Lieut.-Col. in the army and Col. of the Worcestershire Yeomanry. Was Under Secretary of State for the Home Department from Apr. 1818-Jan. 1822. Patron of 1 living. A Conservative, but in favour of free trade. Sat for Ludlow from 1818-32 when he was returned for the county of Salop S., and sat until his death on 20 Jan. 1854. [1853]

CLIVE, Hon. Robert Windsor. 53 Lower Grosvenor Street, London. Oakley Park, Salop. Hewell Grange, Nr. Bromsgrove. Carlton. Eld. s. of Hon. Robert Henry Clive, of Oakley Park (who was 2nd s. of the 1st Earl of Powis), by Lady Harriet, 2nd d. of the 5th Earl of Plymouth, who became Baroness Windsor. B. in Grosvenor Street, London 1824; m. 1852, Lady Mary, young. d. of 2nd Earl of Bradford. Received honorary degree of M.A. from Cambridge in 1845. A Magistrate for Salop. Appointed Capt. Worcestershire Yeomanry Cavalry 1848. A Conservative supporting education on a religious basis, an extension of the franchise, conditionally upon the spread of education. Sat for Ludlow from July 1852-Jan. 1854, when he was elected for Salop S. without opposition. MP until his death 4 Aug. 1859. [1859]

CLIVE, Visct. D.C.L. (I). 29 Hill Street, London. Powis Castle, Montgomeryshire. Athenaeum, and Carlton. Eld. s. of the Earl of Powis. B. 1785; m. 1818, Lucy, 3rd d. of Duke of Montrose. Lord-Lieut. of Montgomeryshire. An East India Proprietor. Patron of 3 livings. A Conservative, sat for Ludlow in six Parliaments before the Reform Act and from 1832 until he succeeded as 2nd Earl of Powis May 1839. Died 17 Jan. 1848. [1838]

CLIVE, Visct. (II). 45 Berkeley Square, London. Walcot Hall, Shropshire. Eld. s. of 2nd Earl of Powis by 3rd d. of 3rd Duke of Montrose. B. 5 Nov. 1818. Received honorary degree of D.C.L. from the University of Cambridge in 1842. Appointed Dept.-Lieut. of Shropshire 1846. A Conservative, voted for agricultural protection 1846. Was first returned for Shropshire N. in 1843, on the succession of Sir Rowland Hill to the Peerage. Sat until he succeeded as 3rd Earl Jan. 1848. Died 7 May 1891. [1847]

CLOSE, Maxwell Charles. Drumbanagher, Newry, Ireland. Carlton. Eld. s. of Col. Close, of Drumbanagher, Co. Armagh, by Anna Elizabeth, sister of 1st Lord Lurgan. B. 1827; m. 1852, Catherine, d. of Henry Close, Esq., of Newtown Park, Co. Dublin. Educ. at Eton and at Christ Church, Oxford; graduated B.A. 1849, M.A. 1856. A Dept.-Lieut. of Armagh, of which Co. he was High Sheriff in 1854. A Conservative. Sat for the Co. of Armagh from 1857 to 1864; re-elected Feb. 1874. Sat until he retired 1885. Died 1903. [1885]

CLOWES, Samuel William. 5 Park Street, London. Norbury, Ashbourne, Derbyshire. Woodham Eaves, Loughborough, Leicestershire. Carlton, Arthur's, and Boodle's. S. of Lieut.-Col.

W.L. Clowes, of the 3rd Dragoons, by the d. of the Rev. Robert Holden, of Aston Hall, Derby. B. at Sutton-on-the-Hill, Derbyshire 1821; m. 1st, 1852, Anne Georgiana, 2nd d. of Sir Richard Sutton, Bart. (she died 1853); 2ndly, 1863 Hon. Adelaide, 2nd d. of the 2nd Baron Waterpark. Educ. at Rugby and at Brasenose Coll., Oxford, where he graduated B.A. A moderate Conservative. Unsuccessfully contested Derbyshire S. 4 Apr. 1857. Sat for N. Leicestershire from Dec. 1868 until he retired 1880. Sheriff of Derbyshire 1888. Died 31 Dec. 1898.   [1880]

COBBETT, John Morgan. 4 Hare-court, Temple, London. Skeynes, Edenbridge, Kent. 2nd s. of William Cobbett, Esq., the well-known author of the *Political Register*, etc. (who sat for Oldham from 1832 till his death in 1835). B. 1800; m. 1851, Mary, d. of John Fielden, Esq., of Todmorden. Was called to the bar at Lincoln's Inn 1830, and joined the Home Circuit. A Magistrate for Sussex, and for many years Chairman of Quarter Sessions for W. Sussex. Was presented with the freedom of the City of London 1861. A Conservative, formerly ranked as a Liberal; was favourable to annual parliaments, universal suffrage, etc. Sat for Oldham in the Liberal interest from July 1852 to July 1865; re-elected June 1872; stood unsuccessfully for Coventry Apr. 1833, for Chichester Jan. 1835, for Oldham July 1835 and again July 1847, July 1865 and Dec. 1868. MP until his death 13 Feb. 1877.   [1876]

COBBETT, William. 23 Crown Street, London. B. at Farnham in 1762. Mr. Cobbett, the great controversialist and author of *Rural Rides* (1830), rose from the humble condition of a farmer's boy in Hampshire, through the various grades of a private soldier, a sergeant, a farmer, and a political and general writer, to his situation as Member for Oldham. His political opinions were given to the world through the medium of his *Register*, and his various other publications. Unsuccessfully contested Manchester 15 Dec. 1832. Sat for Oldham from 1832 until his death 18 June 1835.   [1835]

COBBOLD, John Chevallier. 54 St. George's Road, London. Holywells, Ipswich. Carlton, and Athenaeum. S. of John Cobbold, Esq., a Brewer and Merchant at Ipswich, by the d. of the Rev. Temple Chevallier, of Aspal Hall, Suffolk. B. at Ipswich 1797; m. Lucy, 3rd d. of the Rev. Henry Patteson, of Drinkstone, Suffolk and sister to Mr. Justice Patteson. Educ. at the Bury St. Edmund's Grammar School. A Banker at Ipswich and Harwich; Chairman of the Eastern Union, the Ipswich and Bury St. Edmund's Railways. A

Conservative, in favour of a 'judicious' extension of the franchise; opposed to concessions to the Roman Catholics. First returned for Ipswich in 1847. Sat until defeated in 1868. Died 6 Oct. 1882.   [1867]

COBBOLD, John Patteson. Eld. s. of John Chevallier Cobbold, Esq., (who represented Ipswich from 1847-68) by Lucy, d. of the Rev. Henry Patteson, of Drinkstone, Suffolk. B. in Ipswich 1831; m. 1858, Adela Hariette, d. of Rev. George John Bupuis, vice-Provost of Eton Coll. Educ. at Eton. A Banker and Brewer at Ipswich. A Maj. in the 2nd Administrative Batt. of the Suffolk Rifle Volunteers. A Conservative. Sat for Ipswich from Feb. 1874. MP until his death 10 Dec. 1875.   [1874]

COBBOLD, Thomas Clement. 14 King Street, St. James's, London. Holywells, Ipswich. 3rd s. of John Chevallier Cobbold, Esq., of the Holywells, Suffolk (who represented Ipswich from 1847-68), by Lucy, 3rd d. of Rev. Henry Patteson, of Drinkstone, Suffolk. Bro. of John Patteson Cobbold, Esq., who sat for Ipswich from Feb. 1874 until his death in Dec. 1875. B. at Ipswich 1833. Educ. at the Charterhouse. Entered the diplomatic service and proceeded to Constantinople in 1854. Was unpaid attaché at Lisbon, and afterwards at Oporto. Appointed paid attaché at Lisbon Jan. 1859. A Second Sec. in the diplomatic service, Oct. 1862, transferred to Turin Nov. 1862, to Stuttgart Aug. 1864. Was acting Chargé d'affaires at Baden-Baden from June-Oct. 1867. Appointed July 1869 Sec. of Legation at Rio de Janeiro, where he was acting Chargé d'affaires from June and was acting Chargé d'affaires there from June 1874-May 1875. A Conservative, but said he would 'support and encourage every well-considered measure for progress.' Sat for Ipswich from Dec. 1875. MP until his death 21 Nov. 1883.   [1883]

COBDEN, Richard. Dunford, Midhurst, Sussex. Athenaeum. S. of William Cobden, Esq., of Dunford, near Midhurst, Sussex, by Milly, his wife. B. at Dunford 1804. Was a Cotton Printer in Lancashire. A Director of the Manchester Chamber of Commerce, and well known as a leading member of the Anti-Corn Law League; author of pamphlets entitled *England, Ireland, and America*, and *Russia, by a Manchester Manufacturer*. Was presented with the freedom of the city of London 1862. In favour of the ballot, extension of the suffrage, and short Parliaments; supported Lord Palmerston on the vote of censure 1864. Unsuccessfully contested Stockport in 1837; sat for Stockport from July 1841-July 1847, and the West

Riding of Yorkshire from the last date until April 1857, when he was an unsuccessful candidate at Huddersfield; elected for Rochdale May 1859 and sat until his death 2 Apr. 1865.   [1865]

COCHRANE, Alexander Dundas Wishart Ross Baillie-. 26 Wilton Crescent, London. Lamington, Biggar, Lanarkshire. Carlton. Eld. s. of Admiral Sir Thomas John Cochrane, K.C.B., by his 1st wife, d. of Lieut.-Col. Sir Charles Ross, Bart. M. 1844, Annabella Mary Elizabeth, eld. d. of Andrew Robert Drummond, Esq., of Cadlands, Hampshire, and grand-d. of 5th Duke of Rutland. Appointed Capt. 1st Lanark Rife Volunteers 1860. Author of *The Morea*. A Conservative. Sat for Bridport from Sept. 1841-Apr. 1846 (when he was unseated on petition), and from July 1847-July 1852; unsuccessfully contested Bridport June 1841 and Southampton Jan. 1853. Sat for Lanark from Jan-Apr. 1857. Sat for Honiton from May 1859-Nov. 1868, when it was disfranchised, and sat from June 1870 for the Isle of Wight, which he had unsuccessfully contested Nov. 1868. Retired at 1880 general election. Created Baron Lamington 3 May 1880. Died 15 Feb. 1890.   [1880]

COCHRANE, Sir Thomas James, K.C.B. Carlton, and United Service. S. of Sir Alex. Cochrane, who was s. of the 8th Earl of Dundonald; m. d. of Sir C. Ross. A Capt. in the navy; was Governor of Newfoundland. A Conservative. Stood for Westminster in 1835. Sat for Ipswich from 1839 until he unsuccessfully contested Greenock 7 July 1841. Died 19 Oct. 1872. [1840]

COCKBURN, Sir Alexander James Edmund. 40 Hertford Street, London. 3 Harcourt Buildings, Temple, London. Wakehurst Place, Sussex. Eld. s. of Alexander Cockburn, Esq., of Hertford Street, Mayfair (once British Minister in Columbia), by the d. of Visct. de Viguier of St. Domingo. Nephew and heir presumptive to Rev. Sir William Cockburn, Bart. Was a Fellow of Trinity Hall, Cambridge, where he graduated LL.B. 1829. Called to the bar at the Middle Temple, Feb. 1829 and joined the Western Circuit. Became a Queen's Counsel 1841, and was a Bencher of the Middle Temple. Appointed Recorder of Bristol Apr. 1854. Was one of the Municipal Corporation Commissioners; from July 1850-Mar. 1851 was Solicitor-Gen., and then Attorney-Gen. until Mar. 1852. Was re-appointed Attorney-Gen. the following Dec. Appointed Lord Chief Justice of Common Pleas 21 Nov. 1856, Queen's Bench 1859, Lord Chief Justice of England 2 Nov. 1874. On 30 Apr. 1858 he succeeded his uncle as 10th Bart. A Liberal, voted for the ballot. Sat for Southampton from

July 1847 to Nov. 1856. Died 20 Nov. 1880. [1856]

COCKBURN, Rt. Hon. Sir George, G.C.B. High Beech, Essex. Carlton. 2nd s. of Sir J. Cockburn. M. Miss Mary Cockburn. A Conservative, but in favour of free trade. An Admiral of the Red, and Maj.-Gen. of Marines. Was a Lord of the Admiralty. Sat for Portsmouth before 1832. Contested Plymouth in 1837. Contested Portsmouth 26 July 1837 and Greenwich 1 July 1841. Returned for Ripon in 1841. Retired 1847. Died 19 Aug. 1853.   [1847]

COCKERELL, Sir Charles, Bart. 147 Piccadilly, London. Sezincot House, Gloucestershire. Travellers'. B. 1755; m. 1st, 1789, Mary Tryphoena, sister of Sir Charles William Blunt; 2ndly, 1808, Harriet, sister of Lord Northwick. A Banker in London, and a Director of the Globe Insurance Office. An Honorary Member of the India Board of Control. An East India Proprietor and Agent. Patron of 1 living. Went to India in 1776, attached to the Surveyor's Office; and in 1804 was appointed Postmaster-Gen. in Bengal. Voted for the Reform Act; but was against Catholic emancipation, and generally supported the Liverpool and the Wellington Administrations. In favour of the Corn Laws and opposed to short Parliaments. Sat for Evesham from 1820. MP until his death Jan. 1837.   [1836]

COCKS, Thomas Somers-. 15 Hereford Street, London. 43 Charing Cross, London. Carlton, and Alfred. Eld. s. of Thomas Somers-Cocks, Esq., of Thames Bank, Buckinghamshire, by the 5th d. of Rt. Hon. Reginald Pole-Carew, of Anthony House, Cornwall. B. 1815; m. d. of C.W.G. Wynne, Esq., formerly MP for Carnarvonshire. Educ. at Westminster and at Christ Church, Oxford. A Partner in the Banking firm of Cocks, Biddulph and Company, Charing Cross. A Director of Western Life Assurance Office. A Dept.-Lieut. for London and a Magistrate for Middlesex. A Conservative, said he would 'carry out all needful reforms in a rational spirit, and support the great cause of Conservative progress.' First returned for Reigate 1847, without opposition. Sat until he retired 1857. Died 30 Aug. 1899.   [1857]

CODDINGTON, W. Continued in House after 1885: full entry in Volume II.

CODRINGTON, Sir Christopher William. 3 Park Place, St. James's, London. Doddington Park, Gloucestershire. Carlton. Nephew of Sir Edward Codrington, eld. s. of Christopher Bethel Codrington, Esq., (who claimed to be a Bart.) by the Hon. Catherine Foley, sister of the 2nd Lord

Foley. Claimed to inherit the Baronetcy of his great-grandfather on the ground that the 3rd Bart. of the family left no legitimate issue; but the Herald's Coll. confirmed the s. of the latter (Sir William Raimond Codrington) in the Baronetcy. M. 1836 Lady Georgiana, d. of 7th Duke of Beaufort. Patron of 3 livings. Appointed a Dept.-Lieut. of Gloucestershire 1852. A Conservative, voted for inquiry into Maynooth 1853. Sat for Gloucestershire E. from 1834 and sat until his death 24 June 1864.   [1864]

CODRINGTON, Sir Edward, G.C.B., K.S.L., K.S.G., F.R.S. 92 Eaton Square, London. Hampton Lodge, Sussex. Reform. Cousin of Sir William Raimond Codrington, Bart. M. Miss Hall. An Admiral of the Blue; an E. & W. India Proprietor. Commanded the allied squadrons at Navarino, and was Capt. of a line of battleships at Trafalgar. A Reformer, an advocate of free trade, repeal of the Corn Laws, the assessed taxes, vote by ballot and shortening the duration of Parliaments. Sat for Devonport from 1832 until he accepted Chiltern Hundreds in 1839. C.-in-C. at Portsmouth Nov. 1839 to Dec. 1842. Died 28 Apr. 1851.   [1838]

CODRRINGTON, Sir William John, K.C.B. 110 Eaton Square, London. Eld. surviving s. of Admiral Sir Edward Codrington, G.C.B., by his marriage with Miss Jane Hall, of Old Windsor. B. 1804; m. 1836, Mary, d. of Levi Ames, of the Hyde, Hertfordshire (she was made a bedchamber woman in ordinary to the Queen, 1856). Entered the army in 1821; appointed Col. of the 54th Foot and a Lieut.-Gen. in 1856, 'as a mark of royal approbation.' Commanded a brigade of the light division, and afterwards a division, throughout the Eastern campaign of 1854-55. Was Commander-in-Chief of the Eastern army from Oct. 1855 till the evacuation of the Crimea. Received a medal and clasps, and was Commander of the Legion of Honour, Grand Cross of the Order of Savoy, etc. A Liberal, and a supporter of Lord Palmerston's foreign policy; in favour of 'progressive reform', 'civil and religious liberty', etc., but opposed to the ballot. First returned for Greenwich, on the occurrence of a vacancy, in Feb. 1857. Retired in 1859. Contested Westminster in 1874 and Lewes in 1880. Governor of Gibraltar 1859-65. Died 6 Aug. 1884.   [1858]

COFFIN, Walter. Llandaff, Glamorganshire. Reform. S. of Walter Coffin, Esq., of Bridgend, Glamorganshire. B. 1764. Unmarried. A Magistrate for Glamorganshire. Chairman of the Taff Vale Railway and Chairman of the Poor Law Guardians of Cardiff Union. A Liberal, in favour

of an extension of the suffrage and vote by ballot; opposed to all State endowments of religion. First returned for Cardiff, July 1852. Retired 1857. Died 15 Feb. 1867.   [1856]

COGAN, Rt. Hon. William Henry Ford. 9 St. James's Street, London. 93 St. Stephen's Green South, Dublin. Tinode, Blessinton, Co. Wicklow. Reform, and Garrick. Only s. of Bryan Cogan, Esq., of Dublin and Athgarret, Co. Kildare. B. in Dublin 1823; m. 1858, Gertrude, only d. of Francis Kyan, Esq., and grand-d. of the late Major-Gen. Kyan E.I.C.S. A Fellow Commoner of Trinity Coll., Dublin, where he graduated M.A., obtained honours in science and gained the large gold medal at the degree examination. Was first senior moderator in metaphysics and ethics 1843. Called to the bar in Ireland 1845, but relinquished practice. A Magistrate for Wicklow, Kildare and Carlow. A Liberal. First elected for Kildare Mar. 1852. Sat until he retired 1880. Commissioner on Irish Board of National Education 1880 until his death 28 Sept. 1894.   [1880]

COHEN, Arthur, Q.C. Continued in House after 1885: full entry in Volume II.

COKE, Hon. Edward Keppel Wentworth. 1 St. James's Street, London. Holkham Hall, Norfolk. 2nd s. of the 1st Earl of Leicester, by his 2nd wife, the 3rd d. of the 4th Earl of Albemarle (who m. subsequently Rt. Hon. Edward Ellice, MP). B. 1824; appointed Lieut. Scots Fusilier Guards in 1843. A Liberal, voted for the abolition of the malt tax; supported Lord John Russell on the education question. First returned for Norfolk W. in 1847. Retired in 1852. Died 26 May 1889.   [1852]

COKE, Hon. Wenman Clarence Walpole. 131, Piccadilly, London. Holkham, Wells, Norfolk. Brooks's, and Guards'. 4th s. of 1st Earl of Leicester, by his 2nd wife, Lady Anne Amelia, 3rd d. of 4th Earl of Albemarle. B. at Holkham, Norfolk, 1828. Educ. at Rugby. Entered the Scots Fusilier Guards 1846, became Lieut. and Capt. 1853, Lieut.-Col. 1858, served in the Crimea, and was wounded in the trenches there; made Brevet-Maj. for distinguished services; and for some time on the staff of the 1st Division. A Liberal, and in favour of moderate reform, but opposed to the ballot. First elected for Norfolk E. July 1858. Sat until defeated 1865. Died 10 Jan. 1907.   [1865]

COLBORNE, Nicholas William Ridley. West Harling Hall, Norfolk. Athenaeum. Bro. of Sir Matthew White Ridley, Bart. Assumed the additional surname of Colborne, upon succeeding to the estates of his maternal uncle William Colborne, Esq. M. 1808, Charlotte, eld. d. of the Rt. Hon. Thomas Steele, joint Sec. to the Treasury in 1784. Patron of 3 livings. A moderate Reformer, opposed to short Parliaments and the admission of Dissenters to the Universities. Sat for Horsham in five Parliaments previous to 1832; unsuccessfully contested Wells in 1832, but was elected on the death of Norman Lamont, Esq., in 1834. Retired in 1837. Created 1st Baron Colborne 15 May 1839. Member of Fine Arts Commission 1841. Died 3 May 1854.   [1837]

COLBORNE, Hon. William Nicholas Ridley. 19 Hill Street, London. West Harling Hall, Norfolk. Reform. B. 1814, the eld. s. of Lord Colborne. A Liberal; voted against the abolition of the Corn Laws. Sat for the borough of Richmond from 1841 until his death in 1846. [1845]

COLE, Hon. Arthur Henry. 3 Cork Street, London. B. 1780, bro. of the 2nd Earl of Enniskillen. Once resident at Mysore. A Capt. in the Fermanagh Militia. A Conservative. Sat for Enniskillen from 1828 until he accepted Chiltern Hundreds May 1844. Died 1844.   [1844]

COLE, Hon. Henry Arthur. 97 Mount Street, London. Florence Court, Enniskillen, Ireland. Carlton. Sackville Street Club, Dublin. 2nd s. of 2nd Earl of Enniskillen, by Lady Charlotte, 4th d. of 1st Earl of Uxbridge. B. in Dover Street, Piccadilly, London 1809. Entered the army in 1828, became Capt. 1835, was retired on half-pay from 1841-July 1868, when he was appointed Capt. 12th Foot and to the Brevet rank of Col. in the army. A Conservative; 'a strong supporter of our Protestant institutions in Church and State.' Sat for Enniskillen from May 1844 until he accepted Chiltern Hundreds Apr. 1851. First elected for Fermanagh Dec. 1854. Sat until he retired 1880. Died 2 July 1890.   [1880]

COLE, Henry Thomas. 17 Prince of Wales's Terrace, Kensington, London. Reform. S. of George Cole Esq., M.A., of St. John's Coll., Cambridge, many years Capt. Cornwall Militia, by Sally, d. of A.S. Crozier, Maj. Royal Marines. B. at Bath 1816; m. 1846, Georgina, d. of John Stone, Esq., Barrister-at-Law of the Western circuit, and of Bulland Lodge, Somerset. Was called in 1842 to the bar at the Middle Temple, of which he became a bencher, and was made a Queen's Counsel Jan. 1867. Was one of the leaders of the Western Circuit, and Recorder of Plymouth and Devonport. Had published several Law Reports. A Liberal, in favour of the enactment of a Permissive Bill, and the abolition of the law of Primogeniture in cases of intestacy; in favour also

of the system of compulsory pilotage. Sat for Penryn from Feb. 1874 until he retired 1880. Died 5 Jan. 1885.   [1880]

COLE, Hon. John Lowry. 97 Mount Street, Grosvenor Square, London. Florence Court, Enniskillen, Ireland. Carlton. Sackville Street Club, Dublin. 3rd s. of 2nd Earl of Enniskillen, by Lady Charlotte, 4th d. of 1st Earl of Uxbridge. B. 1813. Educ. at Winchester Coll. A Dept.-Lieut. of Fermanagh. A Conservative, who said he would give a general support to Lord Derby. Sat for Enniskillen from Feb. 1859 until defeated in 1868 (perhaps withdrew before the poll). Died 29 Nov. 1882.   [1867]

COLE, Visct. (I). Florence Court, Fermanagh. Carlton, White's, Travellers' and Athenaeum. Eld. s. of the Earl of Enniskillen, and nephew of the Member for Enniskillen. B. 1807. Col. of the Fermanagh Militia. Was not in the Parliament of 1830, but was elected for Fermanagh at the dissolution of 1831 on the Conservative interest, and having voted against the Reform Bill was re-elected in 1832 without opposition and sat until he succeeded to the Peerage (3rd Earl of Enniskillen) in Mar. 1840. Died 12 Nov. 1886.   [1838]

COLE, Visct. (II). Cassia, Winsford, Cheshire. Carlton, and Travellers'. Sackville Street Club, Dublin. Eld. s. of the Earl of Enniskillen, by his 1st wife, Jane, eld. d. of James Archibald Casamajor, Esq. B. in Mount Street, London; m. 1869, Charlotte Marion, d. of Douglas Baird, Esq., of Closeburn, Scotland. Was educ. at Eton. Appointed Ensign Rifle Brigade 1865, retired from the army 1868. A Magistrate and Dept.-Lieut. for Fermanagh, of which he was High Sheriff in 1870. A Conservative. Sat for Enniskillen from Apr. 1880. Retired 1885. Succeeded father as 4th Earl in 1886. Died 28 Apr. 1924.   [1885]

COLEBROOKE, Sir Thomas Edward, Bart. 14 South Street, London. Abington House, Abington, Lanarkshire. Athenaeum. Only s. of Henry Thomas Colebrooke, Esq., F.R.S. (Member of Council at Calcutta), by Elizabeth, d. of Johnson Wilkinson, Esq., of Portman Square. B. 1813; m. 1857, 2nd d. of John Richardson, Esq., of Kirklands, Roxburghshire. Lord-Lieut. of Lanarkshire. A Liberal, voted against the abolition of the corn laws in 1842, but in 1846 supported their repeal. Sat for Taunton from Feb. 1842 to July 1852, and for Lanarkshire from Apr. 1857 to Dec. 1868, when, on the division of the Co., he was elected for North Lanarkshire. Sat until he retired at 1885 gen. election; contested Lanarkshire North-East in 1886 as a Liberal Unionist. Died 11 Jan 1890.   [1885]

COLERIDGE, Sir John Duke. 1 Sussex Square, Hyde Park, London. 1 Brick Court, Temple, London. Athenaeum, and Reform. Eld. s. of the Rt. Hon. Sir John Taylor Coleridge, of Heath's Court, Ottery St. Mary, Devon (a Judge of the Court of Queen's Bench), by Mary, d. of Dr. Albert Buchanan, Vicar of Woodmansterne and Rector of Northfleet. B. 1821; m. 1846, Jane Fortescue, 3rd d. of the Rev. George Turner Seymour of Farringford Hill, Isle of Wight. Educ. at Eton and Oxford, where he was a Scholar of Balliol, Fellow of Exeter and graduated M.A. Called to the bar 1847, made a Queen's Counsel 1861. Was Solicitor-Gen. from Dec. 1868-Nov. 1871, when he was appointed Attorney-Gen. Was Recorder of Portsmouth from 1855-65, when he resigned. A constant contributor to the *Edinburgh Review* and other publications. A 'decided Liberal', in favour of a much larger distribution of Parliamentary seats and the repeal or modification of the rating clauses of the Reform Act. Unsuccessfully contested Exeter Aug. 1864; first elected for Exeter July 1865 and sat until appointed Lord Chief Justice of Common Pleas Nov. 1873. Created 1st Baron Coleridge 10 Jan. 1874. Lord Chief Justice of England Nov. 1880, until his death 14 June 1894.   [1873]

COLES, Henry Beaumont. 36 Portman Square, London. Middleton House, Whitchurch, Hampshire. Carlton, and Athenaeum. Only s. of Philip Coles, Esq., by Catherine, only sister of Francis Const, Esq., for many years chairman of the Middlesex and Westminster Sessions. B. in London, 1794; m. 1814, Mary, eld. d. of Robert Bird, Esq. Was called to the bar at Gray's Inn, 1836. Was for many years a Magistrate for Middlesex and Hampshire, and a Dept.-Lieut. for the latter from 1848. A 'decided Conservative', and a supporter generally of Lord Derby; opposed to the endowment of the Roman Catholic Clergy. Sat for Andover from July 1847 till Apr. 1857; re-elected July 1861. MP until his death 23 Nov. 1862.   [1862]

COLLETT, John. 7 Upper Belgrave Street, London. Reform, Union, Portland, and Graham's. Eld. s. of E.J. Collett, Esq., of Locher's House, Hertfordshire, many years MP for Cashel. B. 1798; m. 1st 1826, Emma, d. of Sir Thomas Gage, Bart., 2ndly 1846, Ermingarde, only d. of William Radclyffe, Esq., of Darley Hall, Yorkshire. Of Liberal politics, in favour of reform generally, and particularly as respected the Church. First returned to Parliament for Athlone in 1843. Sat until he unsuccessfully contested Tipperary 27 Nov. 1869.   [1847]

COLLETT, William Rickford. 2A St. James's Square, London. Carlton, Conservative, and Albion. S. of E.J. Collett, Esq., many years MP for Cashel. B. 1810. Unsuccessfully contested Boston in 1837. First returned for Lincoln in 1841. Sat until defeated July 1847.   [1847]

COLLIER, John. 48 Craven Street, Strand, London. Grimstone Hall, Devon. Reform. B. 1769; m. Emma, 4th d. of Robert Porrett, Esq., of North Hill, Devon. A Merchant, Shipowner, Agent for Lloyds and Portuguese Vice-Consul at Plymouth. Dept.-Lieut. of the county. A Reformer, inclined to support Lord Melbourne's administration. In favour of the ballot, shortening the duration of Parliaments, the abolition of Church rates, the Bank monopoly and every other. Sat for Plymouth from 1832 until he retired 1841.   [1838]

COLLIER, Sir Robert Porrett. 104 Eaton Place, London. 1 Mitre Court Buildings, Temple, London. Grimstone, Tavistock, Devon. Brooks's, Oxford & Cambridge, and Reform. S. of John Collier, Esq., (who was MP for Plymouth from 1832-41), by Emma, 4th d. of Robert Porrett, Esq., of North Hill House, Nr. Plymouth. B. at Mount Tamar, Nr. Plymouth 1817; m. 1844, Isabella, d. of William Rose (sic) Esq., of Eaton Place, W. London and of Wolston Heath, Warwickshire. Educ. at Plymouth Grammar School and at Trinity Coll., Cambridge, where he graduated B.A. 1841. Called to the bar at the Inner Temple Jan. 1843; received a patent of precedence 1854; on the Western circuit; a Dept.-Lieut. of Devon. Appointed Judge Advocate of the Fleet and Counsel to the Admiralty, Dec. 1859; Solicitor-Gen. Oct. 1863, resigned July 1866. Attorney-Gen. 1868. Appointed Recorder of Bristol July 1870, but resigned that appointment on standing a fresh election at Bristol immediately afterwards. Author of works on *The Law of Railways,* and *The Law of Mines.* A Liberal; voted for the ballot 1853. First returned for Plymouth in July 1852. Sat until appointed a Judge Oct. 1871.   [1871]

COLLINGS, Jesse. Continued in House after 1885: full entry in Volume II.

COLLINS, Eugene. 38 Porchester Terrace, Bayswater, London. Kinsale, Ireland. Devonshire. Eld. s. of Daniel Collins, Esq., of Kinsale, by Catherine, d. of Martin Kenefick, Esq., of Clontead, Co. Cork. B. at Kinsale 1822; m. 1854, Marianne, d. of Thomas Henry Taunton, Esq., of Grandpont House, near Oxford, and niece of Sir William Elias Taunton, Judge of the

Court of Queen's Bench. A moderate Liberal, and in favour of denominational education. Sat from Feb. 1874 for Kinsale, which he had unsuccessfully contested July 1865. Sat until he retired in 1885 when Kinsale disfranchised. Died 10 March 1895.
[1885]

COLLINS, Thomas. 2 Hare Court, Temple, London. Knaresborough, Yorkshire. Carlton. Eld. surviving s. of the Rev. Thomas Collins of Knaresborough, where the family had been settled for 200 years, by Anne, d. of Richard Ramsden Bromley, Esq., of Addingham, Yorks. Educ. at the Charterhouse, and at Wadham Coll., Oxford. Graduated 1847. Called to the bar at the Inner Temple 1849 and joined the Northern Circuit. A Magistrate and Dept.-Lieut. of Yorks. A Liberal-Conservative. Sat for Knaresborough for a few months in 1851 and again from Apr. 1857-July 1865. Sat for Boston from Dec. 1868-Jan. 1874, when he stood unsuccessfully. Was also an unsuccessful candidate for Knaresborough in July 1852 and July 1865, and also for Derby Apr. 1880. Was again returned for Knaresborough May 1881. MP until his death 26 Nov. 1884.
[1884]

COLLINS, William. 12 Walton Place, Hans Place, London. Warwick. Reform. M. d. of John Tomes, Esq., formerly member for Warwick. A resident in Warwick and engaged in business there as a Tanner. Was the first mayor of the borough under the Municipal Reform Act. A radical Reformer. First returned for Warwick, Mar. 1837, on the accession of the previous member, Mr. Canning, to the Peerage. Sat until he retired in 1852.
[1852]

COLMAN, J. J. Continued in House after 1885: full entry in Volume II.

COLQUHOUN, Sir James, Bart. Ross-dhu and Arden-connely, Dumbartonshire. S. of Sir James Colquhoun, of Luss, Bart. by Janet, d. of Rt. Hon. Sir John Sinclair, of Ulster, Bart. Both a Bart. of England and Scotland, and Chief of the Colquhouns, of Luss, who have resided at Ross-dhu for about a thousand years. Holds the patronage of 8 livings in the Church of Scotland. A Whig. Returned for Dumbartonshire in 1837. Retired in 1841. M. 14 June 1843, Jane, 2nd d. of Sir Robert Abercrumby. Died 18 Dec. 1873.
[1838]

COLQUHOUN, John Campbell. 8 Chesham Street, Belgrave Square, London. Killermont, Lanarkshire. Athenaeum. S. of A.C. Colquhoun, Esq., Lord Registrar of Scotland. B. 1802; m.

1827, d. of 2nd Lord Lilford. Was a first class man at Oxford. Sat for Dumbarton after the passing of the Reform Act, but in 1834-5 declined to come forward on account of ill health. Author of some pamphlets on 'Reform', 'Ireland', etc. Professed to belong to no political party, but said he would 'endeavour to promote the diffusion of sound knowledge and scriptural principles throughout the country, as one great end of political well-being.' Conservative. Voted against an abolition of the Corn Laws 1846. Sat for the Kilmarnock district of burghs from 1837 until defeated in 1841. The return made at Newcastle-under-Lyme in 1841, having been declared void, so far as regarded Mr. Harris, a new election took place in July 1842, and Mr. Colquhoun subsequently succeeded on petition (July 23, 1842). Retired 1847. Died 17 Apr. 1870.
[1847]

COLTHURST, David La Touche. 24 Pall Mall, London. Adelaide Place, Cork. Reform. 3rd s. of Sir Nicholas Conway Colthurst, 4th Bart., by Elizabeth, only d. of Col. George Vesey, of Lucan House, Co. Dublin. B. at Lucan, Co. Dublin, 1828. Was educ. at Eton. Entered the army in 1847, and served in the 17th Foot in the Crimea and at Sebastopol. Commanded the 20th Foot during 3 years; retired as Lieut.-Col. in 1872. A Liberal, and in favour of 'Home Rule for Ireland', also of denominational education. Sat for Co. Cork from 1879. Retired in 1885.
[1885]

COLTHURST, Sir George Conway. 36 Wilton Crescent, London. Ardrum, Inniscarra, Co. Cork. Eld. s. of Sir Nicholas Conway Colthurst (4th Bart.), who represented Cork for several years, by Elizabeth only d. of Col. George Vesey, of Lucan House, Co. Dublin. B. 1824; m. 1846, Louisa Jane, only d. of St. John Jeffreys, Esq., of Blarney Castle, Co. Cork. Educ. at Harrow. A Liberal, voted for the disestablishment of the Irish Church 1869. First elected for Kinsale June 1863. Sat until he retired 1874. Died 24 Sept. 1878. [1873]

COLVILE, Charles Robert. 27 Eccleston Square, London. Lullington Hall, Burton-on-Trent, Derbyshire. Arthur's. Only s. of Sir Charles H. Colvile, by Harriet Anne, only d. of Thomas Porter Bonel, Esq., of Duffield Hall, Derbyshire. B. in London 1815; m. 1850, Hon. Katherine, eld. d. of Capt. John Russell, R.N., and the Baroness de Clifford. Educ. at Eton and Christ Church, Oxford. A Magistrate for the counties of Derby, Stafford, and Leicester, and a Dept.-Lieut. of Derbyshire. Patron of 1 living. Lieut.-Col. Commandant Derbyshire Yeomanry Cavalry. A Liberal, formerly ranked as a Liberal-Conservative, prepared to amend 'the anomalies of our representative system', especially by the 'disfranchisement of small boroughs and a redistribution of the vacant seats'; would not oppose the total abolition of church-rates if a compromise were found impossible. Unsuccessfully contested Derby, July 1837. Sat for Derbyshire S. from July 1841 till Apr. 1859; re-elected July 1865. Defeated in 1868. Died 10 Mar. 1886.   [1867]

COMMINS, A. Continued in House after 1885: full entry in Volume II.

COMPTON, Francis. Continued in House after 1885: full entry in Volume II.

COMPTON, Henry Combe. 13a Cannon Row, London. Minstead Manor House, Lyndhurst, Hampshire. Carlton. S. of John Compton, Esq. B. 1789; m. 1810, d. of William Miles, Esq., of Bristance, Hampshire (she died 1855). Patron of 3 livings. A Conservative, opposed to the endowment of the Roman Catholic Clergy. Sat for Hampshire S. from 1835 until he retired 1857. Died 27 Nov. 1866.   [1857]

CONINGHAM, William. 20 Sussex Square, Kemp Town, Brighton. Oxford & Cambridge. S. of Rev. Robert Coningham, of the Co. of Londonderry, Ireland, by Louisa, d. of Col. James Capper, of the Madras army; descended from a Suffolk family. B. at Penzance, Cornwall, 1815; m. 1840, Elizabeth, d. of Rev. William Meyrick, who was grands. of William Meyrick, Esq., Bodorgan, Anglesea. Entered the army in 1834, and served in the 1st Royal Dragoons, but later sold out. A Liberal; 'a general and independent supporter of Lord Palmerston'; in favour of the ballot, and a gradual extension of the suffrage; opposed to the Maynooth grant and to church-rates; an advocate for 'free trade, reform, and retrenchment'. Was an unsuccessful candidate for Brighton in July 1847, and for Westminster in July 1852. First returned for Brighton in Apr. 1857. Accepted Chiltern Hundreds 1864. Died 20 Dec. 1884.   [1863]

CONOLLY, Col. Edward Michael, D.C.L. 53 Jermyn Street, London. Castle Town, Kildare. Cliff, Co. Donegal. Carlton, and University. Eld. s. of the Hon. Adm. Sir Thomas Pakenham. B. 1786; m. 1819, Catherine, eld. d. of Chambre Brabazon Ponsonby Barker, Esq. Assumed the name of Conolly on inheriting the estates of the Rt. Hon. Thomas Conolly, of Castletown. Patron of 1 living. Was Lieut.-col. in the Donegal Militia, and Capt. of Artillery. A Conservative, voted for

agricultural protection 1846. First sat for Co. Donegal in 1831. MP until his death 1849. [1847]

CONOLLY, Thomas. 19 Hanover Square, London. Castletown House, Celbridge, Kildare. Cliff, Ballyshannon, Co. Donegal. Carlton, and Boodle's. Sackville Street Club, Dublin. Eld. s. of Col. Edward M. Conolly (who represented Donegal from 1831 till his death in 1849), by the d. of Chambre Brabazon Ponsonby Barker, Esq., of Kilcooly Abbey, Co. Tipperary. B. at Kilcooly Abbey 1823; m. 1868, Sarah Eliza, eld. d. of Joseph Shaw, Esq., of Temple House, Celbridge, Co. Kildare. Educ. at Harrow and Christ Church, Oxford. A patron of 1 living. A Conservative. Sat for Donegal from Jan. 1849 when he was returned on the death of his father. MP until his death 10 Aug. 1876.   [1876]

CONYNGHAM, Lord Albert Denison, K.C.H. Bitrons, Kent. 90, Pall Mall, London. Junior United Service, White's, and Brooks's. B. 1805, the 2nd s. of the 1st Marq. Conyngham, by the d. of Joseph Denison, Esq., of Denbies, Surrey. Married 1st, 1833, Hon. Henrietta, 4th d. of the 1st Lord Forester (she died 1841); 2ndly, 1847, Amelia, the eld. d. of the Hon. Capt. Bridgeman, R.N. Was for a short time Secretary of Legation at Berlin. A Dept.-Lieut. of Donegal. A Liberal, opposed to the Poor Laws, in favour of the ballot and short Parliaments. Assumed the name of Denison in place of Conyngham 4 Sept. 1849. Sat for Canterbury from 1835-Feb. 1841, when he retired through ill-health. Resumed his seat on a vacancy occuring Mar. 1847 and was also rechosen at the general election in that year. Sat until 1850 when he accepted Chiltern Hundreds. Created Baron Londesborough 4 Mar. 1850 and purchased the Selby Estate in Yorkshire 1853. Became F.R.S. 1850 and was an unsuccessful racehorse owner. Died 15 Jan. 1860.   [1849]

CONYNGHAM, Lord Francis Nathaniel. 46 Half Moon Street, London. The Mairshiel, Lochwinnoch, Renfrewshire. Reform. 2nd s. of the 2nd Marq. Conyngham, by Lady Jane, 2nd d. of the 1st Marq. of Anglesey. B. at Goodwood 1832; m. 1857, 5th d. of the 1st Lord Tredegar. Became Lieut. R.N. 1854. Appointed Lieut. London Irish Rifle Volunteers 1860, resigned 1861. A Magistrate and Dept.-Lieut. of the Co. of Donegal. A Liberal, in favour of the system called 'Home Rule' for Ireland. Sat for Clare Co. from Apr. 1857-May 1859; re-elected Feb. 1874. Retired 1880. Died 14 Sept. 1880.   [1880]

COOKES, Thomas Henry. Bentley Hall, Worcestershire. A Capt. in the Worcestershire

Yeomanry. Of Whig principles. In favour of the Malt Tax. Sat for Worcestershire E. from 1832. Retired in 1837.   [1837]

COOPE, Octavius Edward. 41 Upper Brook Street, London. Rochetts, Brentwood, Essex. Berechurch Hall, Colchester. Carlton. S. of John Coope, Esq., of Great Cumberland Street, London, by Anna Maria, d. of J.C. Doorman, Esq. B. at Leyspring, Essex; m. 1848, Emily Mary, only d. of Capt. R. Fulcher. A well-known Brewer; Partner in the firm of Messrs. Ind, Coope, and Co., Romford, and Burton-on-Trent. A Magistrate and Dept.-Lieut. for Essex, and Hon. Col. Essex Rifle Volunteers. A Conservative, in favour of a re-adjustment of local taxation. Sat for Yarmouth from July 1847 to July 1848. Was an unsuccessful candidate for the Tower Hamlets, Dec. 1868. Sat for Middlesex 1874-85 and from that date for the Brentford division. MP until his death 27 Nov. 1886.   [1886]

COOPER, Hon. Anthony Henry Ashley, D.C.L. St. Leonards, Berkshire. Carlton. 3rd s. of the Earl of Shaftesbury, bro. of Lord Ashley, a member for the County (Dorset). B. 1807; m. 1835, Jane Frances, only d. of Rbt. Pattison, of Wrackleford House, Dorset. A Capt. in the army. A Conservative. Sat for Dorchester from 1831 until he retired 1847. Died 30 Nov. 1858.   [1847]

COOPER, Charles William. Cooper's Hill, Ballymole, Sligo Co. Son of the late Arthur Brooke Cooper, Esq., of Cooper's Hill, by Jane Frances, daughter of Charles O'Hara, Esq., of Annachmore, County of Sligo (who was member of Parliament for the county of Sligo for forty years). Born at Cooper's Hill in 1817; he was married in 1858 to Annie Charlotte, the eldest daughter of Richard Streatfeild, Esq., late of the Rocks, Uckfield, Sussex. Graduated at Trinity College, Dublin in 1838. He was made High Sheriff for Sligo in 1849. He was at one time a Magistrate and Deputy-Lieutenant for Sligo. A Conservative. He was first elected for the county of Sligo in May 1859, and he continued to sit until he retired in July 1865.   [1863]

COOPER, Edward Henry. 5 Bryanston Square, London. Markree Castle, Collooney, Ireland. Guards'. S. of Richard Wordsworth Cooper, Esq., of Dunboden, Mullingar, Ireland, by Emilia Eleanor, d. of 1st Visct. Frankfurt de Montmorency. Nephew of E.J.Cooper, Esq., who represented the Co. of Sligo for many years. B. at Lough Park, Co. Westmeath, 1827; m. 1858, Charlotte Maria, d. of Edward W. Mills, Esq. Educ. at Eton.

Entered the 7th Hussars, 1845; exchanged into the Grenadier Guards, 1852, and retired 1863 as Capt. and Lieut.-Col. A Conservative, and supported all measures that tended 'to develop the resources of Ireland.' First elected for the Co. of Sligo, July 1865. Defeated in 1868. Died 26 Feb. 1902.   [1867]

COOPER, Edward Joshua, F.R.S. Markree Castle, Co. Sligo. National. Eld. s. of Edward Synge Cooper, Esq. (who sat for the Co. of Sligo from 1806 till his death), by Anne, d. of Harry Verelst, Esq. B. in Dublin 1798; m. 1st, 1822, Sophia, 3rd d. of Col. Henry Paisley L'Estrange; 2ndly, 1827, Sarah Frances, d. of Owen Wynne, Esq., of Haslewood. Educ. at Armagh, Eton, and Christ Church, Oxford. Was Capt. Sligo Militia. A member of the Royal Irish Academy, and of several Foreign Artistical Institutions. Patron of 1 living. A Conservative, voted against the repeal of the malt tax. Sat for Sligo Co. from 1830 till July 1841; re-elected Apr. 1857. Retired in 1859. Died 23 Apr. 1863.   [1858]

COOTE, Sir Charles Henry, Bart. 5 Connaught Place, London. Ballyfin, Mountrath, Queen's Co. Carlton, Junior United Service, and Boodle's. Eld. s. of Childley Coote, Esq., of Ash Hill, by his 2nd wife, Elizabeth Ann, d. of the Rev. Ralph Carr, of Bath. M. Anne, d. of John Whaley, Esq., of Whaley Abbey, Co. Wicklow, and grandd. maternally of the 1st Earl of Clanwilliam (she died 1837). Was Col. of the Queen's Co. Militia from 1825. Premier Bart. of Ireland. Of moderate Conservative opinions, but voted in favour of the Reform Bill of 1831, and for Lord Palmerston's policy in China 1857. Was an unsuccessful candidate for Queen's Co. in 1818 and 1820; sat for that Co. from 1821 till 1847; regained his seat in July, 1852. Retired in 1859. Died 5 Oct. 1864.   [1858]

COPELAND, William Taylor. 160 New Bond Street, London. Russell Farm, Watford, Hertfordshire. Only s. of William Copeland, Esq., (partner of Josiah Spode, Esq., of the Stoke Potteries, Staffordshire, and of Portugal Street, London, Porcelain Manufacturers and Merchants). B. 1797; m. 1826, Sarah, d. of John Yates, Esq., of Shelton, Staffordshire (she died 1860). Succeeded his father as head of the firm in Portugal Street, and subsequently purchased the interest of the Spode family in the Potteries and in London. Was Sheriff of London in 1828-29. An Alderman of the City of London, a Dept.-Lieut. for London, and filled the office of Lord Mayor 1835-36. Treasurer of the Hon. Artillery Company. A Liberal-Conservative, supported the vote of censure on Lord Palmerston 1864; in favour of a moderate extension of the suffrage coincident with education. Contested Coleraine in 1831 and 1832 unsuccessfully, but was seated on petition in both years. Again elected for Coleraine 12 Jan. 1835. Sat for Stoke-upon-Trent from July 1837-July 1852, when he was unsuccessful; regained his seat in Mar. 1857. Retired 1865. Died 12 Apr. 1868. [1865]

CORBALLY, Matthew Elias. 35 Pall Mall, London. Corbalton Hall, Tara, Co. Meath. Brooks's, Arthur's, and Reform. Only s. of Elias Corbally, Esq., of Corbalton. Bro.-in-law of 9th Earl of Fingall. B. 1797; m. 1842, Hon. Matilda, d. of 12th Visct. Gormanston. An owner of tithes, 'but would never receive them.' High Sheriff of the Co. in 1838. A Liberal; voted for Lord Derby's Reform Bill Mar. 1859; in favour of the ballot, and tenant-right in Ireland. Opposed to the Ecclesiastical Tithes Act. Sat for the Co. of Meath from Feb. 1840 to July 1841; re-elected 1842. MP until his death 25 Nov. 1870. [1870]

CORBET, W.J. Continued in House after 1885: full entry in Volume II.

CORBETT, Col. Edward. Longnor Hall, Near Shrewsbury. Carlton. Eld. s. of Parton Corbett, Esq., of Longnor Hall, by Lucy Favoretta, d. of Mr. Jones, M.D., of Lichfield. B. at Sidmouth, Devon 1817; m. 1842, Elizabeth Anne Teresa, d. of Robert Shell, Esq. Educ. at Eton. Appointed Ensign 51st Light Infantry Mar. 1837; promoted to Lieut. July 1839. Retired from the army Oct. 1844. Lieut.-Col. of the Shropshire Militia since 1855. Patron of 1 living. A Conservative and voted against the disestablishment of the Irish Church 1869; in favour of the abolition of the malt tax, and its imposition in a reduced form upon beer. Sat for S. Shropshire from Dec. 1868 until he accepted Chiltern Hundreds July 1877. [1877]

CORBETT, J. Continued in House after 1885: full entry in Volume II.

CORBETT, Thomas George. Darnhall, Cheshire. Elsham Hall, Lincolnshire. Athenaeum. Patron of Elsham Vicarage. In 1826 contested Lincoln on the Reform interest, but later a Conservative. Sat for Lincolnshire N. from Jan. 1835 until he retired in 1837. [1837]

CORDES, Thomas. 14 St. James's Place, London. Bryn Glas, Newport, Monmouthshire. Carlton, and Windham. S. of James J. Cordes, Esq., by Mary, eld. d. of I. Lucas, Esq., of Hatcham Grove, Surrey. B. at Hatcham Grove 1826. A Dept.-Lieut. and Magistrate for the Co. of Monmouth, for which he was High Sheriff in

1871. A Conservative, and willing to give an Independent support to that party, in favour of a careful economy being observed in the public departments. Sat for the district of Monmouth from Feb. 1874 until defeated 1880. Contested the district of Monmouth 28 Nov. 1885. Died 16 Aug. 1901. [1880]

CORNISH, James. 35 Connaught Place, Blackhall, Nr. Totnes, Devon. A Solicitor at Totnes in partnership with his father. A Reformer. Returned for Totnes in 1832. Accepted Chiltern Hundreds in Feb. 1834. Sheriff of Devon 1852-53. Died 7 Sept. 1865. [1833]

CORRANCE, Frederick Snowdon. Broadwater, Framlingham, Suffolk. Carlton, and Junior United Service. Eld. s. of Frederick White, Esq., of Parham Hall, Suffolk (who in 1837 assumed the name of Corrance in lieu of his patronymic), by Frances, d. of William Woodley, Esq., Gov. of Berbice. B. 1822; m. 1860, Frances Maria, 2nd d. of Capt. du Cane, R.N., of Broxted Park, Essex. Educ. at Harrow and Trinity Coll., Cambridge. Entered 11th Hussars 1842, retired 1844. Dept.-Lieut. and a Magistrate for Suffolk. Patron of 1 living. A Conservative, gave a conscientious support to Mr. Disraeli, was in favour of substantial reforms being effected in the Irish Church, but voted against the disestablishment 1869. In favour also of the abolition of the malt tax. Elected for Suffolk E. Feb. 1867 until he retired 1874. Died 31 Oct. 1906. [1873]

CORRIGAN, Sir Dominick John, Bart. 4 Merrion Square West, Dublin. Inniscorrig, Dalkey, Ireland. S. of John Corrigan, Esq., of Dublin, Merchant. B. 1802; m. 1829, Joanna Mary, d. of William Woodlock, Esq., of Dublin. Graduated M.D. at Edinburgh University 1825, and at Dublin 1849. Became a member of the Coll. of Surgeons, England 1843. Physician in ordinary to the Queen in Ireland. A member of the Senate and Vice-chancellor of the Queen's University, Ireland. Was repeatedly elected President of the King's and Queen's Coll. of Physicians. President of the Pathological Society, Ireland, and Physician to the House of Industry Hospitals, Dublin, from which he retired in 1866. Author of numerous contributions to medical journals on *The Nature of Fever;* on *Famine and Fever as Cause and Effect in Ireland.* A Liberal. Unsuccessfully contested Nov. 1868, the city of Dublin for which he sat from Aug. 1870. Retired 1874. Died 1 Feb. 1880. [1873]

CORRY, Rt. Hon. Henry Thomas Lowry-. 68 Grosvenor Street, London. Carlton, and Travellers'. 2nd s. of 2nd Earl of Belmore, by 2nd

d. of 2nd Earl of Carrick. B. in Dublin 1803; m. 1830, Lady Harriet Anne, 2nd d. of 6th Earl of Shaftesbury (she died 1868). Educ. at Christ Church, Oxford, where he graduated M.A. 1829, was 2nd class in classics 1823. Was Controller of the Household in 1834 and 1835, a Lord of the Admiralty Sept. 1841-Feb. 1845, Sec. to the Admiralty Feb. 1845-July 1846 and from Mar. 1858-June 1859. Pres. of the Board of Health and Vice-Pres. of the Council from July 1866-Mar. 1867, and First Lord of the Admiralty from the last date until Dec. 1868. A Conservative. Sat for Tyrone from 1826. MP until his death 6 Mar. 1873. [1873]

CORRY, Hon. Henry William Lowry-. 95 Eaton Place, London. Edwardstone Hall, Boxford, Suffolk. Carlton, and Guards'. Youngest s. of the 3rd Earl of Belmore, by Emily Louise, youngest d. and co-heir of William Shepherd, Esq., of Bradbourne, Kent. Nephew to Rt. Hon. Henry Thomas Lowry-Corry, who sat for Tyrone from 1826 until his death in 1873. B. at Castlecool, Ireland 1845; m. 1876, Hon. Blanche Edith, d. of the 1st Visct. Halifax (she was born 1851). Was educ. at Trinity Coll., Cambridge. Entered the army as Ensign and Lieut. Coldstream Guards 1866, became Lieut. and Capt. 1868, Capt. and Lieut.-Col. 1877. Patron of 1 living. A Conservative. Sat for Tryone from Mar. 1873 until he retired 1880. Died 6 May 1927. [1880]

CORRY, Sir J.P. Continued in House after 1885: full entry in Volume II.

COTES, Charles Cecil. 12 Grosvenor Street, London. Woodcote, Newport, Shropshire. Devonshire, Brooks's, and Reform. Eld. s. of John Cotes, Esq., of Woodcote, near Newport, Shropshire, by Lady Louisa Harriett, 3rd d. of the 3rd Earl of Liverpool. B. at Woodcote 1846. Unmarried. Educ. at Eton and at Christ Church, Oxford; graduated B.A. 1869. Appointed a Lord of the Treasury Apr. 1880 (salary £1000). A Magistrate and a Dept.-Lieut. for Shropshire and Staffordshire. Appointed Capt. Shropshire Yeomanry Cavalry 1869; retired 1880. A Liberal, and in favour of 'progressive reform.' Sat from Feb. 1874 for Shrewsbury which he unsuccessfully contested Sept. 1870. Sat until he retired in 1885. Died 9 Aug. 1898. [1885]

COTES, John. Wood-cote, Shropshire. Of Whig principles, was elected in opposition to Mr. Gore, a Conservative. He was the first who had for a hundred years contested an election in Shropshire. Sat for Shropshire N. from 1832. Retired in 1835. Died 10 Jan. 1874. [1833]

COTTERELL, Sir Geers Henry, Bart. 9 Stratton Street, London. Garnons, Herefordshire. Reform. 3rd s. of John Henry Cotterell, Esq. (who was eld. s. of the 1st Bart. in this family), by the eld. d. of the 20th Lord Dacre (she m. 2ndly, Granville Harcourt Vernon, Esq.). B. in Mayfair, London 1834. Appointed a Dept.-Lieut. of Herefordshire 1856. Patron of 3 livings. A Liberal, giving 'a decided but independent support to Lord Palmerston's government'; in favour of extension of the franchise, and of 'a system of sound religious and secular education'; rejoiced 'over the excellent appointments to the Church made by Lord Palmerston.' First returned for Herefordshire in Apr. 1857. Retired in 1859. Sheriff of Herefordshire 1865; died 17 Mar. 1900. [1858]

COTTON, Hon. Wellington Henry Stapleton. 48 Belgrave Square, London. Combermere Abbey, Cheshire. Carlton, and White's. B. at Barbados 1818, the eld. s. of Lord Combermere, by the 2nd d. of William Fulke Greville. M. 1844, Susan Alice, eld. d. of Sir George Sitwell, Bart., of Renishaw, Derbyshire. Educ. at Eton. Entered the army in 1837 as Cornet and Sub-Lieut. in the 1st Life Guards. Became a Lieut. in 1841, Capt. in 1846 and Major unattached in 1850. A Conservative, first returned for Carrickfergus 1847, without opposition; he held this seat until his retirement in 1857. In Feb. 1865 he succeeded as 2nd Visct. Combermere. Died 1 Dec. 1891. [1856]

COTTON, William James Richmond. 27 St. Mary Axe, London. Woodside, Whetstone, Middlesex. Eld. s. of William Cotton, Esq., and Caroline his wife B. at Stratford-le-Bow 1822. Was for some time engaged in the office of a Solicitor and afterwards became a Partner in the firm Culverwell, Brooks, and Cotton, St. Mary Axe, established in 1824. Elected an Alderman of London 1866. Was Sheriff of London and Middlesex in 1868-9. A Magistrate for London, and for Middlesex and Hertfordshire, a Commissioner of Lieutenancy for London, Chairman of the City Police Committee, a Commissioner of inland revenue for Hertfordshire, Director of the London and Liverpool and Globe Fire and Life Offices, and Chairman of the Staines and West Drayton Railway Co. Elected to the first London School Board in 1870. Lord Mayor of London 1875-6. A Governor of Queen Anne's Bounty. Owner of extensive iron ore mines, situate on the West Coast of Norway. Wrote poems, and a brochure entitled *Smash*, referring to railway speculations, and also occasional contributions to the press. A Conservative. Was an unsuccessful candidate for Southwark, Dec. 1868; sat as Senior Member for London from Feb. 1874. Sat until defeated in 1885 after representation of City of London had been reduced from four members to two. Chamberlain of City of London from 1892. Died 4 June 1902. [1885]

COURTAULD, George. 39 St. James's Place, London. Cut Hedge, Halstead, Essex. Reform. S. of George Courtauld, Esq., of Bocking, Essex, and nephew of Samuel Courtauld, Esq., of Gosfield Hall, Essex. Of a French Huguenot family, his great-great-grandfather, Augustine Courtauld, having been driven from France at the revocation of the Edict of Nantes. B. 1830. Educ. at University Coll., London. A Liberal. Sat for Maldon from Dec. 1878. Retired in 1885. [1885]

COURTENAY, Lord. (I). 4 Bryanston Square, London. Powderham Castle, Devonshire. Carlton. Eld. s. of the Earl of Devon. B. 1807; m. 1830, d. of 3rd Earl Fortescue. A Dept.-Lieut of Devon. A Conservative, voted for agricultural protection 1846. First returned for Devonshire S. in 1841. Sat until he accepted Chiltern Hundreds Jan. 1849. Succeeded as 12th Earl Mar. 1859. Sec. to Poor Law Board 1852-58. Chancellor of Duchy of Lancaster 1866-67. President of Poor Law Board 1867-68. Died 18 Nov. 1888. [1847]

COURTENAY, Lord. (II). 23 Brook Street, London. Powderham Castle, Exeter. Carlton, White's, Boodle's and Travellers'. Eld. s. of the Earl of Devon, by Lady Elizabeth, 7th d. of 1st Earl Fortescue. B. in London 1836. Educ. at Christ Church, Oxford. Capt. South Devon Yeomanry Cavalry. Appointed a Dept.-Lieut. of Devon 1858. A Conservative, voted against the Irish Church being disestablished 1869, and opposed any measure which would weaken the union between Church and State. Sat for Exeter from Aug. 1864-Dec. 1868, from which date he sat for E. Devon. Accepted Chiltern Hundreds 1870. Succeeded as 12th Earl 18 Nov. 1888. Died 15 Jan. 1891. [1870]

COURTENAY, Philip. 13 Montague Street, Russell Square, London. M.A. of Cambridge; one of Her Majesty's Counsel and practised many years on the Northern Circuit. A Conservative. Returned for Bridgwater in 1837. Retired 1841. [1841]

COURTENAY, Visct. See COURTENAY, Lord. (I).

COURTNEY, L.H. Continued in House after 1885: full entry in Volume II.

COWAN, Charles. 32 Royal Terrace, Edinburgh. Valleyfield, Pennycuick, Scotland.

Reform. Eld. s. of Alexander Cowan, Esq., of Edinburgh, Merchant. B. in Edinburgh 1801; m. 1824, Catherine, 2nd d. of the Rev. William Menzies, Minister of Lanark. Educ. at the parish school of Pennycuick, at the High School of Edinburgh, at the University of Edinburgh, and at the University or 'Auditoire' of Geneva. From Oct. 1822, was a Paper-Manufacturer at different mills on the Esk and Water of Leith: author of the article on the manufacture of paper in the *Encyclopaedia Britannica*, also of some pamphlets. Was an elder in the Church of Scotland from May 1830, to May 1843, and an acting elder in the Free Church. A Director of the Chamber of Commerce in Edinburgh. A Liberal, voted for the ballot, 1853, and against church-rates 1855; took a prominent part in the National Anti-Excise Association, and was 'desirous of relieving all useful trades and manufactures from the fetters of the Excise.' First returned for Edinburgh City in 1847. Sat until he retired in 1859. Died 29 Mar. 1889. [1858]

COWAN, James. 100 St. George's Square, London. 35 Royal Terrace, Edinburgh. Devonshire, and University, Edinburgh. S. of Alexander Cowan, Esq., of Penicuik, Nr. Edinburgh, by Elizabeth, d. of George Hall, Esq., of Liverpool, Merchant. Bro. of Charles Cowan, Esq., who sat for Edinburgh from 1847-59. B. 1816; m. 1841, Charlotte, d. of Duncan Cowan, Esq. Educ. at the High School and Univ. of Edinburgh. A Paper Manufacturer. Was Lord Provost of Edinburgh from Nov. 1872-Mar. 1874. A Liberal; in favour of the amendment of the Land Laws so as to simplify the transfer of land. Sat for the City of Edinburgh from Feb. 1874 until he accepted Chiltern Hundreds Oct. 1882. Died 24 Nov. 1895. [1882]

COWEN, Joseph. 23 Onslow Square, London. Stella Hall, Blaydon-on-Tyne. B. at Blaydon Barn, Co. Durham 1831, the s. of Sir Joseph Cowen (MP for Newcastle-on-Tyne July 1865 until his death Dec. 1873), by Mary, d. of Anthony Newton, Esq., of Winlaton. M. Jane, d. of John Thompson, Esq., of Fatfield. Educ. at Edinburgh University. A Coal-owner and Fire-brick and Clay retort Manufacturer. Proprietor of the *Newcastle Weekly Chronicle* and the *Newcastle Daily Chronicle*. Wrote numerous political pamphlets. A 'Radical Reformer', seeking the disestablishment of the Church, the abolition of the game laws, short Parliaments etc. In favour of Home Rule for Ireland. Sat for Newcastle-on-Tyne from Jan. 1874 to 1886, when he retired. Died 17 Feb. 1900. [1886]

COWEN, Sir Joseph. 3 Redcliffe Square,

London. Brompton, London. Stella Hall, Blaydon-on-Tyne. Reform. Eld. s. of John Cowen, Esq., of Winlaton, Durham, by Mary, his wife. B. at Greenside, Durham 1800; m. 1822, Mary, d. of Anthony Newton, Esq., of Winlaton (she died 1851). A Coal-owner, also a Fire-brick and Clay-retort Manufacturer. An Alderman of Newcastle and a Magistrate for the Co. of Durham. Was Chairman of the Gateshead Board of Guardians for 13 years and for 13 years Chairman of the Tyne Improvement Commission, of which he was a life member appointed by Act of Parliament. A 'Radical Reformer'; in favour of shorter Parliaments and a more equitable apportionment of members to population, the reduction of the county franchise to the same amount as boroughs etc. First elected for Newcastle July 1865. MP until his death 19 Dec. 1873. [1873]

COWPER, Hon. Henry Frederick. 4 St. James's Square, London. Penshanger, Hertford. Devonshire. 2nd s. of 6th Earl Cowper, by the eld. d. and co-heir of 1st Earl De Grey. B. 1836. Appointed a Dept.-Lieut. of Kent 1848; Capt. in 1st Hertfordshire Rifle Volunteers 1860. A Liberal, in favour of the revision of local taxation. Unsuccessfully contested Tamworth 12 Oct. 1863. In Feb. 1864 unsuccessfully contested Hertfordshire for which he sat from July 1865 until defeated in 1885 contesting East Hertfordshire. Died 10 Nov. 1887. [1885]

COWPER, W. See COWPER-TEMPLE, Rt. Hon. W.F.

COWPER-TEMPLE, Rt. Hon. William Francis. 15 Great Stanhope Street, London. Brockett Hall, Hertfordshire. Broadlands, Hampshire. Brooks's, Reform, Travellers' and Boodle's. 2nd s. of 5th Earl Cowper, by Hon. Emily Mary, d. of 1st Visct. Melbourne (she m. 2ndly, the celebrated Visct. Palmerston.). B. at Brockett Hall 1811; m. 1st, d. of Daniel Gurney, Esq., (dead); 2ndly, 1848, Elizabeth, youngest d. of Admiral and Lady Elizabeth Tollemache. Formerly a Lieut. in the Royal Horse Guards, became a Major in the army 1852, was Aide-de-Camp to the Lord-Lieut. of Ireland, Private Sec. to. Visct. Melbourne, a commissioner of Greenwich Hospital, and a Lord of the Treasury. Was a Lord of the Admiralty from July 1846-Mar. 1852, and from Dec. following until Feb. 1855. Under-Sec. of State for the Home Dept. from the last date until Aug. 1855. Pres. of the Board of Health from Aug. 1855-Feb. 1857, and from Sept. 1857-Mar. 1858, and Vice Pres. of the Education Committee of the Privy Council from Feb. 1857-Mar. 1858. Vice-Pres. of the Board of Trade, and Paymaster-Gen. from Aug.

1859-Feb. 1860, and Commissioner of Works and Buildings from the last date until July 1866. A Liberal, in favour of local taxation being 'relieved of its heavy burdens', also of tenant farmers being secured the value of their improvements. Sat for Hertford from 1835 to Dec. 1868, from which date he sat for Hampshire S. Sat until he retired 1880. Created Baron Mount Temple May 1880. Died 17 Oct. 1888. [1880]

COX, E.W. B. at Taunton 1809. Barrister 1843. Recorder of Helston and Falmouth 1857-68. MP for Taunton Nov. 1868 to Jan. 1869, when he was unseated on petition. Chairman of Second Court of Middlesex Sessions 1870 until his death 24 Nov. 1879.

COX, William. Pinners Hall, Old Broad Street, London. S. of William Cox, Esq., by Olive, d. of — Best, Esq. B. in London 1817; m. 1840, Emma, d. of Francis William Angeil, Esq., Solicitor. Practised as a Solicitor from 1840. Elected a member of the Common Council of London 1851. A Liberal, in favour of the ballot, of shortening the duration of Parliaments, a large extension of the franchise, and redistribution of seats. Sat for Finsbury from Mar. 1857 to Apr. 1859, when he was an unsuccessful candidate; re-elected Dec. 1861. Defeated 1865. Contested same seat in 1868. Died 12 Dec. 1889. [1865]

COX, William Thomas. Spondon Hall, near Derby. 2nd s. of Roger Cox, Esq., of Spondon Hall, near Derby, by Frances, d. of George Richardson, Esq., of Derby. B. at Derby 1808; m. 1839, Maria, d. of the Rev. Edward Edwards, of Lynn, Norfolk. A Merchant. A Magistrate for the bor. and Co. of Derby. High Sheriff of the latter 1861; Mayor of Derby 1860, and again 1861. A Conservative, in favour of a wide extension of the suffrage, and of 'a compromise' on the church-rate question. First elected for Derby, July 1865. Defeated in 1868. Contested same seat in 1874. [1867]

CRAIG, Rt. Hon. Sir William Gibson, Bart. 22 Lowndes Street, London. Riccarton, Midlothian. Brooks's. Eld. s. of Sir Jas. Gibson Craig, 1st Bart., of Riccarton, by the d. of James Thompson, Esq., of Edinburgh. B. 1797. M. 1840, d. of J.H. Vivian, Esq., of Singleton, Glamorganshire. An Advocate at the Scottish Bar. Appointed a Lord of the Treasury, July 1846, salary, £1,200. A Liberal. Represented the county of Edinburgh from 1837 to 1841, having been an unsuccessful candidate in 1835. Sat for the city of Edinburgh from 1841 until he retired in 1852. Lord Clerk Register 1862-78, and Keeper of Signet for Scotland. Died 12 Mar. 1878. [1852]

CRAIG, William Young. Milton House, Alsager, Stoke-on-Trent. Reform, and National Liberal. S. of Mr. John Craig, of Burntisland, by Jane, d. of Mr. William Young. B. at Haggerston, Northumberland, 1827; m. 1857, Harriet Milton, d. of Mr. Richard Donaldson Stanney, of the Isle of Wight. A Mining Engineer in London, and a Coal and Ironstone Master. Was elected President of North Staffordshire Institute of Mining and Mechanical Engineers for 1870 and 1880. Wrote several papers on mining subjects. A Liberal, in favour of the extension of the county franchise, and of a redistribution of seats, a reform of the Land Laws, and the placing of real and personal estates on the same footing in the eye of the law. Sat for North Staffordshire from Apr. 1880 until he retired in 1885.   [1885]

CRANBORNE, Rt. Hon. Visct. 1 Mansfield Street, Portland Place, London. Carlton, and Junior Carlton. B. at Hatfield 1830, the eld. surviving s. of Marq. of Salisbury, by his 1st wife, Frances Mary, only d. and heir of Bamber Gascoigne. M. 1857, Georgiana Caroline, eld. d. of Hon. Baron Alderson. Educ. at Eton and at Christ Church, Oxford, obtaining a fellowship at All Soul's in 1853. Appointed Sec. of State for India (salary £5,000), July 1866, and again 1874-78; Sec. of State for Foreign Affairs 1878-80; Prime Minister June 1885-Feb. 1886, and from June 1886-1902. Was also a Dept.-Lieut. and Magistrate of Middlesex. A Conservative; opposed any fundamental change in the constitution, and any system of national education not 'based on the truths of Revelation.' Sat for Stamford from Aug. 1853 until he succeeded as 3rd Marq. of Salisbury in Apr. 1868. Died 22 Aug. 1903.   [1867]

CRAUFURD, Edward Henry John. 89 Belgrave Road, London. 3 Essex Court, Temple, London. Crosby Castle, W. Kilbryde, Ayrshire. Brooks's, and Oxford & Cambridge. Eld. s. of John Craufurd, Esq., of Auchinames and Crosbie, Ayrshire (formerly Trearurer Gen. of the Ionian Islands), by Sophia Marianna, d. of Maj-.Gen. Horace Churchill, and great grand-d. of Sir Robert Walpole. B. in London 1816; m. 1863 Frances, only d. of the Rev. William Molesworth, incumbent of St. Breoke, Cornwall, and sister of Sir Paul William Molesworth, Bart., of Pencarrow. Educ. at Trinity Coll., Cambridge, where he obtained a Scholarship, was 12th Senior Optime 1841, and graduated M.A. 1844. Was called to the bar at the Inner Temple Nov. 1845. Formerly editor of *The Legal Examiner*. A Magistrate for Ayrshire and a Dept.-Lieut. of Buteshire. A Liberal, voted for the disestablishment of the Irish Church 1869. In favour of the repeal of the rate-paying clause of the Reform Act and of the assimilation of the county to the borough franchise. First returned for Ayr district July 1852. Sat until defeated 1874. Died 29 Aug. 1887.   [1873]

CRAWFORD, James Sharman. Crossgar, Ireland. Reform. Ulster Club, Belfast. 3rd s. of William Sharman Crawford, Esq., who sat for Dundalk and for Rothdale, by Mabel, 4th d. of John Crawford, Esq., of Crawfordstown, Co. Down. He assumed the name of Crawford under the will of his father-in-law. B. at Waringstown 1812. Was educ. at Trinity Coll., Dublin. Was engaged as a land-agent from 1835. A Liberal, was in favour of a system of tenant-right more complete than that given by the Irish Land Act of 1870; also favoured an amendment of the Grand Jury Laws and economy in the public finances. Sat for the Co. of Down from Feb. 1874. MP until his death Apr. 1878.   [1878]

CRAWFORD, Robert Wigram. 20 Eaton Square, London. Crum Castle, Newtownbutler, Ireland. Carlton. 4th s. of William Crawford, Esq., who sat for London from 1833-41. B. 1813; m. 1836, d. of the Rev. John Cruickshank, of Turriff, Scotland. A Partner in the firm of Crawford, Colvin and Company, E. India Merchants and Agents. A Director of the Bank of England, of which he had been Dept.-Gov. Chairman of the E. Indian Railway. A Commissioner of Lieutenancy for London and an E. India Proprietor. A Reformer, voted for the disestablishment of the Irish Church 1869. Unsuccessfully contested Harwich Mar. 1851, but was elected May following, when the seat became vacant on petition. In July of the same year was displaced on petition, in consequence of the premature removal of a polling booth. First elected for the City of London Apr. 1857. Sat until he retired 1874. Died 30 July 1889.   [1873]

CRAWFORD, William. 14 Upper Wimpole Street, London. 71 Broad Street, London. Reform. S. of Mr. Crawford of Brighton. A Director of the Alliance Assurance Company. Early in life went out to India in the service of the East India Company and returned after having realised a handsome fortune. Was a Partner in the East India Mercantile House of Crawford, Colwin and Company, formerly Bazett & Farquhar. Of Whig principles, in favour of the abolition of the Window Taxes; opposed to short Parliaments, and the Corn Laws. Was an unsuccessful candidate for Brighton at the general election in 1832; but was returned for London in Aug. 1833 and sat until he was defeated in June 1841.   [1841]

CRAWFORD, William Sharman. 5 Radnor Place, Hyde Park Gardens, London. Crawfordsburn, Co. Down. Reform. Took the surname of Crawford in addition to and after that of Sharman, in pursuance of the will of John Crawford, Esq., to whose estates he succeeded. A Liberal, in favour of the ballot. Contested Belfast in 1832. Sat for Dundalk from 1834 till 1837. Represented Rochdale from 1841. Sat until he retired in 1852. [1852]

CRAWLEY, Samuel. 59 Portland Place. Stockwood, Bedfordshire. Of Whig principles. In favour of the ballot; a fixed duty on corn. Patron of 1 living. Sat for Bedford from 1832. Defeated in 1837. [1837]

CREMORNE, Visct. 30 Curzon Street, London. Dartrey, Rockcorry, Ireland. Guards'. Eld. s. of the Earl of Dartrey, by Augusta, 2nd d. of Edward Stanley, Esq. B. 1842. Educ. at Eton. Became Ensign and Lieut. Coldstream Guards 1859, Lieut. and Capt. 1865. A Liberal. First elected for Monaghan July 1865. Retired 1868. Succeeded as 2nd Earl 12 May 1897. Died 1920. [1868]

CRESSWELL, Addison John Baker. 6 Sackville Passage, Conduit Street, London. Cresswell, Northumberland. Carlton. Eld. s. of Francis Cresswell, Esq., of Cresswell, and therefore bro. to the Judge. B. 1788; m. 1818, d. of G.L. Reid, Esq. Was High Sheriff of Northumberland 1821. Patron of 1 living. A Conservative, voted for agricultural protection 1846. First returned for Northumberland N. in 1841. Retired 1847. Died 5 May 1879. [1847]

CRESSWELL, Cresswell. Fleming House, Old Brompton, London. 1 Mitre Court Buildings, London. S. of F. Easterby, Esq., of Blackheath who assumed the name of Cresswell, and therefore bro. to the Member for Northumberland. A Barrister and a Queen's Counsel. A Conservative. Elected for Liverpool after the dissolution in 1837, defeating Mr. Ewart, the former member. Sat until appointed Judge 22 Jan. 1841. Knighted 4 May 1842. Died 29 July 1863. [1841]

CREWE, Sir George Harpur, Bart. 21 Hyde Park Terrace, London. Calke Abbey, Derbyshire. Carlton. Grands. of Sir Henry Harpur, MP for Derbyshire, whose estates he inherited. B. 1795; m. 1819, d. of Rev. Thomas Whitaker. Patron of 8 livings. A Conservative. Returned for Derbyshire S. in 1835. Retired 1841. Died Jan. 1844. [1838]

CREYKE, Ralph. Queen Anne's Mansions, London. Rawcliffe Hall, Selby. Marton Hall, Burlington. Devonshire, and Brooks's. Only s. of Ralph Creyke, Esq., of Morton and Rawcliffe Hall, Yorkshire, by Louisa 2nd d. of Col. Croft, of Stillington Hall, Yorkshire. B. at Rawcliffe Hall 1849; m. 1882, Frances Elizabeth, eld. surviving d. of Sir Henry Hickman Bacon, Bart., of Thonock Hall, Lincolnshire. Was educ. at Eton and at Cambridge. A Magistrate for the East and West Ridings of Yorkshire, and for Middlesex and Westminster. A Liberal, in favour of the assimilation of the borough and county franchise, and the full compensation of tenants for improvement. Sat for York City from Apr. 1880. Retired 1885. Chairman of the Yorkshire Liberal Unionist Federation. High Sheriff of Yorkshire 1894. Died 17 Apr. 1908. [1883]

CRICHTON, Visct. 12 St. George's Place, London. Crum Castle, Newton Butler, Ireland. Carlton. Eld. s. of the 3rd Earl of Erne, by Selina, 2nd d. of the Rev. Charles Cobbe Beresford, and cousin to the Marq. of Waterford. B. in Dublin 1839; m. 1870, Lady Florence Mary, d. of the 3rd Earl of Enniskillen. Educ. at Eton and at Christ Church, Oxford, where he graduated B.A. 1861. Was a Lord of the Treasury from Feb. 1876 to Apr. 1880. Appointed Capt. Fermanagh Militia 1862. A Conservative. Sat for Enniskillen from Dec. 1868 to Apr. 1880, from which date he sat for Fermanagh. Sat until he succeeded as 4th Earl of Erne Oct. 1885. Died 2 Dec. 1914. [1885]

CRICHTON-STUART, James Frederick Dudley. See STUART, James Frederick Dudley Crichton-.

CRIPPS, Joseph. 85 St. James's Street, Cirencester. A Banker in Cirencester, and an East India Proprietor. Dept.-Gov. of the Van Diemen's Land Co. Was a Col. of Volunteers. A Conservative. Sat for Cirencester from 1807 until he retired in 1841. [1840]

CRIPPS, William. 38 St. James's Place, London. Cirencester. S. of Joseph Cripps, Esq., who represented Cirencester from 1807 till 1841. M. d. of Benjamin Harrison, Esq., Chairman of the Exchequer Loan Commission. A Barrister, M.A. of Trinity Coll., Oxford, and Vinerian Fellow. A Conservative, but in favour of free trade. Was a Lord of the Treasury. Sat for Cirencester from 1841. MP until his death in 1848. [1847 2nd ed.]

CROFT, Sir Herbert George Denman, Bart. Lugwardine Court, Herefordshire. Oxford & Cambridge. Only s. of Sir Archer Denman Croft

(8th Bart.), of Croft Castle, by Julia Barbara, d. of Maj-Gen. John Carstin, of Calcutta, and widow of Athelstan Corbet, Esq., of Ynys-y-Maengwyne, Merionethshire. B. at Acton 1838; m. 1865, his cousin, Georgina Eliza Lucy, eld. d. of Matthew H. Marsh, Esq. (formerly member for Salisbury), of Ramridge House, Hampshire. Educ. at Eton and Merton Coll., Oxford, graduated B.A. 1860, M.A. 1864. Called to the bar at the Inner Temple Nov. 1861 and joined the Oxford Circuit. A Magistrate and Dept.-Lieut. for Herefordshire and a Lieut. Herefordshire Militia. A Conservative, voted against the disestablishment of the Irish Church 1869. Sat from Dec. 1868 for Herefordshire, which Co. had been represented by members of his family fifteen times in Parliament from 1307-1695. Retired 1874. Died 11 Feb. 1902. [1873]

CROMPTON, Joshua Samuel. Limmer's Hotel, London. Sion Hill, Yorkshire. Of Whig principles, in favour of the immediate abolition of slavery. Sat for Derby in the Parliament of 1826. Returned for Ripon in 1832. Retired in 1835. Died 17 June 1881. [1883]

CROMPTON, Samuel. Woodend, Yorkshire. University. S. of S. Crompton, Esq., of Wood End, and of Sarah, d. of S. Fox, Esq., of Derby. M. 1829, Isabella, d. of the Hon. and Rev. Archibald Hamilton Cathcart, of Kippax, Yorkshire. A moderate Reformer, voted for Lord John Russell's Reform motion in the Parliament; was friendly to Lord Melbourne's administration, opposed to the ballot and to shortening the duration of Parliaments; in favour of Corn Laws and a modified poor-rate in Ireland. Sat for Retford from 1818-1826; from then for Derby until 1830; was elected for Thirsk in 1834. Sat until he retired in 1841. Died 1849. [1838]

CROOK, Joseph. Chamber Hall, Nr. Bolton. Reform. Eld. s. of Joshua Crook, Esq., of Whitebank, near Bolton. B. at Bolton 1809; m. 1856, Mary, eld. d. of Thomas Biggs, Esq., of Upper Bedford Place, Russell Square, London. A Cotton-Spinner at Bolton. A Liberal, in favour of 'manhood suffrage', vote by ballot, direct taxation, annual Parliaments, and a more equal distribution of electoral districts; voted, however for Lord Derby's Reform Bill, Mar. 1859. First returned for Bolton in July 1852. Accepted Chiltern Hundreds 1861. Died 8 Dec. 1884. [1860]

CROPPER, James. Eller Green, Kendal. Reform. Eld. s. of John Cropper, Esq., of Dingle Bank, Liverpool, by Anne, d. of John Wakefield,

Esq., of Kendal. B. at Liverpool 1823; m. 1845, Fanny, d. of John Wakefield, Esq., of Sedgewick, Westmorland. Educ. at the Royal Institution, Liverpool, and University of Edinburgh. Formerly a Paper Manufacturer at Kendal. A Magistrate and Dept.-Lieut. for Westmorland, of which Co. he was High Sheriff 1875. A Liberal. Sat for Kendal from Dec. 1880; defeated in 1885 contesting Kendal division of Westmorland. Chairman of Westmorland County Council 1889, until he died 16 Oct. 1900. [1885]

CROSLAND, Thomas Pearson. Gledholt, Huddersfield. Eld. s. of George Crosland, Esq., of Crosland Lodge, near Huddersfield, by Mary Ann, d. of John Pearson, Esq., of Crosland Hill. B. at Crosland Moor, near Huddersfield 1815; m. 1st, Ann, d. of William Kilner, Esq.; 2ndly, Matilda, d. of William Cousins, Esq., of Bristol; 3rdly, in Prussia, Julia, another d. of William Cousins, Esq. A Merchant and Woollen Manufacturer. A Magistrate, and Dept.-Lieut. of the West Riding of York. Lieut.-Col. of the 5th Administrative batt. of West York Volunteers. A Liberal, and in favour of a 6/- rating franchise in boroughs and 10/- in counties, and the eventual extension of the right of voting to all payers of income-tax; voted however against Lord Russell's Reform Bill 1866; opposed to the ballot. First elected for Huddersfield July 1865 and sat until his death 8 Mar. 1868. [1867]

CROSS, John Kynaston. 19 Eaton Square, London. Fernclough, Bolton. Reform, and Devonshire. Eld. s. of John Cross, Esq., of Gartside House, Bolton, by Hannah, only d. of Richard Kynaston, Esq., of Bolton. B. 1832; m. 1858, Emily, d. of James Carlton, Esq., of Manchester. A Cotton Spinner at Bolton. A Magistrate for Bolton. Appointed Under-Secretary for India, Jan. 1883 (salary £1500). A 'Radical, in favour of Ireland having extended to her all privileges enjoyed by England, while opposing any measure tending to the disintegration of the Empire.' Sat for Bolton from Feb. 1874. Sat until defeated in 1885. Died (suicide) 20 Mar. 1887. [1885]

CROSS, Rt. Hon. Sir Richard Assheton, G.C.B., F.R.S. 12 Warwick Street, London. Eccle Riggs, Broughton-in-Furness. Carlton, Athenaeum, and St. Stephen's. B. at Redscar 1823, s. of William Cross, Esq., of Redscar, Nr. Preston (a Dept.-Lieut. for Lancashire), and Ellen, his wife. M. 1852, Georgiana, d. of Thomas Lyon, Esq., of Appleton Hall, Warrington. Educ. at Rugby and at Trinity Coll., Cambridge. Created D.C.L. Oxon. 1877, Hon. LL.D. Cambridge 1878, Hon. LL.D. St. Andrew's 1885. Called to the bar 1849 at the Inner Temple, became a Bencher and joined the Northern Circuit. Was Sec. of State for the Home Dept. Feb. 1874-Apr.1880, and again 1885. An Ecclesiastical Commissioner for England, a Magistrate for Cheshire and Lancashire, a Dept.-Lieut. for Lancashire and Chairman of the Lancashire Quarter Sessions. Presented with the Freedom of the City of Glasgow 1876, and of the City of Aberdeen and of Paisley 1883. A Conservative. Sat for Preston Mar. 1857 to Mar. 1862 and for S.W. Lancashire from Dec. 1868 to July 1886, when he was created 1st Visct. Cross. Became Sec. for India 1886-92. Died 8 Jan. 1914.   [1886]

CROSSE, Thomas Bright. Shaw Hill, Lancashire. Carlton, University, and Athenaeum. Only s. of Thomas Iken, Esq. B. 1796; m. 1828, d. of Richard Legh, Esq., (formerly Richard Crosse, Esq.) Assumed the name and arms of Crosse by royal licence on his marriage, his lady having succeeded to the Lancashire estates of the family of Crosse, which had been settled in that Co. since the reign of Edward I. A Dept.-Lieut. of Lancashire, and served the office of High Sheriff in 1837. A Conservative. First returned for Wigan in 1841. Unseated on petition Apr. 1842. Died 21 Mar. 1886.   [1842]

CROSSLEY, Sir Francis, Bart. Belle Vue, Halifax. Somerleyton, Lowestoft, Suffolk. Reform, and Brooks's. S. of John Crossley, Esq., of Halifax, Carpet Manufacturer. B. at Halifax 1817; m. 1845 Martha Eliza, d. of Henry Brinton, Esq., of Kidderminster. A Carpet Manufacturer in Halifax. A Magistrate and Dept.-Lieut. for the W. Riding of Yorkshire. A Magistrate for E. Suffolk. A Liberal; voted in favour of the disestablishment of the Irish Church 1869; in favour of vote by ballot. Sat for Halifax from July 1852 to Apr. 1859, and for the whole of the W. Riding of Yorkshire from the last date till July 1865, when he was elected for the Northern div. MP until his death 5 Jan. 1872.   [1871]

CROSSLEY, John. Manor Heath, Halifax. S. of John Crossley, Esq., Carpet Manufacturer, by Martha, d. of Abraham Turner, Esq., of Scout Hall, Halifax. Brother to Sir Francis Crossley, Bart., who sat for Halifax from 1852-9, and afterwards for the North Riding of Yorkshire. B. at Halifax 1812; m. 1st, Anne, d. of Kitchenman Child, Esq., of Ovenden, Halifax; 2ndly, Sarah, d. of Josiah Wheatley, Esq., of Minefield. Magistrate for the W. Riding of Yorkshire and Halifax, was 4 times Mayor of the latter town. Governing Director of the John Worsley and Son's Co. (Ltd.) and Chairman of the Halifax Commercial Banking Co. (Ltd.). A Liberal; supported Mr. Gladstone; was in favour of the amendment of the Educational Act, not only by the repeal of the 25th clause, but by other alteration; was in favour also of religious equality. Sat for Halifax from Feb. 1874. Accepted Chiltern Hundreds Feb. 1877. Died 16 Apr. 1879. [1876]

CROWDER, Richard Budden. 17 Carlton House Terrace, London. 1 Brick Court, Temple, London. Athenaeum. Reform, and Brooks's. B. in London, the s. of William Henry Crowder of Montague Place. Unmarried. Educ. at Eton and at Trinity Coll., Cambridge. Was called to the bar at Lincoln's Inn in 1821 and joined the Western Circuit. Became Queen's Counsel 1837. Made Recorder of Bristol in Aug. 1846. Counsel for the Admiralty, Judge-Advocate to the Fleet and Dept.-Lieut. of Cornwall. A Reformer, in favour of extension of the suffrage, in proportion as the people become better educated and 'decidedly opposed to the arrogant assumption of dominion by the Priesthood, whether Roman Catholic or Protestant.' Unsuccessfully contested Winchester in 1841. First returned for Liskeard in Jan. 1849, without opposition, and sat until 1854, when in Mar. he was appointed Judge and on 3 May he was Knighted. Died 5 Dec. 1859. [1853]

CRUM, Alexander. 10 Park Place, St. James's, London. Thornliebank, Near Glasgow. Kelburne, Nr. Greenock. Windham, and Devonshire. Eld. s. of Walter Crum, Esq., F.R.S., of Thornliebank, near Glasgow, by Jessie, d. of William Graham, Esq., of Burntshiel, Renfrewshire. B. 1828; m. 1863, Margaret Nina, eld. d. of the Rt. Rev. Alexander Ewing, LL.D., D.C.L., Bishop of Argyll. Educ. in Germany and at Glasgow University. A Merchant. A Magistrate and Dept.-Lieut. of Lanark and Renfrewshire. A Liberal. Was an unsuccessful candidate for Glasgow Feb. 1874; sat for Renfrewshire from Nov. 1880. Retired in 1885. Died 23 Aug. 1893.   [1883]

CRUM-EWING, H.E. See EWING, H.E. Crum-.

CUBITT, Rt. Hon. George. Continued in House after 1885: full entry in Volume II.

CUBITT, William. 20 Abchurch Lane, London. Penton Lodge, Nr. Andover, Hampshire. Carlton. B. at Buxton, Norfolk, 1791; m. 1814, Elizabeth, 2nd d. of William Scarlett, Esq., of Norfolk (she died 1854). In early youth served for a short time in the navy; subsequently became a Builder; and for many years carried on that business on a large scale at Gray's Inn Road, London. Elected Sheriff of London and Middlesex 1847, and an Alderman of the city of London 1851; elected Lord Mayor

1860-61, re-elected 1861-62. A Commissioner of Lieutenancy for London. A Magistrate for Middlesex and for Surrey. A Conservative, and a supporter of Church and State, but voted for the abolition of church-rates 1855; in favour of the repeal of the malt tax. Sat for Andover from Aug. 1847 till July 1861, when he accepted Chiltern Hundreds to stand unsuccessfully for the city of London. Again elected for Andover 17 Dec. 1862 and was MP until his death 28 Oct. 1863. [1863]

CUNINGHAME, Sir William James Montgomery. 16 Eccleston Square, London. Gleumvoir, Ayrshire. Carlton. Eld. s. of Sir Thomas M. Cuninghame, 7th Bart., by Charlotte, the only child of Hugh Hutcheson, Esq., of Southfield, Renfrewshire. B. 1834; m. Elizabeth, d. of E.B. Hartopp, Esq., of Dalby Hall, Melton Mowbray. Educ. at Harrow. Entered the army 1853, appointed Capt. Rifle Brigade 1855, served throughout the Russian War, for which he received a medal and 4 clasps, the 5th class of the Order of the Medjidie, and the Victoria Cross for personal valour; became a Major Aug. 1867, and placed on half-pay Aug. 1871. A Conservative. Sat for the district of Ayr from Feb. 1874. Defeated 1880. Contested the College division of Glasgow 27 Nov. 1885. Died 11 Nov. 1897. [1880]

CUNLIFFE, J.C.P. A Conservative. First elected for Bewdley 11 Mar. 1869 but on petition and scrutiny the election was declared void and he did not stand at the subsequent election on 30 Apr. 1869.

CUNLIFFE, Sir Robert Alfred, Bart. 37 Lowndes Street, London. Acton Park, Wrexham, North Wales. Travellers', and Brooks's. Eld. s. of Robert Ellis Cunliffe, Esq., of the Bengal Civil Service (eld. s. of Sir Robert Cunliffe, the 4th Bart.), by Charlotte, eld. d. of Iltid Howel, Esq. B. 1839; m. 1869, Eleanor Sophia Egerton, only d. of Col. Egerton Leigh, of West Hall, High Leigh, and Jodrell Hall, Cheshire. Was educ. at Eton. Appointed Ensign and Lieut. Scots Fusilier Guards 1857, Lieut. and Capt. 1862, and retired the same year. Appointed Lieut.-Col. Commandant of Denbighshire Militia 1872. A Magistrate and Dept.-Lieut. of Denbighshire, of which he served as High Sheriff in 1868. A Liberal, and a supporter of Mr. Gladstone, in favour of an extension of the franchise. Sat for Flint district from Oct. 1872 to Jan. 1874, when he stood unsuccessfully; sat for Denbighshire district from Apr. 1880; defeated in 1885; contested Flintshire as a Liberal Unionist in 1892. Died 18 June 1905. [1885]

CURRIE, Sir D. Continued in House after 1885: full entry in Volume II.

CURRIE, Henry. 69 Park Street, Grosvenor Square, London. 29 Cornhill, London. West Horseley Place, Guildford, Surrey. Travellers', and Boodle's. 2nd s. of William Currie, Esq., of East Horseley Park, Surrey, by the d. of Francis Gore, Esq. Cousin to Raikes Currie, Esq., MP for Northampton. B. at Westminster, 1798; m. Emma, d. of Col. Knox, of the Grenadier Guards. Educ. at Eton. A Banker in London. A 'Liberal Conservative'. Unsuccessfully contested Guildford in 1841; returned at the head of the poll in 1847. Retired in 1852. Contested Surrey W. 6 Apr. 1857. Died 26 May 1873. [1852]

CURRIE, Raikes. 4 Hyde Park Terrace, London. Sandling Park, Hythe, Kent. Athenaeum, and Reform. 2nd. s. of Isaac Currie, Esq., of Bush Hill, Middlesex, by the eld. d. of William Raikes, Esq. Cousin of the Rt. Hon. C.S. Lefevre, and of Sir Frederick Currie, Bart. B. 1801; m. 1825, Hon. Sophia, d. of 2nd Lord Wodehouse. Educ. at Eton. A Banker in London, a Bank and East India Proprietor, Director of the Sun Fire Office, a Magistrate for Buckinghamshire and Essex. A Magistrate and Dept.-Lieut. of Middlesex. A Liberal, advocated national education, Church reform, and vote by ballot. Was first elected for Northampton July 1837. Sat until he unsuccessfully contested London 27 Mar. 1857. Died 16 Oct. 1881. [1857]

CURRY, William. 37 Summer Hill, Dublin. Only s. of William Curry, Esq. B. 16 Aug. 1784. A Queen's Counsel in Ireland. Of Liberal opinions. Returned for City of Armagh in 1835. Accepted Chiltern Hundreds in 1839. [1839]

CURTEIS, Ed. Barrett. Windmill Hill, Sussex. 2nd s. of Ed. Jer. Curteis, of Windmill Hill, Sussex; and bro. of the Member for Sussex. Major in the 7th Dragoon Guards. An East India Proprietor. Col. Evans, after his defeat in Westminster, contested the election with Mr. Curteis. A Reformer, opposed to the ballot and short Parliaments. Sat for Rye from 1832. Retired in 1837. Author of *Exposure of the Corrupt System of Elections at Rye* (1853). Died 14 Dec. 1879. [1837]

CURTEIS, Herbert Barrett. Peasmarsh, Sussex. Reform, and Wyndham. Eld. s. of Ed. Jer. Curteis, Esq., of Windmill Hill, Co. Sussex. Member for the Co. in the Parliaments of 1820 and 1826. B. 1793; m. 1821, his cousin, Caroline Sarah, d. and co-heiress of Robert Mascall, Esq., Peasmarsh Place, Sussex (dead). A Trustee of the Agricultural Employment Institution. A Liberal, in favour of agricultural protection, but voted against the Corn Laws in 1846. Represented Sussex from 1830-32, before it was divided under the Reform Act, and from 1832-37, sat for the Eastern div. of the county; remained out of Parliament from 1837-1841, when he was returned for Rye. MP until his death in 1847.   [1847]

CURTEIS, Herbert Mascall. Windmill Hill, Hurstmonceaux Place, Sussex. Peasmarsh Place, Sussex. Wyndham, and Reform. Only s. of Herbert Barrett Curteis, Esq., many years MP for Rye, by the d. and co-heir of Robert Mascall, Esq., of Peasmarsh, Sussex. B. at Florence, 1823; m. 1848, Paulina, youngest d. of the Rev. Sir John Godfrey Thomas (6th Bart.), of Bodiam, Sussex. Educ. at Westminster, and at Christ Church, Oxford. A Liberal. First returned for Rye on the death of his father, in Dec. 1847, without opposition. Retired in 1852. Master of the Hunt. Died 16 June 1895.   [1852]

CURZON, Hon. Montagu. 31 Clarges Street, London. Carlton, and White's. S. of the 1st Earl Howe, by Anne, d. of Vice-Admiral Sir John Gore, K.C.B. B. in London, 1846. Educ. at Eton. Became Ensign Rifle Brigade in 1865, Lieut. in 1870, Captain in 1878, and Mayor in 1882. A Conservative. Sat for Leicestershire N., from June 1883; defeated in 1885 contesting the new Loughborough division. Served on North-West Frontier, India until retired in 1897. Died 1 Sept. 1907.   [1885]

CURZON, Visct. 8 South Audley Street, London. Gopsall, Atherstone, Leicestershire. Penn, Amersham. Eld. s. of 1st Earl Howe, by his 1st wife, the 2nd d. of the 6th Earl of Cardigan. B. 1821; m. 1846, Harriet Mary, the 2nd d. of Henry Charles Sturt, Esq., of Critchill House, Wiltshire and niece of 7th Earl of Cardigan. Appointed Lieut.-Col. in Leicestershire Yeomanry Cavalry 1860. A Conservative, 'a firm supporter of the Protestant church.' First returned for Leicestershire S. Mar. 1857. Sat until he succeeded as 2nd Earl May 1870. Died 4 Feb. 1876.   [1870]

CUSACK-SMITH, Rt. Hon. T.B. See SMITH, Rt. Hon. Thomas Berry Cusack-.

CUST, Hon. A.W. Parliamentary Sec. to Local Government Board from 1885-86; Paymaster Gen. 1887-89; Under-Sec. of State for War 1889-92. A Conservative. MP for Shropshire N. from Aug. 1866. Sat until he succeeded bro. as 3rd Earl Brownlow. Feb. 1867. Died 19 Apr. 1927.

CUST, Hon. Charles Henry. 13 Great Stanhope Street, London. Arthingworth, Northampton. 2nd s. of 1st Earl Brownlow, by his 1st wife, Sophia, 2nd d. and co-heir of Sir Abraham Hume, Bart. B. 1813; m. 1842, Caroline Sophia, eld. d. of Reginald George Macdonald, Esq., Chief of Clanronald. Educ. at Christ Church, Oxford. Appointed Capt. Royal Horse Guards 1845; retired 1847. A Dept.-Lieut. of Lincolnshire and a Maj. N. Shropshire Yeomanry. Was Sheriff of Northamptonshire 1859. A Conservative. Contested Lincolnshire N. 5 July 1841. First elected for N. Shropshire July 1865. Accepted Chiltern Hundreds Aug. 1866. Died 19 May 1875.   [1865]

CUST, Henry Francis Cockayne. 16 Eccleston Square, London. Cockayne Hatley, Sandy, Bedfordshire. Ellesmere House, Ellesmere, Shropshire. Carlton, and Travellers'. Eld. s. of Hon. and Rev. Henry Cockayne Cust, Canon of Windsor, of Cockayne Hatley, Co. Bedford (who was 2nd s. of 1st Baron Brownlow), by Lady Anna Maria, eld. d. of 1st Earl of Kilmorey. B. at Cockayne Hatley 1819; m. 1852, Sarah Jane, d. of Isaac Cookson, Esq., of Meldon Park, Northumberland, and widow of Major Sidney Streatfield. Educ. at Eton. Entered the army in 1838 as Ensign in the 25th Foot, became Capt. 8th Hussars, and served on the staff in India, retired. Major North Salopian Yeomanry Cavalry. A Magistrate for Shropshire, Lincolnshire and Bedfordshire. Was High Sheriff of Bedfordshire in 1869. Private Sec. to the Earl of Eglinton while Lord-Lieut. of Ireland 1852. Patron of 1 living. A Conservative. Sat for Grantham from Feb. 1874. Defeated 1880. Died 5 Apr. 1884.   [1880]

DALBERG-ACTON, Sir John Emerich Edward. See ACTON, Sir John Emerich Edward Dalberg-.

DALBIAC, Sir Charles James, K.G.H. 34 Cavendish Square, London. Carlton. A Maj. Gen. in the army, the Inspecting General Officer of Cavalry. M. Susanna Isabella, d. of John Dalton, Esq., of Sleningford, Yorkshire, and of Fillingham Castle, Lincoln. A Conservative. He presided at the court martial held at Bristol after the riots there in 1831. Unsuccessfully contested Ripon in 1832. Sat for Ripon from 1835 until he retired in 1837. Lieut.-Gen. in 1838; Col. of 3rd Dragoon Guards Jan. 1839.   [1837]

DALGUISH, Robert. 29 St. Vincent Place, Glasgow. Kilmardinny, Milnganie, Dumbartonshire. Reform. S. of Robert Dalguish, Esq. B. at Glasgow 1808. Educ. at Glasgow University. A

Calico-printer at Glasgow, a member of the firm of Dalguish, Falconer and Company. A Liberal, voted for the disestablishment of the Irish Church 1869; in favour of the withdrawal of all State Grants for religious purposes, and also of the assimilation of the county and borough franchise. First elected for Glasgow Apr. 1857 and sat until he retired 1874. Died 20 June 1880.   [1873]

DALKEITH, Earl of. 3 Hamilton Place, London. Dalkeith Palace, Dalkeith. Carlton. Eld. s. of the Duke of Beccleuch, by Lady Charlotte Anne, youngest d. of the 2nd Marq. of Bath. B. at Montagu House 1831; m. 1859, Lady Louisa, 3rd d. of the 1st Duke of Abercorn. Appointed Lieut.-Col. Mid-Lothian Yeomanry Cavalry 1856, a Dept.-Lieut. of Selkirkshire 1853, Lord-Lieut. of Dumfriesshire 1858. Attached to a special mission to Russia 1856. A Conservative; said he would uphold 'the Protestant institutions of the country.' Sat for Edinburghshire from June 1853-Dec. 1868; re-elected Feb. 1874 and sat until defeated in the 1880 gen. election by Mr. Gladstone. Succeeded father as 6th Duke in 1884. Died 5 Nov. 1914.   [1880]

DALMENY, Lord. 20 Charles Street, Berkeley Square, London. Dalmeny Park, Linlithgow. Reform. Eld. s. of the Earl of Rosebery. B. 1809. A Lord of the Admiralty from Apr. 1835-Sept. 1841. A Liberal. Sat for Stirling district from 1832 until he retired 1847. Died 23 Jan. 1851. [1847]

DALRYMPLE, Sir Adolphus John, Bart. 129 Park Street, Grosvenor Square, London. Delrow House, Hertfordshire. Brunswick Terrace, Brighton. United Service. S. of Gen. Sir Hew Whiteford Dalrymple, Bart. and grands. of James, Visct. Stair. M. Anne, only d. of Sir James Graham, Bart., of Kirkstall, Yorkshire. A Col. in the army, and Aide-de-Camp to the Queen. A Conservative. Sat for Weymouth in 1817; for Appleby in 1819 and 1820; and for the Haddington district of Burghs from 1826 to 1831. Unsuccessfully contested Brighton in 1832 and 1835, but was successful at Brighton Aug. 1837 and sat until he was again defeated in July 1841. Appointed General 11 Apr. 1860. Died 3 Mar. 1866.
[1841]

DALRYMPLE, C. Continued in House after 1885: full entry in Volume II.

DALRYMPLE, Donald. Thorpe Lodge, Norwich. Athenaeum, and Reform. S. of William Dalrymple, Esq., by Marianne, d. of Benjamin Bertram, Esq., of Norwich. B. at Norwich 1814; m. 1841, Sarah, only d. of Thomas Osborne Springfield, Esq., of Norwich. Educ. at Norwich

Grammar School and at Guy's Hospital, London. Became a member of the Coll. of Surgeons 1836, Fellow 1854. Licentiate of the Society of Apothecaries 1835. Member of the Coll. of Physicians, London, by examination 1859, retired from the profession 1862. A Magistrate and Dept.-Lieut. for Norfolk and Chairman of the Governors of King Edward Schools at Norwich. Published in 1861 a work *On the Climate of Egypt*. A Liberal, and supported Mr. Gladstone on the Irish Church 1869; considered the Reform Bill incomplete without a further distribution of seats. Sat for Bath from Nov. 1868. MP until his death circa Sept. 1873.   [1873]

DALRYMPLE, John. See Dalrymple, Visct. John.

DALRYMPLE, Visct. John. 31 Albermarle Street, London. Guards', Brooks's, and Reform. B. 1819, the eld. s. of the 9th Earl of Stair, by his 1st wife, d. of James Penny, Esq. M. 1846, eld. d. of the Duke de Coigney, grand-d. of Sir Hew Dalrymple Hamilton, Bart. An officer in the Guards. Appointed Dept.-Lieut. of Lanarkshire 1844; and Lord Lieut. of Wigton 1851, Wigtonshire 1857, and Ayrshire 1870. Succeeded as 10th Earl Stair on 9 Nov. 1864. A Whig, at one time voted against the abolition of the Corn Laws, but in 1846 supported their repeal. Sat for Wigtonshire from 1841 until he accepted Chiltern Hundreds in Feb. 1856. Died 3 Dec. 1903. [1855]

DALRYMPLE, Lieut.-Gen. Sir John Hamilton, Bart. 6 King Street, St. James's, London. Consland. B. 1771; m. 1st 1795, Henrietta, eld. d. of the Rev. R.A. Johnson, Kenilworth, Warwick, and, 2ndly, Adamina, sister of Admiral Lord Duncan. Colonel of the 92nd Foot. Of Whig principles, and was in favour of the immediate abolition of slavery. Was elected for Edinburghshire in 1832 in opposition to Sir G. Clerk, with whom he unsuccessfully contested Edinburghshire several times. Sat until he retired in 1835. Succeeded his kinsman as 8th Earl Stair 22 Mar. 1840. Created Baron Oxenfoord, (U.K. Peerage) 16 Aug. 1841. Died 10 Jan. 1853. [1853]

DALWAY, Marriott Robert. 12 Little Queen Street, Westminster, London. Belmont, Carrickfergus, Co. Antrim. Ulster Club, Belfast. S. of Marriott Dalway, Esq., a Justice of the Peace and Mayor of Carrickfergus, by Euphemia, d. of Thomas Henry, Esq., of Castle Dawson. B. at Bella Hill, Co. Antrim 1832; m. 1859, Elizabeth, only d. of Col. Andrew Armstrong Barnes of the 6th Royals. Educ. at Larwin Hall, Chester. A Magistrate for the Co. of Antrim and the Co. of the town of Carrickfergus from 1858; was High

Sheriff of Carrickfergus 1859. A Liberal-Conservative, voted against the disestablishment of the Irish Church 1869. Sat for Carrickfergus from Dec. 1868 until he was defeated 1880. Contested the East division of Antrim 5 Dec. 1885. [1880]

DALY, James. A Retired Commander in the army. Of Conservative principles, supported the Duke of Wellington's Administration, and was to have been raised to the peerage by the title of Lord Dunsandale; it is said the patent was actually made out when the Duke resigned. Sat for Galway Co. from 1802 to 1826. Regained his seat in 1832 and sat until he retired in 1835. [1833]

DALY, John. Rookhurst, Monkstown, Co. Cork. S. of John Daly, Esq., of Cork, by Mary, d. of Charles O'Connell, Esq., of Cork. B. at Cork 1834. Educ. at Conglowes Coll., Co. Kildare. A Merchant at Cork. A Magistrate for the Co. and City of Cork. An Alderman of Cork, of which city he, for three consecutive years served in the office of Mayor – 1871, 1872 and 1873. A Chevalier of the Legion of Honour. A Liberal, and in favour of the system called 'Home Rule for Ireland', believing self-government to be indispensible to a healthy national life; also of 'a peasant proprietary' etc. Unsuccessfully contested Tralee Feb. 1874 and Cork June 1876. Sat for Cork from Apr. 1880 until he accepted Chiltern Hundreds Feb. 1884. Died Aug. 1888. [1883]

DAMER, Rt. Hon. George Lionel Dawson, C.B. 23 Wilton Crescent, London. Carlton. 2nd s. of the 1st Earl of Portarlington, and bro.-in-law of 1st Lord Congleton. B. 1788; m. in 1825, 2nd d. of Lord Hugh Seymour. Was Comptroller of the Household; resigned July 1846. Was a Col. in the army. Was at the battle of Waterloo. Assumed the name of Damer in 1829, on the death of his aunt, Lady Caroline Damer, when he succeeded to considerable estates in Dorset. Patron of 2 livings. A Conservative, but in favour of free trade. Contested Portarlington unsuccessfully in 1832, but sat for that borough from 1835 to 1847, when he was returned for Dorchester. Sat until he was defeated in 1852. Died 14 Apr. 1856. [1852]

DAMER, Lionel Seymour William Dawson-. 2 Chapel Street, Grosvenor Square, London. Came House, Dorchester. Carlton, White's, and Guards'. S. of the Rt. Hon. Col. G. Dawson-Damer, C.B. (who sat for Portarlington and Dorchester), by Mary Emma, d. of Lord Hugh Seymour. B. at Brighton 1832; m. 1855, Hon. Harriet, 2nd d. of 6th Lord Rokeby. Educ. at Eton. Entered the army 1849, became Lieut. and Capt. Scots Fusilier Guards 1854, served in the Crimea and was present at the battles of the

Alma, Balaklava, Inkerman and the siege of Sebastopol, left the army 1856. A Magistrate for Dorset, Queen's Co., Ireland, and for Middlesex; a Dept.-Lieut. for Queen's Co., and a Lieut. Dorset Yeomanry. Patron of 2 livings. 'Of Conservative principles, free and uncontrolled.' Sat for Portarlington from Apr. 1857-July 1865, when he was unsuccessful; re-elected Nov. 1868 and sat until he retired 1880. Succeeded as 4th Earl Portarlington Mar. 1889. Died 17 Dec. 1892. [1880]

DARBY, George. 21 Duke Street, Westminster, London. 10 King's Bench Walk, Temple, London. Monkley, Sussex. S. of John Darby, a London Merchant. A Barrister. Of Conservative principles. First sat for Sussex East at the general election in 1837, when he came in at the head of the poll, defeating H.B. Curteis, the late member. Sat until he accepted Chiltern Hundreds in Jan. 1846. Became enclosure commissioner in 1846 to 1852, when he became tithe commissioner until his death on 16 Nov. 1872. [1845]

D'ARCY, Matthew Peter. Shananagh House, Loughlinstown, Co. Dublin. Reform, and Garrick. Royal Irish Yacht and Stephen's Green Clubs, Dublin. S. of John D'Arcy, Esq., of Raleny, Co. Dublin (a Dept.-Lieut. of that Co.). B. 1821; m. 1st, 1853, Emma, d. of William Knaresborough, Esq., R.M. of Inch House, Kilkenny; 2ndly, 1860, Christina, d. of James Daly, Esq., of Castle Daly, Co. Galway. Educ. at Trinity Coll., Dublin, where he graduated M.A. 1847. A Brewer in Dublin, Proprietor of Anchor Brewery. A Liberal. Sat for Co. Wexford from Dec. 1868 until he retired 1874. Died (suicide) 28 Nov. 1889. [1873]

DARE, Robert Westley Hall. 16 Carlton Terrace, London. Cranbrook House, Essex. Carlton. S. of Robert Hall, Esq., a West India Proprietor; assumed the name of Dare on marrying the d. of Capt. Grafton Dare, of Cranbrook House, Ilford, who, on his marriage with her mother, had in like manner assumed the name of Dare. Patron of 1 living. A Conservative, opposed to free trade in corn, and in everything else. In favour of the repeal of the assessed and other 'taxes pressing on the springs of industry, and the imposition in their stead of a tax upon property'; also in favour of the extension of the currency. Sat for Essex S. from 1832. MP until his death in 1836. [1836]

DARLINGTON, Earl of. Snettisham Hall, Norfolk. 40 Upper Brook Street, London. Carlton. Eld. s. of the Duke of Cleveland; b. 1788; m. 1809, Sophia, sister of Earl Poulett. A

Lieut.-Col. in the army. A Conservative. Patron of 4 livings. Opposed the first Reform Bill, though his father supported Ministers throughout the debates in the House of Lords. In Parliament for twenty years, with the exception of the Parliament of 1831, in which he had no seat. Sat for Durham County 1812-15 (accepted commission); for Winchelsea 12 Feb. 1816-18; for Tregony 1818-26 (two parliaments); for Totnes 1826-30; for Saltash 1830-32; and for Salop S. from 1832. Sat until he succeeded as 2nd Duke of Cleveland Jan.1842. Died 18 Jan. 1864.   [1841]

DASHWOOD, Sir George Henry, Bart. West Wycombe, Buckinghamshire. Reform. Eld. s. of Sir John Dashwood King, 4th Bart. (whose father assumed the name of King). M. in 1823, his cousin, Elizabeth, d. of Theodore Henry Broadhead, Esq. A Liberal, voted for the ballot, 1853. Sat for Buckinghamshire from 1832 to 1835; was an unsuccessful candidate there in 1835 and 1837. Sat for Wycombe from 1837. MP until his death 4 Mar. 1862.   [1861]

DAUNT, William Joseph O'Neil Kilkaskin. A Repealer. The election of this gentleman for Mallow may be noted as perhaps the most extraordinary of all the extraordinary instances of Daniel O'Connell's influence at the elections for the Parliament of 1833. Mr. Jephson, who represented it from the time of his attaining his majority downwards, possessed every house in the town, with the exception of a few belonging to a family not usually opposed to him, and his principles were by no means considered unpopular. He would not, however, pledge himself to a repeal of the Union, and Mr. Daunt, a gentleman of small landed property in the neighbourhood was elected for Mallow Dec. 1832. On petition he was unseated and his opponent was seated 24 Apr. 1833.   [1833]

DAVENPORT, Edward Gershour. 28 Lancaster Gate, London. Tregenna Castle, St. Ives, Cornwall. St. Stephen's Club. S. of George Davenport, Esq. B. 1838; m. 1863, Louisa, d. of Edward Oxenford, Esq. Was educ. at King's Coll. School, London, and at Trinity Coll., Cambridge. Capt. Duke of Cornwall's Artillery Volunteers. A Liberal-Conservative; favoured a 'thorough reconstruction of the present system of local taxation'; also the enactment of a Permissive Bill. Sat for St. Ives from Feb. 1874. MP until his death 4 Dec. 1874.   [1874]

DAVENPORT, H.T. Continued in House after 1885: full entry in Volume II.

DAVENPORT, John. 28 Parliament Street, London. Westwood Hall, Staffordshire. An extensive Manufacturer in Stoke-upon-Trent. A Magistrate and Dept.-Lieut. of Staffordshire. A Conservative, in favour of a fixed duty on corn and short Parliaments. Sat for Stoke-upon-Trent from 1832 until he retired 1841.   [1838]

DAVENPORT, William Bromley. 1 Belgrave Place, London. Capesthorne, Chelford, Crewe. Baginton Hall, Coventry. White's, and Carlton. S. of the Rev. Walter Davenport Bromley, by Caroline Barbara, d. of Archdeacon Gooch. B. at Capesthorne, Cheshire 1821; m. 1858, Augusta Elizabeth, eld. d. of Walter Campbell, Esq., of Islay. Educ.at Harrow and Christ Church, Oxford. Assumed by Royal License the name Davenport in addition to Bromley 1868, in compliance with the will of his cousin. A Dept.-Lieut. of Stafford and Lieut.-Col. Staffordshire Yeonmanry Cavalry. A Liberal-Conservative, in favour of tenant farmers being secured the value of inexhausted improvements. Sat for Warwickshire N. from Dec. 1864. MP until his death 15 June 1884.   [1884]

DAVEY, Horace. Continued in House after 1885: full entry in Volume II.

DAVEY, Richard. 11 St. James's Place, London. Bockym House, Helston. Brooks's, and Reform. S. of William Davey, Esq., of Redruth, Cornwall. B. at Redruth 1799. Unmarried. Educ. at Tiverton School, and at the University of Edinburgh. A Dept.-Lieut. and Magistrate for Cornwall. A Liberal, in favour of a large extension of the franchise, a 'settlement' of the church-rates question, and a 'sound system' of education. First returned for Cornwall W. Apr. 1857 and sat until he retired in 1868. Died 24 June 1884.   [1867]

DAVIE, Sir Henry Robert Ferguson, Bart. 48 Wilton Crescent, London. Creedy Park, Crediton. Devon. Brooks's, Travellers', and United Service. S. of Robert Ferguson, Esq., MP of Raith, Fifeshire. M. 1823, Frances Juliana, only sister and heir of Sir John Davie, Bart., of Creedy Park, Devon; and at the death of her uncle Sir Humphrey Phineas Davie, assumed that name by Royal Licence, obtaining also a revival in his own favour of the baronetcy which had then become extinct. Entered the army in 1818; became Maj.-Gen. 1854; Col. of 73rd Foot 1865. A Liberal. Sat for Haddington district from 1847 until he accepted Chiltern Hundreds 1878. Died 30 Nov. 1885.   [1878]

DAVIE, John Davie Ferguson. 48 Wilton Crescent, London. Creedy Park, Crediton, Devon. Brooks's, and Travellers'. Eld. s. of Sir

Henry Robert Ferguson Davie, Bart., by Frances Juliana, only surviving d. of Sir John Davie, Bart., of Creedy Park, Devon. B. at Creedy Park, Devon 1830; m. 1859, Edwina Augusta, d. of Sir James Hamlyn Williams, Bart., of Clovelly Court. Educ. at Eton. Appointed Lieut. and Capt. Grenadier Guards 1853, but retired. Lieut.-Col. Commandant of the 1st Devon Militia, and a Dept.-Lieut. for Devon. A Liberal, in favour of 'real progress, and an extensive measure of reform.' First elected for Barnstaple May 1859, and sat until he retired 1865. Succeeded father as 2nd Bart. 1885. Died 16 June 1907.   [1865]

DAVIES, David. Bronierian, Llandinan, Montgomeryshire. B. at Llandinan 1818, the s. of Mr. David Davies, and Elizabeth, his wife. M. 1851, d. of Mr. Edward Jones of Llanfair. Educ. at Llandinan School. Was a Railway Contractor and Coal-owner. Director and Vice Chairman of the Barry Dock and Railway, and Chief Projector of Barry Docks, opened 1889. A Magistrate for Montgomeryshire and Cardiganshire. A Liberal and supporter of Gladstone. Unsuccessfully contested Cardiganshire 20 July 1865. Sat for Cardigan district from Feb. 1874 to 1886, when he was defeated. Died 28 Feb. 1893.   [1886]

DAVIES, David Arthur Saunders. Pentre, Newcastle Emlyn, Pembrokeshire. Carlton, Conservative, and United University. B. 1792, the s. of D. Davies, M.D. by Susanna, d. of Erasmus Saunders, Esq., of Pentre, Pembrokeshire. M. 1826 Elizabeth Maria, d. of Col. Philipps of Williamston, Pembrokeshire (she died 1851). Graduated M.A. at Christ Church, Oxford, and became a barrister-at-law. Was for some years Chairman of the Cardiganshire Quarter Sessions. A Conservative, voted against the Chinese War, but would have supported Lord Palmerston 'if it had been intimated that a Plenipotentiary would be sent out'. Sat for Carmarthenshire from 1842 until his death on 22 May 1857. [1857 2nd ed.]

DAVIES, John Lloyd. Blaendyffryn, and Alltyr Odin, Cardiganshire. Conservative. S. of Thomas Davies, Esq., and Elizabeth, his wife. B. at Aberystwith 1801; m. 1825, Anne, only surviving child of John Lloyd, Esq., and grand-d. of David Lloyd, Esq., of Alltyr Odin, Cardiganshire, one of whose ancestors was the first member returned to Parliament for the Co. of Cardigan, *temp.* Henry VIII. A Magistrate and Dept.-Lieut. for the Cos. of Cardigan and Carmarthen; High Sheriff for Cardigan 1845. Patron of 2 livings. A Conservative, opposed to the Maynooth Grant. First returned for Cardigan district Feb. 1855 and sat until he retired 1857. Died 21 Mar. 1860. [1856]

DAVIES, Richard, Trebarth, Bangor, North Wales. Reform. B. 1818, the s. of Richard Davies of Llangefui, Anglesey. M. 1855 Annie, only child of the Rev. Henry Rees, of Liverpool. Unsuccessfully contested Carnarvon bor. in 1852. A Magistrate for Anglesey and Carnarvonshire. Sheriff of Anglesey 1858. Lord Lieut. 1884. A Liberal. Sat for Anglesey from 1868 to 1886, when he retired. Died 27 Oct. 1896.   [1886]

DAVIES, Col. Thomas Henry Hastings. Elmley Park, Worcestershire, Brooks's, Crockford's, United Service. M. 1824 Miss de Crespiguy. A Col. in the army; was at Waterloo. Of Liberal politics. Sat for Worcester from 1818-1835. Defeated in 1835; returned unopposed in 1837. Sat until he retired 1841.   [1386]

DAVIES, Sir W. Continued in House after 1885: full entry in Volume II.

DAVISON, Rt.Hon. John Robert. 61 Lancaster Gate, Hyde Park, London. Under-river House, Sevenoaks, Kent. Windham, and Brooks's. 2nd s. of the Rev. Edward Davison, Rector of Harlington, Middlesex, and Incumbent of St. Nicholas, Durham. B. 1826; m. 1860, Jane, eld. d. of Nicholas Wood, Esq., of Hetton Hall, Durham (she died 1869). Educ. at Durham Grammar School and at the University of Durham. Was called to the bar at the Middle Temple, and joined the Northern circuit; appointed a Queen's Counsel 1866. Appointed Judge Advocate-Gen. Dec. 1870, (salary £2,000). Chairman of Quarter Sessions of the Co. of Durham. A Liberal. Sat for Durham from Dec. 1868. MP until his death 15 Apr. 1871.   [1871]

DAVISON, Richard. 66 Warwick Square, Belgrave Road, London. Donegall Place, Belfast. The Abbey, White Abbey, Belfast. Carlton. S. of Alexander Davison, Esq., of Knockboy, Co. Antrim, by Mary d. of — McKillop, Esq., of Glenarm, Co. Antrim. B. at Knockboy 1796; m. 1822, Margaret, youngest d. of George Casement, Esq., M.D., of Larne, Co. Antrim, and sister of Sir William Casement, K.C.B., of Calcutta. Admitted a Solicitor in Jan. 1818, and practised in Belfast, being a senior partner in the firm of Davison and Torrens; Solicitor to several Railways and public companies. A Conservative, would 'ever support the interest of the Established Churches' in the United Kingdom; against the Maynooth grant, and in favour of compensation to tenants for improvements, but against general tenant right where no improvements have been made. First returned for Belfast in July 1852, and sat until he accepted Chiltern Hundreds 1860.   [1860]

DAVITT, Michael. Continued in House after 1885: full entry in Volume II.

DAWES, Edward. 33 Portland Place, London. St. Helen's House, near Ryde, Isle of Wight. Eld. s. of Mr. James Dawes of St. Helen's, Isle of Wight. M. 1st, d. of John Beech, Esq., Surgeon, R.N. (dead); 2ndly, youngest d. of Dr. Thomas, Archdeacon of Bath. Was for several years a first class member of the Royal Victoria Yacht Club at Ryde, Isle of Wight. Succeeded to the Niton estate in the Isle of Wight, on the death of his father. A Liberal, in favour of free trade being carried out more extensively, the extension of the suffrage to the £10 county renters, vote by ballot, and a gradual reduction of the malt tax. First returned for the Isle of Wight May 1851 and sat until defeated in 1852. [1852]

DAWNAY, Hon. Guy Cuthbert. Bookham Grove, Leatherhead. 4th s. of the 7th Visct. Downe, by Mary Isabel, 4th d. of the Hon. and Rt. Rev. Richard Bagot, Bishop of Bath and Wells. B. 1848. Educ. at Christ Church, Oxford, and graduated M.A. 1875. A Conservative. Sat for the North Riding of Yorkshire from Jan. 1882 until he was defeated in 1885 contesting Cleveland division. Surveyor general of ordnance June 1885 to Feb. 1886. Killed by buffalo 28 Feb. 1889. [1885]

DAWNAY, Hon. L.P. Continued in House after 1885: full entry in Volume II.

DAWNAY, Hon. William Henry. 30 Upper Brooke Street, London. Benningborough Hall, Yorkshire. Carlton. the eld. s. of Visct. Downe, b. 1812. A Conservative. Sat for the county of Rutland from 1841, until he accepted Chiltern Hundreds in Jan. 1846. He succeeded as 7th Visct. Downe on 23 Mar 1846. Died 26 Jan. 1857. [1845]

DAWSON, Charles. Palmerston Park, Dublin. 27 Lower Stephen's Street, Dublin. 28 Lower Mallow Street, Limerick. S. of Michael Dawson, Esq., Alderman of Limerick, by Maryanne, d. of Thomas Clarke, Esq., of Limerick. B. at Limerick 1842; m. 1873, d. of William Carroll, Esq., Secretary to the Chamber of Commerce at Limerick. Was educ. at 'The Catholic University' of Ireland. Was High Sheriff of Limerick 1876-77. Was Lord Mayor of Dublin for 1882 and 1883. Wrote various pamphlets on education and articles on the franchise in the *Fortnightly Review* etc. A Liberal, in favour of 'a government in Ireland administered by Irishmen.' Sat for Carlow bor. from Apr. 1880 until he retired 1885. [1885]

DAWSON, Edward. Whatton House, Leicestershire. A Reformer, in favour of the ballot, short Parliaments, a revision of the corn laws, a thorough reform in the Church, and the immediate abolition of slavery. Sat for Leicestershire S. from 1832 until he retired in 1835. [1833]

DAWSON, Col. Robert Peel. Moyola Park, Castle Dawson, Co. Londonderry. Carlton. Eld. s. of Rt. Hon. George Robert Dawson of Castle Dawson, Co. Londonerry (who sat for the Co. of Londonderry for many years), by Mary, d. of Sir Robert Peel (1st Bart.), of Drayton Manor. B. in London 1818; m. 1848, Hon. Mary Elizabeth, eld. d. of 1st Lord Lurgan. Educ. at Harrow and at Christ Church, Oxford. Entered the Grenadier Guards as Ensign and Lieut. Aug. 1837, became Capt. 1842, retired 1847. Lord-Lieut. and Custos-Rot. for the Co. of Londonderry, for which he was High Sheriff in 1850. Col. of the Londonderry Militia from Apr. 1871. Patron of 1 living. A Liberal-Conservative, and in favour of all measures of social progress. First elected for Londonderry Co. May 1859 and sat until he retired 1874. Died 2 Sept. 1877. [1873]

DAWSON, Hon. Thomas Vesey. 3 Great Stanhope Street, London. Guards', and Reform. S. of 2nd Lord Cremorne, by the d. of John Whaley, Esq., of Whaley Abbey, Co. Wicklow; b. 1819; m. 1851 Augusta, 2nd d. of the Rt. Hon. John Wilson Fitz-Patrick. Became Lieut. and Capt. in the Coldstream Guards, 1843, and a Col. unattached in 1845. A Liberal, voted against the abolition of the Corn Laws, but in 1846 supported their repeal. Sat for the county of Louth from 1841 to 1847, when he was first elected for Monaghan. Sat until he retired in 1852. Died in Battle of Inkerman 5 Nov. 1854. [1852]

DEAKIN, James Henry. 3 Elm Court, Temple, London. The Hollies, Snaresbrook, Essex. Eld. s. of James Henry Deakin, Esq., of Mosely Park, Cheadle, by Martha, d. of John Newton, Esq., of Cheshire. B. near Manchester 1851; m. 1872, Kate, youngest d. of John W. Makin, Esq., of The Brook, Sandbach, Cheshire (a Magistrate for Cheshire). Educ. abroad and at Wadham Coll., Oxford. Entered a Student of the Middle Temple, Apr. 1872. A Conservative, opposed any encroachments on the privileges of the Church of England; was in favour of popular education, based upon religion, of economy in public expenditure, the equilisation of taxation etc. Sat for Launceston from July 1874 when he was elected on the displacement of his father. Sat until he accepted Chiltern Hundreds in Feb. 1877. Died 8 Nov. 1881. [1877]

DEAKIN, Lieut.-Col. J.H. A Conservative. First elected for Launceston 9 Feb. 1874 but shortly afterwards unseated on petition.

DEASE, Edmund. 2 Savile Row, London. Rath House, Ballybrittas, Queen's Co. 2nd s. of Gerald Dease, Esq., of Turbotston, Co. Westmeath, by Elizabeth, d. and co-heir of Edmund O'Callaghan, Esq., of Kilgorey, Co. Clare. B. at Turbotston 1829; m. 1859, Mary, 3rd d. of Henry Gratten, Esq., of Celbridge Abbey, Co. Kildare, who formerly sat for Meath. A Magistrate and Dept.-Lieut. for Queen's Co., of which he had been High Sheriff. A moderate Liberal, in favour of the system called 'Home Rule' for Ireland. Sat for Queen's Co. from Jan. 1870 until he retired 1880. Died 17 July 1904. [1880]

DEASE, Matthew O'Reilly. Dee Farm, Dunleer, Co. Louth. Only s. of Richard Dease, Esq., M.D., of Lisney, Co. Cavan, by Anne Maria, only d. and heir of Matthew O'Reilly, Esq., of Thomastown, Co. Louth. B. 1819. A Magistrate and Dept.-Lieut. of Louth. A Liberal. Contested Cavan 13 Apr. 1857. Sat for the Co. of Louth from Dec. 1868 until he was defeated 1874. Died 17 Aug. 1887. [1873]

DEASY, J. Continued in House after 1885: full entry in Volume II.

DEASY, Rickard. 184 Brunswick Street, Dublin. Reform, London, University, and Stephen's Green, Dublin. 2nd s. of Rickard Deasy, Esq., of Clonakilty, Co. Cork by Mary Anne, d. of — Caller, Esq. Unmarried. Educ. at Trinty Coll., Dublin, where he graduated M.A. Called to the bar in Ireland 1835, made Queen's Counsel 1849, and joined the Munster Circuit. Appointed Solicitor-Gen. for Ireland, June 1859. A Liberal, in favour of a 'settlement of the tenant-right question', vote by ballot, and progressive reform; said he would resist any attempt to disturb the present grant to Maynooth. First elected for Cork Co. Apr. 1855 and sat until 1861 when he was appointed a Baron of the Exchequer in Ireland. Attorney Gen. for Ireland Feb. 1860-Jan. 1861. Judge of Court of Appeal Jan. 1878 until his death 6 May 1883. [1860]

DEEDES, William. 21 Lower Belgrave Street, London. Sandling Park, Hythe, Kent. Travellers', and Carlton. Eld. s. of William Deedes, Esq., of Sandling Park, Kent, who was MP for Hythe in 1807. B. 1796; m. in 1833, Emily Octavia, d. of Edward Taylor, Esq., formerly of Bifrons, Kent. Was educ. at Winchester and Corpus Christi Coll., Oxford, afterwards elected a Fellow of All Souls' Coll., Oxford. Appointed a Commissioner of Church Estates, May 1858, salary £1000. Chairman of Quarter Sessions, a Dept.-Lieut. for Kent, and Lieut.-Col. Commandant of the East Kent Yeomanry Cavalry. Of Conservative principles, voted for inquiry into Maynooth, 1853. Sat for E. Kent from Feb. 1845 till Apr. 1857, when he was an unsuccessful candidate; re-elected Dec. following. MP until his death 30 Nov. 1862. [1862]

DEEDES, Col. William. Sandling Park, Hythe, Kent. Carlton. Eld. s. of William Deedes, Esq., of Sandling Park, Kent (who sat for East Kent from 1845 until his death in 1863), by Emily Octavia, d. of Edward Taylor, Esq., of Bifrons, Kent. B. at Sandling 1834; m. 1861, Sarah Mary Sophia, eld. d. of William Bernard Harcourt, Esq., of St. Leonard's Hill, Windsor. Educ. at Harrow. Entered the Rifle Brigade in 1852, became Capt. Mar. 1855 and retired. Was Lieut.-Col. Commandant East Kent Militia from 1865-1869. A Conservative, and opposed to the utmost any measure tending to the separation of Church and State. Sat for kent E. from July 1876 until he retired 1880. Died 27 May 1887. [1880]

DEERING, John Peter. 40 South Street, Park Lane, London. The Lee, Great Missenden, Buckinghamshire. Travellers', and United University. Educ. at Bristol under Mr. Bowles, minor Canon of the Cathedral. Unmarried. Succeeded to the estates of Henry Deering, Esq., within the hundreds which surround Aylesbury. A Dept-Lieut. and Magistrate for Buckinghamshire, and High Sheriff of the Co. in 1840-1. A Member of the Dilettanti Society, for which he travelled a voyage of research in Greece, under the auspices of George IV, then Prince Regent. Practised as an architect, and was attached to the Household of Queen Caroline at the period of her death. Wrote about the remains of Pompeii, and the antiquities of Attica. Edited the 6th Edition of *Eustace's Classical Tour in Italy*. Patron of 2 livings. A Conservative, supported the agricultural interest, opposed to the endowment of the Roman Catholic Clergy, and the policy of Sir Robert Peel's administration. Sat for Aylesbury from 1847 until he was unseated on petition in Mar. 1848. [1847 2nd ed.]

DE FERRIÈRES, Charles Conrad Adolphus Du Bois (commonly called Baron de Ferrières). Bays Hill House, Cheltenham. Union. Only s. of Baron Du Bois de Ferrières, of the Netherlands, by Henrietta, d. of C. A. Peterson, Esq., of Northallerton, Yorkshire. B. 1823; m. 1851, Annie, youngest d. of W. Sheepshanks, Esq., of Arthington Hall, Yorkshire. In 1867, on the death of his father, was granted letters of

105

naturalisation by Act of Parliament. A Magistrate for Gloucester. A Liberal. Sat for Cheltenham from Apr. 1880 until he retired in 1885. Died 18 Mar. 1908. [1885]

DE GREY, Earl. 1 Carlton Gardens, London. Studley Royal, Ripon. White's. Eld. s. of the Marq. of Ripon, by Henrietta Ann Theodosia, eld. d. of Capt. Henry and Lady Mary Vyner. B. in London 1852. Unmarried. Educ. at Eton. Was Attaché to the Joint High Commission at Washington 1871. Capt. Commandant 27th West Riding of Yorkshire Rifle Volunteers. A Dept.-Lieut. for the North Riding of Yorkshire. A Liberal. Sat for Ripon from Feb. 1874 until he retired 1880. Succeeded as 2nd Marq. 1909. Died 23 Sept. 1923. [1880]

DE GREY, Hon. Thomas. 23 Arlington Street, London. Merton Hall, Thetford, Norfolk. White's. Eld. s. of Lord Walsingham, by his 1st wife, Augusta Louisa, eld. d. of Sir R. Frankland Russell, Bart. B. in London 1843. Educ. at Eton and at the Univ. of Cambridge. Appointed Dept.-Lieut. of Norfolk 1863. A Conservative, voted against the disestablishment of the Irish Church 1869. First elected for W. Norfolk July 1865. Sat until he succeeded as 6th Baron Dec. 1870. A Fellow of many foreign and learned societies. Died 3 Dec. 1919. [1870]

DE HORSEY, Spencer Horsey. 8 Upper Grosvenor Street, London. Glemham, Suffolk. Only s. of the Rev. Dr. Kilderbee, by Caroline, only d. and heiress of S. Horsey, Esq., M. 23 Feb. 1824, Lady Louisa Maria Judith, 2nd surviving d. of the Earl of Stradbroke. Assumed the name of de Horsey in 1832. A Conservative. Returned in 1837 for Newcastle-under-Lyme and sat until he retired 1841. Died 20 May 1860. [1838]

DELAHUNTY, James. 2 Savile Row, London. Mary Street, Waterford. S. of Tobias Delahunty, Esq., Merchant of Waterford, by Bridget, d. of Martin Kelly, Esq., of Thomastown. B. at Waterford 1808. Educ. at St. John's Coll., Waterford. A Merchant at Waterford. Was an Alderman of Waterford from 1842-1845. Coroner for the Co. of Waterford from 1850-1867, and for several years Treasurer of the Co. of Waterford. A Liberal, in favour of 'Home rule' for Ireland. Sat for the City of Waterford from Dec. 1868-Feb. 1874, when he was defeated. Sat for the Co. of Waterford from Jan. 1877 until he retired 1880. Died 15 June 1885. [1880]

DE LA POER, Edward. Gurteen, Clonmel. Brooks's, and Reform. Kildare St. Club, Dublin. S. of John Power, Esq., of Gurteen, Co. Water-ford, a Magistrate and Dept.-Lieut. , by Frances, d. of Sir John Power, Bart., of Kifane, Co. Kilkenny. Was created a Count by the Pope in 1864. Male representative of John 'More' Lord Power of Curraghmore, who died in 1592, being descended from the Hon. Piers Power of Clandonell, his 2nd son. Resumed, by Royal License 1863, the name of De la Poer in lieu of his patronymic. A Liberal, voted for the disestablishment of the Irish Church 1869. First elected for the Co. of Waterford Jan. 1867 and sat until he accepted Chiltern Hundreds 1873. Died 30 Aug. 1915. [1873]

DENISON, Christopher Beckett. 43 Victoria Street, London. Grimthorpe, Doncaster. Carlton, and Garrick. 2nd s. of Sir Edmund Beckett (4th Bart.), of Grimthorpe, Yorkshire, who sat for the W. Riding of Yorkshire before its division as Mr. Beckett-Denison, by Maria, d. of William Beverley, Esq., of Beverley. B. 1825. Educ. at Uppingham School, Durham and Haileybury. Entered the Indian Civil Service in the 2nd class 1845, held various offices in the N.W. province of Bengal, the Punjab and Oude, resigned 1865. A Magistrate for the W. Riding of Yorkshire. A Conservative, voted against the disestablishment of the Irish Church 1869. Unsuccessfully contested the Southern division of the W. Riding July 1865; sat for the Eastern division of that Riding from Dec. 1868 until defeated 1880. Deputy Chairman Great Northern Railway 1880 until his death 30 Oct. 1884. [1880]

DENISON, Edmund Beckett. 7 Stone Buildings, Lincoln's Inn, London. Grimthorpe, Yorkshire. Carlton. 6th s. of Sir John Beckett (1st Bart.), by Mary, d. of Bishop (Wilson) of Bristol. B. 1787; m. 1814 Maria, d. of William Beverley, Esq., of Beverley, and great-niece of Sir Thos. Denison. Assumed the additional name of Denison by Royal License, 1816. A Dept.-Lieut. and Magistrate for the East and West Ridings of Yorkshire. A Liberal, gave his general support to Lord Palmerston's government, but was formerly ranked as a Conservative; voted for the Chinese war 1857; voted for the repeal of the Maynooth grant; and for the sound religious education of the lower classes. Sat for the West Riding of Yorkshire from July 1841 till July 1847; again returned Dec. 1848 and sat until he retired in 1859. Succeeded bro. as 4th Bart. Nov. 1872 and resumed name of Beckett. Died 24 May, 1874. [1858]

DENISON, Edward. 16 Chesham Place, London. Only s. of Dr. Edward Denison, Bishop of Salisbury, by his 1st wife Louisa Maria Ker, 2nd d. of Henry Ker Seymer, Esq., of Hanford House, Co. Dorset. B. at Salisbury 1840. Educ. at

Eton and at Christ Church Coll., Oxford. Called to the bar at Lincoln's Inn 1867. A Liberal; in favour of the disestablishment of the Irish Church and of tenants in Ireland being granted compensation for their improvements. Opposed to the ballot. Sat for Newark from Dec. 1868 until his death on 26 Jan. 1870, having left England for Australia in Oct. 1869.   [1869]

DENISON, Rt. Hon. John Evelyn. Speaker's House, Palace Yard, Westminster, London. Ossington Hall, Newark, Nottinghamshire. Reform, Travellers', and Brooks's. Eld. s. of John Denison, Esq., of Ossington, by his 2nd wife, d. of Samuel Estwicke, Esq. B. 1800; m. 1827, Lady Charlotte, 3rd d. of 4th Duke of Portland. Educ. at Eton and Christ Church, Oxford, where he graduated M.A. 1828, and was created honorary D.C.L. 1870. Lord of the Admiralty from May 1827-Feb. 1828. Was chosen Speaker of the House without opposition in 1857; again elected unanimously 1859; a third time Feb. 1866; a 4th time Dec. 1868 (salary £5,000). Patron of 2 livings. Appointed Dept.-Lieut. Nottinghamshire 1854. A Liberal 'careful to maintain the principles and balances of the constitution'; voted against the ballot 1853. Sat for Newcastle-under-Lyme from July 1823-26; for Hastings from Dec. 1826-30; for Nottinghamshire from 1831 (when he was also elected for Liverpool) to Dec. 1832; then for Nottinghamshire S. till July 1837; next for Malton from June 1841 to Mar. 1857, when he was returned for Nottinghamshire N. Sat until created Visct. Ossington Jan. 1872. Died in 1873.
                                                              [1872]

DENISON, William Beckett. 43 Lowndes Square, London. Meanwood Park, Leeds. Carlton, Junior Carlton, and Garrick. 3rd s. of Sir Edmund Beckett, 4th Bart., of Grimthorpe, Yorkshire (who assumed the name of Beckett), by Maria, d. of William Beverley, Esq., of Beverley. B. at Doncaster 1826; m. 1855, Hon. Helen, d. of the 2nd Baron Feversham. Educ. at Rugby and at Trinity Coll., Cambridge. A Banker, head of the firm of Messrs. Beckett and Company, Leeds, Beverley, and other parts of Yorkshire. A Conservative, and gave a general support to the Conservative government. Sat for E. Retford from Feb. 1876 until defeated 1880.   [1880]

DENISON, William Evelyn. 40 South Street, London. Junior United Service. St. Stephen's Dublin. S. of Lieut.-Gen. Sir William Thomas Denison, K.C.B., by Caroline, 2nd d. of Admiral Sir Phipps Hornby, K.C.B. Was therefore newphew to Lord Ossington. B. at Woolwich 1843; m. 1877, Lady Elinor, d. of the 2nd Earl Amherst. Educ. at Eton and at the Military Academy, Woolwich. Entered the Royal Artillery

as Lieut. Feb. 1864, and was attached to the Depot Brigade. Patron of 2 livings. A Conservative. Sat for the bor. of Nottingham from Feb. 1874. Defeated contesting Nottingham N. Apr. 1880. President of M.C.C. 1892. Died 24 Sept. 1916.   [1880]

DENISON, Hon. William Henry Forester. 8 Carlton House Terrace, London. Grimston, Tadcaster, Yorkshire. Brooks's. Eld. s. of Lord Londesborough, by his 1st wife, Hon. Henrietta Maria, 4th d. of the 1st Lord Forester. B. 1834. Appointed a Dept.-Lieut. of the N. Riding of Yorkshire 1856. A Liberal, in favour of a wide extension of the suffrage, reform in taxation, and the abolition of Church rates. Sat for Beverley from Apr. 1857 to May 1859, when he was elected for Scarborough. Sat until he succeeded as 2nd Baron Londesborough Jan. 1860. Advanced to an Earldom 1887. Died 19 Apr. 1900.   [1859]

DENISON, William Joseph. 90 Pall Mall, London. Denbies, Surrey. Reform. B. 1770, the only s. of Joseph Denison, Esq., a London Banker. Uncle to the 2nd Marq. of Conyngham. Patron of 2 livings. A Banker of Whig principles. Voted for agricultural protection 1846 and in favour of short Parliaments, the repeal of the Assessed Taxes, and the substitution of a graduated property tax, and a currency based on gold or silver. Sat for the county of Surrey W. from 1818 until his death in 1849.   [1848]

DENMAN, Hon. George, Q.C. 1 Tamfield Court, Temple, London. Athenaeum. 4th s. of 1st Lord Denman, by Theodosia, eld. d. of the Rev. Richard Vevers, Rector of Kettering. B. in Russell Square, London 1819; m. 1852 Charlotte, d. of Samuel Hope, Esq., Banker of Liverpool. Educ. at Repton School, Derbyshire and at Trinity Coll., Cambridge, was senior classic and captain of the Poll 1842. Elected Fellow of Trinity Coll. 1848 and Auditor of the same Coll. 1852; one of the University Council 1857. Called to the bar at Lincoln's Inn 1846, joined the home circuit; made a Queen's Counsel 1861. A Liberal, believed there was 'no necessity' for the ballot. Unsuccessfully contested Cambridge University Feb. 1856; sat for Tiverton from May 1859 to July 1865; re-elected Feb. 1866. Sat until appointed a Judge 17 Oct. 1872; retired 24 Oct. 1892. Author of various works. Died 21 Sept. 1896.   [1872]

DENNISTOUN, Alex. Mid Calder, Edinburgh. Westminster Club. S. of James Dennistoun, Esq., Banker, of Golf Hill, Glasgow. A Merchant at Glasgow, and had property in Louisiana. A radical Reformer. Sat for Dumbartonshire from 1835 until he retired in 1837. J.P. in Dumbarton and Lanark. Died 15 July 1874.   [1836]

DENNISTOUN, John. 3 Grosvenor Place Houses, London. Brooks's. S. of James Dennistoun, Esq., Banker, of Golf Hill, Glasgow. B. 1803; m. 1838, d. of Sir H. Onslow, Bart. A Banker. A Dept.-Lieut. of Lanarkshire. Had property in Louisiana. A radical Reformer. A member of the Free Trade Club. First returned for Glasgow in 1837 and sat until defeated 1847. Died 9 Sept. 1870.   [1847]

DENT, John Dent. 5 Stanhope Place, London. Ribston Hall, Wetherby, Yorkshire. Reform, and Oxford & Cambridge. Eld. s. of Joseph Dent, Esq., of Ribston Hall, Yorkshire and Winterton, Lincolnshire (who assumed that name in 1834 in lieu of his patronymic Tricket), by Martha, d. of Joseph Birley, Esq. B. 1826; m. 1855, Mary, eld. d. of John Woodhall, Esq., of St. Nicholas House, Scarborough. Educ. at Eton and at Trinity Coll., Cambridge, where he was 16th Senior Optime 1848. Was called to the bar at Lincoln's Inn 1851, but did not practise. Appointed a Dept.-Lieut. of the W. Riding of Yorkshire 1853. A Liberal; in favour of the abolition of Church rates, voted against the ballot 1853. Sat for Knaresborough from 1852-Mar. 1857, when he chose not to contest the seat again. Returned for Scarborough at a by-election 14 Dec. 1857; defeated in 1859 but returned at another by-election 1 Feb. 1860 and sat until defeated again in 1874. Chairman of North Eastern Railway 1880 until his death 22 Dec. 1894.   [1873]

DERING, Sir Edward Cholmeley, Bart. Surrenden Dering, Ashford, Kent. Travellers'. Only s. of Edward Dering, Esq., by Henrietta, eld. d. and co-heir of Richard Neville, Esq., of Furness, Co. Kildare. B. at Barham, Kent, 1807; m. 1832, Hon. Jane, d. of 2nd Lord Kensington. A Dept.-Lieut. of Kent. Appointed Lieut.-Col. East Kent Yeomanry Cavalry, 1861. A Liberal, in favour of the abolition of 'compulsory' church-rates, but 'would strongly deprecate any severance of the existing tie between Church and State'; in favour also of such an extension of the franchise as 'would not confer an undue share of power on any one class.' Sat for East Kent from July 1852 till Oct. 1857; was an unsuccessful candidate there Feb. 1852; re-elected Jan. 1863 and sat until he retired in 1868. Died 1 Apr. 1896.   [1867]

DESART, Earl of. A Conservative. First elected for Ipswich 3 June 1842, but on petition the election was declared void in Aug. 1842. A representative Peer for Ireland from 19 Jan. 1847. Under Secretary of State for the Colonies Mar.-Dec. 1852. Died 1 Apr. 1865.

DE VERE, Stephen Edward. 10 Chapel Street, Grosvenor Square, London. Currah Chase, Adare, Ireland. 2nd s. of Sir Aburey de Vere (2nd Bart.), by Mary, eld. d. of Stephen Edward Rice, Esq., of Mount Trenchard, Co. Limerick, and sister to 1st Lord Monteagle. B. 1812. Unmarried. Educ. at Trinity Coll., Dublin. Called to the bar in Ireland. Of Liberal opinions, in favour of 'tenant-right'; 'opposed the pertinacious assaults on the college of Maynooth'; voted against church rates 1855. First elected for Limerick Co. Dec. 1854, without opposition and sat until he retired 1859.   [1859]

DEVEREUX, John Thomas. Rocklands, Wexford. Reform, and Stafford Street. B. in Wexford. A Liberal, formerly a member of the 'Repeal party'; in favour of the ballot, the admission of Jews to parliament, and 'tenant-right'. First returned for Wexford bor. 1847 and sat until he retired in 1859. Died 31 Dec. 1885.   [1858]

DEVEREUX, Richard Joseph. Wexford. S. of Nicholas Devereux, Esq., by Anne, d. of — Scallan, Esq. B. at Wexford, 1829; m. 1850, Kate, d. of William Hagarty, Esq., R.N. Educ. at Oscott, Mount St. Mary's and Namur. A Merchant. A Liberal. Sat for Wexford from July 1865 to Jan. 1869, when he was unseated on petition; regained his seat Feb. following and sat until he accepted Chiltern Hundreds in 1872.   [1872]

DE WORMS, Baron H. Continued in House after 1885: full entry in Volume II.

D'EYNCOURT, Rt. Hon. Charles Tennyson, F.R.S., F.S.A. Bayons Manor and Usselby, Lincolnshire. Aincourt en Vexin, France. Brooks's, and Reform. S. of George Tennyson, Esq., of Bayons Manor and Usselby, Lincolnshire; m. Frances Mary, only child of the Rev. John Hutton, of Morton, Lincolnshire. Assumed the surname of d'Eyncourt, by royal license, July 31, 1835. Graduated M.A. at St. John's Coll., Cambridge. Called to the bar at the Inner Temple in 1806. Was clerk of the Ordnance from 1830 till 1832, when he was sworn in a P.C. A Magistrate and Dept.-Lieut. for Lincolnshire. High Steward of Louth. Patron of 2 livings. A Liberal, in favour of household suffrage, election by ballot, and religious liberty 'in its full extent', but supported the Church Establishment; brought forward motions in 1833, 34, 37 for shortening the duration of parliaments, which failed by small majorities, but in 1849 succeeded in bringing a bill through the first reading; in 1827, originated the act prohibiting spring guns, etc. in the preservation of game; in 1827, 28, 29, 30 conducted a bill for transferring the franchise from East Retford to

Birmingham, the discussions on which led to important secessions from the Wellington ministry. Was returned for Great Grimsby in 1818 and 1820; for Bletchingley in 1826 and 1830; unsuccessfully contested Stamford in the latter year, but was returned in 1831; this election led to a duel with Lord Thomas Cecil. Sat for Lambeth from 1832 until he retired in 1852. Died 21 July 1861.   [1852]

DICK, Quintin. 20 Curzon Street, London. Layer Marney Tower, Essex. Carlton, White's, Conservative, and Athenaeum. S. of an eminent Merchant. B. 1780; graduated at the University of Dublin; was called to the Irish bar. An East India Proprietor. Patron of 1 living. Lieut.-Col. of the North Essex Militia. Of Conservative principles, voted for agricultural protection, 1846. In favour of the repeal of the Malt Tax and of the substitution of a Property Tax. Sat for West Looe in 1804; for Cashel in 1807; vacated his seat in 1809, and remained out of Parliament till 1826, when he was returned for Oxford; sat for Maldon from 1830 till 1847; first returned for Aylesbury in 1848 and sat until he was defeated at Maldon in 1852. Left between 2 and 3 million pounds at death. Died 26 Mar. 1858.   [1852]

DICK, William Wentworth Fitz-William. 20 Curzon Street, London. Hume Wood, Baltinglass, Co. Wicklow. Carlton, Sackville Street Club, Dublin. Eld. s. of William Hoare Hume, Esq., of Hume Wood (who formerly sat for Wicklow), by Charlotte Ann, d. of the late Samuel Dick, Esq., of Dublin (and sister to Quintin Dick, Esq., who sat for Maldon for several years). Assumed the name of Dick in lieu of Hume by Royal License, June 1864. B. 1805; m. 1829, Margaret Bruce, eld. d. of Robert Chaloner, Esq., of Guisborough, Yorkshire. A Magistrate and Dept.-Lieut. for Wicklow, of which he was High Sheriff 1844. A Conservative, and a firm supporter of the Established Church. First returned for Wicklow July 1852 and sat until defeated 1880. Contested Wicklow W. 5 Dec. 1885 and 13 July 1886.   [1880]

DICKINSON, Francis Henry. 8 Upper Harley Street, London. King's Weston, Somersetshire. Carlton. M. d. of Gen. Carey. A Magistrate and Dept.-Lieut. of Somersetshire. A Conservative, but in favour of free trade; first returned for Somersetshire in 1841, having been an unsuccessful candidate at the general election in 1837, and sat until he retired 1847. Sheriff of Somerset 1854. Died 17 July 1890.   [1847]

DICKINSON, Sebastian Stewart. Brown's Hill, Stroud. Union. S. of Maj.-Gen. Thomas Dickin-

son, of the E.I.C. Engineers, by his marriage with Miss Catherine Dear. B. at Bombay 1815; m. 1856, Frances Stephana, eld. d. of William Henry Hyett, Esq., of Painswick, Gloucestershire, who had sat for Stroud. Educ. at Eton. Called to the bar at the Inner Temple June 1839. A Liberal and Reformer, gave a general support to Mr. Gladstone and voted for the disestablishment of the Irish Church 1869. Sat for Stroud from Dec. 1868. Also returned in Jan. and Feb. 1874, but elections were declared void. Died 23 Aug. 1878.   [1873]

DICKSON, Maj. Alexander George. 10 Duke Street, St. James, London. Glemham Hall, Wickham Market. Carlton, Army & Navy, United Service, and Garrick. S. of George Dickson, Esq., of Belchester, Berwickshire, by Jane, eld. d. of Gen. Sir Martin Hunter, G.C.M.G., of Meadowsley, Durham, and Anton's Hill Berwickshire. B. at Belchester, 1834; m. 1861, Charlotte Maria, 3rd d. of Hon. the Rev. William Eden and widow of Lord North. Educ. at Rugby. Entered the army as Ensign 1853, became Lieut. 1854, afterwards Capt. 6th Dragoon Guards Carabineers, Major 13th Hussars 1860, served with the 62nd Foot at Sebastopol 1854-5, including the attack on the Quarries and on the Redan, for which he received a medal and clasp, was present with the Carabineers at Meerut during the Sepoy mutiny 1857, and at the operations before Delhi, for which he also received a medal and clasp. Chairman of the Crystal Palace Company, and a Director of the London, Chatham and Dover Railway. A moderate Conservative. Sat for Dover from 1865. MP until he died in 1889.   [1889]

DICKSON, James. Howard Terrace, Dungannon. Reform. Ulster Reform. Eld. s. of Thomas Alexander Dickson, Esq., MP, Co. Tyrone, of Miltown House, Dungannon, by Elizabeth Greer, d. of John McGeugh, Esq., of Cookstown. B. at Dungannon 1850. Educ. at the Royal School, Dungannon. M. 1884, Ella, youngest d. of William Tillie, Esq., of Duncreggan, Londonderry. JP for Co. Tyrone. A Liberal. Sat for Dungannon from June 1880 until he retired in 1885.   [1885]

DICKSON, Samuel Auchmuty. Croom Castle, Limerick. Carlton, White's, and Army & Navy. Eld. s. of Maj.-Gen. William Dickson, C.B., (Madras Army), by Harriet, 2nd d. of Maj.-Gen. Sir Thomas Dallas, K.C.B. B. at Madras 1817; m. 1849, Maria Theresa, d. of N. Sanders, Esq. Educ. at Rugby. Entered the army as Ensign 32nd Foot 1835; afterwards became Capt. 13th Dragoons. Appointed Lieut.-Col. Limerick

Militia, May 1854. A Liberal, supported the vote of censure on Lord Palmerston 1864. First elected for the Co. of Limerick May 1859, and sat until he retired in 1865. Died 1870.   [1865]

DICKSON, T.A. Continued in House after 1885: full entry in Volume II.

DIGBY, Hon. Edward Henry Trafalgar. 39 Belgrave Square, London. Minterne House, Cerne, Dorset. Carlton, Guards', White's, and Travellers'. Eld. s. of Lord Digby, by Lady Theresa, eld. d. of the 3rd Earl of Ilchester. B. 1846. Appointed Lieut. and Capt. Coldstream Guards 1868; was Instructor of Musketry from 1869 to 1872; Adjutant from Apr. 1874 to Mar. 1876, Capt. and Lieut.Col. 1877. A Conservative. Sat for Dorset from Jan. 1876 and sat until he retired in 1885. Succeeded as 10th Baron Oct. 1889. Died 11 May 1920.   [1885]

DIGBY, J.K.D.W. See WINGFIELD-DIGBY, J.K.D. Continued in House after 1885: full entry in Volume II.

DIGBY, Kenelm Thomas. Shaftesbury House, The Terrace, Kensington, London. Windham. Only s. of Kenelm Henry Digby, Esq., of Shaftesbury House, The Terrace, Kensington, by Jane Mary, 2nd d. of Thomas Dillon, Esq., of Mount Dillon, Co. Dublin. Was of the same family with Lord Digby. M. 1870, Elizabeth, 2nd d. of Hon. W. Groesbeck, of Cincinnati, Ohio, United States of America. A Liberal, in favour of the system called 'Home Rule' for Ireland, and a 'National Parliament'; also in favour of denominational education. Sat for Queen's Co. from Dec. 1868 until defeated 1880.   [1880]

DILKE, Ashton Wentworth. 1 Hyde Park Gate, London. 2nd s. of Sir Charles Wentworth Dilke, 1st Bart. (who represented Wallingford from 1865-68) by Mary, only d. of Capt. William Chatfield, of the Madras Cavalry. B. in London 1850; m. 1876, Margaret Mary, d. of T. Eustace Smith, Esq., MP, of Gosforth House, Northumberland. Educ. at Trinity Hall, Cambridge, of which he was a scholar. An Author and Journalist. An advanced Liberal. Sat for Newcastle-upon-Tyne from Apr. 1880 until he accepted Chiltern Hundreds Feb. 1883. Died 12 Mar. 1883.   [1882]

DILKE, Sir C.W. Continued in House after 1885: full entry in Volume II.

DILLON, J. Continued in House after 1885: full entry in Volume II.

DILLON, John Blake. 51 Fitzwilliam Square, Dublin. S. of Luke Dillon, Esq., by his marriage with Miss Ann Blake. B. at Ballyhaderran, Co. Mayo 1814; m. 1847, Adelaide, d. of William Hart, Esq. Educ. at Trinity Coll., Dublin. Was called to the bar in Ireland 1841. An Alderman of Dublin, and one of the secretaries and founders of the National Association. A Liberal, directed his efforts to secure 'substantial self-government for Ireland.' First elected for the Co. of Tipperary July 1865 and sat until his death 15 Sept. 1866.
[1865 2nd ed.]

DILLWYN, Lewis Llewelyn. 10 King's Bench Walk, London. Hendrepohan, Nr. Swansea. Athenaeum. 2nd s. of Lewis Weston Dillwyn, Esq., of Skelty Hall, (who sat for Glamorganshire from 1832-37, and was well known for his works on Botany and Natural History), by Mary, d. of John Llewelyn, Esq., of Penllergaer, Glamorganshire. B. at Swansea, 1814; m. 1838, d. and heir of Sir H.T. De la Beche, C.B. (she died 1866). A Magistrate and Dept.-Lieut. for Glamorgan and Hon. Colonel 3rd Glamorgan Regt. A Liberal, in favour of 'Home Rule' for Ireland. Sat for Swansea from Feb. 1855 until he retired in 1892. Died 19 June 1892.   [1891]

DILLWYN, Lewis Weston, F.R.S. Sketley Hall, Glamorganshire. Athenaeum. B. 1778; m. in 1807 Mary, d. of John Llewelyn, Esq., of Penllengare, Glamorganshire. Published several botanical works. A Manufacturer. Of Whig principles, opposed to the ballot and short Parliaments. Sat for Glamorganshire from 1832 until he retired in 1837. Died 31 Aug. 1855.   [1837]

DIMSDALE, Robert. Continued in House after 1885: full entry in Volume II.

DISRAELI, Rt. Hon. Benjamin. 1 Grosvenor Gate, Park Lane, London. Hughendon Manor, High Wycombe, Buckinghamshire. Carlton and Junior Carlton. Eld. s. of Isaac D'Israeli, Esq., D.C.L. of Bradenham Manor, Bucks. (the author of *Curiosities of Literature*). B. Dec. 1805; m. 1839, Marian, d. of Capt. Viney Evans, R.N., and niece of Gen. Sir James Viney, K.C.B., of Taynton Manor, Gloucestershire, and widow of Wyndham Lewis, Esq., MP. Was Chancellor of the Exchequer from Mar.-Dec. 1852, and from Mar. 1858-June 1859, and from July 1866-Feb. 1868. First Lord of the Treasury from the last date to Dec. following; re-appointed First Lord of the Treasury Feb. 1874 (Salary £5,000). Also a member of the Council on Education. Elected Lord Rector of Glasgow University from 1872-73. Author of *Coningsby* and numerous other works of imagination. A Dept.-Lieut. for Buckinghamshire. A trustee of the British

Museum, D.C.L. of the University of Oxford, LL.D. of Edinburgh, a Governor of Wellington Coll., an elder brother of the Trinity House, etc. A Conservative; he said he would 'uphold the constitution in Church and State.' Was an unsuccessful candidate for Wycombe 12 Dec. 1832 and again 7 Jan. 1835; also unsuccessful at Taunton 29 Apr. 1835. Represented Maidstone from July 1837 till June 1841; then Shrewsbury till July 1847, and Buckinghamshire since the last date. Sat until created Earl of Beaconsfield and Visct. Hughendon 21 Aug. 1876. PM 1874-80. Died 19 Apr. 1881.   [1876]

DIVETT, Edward. 97 Eaton Square, London. Bystock, Sidmouth, Devon. Brooks's, and Reform. M. 1836, Anne, d. of G. Ross, Esq., (she died 1856). A Magistrate for Devon. A Liberal, in favour of the ballot and short Parliaments, and the abolition of Church rates. Sat for Exeter from 1832, and sat until his death 25 July 1864. [1864]

DIXON, G. Continued in House after 1885: full entry in Volume II.

DIXON, John. The Knells, Nr. Carlisle. Reform, and Free Trade. B. at Whitehaven 1785, the eld. s. of Peter Dixon, Esq., of Whitehaven, by the d. of Richard Ferguson, Esq., of Carlisle. M. 1814, Mary, d. of Capt. Stordy, of 31st Regiment. Educ. at Kirklington, Nr. Carlisle. A Manufacturer in Carlisle from 1801. Was High Sheriff of Cumberland in 1838, and Mayor of Carlisle in 1839 and in 1840. A Magistrate for Cumberland; Director of the Lancaster and Carlisle, and the Newcastle and Carlisle Railways, and the Carlisle Canal Co. A Reformer, and was one of the Council of the Anti-Corn Law League. Opposed to all further religious endowments. Returned for Carlisle in 1847, but on petition the election was declared void, and he was defeated in the election held there Mar. 1848.   [1847 2nd ed.]

DIXON-HARTLAND, F.D. Continued in House after 1885: full entry in Volume II.

DOBBIN, Leonard. Armagh. Was a Mill Owner and an Agent to the Bank of Ireland, in Armagh. A Dept. Governor and Magistrate for the Co. of Armagh. Of Whig principles; in favour of short Parliaments, and the ballot. Sat for Armagh from 1832 until he retired in 1837.   [1836]

DOBBS, C.R. Acton House, Armagh. A Lieut. in the navy. A Conservative. Returned for Carrickfergus in 1832; unseated on petition in Mar. 1833. Sheriff of Antrim 1841. Died 28 Feb. 1886.   [1833]

DOBBS, William Cary. 21 Fitzwilliam Place, Dublin. Ashurst Dalkey, Co. Dublin. Carlton. Only s. of the Rev. Robert Dobbs (2nd s. of Conway Richard Dobbs, Esq., who was MP for Carrickfergus in the Irish Parliament), by Wilhelmina Josepha, youngest d. of the Rev. William Bristow, D.D., Rector of Belfast. B. in Belfast 1806; m. 1834, Elinor Jones, eld. d. of Henry Sheares Westropp, Esq., of Richmond Villa, Limerick. Educ. at Trinity Coll., Cambridge, of which he was a scholar; took a wrangler's degree in 1827; and graduated M.A. 1830. Called to the bar in Ireland 1833. Appointed Crown Prosecutor for Drogheda and Dundalk on the north-east circuit in Ireland, July 1851. A Conservative, 'being sincerely attached in the Church of England', considered himself thereby 'able to serve his presbyterian and other dissenting fellow subjects most efficiently.' First returned for Carrickfergus, Apr. 1857 and sat until he retired in 1859. A Judge of Landed Estates Court 1859 until his death in London 17 Apr. 1869.   [1858]

DOD, John Whitehall. Cloverley Hall, Whitchurch, Shropshire. Carlton. Only s. of John Dod, Esq., of Cloverley Hall, Shropshire (which the family held uninterruptedly from 1380, having been settled at Calverhall, the adjoining manor, for three centuries. B. at Cloverly, 1797; m. 1st, 1822, Elizabeth, eld. d. of the Rev. George Allanson, of Middleton Quernhow, Yorkshire (she died 1837); 2ndly, 1841, Anne Caroline, 2nd d. of the Venerable Francis Wrangham, Archdeacon of the East Riding of York. Graduated B.A., Christ's Coll., Cambridge, 1820; was appointed Capt. North Shropshire Yeomanry Cavalry, 1823; served the office of Sheriff of Shropshire 1825; appointed a Dept.-Lieut. of Shropshire in 1846. A Conservative, supported the Church in its integrity in England and in Ireland; resisted further concessions to the Church of Rome, and opposed to the admission of the Jews to our Christian legislature. First returned for Shropshire N. without opposition, Feb. 1848 and sat until he retired in 1859. Died 8 July 1863.   [1858]

DODD, George, F.S.A. 9 Grosvenor Place, London. Carlton, Conservative. S. of George DoHof Lieutenant for London, a Magistrate and Dept.-Lieut. for Middlesex, and a Director of several public companies. One of the gentlemen of Her Majesty's Privy Chamber. A Conservative, voted for agricultural protection, 1846. First elected for Maidstone 1841. Sat until he was unseated May 1853. Died 15 Dec. 1864.

[1852 2nd ed.]

DODDS, Joseph. 105 Pall Mall East, London.

Ragworth, Stockton-upon-Tees. Reform. S. of Matthew Dodds, Esq., of Whorley Hill, Co. Durham, by his marriage with Miss Margaret Richardson. B. at Winston, Co. Durham 1819; m. 1847, Anne, only d. of William Smith, Esq., and cousin and co-heiress of Mrs. Elizabeth Starkey, of Stockton-upon-Tees (she died 1876). Was admitted a Solicitor Sept. 1850. A Dept.-Lieut. for the Co. of Durham; Mayor of Stockton 1857-8. Pres. of the Stockton Athenaeum and other local institutions. A Liberal, was in favour of Home Rule. Sat for Stockton from Dec. 1868 until he accepted Chiltern Hundreds Dec. 1888. Name struck off list of Solicitors for embezzlement 18 Feb. 1889. Died 12 Dec. 1891. [1888]

DODSON, Rt. Hon. John George. 6 Seamore Place, London. Conyboro', Lewes, Sussex. University, Reform, Devonshire, and Brooks's. Only s. of the Rt. Hon. Sir John Dodson, by Frances Priscilla, d. of George Pearson, Esq., M.D. B. 1825; m. 1856, Florence, 2nd d. of W.J. Campion, Esq., of Danny, Sussex. Educ. at Eton, where he gained the Prince Consort's prizes for modern languages 1841 and 1842, and at Christ Church, Oxford, where he was 1st class in classics 1847. Called to the bar at Lincoln's Inn 1853. Chairman of Committees of the Whole House from Feb. 1865-Apr. 1872. Was Financial Sec. to the Treasury from Aug. 1873-Feb. 1874. Pres. of the Local Government Board from Apr. 1880-Dec. 1882, when he became Chancellor of the Duchy of Lancaster (salary £2,000). Appointed a member of the Committee of Council on Agriculture 1883. A Liberal. Unsuccessfully contested Sussex E. July 1852 and Mar. 1857. First elected for E. Sussex Apr. 1857 and sat until Feb. 1874. Sat for Chester from Feb. 1874 to Apr. 1880, when he was unseated on petition. Sat for Scarborough from July 1880 until he was created Baron Monk Bretton Nov. 1884. Died 25 May 1897. [1884]

DONKIN, Sir Rufane Shaw, G.C.B. 33 Park Street, Grosvenor Square, London. Caversham, Berkshire. M. in 1832, d. of the 2nd Earl of Minto. Surveyor-Gen. of the Ordnance, and a Major-Gen. in the army. Of Liberal politics. Sat for Berwick in 1832 and 1835, elected for Sandwich 1839. MP until he died Apr. 1841. [1840]

DORINGTON, J.E. Continued in House after 1885: full entry in Volume II.

DOTTIN, Abel Rons. 31 Argyle Street, London. Bugle Hall, Hampshire. Carlton. Formerly a Capt. in the 2nd Life Guards. M. Dorothy, sister of Mary, Dowager Lady Arundel, and eld. d. of Robert Burnett Jones, Esq., of Ades, Sussex, late Attorney-Gen. in the Island of Barbados. A Dept.-Lieut. for the town and Co. of Southampton. The founder of the family was William Dottin, Esq., of Granada Hall, Barbados. A Conservative. Sat for Southampton in several Parliaments before and after the passing of the Reform Act. He did not stand in 1832, but regained his seat in 1835. Sat until he retired in 1841. Died 7 June 1852. [1838]

DOUGLAS, A. Akers. See AKERS-DOUGLAS, A. Continued in House after 1885: full entry in Volume II.

DOUGLAS, Sir Charles Eurwicke, K.C.M.G. 27 Wilton Crescent, London, White's, and Brooks's. S. of the Rt. Hon. Charles Yorke. B. 1806; m. 1832, Jane, eld. d. of Sir Charles Des Voeux, Bart. Educ. at Harrow and St. John's Coll., Cambridge, where he graduated B.A. 1828, M.A. 1831. Was private Sec. to the Earl of Ripon from 1830-1834, when his Lordship was Sec. of State for the Colonies. Was a Commissioner of Greenwich Hospital from Aug. 1845-July 1846. Formerly held the honorary office of King of Arms of the Order of St. Michael and St. George. A Liberal, in favour of a wide extension of the franchise, vote by ballot, and the abolition of Church rates. Sat for Warwick from July 1837 to July 1852; unsuccessfully contested Durham City 1853. Elected for Banbury Apr. 1859 and sat until he retired 1865. Died 21 Feb. 1887. [1865]

DOUGLAS, Sir George Henry Scott, Bart. Springwood Park, Kelso, Scotland. Army & Navy, and Carlton. S. of Sir John James Scott Douglas, (3rd) Bart., by Hannah Charlotte, only d. and heir of Henry Scott, Esq., of Belford, Roxburghshire. B. at Edinburgh 1825; m. 1851, Marquita, eld. d. of Francisco Sancherz di Pina, Esq., of Gibraltar. Was appointed Capt. 34th Foot in 1850, retired 1851. Became Major 2nd Batt. Roxburghshire Rifle Volunteers 1862. A Conservative, in favour of maintaining the Established Church of Scotland, but said he would willingly have supported a change of the law of patronage; in favour also of an alteration of the Game Laws as regards ground game. Sat for Roxburghshire from Feb. 1874 until defeated 1880. [1880]

DOUGLAS, Sir Howard, Bart., G.C.B., G.C.M.G., K.C.H., F.R.S. 15 Green Street, London. Carr, Perthshire. Carlton. 3rd s. of the 1st Bart., by the d. of John Baillie, Esq. M. 1799, eld. d. of James Dundas, Esq., succeeded his bro. as 3rd Bart. in 1809. A Lieut.-Gen. in the army, and Col. of the 99th Foot. Served in Spain and Portugal. Was Lord High Commissioner of the Ionian Islands from 1835-1840. A Conservative, voted for agricultural protection 1846. First returned for Liverpool in Feb. 1842, on the elevation of Mr. Cresswell to the Bench, having been unsuccessful in 1832 and 1835, and sat until he retired 1847. Died 9 Nov. 1861. [1847]

DOUGLAS, James Douglas Stoddart. 16 Hyde Park Square, London. Chelston Park, Kent. Carlton, Junior United Service, and Colonial. A Lieut. R.N. A Conservative, voted for agricultural protection 1846. Unsuccessfully contested Rochester in 1837. First returned for it in 1841 and sat until defeated 1847. [1847]

DOUGLAS-PENNANT, Hon. Edward Gordon. See PENNANT, Hon. Edward Gordon Douglas-.

DOUGLAS-PENNANT, Hon. George Sholto. See PENNANT, Hon. George Sholto Douglas-.

DOULTON, Frederick. High Street, Lambeth, London. Alleyn House, Dulwich Common, Surrey. Reform. S. of Mr. John Doulton and Jane his wife. B. in Lambeth 1824; m. 1848, Sarah, d. of John Meredith, Esq., of Lambeth. A Manufacturer in Lambeth of earthenware, terra cotta, etc. Was a Member of the Metropolitan Board of Works from its first formation. A Liberal, strongly in favour of an extension of the franchise, but voted against Lord Russell's Reform Bill 1866; in favour of the ballot, 'the unconditional repeal' of church-rates, and 'the economical application of the public revenues.' Contested Reigate 6 Feb. 1858. First elected for Lambeth May 1862 and sat until he retired in 1868. Died 21 May 1872. [1867]

DOURO, Marq. of. 3 Upper Belgrave Street, London. White's, Travellers', Junior United Service, and Carlton. Eld. s. of the Duke of Wellington; grands. on the paternal side of the Earl of Mornington, and on the maternal of the Earl of Longford. B. in Harley Street, 1807; m. d. of the 8th Marq. of Tweeddale (she was a Lady of the Bedchamber to the Queen). M.A. and D.C.L. of Cambridge. A Col. in the army, and Aide-de-Camp to the Commander-in-Chief. A Conservative, but in favour of free trade. Sat in 1829, 1830 and 1831 for Aldborough, in Suffolk, for which he was elected three times. Contested Hampshire N. 14 Dec. 1832. First elected for Norwich in 1837 and sat until he was defeated in 1852. Succeeded as 2nd Duke Sept. 1852. Died 13 Aug. 1884. [1852]

DOWDESWELL, William. 7 Park Place, St. James's, London. Pull Court, Gloucestershire.

Athenaeum, and Carlton. Eld. s. of John Edmund Dowdeswell, Esq., the Master in Chancery, (formerly MP for Tewkesbury), and grands. of the Rt. Hon. William Dowdeswell, Chancellor of the Exchequer during the Rockingham Administration. M. 1839, the youngest d. of Robert Graham, Esq. Some member of the Dowdeswell family had represented Tewkesbury for many years. A Conservative, voted for agricultural protection 1846. Unsuccessfully contested Tewkesbury in 1832, but was elected in 1835, and sat until he retired 1847. Sheriff of Worcestershire 1855. Died 5 Feb. 1870. [1847]

DOWDESWELL, William Edward. Pull Court, Tewkesbury. Athenaeum, and Carlton. Eld. s. of William Dowdeswell, Esq., of Pull Court, Worcestershire, who represented Tewkesbury for many years, by Amelia Letitia, youngest d. of Robert Graham, Esq., of Cossington Hall, Somersetshire. B. 1841; m. 1868, Emily, 2nd d. of Sir Thomas G.A. Parkyns, Bart. A Dept.-Lieut. of Worcestershire. A Conservative, in favour of the establishment of County financial boards. Sat for Tewkesbury from July 1865 to Mar. 1866, since which date he sat for W. Worcestershire. Sat until he accepted Chiltern Hundreds about 1 June 1876. Died 12 July 1893. [1876]

DOWNING, McCarthy. Bessborough Gardens, London. Prospect House, Skibbereen, Co. Cork. S. of Eugene Downing, Esq., of Kenmore, Co. Kerry, by Helena, 5th d. of Timothy McCarthy, Esq., of Kilgadamore in the same Co. B. at Kenmore 1814; m. 1837, Jane, youngest d. of Daniel McCarthy, Esq., of Ave Hill, Co. Cork. Admitted a Solicitor in Ireland 1836. Was for 6 years in succession Chairman of the Skibbereen Town Commissioners. A Liberal, in favour of a system called 'Home Rule' for Ireland, the amendment of the Grand Jury Laws, and denominational education. Sat for the Co. of Cork from Dec. 1868. MP until his death 9 Jan. 1879. [1878]

DOWSE, Richard, Q.C. 38 Mountjoy Square, S. Dublin. University Club, Dublin. S. of William Henry Dowse, Esq., of Dungannon, C. Tyrone, by Maria, d. of Hugh Donaldson, Esq. B. at Dungannon 1824; m. 1852, Kate d. of George Moore, of Dualore, Clones, Ireland. Educ. at Dungannon Royal School; also at Trinity Coll., Dublin, where he was first in honours and a scholar. Was called to the bar in Ireland 1852; appointed a Queen's Counsel 1863, made 3rd Queen's Serjeant there by patent 1869, and Solicitor-Gen. for Ireland Feb. 1870. A Liberal, who promised to give general support to Mr. Gladstone. Sat for Londonderry City from Dec. 1868 until appointed Baron of Exchequer 1 Nov. 1872. Died 14 Mar. 1890. [1872]

DRAX, John Samuel Wanley Sawbridge Erle-.
20 King Street, St. James's, London. Charborough Park, Blandford. Holnest House, Sherborne, Dorsetshire. Ellerton Abbey, Richmond, Yorkshire. Olantigh House, Wye, Kent. Carlton, and Wyndham. Eld. s. of Samuel Elias Sawbridge, Esq., of Olantigh House, Co. Kent, by Elizabeth, d. of Brabazon Ellis, Esq., of Wyddiall Hall, Hertfordshire. Grands. of Alderman Sawbridge, who sat for London upwards of 30 years. Assumed the names Erle Drax 1828. B. 1800; m. 1827, only d. of Richard Erle Drax Grosvenor, Esq. Appointed Dept.-Lieut. of Dorset 1852. Patron of 5 livings. A Conservative. Unsuccessfully contested Wareham Dec. 1832, and again July 1837. Sat for Wareham from July 1841 to July 1857 (when he was again an unsuccessful candidate), and from Apr. 1859 to July 1865, when he was defeated. Was unsuccessful Nov. 1868, but was re-elected Jan. 1869. Sat until he was defeated 1880. Died 7 Jan. 1887.   [1880]

DRUMLANRIG, Rt. Hon. Visct. Kinmount and Glen Stenart, Dumfriesshire. Arthur's, and St. James's. B. in Edinburgh 1818, the only s. of the Marq. of Queensberry. M. 1840, Caroline, the d. of Sir William Robert Clayton, Bart. Educ. at Eton. Was a Cornet in the 2nd Life Guards, but retired in 1844. Lord Lieut. of Dumfriesshire and a Col. in the Dumfries Militia. Appointed Comptroller of the Household, Dec. 1852. 'A Tory, but a Liberal one', who supported any well-considered measure for the extension of the franchise. Voted against the ballot 1853; opposed any endowment of the Roman Catholic Clergy, but was an advocate of entire religious liberty. Represented Dumfriesshire from 1847 until he succeeded as 7th Marq. in Dec. 1856. Died 6 Aug. 1858.   [1856]

DRUMMOND, Henry, F.R.S. 33 Albermarle Street, London. Albury Park, Guildford, Surrey. Travellers'. Eld. s. of Henry Drummond, Esq., Banker in London, by the d. of the 1st Visct. Melville (she m. 2ndly James Strange, Esq.). Represented a Junior branch of Visct. Strathallan's family. B. 1786; m. 1807, Lady Henrietta eld. d. of the 9th Earl of Kinrouh (she d. 1854). Member of the Royal Academy of Fine Arts at Florence, founded the Professorship of Political Economy at Oxford. A Magistrate of Surrey, President of the Western Literary Institution. A Conservative. Held that 'the beverage of the people should be as free from taxation as their bread.' First elected for West Surrey in 1847, without opposition. MP until his death 20 Feb. 1860.   [1859]

DRUMMOND,   Henry   Home. Blair-Drummond, Perthshire, Carlton, and Union. S. of George Home Drummond, Esq., and grands. of Henry Home Lord Kames. B. 1783; m. in 1812 d. of C.M. Stirling, Esq. Took the degree of B.C.L. at Oxford. Director of the Royal Bank of Scotland. Appointed in Sept. 1845 one of the Board of Supervision for the Relief of the Poor in Scotland. Was called to the Scottish bar. Vice-Lieut. of Perthshire. Author of a work on the Course of Education pursued in the University of Oxford, in reply to an article in the *Edinburgh Review*. A Conservative, but in favour of free trade. Sat for Stirlingshire in the Parliaments of 1821, 1826, and 1830. First returned for Perthshire in 1840. Sat until he retired in 1852. Died 12 Sept. 1867.   [1852]

DU CANE, Sir Charles. 54 Queen's Gate Terrace, South Kensington, London. Braxted Park, Witham, Essex. Arthur's, and Carlton. S. of Capt. Charles Du Cane, R.N., of Braxted Park, Witham, Essex, by Frances, 2nd d. of the Rev. Charles Prideaux Brune, of Prideaux Place, Padstow, Cornwall. B. at Ryde, Isle of Wight, 1825; m. 1863 Hon. Georgina Susan, d. of Lord Lyndhurst. Educ. at the Charterhouse, and at Exeter Coll., Oxford, where he was fourth class in classics and mathematics in 1847. Appointed a Lord of the Admiralty July 1866 (salary £1000). A Magistrate and Dept.-Lieut. for Essex. Patron of 1 living. A Conservative, in favour of extending the franchise to the 'industrious and intelligent portion of the working classes'; opposed to the malt-tax as being 'oppressive to both producer and consumer'; against all compulsory education-rates. Sat for Maldon from July 1852 till Mar. 1853, when the election was declared void for bribery and treating. First returned for Essex N. in Mar. 1857. Sat until he retired in 1868. Governor of Tasmania 1869-74; K.C.M.G. 1875; Chairman of Board of Customs May 1878, until his death on 25 Feb. 1889.   [1867]

DUCKHAM, Thomas. Continued in House after 1885: full entry in Volume II.

DUCKWORTH, Sir John Thomas Buller, Bart. Wear House, Devonshire. Carlton, Travellers', and Oxford & Cambridge. S. of Admiral Sir John T. Duckworth, 1st Bart., by his 2nd wife, Susannah, d. of Bishop (Buller) of Exeter. B. at Downes, in Crediton parish, Devon 1809; m. 1850, Mary Isabella, youngest d. of John Buller, Esq., of Morval, Cornwall. Educ. at Eton and at Oriel Coll., Oxford, where he graduated B.A. 1829. Appointed Major of the 1st Devon Yeomanry Cavalry 1844, and Dept.-Lieut. of Devon 1848. A Conservative, voted for inquiry into Maynooth 1853. First returned for Exeter

1845. Sat until he retired 1857. Sheriff of Devon 1861. Died 29 Nov. 1887. [1857]

DUCKWORTH, Samuel. 35 Woburn Place, Old Square, Lincoln's Inn. S. of a Solicitor at Manchester and bro.-in-law of Sir Thomas Coltman, one of the Judges of the Court of Common Pleas; he practised at the Chancery Bar. A radical Reformer. Returned for Leicester in 1837 and sat until appointed Master in Chancery Feb. 1839. [1838]

DUFF, George Skene. 130 Piccadilly, London. Milton Duff, Elginshire. Delgaty Castle, Turriff, Aberdeenshire. Brooks's, Boodle's, and Army & Navy. B. at Edinburgh 1816, the 2nd s. of Gen. the Hon. Sir Alexander Duff, by the youngest d. of James Skein, Esq. Was bro. to the 5th Earl of Fife. Unmarried. Was successively attaché to the embassies of Paris and Vienna, during a period of 6 years. Appointed Lord Lieut. of Elginshire 1856. A Liberal, opposed to the ballot, and in favour of a system of United National Education, on religious principles, for Scotland. Sat for the Elgin district of Burghs from 1847 until he accepted Chiltern Hundreds 19 Dec. 1857. Died 15 Mar. 1889. [1857 2nd ed.]

DUFF, James. 41 Eaton Place, London. Skene House, and Corriemulzie, Aberdeenshire. Brooks's, and Reform. Eld. s. of Gen. the Hon. Sir Alexander Duff, G.C.H., and heir presumptive to his uncle, the 4th Earl of Fife. B. in Edinburgh 1814; m. 1846, Lady Agnes Georgiana, 2nd d. of 16th Earl of Erroll. A Dept.-Lieut. of Banff, of Aberdeenshire and of Elginshire. Appointed Lord-Lieut. of Morayshire 1851. Of Liberal politics, voted against the ballot 1853. Sat for Banffshire from 1837 until he succeeded as 5th Earl of Fife June 1857. Created Baron Skene (U.K. Peerage) 1 Oct. 1857. Died 7 Aug. 1879. [1857]

DUFF, Col. James. 36 Upper Brook Street, London. Westwick House, Norwich. Junior United Service, Army & Navy, and Carlton. S. of James Duff, Esq., (only s. of Gen. Sir James Duff) by Eliza Charlotte, eld. d. of Sir George Beeston Prescott, Bart. B. at Innes House, Elgin, 1831; m. 1859, Mary Laura, d. of Edward Dawkins, Esq., of Upper Brook Street, London. Was Educ. at Rugby. Entered the army as Ensign in 1851; became Capt. 23rd Fusiliers Dec. 1854, and retired as Major 1858; served in the Crimea 1854 and at Sebastopol and Inkermann, where he was taken prisoner; received the Crimean Medal with two clasps, the Turkish Medal, the 5th class of the Medjidie etc. Magistrate for Norfolk. A Conservative. Sat for N. Norfolk from Apr. 1876. MP until his death 22 Dec. 1878. [1878]

DUFF, Lachlan Duff Gordon-. Park House, Banffshire. Senior United Service. S. of Thomas Gordon, Esq., of Park, Banffshire, by Joan Maria, eld. d. of D. Macdowall Grant, Esq., of Arndily. B. at Park, 1817; m. 1847, Jane, d. of Thomas Bullerfield, Esq., of Bermuda. Educ. at Edinburgh and on the Continent. Entered the army in 1834 (20th Foot); retired as Major 1851. A Liberal, and supporter of Lord Palmerston. First elected for Banff July 1857, and sat until he accepted Chiltern Hundreds 1861. [1861]

DUFF, Rt. Hon. Monntstuart Elphinstone Grant. York House, Twickenham, Middlesex. Athenaeum, and Brooks's. S. of James Cunninghame Grant Duff, Esq., by Jane Catherine, only child of Sir Whitelaw Ainshe, M.D. B. at Eden, Nr. Banff, 1829; m. 1859, Anna Julia, only d. of Edward Webster, Esq., of North Lodge, Ealing. Was educ. at Edinburgh and Balliol Coll., Oxford where he was 2nd class in classics 1850, and graduated M.A. 1853; gained a Law Studentship offered for competition by the Inns of Court 1853; graduated LL.B. with honours at the University of London 1854. Was called to the bar at the Inner Temple Nov. 1854 and went for a short time the Midland Circuit. Was Lord Rector of Aberdeen University from Dec. 1866-Dec. 1872. Under-Secretary of State for India from Dec. 1868-Feb. 1874. Appointed Under-Secretary of State for the Colonies Apr. 1880 (Salary £1,500). A member of the Committee of Council on Education in Scotland. Dept.-Lieut. of Moray and a Magistrate for Banff, Moray and Aberdeen S. A Liberal, and voted for the disestablishment of the Irish Church 1869, as being 'a monster injustice'; in favour of the amelioration of the State of Ireland, and amendment of the Land Laws, the lowering of the county franchise, and a system of self-government for counties. Sat for Elgin district from Dec. 1857 until appointed Governor of Madras, July 1881. [1881]

DUFF, Robert William. Fetteresso Castle, Stonehaven, Scotland. Glassangh Portson, Banffshire. Culter, Aberdeenshire. Brooks's. Only s. of Arthur Duff, Esq., of Fetteresso (who assumed the name of Abercromby on succeeding to the estates of his mother), by Elizabeth, d. of John Innes, Esq., of Cowie, Kincardineshire. B. at Banff, 1835; m. 1871, Louisa, youngest d. of Sir William Scott, Bart., of Ancrum. Educ. at Blackheath School. Entered the navy 1848; attained the rank of Lieut. 1856 ; retired as Commander 1870. Appointed Lord of the Treasury June 1882, and Civil Lord of the Admiralty 1886. A Dept.-Lieut. of Banffshire, Aberdeen and Kincardineshire. Assumed the name Duff *in lieu* of Abercromby on succeeding to the estates of his uncle, Dec. 1861. A Liberal, in favour of 'Home Rule' for Ireland, the Reform of the land laws, and the maintenance of an efficient Navy. Sat for Banff from May 1861 until appointed Governor of New South Wales 8 Mar. 1893. Remained Governor until his death 18 Mar. 1895.   [1891]

DUFFIELD, Thomas, D.C.L. Marcham Park, Berkshire. Carlton. M. 1st, d. of Robert Cary Elwes, Esq., 2ndly, 1838, d. of Lieut.-Col. Rushbrooke. A Dept.-Lieut. of Berkshire. A Conservative. From 1832 he sat for Abingdon, succeeding Mr. John Maberly, who represented the borough from 1818-32. Sat until he accepted Chiltern Hundreds Apr. 1844.   [1844]

DUFFY, Sir Charles Gavan. 21 Eccleston Street, London. 15 Waltham Terrace, Blackrock, Dublin. S. of Mr. Duffy, a Farmer, in the Co. of Monaghan. B. in Monaghan 1816; m. 1st, 1842, Emily, d. of Francis McLaughlin, Esq., of Belfast, Merchant, and grand-d. of the McDermott of Coolavin (she died 1845); 2ndly, 1846, Susan, d. of Philip Hughes, Esq., of Newry, Merchant. Educ. at the Belfast Institution. Was called to the bar in Ireland 1845. Founder and editor of the *Nation* newspaper. Edited the *Ballad Poetry of Ireland*, and other volumes of the *Library of Ireland*. Of extreme Liberal opinions, was one of the founders of the Irish tenant league; was one of the State Prisoners with Daniel O'Connell, Esq., in 1844, and one of the prisoners prosecuted for treason and felony in 1848. First returned for New Ross in July 1852. Accepted Chiltern Hundreds in 1856.   [1856]

DUGDALE, William Stratford. Blyth Hall, Warwickshire. Carlton. Only s. of Dugdale Stratford Dugdale, Esq., of Merevale Hall, Warwickshire, (Patron of 1 living), who married Charlotte, d. of Visct. Curzon. B. 1801; m. 1827, Harriet-Ella, d. of E.B. Portman, Esq., of Bryanstone, Co. Dorset, and sister of Lord Portman. A Trustee of Rugby School, and Capt. of the Warwickshire Yeomanry. A Conservative, but in favour of free trade. Sat for Bramber in 1831, and before that for Shaftesbury. Sat for Warwickshire N. from 1832 until he retired 1847. Died 15 Sept. 1871.   [1847]

DUKE, Sir James, Bart. 43 Portland Place, London. Laughton Lodge, Lewes, Sussex. Reform, and City. S. of John Duke, Esq., Merchant, of Montrose. B. at Montrose; m. 1802, Jane Amelia, eld. d. of William Bennett, Esq., of Aberdeen Park, Highbury. Entered the Civil Dept. of the Royal Navy at an early age, under Capt. Sir Peter Parker, Bart. Was with Lord Exmouth when Commander in Chief in the Mediterranean, and was Sec. to Admiral Sir John Gore at the close of the war. Commenced his commercial career in London 1819, was chosen Sheriff of London and Middlesex in 1836, having the previous year been appointed a Magistrate for Middlesex. Elected Lord Mayor of London 1848-9. A Dept.-Lieut. for Lincolnshire and for Middlesex; an Alderman of London (elected 1840 for Farringdon-without); a Magistrate for Sussex, and a Commissioner of the Lieutenancy of London. A Liberal, favourable to the ballot, and to the shorter duration of Parliaments. Sat for Boston from 1837 to July 1849, when he was returned for London without opposition. Sat until he retired 1865. Died 28 May 1873.   [1865]

DUNBAR, George. 5 St. James's Square, London. Belfast. Landmore, Co. Londonderry. Carlton, and Junior University. Only s. of Alex. Orr, Esq., of Landmore. In 1833 assumed the name of Dunbar. A Barrister. A Conservative, totally unpledged. First elected for Belfast towards the close of 1835, on the death of Mr. McCance the former member; defeated at the general election in 1873, but seated on petition in Mar. 1838. Retired in 1841. Died 17 Aug. 1875.   [1840]

DUNBAR, John. 4 Garden Court, Temple, London. Garrick. 3rd s. of Joseph Dunbar, Esq., of Cork, by Bridget, d. of T. Murray, Esq., of Cork. B. at Cork 1827. Unmarried. Was educ. at Clongowes Wood and at Trinity Coll., Dublin, where he graduated B.A. 1849, M.A. 1865. Was called to the bar in Ireland June 1849, and at the Middle Temple Nov. 1854. Joined the Home Circuit, practised for some years at the Bombay bar, and was a Fellow of the Bombay University. A Liberal, was in favour of the establishment of a system of union rating, the amendment of Grand Jury Laws in Ireland; also of denominational education, and of the system called 'Home Rule' for Ireland etc. Sat for New Ross from Feb. 1874. MP until his death 3 Dec. 1878.   [1878]

DUNBAR, Sir William, Bart. Merton Hall, Newton Stewart, Scotland. Brooks's. Eld. s. of James Dunbar, Esq., sometime an officer in the 21st Light Dragoons, by Anna Catharina, d. of William Ferdinand Baron de Reede D'Oudtshoorn, in the Netherlands. B. 1812; m. 1842, Catherine Hay, eld. d. of James Paterson, Esq., of Carpow, Perthshire. Educ. at the University of Edinburgh. Admitted an advocate at the Scottish bar 1835, but never practised. Appointed a Lord of the Treasury June 1859, salary £1,000; Keeper of the Privy Seal to the Prince of Wales July following, and one of the Council of His Royal Highness Jan. 1863. Had been a

Dept.-Lieut. of Wigton from 1856. A Liberal, in favour of extension of the suffrage, but opposed to the ballot; in favour also of an extended measure of education, and of improving the condition of schoolmasters. First elected for Wigton district Apr. 1857 without opposition and sat until he was appointed Commissioner for Auditing Public Accounts in 1865. Comptroller and Auditor General 1867-88. Died 18 Dec. 1889.

DUNCAN, George. 1 Belgrave Street South, London. The Vine, Dundee. Reform. B. 1791. Was a Merchant in Dundee, but retired 1831. Was mainly instrumental in introducing Steam Navigation between Dundee and London. A Liberal, voted in 1853 for the ballot, opposed to any grant to Maynooth. First returned for Dundee 1841, and sat until he retired 1857. Died 6 Jan. 1878.   [1857]

DUNCAN, Visct. 15 Hill Street, London. Camperdown, Forfarshire. Gleneagles, Perthshire. Brooks's, and Travellers'. Eld. s. of the Earl of Camperdown and Grandson of Admiral, 1st Visct. Duncan. B. at Edinburgh, 1812; m. 1839, Juliana Cavendish, d. of Sir Geo. Richard Philips, Bart. Educ. at Trinity Coll., Cambridge, where he graduated M.A. 1834. A Dept.-Lieut. for Forfarshire and Perthshire. Lord of the Treasury from Mar. 1855-Mar. 1858. A Liberal, in favour of the ballot, the abolition of Church rates and of the removal of all religious disabilities. Sat for Southampton from July 1837 to July 1841, and for Bath from the latter date until July 1852, when he was an unsuccessful candidate for Bury. First elected for Forfarshire, Oct. 1854, without opposition, and sat until he succeeded father as 2nd Earl of Camperdown 22 Dec. 1859. Died 30 Jan. 1867.   [1859]

DUNCANNON, Lord. 3 Cavendish Square, London. Brooks's, White's, and Travellers'. Eld. s. of the Earl of Besborough, related to the Duke of Devonshire, whose family interest in Derby he was understood to represent. B. 1809; m. 1835, d. of the Earl of Durham. Lord-Lieut. of Carlow. Of Whig principles, in favour of the ballot. Was opposed, on conservative principles, by Mr. Pole. Sat for Bletchingly in May 1831, and for Higham Ferrers in Nov. of the same year. First elected for Derby in Jan. 1835. Sat until he succeeded as 5th Earl of Besborough (2nd Baron Duncannon in U.K. Peerage) May 1847. Died 28 Jan. 1880.   [1847]

DUNCOMBE, Hon. Arthur. 58 Grosvenor Street, London. Kilnwick Percy, Pocklington, Yorkshire. Carlton, and Conservative. 2nd surviving s. of 1st Lord Feversham, by Lady Charlotte, d. of 2nd Earl of Dartmouth. B. 1806; m. in 1836 Delia, youngest d. of John Wilmer Field, Esq., of Heaton Hall, Yorkshire. Became a Capt. in the navy, 1834; made a Vice-Admiral on the reserved list 1863. Was Groom in Waiting to the Queen. Was a Lord of the Admiralty from Mar. 1852 till Dec. of the same year. Appointed Dept.-Lieut. of the East Riding of Yorkshire, 1852. A Conservative, opposed to the grant to Maynooth, in favour of education being 'based on Scripture'; voted for the abolition of church-rates 1855. Sat for East Retford, in 1830; re-elected in 1835, and sat from that date until Oct. 1851, when he was returned without opposition for the East Riding of Yorkshire. Sat until he unsuccessfully contested Leeds 17 Nov. 1868. Sheriff of Yorkshire 1874. Died 6 Feb. 1889.   [1867]

DUNCOMBE, Hon. Octavious. 84 Eaton Square, London. Westerdale, Grosmont. Waresley Park, Huntingdonshire. Carlton. Youngest s. of 1st Baron Feversham, by Lady Charlotte, only d. of 2nd Earl of Dartmouth. B. 1817; m. 1842, Lady Emily Caroline, eld. d. of 1st Earl of Cawdor. Once Lieut. in 1st Life Guards. A Dept.-Lieut. of Huntingdonshire. Appointed Col. of Cambridge Militia 1852 and a Dept.-Lieut. of the same Co. Oct. 1853. A Conservative. Sat for the N. Riding of Yorkshire from Sept. 1841 to Apr. 1859; re-elected Feb. 1867 and sat until he retired 1874. Died 3 Dec. 1879.   [1873]

DUNCOMBE, Thomas Slingsby. 88 St. James's Street, London. Reform. Eld. s. of Thos. Duncombe, Esq., of Copgrove, near Boroughbridge (bro. of 1st Lord Feversham), by the d. of Bishop (Hinchcliffe) of Peterborough. A radical Reformer. In favour of triennial Parliaments, and the ballot. Sat for Hertford from 1824 to 1832, in which year he was ejected by Lords Mahon and Ingestre, but the election was subsequently declared void, though no new writ was issued. Sat for Finsbury from 1834. MP until his death 13 Nov. 1861.   [1861]

DUNCOMBE, Hon. William. 23 Cavendish Square, London. Hooten Pagnell, Yorkshire. Carlton. Eld. s. of Lord Feversham. B. 1798; m. 1823 Louisa, youngest d. of the Earl of Galloway. A Major of the 3rd West Yorkshire Militia. A Conservative, in favour of protection for agriculture. Sat for Yorkshire in the Parliaments of 1826 and 1830, but lost his seat in 1831 in consequence of his opposition to the first Reform Bill. Sat for Grimsby 1820 to 26, Yorkshire 1826 to 31 (2 Parliaments), and Yorkshire N. since 1832. Sat until he succeeded as 2nd Baron Feversham 16 July 1841. Died 11 Feb. 1867.   [1838]

DUNCOMBE, Hon. William Ernest. 20 Grosvenor Square, London. The Leases, Bedale, Yorkshire. Junior Carlton. Eld. s. of Lord Feversham, by Lady Louisa, 3rd d. of the 8th Earl of Galloway. B. at Hooton Pagnell House, Nr. Doncaster, 1829; m. 1851, Mabel, 2nd d. of the Rt. Hon. Sir James R. Graham, Bart. Appointed Capt. of the Yorkshire Yeomanry Cavalry 1854; Dept.-Lieut. of the N. Riding of Yorkshire 1852; Lieut.-Col. 2nd Batt. N. Riding Rifle Volunteers 1860. A Conservative, and said he would give a general support to Lord Derby; in favour of such a measure of Parliamentary reform 'as would give no undue preponderance to any one class, but would conduce to a fair distribution of political privileges', also of a reduction and the ultimate repeal of the malt-tax. Sat for E. Retford from Feb. 1852 to July 1857. Elected for the N. Riding of Yorkshire May 1859 and sat until he succeeded as 3rd Baron in 1867. Created 1st Earl in 1868. President of Royal Agricultural Society 1891. Died 13 Jan. 1915. [1865]

DUNCUFT, John. Westwood House, Oldham, Lancashire. National. Descended from a family long settled in Oldham. Was a Sharebroker from 1824. A Magistrate for Lancashire, West Riding of Yorkshire, and Cheshire. A Conservative, but in favour of free trade; opposed to the endowment of the Roman Catholic Clergy. First returned for Oldham in 1847. MP until he died 27 July 1852. [1852]

DUNDAS, Charles Whitley Deans. 9 Baker Street, Portman Square, London. Aston Hall, Flintshire. S. of the member for Devizes. M. his cousin, Miss Jardine, grand-d. of the celebrated Bruce, the Abyssinian traveller. Of Whig principles and supported the government. From the ancient family of Whitley of Aston, he succeeded to considerable property in the county of Flint. Returned for Flint district in 1837, and sat until he retired 1841. Died 11 Apr. 1856. [1838]

DUNDAS, Rt. Hon. Sir David. 13 King's Bench Walk, Temple, London. Ochtertyne, Stirling. United University. B. at Edinburgh 1799, the eld. surviving s. of James Dundas, Esq., of Ochtertyne, Perthshire. Educ. at Westminster School and at Christ Church, Oxford, where he graduated B.A. 1820, M.A. 1822. Was called to the bar at the Inner Temple (of which he became a Bencher) and joined the Northern Circuit. Appointed a Queen's Counsel 1840. Was Solicitor-Gen. from July 1846-Mar. 1848, and Judge Advocate Gen. from May 1849-Feb. 1852. A Liberal. Sat for the Co. of Sutherland from Apr. 1840 to July 1852 and again from Apr. 1861 until he accepted Chiltern Hundreds in May 1867. Died 30 Mar. 1877. [1867]

DUNDAS, Frederic. 24 Hanover Square, London. Papdale, Kirkwall, Orkney. Brooks's. Eld. s. of the Hon. Charles Lawrence Dundas by Lady Caroline, 2nd d. of 5th Duke of St. Alban's. B. 1802; m. 1847, Grace, eld. d. of Sir Ralph St. George Gore, Bart., (she died 1868). A Liberal, in favour of the ballot. Sat for Orkney from July 1837 to July 1847, when he was an unsuccessful candidate. Regained his seat in July 1852. MP until his death Jan. 1873. [1872]

DUNDAS, George. 26 Pall Mall, London. Dundas Castle, South Queensferry. Carlton. B. at Dundas Castle 1819, the eld. s. of James Dundas, Esq., of Dundas, Linlithgowshire, by the d. of the celebrated Admiral 1st Visct. Duncan. His father was Chief of the Dundas family, whose ancient castle and lands had descended in the male line since 12th century. A Dept.-Lieut. of Linlithgowshire. Formerly an Officer in the Rifle Brigade, served at Burmuda, in Novia Scotia, and in the Mediterranean. Retired from the army in Dec. 1844. A Conservative, opposed to the admission of Jews to Parliament. Favoured an 'extended system of national education.' Sat for Linlithgowshire from 1847 until he was appointed Lieut. Gov. of Prince Edward's Island, which office he held until 1870. Lieut.-Gov. of St. Vincent 1874-78, and of the Windward Islands 1876 and 1878-9. Died 18 Mar. 1880. [1857]

DUNDAS, James Whitley Deans, G.C.B. Admiralty, London. Barton Court, Buckinghamshire. B. 1785, the s. of James Deans, Esq., M.D. of Calcutta. Assumed the names of Whitley and Dundas on his m. with his first cousin, Janet, only d. of Lord Amesbury (she died 1846). M. again in 1847 Lady Emily, born in 1809 the d. of the 1st Earl of Ducie. Was Rear-Admiral of the Red, Clerk of the Ordnance and in July 1846 was appointed a Lord of the Admiralty. (salary £1,200). A Dept.-Lieut. for Berkshire, and patron of 1 living. Of Whig principles. Unsuccessfully contested Queensborough in 1831, but represented Greenwich in 1832. Unsuccessfully contested Devizes in Nov. 1835 with Mr. Estcourt but succeeded in Feb. 1836 on the resignation of Sir P. Durham and sat until 1838. Sat for Greenwich from 1841 until he accepted Chiltern Hundreds 1852. On 17 Jan. 1852 he was appointed to Command the Mediterranean Fleet and was awarded G.C.B. 1855. Died 3 Oct. 1862. [1851]

DUNDAS, Hon. John Charles, sen. 43 Harley Street, London. Travellers'. B. 1808, 4th s. of 1st Earl of Zetland, by Harriet, d. of Gen. Hale. M. 1843, d. of James Talbot, Esq., of Talbot Hall, Co. Wexford. Educ. at Trinity Coll., Cambridge.

Called to the bar at the Middle Temple, 1834. A Dept.-Lieut. of Yorkshire. Appointed Lord-Lieut. of Orkney and Shetland 1839. A Liberal, opposed to Church rates, and in favour of the ballot. Sat for Richmond 1830 to 35, for York 1835 to 37, for Richmond 1841 to 47, and again for Richmond 1865 until his death 14 Feb. 1866. [1865 2nd ed.]

DUNDAS, Hon. John Charles, jun. Mount St. John, Thirsk. Brooks's. 2nd s. of the Hon. John Charles Dundas (youngest s. of the 1st Earl of Zetland), by Margaret Matilda, d. of James Talbot, Esq., of Talbot Hall, Co. Wexford. B. at Edinburgh 1845; m. 1870, Hon. Alice Louisa, 2nd d. of the 1st Visct. Halifax. Was educ. at Harrow and at Trinity Coll., Cambridge. Was called to the bar at Lincoln's Inn 1869. Lord Lieut. of Orkney and Shetland. A Dept.-Lieut. and Chairman of Quarter Sessions of the North Riding of Yorkshire. A Liberal. Unsuccessfully contested Yorkshire N.R. 1 Apr. 1857. Sat for Richmond from June 1873 until he retired in 1885. Contested York in 1886, standing as a Liberal Unionist. chairman of North Riding County Council 1889, until he died 13 Sept. 1892. [1885]

DUNDAS, Lawrence. Waplington Hall, Allerthorpe, Yorkshire. B. 1844, the eld. s. of Hon. John Charles Dundas, (youngest s. of 1st Earl of Zetland), by Margaret Matilda, eld. d. of James Talbot, Esq., of Talbot Hall, W. Wexford. M. 1871, Lady Lillian Elizabeth Selina, 3rd d. of 9th Earl of Scarborough. Appointed Cornet Royal Horse Guards Aug. 1866, Lieut. July 1869. Was Lord Lieut. of Ireland from 1889-92. A Liberal. Sat for Richmond from Nov. 1872 until he succeeded his uncle as 3rd Earl of Zetland in May 1873. Promoted to a Marquisate in Aug. 1892. Died 11 Mar. 1929. [1873]

DUNDAS, Lord. 17 Hertford Street, London. Upleatham, Lincolnshire. Eld. s. of Lord Dundas, who had church patronage. B. 1795; m. 1823, Sophia Jane, youngest d. of Sir Hedworth Williamson, Bart. of Whig principles; was in favour of the ballot and shortening the duration of Parliaments. Sat for Richmond from 1818-1830, when he was elected for York. Lost his seat in 1832, but on the election occasioned by the death of Capt. Bayntun was again returned for York in 1833 until 1835 when he sat again for Richmond. Sat until he succeeded as 2nd Earl Feb. 1839. Died 6 May 1873. [1838]

DUNDAS, Robert Adam. 97 Eaton Square, London. Eld. s. of Philip Dundas, Esq., who was the youngest s. of Robert Dundas, of Aunston, Lord President of the Court of Session, and eld. bro. of Henry, First Viscount Melville. M. in

1828, Mary, eld. d. of the Earl of Elgin. Seconded the Address in 1820. A Conservative. Sat for Ipswich in 1826 and 1830; for Edinburgh in 1831; was not in the following Parliament and, though returned in 1835 for Ipswich, he lost his seat when the result was declared void. [1835]

DUNDAS, Hon. Sir Robert Lawrence, K.C.B. 19 Arlington Street, London. Uncle to the Earl of Zetland; b. 1780. A Major-Gen. in the army. A Reformer. Sat for Richmond from 1828 to 1835; was again returned in 1839, when his nephew succeeded to a peerage. Retired in 1841. [1840]

DUNDAS, Hon. Thomas. See DUNDAS, Lord.

DUNGANNON, Visct. A Conservative. First elected for Durham 5 Apr. 1843 but unseated on petition 26 July 1843. Representative Peer of Ireland 11 Sept. 1855 until his death 11 Aug. 1862.

DUNGARVAN, Visct. 3 Hamilton Place, Piccadilly, London. White's. S. of Visct. Dungarvan, by Lady Catherine, 5th d. of 2nd Earl of Howth, and grands. of the Earl of Cork and Orrery. B. in Dublin, 1829, and m. in 1853, the Lady Emily, 2nd d. of 1st Marq. of Clanricarde. Appointed Capt. North Somerset Yeomanry Cavalry and a Dept.-Lieut. of Somerset, 1850. A Liberal, was in favour of Parliamentary Reform and civil and religious liberty, and avowed himself a staunch supporter of 'Sound Protestant Principles.' Sat for Frome from Oct. 1854 (on the death of his Uncle, Hon. R. Boyle, who had represented it from July 1847), until he succeeded his grandfather as 9th Earl in June 1856. Became a Speaker of the House of Lords 1882. Died 22 June 1904. [1856]

DUNKELLIN, Lord. 2 Carlton House Terrace, London. Portumna Castle, Co. Galway. Eld. s. of the 1st Marq. of Clanricarde, by the only d. of the Rt. Hon. George Canning and the Viscountess Canning. B. in St. James's Square, London 1827. Appointed Capt. and Lieut.-Col. in the Coldstream Guards in 1854, Was Aide-de-Camp to the Lord-Lieut. of Ireland from 1846 to 1852; appointed State Steward to the same Jan. 1853; Military Secretary to the Governor-General of India, June, 1856. Served the Eastern campaign, including Alma, etc., till he was taken prisoner before Sebastopol, Oct. 1854. A Liberal. First returned for Galway bor. Mar. 1857 (was an unsuccessful candidate in July 1852). Sat until defeated in 1859. Died 16 Aug. 1867. [1858]

DUNLOP, Alexander Murray. 8 Albion Street, Hyde Park, London. Corsock House, Corsock,

Dumfries. S. of Alexander Dunlop, Esq., of Keppoch, Dumbartonshire (some time a Banker in Greenock), by Margaret, d. of William Colquhoun, Esq., of Kenmure, Lanarkshire. B. at Greenock 1798; m. 1844, Eliza Esther, only child of John Murray, Esq., of Ainslie Place, Edinburgh. Educ. at Greenock Grammar School, and the University of Edinburgh; received the honorary degree of LL.D. from Princeton University, United States of America. Was called to the bar in Scotland in 1820. Was for several years Assessor to the town of Greenock. Author of treatises on Scottish Poor Law and Parochial Law, pamphlets on the Scottish Church controversy (in which he took part, as a member of the General Assembly); was legal adviser to the Free Church of Scotland from its establishment. A Liberal, voted against Church-rates 1855; in favour of an extension of the suffrage. Was an unsuccessful candidate for Greenock in Mar. 1845, and July 1847. First returned for Greenock in July 1852. Sat until he retired in 1868. Died 1 Sept. 1870.   [1867]

DUNLOP, Colin. Folcross, Lanarkshire. Brooks's. B. 1775. Unmarried. Of the family of Dunlop of Dunlop. An advocate but retired from practice at an early period of his life. Proprietor of the Clyde Iron Works. Principal Patentee of the Hot Air Blast. President of the Glasgow Anti-Corn Law Association. A radical Reformer. Sat for Glasgow from 1835 until he accepted Chiltern Hundreds Feb. 1836. Died 27 July 1837. [1836]

DUNLOP, John. Dunlop, Ayrshire. Reform. Eld. s. of Gen. Dunlop, MP for Kirkcudbright in 1812, and the two ensuing Parliaments. B. 1806; m. 1829, Charlotte Constance, d. of Maj.-Gen. Sir Richard Downs Jackson, K.C.H. Capt in the army, and Dept.-Lieut. for Ayrshire. A Reformer. Sat for Kilmarnock from 24 Dec. 1832 until 17 Jan. 1835 when he was defeated. Elected for Ayrshire in June 1835, on the resignation of Mr. Oswald. MP until his death Mar. or Apr. 1839.
                                                      [1838]

DUNN, John. 37 Lowndes Square, London. Berrywood, Near Southampton. Oriental. S. of John Dunn, Esq., of Tasmania, Banker, by Catherine, d. of William Colville, Esq., of Aberdeen. B. at Aberdeen 1820; m. 1858, Alicia Caroline, d. of B. Kingston, Esq. Educ. in Tasmania. Was a member of the legislative council in Tasmania from 1845-1855. A Merchant and Shipowner in London, largely engaged in the Australian trade. A Conservative, and a supporter generally of Lord Derby's policy. Unsuccessfully contested Totnes May 1859. First elected for Dartmouth Aug. 1859 and sat until his death 10 Sept. 1860.   [1860]

DUNNE, Rt. Hon. Francis Plunket. Brittas, Cloneslie, Queen's Co. Senior and Junior United Service. Eld. s. of Gen. Edward Dunne, of Brittas, Queen's Co., by the d. of Simon White, Esq., and sister to the 1st Lord Bantry. Was educ. at Sandhurst Military Coll., and at Trinity Coll., Dublin, where he was first class. Entered the army as Ensign in 1823; served in the 7th Dragoon Guards, in the 10th Foot, and on the Staff, in Greece and at home; was made a Maj. in the army in 1840; a Lieut.-Col. 1851, a Maj.-Gen. 1866. A Brevet-Col. in the army, and was private Secretary and Aide-de-camp to the Earl of Eglinton, when Lord-Lieut. of Ireland. Lieut.-Col. of Queen's Co. Militia, and a Dept.-Lieut. of Queen's Co. Was Clerk of the Ordnance from Mar. till Dec. 1852. A 'very Liberal-Conservative', and in favour of the ballot. Was an unsuccessful candidate for Portarlington, July 1837. Sat for that bor. from July 1847 till Apr. 1857. Elected for Queen's Co. May 1859 and sat until he retired in 1868. Died 6 July 1874.   [1867]

DUNNE, Michael. Ballymanus, Stradbally, Queen's Co. S. of William Dunne, Esq. B. at Ballymanus, Queen's Co., 1800; m. 1838, d. of John Cassidy, Esq., of Monasterevan, Co. Kildare. Educ. at Stoneyhurst Coll., Lancashire. A Magistrate for Queen's Co. A Liberal, in favour of tenant right in Ireland. First returned for Queen's Co. in July 1852. Retired 1865. Died 20 Sept. 1876.   [1865]

DUNRAVEN, Earl of. A Conservative. Successfully contested Glamorganshire in the general elections of 1837 and 1841 coming top of the poll on both occasions. Was again successful in 1847. Later became Earl of Dunraven. Sat until he accepted Chiltern Hundreds Jan. 1851. Created Baron Kenry (U.K. Peerage) 12 June 1866; Lord-Lieut. Co. Limerick 1864. Died 6 Oct. 1871.   [1850]

DU PRE, Caledon George. 40 Portland Place, London. Wilton Park, Beaconsfield. Carlton, Conservative, Junior United Service, Travellers', and Boodle's. Eld. s. of James du Pré, of Wilton Park, Buckinghamshire, by the d. of Sir William Maxwell, 4th Bart. Cousin of the Earl of Caledon. M. Louisa Cornwallis, 3rd d. of Sir William Maxwell, 5th Bart. A Magistrate and Dept.-Lieut. for Buckinghamshire. A Conservative, strongly resisted any measure calculated to disturb the union of Church and State. Sat for Buckinghamshire from 1839 until he retired in 1871. Died 7 Oct. 1886.   [1873]

DURHAM, Sir Philip C. Henderson, G.C.B. Hill Street, Berkeley Square, London. Bro. of

General Durham, of Largo in Fifeshire, representative of an old Scottish family, which laid claim to the Rutherford Peerage. Admiral of the Blue. A Conservative. Before the passing of the Reform Act, he unsuccessfully contested Queenborough, and Devizes in 1832. Elected for Devizes in 1834, on the resignation of Mr. Montagu Gore. Accepted Chiltern Hundreds Jan. 1836. [1835]

DUTTON, Hon. Ralph Heneage. 16 Halkin Street, West, London. Timsbury Manor, Romsey, Hampshire. Boodle's. Youngest s. of the 2nd Lord Sherborne, by the Hon. Mary, only child of the 2nd Lord Stawell (extinct). B. 1821; m. 1848, Isabella, youngest d. of John Mansfield, Esq., of Digswell House, Hertfordshire. Educ. at Trinity Coll., Cambridge. Appointed a Dept.-Lieut. of Hampshire 1852. A Liberal-Conservative, in favour of the abolition of church-rates 'as soon as practicable', and opposed to the ballot. Sat for Hamshire S. from Apr. 1857 till July 1865, when he was elected for Cirencester. Sat until he retired in 1868 when constituency became single seat. Contested Salisbury 1880. Died 8 Oct. 1892. [1867]

DYKE, Rt. Hon. Sir W. Hart. Continued in House after 1885: full entry in Volume II.

DYKES, Fretchville Lawson Ballantine. Dovenby Hall, Cockermouth. 1 Elm Court, Temple, London. Eld. s. of Joseph Dykes Ballantine, Esq. Assumed the name Dykes. A Reformer, in favour of the vote by ballot, tri-ennial Parliaments, commutation of tithes, of poor laws in Ireland, and the repeal of the window tax. Opposed to the Bishops being in the House of Lords, to the severity of the criminal code, and the corn laws, but thought that agriculture would decline without a fixed duty on foreign grain. Mr. Dykes and his family possessed impropriate tithes. Sat for Cockermouth from 1832 until he accepted Chiltern Hundreds in 1835. [1835]

DYOTT, Richard. 31 Grosvenor Place, London. Freeford Hall, Lichfield. Carlton. S. of Gen. William Dyott, by Eleanor, d. and co-heir of Samuel Thompson, Esq., of Greenmount, Co. Antrim. B. at Freeford 1808; m. 1849, Ellen Catherine, d. of Charles Smith Foster, Esq., of Lysway Hall, Lichfield. Educ. at Westminster and at Trinity Coll., Cambridge. Entered the army 1827, and retired on half-pay as Lieut.-Col. 1842. Lieut.-Col. of Stafford Militia. A Conservative. Unsuccessfully contested Staffordshire S. Aug. 1837 and in July 1841 Lichfield. He was elected for Lichfield July 1865. Sat until 1880 when he was returned again, but election declared void. Died 13 Feb. 1891. [1880]

EARLE, Ralph Anstruther, 116 Park Street, Grosvenor Square, London. Carlton. 2nd s. of Charles Earle, Esq., of Everton, Lancashire, by Emily, d. of Primrose Maxwell, Esq., of Tuppendence, Kent. B. at Edinburgh 1835. Educ. at Harrow. Was unpaid attaché subsequently promoted and attached to the Embassy at Vienna. Private Sec. to the Rt. Hon. Benjamin Disraeli, while Chancellor of the Exchequer in 1858. Appointed Parliamentary Sec. to the Poor Law Board, July 1866 (salary £1000). A Conservative, and a supporter generally of Lord Derby's party; in favour of the reduction and ultimately the repeal of the malt-tax; opposed to the unconditional abolition of church-rates. Sat for Berwick from Apr. till Aug. 1859. Elected for Maldon, July 1865. Retired in 1868 when Maldon lost one of its members. Died 10 June 1879. [1867]

EARP, Thomas. Trent View, Newark. S. of Mr. William Earp, by Sarah Ann, d. of Mr. James Taylor, of Muskham, Newark. B. at Derby 1830; m. 1855, Martha, d. of Mr. Thomas Weightman, of Langford Moor, Nottinghamshire. Educ. at Derby Diocesan School. A Maltster and Brewer at Newark. Elected Mayor of Newark for 1869-70. An 'advanced' Liberal, in favour of household franchise in counties, etc. Sat for Newark from Feb. 1874 until defeated in 1885, contesting the Newark division of Nottinghamshire. [1885]

EAST, Sir James Buller, Bart., D.C.L. 117 Eaton Square, London. Bourton House, Moreton in Marsh, Gloucestershire. Carlton. Eld. s. of the Rt. Hon. Sir Edward Hyde East, Bart. (who sat for Winchester from 1823 till 1830), by the d. of Joseph Chaplin Hankey, Esq., of East Bergholt, Suffolk. B. in Bloomsbury, London 1789; m. in 1822 Caroline Eliza, 2nd d. of J. Henry Leigh, Esq., of Stoneleigh Abbey, Warwickshire. Educ. at Harrow School and at Christ Church, Oxford. Was called to the bar at the Inner Temple 1813. A Liberal-Conservative, prepared to 'rescind the grant to Maynooth.' Sat for Winchester from 1831 till Dec. 1832; re-elected Jan. 1835 and sat until he accepted Chiltern Hundreds 1864. Died 19 Nov. 1878. [1863]

EASTHOPE, Sir John, Bart. 19 Grafton Street, London. Firgrove, Weybridge. Reform, and Wyndham. B. 29 Oct. 1784; m. 1st, 1807, Ann, d. of Jacob Stokes, Esq., of Leopard, near Worcester; 2ndly, 1843, eld. d. of Co. Skyring and widow of Maj. Longley. Proprietor of the *Morning Chronicle* newspaper, a Director of the Canada Land Company, and Chairman of the United Mexican Mining Company. Of Liberal opinions, gave no pledges. Before 1832 was Member successively for St. Alban's and Banbury. Unsuccessfully contested Southampton 9 Jan. 1835. Contested Lewes without success 12 Apr. 1837, prior to the 1837 general election, when he was returned for Leicester, and sat until he retired 1847. Contested Bridgnorth 29 July 1847. Died 11 Dec. 1865.				[1847]

EASTNOR, Visct. Charles. 45 Grosvenor Place, London. Reigate Priory, Surrey. Carlton. Eld. s. of Earl Somers. B. 1819. A Conservative, but in favour of free trade. First returned for Reigate in 1841, when his father succeeded to a Peerage. Sat until he retired 1847. Succeeded as 3rd Earl Oct. 1852. Died 26 Sept. 1883.				[1847]

EASTNOR, Visct. John. 3 St. James's Square, London. Reigate Priory, Surrey. Carlton, Alfred, and Athenaeum. Eld. s. of Earl Somers; b. 1788; m. in 1815 Caroline, 4th d. of the 3rd Earl of Hardwicke. Lieut.-Col of the Herefordshire Militia. A Conservative, sat for Hereford from 1820 till 1832. Sat for Reigate from 1832 until he succeeded as 2nd Earl Somers in 1841. Died 5 Oct. 1852.				[1840]

EASTWICK, Edward Backhouse. 38 Thurloe Square, London. Place House, St. Anthony, Cornwall. Athenaeum, and Junior Carlton. S. of R.W. Eastwick, Esq., of Thurloe Square, London, by Lucy, d. of John King, Esq. B. at Watfield, Berkshire 1814; m. 1847, Rosina Jane, d. of James Hunter, Esq., of Hapton House, Argyllshire. Educ. at the Charterhouse, also at Balliol and Merton Colls., Oxford. Became a Cadet of Infantry 1836, Assist. Sec. India Office 1859, Sec. of Legation 1860, Chargé d'Affaires 1862, Private Sec. to Lord Cranborne from July 1866-Mar. 1867. Called to the bar at the Middle Temple 1860. Author of works entitled *Lutfullah, Handbook of India, Journal of a Diplomate, Venezuela; or, Sketches in the Life of a South American Republic.* A Liberal-Conservative, voted against the disestablishment of the Irish Church 1869 and not in favour of disturbing the Reform question. Sat for Penryn from Dec. 1868 until defeated 1874. Died 16 July 1883.				[1873]

EATON, Henry William. 16 Prince's Gate, Hyde Park, London. Carlton, Junior Carlton, St. Stephen's, and Union. B. 1816; m. 1839, only d. and heir of Thomas Lender Harman, Esq., of New Orleans (she died 1877). Educ. at Enfield and at the College Rollin, Paris. Largely engaged in the Silk Trade in Old Broad Street, London. A Fellow of the Geographical Society, of the Horticultural Society and of the Botanical Society. A Dept.-Lieut. for Suffolk and for the Tower Hamlets. A Conservative. Sat for Coventry from June 1865, when he was returned just previous to

the general election, till Mar. 1880; re-elected Mar. 1881. Sat until created Lord Cheylesmore, July 1887. Died 2 Oct. 1891.				[1887]

EATON, Richard Jefferson. 6 Chesham Place, London. Stretchworth Park, Cambridgeshire. Carlton, Travellers', and Junior United Service. Eld. s. of Richard Eaton, Esq., who was Patron of 1 living, a Banker at Newmarket, and Magistrate for Cambridgeshire. B. 1806; m. 1839, d. of J. Conyers, Esq. A Capt. in the army. Had Church patronage. A Conservative, voted for agricultural protection 1846. Sat for Cambridgeshire from 1835 until he retired in 1847.				[1847]

EBRINGTON, Visct. (I). 17 Grosvenor Square, London. Castle Hill, Devon. Eld. s. of Earl Fortescue. B. 1783; m. 1817, Lady Susan Ryder, d. of the Earl of Harrowby (dead); Col. of the E. Devon Militia, and since 1830 Vice-Lieut. of Devon. Of Whig principles. Bro.-in-law of his colleague Mr. Newton Fellowes. His Lordship distinguished himself in the Parliament of 1831 by moving the address to the King, of confidence in Lord Grey's Administration, when that noble Lord and colleagues resigned upon their defeat in the House of Lords on Lord Lyndhurst's motion for changing the order of proceeding in the Committee on the Reform Act. Sat for Tavistock from 1820-31 when he was elected for the county Devon, as he had been in 1830, but sat for Tavistock. Sat for Barnstaple 4 Aug. 1804-07 (2 Parliaments); for St. Mawes 22 July 1807-09; for Buckingham 1812-17 (Chiltern Hundreds); for Devonshire 1818-20; for Tavistock 22 May 1820-30, when he was re-elected but chose to sit for Devonshire again, 1830-32. Sat for Devonshire N. from 1832 until summoned to House of Peers in his father's barony of Fortescue on appointment as Lord Lieut. of Ireland 1 Mar. 1839. Succeeded as 2nd Earl 1841; Parliamentary Sec. to Poor Law Board 1847-51. Died 14 Sept. 1861.				[1838]

EBRINGTON, Visct. (II). 17 Grosvenor Square, London. Castle Hill, Devon. Brooks's. Eld. s. of Earl Fortescue. B. in Upper Brook Street, London 1818; m. 1847, Georgiana, eld. d. of Rt. Hon. Col. Dawson Damer. Educ. at Harrow School. Was Lord of the Treasury from July 1846 till Dec. 1847; and for some years secretary to the Poor Law Board, resigned Feb. 1851. Appointed Lieut.-Col. North Devon Yeomanry Cavalry, 1851. A Dept.-Lieut. of Devon. A Liberal, in favour of extension of the franchise and general education; voted against church rates 1855. Sat for Plymouth from July 1841 to July 1852. First elected for Marylebone, Dec. 1854. Sat until he accepted Chiltern Hundreds Jan. 1859. Succeed-

ed as 3rd Earl in 1861; called to House of Lords in 1859; author of several books. Died 10 Oct. 1905.
[1858]

EBRINGTON, Visct. (III). Continued in House after 1885: full entry in Volume II.

ECCLES, William. 8 Salisbury Street, London. Spring Mount, Blackburn. B. 1794. Educ. as an Attorney and practised for 20 years. Quit that profession in 1840, and became a Cotton Spinner and Manufacturer. Took a prominent part at Blackburn during the Reform agitation, and was Chairman of Sir William Feilden's Committee at the first election for Blackburn. Was Chairman of the Blackburn Anti-Corn-Law Association from 1841-46. A Liberal, in favour of the extension of the suffrage, vote by ballot, and a system of national education. First returned for Blackburn in July 1852 and sat until he was unseated for bribery on 25 Feb. 1853. Died 17 June 1853.
[1853]

ECKERSLEY, Nathaniel. Standish Hall, Wigan. Carlton Manor, Guisely, Yorkshire. Carlton. S. of James Eckersley, Esq., of Wigan, by Elizabeth, d. of James Ditchfield, Esq., of Wigan. B. at Wigan, 1815; m. 1st, 1841 Mary, d. of Christopher Fell, Esq., of Sharples, near Bolton; 2ndly, 1852, Elizabeth d. of Henry Ffarington, Banker of Mariebonne, Wigan. Educ. at Wigan Grammar School. A Banker, Cotton Manufacturer, and Colliery Proprietor. A Magistrate and Dept.-Lieut. of Lancashire. High Sheriff of Lancashire in 1878. Was chosen Mayor of Wigan on six different occasions - 1851, 1852, 1870, and three following years. Patron of 1 living. A Conservative. Sat for Wigan from Mar. 1866 to Oct. 1868; re-elected Dec. 1883. Retired in 1885. Died 15 Feb. 1892.
[1885]

ECROYD, William Farrer. Lomeshaye, Burnley, Lancashire. Creden Hill Court, Hereford. Carlton. Eld. s. of William Ecroyd, Esq., of Lomeshaye, near Burnley, Lancashire, by Margaret, eld. d. of William Farrer, Esq., of Lambrigg, Westmoreland. B. at Lomeshaye, near Burnley, 1827; m. 1st, 1851, Mary, eld. d. of Thomas Backhouse, Esq., of York (she died 1867); 2ndly, 1869, Anna Maria, eld. d. of George Foster, Esq., of The Whins, near Whalley, Lancashire. A Worsted Manufacturer, head of the firm of Messrs. William Ecroyd and Sons, Lomeshaye Mills, Burnley, Lancashire. A Magistrate for Lancashire. Author of various pamphlets on Education, Freedom of Trade, etc. Patron of 1 living. A Conservative, and a firm supporter of the constitution in Church and State. Unsuccessfully contested Carlisle 6 Feb. 1874 and

North-East Lancashire, Apr. 1880. Sat for Preston from May 1881. Retired in 1885. Contested Rossendale (Lancashire) in 1885. Died 9 Nov. 1915.
[1885]

EDGE, Samuel Rathbone. Pitfield House, Newcastle-under-Lyme. S. of Stephen Edge, Esq., of Pitfield House, Newcastle-under-Lyme, by Elizabeth, d. of Samuel Rathbone, Esq., of Tunstall, Staffordshire. B. at Tunstall, Staffordshire 1848. Educ. at the Wesleyan Coll., Sheffield, and at Queen's Coll., Oxford, graduated B.A. 1873, M.A. 1876. A Liberal. Sat for Newcastle-under-Lyme from Aug. 1878. Defeated 1880.
[1880]

EDMONSTONE, Sir William Bart., C.B. Colzium House, Kilsyth. Duntreath, Stirlingshire. Carlton. 2nd s. of Sir Charles Edmonstone, (2nd Bart.), who was for many years MP for Stirling, by his 2nd wife Hon. Louisa, d. of 2nd Lord Hotham. B. at Hampton, Middlesex, 1810; m. 1841, Mary Elizabeth, eld. d. of Lieut.-Col. T.W. Parsons, C.M.C. Resident of the Island of Zante. Was severely wounded when Midshipman of the 'Sybille' by pirates in the Archipelago 1826. Became a Commander R.N. 1841. Was Inspecting Commander in the Coast-Guard from 1844-1852. Appointed to the 'St. George' 120 guns Guardship at Devonport 1852, transferred to the 'Arrogant' with the rank of Commodore on the West Coast of Africa 1859. A Dept.-Lieut. of Stirlingshire. A Conservative, in favour of congregations in the Scottish Church having the choice of their ministers, also of Tenant-farmers having a right to the ground game, of the abolition of the law of Hypothec in Scotland. Sat for Stirlingshire from Feb. 1874 until defeated 1880. Died 18 Feb. 1888.
[1880]

EDWARDES, Hon. W. See Kensington, Rt. Hon. Lord.

EDWARDS, Charles. 12 St. George's Place, Hyde Park, London. Beaumont Manor, Wormley, Hertfordshire. Dolserau, Near Dolgelley, Merionethshire. S. of Edward Edwards, Esq., of Dolserau, Merionethshire, by Margaret, d. of the Rev. Watkin Williams, Rector, Henllan, Denbighshire. B. in London 1825; m. 1848, Mary, only d. of William Tate, Esq., of Frognal, Hampstead. A Magistrate and Dept.-Lieut. of Merionethshire. A Liberal, and an earnest supporter of Lord Russell's party, in favour of the abolition of Church rates. First elected for Windsor Apr. 1866. Retired 1868. Contested Canterbury 8 May 1879 and again in Apr. 1880. Died 22 Feb. 1889.
[1868]

EDWARDS, Sir Henry, Bart. 32 Dover Street, London. Pye Nest, Nr. Halifax, Yorkshire. Carlton, Junior Carlton, and Boodle's. Eld. s. of Henry Lees Edwards, Esq., of Pye Nest, by Lea, d. of Joseph Priestley, Esq., of Sowerby, Yorkshire. Descended from a Warwickshire family, a branch of which settled in Yorkshire in 1749. B. at Pye Nest, 1812; m. 1838, Maria Churchill, eld. d. of Thomas Coster, Esq., of Marchwood and of Regent's Park. A Dept.-Lieut. and Magistrate for the West Riding of Yorkshire, Lieut.-Col. Commandant of the 2nd West York Yeomanry Cavalry. A Conservative, and in favour of the reduction of those taxes which press upon the working classes. Sat for Halifax from July 1847 till July 1852; contested that bor. unsuccessfully in 1852, 1853, and Apr. 1857. First returned for Beverley Aug. 1857. Returned in 1868, but the election was declared void and Beverley disfranchised. Sheriff of Yorkshire 1871. Died 23 Apr. 1886. [1867]

EDWARDS, Sir Henry. 53 Berkeley Square, London. King's Mill House, Nutfield, Surrey. Union Club, Brighton. Wyndham, and Reform. Eld. s. of John Edwards, of Somerton, Somersetshire, by Elizabeth, 2nd d. of James Brayley, of Southmolton, Devon. B. in London, 1820. Unmarried. A Merchant in London. Was a Magistrate for Middlesex from 1863, and a Dept.-Lieut. for the Tower Hamlets, from 1864; also a Magistrate for Surrey, and a Dept.-Lieut. for Dorset. A Liberal. Sat for Weymouth from June 1867 until he retired in 1885. Knighted 29 Dec. 1885. Died 4 Feb. 1897. [1885]

EDWARDS, Col. Sir John. Dolefergan, Montgomeryshire. Reform. S. of John Edwards, Esq., of Greenfields, who m. Cornelia, d. and heiress of Richard Owen, Esq., of Garth, Montgomeryshire. Grands. of Humphrey Edwards, Esq., of Halgarth, Merionethshire. B. 1770; m. 1st, Catherine, d. and co-heiress of Col. Browne of Millington; 2ndly, Harriet, widow of John Owen Herbert, Esq., of Dolvorgan. Was at Queen's Coll., Oxford. Lieut.-col. of Montgomeryshire local Militia. A Reformer, contested Montgomery district in 1832 with Major Pugh, a Conservative, who was returned, but on petition election declared void. Returned in 1833 and petitioned against unsuccessfully. Sat until defeated in 1841. [1838]

EDWARDS, John Passmore. 20 Queen Anne's Gate, London. Devonshire. S. of Mr. William Edwards, of Blackwater, Cornwall. B. at Blackwater, Cornwall, 1824; m. d. of Henry Humphreys, Esq., of Brixton. A Newspaper Proprietor. A Liberal. Unsuccessfully contested

Truro 17 Nov. 1868. Sat for Salisbury from Apr. 1880 to 1885. Contested Rochester 24 Nov.1885. Died 22nd Apr. 1911. [1885]

EGERTON, Hon. A. de T. Continued in House after 1885: full entry in Volume II.

EGERTON, Hon. Algernon Fulke. 28 Ennismore Gardens, London. Worsley Old Hall, Manchester. Carlton. 3rd s. of the 1st Earl of Ellesmere, by Harriet Catherine, d. of Charles Greville, Esq. B. 31st Dec. 1825; m. 1862, Alice Louisa, eld. d. of Lord George Cavendish. Appointed Lieut.-Col. Commandant Lancashire Yeomanry Cavalry 1881, Col. 1882, and a Dept.-Lieut. of the County Palatine of Lancaster 1860. Was Secretary to the Admiralty from May 1859 to Dec. 1868. A Conservative. Sat for South Lancashire from May 1859 to Dec. 1868, and for the South-Eastern Division of Lancashire from Nov. 1868 to Apr. 1880; sat for Wigan from Dec. 1882. Retired in 1885. Lancashire Alderman 1888 until he died 14 July 1891. [1885]

EGERTON, Edward Christopher. 45 Eaton Place, London. Mountfield Court, Hurst Green, Sussex. Travellers', and Carlton. B. at Tatton Park 1816, the 4th s. of Wilbraham Egerton, Esq., of Tatton Park, by Elizabeth, 2nd d. of Sir Christopher Sykes, Bart., of Sledmere House, Yorkshire. Therefore bro. to Lord Egerton. M. 1845, Lady Mary Frances, d. of the 2nd Earl Manvers. Educ. at Harrow and at Christ Church, Oxford, where he graduated B.A. 1837. Obtained a Fellowship at All Soul's Coll. and graduated B.C.L. 1841. Was called to the bar at the Inner Temple June 1840. Was Under Secretary for Foreign Affairs from July 1866 to Dec. 1868. A 'Liberal-Conservative', and voted against the ballot 1853. Was an unsuccessful candidate for Chester in July 1850. Sat for Macclesfield from July 1852-Nov. 1868, when he was elected for East Cheshire and sat until his death on 27 Aug. 1869. [1860]

EGERTON, Hon. Francis. 78 Piccadilly, London. St. George's Hill, Weybridge, Surrey. Devonshire. B. 1824, the 2nd s. of 1st Earl Ellesmere, by Harriet Catherine, d. of Charles Greville, Esq. M. 1865, Lady Louisa Caroline, only d. of 7th Duke of Devonshire. Became a Capt. R.N. 1855, Rear-Admiral 1873 and appointed Naval Aide-de-Camp to the Queen 1865. A Magistrate for Surrey. A Liberal. Sat for E. Derbyshire 1868-85; and for N.E. div. 1885-86. Retired 1886. Died 15 Dec. 1895. [1886]

EGERTON, Rt. Hon. Lord Francis. 18 Belgrave Square, London. Bridgewater House, St. James's,

London. Oatlands, Surrey. Carlton, and Athenaeum. B. in 1800, the 2nd surviving s. of the 1st Duke of Sutherland. Took the name of Egerton pursuant to the will of the Duke of Bridgewater. M. 1822, Harriet, youngest d. of Charles Greville, Esq., of Warwick, by Lady Charlotte, sister of the Duke of Portland. Was Secretary for Ireland and acquired considerable literary distinction as Lord Francis Leveson Gower. A Conservative. Sat for Bletchingley and the county of Sutherland before the Reform Act. Sat for Lancashire S. from 1835 until he was created 1st Earl of Ellesmere in July 1846. Died 18 Feb. 1857.   [1845]

EGERTON, Sir Philip de Malpas Grey, Bart. 28B Albermarle Street, London. Onton Park, Taporley, Cheshire. Carlton, and Athenaeum. S. of the Rev. Sir Philip Grey Egerton, (9th Bart.) B. at Malpas 1806; m. 1832 Anna Elizabeth, 2nd d. of George J. Legh, Esq. Educ. at Christ Church, Oxford, where he graduated B.A. 1828. Patron of 1 Sixth of Taporley rectory; a Dept.-Lieut. of Cheshire and Lieut.-Col. Cheshire Yeomanry Cavalry. Elected Antiquary to the Royal Academy, Mar. 1876. A Conservative, said he would 'maintain in full integrity the union of Church and State'; favoured the amendment of local taxation, and would not support a Permissive Bill. Sat for Chester in the Parliament of 1830. Contested Cheshire S. unsuccessfully in 1832; but was elected for Cheshire S. in 1835, and in 1868 for the Western division. MP until his death 5 Apr. 1881.   [1881]

EGERTON, Hon. Wilbraham. 23 Rutland Gate, London. Rostherne Hall, Knutsford, Cheshire. Travellers', and Carlton. Eld. s. of Lord Egerton (who sat for N. Cheshire for 26 years), by Lady Charlotte, eld. d. of 2nd Marq. of Ely. B. 1832; m. 1857, Lady Mary Sarah, eld. d. of 2nd Earl Amherst. Educ. at Eton and at Christ Church, Oxford. Appointed Ecclesiastical Commissioner for England Apr. 1880. Capt. Earl of Chester's Yeomanry Cavalry 1863. A Liberal-Conservative, in favour of local taxation being relieved out of Imperial resources; also of denominational education. Sat for Cheshire N. from July 1858-Dec. 1868; from that date he sat for Cheshire Mid division and sat until he succeeded father as 2nd Baron in 1883; Chairman of Manchester Ship Canal 1887-94; created 1st Earl 1897. Died 16 Mar. 1909.   [1882]

EGERTON, William Tatton. 43 Wilton Crescent, London. Tatton Park, Cheshire. Carlton, and Travellers'. S. of Wilbraham Egerton, Esq., by the d. of Sir Christopher Sykes (2nd Bart.), of Siedmere, and grands. of William Eger-

ton, Esq., of Tatton Park, who each represented Cheshire for upwards of 20 years. B. 1806; m. 1830, Lady Charlotte Elizabeth, eld. d. of the 2nd Marq. of Ely. A Conservative. Sat for Lymington in 1830. Sat for Cheshire N. from 1832 until he accepted Chiltern Hundreds July 1858. Created 1st Baron Egerton of Tatton May 1859. Died 21 Feb. 1883.   [1858]

ELCHO, Lord F. 23 St. James's Place, London. Amisfield, Haddington. Gosford House, Longniddry, Edinburgh. Carlton. Eld. s. of Earl of Wemyss. B. 1818; m. 1843, Lady Anne Frederica, 2nd d. of 1st Earl of Lichfield. Educ. at Christ Church, Oxford, where he graduated B.A. 1841. Appointed a Dept.-Lieut. of Haddingtonsh. 1846, and Lieut.-Col. in the London Scottish Rifle Volunteers Feb. 1860. Was a Lord of the Treasury from Dec. 1852 to Feb. 1855. A Liberal-Conservative, voted for Lord Derby's Reform Bill Mar. 1859, and against Lord Russell's Reform Bill 1866; voted against the disestablishment of the Irish Church 1869; in favour of a measure for 'the simplification of the land laws'. Sat for E. Gloucestershire from 1841-Feb. 1846. Sat for Haddingtonshire from July 1847 until he succeeded as 10th Earl Jan. 1883. A.D.C. to H.M. until his death 30 June 1914.   [1882]

ELCHO, Lord H. Continued in House after 1885: full entry in Volume II.

ELIOT, Lord. (I). 36 Dover Street, London. Port Eliot, Cornwall. Carlton, White's, and Travellers'. B. 29 Aug. 1798, eld. s. of the Earl of St. German's and nephew of the 1st Duke of Sutherland. M. 2 Sept. 1824, Lady Jemima, 3rd d. of 2nd Marq. Cornwallis. Dept.-Lieut. of Cornwall, at one time engaged in the Diplomatic service. A Lord of the Treasury 1827-30; and in fulfillment of his mission to Spain in May 1835, concluded the celebrated 'Eliot Convention'. Chief Sec. to the Lord-Lieut. of Ireland. Sat for Liskeard 1824-32. Unsuccessfully contested Bodmin 6 Jan. 1835. Returned as a Conservative for Cornwall E. in 1837 and sat until he succeeded as 3rd Earl St. Germans Jan. 1845. Became Postmaster Gen. Nov. 1845, Lord-Lieut. of Ireland Dec. 1852-Mar. 1855. Died 7 Oct. 1877. [1844]

ELIOT, Lord. (II). 36 Dover Street, London. Travellers'. Eld. s. of Earl St. Germans, by the 3rd d. of the 2nd Marq. of Cornwallis. B. at Port Eliot 1829. Appointed 1853, 2nd paid attaché to the Embassy at Berlin, having previously served in the Foreign Office at Madrid and at Lisbon. Subsequently 1st paid attaché at St. Petersburg. In 1859 Secretary of Legation at Rio de Janiero; transferred to Athens same year; returned to Rio

1861; transferred June 1861 to Lisbon, where he remained till 1866. A Liberal. Unsuccessfully contested Cricklade 13 July 1865. First elected for Devonport, May 1866. Retired in 1868. Summoned to the Lords Sept. 1870. Succeeded father as 4th Earl Oct. 1877. Died 19 Mar. 1881.   [1867]

ELLEY, Sir John, K.C.B. Carlton. A Maj. Gen. in the army; Governor of Galway; Col. of 17 Dragoons. Was at Waterloo. A Conservative. Contested Windsor in 1835 with Sir John de Beauvoir, who was returned, but on petition unseated. Seat assigned to Elley 6 Apr. 1835. Retired in 1837.   [1837]

ELLICE, Alexander. Bro. of the member for Coventry, and uncle to the member for the St. Andrew's district of Burghs. A Capt. in the navy. Of Liberal opinions. Returned for Harwich in 1837. Retired 1841.   [1838]

ELLICE, Edward. 28 Grosvenor Square, London. Ivergarry, Scotland. Reform, and Brooks's. S. of the Rt. Hon. Edward Ellice, many years MP for Coventry, and nephew of Capt. Ellice, R.N. M. 1st, d. of Gen. Balfour (she died Apr. 1864); 2ndly, 1867, Eliza Stewart, eld. d. of Thomas Campbell Hagart, Esq., of Bantaskine, and widow of Alexander Speirs, Esq., of Elderslie. Educ. at Trinity Coll., Cambridge, where he graduated M.A. 1831. Of strong Liberal opinions, voted in favour of the disestablishment of the Irish Church 1869. Unsuccessfully contested Inverness district 1835. Sat from May-July 1837 for Huddersfield. Represented St. Andrew's from the last date and sat until he retired 1880. Died 2 Aug. 1880.   [1880]

ELLICE, Rt. Hon. Edward. 18 Arlington Street, London. Horsley Park, Ripley, Surrey. Reform, and Brooks's. M. 1st, 1809, Hannah Althea, youngest sister of 2nd Earl Grey, and widow of Capt. Bettesworth, R.N.; 2ndly, 1843, the Countess of Leicester (relict of the 1st Earl), 3rd d. of 4th Earl of Albemarle, (she died 1844). Was a Merchant in London. Was Joint Secretary of the Treasury from Nov. 1830, till Aug. 1832; and Secretary at War from Apr. 1833, till Dec. 1834. Founding Chairman of Reform Club in 1836. A Dept-Lieut. of Inverness. A Liberal. Sat for Coventry from 1818, with the exception of the period from 1826 to 1830.   [1863]

ELLIOT, Hon. A.D. Continued in House after 1885: full entry in Volume II.

ELLIOT, Hon. Capt. George, R.N. Admiralty. Bro. of the Earl of Minto. B. 1784; m. 1810, to Eliza Cecilia, youngest d. of James Ness, Esq.

Governor of the Mint in Scotland, and Secretary to the Admiralty, and as such a Member of the Government. Sat for Roxburghshire from 1832 until he was defeated in 1853. C.-in-C. at Cape of Good Hope 1837-40; Admiral 1853; K.C.B. Nov. 1862. Died 24 June 1863.   [1833]

ELLIOT, Rear-Adm. George. 17 St. George's Square, London. Carlton, and Junior United Service. Eld. s. of Admiral Hon. Sir George Elliot, K.C.B. (2nd s. of 1st Earl of Minto), by Eliza Cecilia, youngest d. of James Ness, Esq., of Osgodvie, Yorkshire. B. at Calcutta 1813; m. 1842, Hersey Susan Sidney, d. of Col. William Wauchope, of Niddrie Marischall, Scotland. Entered the navy in 1827; became Rear-Admiral 1858, Admiral Sept. 1869. Commanded the line-of-battle ship 'James Watt', two years in the Baltic during the Russian War, and was present at the capture of Bomarsund, having completed 11 years sea time as Capt. Served as Capt. of the Fleet under Sir C. Freemantle in the Channel Squadron and for a short time commanded the Squadron. Admiral-Superintendent of Portsmouth Dockyard. A Conservative. Sat for Chatham from Feb. 1874. Accepted Chiltern Hundreds 1875 on appointment as C.in-C. at Portsmouth. Author of *A Treatise on Future Naval Battles* (1888). Died 13 Dec. 1901.   [1875]

ELLIOT, Sir G. Continued in House after 1885: full entry in Volume II.

ELLIOT, Sir G.W. Continued in House after 1885: full entry in Volume II.

ELLIOT, Hon. John Edmund. 8 Wilton Crescent, London. Minto Castle, Roxburghshire. Reform. 3rd s. of the 1st Earl of Minto, by the eld. d. of Sir George Amyand, Bart. B. 1788; m. 1809, Amelia, 3rd d. of James Henry Casamajor, Esq., of Madras. Was formerly in the civil service of the East India Company in Bengal. Was Secretary to the Board of Controul, resigned Mar. 1852. A Liberal, voted in favour of the ballot; voted against that measure, 1853. Sat for Roxburghshire from 1837 to 1841, when he was an unsuccessful candidate; again returned July 1847 and sat until he retired in 1859. Died 4 Apr. 1862.   [1858]

ELLIS, John. (I). Belgrave, Nr. Leicester. S. of Joseph Ellis, Esq., by Rebecca, d. of John Burgess, Esq., of Wigston, Leicestershire. B. at Frisk House, near Leicester, 1789; m. 1st, 1816, d. of John Shipley, Esq., of Uttoxeter, Staffordshire; 2ndly, 1820, d. of Daniel Evans, Esq., of Goodrest Lodge, Warwickshire. Educ. at Hartshill, Warwickshire. Deputy-Chairman of the Midland

Railway and Director of the London and North-Western Railway. A Liberal, against any endowment of the Roman Catholic Clergy. First returned for Leicester Aug. 1848. Retired in 1852. Died 26 Oct. 1862. [1852]

ELLIS, John. (II). 5 Hereford Street, Grosvenor Square, London. Carlton. A younger s. of John Ellis, Esq., who was a Barrister-at-Law, an active Magistrate for many years in the Co. of Cornwall and descended from an ancient Cornish family. Born 21 Nov. 1812; m. 12 Dec. 1835, Ellen, eld. d. of John Weldale Knollys, Esq., who succeeded as heir to the estates of Sir Francis Knollys, Bart. of Fernhill, Berkshire. His eld. bro. unsuccessfully contested the borough of Bodmin at the late general election. A Conservative, who was returned in 1837 for Newry by the Protestant interest, in opposition to Mr. Brady, the late member. Retired 1841. Contested Lancaster 9 July 1852. [1838]

ELLIS, Sir J.W. Continued in House after 1885: full entry in Volume II.

ELLIS, Hon. Leopold George Frederick Agar. 99 Belgrave Road, London. Gowan Castle and Ringwood, Co. Kilkenny. B. 1829, 2nd s. of 1st Lord Dover, by Lady Georgiana, 2nd d. of 6th Earl of Carlisle. Uncle and heir presumptive of Visct. Clifden. M. 1864, Hon. Harriet, 6th d. of 3rd Baron Camoys. Called to the bar at the Inner Temple 1854. Appointed Capt. Kilkenny Fusiliers 1854, Major 1860. Was Aide-de-Camp to the Lord Lieut. of Ireland, 1859. A Liberal-Conservative who voted against Lord Russell's Reform Bill 1866. Unsuccessfully contested Kilkenny Co. July 1852, but was elected in Apr. 1857. Sat until his defeat in 1873. Succeeded his nephew as 5th Visct. Clifden, Mar. 1895. Died 10 Sept. 1899. [1873]

ELLIS, Wynn. 30 Cadogan Place, London. Ponsbourne Park, Hertfordshire. Tankerton Tower, Kent. Reform. Descended lineally from Hugh Ellis, Esq., of Flintshire. M. d. of J. Smithson, Esq., and niece of Charles Pearson, Esq., of Tankerton. Of Liberal politics, in favour of ballot and an extension of the suffrage. A member of the Free Trade Club. Was first returned for Leicester in 1831, but did not come into Parliament in 1835. Was returned in 1839 on the retirement of Mr. Duckworth. Sat until he retired 1847. Sheriff of Hertfordshire 1851-52. Died 20 Nov. 1875. [1847]

ELMLEY, Visct. 16 Grosvenor Place, London. Madresfield Court, Worcester. Carlton. Eld. s. of Earl Beauchamp, who sat for Worcestershire W.

as Hon. H.B. Lygon, for 30 years before his succession to the peerage. B. 1829. Appointed Cornet in 1st Life Guards, 1843, and Capt. 1854; and a Dept.-Lieut. of Worcester July 1859. A Conservative, 'a firm supporter of our institutions in Church and State'; and 'reserved to himself the right of opposing hasty or ill-considered change in the fundamental principles of the constitution'; voted against the ballot, 1853. First returned for Worcestershire W. Mar. 1853, without opposition, on his father becoming Earl Beauchamp. Sat until he succeeded to the Peerage (Earl Beauchamp) 1863. Died 4 Mar. 1866. [1863]

ELPHINSTONE, Sir Howard, D.C.L., F.R.S. 19 Eaton Place, London. 1 College, Doctors Commons, London. Ore Place, Hastings. Athenaeum, and Reform. B. 1804, the only s. of Maj.-Gen. Sir Howard Elphinstone, Bart., and grands. of Admiral Elphinstone, who defeated the Turkish fleet at the battle of Tchesme. Also the only nephew of H. Warburton, Esq. M. 1829, Elizabeth Julia, youngest sister of H.B. Curteis, Esq., of Windmill Hill, Sussex. Was a Magistrate and Dept.-Lieut. for the Co. of Sussex. A Barrister, and formerly practised as an Advocate at Doctors Commons. A radical Reformer. Voted for the ballot, short Parliaments, the extension of the suffrage, the repeal of the corn laws, and free trade. Considered that land should be liable to the Probate and Legacy duties. Unsuccessfully contested Hastings in 1832, but represented that borough from 1835-37. Contested Liverpool in 1837, but was defeated by only a few votes. Sat for Lewes from 1841 until he accepted Chiltern Hundreds Mar. 1847. Succeeded his father as 2nd Bart. on 28 Apr. 1846. Died 16 Mar. 1893. [1846]

ELPHINSTONE, Sir James Dalrymple-Horn-, Bart. 104 St. George's Square, London. Logie Elphinstone, Pitcaple, Aberdeenshire. St. Stephen's, Travellers', and Carlton. 3rd s. of Sir Robert Dalrymple-Horn-Elphinstone, Bart., of Horn and Logie Elphinstone, Aberdeenshire, by Graeme, d. of Col. David Hepburn, of Keith Mareschal, Co. Haddington. B. at Logie-Elphinstone, Aberdeenshire 1805; m. 1836, Mary, the 4th d. of Lieut.-Gen. Sir John Heron Maxwell, Bart., of Springkell (she died 1876). Appointed a Lord of the Treasury Feb.1874 (salary £1,000). A Dept.-Lieut. for Aberdeenshire and patron of 1 living. Was Capt. of the Ship 'Orwell' in the E.I. Co's service at the time their maritime service was reduced 1835. A Liberal-Conservative, and supported the constitution of the country in Church and State, in favour of a revision of rating generally, and of government property being assessed for municipal rates; was opposed to the construction of the Queen's ships

127

at private yards. Unsuccessfully contested Greenock 14 July 1852 and Aberdeenshire 15 May 1866. Represented Portsmouth from Apr. 1857-July 1865, and sat for it from Dec. 1868 until he retired 1880. Died 26 Dec. 1886.   [1880]

ELTON, Sir Arthur Hallam, Bart. 35 Eaton Place, London. Clevedon Court, Nr. Bristol. Athenaeum. Eld. s. of Sir Charles Abraham Elton, Bart., by the eld. d. of Joseph Smith, Esq., of Bristol. B. at Belle Vue Place, Clifton, near Bristol, 1818; m. 1841, Rhoda Susan, d. of James Willis, Esq., of Hampton Court Palace, and widow of Capt. James Baird of the 15th Hussars. Educ. at the Royal Military Coll., Sandhurst, where he obtained a commission, and served in the 14th Foot till 1841; appointed a Dept.-Lieut. of Somerset in 1852; High Sheriff in 1857. A Liberal, promised 'a general support' to Lord Palmerston's ministry, but regarded 'much of his foreign policy with strong disfavour'; considered that 'justice and humanity were alike disregarded in the attack on Canton'; in favour of the ballot, extension of the franchise, and a re-distribution of electoral districts; would not 'meddle with the Maynooth grant except as part of a general scheme for settling such questions.' Was an unsuccessful candidate for Somerset E. in 1852. First returned for Bath 1857. Retired in 1859. Died 14 Oct. 1885.   [1858]

ELTON, C.I. Continued in House after 1885: full entry in Volume II.

ELWES, John Payne. Grove House, Essex. A Conservative. Elected to Essex N. in 1835, on the elevation of Mr. A. Baring to the peerage. Retired in 1837.   [1837]

EMLYN, Visct. (I). 3 Tilney Street, South Audley Street, London. Golden Grove, Llandilo, South Wales. Travellers', and White's. Eld. s. of the Earl Cawdor. B. in Grosvenor Square 1817; m. 1842, d. of Hon. Col. Cavendish, and grand-d. of 1st Earl of Burlington. A Dept.-Lieut. of Carmarthenshire and of Nairn. Educ. at Christ Church, Oxford, where he graduated M.A.1840. Was précis writer to Lord Aberdeen (when Foreign Sec.) in 1842. A Conservative, but ready to 'consider measure for the correction of proved abuses.' First returned for Pembrokeshire in 1841 and sat until he succeeded to the Peerage (Earl Cawdor) 7 Nov. 1860. Died 29 Mar. 1898. [1860]

EMLYN, Visct. (II). 22 Ennismore Gardens, London. Golden Grove, Carmarthen, South Wales. Carlton, and White's. Eld. s. of the Earl of Cawdor, by Sarah Mary, 2nd d. of Gen. Hon. Henry Frederick Compton Cavendish (a maid of

honour to the Queen). B. 1847; m. 1868, Edith Georgiana, d. of Christopher Turnor, Esq., and Lady Caroline Turnor. Educ. at Eton and at Christ Church, Oxford. A Magistrate and Dept.-Lieut. for Carmarthenshire and Pembrokeshire. Appointed an Ecclesiastical Commissioner for England 1880. A Conservative. Sat for Carmarthenshire from Feb. 1874 until defeated in 1885. Contested Manchester South July 1892 and Wiltshire North 24 Feb.1898. Succeeded as 3rd Earl in Mar. 1898. Chairman of Great Western Railway 1895-1905; First Lord of the Admiralty 1905. Died 8 Feb. 1911.   [1885]

ENFIELD, Rt. Hon. Visct. (I). 82 Eaton Square, London. Eld. s. of the 1st Earl of Strafford. B. 1806; m. 1st, 1829, Agnes, 5th d. of 1st Marq. of Anglesey (she died 1845); 2ndly, 1848, Harriet Elizabeth, 2nd d. of the Hon. Charles and Lady Catherine Cavendish. A Capt. in the army. Had been Comptroller of the Household. Appointed Secretary to the Board of Controul, July 1846; resigned Nov. 1847. A Whig. Sat for Milbourne Port in 1830. Was elected for Chatham in June 1834 (having been appointed Lord of the Treasury) on the retirement of Col. Maberley (as a Commissioner of Customs). Was defeated in the general election following. Next succeeded his father in the representation of Poole in May 1835 and sat for that borough until 1837, when he was returned for Chatham. Sat until he retired in 1852.   [1851]

ENFIELD, Visct. (II). 7 Charles Street, Berkeley Square, London. Boodle's, White's, and Brooks's. B. in Upper Brook Street, London 1830, the eld. s. of the Earl of Stafford, by his 1st wife the 5th d. of the Marq. of Angelsey. M. 1854, Lady Alice Harriet Frederica, eld. d. of 1st Earl of Ellesmere. Educ. at Eton, where he gained the Prince Consort's prizes for modern languages, 1846 and 1847; and at Christ Church, Oxford, where he was an honorary 4th in classics 1852, and graduated M.A. 1854. Became Hon. Col. of 29th North Middlesex Rifle Volunteers 1862, Lieut.-Col. Commandant of 2nd Middlesex Militia 1859, and Dept.-Lieut. of that Co. 1854. Was Parliamentary Sec. to the Poor Law Board Feb. 1865-July 1866, Under-Sec. of State for Foreign Affairs Dec.1870 (salary £1,500). A Liberal, voted in favour of the disestablishment of the Irish Church 1869. Favoured financial reform. Sat for Tavistock from July 1852 to Sept. 1857; then sat for Middlesex until 1874, when he was defeated. Summoned to the Lords in 1874 and succeeded his father as 3rd Earl in Oct. 1886. Died 28 Mar. 1898.   [1873]

ENNIS, Sir John. Ballinahoen Court, Athlone. S.

of Andrew Ennis, Esq., of Ballinahoen (who was extensively engaged in mercantile pursuits), by his wife, Miss M'Manus. B. 1809; m. 1834, Anna Maria, eld. d. of David Henry, Esq., of Dublin. Educ. at Stonyhurst Coll. Governor of the Bank of Ireland. Chairman of the Midland Great Western Railway, and a Commissioner of Charitable Bequests. Was High Sheriff of Westmeath in 1837, and of the Co. of Dublin in 1849. A Liberal. Unsuccessfully contested Athlone Apr. 1856; first elected for Athlone Apr. 1857. Sat until he was defeated 1865. Created 1st Bart. July 1866. Died 8 Aug. 1878. [1865]

ENNIS, Sir John James. 36 Curzon Street, London. Ballinahoen Court, Athlone. Reform. Eld. s. of John Ennis, Esq., 1st Bart. (who sat for Athlone from Apr. 1857-July 1865), by Anna Maria, eld. d. of David Henry, Esq., of Dublin. B. in Dublin 1842. Educ. at Christ Church, Oxford. A Magistrate and Dept.-Lieut. of Westmeath, of which he served as High Sheriff in 1866. A Liberal. Sat for Athlone from Dec. 1868 to Feb. 1874, when he polled the same number of votes as his opponent, who on petition obtained the seat. Re-elected Apr. 1880. MP until his death 28 May 1884. [1884]

ENNIS, Nicholas. Claremont, Julianstown, Drogheda, Ireland. A Farmer in Meath. A Liberal, in favour of the system called 'Home Rule' in Ireland, believing that without a 'Native Parliament' there could never be peace, prosperity, or happiness in Ireland; in favour also of education being based upon religion, and of an amendment of the Irish Land Laws so as to ensure fixity of tenure. Sat for Meath from Feb. 1874 until he retired 1880. [1880]

ENTWISLE, John. 35 York Terrace, Regent's Park, London. Foxholes, Lancashire. Was the first President of the South Lancashire Conservative Association. He contested Rochdale unsuccessfully in 1832. Was successful there in 1835 and MP until his death in 1837. [1836]

ENTWISLE, William. 1 Sussex Square, Hyde Park, London. Rusholme, Nr. Manchester. Cousin of John Smith Entwisle, Esq., of Foxholes, Lancashire. M. d. of Edward Lloyd, Esq., Banker. A Barrister, Chairman of the Board of Directors of the Leeds and Manchester Railway Company. A Conservative, voted for agricultural protection 1846; opposed to the Poor Law. Was an usuccessful candidate for Manchester in 1841. First elected for S. Lancashire, on the death of the Hon. Richard Bootle Wilbraham in 1844. Retired 1847. Director of the re-united Chamber of Commerce (including the Commercial Association) until 1862. [1847]

ERLE, William. 20 Bedford Square, London. Athenaeum. S. of the Rev.— Erle, one of a family of some antiquity in Dorset and Somerset. B. 1 Oct. 1793; m. 1834 the eld. d. of the Rev. Dr. Williams, Prebendary of Winchester. A Queen's Counsel. A 'Constitutional Reformer and supporter of the present ministery'. First elected for Oxford in 1837. Retired 1841. Judge 1844; Knighted 1845; F.R.S. 1860; Member of Trades Union Commission 1867-68. Died 28 Jan. 1880. [1838]

ERRINGTON, Sir George, Bart. 6,I., Albany, London. Casino, Co. Dublin. Reform. S. of Michael Errington, Esq., of Clintz, in Yorkshire, afterwards of Casino, Co. Dublin, by Rosanna, d. of Ambrose More O'Ferrall, Esq., of Balyna, Co. Kildare. B. at Dublin 1839. Educ. at Ushaw Coll., Durham, and at the Roman Catholic University of Ireland. A Knight of St. John of Jerusalem (Order of Malta). A Liberal, and on his first election was in favour of the system called 'Home Rule' for Ireland, but in 1881 withdrew his adherence from the Home Rule party 'in the interests of the tenants.' Sat for the Co. of Longford from Feb. 1874 until he retired in 1885. Contested Newton div. of Lancashire 8 July 1886. [1885]

ERSKINE, John Elphinstone. Albany, London. United Service, Brooks's, and Travellers'. S. of David Erskine, Esq., of Cardross, by Hon. Keith (sic.) youngest d. of 11th Lord Elphinstone. B. Nr. Edinburgh 1806. Educ. at the Royal Naval Coll., Portsmouth. Entered the navy 1819, became a Vice-Admiral 1864 and received a medal. Author of a *Journal of a Cruise among the Islands of the Western Pacific*. A Liberal. First elected for Stirlingshire July 1865. Sat until he retired 1874. Died 23 June 1887. [1873]

ESCOTT, Bickham. 9B John Street, Berkeley Square, London. Harstrow, Somerset. Carlton. Eld. s. of Rev. T. Sweet Escott. B. 1800; m. 1825, d. of Rev. Walter Trevelyan; was in the same year called to the bar. Author of a reply to Lord Brougham on Parliamentary Reform; and a letter to the farmers on the same subject. 'A Tory, but no pledges; a strong supporter of agriculture, and trade', but in 1846 voted for the abolition of the corn laws. Contested Somerset W. in Dec. 1832 and again in Jan. 1835, and Westminster in May 1833. Contested Winchester in July 1837. First returned for Winchester June 1841. Sat until he was defeated 1847. Contested Cheltenham Sept. 1848 and Plymouth July 1852. [1847]

ESLINGTON, Lord. 9 Marsfield Street, London. Ravensworth Castle, Durham. Carlton. Eld. s. of the Earl of Ravensworth, by Isabella Horatia, eld. d. of Lord George Seymour. B. at

129

Edinburgh 1821; m. 1852, Diana, only d. of Capt. Gunning Sutton, R.N. Educ. at Eton. Appointed Dept.-Lieut. of Northumberland 1852. A Liberal-Conservative, voted against the disestablishment of the Irish Church 1869. Sat for Northumberland S. from July 1852 until he succeeded as 3rd Baron and 2nd Earl of Ravensworth March 1878. Died 22 July 1903. [1878]

ESMONDE, Sir John, Bart. Ballynestragh, Gorey, Ireland. Reform. S. of Lieut. James Esmonde, R.N. of Pembrokestown, Co. Waterford, by Anna Maria, d. of James Murphy, Esq., of Ring Manor Castle, Cork. B. at Kilmarnok, W. Wexford 1826; m. 1861, Louisa, 4th d. of Henry Grattan, Esq., and Grand-d. of Rt. Hon. Henry Grattan. Educ. at Conglowes Wood, and at Trinity Coll., Dublin, where he graduated B.A. Was called to the bar in Ireland 1850. A Magistrate for the Cos. of Waterford, Wexford and Wicklow. Major Waterford Militia Artillery. Was High Sheriff of the Co. of Wexford 1866, of which Co. he became a Dept.Lieut. Was a Lord of the Treasury June and July 1866. A Member of the Royal Irish Academy. A Liberal. Sat for Waterford from July 1852. MP until his death 9 Dec. 1876. [1876]

ESMONDE, Sir Thomas, Bart. 151 Regent Street, London. Ballynastra, Co. Wexford. Reform. S. of John Esmonde, Esq. (2nd s. of 6th Bart.). B. 1786; m. d. of—Payne, Esq. (she died 1840). A Dept.-Lieut. of the Co. of Wexford. A Liberal, voted against an abolition of the Corn Laws, but in 1846 supported their repeal. First returned for Wexford in 1841. Sat until he retired 1847. Died 31 Dec. 1868. [1847]

ESTCOURT, George Sotheron-. Newnton House, Tetbury, Wiltshire. Carlton. S. of the Rev. Edmond H. Bucknall Estcourt, of Eckington Rectory, Derbyshire, by Anne, d. of Sir John Lowther Johnstone, Bart., of Westerhall, Dumfriesshire. B. at Hartshorne, Derbyshire, 1839; m. 1863, Monica, d. of the Rev. Martin Stapylton, rector of Barlborough, Derbyshire. Educ. at Harrow and at Balliol Coll., Oxford. Capt. Royal Wiltshire Yeomanry. Assumed the name of Sotheron before his patronymic in 1876. A Conservative, not in favour of the 'Permissive Bill', but would give greater discretion to Magistrates in respect of licences; in favour of the re-adjustment of local taxation. Sat for N. Wiltshire from Feb. 1874 until he retired in 1885. Created 1st Baron Estcourt in 1903. Died 12 Jan 1915. [1885]

ESTCOURT, Col. James Bucknall Bucknall-. 90 Ebury Street, Pimlico, London. Junior United Service. 2nd s. of T.G. Bucknall-Estcourt, Esq. (who sat for Devizes from 1805 till 1826, and for Oxford University from 1826 till 1847), by Eleanor, d. of James Sutton, Esq., of New Park, Wiltshire. Was therefore bro. to Mr. Sotheron, MP for Wiltshire N. B. 1802; m. 1837 Caroline, d. of the Rt. Hon. Reginald Pole Carew, of East Anthony, Cornwall. Educ. at Harrow and at Sandhurst Coll. Entered the army in 1820, became a Lieut.-Col. in 1839, and a Col. in 1851; served in the Euphrates expedition from 1835 till 1837, and was employed to trace and survey the line of boundary determined by the treaty of Washington 1842. A Conservative, opposed a return to agricultural protection, 1850. First returned for Devizes, Feb. 1848, without opposition. Retired in 1852. Died on active service 23 June 1855. [1852]

ESTCOURT, Thomas Grimston Bucknall, D.C.L. 82 Eaton Place, London. Estcourt, Gloucestershire. Carlton, and Athenaeum. B. 1775. Was Father of Mr. Sotheron, MP for Devizes. M. 1800, d. and heiress of Jos. Sutton, Esq., of New Park, Wiltshire, assumed the name of Bucknall in compliance with the will of his uncle, W. Bucknall, Esq., of Oxley, Hertfordshire. Was Chairman of Wiltshire Quarter Sessions, resigned in 1837. A Barrister. Patron of 3 livings. A Conservative, but in favour of free trade. Sat for Oxford University from 1826; before that for Devizes. MP until he retired 1847. Died 26 July 1853. [1847]

ESTCOURT, Rt. Hon. Thomas Henry Sutton Sotheron-. 51 Eaton Place, London. Estcourt, Tetbury. Carlton, and United University. S. of Thomas Grimston Bucknall-Estcourt, Esq., many years MP for Oxford University, by the d. and heiress of Joseph Sutton, Esq., of New Park, Wiltshire. B. 1801; m. d. and heiress of Admiral Sotheron. Assumed the name of Sotheron on the death of his father-in-law in 1839, instead of that of Bucknall-Estcourt, and in 1855, resumed by royal licence, the name of Estcourt. Educ. at Oriel Coll., Oxford, where he graduated M.A. 1826, and received the honorary degree of D.C.L. 1857. Was President of the Poor Law Board from Mar. 1858-Mar. 1859, and Secretary of State for the Home Department from the latter date till June 1859. A Maj. in the Wiltshire Yeomanry. A Magistrate and Dept.-Lieut. of Wiltshire. A Liberal-Conservative, in favour of a moderate extension of the franchise; opposed to the ballot; would not support the total abolition of Church rates. Sat for Marlborough from Mar. 1829 to 1832; for Devizes from Nov. 1835 to 1844, when he was chosen for N. Wiltshire. Sat for N. Wiltshire from 1844 to 1865 when he accepted

Chiltern Hundreds. Died 6 Jan. 1876.   [1864]

ETWALL, Ralph. Longstock Down, Hampshire. Brooks's, Oxford & Cambridge, and Reform. S. of R. Etwall, Esq. B. 1804. Of Whig principles, inclining to Radicalism; in favour of short Parliaments. Was first elected for Andover, in which he had sufficient influence to be called one of its Patrons, in 1831, and voted for the Reform Act; voted also for Lord Ebrington's motion. Sat until he retired 1847. Kept a racing stud until about 1849. Died 15 Dec. 1882.   [1847]

EUSTON, Earl of. (I). 7 Grosvenor Place, London. Salsay, Northamptonshire. Eld. s. of the Duke of Grafton. B. 1790; m. 1812, Mary Caroline, 3rd. d. of the Hon. Admiral Sir G. Cranfield Berkeley. Col. of the West Suffolk Militia; Ranger of Salsay Forest. A moderate Reformer. Succeeded his younger bro. Lord J.H. Fitzroy (died) in Thetford in 1834; but had previously sat in two Parliaments for Bury St. Edmunds; was again returned for Thetford in conjunction with Sir Jas. Flower, at the general election in 1841, having polled the same number of votes; neither could vote till after the report of a Committee. Declared not duly elected 1842. Succeeded as 5th Duke 28 Sept. 1844. Died 26 Mar. 1863.   [1842]

EUSTON, Earl of. (II). Clarges Street, London. Wakefield Lodge. Stoney Stratford. Euston Hall, Thetford, Norfolk. Reform, and Travellers'. Eld. s. of the Duke of Grafton (who formerly sat for Thetford). B. in Grosvenor Place, 1819. Was attaché to the British Legation at Naples in 1841. Was Col. of the West Suffolk Militia for a short period in 1846. A Liberal, voted against the ballot, 1853. First returned for Thetford July 1847. Sat until he succeeded to the Peerage (Duke of Grafton) in 1863.   [1857 2nd ed.]

EVANS, Sir De Lacy, G.C.B. S. of John Evans, Esq., of Miltown, Ireland. B. at Moig in Ireland 1787; m. 1834, Jesette, d. of Col. R. Arbuthnot, and widow of P. Hughes, Esq. (she died 1861). Appointed Gen. in the army 1861; and a Lieut.-Gen. in the Spanish National Army. Appointed Col. of 21st Fusiliers 1853. Was at Waterloo. In 1835 was appointed to the command of the British Auxiliary Force in Spain; and in 1854 to the command of a division of the forces sent to the E.; was slightly wounded at the battle of the Alma, and eulogised in the despatches of the Commander in Chief. Returned home invalided Dec. 1854, and received the thanks of Parliament for his services in the Crimea. Made Grand Officer of the Legion of Honour 1856. A Liberal, in favour of the enfranchisement of large towns, vote by ballot, abolition of Church rates, etc. Opposed to the system of sale of commissions in the army. Sat for Rye for a few months in 1830; was an unsuccessful candidate there at the general election same year, re-elected in 1831. Unsuccessfully contested Rye as well as Westminster in 1832. Sat for Westminster from 1833-1841, and from Feb. 1846 until he retired 1865. Died 9 Jan. 1870.   [1865]

EVANS, George. Portrane, Co. Dublin. Reform. S. of Hampden Evans, Esq., of Portrane, a branch of Lord Carbery's family, which assumed the name of Freke in addition to that of Evans. Bro. of Joshua Evans, Esq., a Commissioner of the Court of Bankruptcy. M. 1805, Sophia, sister of the Rt. Hon. Sir Henry Parnell, Bart. Was in favour of the ballot, the abolition of tithes, but considered lay tithes as private property; also favoured a revision of the laws relating to Juries, and said if justice be not speedily done to Ireland, he would vote for a repeal of the Union. Sat for Dublin Co. from 1832 until defeated 1841.   [1838]

EVANS, John, Q.C. 30 Cumberland Terrace, Regent's Park, London. 11 South Crown Office Row, Temple, London. Clareston, near Haverfordwest. Was educ. at Glasgow, and at Geneva; graduated B.A. at the former University; was called to the bar at the Inner Temple in 1820; made a Queen's Counsel in 1837; elected a Bencher of the Inner Temple in 1837; went the Oxford circuit. A Liberal. First returned for Haverfordwest in 1847, without opposition. Sat until he retired in 1852. Unsuccessfully contested Cardigan 24 Feb. 1855. Died 17 Oct. 1864.   [1852]

EVANS, Thomas William. 2 Queen Anne's Gate, London. Allestree Hall, Derby. Reform, Devonshire, and Brooks's. S. of William Evans, Esq., of Allestree Hall, near Derby (who once sat for Derbyshire North), by Mary, d. of the Rev. Thomas Gisborne, of Yoxall Lodge, Staffordshire. B. in London 1821; m. 1845, Mary, eld. d. of Thomas John Gisborne, Esq., of Holme Hall, Bakewell, Derbyshire. Educ. at Trinity Coll., Cambridge. A Dept.-Lieut. and Magistrate for Derbyshire. Patron of 4 livings. A sincere though moderate Liberal, and was willing to give an independent support to Mr. Gladstone. Unsuccessfully contested Derbyshire N. 22 July 1853 and Stafford 7 June 1869. Unsuccessfully contested South Derbyshire Dec. 1868 and Jan. 1869; sat for South Derbyshire from Apr. 1857 to Nov. 1868; re-elected Feb. 1874 and sat until he retired in 1885; contested Derby in 1886. Created Baronet July 1887; Chairman of Derbyshire County Council 1889 until his death on 4 Oct. 1892.   [1885]

131

EVANS, William. Park House, Kensington Gore, London. Allestree Hall, Derbyshire. B. in Jan. 1788, the eld. s. of William Evans, Esq., of Darley, by the d. of Jedediah Strutt, Esq. M. 1820, Mary d. of the Rev. Thomas Gisborne, of Yoxhall Lodge, Staffordshire and sister of Thomas Gisborne, Esq., many years member for Derbyshire. Was Sheriff of Derbyshire in 1829. Held Liberal opinions, was in favour of an extension of the suffrage and the enfranchisement of smaller boroughs, of some moderate and cautious reform in the Church and more extensive public education. Formerly voted against the abolition of the Corn Laws, but in 1846 supported their repeal. Sat for Retford from 1818-26, for Leicester from 1830-35, having been unsuccessful there in 1826 and 1835. Sat for Derbyshire N. from 1837 until he accepted Chiltern Hundreds in 1853. Died 8 Apr. 1856. [1853]

EVELYN, W.J. Continued in House after 1885: full entry in Volume II.

EWART, Joseph Christopher. New Brighton, Liverpool. Reform. 3rd s. of William Ewart, Esq., a Liverpool Merchant. B. at Liverpool 1799. Unmarried. Educ. at Eton. Was engaged in trade in Liverpool, but retired. A Dept.-Lieut. of Lancashire; a Director of the London and North-Western Railway, and of the Peninsular and Oriental Steam Navigation Company, of the latter he was one of the original founders. A Liberal, in favour of a measure of national education, and 'a further extension of the suffrage, suited to the advancing spirit of the age'. Unsuccessfully contested Liverpool July 1852; first elected there Mar. 1855. Sat until he was defeated 1865. Died 14 Dec. 1868. [1865]

EWART, William. 6 Cambridge Square, Hyde Park, London. Broadleas, Devizes. United University, and Reform. 2nd s. of William Ewart, Esq., an extensive Merchant at Liverpool. B. at Liverpool 1798; m. 1829 his cousin, Mary Ann, d. of G.A. Lee, Esq., of Manchester. Educ. at Eton and at Christ Church, Oxford, where he graduated B.A. 1821; gained the University prize for English verse 1819. Called to the bar at the Middle Temple, Jan. 1827. A radical Reformer, in favour of triennial Parliaments, the ballot, and the total abolition of capital punishment; in favour of all classes being represented, without undue preponderance being given to any. Was instrumental in procuring the abolition of capital punishment in cases of cattle stealing, sacrilege etc. in 1833; also introduced the Prisoners' Counsel Act in 1833, and the Act for Free Public Libraries in 1850. Sat for Bletchingley from 1828 till 1830; for Liverpool from 1830 to 1837. Un-

successfully contested Kilkenny 7 Aug. 1837 and Marylebone Mar. 1838. Sat for Wigan from 1839 till 1841, when he was returned for Dumfries district. MP until he retired in 1868. Died 23 Jan. 1869. [1867]

EWART, Sir William, Bart. Glenmachan House, Strandtown, Belfast. Sackville Street, Dublin. Carlton. S. of Alderman William Ewart, of Glenbank, Co. Antrim. B. at Belfast 1817; m. 1840, Isabella, d. of the late Lavers Mathewson, Esq., of Newton Stewart, Co. Tyrone. Educ. at Belfast Academy. A Merchant and Linen Manufacturer at Belfast. Was Mayor of Belfast in 1859 and 1860, and was one of the deputies from Belfast for the arrangement of a treaty of commerce with France in 1864. JP for the counties of Antrim and Down and for the borough of Belfast. Baronetcy conferred in 1887. A Conservative. Sat for Belfast from Mar. 1878 and for Belfast N. from 1885 until his death in 1889. [1888]

EWING, Sir A. Orr. Continued in House after 1885: full entry in Volume II.

EWING, Humphrey Ewing Crum-. 28 Cornwall Gardens, South Kensington, London. Ardencaple Castle, Helensburgh, Dumbartonshire. Union, and Reform. S. of Alexander Crum, Esq., of Thornliebank, by Jane, d. of Walter Ewing Maclae, Esq., of Cathkin. B. at Thornliebank, Renfrewshire 1802; m. 1826, Helen, d. of Rev. John Dick, D.D., of Glasgow, and a W. India Proprietor. A Dept.-Lieut. of Dumbartonshire and a Magistrate for the Cos. of Argyll, Lanark, Renfrew and Dumbarton. Assumed the name of Ewing in accordance with the will of his uncle, James Ewing, Esq., of Strathleven. A Liberal. Unsuccessfully contested Paisley, Apr. 1857. Sat for Paisley from Dec. 1857 until he retired 1874. Made Lord-Lieut. of Dumbartonshire Feb. 1874 until his death 3rd July 1887. [1873]

EWING, James, LL.D., F.R.S.E. 19 Downing Street, London. Dunoon Castle, Argyllshire. Lord Provost of Glasgow. A Banker and Merchant. A Reformer, opposed to restraints on knowledge, the Corn Laws, the East India monopoly, flogging in the army, and the impressment of seamen; in favour of the repeal of the Assessed Taxes, a revision of the excise laws, a commutation of tithes in Ireland and England, and the abrogation of patronage in the Church of Scotland; but a decided preserver of the constitution as established in 1688. Sat for Glasgow from 1832 until defeated in 1835. Died 6 Dec. 1853. [1833]

EYKYN, Roger. 13 Upper Grosvenor Street,

London. The Willows, Windsor. Reform. S. of Richard Eykyn, Esq., of Hornsey, Middlesex and Ackleton, Shropshire, by Susannah, d. of Sir William Stan. B. at Hornsey 1828; m. 1st, 1851, Maria Prinald, d. of George Schoted, Esq., of Essex Lodge (she died 1866); 2ndly, 1868, Hon. Mary Caroline, eld. d. of 6th Baron Vaux. Lieut. Royal Buckinghamshire Yeomanry Lancers. A Dept.-Lieut. and Magistrate for Berkshire. A Liberal. A 'staunch supporter' of the Established Church, but in favour of the total abolition of Church rates; voted for the disestablishment of the Irish Church 1869, and for the ballot 1866. First elected for Windsor Apr. 1866 and sat until defeated 1874. Contested Taunton 1880. Died 14 Nov. 1896. [1873]

EYTON, Peter Ellis. 34 Edwardes Square, Kensington, London. Englefield House, Rhyl, North Wales. S. of James Eyton, Esq., by Mary, only d. of David Parry, Esq., of Rhydycilgwn, Denbighshire. B. at Flint 1827. Unmarried. Was educ. at the High School, Liverpool Institute. Commenced practice as an Attorney-at-law 1856. Had been town clerk and clerk to the Magistrates of the borough of Flint since 1856. Author of a *Trip to the Isle of Man*. An 'advanced Liberal', in favour of the disestablishment and disendowment of the Church of England. Also in favour of the system called 'Home Rule' for Ireland. Sat for the district of Flint from Feb. 1874. MP until his death 17 or 19 June 1878. [1878]

EAGAN, James. 49 Upper Mount Street, Dublin. Reform. S. of James Fagan, Esq., a Timber Merchant. B. in Dublin 1800. Unmarried. Educ. at Baymount, Co. Dublin. A Timber Merchant and Shipowner. Had an extensive factory in Bridgefoot Street, Dublin, for railway carriages, waggons, trucks, etc. A Liberal and Repealer. First elected for Wexford Co. in 1847. Retired in 1852. [1852]

FAGAN, Capt. William Addis. Junior United Service. B. at Feltrim, Co. Cork 1832, the s. of William Trant Fagan, Esq., of Feltrim (who sat for the City of Cork for many years), by Mary, d. of Charles Addis, Esq., of London. M. 1871, Frances Anne, 2nd d. of Daniel Mahony, Esq., of Dunloe Castle, Co. Kerry. Educ. at Stonyhurst Coll., Lancashire. Entered the army as Cornet 12th Lancers 1855, and became Capt. November 1860. Retired Aug. 1867. A Liberal, voted for the disestablishment of the Irish Church 1869. Sat for the bor. of Carlow from Dec. 1868 until his retirement in 1874. [1873]

FAGAN, William Trant. Feltrim, Co. Cork. Reform. Eld. s. of James Fagan, Esq., of Cork, by the d. of Ignatius Trant, Esq., of Cork. B. in Cork 1801; m. 1827, Mary d. of Charles Addis, Esq., of London. Was educ. at Southall Park, Middlesex; a Merchant and an Alderman of Cork, of which city he filled the office of Mayor; author of *The Life and Times of Daniel O'Connell*. A Liberal, formerly a member of the 'Repeal' party; voted for the ballot, 1853. First elected for Cork city in 1847; vacated his seat Apr. 1851; re-elected July 1852. MP until his death on 9 or 16 May 1859. [1858]

FAIRBAIRN, Sir Andrew. 15 Portman Square, London. Brooks's, Reform, Devonshire, Boodle's, Marlborough. St. James's, and United University. B. at Glasgow 1828, only s. of Sir Peter Fairburn of Woodsley, Yorkshire., by his 1st Wife, Margaret, d. of Robert Kennedy of Glasgow. M. 1862 Clara Frederica, youngest d. of Sir John Lambton Loraine, Bart. Educ. at Geneva and at Glasgow Schools, and St. Peter's Coll., Cambridge. Graduated as 37th Wrangler 1850, M.A. 1853. Called to the bar at the Inner Temple April 1852, and went the Northern Circuit; but relinquished practice in 1856, and became Chairman of the firm of Fairburn, Naylor Machpherson & Co. Ltd., machine makers at Leeds. Twice Mayor of Leeds School Board from its formation in 1870-1878. A Magistrate and Dept.-Lieut. of Yorkshire (W. Riding), and a Magistrate for Leeds. High Sheriff of Yorkshire 1892. Capt. Yorkshire Hussar Yeomanry. A member of the Executive of the Leeds Exhibiton 1868, and a Royal Commissioner for the Paris Exhibition 1878. A Liberal, and general supporter of that party. Unsuccessfully contested Leeds 17 Nov. 1868 and Knaresborough 5 Feb. 1874. Sat for the Eastern div. of the W. Riding of Yorkshire from April 1880-1886, when he was defeated, standing as a Liberal Unionist. Died 30 May 1901. [1886]

FAITHFUL, George. 5 King's Road, Brighton. Mr. Faithful and his bro. Henry took up their abodes at Brighton as Attornies. The Hon. Member was a Dissenter, and soon acted as Minister at a Dissenting Chapel; his congregation increasing, a Chapel was built for him in Church Street, Brighton, in which he continued to preach till ill health obliged him to resign. It was whilst he acted as a Dissenting Minister that Mr. Kemp, the Member for Lewes, himself a Dissenting Preacher, appointed the Messrs. Faithful his solicitors. Mr. George Faithful had been always an active commissioner under the Brighton Paving Act, in which capacity he was able to make the principal part of the inhabitants acquainted with his political opinions. He was an advocate for the immediate abolition of slavery, of all unmerited pensions, and sinecures, the standing army, all useless expense, the Corn Laws, and every other monopoly. He said that if the extent of suffrage at that time was not found efficient he would vote for universal suffrage; and if triennial Parliaments did not succeed, would vote for having them annual; he was an advocate of the ballot. Elected for Brighton 13 Dec. 1832. Defeated in 1835, and again in 1837.   [1833]

FANCOURT, Major Charles St. John. 13 Grafton Street, Bond Street, London. Nephew to Mr. Greenwood, of the house of Greenwood, Cox and Hammersley. A Reformer, considered as inclined to Conservative principles; in favour of the removal of the Jewish disabilities. In 1834 he moved the abolition of flogging in the army. Sat for Barnstaple from 1832. Retired in 1837. [1836]

FANE, Col. Henry Hamlyn. Avon Tyrrell, Ringwood, Hampshire. Clovelly Court, Bideford, Devon. Travellers', and United Services. Eld. s. and heir of the Rev. Edward Fane, of Fulbeck, Lincolnshire, and Avon Tyrrel, Ringwood, Hampshire. B. at Fulbeck Hall, 1817; m. 1850, Susan, eld. d. and co-heir of Sir James Hamlyn Williams, of Clovelly Court, Devon. Educ. at the Charterhouse. Entered the army 1834; became Maj. 4th Dragoons 1846, and retired. Served in the campaign in Afghanistan, and was present at the storm and capture of Chuznee, for which he had a medal. Lieut.-Col. Commandant Lincolnshire Militia. Author of a work entitled *Five Years in India*. Patron of 1 living. A Conversative, not opposed to the reduction of the malt duty. First elected for South Hampshire, July 1865. Retired in 1868. Died 27 Dec. 1868.   [1867]

FANE, Col. John William. Wormsley Park, Stokenchurch, Oxfordshire. Carlton, and Junior Carlton. Eld. s. of John Fane, Esq., of Wormsley Park, Oxfordshire, by Elizabeth, d. of William Lowndes Stone, Esq., of Brightwell Park, Oxfordshire. B. 1804; m. 1st, 1826, Catherine, 7th d. of Sir Benjamin Hobhouse, Bart., and sister of Lord Broughton (she died 1828), 2ndly, 1829, Lady Ellen Catherine, 3rd d. of 5th Earl of Macclesfield (she died 1844); 3rdly, 1845, Charlotte, youngest d. of Theodore Henry Broadhead, Esq. (she died 1855); 4thly, 1856, Victoria, eld. d. of Sir William Temple. Was educ. at Rugby. Lieut.-Col. of the Oxfordshire Militia. A Conversative, voted against the abolition of church-rates May 1862. First elected for Oxfordshire Feb. 1862. Retired in 1868. Died 19 Nov. 1875.   [1867]

FARMER-ATKINSON, H.J. Continued in House after 1885: full entry in Volume II.

FARNHAM, Edward Basil. 63 St. James's Street, London. Quorndon House, Leicestershire. Carlton, and United University. Eld. s. of Edward Farnham, Esq., of Quorndon, by the d. and co-heiress of the Rev. Dr. Rhudde, one of the chaplains in ordinary to George III. The family held the Quorndon estates since the reign of Edw. I. B. 1799; m. 1851, Gertrude Emily, 2nd d. of Sir William Hartopp (3rd Bart.), of Four Oaks Hall, Warwickshire. A Dept.-Lieut. for Leicestershire. Appointed major in the Leicestershire Yeomanry Cavalry, May, 1852. A Conversative; supported 'a careful revision of taxation', and a system of 'education based on religion'; opposed to the Maynooth grant; in favour of a repeal of the malt tax, and the extinction of the income tax in 1860. First returned for Leicestershire N. 1837. Sat until he retired in 1859. Sheriff of Leicestershire 1870. Died 13 May, 1879.   [1858]

FARQUHAR, Sir Walter Minto Townshend-. 4 Berkeley Street, Berkeley Square, London. Hertford. Carlton, and Arthur's. S. of Sir Robert Townshend-Farquhar, Bart., by Maria Frances Geslip, 2nd d. of Joseph Francis Louis de Lantour of Madras (she married 2ndly, Thomas Hamilton, Esq.,). B. at Madras 1809; m. 1835, d. of the 7th Lord Reay. Educ. at Christ Church, Oxford, where he was 3rd class in classics 1829; was for some years attached to the embassy at Vienna. An 'independent Conservative', in favour of admitting the working classes to a large share of the franchise, but opposed to 'sudden and organic changes'; said he would not vote for the total abolition of Church rates unless some provision be made for the fabrics of Churches. Was an unsuccessful candidate for Hertford in May 1839; first returned for that bor. 1857. MP until his death May 1866.   [1865]

FARQUHARSON, Dr. Continued in House after 1885: full entry in Volume II.

FARRAND, Robert. 19 Park Crescent, Regents Park, London. Hale Hall, Norfolk. Carlton. A Merchant in London. A Conversative. Sat for Hedon, Yorkshire, previously to the passing of the Reform Bill. First elected for Stafford prior to the dissolution of Parliament in 1837, when, by a resolution of the House of Commons, a new writ was issued after it had been suspended after the resignation of Sir F.L.H. Goodricke, Bart. in May 1835. Again chosen at the general election in 1837. Retired 1841.   [1841]

FARRER, James. 14 Queen Street, Mayfair, London. Ingleborough, Lancaster. Carlton. Eld. s. of James William Farrer, Esq., of Ingleborough (for many years Master in Chancery), by

Henrietta, relict of the Hon. John Scott, and only d. of Sir Matthew White Ridley, Bart.; was therefore half-bro. to 2nd Earl of Eldon. B. in London 1812. Educ. at Winchester, and at New Coll., Oxford. A Dept.-Lieut. for Durham and the W. Riding of Yorkshire, and a Magistrate for Durham, Westmorland, and the W. Riding. A Conversative, 'ready to support Parliamentary Reform with no illiberal hand'. Was an unsuccessful candidate for Durham S. in 1841; sat for Durham S. from July 1847 to Apr. 1857, when he was again defeated, but regained his seat in May 1859, and sat until he retired 1865. Died 13 June 1879.   [1865]

FAWCETT, Rt. Hon. Henry. 51 The Lawn, South Lambeth Road, London. Trinity Hall, Cambridge. Reform, and Athenaeum. S. of William Fawcett, Esq., of Longford, Salisbury, by Mary, d. of W. Cooper, Esq., of Salisbury. B. at Salisbury 1833; m. 1867, Millicent, d. of Newson Garrett, Esq., of Alde House, Aldeburgh, Suffolk. Educ. at King's Coll. School, London, and at Trinity Hall, Cambridge, where he graduated 7th Wrangler 1856 and was elected to a Fellowship in his College the same year. Elected Professor of Political Economy at Cambridge Nov. 1863 and elected Lord Rector of Glasgow Univ. 1883. Appointed Postmaster Gen. Apr. 1880. Author of a *Manual of Political Economy, Pauperism, its causes and remedies*, and various articles on Economic Science. A Liberal. Contested Cambridge unsuccessfully Feb. 1863; and in Feb. 1864 Brighton, for which latter place he sat from July 1865 to Jan. 1874, when he stood unsuccessfully. Sat for Hackney from Apr. 1874. MP until his death 6 Nov. 1884.   [1884]

FAY, Charles Joseph. Granite Lodge, Kingstown, Co. Dublin. Devonshire. S. of Thomas Fay, Esq., by Mary Herbert, d. of P. Maccabe, Esq., B. at Cootehill, Co. Cavan, 1842; m. 1870, Susan, d. of James Fay, Esq., of Moyne Hall, near Cavan. Educ. at Clongowes Wood and at Castleknock. Was admitted a Solicitor in 1866. A Magistrate for the Co. of Dublin. A 'Conservative-Liberal.' Sat for the Co. of Cavan from Feb. 1874 until he retired in 1885. Died, by drowning, 20 Sept. 1895.   [1885]

FAZAKERLEY, John Nicholas. 18 Upper Brook Street, London. Stoodley, Bampton, Devon. Of Whig principles. Patron of 1 living. Sat for Great Grimsby in 1809; for Lincoln 1812-18; for Great Grimsby 1818-20; for Tavistock in 1820. Accepted Chiltern Hundreds May 1820. Sat again for Lincoln 1826 to 30, and for Peterborough from Nov. 1830 until he retired in 1841. Died 16 July 1852.   [1838]

FECTOR, John Minet. Kearnsey Abbey, Kent. S. of John Minet Fector, Esq., Banker at Dover, by Anne Wortley Montague, d. of Lieut.-Gen. Sir Robert Laurie, Bt., MP for Dumfriesh. B. 1812. A Banker. A Conservative. Sat for Dover 1835-37. Was elected for Maidstone in Mar. 1838, on the death of Wyndham Lewis, Esq., the previous member, by a considerable majority over Mr. Robarts, who formerly represented it. Retired 1841.   [1841]

FEILDEN, Henry Master. 13 Palace Gate, Kensington W., London. Carlton, and Junior United Service. St. Stephen's Club, Wilton Park, Blackburn. Eld. s. of Joseph Feilden, Esq., of Whitton Park (who represented Blackburn from July 1865-March 1869), by Frances Mary, d. of the Rev. S. Master, Rector of Crofton, Lancashire. B. at Witton Park, Blackburn, 1818; m. 1st, 1843, Caroline, d. of Sir O. Mosely, Bart. (she d. 1862); 2ndly, Hannah, d. of John Fox Esq., of Haverigg. Educ. at Christ Church Coll., Oxford. Was a Magistrate for the Co. of Lancaster, and the W. Riding of Yorkshire. Appointed a Dept.-Lieut. for the Co. of Lancaster 1853. A Major and Hon. Lieut.-Col. 1st Duke of Lancaster's Own Militia. A Conservative, who said he would act with the Conservative Party; though 'not opposed to necessary reforms', he was 'averse to rash or sudden changes in the constitution'. Sat for Blackburn from March 1869. MP until his death 5 Sept. 1875.   [1875]

FEILDEN, Joseph. Wilton Park, Blackburn, Carlton. B. at Blackburn 1792, the s. of Henry Fielden, Esq., of Witton Park, Blackburn, by Fanny, d. of William Hill, Esq., of Blythe Hall, Nr. Ormskirk. M. 1817, Frances Mary, d. of the Rev. S. Master, Rector of Croston, Lancashire. Was Capt. 1st Lancashire Militia from 1812-16. A Magistrate and Dept.-Lieut. of Lancashire, for which he was High Sheriff 1818. A Liberal-Conservative. First elected for Blackburn July 1865 and sat until he was unseated in 1869.   [1869]

FEILDEN, Montague Joseph. Feniscowles, Nr. Blackburn, Lancashire. 2nd. s. of Sir William Feilden (1st. Bart.), who sat for Blackburn from 1832 till 1847, by Mary Haughton, d. of the late Edmund Jackson, Esq., member of the House of Assembly at Jamaica. B. at Feniscowles, near Blackburn, 1816; m. 1846, Mary Anne, only d. and heir of William Valentine, Esq., of Samlesbury, Lancashire. Educ. at the Free Grammar School, Blackburn, and subsequently under the Rev. Canon Casson, of Chester. A Merchant and Cotton Spinner, head of the firm of Messrs. Feilden and Jackson, the well-known and extensive manufacturing house. A Magistrate, and Dept.-Lieut. for the county of Lancaster, Director of the East Lancashire Railway, President of the Blackburn Commercial Association, and senior Maj. in 3rd. Royal Lancashire Militia. A Liberal, in favour of financial and Parliamentary reform, vote by ballot, and and a gradual extension of the suffrage. First returned for Blackburn Mar. 1853. Sat until he retired 1857. Contested Blackburn Nov. 1868.   [1857]

FEILDEN, Gen. R.J. Continued in House after 1885: full entry in Volume II.

FEILDEN, Sir William, Bart. 18 Hanover Square, London. Feniscowles, Lancashire. 3rd s. of Joseph Feilden, Esq., of Witton House, near Blackburn, B. at Blackburn 1772; m. 1797, Mary Haughton, d. of Edmund Jackson, Esq., Member of the House of Assembly, Jamaica. Graduated at Brasenose Coll., Oxford. A Manufacturer, and a Merchant at Blackburn. A Dept.-Lieut. for the Co. of Lancaster. Frequently voted with the Conservative party, but was favourably inclined to the ballot; did not think household suffrage and shortening the duration of Parliament necessary at that time. Sat for Blackburn from 1832 until he retired 1847.   [1847]

FELLOWES, Edward. 3 Belgrave Square, London. Ramsey Abbey, Huntingdon. Haverland Hill, Norwich. Carlton, and Junior United Service. 2nd s. of William Henry Fellowes, Esq., MP of Ramsey Abbey, Huntingdon, by Emma, 4th d. of Richard Benyon, Esq., of Englefield House, Berkshire. B. 1809; m. 1845, Hon. Mary Julia, eld. d. of the 4th Lord Sondes. Served for some time in the 15th Hussars. A Magistrate and Dept.-Lieut. for Huntingdonshire. Appointed a Dept.- Lieut. for Norfolk 1847. A Conservative, voted against the disestablishment of the Irish Church. First elected for Huntingdonshire 1837, and sat until he retired 1880. Created Baron De Ramsay July 1887. Died 9 Aug. 1887.   [1880]

FELLOWES, Henry Arthur Wallop. 41 Bryanston Square. Nephew to the Earl of Portsmouth and s. of Newton Fellowes (bro. to the Earl.) B. in 1799. A Reformer; in favour of the ballot. He was first elected for Andover in 1831. Retired in 1835.   [1833]

FELLOWES, Hon. Newton. 11 Bryanston Square, Eggesford, Devon. Bro. and heir presumptive to the Earl of Portsmouth, and father of the member for Andover. B. 1772; assumed, in 1795, the surname and arms of Fellowes, upon succeeding to the estates of his maternal uncle, Henry Arthur Fellowes, Esq., of Eggesford. M.

1st,1795, Frances, 4th d. of the Rev. Castel Sherrard, of Huntingdonshire, 2ndly, 1820 Catharine, 2nd d. of Earl Fortescue, and therefore bro.-in-law of Lord Ebrington. A Capt. in the East Devon militia, and patron of 4 livings. Of Whig principles, in favour of the ballot. Sat for Andover in several parliaments. Sat for Devon N. from 1832. Retired in 1837.   [1837]

FELLOWES, W.H. Continued in House after 1885: full entry in Volume II.

FENTON, John. Rochdale, Lanchashire. A Banker in Rochdale. Unsuccessfully contested Rochdale at the general election in 1835. Chosen in 1837 by a majority of 25. A Liberal. Sat for Rochdale 1832 to 1835 and from 19 Apr. 1837. Retired 1841. Died 25 July 1863.   [1838].

FENTON, Capt. Lewis. 35 Jermyn Street, London. Spring Grove, Huddersfield. Of Whig principles; in favour of the Factories Bill. Returned for Huddersfield in 1832; was an MP until he died, Dec. 1833.   [1833]

FENWICK, Edward Matthew. 11 Kings Bench Walk, Temple, London. Burrow Hall, Kirkby, Lonsdale. Reform. S. of Edward James Reid, Esq., of Jamaica. B. in Jamaica; m. 1841, Sarah, grand-d. and heir of Thomas Fenwick, Esq., of Burrow Hall, Lancaster. Assumed the name of Fenwick and the arms of that family by Royal Licence 1854. Called to the bar at the Middle Temple. A Magistrate for the Cos. of York and Lancaster. Patron of 1 living. First elected for Lancaster Apr. 1864. On petition the election was declared void. Lancaster defranchised in 1867. Died 16 Oct. 1877.   [1865]

FENWICK, Henry. Southill, Chester-le-Street. Brooks's, Reform, and Oxford & Cambridge. B. 1820, the eld. s. of Thomas Fenwick, Esq., of Southill, Co. Durham. M. 1861, Jane Lutwidge, eld. d. of John Cookson, Esq., of Meldon Park, Northumberland. Educ. at St. John's Coll., Cambridge, where he graduated B.A. 1842, M.A. 1845. Called to the bar 1845 and joined the Northern Circuit until 1851, when he retired. Appointed Dept.-Lieut. of Durham 1855. A Liberal, in favour of an 'extension of the suffrage proportioned to the increasing intelligence of the people', vote by ballot, the 'voluntary system of education assisted by the State' and the abolition of Church rates. Unsuccessfully contested Sunderland July 1852, and Durham City Dec. following. Sat for Sunderland from Jan. 1855 until he was defeated at a by-election 28 Feb. 1866, subsequent to appointment as a Lord of the Admiralty. Died 16 Apr. 1868.   [1865 2nd. ed.]

FERGUS, John. Kirkcaldy and Strathore, Fifeshire. Brooks's, and Reform. S. of Walter Fergus, Esq., for many years Provost of Kirkcaldy. A Manufacturer and Merchant at Kirkcaldy. A Dept.-Lieut. of Fifeshire. A Liberal, voted against the repeal of the malt tax in 1835, and for the ballot 1853; said he would 'always be anxious to promote measures for the education of the masses of the people'. Represented the Kirkcaldy district of burghs from 1835 till 1837. First returned for Fifeshire in 1847. Sat until he retired in 1859. Died 23 Jan. 1865. [1858]

FERGUSON, George. 37 Charles Street, Berkeley Square, London. Pitfour, Aberdeenshire. Carlton. M. 1825, Elizabeth, d. of Lord Langford. A Post Capt. in the Navy. A Conservative. Sat for Banffshire for 1832. Defeated in 1837. Died 15 Mar. 1867. [1836]

FERGUSON, Joseph. Carlisle. Reform. S. of Robert Ferguson, Esq., B. at Whitehaven 1788; m. 1815, d. of John Clerk, Esq., of Bebside House, Northumberland. Educ. at Carlisle Grammar School. A sleeping partner in a Manufacturing concern at Carlisle. Mayor of that city 1837, a Magistrate for Cumberland from 1840, President of the Carlisle Mechanics' Institute from 1833. Of 'decidedly Liberal opinions; in favour of Parliamentary Reform, opposed to the Maynooth Grant'. Voted for the ballot 1853. First returned for Carlisle in July 1852. Defeated 1857. Died 17 Feb. 1863. [1857]

FERGUSON, Lieut.-Col. Robert. 8 Curzon Street, London. Raith House, Fifeshire. Brooks's, and Reform. S. of Sir Ronald Ferguson, and nephew of Robert Ferguson Esq., of Raith. M. 1859, Emma, d. of James Henry Mandeville, Esq., and grand-d. of J.H. Mandeville, Esq., of Rutland Gate, London. Formerly a Lieut.-Col. in the army. A Liberal, 'favourable to extension of the suffrage, and education to all classes and creeds'; voted for the ballot 1853. Succeeded his uncle in the representation of Kirkcaldy district in 1841. Sat until he accepted Chiltern Hundreds 1862. Died 28 Nov. 1868. [1862]

FERGUSON, Robert. (I). 18 Portman Square, London. Raith, Fifeshire. Athenaeum, and Reform. Eld. s. of William Ferguson, Esq., of Raith, by Jane, d. of Ronald Crawford, of Redalrig, sister of Margaret Countess of Dumfries; bro. of Gen. Sir R.C. Ferguson, member for Nottingham; m. Mary, only daughter of Wm. Hamilton Nisbet, Esq., of Direleton, Haddingtonshire, divorced from the Earl of Elgin in 1808. Lord-Lieut. of Fifeshire. A Reformer, opposed to the ballot. Sat for Fifeshire in 1806; for the Kirkcaldy district of Burghs from 1831 till 1835, when he retired from its representation for the purpose of contesting Haddingtonshire. Returned for Haddingtonshire in 1835; he was defeated in 1837 but successful in standing for Kirkcaldy at the same election, he continued as MP until his death Jan. 1841. [1840]

FERGUSON, Robert. (II). 45 St. James's Place, London. Morton, Carlisle. B. at Carlisle 1817, the s. of Joseph Ferguson of Carlisle (MP for Carlisle 1852-57), by the d. of John Clerk of Bebside House, Northumberland. A Manufacturer at Carlisle. Author of *The Teutonic Name System, River Names of Europe*, etc. A Liberal. Sat for Carlisle from Feb. 1874 until 1886, when he retired. Died 1 Sept. 1898. [1886]

FERGUSON, Sir Robert Alexander, Bart. The Farm, Co. Derry. United University. S. of Sir Andrew Ferguson (1st Bart.), by the d. of Robert Alexander, Esq., of Broomhall, Londonderry. B. in Londonderry 1795. Educ. at Trinity Coll., Cambridge, where he graduated M.A. 1817. Lord-Lieut. of Londonderry Co. and Col. of that Co. Militia. A Liberal, voted in favour of Lord Derby's Reform Bill, Mar. 1859. Sat for Londonderry city from 1830 until his death 13 Mar. 1860. [1860]

FERGUSON, Sir Ronald Craufurd, G.C.B. 5 Bolton Row, London. Muirtown, Fifeshire. Athenaeum, and Reform. 2nd s. of William Ferguson, Esq., of Raith, and bro. and heir presumptive of the member for Kirkcaldy. A Gen. in the army, and Col. of the 79th Foot. A Reformer, in favour of the ballot, triennial parliaments, a revision of the Corn Laws, the abolition of the taxes upon knowledge, and of Church reform. Sir Ronald pledged himself to resign his seat whenever his general conduct should displease the majority of his constituents. Sat for some time for the Kirkcaldy district of Burghs. Sat for Nottingham from 1830. MP until he died in Mar. 1841. [1840]

FERGUSON, R.C. Munro-. Continued in House after 1885: full entry in Volume II.

FERGUSSON, Sir J. Continued in House after 1885: full entry in Volume II.

FERGUSSON, Rt. Hon. Robert Cutlar. 38 Portman Square, London. Craigdaroch, Dumfrieshire. Orraland House, Kirkcudbrightshire. Reform. Eld. s. of Alex Fergusson, Esq., of Craigdaroch, an eminent advocate. A Barrister, practised upwards of 30 years in the Supreme Court of Judicature at Calcutta, returned from

India in 1825. Was an E. India Director. Succeeded Sir Robert Grant as Judge Advocate Gen. in 1834, but lost his office in Nov. of that year; resumed it in Apr. 1835. Was appointed in Mar. 1835 a Commissioner for inquiring into Army Punishments. Sat for Kirkcudbrightshire from 1826. MP until his death 31 Dec. 1838. [1838]

FERMOY, Lord. 5 Clarendon Place, Hyde Park, London. Trabolgan, Cloyne. Kilshanic, Rathcormac, Ireland. Reform. B. 1815; m. 1848, Eliza Caroline, eld. d. of J.B. Boothby, Esq., of Twyford Abbey, Middlesex. An Irish Peer. Lord-Lieut. of the Co. of Cork. A Reformer, and formerly belonged to the 'Repeal' party; in favour of the ballot and the abolition of Church rates; supported Lord Palmerston on the vote of censure 1864. First elected for Marylebone July 1859. Sat until he was defeated 1865. Died 17 Sept. 1874, [1865]

FERRALL, Daniel Henry. A Liberal. Contested Athlone in July 1841. In 1842 on petition and scrutiny, the committee of the House of Commons altered the poll and Mr. Ferrall was returned. On the presentation of a counter petition he was unseated, the election declared void and a new writ issued.

FERRAND, William. St. Ives, Bingley, Yorkshire. Carlton. Eld. s. of Currer Fothergill Busfield, Esq., by Sarah, d. of John Ferrand, Esq., and nephew of Walker Ferrand, Esq., of Harden Grange, upon whose death he assumed the name of Ferrand. B. 1809; m. 1st, Sarah, d. of Capt. Priestley (she died 1832); 2ndly, 1847, Hon Fanny Mary, 2nd d. of 11th Lord Blantyre. A Conservative, voted for agricultural protection 1846; a supporter of Lord Derby; looked 'upon Labour as the source of all wealth, and the well-being of the productive classes as a chief duty of government.' Sat for Knaresborough from June 1841 to July 1847; unsuccessfully contested Aylesbury Apr. 1851, Devonport Apr. 1859, and a second and third time in July and Aug. following. Elected for Devonport Feb. 1863. Unseated in May 1866. Unsuccessfully contested Coventry 23 July 1867. President of Bradford Working Men's Conservative Association 1866. Died 31 Mar. 1889. [1865]

FFOLKES, Sir William Hovell Browne. Hillington Hall, Lynn. Brooks's. Eld. s. of Martin Ffolkes, Esq., by Henrietta Bridget, d. of Sir Charles Wale, K.C.B., grands. of Sir William Ffolkes, Bart. B. at Congham 1847; m. 1875, Emily Charlotte, 3rd d. of Robert Elwes, Esq., of Congham House, Norfolk. Was educ. at Harrow and at Trinity Coll., Cambridge; graduated B.A.

1868, and subsequently M.A. A Magistrate and Dept.-Lieut. for Norfolk, of which he was High Sheriff 1876. Patron of 2 livings. A Liberal. Sat for Lynn Regis from Apr. 1880 until his defeat in 1885. Contested N.W. Norfolk in 1900. Chairman of Norfolk County Council. Died 9 May 1912. [1885]

FFOLKES, Sir William John Henry Browne, Bart. 30 Cavendish Square. Hillington Hall, Norfolk. B. 1786; M. 1818 Charlotte, youngest d. of D.G. Browne, Esq., of Castle M'Garrett, Ireland. Patron of 2 livings. A Whig, was a strong supporter of the £50 tenant-at-will clause. Was nominated by Mr. Coke, who at the same time took his farewell of the constituency of a county he had represented 47 years. Sat for Norfolk W. from 1830. Defeated in 1837. Contested Norfolk E. in 1841. [1837]

FFOLLIOTT, John. Hollybrook, Co. Sligo. Conservative. Descended from a common ancestor with the Ffolliotts of Worcestershire. B. 1798; m. the daughter of Herbert R. Stepney, Esq., of Durrow, King's Co. Patron of 1 living. A Conservative and voted for agricultural protection 1846. Sat for the county of Sligo from Sept. 1841 until he accepted Chiltern Hundreds circa 1 Mar. 1850. Died 11 Feb. 1868. [1849]

FIELDEN, John. Todmorden, Yorkshire. Reform. A Merchant and Manufacturer. A radical Reformer, in favour of the ballot, short Parliaments, and universal suffrage. Sat for Oldham in the Parliament of 1832. Sat until defeated 1847. Died 1849. [1847]

FIELDEN, Joshua. Red Hill, Surrey. Stansfield Hall, Todmorden. Youngest s. of John Fielden, Esq., of Todmorden, Yorkshire, who sat for Oldham from 1832-1847, and who in the latter year introduced and carried the celebrated Ten Hours Bill. B. at Todmorden 1827; m. 1851, Ellen, eld. d. of Thomas Brocklehurst, Esq., of The Fence, Macclesfield. A Cotton Manufacturer and Merchant at Todmorden and Manchester; a Partner in the firm of Messrs. Fielden, Brothers. A Magistrate for Lancashire and for the W. Riding of Yorkshire. Author of a Pamphlet in favour of *The Repeal of the Malt-Tax*, also one on *The Union of Church and State*. A Conservative, was as much opposed as any Churchman can be to the separation of Church and State; voted against disestablishment of the Irish Church 1869, was in favour of the repeal of the malt-tax, and a large reduction in the national expenditure. Sat for the Eastern division of the W. Riding of Yorkshire from Dec. 1868 until he retired 1880. Died 9 Mar. 1887. [1880]

FIFE, Earl of. 41 Eaton Place, London. Skene House, and Corriemuizie, Aberdeenshire. Brooks's, and Reform. A Scottish Peer. B. in Edinburgh 1814, the eld. s. of Gen. the Hon. Sir Alexander Duff, G.C.H., by Anne, youngest d. of James Stein of Kilbagie. M. 1846 Lady Agnes Georgiana, 2nd d. of the Earl of Erroll. A Dept.-Lieut. of Banffshire, and of Aberdeenshire, and appointed Lord Lieut. of Elginshire 1851. Of Liberal politics, voted against the ballot 1853. Sat for Banffshire from 1837 until he accepted Chiltern Hundreds in June 1857. Succeeded his uncle as 5th Earl on 9 March 1857. Created Baron of Skene 1 Oct. 1857. Died 7 Aug. 1879. [1857 2nd ed.]

FIGGINS, James. 35 Russell Square, London. Fair Lawn, Forest Hill, Surrey. City, and Carlton. S. of Vincent Figgins, Esq., by Elizabeth, his wife. B. at West Smithfield, London 1811; m. 1836, d. of W.A. Beckwith, Esq. Educ. at a Private School at Esher, Surrey. A Type-founder at Farringdon Road, London. A Magistrate for Middlesex, and Sheriff of London and Middlesex 1865-6. A Conservative; voted against the disestablishment of the Irish Church 1869, as an 'act of injustice' and as tending to the separation of Church and State; a 'strong advocate for economy' in the public expenditure. Sat for Shrewsbury from Dec. 1868 until defeated 1874. Alderman of Farringdon 1873-82. Died 12 June 1884. [1873]

FILDES, John. Woodlands, Crumpsall, Nr. Manchester. S. of Mr. Thomas Fildes, by Martha, his wife. B. at Dorton, Lancashire 1811; m. 1838, Mary, d. of Mr. Joseph Moore of Manchester. Was a Stockbroker at Manchester from 1846. Elected a Member of the Manchester City Council 1857, and for some years exerted himself to promote the abolition of capital punishment. A Liberal, in favour of direct taxation, and 'strict neutrality as regards the domestic policy of other countries.' First elected for Great Grimsby, July 1865. Defeated in 1868. Died 6 July 1875. [1867]

FILMER, Sir Edmund, Bart., sen. 90 Eaton Square, London. East Sutton, Kent. B. 1809, the s. of Capt. Filmer, and nephew of the Rev. Sir John Filmer, whom he succeeded in the Baronetcy 1834. M. 1831, Helen, d. of David Monro, Esq., of Quebec. Appointed a Dept.-Lieut. of Kent 1849. Patron of 1 living. A Conservative, opposed to all concessions to the Roman Catholics. Sat for Kent W. from Mar. 1838 until he died 8 Jan. 1857. [1856]

FILMER, Sir Edmund, Bart., jun. East Sutton Place, Staplehurst, Kent. Carlton, Guards', and Army & Navy. Eld. s. of Sir Edmund Filmer, Bart., of East Sutton Place, Kent (who sat for W. Kent from 1838-1857), by Helen, 2nd d. of David Munro, Esq., of Quebec. B. 1835; m. 1858, Hon. Mary Georgiana, eld. d. of 2nd Baron Sandys. Was for a short time in the Grenadier Guards and had been Capt. W. Kent Militia. Was High Sheriff for Kent 1870. Patron of 1 living. A Conservative. Sat for Kent. W. from May 1859 to July 1865. Elected for mid Kent Apr. 1880. Accepted Chiltern Hundreds 1884. Died 17 Dec. 1886. [1884]

FINCH, Francis. Great Barr, Warwickshire. Reform. S. of Charles Finch, Esq., of Cambridge. A Reformer, contested Lichfield twice without success. Sat for Walsall from 1837. Accepted Chiltern Hundreds Jan. 1841. [1840]

FINCH, George. Burley-on-the-Hill, Rutlandshire. A Magistrate and Dept.-Lieut. of Rutlandshire. A Conservative, and in favour of protection. Elected for Stamford 12 Dec. 1832 until 25 July 1837. First returned for Rutlandshire Feb. 1846. Retired 1847. Died 29 June 1870. [1847]

FINCH, G.H. Continued in House after 1885: full entry in Volume II.

FINCH-HATTON, Hon. M.E.G. Continued in House after 1885: full entry in Volume II.

FINDLATER, William. 22 Fitzwilliam Street, Dublin. Fernside, Killiney, Co. Dublin. Stephen's Green, and Law Club, Dublin. Only s. of William Findlater, Esq., of Londonderry, and formerly of Greenock, Merchant, by his m. with Miss Sophia Huffington, of Londonderry. B. at Londonderry 1824; m. 1st, 1853, Mary Jane, d. of John Wolfe, Esq., Solicitor, of Fitzwilliam Street, Dublin; 2ndly, 1878, Marion, eld. d. of Lieut. Col. Archibald Park, of the Bengal Army, and grand-d. of Mungo Park, the celebrated African traveller. Was admitted a Solicitor in Ireland 1846. Was elected President of the Incorporated Law Society of Ireland for 1878. A Member of the firm of Findlater and Co., Brewers, Dublin. A Liberal. In favour of reform of the Grand Jury Laws. Sat for Monaghan from Apr. 1880. Retired 1885. [1883]

FINIGAN, James Lysaght. 5 King's Bench Walk, Temple, London. A Liberal and advanced Nationalist. Sat for Ennis from July 1879. Accepted Chiltern Hundreds in 1882. [1882]

FINLAY, Alexander Struthers. Castle Toward, Inellan, Argyllshire. Union. B. 1806, the s. of

Kirkman Finlay, Esq., of Castle Toward, many years MP for Glasgow. M. 1840, Marion, d. of Colin Campbell, Esq., of Colgrain, Dumbartonshire (she died Jan. 1865). Educ. at Harrow. A Commissioner of Supply, a Dept.-Lieut. of Bute and Argyll and a Magistrate for Argyllshire. A Liberal, voted for Lord Derby's Reform Bill 1859. Sat for Argyllshire from Apr. 1857 until he accepted Chiltern Hundreds in Feb. 1868. Died in Greenock 9 June 1886. [1867]

FINN, William Francis. Tullarone, Co. Kilkenny. S. of an opulent Tanner at Carlow. M. Alicia, sister of D. O'Connell, Esq. A Barrister. A Repealer. Sat for Co. Kilkenny from 1832 until he retired in 1837. [1837]

FINNIE, William. Newfield, Dundonald, Ayrshire. Reform. B. 1827, the 3rd s. of James Finnie, Esq., of Newfield, Ayrshire, by Mary Ann, eld. d. of Provost Brown, of Kilmarnock. M. 1853, Antoinette, youngest d. of George Burnand, Esq., of Tewin Water, Hertfordshire. Educ. at Edinburgh and at King's Coll., London, and graduated at Trinity Coll.,Cambridge, LL.B. 1850. Was called to the bar at the Inner Temple, Jan. 1853, but never practised. A Liberal, voted in favour of the disestablishment of the Irish Church 1869, and favoured a more effective redistribution of Parliamentary Seats and a reduction of the county franchise. Sat for N. Ayrshire from Dec. 1868 until his defeat in 1874. Died 3 Sept. 1899. [1873]

FIRTH, Joseph Firth Bottomley. 2 The Grove, Boltons, South Kensington, London. New Court, Temple, London. Reform, National Liberal, and Cobden. Eld. s. of J. Bottomley-Firth, Esq., of Matlock, Derbyshire. B. Nr. Huddersfield, West Riding of Yorkshire 1842; m. 1873, Elizabeth, youngest d. of George Tatham, Esq., of Leeds, (Mayor of Leeds 1880-3). Assumed the name of Firth by royal license 1873. Graduated LL.B. at London 1875. Was called to the bar at the Middle Temple June 1866, and joined the North-Eastern circuit. A member of London School Board, for Chelsea 1876-9. A Liberal, in favour of 'Home Rule' for Ireland, 'shortening the period of residential qualification for voters', and of making 'registration the compulsory duty of a public officer in each borough', and of 'the re-appropriation for public purposes of the funds of the London Livery Companies'. Pres. of the Municipal Reform League. Sat for Chelsea from Apr. 1880 to Nov. 1885. Elected for Dundee Feb. 1888. MP until he died in 1889. [1885]

FITZALAN, Lord. See ARUNDEL AND SURREY, Earl of.

FITZ-GERALD, Rt. Hon. John David. 11 Half-Moon Street, Piccadilly, London. 7 Merrion Square East, Dublin. Kilmanoili, Killiney, Co. Dublin. Brooks's and Reform. St. Stephen's Green Club, Dublin. Clare County Club. S. of David Fitzgerald, Esq., of Dublin, Merchant, by Catherine, eld. d. of David Leaby, Esq., of London. B. in Dublin 1815; m. 1846, Rose, 2nd d. of John O'Donohoe, Esq., of Fitzwilliam Square, Dublin, Distiller. Educ. at Trinity Coll., Dublin, called to the bar in Ireland 1838. Created a Queen's Counsel in 1847 and became leader of the Munster Circuit. Solicitor-Gen. for Ireland from Feb. 1855-Mar. 1856, and Attorney Gen. from the latter date until Mar. 1858. A Liberal, in favour of comprehensive reform, and of tenant-right in Ireland; voted for the ballot 1853, and against Church rates 1855. First returned for Ennis in July 1852 and sat until appointed Judge of Queens Bench, Ireland, Feb. 1860. Lord of Appeal. May 1882. Created Baron Fitzgerald June 1882. Died 16 Oct. 1889. [1859]

FITZGERALD, Sir John Forster, K.C.B. Worthing, Sussex. Union. 4th s. of Edward Fitz-Gerald, Esq., of Carrigoran (who was MP for Clare in the Irish Parliament), by Anne Catherine, d. of Capt. Thomas Burton, of the 5th Dragoons; was uncle to Sir Edward FitzGerald Bart. M. 1st, Charlotte, d. of M. Hazen, Esq., of St. John's, New Brunswick; 2ndly, 1839, Jean, eld. d. of the Hon. Donald Ogilvy of Clova. Educ. at Manchester, received a commisson in the army in 1793, but did not join any regiment until 1801. Became a Gen. 1854, Col. 18th Foot 1850, received a cross for his services in command of a light battalion and a brigade at Badajos, Salamanca, Vittoria, and the Pyrenees. A Liberal, in favour of 'tenant-right.' First returned for Clare in July 1852 and sat until defeated 1857. Died 24 Mar. 1877. [1857]

FITZ-GERALD, Rt. Hon. Lord Otho Augustus. 8 Carlton House Terrace, London. West Park, Fordingbridge, Salisbury. Londesborough Lodge, Scarborough. White's, and Army & Navy. Youngest s. of 3rd Duke of Leinster, by Lady Charlotte, 3rd d. of 3rd Earl of Harrington. B. at Carton, Maynooth, 1827; m. 1861, the Dowager Lady Londesborough, eld. d. of Rear-Admiral Charles Orlando Bridgeman. Educ. at Carton, Maynooth. Entered the Royal Horse Guards Blue 1845; retired as Lieut. 1854. Master of the Horse, Aide-de-Camp, and Gentlemen in Waiting to the Lord-Lieut. of Ireland from 1855-1862, when he resigned and was Treasurer of the Queen's Household from May-July 1866. Appointed Controller of the Queen's Household Dec. 1868. Capt. of the London Irish Volunteers, Capt. Lancashire Hussars and a Lieut. in the Royal Naval Reserve. A Liberal; in favour of the further improvement of the system of National Education in Ireland. First elected for Kildare Co. July 1865. Sat until defeated 1874. Died 19 Nov. 1882. [1873]

FITZ-GERALD, Richard Albert. 11 Air Street, Piccadilly, London. North Great George's Street, Dublin. Muckridge House, Co. Cork. Garnavella House, Co. Tipperary. '82 Club. Dublin. S. of Richard Fitz-Gerald, Esq., of Muckridge House, Co. Cork, by the d. of Richard Nagle, Esq., of Garnavella House, Co. Tipperary. Descended from a younger branch of the Leinster family. B. at Clonmell 1806; m. 1836, the Signora Donna Emilia, d. of the Signor Daniel Frizoni of Lisbon. Received his early education at Clongowes Wood and Carlow Coll., Ireland, and completed it in Paris. A Repealer. First elected for Tipperary in Feb. 1845, without a contest. MP until his death in 1847. [1847]

FITZ-GERALD, Thomas. 22 Parliament Street, London. Fanevalley. A West India Proprietor. A Repealer. Sat for Louth Co. from 1832. MP until his death in 1834. [1833]

FITZ-GERALD, Rt. Hon. Sir William Robert Seymour Vesey, G.C.S.I. Holbrook, Horsham. Ballylinch, Thomastown, Kilkenny. B. 1817; m. 1840, Maria Tryphera, eld. d. of Dr. Seymour. Educ. at Oriel Coll., Oxford, where he was 2nd class in classics 1837, and gained the Newdegate prize 1835; graduated M.A. 1844, and received the Hon. degree D.C.L. 1863. Was called to the bar at Lincoln's Inn, Jan. 1839 and went the Northern Circuit; was Under-Sec. of State for Foreign Affairs from Mar. 1858-June 1859;Governor of Bombay from Jan. 1867 to March 1872. A Liberal-Conservative, voted against the Church rates 1855. Sat for Horsham from June-Sept. 1848 (when he was unseated on petition, and from July 1852 to July 1865. Re-elected Feb. 1874. MP until appointed Chief Commissioner of Charities 30 Nov. 1875 to 1885. Died 28 June 1885. [1875]

FITZ-GIBBON, Hon. Richard Hobart. 44 Belgrave Square, London. Mount Shannon, Co. Limerick. Bro. of the Earl of Clare. B. 1793; m. 1825, Diana, d. of Charles Woodcock, Esq., Lord Lieut. of the Co. of Limerick. Col. of the Limerick Militia; Usher and Registrar of Affidavits in the Court of Chancery in Ireland from 1797; duties performed by deputy; fees 3245/-. Was in the army and was present at the battles of Oporto, Talavera, etc. Of Whig principles. Sat for Limerick Co. from 1818. Sat until he retired 1841. Succeeded bro. as 3rd Earl 1851. Died 10 Jan. 1864 [1841]

FITZ-HARRIS, Visct. Heron Court, Hampshire. Whitehall Gardens, London. Carlton. Eld. s. of the Earl of Malmesbury. B. 1807; m. in 1830, only d. of 5th Earl of Tankerville. A Conservative. Unsuccessfully contested Portsmouth 26 July 1837. First returned for Wilton in 1841 and sat until succeeded as 3rd Earl Sept. 1841. Died 17 May 1889. [1841]

FITZMAURICE. Lord E.G. Petty-. Continued in House after 1885: full entry in Volume II.

FITZMAURICE, Hon. William Edward. 4 Chesham Street, Belgrave Square, London. Taplow, Buckinghamshire. Junior United Service. Only bro. of the 2nd Earl of Orkney, being s. of Visct. Kirkwall. B. 1805; m. 1837, Esther, d. of Henry Harford, Esq. Was a member of the Queen's Royal Lancers, and was a Capt. in the 2nd Life Guards. A Major in the army. Author of *Cruise to Egypt, Palestine, and Greece,* and contributed many drawings for the *Landscape Illustrations of the Bible,* and for Mr. Murray's edition of *Childe Harold.* A Conservative, voted for agricultural protection 1846. Was first returned for Buckinghamshire in July 1842, on the death of Sir William Young, Bart. Sat until he retired 1847. Died 18 June 1889. [1847]

FITZPATRICK, Hon. Bernard Edward Barnaby. Granston Manor, Abbeyleix, Ireland. Travellers'. Kildare Street, Dublin. Only surviving s. of 1st Lord Castletown, of Upper Ossory, by Augusta, only d. of the Rev. Archibald Douglas of Cook Hill, Co. Cavan. B. in London 1848; m. 1874, Hon. Ursula Clare Emily, only d. of 4th Visct. Doneraile. Was educ. at Eton and Brasenose Coll., Oxford, graduated B.A. 2nd class in Law and Modern History 1870. A Magistrate for Queen's Co. A Liberal-Conservative. Sat for Portarlington from Apr. 1880 until he succeeded as 2nd Baron Jan. 1883. [1882]

FITZ-PATRICK, Rt. Hon. John Wilson. 38 Portman Square, London. Lisduff, Rathdowney, Queen's Co. Grantstown Manor, Abbeyleix, Ireland. Brooks's and Travellers'. Sackville Street Club, Dublin. Representative of a younger branch of the Fitz-Patricks, Earls of Ossory, whose title in 1869 was extinct. B. in London. M. 1830, only d. of the Rev. Archibald Douglas, Rector of Coolehill, grand-d. maternally of the 4th Earl of Dunmore. Educ. at Eton. Served in the army. Appointed Lord-Lieut. of Queen's Co. 1855. Patron of 2 livings. Once ranked as a Whig, and supported the Corn Laws. Opposed to the ballot, and favoured the 'improvement of the condition of the tenant farmer in Ireland.' Sat for Queen's Co. from July 1837 to July 1841; from

July 1847 to July 1852; and from 1865 until he was created 1st Baron Castletown (U.K. Peerage) in Dec. 1869. Died 22 Jan. 1883.   [1869]

FITZ-ROY, Rt. Hon. Lord Charles. Reform. 2nd s. of the 4th Duke of Grafton. B. 1791; m. 1825, Anne, eld. d. of the 1st Earl of Burlington. A Lieut.-Col. in the army. Appointed in 1835, Vice-Chamberlain of his Majesty's household. Of Whig principles. A member of the Free Trade Club. Sat for Thetford in several Parliaments. Sat for Bury St. Edmunds from 1831 until he retired 1847. Died 17 June 1865.   [1847]

FITZ-ROY, Lord Frederick John. 23 Grosvenor Street, London. Travellers'. 3rd s. of 5th Duke of Grafton, by Mary Caroline, 3rd d. of the Hon. Col. Sir George Cranfield Berkeley, G.C.B. B. 1823; m. 1853, Catherine Sarah Wilhelmina, d. of the Rev. William Westcomb, Rector of Longford, Essex. Became Capt. and Lieut.-Col. Grenadier Guards 1855; retired 1862. A Liberal. First elected for Thetford Apr. 1863. Retired 1865. Unsuccessfully contested Northamptonshire S. 20 July 1865 and again on 25 Nov. 1868. Died Feb. 1919.   [1865]

FITZ-ROY, Rt. Hon. Henry. 42 Upper Grosvenor Street, London. Whittlebury Lodge, Northamptonshire. Brooks's. S. of 2nd Baron Southampton, by his 2nd wife, d. of Lord Robert Seymour. Heir pres. to Lord Southampton. B. in Stanhope Street, London 1807; m. 1839, d. of the Baron N.M. Rothschild. A Magistrate for Middlesex. A Lord of the Admiralty from Jan. 1845-July 1846, Under Secretary of State for the Home Dept. from Dec. 1852-Feb. 1855. Became Chairman of Committees of the Whole House, March 1855. Lieut.-Col. of the London Artillery Co. A Liberal, in favour of 'reform and progress'; formerly ranked as Conservative; voted against Church rates in 1855. Sat for Great Grimsby in 1831. Unsuccessfully contested Northampton Dec. 1832. Sat for Lewes from Apr. 1837 to Mar. 1841, when he was an unsuccessful candidate, but succeeded on petition 1842. First Commissioner of Board of Works 1859. MP until his death 22 Dec. 1859.   [1859]

FITZ-ROY, Lord James Henry. 47 Clarges Street, London. 3rd Surviving s. of the Duke of Grafton. B. in 1804. A captain in the 10th Hussars. A Reformer, in favour of the ballot. First sat for Thetford in 1831. MP until his death 26 July 1834.   [1833]

FITZ-ROY, Robert. 25 Lowndes Street, Belgrave Square, London. Carlton. Senior United Service. 3rd s. of Lord Chas. Fitz-Roy, and grand-s. of the 3rd Duke of Grafton. B. 1805; m. 1836, d. of Gen. O'Brien. Capt. R.N., an elder brother of the Trinity House. Author of *Voyages of the Adventure* and *Beagle*. A Conservative. Unsuccessfully contested Ipswich in 1831. First returned for Durham City in 1841 and sat until appointed Governor of New Zealand 1843. Disagreed with Colonists and was superseded Nov. 1843. F.R.S. 1851. Superintendent of the Meteorological Dept. of the Board of Trade 1854. Instituted system of storm warnings 1862. Died (suicide) 29 Apr. 1865.   [1843]

FITZ-SIMON, Christopher. Merrion Square, Dublin. Glencullen, Co. Dublin. Westminster Club. M. Ellen, eld. d. of D. O'Connell, Esq. A Barrister. A Repealer; an advocate of the total abolition of tithes. Sat for Dublin Co. from 1832. Retired in 1837.   [1837]

FITZ-SIMON, Nicholas. Castlewood, King's Co. M. d. of — Power, Esq. A Distiller. A Repealer. Sat for King's Co. from 1832. Sat until he accepted Chiltern Hundreds in 1840.   [1840]

FITZ-WILLIAM, Hon. Chas. William Wentworth-. Alwalton, Peterborough. Brooks's. 2nd surviving s. of the 5th Earl Fitz-William, by his cousin, the 4th d. of the 1st Lord Dundas. B. at Wentworth House, Yorkshire. 1826; m. 1854, Anne, youngest d. of the Hon. and Rev. T.L. Dundas. Educ. at Trinity College, Cambrige. Appointed Capt. in the 1st West York Yeomanry Cavalry in 1846. A Liberal-Conservative, but voted against Lord Russell's Reform Bill 1866. First returned for Malton in July 1852. Sat until he retired in 1885. Died 20 Dec. 1894. [1885]

FITZ-WILLIAM, Hon. George Wentworth. Mortimer House, Halkin Street, London. Wentworth House, Yorkshire. Travellers', and Brooks's. 2nd s. of 3rd Earl Fitz-William, by the 4th d. of the 1st Lord Dundas. B. 1817. Graduated at Trinity Coll., Cambridge, M.A. 1838. A Liberal, in favour of 'progressive reform'; voted against the ballot 1853. Sat for Richmond from Feb. to July 1841, and for Peterborough from the latter date until he retired in 1859. Died 4 Mar. 1874.   [1858]

FITZWILLIAM, Hon. J.W. Continued in House after 1885: full entry in Volume II.

FITZWILLIAM, Hon. Wentworth. See MILTON, Visct. (I).

FITZWILLIAM, Hon. W.H.W. Continued in House after 1885: full entry in Volume II.

FITZ-WYGRAM, Sir F. Continued in House after 1885: full entry in Volume II.

FLEETWOOD, Sir P. Hesketh, Bart. Hill House, Windsor Forest, Berkshire. Fleetwood, Lancashire. Athenaeum, Boodle's, and Reform. Eld. s. of Robert Hesketh, Esq., of Rossall. B. 1801; m. 1st Eliza Debonaire, only child of heiress of Sir Theophilus John Metcalfe, Bart., of Fernhill, Berkshire; 2ndly Virginie Marie, d. of Señor Pedro Garcia, who was descended from the ancient family of the Garcias, Counts of Castile. Assumed the name of Fleetwood for self and issue, in addition to that of Hesketh in 1831. Was the great grands. of Roger Hesketh, Esq., of North Meols, who m. Margaret, d. and heiress of Edward Fleetwood, Esq., of Rossall; thus two families, who trace their respective descents from a very remote period of our history, were united. Was therefore connected with the ancient branch of the Fleetwood family, formerly of Clapham, Surrey, and with the celebrated Gen. Fleetwood of the time of Charles I. Patron of 5 livings. Dept.-Lieut. of Lancashire, Chairman of the Preston and Wyre Dock and Harbour Company. Was High Sheriff of Lancashire. Author of *Observations on Capital Punishment,* translation of *The Last Days of a Condemned,* etc. Was elected for Preston in 1832, without giving pledges, in consequence of his character in the town and neighbourhood. A Reformer. Was re-elected in 1835, 1837, and 1841, by large majorities, and in each instance at the head of the poll. MP until he retired 1847. Died 12 Apr. 1866. [1847]

FLEMING, Hon. Vice-Admiral Charles Elphinstone. United Service Club. Of Whig Principles. Returned for Stirlingshire in 1832. Defeated in 1835. Governor of Greenwich Hospital in 1839. Died 30 Oct. 1840. [1833]

FLEMING, John. 15 Upper Hyde Park Gardens, London. Brigadon, Buckfastleigh, S. Devon. Conservative, and Junior Carlton. 2nd s. of Alexander Fleming, Esq., of Lethendy, Perthshire. M. 1859, Charlotte Mary, only d. of John Blythe, Esq., of London. A Merchant and Shipowner at Austin Friars, London. A Conservative. Was an unsuccessful candidate for Devonport June 1865; but succeeded at the general election July following. Unseated 1866. Unsuccessfully contested Barnstaple 3 Feb. 1874. [1865]

FLEMING, John Willis. Stoneham Park, Hampshire. Carlton. Great grands. of Browne Willis, Esq. M. Christophena, d. of James Buchanan, Esq. Assumed the name of Fleming upon succeeding to the Stoneham estates. Patron of 4 livings. Was High Sheriff of Hampshire in

1817. A Conservative. Sat for Hampshire S. in several Parliaments before 1832, when he lost his seat. He was placed at the head of the poll for Hampshire S. in 1835. Sat until he accepted Chiltern Hundreds July 1842. [1842]

FLEMING, Thomas Willis. 10 Lancaster Gate, London. South Stoneham, Southampton. Carlton, and Union. 2nd s. of John Willis Fleming, Esq., many years MP for Hampshire and S. Hampshire, by Christophena, d. of James Buchanan, Esq. B. at South Stoneham, Southampton 1810; m. 1845, Caroline, only d. of Peter Hunter, Esq., of Abele Grove, Epsom. Educ. at Eton. Called to the bar 1843, but never practised. A Magistrate and Dept.-Lieut. for Hampshire and Dorset. Published in 1846 a pamphlet entitled *A Marine Militia.* A Conservative, and a supporter of Lord Derby; was 'for a progressive, but at the same time a Conservative policy.' Unsuccessfully contested Isle of Wight 10 Aug. 1847 and again on 6 Apr. 1857. First elected for Winchester Feb. 1864. Defeated 1865. [1865]

FLETCHER, Sir H. Continued in House after 1885: full entry in Volume II.

FLETCHER, Isaac, F.R.S. Tarnbank, Cockermouth. City Liberal and Reform. S. of John Wilson Fletcher, Esq., of Tarnbank, Cumberland, by his marriage with Miss Mary Allason, of Beech Hill, Cumberland. B. at Greysowthen, Cumberland, 1827; m. 1861, Esther, only surviving d. of Joseph King, Esq., of Wassen Grove, Worcestershire. A Magistrate for that Co. Educ. at York and at Tottenham. A Coal-Owner, and Iron-master in Cumberland. A Magistrate for Cumberland. A 'moderate Liberal'; voted for the disestablishment of the Irish Church 1869; favoured a further distribution of parliamentary seats. Unsuccessfully contested Cockermouth Apr. 1868; sat for that place from Dec. 1868. MP until his death Apr. 1879. [1879]

FLETCHER, William. Brigham Hall, Carlisle. Reform. Eld. surviving s. of John Wilson Fletcher, Esq., of Tarnbank, Cumberland, by his marriage with Miss Mary Allason, of Beech Hill, Cumberland. Bro. to Isaac Fletcher, Esq., who sat for Cockermouth from 1868 until his death 1879. B. at Greysowthen, Cumberland 1831; m. 1863, Caroline, d. of Frederick Ashby, Esq., of Staines. An extensive Coal-Owner and Iron-Master in W. Cumberland. A Magistrate for Cumberland. A Liberal, in favour of household suffrage in counties, a redistribution of seats and the disestablishment of the Church. Sat for Cockermouth from Apr. 1879. Retired 1880. Chairman of Cumberland County Council

1889-92. Died 6 Aug. 1900. [1880]

FLOWER, Cyril. Continued in House after 1885: full entry in Volume II.

FLOWER, Sir James, Bart. 15 Wimpole Street, London. Lobb Farm, Oxfordshire. Woodford, Essex. S. of the 1st Bart., by the eld. d. of Joseph Squire, Esq., of Portsmouth. B. 1794; m. 1816, eld. d. of Sir Walter Stirling, Bart. Filled the office of Sheriff of Norfolk in 1838. A Conservative, but in favour of free trade. Was returned for Thetford in 1841 in conjunction with the Earl of Euston (having polled the same number of votes); was declared duly elected by a committee, and the Earl of Euston unseated. Sat until he retired 1847. [1847]

FLOYER, John. 5 Old Palace Yard, London. West Staffod, Dorchester. Carlton. S. of the Rev. William Floyer, Rector of West Stafford, and Vicar of Stinsford, Dorset, by Elizabeth, youngest d.and co.-heir of Stephen Barton, Esq., of Bland-ford. B. at Stinsford, 1811; m. 1844, Georgina Charlotte Frances, eld. d. of the Right Hon. George Bankes. Educ. at Winchester, and at Balliol Coll., Oxford, graduated B.A. 1831. Appointed Capt. in the Dorset (Queen's Own) Regiment of Yeomanry Cavalry, Dec. 1852. Patron of 1 living. A Conservative. Sat for Dorset from Feb. 1846. till Apr. 1857; re-elected Feb. 1864. Sat until he retired in 1885. Died 4 July 1887. [1885]

FOLEY, Edward Thomas. 16 George Street, Hanover Square, London. Stoke Edith Park, Herefordshire. Carlton. A cousin of Lord Foley. B. 1791; m. 1832, Emily 4th d. of the Duke of Montrose. A Conservative, in favour of protection to agriculture. Patron of 4 livings. Sat for the disfranchised borough of Ludgershall from 1826-1832. Sat for Herefordshire from 1832 until he retired 1841. [1838]

FOLEY, Henry John Wentworth Hodgetts-. Prestwood, Stourbridge, Worcestershire. Travellers'. Only s. of John Hodgetts Hodgetts-Foley, Esq., of Prestwood, by Charlotte Margaret, d. of John Gage, Esq. B. 1828; m. 1854, Hon. Jane Francis Anne, 2nd d. of 1st Lord Vivian. Educ. at Eton, and at Christ Church, Oxford. Appointed Dept.-Lieut. of Worcestershire Nov. 1859. A Liberal, in favour of the ballot and the abolition of church rates, and the removal of 'the anomalies of our present electoral system.' First elected for the Staffordshire S. Apr. 1857. Sat until defeated in 1868 contesting Staffordshire W. [1867]

FOLEY, John Hodgetts Hodgetts. Prestwood, Stourbridge, Worcestershire. Travellers', Brooks's, and Athenaeum. 2nd s. of the Hon. Edward Foley, (bro. to 2nd Lord Foley,) by the d. and heir of John Hodgetts, Esq., of Prestwood. Born Prestwood, Worcestershire, 1797; m. 1825, Charlotte Margaret, 2nd d. of John Gage, Esq., of Rogate Lodge, Hampshire (she died 1855). Was educ. Christ Church, Oxford. A Magistrate and Dept.-Lieut, for Worcestershire and for several years Chairman of the Poor Law Union; was President of the Stourbridge Mechanics' Institution, and many other local associations. A Liberal, a supporter of the Established Church, but a friend to civil and religious liberty; voted against church rates 1855; in favour of a 'gradual extension of the suffrage'. Represented Droitwich from 1821 till 1834. First returned for Worcestershire E. in 1847, without opposition. MP until his death in 1861. [1861]

FOLEY, Joseph William. Mountown House, Kingstown, Ireland. 2nd s. of William Foley Esq., of Dromore, Co. Waterford, and of New Ross. B. at New Ross 1821; m. 1865, Julia, 2nd d. of George William Cram, Esq., of Croft House, Ovingham, Northumberland. Educ. at Ushaw Coll., Durham. Was admitted a Solicitor in Ireland in 1841, and practised in Dublin. A Magistrate for the Co. of Dublin. A Nationalist and Home Ruler. Sat for New Ross from Apr. 1880 until his death in 1890. [1880 2nd ed.]

FOLEY, Hon. Thomas Henry. Witley Court, Worcestershire. 16 Bruton Street, London. B. 1808. Returned for Worcestershire W. in 1832 and sat until he succeeded his father as 4th Baron 16 Apr. 1833. Died 20 Nov. 1869. [1833]

FOLJAMBE, Cecil George Savile. Continued in House after 1885: full entry in Volume II.

FOLJAMBE, Francis John Savile. Aldwark, near Rotherham, Yorkshire. Brooks's. Eld. s. of George Savile Foljambe, Esq., of Osberton, Nottinghamshire, and of Aldwarke, Yorkshire, by his first wife, Harriet Emily Mary, d. of Sir William Mordaunt Sturt Milner, Bart. B. at Osberton 1830; m. 1856, Lady Gertrude Emily, eld. d. of the 3rd Earl of Gosford. Educ. at Eton, and at Christ Church, Oxford. Appointed Lord High Steward of East Retford 1880. 'Attached to the old Whig principles.' Sat for East Retford from April 1857 until 1885. Contested Bassetlaw division of Nottinghamshire 5 Dec. 1885. Contested the Rotherham division of W. Riding of Yorkshire 7 July 1886. In July 1892 he contested the Barnsley division of W. Riding of Yorkshire. Died 5 Feb. 1917. [1885]

FOLKSTONE, Visct. Continued in House after 1885: full entry in Volume II.

FOLLETT, Brent Spencer. 10 New Square, Lincoln's Inn, London. Athenaeum. Youngest s. of Benjamin Follett, Esq., (a Timber Merchant at Topsham, Devon, who had previously been in the 13th Foot), by the d. of John Webb, Esq., of Kinsale, Ireland. Bro. of Sir William Webb Follett. B. at Topsham 1810; m. 1847, Caroline Amelia, youngest d. of Walker Skirrow, Esq., Q.C., of Reddish House, Nr. Stockport. Called to the bar at Lincoln's Inn 1833, and a Queen's Counsel. A Conservative, an advocate for extensive Chancery reform. First returned for Bridgewater in July 1852. Sat until defeated 1857. Unsuccessfully contested Cirencester 30 Apr. 1859. Died 23 Jan. 1887. [1857]

FOLLETT, Sir William Webb. 6 Park Street, Westminster, London. 10 King's Bench Walk, Temple, London. Carlton, and Athenaeum. S. of Benjamin Follett, Esq., M. 1830, d. of Sir Harding Giffard, once Chief Justice of Ceylon. Solicitor-Gen. Nov. 1834-Apr. 1835, and re-appointed Sept. 1841. A Conservative. Unsuccessfully contested Exeter 1832; but was successful there in 1835. MP for Exeter until his death in 1845. [1844]

FORBES, Visct. Bryant's Hotel, London. Castle Forbes, Longford Co. Eld. s. of the Earl of Granard. B. 1785; m. in 1832, Frances, d. of William Ferritt, Esq., of Chilton, Suffolk. A Maj.-Gen. in the army, was Aide-de-Camp to the King; Lord-Lieut. and Custos Rot. of Longford Co. A Conservative, sat for Longford Co. from 1812. At the election in 1832, two Repealers were returned, but on petition, Lord Forbes and A Lefroy, Esq., the old members, succeeded in ousting them and he sat until his death 13 Nov. 1836. [1836]

FORBES, William. Callendar House, Stirlingshire. B. 1806; m. 1832, Lady Louisa Antoinetta, d. of 7th Earl of Wemyss (she died 1845). Vice-Lieut. of Stirlingshire. A Conservative, voted for agricultural protection 1846, and favoured 'relief' to the agricultural and commercial classes. Wanted a withdrawal of the Maynooth Grant. Represented Stirlingshire 1835-37, when he was unseated on petition, and again from 1841 to Mar. 1854, when he died. [1854]

FORDE, Col. William Brownlow. 8 Charles Street, Berkeley Square, London. Seaforde, Clough, Co. Down. Carlton, and Sackville Street, Dublin. S. of the Rev. William Brownlow Forde, by Theodosia Helena, d. of Thomas Douglas,

Esq., of Grace Hall. B. at Annahilt 1823; m. 1855, Adelaide, 5th d. of Gen. the Hon. Robert Meade, and grand-d. of the 1st Earl of Clanwilliam. A Magistrate and Dept.-Lieut. of the Co. of Down, of which he was High Sheriff in 1853. Entered the army in 1843; served in the 67th foot; retired 1847. Appointed Lieut.-Col. of the Royal South Down Militia 1854. A Conservative, not opposed to the removal of abuses from the Irish Church, but voted against its disestablishment 1869. First returned for the Co. of Down, Apr. 1857. Sat until defeated Feb. 1874. [1873]

FORDWICH, Visct. 11 Little Maddox Street, London. Mote House, Kent. Eld. s. of the Earl Cowper. B. 1806; m. 1833, Anne Florence, eld. d. of Earl de Grey, and niece to the Earl of Ripon. A Lieut. in the Blues. Entertained Whig opinions. Was first elected for Canterbury in 1830. Retired 1835. Succeeded as 6th Earl 21 June 1837. Died 15 Apr. 1856. [1834]

FORDYCE, Alexander Dingwall. 83 Spring Gardens, London. Albyn Place, Aberdeen. Brucklay Castle, Aberdeenshire. S. of William Dingwall Fordyce, Esq., of Techminry, Aberdeenshire. and cadet of the families of Dingwall of Brucklay, and Lindsay of Downhill. B. at Aberdeen 1800; m. 1835, Barbara, d. of James Thom, Esq., of Aberdeen. Was educ. at the Aberdeen Grammar School; entered the navy as Midshipman in 1813; became a Lieut. in 1826, and a Commander in 1841; author of *Outlines of Naval Routine.* A Dept.-Lieut. of the Co. of Aberdeen. Of Liberal opinions, opposed to any further religious endowments. First returned for Aberdeen in 1847, when he was strongly supported by the Free Church party. Sat until he retired in 1852. Died 16 July 1864. [1852]

FORDYCE, William Dingwall. 16 Suffolk Street, London. Albyn Place, Aberdeen. Brucklay Castle, Mintlaw, Scotland. Eld. s. of Alexander Dingwall Fordyce, of Brucklay, Capt. R.N., who sat for the city of Aberdeen, from 1847-1852, by Barbara, d. of James Thom., Esq., of Novia Scotia. B. at Rubielan Cottage, Aberdeen, 1836 (twin with his bro. James); m. 1870, Christina, eld. d. of Robert Horn Esq., of Edinburgh. Educ. at the Propietary School, Blackheath and at Edinburgh University. Was admitted an advocate at the Scottish bar 1861. Was Dept.-Lieut. of Aberdeenshire and a Capt. of Volunteers. Patron of 1 living. A Whig, in favour of the abolition of the 'Law of Hypothec' in Scotland, etc. Sat for Aberdeenshire from May 1866 to Dec. 1868, and from that date for E. Aberdeenshire. MP until his death 27 Nov. 1875. [1875]

FORESTER, Cecil Theodore Weld. 54 Seymour Street, Portman Square, London. Gedling Rectory, Nottingham. Carlton. Only s. of the Hon. and Rev. Orlando Watkin Weld Forester (Canon and Chancellor of York, and Rector of Gedling, Nottinghamshire), by Sophia Elizabeth, d. of Richard Norman, Esq., (and Lady Elizabeth), of Melton Mowbray. Nephew to Lord Forester, who as Right Hon. George Cecil Weld Forester sat for Wenlock uninterruptedly from 1828 till his succession to the peerage in 1874. B. at Broseley, Shropshire. 1842; m. 1866, Emma Georgina, 3rd d. of Sir Willoughby Wolstan Dixie, 8th Bart., of Bosworth Park, Leicestershire. Educ. at Harrow and at Trinity Coll., Cambridge. A Conservative, and strongly attached to our constitution in Church and State; in favour of an amendment of the Masters and Servants' Act. Sat for Wenlock from Nov. 1874 until he retired in 1885. Succeeded as 6th baron in 1894. Died 20 Nov. 1917. [1885]

FORESTER, Rt. Hon. George Cecil Weld. 3 Carlton Gardens, London. Meaford Hall, Stone, Staffordshire. Carlton. 2nd s. of 1st Lord Forester, by the 2nd d. of 4th Duke of Rutland. Heir pres. to the 2nd Lord Forester. B. in Sackville Street 1807; m. 1862, the Hon. Mary Anne, d. of 2nd Visct. St. Vincent, and widow of D.O. Dyce Sombre, Esq. Became a Major in the Horse-Guards, 1846 and Lieut.-Col. 1853; Lieut.-Gen. in the army 1871; Groom of the Bedchamber. Was comptroller of the Household from Mar.-Dec. 1852, and from Mar. 1858- June 1859. A Conservative, 'strongly attached to our constitution in Church and State.' Sat for Wenlock from 1830 until he succeeded brother as 3rd Baron 10 Oct. 1874. Died 14 Feb. 1886. [1874]

FORMAN, Thomas Seaton. 6 Albany Court Yard, London. Penydarran Place, Glamorganshire. Carlton, Union, Wyndham, and Parthenon. An Ironmaster. A Conservative, voted for agricultural protection 1846. First returned for Bridgewater in 1841 and sat until he retired 1847. [1847]

FORSTER, Sir C. Continued in House after 1885: full entry in Volume II.

FORSTER, Charles Smith. 2 Queen's Square, Westminster. Walsall. S. of Mr. Forster, many years a Banker in the Borough. B. 1784; m. 1813, Elizabeth, d. of R. Emery, Esq. A Banker at Walsall. He was elected in opposition to Mr. de Boscoe Attwood, son of the Member for Birmingham. A Conservative. Voted against the legal tender clause of the Bank Charter Bill. Sat for Walsall from 1832 until defeated in 1837. Died 17 Nov. 1850. [1837]

FORSTER, Sir George, Bart. 33 Duke Street, St. James's, London. Coolderry, Carrickmacross, Co. Monaghan. Carlton. Only s. of the Rev. Sir Thomas Forster, 1st Bart., by Dorcas, only d. of the Rev. George Howse, D.D., of Cork. B. at Baronstown Glebe, Co. Louth 1796; m. 1st, 1817, Anna Maria, eld. d. of Matthew Fortescue, Esq., of Stephenstown, Co. Louth, 2ndly, Charlotte Jane, youngest d. of William Hoare Hume, Esq., of Humewood. Was called to the bar in Ireland 1830. A Magistrate for the Cos. of Meath, Louth, and Monaghan; and a Dept.-Lieut. for the two last. A Conservative, voted for inquiry into Maynooth 1853. First returned for Monaghan July 1852. Sat until defeated July 1865. Died 4 Apr. 1876. [1865]

FORSTER, John. York Chambers, St. James's Street, London. Reform. S. of Matthew Forster, Esq., who sat for Berwick from 1841 till 1853. B. 1817. A Reformer, voted for the ballot, June 1853. First returned for Berwick, May 1853, on his father, Mr. Matthew Forster, being unseated on petition. Sat until defeated 1857. [1857]

FORSTER, Matthew. 5 New City Chambers, London. Belsise House, Hampstead. Reform B. in Durham. A London Merchant. A Liberal. An advocate for free trade and a friend to direct taxation in preference to excise duties. First returned for Berwick-on-Tweed in 1841 and sat until Apr. 1853 when the election was declared void for bribery. [1853]

FORSTER, Rt. Hon. William Edward. 80 Ecclestone Square, London. Burley, Nr. Leeds, Yorkshire. Reform, and Devonshire. B. at Bradpole, Dorset, 1818, only s. of William Forster (who was for more than 50 years a Minister of the Society of Friends and died on an Anti-Slavery Mission in Tennessee), by Anna, sister of Sir Thomas Fowell Buxton (1st Bart.). M. 1850 Jane Martha, eld. d. of Rev. Thomas Arnold, D.D., Headmaster of Rugby. Created D.C.L. Oxon. 1879. A worsted manufacturer at Bradford. A Magistrate and Dept.-Lieut. of the W. Riding of Yorkshire, and Capt. 23rd W. Riding Volunteers. Was Under-Secretary for the Colonies from November 1865-July 1866, Vice-President of the Committee of Council on Education, and Fourth Charity Commission Dec. 1868-Feb. 1874. Chief Secretary of Ireland April 1880-May 1882. Presented with the freedom of the city of Edinburgh, Nov. 1875. A Liberal. Unsuccessfully contested Leeds Apr. 1859. Sat for Bradford from February 1851 until his death on 5 Apr. 1886. [1886]

FORSYTH, William, LL.D., Q.C. 61 Rutland Gate, London. The Firs, Mortimer, Berkshire. Athenaeum, and Carlton. S. of Thomas Forsyth, Esq., of Liverpool. B. at Greenock 1812; m. 1st, 1843, Mary. d. of George Lyall, Esq. (she died 1864); 2ndly, 1866, Georgiana Charlotte, d. of T. Plumer, Esq. Educ. at King's School, Sherborne, Dorset, and at Trinity Coll., Cambridge, where he graduated B.A. 1834. Was 3rd in the first class of the classical tripos, was Chancellor's Medallist and Fellow of Trinity, and proceeded to M.A. 1837. Called to the bar at the Inner Temple 1839. Commissary to the University of Cambridge. Was standing Counsel to the Sec. of State for India from 1859-1872. A Bencher of the Inner Temple, a member of the Council of Law Reporting from its foundation. Became a Queen's Counsel 1857. A Magistrate for Middlesex. Author of *The Life of Cicero, Hortensius or the Duty and Office of an Advocate* and *The History of Trial by Jury*, besides several other important works, and contributed to the *Quarterly* and *Edinburgh Reviews*. A Conservative, and supported the constitution in Church and State, opposed to the principles of the Permissive Bill as arbitrary and tyrannical. Elected for the borough of Cambridge 1865, but was decided to be legally disqualified from sitting; was an unsuccessful candidate for Bath Oct. 1873. Sat for Marylebone from Feb. 1874 until he retired 1880. Died 26 Dec. 1899. [1880]

FORT, John. Reid Hall, Lancashire. Reform. A Manufacturer at Blackburn. Entertained Whig principles; in favour of short Parliaments. Sat for Clitheroe from 1832 until he retired in 1841. [1840]

FORT, Richard, sen. 24 Queen's Gate Gardens, South Kensington, London. Read Hall, Whalley, Blackburn. Reform, and Brooks's. S. of John Fort, Esq., of Read Hall, many years MP for Clitheroe, by Mary, d. of James Kay, Esq., of Bass Lane, near Bury. B. at Oakenshaw 1822; m. 1853, Margaret Ellen, d. of Maj.-Gen. J.N. Smith, E.I.C.S. Educ. at Eton and at Christ Church, Oxford. A Magistrate and Dept.-Lieut. for Lancashire; was High Sherriff of that co. 1854. A Liberal. Unsuccessfully contested Clitheroe, May 1853. First elected for Clitheroe July 1865. MP until his death on 2 July 1868. [1867]

FORT, Richard, jun. 40 Clarges Street, London. Read Hall, Whalley, Lancashire. Arthur's. S. of Richard Fort, Esq., of Read Hall, Lancashire, who sat for Clitheroe from 1865 to 1868, by Margaret Ellen, d. of Maj.-Gen. John N. Smith, of the E.I.C.S. B. 1856. Educ. at Eton, and at Brasenose Coll., Oxford. Became Lieut. 11th

Hussars Jan 1878. A Liberal. Sat for Clitheroe from Apr. 1880. Retired in 1885. Master of the Hunt. Died 30 June 1918. [1885]

FORTESCUE, Rt. Hon. Chichester Samuel. 7 Carlton Gardens, London. Strawberry Hill, Teddington, London. Dudbrooke, Essex. Red House, Ardee, Ireland. Reform, Brooks's, Travellers'. Sackville Street, Dublin. B. 1823, the youngest s. of Lieut.-Col. Chichester Fortescue of Dromisken, Co. Louth, by the d. of Samuel Hobson, Esq., of Waterford. Bro. of Lord Clermont, who sat for Louth in 1840. M. 1863, Frances, Dowager Countess Waldegrave. Educ. at Christ Church, Oxford, where he was 1st class in classics in 1844, and obtained the Chancellor's Prize for the English Essay in 1846. Was Lord of the Treasury Jan. 1854-Apr. 1855; Under-Sec. of State for the Colonies June 1857-Mar. 1858 and June 1859-Nov. 1865; Chief Sec. of Ireland 1865-July 1866, and again Dec. 1868-Dec. 1870, when he became Pres. of the Board of Trade (Salary £2,000). A Liberal, voted for the ballot 1853, but against Church rates 1855. Sat for Louth from July 1847 untill he was defeated in 1874. [1873]

FORTESCUE, Hon. Dudley Francis. 9 Hatford Street, London. Summerville, Tramore, Co. Waterford. Brooks's, and Travellers'. 3rd s. of 2nd Earl of Fortescue, by his 1st wife, Lady Susan, eld. d. of 1st Earl of Harrowby. B. 1820; m. 1852 Lady Camilla Eleanor Wallop, 6th d. of 4th Earl of Portsmouth. Educ. at Trinity Coll., Cambridge. Appointed a Dept.-Lieut. of Devon in 1849, and Capt. 1st Devon Militia in 1855, but retired from that Corps. A Liberal. First returned for Andover Apr. 1857, and sat until he retired 1874. Died 2 Mar. 1909. [1873]

FORTESCUE, Hon. John William. 17 Grosvenor Square, London. Castle Hill, South Molton, Devon. Travellers', Coventry, and Reform. 2nd s. of 2nd Earl Fortescue, by the eld. d. of 2nd Lord Harrowby. B. 1819. Was formerly in the army. Appointed a Dept.-Lieut. of Devon in 1845, and Maj. in the Devon Militia in 1846. A Liberal. Unsuccessfully contested Barnstaple in 1841. Was first returned for Barnstaple in 1847. Retired in 1852. Died 25 Sept. 1859. [1852]

FORTESCUE, T. A Liberal. Returned for Louth Co. 31 July 1840. Retired in 1841.

FOSTER, William Henry. 6 Belgrave Square, London. Spratton Grange, Northampton. Apley Park, Bridgnorth, Shropshire. Carlton. Eld. s. of William Orme Foster, Esq., of Apley Park, Shropshire (who sat for South Staffordshire from 1857 to 1860), by Isabella, d. of Henry

Grazebrook, Esq., of Liverpool. B. 1846; m. 1874, Henrietta Grace, eld. d. of H.S. Pakenham Mahon, Esq., of Strokestown House, Roscommon, Ireland. Educ at Eton and at Christ Church, Oxford. A Magistrate for Shropshire and Northamptonshire, also a Dept.-Lieut for Shropshire. Sat for Bridgnorth from Feb. 1870, and sat until he retired in 1885.   [1885]

FOSTER, William Orme. 35 Lowndes Square, London. Stourton Castle, Stourbridge, Worcestershire. Brooks's. Eld. s. of William Foster, Esq., and nephew of James Foster, Esq., who was MP for Bridgnorth in 1831-32. B. 1814; m. 1843, Isabella, d. of Henry Grazebrook, Esq., of Liverpool. An Ironmaster at Stourbridge. A Dept.-Lieut. of Staffordshire and Worcestershire. A Liberal, in favour of 'a large and comprehensive measure' of parliamentary reform, but did not vote for Mr. Baines's £6 franchise, as not being 'a satisfactory solution of the question', opposed to the ballot; in favour of a reduction of the malt tax. First elected for Staffordshire S. Apr. 1857. Sat until defeated contesting Staffordshire W. in 1868. Died 29 Sept. 1900.   [1867]

FOTHERGILL, Richard. Abernant House, Aberdare, Glamorganshire. City Liberal. S. of Richard Fothergill, Esq., of Lowbridge House, Westmoreland, by Charlotte, d. of Charles Elderton, Esq., of London. B. at Caerleon, Monmouthshire 1822; m. 1st, 1848, Elizabeth, d. of Edward Lewis, Esq.; 2ndly, 1850, Mary, d. of William Boden, Esq. Educ. at the Military Academy, Edinburgh. Proprietor and Manager of the Aberdare Extension Iron-Works and Collieries in S. Wales. A Magistrate for Glamorganshire and Pembrokeshire and a Dept.-Lieut. for Glamorganshire. A Liberal, voted for the disestablishment of the Irish Church 1869. Sat for Merthyr Tydvil for Dec. 1868 until he retired 1880.   [1880]

FOWLER, H.H. Continued in House after 1885: full entry in Volume II.

FOWLER, Sir R.N. Continued in House after 1885: full entry in Volume II.

FOWLER, William. 38 Grosvenor Square, London. Forest House, Leytonstone, Essex. Reform, and City Liberal. Fourth s. of John Fowler, Esq., of Chapel Ness, Melksham, Wiltshire, by Rebecca, d. of William Hull, Esq., of Uxbridge, Middlesex. B. at Melksham 1828; m. 1st, 1855, Rachel Maria, d. of Robert Howard, Esq., of Tottenham Middlesex, and Ashmore Manor, Dorset (she died 1868); 2ndly, 1871, Elizabeth Fox, eld. d. of Francis Tuckett, Esq., of

Frenchays, Gloucester (she died 1872); 3rdly, 1875, Rachel, 3rd d. of Joseph Pease, Esq., of Southend, Durham, and widow of Charles Albert Leatham, Esq., of Gunnergate, York. Was Educ. at University Coll., London; graduated there LL.B. and was also University Law Scholar. Called to the Bar at the Inner Temple 1852. Was a Partner in the firm of Messrs. Alexander and Co. (afterwards Messrs. Alexander and Cunliffe) from 1856 till the dissolution of that firm in 1877. Was a Magistrate for Essex from 1866. Author of various works, including *The Crisis of 1866, Mozley and Tyndall on Miracles, Thoughts on Free Trade in Land* (1869), etc. A Liberal, in favour of a reform in the laws as to the ownership and tenure of land. Sat for Cambridge bor. from Dec. 1868 to Feb. 1874. Unsuccessfully contested Northampton 7 Oct. 1874. Re-elected for Cambridge bor. Apr. 1880. Retired in 1885. Died Sept. 1905.   [1885]

FOX, Charles. A Conservative. Unsuccessfully contested Longford 30 Dec. 1836, but on petition his opponent Luke White, Esq., was unseated and Mr. Fox sat for Longford from 5 May 1837 until 18 Aug. 1837, when he again contested the seat unsuccessfully.

FOX, Gen. Charles Richard. 1 Addison Road, Kensington, London. Reform. S. of 3rd Lord Holland. B. 1801; m. 1824, Lady Mary Fitzclarence. A Maj.-Gen. in the army. Was Surveyor-Gen. of the Ordance from July 1846. A Liberal. Sat for Horsham, for Calne, and for Tavistock, before 1832. Was returned for Stroud in 1831. Retired 1832. Was returned for Tavistock 10 Dec. 1832 and sat until 8 Jan. 1835, when he was re-elected for Stroud but shortly afterwards accepted Chiltern Hundreds to make room for Lord John Russell. Unsuccessfully contested Sandwich on the death of Sir. R.S. Donkin, a short time previous to the dissolution in 1841. First returned for the Tower Hamlets in 1841 and sat until defeated 1847. Possessed finest private collection of Greek Coins in the world, purchased by Royal Museum in Berlin 1873. Died 13 Apr. 1873.   [1847]

FOX, George Lane. Bramham House, Yorkshire. White's, St. James's, and Union. S. of James Fox, Esq., who was nephew to Lord Bingley, and who m. the sister of George Pitt, Lord Rivers. B. 1794; m. Georgiana, d. of Edward Pery Buckley, Esq., and Lady Georgiana Buckley. Was M.A. of Cambridge. Of Conservative principles, but independent and unpledged. Elected for Beverley in 1818, and again after the dissolution in 1837. Accepted Chiltern Hundreds in 1840.   [1838]

FOX, Richard Maxwell. 48 Duke Street, St. James's, London. Fox Hall, Rathowen, Longford. Eld. s. of the Rev. Francis Fox, and nephew to the 6th Lord Farnham. B. at Raheny Glebe, Co. Dublin 1816; m. 1835, Susan Amelia, 2nd d. of Admiral Sir Lawrence Halsted, G.C.B., and grand-d. of the celebrated Admiral Visct. Exmouth. Was educ. at Winchester and at University Coll., Oxford. Was a Government Inspector for the Dungannon Union, Co. Tyrone, under the Irish Relief Act. A Magistrate and Dept.-Lieut. of Longford. A Liberal, voted for the ballot 1853. In favour of the repeal of the Union with Ireland, the extension of the franchise, etc., but opposed to the endowment of the Roman Catholic Clergy. First returned for Longford July 1847 and sat until his death 26 Apr. 1856.   [1856]

FOX, Sackville Walter Lane. 3 St. James's Square, London. Oran House, Yorkshire. Carlton. 3rd s. of James Lane Fox, Esq., by the only d. of the 1st Lord Rivers; m. in 1826, the Lady Charlotte Mary Anne Georgiana, only d. of the 6th Duke of Leeds (she died 1836). A Dept.-Lieut. of the North Riding of Yorkshire. A Conservative, voted for agricultural protection in 1846. Sat for Helstone from 1831 to 1835; for Beverley from 1837 to 1841; for Ipswich from 1842 to 1847; and was elected again for Beverley in the latter year and sat until he retired in 1852. Died 18 Aug. 1874.   [1852]

FOX, William Johnson. 3 Sussex Place, Regent's Park, London. Reform. S. of a Suffolk farmer, afterwards a Cotton-Weaver in Norwich. B. at Uggeshal Farm, near Wrentham, Suffolk, 1786; m. 1820, d. of James Florance, Esq., of Chichester, Barrister. Educ. for the Dissenting ministry at Old Coll., Homerton, under the Rev. J. Pye Smith, D.D. Was well known as a political writer and lecturer, who took a prominent part in the proceedings of the Anti-Corn-Law League. Author of 3 Vols. of *Lectures chiefly addressed to the Working Classes; Letters of a Norwich Weaver Boy*, in the *League* Newspaper, etc. A radical Reformer, in favour of a separation of Church and State, and opposed to all religious endowments; voted for the ballot 1853. Sat for Oldham from July 1847 till July 1852, and from Dec. following till Apr. 1857, when he was an unsuccessful candidate; re-elected Oct. 1857. Sat until he accepted Chiltern Hundreds 1862. Died 3 June 1864.   [1862]

FRANKLAND, Sir Robert, Bart. Thirkleby Park, Yorkshire. 15 Cavendish Square, London. B. July 1784; m. in 1815 Louisa, 3rd d. of Lord George Murray, Bishop of St. David's, and cousin of the Duke of Atholl. A moderate Reformer, he was absent from the division on Lord Ebrington's

motion, as also from every other division connected with the Reform Act. First returned for Thirsk 31 March 1815. Sat until he accepted Chiltern Hundreds in 1834. Died 11 March 1849.   [1833].

FRANKLYN, George Woodroffe. Lovel Hill, Nr. Windsor. Carlton. 2nd s. of George Franklyn, Esq., of Clifton, by the d. of Thomas Ward, Esq., of London, Solicitor. B. at Bristol 1800; m. 1825, Mary Jane, d. of the Rev. John Arden, of Longcroft Hall, Staffordshire (she died 1862). Formerly a Merchant at Bristol; Mayor of that City 1842-3. Elected Warden and Master of the Guild of Merchant-Venturers there 1849-50. Appointed a Dept.-Lieut. of Middlesex 1855. A Conservative, and a supporter generally of Lord Derby's policy. First returned for Poole July 1852, and sat until he retired 1865. Died 5 Nov. 1870.   [1865]

FRASER, Sir William Augustus, Bart. 88 St. James' Street, London Carlton, and White's. Eld. s. of Lieut.-Col. Sir James John Fraser 3rd Bart., by Charlotte Anne, grand-d. of Sir Alexander Craufurd, Bart., of Kilbirnie. B. 1826. Educ. at Eton and at Christ Church, Oxford, where he graduated B.A. 1849, and M.A. subsequently. Formerly Capt. 1st Life Guards. One of the Queen's Bodyguard for Scotland. Author of *London Self-Governed* and other works. A Conservative, but not opposed to such changes as 'the progressive spirit of the age renders necessary.' Sat for Barnstaple from July 1852-Apr. 1853, when he was unseated on petition. Unsuccessfully contested Harwich 21 June 1853. Re-elected for Barnstaple Mar. 1857. Defeated May 1859. Sat for Ludlow from Aug. 1863-July 1865. Sat for Kidderminster from Aug. 1874. until he retired 1880. Died 17 Aug. 1898.   [1880]

FREELAND, Humphrey William. 16 Suffolk Street, Pall Mall, London. Oaklands, Chichester. Athenaeum, and Oxford & Cambridge. Only surviving s. of James Bennett Freeland, Esq., of Chichester, by Ann, d. of William Humphrey, Esq., late of Chichester. B. 1814. Educ. at Midhurst and at Christ Church Coll., Oxford, where he was 2nd class in classics 1835, and graduated M.A. Called to the bar at Lincoln's Inn, 1841, but did not practise. A Magistrate and Dept.-Lieut. for Sussex. Author of a volume of *Lectures, Life and Writings of Lamartine*, etc. also a volume of *Poems with translation from Lamartine*. A Fellow of the Royal Botanical, Geological, and Statistical Societies, a Life Governor of the Agricultural Society, Titular Life Member of 'Institut d'Afrique', etc. A Liberal, and in favour

149

of a 10/- franchise in counties, and a 6/- franchise in boroughs; in favour also of the ballot. First elected for Chichester Apr. 1859. Accepted Chiltern Hundreds 1863.   [1862].

FREESTUN, Col. William Lockyer. 22 Gloucester Square, Hyde Park, London. The Belvidere, Weymouth, Dorset. Reform, and Junior United Service. 2nd s. of Edward Freestun, Esq., of Primrose Hill, Co. Waterford, by Mary, only d. of William Lockyer, Esq., of Wembury House, Devon. B. at May Park, Co. Waterford, 1804; m. 1846, Josefa Benita, relict of Charles Pratt, Esq., of Totton House, Hampshire, and the Belvidere, Weymouth. Entered the army as Ensign in the 5th Foot, and served for 23 years; was on the staff of the British Legion under Sir de Lacy Evans in 1835-36-37, in which service he became a Col., and was three times wounded. Received permission to accept and wear the Order of Charles III. (Knight Commander), as also the first class of the Orders of San Fernando and of Isabella the Catholic. Served in Syria in 1840 and 1841 with the local rank of Major and Assistant-Adjutant General, where he was presented with a gold medal by the Sultan, which he received royal permission to wear. Also a Knight Grand Cross of the Order of St. John of Jerusalem. A Dept.-Lieut. and Magistrate for the county of Dorset. A Liberal, in favour of vote by ballot, and 'either the endowment of all religious bodies or of none'; voted for inquiry into Maynooth, 1853, and against church-rates 1855. First returned for Weymouth in 1847. Sat until defeated in 1859. Knighted 1860. Died 16 Apr. 1862.   [1858]

FREMANTLE, Hon. Thomas Francis. 22 Chesham Place, London. Swanbourne, Winslow, Buckinghamshire. Travellers', and Carlton. Eld. s. of Lord Cottesloe (who sat for Buckingham from 1826 to 1846), by Louisa Elizabeth, eld. d. of Sir George Nugent, Bart. B. at Westhorpe 1830; m. 1859, Lady Augusta Henrietta, 2nd d. of the 2nd Earl of Eldon. Educ. at Eton, where he obtained the Newcastle Medal 1848, and at Balliol Coll., Oxford, where he obtained the Balliol Scholarship 1847; gained the Hertford University Scholarship 1849; graduated B.A. 1st class in classics 1852. and subsequently M.A. A Conservative. Sat for Buckinghamshire from Sept. 1876 to 1885. Succeeded father as 2nd baron in 1890. Died 13 April 1918.   [1885]

FREMANTLE, Rt. Hon. Sir Thomas Francis, Bart. 2 Eaton Place, London. Swanburn, Buckinghamsire. Carlton. B. in 1798. M. in 1824, Louisa, eld. d. of Gen. Sir George Nugent, Bart., of Westhorpe House, Buckinghamsire. A Baron of

the Austrian Empire. A Director of London and Westminster Joint Stock Bank; and a Metropolitan Commissioner of Lunacy. Secretary to the Treasury from Dec. 1834-Apr. 1835, and again appointed in Sept. 1841-1844. Then appointed Secretary at War, but relinquished the office on being appointed Chief Secretary to the Lord Lieut. of Ireland in Feb. 1845. Was appointed deputy Chairman of the Board of Customs from Feb. 1846-Jan. 1874. Was Visitor of Maynooth Coll. Sat for the borough of Buckingham from 1826 until he accepted Chiltern Hundreds in Feb. 1846. Created Baron Cottesloe on 2 Mar. 1874. Died 3 Dec. 1890.   [1845]

FRENCH, Hon. Charles. 22 Jermyn Street, London. French Park, Roscommon. S. of the 3rd Lord de Freyne. B. at Cahir House, Roscommon 1851. Educ. at Downside Coll., Bath. A Liberal, and declared himself a supporter of 'Home Rule' for Ireland. Sat for Roscommon from June 1873 until he retired 1880. Died 27 Oct. 1925. [1880]

FRENCH, Col. Rt. Hon. Fitzstephen. 68 Warwick Square, London. Lough Erritt, Co. Roscommon. Brooks's, and Junior United Service. Sackville Street Club, Dublin. 3rd s. of Arthur French, Esq., of French Park, Co. Roscommon, by Margaret, d. of Edmund Costello, Esq. B. 1801; m. 1839, Charlotte, eld. d. of the Hon. Henry Grey Bennett, and niece of the 4th Earl of Tankerville. Obtained several science premiums in Coll. Appointed Col. of the Roscommon Militia 1854. A Liberal, in favour of short Parliaments. Unsuccessfully contested Sligo 1829. Sat for Roscommon Co. 1832. MP until his death 4 June 1873.   [1873]

FRESHFIELD, Charles Kaye. 21 Half Moon Street, London. Upper Gatton Park, Merstham, Surrey. Carlton, and Union. S. of James William Freshfield, Esq., F.R.S., of Mynthurst, Surrey. (who represented Falmouth for many years, and was High Sheriff of Surrey in 1850), by Mary, d. of John Blackett, Esq. B. in London 1812; m. 1834, Elizabeth, only d. of Daniel Stephenson, Esq., an Elder Brother of the Trinity House (she died 1849). Was educ. at Charterhouse School. A Solicitor in London, and was for many years Solicitor to the Bank of England. A Commissioner of Lieutenancy for London. A Liberal-Conservative. Sat for Dover from July 1865-Nov. 1868. when he stood unsuccessfully; re-elected Jan. 1874 and again in Apr. 1880. Sat until he retired 1885. Died 6 June 1891.   [1885]

FRESHFIELD, James William, F.R.S. 6 Devonshire Place, Portland Place, London. Moor Place, Betchworth, Sussex. Carlton, National,

150

and Athenaeum. Eld. s. of James Freshfield, Esq., of Chertsey, and said to be descended from the family of Frescheville, Barons by writ of summons. B. at Windsor 1775; m. 1st, Miss Blacket, of Durham; 2ndly, eld. d. of John Sims, Esq., of Walthamstow, Essex. Was entered a pensioner at Peterhouse, Cambridge. Was admitted an Attorney 1796, and was a Solicitor to the Bank of England for 20 years, but retired in 1840. Called to the bar at Gray's Inn 1842. Chairman of the Easter Quarter Sessions in Surrey, a Magistrate for Middlesex, Surrey, Sussex and the City of Westminster, a Dept.-Lieut. for the first two Cos., and was High Sheriff of Surrey 1850. Chairman of the Globe Insurance Company, a Director of the Canada Company, and joint Treasurer of the Corporation of the Sons of the Clergy. For more than 20 years Major in the City-Artillery, and on resigning his commission in 1845, received permission to retain his nominal rank, etc. A Conservative, of 'Protestant principles.' Sat for Penryn from 1830-1832,for Penryn and Falmouth from 1835 until the general election 1841. Unsuccessfully contested Wycombe, 1841, London 1847, and Derby 1848. Sat for Boston from Apr. 1851-July 1852, when he was again elected for Penryn and Falmouth. Sat until he retired 1857. Died 27 June 1864.   [1857]

FREWEN, Charles Hay. Cold Overton Hall, Leicestershire. Northiam, Staplehurst, Kent. Innishannon, Co. Cork. Carlton, and National. B. 1813, the 2nd s. of John Frewen Turner, Esq. (MP for Athlone in 1807), and bro. of Thomas Frewen Turner, Esq., who represented S. Leicestershire in 1835. This family, having succeeded to the Turner estates in Leicestershire about the middle of the last century, assumed the name of Turner, but in 1837 they reverted to the use of their patronymic Frewen only. Was Fellow Commoner of Trinity Coll., Cambridge. A Magistrate for the Cos. of Leicester and Rutland, and one of the Governors of Christ's Hospital. Appointed Dept.-Lieut. of Rutland 1848, and of Sussex 1852. 'A Protestant Conservative', opposed to concessions to the Roman Catholic Church. Favoured the repeal of the malt tax and hop duty, and the removal of direct taxes generally, for he considered customs duties as the best source of revenue. Unsuccessfully contested Leicester in 1839 and Rye in 1841. Represented E. Sussex from Jan. 1846 until he accepted Chiltern Hundreds 1857. Unsuccessfuly contested Leicestershire N. 1857, 1859, 1865 and again in 1868. Died 1 Sept. 1878.   [1856]

FRY, Lewis. Continued in House after 1885: full entry in Volume II.

FRY, Theodore. Continued in House after 1885: full entry in Volume II.

FRYER, Richard. 23 Downing Street, London. Weys, Tottenhall, Staffordshire. A Banker and Iron-Master, residing in Wolverhampton. A radical Reformer, in favour of the ballot, triennial Parliaments, free-trade, the immediate abolition of slavery, and no corn laws. Sat for Wolverhampton from 1832. Retired in 1835.   [1833]

FULLER, Augustus Eliott. 16 Clifford Street, London. Rose Hill and Ashdown House, Sussex. United University, and Alfred. Eld s.of John Trayton Fuller, Esq., formerly of Heathfield Park, Sussex, by the only d. of the 1st Lord Heathfield; was eld bro. of Sir T.T.F.E. Drake, Bart. B. 1777; m. 1801, d. of Owen P. Meyrick, Esq. (she died 1856). A Magistrate and Dept.-Lieut. of Sussex. Patron of 1 living. A Conservative. Was an unsuccessful candidate for E. Sussex 1837. First returned for E. Sussex in 1841. Sat until he retired 1857. Died 5 Aug. 1857.   [1857]

FULLER-MAITLAND, W. See MAITLAND, W. Fuller-.

GABBETT, Daniel FitzGerald. Cahirconlish House, Lisnagar, Co.Limerick. United Service Club, Dublin. S. of Daniel Gabbett, Esq., of Bellefield, by Susannah, d. of Rev. Windham Magrath-FitzGerald, of Ballinard, Co. Limerick. B. 1841. Educ. at St. Columba's College and Trinity Coll., Dublin. Was Lieut. 10th Hussars and 2nd Life Guards. A Magistrate for the Co. of Limerick. A Liberal, and in favour of 'Home Rule for Ireland.' Sat for Limerick City from May 1879. Sat until he retired in 1885. Bankrupt 1896. Died 4 Aug. 1898   [1885]

GALLWEY, Sir William Payne, Bart., 2 Buckingham Gate, London. Thirkleby Park, Thirsk. Travellers'. Only s. of Sir William Payne Gallwey, (1st Bart.), by the only d. of 1st Earl of Dunraven. M. 1847, Emily, 3rd d. of Sir Robert Frankland-Russell, Bart., of Thirkleby Hall, Yorkshire. Was once Major in the 7th Fusiliers. Appointed Dept.-Lieut. of the N. Riding of Yorkshire 1853. A Liberal-Conservative, initially voted in favour of the late Lord Derby's policy, but afterwards gave 'an independent support' to Lord Palmerston. Voted however with Lord Derby on Parliamentary Reform, Mar. 1859, and against Lord Palmerston on the vote of censure 1864. Sat for Thirsk from Mar. 1851 until he retired 1880. Died 19 Dec. 1881.   [1880]

GALWAY, Visct.(I). Serlby Hall, Bawtry, Nottinghamshire. Carlton, Boodle's, and

Travellers'. An Irish Peer. B. at Knutsford, Cheshire, 1805; m. 1838, his cousin Henrietta Eliza, only d. of Robert Pemberton Milnes, Esq., of Fryston Hall, Yorkshire, and sister of 1st Lord Houghton. Was educ. at Harrow, and graduated at Christ Church, Oxford. Was a Lord in Waiting to the Queen from Feb.-Dec. 1852. A Conservative opposed to the disestablishment of the Irish Church 1869. First returned for E. Retford in 1847. MP until his death 6 Feb. 1876.   [1875]

GALWAY, Visct.(II). Serlby Hall, Bawtry, Yorkshire. Carlton, and Travellers'. An Irish Peer. B. in Grafton Street, 1844; m. 1879, Vere, only d. of Ellis Gosling, Esq., of Bushridge Park, Godalming, Surrey. Educ. at Eton, and at Christ Church, Oxford; graduated B.A. 1866, 2nd class in law and modern history; M.A. 1877. A Dept.-Lieut. and Magistrate for Nottinghamshire and Capt. Sherwood Rangers Yeomanry. A Conservative. Sat for North Nottinghamshire from Feb. 1872. Sat until he retired in 1885. Created Baron Monckton July 1887. A.D.C. to three monarchs 1897 to 1920. Died 7 March 1931.   [1885]

GALWEY, John Matthew. Duckspool, Co. Waterford. A Repealer. Contested Dungarvan in 1832. Sat for Co. Waterford from 1832. Retired in 1835. Unsuccessfully contested Dungarvan again in Jan. 1835 and Feb. 1837.   [1834]

GARD, Richard Sommers. Rougemont House, Exeter. Carlton, and National. S. of Jonas Gard, Esq., Woollen Manufacturer, of North Tawton, Devon, and Elizabeth his wife. B. at North Tawton, Devon 1797; m. 1829, d. of Richard Parr, Esq., of Kirton, Lincolnshire. Formerly a partner in the firm of Messrs. Sanderson and Company, Discount Brokers, King William Street, London. A Magistrate and Dept.-Lieut. of Devon, and a Dept.-Warden of the Stannaries of Cornwall and Devon. Was High Sheriff of Devon 1854. A Conservative, in favour of 'local municipal government as opposed to centralization.' Unsuccessfully contested Honiton July 1852; first elected for Exeter Apr. 1857. Sat until he retired 1865. Died 16 Dec. 1868.   [1865]

GARDNER, John Dunn. 14 Lower Grosvenor Street, Grosvenor Square, London. Chatteris, Cambridgeshire. B. 1811, and claimed to be the eld. s. of the 3rd Marq. Townshend, assuming the courtesy title of Earl of Leicester, which he dropped in 1843. Took the name of Dunn Gardner by royal license. A Conservative. Sat for the borough of Bodmin from 1841 until his retirement in 1846. Became JP for the Isle of Ely. Died 11 Jan 1903.   [1845]

GARDNER, J.T. Agg-. See AGG-GARDNER, J.T. Continued in House after 1885: full entry in Volume II

GARDNER, Richard. 130 Piccadilly, London. Chaseley Hall, Manchester. Reform. B. in London 1813, the eld. s. of Robert Gardner, Esq., a Merchant and Magistrate of Lancashire. M. 1850, Lucy, only d. of Count de Mandelsloh, formerly Minister Plenipotentiary from Wurtemburg. Educ. at Charterhouse and Wadham Coll., Oxford, where he graduated B.A. 1838. Author of several political pamphlets and contributions to magazines, newspapers etc. Of Radical opinions, and favoured an extension of the suffrage. Voted for the ballot 1853. Objected 'to the alliance of Church and State under any circumstances', and was opposed to public endowments for religious purposes under any pretexts. Returned for Leicester in July 1847, but unseated on petition. Again returned in July 1852, and sat until he died 4 June 1856.   [1856]

GARDNER, Col. R. Richardson. Continued in House after 1885: full entry in Volume II

GARFIT, Thomas. Boston. Little Grimsby Hall, Louth. S. of William Garfit, Esq., of Boston, by Harriet, d. of Rev. William Draper. B. at Boston 1815; m. 1846, Elizabeth Boyd, only d. of Thomas Broadbent, Esq., of Grove House, Longsight, Lancashire. Called to the bar at the Middle Temple 1846. A Banker at Boston and Louth, a Partner in the firm of Messrs. Garfit, Claypon and Company. A Magistrate and Dept.-Lieut.   for   Lincolnshire.   A Moderate-Conservative. Sat for Boston from Aug. 1878. Unseated 1880. Died 29 May 1883. [1880]

GARLIES, Lord. Galloway House, Wigtonshire. Eld. s. of Earl of Galloway, by Lady Harriet Blanche, 7th d. of 6th Duke of Beaufort. B. in Grosvenor Square, 1835. Entered the army as cornet Royal Horse Guards 1855; became Lieut. 1857, Capt. 1861. Capt. Galloway Militia. A Conservative, 'but quite prepared to support measures for the progressive improvement of our institutions.' Sat for the Co. of Wigton from Dec. 1868 until he succeeded as 10th Earl of Galloway 2 Jan. 1873. Lord High Commissioner to the Kirk of Scotland 1876. Died 7 Feb. 1901.   [1872]

GARNETT, William James. Bleasdale Tower, Garstang. Quernmore Park, Lancaster. University. S. of William Garnett, Esq., of Quernmore Park, Lancaster (many years a Merchant in Manchester, and High Sheriff for Lancashire in 1843), by Margaret, d. of — Carson, Esq. B. at Manchester 1818; m. 1846, Frances Anne, d. of the Rev. Henry Hale, of King Walden, Hertfordshire. Educ. at Eton, and at Christ Church, Oxford, where he graduated M.A. 1844. Called to the bar at the Inner Temple 1845, but never practised. A Magistrate and Dept.-Lieut. of Lancashire. Appointed Capt. 3rd Lancashire Militia 1846; retired on the regiment going on foreign service, June 1855. Chairman of the Board of Guardians of Garstang Union from 1850. A Dept.-Forester of the Royal Forest of Bleasdale. Author of a Report on Lancashire farming, for which he received a prize of 50/- from the Agricultural Society. A Liberal, desired a moderate extension of the franchise, and voted in favour of Lord Derby's Reform Bill, Mar. 1859, but opposed to the ballot and to the abolition of the Maynooth grant; in favour of 'industrial and religious education.' First elected for Lancaster, Apr. 1857. Sat until he accepted Chiltern Hundreds 1864. Died 15 Sept. 1873. [1864]

GARNIER, John Carpenter. 42 St. James's Place, London. Mount Tavy, Tavistock, Devon. Rookesbury Park, Fareham, Hampshire. Carlton. Only s. of John Carpenter, Esq., of Mount Tavy, Tavistock, by Lucy, d. of the Rev. William and Lady Harriet Garnier, of Rookesbury Park, Hampshire. B. at Mount Tavy, Tavistock 1839; m. 1868, Hon. Mary Louisa, 2nd d. of 18th Baron Clinton. Educ. at Harrow and at Christ Church, Oxford. Assumed by royal license in 1864 the name of Garnier in addition to his patronymic Carpenter under the will of his Uncle William Garnier, Esq., to whose estate of Rookesbury Park he succeeded. A Magistrate for Hampshire and Devon; also a Dept.-Lieut. of the latter. Patron of 2 livings. A Conservative. Unsuccessfully contested South Hampshire Dec. 1868; sat for S. Devon from June 1873 until he accepted Chiltern Hundreds July 1884. [1884]

GARTH, Sir Richard. Wimbledon, London. Junior Carlton. S. of Rev. Richard Garth, of Morden, Surrey, by his marriage with Miss Mary Douglas. B. at Lasham, Hampshire, 1820; m. 1847, Clara, 2nd d. of W. Loftus Lowndes, Esq., Q.C. Educ. at Eton and at Christ Church, Oxford. Was called to the bar at Lincoln's Inn, 1847, and went the Home Circuit; made a Queen's Counsel, 1866. Patron of 1 living. A Conservative, in favour of moderate reform and of 'an adjustment of the church-rate question', so as to secure 'civil and religious liberty.' First elected for Guildford, Dec. 1866. Defeated in 1868. Created Bart. 1875; K.C., P.C. 1888; Chief Justice of Calcutta 1875-86. Died 25 Mar. 1903. [1867]

GASELEE, Stephen. 2 Cambridge Square, Hyde Park, London. 3 Serjeants' Inn, Fleet Street, London. Reform. Eld. s. of Sir Stephen Gaselee, one of the Justices of the Common Pleas, by Henrietta, d. of James Harris, Esq., of the East India Company Service. B. in London, 1807; m. 1841, Alma Mary, eld. d. of Vice-Admiral Sir John Tremayne Rodd, K.C.B. Educ. at Winchester, and at Balliol Coll., Oxford, where he was 2nd class in Classics and graduated B.A. 1828, M.A. 1832. Was called to the bar at the Inner Temple 1832, made a Sergeant-at-Law 1840, and went the Home Circuit. A Liberal. Unsuccessfully contested Bridgwater 29 July 1847 and Oxford 31 Mar. 1857. First elected for Portsmouth July 1865. Defeated in 1868. Died 20 Oct. 1883. [1867]

GASKELL, Daniel. Westminster Club. Lupset Hall, Yorkshire. A Reformer, in favour of free trade, the repeal of all taxes pressing upon industry, and the substitution of a graduated property tax; the abolition of all monopolies; the fixing a small duty on corn for one year, and then its perfectly free admission; vote by ballot, and triennial Parliaments. Sat for Wakefield from 1832. Defeated in 1837. Died 20 Dec. 1875. [1837]

GASKELL, James Milnes. 12 Stratford Place, London. Wenlock Abbey, Wenlock, Shropshire. Thornes House, Wakefield, Yorkshire. Carlton, and Oxford & Cambridge. Only s. of Benjamin Gaskell, Esq., of Thornes House, Yorkshire (who sat for Maldon for many years), by the eld. d. of Dr. Brandreth, of Liverpool. B. 1810; m. 1832, Mary, 2nd d. of the Rt. Hon. C.W.W. Wynn. Was a Lord of the Treasurey; resigned Feb. 1846. A Conservative, and in favour of 'the basis of our representative system being extended', but opposed to 'any sudden or sweeping alteration'; in favour of complete 'religious freedom'. Sat for Wenlock from 1832 until he retired in 1868. Died 5 Feb. 1873. [1867]

GATHORNE-HARDY, Hon. A.E. See HARDY, Hon. A.E. Gathorne-.

GATHORNE-HARDY, Hon. J.S. Continued in House after 1885: full entry in Volume II.

GAVIN, C. Major. A Liberal. Returned for Limerick at a by-election 15 Feb. 1858; but was unseated on petition shortly afterwards.

GAVIN, George. Kilpeacon House, Limerick. United Service. S. of Michael Gavin, Esq., of Limerick, by Margaret, d. of J.O.Halloran, Esq. B. at Limerick 1810; m. 1855, Jane, d. of Montjord Westropp, Esq. Entered the 16th Lancers 1837, became Maj. 1846, retired 1850. A Magistrate for the Co. of Limerick. A Liberal. First elected for Limerick May 1859. Sat until he retired 1874. Died 23 Oct. 1880.   [1873]

GEACH, Charles. 10 Park Street, London. Dale, Nr.Birmingham. Reform. B. at St. Ansell, Cornwall 1808. M. 1832, d. of John Skully, Esq., of Birmingham. Managing Director of the Birmingham and Midland Bank at Birmingham, having been a clerk in the Bank of England. A Director of the Manchester, Sheffield and Lincolnshire Railway, and of the Shrewsbury and Birmingham Railway. A Liberal, in favour of free trade, extension to the suffrage, vote by ballot. 'Attached to the doctrines of the Established Church, but opposed to compulsory payment from one denomination to support another.' Sat for Coventry from Apr. 1851 until his death 1 Nov. 1854.   [1854]

GEARY, Sir William Richard Powlett, Bart. 3D Albany, London. Oxon Hoath, Kent. Carlton. B. 1810; m. 1835, Louisa, d. of Charles Andrew Bruce. A Conservative. Possessed considerable property in Wexford. Contested Kent W. unsuccessfully in 1832, but was at the head of the poll in 1835. His father had represented the county in the Parliaments of 1796, 1802 and 1812. Sat until he accepted Chiltern Hundreds 1837. Died 19 Dec. 1877.   [1837]

GEORGE, John. Cahore House, Gorey, Wexford. Carlton. Kildare Street Club, Dublin. S. of John George, Esq., Merchant, by Emily Jane, d. of — Fox, Esq. B. in Dublin 1804; m. 1st, 1832, Miss Sarah Rosania D'Olier; 2ndly, 1848, Miss Mary Carleton L'Estrange. Educ. at Frascati School, and at Trinity Coll., Dublin. Called to the bar at Gray's Inn 1827; made a Queen's Counsel 1844. Was Solicitor-Gen. for Ireland. A Magistrate for the Co. of Wexford. A moderate Conservative, and said he would give a general support to Lord Derby. Unsuccessfully contested the Co. of Wexford Apr. 1857. First elected for the Co. of Wexford May 1859 and sat until appointed Judge of Queen's Bench, Ireland 1866. Died 15 Dec. 1871.   [1865]

GERVIS, Sir G.W.T. See TAPPS-GERVIS, Sir George William.

GETTY, Samuel Gibson. 15 Onslow Square, London. Ulster Club, Belfast. A Conservative, and voted against Lord Palmerston on the vote of censure 1864. First elected for Belfast, June 1860. Sat until he retired in 1868. Died 15 Dec. 1877.   [1867]

GIBSON, Right Hon. Edward. 23 FitzWilliam Square South, Dublin. Carlton, and Garrick. University Club, Dublin. S. of William Gibson, Esq., of Merrion Square, Dublin, and Rockforest, Co. Tipperary, by Louisa, d. of Joseph Grant, Esq., Barrister-at-Law. B. at Dublin 1837; m. 1868, Fanny, d. of Henry Colles, Esq., Educ. at Trinity Coll., Dublin, where he graduated B.A. 1858 with honours and obtained the first Gold medal for history, political science, and composition; graduated M.A. 1861; created hon. LL.D. at Dublin 1881. Was called to the bar in Ireland 1860, and went the Leinster circuit; made a Queen's Counsel July 1872. Was Attorney-gen. for Ireland from Jan. 1877 to Apr. 1880. A Magistrate for Meath. A Conservative. Unsuccessfully contested Waterford city 1874. Sat for Dublin University from Jan. 1875 until he was appointed Lord Chancellor of Ireland in 1885 and created Lord Ashbourne July 1885. Lord Chancellor of Ireland with a seat in the Cabinet 1885-86, 1886-92, and 1895-1905. Died 22 May 1913.   [1885]

GIBSON, James. A Barrister at Law. Of Whig politics. First elected for Belfast in Aug. 1837, but shortly afterwards unseated on petition. Q.C. 1869. Commissioner of National Education in Ireland from 1848. Legal Adviser to Irish Presbyterian Church. Died 5 Feb. 1880.

[1838 2nd ed.]

GIBSON, Rt.Hon Thomas Milner. 3 Hyde Park Place, Cumberland Gate, London. Theberton House, Saxmundham, Suffolk. Oxford & Cambridge. Only s. of Maj. Thomas Milner Gibson, of the 78th regt. B. at Trinidad 1807; m. 1832, d. of the Rev. Sir Thomas G. Cullum, Bart. Educ. at Trinity Coll., Cambridge, where he took a wrangler's degree 1830. Was Vice-President of the Board of Trade from July 1846 till Apr. 1848. Was President of the Poor Law Board for a few weeks in June 1859; and President of the Board of Trade from July following till June 1866. A Liberal, voted for the ballot, 1853. Sat for Ipswich from July 1837 till July 1839, when he accepted the Chiltern Hundreds, stood a contest, and was not elected; unsuccessfully contested Cambridge in 1839. Sat for Manchester from June 1841 till Apr. 1857. First returned for Ashton-under-Lyne, Dec. 1857, and sat until he was defeated in 1868. Died 25 Feb. 1884.   [1867]

GIFFARD, Sir Hardinge Stanley. 99 Gloucester Place, Hyde Park, London. S. of S.L. Giffard, Esq., LL.D. B. 1825. Graduated at Merton Coll., Oxford 1852. M. 1st, 1852, Caroline Louisa, eld. d. of William Conn Humphreys, Esq., (dead); 2ndly, 1874, Lynie, 3rd d. of Henry Woodfall, Esq. Was called to the bar at the Inner Temple Jan. 1850, and went the South Wales circuit. Was appointed a Queen's Counsel in 1865. Was

Solicitor-Gen. from Nov. 1874 to Apr. 1880. Treasurer of the Inner Temple for 1881, appointed Constable of Launceston Castle Jan. 1883. A moderate Conservative. Unsuccessfully contested Cardiff Dec. 1868, and again Feb. 1874, also Horsham Feb. 1876. Sat for Launceston from Feb. 1877 until he was appointed Lord Chancellor, as Baron Halsbury, June 1885; held the same office 1886-92 and 1895-1905. Promoted to an earldom Jan. 1898. Died 11 Dec. 1921.

[1885]

GIFFORD, Earl of. 2 Wilton Place, London. Brooks's. Eld. s. of Marq. of Tweeddale, by Lady Susan, 3rd d. of 5th Duke of Manchester. B. at Yester House, Haddingtonshire, 1822. Educ. at Trinity Hall, Cambridge, where he graduated M.A. 1845. Appointed a Dept.-Lieut. of Haddington, 1846, and Capt. East Lothian Yeomanry Cavalry, 1850. Was Private Secretary to Lord Panmure (Secretary at War) for a short time, 1854. A Liberal, avowed himself 'a sincere friend to the Established Church,' but in favour of the abolition of church-rates, as vexatious and anomalous; opposed to the ballot. First returned for Totnes, Nov. 1855. M.P. until his death in 1862/63. [1862]

GILES, A. Continued in House after 1885: full entry in Volume II

GILL, Henry Joseph. Continued in House after 1885: full entry in Volume II.

GILL, Thomas. Buckland Abbey, Devon. Crescent, Plymouth. Reform. S. of John Gill, Esq., Banker. B. 1788. A Merchant and Manufacturer, a Magistrate and Dept.-Lieut. of Devon. A Director of the West of England Assurance Company. Opposed to monopolies and protective duties, except for the purposes of revenue; formerly voted against the abolition of the Corn Laws, but in 1846 supported their repeal; hostile to Church rates as far as dissenters were concerned, also to the building of Churches at the public expense, considering the property of the Church ample for every legitimate object. A supporter of the ballot, if electors could not otherwise be protected. Sat for Plymouth from 1841 until he retired 1847. Died 20 Oct. 1861. [1847]

GILLON, William Downe. Wallhouse, Linlithgowshire. Hurstmonceaux, Sussex. Union, Albion, and Reform. Only s. of Col. Andrew Gillon, of Wallhouse, by Mary Anne, d. of William Downe, Esq., of Downe Hall, Dorset. A radical Reformer. In favour of the ballot, triennial Parliaments, and extension of the suffrage. First sat for Falkirk district in the Parliament of 1831,

and sat until defeated in 1841. Died 7 Oct. 1846.

[1840]

GILPIN, Charles. 14 Moorgate Street, London. 10 Bedford Square, London. S. of Mr. James Gilpin, by Mary, sister of Mr. Joseph Sturge, of Birmingham. B. at Bristol 1815; m. 1840, Anne, d. of William Crouch, Esq., of Falmouth. Had been a publisher in London; retired in 1853. Chairman of the National Freehold Land Society. Was Parliamentary Sec. to the Poor Law Board from July 1859-Feb. 1865. An 'earnest and thorough Liberal', in favour of 'the modification or repeal' of the income tax, and greater economy in the public expenditure; opposed to all State endowments of religion. Unsuccessfully contested Perth, May 1852. Sat for Northamptonshire from Apr. 1857. MP until his death 8 Sept. 1874.

[1874]

GILPIN, Sir Richard Thomas, Bart. Hockliffe Grange, Leighton Buzzard. Carlton. Only s. of Richard Gilpin, Esq., of Hockliffe (who was Lieut.-Col. of the Bedfordshire Militia for more than 40 years), by his 2nd wife, Sarah, 4th d. of William Wilkinson, Esq., of Westmoreland. B. in Manchester Street, Manchester Square, 1801; m. 1831, Louisa, d. of General Gore Browne, of Weymouth (she died 1871). Educ. at Rugby and at Christ's Coll., Cambridge. Appointed Lieut.-Col. Rifle Brigade 1851, retired; once served with the 14th Light Dragoons. A Magistrate and Dept.-Lieut. of Buckinghamshire and Bedfordshire High Sheriff of the latter in 1850, also Col. of the Bedfordshire Militia. A Conservative, a strong supporter of the Protestant constitution in Church and State, but in favour of civil and religious liberty. Sat for Bedfordshire from Feb. 1851 until he retired 1880. Died 8 Apr. 1882.

[1880]

GIPPS, Henry Plumptre. 9 Montagu Place, Bryanstone Square, London. Carlton. Eld. s. of Rev. Henry Gipps, (whose father, George Gipps, sat for Canterbury 1785-1805), by Emma Maria, 2nd d. of John Phimptre, Esq. of Fredville, Kent. B. at Norton Court, Kent, 1813; m. 1835, Mary Anne, 2nd d. of the late Sir William Lawrence Young, Bart., of Bradenham, Buckinghamshire. Educated at St. Johns Coll., Cambridge where he was 22nd Wrangler in 1835, and graduated M.A. in 1838. Called to the bar at Lincoln's Inn, November 1838. A Conservative and a supporter generally of Lord Derby's Government, but opposed to the reimposition of protective duties on corn, and to the Maynooth Grant (in favour of a moderate parliamentary reform). An unsuccessful candidate for Canterbury in July 1837, but failed only by three votes. First returned for Canterbury in July 1852 but unseated on petition in 1853.

[1852 2nd ed.]

GISBORNE, Thomas. Park House, Kensington Gore, London. Horwick House, Co. Derby. S. of the Rev. Thomas Gisborne, of Yoxhall Lodge, Staffordshire, a Prebendary of Durham. Bro.-in-law of William Evans, Esq., once member for Leicester. M. 1st, sister of Charles Fysche Palmer, Esq., MP; 2ndly, 1826, relict of Francis Dunkinfield Astley, Esq., of Dunkinfield, Cheshire. A Dept.-Lieut. of Derbyshire. A Reformer, in favour of the relief of the Dissenters from payments to the Established Church, also in favour of the ballot, and an extension of the currency. Represented Stafford in the Parliaments of 1830 and 1831, sat for Derbyshire from 1832-37. In Feb. 1839, Mr. Maule, who had been the member for Carlow, was raised to the Bench, when Col. Bruen and Mr. Gisborne became candidates. The former was returned, but the latter succeeded in unseating him on petition. Contested Totnes Apr. 1840. At the general election in 1841 contested Leicestershire S. and Newport, Isle of Wight, but was not returned. Contested Ipswich June 1842. First elected for Nottingham in 1843. Defeated 1847. Contested Kidderminster 1849. Author. Died 20 July 1852.

[1847]

GIVAN, John. 7 Upper Fitzwilliam Street, Dublin. Ivy Hill, Co. Monaghan. Reform. Stephen's Green Club, Dublin. S. of John Givan, Esq., of Castlecaulfield, Co. Tyrone, Linen Manufacturer, a Magistrate for that Co., by Margaretta, d. of James Macdonnell, Esq. B. at Castlecaulfield 1837; m. 1st, Eliza, d. of Samuel Hopper, Esq., of Crewe, Co. Tyrone; 2ndly, Arminta Read, d. of James M. Ross, Esq., of Liscarney, Monaghan. Admitted a Solicitor in Ireland May 1870. A Magistrate of Co. Tyrone, and Chairman of Town Commissioners of Aughnacloy, in that Co. A Liberal of advanced views, in favour of the creation of a peasant proprietary in Ireland, the reform of the present Grand Jury Laws, and the establishment of elective county boards. Sat for Monaghan from Apr. 1880 until appointed Crown Solicitor in 1883.

[1883]

GLADSTONE, Herbert John. Continued in House after 1885: full entry in Volume II.

GLADSTONE, John Neilson. 42 Upper Brook Street, London. Bowden Park, Chippenham, Wiltshire. Carlton, and United Service. 3rd s. of Sir John Gladstone, Bart. (who was for 60 years a Liverpool merchant), by his 2nd wife, Anne, d. of Andrew Robertson, Esq., Provost of Dingwall. B. 1807; m. 1839, Elizabeth Honoria, d. of Sir Robert Bateson, Bart., of Belvoir Park, Belfast. Entered the navy in 1820, and became a Commander in 1842. High Sheriff for Wiltshire for 1859. A Conservative, supported a system of national education based on religion, and voted for an inquiry respecting Maynooth. Sat for Walsall from Feb. to July 1841. Returned for Ipswich in Aug. 1842, after two previous elections there had been declared void, and sat till 1847. Sat for Devizes from July 1852 till Apr. 1857, when he was an unsuccessful candidate; was re-elected, however, Apr. 1859. MP until his death in 1863.

[1862]

GLADSTONE, Thomas. 6 Albany, London. Fettercairn, Scotland. Carlton, and Athenaeum. Eld. s. of Mr.Gladstone, the Liverpool Merchant, and bro. to the member for Newark. A Conservative. Sat for Queenborough in the Parliament of 1830, and for Portarlington in that of 1832. Sat for Leicester from 1835. Defeated in 1837. Unsuccessfully contested Peterborough 29 June 1841. Returned for Ipswich 1842, but unseated on petition. Lord Lieut. of Kincardineshire. Died 20 Mar. 1889.

[1837]

GLADSTONE, Rt. Hon. William Ewart. Hawarden Castle, Chester. United University. 4th s. of Sir John Gladstone (1st Bart.), a Liverpool Merchant. Grandson maternally of Andrew Robertson, Esq., Provost of Dingwall. B. at Liverpool 1809; m. 1839, Catherine, eld. d. of Sir Stephen Richard Glynne, Bart., of Hawarden Castle, Flintshire. Was educ. at Eton and Christ Church, Oxford, where he obtained a double first class in 1831, graduated M.A. 1834 and received the honorary degree of D.C.L. 1848. A Dept.-Lieut. of Wiltshire. Was appointed Lord of the Treasury in Dec. 1834; was Under-Sec. for the Colonies from Jan. 1835-Apr. same year; Vice Pres. of the Board of Trade and Master of the Mint from Sept. 1841-May 1843, when he became Pres. of that Board, retaining the office of Master of the Mint. Resigned both Feb. 1845. Was Sec. of State for the Colonies from Dec. 1845-July 1846, Chancellor of the Exchequer from Dec. 1852-Feb 1855 and from June 1859-July 1866. Was first Prime Minister from Dec. 1868- Feb. 1874; having been from Aug. 1873 Chancellor of the Exchequer in addition to his other offices. Re-appointed to the Premiership, and in conjunction with that office, Chancellor of the Exchequer Apr. 1880. In Dec. 1882 he resigned the latter office to the Rt. Hon.H.C.E. Childers, and in June 1885, on an adverse vote in the House of Commons, the whole Liberal Ministry resigned. In Jan. 1886 he returned to office as 1st Lord of the Treasury and Lord Privy Seal in his third administration, but after an adverse vote for his Bill for the Government of Ireland, Parliament was again dissolved and he shortly afterwards resigned office. Took office as Premier for the 4th time Aug. 1892, but resigned and was succeeded by Lord Rosebery, 3 Mar. 1893. Went on a special mission to the Ionian Islands as Lord High Commissioner Extraordinary, Nov. 1858. Elected Lord Rector of the University of Edinburgh Nov. 1859, and again 1862. Lord Rector of the University of Glasgow 1877. A Prof. of Ancient History to the Royal Academy, Mar. 1876. Author of *The State and its Relations with the Church, Church Principles considered in their Results,* and other works. A Liberal. Sat for Newark from 1832 till his acceptance of office in Dec. 1845. Unsuccessfully contested Manchester 28 July 1837. Sat for the University of Oxford from 1847-July 1865, when he was returned for S. Lancashire. Was unsuccessful at the last place Dec. 1868, but obtained a seat for Greenwich which he held until returned Apr. 1880 for Edinburghshire (Midlothian) and Leeds and elected to sit for the former, which he continued to represent. Retired in 1895. Died 19 May 1898.   [1895]

GLADSTONE, William Henry. 41 Berkeley Square, London. Hawarden Castle, Chester. Devonshire. Eld. s. of the Rt. Hon. William Ewart Gladstone, by Catherine, eld. d. of Sir Stephen Richard Glynne, 8th Bart. B. 1840; m. 1875, Hon. Gertrude, d. of the 12th Baron Blantyre. Educ. at Eton and at Christ Church, Oxford, where he was 1st class in classics at Moderation 1860, and 2nd class in classics 1862. Was a Lord of the Treasury from Nov. 1869-Feb. 1874. A Liberal, in favour of giving ratepayers a control over local expenditure, also of an amendment of the Land Laws, etc. Sat for Chester from July 1865-Dec. 1868, and for Whitby from that date to Apr. 1880, when he was returned for Worcestershire E. Retired 1885. Member of Flintshire County Council until his death 4 July 1891.   [1885]

GLASS, Sir R.A. A Conservative. Successfully contested Bewdley at the general election of 1868 but was later unseated on petition.

GLOVER, Edward Auchmuty. 28 Grosvenor Street West, Eaton Square, London. The Oaks, Ospringe, Kent. B. at Mount Glover, Co. Cork, the eld. s. of James Glover, Esq., by Ellen, d. of John Power, Esq., of Roskeen, Co. Cork (maternally descended from the same family as Anne Boleyn, Queen of Henry VIII). Unmarried. Educ. at Trinity Coll., Dublin, where he graduated B.A. Called to the bar in Ireland and in England, but did not practise for long. Assumed the name of

Auchmuty in compliance with a request of Sir Samuel Auchmuty, K.C.B. A Magistrate for Middlesex and the City of Westminster. A Fellow of the Royal Geographical Society and of the Society of Arts, and a member of the Middlesex Archeological Society. A Liberal, and supporter of Lord Palmerston's Government, while its foreign policy was 'temperate, dignified and conciliatory, and at the same time firm, frank and truly English.' and its domestic policy 'marked by rational and well-considered measures of Reform.' Favoured economy in the public expenditure. Unsuccessfully contested Beverley July 1852, Canterbury July 1854 and Abingdon Nov. 1854, but in the last instance did not go to poll. Elected for Beverley in Mar. 1857, but unseated 3 Aug. 1857. On 13 Apr. 1858 was sentenced to three months imprisonment for having made a false declaration as to his property. This was the last such prosecution, as the qualification was abolished in 1858. Died 17 Mar. 1862.
                    [1857 2nd ed.]

GLYN, George Carr. 1 Upper Eccleston Street, Belgrave Square, London. 7 Lombard Street, London. Stanmore Park, Stanmore, Middlesex, London. Reform, Brooks's, and City. 4th s. of Sir Richard Carr Glyn, Bart., by the only d. of John Plumptre, Esq., of Fredville, Kent, former member for Nottingham. B. in London, 1797; m. 1823, Marianne, d. of Pascoe Grenfell, Esq., MP, of Taplow House, Bucks. Was educ. at Westminster. Partner in the well-known banking firm, Glyn, Halifax and Co. A Trustee of the City Club. A Commissioner of Lieutenancy for the city of London. A Liberal, voted for the ballot, 1853; in favour of the 'entire abolition of church-rates', believing that the Church of England would be 'secure without them.' First returned for Kendal in 1847. Sat until he retired in 1868. Created 1st Baron Walverton 14 Dec. 1869. Died 24 July 1873.   [1867]

GLYN, Hon. George Grenfell. 51 Berkeley Square, London. Banstead Place, Epsom. Brooks's, Travellers' and City. B. in London 1824, the eld. s. of Lord Wolverton, by Marianne, d. of Pascoe Grenfell, Esq., of Taplow House, Buckinghamshire. M. 1848, Georgiana Maria, eld. d. of the Rev. George Tuffnell of Watlass, Bedale. Educ. at Rugby and at University Coll., Oxford. A partner in the Banking firm Glyn, Mills and Co., London. A Commissioner of Lieutenancy in London. Appointed Patronage Sec. to the Treasury, Dec. 1868 (salary £2,000). A 'decided Liberal.' Represented Shaftesbury from Apr. 1857 until he succeeded as 2nd Baron in July 1873. Died 6 Nov. 1887.   [1873]

GLYN, Hon. Sidney Carr. 6 Hyde Park Street, London. Army & Navy, and Brooks's. Seventh s. of 1st Lord Wolverton, by Marianne, d. of Pascoe Grenfell, Esq., MP, of Taplow House, Buckinghamshire. B. in London 1835; m. 1868, Fanny, d. of M. Adolphe Marescaux, of St. Omer, France. Was educ. at Harrow and at Trinity Coll., Cambridge. Entered the Rifle Brigade April 1855, served in the Crimea, became Capt. April 1863, and retired 1872. A Liberal. Sat for Shaftesbury from April 1880 until he retired in 1885. Died 26 Feb. 1916.   [1885]

GLYNNE, Sir Stephen Richard, Bart. 13 Carlton House Terrace, London. Hawarden Castle, Flintshire. Carlton. B. 1807. A Dept.-Lieut. and Custos Rot. of Flintshire. A Conservative, but in favour of free trade. Sat for Flintshire in the Parliaments of 1831, 1832, 1835 and 1837; was not returned in 1841, but succeeded on petition. Sat until he retired 1847. Died 17 June 1874.   [1847]

GODDARD, Ambrose. Fenton's Hotel, St. James Street, London. Swindon, Wilts. Pilwath, Carmarthenshire. Carlton. S. of Ambrose Goddard, Esq., who was MP for Wiltshire in six successive parliaments. B. 1779; m. 1819, d. of Sir T.B. Lethbridge,, Bart. Chairman of the Wiltshire and Berkshire Canal Company. Dept.-Lieut. of Wiltshire. A Conservative. Patron of 1 living. Returned for Cricklade in 1837. Retired 1841. Died 29 Nov. 1854.   [1838]

GODDARD, Ambrose Lethbridge. The Lawn, Swindon, Wiltshire. Carlton, and Boodles. Eld. s. of Ambrose Goddard, Esq., of Swindon, Wiltshire, by Jessie Dorothea, eld. d. of Sir Thomas Buckler Lethbridge, Bart. B. in London 1819; m. 1847, Charlotte, eld. d. of Ayshford Sanford, Esq., of Nynehead Court, Somerset. Educ. at Harrow and at St.John's Coll., Cambridge. A Magistrate for Wiltshire. Major in the Wiltshire Yeomanry Cavalry, appointed Dept.-Lieut. of Wiltshire 1852. A Conservative. Sat for Cricklade (which his father had represented from 1837-1841) from 1847 to Dec. 1868, when he was an unsuccessful candidate; re-elected Feb. 1874. Sat until he retired 1880. Died 15 Nov. 1898.   [1880]

GODERICH, Visct. 1 Carlton Gardens, London. Reform, and Brooks's. Eld. s. of the 1st Earl of Ripon, by the only d. of the 4th Earl of Buckinghamshire. B. in London, 1827; m. 1851, Henrietta Anne Theodosis, eld. d. of Capt. Henry Vyner, and grandd. of the 1st Earl de Grey. Appointed a Dept.-Lieut. of Lincolnshire in 1849. A Liberal, voted against the Chinese war; in favour

of extension of the suffrage, vote by ballot, and the abolition of church-rates. Sat for Hull from July 1852 till Mar. 1853; and for Huddersfield from Apr. 1853 to Mar. 1857; first returned for the West Riding of Yorkshire Apr. 1857 and sat until he succeeded as 3rd Earl of Ripon Nov. 1859. Under-Secretary at War, June 1859; Secretary of State for War, 1863; Secretary of State for India, 1866; Lord President of the Council, 1868-73; Viceroy of India, 1880-84; Secretary of State for Colonies, 1892; raised to Marquessate of Ripon, June 1871. Died 22 Sept. 1923.   [1858]

GODSON, Richard. 11 King's Bench Walk, London. 30 Grosvenor Place, London. Springfield Hall, Nr.Lancaster. Carlton. B. on 19 June 1797, the 5th s. of W. Godson, Esq., one of the Coroners for Worcestershire. M. 1825, Mary, the only d. of Henry Hargreaves, Esq., of Springfield Hall, Nr. Lancaster. Was a Wrangler at Cambridge. A Queen's Counsel and a Bencher of Lincoln's Inn. Author of a Practical Treatise on the law of patents for inventions, and on that of copyright. Appointed Judge Advocate of the Fleet and Counsel to the Admiralty in Feb. 1845. A 'Conservative Reformer', and in favour of free trade. Voted for the Reform Bill, the emancipation of Jews and of Negroes, but against both the admission of Dissenters to the Universities, and the Appropriation Clause. Sat for St. Alban's in 1831, and for Kidderminster in 1832, which he then unsuccessfully contested in 1835. Was again returned for Kidderminster in 1837 and sat until his death in 1849.   [1848]

GOFF, Thomas William. A Conservative. First returned for Roscommon 16 May 1859, having bought out of the army in 1858. Unseated in Mar. 1860. Died 3 June 1876.

GOLDNEY, Sir Gabriel, Bart. 27 South Street, London. Beechfield House, Nr. Chippenham. Bradenstoke Abbey, Wiltshire. Carlton, Brooks's, and Conservative. Eld. s. of Harry Goldney, Esq., by Elizabeth Reade, d. and heir of Michael Burrough, Esq., of Salisbury. B. 1813; m. 1839, Mary-Anne, only d. of R.H. Alexander, Esq., of Corsham, Wiltshire. A Magistrate and Dept.-Lieut. for Wiltshire. Patron of 1 living. A Conservative and opposed Mr. Gladstone's measures on the Irish Church 1869. Sat for Chippenham from July 1865. Sat until he retired in 1885. Sheriff of Wiltshire 1893; grand Warden of Freemasons 1887. Died 8 May 1900.   [1885]

GOLDSMID, Sir Francis Henry, Bart. St. John's Lodge, Regent's Park, London. Rendcombe Park, Cirencester. Athenaeum, and Reform. Eld s. of Sir Isaac Goldsmid, Bart., by the 2nd d. of Abraham Goldsmid, Esq., of Morden, Surrey. B. in Spital Square 1808; m. 1839 d. of Moses Asher Goldsmid, Esq., of Gloucester Place. Was called to the bar at Lincoln's Inn 1833; made a Queen's Counsel 1858. Was a Dept-Lieut. and a Magistrate for Berkshire. A Liberal, and opposed to all religious endowments. Unsuccessfully contested Yarmouth July 1847. Sat for Reading from Jan. 1860. MP until his death 2 May 1878. [1878]

GOLDSMID, Frederick David. 20 Portman Square, London. Somerhill, Tunbridge, Kent. Reform. 4th s. of Sir Isaac Lyon Goldsmid, Bart., by Isabel, d. of Abraham Goldsmid, Esq., of Morden, Surrey. B. in London 1812; m. 1834, Caroline, only d. of Philip Samuel, Esq., of Bedford Place, Russell Square, London. Educ. at University Coll., London. A Magistrate for Kent. A Liberal, and a supporter of Lord Palmerston; considered 'the victories already gained by religious liberty are but the heralds of those remaining to be won.' Unsuccessfully contested Brighton 16 July 1860. First elected for Honiton July 1865. MP until his death 18 Mar. 1866. [1865]

GOLDSMID, Sir Julian. Continued in House after 1885: full entry in Volume II.

GOOCH, Sir Daniel, Bart. See page 424 for the full entry.

GOOCH, Sir Edward Sherlock, Bart. Beacon Hill, Suffolk. Boodle's, and Carlton. B. at Holbecks, Suffolk 1802, the eld. s. of Sir T.S.Gooch, 5th Bart., by the d. of Abraham Whitaker, Esq., of Lyster House, Herefordshire. M. 1st, 1828, 2nd d. of Sir George Beeston Prestcott, Bart. (she died 1838); 2ndly, 1839, Harriet, 3rd d. of James Joseph Hope Vere of Craigie Hall, Linlithgowshire. Educ. at Westminster. Obtained a Commission in the 14th Light Dragoons in 1819, but sold out as Capt. in 1837. A J.P. and Dept.-Lieut. of Suffolk. A Conservative, pledged to oppose the endowment of the Roman Catholic Clergy. Sat for East Suffolk from Feb. 1846, until he died 9 Nov. 1856. [1856]

GOODMAN, Sir George. Leeds. Unmarried. A Woolstapler in Leeds. Was the first Mayor of Leeds, and four times successively elected to that office; knighted in 1852, after his fourth mayoralty. A Magistrate and Dept.-Lieut. for the West Riding of Yorkshire. A Liberal, in favour of an extension of the franchise; voted for the ballot, 1853. First returned for Leeds in July 1852. Retired in 1857. Died 13 Oct. 1859. [1857]

GOODRICKE, Sir Francis Lyttelton Holyoake, Bart. 19 Arlington Street, London. Studley Castle, Warwickshire. Eld. s. of Francis Holyoake, Esq., of Tettenham Hall, Staffordshire. B. 1797; m. 1827, Elizabeth Martha, d. of George Payne, Esq., of Sulby Hall, Wellford. Assumed the name of Goodricke in 1833, on the late Sir Harry Goodricke (to whom he was not related) bequeathing to him a large portion of his estates. Created a Bart. in 1835. A Conservative. Was returned for the bor. of Stafford at the 1835 gen. election; but in May, 1835, accepted the Chiltern Hundreds, in order to sit for South Staffordshire, on the elevation of Mr. Littleton to the peerage. Patron of 1 living. Retired in 1837. Died 29 Dec. 1865. [1837]

GOODSON, James. 22 Kensington Gardens Square, London. Carlton, and Junior Carlton. S. of Thomas Goodson, Esq. Was called to the bar at Gray's Inn 1855. Chairman of the Great Eastern Railway Company, a Magistrate for Middlesex and Westminster, and a Dept.-Lieut. of Norfolk. A Conservative. First elected for Yarmouth July 1865 but on petition the election was declared void and a new writ suspended. Yarmouth was disfranchised in 1868. [1868]

GOOLD, Wyndham. 21 Bury Street, London. 21 Merrion Square, North Dublin, Carlton. 3rd s. of Thomas Goold, Esq., Master in Chancery (Ireland). Unmarried. Educ. at Westminster School and at the University of Dublin, where he obtained honours in classics. Called to the Irish bar, 1837. A Liberal, was 'prepared to support such measures as will secure to the tenant an ample compensation for all useful and permanent improvements.' First returned for the Co. of Limerick Dec. 1850. MP until his death 27 Nov. 1854. [1854]

GORDON, Hon. Sir Alexander Hamilton. K.C.B. 50 Queen's Gate Gardens, South Kensington, London. 2nd s. of the 4th Earl of Aberdeen, by his 2nd wife Harriet, 2nd d. of Hon. John Douglas. B. 1817; m. 1852, Caroline Emilia Mary, eld. d. of Sir J.P. Herschel, Bart. (appointed a bedchamber woman to the Queen 1855). Educ. at Trinity Coll., Cambridge. Was a précis writer in the Foreign Office from 1843 to 1845. Equerry to the Prince Consort from 1846 to 1854, when he became an extra equerry. Appointed hon. equerry to the Queen 1862. Became Capt. and Lieut. Col. Grenadier Guards 1849, Col. in the army 1855, and distinguished himself at the battle of the Alma. Received the Medjidie and the legion of honour. Was Dept.- Quartermaster at the Horse Guards, from 1855 to 1860. Appointed to command the camp at Colchester in 1860; to the command of a division in India 1861, and to the command of the eastern district of England, Jan. 1872, but vacated the appointment on his promotion to Lieut.Gen. in the army the same year. Appointed Col. 100th Foot July 1872. A Liberal, was formerly ranked as a Conservative. Sat for E. Aberdeenshire from Dec. 1875. Sat until he retired in 1885. Died 18 May 1890. [1885]

GORDON, Hon. Arthur Hamilton-. Argyll House, Argyll Street, London. 4th s. of 4th Earl of Aberdeen, by his 2nd wife, Harriet, sister of the 18th Earl of Morton, and widow of James Visct. Hamilton. B. at Argyll House, 1829. Educ. at Trinitiy Coll., Cambridge, where he graduated M.A. 1850. A Liberal, in favour of a large increase for the suffrage, and vote by ballot. First elected for Beverley, July 1854. Retired in 1857. Unsuccessfully contested Liskeard 27 Mar. 1857 and Aberdeenshire 13 Feb. 1861. Died 15 Jan. 1864. [1857]

GORDON, Charles William. 26 Pall Mall, London. Carlton. 3rd s. of Charles Gordon, Esq., of Fyvie Castle, Aberdeenshire (who was cousin of the 4th Earl of Aberdeen), by Elizabeth, widow of William Clutton, Esq. B. 1817. Unmarried. Formerly Capt. Madras Light Cavalry in the E.I. Co's Service. A Conservative, and a supporter of Lord Derby. First returned for Berwick, May 1859, having been an unsuccessful candidate there Mar. 1857. MP until his death 15 June 1863. [1863]

GORDON, Lord Douglas William Cope. Guards'. 3rd s. of the 10th Marq. of Huntly, by his 2nd wife, Mary Antoinetta, only d. of the Rev. P. William Pegus. B. 1851. Appointed Ensign and Lieut. Goldstream Guards Oct. 1871. Lieut. and Capt. May 1874. A Liberal, in favour of the re-arrangement of local taxation and highway administration, and the lowering of the county franchise. Sat for W. Aberdeenshire from May 1876 to Apr. 1880, when he was elected for Huntingdonshire. Sat until he retired in 1885. Died 4 Aug. 1888. [1885]

GORDON, Rt. Hon. Edward Strathearn. 2 Randolt Court, Edinburgh. Carlton. S. of Maj. John Gordon, 2nd Queen's Royal Regiment, by Katherine, d. of Alexander Smith Esq. B. at Inverness 1814; m. 1845, Agnes, only d. of John McInnes, Esq. of Auchennock. Educ. at Inverness Royal Academy, and at Edinburgh University. Called to the bar in Scotland 1835. Was Sheriff of Perthshire from 1858-July 1866. Was Solicitor Gen. for Scotland from 1866-Mar. 1867. Lord Advocate of Scotland from 1867-Dec. 1868; re-ap-

pointed Feb. 1874. Elected Dean of the Faculty of Advocates in Scotland Nov. 1869. A Queen's Counsel, LL.D. of Edinburgh, and as Chancellor's Assessor was a member of the Court of that University. Lieut.-Col. Queen's City of Edinburgh Rifle Volunteer Brigade. A Conservative. Sat for Thetford from Dec. 1867 till its disenfranchisement in Dec. 1868; sat for the Glasgow and Aberdeen Universities (for which he was an unsuccessful candidate Dec. 1868) from Nov. 1869 until created Lord Gordon of Drumearn, a Lord of Appeal, Oct. 1876. Died 21 Aug. 1879. [1876]

GORDON, Lachlan Duff-. See DUFF, Lachlan Duff Gordon-.

GORDON, Robert. 29 Dover Street, London. Kemble House, Gloucestershire. Lewston House, Dorset. Reform. S. of William Gordon, Esq., a Merchant of Bristol; m. d. of C. Westley Coxe, Esq. A Commissioner of the Board of Control from 1832-Nov. 1834, with a salary of £1,200 per annum, paid by the East India Company. Sec. to the Board from Apr. 1835 (salary £1,500). Patron of 1 living. A Metropolitan Lunacy Commissioner; a W. India Proprietor. Chairman of the Commission of inquiry into the fees in public offices. Sat for Windsor from 1807. Sat for Wareham 1812- 18; for Cricklade 1818-37; for Windsor from 1837. Retired 1841. Died 16 May 1864. [1838]

GORDON, Hon. William. Argyll House, Argyll Street, London. Haddo House, Aberdeenshire. Carlton. B. 1785, the 2nd s. of Lord Haddo (who was eld. s. of 3rd Earl of Aberdeen), by Charlotte, youngest d. of William Baird, Esq., of Newbyth, Co. Haddington. Became Rear-Admiral of the Red 1851. A Lord of the Admiralty Sept. 1841-Feb. 1846, and Commander in Chief at the Nore 1 July 1854-1 July 1857. A Conservative, voted for agricultural protection 1846. Sat for Aberdeenshire from 1820 to 1854, when he accepted Chiltern Hundreds. Died 3 Feb. 1858. [1854]

GORDON, William. 11 Leinster Gardens, London. Carlton, and Junior Carlton. Youngest s. of Alexander Gordon, Esq., of Wandsworth Common, by Harriet d. of Hastings Elwin, Esq., of Bath. B. in London 1818; m. 1852, Frances, 2nd d. of John Hey Puget, Esq., of Totteridge Park, Hertfordshire. Practised as a Solicitor in London for many years. A Conservative, and said he would 'steadfastly oppose every attempt to disestablish or disendow the Church of England.' Sat for Chelsea from Feb. 1874 until he retired 1880. Unsuccessfully contested Dumfries Apr.

1880. Died 9 June 1894. [1880]

GORDON-HALLYBURTON, Lord J.F. See HALLYBURTON, Lord J.F. Gordon-.

GORE, John Ralph Ormsby. Porkington, Oswestry, Salop. Carlton, and Junior Carlton. Eld. s. of William Ormsby-Gore, Esq. of Porkington, Shropshire, (many years MP for N. Shropshire), by Mary Jane, only d. and heir of Owen Ormsby, Esq., of Willowbrook, Co. Sligo, 1816; m. 1844, Sarah, youngest d. of Sir John T. Tynell, Bart. A Dept.-Lieut. of Shropshire. Had been a groom in waiting to the Queen. A Conservative. Sat for Carnarvonshire from July 1837 till July 1841. Elected for N. Shropshire May 1859, and sat until created 1st baron Harlech 14 Jan. 1876. Died 15 June 1876. [1875]

GORE, Montagu. 39 Mount Street, Grosvenor Square, London. Barrow Court, Somerset. Tilset, Wiltshire. Carlton, and Arthur's. B. 1811, one of the family of the Gores of Barrow Court. Author of an *Essay on the Corn Laws, Letter to the Duke of Wellington on the present Crisis, Remarks on Foreign Policy*, etc. A Conservative, but favoured free trade. Sat for Devizes 1833, 1834 and 1839. Sat for Barnstaple from 1841. Accepted Chiltern Hundreds 1847. Died 5 Oct. 1864. [1847]

GORE, Hon. Robert. 21 Wilton Crescent, London. Saunders Court, Co. Wexford. Brooks's, Travellers', Naval, and Crockford's. 4th bro. of the Earl of Arran. B. 1810. A Capt. in the navy. Declared himself to be 'a cordial supporter of the Melbourne ministry, the only government that ever endeavoured to do justice to Ireland.' Was an 'advocate for free trade and abolition of monopolies.' Insisted that 'Ireland should be placed on an equal footing with England and Scotland.' First returned for New Ross in 1841. Retired 1847. Appointed Chargé d'affaires at Montevideo 23 Oct. 1846, and at Buenos Aires from 29 Aug. 1851 until he died 4 Aug. 1854. [1847]

GORE, William Ormsby. 66 Portland Place, London. Porkington, Shropshire. Glyn, Merionethshire. Willowbrook, Co. Sligo. Carlton. S. of William Gore, Esq., B. 1779; m. 1815, Mary Jane, only d. and heiress of Owen Ormsby, Esq., of Willowbrook, in the Co. of Sligo, and Porkington, Shropshire; upon which occasion he assumed, by sign manual, the additional surname and arms of Ormsby. Patron of 1 living. A Conservative. Sat for Leitrim in the Parliament of 1806, his ancestors having represented that county for nearly a century. Sat for Carnarvon in that of 1830, but unsuccessfully contested it in 1831.

Contested Shropshire N. in 1832, but in Jan. 1835 was returned without opposition. Sat until retired in 1857. Died 1860. [1857]

GORE, William Richard Ormsby. Derrycarne, Co. Leitrim. Carlton. 2nd s. of William Ormsby-Gore, Esq., of Porkington, Shropshire, by Mary Jane, only d. and heir of Owen Ormsby, Esq., of Willowbrook, Co. Sligo. B. 1819; m. 1850 Lady Emily, 2nd d. of Admiral Sir George Francis Seymour, K.C.B. and sister of 5th Marq. of Hereford. Formerly served in the 13th Light Dragoons. Made Maj. in the army 1852, and retired. A Conservative. Sat for Sligo Co. from July 1841 to July 1852, when he was an unsuccessful candidate there. Sat for Leitrim from Apr. 1858, until he succeeded his bro. as 2nd Baron Harlech in June 1876. Died 27 June 1904. [1875]

GORE-LANGTON, William. See LANGTON, William Gore-.

GORE-LANGTON, William Henry. See LANGTON, William Henry Gore-.

GORE-LANGTON, William Henry Powell. See LANGTON, William Henry Powell Gore-.

GORE-LANGTON, William Stephen. See LANGTON, William Stephen Gore-.

GORING, Charles. Wiston Park, Sussex. Carlton. B.1817. A Conservative, voted for agricultural protection 1846. First returned for Shoreham in 1841. MP until his death 19 Apr. 1849. [1848]

GORING, Harry Dent. 17 New Street, Spring Gardens, London. Yapton Place, Sussex. Eld. s. of Sir Charles Forster Goring, Bart., of Highden, Sussex, who was patron of 3 livings. B. 1802; m. Augusta, d. of Lieut.-Col. Harvey, of Thorpe Lodge, Norfolk. A Trustee of the Agricultural Employment Institution. Inclined to Conservative principles, in favour of a moderate property tax, opposed to triennial Parliaments and the ballot. Sat for Shoreham from 1832 until he retired in 1841. [1841]

GORST, Sir J.E. Continued in House after 1885: full entry in Volume II.

GOSCHEN, Rt. Hon. G.J. Continued in House after 1885: full entry in Volume II.

GOULBURN, Edward. 3 Serjeant's Inn, London. 21 Park Street, London. Carlton. Bro. of the Rt. Hon. Henry Goulburn. B. 1787; m. 1st,

1825, Esther, 2nd d. of Richard, 5th Visct. Chetwynd (dead), 2ndly, 1831, Catherine, d. of Matthew, 4th Lord Rokeby. A Serjeant at Law; was a Welsh Judge, and Commissioner of Bankrupts; was Recorder of Leicester, but resigned the situation on his election. A Conservative. In 1832, he unsuccessfully contested Ipswich. Sat for Leicester from 1835. Defeated in 1837. Commissioner of Court of Bankruptcy 21 Oct. 1842 to 1868. Died 24 Aug. 1868.   [1837]

GOULBURN, Rt. Hon. Henry. 18 Montagu Square, London. Beechworth House, Surrey. Carlton, and United University. B. in Marylebone 1784, the s. of Munbee Goulburn, Esq. of Portland Place, and the Hon. Susan, sister of Visct. Chetwynd. M. 1811, Hon. Jane, 3rd d. of 4th Lord Rokeby. Educ. at Trinity Coll., Cambridge, where he graduated M.A. 1808. Was created D.C.L. at Oxford 1834. A West India Proprietor. Was Under-Sec. for the Home Dept. Feb. 1810-Aug. 1812 and Dec. 1834-Apr. 1835; for the Colonies from 1812- 21; Sec. for Ireland from Dec. 1821-28; Chancellor of the Exchequer from 1828-1830 and from 1841-46. In 1839 was proposed for the office of Speaker and had 299 votes. Appointed Church Estates Commissioner in 1850 with a salary of £1,000. A Conservative, but favoured free trade. 'Strenuously resisted all encroachments on the authority and rights of the established Church.' Sat for St. Germains, West Looe and other boroughs until 1826, when he sat for Armagh until 1831. Was then in 1831 elected for Cambridge University, which he had previously unsuccessfully contested in 1826. In 1831, Lord Palmerston and Lord Cavendish having voted for Reform, he and Mr. Yates Peel succeeded in ousting them. Sat for the University from 1831 until he died 10 Jan. 1856.   [1855]

GOULDING, William. Summerhill House, Cork. Carlton, and Junior Carlton. Eld. s. of Joshua Goulding, Esq., of Birr, Ireland, by Sarah, d. of H. Manders, Esq. B. in Dublin 1817; m. 1849, d. of Isaac Smallman, Esq. Educ. at the Grammar School, Mountmellick, Queen's Co. A Merchant and Shipowner, also a Manufacturer of Chemical Manures at Cork and Dublin. A Magistrate for the borough of Cork. A Conservative. Unsuccessfully contested Cork City Feb. 1874. Sat for Cork city from May 1876. Defeated 1880. Died 8 Dec. 1884.   [1880]

GOURLEY, E.T. Continued in House after 1885: full entry in Volume II.

GOWER, Hon. Edward Frederic Leveson-. 14 South Audley Street, London. Holmbury, Dorking. Travellers', Brooks's, and Turf. 2nd surviving

s. of the 1st Earl Granville, by the 2nd d. of the 5th Duke of Devonshire. B. in London 1819; m. 1853 Lady Margaret, d. of 2nd Marq. of Northampton (she died 1858). Educ. at Christ Church, Oxford, where he graduated M.A. 1844. Called to the bar at the Inner Temple, Nov. 1845. Was a précis writer in the Foreign Office from Dec. 1851 till Feb. 1852. A Magistrate for Surrey. A Liberal, a supporter of Mr.Gladstone. Elected for Derby in May 1847; returned again for that borough in July 1847, which election, however, was declared void; sat for Stoke-upon-Trent from July 1852 till Mar. 1857, when he was an unsuccessful candidate. Sat for Bodmin from May 1859. Sat until he retired in 1885. Died 30th May, 1907.   [1885]

GOWER, Granville William Gresham Leveson-. 33 Brook Street, London. Titsey Park, Godstone, Surrey. Oxford & Cambridge. S. of William Leveson-Gower, Esq., by Emily, d. of Sir Francis Hastings Doyle, Bart. B. at Titsey Park, Godstone; m. 1861, Hon. Sophia, youngest d. of 1st Lord Leigh. Educ. at Eton and at Christ Church, Oxford, where he graduated M.A. 1862. Patron of 3 livings. A Liberal, 'a firm supporter of the Liberal party, and prepared to vote for any measure of reform which may considerably extend the electoral franchise'; in favour of the abolition of Church rates, and 'the strictest neutrality' in the American War. First elected for Reigate Feb. 1863. Returned 1865, but election declared void and Reigate disfranchised in 1867. Unsuccessfully contested Surrey E. 26 Aug. 1871.   [1865]

GOWER, Lord Ronald Charles Sutherland Leveson-. Stafford House, St. James's, London. Youngest s. of 2nd Duke of Sutherland, by Lady Harriet Elizabeth, 3rd d. of 6th Earl of Carlisle. B. 1845. A Liberal, in favour of measures of progress and improvement. Elected for Sutherlandshire May 1867. Sat until he retired 1874. Died 9 Mar. 1916.   [1873]

GRACE, Oliver Dowell John. Mantua House, Elphin, Co. Roscommon. Gracefield, Queen's Co. Brooks's. Only s. of John Grace, Esq., of Mantua, Co. Roscommon, by the 2nd d. and co-heir of Patrick Hussey, Esq., of Ardimore, Co. Kerry. Male representative of the feudal barons of Courtstown. B. at Mantua 1791; m. 1819, Frances Mary, eld. d. of Sir Richard Nagle, Bart., of Jamestown, Co. Westmeath (she died June, 1828). Was educ. at Celbridge and at Maynooth, where he obtained several premiums. A Magistrate for Roscommon, of which county he was High Sheriff in 1830. A Liberal. First returned for Roscommon Co. in 1847. Sat until he retired in 1859. Died 25 Jan. 1871.   [1858]

GRAFTON, Frederick William. Hope Hall, Pendleton, Manchester. Heysham Hall, Lancaster. Devonshire. B. at Manchester 1816, s. of Mr. Joseph Smith Grafton. M. 1850 Emily Sophia, d. of William Howard. A Merchant and calico-printer at Manchester. A Liberal. Sat for Lancashire N.E. from 1880 and was returned for the Accrington division in 1885. Retired in 1886. Died 27 Jan. 1890.   [1886]

GRAHAM, Rt. Hon. Sir James Robert George, Bart. 46 Grosvenor Place, London. Netherby, Longtown, Cumberland. Boodle's and Arthur's. Eld. s. of Sir James Graham (1st Bart.), by Lady Catherine, eld. d. of 7th Earl of Galloway. B. 1792; m. 1819, Fanny Callender, youngest d. of Jas Campbell, Esq., of Ardinglass (she died 1857). Created LL.D. at Cambridge, 1835. Was Lord Rector of the University of Glasgow, 1840. Was First Lord of the Admiralty from 1830 till 1834, when he retired on account of the extent to which it was intended to carry the Reform of the Irish Church. Was Secretary of State for the Home Department from Sept. 1841 to July 1846. First Lord of the Admiralty from Dec. 1852 till Feb. 1855. One of the Council of the Duchy of Lancaster. A Dept.-Lieut. of Hertfordshire. Patron of 2 livings. For many years ranked as a Conservative, but later inclined again towards the Liberal party. Sat for Hull from 1818 till 1820; for Carlisle from 1826 to 1829; for Cumberland E. from 1830 to 1837; for Pembroke district from 1838 till 1841; for Dorchester from 1841 till 1847; and for Ripon from 1847 till July 1852, when he was returned for Carlisle. MP until his death 25 Oct. 1861.   [1861]

GRAHAM, Lord Montagu William. Stoke Edith Park, Ledbury, Herefordshire. Carlton. Youngest s. of the 3rd Duke of Montrose, by his 2nd wife, eld. d. of 4th Duke of Manchester. B. in Grosvenor Square 1807. Became Capt. Coldstream Guards 1830, but retired from the army. A Liberal-Conservative, voted for inquiry into Maynooth 1853, and for the vote of censure on Lord Palmerston 1864; in favour of the national defences being 'kept in full efficiency.' Sat for Grantham from July 1852-Apr. 1857. Elected for Herefordshire Dec. 1858. Sat until he retired 1865. Died 21 June 1878.   [1865]

GRAHAM, William. 44 Grosvenor Place, London. Urrard, Pittochrie, Scotland. Reform and Windham. Eld. s. of William Graham, Esq., of Burnshields, by Catherine, d. of J. Swanston, Esq. B. in Glasgow 1817; m. Jane Catherine, d. of John Lowndes, Esq., of Arthurlie, Renfrewshire.

Educ. at Glasgow University. A Merchant and Partner in the firm of Messrs. W. Graham and Company. A Magistrate and Dept.-Lieut. for Lanarkshire. A Liberal, but not in favour of 'extensive change', opposed to any interference of governments with religious questions, whether as to 'endowment or State connexion.' Sat for Glasgow from July 1865 until he retired 1874. Died 16 July 1885.   [1873]

GRAHAM-MONTGOMERY, Sir Graham. See MONTGOMERY, Sir Graham Graham-.

GRANBY, Marq. of. 5 Hyde Park Gate, London. Belvoir Castle, Leicestershire. Carlton. B. in Arlington Street, London, 1815, the eld. surviving s. of the Duke of Rutland. Educ. at Trinity Coll., Cambridge, where he graduated M.A. 1835. Was a Lord of the Bedchamber to Prince Albert from Dec. 1843-Aug. 1846. A Major in the Leicestershire Militia. Appointed Lord Lieut. and Custos Rot. of Lincolnshire, 1852. A Conservative; returned for Stamford 1837-52, and sat for Leicestershire N. from 1852 until he succeeded as 6th Duke in Jan. 1857. Died 3 Mar. 1888. [1856]

GRANGER, Thomas Colpitts. 11 Crown Office Row, Temple, London. Was called to the bar at the Inner Temple in 1830, and engaged on the Northern Circuit. A Queen's Counsel. A Liberal, who said he 'most strenuously opposes any attempt that may be made, either openly or covertly, to reverse or undermine free-trade measures.' First returned Durham City in 1841, having been an unsuccessful candidate at the elections in 1835 and 1837. MP until his death 13 Aug. 1852.   [1852 2nd ed.]

GRANT, Albert, F.S.A. Roseau House, Addison Road, Kensington, London. Conservative. B. in Dublin 1830; m. 1856, Emily Isabella, d. of Skeffington Robinson, Esq., of London. Educ. in London and afterwards at Paris. A Liberal-Conservative, said he would give 'his strenuous support to a well-digested voluntary scheme of reform', but was against the ballot; in favour of the principle of 'non-intervention', but of armaments being always prepared for war, especially the navy. First elected for Kidderminster, July 1865. Retired in 1868; returned for same seat in 1874, but election declared void; contested seat again in 1880. Died 30 Aug. 1899.   [1867]

GRANT, Sir Alexander Cray, Bart. 16 Grosvenor Street, London. B. 1782. Was descended from the Grants of Dalvey. Was educated at St. John's Coll., Cambridge. Chairman of Committee of Ways and Means from 1826-32, and one of the Commissioners of the

Board of Control during the administration of Sir R. Peel. Was in Parliament during the 20 years antecedent to the Reform Act. Contested Great Grimsby in 1835 and Honiton in 1837; first returned for Cambridge in 1840. Accepted Chiltern Hundreds 1843. Member of the Board of Control for India 1834-35. Commissioner for auditing public accounts 1843 until his death 29 Nov. 1854. [1843]

GRANT, Andrew. Invermay House, Bridge of Earn, Perthshire. Reform, and Oriental. S. of the Rev. James Grant, D.D., D.C.L., Oxfordshire. B. at Leith 1830; m. 1872, eld d. of Joseph Townsend, Esq., of Glasgow. Was educ. at the High School and at the University of Edinburgh. A Fellow of the Geographical Society, and a Fellow of the University of Bombay. Was for many years an East India merchant in Bombay and Liverpool, from which business he retired in 1868. A Liberal, and in favour of the equalization of the county and borough franchise; opposed to all religious endowments by the State. Sat for the district of Leith from Jan. 1878 until he retired at 1885 gen. election. [1885]

GRANT, Rt. Hon. Charles. Glanely, Co. Inverness. 11 Great George Street, London. S. of C. Grant, Esq., once chairman of the Court of Directors, East India Company; bro. to the Rt. Hon. Robert Grant, MP for Finsbury in the Parliament of 1832, subsequently Governor of Bombay. B. 1783. Was Secretary for Ireland; was President of the Board of Control from 1830 till November 1834; a Commissioner of the Church and Corporation Land Tax; an East India proprietor. Before 1818 sat for the Inverness district of Burgus. Sat for Inverness-shire from 1818 until created Baron Glenelg 8 May 1835. Principal Secretary of State, Colonial Department, 1835-39. Died 23 Apr. 1866. [1835]

GRANT, D. Continued in House after 1885: full entry in Volume II.

GRANT, Hon. Francis William, sen. 42 Belgrave Square, London: Cullen House, Inverness-shire. Carlton, and Athenaeum. Bro. and heir presumptive to the Earl of Seafield. B. 1778; m. 1811, Mary Anne, only d. of J.C. Dunn, Esq. Lord Lieut. of Inverness-shire. Col. of the Militia of that Co., and a retired Col. of the Army. A Conservative. Sat for the counties of Elgin and Nairn from Dec. 1832 until he accepted Chiltern Hundreds 1840. Succeeded bro. as 6th Earl of Seafield 26 Oct. 1840. Representative Peer 1841-1853. Died 30 July 1853. [1839]

GRANT, Francis William, jun. Cullen House, Inverness-shire. S. of the member for Elginshire

and Nairnshire and nephew to the Earl of Seafield. B. 1814. A Conservative. MP for Inverness-shire from 12 June 1838 until his death 11 Mar. 1840. [1839]

GRANT, Sir George MacPherson, Bart. Ballindalloch Castle, Elginshire. Invereshie House, Inverness-shire. Brooks's. B. in Inverness-shire 1839, the eld. s. of Sir John MacPherson Grant, 2nd. Bart., by Marion Helen, eld. d. of Mungo Nutter Campbell, Esq., of Ballimore, Argyllshire. M. 1861, Frances Elizabeth, younger d. of Rev. Roger Pocklington, Vicar of Walesby, Nottinghamshire. Educ. at Harrow and at Christ Church, Oxford, and graduated B.A. 1861. Appointed Dept.-Lieut. of Banffshire 1860, of Inverness-shire 1861 and of Elginshire 1866. A Liberal. Unsuccessfully contested Inverness-shire 1865. Sat for the united Cos. of Nairn and Elgin from Sept. 1879-1886, when he was defeated, standing as a Liberal-Unionist. Died 5 Dec. 1907. [1866]

GRANT, Hon. James Ogilvie. Invererne, Forres, Scotland. Carlton. B. 1817, the 4th s. of 6th Earl of Seafield, by his 1st wife, Mary Anne, only d. of John Charles Dunn, Esq., of Higham House, Surrey. M. 1st, 1841, Caroline Louisa, 2nd d. of Eyre Evans, Esq., of Ashill Towers, Co. Limerick (she died 1850); 2ndly, 1853, Constance Helena, 4th d. of Sir Robert Abercromby, Bart. (she died 1872). Appointed Capt. 42nd Foot 1854 and retired 1855. Became Major, Inverness Militia 1857, and was a Lieut.-Col. of Elginshire Volunteers. A Conservative, sat for Elginshire and Nairnshire from Dec. 1868 until his defeat in 1874. Succeeded nephew as 9th Earl Seafield in Mar. 1884, Baron in U.K. Peerage, June 1884. Died 3 Dec. 1888. [1873]

GRANT, Rt. Hon. Robert. 11 Great George Street, Westminster, London. Bro. of the President of the Board of Control, a Commissioner of the Board, Judge-Advocate-General, King's Serjeant in the Duchy Court of Lancaster, an East India Proprietor, and formerly a Commissioner of Bankrupt. Sat for Norwich in the Parliaments of 1830 and 1831, and previously for the Inverness district. Sat for Finsbury from 1832 until appointed Governor of Bombay June? 1834. [1833]

GRANTHAM, W. Continued in House after 1885: full entry in Volume II.

GRATTAN, Henry. Motrahy, Co. Meath. Reform. S. of the celebrated Hen. Grattan. M. d. of Dr. Harvey. Called to the Irish Bar 1810. A Repealer. Sat for the city of Dublin in 1826, hav-

ing before unsuccessfully contested it; in 1830 he was thrown out by Mr. Shaw, the Recorder of Dublin. Was unsuccessful for the Co. of Meath in 1831. Sat for it from 1832 until defeated in 1852.
[1852]

GRATTAN, James, Tinnehinch, Co. Wicklow. Reform. Eld. s. of the celebrated Henry Grattan, Esq., and bro. to the member for Meath. B. 1783. A Lieut. in the army, served at Walcheren and on the Peninsula. Was introduced to public life by the late Earl Fitzwilliam and it is chiefly through the influence of that nobleman's family, who had vast estates in Wicklow, that he was returned of Whig principles. Sat for Wicklow from 9 Feb. 1821 until defeated 1841. Died 21 Oct. 1854.
[1838]

GRAVES, Samuel Robert. 5 Cleveland Row, London. The Grange, Wavertree, Liverpool. Conservative. 2nd s. of William Graves, Esq., of New Ross, a Magistrate, by Sarah, d. of Samuel Elly, Esq., of The Walks, Co. Wexford. B. at Blackwell Lodge, Kilkenny 1818; m. 1848, Elizabeth, d. of Samuel Haughton, Esq., of Carlow. Educ. at a private school at New Ross. A Merchant and Shipowner at Liverpool. Appointed Chairman of the Liverpool Shipowners Assoc. and of the local Marine Board 1856. Member of the Royal Commission to inquire into the management of Lights, Buoys and Beacons 1858. Elected Mayor of Liverpool 1860. Author of *A Yachting Cruise in the Baltic.* A Conservative and supporter of Mr. Disraeli; said he would 'uncompromisingly oppose any attempt to diminish the influence of the church, or to weaken its connection with the State.' Unsuccessfully contested New Ross 2 Apr. 1857. First elected for Liverpool, July 1865. MP until his death 18 Jan. 1873.
[1872]

GRAVES-SAWLE, Charles Brune. See SAWLE, Charles Brune Graves-.

GRAY, E.D. Continued in House after 1885: full entry in Volume II.

GRAY, Sir John. 39 Bedford Square, London. Charleville House, Rathinnes, Nr. Dublin. Chairman of the Waterworks Committee of the city of Dublin; Proprietor and Editor of the *Freeman's Journal,* Dublin Newspaper. A Liberal of advanced views, in favour of the granting of a charter to the Roman Catholic University etc. Voted in favour of 'Home Rule' for Ireland. First elected for the city of Kilkenny, July 1865. MP until his death in 1875.
[1875]

GRAY, William. 26 Prince's Gardens, London.

Darcy Lever Hall, Bolton. Carlton, Junior United Service, and Conservative. 2nd s. of William Gray, Esq., Merchant at Bolton, by Frances, d. of Dorning Rasbotham, Esq., of Birch House, near Bolton. Grands. of John Gray, Esq., of Finedon, Northamptonshire. B. at Darcy Lever, Nr. Bolton 1814; m. 1861, Magdalene, d. of John Robin, Esq., of Grove Hill, West Kirby, Cheshire. Mayor of Bolton in 1850-1 and 1851-2. A Magistrate and Dept.-Lieut. of Lancashire, and a Magistrate for the borough of Bolton. Appointed Capt. 4th Royal Lancashire Militia 1853 and Lieut. Col. 27th Lancashire Rifle Volunteers 1861. Previously held a Commission in the 'Duke of Lancaster's Own' Yeomanry Cavalry. A 'Liberal-Conservative'. First returned for Bolton Apr. 1857. Sat until he was defeated at 1874 general election. Sheriff of Berkshire 1882. Died 6 Feb. 1895.
[1873]

GREAVES, Edward. 22 Ashley Place, London. Avonside, Barford, Warwickshire. Carlton. 2nd s. of John Greaves, Esq., of Radford Semele, Warwickshire, who was descended from the family of Greaves of Moseley, Worcestershire. B. 1803; m. 1826, Anne, d. and sole heir of John Hobbins, Esq., of Barford, and relict of Thomas Ward, Esq., of Moreton Morrell, Warwickshire (she died 1862). Was in the Commission of the Peace for Warwickshire and County Treasurer; also a Magistrate for the borough of Warwick and Mayor there 1840. Appointed a Dept.-Lieut. of Warwickshire 1852. Formerly a Banker at Warwick (head of the firm of Greaves and Greenway). A Conservative, voted against the disestablishment of the Irish Church 1869. Sat for Warwick from July 1852 to July 1865, when he was unsuccessful; re-elected Dec. 1868. Retired 1874. Died 6 July 1879.
[1873]

GREEN, E. Continued in House after 1885: full entry in Volume II.

GREENALL, Sir Gilbert. Continued in House after 1885: full entry in Volume II.

GREENALL, Peter. St. Helen's, New Brighton, Cheshire. S. of Edward Greenall, Esq., of Wilderspool. B. 1796; m. 1821, d. of William Pilkington, Esq. A Glass Manufacturer and Brewer, Director of the Union Plate Glass Company, and of the St. Helen's and Runcorn Gap Railway. Patron of 1 living. A Conservative. First returned for Wigan in 1841, having been an unsuccessful candidate at the election in 1837. MP until he died in 1845.
[1844]

GREENAWAY, Charles. Barrington Grove, Gloucestershire. Burford Priory, Oxfordshire.

Reform. The only s. and heir of G. Greenaway, Esq., of Barrington Grove, Gloucestershire. In 1813 he m. Charlotte Sophia, the youngest d. of R.H. Hirst, Esq. Was a Magistrate and Dept.-Lieut. for Gloucestershire. Of independent Whig principles and gave no pledges. Voted against the abolition of the Corn Laws. Was B.A. of Cambridge. Sat for Leominster from 1837 until he accepted Chiltern Hundreds Apr. 1845. Died 25 Nov. 1859.   [1844]

GREENE, E. Continued in House after 1885: full entry in Volume II.

GREENE, John. 4 Charles Street, St. James's, London. Greenville, Waterford, Ireland. Reform, and Army & Navy. Only s. of John Greene, Esq., of Greenville, Co. Kilkenny. Was Lieut. 7th Dragoon Guards. A Liberal, and member of the 'Repeal', and 'Old Ireland' parties. Voted against Lord Derby's Reform Bill Mar. 1859. Sat for Kilkenny Co. from 1847 to 1865, when he was defeated. Died 16 June 1883.   [1864]

GREENE, Thomas. 19 Duke Street, Westminster, London. Whittington Hall, Westmoreland. Slyne, Lancashire. United University, and Travellers'. S. of Thomas Greene, Esq., of Slyne. B. 1794; m. 1820, Henrietta, 3rd d. of the Rt. Hon. Sir Henry Russell, Bart. Was Chairman of Committees of the whole House from 1841-1847. Was a Gentleman-Commoner of Oriel Coll., Oxford, where he graduated M.A. Called to the bar at Gray's Inn 1819, but never practised. A Bencher of Gray's Inn. A Conservative, opposed to Dissenters graduating at the Universities; in favour of withdrawing from Maynooth the recent, but not the first, grant of money; brought in bills for the commutation of tithes in 1826, 1827 and 1829. Sat for Lancaster from 1824 to July 1852, when he was an unsuccessful candidate; re-elected Apr. 1853. Defeated 1857. Died 8 Aug. 1872.   [1857]

GREEN-PRICE, Sir Richard. See PRICE, Sir Richard Green-.'

GREENWOOD, John. Swarcliffe Hall, Ripley, Yorkshire. Brooks's. Eld. s. of Frederick Greenwood, Esq., of Keighley and Norton Conyers, Yorkshire, by Sarah, only d. of Samuel Staniforth, Esq., of Liverpool and Darnall. B. at Ryshworth Hall, Yorkshire 1829; m. 1852, Louisa Elizabeth, eld. d. of Nathanial C. Barnardiston, Esq., of the Ryes, Sudbury, Suffolk. Educ. at Eton and at Christ Church, Oxford, where he graduated M.A. A Magistrate and Dept.-Lieut. of the N. and W. Ridings of Yorkshire. Appointed Cap. in the Yorkshire Hussar Yeomanry Cavalry

1852. Patron of 1 living. A Liberal, and an adherent of Lord Palmerston. Voted against the ballot. A firm supporter of the Established Church, but thought it 'undesirable to maintain the compulsory exaction of Church rates.' In favour of an extended system of education for the poor, 'based upon religion'. First elected for Ripon Apr. 1857. Sat until defeated 1865. Died 21 Feb. 1874.   [1865]

GREER, Samuel Macurdy. 2 Warwick Terrace, Pimlico, London. 21 North Frederick Street, Dublin. Spring Vale, Coleraine. S. of the Rev. Thomas Greer, Presbyterian minister of Dunbar, Co. Derry, by Elizabeth, d. of Mr. Caldwell. B. at Spring Vale, near Coleraine, 1809; m. 1845, Marion Fletcher, eld. d. of James McCrone, Esq., of Rockville, Isle of Man. Educ. at Coleraine, under Rev. Dr. Bryce (later Principal of the Belfast Academy); graduated M.A. at Glasgow 1828, where he took the highest honours. Called to the bar in Ireland 1835, and went the North Western Circuit. Author of letters on the Tenant right question. A Liberal. First returned for Londonderry Co. Apr. 1857; was an unsuccessful candidate there in July 1852, and Feb. 1857. Defeated in 1859. Unsuccessfully contested Londonderry 2 Apr. 1860 and again in July 1865. Recorder of Londonderry 1870-78; County Court Judge 1878. Died 3 Nov. 1880.   [1858]

GREER, Thomas. Grove House, Regent's Park, London. Sea Park, Carrickfergus. St. Stephen's, National, Kildare Street, Dublin. S. of Alfred Greer, Esq., of Dripsey House, Co. Cork, a Magistrate for that Co., by Helena, eld. d. of Joshua Carroll, Esq., of Sydney Place, Co. Cork. B. at Sydney Place, Co. Cork 1837; m. 1864, Margaret, only d. of John Owden, Esq., of Sea Park, Carrickfergus. Educ. at a private school at Clifton. A Magistrate for the Co. of Antrim, and for Carrickfergus, of which town he was High Sheriff in 1870; also High Sheriff for the Co. of Tyrone 1876. A Conservative, he said he would support in Parliament the Harbour and other local improvements for Carrickfergus. Sat for Carrickfergus from Apr. 1880. Retired after his seat was disfranchised 1884. County Solicitor for Antrim 1900; Senator of Parliament of N. Ireland 1921. Died 19 Feb. 1928.   [1884]

GREGG, Robert Hyde. Manchester. S. of Samuel Gregg, Esq., in partnership with whom he for many years carried on business in Manchester as a Cotton-Spinner and Merchant. A Whig. Unsuccessfully contested Macclesfield in 1837, but was successful in 1839 standing for Manchester. Retired in 1841. An author. Died 21 Feb. 1875.   [1841]

GREGORY, George Burrow. The Foundling Hospital, Guilford Street, London. 1 Bedford Row, London. Boarzell, Hurst Green, Sussex. Carlton, and Oxford & Cambridge. B. 1813. Educ. at Eton and at Trinity Coll., Cambridge, where he graduated B.A. 1835, M.A. 1839. Admitted a Solicitor and Attorney 1841. A member of the firm of Messrs. Gregory and Rowcliffes. Treasurer of the Foundling Hospital. A Conservative. Sat for East Sussex from 1868 and was returned for the East Grinstead division in 1885. Sat until he retired in 1886. Died 5 Mar. 1893.
[1886]

GREGORY, Sir William Earle Welby-, Bart. Newton Hall, Folkingham, Carlton, and St. Stephen's. Eld. s. of Sir Glynne Earle Welby-Gregory, Bart. (who was MP for Grantham from 1830-57 and who assumed the name of Gregory in 1861), by Frances, youngest d. of Sir Montagu Cholmeley, Bart. B. at Rome 1829; m. 1863, Victoria Alexandrina, only d. of the Hon. Charles, and Lady Emmeline Stuart Wortley. Educ. at Eton and at Christ Church, Oxford, where he graduated 2nd class in classics 1851. Assumed by royal license the name of Gregory in addition to his patronymic in 1876. A Magistrate and Dept.-Lieut. of Lincolnshire. Appointed Lieut. in the Leicestershire Yeomanry Cavalry 1856; and Capt. Commandant of the 3rd Lincolnshire Rifle Volunteers 1860. A Conservative, 'deeply attached to the union of Church and State.' Sat for Grantham from Apr. 1857 to Apr. 1868, since when he represented S. Lincolnshire. Sat until he accepted Chiltern Hundreds Feb.1884. Died 26 Nov. 1898. [1883]

GREGORY, Rt. Hon. Sir William Henry. 19 Grosvenor Street, London. Coole Park, Gort, Ireland. Carlton. Only s. of Robert Gregory, Esq., of Coole Park, Co. Galway, by Elizabeth d. of —O'Hara, Esq. B. 1817. Educ. at Harrow and at Christ Church, Oxford. a Magistrate and Dept.-Lieut. of the Co. of Galway, of which he was High Sheriff in 1849. A 'Liberal-Conservative', voted with Lord Derby on his Reform Bill, and against Lord Russell's Reform Bill 1866; favourable to endowments in Ireland being granted to all creeds equally. Sat for Dublin City from Jan 1842 to July 1847, when he was unsuccessful. Unsuccessfully contested Dungarvan 26 Aug. 1853. First returned for Galway Co. Apr. 1857 and sat until appointed Governor of Ceylon Jan. 1872-May 1876.; K.C.M.G. Aug. 1875. Died 6 Mar. 1892. [1871]

GREGSON, Samuel. 32 Upper Harley Street, London. Moorlands, Lancaster. Overton Hall, Maplas, Cheshire. Reform, Oriental, and City. B. at Lancaster 1795; m. Ellen, d. of M. Gregson, Esq., of Overton Hall, Malpas, Cheshire (she died 1857). Formerly head of the firm of Gregson and Company, East India and China Agents, Austin Friars. A Commissioner of Lieutenancy for London; a Magistrate for Middlesex and Westminster; a Magistrate and Dept.-Lieut. for Lancashire; Director of the London Assurance Corporation, and the East and West India Dock Company; Chairman of the East India and China Association. Patron of 1 living. An 'advanced Liberal', voted for the ballot 1853, and against Church rates 1855. Unsuccessfully contested Lymington in 1837. Sat for Lancaster from July 1847 to Mar. 1848. when he was unseated on petition. Re-elected July 1852 and sat until his death 8 Feb. 1865. [1864]

GREIG, David. Perth. A Whig. Was Provost of Perth. A Watch-maker and Jeweller. Was connected with the shipping interest of the port. Sat for Perth from Aug. 1839 until July 1841. [1841]

GRENFELL, Charles Pascoe. 38 Belgrave Square, London. Taplow Court, Maidenhead. White's, Brooks's, and Travellers'. S. of Pascoe Grenfell, Esq., MP of Belgrave Square and Taplow House, Buckinghamshire. B. in London; m. 1819, Lady Georgiana Isabella, eld. d. of 2nd Earl of Sefton (she died 1826). Educ. at Harrow and at Christ Church, Oxford. A Copper Master; a Director of the Bank of England; a Commissioner of Lieutenancy for London; was Chairman of the Brighton Railway in 1846; Director of the St. Katharine's Dock Company. A Liberal, Was an unsuccessful candidate for Wigan in 1841. First returned for Preston 1847; was unsuccessful there in July 1852, but regained the seat in Mar. 1857, and sat until he retired 1865. Died 21 Mar. 1867. [1865]

GRENFELL, Charles William. 38 Belgrave Square, London. Travellers', and Brooks's. Eld. s. of Charles Pascoe Grenfell, Esq., MP for Preston, by Lady Georgiana, eld. d. of the 2nd Earl of Sefton. B. in London 1823; m. 1852, Georgiana Caroline, d. of the Rt. Hon. William S. Lascelles, and grandd. of the 6th Earl of Carlisle. Educ. at Harrow, and at Christ Church, Oxford, where he graduated B.A. 1846. Appointed Capt. of the West Middlesex Militia, 1848. A Liberal, and in favour of extension of the suffrage; voted for the ballot 1853. Sat for Sandwich from 1847 till May 1852, when he was elected for Windsor. Sat until defeated in 1859. Died 4 May 1861. [1858]

GRENFELL, Henry Riversdale. 15 St. James's Place, London. Taplow Court, Maidenhead.

167

Brooks's, and Travellers'. 2nd s. of Charles Pascoe Grenfell, Esq., by Lady Georgiana Isabella, eld. d. of 2nd Earl of Sefton. B. in London 1824. Unmarried. Educ. at Harrow and at Christ Church, Oxford. A Partner in the firm of Pascoe Grenfell and Sons, Copper Smelters and Manufacturers. Was Private Secretary to Lord Panmure during the Crimean War, and to Sir Charles Wood at the India Office. A Liberal, and in favour of extension of the suffrage, a redistribution of seats, and the ballot. Contested Chester Mar. 1857 and Lymington May 1860. First elected for Stoke-upon-Trent, Aug. 1862. Sat until he retired in 1868. Contested Lancashire S.W. Nov. 1868 and Barnstaple Apr. 1880. Governor of the Bank of England 1881. Author. Died 11 Sept. 1902.   [1867]

GRENFELL, W.H. Continued in House after 1885: full entry in Volume II.

GRENVILLE, Ralph Neville. 36 Queen Anne's Gate, Westminster, London. Butleigh Court, near Glastonbury. Carlton. Eld. s. of Hon. and Very Rev. George Neville Grenville, Dean of Windsor, by Lady Charlotte, 2nd d. of 3rd Earl of Dartmouth. B. at Hawarden, 1817; m. 1845, Julia, d. of Sir Robert Frankland Russell, Bart. Educ. at Eton and at Magdalen Coll., Cambridge, where he graduated M.A. A Dept.-Lieut. of Somerset. Was a Lord of the Treasury 1846. Patron of 1 living. A Conservative. Sat for Windsor as Mr. Neville, from June 1841 to July 1847, for East Somerset from July 1865 to Dec. 1868, from which date he sat for the Mid div. of Somerset until he accepted Chiltern Hundreds 1878. Died 20 Aug. 1886.   [1877]

GRESLEY, Sir Roger, Bart. 11 Upper Grosvenor Street, London. Drakelow Hall, Lincolnshire. B. 1799; m. in 1821 Sophia Katherine, youngest d. of the Earl of Coventry. Wrote *The Life and Pontificate of Gregory VII.* A Conservative, in favour of a paper currency, properly secured, or at all events of an enlarged circulation of silver coin. Unsuccessfully contested Lichfield in 1826, Newark in 1831, and Debyshire S. in 1832. Sat for Durham in the Parliament of 1830, for New Romney in that of 1831. Was elected for Derbyshire S. in 1835. Retired in 1837. Died 1837.   [1837]

GRESLEY, Sir T. A Conservative. Returned for Derby S. in 1868. MP until his death 18 Dec. 1868.

GREVILLE, Hon. Algernon William Fulke. 14 Beaufort Gardens, London. White's, and Brooks's. Kildare Street Club, Dublin. Eld. s. of

Lord Greville, by Lady Rosa Emily, only d. of 1st Marq. of Westmeath. B. in London 1841; m. 1863 Lady Violet Beatrice, 2nd d. of 4th Duke of Montrose. Became a Lieut. 1st Life Guards Aug. 1859, Capt. July 1867. Was a Groom in Waiting to the Queen from Dec. 1868-Apr. 1872. A Liberal, First elected for Westmeath July 1865. Sat until defeated 1874. Unsuccessfully contested Perthshire 4 Feb. 1878. Died 2 Dec. 1910.   [1875]

GREVILLE, Hon. Sir Charles John, K.C.B. 15 Chesterfield Street, London. Carlton. Bro. of the Earl of Warwick; a Major-Gen. in the army, and Col. of the 98th Foot. Patron of 1 living. A Conservative. Represented Warwick from 1812 to 1831; was returned in 1832, but unseated on petition. Sat again for Warwick from 1835 until accepted Chiltern Hundreds July 1836. Died later that year.   [1836]

GREVILLE-NUGENT, Hon. A.W.F. See GREVILLE, Hon. A.W.F.

GREVILLE-NUGENT, Col. F.S. See NUGENT, Col. F.S.G-.

GREVILLE-NUGENT, Hon. George Frederick Nugent. See NUGENT, Hon. George Frederick Nugent Greville-.

GREVILLE-NUGENT, Hon Reginald James Macartney. 2 Albert Gate, Hyde Park, London. 4th s. of the 1st Lord Greville (who sat for Longford from 1852 to 1869), by Lady Rosa Emily Mary Anne, only d. of the 1st Marq. of Westmeath. B. 1848. Appointed Lieut. Coldstream Guards June 1868. A Liberal. Sat for Longford from Dec. 1869, but the election was later declared void.   [1870]

GREY, Albert Henry George. Dorchester House, Park Lane, London. Howick, Alnwick, Lesbury, Northumberland. Brooks's. Eld. s. of Gen. Hon. Charles Grey, Private Secretary to the Queen (2nd s. of 2nd Earl Grey), by Caroline, eld. d. of Sir Thomas Harvie Farquhar, Bart. B. 1851; m. 1877, Alice, 3rd d. of Robert Stayner Holford, Esq., of Westonbirt, Gloucester, and Dorchester House, Park Lane. Was educ. at Harrow, and at Trinity Coll., Cambridge; graduated B.A. and was Senior in the Law and History Tripos 1874. A Liberal. Was a candidate for S. Northumberland, Apr. 1878, when he polled the same numbers as his opponent, to whom he afterwards relinquished the seat. Sat for S. Northumberland from Apr. 1880 until defeated July 1886.   [1885]

GREY, Hon. Charles. 48 Berkeley Square, London. Sheen, Surrey. 2nd s. of Earl Grey. B. 1804. A Lieut.-Col. in the army; was private Secretary to his father, when First Lord of the Treasury. Of Whig principles. Sat for Wycombe, Chipping in the Parliament of 1831. Sat until he retired in 1837. Treasurer and Private Secretary to Prince Albert 1849-61; Private Secretary to the Queen 1866 until his death on 31 Mar. 1870.
[1837]

GREY, Sir Charles. The Oaks, Surrey. Formerly a Judge in India, was one of the Commissioners to Canada with the Earl of Gosford and Sir George Gipps. A Whig. Contested Tynemouth at the general election in 1837 with G.F. Young, Esq., whom he subsequently unseated on petition. Retired 1841. Governor of Barbados and Trinidad 1841-46; Governor of Jamaica 1846-53. Died 1 June 1865.
[1838]

GREY, Rt. Hon. Sir George, Bart. 34 Eaton Place, London. Falloden, Chathill. Reform. Nephew of 2nd Earl Grey, and s. of Sir G. Grey, Resident Commissioner of Portsmouth Dockyard, by Mary, sister of Samual Whitbread, Esq., MP. B. at Gibraltar 1799; m. 1827, Anna Sophia, eld. d. of Bishop (Ryder) of Lichfield, and niece of 1st Earl of Harrowby. Educ. at Oriel Coll., Oxford, where he was 1st class in classics 1821 and graduated M.A. 1824. Called to the bar at Lincoln's Inn 1826. Under-Sec. for the Colonies from July-Nov. 1834 and from Apr. 1835-39. Was Judge-Advocate-Gen. from 1839-June 1841, and Chancellor of the Duchy of Lancaster from June-Sept. 1841. Was Sec. of State for the Home Dept. from July 1846-Feb. 1852, and for the Colonies from June 1854-Feb. 1855, when he was again Sec. of State for the Home Dept. until Mar. 1858. Was 2nd time Chancellor of the Duchy of Lancaster from June 1859-July 1861, and a third time Sec. of State for the Home Dept. from the last date until July 1866. A Liberal. Sat for Devonport from 1832-47 and for Northumberland N. from July 1847 to July 1852, when he was an unsuccessful candidate. First returned for Morpeth Jan. 1853 without opposition, and sat until he retired 1874. Died 9 Sept. 1882. [1873]

GREY, Ralph William. 16 Carlton House Terrace, London. Chipchase Castle, Northumberland. Brooks's, and Travellers'. S. of Ralph William Grey, Esq., of Backworth House, Northumberland, by the d. of Rev. Sir Samual Clarke Jervoise, Bart. of Idsworth Park, Hampshire. B. 1819. Unmarried. Was educ. at Eton and at Trinity Coll., Cambridge, where he graduated B.A. 1840. Was Private Sec. to the late Lord Sydenham when Gov.-Gen. of Canada, sub-

sequently Private Sec. to Lord John Russell and afterwards appointed in the same capacity to Lord Palmerston. Was Sec. to the Poor Law Board from Apr. 1851-Dec.1852; re-appointed May 1856. A Dept.-Lieut. of Northumberland. A Liberal. Sat for Tynemouth from July 1847 to July 1852, when he was an unsuccessful candidate there. First elected for Liskeard Mar. 1854 and sat until appointed Commissioner of Customs in 1859. Died 1 Oct. 1869.
[1859]

GREY DE WILTON, Visct. 7 Grosvenor Square, London. White's, and Carlton. Eld. s. of Earl Wilton, by Lady Mary, 4th d. of 12th Earl of Derby. B. at Heaton House, Lancashire, 1833; m. 1858, Lady Elizabeth, eld. d. of the 2nd Earl of Craven. Educ. at Eton, and at Christ Church Coll., Oxford. Entered the 1st Life Guards 1854, became Lieut. 1856, retired Aug. 1859. Lieut.-Col. Commandant 6th Lancashire Rifle Volunteers. A Conservative, and a supporter of Lord Derby's policy. First elected for Weymouth, Apr. 1859. Defeated in 1865; returned for Bath at by-election 28 June. 1873; defeated at 1874 general election. Created Baron Grey de Radcliffe 14 Jun. 1875. Succeeded father as 3rd Earl of Wilton 7 Mar. 1882. Died 18 Jan. 1885. [1873]

GRIDLEY, Henry Gillett. 49 Wilton Crescent, Belgrave Square, London. Reform, and Oriental. B. at Norwich 1820, the only s. of Henry Gridley, Esq., by Amelia, d. of John Gillett, Esq., of Halvergale Hall, Norfolk. M. 1853, Elizabeth, youngest d. and co-heir of T.G. Adams, Esq. Was called to the bar at the Middle Temple in 1856, but never practised. A Dept.-Lieut. and Capt. 'King's Own' Light Infantry Militia. An 'Independent' Liberal, and as a sincere member of the Church of England considered that the complete abolition of Church rates was the only alternative. Also favoured the principle of 'non-intervention', and where practicable, a reduction of the public expenditure. Unsuccessfully contested Beverley in Jan. 1860. Sat for Weymouth from July 1865 until he accepted Chiltern Hundreds May 1867.
[1867]

GRIEVE, James Johnston. Levan, Gourock, Scotland. S. of Robert Grieve, Esq., a Farmer in Renfrewshire, by Margaret, his wife. B. at Kirlator, in the Parish of Killin, Perthshire, 1810; m. 1st, 1833, Mary, d. of Andrew Richardson, Esq., of Halifax, Nova Scotia; 2ndly, 1846, Annie, d. of Charles J. Hill, Esq., of Halifax, Nova Scotia. Educ. at the High School, Moffat, and at Caslaverock Academy, Dumfriesshire. A Merchant trading at Greenock and New-

169

foundland. A Liberal. Sat for Greenock from Dec. 1868 until he accepted Chiltern Hundreds Jan 1878. Died 20 Aug. 1891. [1877]

GRIFFITH, Christopher Darby. Padworth House, Reading, Berkshire. Carlton, Union, and Windham. Eld. s. of Major Gen. Darby Griffith, of Padworth House, Berkshire, by Louisa, d. of Thomas Hankey, Esq., of Fetcham Park, Surrey. M. 1855, Arabella, only d. of Edward Francis Colston, Esq., of Roundway Park, Wiltshire. Educ. at Eton, and at Christ Church, Oxford, where he graduated B.A. 1826. A Magistrate and Dept.-Lieut. of Berkshire. A Liberal-Conservative, 'not bound to the absolute support of any party or minister'; voted against Lord Palmerston on the vote of censure 1864; 'opposed to any advance in the direction of the Church of Rome, and in favour of an equitable settlement of the Church rate question.' First returned for Devizes Apr. 1857. Sat until defeated in 1868 when Devizes became a single-member seat; contested seat again in 1874. Unsuccessfully contested Berkshire 24 Feb. 1876. [1867]

GRIMSDITCH, Thomas. Park Brook, Macclesfield. A Lineal descendant of the family of Grimsditch, of Grimsditch, seated there in the reign of Henry III, and possessor, by purchase, of Grimsditch Hall, the direct male line having become extinct. B. 1786. A Solicitor of eminence in Macclesfield, the representation of which he contested in 1835, but lost his election by a small majority. A Conservative, 'opposed to the new Poor Laws, but not tied down by any pledges.' In favour of free trade. Contested Macclesfield in 1832 and 1835. First returned for Macclesfield in 1837. Sat until defeated in 1847. [1847]

GRIMSTON, Hon. Edward Harbottle. 42 Grosvenor Square, London. Carlton. 2nd s. of the 1st Earl of Verulam. B. 1812. A Conservative. Sat for St. Alban's from 1835. Accepted Chiltern Hundreds 1841. Rector of Pebmarsh, Essex, 1841 until his death on 4 May, 1881 [1840]

GRIMSTON, Visct. 42 Grosvenor Square, London. Gorhambury, Hertfordshire. Carlton. The eld. s. of the Earl of Verulam, and born in 1809. In 1844, married the d. of Major Weyland, of Wood Eaton, Oxfordshire. A Conservative. In 1830 he sat for St. Albans, in 1831 for Newport, having been unsuccessful at St. Albans. He then sat for the county of Hertford from 1832 until he succeeded as the 2nd Earl of Verulam in Nov. 1845. Died 27 July 1895. [1845]

GROGAN, Sir Edward, Bart. 1 Grosvenor Terrace, Belgrave Road, London. 10 Harcourt Street, Dublin. Carlton. eld. s. of John Grogan, Esq., Barrister-at-Law. Graduated M.A. at Trinity Coll., Dublin, where he took honours. Called to the bar in Ireland 1840. A Conservative, and 'a firm supporter of the Established Church'; voted for inquiry into Maynooth 1853. First elected for Dublin in 1841. Sat until he retired 1865. Contested Dublin University 1868. Died 26 Jan. 1891. [1865]

GRONOW, Capt. R.H. A Liberal. Sat for Stafford from Dec. 1832, but in Mar. 1833 the election was declared void and he was defeated at the next election on 6th Jan. 1835. Died 20 Nov. 1865.

GROSVENOR, Earl. (I). 15 Grosvenor Square, London. Eaton Hall, Cheshire. Eld. s. of the Marq. of Westminster. B. 1795; m. 1819, Elizabeth Mary, youngest d. of the Duke of Sutherland. Of Whig principles. Sat for the city of Chester from 1818 to 1830, when he was elected by the County for which he sat until he retired in 1835. Succeeded as 2nd Marquess in 1845. Died 31 Oct. 1869. [1833]

GROSVENOR, Earl. (II). 28 Princes Gate, London. Calveley, Tarporley, Chester. Brooks's, and Travellers'. B. at Eaton, Cheshire in 1825, the eld. s. of the Marq. of Westminster. M. 1852, Lady Constance Gertrude, youngest d. of 2nd Duke of Sutherland. Educ. at Eton and at Balliol Coll., Oxford. Appointed Capt. Cheshire Yeomanry Cavalry in 1847, Lieut.-Col. in the Queen's Rifle Volunteers in Feb. 1860, and Lieut.-Col. Commandant in the same corps, Apr. 1861. A Whig, and voted against Lord Russell's Reform Bill 1866. Sat for Chester from Jan. 1847 until he succeeded as 3rd Marq. Oct. 1869. Advanced to a Dukedom Feb. 1874. Died 22nd Dec. 1899. [1869]

GROSVENOR, Hon. Norman de L'Aigle. 107 Park Street, Grosvenor Square, London. 3rd s. of the 1st Lord Ebury, by Hon. Charlotte 2nd d. of the 1st Lord Cowley; bro. of Earl Grosvenor, who sat for Chester from Jan. 1847-Dec. 1869. B. 1845. Appointed Ensign Grenadier Guards 1863; Lieut. 1867. A Liberal, and gave a general support to a Liberal Government. Sat for Chester from Dec. 1869 until he retired 1874. Died 21 Nov. 1898. [1873]

GROSVENOR, Rt. Hon. Lord Richard de Aquila. 12 Upper Brook Street, London. Devonshire, Reform, and Brooks's. Youngest s. of the 2nd Marq. of Westminster, by Lady Elizabeth

Mary, d. of 1st Duke of Sutherland. B. at Motcombe House, Dorset, 1837; m. 1st, 1874, Hon. Beatrix, 3rd d. of 3rd Visct. de Vesci (she died 1875); 2ndly, 1879, Eleanor Frances Beatrice, d. of Robert Hamilton Stubber, Esq., of Moyne, Queen's Co. Educ. at Westminster and at Trinity Coll., Cambridge, graduated M.A. 1858. Was Vice-Chamberlain of the Queen's Household from Feb. 1872 to Feb. 1874. Appointed (patronage) Secretary to the Treasury Apr. 1880. A Liberal. Sat for Flintshire from May 1861 until he accepted Chiltern Hundreds Feb. 1886. Created Baron Stalbridge Mar. 1886. Chairman of London and North Western Railway 1891-1911. Died 18 May 1912.   [1885]

GROSVENOR, Rt. Hon. Lord Robert. 107 Park Street, Grosvenor Square, London. Moor Park, Hertfordshire. 3rd s. of the 1st Marq. of Westminster. B. at Milbank House, Westminster 1801; m. 1831, Hon. Charlotte, eld. d. of 1st Lord Cowley. Educ. at Christ Church, Oxford, where he graduated B.A. 1821. Comptroller of the Household from 1830-Nov. 1834. Treasurer of the Household from July 1846-July 1847. A Whig. Sat for Chester from 1826 to Jan. 1847, when he was first elected for Middlesex on the death of Mr. Byng. Sat until created 1st Baron Ebury 15 Sept. 1857. Founded Prayer Book Revision Society 1854. Author. Died 18 Nov. 1893.   [1857]

GROSVENOR, Hon. Robert Wellesley. 107 Park Street, London. Moor Park, Rickmansworth, Hertfordshire. Travellers', and Brooks's. B. 1834, eld. s. of Lord Ebury, by the Hon. Charlotte, eld. d. of 1st Lord Cowley. M. 1867, Hon. Emelie Beaujolais, d. of 1st Lord Annaly. Educ. at Harrow and at King's Coll., London. Entered the 1st Life Guards 1853, appointed Capt. 1859. A Liberal, sat for Westminster from July 1865 until his retirement in 1874. Succeeded as 2nd Baron of Ebury, Nov. 1893. Died 13 Nov. 1918.   [1873]

GROTE, George. 62 Threadneedle Street, London. Dulwich Wood, Surrey. Reform. Eld. s. of George Grote, Esq., a Magistrate for the counties of Kent and Oxfordshire, and Sheriff of the former in 1809. B. 1794; m. 1820, Harriet, d. of Thomas Sewin, Esq., of the Hollies, in Kent, and grand-d. of Gen. Hale of Guisborough, Yorkshire. A Banker. An E. India Proprietor. The author of publications on the Bank Charter, Greek History, Reform, etc. etc. A radical Reformer, in favour of free-trade, vote by ballot, triennial Parliaments, the repeal of the Corn Laws, removing the Bishops from the House of Lords, a reduction of expenditure down to the scale of 1792, the repeal

of the assessed taxes and the taxes on knowledge, and Church reform. Sat for the City of London from 1832 until he retired 1841. Vice-Chancellor of London University 1862. A distinguished author and historian. Died 18 June 1871. [1838]

GROVE, Sir T. F. Continued in House after 1885: full entry in Volume II.

GUERNSEY, Lord. 15 Curzon Street, London. Offchurch, Bury, Warwickshire. Eld. s. of the Earl of Aylesford. B. at Packington Hall, Coventry, 1824; m. 1846, only d. and heir of John Wrightwick Knightley, Esq., of Offchurch, Warwickshire. Appointed Major in the Warwickshire Yeomanry Cavalry, 1848. A Conservative, declared himself 'a firm upholder of the Established Church', and 'an unflinching advocate for protection of agriculture.' First returned for Warwickshire S. May 1849, without opposition, on the retirement of Mr. Evelyn J. Shirley. Retired in 1852. Succeeded father as 6th Earl Aylesford, Jan. 1859. Died 10 Jan. 1871. [1852]

GUEST, Arthur Edward. Canford Manor, Wimborne, Dorset. Boodle's. B. at Dowlais House, Merthyr Tydvil 1841, the 5th s. of Sir Josiah John Guest, 1st Bart., of Dowlais, by his 2nd wife, Lady Charlotte Elizabeth, only d. of 9th Earl of Lindsey. M. 1867, Adeline Mary, 2nd d. of D.B. Chapman, Esq., of Roehampton, Surrey. Educ. at Harrow and at Trinity Coll., Cambridge. A Magistrate and Dept.-Lieut. of Glamorgan. A Liberal-Conservative. Sat for Poole from Dec. 1868 to 1874, when he was defeated. Contested Cardiff 1880, and Southampton 23 May 1888. Director of London and South Western Railway Company 1878 until his death 17 July 1898.   [1873]

GUEST, Sir Josiah John, Bart. 8 Spring Gardens, London. Bowlais House, Glamorganshire. Canford, Dorsetshire. Athenaeum, and Reform. Only surviving s. of Thomas Guest, Esq., of Dowlais, Glamorganshire, by the d. of Thomas Philipps, Esq., of Shiffnar, Salop. B. at Dowlais, 1785; m. 1st, 1817, d. of William Ranken, Esq. (she died 1818); 2ndly, 1833, 2nd d. of the 9th Earl of Lindsey. An Ironmaster at Merthyr Tydvil. A Whig. Sat for Honiton in the Parliaments of 1826 and 1830, and for Merthyr Tydvil from 1832 until his death 26 Nov. 1852.

[1852 2nd ed.]

GUEST, Montague John. 3 Savile Row, London. Bere Regis, Wareham. Travellers', White's, and Brooks's. 3rd s. of Sir Josiah John

Guest, (1st) Bart., of Dowlais, MP for Merthyr Tydvil, by his 2nd wife, Lady Charlotte Elizabeth, only d. of the 9th Earl of Lindsey. B. at Grosvenor Square, London 1839. Was educ. at Harrow. Entered the Rifle Brigade May 1855, and retired as Lieut. 1859. A Magistrate and Dept.-Lieut. for Dorset, and Capt. Dorset Yeomanry Cavalry. A moderate Liberal, opposed to Home Rule and all 'measures tending to the severance of those ties which unite Ireland to this country.' Sat for Youghal from May 1869 to Jan. 1874, when he was an unsuccessful candidate for Wareham. Sat for Wareham from Apr. 1880 until he retired in 1885. Became a Liberal Unionist. Member of Dorset County Council. Died 9 Nov. 1909.   [1885]

GUINNESS, Sir Arthur Edward, Bart. 11 Carlton House Terrace, London. 18 Lower Leeson Street, Dublin. St. Anne's, Clontarf, Co. Dublin. Ashford, Co. Galway. Eld. s. of Sir Benjamin Lee Guinness, the 1st Bart. (who sat for Dublin from 1865 until his death 1868), by Elizabeth, d. of Edward Guinness, Esq. B. at St. Anne's, Co. Dublin 1840; m. 1871, Lady Olivia Charlotte, d. of the 3rd Earl of Bantry. Was M.A. of Trinity Coll., Dublin. Patron of 1 living. A Conservative. Sat for Dublin from May 1868 to Jan. 1869, when he was unseated on petition; re-elected Feb. 1874. Sat until he was defeated 1880.   [1880]

GUINNESS, Benjamin Lee. 27 North Street, Park Lane, London. 80 Stephen's Green, Dublin. St. Anne's, Clontarf, Co. Dublin. Ashford, Co. Galway. S. of Arthur Guiness, Esq., of Beaumont, Co. Dublin, by Anne, d. of Benjamin Lee. Esq., of Merrion, Co. Dublin. B. in Dublin, 1798; m. 1837, Elizabeth, d. of Edward Guiness, Esq. (she died 1865), the well-known Brewer, head of the firm of Arthur Guinness and Co., Dublin. Made Hon. LL.D. by the University of Dublin. Was Lord Mayor of Dublin. A Magistrate and Dept.-Lieut. for the city of Dublin, and an Ecclesiastical Commissioner for Ireland. Patron of 1 living. A Liberal-Conservative, protected the interests of the Established Church, but in favour of 'complete civil and religious liberty' for all creeds. First returned for Dublin July 1865. MP until his death on 19 May 1868.   [1867]

GUINNESS, Richard Samuel. Deepwell, Blackrock, Dublin. Carlton. Kildare Street Club, Dublin. 2nd s. of Richard Guinness, Esq., a Barrister in Ireland, by Mary, eld. d. of George Darley, Esq., of The Scalp, Co. Wicklow. B. in Dublin 1797; m. 1833, Katherine, 2nd d. of Sir Charles Jenkinson, Bart., of Hawkesbury,

Gloucestershire (formerly MP for Dover), and grand-niece to the 1st Earl of Liverpool. Educ. at Trinity Coll., Dublin, where he graduated B.A. 1818, called to the bar in Ireland 1821; an extensive Land Agent and Auditor of Estates. Head of the firm of Guinness and Company, Dublin. A Conservative, relied on Protestantism as the safeguard of the country. Sat for Kinsale from July 1847 to Mar. 1848; first elected for Barnstaple Aug. 1854, but in consequence of an informality in the return made by the Mayor to the Clerk of the Crown, he did not take his seat until Dec. following. Retired 1857. Died 28 Aug. 1857.   [1857]

GUISE, Sir Berkeley William, Bart. Higham Park, Gloucestershire. B. 14 July 1775. Of Whig principles, in favour of the immediate abolition of slavery. Sat for Gloucestershire E. from 1812. MP until his death 23 July 1834.   [1833]

GULLY, John. Ackworth Park, Yorkshire. Westminster. His father, it is said, kept a public house in a small village of Gloucestershire, and he himself originally kept a butcher's shop. Was for a time the champion of the ring, and kept a public house, (the Plough, in Carey Street), as was the practice of most successful prize-fighters. He subsequently went upon the Turf, where he made a large fortune, which was considerably increased by bequests. After having said thus much, it is but justice to record a remark made by a person competent to speak upon the subject; namely, that although our informant had heard the characters of all so connected with the Turf, more or less impugned, he had never heard a whisper against that of Gully. Principal Proprietor of the Hetton Colliery, near Sunderland. A Reformer; in favour of the ballot, and short Parliaments. Sat for Pontefract from 1832. Retired in 1837. Contested seat again in 1841. Colliery owner 1862. Died 9 Mar. 1863.   [1837]

GUNTER, R. Continued in House after 1885: full entry in Volume II.

GURDON, J. Brampton. 19 Hill Street, Berkeley Square, London. Letton, Thetford, Norfolk. Grundisburgh, Woodbridge, Suffolk. Brooks's, and Boodle's. Eld. s. of Lieut.-Col. Theophilus Thornhagh Gurdon, of Letton, Norfolk, and Grundisburgh, Suffolk, by Anne,d. of William Mellish, Esq., MP of Blyth, Nottinghamshire. Bro. of John Gurdon Rebow, Esq., formerly MP for Colchester. B. in London 1797; m. 1828, Hon. Henrietta Susannah, eld. d. of the 1st Lord Colborne. Educ. at Eton and at Cambridge. Patron of 6 livings. A Liberal, in favour of 'progressive reform', and the extension of the borough franchise to skilled mechanics. First returned for Norfolk W. in Apr. 1857. Sat until he was defeated 1865. Died 28 Apr. 1881.   [1865]

GURDON, R.T. Continued in House after 1885: full entry in Volume II.

GURNEY, John Henry. 1 Victoria Street, Westminster, London. Catton Hall, Norwich. Only s. of Joseph John Gurney, Esq., of Earlham Hall, Norwich, by Jane, only d. of John Birkbeck, Esq., of King's Lynn. B. at Earlham Hall 1819; m. 1846, Mary, only d. of Richard Hanbury Gurney, Esq., of Thickthorn, Norfolk, which marriage was dissolved 1861. A Banker at Norwich and at other towns in the Co. of Norfolk. A Magistrate for Norwich and for Norfolk. Of moderate Liberal opinions, voted in favour of Church rates 1855; in favour of a limited Parliamentary reform, and voted for Lord Derby's Reform Bill Mar. 1859, but opposed to the ballot and the grant to Maynooth; supported Lord Palmerston on the vote of censure 1864. First elected for Lynn Regis Sept. 1854, without opposition. Sat until he retired 1865. Died 21 Apr. 1890.   [1865]

GURNEY, Rt. Hon. Russell. 8 Palace Gardens, London. 1 Paper Buildings, Temple, London. Oxford & Cambridge. S. of Sir John Gurney, one of the Barons of the Exchequer, by Maria, d. of William Hawes, Esq., M.D. B. at Norwood, Surrey, 1804; m. 1852, Emelia, d. of Rev. Ellis Batten, one of the Masters of Harrow. Educ. at Trinity Coll., Cambridge. Called to the bar at the Inner Temple, 1828; made a Queen's Counsel, 1845; appointed Recorder of London 1856, and one of the Commission to inquire into the disturbances in Jamaica Jan. 1866. A Commissioner on behalf of Great Britain 'for the settlement of British and American claims under the Treaty of Washington of May 1871.' Was a Commissioner of Lieutenancy for London. A Conservative; voted against the disestablishment of the Irish Church 1869. Sat for Southampton from July 1865. MP until his death 31 May 1878.   [1878]

GURNEY, Samuel. 25 Princes Gate, London. The Culvers, Carshalton, Surrey. City. 2nd s. of Samuel Gurney, Esq., of Upton, Essex (a younger s. of the Norfolk family), by Elizabeth, d. of James Sheppard, Esq. B. at Upton, near West Ham, 1816; m. 1837, Ellen, d. of William Reynolds, Esq., of Carshalton, Surrey. Partner in the firm of Overend, Gurney and Company, Money-Dealers. A Liberal, said he would give a 'general, but independent support' to Lord Palmerston; 'a

member of the Society of Friends, and conscientiously respects the rights of conscience of all religious denominations.' First returned for Penryn and Falmouth Apr. 1857. Sat until he retired 1865. Died 4 Apr. 1882.   [1865]

GWYN, Howel. 12 St. James's Place, London. Duffryn, Neath, Glamorganshire. Carlton, and Oxford & Cambridge. S. of William Gwyn, Esq., of Neath, Glamorganshire, by his 1st wife, the eld. d. of Edward Roberts, Esq., of Barnstaple, Devon. B. at Neath, 1806; m. 1851, Ellen, only d. of John Moore, Esq., of Plymouth. Educ. at Trinity Coll., Oxford, where he graduated M.A. A Magistrate for the counties of Brecknock, Carmarthen, and Glamorgan, and a Dept.-Lieut. of the last. Was High Sheriff of Glamorganshire, in 1837-38, and for Carmarthenshire in 1838-39. Patron of 2 livings. A Conservative, in favour of a £6 rating borough franchise, and the relief of dissenters from church-rates. Sat for Penryn from July 1847 till Apr. 1857, having stood unsuccessfully in 1841. Unsuccessfully contested Barnstaple 12 June 1865. Elected for Brecknock, Sept. 1866. Unseated in 1868. Contested Brecon Co. 1875. Died 25 Jan. 1888.   [1867]

HACKBLOCK, William. The Rock. Reigate Hill, Surrey. Reform, and City. B. at Clapton 1805, the s. of William Hackblock, Esq. of Clapton, Middlesex, by Winifred, d. of John Webber, Esq. of Morton Hampstead, Devon. M.1833 Caroline Matilda, d. of William Lee, Esq., Alderman of the City of Exeter (she died 1842). Was a Merchant in the City of London, but retired in 1855. A Director of the City Bank. 'An ardent Reformer', believing that 'judicious retrenchment' may be made in public expenditure. Favoured Lord Palmerston's foreign policy. Sat for Reigate from April 1857 until his death on 2nd Jan. 1858.   [1857 2nd ed.]

HADDO, Lord. 7 Argyll Street, London. Eld. s. of the Earl of Aberdeen. B. at Stanmore Priory 1816; m.1840, Mary, 2nd d. of George Baillie, Esq., of Jerviswood. A Liberal, declared in 1857 that his votes were given 'in a Conservative spirit', and that he 'always endeavoured to preserve unimpaired the great interests of the State', in favour of a national education combining religious secular instruction; opposed to the ballot, but in favour of Parliamentary reform. First elected for Aberdeenshire, without opposition, Aug. 1854, on the retirement of his uncle, Hon. Admiral Gordon, who had represented it for 34 years. Sat for Aberdeenshire until he succeeded to the Peerage (Earl of Aberdeen) in Dec. 1860. Died 22 Mar. 1864.   [1860]

HADFIELD, George. 9 Gloucester Street, Belgrave Road, London. Victoria Park, Manchester. Reform. S. of Robert Hadfield, Esq., of Sheffield. Merchant, by Anne, d. of — Bennett, Esq. B. at Sheffield 1787; m. 1814, Lydia, d. of Samuel Pope, Esq., of Cheapside, London. Educ. at Sheffield. Admitted a Solicitor 1810 and practised in Manchester for 40 years. For many years Treasurer of the Coll. for the Education of Independent Ministers at Blackburn, later removed to Manchester. A Liberal, voted for the ballot 1853. Was one of the founders of the Anti-Corn Law League. A supporter of the peace movement, of financial and Parliamentary reform, etc., opposed to all religious endowments as well as to the union of Church and State. Was an unsuccessful candidate for Bradford in Jan. 1835. First returned for Sheffield July 1852. Sat until he retired 1874. Died 21 Apr. 1879.   [1873]

HAGGITT, Francis Richard. Belmont, Herefordshire. Conservative. S. of the Rev. Francis Haggitt, D.D., Prebendary of Durham, and Rector of Nuneham Courtenay, Oxfordshire. B. 1824. Unmarried. Was educ. at Eton, and at Balliol Coll., Oxford, where he was first class in mathematics. A Magistrate and Dept.-Lieut. of Herefordshire. 'Of Tory principles', and a strong supporter of Church and State. First returned for Herefordshire, standing as a Liberal-Conservative, in 1847 without opposition. Sat until he retired in 1852.   [1847 2nd ed.]

HALCOMB, John. Hall Stairs, Inner Temple, London. S. of the Coach Proprietor of that name. A Barrister. A Conservative. Mr. Halcomb first became known as the Anti-Catholic candidate for Dover, which place he several times unsuccessfully contested. Was returned in 1833 in the room of Mr. Poulett Thomson, who made his election to sit for Manchester. Retired in 1835. Contested Warwick 1835. Author. Died 3 Nov. 1852. [1833]

HALE, Robert Blagden. 15 Bolton Street, London. Alderley Park, Gloucestershire. Carlton and Boodle's. S. of R.H.B. Hale, Esq., by Lady Theodosia Eleanor, youngest d. of 3rd Earl of Mayo. A descendant of the celebrated Sir Matthew Hale. B. 1807; m. 1832, Anne Jane, eld. d. of G.P. Holford, Esq. Educ. at Corpus Christi Coll., Oxford, where he graduated B.A. 1829. A Conservative, was 'not prepared to sanction any additional grant of public money to the Church of Rome'. Patron of 1 living. First elected for Gloucestershire W. in Jan. 1836. Sat until he retired 1857. Sheriff of Gloucester 1870. Died 22 July 1883.   [1857]

HALFORD, Sir Henry, Bart. 1 Cambridge Terrace, Regent's Park, London. Newton Harcourt, Leicestershire. Carlton. S. of Sir H. Halford, Bart., of Wistow Hall, Co. of Leicester (formerly known as Dr. Vaughan, the favourite physician of George IV). B. in London 1798; m. 1824, his cousin, Barbara, 2nd d. of Mr. Justice Vaughan. A Conservative, voted for inquiry into Maynooth 1853. Patron of 2 livings. Sat for Leicestershire S. from 1832 until he retired 1857. His researches in French Revolutionary History were not published. Died 22 May 1868. [1857]

HALIBURTON, Thomas Chandler. Gordon House, Isleworth, Middlesex. Athenaeum. S. of the Hon. Mr. Justice Haliburton, of Nova Scotia, by Lucy, d. of Maj. Grant. B. at Windsor, Nova Scotia 1796; m. 1st, Louisa, d. of Capt. Neville, of 19th Light Dragoons; 2ndly, Sarah Harriet, d. of William Mostyn Owen, Esq., of Woodhouse, Shropshire, and widow of Edward Hosier Williams, Esq., of Eaton Mascott, Shrewsbury. Educ. at King's Coll., Windsor, Nova Scotia; received the honorary degree of D.C.L. at Oxford 1858. Appointed Chief Justice of the Common Pleas in Nova Scotia in 1829; Judge of the Supreme Court 1840. Author of *History of Nova Scotia, Sam Slick the Clock-maker, Letter Bag of the Great Western,* etc. 'Of Conservative principles, which will be found in practice to combine security with progress', said he would support Lord Derby's policy. First elected for Launceston May 1859. Sat until he retired 1865. Died 27 Aug. 1865.   [1865]

HALL, A.W. Continued in House after 1885: full entry in Volume II.

HALL, Rt. Hon. Sir Benjamin, Bart. 9 Stanhope Street, London. Llanover, Abergavenny, Abercarn, Newport, South Wales. Brooks's, and Arthur's. Eld. s. of Benjamin Hall, Esq., of Hensal Castle, Glamorganshire, and Abercarn, Monmouthshire (some time MP for Glamorganshire). B. 1802; m. 1823, Augusta, d. and co-heir of Benjamin Waddington, Esq., of Llanover. Was Pres. of the Board of Health from Aug. 1854 - July 1855 and First Commissioner of Works and Public Buildings from the latter date until Mar. 1858. A Liberal, in favour of the ballot, a larger and more comprehensive measure of Reform than Lord Derby's and of local self-government, as opposed to centralization; declared in 1852 that 'grants of public money must be confined to secular purposes.' Was elected for Monmouth in 1831, but on petition lost his seat. Was again returned for Monmouth in 1832 and sat for that district until 1837, when he was first returned for Marylebone. Sat until created Baron Llanover, June 1859. Died 27 Apr. 1867. [1859]

HALL, Gen. John. Carlton, and United Service. S. of John Hall, Esq., of Weston Colville, Cambridgeshire (a Dept.-Lieut. of that county), and grands. of Lieut. Gen. John Hall. Entered the army in June, 1817; became Lieut.-Col. lst Life Guards in Dec. 1837, and was Col. from 1846 till 1854, when he became a Major-Gen. in the army. A Conservative, voted against the Chinese war. First elected for Buckingham bor. in 1845, without a contest. Sat until he retired in 1859. Died 5 May 1872. [1858]

HALL, Robert. The Terrace, Dean's Yard, Westminster, London. New Court, Middle Temple, London. B. at Leeds 1801, the s. of Henry Hall, of Leeds, by Grace, eld. d. of Robert Butterfield of Halifax. M. 1829 Maria Clay, 2nd d. of Thomas Tennant of Leeds. Educ. at Heath, near Halifax, at the Leeds Grammar School, and at Christchurch, Oxford, where he graduated B.A. (lst class in classics and 2nd class in mathematics) 1823, and M.A. 1826. Called to the bar at Lincoln's Inn 1828, and went the Northern Circuit. Author of *Mettray*, a lecture, *Visits to Continental Reformatories*, a lecture etc. Appointed Recorder of Doncaster 1845, was Assistant Barrister at Leeds 1842-January 1857, and Lecturer on Common Law at the Inner Temple 1848-52. Patron of 1 living. A Conservative, 'firmly attached to the Church' and 'friend of civil and religious liberty'. Favoured education 'based on religion', and 'adjustment' of direct and indirect taxation, but considered income-tax a 'regular source of national revenue'. Supported the admission of Jews to Parliament. Sat for Leeds from April 1857 until his death on 25th May, 1857. [1857 2nd ed.]

HALLEWELL, Edmund Gilling. 6 Royal Crescent, Cheltenham, Gloucestershire. 2nd s. of the Rev. John Hallewell, B.D., of Farnham, Yorkshire. B. at Boroughbridge, Yorkshire, 1796; m. 1821, Martha, sole d. and heir of Joseph Watts, Esq., of Stratford House, near Stroud, Gloucestershire. Educ. at the Grammar School, Ripon. A Magistrate for Gloucestershire. A Conservative, and formerly opposed to the Reform Bill as being 'too sweeping', supported 'reciprocated free trade under careful revision' and thought 'that revealed truth should be the basis of every system of national education.' Published a long series of letters on various questions of social and political economy in the *Gloucestershire Chronicle* and other newspapers, under the signature of 'A True Conservative'. First

returned for Newry, where he possessed property, June 1851, without opposition. Defeated in 1852. Unsuccessfully contested Cheltenham 8 May 1856. Died 5 Nov. 1881. [1852]

HALLYBURTON, Lord Douglas Gordon. Pitcur, Forfarshire. Reform. S. of the 4th Earl of Aboyne, by his 2nd wife, Mary, d. of the 14th Earl of Morton. Half-bro. of the Marq. of Huntley; took the name of Hallyburton upon succeeding to the extensive possessions of his maternal ancestors, the Hallyburtons of Pitcur, at the decease of his cousin, the Hon. Hamilton Douglas Hallyburton, in 1784. B. 1777; m. in 1807, Louisa, only d. of Sir Edward Leslie, Bart., of Tarbut, Tralee. Obtained by royal licence precedency as the younger s. of a Marq. on the accession of his bro. to the Marquisate of Huntley. A Director of the National Bank of Scotland. Of Whig principles. Sat for Forfarshire from 1831. Sat until he retired in 1841. Died late Dec. 1841. [1840]

HALLYBURTON, Lord John Frederick Gordon, G.C.H. Kensington Palace, London. Reform. S. of the 9th Marq. of Huntly, by the 2nd d. of Sir Charles Cope, Bart. B. 1799; m. 1836, sister of the 1st Earl of Munster, and relict of the Hon. J. Kennedy Erskine. Assumed the name of Hallyburton in 1843. Capt R.N. Became Dept.-Lieut. of Forfar 1847. A Liberal. First returned for Forfarshire in 1841. Sat until he retired in 1852. Died 29 Sept. 1878. [1852]

HALSE, James. St. Ives, Cornwall. Wyndham, and Carlton. B. 1776. Descended from the historian of Cornwall of the same name. M. 1810, Mary, only d. of Thomas Hickens, Esq. Was called to the bar, an owner of mines in the neighbourhood of St. Ives, raised a regiment of volunteers during the war which he commanded. A Conservative, with exception of the Parliament of 1830. Sat for St. Ives from 1826. MP until his death 1838. [1838]

HALSEY, T.F. Continued in House after 1885: full entry in Volume II.

HALSEY, Thomas Phimer. 10 Albany, London. Gaddesden Park, Hertfordshire. The Hall, Great Berkhampstead. B. 1815, the eld. s. of Sir Joseph Thompson Whately, who on his marriage with Sarah, sole heir of the Halseys of Great Gaddesden, assumed that name. Nephew to the Archbishop (Whately) of Dublin. M. 1839, Frederica, d. of Lieut.-Col. Frederic Johnstone of Hilton. A Magistrate for Hertfordshire and a Major of the South Hertfordshire Yeomanry Cavalry. A Conservative, voted for agricultural protection 1846, and opposed to the Maynooth Grant. Sat for Hertfordshire from Jan. 1846 until his death 24 Apr. 1854.   [1854]

HAMBRO, Col. Charles Joseph Theophilus. Continued in House after 1885: full entry in Volume II.

HAMILTON, Charles John Baillie. 2nd s. of the Rev. C. Baillie Hamilton, and cousin to the Earl of Haddington. B. 1800; m. 1821, d. of the 5th Earl of Abingdon. A Conservative. First returned for Aylesbury at a by-election 31 July 1839. Sat until he retired 1847. Contested Buckinghamshire 23 Dec. 1857.   [1847]

HAMILTON, Rt. Hon. Lord Claud. 19 Eaton Square, London. Baron's Court, Newtown Stewart, Tyrone. Carlton, and Travellers'. B. in Lower Grosvenor Street, London, 1813, the s. of Visct. Hamilton and grands. of 1st Marq. of Abercorn. M. 1844, 2nd d. of Admiral the Hon. Granville Leveson Proby. Educ. at Trinity Coll., Cambridge. A Dept.-Lieut. of Tyrone. Treasurer of the Household, Mar.-Dec. 1852 and Mar. 1858-June 1859; Vice-Chamberlain July 1866-Dec. 1868. A Conservative, generally supported Disraeli's policy. Sat for Tyrone Jan. 1835 to July 1837, and May 1839 to 1874, when he was defeated. Unsuccessfully contested the same seat in 1880. Died 3 June 1884.   [1873]

HAMILTON, Lord C.J. Continued in House after 1885: full entry in Volume II.

HAMILTON, Edward William Terreck. 32 Upper Brook Street, London. Oxford & Cambridge, and Arthur's. B. in London 1809, the younger s. of the Ven. Anthony Hamilton, Archdeacon of Taunton and Rector of Loughton, Essex, by the 3rd d. of Sir Walter Farquihar, 1st Bart. Only bro. of the Bishop of Salisbury and a descendant of William Hamilton of Wishaw. M. 1844, 2nd d. of John Tacker, Esq., a Merchant in Sydney, New South Wales. Educ. at Eton and at Trinity Coll., Cambridge, where he graduated B.A. 1832, M.A. 1835, being 5th Wrangler and Fellow of his College. Read for the bar, but was not called. Was a resident of New South Wales from 1839-55. A Liberal, and in favour of the reduction of the public expenditure, the abolition of University Tests, and the removal of the Irish Church; also the reduction, with a view to the total abolition, of the Income Tax. Sat for Salisbury from July 1865 until he accepted Chiltern Hundreds July 1869. Appointed Sheriff of Berkshire 1879. Died 28 Sept. 1898.   [1869]

HAMILTON, Rt. Hon. Lord G. Continued in House after 1885: full entry in Volume II.

HAMILTON, Rt. Hon. George Alexander. 20 Chester Square, Pimlico, London. Hampton Hall, Balbriggan, Co. Dublin. Carlton, and National. Eld. s. of the Rev. George Hamilton, of Hampton Hall, and grands. of the Hon. George Hamilton, Baron of the Exchequer in Ireland. B. 1802; m. in 1835, Amelia Fancourt, d. of Joshua Uhthoff, Esq., of Bath. Was educ. at Rugby and at Trinity Coll., Oxford; graduated B.A. 1822. Was financial secretary to the Treasury from Mar. till Dec. 1852. A Conservative, in favour of 'sound scriptural education', the withdrawal of the grant to Maynooth, and the 'protection of the Established Church against spoliation'. Unsuccessfully contested the Co. of Dublin in 1826, in 1830, and in 1832, and the City of Dublin in 1835, but was seated on petition, after an investigation which lasted 14 months. Once more an unsuccessful candidate in 1837. First returned for the University of Dublin in 1842. Sat until he accepted Chiltern Hundreds Jan. 1859. Appointed Permanent Secretary of the Treasury 1859. Died 17 Sept. 1871.   [1858]

HAMILTON, Ion Trant. Hacketstown, Co. Dublin. Abbotstown, Castleknock, Ireland. Carlton Club. Sackville Street Club, Dublin. S. of James Hans Hamilton, Esq. (who represented Dublin co. from 1841 till 1863), by Caroline, d. of John Trant, Esq., of Dover. Grands. of Hans Hamilton, Esq., who sat for Dublin Co. for 30 years. B. 1839; m. 1877, Victoria Alexandrina, d. of Major-Gen. Lord Charles Wellesley. Educ. at Trinity Coll., Cambridge. A Conservative. Sat for Dublin co. from Apr. 1863 until defeated in 1885 standing in the South division of the county. Lord Lieut. of county and city of Dublin 1892. Created Baron Holmpatrick July 1897. Died 6 Mar. 1898.   [1885].

HAMILTON, James Hans. 11 Lowndes Street, London. Abbotstown and Holmpatrick, Balbriggan, Ireland. Carlton, Conservative, and Travellers'. S. of Hans Hamilton, Esq., who represented Dublin Co. for nearly 30 years. B. 1810; m. in 1833, d. of J.F. Trant, Esq. (she died Mar. 1845). Patron of 1 living. A Conservative, voted for inquiry into Maynooth 1853. Unsuccessfully contested the Co. of Dublin in 1835; sat for it from 1841 until he accepted Chiltern Hundreds Apr. 1863. Died 30 June 1863. [1863]

HAMILTON, Sir James John. B. 1 Mar. 1802. Educ. at Harrow and Christ Church, Oxford. Became 2nd Lieut. Rifle Brigade 10 July 1823. 2nd Bart. MP for Sudbury 25 July to Dec. 1837.

Contested Marylebone in 1841 and 1847. Died 12 Jan. 1876.

HAMILTON, John Glencairn Carter. 54 Eaton Place, London. Dalzell, Motherwell, Scotland. Brooks's, and Arthur's. B. at Marseilles 1829, the only surviving s. of Archibald James Hamilton, of Dalzell, by his 2nd wife, Ellinor, d. of David Hamilton of Gilkerscleugh. M. 1864 Lady Emily, youngest d. of 8th Earl of Leven and Melville (she died 1882). Educ. at Eton. Entered the 2nd Life Guards 1847, and retired as Capt. 1860. Col. of Queen's Own Glasgow Yeomanry. Made Vice-Lieut. of Lanarkshire 1865. A Liberal. Sat for Falkirk August 1857 to April 1859, and for South Lanarkshire December 1868 to Feb. 1874, when he was unsuccessful. Re-elected April 1880, but defeated 1886, standing as a Gladstonian Liberal.   [1886]

HAMILTON, Marq. of. 2 Belgrave Square, London. Baron's Court, Newtown Stewart, Ireland. Carlton, and White's. Sackville Street Club, Dublin. Eld. s. of the Duke of Abercorn, by Lady Louisa Jane, 2nd d. of 6th Duke of Bedford. B. at Brighton 1838; m. 1869, Lady Mary, d. of 1st Earl Howe. Educ. at Harrow and at Christ Church, Oxford, where he graduated B.A. 1860. Appointed a Lord of the Bedchamber to the Prince of Wales, June 1866, Ensign London Scottish Rifle Volunteers 1860. Hon. Col. Donegal Militia same year. A Conservative. Sat for Donegal from July 1860 until defeated 1880. Succeeded as 2nd Duke in 1885. Died 3 Jan. 1913.   [1880]

HAMILTON, Hon. Robert Baillie-. 21 Dover Street, London. Langton Dunse, Berwickshire. 2nd s. of the 10th Earl of Haddington. B. 1828; m. 1861, Mary Gavin, eld. d. of Sir John Pringle, Bart. Appointed Capt. 44th Foot 1855; became Maj. in the army 1861, retired 1864. A Conservative. Sat for Berwickshire from Feb. 1874 until defeated Apr. 1880. Died 5 Sept. 1891.   [1880]

HAMILTON, Maj. Walter Ferrier. 13 Royal Terrace, Edinburgh. Cairn Hill, Kilmarnock. Junior United Service. New Club, Edinburgh. Eld. s. of Col. John Ferrier Hamilton, of Cairn Hill, Ayrshire, and Westport, Linlithgowshire, by the Hon. Georgina, 2nd d. of 2nd Visct. Gort. B. at Cairn Hill 1819. Entered the army in 1837, and became Lieut. 83rd Foot. Major in Ayr Rifle Militia and a Dept.-Lieut. of Linlithgow. Aide-de-Camp to the Lord-Lieut. of Ireland. A Liberal, opposed to many of the clauses of Lord Derby's Reform Bill, but would have voted for it with a view to its amendment in committee; supported the vote of censure on Lord Palmerston

1864. First elected for Linlithgowshire May 1859. Sat until he retired 1865. Died 8 Apr. 1872.   [1865]

HAMILTON, William John. 14 Chesham Place, Belgrave Square, London. Travellers', Athenaeum, and Carlton. Eld. s. of William R. Hamilton, Esq., Minister at the Court of Naples. B. 1805; m. 1st, 1832 d. of John Trotter, Esq.; 2ndly, 1838, d. of Visct. Dillon. Formerly in the diplomatic line; called to the bar in 1840. 'A Moderate Conservative', in favour of the principle of the Corn Laws, but supported their abolition in 1846. First returned for Newport, Isle of Wight, in 1841. Sat until he retired 1847. Director of Great Indian Peninsular Railway 1849 until his death 27 June 1867.   [1847]

HAMOND, C.F. Continued in House after 1885: full entry in Volume II.

HAMPDEN, Renn. 59 St. James Street, London. Manor House, Little Marlow, Buckinghamshire. Unsuccessfully contested Lyme Regis at the general election in 1837. A Conservative. Was not returned at a general election in 1841, but in 1842 was seated for Great Marlow on petition, ousting Sir William Clayton. Sat until he retired 1847.   [1847]

HANBURY, Hon. Charles Spencer Bateman-. See LENNOX, Hon. Charles Spencer Bateman-Hanbury Kincaid-.

HANBURY, Robert Culling. 10 Upper Grosvenor Street, London. Brick Lane, Spitalfields, London. Frohsdorf, Eastbourne, Sussex. Poles, Ware, Hertfordshire. Brooks's. Eld. s. of Robert Hanbury, Esq., of Poles, Hertfordshire (High Sheriff of that Co. in 1854), by Emily, d. of William Hall, Esq. B. in London 1823; m. 1st, 1849, Caroline, eld. d. of Abel Smith, Esq., of Woodhall Park, Hertfordshire (she died 1863); 2ndly, 1865, Frances Selena, eld. d. of Sir Culling E. Eardley, Bart., of Bedwell Park, Hertfordshire. A Partner in the firm of Truman, Hanbury, Buxton, and Company, Brewers. A Liberal, said he would give Lord Palmerston a 'hearty support', in favour of extension of the franchise, the total abolition of Church rates, and a system of 'education based upon the Bible'. First returned for Middlesex, Apr. 1857. MP until his death 29 Mar. 1867. [1865 2nd ed.]

HANBURY, R.W. Continued in House after 1885: full entry in Volume II.

HANBURY-TRACY, C. See TRACY, Hon. C. Hanbury-.

HANBURY-TRACY, Hon. C.D.R. See TRACY, C.D.R. Hanbury-.

HANBURY-TRACY, Hon. C.R. See TRACY, Hon. C.R.H-.

HANBURY-TRACY, Hon. F. See TRACY, Hon. F.H-. Continued in House after 1885: full entry in Volume II.

HANDCOCK, Hon. Henry. Moydrum Castle, Athlone. Army & Navy. 3rd s. of the 3rd Lord Castlemaine, by Margaret, 2nd d. of Michael Harris, Esq., of Dublin. B. at Athlone 1834. Unmarried. Educ. at Cheltenham Coll. Appointed Capt. 44th Foot 1854. A Conservative. First elected for Athlone Apr. 1856. Defeated 1857. Killed by a tiger 1 Dec. 1858.   [1857]

HANDLEY, Maj. Benjamin. United Service. Was a relation of the Member for Lincolnshire. Entertained Whig opinions, inclining to Radicalism. Was an advocate of the ballot. Returned for Boston at the Dec. 1832 election, but was defeated in 1835 and again in 1837.
                                                                    [1834]

HANDLEY, Henry. Culverthorpe Hall, Lincolnshire. Travellers', and University. Cousin of the one-time member for Boston and Newark, of the same name. B. 1797; m. 1825, Caroline, eld. d. of Lord Kensington. Patron of 1 living. A Reformer, was in favour of the Corn Laws, the repeal of the Malt Duty and assessed taxes, of property tax in lieu, and of shortening the duration of Parliaments. Sat for Heytesbury in the Parliament of 1820 and was first elected for Lincolnshire in 1832. Sat until defeated 1841. [1838]

HANDLEY, John. Wiverton Hall, Bingham, Nottinghamshire. Oxford & Cambridge. Eld. s. of John Handley, Esq., of Muskham Grange, Nottinghamshire, by Martha, 2nd d. of Philip Story, Esq., of Lockington Hall, Leicestershire. B. at Stoke, Nottinghamshire 1807. Unmarried. Educ. at Eton and at Trinity Coll., Cambridge. Called to the bar at the Inner Temple 1834. A Magistrate and Dept.-Lieut. of Nottinghamshire. Patron of 1 living. A Liberal, in favour of a considerable extension of the franchise, and a scheme of 'religious and moral education'. First elected for Newark Apr. 1857. Sat until he retired 1865. Sheriff of Nottingham 1869. Died 8 Dec. 1869.
                                                                    [1865]

HANDLEY, William Farnworth. 1 Clifford Street, London. A Banker at Newark. A Reformer, voted for the Reform Act, which he considered a final measure, but thought what had taken place throughout the Country would force the adoption of the ballot; in favour of the immediate abolition of slavery. Sat first for Newark-upon-Trent in 1831. Sat until he retired in 1835.   [1833]

HANKEY, Thomson. 59 Portland Place, London. Shipborne Grange, Tunbridge. Travellers', United, City Liberal, and Brooks's. S. of Thomas Hankey, Esq., of Portland Place, a Merchant in London, by Martha, d. of Benjamin Harrison, Esq. B. at Dalston, near London 1805; m. 1830, Miss Appolina Agatha Alexander. Was a W. India Merchant. A Director of the Bank of England, of which he was Governor from 1851-1853. A Commissioner of Lieutenancy for London. A Liberal. Unsuccessfully contested Boston July 1852 and Peterborough June 1853, but was seated for the latter by decision of a committee Aug. following, and sat until Dec. 1868 when he was unsuccessful; re-elected Feb. 1874 and sat until he was defeated 1880. Died 13 Jan. 1893.   [1880]

HANMER, Lieut.-Col. Henry, K.H. 7 Devonshire Place, London. Stockgrove, Buckinghamshire. Carlton. Uncle of Sir John Hanmer, Bart.; m. in 1815 Sarah, only d. of Sir M. Ximenes. Was a Lieut. Col. in the Royal Horse Guards; served in Spain. A Conservative. He was returned for Westbury in the Parliament of 1831, but shortly afterwards accepted the Chiltern Hundreds. Was elected for Aylesbury in 1832, in opposition to Mr. T.B. Hobhouse, half-bro. of Sir J. Hobhouse. Sat until he retired in 1837. Sheriff of Buckinghamshire 1854; Knight of Hanover 1837. Died 2 Feb. 1868.   [1837]

HANMER, Sir John, Bart. 59 Eaton Place, London. Bettisfield Park, Flintshire. Athenaeum, Travellers', and Brooks's. B. 1809; m. 1833, Georgiana, youngest d. of Sir George Chetwynd, Bart., of Grendon Hall, Warwickshire. His ancestor, Sir Thomas Hanmer, was Speaker in 1713 and represented Suffolk in 5 Parliaments. Patron of 2 livings. A Magistrate for Flintshire. Appointed Dept.-Lieut. of Flint 1852. A Liberal, voted against the ballot 1853. Sat for Shrewsbury from 1832-37, for Hull from 1841-47, and for Flint from the last date. MP until created 1st Baron Hanmer 1 Oct. 1872. Died 8 Mar. 1881. [1872]

HARCOURT, E.W.V. Continued in House after 1885: full entry in Volume II.

HARCOURT, Col. Francis Vernon. 40 Grosvenor Square, London. Buxton Park, Sussex. St. Clare, Ryde, Isle of Wight. 9th s. of the

Archbishop (Harcourt) of York, by Lady Anne, 3rd d. of the 1st Marq. of Stafford. B. at Rose Castle, near Carlisle 1801; m. 1837, Lady Catherine Julia, eld. d. of the Earl of Liverpool (extinct). Educ. at the Military Coll., Sandhurst, entered the army in 1816, and eventually became a Col., but retired from the service. A Magistrate and Dept.-Lieut. of Hampshire. Appointed Dept.-Lieut. of the Isle of Wight 1852. A Conservative, would not support the repeal of the Maynooth Grant, 'because a grant was guaranteed at the period of the Union with Ireland'. First returned for the Isle of Wight July 1852. Sat until he retired 1857. Sheriff of Sussex 1867. Died 23 Apr. 1880.   [1857]

HARCOURT, George Granville Vernon. 102 Eaton Square, London. Nuneham Courtenay, Oxford. Travellers' and Athenaeum. Eld. s. of Archbishop (Harcourt) of York, by Anne, 3rd. d. of 1st Marq. of Stafford. Cousin of Lord Vernon. B. 1785; m. 1st, 1815, Lady Elizabeth, d. of the 2nd Earl of Lucan (dead); 2ndly, 1846, Frances, Dowager Countess of Waldegrave. Educ. at Christ Church, Oxford, where he graduated B.A. 1808; M.A. 1810. A Liberal-Conservative, voted in favour of the principle of the first Reform Act, but was opposed to many of its details; voted against church-rates 1855. Sat for Lichfield from 1806 till 1830, and for Oxfordshire from 1831. MP until his death 19 Dec. 1861.   [1861]

HARCOURT, George Simon. 13 Clarges Street, London. Ankerwycke House, Buckinghamshire. Cooper's Hill, Surrey. Shoolstwode Lodge, Sussex. Senior and Junior University, and Carlton. Only s. and heir of John Simon Harcourt, Esq., of Ankerwycke, Buckinghamshire, by Elizabeth Dale Henniker, sister of Lord Henniker and of the late Lady Sykes (wife of Sir Francis Sykes, Bart.), and aunt to the member for East Suffolk. J.S. Harcourt, Esq., who sat for Westbury in 1801-2, was eld. s. of John Harcourt, Esq., of Ankerwycke, by Margaret Jane Sarney, sometime Baroness Shuldham, and afterwards Countess Clanwilliam, grands. of Philip Harcourt, Esq., of Ankerwycke, and great-grands. of Sir Philip Harcourt, of Stanton Harcourt, the father of Simon, 1st Visct. and Baron Harcourt, and Lord High Chancellor of England. George Simon Harcourt was b. 28th Feb. 1807, and m. 24 June 1833, Jessy, 2nd d. of John Rolls, Esq., of Bryanston Square, London, and the Hendrée, Monmouthshire. Was educ. at Eton, and at Christ Church, Oxford; was High Sheriff of Buckinghamshire in 1834. Was returned member for Buckinghamshire by a large majority on 13 Feb. 1837 at a by-election, and again after the dis-

solution of Parliament in the same year. Mr. Harcourt was 24th in lineal descent from Robert de Harcourt, whose bro. Angurrand de Harcourt was one of the followers of William the Conqueror in 1066. On the death, in 1830, of William, last Earl Harcourt, Mr. G.S. Harcourt became his heir male and head of the Harcourt family in England, and would have succeeded to their ancient estates, had not the entail been cut off in favour of the Vernon family, by whom, on their succession to the property, the name and arms of Harcourt were assumed by Royal licence in 1831. His political opinions were 'liberally Conservative, and he was warmly attached to the agricultural cause'. Retired in 1841. Died 24 Oct. 1871.   [1840]

HARCOURT, Rt. Hon. Sir W. Vernon. Continued in House after 1885: full entry in Volume II.

HARDCASTLE, E. Continued in House after 1885: full entry in Volume II.

HARDCASTLE, Joseph Alfred. 54 Queen's Gate Terrace, London. The Lodge, Holt, East Dereham, Norfolk. Brooks's, Reform, and Oxford & Cambridge. Eld. s. of Alfred Hardcastle, Esq., of Hatcham House, Surrey. B. 1815; m. 1st, 1840, Frances, only d. of H.W. Lambirth, Esq., (she died 1865); 2ndly, 1869, Hon. Mary Scarlett, d. of the Baroness Stratheden and Lord Campbell. Educ. at Bury School and at Trinity Coll., Cambridge, of which he was a scholar; was 1st class in classics and senior optime 1838. Was called to the bar at the Inner Temple 1841, but never practised. A Magistrate for Norfolk, Essex and Suffolk and a Dept.-Lieut. for Surrey. A Liberal. Sat for Colchester from July 1847 to July 1852, when he was an unsuccessful candidate there. Sat from Apr. 1857 to Feb. 1874 for Bury St. Edmunds, which he unsuccessfully contested Dec. 1852, and Feb. 1874; re-elected for Bury St. Edmunds Apr. 1880. Defeated 1885.   [1885]

HARDINGE, Hon. Charles Stewart. 15 Great Stanhope Street, London. South Park, Penshurst, Kent. White's, and Carlton. B. 1822, the eld. s. of Visct. Hardinge, by the d. of 1st Marq. of Londonderry. Educ. at Eton and at Christ Church, Oxford, where he was 3rd class in classics 1844. Was Private Sec. to Lord Hardinge while he was Gov.-Gen. of India from 1844-48. Appointed a Dept.-Lieut. of Kent in 1848, and Major in the Kent Militia Artillery 1853. A Conservative, but favoured an amendment in the laws affecting landlord and tenant. Voted for inquiry into Maynooth 1853. First returned for Downpatrick Aug. 1851, without opposition, and sat until he succeeded as 2nd Visct. in Sept. 1856. Died 28 July 1894. [1856]

HARDINGE, Rt. Hon. Sir Henry, K.C.B. 3 Whitehall Gardens, London. Ketton, Co. Durham. Carlton, and Athenaeum. B. 1775, the bro. of Rev. Sir Charles Hardinge, Bart., of Bellisle, Co. Fermanagh. M. 1821, Emily Jane, widow of John James, Esq., and 6th d. of 1st Marq. of Londonderry. A Commissioner of Sandhurst Coll. Served in the Peninsula and lost an arm, for which he received a pension of £300. A Lieut.-Gen. in the army, and Col. of 97th Foot. Was at Waterloo. Clerk of the Ordnance 1823-28, Sec. at War 1828-30, Sec. of Ireland 1830 until the dissolution of the Wellington Administration. Again Sec. of Ireland 1834-Apr. 1835, when he resigned. Appointed Sec. at War 1841. Sat for Durham 1826, St. Germains 1830, Newport (Cornwall) 1831 and Launceston 1832 until 6 May 1844, when he was appointed Gov.-Gen. of India, which office he held until Jan. 1848. Created Visct. Hardinge 2 May 1846, Field Marshall Oct. 1855. Died 2 Oct. 1856. [1844]

HARDY, Hon. A.E. Gathorne. Continued in House after 1885: full entry in Volume II.

HARDY, Rt. Hon. Gathorne. 17 Grosvenor Crescent, London. Hemsted, Staplehurst, Kent. Carlton, and Oxford & Cambridge. 3rd s. of John Hardy, Esq., (who represented Bradford for 10 years) by the d. of Richard Gathorne, Esq. B. at Bradford 1814; m. 1838, Jane, d. of James Orr, Esq. Educ. at Shrewsbury School and at Oriel Coll., Oxford, where he was 2nd class in classics, and graduated B.A. 1836; made Hon. D.C.L. Oxford 1866. Called to the bar at Inner Temple 1840; but ceased to practise. Was Under Secretary for the Home Dept. from Mar 1858-June 1859; Pres. of the Poor Law Board from July 1866-May 1867, and Sec. of State for the Home Dept. from the last date till Dec. 1868. Appointed Sec. of State for War Feb. 1874; also a member of the Council on Education. Became a Dept.-Lieut. of the W. Riding of Yorkshire, May 1856, for which he was also a Magistrate. A Conservative; was opposed to systems of centralization. Unsuccessfully contested Bradford, July 1847; sat for Leominster from Feb. 1856 to July 1865; when being returned both for the Univ. of Oxford and for Leominster he elected to sit for Oxford. Sat until created Visct. Cranbrook April 1878; Secretary for State for India 1878-80; Lord President of Council 1885-86 and 1886-92; took additional surname of Gathorne 1878; advanced to an earldom 1892. Died 30 Oct. 1906. [1878]

HARDY, John. (I). 3 Portland Place, London.

Low Moor, Yorkshire. Carlton. Eld. s. of John Hardy, Esq. B. 1773; m. 1804, d. of Richard Gathorne, Esq. (dead). A Barrister. Recorder of Leeds from 1806-34, which office he then resigned in order to attend to his Parliamentary duties. A Bencher of the Inner Temple. A Dept.-Lieut. and Magistrate of the West Riding of Yorkshire. Patron of 2 livings. A Conservative, 'on the principles and opinions expressed by Sir Robert Peel in his Address of 1835'. Sat for Bradford from 1832-37; defeated in 1837; returned 1841 and sat until he retired 1847. Gave £6000 for erection of Churches in Bradford in 1848. Died 29 Sept. 1855. [1847]

HARDY, John. (II). 7 Carlton House Terrace, London. Dunstall Hall, Burton-on-Trent, Staffordshire. Carlton, and Oxford & Cambridge. Eld. s. of John Hardy, Esq., by Isabella, d. of R. Gathorne, Esq. B. 1809; m. 1846, Laura, d. of William Holbech, Esq., of Farnborough, Warwickshire. Educ. at Oriel Coll., Oxford. Patron of 1 living. A Conservative, and a 'sincere supporter of those constitutional principles in Church and State, which have so long secured for us the blessings of civil and religious liberty'. Contested Plymouth Mar. 1857 and Banbury Feb. 1859. Sat for Midhurst from 3 Mar. 1859 until 30 Apr. 1859. Sat for Dartmouth from Nov. 1860-Dec. 1868, from which date he sat for Warwickshire S. Sat until he retired 1874. Created Baronet Feb. 1876. Contested Staffordshire E. Apr. 1880. Died 9 July 1888. [1873]

HARDY, Hon. J.S. Gathorne. See GATHORNE-HARDY, Hon. J.S. Continued in House after 1885: full entry in Volume II.

HARFORD, Summers. Sirhoury, Monmouthshire. Reform. S. of R.S. Harford, Esq. An Iron Master; a Magistrate of Monmouthshire; Sheriff for the year 1840-41. A Liberal. First returned for Lewes in 1841. Unseated Mar. 1842. Unsuccessfully contested Brighton 5 May 1842. Died 2 June 1873. [1842]

HARLAND, William Charles. Sutton Hall, Yorkshire. Bailey, Durham, Brookes's, Clarence, and Reform. S. of William Harland, Esq., a Bencher of Lincoln's Inn. B. 1803; m. 1827, Catherine, only d. of Robert Eden Duncombe Shafto, Esq., of Whitwork Park, Co. Durham, and of Catherine, d. of Sir John Eden, Bart., of Windlestone Hall, same Co. A cousin of Lord Auckland. A Reformer, in favour of a thorough reform of the Church, of 'an extension of civil and religious liberty to every class in the community', of the repeal of the house and window duties, and a reduction of the taxes on the necessaries and comforts of life. Opposed to the ballot and short Parliaments. Sat for the city of Durham from 1832 until he retired 1841. Died 10 Mar. 1863. [1838]

HARMAN, Col. E.R. King-. See KING-HARMAN, Col. E.R. Continued in House after 1885: full entry in Volume II.

HARRINGTON, T. Continued in House after 1885: full entry in Volume II.

HARRIS, Hon. Edward Alfred John. 8 Whitehall Gardens, London. Senior United Service. 2nd s. of the 2nd Earl of Malmesbury, and heir-presumptive to the peerage. B. in Spring Gardens, London, 1808; m. in 1841, youngest d. of Capt. Samuel Chambers, R.N. Was educ. at Eton and at the Royal Naval Coll. A Capt. in the navy, which he entered in 1821. A Conservative, but was 'unpledged'; voted for agricultural protection, 1846. First elected for Christchurch in Mar. 1844. Sat until he retired in 1852. Consul Gen. in Chile 1853-58; Minister at Berne 1858; Envoy extraord. at Amsterdam 1867-77; K.C.B. 1872. Died 17 July 1888. [1852]

HARRIS, John Dove. 130 Cambridge Street, Warwick Square, London. Ratcliffe Hall, Ratcliffe-on-Wreake, Leicester. Reform. Eld. s. of Richard Harris, Esq., who sat for Leicester from 1848-1852, by Fanny, d. of William Dove, Esq., of Moulton, Northamptonshire. B. at Leicester 1809; m. 1831, Emma, eld. d. of George Shinley, Esq., of Tamworth. A Manufacturer, and head of the firm of Harris and Sons, Leicester. A Magistrate and Dept.-Lieut. for that Co. Elected Mayor of Leicester 1850 and 1856. A Liberal, voted for the disestablishment of the Irish Church 1869. Sat for Leicester from Apr. 1857 to Apr. 1859, when he was unsuccessful; re-elected July 1865. Sat until he retired 1874. Died 20 Nov. 1878. [1873]

HARRIS, John Quincey. Winchester House, Southwark. The Parthenon, Branchley, Kent. Eld. s. of J.R. Harris, Esq., MP for Southwark. B. 1815. A Hat Manufacturer and Fur Cutter. A Reformer. First returned for Newcastle-under-Lyne in 1841. Unseated in 1842. Returned again at the subsequent by-election, but unseated once more immediately afterwards. [1842]

HARRIS, Richard. 36 Woburn Square, London. Leicester. B. at Leicester 1777. An Alderman and Justice of the Peace for Leicester; elected Mayor of Leicester 1844-45. 'A Liberal Whig'. First returned for Leicester Aug. 1848. Sat until he

retired in 1852. Died 2 Feb. 1854. [1852]

HARRIS, William James. Halwill Manor, Highhampton, Devon. 75 Linden Gardens, London. Carlton, and City Carlton. S. of E. Harris, Esq., of London, by Isabella, d. of John Tindall, Esq., of Knapton Hall, Yorkshire. B. 1835; m. 1858, Catherine, d. of R.I. Thornhill, Esq., of Clapton, Middlesex. A merchant in London, and a J.P. for Devon. Author of *Protection from the Workman's Point of View,* and other fiscal treatises. A Liberal-Conservative. Elected for Poole in April 1884. Defeated in 1885 standing for mid-Devon after disfranchising of Poole. Died 29 Oct. 1911. [1885]

HARRISON, Charles. Areley Court, Stourport, Worcestershire. National. Youngest s. of Benjamin Harrison, Esq., of Liverpool, by Hannah, d. of William King, Esq., of Stourbridge. B. in Liverpool 1830; m. 1858, Elizabeth Augusta, d. of Samuel Kempson, Esq., of Birmingham. A Magistrate for Worcestershire. A Liberal, in favour of the reduction of the national expenditure. Sat for Bewdley from Feb. 1874 until unseated June 1880. Died 11 May 1888. [1880]

HARRISON, James Fortescue. 88 Cornwall Gardens, London. Crawley Down Park, Sussex. Reform. S. of Henry Fortescue Harrison, Esq., by his m. with Miss Elizabeth Pepper. B. 1819; m. 1837, Anne, d. of William Humphries, Esq., of Oxford. Called to the bar at Lincoln's Inn June 1864, and was a member of the Home Circuit. A Magistrate for Surrey. 'A thorough Liberal', in favour of the abolition of the Game Laws, the repeal of the law of Hypothec, and of tenant-farmers being secured the full value of their improvements; opposed to all State endowments for religious purposes and to the law of primogeniture and entail. Sat for the district of Kilmarnock from Feb. 1874 until he retired 1880. [1880]

HARTINGTON, Marq. of. Continued in House after 1885: full entry in Volume II.

HARTLAND, F.D. Dixon. See DIXON-HARTLAND, F.D.

HARTLEY, James. 13 Chatham Place, Blackfriars, London. High Barnes, Sunderland. Junior Carlton. S. of James Hartley, Esq., Glass Manufacturer of West Bromwich, by Margaret, his wife. B. in Dumbarton, Scotland, 1811; m. 1837, Annie, only d. of Thomas Blenkinsop, Esq., of Felling. Educ. at private schools at Banwell and Bristol. A Glass Manufacturer, and established

181

the Wear Glass Works, Sunderland. A Magistrate for the co. of Durham, also for Sunderland; Alderman of the latter, and a Commissioner of the River Wear. A Liberal-Conservative, in favour of an extension of the franchise, including a redistribution of seats, but against the ballot; not opposed to the abolition of church-rates. First elected for Sunderland, July 1865. Retired in 1868. Unsuccessfully contested Staffordshire E. 17 Nov. 1868. Died 24 May 1886.   [1867]

HARTOPP, Edward Bourchier. 22 Wilton Crescent, London. Dalby Hall, Melton Mowbray. Travellers', and Carlton. Eld. s. of Edward Hartopp, Esq., of Dalby, Leicestershire, by Anna Eleanora, eld. d. of Sir Bourchier Wrey, Bart., of Tawstock Court, Barnstaple. B. in London 1809; m. 1834, Honoria, d. of Gen. Gent. Educ. at Eton, and at Christ Church, Oxford. A Magistrate and Dept.-Lieut. for Leicestershire; High Sheriff of that county 1832. Patron of 2 livings. A Conservative. First elected for North Leicestershire, May 1859. Sat until he retired in 1868.   [1867]

HARVEY, Daniel Whittle. 7 Great George Street, London. Brixton Hill, Surrey. Reform. Eld. s. of Matthew Barnard Harvey, Esq., of Witham, Essex, who m. the heiress of Major Whittle, of Feering House, Essex. B. 1786; m. 1809, only d. of Ebenezer Johnston, Esq., of Stamford Hill. A retired Solicitor. Was admitted a student of the Inner Temple, but the Benchers of that Inn refused to call him to the bar, on account of more than one verdict having gone against him in actions affecting his character. At his request they examined into the particulars of the charges brought against him, and came to a resolution that they saw no reason to alter their determination. After several ineffectual attempts to attain that object, he procured a committee of the House of Commons to be appointed in 1834, at the head of which was Mr. O'Connell, to examine the evidence upon his case, and that committee reported in his favour. Was the originator of the *Sunday Times*, the copyright of which he sold, after conducting it for two years. Was the Proprietor of the *True Sun* and *Weekly True Sun* newspapers. An ultra radical Reformer, recommended an 'equitable adjustment' of the National Debt. Contested Colchester in 1812 unsuccessfully, against Robert Thornton, Esq., Chairman of the India Company; sat for it from 1818-1834, when he was elected for Southwark. Sat for Southwark from 1834 until Jan. 1840 when he was appointed Commissioner of Metropolitan Police. Died 24 Feb. 1863.   [1838]

HARVEY, Sir Robert Bateson, Bart. Langley Park, Slough. Carlton. S. of Robert Harvey, Esq.,

of Langley Park, by Jemima Jane, d. and heir of J.R. Collins, Esq., of Hatch Court, Somerset. B. at Langley Park, Slough, 1825; m. 1st, 1855, Diana Jane, d. of Archdeacon Creyke (she died 1866); 2ndly, 1874, Magdalen Breadalbane, widow of A. Anderson, Esq., and d. of Lady Elizabeth Pringle. Educ. at Eton, and at Christ Church, Oxford. Capt. in the Buckinghamshire Rifle Volunteers. Patron of 2 livings. A Conservative. Sat for Buckinghamshire from Nov. 1863 to Nov. 1868; re-elected Feb. 1874 and sat until he retired in 1885. Died 23 Mar. 1887.   [1885]

HARVEY, Sir Robert John Harvey. Brundall House, Blofield, Norwich. St. Mary's House, Thetford, Norfolk. Athenaeum. S. of Gen. Sir Robert Harvey, C.B., of Monsehold House, Nr. Norwich. B. 1816, of Charlotte, d. and heir of Robert Harvey, of Watton. M. 1845, Lady Henrietta, d. of George, Visct. Kilcoursie, and sister of 8th Earl of Cavan. Was High Sheriff of Norfolk in 1863. A Liberal-Conservative, in favour of 'progress carried out in a Conservative spirit'. Voted for Lord Russell's Reform Bill 1866. Sat for Thetford from July 1865 until its disfranchisement in 1868. Was created a Bart. on 8 Dec. 1868. Committed suicide on 19 July 1870.   [1867]

HASSARD, Michael Dobbyn. 7 Onslow Crescent, South Kensington, London. Glenville, Waterford. Oxford & Cambridge. S. of Richard Hassard, Esq., a Lieut. in the Royal Irish Artillery, and afterwards Capt. Waterford Militia, by Margaret Frances, d. of Michael Dobbyn, Esq., of the City of Waterford. B. at Waterford 1817; m. 1846, Anne, d. of Sir Francis Hassard. Educ. at Waterford School, and at Trinity Coll., Dublin, where he graduated, and gained the Gold Medal. A Magistrate for the City and Co. of Waterford; served the office of Sheriff 1853. A Liberal, opposed to the impost called 'Ministers' Money' in Ireland, and especially to the mode of levying it; supported the vote of censure on Lord Palmerston 1864. First elected for Waterford Apr. 1857. Sat until he retired 1865. Died 7 Apr. 1869.   [1865]

HASTIE, Alexander. 8 Sumner Terrace, Fulham Road, London. Adelaide Place, Glasgow. Reform. S. of Robert Hastie, Esq., Merchant of Glasgow. B. 1805; m. 1851, d. of Robert Napier, Esq., of Shandon, Nr. Glasgow. A Merchant at Glasgow. Elected Lord Provost of Glasgow 1846. A Liberal, in favour of 'an extension of the franchise, equal electoral districts, and the ballot, opposed to the Maynooth and all other ecclesiastical grants'. First elected for Glasgow 1847. Sat until defeated 1857. Died 13 Aug. 1864.   [1857]

HASTIE, Archibald. 5 Rutland Gate, Knightsbridge, London. Reform. S. of W. Hastie, Esq. B. 1791. An East India Agent in London. A Reformer, desired a large modification in the excise laws, voted for the ballot 1853, also for inquiry into Maynooth, same year. First elected for Paisley Mar. 1836. MP until his death 11 Dec. 1857. [1857]

HASTINGS, G.W. Continued in House after 1885: full entry in Volume II.

HATCHELL, John. 12 Merrion Square South, Dublin. Fortfield, Rathfarnham, Co. Dublin. Kildare Street, and University. Only s. of the Rt. Hon. John Hatchell, Dublin, by the d. of Richard Waddy, Esq., of Kilmacoe, Co. Wexford. B. in Dublin 1825; unmarried. Educ. at Rugby, and graduated at Trinity Coll., Dublin, as a Fellow Commoner. Called to the bar in Ireland 1847. A Liberal. First elected for Wexford Apr. 1857. Defeated 1859. [1859]

HATCHELL, Right Hon. John. 12 Merrion Square, Dublin. Kildavin, Co. Carlow. Reform. B. 1788; m. 1815, Elizabeth, d. of Richard Waddy, Esq. (whose son, Cadwallader Waddy, Esq., was member for Wexford, for a few months, in 1834). Educ. at the University of Dublin, where he graduated, and obtained premiums and a scholarship. Was called to the Irish bar, 1809; made a King's Counsel, 1835; appointed Solicitor-Gen. for Ireland Dec. 1847, and Attorney-Gen. for Ireland Sept. 1850. Of 'Old Whig principles', in favour of free trade, and 'a zealous advocate of civil and religious liberty', in favour of economy and retrenchment in every department of the State. First returned for Windsor Feb. 1850, without opposition. Retired in 1852. Commissioner of insolvent debtors' court, Dublin 1854. Died 14 Aug. 1870. [1852]

HATTON, Hon. M. Finch. See FINCH-HATTON, Hon. M.E.G. Continued in House after 1885: full entry in Volume II.

HATTON, Capt. Villiers Francis. 81 Eaton Place, London. Delgany, Co. Wicklow, United Service. S. of George Hatton, Esq., formerly MP for Lisburne, and grand-s. maternally of the 1st Marq. of Hertford. B. 1787; m. 1817, 2nd d. of Rt. Hon. D. Latouche, and grand-d. of the 1st Earl of Miltown. A Cap. R.N. of the date of 1812. Had a pension of £300 a year for the loss of an arm in action off Norway in 1808. A Liberal. Formerly voted against the abolition of the Corn Laws, but in 1846 supported their repeal. First returned for Wexford Co. July 1841. Sat until he retired Aug.

1847. Died 8 Feb. 1859. [1847]

HAVELOCK-ALLAN, Sir Henry Marsham, Bart., V.C., K.C.B. Continued in House after 1885: full entry in Volume II.

HAWES, Sir Benjamin. 9 Queen Street, Westminster, London. Athenaeum, and Reform. Married the d. of Sir Marc Isambart Brunel. At one time Soap Manufacturer. Appointed Under Sec. of State for the Colonies July 1846, Deputy Sec. at War 1851-57, permanent Under Sec. in 1857 and made K.C.B. Feb. 1856. A Reformer and in favour of triennial Parliaments, the ballot, a property tax, and free trade generally. Sat for Lambeth from 1832 to 1847, and for Kinsale from Mar. 1848 until he accepted Chiltern Hundreds in Oct. 1851. [1851]

HAWKES, Thomas. Himley House, Staffordshire. Carlton. B. 1778; m. 1814, d. of John Blackburne, Esq. Was extensively engaged, as were his ancestors, in Mercantile and Mineral pursuits in Worcestershire and Lancashire. High Sheriff of Worcestershire 1810. Capt. of the Himley Troops of Staffordshire Yeomanry and Magistrate of the Cos. of Stafford and Worcester. A Conservative. Returned for Dudley when he successfully opposed Sir John Campbell in 1834 after the latter's appointment to the office of Attorney Gen. Sat until he accepted Chiltern Hundreds 1844. [1844]

HAWKINS, John Heywood. Bignor Park, Sussex. Athenaeum, and Reform. S. of B. Hawkins, Esq., of Bignor Park, and nephew of Sir Christopher Hawkins of Trewithen, Cornwall, for whose borough of St. Michael, now disfranchised, he sat in 1830. A Barrister. Of Whig politics; in favour of the ballot. Was elected for Tavistock on the dissolution in 1831. Sat for Newport from 1832. Sat until he retired 1841. Died 27 June 1877. [1838]

HAWKINS, William Warwick. 3 Berkeley Square, London. Alresford Hall, Colchester, Essex. Carlton. Eld. s. of William Hawkins, Esq., of Colchester (a Merchant and Magistrate), by Mary Anne, d. of John Warwick, Esq., of Cumrue, Cumberland. B. at Colchester 1816; m. 1842, Jane Harriet, only surviving d. of Francis Smythies, Esq., of Hereford Street, London, and of the Turrets, Colchester. Educ. at Queen Elizabeth's Grammar School, Dedham, Essex. A Magistrate for the Co. of Essex, Chairman of the Colchester and Stour Valley Railway, Director of the Eastern Union Railway. Patron of 1 living. A Conservative, said he would 'vote for an inquiry into the education and practices at Maynooth'.

First returned for Colchester in July 1852. Sat until he retired 1857.   [1857]

HAY, Sir Andrew Leith, K.H. 2 Great Ryder Street, St. James's, London. Rannes and Leith Hall, Aberdeenshire. United Service. Eld. s. of Gen. Alex. Leith Hay, of Rannes. M. 1816, Mary Margaret, d. of W. Clark, Esq., of Buckland House, Devonshire. A Lieut.-Col. in the army, and a Director of the National Bank of England. Served in Spain, Portugal, France, and the West Indies, was present at Corunna, Talavera, Busaco, Salamanca, Vittoria, and St. Sebastian, and published an account of the Peninsular War. Was Clerk of the Ordnance during the Melbourne administration of 1834. Resumed his office in Apr. 1835. A Liberal. Sat for Elgin district from 1832 until his appointment to the governorship of Bermuda in 1838; was re-elected in 1841 and sat until defeated 1847. Unsuccessfully contested Aberdeen 10 July 1852. Died 13 Oct. 1862.   [1847]

HAY, Lord John, C.B. (I). Admiralty, London. Reform. B. in 1793, the 3rd s. of the 7th Marq. of Tweeddale, by the 4th d. of the 7th Earl of Lauderdale. M. in 1846, Mary Anne, the eld. d. of Donald Cameron, Esq., of Lochiel. A Dept.-Lieut. of Haddingtonshire. A Lord of the Admiralty, and Capt. R.N. from 1818. Lost his arm while Midshipman of the 'Seahorse', when serving in her boats in the Mediterranean. Served as Commodore in command of a small squadron and a battalion of marines on the N. coast of Spain during the Civil War, and was frequently engaged with the Carlist forces. Received the Grand Cross of the Spanish Order of Charles III, and was nominated a C.B. 1837. A Liberal, and sat for Windsor from 1847 until he accepted Chiltern Hundreds in 1850. Died on either 26 or 27 Aug. 1851.   [1849]

HAY, Lord John. (II). 15 Cromwell Road, S. Kensington, London. Yester House, Haddington, Scotland. Reform. 4th s. of 8th Marq. of Tweeddale, by Lady Susan, 3rd d. of 5th Duke of Manchester. B. 1827. Appointed Capt. R.N. Nov. 1855. C.B. the same year and Knight of the Legion of Honour 1856. Received the 4th class medal of the Medjidie 1858. Lord of the Admiralty April-June 1866, reappointed Dec. 1868 (salary £1,000). A Liberal, opposed to the ballot; voted in favour of the disestablishment of the Irish Church 1869. Sat for Wick from Apr. 1857 till May 1859. Contested Belfast 15 July 1865. Elected for Ripon Feb. 1866, and sat until he accepted Chiltern Hundreds Jan. 1871. A Lord of the Admiralty 1880-83. Comm.-in-Chief in Mediterranean 1883-86, at Devonport 1887-88. Died 4 May 1916.   [1870]

HAY, Sir John, Bart. 103 Pall Mall, London. Smithfield and Hayston, Peebleshire. Carlton. Eld. s. of the former Bart., by Mary Elizabeth, d. of James, 16th Lord Forbes. B. 1788; m. Miss Anne Preston, niece and co-heiress of Sir Robert Preston, of Vallyfield. Bro. of Mr. Adam Hay, formerly MP for Peebles. A Partner in the firm of Forbes and Co., Bankers at Edinburgh. A Conservative. Sat for Peebleshire from 1831 until he retired in 1837. Died 1 Nov. 1838.   [1837]

HAY, Rt. Hon. Sir John Charles Dalrymple, Bart., C.B., F.R.S. 108 St. George's Square, London. Craigenveoch, Glenluce, Scotland. Carlton, St. Stephen's, and United Service. S. of Sir James Dalrymple Hay (2nd Bart), by Elizabeth, d. of Lieut.-Col. Sir John Heron Maxwell, Bart., of Springkell, B. in Princes Street, Edinburgh, 1821; m. 1847, Hon. Eliza, 3rd d. of the 8th Lord Napier. Educ. at Rugby. Created Honorary D.C.L. at Oxford 1870. Entered the navy 1834, and became a Capt. 1850; Rear-Admiral 1866; served on the coast of Africa and at the Cape of Good Hope during the first Caffre war, and afterwards in the Mediterranean during the Syrian war; was at the capture of Beyrout and St. Jean d'Acre. Served from 1842 to 1850 on the East India and China Stations, in the squadrons which destroyed the pirate fleets in Bias Bay and in the Tonquin River, 1849; and commanded the Hannibal during the Russian war, at the sieges of Sebastopol, Kertch, and Kinburn. Received three war medals and a clasp, and the Medjidie 4th class. Became an Admiral on the retired list March 1878. Was a Lord of the Admiralty from June 1866 to Dec. 1868. A Magistrate and Dept.-Lieut. for Wigtownshire. A Liberal-Conservative, in favour of preserving 'a just union' between Church and State. Sat for Wakefield from Mar. 1862 till July 1865, when he was unsuccessful. Unsuccessfully contested Tiverton 28 Feb. 1866. Sat for Stamford from May 1866 to Mar. 1880, when he was an unsuccessful candidate there; sat for Wigtown from July 1880 until he retired in 1885. Died 28 Jan. 1912. [1885]

HAY, Lord William Montagu. Yester House, Haddington. Boodle's, and Garrick. 3rd s. of 8th Marq. of Tweeddale, by Lady Susan, 3rd d. of 5th Duke of Manchester. B. 1826, Educ. at Haileybury Coll. Entered the Civil Service of the E.I.C. at Bengal, 1845, returned to England, 1862. Was a dept.-commissioner of Simla and superintendent of Hill States in Northern India. A Liberal, and stated himself to be such 'by observation, reflection, and conviction'. First elected for Taunton, July 1865. Defeated in 1868 contesting Haddingtonshire; unsuccessfully contested Edinburghshire 10 Feb. 1874. Returned for Haddington district at a by-election 3 Aug. 1878. Sat until he succeeded bro. as 10th Marq. Dec. 1878; created Baron of U.K. Oct. 1881; Lord High Commissioner to Church of Scotland 1888-92 and 1896-97. Died 25 Nov. 1911. [1867]

HAYES, Sir Edmund Samuel, Bart. 15 Chesham Street, London. Drumboe Castle, Stranorlar, Co. Donegal. Carlton. Only s. of Sir Samuel Hayes (2nd Bart.), by the eld. d. of Sir Thos. Leighton, Bart. B. in Dublin 1806; m. in 1837, eld. d. of Hon. H. Pakenham. Graduated at Trinity Coll., Dublin. A Dept.-Lieut. of Donegal. A Conservative. Sat for Co. of Donegal from 1831 and sat until his death 30 June 1860. [1860]

HAYTER, Sir Arthur Divett, Bart. Continued in House after 1885: full entry in Volume II.

HAYTER, Rt. Hon. Sir William Goodenough, Bart. 19 Hyde Park Terrace, London. South Hill Park, Bracknell, Berkshire. Wells, Somersetshire. Brooks's, United University, and Reform. Youngest s. of John Hayter, Esq., of Winterbourne-Stoke, Wiltshire. B. at Winterbourne-Stoke; m. 1832, Ann, eld. d. of William Pulsford, Esq., of Wimpole Street, London. Educ. at Winchester and at Trinity Coll., Oxford, where he was second class man. A Queen's Counsel, and a Bencher of Lincoln's Inn; called to the bar Nov. 1819, but retired from practice in 1839. Was Judge-Advocate-Gen. from Dec. 1847-May 1849; Financial Sec. to the Treasury from the latter date until July 1850, when he became Parliamentary Sec. until Mar. 1852; again filled the last office from Dec. 1852-Mar. 1858. A Magistrate for Wiltshire and Somersetshire, and a Dept.-Lieut. of Berkshire. A Liberal. First returned for Wells Aug. 1837. Sat until he retired 1865. Died 26 Dec. 1878. [1865]

HEADLAM, Rt. Hon. Thomas Emerson. 27 Ashley Place, London. 35 Great George Street, London. Gilmouby Hall, Barnard Castle, Durham. Oxford & Cambridge. Eld. s. of the Rev. John Headlam, Archdeacon of Richmond and Rector of Wycliffe, Yorkshire. B. at Wycliffe Rectory 1813; m. 1854, Emma Perceval, eld. d. of Maj. Von Straubenzee, R.A. of Eastfield House, Yorkshire. Educ. at Shrewsbury School and at Trinity Coll., Cambridge, where he was 16th Wrangler in 1836. Called to the bar in 1839 at the Inner Temple of which he was a Bencher; made a Queen's Counsel 1852. Author of a *Treatise on the Practise of the Court of Chancery,* and carried through Parliament the Trustee Act. A Magistrate and Dept.-Lieut. for the N. Riding of Yorkshire. Chancellor of the dioceses of Durham and Ripon

from 1854. Was Judge-Advocate-Gen. from June 1859-July 1866. A Liberal, 'in favour of greater economy in the public expenditure'. Voted for the ballot 1853. First returned for Newcastle-upon-Tyne 1847. Sat until defeated 1874. Died 3 Dec. 1875. [1873]

HEALD, James. Parr's Wood, Didsbury, Lancashire. National. 2nd s. of James Heald, Esq. (Merchant and Calico-printer), of Brinnington, and Disley, Cheshire. B. at Brinnington, near Stockport, 1796. Unmarried. A Magistrate for Lancashire and Cheshire, and a Dept.-Lieut. of Cheshire. A Conservative, but in favour of free trade; opposed to the endowment of the Roman Catholic Clergy. First returned for Stockport in 1847. Sat until defeated in 1852. Unsuccessfully contested Oldham 3 Dec. 1852. Died 26 Oct. 1873. [1852]

HEALY, T.M. Continued in House after 1885: full entry in Volume II.

HEARD, John Isaac. Kinsale, Co. Cork. Union. S. of John Heard, Esq., of Kinsale, Co. Cork, by Rachel, d. of—Servatt, Esq. B. at Kinsale 1788; m. 1808, Mary, d. of Hope Wilkes, Esq., of Lofts Hall, Essex. Educ. at Peterhouse, Cambridge, where he graduated B.A. 1808. A Magistrate and Dept.-Lieut. for the Co. of Cork, of which he was High Sheriff in 1849. Of moderate Whig principles. First elected for Kinsale on the retirement of Mr. Hawes, Feb. 1852, and again returned without opposition at the general election July 1852. Sat until he retired in 1859. Died 1 Sept. 1862. [1858]

HEATH, Robert. 41 Portman Square, London. Biddulph Grange and Greenway Bank, Stoke-upon-Trent. Conservative. S. of Robert Heath, Esq. B. at Sneyd House, Nr. Burslem; m. Anne, d. of James Beech, Esq., of the Staffordshire Potteries. Educ. at Etruria Hall, by G.E. Maguns, Foreign Correspondent to Josiah Wedgwood. A Coal and Iron-Master of the Biddulph Valley Ironworks. Patron of 1 living. A Conservative. Sat for Stoke-upon-Trent from Feb. 1874. Defeated 1880. Sheriff of Staffordshire 1885. Died 7 Oct. 1893. [1880]

HEATHCOAT, John. 5 Warwick Street, Charing Cross, London. Tiverton. Reform. Proprietor of the Lace Manufactory at Tiverton, of the machinery of which he was the sole inventor and patentee. Of Whig principles, in favour of 'the abolition of useless places, pensions, and sinecures; of a more equal and just system of taxation,' etc. Sat for Tiverton from 1832 until he retired in 1859. Died 18 Jan. 1861. [1858]

185

HEATHCOTE, Sir Gilbert, Bart. 12 Langham Place, London. Normanton Park, Rutlandshire. B. 1773. M. 1st, 1793, Catherine, d. of John Manners, Esq., of Grantham Grange, ein-colnshire and of the Countess of Dysart; 2ndly, 1825, Mrs. Eldon of Park Crescent, Portland Place, London. A remote connection of Sir William Heathcote's. Patron of 11 livings. A Moderate Reformer. Was returned for Gatton 1796 (resigned for county); for Lincolnshire 1796-1807; for Rutlandshire from 1812 until he retired 1841. Died 27 Mar. 1851.   [1838]

HEATHCOTE, Hon. Gilbert Henry. 12 Belgrave Square, London. Normanton Park, Oakham, Rutlandshire. Bulby, Bourne, Lincolnshire. White's. B. in London 1830, the eld. s. of Lord Aveland, by the Hon. Clementina Elizabeth, eld. d. of 19th Lord Willoughby d'Eresby. M. 1863, Lady Evelyn Elizabeth, 2nd d. of 10th Marq. of Huntly. Educ. at Harrow and at Trinity Coll., Cambridge. A Liberal, opposed to the ballot, but supported 'constitutional reform'. Voted for Lord Derby's Reform Bill Mar. 1859, and against that of Lord Russell, 1866. Sat for Boston July 1852 to Mar. 1856, when he was elected for Rutlandshire. Sat until Sept. 1867, when he succeeded as 2nd Baron Aveland. Was created Earl of Ancaster in Aug. 1892. Died 24 Dec. 1910.   [1867]

HEATHCOTE, Sir Gilbert John, Bart. 12 Langham Place, London. Normanton Park, Rutlandshire. Stocken Hall, Stamford, Rutlandshire. Travellers', White's, Boodle's, and Brooks's. B. at Normanton Park 1795, the eld. s. of Sir G. Heathcote, 3rd Bart. M. 1827, Hon. Clementina Elizabeth, eld. d. of 19th Lord Willoughby d'Eresby. A Magistrate and Dept.-Lieut. for Lancashire and Rutlandshire. Patron of 11 livings. Voted for agricultural protection 1846, but was a moderate Reformer in other respects. Voted for inquiry into Maynooth 1853. Sat for Boston from 1820-31, and for Lincolnshire from 1832-41, after which time he sat for Rutlandshire until he was created Baron Aveland in Feb. 1856. Died 6 Sept. 1867.   [1855]

HEATHCOTE, Richard Edenson. Longton Hall, Staffordshire. Eld. s. of Sir John Edenson Heathcote of Longton Hall. B. 1780, m. 1st, Emma Sophia, 2nd d. of Sir Nigel Bowyer Gresby, Bart., of Drakelow Park, Co. Derby; 2ndly, 1815, Elizabeth Keith (Dec. 1825), eld. d. of the Earl of Balcarres. A Reformer, supported Catholic emancipation and other liberal measures. Sat for Coventry in the Parliament of 1826; unsuccessfully contested Stoke-upon-Trent in 1832. Was elected for Stoke-upon-Trent without opposition in 1835. Accepted Chiltern Hundreds, Jan. 1836.   [1835]

HEATHCOTE, Sir William, Bart. 91 Victoria Street, London. Hursley Park, Winchester. United University, and Oxford & Cambridge. Only s. of the Rev. William Heathcote, Prebendary of Winchester, by Elizabeth, d. of Lovelace Bigg Wither, Esq., of Manydown, Hampshire. B. at Worting, Hampshire, 1801; m. 1st, 1825, Hon. Caroline Frances, youngest d. of 1st Lord Arden; 2ndly, 1841, Selina, eld. d. of Evelyn John Shirley, Esq., of Lower Eatington, Warwickshire. Educ. at Winchester and at Oriel Coll., Oxford, where he was 1st class in classics, 1821, became Fellow of All Souls', and graduated B.C.L. 1824, D.C.L. 1830. A Dept.-Lieut. of Hampshire and Chairman of Quarter Sessions. Patron of 1 living. A Conservative. Sat for Hampshire from 1826 till 1832, and for the northern division from July 1837 till Apr. 1849; first elected for the University of Oxford, Feb. 1854. Sat until he retired in 1868. Died 18 Aug. 1881.   [1867]

HECTOR, Cornthwaite John. Petersfield. A Banker and Brewer in Petersfield; was Steward of the Jolliffe family for upwards of 30 years, but was elected at Petersfield in 1835 in opposition to Col. Jolliffe. At the general election of 1837 he was defeated by Sir W.G.H. Jolliffe, Bart. by one vote, but was subsequently seated on petition. A radical Reformer Sat until he retired 1841. [1838]

HELMSLEY, Visct. Duncombe Park, Helmsley, Yorkshire. Boodle's and Carlton. Eld. s. of the Earl of Feversham, by Mabel Violet, 2nd d. of the Rt. Hon. Sir James Graham, Bart. B. 1852; m. 1876, Lady Muriel Frances Louisa, d. of the 19th Earl of Shrewsbury and Talbot. Appointed Sub-Lieut. 1st Life Guards, July 1872; resigned June 1876. A Conservative. Sat for the N. Riding of Yorkshire from Feb. 1874. MP until his death 24 Dec. 1881.   [1881]

HENCHY, David O'Connor. 112 Jermyn Street, London. Stonebrook, Ballymore-Eustace, Co. Kildare. Reform. 2nd s. of Valentine O'Connor, Esq., of Rockfield, Co. Dublin, and Great Denmark Street, in the city of Dublin, by Margaret, only child of David Henchy, Esq., of Rockfield (whose name he assumed). B. in Rutland Square West, Dublin, 1810; m. 1850 Elizabeth, d. of Sir John Burke, Bart., of Marble Hill, Co. Galway. Educ. at Oscott Coll., and at Trinity Coll., Dublin, where he graduated M.A. A Liberal, in favour of tenant right in Ireland. First returned for Kildare in July 1852. Sat until he retired in 1859. Died 1 Dec. 1876.   [1858]

HENDERSON, Frank. 34 Duke Street, St. James's, London. 4 Clarendon Terrace, Dundee. S. of Mr. Henry Henderson, Leather Merchant, of Dundee, by Anne, d. of Mr. James Lindsay, of Dundee, Manufacturer. B. at Dundee 1836; m. 1863, Ellen Isabella, d. of Mr. David Scroggie, of Beechwood, Lawrancekirk, Kincardineshire. Educ. at the High School, Dundee. Elected a member of the Town Council of Dundee 1868, and Convener of the Improvement Committee there 1871. A Liberal, in favour of a redistribution of seats so as to give to Scotland increased representation, the facilitation of the transfer of land, and of the control of the liquor traffic being vested in the ratepayers. Sat for Dundee from Apr. 1880. Retired in 1885. Died 21 July 1889.   [1885]

HENDERSON, John. Leazes House, Durham. Reform. B. at Durham 1807, the s. of Gilbert Henderson, Esq., of Durham, and Ann, his wife. M. 1846, Hannah, d. of Alexander Thomas Chipchase, Esq. Educ. at the Grammar School, Durham. A Carpet Manufacturer and Coal Owner. A Liberal, favoured 'neutrality and non-intervention' in foreign policy, and the unconditional abolition of Church rates. Sat for Durham from Feb. 1864 to 1874, when the entire poll of 5th Feb. 1874 in Durham was declared void, and Henderson retired thereafter. Died 4 Apr. 1884.   [1873]

HENEAGE, Edward. 39 Charles Street, Berkeley Square, London. Hainton, Lincolnshire. Reform. 2nd s. of Geo. Robt. Heneage, Esq., Bro. to George Fieschi Heneage, Esq., once member for Lincoln, who had himself sat for Great Grimsby. There was much church patronage in the family. Of Whig principles. Voted for agricultural protection, 1846. Sat for Great Grimsby from 1835 until defeated in 1852. Died 25 June 1880.   [1852]

HENEAGE, Rt. Hon. E. Continued in House after 1885: full entry in Volume II.

HENEAGE, George Fieschi. 39 Charles Street, Berkeley Square, London. Hainton Hall, Louth, Lincolnshire. Reform, Travellers', United University, and Brooks's. Eld. s. of George Robert Heneage, Esq., of Hainton, Lincolnshire, by Frances Anne, 2nd d. of Lieut.-Gen. George Ainslie. B. in Welbeck Street, 1800; m. 1833, Frances, d. of Michael Tasburgh, Esq., of Burghwallis, Yorkshire. Educ. at Trinity Coll., Cambridge, where he graduated B.A. 1822, M.A. 1826. A Magistrate and Dept.-Lieut. for Lin-

colnshire. A Liberal, in favour of 'widening and strengthening the foundations of all constitutional rights and privileges'; said he would support a 'sound system of national education, acceptable alike to Churchman and Nonconformist.' Was MP for Great Grimsby from 1826 to 1830, and for Lincoln from 1831 to 1835. Again returned for Lincoln in July 1852 and sat until he accepted Chiltern Hundreds 1862. Unsuccessfully contested Great Grimsby 14 Feb. 1862. Died 11 May 1868.   [1861]

HENEAGE, George Heneage Walker. 19 Park Street, Grosvenor Square, London. Compton Basset, Wiltshire. Carlton, and Travellers'. Eld. s. of the Rev. George Wyld, of Speen, Berkshire. B. 1799, assumed the names of Walker Heneage in 1818; m. 1824, eld. d. of William Webber, Esq., of Binfield Lodge, Berkshire. Educ. at Christ Church, Oxford, where he graduated M.A. 1823. A Magistrate and Dept.-Lieut. of Wiltshire. Hereditary Chief Usher of the Court of Common Pleas. A Conservative. Patron of 5 livings. Sat for Devizes from 1838, when he succeeded on petition, until he retired 1857.   [1857]

HENLEY, Rt. Hon. Joseph Warner. Waterpenny, Wheatley, Oxfordshire. Carlton. Only s. of Joseph Henley, Esq., by the d. of C. Rooke, Esq., of Wandsworth. B. 1793; m. 1817, d. of John Fane, Esq., and Lady Elizabeth Fane (she died 1864). Educ. at Magdalen Coll., Oxford, where he graduated B.A. 1815; M.A. 1834 and made honorary D.C.L. 1854. Was Pres. of the Board of Trade from Mar.-Dec. 1852; and from Mar. 1858-Feb. 1859, when he relinquished the office as a consequence of his dissatisfaction with the government Reform Bill, especially the clauses referring to the 40s. freeholders. A Magistrate and Dept.-Lieut. of Oxfordshire. A Conservative, voted against the disestablishment of the Irish Church 1869. Sat for Oxfordshire from 1841 until he accepted Chiltern Hundreds 1878. Died 8 Dec. 1884.   [1877]

HENLEY, Lord. 53 Eccleston Square, London. Watford Court, Rugby. B. in Whitehall Yard 1825; m. 1st, 1846, Julia Emily Augusta, only d. of the Very Rev. John Peel, Dean of Worcester (she died 1862); 2ndly, 1870, Clara Campbell Lucy, 2nd d. of Joseph H.S. Jekyll, Esq. Educ. at Eton and Christ Church, Oxford. An Irish Peer. Appointed Dept.-Lieut. of Northamptonshire 1846, Sheriff of that Co. 1854. A Liberal, in favour of strict neutrality in foreign politics, and insisted on 'the absolute necessity of greater economy in our public departments.' Unsuccessfully contested S. Northamptonshire July 1847 and Bridgwater 7 July 1852. Contested S. Northamptonshire again Feb. 1858. First elected for Northampton July 1859. Sat until defeated 1874. Created Baron Northington June 1885. Member of Northamptonshire County Council 1889-95. Died 27 Nov. 1898. [1873]

HENNESSY, John Pope, F.G.S., F.R.A.S. 2 Harcourt Buildings, Temple, London. Ballymacmoy House, Kilavullen. S. of John Hennessy, Esq., of Ballyhennessy. B. at Cork 1834. Unmarried. Educ. at St. Vincent's Seminary, Cork, and at Queen's University, Ireland. Called to the bar at the Inner Temple 1861. A Conservative, and a supporter generally of Lord Derby; said he would support a 'practical system of tenant--right'; opposed to every form of 'Mixed Education.' First elected for King's Co. May 1859. Sat until defeated 1865. Contested Wexford Co. 1866. Governor of Labuan 1867-71. Various Colonial governorships until retired in 1889. K.C.M.G. 1880. Author. Elected for the N. division of Kilkenny Co. from Dec. 1890 and sat until his death 7 Oct. 1891. [1865]

HENNIKER, Hon. John Major. 6 Grafton Square, London. Thornham Hall, Eye, Suffolk. Eld. s. of Lord Henniker (who represented E. Suffolk for 25 years until he received an English Peerage), by Anna, eld. d. of Sir Edward Harrison, Bart. B. in Belgrave St., London, 1842; m. 1864, Alice Mary, only d. of 3rd Earl of Desart. Appointed Lieut. 10th Suffolk Rifle Volunteers 1860; a Dept.-Lieut. of Suffolk 1863. A Conservative, voted against the disestablishment of the Irish Church 1869; in favour of 'the reduction, and if possible the repeat of the malt tax.' First elected for E. Suffolk July 1866. Sat until he succeeded as 5th Baron Henniker (and to Barony of Hartismere, U.K. Peerage), Apr. 1870. Died 27 June 1902. [1870]

HENNIKER, Lord. 6 Grafton Street, London. Thornham Hall, Eye, Suffolk. Carlton, and Athenaeum. An Irish Peer. B. at Stratford Green, Essex 1801. M. 1837, eld. d. of Sir Edward Kerrison, Bart. Educ. at St. John's Coll., Cambridge, where he graduated M.A. 1822. Called to the bar at Lincoln's Inn 1824. High Sheriff of Suffolk 1853. Patron of 7 livings. A Conservative, but favoured 'progress and reforms where they can be effected with safety and justice.' Sat for Suffolk E. 1832 to Feb. 1847 and Dec. 1856 to July 1866, when he was created Baron Hartismere. Died 16 Apr. 1870. [1865 2nd ed.]

HENRY, Alexander. 56 St. James's Street, London. Woodlands, Nr. Manchester. Reform. B. at Loughbrickland, Co. Down, Ireland. Head of the mercantile firm of A. and S. Henry and Co.,

of Manchester, Leeds, Huddersfield, etc. A Liberal, in favour of the further extension of free trade, the ballot, and the diffusion of education unconnected with religious opinions; opposed to grants of money for religious endowments. First returned for Lancashire S. in Dec. 1847, without opposition. Retired in 1852. Died 4 Oct. 1862. [1852]

HENRY, John Snowdon. 142 Piccadilly, London. East Dens, Bonchurch, Isle of Wight. Kirouchtree, Newton Stewart, Scotland. Union, Carlton, and Junior Carlton. S. of Alexander Henry, Esq., who sat for the Southern div. of Lancashire from Dec. 1847-July 1852, by Elizabeth, d. of Henry Brush, Esq., of Willow Bank, Co. Down. B. at Ardwick, near Manchester 1824; m. 1851, d. of Thomas Wood, Esq., of Bishopswearmouth and Masham. Partner in the firm Messrs. Henry and Company, of Manchester, Huddersfield, etc. A Conservative, and in favour of full religious liberty, but voted against the disestablishment of the Irish Church 1869. Sat for S.E. Lancashire from Dec. 1868 until he retired 1874. Died 30 Oct. 1896. [1873]

HENRY, Mitchell. Continued in House after 1885: full entry in Volume II.

HEPBURN, Sir Thomas Buchan, Bart. Hepburn, Haddingtonshire. Carlton, and Smeaton. B. 1804; m. 1833, Helen, d. of A. Little, Esq., of Shelden Park, Surrey. Contested the Haddington district of Burghs at the general election in 1837. In Apr. 1838 was returned without opposition for Haddingtonshire, on the elevation of Lord Ramsey to the Peerage. A Conservative. Sat until he retired 1847. Died 17 Dec. 1893. [1847]

HERBERT, Hon. Auberon Edward William Molyneux. 13 St. Johns Terrace, North Gate, Regent's Park, London. Youngest s. of the 3rd Earl of Carnarvon, by Henrietta Anna, d. of Lord Henry Molyneux Howard. B. 1838; m. 1871, Lady Florence, d. of 6th Earl Cowper. Was educ. at St. John's Coll., Oxford, where he was 2nd class in classics at Moderations in 1857, gained a Fellowship, and graduated B.C.L. Appointed Lieut. 7th Dragoons 1859, retired 1862. A Liberal. Unsuccessfully contested Newport 12 July 1865 and Berkshire Nov. 1868. Sat for Nottingham from Feb. 1870 until he retired 1874. Died 5 Nov. 1906. [1873]

HERBERT, Henry Arthur. 53 Victoria Street, London. Hitcham Grange, Taplow. Muckross Abbey, Killarney. Brooks's, and Travellers'. Eld. s. of Rt. Hon. Henry Arthur Herbert, of

Muckross, Killarney (who sat for Kerry from 1847 until his death in 1866), by Mary, d. of James Balfour, Esq., of Wittinham, Co. Berwick. Was lineally descended from Sir William Herbert, who was knighted by Henry V. B. at Whittingham, Scotland 1840; m. 1866, Hon. Emily Julia, only d. of the 2nd Baron Keane. Entered the army Jan. 1857 as Ensign Coldstream Guards, became Lieut. and Capt. Nov. 1862, retired Mar. 1866. A Liberal. Sat for Kerry Co. from Mar. 1866 until he retired 1880. [1880]

HERBERT, Rt. Hon. Henry Arthur. 3 Grosvenor Crescent, Belgrave Square, London. Muckross, Killarney, Ireland. Travellers', and White's. B. at Muckross, the only s. of Charles John Herbert, Esq. Was representative of the Herberts of Muckross, Co. Kerry, and lineally descended from Sir William Herbert who was knighted by Henry V. M. 1837, d. of James Balfour, Esq., of Whittingham, Co. Berwick. Educ. at Trinity Coll., Cambridge. Was Chief Sec. for Ireland June 1857-Mar. 1858. A Magistrate for Kerry and Lord-Lieut. of the Co. since 1853. A Liberal, once ranked as a Conservative. Supported Lord Palmerston on the vote of censure 1864. Sat for Kerry Co. 1847 until his death 26 Feb. 1866. [1865 2nd ed.]

HERBERT, Rt. Hon. Sir Percy Egerton, K.C.B. 43 Charles Street, Berkeley Square, London. Carlton, and Travellers'. 2nd s. of 2nd Earl Powis by Lady Lucy, 3rd d. of 3rd Duke of Montrose. B. at Powis Castle 1822; m. 1860 , Lady Mary, only d. of the late Earl of Keary, and grand-d. of 3rd Marq. of Lansdowne. Educ. at Eton and the Military Coll., Sandhurst. Entered the army as Ensign 43rd Foot 1840; appointed Maj. 43rd Foot 1853, Col. in the army 1855, and wounded at the battle of the Alma. Appointed Dept. Quartermaster Gen. at Head Quarters 1860. Maj.-Gen. in the army 1868. Was Treasurer of the Queen's Household from March 1867-Dec. 1868. A Conservative; voted against the disestablishment of the Irish Church 1869. In favour of the repeal of the malt tax. Sat for Ludlow from Feb. 1854 to Sep. 1860; sat for S. Shropshire from July 1865. MP until his death 7 Oct. 1876. [1876]

HERBERT, Rt. Hon. Sidney. 49 Belgrave Square, London. Wilton House, Wiltshire. Carlton, and Travellers'. S. of the 11th Earl of Pembroke, by his 2nd wife, only d. of Simon, Count Woronzow. B. at Richmond 1810; m. 1846, d. of Major Gen. à Court, and niece of the 1st Lord Heytesbury. Educ. at Harrow School and at Oriel Coll., Oxford, where he was 4th class

in classics 1831. Was patron of 1 living. Was Secretary to the Admiralty from 1841-Feb. 1845, Secretary at War from the latter date till July 1846, and again from Dec. 1852, till the office was abolished, Feb. 1855, when he became Secretary of State for the Colonies, but resigned after a few weeks. Appointed Secretary of State for War June 1859. A Dept.-Lieut. of the counties of Shropshire, Wiltshire, and Dublin. A Liberal-Conservative, in favour of extension of the franchise 'to the better part of the working classes.' Sat for S. Wiltshire from 1832. MP until created Peer (Lord Herbert of Lea) 1861. Died 2 Aug. 1861. [1860]

HERBERT, Hon. Sidney. Continued in House after 1885: full entry in Volume II.

HERBERT, Sir Thomas, K.C.B. Torc Cottage, Killarney. 2nd s. of Richard Townsend Herbert, Esq., of Cahirnane, Co. Kerry (who was a member of the Irish Parliament, and descended from a branch of the Pembroke family). B. at Cahirnane 1793. Unmarried. Entered the navy in 1803, and became a Capt. in 1822, created a K.C.B. for his services in command at the destruction of the Chinese forts in 1841, appointed Commodore on the S.E. coast of America 1846. A Lord of the Admiralty from Feb.-Dec. 1852, made Rear-Admiral of the White 1854. A Magistrate and Dept.-Lieut. of Kerry, High Sheriff of that Co. in 1829. A Conservative, said he would 'oppose any further concession to the Roman Catholics.' First returned for Dartmouth July 1852. Retired 1857. Died 4 Aug. 1861. [1857]

HERMON, Edward. 1 Wilton Place, London. Wyfold Court, Henley-on-Thames. Preston. Carlton. B. in London. M. Emily, youngest d. of George Udney, Esq., of the Bengal Civil Service, formerly member of the Supreme Council. A Cotton Manufacturer and E. India Merchant. A Conservative. Sat for Preston from Dec. 1868. MP until his death 6 May 1881. [1881]

HERON, Denis Caulfeild, LL.D. 7 Upper Fitzwilliam Street, Dublin. Reform. St. Stephen's Green, and University Clubs, Dublin. Eld. s. of W. Heron, Esq., by Mary, d. of Thomas Maguire, Esq., Merchant of Enniskillen. B. in Dublin 1826; m. 1854, Emily, d. of David FitzGerald, Esq., and sister of Rt. Hon Judge FitzGerald (she died 1863). Educ. at the Coll. of St. Gregory, Downside, near Bath, and at Trinity Coll., Dublin. Obtained first classical honours, first prizes in history and political economy, a senior classical moderatorship, gained a gold medal, etc., was the first Roman Catholic elected by the students to be auditor of the Historical Society; obtained a university scholarship in 1845, but was precluded from enjoying it on account of being a Roman Catholic. Was called to the bar in Ireland 1848; appointed a Queen's Counsel there 1860, and joined the Munster circuit. Was Professor of Jurisprudence at Queen Coll., Galway from 1849-1859; was law adviser to the Crown in Ireland from Apr. to July 1866. Author of *History of Jurisprudence* and other works. A Liberal. Sat for Tipperary from Feb. 1870. Retired 1874. 3rd Sergeant at Law 1880 until his death 15 Apr. 1881. [1873]

HERON, Sir Robert, Bart. Stubton Hall, Lincolnshire. Reform. B. 1765; m. 1792, Amelia, d. of Sir Horatio Mann, and grand-d. of the Earl of Gainsborough. Patron of 1 living. A Whig. Sat for Peterborough from 1820 until he retired 1847. Died 29 May 1854. [1847]

HERRIES, Rt. Hon. John. 20 Duke Street, Westminster, London. St. Julian's, Sevenoaks, Kent. Carlton. Eld. s. of Col. Charles Herries, who was distinguished as among the first to set the example of raising volunteer companies during the last war. Bro. to Maj.-Gen Sir William Lewis Herries, K.C.H., Chairman of the Audit Board. Was educ. at the University of Leipsig. M. 1814, d. of John Dorington, Esq., principal Committee Clerk to the House of Commons, (she died 1821). Was Private Sec. to Mr. Perceval during the greater part of his administration, and has filled the office of Commissary in Chief and Auditor of the Civil List (for the abolition of the former office he was entitled to a pension of £1,350 p.a. being half the emoluments). Was Sec. to the Treasury from 1823-Sept. 1827, Chancellor of the Exchequer from the latter date until Jan. 1828, Master of the Mint from 1828-30, President of the Board of Trade from Feb.-Nov. 1830, Sec. at War from Dec. 1834-Apr. 1835 and Pres. of the Board of Control from Mar.-Dec. 1852. A Conservative and Protectionist. Sat for Harwich from 1823 to 1841, when he was an unsuccessful candidate for Ipswich. Sat for Stamford from 1847 until he accepted Chiltern Hundreds in 1853. Died 24 Apr. 1855. [1853]

HERSCHELL, Sir Farrer. 46 Grosvenor Gardens, London. 3 Harcourt Buildings, Temple, London. Devonshire, Brooks's, and Windham. S. of the Rev. R.H. Herschell, of Gloucester Terrace, London, by Helen, d. of William Mowbray, Esq., of Edinburgh. B. 1837; m. 1876, Agnes Adela, 3rd d. of Edward Leigh Kindersley, Esq., of Clyffe, Dorchester. Educ. at University Coll., London, and the University of Bonn. Called to the bar at Lincoln's Inn 1860; became a

Queen's Counsel 1872, and a Bencher of Lincoln's Inn in the same year. Appointed Solicitor-Gen. Apr. 1880. Recorder of Carlisle in 1873, and Examiner in Common Law at the University of London in 1872. A Liberal. Sat for Durham city from June 1874 until defeated in 1885 contesting North Lonsdale division, Lancashire. Lord Chancellor 1886; created Baron Herschel Feb. 1886. Died 1 Mar. 1889. [1885]

HERVEY, Lord Alfred. 6 St. James's Square, London. Carlton. Youngest s. of 1st Marq. of Bristol, by the Hon Elizabeth Albana, 2nd d. of 1st Lord Templetown. B. 1816; m. 1845, Sophia Elizabeth, d. of Maj.-Gen. John Chester. Educ. at Trinity Coll., Cambridge, where he graduated M.A. 1837. Was called to the bar at the Inner Temple 1843. Was a Lord of the Treasury from Dec. 1852-Feb. 1855. Had been Keeper of the Privy Purse to the Prince of Wales. Appointed a Lord of the Bedchamber to the Prince of Wales, 1862. A Liberal-Conservative, supported Lord Palmerston on the vote of censure 1864; opposed to organic changes. Sat for Brighton from May 1842 to Apr. 1857. Sat for Bury St. Edmunds from Feb. 1859 until defeated July 1865. Receiver General of Inland Revenue from 1871 until his death 15 Apr. 1875. [1865]

HERVEY, Lord Augustus Henry Charles. 5 Chesham Street, London. Ickworth, Bury St. Edmunds, Suffolk. Carlton. 2nd s. of Marq. of Bristol by Lady Katherine, 4th d. of 5th Duke of Rutland. B. 1837; m. 1861, Mariana, youngest d. of William P. Hodnett, Esq., of Kensington, and widow of Ashton Benyon, Esq. Appointed a Lieut. in the W. Suffolk Militia, 1859. Made an Hon. M.A. Trinity Coll., Cambridge, 1859. A Conservative, and a supporter of Mr. Disraeli's policy. Sat for Suffolk W. from Nov. 1864. MP until his death 28 May 1875. [1875]

HERVEY, Lord Francis. Continued in House after 1885: full entry in Volume II.

HESKETH, Sir Thomas George Fermor, Bart. Rufford Hall, Ormskirk, Lancashire. Carlton, and Junior Carlton. S. of Sir Thomas Henry Hesketh, Bart., by Annette Maria, d. of Robert Bomford, Esq., of Robinstown House, Co. Meath. B. at Rufford Hall, 1825; m. 1846, Lady Anna Maria Arabella, eld. d. of 4th Earl of Pomfret (she died 1870). Appointed Col. of Duke of Lancaster's Militia 1853, Lieut.-Col. 6th Lancashire Rifle Volunteers 1861. A Dept.-Lieut. of Lancashire since 1846. Was High Sheriff of that County in 1848. A Conservative, voted against the abolition of Church-rates, May 1862. Unsuccessfully contested Lyme Regis 28 Mar. 1857.

First elected for Preston, March 1862. MP until his death 20 Aug. 1872. [1872]

HEYGATE, Sir Frederic William, Bart. 43 Eaton Square, London. Bellarena, Londonderry, Ireland. Carlton. Eld. s. of Sir William Heygate, Bart. (who represented Sudbury in 2 Parliaments), by Isabella, 4th d. of Edward Longdon Macmurdo, Esq., of Upper Clapton, Middlesex. B. at Holwood, Keston, Kent, 1822; m. 1851, Marianne, only d. of Conolly Gage, Esq., of Ballarena, Co. Derry. Educ. at Eton and at Trinity Coll., Cambridge, where he graduated M.A. 1847. Appointed Lieut. Leicestershire Yeomanry Cavalry 1851. A Dept.-Lieut. of Leicestershire 1852 and of Londonderry 1853. A Conservative, though 'opposed to violent and unnecessary change, will lend his aid to reform all proved abuses.' First elected for the Co. of Londonderry May 1859. Sat until he retired 1874. Author. Died 14 Nov. 1894. [1873]

HEYGATE, William Unwin. Roecliffe, Loughborough. Carlton. 2nd s. of Sir William Heygate, 1st Bart. (who represented Sudbury in two Parliaments), by Isabella, 4th d. of Edward Longdon McMurdo, Esq., of Upper Clapton, Middlesex. B. in London 1825; m. 1852, Constance Mary, only d. of Sir George Beaumont, Bart., of Cole Orton Hall, Leicestershire, and grand-d. of the late Dr. Howley, Archbishop of Canterbury. Educ. at Eton and at Merton Coll., Oxford, where he took classical honours in 1847, graduated M.A. 1850. Called to the bar at Lincoln's Inn 1850. Capt. Leicestershire Yeomanry Cavalry. A Magistrate for Hertfordshire and Leicestershire and a Dept.-Lieut. of the latter. A Conservative. Unsuccessfully contested Bridport 28 Mar. 1857. Sat for Leicester from Jan. 1861 to Aug. 1865, for Stamford from June-Nov. 1868, and for South Leicestershire from May 1870 until he was defeated 1880. Died 2 Mar. 1902. [1880]

HEYWOOD, James, F.R.S. 5 Eaton Place, London. The Headlands, Nr. Manchester. Athenaeum, United University, and Reform. 5th s. of Nathaniel Heywood, Esq., Banker of Manchester, by the d. of Thomas Percival, Esq., M.D. of Manchester. Bro. to Sir Benjamin Heywood, Bart., who represented Lancashire in 1831. B. at Liverpool 1810; m. 1853, Annie, d. of John Kennedy, Esq., of Ardwick Hall, Nr. Manchester, and widow of G. Albert Escher, Esq., of Zurich. Educ. at Trinity Coll., Cambridge, where he was Senior Optime in 1833. A Liberal, in favour of the ballot, and a moderate extension of the suffrage, the reduction of duties on tea, coffee and sugar; considered that the Irish Roman Catholic Clergy should be maintained by taxes on Irish land, and that the Irish Protestant Church required reform. First returned for Lancashire N. 1847, without opposition. Sat until he retired 1857. Pioneer of Free Library Movement. Died 17 Oct. 1897. [1857]

HEYWORTH, Laurence. Yew Tree, Nr. Liverpool. Reform. Youngest s. of Peter Heyworth, Esq., of Greensnook, Nr. Rochdale, Lancashire. B. at Greensnook 1786; m. 1820, d. of Mr. Aked, of Liverpool. Educ. at Hipperholme Grammar School, Nr. Halifax. A Partner in the firm of Ormerod, Heyworth and Company, Liverpool, General Merchants. Author of pamphlets on the Corn Laws, Direct Taxation, and other subjects connected with free trade. A Magistrate for Lancashire, formerly a Director of the Midland Railway and of the Eastern Counties Railway. A Liberal, in favour of universal suffrage, vote by ballot, direct taxation, and financial reform. Opposed to Church Rates. Sat for Derby from Aug. 1848 to July 1852, when he was unsuccessful candidate, but on investigation by Committee was substituted for his opponent, Mar. 1853. Retired 1857. Died 17 Apr. 1872. [1857]

HIBBERT, J.T. Continued in House after 1885: full entry in Volume II.

HICK, John. 4 St. James's Place, London. Mytton Hall, Whalley, Lancashire. Highfield, Bolton. Carlton. S. of Benjamin Hick, Esq., by Elizabeth, d. of William Routledge, Esq. B. at Bolton 1815; m. 1846, Margaret, eld. d. of William Bashall, Esq., of Farington Lodge, Nr. Preston. Educ. at Bolton Grammar School, and subsequently at a private school. A Civil Engineer, a member of the Institute of Civil Engineers, London, and of the Society of Arts. A Magistrate for Lancashire and a governor of Bolton Grammar School. A Liberal-Conservative, voted against the disestablishment of the Irish Church 1869. Sat for Bolton from Dec. 1868 until he retired 1880. Died 2 Feb. 1894. [1880]

HICKS, Edward. Wilbraham Temple, Cambridge. Carlton, Oxford & Cambridge, and Garrick. Only s. of Edward Simpson, Esq., of Lichfield, by Elizabeth, d. of William Anderton, Esq., and grand-d. of Gregory Hicks, Esq., of Wilbraham Temple. B. 1814; m. 1838, Grace, d. of Stanley Pipe Wolferstan, Esq., of Statfold and Pipe. Was educ. at the Charterhouse and at Oxford (Corpus Christi Coll.); entered at the Inner Temple 1834. Assumed by Royal licence in 1835 the name of Hicks in lieu of his patronymic on succeeding to the estates of that family. Chairman of Quarter Sessions for Cambridgeshire, and Chairman of Finance Committee for 30 years. A Conservative, opposed to the increase of local burdens and to centralization. Sat for Cambridgeshire from Jan. 1879 until he was defeated in 1885 contesting the Newmarket division. Died 13 Jan. 1889. [1885]

HICKS-BEACH, Sir M.E. Continued in House after 1885: full entry in Volume II.

HICKS-BEACH, Sir M.H. See BEACH, Sir M.H. Hicks-.

HIGGINS, George Gore Ouseley. 41 St. James's Place, London. Glen-Corrib, Co. Mayo. Alfred, and Turf. 2nd s. of Fitzgerald Higgins, Esq., of Westport, Co. of Mayo, by the d. of William Ouseley, Esq., of Rushbrooke. B. 1818. Unmarried. Educ. at Trinity Coll., Dublin. Was in the civil service in Jamaica. A Magistrate for Mayo, and Lieut.-Col. of the North Mayo Militia. A Liberal, in favour of 'tenant-right, and every measure for the advancement of civil and religious liberty.' First returned for Mayo July 1850. Sat until defeated 1857. Died 8 May 1874. [1857]

HILDYARD, Robert Charles. 24 Lowndes Street, London. Manor House, Catherston, Dorset. Carlton. B. at Winestead 1800, the 3rd s. of Rev. William Hildyard, Rector of Winestead, Yorkshire, by Catherine, 3rd d. of Isle Grant of Ruckland, Lincolnshire. Educ. at Oakham, Rutlandshire and at Catharine Hall, Cambridge, of which he was a Fellow. Was Senior Optime in 1823, and graduated M.A. 1826. Was called to the bar at Lincoln's Inn in 1827, was a Queen's Counsel and joined the Northern Circuit. A Bencher of the Inner Temple. Was Counsel to the Duchy of Lancaster, but resigned 1846. A Conservative, supported inquiry into Maynooth. Returned for Whitehaven, without opposition, in 1847, and sat until his death 7 Dec. 1857.

[1852 2nd ed.]

HILDYARD, Thomas Blackborne Thoroton-. 24 St. James Street, Pimlico, London. Winestead Hall, Hull. Flintham Hall, Newark. Carlton. Eld. s. of Col. Thomas Thoroton, of Flintham Hall, Nottinghamshire, by Anne Catherine Whyte, niece and heir of Sir Robert D'Arcy Hildyard (last Bart.), of Winestead Hall, Yorkshire, whose name Col. Thoroton assumed. B. at Flintham, Nottinghamshire, 1821; m. 1842, Anne Margaret, 2nd d. of Col. Rochfort, of Clogrenane, Co. Carlow. Educ. at Eton and at Christ Church, Oxford. A Magistrate for Nottinghamshire. Patron of 2 livings. A Conservative. Sat for S. Nottinghamshire from Feb. 1846 till July 1852;

re-elected June 1866 and sat until he retired in 1885. Died 19 Mar. 1888. [1885]

HILL, Rt. Hon. Lord Arthur Marcus Cecil. 2 Chesham Street, Belgrave Square, London. Reform. 3rd s. of the 2nd Marq. of Downshire. B. in Hanover Square, London, 1798; m. Apr. 12, 1837, Louisa, youngest d. of J. Blake, Esq., related to Admiral Blake. Comptroller of the Household from July 1846 to July 1847, when he became Treasurer. A Liberal. Represented Newry in 1832. Retired in 1835. Sat for Evesham from 1838, when he was seated on petition, having been unsuccessful at the poll. Sat until he retired in 1852. Succeeded bro. as 3rd Baron Sandys July 1860. Died 10 Apr. 1863. [1852]

HILL, Lord Arthur Moyses William. 20 Arlington Street, London. Bro. of the Marq. of Downshire, and s. and heir of the Baroness Sandys. B. 1792. Lieut.-Col. of the Scots Greys; was at Waterloo. Of moderate Whig principles; supported the Reform Act; opposed to a repeal of the Union. Sat for Downshire from 1812. Succeeded mother as 1st Baron Sandys Aug. 1836. Died 16 July 1860. [1836]

HILL, A. Staveley, Q.C. Continued in House after 1885: full entry in Volume II.

HILL, Lord A.W. Continued in House after 1885: full entry in Volume II.

HILL, Matthew Davenport. 44 Chancery Lane, London. S. of Mr. Hill, of Hazelwood School, and bro. of Mr. Hill, of Bruce Castle School, Tottenham. A Barrister. Was a Reporter on the *Morning Herald* when he first came to London; he afterwards became a contributor to magazines; gradually rose in his profession, and was recommended by Lord Brougham to the Livery of London as a fit person to succeed Sir Thomas Denman as Common Serjeant, but was unsuccessful in his attempt to obtain that office. Of Whig principles, inclined to radicalism. Sat for Hull from 1832 until defeated in 1835. Q.C. 1834. Died 7 June 1872. [1833]

HILL, Sir Rowland, Bart. Limmer's Hotel, London. Hawkestone, Shropshire. Carlton. Heir presumptive to his uncle, Lord Hill. B. 1800; m. 1831, Anne, only child and heiress of Joseph Glegg, Esq., of Peplow Hall, Drayton. Patron of 3 livings. A Conservative. Sat for Shropshire N. from 1821 until he succeeded uncle as 2nd Visct. Hill, Dec. 1842. Died 2 Jan 1875. [1842]

HILL, Hon. Rowland Clegg. Hawkstone Park, Shrewsbury. White's. Eld. s. of the 2nd Visct.

Hill, by Anne, only d. and heir of Joseph Clegg, Esq., of Peplow Hall, Shropshire. B. at Hawkstone 1833. Appointed Cornet in the N. Shropshire Yeomanry Cavalry 1853. A Magistrate and Dept.-Lieut. of Shropshire 1857; a Dept.-Lieut. of Ross-shire 1862. A Conservative, 'a firm supporter of the Queen and constitution, and an unflinching advocate of the pure doctrines of the Protestant faith'; opposed to the abolition of Church rates without an equivalent. First returned in Mar. 1857 for Shropshire N, which county his father had represented for 21 years. Sat until he retired 1865. Succeeded as 3rd Visct. Jan. 1875. Died 30 Mar. 1895.   [1865]

HILL, Thomas Rowley. Belgrave Mansions, London. St. Catherine's Hill, Worcester. Reform, and Devonshire. S. of William Hill, Esq., F.R.A.S. B. at Stourport 1816; m. 1842, Mary, d. of Edward Evans, Esq., (a Magistrate of Worcester). Educ. at University Coll., London. Was Mayor of Worcester in 1858, and High Sheriff of Worcestershire in 1870; a Magistrate for Herefordshire and for the co. and city of Worcester; also a Dept.-Lieut. for Worcestershire. A Liberal, and gave independent support to that party; in favour of the amendment of the land laws, etc. Sat for Worcester from Feb. 1874 until he retired in 1885. Died 9 Oct. 1896.
[1885]

HILLSBOROUGH, Earl of. 21 Hanover Square, London. Hillsborough Castle, Downshire. Carlton. The eld. s. of the Marq. of Downshire. B. 1812. Married the d. of the 1st Lord Combermere. A Conservative and first elected for the county of Down in 1836, in the room of his Uncle, Lord Arthur Hill, who succeeded to the Barony of Sandys on the death of his Mother, the Marchioness Dowager of Downshire. Continued to sit until he succeeded as the 4th Marq. in Apr. 1845. He died on 6 Aug. 1868.   [1844]

HILL-TREVOR, Lord A.E. See TREVOR, Lord A.E. Hill.

HINCHINBROOK, Visct. 6 James Street, Pimlico, London. Hinchinbrook House, Huntingdon. Army & Navy, and Travellers'. Edl. s. of Earl of Sandwich by his 1st wife, Lady Mary, 7th d. of 1st Marq. of Anglesey. B. in London 1839. Appointed Lieut. Grenadier Guards 1862, Adjutant 1864, promoted to be Capt. and Lieut.-Col. 1870. A Magistrate for Huntingdonshire. Pres. of the Huntingdon Conservative Assoc. A Conservative. Sat for Huntingdon from Feb. 1876 until he succeeded as 8th Earl in Mar. 1884. Mayor of Huntingdon 1896-98. Died 26 June 1916. [1883]

HINDE, John Hodgson. Elswick, Northumberland. S. of John Hodgson, Esq., of Elswick. Assumed the name of Hinde on succeeding to the estates of that family. B. 1806; m. 1833, d. and co-heir of A. Compton, Esq., of Carham Hall. Returned for Newcastle-upon-Tyne in Dec. 1832. Defeated Jan. 1835. Re-elected for Newcastle-upon-Tyne on the death of Sir M.W. Ridley, Bart. in 1836. Sat until he retired 1847. Died 26 Nov. 1869.   [1846]

HINDLEY, Charles. Dartmouth House, Westminster, London. Portland House, Ashton, Lancashire. Reform, and Brooks's. M. 1839, d. of R. Fort, Esq. (she died 1854). A Liberal; 'peace, economy and reform were his watchwords.' Voted for the ballot 1853. Unsuccessfully contested Ashton 1832. In 1835 he succeeded at Ashton-under-Lyne, and was, at the same time, an unsuccessful candidate at Warrington. Sat for Ashton-under-Lyne until his death 1 Dec. 1857.
[1857 2nd ed.]

HOARE, Sir Henry Ainslie, Bart. Stourhead, Wiltshire. Brooks's. S. of Henry Charles Hoare, Esq., of Wavendon House, Buckinghamshire, by Penelope, d. of Gen. Ainslie and relict of Capt. John Prince, Coldstream Guards. B. in York Place, Portman Square 1824; m. 1845, Augusta Frances, 2nd d. of Sir East George Clayton-East, Bart. Educ. at Eton and at Cambridge. Appointed a Dept.-Lieut. of Somerset 1858. Patron of 8 livings. A Liberal, in favour of the 1867 Reform Act being extended. Sat for Windsor from July 1865 to Apr. 1866, when he was unseated on petition. Sat for Chelsea from Dec. 1868 until defeated 1874. Contested E. Somerset 1885. Died 7 July 1894.   [1873]

HOARE, Joseph. Child's Hill, Hampstead. Oxford & Cambridge. S. of Samual Hoare, Esq., Banker, by Louisa, d. of John Gurney, Esq., of Earlham. B. at Hampstead 1814; m. 1847, Rachel Juliana, d. of Charles Barclay, Esq., of Bury Hill, Dorking. Educ. at Trinity Coll., Cambridge. A Banker in London from 1834. A 'very Liberal-Conservative', opposed to frequent change and therefore supported the 1859 government; averse to the disenfranchisement of county voters in boroughs, and to the equalisation of town and country suffrages; opposed to the ballot and to the Maynooth grant; favoured an extended system of national education 'firmly grounded on religious principles.' First elected for Hull May 1859, but unseated on petition, Aug. 1859. Contested Manchester in 1868. Died 21 Jan 1886.
[1859]

HOARE, Peter Merrick. 3 Hyde Park Gate, Kensington, London. Carlton. S. of Peter Richard Hoare, Esq., (Banker, Fleet Street, London), of Luscombe, Devon, by Lady Sophia, eld. d. of 2nd Earl of Romney. B. in London 1843; m. 1865, Edith Augusta, d. of the Rev. Edward Strong, Rector of Clyst St. Mary, Devon. A Magistrate for Devon. A Conservative, in favour of 'peace, retrenchment and reform', voted against the disestablishment of the Irish Church 1869. Sat for Southampton from Dec. 1868 until he retired 1874. Bankrupt 16 June 1874. Died 22 Feb. 1894. [1873]

HOBHOUSE, Henry William. Fenby House, Somerset. Brooks's, and Reform. Next bro. to Sir John Cam Hobhouse, Bart. Married. A Liberal, in favour of the ballot. Unsuccessfully contested Bath Dec. 1832, Finsbury Jan. 1835 and Warwick Aug. 1836. First elected for Hereford City in 1841. Sat until he accepted the Chiltern Hundreds Sept. 1841. [1841]

HOBHOUSE, Rt. Hon. Sir John Cam, Bart., F.R.S. 42 Berkeley Square, London. Westbury College, Gloucestershire. Enlestoke Park, Wiltshire. Athenaeum, and Reform. B. 1786; m. 1828, Lady Julia, d. of 7th Marquis of Tweeddale (she died 1835). Educ. at Trinity Coll., Cambridge. Partner in the House of Whitbread & Co., the London Brewers. Published his Travels with Lord Byron in Greece. Having been prominently active in the cause of Reform in 1818 and 1819, and having been sent to prison by the House of Commons in the latter year, from which he was only released at the end of three months by the death of George III, he was in 1820 elected for Westminster. Became Secretary-at-War in 1832, was shortly afterwards appointed Secretary for Ireland, but resigned in May 1833, in consequence of the Government resolving not to take off the house and window taxes. Then accepted the Chiltern Hundreds, in order to give his constituents an opportunity of expressing their opinion of his conduct in not voting in favour of that measure. Sir de Lacy Evans, who had unsuccessfully opposed him in 1832, was then returned for Westminster. In 1834 he was appointed Chief Commissioner of Woods and Forests, which office he held until November of that year. President of the Board of Control from Apr. 1835 until Sept. 1841, and from July 1846. Elected for Nottingham 1834, and unsuccessfully contested Bristol in 1835. Sat for Nottingham from 1835 until the general election of 1847. Returned for Harwich 1848, without opposition. Sat until created Baron Broughton, Feb. 1851. Died 3 June 1869. [1850]

HOBHOUSE, Thomas Benjamin. 5 Brick Court, Temple, London. Reform. S. of Sir Benjamin Hobhouse (1st Bart.), by his 2nd wife, d. of the Rev. Joshua Parry, of Cirencester, Gloucestershire. Was called to the bar at the Middle Temple, May 1833, and went the Western circuit. A Reformer. Was an unsuccessful candidate for Aylesbury in 1832, again in 1835, and for Newark in 1841. Sat for Rochester from 1837 till the general election 1841. First returned for Lincoln, Mar. 1848. Sat until defeated contesting Ipswich in 1852. Died 31 Dec. 1876. [1852]

HODGES, Thomas Law. 12 Suffolk Street, Pall Mall E., London. Hemsted, Kent. Reform, and United University. Eld. s. of Thomas Hallett Hodges, Esq., of Hemsted, Kent, by the youngest d. of John Cartwright, Esq., of Marnham, Nottinghamshire. Father of the member for Rochester. B. 1776; m. 1802, Rebecca, only child of Sir Roger Twisden, Bart., of Bradbourn Park, Kent. A Dept.-Lieut. of Kent; a Magistrate for that county and for Sussex; formerly Major in the West Kent Militia. A Liberal, in favour of the ballot, the repeal of the malt tax, and short Parliaments; opposed to the endowment of the Roman Catholic clergy. Sat for Kent from 1830 till the dissolution of Parliament in 1841; again elected in 1847. Sat until defeated in 1852. Died 14 May 1857. [1852]

HODGES, Thomas Twisden. 3 Arlington Street, London. Sandgate, Kent. Reform. Only s. of Thomas Law Hodges, Esq., of Hemsted, Kent, (MP for that county) by the only d. and heir of Sir Roger Twisden, Bart., of Bradbourn Park. M. Mary, d. of Thomas Chandless, Esq., of London; she died 1849. A Liberal, in favour of the ballot; voted for the repeal of the malt tax. First elected for Rochester in 1835 by a majority of one over Lord Charles Wellesley, and defended his seat successfully against the petition which followed his return; sat till 1837; was re-elected in 1847; but in the interval was twice an unsuccessful candidate for Canterbury, viz. in Feb. and in July 1841. Sat for Rochester from 1847 until defeated in 1852. Emigrated to Australia in 1852. Died 12 Mar. 1865. [1852]

HODGKINSON, Grosvenor. 105 Pall Mall, London. North Gate, Newark. Reform. S. of George Hodgkinson, Esq., by Julia, d. of John Beevor, Esq., Rector of Claypole, Lincolnshire. B. at Newark, 1818; m. 1845, Alice, d. of Robert Harvey, Esq. Educ. at King Edward's School, Louth. Admitted an Attorney and Solicitor 1839, retired. A Magistrate for Nottinghamshire. A Liberal, in favour of short Parliaments, voted for the disestablishment of the Irish Church 1869. First elected for Newark Apr. 1859. Sat until he retired 1874. Died 14 Feb. 1881.   [1873]

HODGSON, Frederick. 3 Carlton Gardens, London. Carlton, and Boodle's. B. 1796; m. 1831, d. of John Erskine, Esq. A Brewer and Merchant. Appointed a Dept.-Lieut. of the Tower Hamlets in 1846. A Conservative, and gave no pledge; voted for agricultural protection 1846. Sat for Barnstaple in 1824, 1826, 1831, 1837, and 1841, and continued to sit until defeated 1847. Died 30 Mar. 1854.   [1847]

HODGSON, J. See HINDE, J. Hodgson.

HODGSON, Kirkham Daniel. 67 Brook Street, London, Ashgrove, Sevenoaks, Kent. Brooks's, Travellers', Union, and Athenaeum. Eld. s. of John Hodgson, Esq., of The Elmo, Hampstead. B. in London 1814; m. 1843, Frances, d. of J.L. Butler, Esq., of Southgate (she died 1851). Educ. at the Charterhouse. A Merchant in London. Was Dept.-Gov. of the Bank of England in 1861-63; Gov. in 1863 and 1865. A Director of the Bank. An 'advanced Liberal'. Sat for Bridport from Mar. 1857 to Nov. 1868, when he stood unsuccessfully for Penryn. Sat for Bristol from June 1870 until he accepted Chiltern Hundreds in 1878. Died 11 Sept. 1879.   [1877]

HODGSON, Richard. 48 Eaton Square, London. Carham Hall, Coldstream, Berwickshire. S. of John Hodgson, Esq., of Elswick. Bro. to J. Hodgson Hinde, Esq., member for Newcastle-upon-Tyne. B. 1 Apr. 1812; m. 2nd d. of A. Compton, Esq., of Carham Hall. Chairman to the N. British Railway. A Conservative, voted for agricultural protection 1846; in favour of a £6 franchise, with some restrictions; opposed to the ballot. Sat for Berwick from 1837 to July 1847, when he was an unsuccessful candidate for Newcastle-upon-Tyne; elected for Tynemouth Apr. 1861. Sat until defeated 1865.   [1865]

HODGSON, William Nicholson. 33 Duke Street, St. James's, London. Newby Grange, Nr. Carlisle. Carlton. Eld s. of Joseph Hodgson, Esq., of Carlisle, by Sarah, d. of W. Nicholson Esq., of Batt House, Crosby. B. at Carlisle 1807; m. 1831, Mary, d. of Thomas Irwin Esq., of Justus Fown, Cumberland (she died 1869). Educ. at Richmond School, Yorkshire. A Magistrate and Dept.-Lieut. for Cumberland. High Sheriff of Cumberland, 1863. A Conservative, once in favour of protection to agriculture; voted against the disestablishment of the Irish Church 1869. Sat for Carlisle from 1847 to 1852 when he was unsuccessful; again elected Mar. 1857, and sat till Apr. 1859, when he

was again unsuccessful; also unsuccessful Nov. 1861. Again sat for Carlisle from July 1865 to Dec. 1868 when he was once more defeated. Then obtained a seat for E. Cumberland which he represented until his death 2 Apr. 1876.   [1876]

HODGSON-HINDE, J. See HINDE, J. Hodgson.

HOGG, Sir James Macnaghten McGarel-. See MCGAREL-HOGG, Sir James Macnaghten.

HOGG, Sir James Weir, Bart. 16 Grosvenor Square, London. Carlton. Eld. s. of William Hogg, Esq., by the d. of James Dickey, Esq., of Dunmore, Co. Antrim. Was originally of Scottish descent. B. at Stoneyford, Co. Antrim 1790; m. 1822, Mary, d. of Samuel Swinton, Esq., of Swinton, Co. Berwick. A Barrister. Shortly after he was called to the bar he proceeded to Calcutta where he practised with much success, and latterly held the office of Registrar in the Supreme Court. Elected an East India Director in 1839, and Chairman of the Court in 1846. A Dept.-Lieut. of London. A Conservative. Sat for Beverley from 1834 to 1847, when he was returned for Honiton. Sat until defeated in 1857.   [1857]

HOLDEN, I. Continued in House after 1885: full entry in Volume II.

HOLDSWORTH, Joseph. Bellefield House, Yorkshire. Eld. s. of Joseph Holdsworth, Esq., of Belleisle, near Wakefield. B. 1789; m. 1822, Elizabeth, d. of Thomas Holy, Esq., of Highfield House, Sheffield. A Dyer; a Director of the North Midland Railway; was Chairman of the great West Riding meeting previous to the passing of the Reform Bill; was returning officer for Wakefield till Mar. 1841. A Magistrate of the West Riding. A Whig. First returned for Wakefield in 1841. Unseated since Mr. Holdsworth had himself been the returning officer in Wakefield from 1832 to 1841.   [1842]

HOLFORD, James Price William Gwynne-. 31 Grosvenor Square, London. Cilgwyn, Carmarthenshire. Buckland, Chrickhowell, S. Wales. Carlton, and Junior United Service. Only s. of Co. James Price Holford, of Cilgwyn, Carmarthenshire (High Sheriff of Brecknockshire in 1840), by Anna Maria Eleanor, only d. of Roderick Gwynne, Esq., and grand-d. and heir of Thynne Howe Gwynne, Esq., of Buckland, South Wales. B. at Buckland 1833. Educ. at Eton and at Christ Church, Oxford. Appointed Cornet 16th Lancers 1854; retired. A Magistrate for Brecknockshire and Carmarthenshire, a Dept.-Lieut. of Brecknockshire, of which last named county he was High Sheriff in 1857. A Liberal-Conservative, declared he would never sanction the separation of Church and State. Sat for the bor. of Brecknock from July 1870 until defeated 1880. [1880]

HOLFORD, Robert Stayner. Dorchester House, Park Lane, London. Westonbirt, Tetbury, Gloucestershire. Carlton. Only s. of George Peter Holford, Esq., of Westonbirt, Gloucestershire by Anne, d. of Rev. Averell Daniell, of Lifford, Co. Donegal. B. 1808. Graduated at Oriel Coll., Oxford, B.A. 1829. A Magistrate for Gloucester and for Wiltshire. Was High Sheriff of the latter county in 1843. appointed Capt. Gloucestershire Yeomanry 1857. A Conservative; voted against the disestablishment of the Irish Church 1869, and believed 'that the connection of Church and State is one of the greatest blessings which we possess'; in favour of the malt-tax being altered to a small duty on beer. First elected for Gloucestershire E. Dec. 1854. Sat until he accepted Chiltern Hundreds Mar. 1872. Died 22 Feb. 1892. [1872]

HOLKER, Sir John. 46 Devonshire Street, Portland Place, London. 6 Crown Office Row, Temple, London. Conservative, and St. Stephen's. S. of Samual Holker, Esq., Manufacturer, of Bury, Lancashire, by Sarah, d. of J. Brocklehurst, Esq. B. at Bury 1828. Educ. at Bury Grammar School. Was called to the Bar at Gray's Inn 1854 and on the Northern Circuit; appointed at Queen's Counsel 1868. Was Solicitor-Gen. from Apr. 1874-Nov. 1875, and Attorney Gen. from the latter date to April 1880. A Conservative, was in favour of maintaining 'our ancient constitution in Church and State.' Sat for Preston from Sept. 1872 until appointed Lord Justice of Appeal 14 Jan. 1882. Died 24 May 1882. [1881]

HOLLAND, Edward. Dumbleton Park, Evesham. Union. M. 1857, Frances Maria Hunter, d. of Samuel Christian, Esq., of Malta. A Magistrate for Gloucestershire. Patron of one living. A Liberal, and in favour of a considerable extension of the franchise. Sat for Worcestershire E. from Jan. 1835 till July 1837, when he was an unsuccessful candidate there. Contested Gloucestershire E., unsuccessfully, Jan. 1854. First returned for Evesham, July 1855. Sat until he retired in 1868 after Evesham made a single member seat. Died 5 Jan. 1875. [1867]

HOLLAND, Sir H.T. Continued in House after 1885: full entry in Volume II.

HOLLAND, Samuel. Caerdeon, Merionethshire. Reform. S. of Samuel Holland, Esq., of Liverpool, Merchant, by Catherine, d. of John Menzies, Esq., of Liverpool. B. at Liverpool 1803; m. 1st, 1850, Anne, d. of Mr. Josiah Robins, of Aston, Birmingham (she died 1877); 2ndly, 1878, Caroline Jane, d. of Rev. John Thomas Burt, of Broadmoor. A Quarry Owner in North Wales. A Magistrate for Merioneth. A Liberal, and supported Mr. Gladstone. Sat for Merionethshire from Jan. 1870, until he retired in 1885. [1885]

HOLLOND, John Robert. 1 Upper Berkeley Street, London. The Hall, Stanmore, Middlesex. Wonham, Devon. Reform. 2nd s. of Rev. Edmund Hollond, of Benhall Lodge, Suffolk, by Isabella, youngest d. of the Rev. Sir John Robinson, Bart., of Rokeby Hall, Co. Louth, Ireland, B. at Benhall Lodge 1843; m. 1870, Fanny Eliza, youngest d. of F. Keats, Esq., of Braziors, Oxfordshire. Educ. at Harrow and at Trinity Coll., Cambridge. A Commissioner of the Lieutenancy of London. Was called to the Bar at the Inner Temple 1870. A decided Liberal, regarded the 'reform of the Land Laws as one of the pressing questions of the day'; in favour also of the abolition of the laws of primogeniture and entail, the assimilation of the borough and county franchise, etc. Sat for Brighton from Apr. 1880 until he retired in 1885. Contested East Perthshire in 1886. Died 27 Dec. 1892. [1885]

HOLLOND, Robert. 63 Portland Place, London. Pall Mall, London. Allegria, Sussex. Reform. 4th s. of William Hollond, Esq., of Grosvenor Place, London. B. 5th Jan. 1808; m. in 1840, d. of Thos. Teed, Esq. Formerly of Corpus Christi Coll., Cambridge, where he graduated M.A. 1831; was called to the bar at Lincoln's Inn 1834. A 'Reformer, pledged to support the ballot.' Sat for Hastings from 1837 until he retired in 1852. Died 26 Dec. 1887. [1852]

HOLMES, Rt. Hon. H. Continued in House after 1885: full entry in Volume II.

HOLMES, William. 10 Grafton Street, London. Carlton, Athenaeum, Union, and Colonial. 5th s. of Thomas Holmes, Esq., of Farmhill, Sligo, who was High Sheriff of that Co. in 1810. Descended from an ancient family in the King's. Co. B. 1779; m. Lady Stronge, d. of John Tow, Esq., and widow of Sir James Stronge, Bart. Educ. at Trinity Coll., Dublin. Was a Capt. in the army, and for many years filled the office of Treasurer of the Ordnance; but resigned when Lord Grey became the head of the Government. First returned to Parliament in 1809, and continued uninterruptedly to be a member of the House of Commons for three and twenty years; supported the Perceval, Liverpool and Wellington administrations; voted against the Roman Catholic Relief Act; in July 1837 contested Berwick with Sir Rufane Donkin on the reappointment of the Melbourne ministry and beat him by a small majority. Retired 1841. Stood for Ipswich in 1835, and previously for Queenborough. Contested Stafford in June 1841 and Dungannon July 1852. Died 26 Jan. 1861. [1841]

HOLMES, Hon. William Henry Ashe A'Court. Westover, Isle of Wight. Carlton. Eld. s. of Lord Heytesbury (who m. Maria Rebecca, cousin-german of the Earl of Radnor) and nephew of Capt. A'Court, R.N., member for Tamworth. B. 11 July 1809; m. 3 Oct. 1833, Elizabeth, eld. d. of Sir Leonard Worsley Holmes, Bart., and assumed the name of Holmes. A Conservative, voted for agricultural protection 1846. Sat for Isle of Wight from 1837 until he retired 1847. Succeeded as 2nd Baron Heytesbury May 1860. Died 21 Apr. 1891. [1847]

HOLMESDALE, Visct. 20 Belgrave Square, London. Linton Park, Staplehurst. Carlton. Eld. s. of Earl Amherst, by Gertrude, 6th d. of the Hon. Hugh Percy, Bishop of Carlisle. B. 1836; m. 1862, Lady Julia Mann-Cornwallis, only d. of the last Earl Cornwallis. Entered the army 1854, appointed Lieut. and Capt. Coldstream Guards 1855, served in the Eastern Campaign in 1854, including Balaklava and Inkermann (where he was severely wounded), and the siege of Sebastopol, for which he received a medal and clasps, retired from the army 1862. A Dept.-Lieut. of Kent. A Conservative, opposed all measure which would 'impair the integrity of the Church of England.' Sat for W. Kent from May 1859 to Dec. 1868, from which date he sat for the mid division of Kent. Sat until he retired 1880. Summoned to Lords as Baron Amherst; succeeded father as 3rd Earl 26 Mar. 1886. Died 14 Aug. 1910. [1880]

HOLMS, John. 16 Cornwall Gardens, Queen's Gate, London. Reform and City Liberal. S. of James Holms, Esq., of Saucel Bank, Paisley, by Janet, d. of James Love, Esq., of Paisley. B. at Saucel Bank, Paisley, 1830; m. 1856, Elizabeth, d. of Edward Lyon, Esq., of Kensington. A Spinner at Glasgow; a Partner in the firm of Messrs. W. Holms. Bros., of Glasgow. Was a Lord of the Treasury from Apr. 1880 to May 1882, when he was appointed Parliamentary Secretary to the Board of Trade (salary £1500). A Magistrate for the Co. of Lanark, Middlesex, and Westminster, also a Dept.-Lieut. for the Tower Hamlets. Author of *The British Army in 1837, with Suggestions on its Administration and Organization,* also *Our Military Difficulty,* etc. A Liberal, in favour of a re-adjustment of local taxation, and of the equalization of poor-rates. Sat for Hackney from Dec. 1868 until he retired in 1885. Died 31 Mar. 1891. [1885]

HOLMS, William. 5 Drumsheugh Gardens W., Edinburgh. Reform. Eld. s. of James Holms, Esq., of Saucel Bank, Paisley, by Janet, d. of James Love, Esq. B. at Saucel Bank, Paisley 1827; m. 1857 Mary Lindsay McArthur, d. of the late John Buchanan, Esq., LL.D., Glasgow. Bro. of John Holms, Esq., M.P. for Hackney and a Partner in the firm of William Holms and Brothers, Spinners and Manufacturers, Glasgow and London. A Magistrate for Lanarkshire and Lieut. Col. 1st Lanarkshire Artillery Volunteers. A Liberal, in favour of the abolition of the laws of entail and primogeniture. Sat for Paisley from Jan. 1874 until he accepted Chiltern Hundreds in 1883. [1883]

HOLT, James Maden. Balham House, Balham Hill, London. Stubbylee, Nr. Bacup. Carlton, and National. S. of John Holt, Esq., of Stubbylee (a Magistrate for Lancashire and the W. Riding of Yorkshire), by Judith, d. of James Maden, Esq., of Greene House, Nr. Bacup. B. at Stubbylee, Nr. Bacup 1829. Educ. at Christ Church, Oxford. Patron of 1 living. A Conservative, a 'firm upholder of the Church of England and the Protestant constitution.' Sat for N.E. Lancashire from Dec. 1868 until he retired 1880. Chairman of Church Association Council 1883-85. Died 19 Sept. 1911. [1880]

HOME, Col. David Milne. Paxton House, Berwick-on-Tweed. Carlton. S. of David Milne Home, Esq., LL.D., F.R.S. of Milne Graden, Co. Berwick, by Jean, eld. d. and heir of William Forman Home, Esq., of Wedderburn. B. at Edinburgh 1838; m. 1867, Jane, d. of Sir Thomas Buchan Hepburn, Bart., of Smeaton, Hepburn. Educ. at Cheltenham Coll., Trinity Coll., Cambridge and Edinburgh University. Entered the Royal Horse Guards as Cornet May 1862; became Capt. 1868. A Conservative. Sat for Berwick from Feb. 1874 to Mar. 1880 when he was an unsuccessful candidate there; regained his seat Aug. 1880 and sat until he retired 1885. [1881]

HOOD, Sir Alexander, Bart. 43 Wimpole Street, London. Wooton, Glastonbury, Somerset. Only s. of Captain Alexander Hood, R.N. (who was slain at the capture of 'L'Hercule' 1798), by the daughter of John Perian, Esq., of Butley Wooton, Somerset. Nephew of the distinguished Sir Samual Hood, (whose baronetcy he enjoyed) and cousin to Lord Bridport (whose Peerage is in contingent remainder to this branch of the

197

family). B. at Wooton, Somerset 1793; m. 1815 Amelia Anne, youngest d. and co-heir to Sir Hugh Bateman, Baronet of Harlington Hall, Co. Derby. Graduated at Exeter Coll., Oxford. A Magistrate for Somerset. A Conservative and Protectionist, opposed to the endowment of the Roman Catholic clergy. First returned for Somerset W. in 1847 and MP until his death 7 Mar. 1851.   [1850]

HOOD, Sir Alexander Bateman Periam Fuller-Acland-, Bart. St. Andries, Bridgewater. Wooton House, Glastonbury, Somerset. Conservative. Eld. s. of Sir Alexander Hood, Bart. (who sat for West Somerset from 1847 till his death in 1851), by Amelia Anne, youngest d. and co-heir of Sir Hugh Bateman, Bart. B. at Bath, 1819; m. 1849, Isabel Harriet, only surviving child of Sir Peregrine Palmer Fuller-Palmer-Acland, Bart. Educ. at Rugby. Appointed Capt. Royal Horse Guards Blue, 1846, but retired; made a Dept.-Lieut. of Somerset 1852. Assumed the names of Fuller-Acland by royal licence on his marriage. A Conservative, and gave 'an independent support to Lord Derby'; in favour of 'keeping our army, and especially our navy, in as efficient a state as possible.' First elected for Somerset W., May 1859. Sat until he retired in 1868. Died Apr. 1892.   [1867]

HOOD, Hon. Arthur Wellington Alexander Nelson. 8 Grosvenor Gardens, London. Cricket St. Thomas, Chard, Somerset. Carlton. Eld. s. of Visct. Bridport, by Lady Mary, 2nd d. of the 3rd Marq. of Downshire. B. 1839; m. 1872, Lady Maria Georgiana Julia, only sister of the 5th Earl of Ilchester. Entered the army as Ensign 1857, became Capt. 26th Foot 1862. A Conservative, in favour of an Established Church being preserved throughout the empire. Sat for W. Somerset from Dec. 1868 until he retired 1880. Succeeded as 4th Baron and 2nd Visct. Bridport June 1904. Died 28 Mar. 1924.   [1880]

HOPE, General Hon. Sir Alexander, G.C.B. Chelsea College, London. Craighall. Farnham, Surrey. Uncle of the Earl of Hopetoun. M. in 1805, Georgiana, youngest d. of George Brown, Esq., of Ellistoun. A Lieut.-Gen. in the Army, and Col. of the 47th regiment; Lieut.-Gov. of Chelsea Hospital; enjoyed a pension for the loss of his arm. A Conservative, in favour of the corn laws. Sat for Linlithgowshire from 1790 until he retired in 1835. Died 19 May 1837.   [1833]

HOPE, A.J.B. See BERESFORD-HOPE, Rt. Hon. A.J.B.

HOPE, Hon. Charles. Greenwich Hospital,

London. The bro. of the Earl of Hopetoun, b. in 1808. In 1841 m. Lady Isabella Helen, the eld. d. of the 5th Earl of Selkirk. Was called to the Scottish bar in 1831. Was a Commissioner of Greenwich Hospital and was appointed Lieut. Governor of the Isle of Man from Aug. 1845-60. A Conservative. Sat for Linlithgowshire from 1838 until 1845. Died 31 Oct. 1893.   [1845]

HOPE, George William. 14 Curzon Street, London. Luffness, Drem, Haddingtonshire. Travellers', and Carlton. S. of Gen. the Hon. Sir Alexander Hope (4th s. of 2nd Earl of Hopetoun), by Georgina Alicia, 3rd d. of George Browne, Esq. of Ellistoun. B. at Blackheath, Kent 1808; m. 1836, Caroline Georgina, d. and co-heir of 2nd Lord Montagu, and grand-d. of 3rd Duke of Buccleuch. Educ. at Christ Church, Oxford. Called to the bar at Lincoln's Inn, 1841. Was Under Secretary of State for the Colonies from Sept. 1841 till Dec. 1845. A Liberal-Conservative, had 'no aversion to change (if proved right),' but would 'firmly resist those sweeping and democratic measures of Parliamentary reform, of which the inevitable tendency is to make mere numbers predominate over intelligence and property.' First elected for Windsor, Apr. 1859. MP until his death 18 Oct. 1863.   [1863]

HOPE, Henry Thomas. 116 Piccadilly, London. Deepdene, Dorking, Surrey. Trenant Park, East Looe, Cornwall. Carlton. Eld. s. of Thomas Hope, Esq., of Deepdene, Surrey (the well-known author of *Anastasius*, by the youngest d. of Lord Decies, Archbishop of Tuam (she m. 2ndly Visct. Beresford). B. 1808; graduated at Trinity Coll., Cambridge. A Magistrate for Surrey and Gloucestershire; a Director of the London and Westminster Joint Stock Bank. A Conservative, but in favour of free trade; voted against a repeal of the malt tax in 1835; opposed the Reform Bill. Sat for East Looe in 1830 and 1831. Unsuccessfully contested Marylebone 20 Mar. 1833. Was an unsuccessful candidate for Gloucester in Dec. 1832; returned for that city in 1833, and sat till 1841, when he was defeated; was re-elected for Gloucester in 1847 and sat until defeated in 1852. Contested same seat in 1853 by-election. Died 4 Dec. 1862.   [1852]

HOPE, Hon. James. Chelsea Hospital, Middlesex. Carlton. 2nd. s. of John, 4th Earl of Hopetoun. B. 1807; m. 1833, Charlotte, d. of Admiral Tollemache, nephew of the Hon. Gen. Sir Alexander Hope, Lieut.-Gov. of Chelsea Hospital. A Capt. in the army. A Conservative. Succeeded his uncle Sir Alexander Hope, in the representation of Linlithgowshire in 1835. Accepted Chiltern Hundreds June 1838. Assumed the additional final surname and arms of Wallace in compliance with the will of Thomas Lord Wallace, 3 Apr. 1844. Died 7 Jan. 1854. [1838]

HOPE, Sir John, Bart. 17 Fludyer Street, London. Pinkie House, Edinburgh. Carlton. B. in 1781, the s. of Sir Archibald Hope, 9th Bart. M. in 1805, the youngest d. of Sir John Wedderburn, Bart. Lieut.-Col. Commandant of the Midlothian Yeomanry Cavalry, Vice-Lieut. and Convener of that Co. A Conservative and in favour of protection to agriculture. First elected for the Co. of Edinburgh in 1845 without opposition, and sat until his death in June 1853. [1853]

HOPE-JOHNSTONE, John James (I). See JOHNSTONE, John James Hope. (I).

HOPE-JOHNSTONE, John James (II). See JOHNSTONE, John James Hope (II).

HOPWOOD, C.H. Continued in House after 1885: full entry in Volume II.

HOPWOOD, John Turner. Rock Cliffe, Blackburn, Lancashire. Carlton. S. of Robert Hopwood, Esq., of Blackburn, Lancashire, and Bracewell, Yorkshire, by Elizabeth, eld. d. of John Turner, Esq., of Huddersfield. B. at Blackburn 1829; m. 1858, Mary Augusta, 3rd d. of Hon. Henry Coventry. Educ. at Trinity Coll., Oxford, where he graduated 1854. Called to the bar 1854, and joined the Northern Circuit. Appointed a Dept.-Lieut. of Lancashire 1856. A Conservative, 'warmly attached to the Church of England, and desirous of promoting its efficiency.' First returned for Clitheroe in Apr. 1857. Sat until he retired 1865. Sheriff of Rutland 1877. Died 1 Jan. 1900. [1865]

HORNBY, Edmund George. 3 Bridge Street, Westminster, London. Grands. of the Earl of Derby. Of Whig principles, in favour of the ballot. Sat for Warrington from 1832 until he retired in 1835. Died 26 or 27 Feb. 1865. [1833]

HORNBY, Edward Kenworthy. 24 Pall Mall, London. Poole Hall, Nantwich. Brook House, Blackburn. Carlton. S. of William Henry Hornby, Esq., of Poole Park, Cheshire (who sat for Blackburn from Apr. 1857-Mar. 1869), by Margaret Susannah, d. and sole heir of Edward Birley, Esq., of Kirkham. B. at Blackburn 1839. Educ. at Harrow. A Cotton Spinner and Manufacturer. A Conservative. Sat for Blackburn from Mar. 1869 until he retired 1874. Died 25 June 1887. [1873]

HORNBY, John. 22 Park Crescent, Portland Place, London. University. Youngest s. of John Hornby, of Blackburn, Lancashire, and of Rake's Hall, Blackpool. M. 1844, Margaret, d. of the Rev. C. Bird, of Chollerton, Northumberland. A Conservative, formerly in favour of free trade, but voted for a return to agricultural protection 1850. First returned for Blackburn in 1841; was petitioned against in 1842, but the Committee declared him duly elected. Sat until defeated in 1852. Died 5 Dec. 1892. [1852]

HORNBY, William Henry. 3 Spring Gardens, London. Shrenbridge Hall, Nantwich, Cheshire. Mains Hall, Preston. Carlton, and Windham. 3rd s. of John Hornby, Esq., of Blackburn and Raikes Hall, Lancashire, by Alice, d. of Daniel Backhouse, Esq., of Liverpool, widow of — Kendall, Esq. B. 1805; m. 1831, Margaret Susannah, d. and sole heir of Edward Birley, Esq., of Kirkham. Educ. at Greenwich. A Merchant at Blackburn. A Magistrate for Cheshire and Lancashire, and a Dept. Lieut. for the Co. Palatine of Lancaster. A Conservative, and in favour of 'peace and retrenchment.' First elected for Blackburn, Apr. 1857 (had been an unsuccessful candidate there in Mar. 1853). Sat until he was unseated in 1869. Died 5 Sept. 1884. [1867]

HORNE, Sir William. 49 Upper Harley Street, London. 19 Lincoln's Inn Old Square, London. Epping House, Nr. Hertford. Was appointed Solicitor-Gen. in 1830 on the accession of the Whigs to office, and Attorney-Gen. on the recent elevation of Sir Thomas Denman to the Chief Justiceship of the King's Bench, vacant by the death of Lord Tenterden. Sat for Newton, Hampshire in 1831. Sat for Marylebone from Dec. 1832. Defeated in 1835. Contested seat again in 1837. Died 13 July 1860. [1833]

HORSFALL, Thomas Berry. Liverpool. Bellamour Hall, Lichfield, Staffordshire. Carlton, and National. Eld. s. of Charles Horsfall, Esq., a Liverpool Merchant, by Dorothy, only d. of Thomas Berry, Esq. B. at Liverpool, 1805; m. 1st, 1834, Jane Anne, 3rd d. of T.E. Marsh, Esq., of Llanidloes, Montgomeryshire; 2ndly, 1847, Mary, eld. d. of Edward S. Cox, Esq., of Brailsford Hall, Derbyshire (she died 1862); 3rdly, 1863, Sophia, eld. d. of the Rev. William Leeke, of Holbrooke Hall, Derbyshire. A Dept.-Lieut. and Magistrate for Lancashire and Staffordshire. Mayor of Liverpool during the disturbed period of 1847-48. Elected president of the Liverpool Chamber of Commerce on its foundation in 1849. A Merchant in Liverpool. A Conservative, voted with Lord Derby on his Reform Bill, 1859; opposed to the ballot, and to the tax upon income, though not upon property. Sat for Derby from July 1852 till Mar. 1853. First elected for Liverpool July 1853. Sat until he retired in 1868. Died 22 Dec. 1878. [1867]

HORSMAN, Rt. Hon. Edward. 1 Richmond Terrace, London. Reform, and Brooks's. S. of William Horsman, Esq., by Jane, d. of Sir John Dalrymple (4th Bart.). Nephew to the 9th Earl of Stair; m. 1841 Charlotte Louisa, only d. of John Charles Ramsden, Esq., many years MP for Malton. Educ. at Rugby. Became Advocate at the Scottish bar in 1831. Had been Commissioner of church inquiry in Scotland. Was a Lord of the Treasury from June 1840 till Sept. 1841, and Chief Sec. for Ireland from Feb. 1855-June 1857. A Liberal, voted for Lord Derby's Reform Bill March 1859, and against Lord Russell's Reform Bill 1866. Sat for Cockermouth from Feb. 1836 till July 1852, but was an unsuccessful candidate there in 1835 and 1852. Sat for Stroud from June 1853 till Dec. 1868. Unsuccessfully contested Falkerk 21 Nov. 1868. Sat for Liskeard from May 1869 until his death 30 Nov. 1876. [1876]

HOSKINS, Kedgwin. 90 Sloane Street, London. Birch House, Herefordshire. Reform. M. 1836, d. of — Haynes, Esq. A Banker at Hereford and Ross. Patron of 1 living. Of Whig principles. Voted for agricultural protection 1846. Sat for Herefordshire from 1831 until 1847, when he retired. Died 24 Dec. 1852. [1847]

HOSKYNS, Chandos Wren-. Harewood Park, Ross, Herefordshire. Athenaeum. 2nd s. of Sir Hungerford Hoskyns (7th Bart.) of Harewood, Herefordshire, by Sarah, youngest d. of John Philips, Esq., of Bank Hall, Lancashire. B. at Hereford 1812; m. 1st, 1837 Theodosia, d. and heir of Christopher Wren, Esq., of Wroxhall Abbey, Warwickshire, 2ndly, 1846, Anna Fane, youngest d. of Charles Millet Ricketts, Esq. Educ. at Shrewsbury School and at Balliol Coll., Oxford, where he graduated 2nd class in classics. Was called to the bar at the Inner Temple 1838. Assumed the name of Wren after his 1st marriage. Appointed Capt. 1st Herefordshire Rifle Volunteers 1861. Author of *Talpa; or, Chronicles of a Clay Farm*, also *Inquiry into the History of Agriculture*, etc. Patron of 2 livings. A 'Conservative-Liberal', in favour of civil and religious freedom. Sat for Hereford from Mar. 1869 until he retired 1874. Died 28 Nov. 1876. [1873]

HOTHAM, Lord. 46 Grosvenor Street, London. South Dalton Hall, Beverley, Yorkshire. Carlton, Athenaeum, and Boodle's. An Irish Peer. B. at Lullington, 1794; became a Gen. in the army,

1865; served with the Coldstream Guards in the Peninsula and at Waterloo; was wounded at Salamanca; received the war medal and 4 clasps, the Waterloo medal, etc. Patron of 4 livings. A Conservative, but voted against Lord Derby's Reform Bill, Mar. 1859. Sat for Leominster from 1820 until 1841, when he was first elected for the East Riding of Yorkshire. Sat until he retired in 1868. Died 12 Dec. 1870. [1867]

HOULDSWORTH, Thomas. Sheerwood Hall, Nottinghamshire. Carlton. A Merchant and a Cotton Spinner, at Manchester, and at Rocester, Staffordshire. Unmarried. A Conservative, voted for agricultural protection 1846. Sat for Pontefract from 1818 to 1830. Sat for Newton, Lancashire, from 1830 till 1832. From 1832 sat for Nottinghamshire N. until he retired in 1852. Died 1 Sept. 1852. [1852]

HOULDSWORTH, W.H. Continued in House after 1885: full entry in Volume II.

HOUSTOUN, George. Johnstone Castle, Renfrewshire. Oxford & Cambridge, and Carlton. S. of Ludovic Houstoun, Esq., of Johnstone, and Anne Stirling, eld. d. of John Stirling, Esq., of Kippendavie. B. 31st July, 1810. Contested Renfrewshire unsuccessfully in 1835. Elected by a large majority over Sir. J. Maxwell in Jan. 1837, and again after the dissolution of Parliament in the same year. 'An enemy to every species of corruption, opposed to all useless expenditure, a supporter of the institutions of the country, civil and sacred, although friendly to every practicable reform by which their efficiency can be increased, or their permanency secured. Would firmly oppose any measure which can be considered even an indirect attack on the Protestant interests of the country.' Retired in 1841. Died 14 Sept. 1843. [1840]

HOWARD, Hon. Charles Wentworth George. 1 Palace Green, London. Naworth Castle. Brampton, Cumberland. Travellers', and Brooks's. S. of 6th Earl of Carlisle, by eld. d. of 5th Duke of Devonshire. B. 1814; m. 1842, Mary, 2nd. d. of the Rt. Hon. Sir Jas. Parke, Baron of the Court of Exchequer (she died 1843). Educ. at Trinity Coll., Cambridge when he graduated M.A. 1836. A Liberal. Sat for Cumberland E. From July 1840. MP until his death 11 Apr. 1879. [1879]

HOWARD, Rt. Hon. Lord Edward George Fitz-Alan. 19 Rutland Gate, London. Glossop, Manchester. Travellers', and Brooks's. 2nd s. of 13th Duke of Norfolk, by the eld. d. of 1st Duke of Sutherland. B. in St. James's Square, 1818; m.

1st, 1851, Augusta, only d. and heir of the Hon. George Talbot, and niece of 17th Earl of Shrewsbury (she died 1862); 2ndly, 1863, Winifred Mary, 3rd d. of A.Z.M. Phillips De Lisle, Esq., of Garendon Park, and Gracedieu Manor, Leicestershire. Was Vice-Chamberlain of the Household from July 1846-Mar. 1852. Appointed Dept. Earl Marshal of England, Feb. 1861. A Liberal. Contested Shoreham July 1841. Was unsuccessful at the election for Horsham, June 1848, but having succeeded on Petition, sat for that place from Sept. following till July 1852, when he was returned for Arundel where he sat until the borough was disfranchised in 1868. Contested Preston Nov. 1868. Created Baron Howard of Glossop 9 Dec. 1869. Died 1 Dec. 1883.   [1868]

HOWARD, Hon. Edward George Granville. 86 Eaton Place, London. Castle Howard. S. of the 6th Earl of Carlisle; b. 1809; m. 1842 Diana, only d. of Hon. George Ponsonby. Became a Captain in the navy in 1838. A Dept.-Lieut. of Derbyshire. A Whig, formerly voted against the abolition of the corn laws, but in 1846 supported their repeal. First returned for Morpeth in 1840. Sat until he accepted Chiltern Hundreds, Dec. 1852. Created Baron Lanerton 8 Jan. 1874. Died 8 Oct. 1880.   [1852 2nd ed.]

HOWARD, E.S. Continued in House after 1885: full entry in Volume II.

HOWARD, Hon. Col. Fred. George. 12 Grosvenor Square, London. Ashtead Park, Epsom. Castle Rising, Norfolk. Elford, Lichfield. Levens, Milnthorpe, Westmoreland. 2nd. s. of the Earl of Carlisle, and bro. of Lord Morpeth, Member for Yorkshire. B. 1805. A Reformer, in favour of free-trade, the abolition of monopolies, and throwing open the trade to China. Sat for Morpeth from 1832 and MP until his death 18 Nov. 1834.   [1833]

HOWARD, Frederick John. Burlington Gardens, London. Only surviving s. of Col. the Hon. Frederick Howard (killed at Waterloo) by Frances Susan, sister of the Earl of Durham. B. 1 Mar. 1814. Nephew of his Lordship, and Secretary to his cousin the Earl of Carlisle, whilst the latter was Viceroy of Ireland 1855-58 and 1859-64; also connected with the Duke of Devonshire's family by his mother's 2nd marriage with the Hon. H.F. Compton Cavendish. A Whig, successfully contested Youghal in 1837. Defeated contesting Bridgnorth in 1841. Died 28 Feb. 1897.   [1838]

HOWARD, George James. 1 Palace Green,

Kensington, London. Castle Howard, York. Naworth Castle, Brampton. Brooks's. 4th s. of the Hon. Charles Wentworth George Howard, of Naworth Castle, Cumberland, who sat for East Cumberland from 1840 to his death in 1879, by Mary Priscilla, 2nd d. of Right Hon. Sir James Parke, Baron of the Court of Exchequer, afterwards Lord Wensleydale. B. at Park Street, London, 1843; m. 1864, Hon. Rosalind Frances, youngest d. of 2nd Lord Stanley of Alderley. Educ. at Eton and at Trinity Coll., Cambridge. A trustee of the National Gallery. A Liberal. Sat for E. Cumberland from Apr. 1879 to Mar. 1880; re-elected Feb. 1881 and sat until he retired in 1885.   [1885]

HOWARD, Hon. Henry Thomas. Brooks's. 2nd s. of the 16th Earl of Suffolk. B. 1808; m. 1845, Georgiana Maria, eld. d. of Lieut.-Gen. Sir John W. Guise, Bart. A Capt. in the army. A Whig, voted for agricultural protection 1846. First returned for Cricklade in 1841. Sat until he retired 1847. Died 29 Jan. 1851.   [1847]

HOWARD, James. Clapham Park, Bedford. Reform. Eld. s. of John Howard Esq., JP of Cauldwell, Bedford. B. at Bedford, 1821; m. 1846, Mahala Wendon, d. of P. Thompson, Esq., of Brook House, Great Bentley, Essex. Was educ. at the Bedford Public Schools. Proprietor (with his youngest bro.) of the Britannia Works, Bedford, the celebrated Agricultural Implement Manufactory. A Magistrate and Dept.-Lieut. for Bedfordshire, of which he was High Sheriff in 1878. Chairman of the Bedford and Northampton Railway. Author of *Continental Farming and Peasantry, The History of Steam Ploughing*, and many other works on agricultural and engineering subjects. A Liberal. Sat for Bedford from Dec. 1868 to Jan. 1874; sat for Bedfordshire from April 1880 until he retired in 1885. Died 25 Jan. 1889.   [1885]

HOWARD, Hon. James Kenneth. Charlton, Wiltshire. Reform, and Travellers'. Youngest s. of the 16th Earl of Suffolk and Berkshire, by the eld. d. of 1st Lord Sherborne. B. 1814; m. in 1845, Lady Louisa Fitz-Maurice, only d. of 3rd Marq. of Lansdowne. Was a Groom in Waiting to Her Majesty. A Liberal. First returned for Malmesbury in 1841. Sat until he retired in 1852. Commissioner of Woods and Forests 1855. Died 7 Jan. 1882.   [1852]

HOWARD, Lord. 57 Eaton Place, London. Barbot Hall, Yorkshire. Reform. B. 1806, eld. s. of Earl of Effingham. M. 1832, d. of Sir Gordon Drummond, G.C.B. A Liberal, voted against the abolition of the Corn Laws. Sat for Shaftesbury from 1841 - Feb. 1845, when he succeeded as 2nd

Earl of Effingham. Died 5 Feb. 1889.   [1844]

HOWARD, Philip Henry. 15 Gloucester Place, Portman Square, London. Corby Castle, Cumberland. Foxcote, Warwickshire. Athenaeum, and Brooks's. Eld. s. of Henry Howard, Esq., of Corby Castle, Co. Cumberland, head of a branch of the Duke of Norfolk's family. B. 1801; m. in 1843, Eliza Minto, eld. d. of Major John Canning (some time political agent at the court of Ava), and niece of Francis Canning, Esq., of Foxcote, whose estates she inherited. Of Whig principles, voted for the Reform Act, and against the abolition of the Corn Laws, but in 1846 supported their repeal; in favour of relieving Roman Catholics and Dissenters from Church Rates. In 1851 supported Mr. Locke King's measure for the extension of the suffrage, and opposed the Ecclesiastical Titles Assumption Bill. Patron of 1 living. Sat for Carlisle from the passing of the Roman Catholic Relief Bill in 1830, till the general election 1847, when he was an unsuccessful candidate; again returned for Carlisle Mar. 1848. Sat until he retired in 1852. Sheriff of Cumberland 1860. Died 1 Jan. 1883.   [1852]

HOWARD, Sir Ralph, Bart. 17 Belgrave Square, London. Bushy Park, Wicklow. Athenaeum. Only s. of the Hon Hugh Howard (4th s. of the 1st Earl of Wicklow), by the 2nd d. of Dean (Bligh) of Elphi n. M. 1837 Lady Frazer. A Dept.-Lieut. of Wicklow, and Col. of the Wicklow Militia. Of Whig principles. Sat for Wicklow from 1829 till the general election 1847; re-elected for Wicklow May 1848, and sat until he retired in 1852. Unsuccessfully contested Evesham 29 July 1847. Died 15 Aug. 1873.[1852]

HOWARD, Hon. William. 16 Grosvenor Street, London. 2nd s. of the Earl of Carlisle; uncle of Lord Morpeth and of the Duchess of Sutherland. B. 25 Dec. 1781. Elected for Sutherlandshire without opposition, in the room of R. Macleod, Esq., jun. of Cadbell, the previous member, who then sat for the Inverness Burghs. A Conservative, said he did 'not much care who was destined to be at the head of the government, so that whoever filled that high station would throw the shield of his ministerial protection over the venerable institutions of this country.' Sat for Sutherlandshire from 1837 until accepted Chiltern Hundreds Apr. 1840. Died 25 Jan. 1843.   [1839]

HOWES, Edward. 9 Cle& Cambridge, and Carlton. S. of the Rev. George Howes, Rector of Spixworth, Norfolk, by Elizabeth, d. of Robert Fellowes, Esq., of Shottesham Park, Norfolk. B. at Spixworth 1813; m. 1851, Fanny 4th d. of Robert Fellowes, Esq., of Shottesham Park, Norfolk. Educ. at St. Paul's School and at Trinity Coll., Cambridge, of which he became a Fellow. Was 3rd Church Estates Commissioner. Chairman of Quarter Sessions for Norfolk from 1849. A Magistrate and Dept.-Lieut. for that Co. A Conservative, who said he would never favour any 'attempt to impair the influence of the Church of England', but at the same time was 'thoroughly opposed to all intolerance'; in favour of a repeal of the Malt Tax. Sat for Norfolk E. from May 1859 to Dec. 1868, from which date he sat for Norfolk S. MP until his death 26 Mar. 1871.   [1870]

HOWICK, Rt. Hon. Visct. 6 Pall Mall East, London. 16 Whitehall Place, London. Reform. B. 1802, the eld. s. of Earl Grey. M. 1832, the d. of Sir James Copley, Bart. A Liberal; voted against the corn laws. Under-Sec. for the Colonies from 1830-33, when he resigned, not concurring in the plan proposed for the emancipation of slaves. In the beginning of 1834 was appointed Under-Sec. to the Home Dept., but resigned on the breaking up of the Grey Administration in July of that year. Was Secretary at War from 1835-39, (salary £2,480). Represented Winchelsea in the Parliament of 1826, and Higham Ferrers in that of 1830. Represented Northumberland N. from 1831-41. Sat for the borough of Sunderland from Sept. 1841, when Mr. Alderman Thompson took the Chiltern Hundreds in order to stand for Westmoreland, until he succeeded his father as 3rd Earl on 17 July 1845. From 1846-52 he was again the Secretary of State for the Colonies. An Author. Died 9 Oct. 1894.   [1838]

HOY, James Barlow. 11 Grosvenor Street, London. Midenburg, Hampshire. Took the name of Hoy on succeeding to the property of—Hoy, Esq. A moderate Reformer, voted for transferring the franchise from Retford to Birmingham, against the Bathurst pension, and against the first Reform Bill. Was an unsuccessful candidate for Southampton at four different elections previous to 1830, when he was elected; was unsuccessful in 1831; was returned again for Southampton in 1832, but ousted by Mr. Penleaze on petition. In 1835 he was at the head of the poll, and sat until he retired in 1837.   [1837]

HUBBARD, Egerton. Continued in House after 1885: full entry in Volume II.

HUBBARD, Rt. Hon. John Gellibrand. 24 Prince's Gate, Hyde Park, London. Addington Manor, Winstow, Buckinghamshire. Carlton. S. of John Hubbard, Esq., of Stratford Grove, Essex, by Mariana, d. of John Morgan, Esq., of Bramfield Place, Hertfordshire. B. at Stratford, Essex 1805; m. 1837, Hon. Maria Margaret, eld.

d. of 8th Lord Napier. A Banker and Merchant; also a Director of the Bank of England, and Chairman of Public Works Loan Commission from 1853-1874. A Commissioner of Lieutenancy for London. Published in 1843 *The Currency of the Country*, and in 1853 *How should the Income Tax be Levied*, and *Reform or Repeal the Income Tax*, besides other pamphlets on commercial and financial policy. A Conservative. Sat for Buckingham from May 1859 to Dec. 1868. Sat for London from Feb. 1874 until created Baron Addington 22 July 1887. Died 28 Aug. 1889.   [1887]

HUDDLESTON, John Walter. 19 Prince's Terrace, London. 2 Paper Buildings, London. Carlton, and Garrick. S. of Thomas Huddleston, by Alethea, d. of Henry Hichens, Esq., of St. Ives, Cornwall. B. in Dublin 1817; m. 1872, Lady Diana, d. of 9th Duke of St. Albans. Was educated at Trinity Coll., Dublin. Was called to the bar at Gray's Inn 1839; became Queen's Counsel 1857, and joined the Oxford Circuit, of which he was the leader. A bencher of Gray's Inn, and twice Treasurer of that Society. A member of the Council of Legal Educ. Appointed Judge-Advocate of the Fleet, and Consel to the Admiralty 1865. When member for Canterbury introduced the Hop (prevention of lands) Act 29 Vic. cap.37. A Conservative. Contested unsuccessfully Worcester July 1852, Shrewsbury May 1857, Kidderminster in 1859 and 1861. Sat for Canterbury from July 1865 to Nov. 1868, when he was an unsuccessful candidate. Sat from Feb. 1874 for Norwich (which he had contested unsuccessfully July 1870) until appointed Judge Feb. 1874. Knighted 1875. Died 5 Dec. 1890.   [1874]

HUDSON, Charles Donaldson-. 51 South Audley Street, London. Cheswardine Hall, Market Drayton. Carlton. Younger and only surviving s. of John Donaldson, Esq., of Wigton, Cumberland, by Catherine, d. of Anthony Halliley, Esq., of Wigton. B. 1840; m. 1870, Sarah Marie, only d. of Sidney Robert Streatfield, Esq., Major 52nd Foot. Assumed by Royal licence in 1862 the name of Hudson, in addition to his patronymic, on succeeding to the estates of his great uncle, Thomas Hudson, Esq., MP of Cheswardine, Shropshire. Educ. at Merton Coll., Oxford. A Magistrate for Staffordshire and Shropshire, of which latter he was High Sheriff 1880. A Conservative. Sat for Newcastle-under-Lyne from April 1880 until he retired in 1885. Died 18 Apr. 1893.   [1885]

HUDSON, George. Whitby, Yorkshire. Carlton, and Conservative. B. 1800; m. Elizabeth, d. of James Nicholson, Esq. Well known for his con-

nection with railway undertakings. Was Chairman of the Board of Directors of the Eastern Counties Railway, the York, Newcastle, and Berwick Railway, etc. Chairman of the Sunderland Dock Company. A Magistrate of the East and North Ridings of Yorkshire, and a Magistrate and Dept.-Lieut. of Durham. A Magistrate of the city of York, for which he was elected Lord Mayor, Nov. 1837; again Nov. 1838; and a third time Nov. 1846. A Conservative, voted against church-rates 1855. First returned for Sunderland in Aug. 1845. Sat until defeated in 1859. Released from York castle after contempt of court of exchequer in 1865. Died 14 Dec. 1871.   [1858]

HUDSON, Thomas. 6 Park Crescent, Portland Place, London. A Reformer. An East India Proprietor. Sat first for Evesham in the Parliament of 1831, and MP until he retired in 1835. Died 14 Apr. 1852.   [1833]

HUGESSEN, Rt. Hon. Edward Hugessen Knatchbull-. 30 Upper Grosvenor Street, London. The Paddock, Smeeth, Ashford, Kent. Brooks's, and United University. S. of the Rt. Hon. Sir Edward Knatchbull, Bart., who represented Kent E. for several years, by his 2nd wife, Fanny Catherine, d. of Edward Knight, Esq., of Godmersham Park, Kent and Chawton House, Hampshire. B. at Mersham Hatch, Kent 1829; m. 1852, Anna Maria Elizabeth, youngest d. of the Rev. Marcus R. Southwell. Educ. at Eton and at Magdalen Coll., Oxford, where he graduated 1850. Assumed the name of Hugessen in addition to his patronymic. A Magistrate and Dept.-Lieut. of Kent. Was a Lord of the Treasury from June 1859-May 1866. Was Under-Sec. of State for the Home Dept. from Dec 1868-Jan. 1871, and Under-Sec. for the Colonies from the last named date to Feb. 1874. A Liberal. Sat for Sandwich from Apr. 1857 until created Baron Brabourne May 1880. Died 6 Feb. 1893. [1880]

HUGHES, Henry George. 22 Lower Fitzwilliam Street, Dublin. Cornadrung, Arva, Co. Cavan. Reform. Stephen's Green, Dublin, and Royal Irish Yacht, Kingstown. S. of James Hughes, Esq., Solicitor, by Margaret, d. of Trevor Morton, Esq. B. in Capel Street, Dublin 1812; m. 1835, Sarah Augusta, d. of Francis L'Estrange, Esq., Capt. 3rd Buffs. Called to the bar in Ireland 1834, made Queen's Counsel there 1844. Was Solicitor-Gen. for Ireland from Oct. 1850-Dec. 1852. Appointed a Commissioner of Lunacy in Ireland 1846, a Commissioner of the Board of Bequests there 1853, and Commissioner of Endowed Schools 1854. A Whig, in favour of free trade and 'tenant-right' in Ireland. Unsuccessfully contested Cavan Apr. 1855. First elected for Longford 1856, without opposition. Retired 1857. Was again Solicitor-Gen. for Ireland from Feb. 1858-July 1859. Appointed Judge 1859. Died 22 July 1872. [1857]

HUGHES, Thomas. 113 Park Street, London. 9 Old Square, Lincoln's Inn, London. 2nd s. of John Hughes, Esq., of Downington Priory, Newbury, Berkshire, by Margaret Elizabeth, d. of Thomas Wilkinson, Esq. B. at Uffington, Berkshire 1823; m. 1847, Anne Frances, eld. d. of Rev. James Ford, Prebendary of Exeter. Educ. at Rugby and at Oriel Coll., Oxford. Called to the bar at the Inner Temple 1848. Author of *Tom Brown's School Days, The Scouring of the White Horse,* and numerous other popular works. A Liberal, in favour of 'a real and direct representation of the whole people in Parliament', the abolition of Church rates, etc. Sat for Lambeth from July 1865 to Dec. 1868, from which date he sat for Frome until he retired 1874. Nominated to contest Marylebone 1874 but retired before poll. County Court Judge 1882. Died 22 Mar. 1896. [1873]

HUGHES, William Bulkeley. 17 St. George's Square, London. Plâs-côch, Anglesea, Bangor. Union, and Portland. Eld. s. of Sir W.B. Hughes, of Plâs-côch, by Elizabeth, 2nd d. and co-heir of Rice Thomas, Esq., of Coedlenen, Carnarvonshire. B. 1797; m. 1825, Elizabeth, widow of Henry Wormald, Esq., of Woodhouse, Leeds, d. and heir of J. Nettleship, Esq., of Mattersey Abbey, Nottinghamshire (she died 1865). Called to the bar at Lincoln's Inn 1824 and joined the Oxford and Chester circuits. A Magistrate for Anglesea and Carnarvon and Dept.-Lieut. of the latter Co. A Liberal-Conservative. Sat for the district of Carnarvon from July 1837 to June 1859, when he was unsuccessful; re-elected July 1865. MP until his death 9 Mar. 1882. [1882]

HUGHES, William Hughes, F.S.A., F.L.S. 15 Manchester Buildings, London. Clapham, Surrey. Bellevue House, Isle of Wight. B. 1792; m. 1814, Maria, youngest d. of Rich. V. Field, Esq., of Brixton Rise, Surrey. Mr. Hughes's name was originally Hewitt, but on the death of his maternal grandfather in 1825, he assumed his name and arms by Royal letters patent. He was a Solicitor, and a Barrister, but ceased to practise in 1831; was for a short time in 1832 an Alderman of London, but soon resigned the office; a Vice-President of the Society of Arts; a Magistrate of Hampshire, Middlesex and Westminster; and a Governor of Christ's Hospital. In 1834, he published a new edition of De Lolme's celebrated Treatise on the Constitution of England, with notes, etc. A moderate Reformer; in favour of short Parliaments. Was a candidate for Oxford at six succeeding elections and in 1835 represented that city for a fourth time, being returned by 137 votes more than were ever polled for a candidate at any election for that city. Defeated 1837. Died 10 Oct. 1874. [1836]

HUMBERSTON, Philip Stapleton. 10 Cadogan Place, London. Mollington Bamastre, Nr. Chester. S. of Philip Humberston, Esq., by Catherina, d. of the very Rev. George Cotton, D.D., Dean of Chester. B. at Chester 1812; m. 1840, Henrietta Elizabeth, 3rd d. of Hugh R. Hughes, Esq., of Kinmel, Denbighshire and Bache Hall, Cheshire. Educ. at Westminster School. Practised as a Solicitor in Chester from 1834-1856, when he retired. Was Mayor of Chester in 1852, and again in 1858 Elected a member of the Council of the Royal Agricultural Society 1858. Capt. Cheshire Rifle Volunteers. A Liberal-Conservative, in favour of the franchise being granted to a £5 rental in boroughs, and a £10 rental in counties; said he would give a general support to Lord Derby. First elected for Chester May 1859. Sat until he retired 1865. Sheriff of Cheshire 1878. Died 16 Jan. 1891. [1865]

HUME, Joseph, F.R.S., F.R.A.S. 6 Bryanston Square, London. Burnley Hall, Norfolk. Reform. B. at Montrose 1777. Educ. for the medical profession, but on proceeding to India was, in a few years, employed in the various offices of Surgeon, Persian interpreter to the army during the Mahratta War from 1802-07, Paymaster, Postmaster, etc., discharging the duties attached to them in a way to call for the public thanks of Lord Lake, and other high functionaries. Having realized a competence he returned to his native country in 1808. In 1810 and 1811 he travelled in Spain, Egypt, Turkey, Greece, etc. A Member of the College of Surgeons in Edinburgh and London, Vice-Pres. of the Society of Arts, Dept.-Lieut. of the Co. of Middlesex, a Magistrate in Westminster, Middlesex and Norfolk etc. etc. An East India Proprietor. A radical Reformer. Sat for Weymouth from Jan.-Nov. 1812, for Montrose district 1818 to 1830, for Middlesex from 1830 to 1837, for Kilkenny from 1837 to 1841. Unsuccessfully contested Leeds in 1841, but was again returned for Montrose district in Mar. 1842 until he died Mar. 1855. [1855]

HUME, W.W. Fitzwilliam. See DICK, W.W. Fitz-William.

HUMPHERY, John. Hibernia Wharf, Tooley Street, London. Clapham Common, Surrey.

Reform. M. in 1836, 2nd d. of James Dyson, Esq., of Bedford. Was Lord Mayor of the city of London in 1842-43; a Wharfinger and Merchant in Southwark; a Dept.-Lieut. for London. A radical Reformer, in favour of the ballot, triennial Parliaments, free-trade, the repeal of the taxes on knowledge and industry, the abolition of all monopolies, and such a reform in the Church as will abolish tithes, appropriate Church lands to the purposes for which they were originally intended, do away with pluralities, deprive the Bishops of all share in the temporal government of the country, and place the election of the clergy in the hands of the parishioners, paying them according to their duties and merits. Sat for Southwark from 1832 until he retired in 1852. Died 28 Sept. 1863.   [1852]

HUMPHERY, William John. 14 Somerset Place, Hyde Park, London. 2 Paper Buildings, Temple, London. Penton Lodge, Nr. Andover, Hampshire. B. in London 1827, the s. of John Humphery, Esq., Alderman of London, who at one time represented Southwark, by Mary, d. of W. Burgess, Esq. M. 1850, Maria, youngest d. of William Cubbitt, Esq., who was twice Lord Mayor of London, and who represented Andover for many years. Educ. at Winchester and at Wadham Coll., Oxford, where he graduated B.A. 1850, M.A. 1853. Was called to the bar at the Inner Temple 1852. Appointed Standing Counsel to the Irish Society 1860. Was a Magistrate for Hampshire. Capt. of the Andover Rifle Corps, and Lieut.-Col. of 1st Hampshire Administrative Battalion of Volunteers. A Conservative, but not opposed to moderate alterations to meet the requirements of the age. Opposed to 'weak and ill-judged interference in foreign politics.' Sat for Andover from Nov. 1863 until he accepted Chiltern Hundreds in 1867.   [1867]

HUNT, Rt. Hon. George Ward. Prince of Wales Terrace, Kensington, London. Wadenhoe House, Oundle, Northamptonshire. Carlton, Athenaeum, and St. Stephen's. Only surviving s. of the Rev. George Hunt, of Buckhurst, Berkshire, and Wadenhoe House, Northamptonshire (sometime Rector of Barningham-Cum-Coney-Weston, Suffolk), by Emma, d. of Samuel Gardiner, Esq., of Coombe Lodge, Oxfordshire. B. at Buckhurst 1825; m. 1857, Alice, 3rd d. of Bishop (Eden) of Moray and Ross. Educ. at Eton and Christ Church, Oxford, where he was second class in classics 1848 and graduated M.A. 1851. Created honorary D.C.L. 1870. Called to the bar at Inner Temple (of which he was a bencher) 1851 and joined the Oxford Circuit, but ceased to practise before entering parliament. Was Financial Sec. to the Treasury

from July 1866-Feb. 1868, and Chancellor of the Exchequer from the latter date to Dec. 1868. Appointed 1st Lord of the Admiralty Feb. 1874 (salary £5,000), also a member of the Council on Education. A Magistrate and Dept.-Lieut. for Northamptonshire and Chairman of Quarter Sessions. Patron of 1 living. A Conservative. Unsuccessfully contested Northampton borough July 1852, and again Apr. 1857; sat for Northamptonshire from Dec. 1857. MP until his death 29 July 1877.   [1877]

HURST, Robert Henry, sen. 2 Mitre Court Chambers, Temple, London. Horsham Park, and Nuthurst Lodge, Sussex. Reform. S. of Robert Hurst, Esq., who was Steward to the 14th Duke of Norfolk and MP for Horsham from 1812-1829, when he retired from Parliament to make room for the return of the Earl of Surrey under the Catholic Relief Act. A radical Reformer, in favour of the abolition of tithes; but voted for agricultural protection 1846. Sat for Horsham from 1832 to 1841, in opposition to the Norfolk interest, having defeated F. Blount, Esq., Steward of the 15th Duke. Was again returned for Horsham in 1844, when the Hon. Robert Scarlett became Lord Abinger. Retired 1847.   [1847]

HURST, Robert Henry, jun. Goldsmith Buildings, Temple, London. Horsham Park, Nr. Horsham, Sussex. Oxford & Cambridge. B. 1817, the eld. s. of Robert H. Hurst, Esq., many years MP for Horsham, by Dorothea, d. of John Breynton, Esq., of Haunch Hall, Co. Stafford. M. 1859, Matilda Jane, eld. d. of James Scott, Esq., of The Nunnery, Rusper, Sussex. Educ. at Westminster and at Trinity Hall, Cambridge. A Liberal. Sat for Horsham from July 1865 to Dec. 1868, when he polled the same number of votes as his opponent, Maj. J. Aldridge. Both members were petitioned against in the following Apr., when his opponent declined contesting the seat. He was defeated in 1874, but was again returned for Horsham in the by-election of 17 Dec. 1875. The result however, was declared void on petition.   [1873]

HURT, Francis. Alderwasley, Derbyshire. Carlton. S. and heir of Francis Hurt, Esq., who was High Sheriff for the Co. in 1778. M. to Elizabeth, eld. d. of Richard Arkwright, Esq., and grand-d. of Sir Richard Arkwright the founder of that family, and had by her a s. m. to Cecilia, d. of Richard Norman, Esq., niece of the Duke of Rutland, and cousin-german of the Marq. of Granby, MP for Stamford. A Conservative. Was returned for Derbyshire S. without a contest at the general election in 1837. Sat until he retired 1841.   [1838]

HUSSEY, Ambrose. 4 Upper Woburn Place, London. A Conservative, and voted against the abolition of the Corn Laws. Sat for Salisbury from 1843, when Mr. Brodie accepted the Chiltern Hundreds, until he accepted the Chiltern Hundreds in 1846. [1845]

HUSSEY, Thomas. 40 St. James's Place, London. Lyme Regis, Dorsetshire. Carlton. B. 1814, the eld. s. of John Hussey, Esq., of Lyme Regis. A Conservative, voted for agricultural protection 1846. Contested Lyme Regis at the general election of 1841, and was seated on petition in 1842, ousting Mr. Pinney. Sat until he retired 1847. [1847]

HUTCHINS, Edward John. 25 Eaton Square, London. S. of Edward Hutchins, Esq., of Briton Ferry, Glamorganshire, by the d. of Thomas Guest, Esq., and sister of Sir John Guest, Bart. B. 1809; m. 1838, Isabel Clara, 2nd d. of Chevalier Don Juan de Bernaben of Alicante. Educ. at Charterhouse. A Liberal, in favour of the ballot and opposed to all State endowments of religion. Sat for Penryn and Falmouth from Jan. 1840 until the general election 1841; unsuccessfully contested Southampton 1841; and although his opponents were subsequently unseated on petition, he did not obtain the seat; unsuccessfully contested Poole July 1847. First returned for Lymington Apr. 1850. Sat until he retired 1857. Died 11 Feb. 1876. [1857]

HUTCHINSON, John Dyson. Birks Hall, Halifax. Reform. S. of John Hutchinson, Esq., of Halifax, by Mary, youngest d. of James Dyson, Esq., of Lees, Nr. Oldham. B. at Halifax 1822; m. 1853, Marianne Neville, youngest d. of George Hutchinson, Esq., of Repton, Derbyshire. Educ. at Hipperholme Grammar School. One of the proprietors of the *Halifax Courier,* and served twice as Mayor of Halifax. A Magistrate for Halifax and a member of the School Board there. A 'Radical', and in favour of complete religious equality. Sat for Halifax from Feb. 1877 until he accepted Chiltern Hundreds Aug. 1882. Died 25 Aug. 1882. [1882]

HUTT, Rt. Hon. Sir William, K.C.B. 2 Grosvenor Square, London. Gibside Hall, Gateshead, Co. Durham. United Service, and Oxford & Cambridge. S. of Richard Hutt, Esq., of Appley, Isle of Wight, and nephew of Capt. John Hutt of 'The Queen', to whose memory a public monument was raised in Westminster Abbey. B. 1803; m. 1st, 1831, Mary, Countess of Strathmore, widow of the 10th Earl and d. of Mr. Millner, of Staindrop (she died 1860); 2ndly, 1861, Fanny Anna Jane, d. of the Hon. Sir Francis Stanhope, and niece of 5th Earl of Harrington. Educ. at Trinity Coll., Cambridge, where he graduated B.A. 1827, M.A. 1831. Was Vice-Pres. of the Board of Trade and Paymaster-Gen. from Feb. 1860-Nov. 1865. Appointed to negotiate a commercial treaty at Vienna 1865. Took an active part in Colonial and commercial questions. Received the thanks of the General Shipowners Soc. for his exertions in obtaining the extinction of the sound dues and the dues collected by the Crown of Hanover at Stade. Was Commissioner for the foundation of South Australia. A Liberal, voted for the ballot 1853. Represented Hull from 1832 to 41 and Gateshead from the latter date until he retired 1874. Died 24 Nov. 1882. [1873]

HUTTON, John. Continued in House after 1885: full entry in Volume II.

HUTTON, Robert, M.R.I.A. Putney Park, Roehampton, Surrey. Reform. M. 1821, d. of Dr. Crompton of Eton House, Nr. Liverpool. Formerly in trade in Dublin, but retired. A fellow of, and one of the Secretaries to, the Geological Society; one of the Council of Univ. Coll., London and of the British Assoc. A supporter of Reform and of Lord Melbourne's administration. Returned for Dublin in 1837 and sat until defeated in 1841. Died 23 Aug. 1870. [1838]

HYDE, Lord. 1 Grosvenor Crescent, London. Eld. s. of Earl of Clarendon, by the eld. d. of 1st Earl of Verulam, and relict of John Foster Barham, Esq. B. at the Vice-Regal Lodge, Dublin, 1846. Graduated B.A. at Cambridge 1867. A Liberal. Unsuccessfully contested Warwickshire S. 21 Nov. 1868. Sat for Brecknock from Apr. 1869 until he succeeded father as 5th Earl Clarendon June 1870. Lord Chamberlain of the Household 1900-1905. Died 2 Oct. 1914. [1870]

HYETT, William Henry. 30 Parliament Street, London. A gentleman of landed property near Stroud. Of Whig principles. Sat for Stroud from 1832 until he retired in 1835. Founder of Gloucestershire Eye Institution in 1866. Translator. Died 10 Mar. 1877. [1833]

IBBETSON, Rt. Hon. Sir H.J. Selwin. See SELWIN-IBBETSON, Rt. Hon. Sir H.J. Continued in House after 1885: full entry in Volume II.

ILLINGWORTH, A. Continued in House after 1885: full entry in Volume II.

INCE, Henry Bret. 20 Old Square, Lincoln's Inn, London. 98 Cromwell Road, London.

Reform, and National Liberal. S. of E.B. Ince, by Annie, d, of Mr. John Finnis. B in London 1830, and m. 1862 Annie Jane Grace, d. of Mr. C.J. Muggeridge, a well-known Hop-Merchant. Educ. at London University, and called to the bar at Lincoln's Inn 1857. Published a treatise on the Trustees Act; became a Queen's Counsel, practising at the Chancery bar, and a Bencher of Lincoln's Inn. A Governor of Bradfield College. A Liberal, and 'a firm supporter of the Gladstone government'. Sat for Hastings June 1883 to November 1885, when returned for Islington East. Defeated in 1886. Died 7 May 1889. [1886]

INDERWICK, Frederick Andrew, Q.C. 8 Warwick Square, London. 1 Mitre Court Buildings, Temple, London. Maritean House, Winchelsea, Sussex. Brooks's, Garrick, Devonshire, and Reform. Only s. of Andrew Inderwick, Esq., R.N., by Jane, d. of Joseph Hudson, Esq. B. 1836; m. 1857, Frances Maria, d. of John Wilkinson, Esq., of the Exchequer and Audit Office, Somerset House, Was educ. at Brighton and at Trinity Coll., Cambridge. Was called to the bar Jan. 1868, at the Inner Temple, of which he was a Bencher. Appointed a Queen's Counsel 1874. A Magistrate for Sussex. Wrote several legal treatises, etc. A Liberal. Unsuccessfully contested Cirencester, Dec. 1868, and Dover Feb. 1874. Sat for Rye from Apr. 1880 until defeated 1885. Mayor of Winchester 1892-93 and 1902-03. Author of historical works. Died 16 Aug. 1904. [1885]

INGESTRE, Visct. C.B. (I). 19 Grosvenor Street, London. Ingestre Hall, Staffordshire. Eld. surviving s. of the Earl of Talbot, and bro.-in-law of the Marq. of Lothian. B. Nov. 8, 1803; m. Nov. 8, 1828, Lady Sarah Elizabeth, d. of the 2nd Marq. of Waterford. A Capt. in the navy; Lieut.-Col. of the Queen's Own Regt. of Staffordshire Militia. A Conservative, voted for agricultural protection, 1846. Was elected for Hertford in 1830 and 1832, but unseated on petition in the latter year; was defeated in the bor. in 1831 and 1835; returned for Armagh in 1831; resigned that seat in Aug. 1831 and was elected for Dublin city. Unsuccessfully contested Staffordshire S. in 1833, but sat for that Co. from 1837 until he succeeded as 3rd Earl Talbot Jan. 1849. Succeeded as 18th Earl of Shrewsbury Aug. 1856. Died 4 June 1868. [1847 2nd ed.]

INGESTRE, Visct. (II). Ingestre Hall, Stafford. Eld. s. of the 18th Earl of Shrewsbury and Talbot, by the eld. d. of the 2nd Marq. of Waterford. B. at Gumley, Leicestershire 1830; m. 1855, Anna Theresa, eld. d. of Capt. Richard Howe Cockerell, R.N. (by his wife afterwards Countess

of Eglinton). Appointed Cornet and Sub-Lieut. in the 1st Life Guards in 1851, but retired in 1853; Capt. in the Staffordshire Yeomanry Cavalry in 1851. A Dept.-Lieut. of that co. 1854, and a Magistrate for Middlesex 1859. A Conservative, said he would 'resist all aggression on the Church of England.' Was an unsuccessful candidate for Staffordshire S. in Jan 1854; sat for Stafford from Mar. 1857 to May 1859, when he was elected for Staffordshire N. Sat until defeated 1865. Returned for Stamford 4 May 1868. Sat until he succeeded as 19th Earl of Shrewsbury June 1868. Died 11 May 1877. [1865]

INGHAM, Robert. 13 King's Bench Walk, Temple, London. Westoe, South Shields. Athenaeum, and United University. S. of William Ingham, Esq., of Newcastle-on-Tyne, by Jane, d. of Robert Walker, Esq., of Westoe. B. 1793. Unmarried. Educ. at Harrow School and Oriel Coll., Oxford, where he was 1st class in classics, 1815; graduated M.A. 1818, and was for some years a fellow of Oriel. Was called to the bar at Lincoln's Inn, 1820, removed to the Inner Temple, where he became a bencher and went the Northern Circuit. A Queen's Counsel. Recorder of Berwick. Was Attorney-General for the Co. Palatine of Durham; resigned 1861. A Liberal, but supported the Conservative ministry on several occasions in 1835; in favour of a large measure of parliamentary reform; formerly opposed the ballot, but voted for that measure 1853, and against church-rates 1855; in favour of complete free trade in shipping. Sat for South Shields from 1832 to 1841, when he was an unsuccessful candidate. Again returned for South Shields July 1852. Sat until he retired in 1868. Died 21 Oct. 1875. [1867]

INGILBY, Sir William Amcotts, Bart. 19 Berkeley Square, London. Ripley Castle, Yorkshire. Kettlethorpe, Lincolnshire. B. 1783; m. Louisa, d. of J. Atkinson, Esq., of Maple Hayes, Staffordshire. A Reformer, inclining to Radicalism, in favour of the ballot and the corn laws, or a more efficient protection to the farmer. Sat for Lincolnshire from 1823 until defeated in 1835. Died 14 May 1854. [1833]

INGLIS, Rt. Hon. J. A Conservative. Contested Orkney Aug. 1852 and Lisburn Dec. 1852. Returned for Stamford 3 Mar. 1858. Retired in 1859. Appointed Lord Justice Clerk of Scotland with title of Lord Glencrose 10 July 1858. Lord Justice General 1867. Died 20 Aug. 1891. [1858]

INGLIS, Sir Robert Harry, Bart., D.C.L., F.R.S. 7 Bedford Square, London. United University. B. in London 1786. M. 1807, Mary, eld. d. of Joseph Seymour Biscoe Esq., of Pendhill, Surrey. Graduated at Christ Church, Oxford, M.A. in 1809, and called to the bar at Lincoln's Inn 1818. Dept.-Lieut. of Bedfordshire, one of the Governors of King's College, Senior Treasurer of the Sons of the Clergy, and Vice-Pres. of the Clergy Orphan Society. Elected Professor of Antiquity in the Royal Academy 1850, and was one of the Vice-Presidents of the Society of Antiquities. A Conservative, and voted for agricultural protection 1846. Sat for Dundalk from 1824 to 26, and for Ripon from 1826 to 28. Sat for Oxford University from 1829 — when Sir Robert Peel took the Chiltern Hundreds in order to give his constituents an opportunity of expressing their sentiments upon his change of conduct with respect to Catholic Emancipation — until he accepted Chiltern Hundreds 1854. Died 5 May 1855. [1853]

INGRAM, Herbert. Loudwater, Near Watford, Hertfordshire. Reform.B. at Boston 1811; m. 1843. Educ. at the Public School, Boston. Patron of 1 living. Proprietor and Manager of the *Illustrated London News* Appointed a Dept.-Lieut. of Lincolnshire 1857. A Liberal, in favour of a comprehensive system of national education, extension of the suffrage, and vote by ballot; against disturbing the grant to Maynooth. First elected for Boston Mar. 1856 and sat until his death by drowning in Lake Michigan 8 Sept. 1860. [1860]

INGRAM, Hugo Francis Meynell. 26 Hill Street, London. Cross Hayes, Burton-on-Trent. Only s. of Hugo Charles Meynell Ingram, Esq., of Temple Newsam, Yorkshire, by Georgina, d. of Frederick Pigou, Esq., of London. M. 1863, Hon. Emily Charlotte, eld. d. of 1st Visct. Halifax. Educ. at Harrow and at Christ Church, Oxford. A Conservative. Sat for W. Staffs. from Dec. 1868 MP until his death in 1871. [1871]

INGRAM, Sir W.J. Continued in House after 1885: full entry in Volume II.

INNES, Arthur Charles. Dromantine, Nr. Newry. Junior Carlton. Sackville Street, Dublin, Kildare Street, Dublin. Only s. of Arthur Innes, Esq., of Dromantine, by Mary Jervis, d. and heir of Admiral William Wolseley, Esq. B. 1834; m. 1858, Louisa Henrietta, d. of James Brabazon, Esq., of Mornington, Co. Meath. Educ. at Eton. A Magistrate for Down. A Conservative. First Elected for Newry July 1865. Retired 1868. [1868]

IRELAND, Thomas James, Owsden Hall, Newmarket. Union. B. 1792, the only s. of Thomas Ireland, Esq., by the d. of the Rev. Christopher Hand, B.D. Rector of Aller,

Somerset. M. 1829 Elizabeth, d. of Sir William Earle Welby, Bart., of Denton, Lincolnshire. Educ. at Emmanuel Coll., Cambridge, where he was Junior Optime 1814, and gained the declamation prizes of his Coll. in 2 successive years. Graduated M.A. 1817. A Magistrate for Suffolk. Patron of 1 living. A Conservative, and 'staunch supporter of the connection between Church and State, and as staunch an opponent of the endowment of the Romish Priesthood from any public sources.' Supported 'any modification of the Poor Laws which may conduce to their humanity and justice.' Sat for Bewdley from 1847 until he was unseated 1848. [1847 2nd ed.]

IRTON, Samuel. 35 Piccadilly, London. Irton Hall, Ravenglass, Cumberland. Carlton. Eld. s. of Edmund Lamplugh Irton, Esq., of Irton Hall, Cumberland (the direct representative of Bartram D'Yrton, who lived temp. Henry I), by Harriet, d. of Richard Hayne, Esq., of Ashbourne Green. B. at Irton Hall, 1796; m. 1825, Eleanor, 2nd d. of Joseph Tiffin Senhouse, Esq., of Calder Abbey, Cumberland. Educ. at Shrewsbury school, and at St. John's Coll., Cambridge. A Magistrate and Dept.-Lieut. for Cumberland. Patron of 2 livings. A Conservative, opposed to the Maynooth Grant, and 'to all rash measures of Parliamentary reform.' first returned for Cumberland W. in Mar. 1833 (on Visct. Lowther electing to represent Westmoreland), and sat until July 1847. Again returned in July 1852, without opposition. Sat until he retired 1857. Died 10 July 1866. [1857]

IRVING, John. 1 Richmond Terrace, London. Ashford, Middlesex. Maheramourne, Co. Antrim. Carlton. A Merchant in London, and partner with Sir John Rae Reid, Bart., MP for Dover. Was the first President of the 'Alliance' Assurance Co. A Conservative, unsuccessfully contested Clitheroe Dec. 1832 and Poole Jan. 1835. Sat in several parliaments for Bramber and then for Antrim from 1837. McCalmont suggests that Irving died in 1845, but it seems that he only accepted Chiltern Hundreds in that year and died in 1853. [1844]

ISAAC, Saul, Tollerton Hall, Nottingham. Junior Carlton. S. of Lewis Isaac, of Poole, Dorset, by his marriage with Miss Catherine Solomon, of Margate, Kent. B. at Chatham 1823; m. 1854, Miriam, d. of Stephen Hart, Esq., of Gloucester Place, London. Patron of 1 living. A Conservative, in favour of strong and effective armaments being maintained, the re-adjustment of local taxation, and the extension of the suffrage in counties. Sat for Nottingham from Feb. 1874 until defeated 1880. Contested Finsbury Central 1885. [1885]

JACKSON, Sir Henry Mather, Bart. 61 Portland Place, London. 2 New Square, Lincoln's Inn, London. Eld. s. of Sir William Jackson, Bart., of Birkenhead (who sat for Newcastle-under-Lyme and N. Derbyshire from 1847-68), by Elizabeth, d. of Lieut. Hughes, R.N. B. 1831; m. 1854, Elizabeth, d. of T.B. Blackburne, Esq., of Grange House, Birkenhead, Educ. at Harrow and Trinity Coll. Oxford, where he was 2nd class in classics and graduated B.A. 1853, M.A. 1859. Was called to the bar at Lincoln's Inn Nov. 1855; appointed Queen's Counsel Jan. 1873. Declared himself to be 'a staunch and hearty Liberal.' Unsuccessfully contested Birkenhead July 1865. Sat for Coventry from July 1867 to Nov. 1868; re-elected Feb. 1874. MP until appointed Judge 8 Mar. 1881. Contested Monmouthshire South 1 Dec. 1885 and Flint district 7 July 1886. [1881]

JACKSON, Rt. Hon. Joseph Devonsher. 26 Leeson Street, Dublin. Carlton. Eld. s. of Strettell Jackson, Esq., of Peterborough, Cork, and of Mary Cossins his wife. B. 23 June 1783; m. 1811, Sarah Lucinda, 9th d. of Benjamin Clarke, Esq. Obtained University honours during each year of his course in Trinity Coll., Dublin. Was Queen's 2nd Serjeant in Ireland. Being Chairman of the Co. of Londonderry, (an office inconsistent with a seat in Parliament,) was invited, in Dec. 1834, by the Protestant conservative electors of Bandon, to represent them; resigned his office, and was returned by a large majority to the 1835 Parliament. Returned for Bandon at the general election in 1837 by a majority of 52 out of 241 voters. 'A temperate Politician, but a steady supporter of the Protestant Monarchy and Constitution, of the Protestant Church, and of British connection with Ireland.' Sat for Dublin University from 11 Feb. 1842 until he accepted Chiltern Hundreds Sept. 1842. Judge of Irish Court of Common Pleas in Sept. 1842. Died 19 Dec. 1857. [1842]

JACKSON, Ralph Ward-. 21 Ryder Street, St. James's, London. 1 New Court, Temple, London. Garrick. S. of William Ward-Jackson, Esq., by Susanna Louisa, d. of E. Martin Atkins, Esq., of Kingston Lisle, Berkshire. B. at Normanby Hall, West Riding of Yorkshire 1806; m. 1829, Susanna, 2nd d. of Charles Swainson, Esq., of Cooper Hill, Lancashire. Educ. at Rugby. The founder of the Port and Town of West Hartlepool, Durham. A Conservative, opposed to all rash and hasty innovations, voted against the disestablishment of the Irish Church 1869. Sat for Hartlepool from Dec. 1868, until defeated 1874. Died 6 Aug. 1880. [1873]

JACKSON, Sir William. 44 Portland Place, London. Manor House, Birkenhead. Reform. S. of Peter Jackson, Esq., of Warrington, Lancashire, Surgeon. B at Warrington, 1805; m. 1829, Elizabeth, d. of Lieut. Hughes. Was formerly an African Merchant, but retired in 1842. Was an active promoter of the improvements effected at Birkenhead and other local undertakings, A Magistrate for Cheshire. Appointed Dept.-Lieut. of that Co. 1852. Patron of 1 living. A Liberal, voted for the ballot, 1853. Sat for Newcastle-under-Lyme from 1847 till July 1865, when he was elected for Derbyshire. N. Defeated after redivision of the county in 1868. Created Baronet 4 Nov. 1869. Died 30 or 31 Jan. 1876. [1867]

JACKSON, Rt. Hon. W.L. Continued in House after 1885: full entry in Volume II.

JACOB, E. Returned for Dungarvan 15 Feb. 1834. Of liberal opinions. Retired in 1835. [1834]

JAMES, C.H. Continued in House after 1885: full entry in Volume II.

JAMES, Edward. 24 Upper Wimpole Street, London. 3 Paper Buildings, Temple, London. Dunhill, Petersfield, Hampshire. Reform. B. at Manchester, the s. of Frederick William James, Esq., Merchant, by Elizabeth, d. of William Baldwin, Esq. M. 1835, d. of Edward Mason Crossfield, Esq., of Liverpool. Educ. at Brasenose Coll., Oxford. Called to the bar at Lincoln's Inn 1835, and made a Queen's Counsel 1853. Was an Attorney Gen. and Queen's Serjeant for the County Palatine of Lancaster, and Assessor of the Court of Passage, Liverpool. A Liberal, in favour of 'peace, retrenchment and reform.' Sat for Manchester from July 1865 until he died 3 Nov. 1867. [1867]

JAMES, Edwin, Q.C. 63 Pall Mall, London. 13 King's Bench Walk, Temple, London. Brook's, and Reform. Eld. s. of John James, Esq., (Solicitor, and for many years Secondary of the City of London), by Caroline, eld. d. of Boyce Combe, Esq., and niece of Alderman Harvey Combe, who sat for London for many years. Called to the bar at Lincoln's Inn, 1835; made a Queen's Counsel 1852. Appointed Recorder of Brighton 1855. 'Is sincerely and essentially a reformer' in favour of the ballot, and 'the total, unconditional, and immediate abolition of church-rates.' First elected for Marylebone, Feb. 1859. Accepted Chiltern Hundreds 1861. Visited Garibaldi in 1860. Disbarred in 1861 after accumulating debts of £100,000. Went to New York 1861 and returned in 1872. Died 4 Mar. 1882. [1861]

209

JAMES, Rt. Hon. Sir H. Continued in House after 1885; full entry in Volume II.

JAMES, Sir Walter, Bart. 11 Whitehall Place, London. Langley Hall, Berkshire. Eld. s. of John, 2nd s. of Sir Walter James James, Bart., by the Lady Emily Jane, d. of the 1st Marq. of Londonderry, and later Lady of Maj.-Gen. the Rt. Hon. Sir Henry Hardinge, K.C.B. B. 3 June 1816; m. 1841, d. of C. Ellison, Esq. First elected for Hull at the general election in 1837. Of Conservative principles, but in favour of free trade. Sat until he retired 1847. J.P. in Kent 1852. Sheriff of Kent 1855. Director of National Gallery 1871. Created Baron Northbourne Nov. 1884. Died 4 Feb. 1893.   [1847]

JAMES, William. 15 Regent Street, London. Barrock Lodge, Cumberland. M. d. of W.C. Ruston, Esq. A Whig, for many years represented Carlisle, retiring as its representative in 1835. First elected for Cumberland E. in 1836, *vice* Mr. Blamire, who was appointed Chief Commissioner under the Tithe Commutation Act. Sat until he retired 1847. Died 4 May 1861.   [1847]

JAMES, Hon. W.H. Continued in House after 1885: full entry in Volume II.

JARDINE, Sir Robert. Continued in House after 1885: full entry in Volume II.

JARDINE, W. Ashburton. A Liberal. First returned for Ashburton in 1841. MP until his death in 1842.   [1842]

JEFFREY, Rt. Hon. Francis. 35 Charles Street, Berkeley Square, London. Lord Advocate of Scotland. Mr. Jeffrey was for many years editor of the *Edinburgh Review,* which he and Lord Brougham were said to have been mainly instrumental in establishing, by the encouragement of Mr. Constable, the Edinburgh bookseller. Being a member of the Administration, Dod said nothing of his individual politics. It was his duty to bring into the House of Commons the Scotch Reform Act. Was elected for the Forfar district in the Parliament of 1831, but his election being declared void, he was elected for Earl Fitz-William's bor. of Malton, in the room of Sir James Scarlett. Sat for Edinburgh from 1832 until he was appointed Lord of Session, as Lord Jeffrey, in May or June 1834. Died 26 Jan. 1850. [1833]

JENKINS, David James. 131, Highbury New Park, London. Reform.B. at Exeter 1824, the s. of John Jenkins, Esq., of Haverford West. M. 1st, 1851, Bessie, d. of Ref. John Howe, of Cork (she died 1875); 2ndly, 1877, Alice, youngest d. of Goodwin Nash, Esq., of Malvern Wells. Educ. at Exeter and Teignmouth Grammar Schools. A Merchant and Shipowner in London. A Liberal and supporter of Mr. Gladstone. Unsuccessfully contested Harwich 17 Nov.1868. Sat for Penryn and Falmouth from Feb. 1874 until 1886, when he was defeated standing as a Gladstonian Liberal. Died 26 Feb. 1891.   [1886]

JENKINS, Edward. 20 Southwell Gardens, London. 5 Paper Buildings, Temple, London. Reform, and City Liberal. S. of Rev. John Jenkins, D.D., Presbyterian Minister of St. Paul's Church, Montreal, Canada, by Harriette, d. of James Shepstone, Esq., of Clifton. B. at Bangalore, India 1838; m. 1867, Hannah Matilda, d. of Philip Johnstone, Esq., of Dalriada, Belfast. Educ. at the High School, and McGill Coll., Montreal. Called to the bar at Lincoln's Inn, Sept. 1864. Author of *Lord Bantam, Ginx's Baby, The Coolie, his Rights and Wrongs,* etc. Was retained to watch the proceedings of the British Guiana Coolie Commission in 1870, by the Aborigines' Protection and Anti-Slavery Society. Was agent-general in London for the dominion of Canada from Feb. 1874-Jan.1875. An 'advanced Liberal', and opposed to 'Imperial disintegration.' Unsuccessfully contested Truro 13 Sept. 1871. Sat for Dundee from Feb. 1874, when he was elected during his absence in America. Retired 1880. Contested Edinburgh 1881 standing as an Independent Liberal and Imperialist. Contested Dundee 1885 and 1896 as a Conservative. Died 4 June 1910.   [1880]

JENKINS, Sir J.J. Continued in House after 1885: full entry in Volume II.

JENKINS, Richard. 7 Mansfield Street. Britonhall, Salop, Shropshire. Carlton. Of an old Shropshire family and connected with many of the leading families of that county. B. 18 Feb. 1785; m. 1824, Eliza Helen, eld. d. of Hugh Spottiswoode, Esq. of the E.I. Co's Civil Service. An E. India Director, having formerly been in the Company's Civil Service and employed in a diplomatic character in India. Was highly spoken of by Mr. Canning for his conduct there in 1817-18. Of Conservative opinions, but gave no pledges. Sat for Shrewsbury in 1831, 1832 and 1833 when he voted against the Reform Bill as too sweeping a measure. Returned again for Shrewsbury in 1837 and sat until he retired 1841. Died 30 Dec. 1853.   [1838]

JENKINSON, Sir George Samuel, Bart. 7 Bryanston Square, London. Eastwood Park, Falfield, Gloucestershire. Carlton. Eld. s. of the Rt. Rev. John Bankes Jenkinson, Bishop of St.

David's, by the 2nd d. of Augustus Pechell, Esq., of Berkhampstead. B. at Worcester 1817; m. 1845, eld. d. of Anthony Lyster, Esq., of Stillorgan Park, Dublin. Capt. 8th Hussars. Appointed a Dept.-Lieut. of Gloucestershire 1855, High Sheriff 1862. A Conservative, in favour of lowering the franchise in counties as much as in boroughs, opposed to the malt tax and to the present system of local taxation; voted against the disestablishment of the Irish Church 1869. Unsuccessfully contested Nottingham 11 May 1866 and N. Wiltshire July 1865. Sat for N. Wiltshire from Dec. 1868 until he retired 1880. Died 19 Jan. 1892.   [1880]

JEPHSON, C.D.O. See NORREYS, Sir C.D.O.J.

JERMYN, Rt. Hon. Earl. (I). 47 Eaton Place, London. Ickworth Park, Suffolk. Putney Heath, Surrey. Carlton. Eld. s. of the Marq. of Bristol. B. in Portland Place, London 1800; m. 1830, Lady Catherine, 3rd d. of the 5th Duke of Rutland (she died 1848). Educ. at Trinity Coll., Cambridge, where he graduated M.A. 1822. Was Treasurer of the Household from Sept. 1841 till July 1846. A Dept.-Lieut. of Suffolk. Appointed Col. of the West Suffolk Militia 1846. A Conservative, a supporter of free trade, but 'would consider with favour any measures for the relief of the agricultural interests.' Sat for Bury St. Edmunds from 1830 until he succeeded to the Peerage (Marq. of Bristol) in 1859.   [1855]

JERMYN, Earl. (II). 6 St. James's Square, London. Ickworth, Bury St. Edmunds, Suffolk. White's. Eld. s. of the Marq. of Bristol (who sat for Bury St. Edmunds from 1830 till he became a peer in 1859), by Lady Katherine, 4th d. of 5th Duke of Rutland. B. 1834; m. 1862, Geraldine, youngest d. of Gen. the Hon. George Anson. Educ. at Eton, and at Trinity Coll., Cambridge. Appointed Capt. West Suffolk Militia 1856, and Dept.-Lieut. of Suffolk, 1860. A Liberal-Conservative, and disapproved of many of the clauses of Lord Derby's Reform Bill. First elected for Suffolk W. May 1859. Sat until he succeeded as 3rd Marq. 30 Oct. 1864. Died 7 Aug. 1907. [1864]

JERNINGHAM, Hon. Henry Valentine Stafford. 11 Lower Grosvenor Street, London. Eld. s. of Lord Stafford. B. in 1802; m. in 1828, Juliana, d. of Edward Howard, Esq., and niece of the Duke of Norfolk. Of Whig principles. Sat for Pontefract from 1830. Retired in 1835. Succeeded father as 9th Baron Stafford Oct. 1851. Died 30 Nov. 1884.   [1833]

JERNINGHAM, Hubert Edward Henry. Longridge Towers, Berwick-on-Tweed. Athenaeum, and Brooks's. Eld. s. of Charles Edward Jerningham, Esq., of Painswick, Gloucestershire (cousin of Lord Stafford), by Emma Mary Wynn, youngest d. of Evan Wynn Roberts, Esq., of the Grove, Surrey. B. 1842; m. 1874, Annie, d. of Edward Liddell, Esq., of Bentonpark, Northumberland, and widow of W. Mather, Esq., of Beech Grove and Longridge House, Northumberland. Educ. at Paris University, of which he was Bachelier ès Lettres. Entered the diplomatic service as an attaché in 1866; became 2nd Secretary in 1873, and was appointed successively to Paris, Constantinople, Darmstadt, Carlsruhe, Vienna, and Belgrade, where he was Acting Agent and Consul-Gen. in 1878; retired from the service Aug. 1881. Author of several works, including *To and From Constantinople, Life of Sixtus V., by Baron Hubner, a translation,* etc. A Liberal, and a supporter of Mr. Gladstone; in favour of local taxation and the extension of the borough franchise to counties. Sat for Berwick-on-Tweed from Oct. 1881. Retired 1885. Colonial Sec. in Honduras 1887-89, Mauritius 1889-92, Governor of Mauritius 1893-97 and of Trinidad 1897-1900. Knighted 1893. Died 23 Apr. 1914.   [1885]

JERVIS, Henry Jervis-White-. Carlton. 3rd s. of Sir Henry Meredyth Jervis-White-Jervis, (2nd Bart.), by Marian, 3rd d. of William Campbell, Esq., of Fairfield, Ayrshire. B. 1825; m. 1855, Lucy, eld. d. of John Chevalier Cobbold, Esq., once MP for Ipswich. Educ. at Harrow and at the Royal Military Academy, Woolwich. Capt. in the Royal Artillery, which he entered Dec. 1844. Was employed under the Board of Ordnance in the United States in 1855, and from then in the Small Arms Dept. Author of *Manual of Field Operations, History of Corfu and the Ionian Islands, The Enfield Rifle,* etc. A Conservative. Sat for Harwich from Mar. 1859. until he retired 1880. Died 22 Sept. 1881.   [1880]

JERVIS, Sir John. 47 Eaton Square, London. Beaumaris, Co. Anglesey. United, and Reform. 2nd s. of Thomas Jervis, Esq. QC, late Chief Justice of Chester, and for many years Counsel to the Admiralty; was returned for Yarmouth, through the influence of his 2nd cousin, the late Earl St. Vincent. B. 1802; m. 1824 Catherine, 2nd d. of Alexander Mundell, Esq. of Great George Street, London. Wrote several law works of repute. Attorney-General from July 1846. A bencher of the Middle Temple. A radical Reformer, voted for the revision of the pension list, for triennial parliaments and against the 147th clause of the New Poor Law Act. Opposed the ballot. Sat for Chester from 1832 until appointed Lord Chief Justice of Common Pleas in 1850. Died 1 Nov. 1856. [1850]

JERVIS, John. 47 Luton Square, London. Fairhill, Tunbridge, Kent. Reform, and Coventry. S. of Sir John Jervis, the Attorney-General. B. in London, 1826. was educ. at Westminster and at Trinity Hall, Cambridge. A Liberal, in favour of free trade. First returned for Horsham in 1847. Unseated in 1848. [1847]

JERVIS, Swynfen. 3 Whitehall Place, London. Reform. Cousin to J. Jervis, Esq., MP for Chester. A Reformer, 'in favour of triennial Parliaments, and willing, till such a change take place, to resign his seat at the end of three years, if his constituents should require it. Prepared to examine, with a view to their amendment, the registration, rate paying, and other disqualifying clauses of the Reform Act. A reluctant convert to the necessity for the ballot. Said he would support the repeal of the Corn Laws, Church Reform, the suppression of Church-rates, and the commutation of Tithes. Favourable to a revision of the Pension List, the abolition of sinecures, the reduction of the army, the removal of all taxes on knowledge, to an unsparing retrenchment in all branches of the publical expenditure, and to a revision of our whole system of civil and criminal law.' Sat for Bridport from 1837. Retired at 1841 gen. election. [1840]

JERVOISE, Sir Jervoise Clarke Clarke-, Bart. 22 Bryanston Square, London. Idsworth, Horndean, Hampshire. S. of Rev. Sir Samuel Clarke-Jervoise (1st Bart.), by Elizabeth, d. of the Rev. Nicholas Griffinhoofe, Rector of Woodham Mortimer, Essex. B. at Kensington 1804; m. 1829, Georgiana, youngest d. of George Nesbitt Thompson, Esq., of Chapel Street, Grosvenor Place, London. Appointed a Dept.-Lieut. of Hampshire 1854. A Liberal, and in favour of a very comprehensive system of reform; voted for the abolition of church-rates. First elected for Hampshire S. Apr. 1857, without opposition. Sat until he retired in 1868. Died 1 Apr. 1889. [1867]

JESSEL, Sir George. 8 Cleveland Square, Hyde Park, London. Reform. S. of Z.A. Jessel, Esq., merchant, of Savile Row, London, by Mary, d. of the late Henry Harris, Esq. B. London 1824; M. 1856, Amelia, d. of Mr. Joseph Moses of Leadenhall Street, London. Educ. at Univ. Coll., London. Was called to the bar at Lincoln's Inn May 1847, appointed a Queen's Counsel March 1865. Solicitor-Gen. Nov. 1871. A Liberal, and a strong supporter of Mr. Gladstone; voted for the disestablishment of the Irish Church 1869. Sat

for Dover from Dec. 1868 until appointed Master of the Rolls Aug. 1873-Nov. 1875 (being the first Jewish Judge). Judge of High Court, Chancery division 1875-81. F.R.S. 1881. Died 21 March 1883. [1873]

JOCELYN, Visct. 22 Bruton Street, Kew Green. Carlton. B. in Pall Mall 1816, the eld. s. of the Earl of Roden. M. 1841 the youngest d. of 5th Earl Cowper (she was Lady of the Bedchamber to the Queen). Was Military Secretary to the Chinese expedition, and author of *Six Months in China.* A Secretary to the Board of Control Feb. 1845-July 1846. Was a Lieut. in 15th Hussars, and appointed Lieut. Col. of East Essex Militia 1853. A Conservative, but in favour of free trade. 'A firm friend to religious toleration', but 'steadily maintained the Protestant principles on which the institutions of the country are based'. Unsuccessfully contested Leeds 2 July 1841. Sat for King's Lynn from 1842 until he died on 12 Aug. 1854. [1854]

JOHNSON, Edward. Farringdon House, Exeter. Reform, and Devonshire. Youngest s. of John Johnson, Esq., of St. Osyth's Priory, Essex, by Anne, d. of William Haward, Esq., of Battersea, Surrey. B. 1833; m. 1855, Eliza Matilda, d. of Philip Pellier, Esq., of Jersey. Was educ. at King's Coll., London. Was formerly a Merchant in London. A Magistrate for Devon. A Liberal. Sat from Apr. 1880 for Exeter, which he had unsuccessfully contested Feb. 1874. Sat until he was defeated Nov. 1885. Contested the seat again in July 1886. Died 2 Nov. 1894. [1885]

JOHNSON, John George. Cross Torrington, North Devon. Carlton, Arthur's, and Garrick. S. of Rev. Peter Johnson, Rector of Wembworthy, Devon, and prebendary of Exeter, by Gratiana, d. of Lamborne Palmer, Esq., of Timsbury, Somerset. B. at Wembworthy, Devon, 1829; m 1856, Frances Grace, only d. of Sir Theodore H.L. Brinckman. Was educ. at Eton and at Brasenose Coll., Oxford. A Magistrate and Dept.-Lieut. for Devon, and Capt. N. Devon Hussars. Was High Sheriff of Devon 1872. Patron of 1 living. A Conservative. Sat for Exeter from Feb. 1874 until he retired 1880. [1880]

JOHNSON, John Samuel Willes. Hannington Hall, Highworth, Wiltshire. Carlton, and Senior United Service. S. of the Rev. Charles Johnson, Rector of Barrow, and Prebendary of Wells, by Mary, d. of Archdeacon Willes. B. at Bath 1793; m. 3rdly, Margaret, eld. d. of David Push, Esq., who represented Montgomery Dist. from 1832 till 1861. Educ. at Elmore Court, near Gloucester. Entered the navy in 1807; became a Commander

1846. Author of *A Journey through France and Italy in 1825*. A Liberal-Conservative. First elected for Montgomery district Apr. 1861. MP until his death 25 July 1863. [1863]

JOHNSON, Gen. William Augustus. 21 Suffolk Street, London. Wytham on the Hill, Lincolnshire. A Maj.-Gen. in the army, and formerly in the Ceylon Regt. A Dept.-Lieut. of Lincolnshire. Was Previously Member for Boston. A Liberal. Candidate for Leicestershire N. in Dec. 1832, and for Huddersfield in Jan. 1835. Sat for Oldham from 1837 until he retired 1847. Died 26 Oct. 1863. [1847]

JOHNSON, William Gillilan. Fertfield, Co. Antrim. Youngest s. of William Johnson, Esq., of Fertfield. B. 1808. A Barrister; a Magistrate for Antrim and Down. A Conservative. First returned for Belfast in 1841, but in Aug. 1842 the election was declared void. Mayor of Belfast 1849 and Knighted by the Queen on her visit to Belfast 12 Aug. 1849. Died 9 Apr. 1886. [1841 2nd ed.]

JOHNSON, Rt. Hon. William Moore. 26 Lower Leeson Street, Dublin. Mallow. Reform, University, and Stephen's Green, Dublin. S. of Rev. W. Johnson, M.A. formerly Chancellor of the Diocese of Cloyne, Co. Cork, by Elizabeth Anne, d. of Rev. W. Hamilton, ex-Fellow of Trinity Coll., Dublin. B. 1828, educ. at Trinity Coll., Dublin, where he graduated B.A. 1849, M.A. 1856. Called to the bar in Ireland 1853 and appointed a Queen's counsel there, 1872. Was Law Advisor to the Crown from 1868-74. Solicitor-Gen. for Ireland from Apr. 1880-Nov. 1881, when he was appointed Attorney Gen. A Bencher of the Society of King's Inns. A Magistrate for the Co. of Cork. A Liberal. Unsuccessfully contested Mallow Feb. 1874; sat for Mallow from Apr. 1880 until appointed Judge 1883; retired 1909. Died 9 Dec. 1918. [1882]

JOHNSTON, Alexander. Shield Hall, Lanarkshire. Reform. B. 1790. M. 1815. A Merchant and Manufacturer in Glasgow. President of the Anti-Corn Laws Association of Glasgow, and of the West of Scotland. 'An anti-monopolist', in favour of vote by ballot, household suffrage and short parliaments. Sat for Kilmarnock from 1841 until his death on 9 May 1844. [1844]

JOHNSTON, Andrew, sen. 54 Devonshire Street, London. Rennyhill, Fifeshire. Eld. s. of Andrew Johnston, Esq., of Rennyhill. B. 1798; m. 1st, 1826 Barbara, d. of D. Pearson, Esq., of Edinburgh; 2ndly, 1834 Priscilla, d. of T.F. Buxton, Esq., MP. for Weymouth. An Elder of the Church in Scotland. A Director of the Real del Monte and the Bolanos Companies. Supported Reform in Parliament and the abolition of slavery; opposed to Lord Stanley's plan of education in Ireland, in favour of an abolition of the existing corn laws, would vote for Church Reform, and oppose lay patronage; in favour of the ballot and short Parliaments. Was elected for St. Andrew's district in the Parliament of 1831. Sat until he retired in 1837. Died 24 Aug. 1862. [1837]

JOHNSTON, Andrew, jun. 46 Onslow Square, London. Woodford, Essex. Holton Hall, Halesworth, Suffolk, Reform. S. of Andrew Johnston, Esq., of Holton, Suffolk (formerly of Renny Hill, Fife, who sat for St. Andrew's 1832-37), by his 2nd. wife, Priscilla, eld. d. of Sir Thomas Fowell Buxton, 1st. Bart. B. in London 1835; M. 1858, Charlotte Anne, eld. d. of the Rev. G. Trevelyan of Malden, Surrey. Educ. at Rugby and at Univ. Coll., Oxford. Was a Partner in the firm of Messrs. Morewood & Co., Iron Manufacturers. A Liberal, in favour of a 'modification of the Game Laws.' Sat for S. Essex from Dec. 1868 until he was defeated 1874. [1873]

JOHNSTON, W. Continued in House after 1885: full entry in Volume II.

JOHNSTONE, Sir Frederick George, Bart. Limmer's Hotel. Westerhall, Dumfriesshire. B. in 1810. At the death of Sir George's father, he was only one year of age; and the patronage of the bor., which was vested in his family, had, during his minority, been managed by his guardians. A West India Proprietor. A Conservative. Sat for Weymouth from 1832. Retired in 1835. Died 7 May 1841. [1833]

JOHNSTONE, Sir Frederick John William, Bart. 9 Arlington Street, London. Westerhall, Dumfriesshire. Eld. s. of Sir George Frederick Johnstone (7th) Bart., by Lady Maria Louisa, only d. of the 1st Earl of Craven. B. at Gore House, Kensington, 1841 (posthumous). Appointed Cornet in the Dorset Yeomanry Cavalry 1862. A Conservative. Sat for Weymouth from Feb. 1874 until he retired in 1885. Died 20 June 1913. [1885]

JOHNSTONE, Sir Harcourt, Bart. 34 Belgrave Square, London. Hackness Hall, Scarborough. Eld. s. of Sir John Vanden Bempde Johnstone, 2nd Bart. (who sat for Yorkshire and for Scarborough, holding his seat for nearly 40 years), by Louisa, 2nd d. of Archbishop (Harcourt) of York. B. at the Palace, Bishopsthorpe 1829; m. 1850, Charlotte, 2nd d. of Sir Charles Mills, Bart., of Park Lane, London and Hillingdon House,

Middlesex. Patron of 2 livings. A Liberal, and said he would 'give Mr. Gladstone a firm support.' Was an unsuccessful candidate for Thirsk, Nov. 1868. Sat for Scarborough from Mar. 1869 until he accepted Chiltern Hundreds 1880. Created Baron Derwent Oct. 1881. Died 1 Mar. 1916.   [1880]

JOHNSTONE, Henry Alexander Munro Butler-. See BUTLER-JOHNSTONE, Henry Alexander Munro.

JOHNSTONE, Hon. Henry Butler-. See BUTLER-JOHNSTONE, Hon. Henry.

JOHNSTONE, James. 10 Wilton Place, London. Alva, Stirlingshire. The Hangingshaw, Selkirkshire. Athenaeum, and Windham. Eld s. of James Raymond Johnstone, Esq., of Alva, Stirlingshire, by 3rd d. of Montague Cholmeley, Esq., of Easton, Lincolnshire, and sister of Sir Montague Cholmeley, 1st Bart. B. at Overton, Rutlandshire 1801; m. 1846, Hon Augusta Anne, sister of 3rd Baron Grantley. Educ. at Rugby and at the University of Edinburgh. Admitted an Advocate at the Scotch bar 1824. A Dept.-Lieut. and Magistrate for the Cos. of Stirling, Selkirk, and Clackmannan; a Director of the Stirling and Dumfriesshire Railway. A 'Liberal-Conservative', in favour of withdrawing the grant to Maynooth. First returned for Clackmannan and Kinross June 1851. Sat until he retired 1857. Died 24 Feb. 1888.   [1857]

JOHNSTONE, John James Hope.(I). Raehills, Lockerbie, Scotland. Carlton. Eld. s. of Adm. Sir William Johnstone, G.C.B., by Lady Anne, eld. d. of 3rd Earl of Hopetoun. B. 1796; m. 1816, Alicia, eld. d. of George Gordon, Esq., Keeper of Lochmaben Castle, and niece of Sir David Baird, Bart. Formerly a Lieut. in the navy; claimant of the dormant Earldom of Annandale. A Liberal-Conservative, in favour of extension of the franchise, retrenchment of expenditure, and a national system of education. Sat for Dumfriesshire from 1830 to July 1847, and from Feb. to Apr. 1857, when he was re-elected without opposition. Sat until he retired at the 1865 general election. Died 11 July 1876.   [1865]

JOHNSTONE, John James Hope.(II). 44 St. James's Place, London. Rachills, Lockerbie, Scotland. Guards', and White's. S. of William James Hope-Johnstone, Esq., by the Hon. Octavia Sophia Bosville, youngest d. of 3rd Baron Macdonald; grands. of John James Hope-Johnstone, Esq., of Annandale. B. 1842. Educ. at Eton. Served in the Rifle Brigade and

subsequently became Cornet in the Grenadier Guards Jan. 1862, promoted to Capt. Apr. 1870. A Conservative. Sat for Dumfriesshire from Feb. 1874 until he retired 1880. Died 26 Dec. 1912.   [1880]

JOHNSTONE, Sir John Vanden Bempde, Bart. 34 Belgrave Square, London. Hackness Hall, Scarborough, Yorkshire. Boodle's, and Travellers'. Eld. s. of Sir R.V.B. Johnstone, by the d. of John Scott, Esq., of London. B. at Hackness Hall 1799; m. in 1825, Louisa Venables Vernon, 2nd d. of Archbishop (Harcourt) of York. Was educ. at Rugby, and at Trinity Coll., Cambridge. Appointed Dept.-Lieut. of the North Riding of Yorkshire, 1852. Lieut.-Col. of the West Riding Yeomanry, 1859. Patron of 2 livings. A Liberal, opposed to the ballot; would exempt Dissenters from the payment of church-rates, and extend education by state grant and not by local rates. Sat for Yorkshire from Dec. 1830 till Dec. 1832; for Scarborough from 1832 till 1837; re-elected for Scarborough in 1841. MP until he died on 25 Feb. 1869.   [1867]

JOICEY, Col. John. Newton Hall, Stockfield-on-Tyne, Northumberland. Reform, and Devonshire. 4th s. of George Joicey, Esq. of Newcastle-on-Tyne. B. at Tynemouth, Northumberland 1817; m. 1867, Rose, d. of the Rev. John Ewen of Hopekirk, Roxburghshire. Was High Sheriff of Durham 1878. Patron of 3 livings. A Liberal, said he would oppose every attempt to disintegrate the Kingdom', and that he 'will support every measure calculated to assimilate the laws of the whole United Kingdom'. In favour also of measures to facilitate the sale and transfer of land. Sat for Durham N. from Apr. 1880. MP until his death 15 Aug. 1881.   [1881]

JOLLIFFE, Hon. Hedworth Hylton. 57 Lancaster Gate, London. Tilgate Forest, Horsham, Sussex. Carlton, Junior Carlton, Army & Navy, and Boodle's. B. at Merstham, 1829, the eld. s. of Baron Hylton. M. 1859, Hon. Agnes, eld. d. of Visct. Enfield, and grand-d. of 1st Earl of Strafford. Educ. at Eton and at Oriel Coll., Oxford. Entered the army as Cornet 4th Light Dragoons, 1848; became Lieut. 1851, Lieut. and Capt. Coldstream Guards 1854, and retired 1855. Was at Alma and Inkermann and the Light Cavalry Charge at Balaklava. A Magistrate for Sussex, and appointed Capt. of North Somerset Yeomanry Cavalry 1855. A Conservative, in favour of an extended system of national education. Sat for Wells from Nov 1855 until it was disfranchised in 1868. Succeeded as 2nd Earl Hylton in June 1876. Died 31 Oct. 1899.   [1867]

214

JOLLIFFE, Rt. Hon. Sir William George Hylton, Bart. 16 Stratton Street, London. Merstham House, Surrey. Heath House, Petersfield. Carlton, Boodle's, White's and Arthur's. S. of the Rev. William Jolliffe, by the d. and co-heir of Sir A. Pytches, of Streatham, Surrey. B. in Little Argyll Street, London, 1800; m. 1825, of the Hon. B. Paget (she died 1862). Was Under-Sec. of State for the Home Dept. from Mar-Dec. 1852, and Parliamentary Sec. to the Treasury from Mar. 1858-June 1859. A Dept.-Lieut. of Surrey. A Conservative. Sat for Petersfield in 1830 and 1831. Unsuccessfully contested it in 1832, but was seated on petition the following year; again stood unsuccessfully in 1835; again returned in 1837 and sat until created Baron Hylton July 1866. Died 1 June 1876.
[1865]

JOLLIFFE, Hon. William Sydney Hylton, 43 Charles Street, Berkeley Square, London. Guards', Carlton, and Boodle's. 4th s. of the 1st Lord Hylton (who represented Petersfield for many years previous to his elevation to the Peerage in 1866), by Eleanor, 2nd d. of the Hon. Berkeley Paget. B. in London 1841; m 1870, Gertrude Henrietta, eld. d. of Richard Eaton, Esq., MP, of Stretchworth Park, Cambridgeshire. Educ. at Eton. Was appointed Ensign in the 29th Foot in 1861, exchanged into Scots Fusilier Guards 1867, retired as Capt. 1873. A Conservative. Sat for Petersfield from Feb. 1874 until he was defeated 1880. Died 19 Jan. 1912. [1880]

JONES, David. 2 Queen's Row, Pimlico, London. Pantglâs, Carmarthen. Penylan, Llandilo. Carlton. Eld. s. of John Jones, Esq., of Blaenôs, Llandovery, and grands. and heir of David Jones, Esq., of Pantglâs. B. at Blaenôs, 1810; m. 1845, Margaret Charlotte, eld. d. of Sir George Campbell, of Edenwood, Fifeshire. Educ. at the Charterhouse. Was Sheriff for Carmarthenshire 1845; a Dept.-Lieut. and Magistrate for Middlesex, Carmarthenshire and Brecknockshire. A Conservative, and a supporter generally of Lord Derby's policy; voted for 'an equitable adjustment' of the Church revenue. Unsuccessfully contested Sudbury, June 1841; and at his own sole expense unseated the two members then returned, which led to the disfranchisement of the bor. First returned for Carmarthenshire May 1852 and sat until he retired in 1868. Died 1 July 1869. [1867]

JONES, John. (I). 45 Buckingham Palace Road, London. Blaenôs, Llandovery, Carmarthenshire. Carlton, and Conservative. S. of John Jones, Esq., of Blaenôs, Llandovery, by Mary, d. of William Jones, Esq., of Ystrad-Walter, Carmarthenshire;

younger bro. of David Jones, Esq., who sat for Carmarthenshire from 1852-1868. B. 1815; m. 1841, his 1st cousin, Anne, 2nd d. of David Thomas, Esq., of Welfield, Radnorshire (deceased).Educ. at Shewsbury School under the celebrated Dr. Butler, afterwards Bp. of Lichfield and Coventry. Called to the bar at the Middle Temple 1839. A Magistrate and Dept.-Lieut. for Carmarthenshire, of which he was High Sheriff 1854. A Conservative. Sat for Carmarthenshire from Feb. 1874 until he was defeated 1880. [1880]

JONES, John. (II). Ystrad Lodge, Carmarthenshire. A Conservative. Represented the Carmarthen district of boroughs in a Parliament previous to 1832; was unsuccessful there in the 1832 election. Was a candidate for Carmarthenshire in 1835. First returned for Carmarthenshire at the general election in 1837, when he defeated Sir J.H. Williams, Bart., of Edwinsford who previously sat for it. MP until his death in 1842. [1842]

JONES, Theobald. 30 Charles Street, St. James's London. Dungiven, Bovagh, Co. Derry. Carlton. 2nd. s. of the Rev. James Jones, Rector of Urney, Strabane, by Lydia, d. of Theobald Wolfe, Esq., grands. of the Rt. Hon. Theophilus Jones, of Headfort, formerly member for Leitrim, and nephew of Walter Jones, Esq., of Hayle Place, Kent. B. 1790. A Capt. in the navy. A Conservative. Sat for Londonderry Co. from 1830 until he retired 1857. Died 7 Feb. 1868. [1857]

JONES, Sir Willoughby Bart. Cranmer Hall, Fakenham, Norfolk. Evesham House, Cheltenham. Alfred Club. 2nd s. of Sir John Thomas Jones, K.C.B., by the d. of Effingham Lawrence, Esq., of New York. B. 1820. Unmarried. Became Scholar of Trinity Coll., Cambridge in 1842; took a Wrangler's degree in 1843; studied for the bar for two years. Patron of 1 living. A Conservative, opposed to the endowment of the Roman Catholic Church. First returned for Cheltenham in 1847. Unseated June 1848; contested same seat in 1852. Unsuccessfully contested Norfolk W. 24 July 1865. Chairman of Quarter Sessions 1856. Author. Died 21 Aug. 1884. [1847 2nd ed.]

JONES, Wilson. 5 South Crescent, Bedford Square, London. Hartsheath Park, Flintshire. Carlton. S. of John Jones of Cefn Coch, Denbighshire, and of Elizabeth, d. and co-heiress of Edward Wilson, Esq., of Liverpool. B. 1795; m. 1822, Cecil, d. of John Carstairs, Esq., of Stratford Green, Essex, and Warboys, Huntingdonshire. Was formerly in the 2nd Dragoon Guards. A Magistrate for Denbighshire and

Flintshire. A Conservative. Sat for Denbigh district from 1835 until he retired in 1841. [1840]

JONES-PARRY, Thomas Duncombe Lone.
177 Piccadilly, London. Madryn Castle, Pwllheli, North Wales. Reform, and Junior United Service. B. at Llanbedrog 1832, eld. s. of Lieut.-Gen. Sir Lone Parry Jones-Parry, K.H., of Madryn Park, Carnarvonshire (MP for Horsham 1806-07, and for Carnarvon dist. 1835-37), by Elizabeth, only d. of Thomas Caldecot, Esq., of Holton Lodge, Lincolnshire. Educ. at Rugby and at University Coll., Oxford. High Sheriff of Carnarvonshire 1854 and Magistrate and Dept.-Lieut. from that date. Capt. Royal Anglesey Militia. Patron of 1 living. A Liberal, and supported Gladstone's policy. Sat for Carnarvonshire Dec. 1868 to Feb. 1874, when he was unsuccessful. Sat for Carnarvon district Mar. 1882 to 86, when he was defeated. Created Baronet Aug. 1886. Died 18 Dec. 1891. [1886]

KARSLAKE, Edward Kent. 1 Cambridge Terrace, Regent's Park, London. 4 Stone Buildings, Lincoln's Inn, London. Athenaeum. Eld. s. of Henry Karslake, Esq., Solicitor, of Regent Street, London, who was Solicitor to the Duke of Kent, and Secretary for Charities to the Duke from 1812 till the Duke's death, by Elizabeth, eld. d. of Richard Preston, Esq., Q.C., of Lincolns Inn. M. 1859, Anne Agnes, younger d. of Robert Gillespie, Esq., of London and Springhill, Lanarkshire. Educ. at Harrow. Was student of Christ Church, Oxford, and afterwards Fellow of Balliol. Was 1st class in classics in 1841; and obtained, amongst other honours, Dean Ireland's University Scholarship, and the Eldon Law Scholarship. Was called to the bar at Lincolns Inn May 1846, and was a Queen's Counsel. A Conservative, gave an independent support to Lord Derby's ministry, and was determined to maintain the established church; in favour of a fair representation 'not only of property, but of education and such other qualifications as raise a man in the social scale.' Elected for Colchester Feb. 1867. Defeated 1868. Died 31 May 1892. [1868]

KARSLAKE, Sir John Burgess. 7 Chester Square, London. 2 Essex Court, Temple, London. Carlton, and Conservative. S. of Henry Karslake, Esq., Solicitor, of Regent Street, by Elizabeth Marsh, eld. d. of Richard Preston, Esq., Q.C. of Lincolns Inn. B. at Bencham, Nr. Croydon, 1821. Was educ. at Harrow. Was called to the bar 1846 and the Middle Temple, of which he was a Bencher. Appointed a Queen's Counsel 1861; Solicitor-Gen. 1866; Attorney-Gen. July 1867, resigned Dec. 1868; again held the last

named office from Feb.-Apr. 1874. A Conservative. Sat for Andover from Feb. 1867 to Dec. 1868, when he was a unsuccessful candidate for Exeter. Sat for Huntingdon from Dec. 1873. Accepted Chiltern Hundreds 1876. Died 4 Oct. 1881. [1876]

KAVANAGH, Arthur MacMurrough. 19 Chester Square, London. Borris House, Borris, Co. Carlow. Sackville Street Club, Dublin. S. of Thomas Kavanagh, Esq., of Borris House, Co. Carlow, by Lady Harriet Margaret, d. of the 2nd Earl of Clancarty. B. at Borris 1831; m. 1854, Frances Mary, only surviving d. of the Rev. Joseph Forde Leathley, of Termonfeckin Rectory, Co. Lough. Was High Sheriff of Kilkenny in 1855, of Carlow 1857. A Magistrate for the Cos. of Carlow and Wexford, and Chairman of the New Ross Board of Guardians. Author of *The Cruise of the Eva*. A Conservative, voted against the disestablishment of the Irish Church 1869. Sat for the Co. of Wexford from Nov. 1866 to Dec. 1868, from which date he sat for the Co. of Carlow until defeated 1880. Founded Irish Land Corporation 1883. P.C. (Ireland) 1886. Died 25 Dec. 1889. [1880]

KAVANAGH, Thomas. Borris House, Co. Carlow. S. of Thomas Kavanagh, Esq., of Borris. M. 1st, 1798, his cousin, Elizabeth, eld. d. of the Marq. of Ormonde (dead); 2ndly, 1825, Harriet Margaret, 2nd d. of Richard, 2nd Earl of Clancarty. Father-in-law of Col. Bruen, the other member for Carlow. Counted as one of the wealthiest commoners in Ireland. A Conservative. Sat for Carlow in several Parliaments before 1831, when he unsuccessfully contested it, as also in 1832. Was returned in Jan. 1835, but the election of himself and colleague was declared void on petition; on a new writ being issued, they were defeated, but succeeded on petition. MP until his death in 1837. [1836]

KEANE, Sir Richard, Bart. 13 Charles Street, Haymarket, London. Cappoquin House, Co. Waterford. B. in 1780; m. Mrs. Penrose, relict of Samuel Penrose, Esq., of Waterford. Of Whig principles. Sat for Waterford Co. from 1832. Retired in 1835. Died 16 Feb. 1855. [1833]

KEARSLEY, John Hodgson. Higher Hall, Lancashire. Carlton. A Conservative. Sat for Wigan in the Parliament of 1831; was unsuccessful, and at the bottom of the poll in 1832; returned at the top of the poll for Wigan in 1835. Defeated in 1837. [1837]

KEARSLEY, Robert. Highfield, Ripon. 7th s. of George Kearsley, Esq., of Ripon. B. at Ripon,

1822; m. 1847, 4th d. of Capt. Winterbottom, R.N. Educ. at the Grammar School, Ripon. A Merchant. A Magistrate for Ripon, of which town he was three times chosen Mayor. Became Capt. 1st West Riding Volunteers 1864. A Liberal, in favour of a 'reasonable extension' of the franchise, but not to the extent proposed in Mr. Baines's Bill; in favour also of a 'material reduction' in the national expenditure. First elected for Ripon, July 1865. Retired in 1868, when Ripon became a single member seat.   [1867]

KEATING, Sir Henry Singer. 13 Great Queen Street, Westminster, London. Windham. 3rd s. of Lieut-Gen. Sir Henry Sheely Keating, K.C.B., Col. of the 33rd Foot, by Mary Anne, eld. d. of James Singer, Esq., of Annadale, Co. Dublin. B. in the Co. of Dublin 1804; m. 1843, Gertrude 3rd d. of Maj-Gen. Evans of the Artillery. Educ. at Trinity Coll., Dublin, where he graduated M.A. Was called to the bar at Inner Temple 1832; and on the Oxford Circuit; appointed Queen's Counsel by patent, Feb. 1849 and elected a Bencher of the Inner Temple May 1849. Was Solicitor Gen. from June 1857-Mar. 1858. A Liberal, in favour of the franchise being lowered to a £6 qualification and vote by ballot (though originally opposed to the latter); against the Maynooth Grant and the imposition of Church rates on Dissenters. First returned for Reading in July 1852 and sat until appointed a Judge Dec. 1859. Retired Feb. 1875. Died 1 Oct. 1888. [1859]

KEATING, Robert. Garranlee, Cashel, Co. Tipperary. Erectheum. S. of Leonard Keating, Esq., of Carranlee, Co. Tipperary, by Lucinda, d. of James Scully, Esq., of Kilfeacle, in the same Co. A Repealer, a member of the 'Old Ireland party'; voted for the ballot 1853. Sat for the Co. of Waterford from 1847 to July 1852, when he was elected for Waterford city. Sat until he retired 1857.   [1857]

KEKEWICH, Samuel Trehawke. Peamore House, Nr. Exeter. United University. S. of Samuel Kekewich, Esq., of Peamore (a Magistrate for Devon), by Salome, d. of George Sweet, Esq., B. at Bowden House, near Totnes, 1796; m. 1st, 1820, Agatha, sister of J.H. Langston, Esq.,; 2ndly, 1840, Louisa, only d. of the late Lewis W. Buck, Esq., of Moreton, Devon. Educ. at Eton and at Christ Church, Oxford. Was patron of 1 living. Was Sheriff of Devon 1834. A Magistrate for Devon, and Chairman of Visitors of the County Lunatic Asylum. Was Chairman of the Board of Guardians, at St. Thomas's, Exeter, for 20 years. A Conservative. When formerly in Parliament voted with the Ministry of Lord Liverpool, and supported Mr. Canning and Sir Robert

Peel, and gave a general support to Mr. Disraeli's party. Sat for Exeter from Feb. 1826 to 1830; unsuccessfully contested Liskeard Jan. 1835, and again in July 1837. First elected for Devon S, Aug. 1858. MP until he died 1 June 1873.   [1873]

KELBURNE, Visct. Kelburne House, Ayrshire. Eld. surviving s. of the Earl of Glasgow. B. 1792; m. 1821, d. of Edw. Hay Mackenzie, Esq. A Lieut. in the navy. A Conservative, first elected for Ayrshire in 1839, on the death of Sir J. Dunlop. Sat until he succeeded father as 5th Earl of Glasgow in 1843; Lord-Lieut. and Sheriff Principal of Ayrshire 1844. Died 11 Mar. 1869. [1842]

KELK, Sir John. 80 Eaton Square, London. Bentley Priory, Stanmore, Middlesex. Junior Carlton. S. of John Kelk, Esq., of St. John's Wood, London, by Martha, d. of Thomas German, Esq., of Witney, Oxfordshire. B. in London 1816; m. 1848, his cousin Anne, d. of George Kelk, Esq., of Sutton, Nottinghamshire. Educ. at Dr. Benson's school at Hounslow. Was a well-known contractor for public works. A moderate Conservative, and a supporter of Lord Derby; in favour of the principle of non-intervention, and of the army, navy and defences of the country being maintained in a state of efficiency. First elected for Harwich, July 1865. Retired in 1868 when Harwich became a single-member constituency. Created Baronet 1 May 1874. Died 12 Sept. 1886.   [1867]

KELLY, Sir Fitz-Roy. 8 Connaught Place, London. 2 Kings Bench Walk, Temple, London. The Chauntry, Ipswich. Carlton, and Junior Carlton. S. of Capt. Robert Hawke Kelly, R.N., by Isabel, d. of Capt. Fordyce, Carver and Cupbearer to George III. Grands. of Col. Robert Kelly. B. in London 1796; m. 1st, 1821, eld. d. and co-heir of Capt. Mason of Leith (she died 1851); 2ndly, ·1856, Ann, d. of Mark Cunningham, Esq., of the Co. of Sligo, Ireland. Called to the bar in 1824 at Lincoln's Inn, of which he was elected a Bencher 1835, and made a King's Counsel 1834. Joined the Home and afterwards the Norfolk Circuit. Appointed standing Counsel to the Bank of England May 1845. Was Solicitor-Gen. from July 1845-Aug. 1846; and from July-Dec. 1852. Attorney-Gen. from Mar. 1858-June 1859. A Dept.-Lieut. of Suffolk 1852. A Conservative, firmly attached to the Established Church; considered the franchise should be extended to 'all persons of property, education, and intellect.' Unsuccessfully contested Hythe in 1830, and Ipswich in 1832. Sat for Ipswich from Jan. to June 1835, when he was unseated on petition; was again unsuccessful July 1837, but succeeding by petition, sat from Feb. 1838 to July

1841, when he was once more an unsuccessful candidate. Sat for Cambridge bor. from Mar. 1843 to July 1847, when he was an unsuccessful candidate for Lyme Regis. Was elected for Harwich in Apr. 1852, but accepted the Chiltern Hundreds and was returned for Suffolk E. in May following. Sat until he was appointed Judge July 1866. Died 10 Nov. 1866.   [1865]

KELLY, James. 80 George's Street, Limerick. Erina House, Castleconnel, Co. Clare. Limerick Club. Only s. of John Kelly, Esq., Dept.-Lieut. of Limerick. M. only d. of Edward Roche, Esq., of Kilshannick, Co. Cork. Educ. at Trinity Coll., Dublin. A Liberal, a Repealer, 'favourable to a more extensive and enlightened system of legislation and government, and also a more liberal system of national education than even the present.' Filled the office of High Sheriff of the Co. of Limerick in 1841, and was a Town Councillor of the corporation of Limerick. First returned for the city of Limerick in 1844, when Sir D. Roche retired from Parliament. Retired 1847.   [1847]

KEMBLE, Henry. Grove Hill, Camberwell, Surrey. S. of Edward Kemble, Esq., for many years a member of the Corporation of London, and an active and disinterested supporter of Mr. Pitt's administration. B. 1787; m. 1830, d. of Capt. Melville, Lieut.-Gov. of Pendennis Castle. Retired from business in 1833, a Director of the Equitable Assurance Company. 'A decided Conservative.' Gave no pledges; voted for agricultural protection 1846. First returned for Surrey E. in 1837, and sat until he retired 1847. Died 18 May 1857.   [1847]

KEMP, Thomas Reid. 24 Belgrave Square, London. Brighton, Sussex. The father of Mr. Kemp was originally a Woolstapler at Lewes, and represented Lewes in Parliament for nearly 30 years. B. 1782; m. 1st, Frances, d. of Sir Francis Baring, Bart., sister of Lord Ashburton; 2ndly, 1832, Frances Margarita, only d. of Charles W.J. Shakerley, Esq., of Somerfield Hall, Co. Chester, and widow of Vigers Hervey, Esq., of Killiane Castle, Co. Wexford. A Manager of the London and Brighton Railway. Succeeded his father in the representation of Lewes on his death in 1811; sat for it in the following Parliament, but afterwards resigned his seat to devote himself to the duties of a Dissenting minister. Of Whig principles, in favour of the ballot. Was again elected for Lewes in 1826 and sat for it until he accepted Chiltern Hundreds in Mar. 1837. Succeeded bro. as 11th Bart. 29 May 1874. Died 7 Aug. 1874.   [1874]

KENDALL, Nicholas. Pelyn, Lostwithiel, Cornwall. Carlton, and National. S. of the Rev. Charles Kendall, of Pelyn, near Lostwithiel, by Ann, d. of Francis Hext, Esq. of Tredethy, near Bodmin. B. at Tredethy, 1800; m. 1823. Educ. at Trinity Coll., Oxford, where he graduated B.A. 1830. A Magistrate and Dept.-Lieut. of Cornwall, and Chairman of the Board of Guardians of the Bodmin Union. Appointed Capt. in the Duke of Cornwall's Rangers, Oct. 1826, and a special Dept. Warden of the Stannaries 1852. Patron of 2 livings. A Conservative, in favour of the principle of non-intervention in Continental politics; voted however against Lord Palmerston on the Danish question 1864; opposed to the existing constituencies being swamped by the too sudden lowering of the franchise; in favour of church-rates. First returned for Cornwall E. in July 1852. Sat until he retired in 1868. Police Magistrate of Gibraltar Dec. 1868 to 1875. Died 8 June 1878.   [1867]

KENEALY, Edward Vaughan Hyde. 6 Tavistock Square, London. Lancing, Sussex. Educ. at Trinity Coll., Dublin, where he graduated B.A. 1840, LL.B. 1846, and proceeded to LL.D. Called to the bar in Ireland 1840, to the English bar at Gray's Inn 1847, and joined the Oxford Circuit. Unsuccessfully contested Wednesbury 18 Nov. 1868. Elected for Stoke-on-Trent on 'Independent principles' Feb. 1875. Sat until defeated 1880. Died 16 Apr. 1880.   [1880]

KENNARD, Coleridge John. 39 Upper Grosvenor Street, London. Stockton House, Bath. Fernhill, Lymington. Carlton. Eld. s. of John Pierce Kennard, Esq., of Hordle Cliff, Hampshire, a Banker at Salisbury, by Sophia, d. of Sir John Chapman. B. 1828; m. 1858, Ellen Georgina, only d. of Capt. Rowe. A Magistrate for Hampshire and one of the Commissioners of Lieutenancy for London. A Conservative, was opposed to all measures calculated to restrict 'liberty of debate in Parliament'; in favour of the education of the poor being combined with religious teaching; and of 'avowed atheists' being excluded from the House of Commons. In Apr. 1880 unsuccessfully contested Salisbury for which he sat from Nov. 1882. Defeated in 1885. Died 25 Dec. 1890.   [1885]

KENNARD, Lieut.-Col. Edmund Hegan. 3 Chesterfield Gardens, London. Carlton, and Army & Navy. S. of John Pierce Kennard, Esq., Banker of London, and of Hordle, Cleff, Lymington, Hampshire, by Sophia, eld. d. of Sir John Chapman, of Windsor. B. at Walthamstow, Essex, 1835; m. 1868, 2nd d. of Joseph Hegan, Esq., of Dawpool, Cheshire. Educ. at Radley Coll., near Oxford, and at Balliol Coll., Oxford, graduated B.A. with honours 1858, M.A.

1873. Entered the army Nov. 1858; became Lieut. June 1862; Capt. 8th Hussars Oct. 1866, retired Feb. 1870. Was Aide-de-Camp to the Duke of Abercorn, Lord Lieut. of Ireland from June 1867 to Dec. 1868. Lieut.-Col. Commandant Middlesex 26th Rifle Volunteers. A Conservative. Sat for Beverley from Dec. 1868 to Mar. 1869, when he was unseated on petition. Sat for Lymington from Feb. 1874 until he retired in 1885. Died 9 July 1912.   [1885]

KENNARD, Robert William. 37 Porchester Terrace, Hyde Park, London. Falkirk, Scotland. Carlton, and National. 2nd s. of John Kennard, Esq., of Clapham Common, Surrey, and a Banker in London, by Harriet Elizabeth, d. of William Pierse, Esq., of Windsor. B. in London 1800; m. 1823, Mary Anne, 2nd d. of Thomas Challis, Esq., of Holloway. An Iron-Master in Scotland and South Wales. Was Sheriff of London and Middlesex, 1846-47. A Magistrate for Westminster, for Middlesex, Hertford, and Stirlingshire. A Dept.-Lieut. for London. Patron of 1 living. A Liberal-Conservative, considered church-rates 'objectionable in principle and vexatious in their operation.' Sat for Newport, Isle of Wight, from Feb. till July 1847; re-elected May 1859. Sat until he retired in 1868, when Newport became a single-member seat. Died 10 Jan. 1870.   [1867]

KENNAWAY, Sir J.H. Continued in House after 1885: full entry in Volume II.

KENNEDY, James. 5 Lincoln's Inn, Old Square, London. S. of General M. Kennedy, of the East India Company's service. A Barrister on the Northern Circuit. A radical Reformer, he was the only English member who, in 1834, voted for Daniel O'Connell's motion on the question of Repeal. In 1826 he made an ineffectual attempt to open Tiverton, but was elected in 1832 by the extended constituency of the Reform Act and sat for it until 1835 when he accepted the Chiltern Hundreds. Judge of mixed commission for protection of slaves at Havana, 1837-52. Author. Died 15 May 1859.   [1835]

KENNEDY, Thomas Francis. 9 Chesterfield Street, Mayfair, London. Dunure, Ayrshire. M. d. of Sir Samuel Romily. Was Clerk of the Ordnance for a short period in 1832; appointed in 1833 a Lord of the Treasury. Was first elected for Ayr district in 1818. Sat until he accepted Chiltern Hundreds in 1834. Paymaster of the Civil Services in Ireland 1837-50; Commissioner of Woods and Forests 1850-54. Wrote an open letter to Lord John Russell concerning his removal from that office. Died 1 Apr. 1879. [1833]

KENNEDY, Tristram. 8 Henrietta Street, Dublin. S. of the Rev. John Pitt Kennedy, Rector of Baltea, Co. Londonderry, by Mary, d. of — Cary, Esq. B. at Glebe House, Donagh, Co. Donegal, 1805; m. 1862, Helen, d. of Lieut.-Col. Graham, of Cossington, Somersetshire. Educ. at Foyle Coll., Londonderry. Called to the bar in Ireland, 1834, and founded the Dublin Law Institute 1839. Was High Sheriff of Londonderry 1828. A Liberal, and in favour of 'the fullest protection being conceded to all in the exercise of their social, industrial, political, and religious rights', as the only means of putting an end to party antagonism in Ireland; in favour also of 'justice to tenants without injustice to landlords', and the furtherance of popular education on terms of equality to all denominations. Unsuccessfully contested Kings Co. 19 May 1859. Sat for Louth from Apr. 1865. Retired in 1868. Contested Donegal in 1874. Died 20 Nov. 1885.   [1867]

KENNY, M.J. Continued in House after 1885: full entry in Volume II.

KENSINGTON, Rt. Hon. Lord. 69 Grosvenor Street, London. St. Bride's, Haverfordwest, Pembrokeshire. Brooks's, Travellers', Devonshire, and Reform. An Irish Peer. B. in London 1835; m. 1867, Grace Elizabeth, eld. d. of Robert Johnstone Douglas, Esq., of Lockerbie. Educ. at Eton. Appointed Capt. and Lieut.-Col. Coldstream Guards 1867. Vice-Lieut. of Pembrokeshire 1862. Lieut. and Custos-rot. in 1872. Was a Groom in Waiting to the Queen from Nov. 1873 to Feb. 1874; appointed Controller of the Queen's Household Apr. 1880. A Liberal. Sat for Haverfordwest from Dec. 1868. Sat until defeated in 1885 contesting Hornsey div. of Middlesex. Created Baron Kensington Mar. 1886. Chairman Pembrokeshire County Council 1892-94. Died 7 Oct. 1896.   [1885]

KEOGH, Rt. Hon. William. Rahoon, Galway. 55 Rutland Square, Dublin. Coburg House, Bray, Wicklow. Erectheum. B. at Galway 1817, the eld. s. of William Keogh, Esq., of Corkip, Co. Roscommon, by Mary, d. of Austin Ffrench, Esq., of Rahoon, Galway. M. 1841, Kate, eld. d. of Thomas Roney, Esq., Surgeon. Educ. at the University of Dublin, where he received 1st class honours in science, the Hebrew prize, the Vice Chancellor's prize and the College Historical Society's medals. Was called to the bar in Ireland 1840 and made a Queen's Counsel 1849. Was Solicitor Gen. for Ireland from Dec. 1852-Feb. 1855, when he became Attorney Gen. A Member of Lincoln's Inn. Author of *The Practice of the Court of Chancery in Ireland*, and several political tracts.

219

Appointed Judge in Mar. 1856 and tried the Fenian prisoners in 1865, the Galway County election petition in 1872. A Liberal, favoured a wide extension of the suffrage, the ballot, the Maynooth Grant, the admission of Jews to Parliament, tenant right in Ireland etc., but originally entered Parliament as a supporter of Sir Robert Peel. Sat for Athlone from 1847 to 1856. Died 30 Sept. 1878. [1856]

KEOWN, William. Ballyduggan House, Downpatrick. Carlton. 3rd s. of Richard Keown, Esq., of Downpatrick, by Mary, d. of Henry Keown, Esq., of Tollymoore, Devon. B. in Dublin 1816; m. 1845, Mary, d. of the Rev. Robert Alexander, prebendary of Aghadoey, in the diocese of Derry, and sister of the Bishop of Derry. Educ. at Shrewesbury School and at Emmanuel Coll., Cambridge. Was a Magistrate for the Co. of Down, and was High Sheriff of that county 1849. A Conservative. Elected for Downpatrick Aug. 1867. Sat until he retired in 1874. Became Keown-Boyd in 1873. Died 19 Jan. 1877. [1873]

KEPPEL, Hon. George Thomas. 12 Stanhope Place, London. 10 Downing Street, London. Reform. 2nd s. of the 4th Earl of Albermarle, by his first wife, the 4th d. of the 20th Lord de Clifford. Born 1799; m. 1831, Susannah, d. and co-heir of Sir Coutts-Trotter, Bart. Entered the army in April 1815; served at Waterloo; became a Lieut.-Col. in 1841. Also served in India. Author of *Journey across the Bakan, Journey from India to England.* Groom in Waiting to the Queen, in 1846 appointed one of Lord John Russell's Private Secretaries. A Liberal. Sat for East Norfolk from 1832 to 1835; was an unsuccessful candidate for Lynn Regis 1837. Contested Lymington without success, 1841; returned there in 1847. Accepted Chiltern Hundreds in 1850. Succeeded his bro. as 6th Earl of Albermarle in May 1867. Died 21 Feb. 1891. [1850]

KER, David Steward. Montalto, Ballynahinch, Co. Down. Oxford & Cambridge. Sackville Street Club, Dublin. Only s. of David Ker, Esq., of Portavo and Montalto, Co. Down, by Lady Selina Sarah Juliana, d. of 1st Marq. of Londonderry. M. 1842, Hon. Anna Dorothea, youngest d. of 2nd Lord Dufferin. Educ. at Christ Church, Oxford, where he graduated B.A. 1841. Was a Magistrate for the Cos. of Down and Antrim, and Dept.-Lieut. of Down. A Conservative, who firmly supported Lord Derby's policy. Sat for the Co. of Down from July 1852 to Apr. 1857. He was elected for Downpatrick in May 1859, and sat until he accepted Chiltern Hundreds in 1867. Died 8 Oct. 1878. [1867]

KER, Richard. Portavo, Co. Down. Travellers'. S. of David Ker, Esq., of Portavo, (sho sat for Athlone and Downpatrick), by Lady Selina Sarah Juliana , d. of 1st Marq. of Londonderry. B. 1822; m. 1856, Rose, d. of Nicholson Calvert, Esq., of Quintin Castle, Co. Down. Educ. at Eton and at Oxford. Was attached to the Embassy at Paris from 1844 till 1847, and at St. Petersburgh from 1851 till the declaration of war 1854; at Copenhagen (on special service), and at Madrid; again appointed to the Russian mission in 1856 as 1st Attaché. A 'Liberal-Conservative', voted in favour of Lord Palmerston's policy in China 1857. Sat for Downpatrick from July 1847 till Aug. 1851, and from Feb. till Mar. 1857, when he was re-elected without opposition. Retired in 1859. Died 18 Dec. 1890. [1858]

KER, R.B.W. Continued in House after 1885: full entry in Volume II.

KERRISON, Sir Edward, Bart., G.C.H., K.C.B. 13 Great Stanhope Street, London. Oakley Park and Brome Hall, Suffolk. Carlton. 2nd s. of Matthias Kerrison, Esq., of Hexne Hall, Suffolk by the d. of Edw. Burnes, Esq., of Bursham. B. 1776; m. 1811, Mary, eld. d. of Alexander Ellice, Esq., of Fife. Recorder of Eye, became a Gen. in the army in 1851. Col. of the 14th Light Dragoons, an Inspector of army clothing, and an East India Proprietor; patron of 9 livings; was at Waterloo, and served in Spain, France, and Holland. A Conservative, voted for agricultural protection, 1846. Father-in-law of Lord Mahon, and of Lord Henniker. Sat for Northampton in the Parliament of 1818, previously for Shaftesbury. Sat for Eye from 1824 until he retired in 1852. Died 9 Mar. 1853. [1852]

KERRISON, Sir Edward Clarence, Bart. 40 Piccadilly, London. Broome Hall, Scole, Norfolk. Carlton, Travellers', and Boodle's. Only s. of Gen. Sir Edward Kerrison, 1st Bart., K.C.B. (who sat in Parliament for 37 years), by Mary, eld. d. of Sir Alexander Ellice, of Pittencrief, Fifeshire. B. at The Wick, Brighton, 1821; m. 1844, Lady Caroline Margaret, d. of the 3rd Earl of Ilchester. Appointed Lieut. of the Suffolk Borderers Yeomanry Cavalry in 1843, a Dept.-Lieut. of Suffolk, and Lieut. Suffolk Rifle Volunteers 1860. A Conservative, in favour of a reduction of the malt tax, and would 'not vote for any reform bill that emanates from an individual member.' First returned for Eye, July 1852. Sat until he accepted Chiltern Hundreds 1866. Sat for Suffolk E. from 25 July 1866 until he accepted Chiltern Hundreds 1867. Master of Hunt 1869. Died 12 July 1886. [1865]

KERRY, Earl of. 10 Harley Street, London. Rowood, Wiltshire. Eld. s. of the Marq. of Lansdowne. B. 1811; m. 1834, Augusta, 2nd d. of Visct. Duncannon. Of Whig principles. Sat for Calne from 1832. MP until his death 21 Aug. 1836. [1836]

KERSHAW, James. Manor House, Streatham, Surrey. Reform. B. at Manchester in 1795. A Cotton Spinner, Manufacturer and Calico Printer. A Magistrate of Lancashire, a Magistrate and Alderman of Manchester. Was Mayor of that town in 1843. A Liberal, in favour of short Parliaments, the ballot, the repeal of the rate paying clauses of the Reform Act of 1832 and the repeal of the game laws; was opposed to all religious endowments. First returned for Stockport in Dec. 1847 and sat until his death 27 Apr. 1864. [1864]

KEY, Sir John, Bart. 30 Abchurch Lane, Denmark Hill, Surrey. B. in 1795; m. in 1814 Charlotte, youngest d. of F. Green, Esq., of Dorking. A Wholesale Stationer, and Alderman of London; late Lord Mayor of the City in two consecutive years; was created a Baronet shortly after the accession of William IV. A Reformer, in favour of the immediate abolition of slavery, the repeal of a part of the assessed taxes, the repeal of the corn laws, the adoption of triennial Parliaments, and the vote by ballot. Returned for City of London in 1832. Accepted Chiltern Hundreds Aug. 1833. Died 15 July 1858. [1833]

KILDARE, Marquis of. 24 St. James's Place, London. Carlton House, Maynooth, Co. Kildare. Brooks's. Eld. s. of the Duke of Leinster. B. in Dublin 1819; m. 1847, Lady Caroline, 3rd d. of the 2nd Duke of Sutherland. Graduated at Christ Church, Oxford. A Commissioner of National Education in Ireland; a Magistrate and Dept.-Lieut. of Kildare. Of Liberal principles, in favour of free trade; against a repeal of the Union with Ireland; supported 'tenant-right'. First returned for Kildare in 1847. Retired in 1852. Created Baron Kildare May 1870; succeeded as 5th Duke of Leinster Oct. 1874. Died 10 Feb. 1887. [1852]

KING, Edward Bolton. Chadshunt, Leamington. Eld. s. of Edward King, Esq., of Hungerhill, Yorkshire (Vice-Chancellor of the Duchy of Lancaster), by his 2nd wife, Dorothy, d. of — Myers, Esq. Nephew of Dr. Walker King, Bishop of Rochester. B. 1801; m. 1828, Georgiana, 2nd d. of Robert Knight, Esq., of Barrels, Warwickshire, former MP for Wallingford. Was High Sheriff of Warwickshire in 1830. Appointed Lieut.-Col. of the

Warwickshire Yeomanry Cavalry in 1848. A Liberal, said he would give 'a general support and fair trial to Lord Palmerston's government'; approved of the policy pursued in the Chinese war, and likewise of Lord Palmerston's 'judicious appointments' in the Church; would afford his 'best support to the Protestant Church as established, and to the religious education and social improvement of all classes'; when first in Parliament, was in favour of the ballot. Sat for Warwick from 1831 to July 1837, when he was unsuccessful. First returned for Warwickshire S. in Mar. 1857. Retired in 1859. Died 23 Mar. 1878. [1858]

KING, James King. 97 Eaton Place, London. Staunton Park, Hereford. Carlton. Eld. s. of Rev. James King, of Staunton Park, Herefordshire, by Emma, 4th d. of Edward Vaux, Esq. B. at Weybridge, Surrey, 1806; m. 1835, Mary Cochrane, 4th d. of Kenneth Francis Mackenzie, Esq. (descended from a junior branch of the Mackenzies, of Redcastle, Ross-shire). Educ. at Balliol Coll., Oxford, where he graduated B.A. 1829, M.A. 1865. A Magistrate and Dept.-Lieut. for Herefordshire and formerly Capt. in that county militia. A Conservative, but not against 'any necessary and rational reform'; in favour of the principle of non-intervention in Foreign politics, but supported the vote of censure on Lord Palmerston respecting the Danish war, 1864. First returned for Herefordshire in July 1852. Sat until he retired in 1868. [1867]

KING, John Gilbert. Ballylin, Ferbane, King's Co. Kildare Street Club, Dublin. Sackville Street Club, Dublin. eld. s. of the Rev. Henry King, of Ballylin, King's Co., by Harriet, d. of John Lloyd, Esq., of Gloster, King's Co., who represented that Co. for many years. B. at Ballylin, 1822. Unmarried. Educ. at Trinity Coll., Dublin. A Magistrate and Dept.-Lieut. of King's Co., for which he served as High Sheriff, 1852. A Conservative, and 'as a landlord is in favour of tenants receiving the fair value of their improvements.' First elected for King's Co. July 1865. Retired in 1868. [1867]

KING, Hon. Peter John Locke. 38 Dove Street, London. Brooklands, Weybridge, Surrey. Athenaeum, and Reform. 2nd s. of 7th Lord King, by the eld. d. of 1st Earl Fortescue, was therefore bro. to 1st Earl Lovelace. B. at Ockham, Surrey, 1811; m. 1836 Louisa Elizabeth, d. of William Henry Hoare, Esq., and niece of 1st Earl of Gainsborough. Was educ. at Harrow and at Trinity Coll., Cambridge, where he graduated M.A. 1833. Appointed Vice-Lieut. of Surrey, Dec. 1871. 'An earnest and sincere Liberal', brought forward on several occasions a bill for extending the county franchise to £10 occupiers; opposed to all religious endowments by the State; voted for the ballot 1853. Was an unsuccessful candidate for E. Surrey in 1837. first elected for E. Surrey in 1847. Sat until defeated in 1874. Died 12 Nov. 1885.   [1873]

KING-HARMAN, Col. E.R. Continued in House. after 1885: full entry in Volume II.

KINGLAKE, Alexander William. 9 St. George's Terrace, Marble Arch, London. Wilton House, Taunton. Travellers', Athenaeum, and Oxford & Cambridge. Eld. s. of William Kinglake, Esq., of Wilton House, Taunton, by Mary, eld. d. of Thomas Woodforde, Esq., of Taunton. B. at Taunton. Unmarried. Educ. at Eton and at Trinity Coll., Cambridge. Called to the bar in 1837, and quitted the practice of the profession in 1856. A Dept.-Lieut. of Somerset. Author of *Eothen*, and of the *Invasion of the Crimea*. An 'advanced Liberal', but declined to go to Parliament 'as the pledged adherent of Lord Palmerston or any other minister.' Was an unsuccessful candidate for Bridgewater in July 1852. First returned for Bridgewater in Apr. 1857. Sat until returned in 1868, but election declared void and Bridgewater disfranchised 1869. Died 2 Jan. 1891.   [1867]

KINGLAKE, John Alexander. 2 Serjeants Inn, London. Count Place, Monkton, Taunton, Somerset. Athenaeum, Reform, and Oxford & Cambridge. S. of Robert Kinglake, Esq., M.D., by Joanna, d. of Anthony Apperlay, Esq., of Herefordshire. M. 1835 Louisa Rebecca, only d. of John Liddon, Esq. Educ. at Eton and at Trinity Coll., Cambridge. Called to the bar at Lincoln's Inn 1830 and made Serjeant-at-law, with a patent of precedence, 1844. Was for some time Recorder of Exeter, appointed Recorder of Bristol 1856. A Liberal; supported Mr. Gladstone in his Irish Church, and general policy, and said he would advance to the utmost of his power, Liberal principles; favoured the principle of neutrality in respect of Continental Wars, and vote by ballot. An unsuccessful candidate for Wells, July 1852. First returned for Rochester Apr. 1857. MP until his death 9 July 1870.   [1870]

KINGSCOTE, Col. Robert Nigel Fitzhardinge, C.B. 34 Charles Street, Berkeley Square, London. Kingscote Park, Gloucestershire. Brooks's, Guards', and White's. B. at Kingscote 1830, the eld. s. of Thomas Henry Kingscote of Kingscote, Gloucestershire by his 1st wife, Lady Isabella Frances Anne, 6th d. of the 6th Duke of Beaufort. M. 1st, 1851, Caroline Sophia, 3rd d. of Col. Wyndham; 2ndly, 1856,

Lady Emily Marie, 3rd d. of 1st Earl Howe (a Lady of the Bedchamber to the Princess of Wales). Appointed Capt. in Scots Fusilier Guards in 1880, Aide-de-Camp to Lord Raglan in the expedition to aid Turkey 1854, and Lieut.-Col. in the army 1855. A Dept.-Lieut. of Gloucester, and Bristol, 1856. Was a Groom in Waiting to the Queen June 1859 - Aug. 1866. A Liberal and favoured the 'total' abolition of church-rates. Sat for Gloucestershire West from July 1852 until he was appointed Commissioner of Woods and Forests in 1885. Died 22 Sept. 1908.   [1884]

KINLOCH, George. 55 Parliament Street, Kinloch. As a consequence of proceedings arising out of his advocacy of Reform, Kinloch was declared an outlaw in December 1819, at the Cross of Edinburgh. On the anniversary of that day in 1832, he was elected for Dundee. A radical Reformer. MP until his death 28 Mar. 1833.   [1833]

KINNAIRD, Hon. Arthur Fitzgerald. 2 Pall Mall East, London. 3rd s. of 8th Lord Kinnaird by the 7th d. of 2nd Duke of Leinster. B. at Rossie Priory, Perthshire 1814; m. 1843, Mary Jane, d. of William Henry Hoare, Esq., of Mitcham Grove, Surrey and niece of 1st Earl of Gainsborough. Educ. at Eton. Was attached to the British Embassy at St. Petersburgh in 1835, and was private Sec. to the Earl of Durham. Was a partner in the firm of Ramson, Bouverie & Co., Bankers. A Liberal, in favour of Scotland being granted more representatives; voted for the disestablishment of the Irish Church 1869. Sat for Perth from July 1837 to Aug. 1839. Again returned for Perth May 1852 and sat until he succeeded bro. as 10th Baron Jan. 1878. Died 26 Apr. 1887.   [1877]

KINNEAR, Rev. John, D.D. 6 Beaufort Buildings, London. The Manse, Letterkenny, Donegal. 2nd s. of the Rev. James Kinnear, Presbyterian Minister of Clonaneese, near Dungannon, by Annie, eld. d. of James McKee, Esq., M.D., of Dungannon. B. 1824. Was educ. at the Royal Coll., Belfast. Was ordained to the Presbyterian ministry, and placed in charge of the 1st Presbyterian church at Letterkenny in 1848. Was created a D.D. of Washington, and Lee University in America 1874. Wrote numerous articles in Irish magazines. A Liberal, in favour of the substitution of elected county boards for the 'present anomalous grand jury system.' Sat for Donegal from Apr. 1880; retired in 1885. Died 1894.   [1885]

KIRK, George Harley. 10 Cantlowe Road, London. Clogher Head, Drogheda, Co. Louth.

Newgrange, Co. Meath. S. of Richard Kirk, Esq., of Kilcop House, Co. Waterford, by Julia, d. of Capt. Drury, R.N. B. at Drogheda 1831; m. 1858, Anne, only d. of John Kirk, Esq., of Clogher Head, Co. Louth. Educ. at Esker Coll. Was a tenant-farmer in Louth. Author of Poems and Essays. A Liberal, in favour of the system called 'Home Rule' for Ireland, also of denominational education, as demanded by the Bishops of Ireland, and for such a reform of the Land Code as will 'effectually root the people in the soil.' Sat for Louth from Apr. 1874 until defeated in 1880. [1880]

KIRK, Peter. Thornfield, Carrickfergus. Carlton. S. of Sir P. Kirk. B. 1800; m. 1821, d. of N. Dalway, Esq. A Dept.-Lieut. of Co. Antrim. Sat for Carrickfergus from 1835; filled the office of Mayor for five successive years. A Conservative, but in favour of free trade. Sat until he retired 1847. [1847]

KIRK, William. Ann Vale, Keady, Co. Armagh. S. of Hugh Kirk, Esq., of Larne, Co. Antrim, Merchant, by Eliza, d. of – Millar, Esq., of Burnside, Co. Antrim. B. at Larne, Co. Antrim, 1795; m. 1820 Anne, d. of James McKean, Esq., of Armagh. Educ. at Larne Schools. A Linen Merchant and Bleacher, retired. Appointed a Magistrate for the Co. of Armagh 1840; a Dept.-Lieut. 1862. A Liberal, voted for the ballot 1853, and in favour of the disestablishment of the Irish Church 1869 and also in favour of perfect religious equality being maintained in Ireland; also that the full and just value of improvements should be secured to tenants by Act of Parliament. Sat for Newry from July 1852 to Apr. 1859, when he was an unsuccessful candidate; again stood unsuccessfully, Aug. 1865. Had also unsuccessfully contested Armagh 17 July 1865. Was re-elected for Newry Dec. 1868. MP until his death 20 Dec. 1876. [1870]

KNACHTBULL, Sir Wyndham, Bart. 3 Chesham Place, London. Merstham Hatch, Ashford, Kent. 2nd s. of Sir Norton Knachtbull (10th) Bart., by Mary, eld. d. of Jesse Watts Russell, Esq., of Ilam Hall, Staffordshire, and Biggin, Northamptonshire. Grand-s. of Sir Edward Knachtbull, Bart., who sat for E. Kent from 1832-45, and previously for the whole county. B. 1844. A Conservative. Sat for E. Kent from Jan. 1875. Accepted Chiltern Hundreds 1876. Died 30 July 1917. [1876]

KNATCHBULL, Rt. Hon. Sir Edward, Bart. 39 Dover Street, London. Mersham-hatch, Kent. University, and Carlton. B. 1781. M. 1st, 1806, Annabella, d. of Sir John Honeywood, Bart., 2nd-ly, 1820, Fanny Catharine, eld. d. of Edward Knight of Godmersham Park, Kent. Paymaster General of the Forces from Dec. 1834 - April 1835, and again Sept. 1841. Patron of 1 living. Sat for E. Kent from the death of his father in 1819, with the exception of 1831, until he accepted Chiltern Hundreds, Feb. 1845. Died 24 May 1849. [1844]

KNATCHBULL, William Francis. 7 St. James's Place, London. Babington, Bath. Carlton, and Arthur's. 2nd s. of Wyndham Knatchbull, Esq., by his cousin, Catherine Maria, d. of Sir Edward Knatchbull, Bart. B. in Russell Place, London, 1804; m. 1829, Emma Louisa, d. of Charles Gordon Gray, Esq., of Virgin Valley, in Jamaica. Educ. at Winchester and at Christ Church, Oxford. A Magistrate and Dept.-Lieut. of Somerset, of which Co. he was High Sheriff in 1841; Lieut.-Col. N. Somerset Yeomanry Cavalry. A Conservative, voted for inquiry respecting Maynooth 1853, and said, if necessary, he would vote for the repeal of the grant. First returned for Somerset E. in July 1852. Sat until he retired 1865. Died 2 May 1871. [1865]

KNIGHT, Frederick Winn, C.B. Wolverley House, Kidderminster, Worcestershire. Simonsbath, Exmoor, Somerset. Carlton. Eld. s. of John Knight, Esq., by his 2nd wife, Jane Elizabeth, d. of 1st Lord Headley; descended from Richard Knight, of Madeley in Shropshire, a considerable Ironmaster in the time of the Commonwealth. M. 1850, Maria, d. of E. Gibbs. Esq. A family trustee of the British Museum, as representative of R. Payne Knight, Esq., of Downton; a retired Lieut.-Col. in the Worcestershire Yeomanry, and Col. 1st Battalion Worcestershire Rifle Volunteers. Patron of 1 living. A Conservative. Sat for West Worcestershire from 1841 until he retired in 1885. K.C.B. Feb. 1886. Died 3 May 1897. [1885]

KNIGHT, Henry Gally. 69 Lower Grosvenor Street, London. Firbeck Hall, Yorkshire. A nephew of Lord St. Helens. M. Henrietta, the d. of A.E. Eyre, Esq., of Grove, Nottinghamshire. A Conservative and a patron of 1 living. He published poems and other literary works. Sat for Nottinghamshire N. from 1834 until his death in 1846. [1845]

KNIGHTLEY, Sir Charles, Bart. 10 Upper Brook Street, London. Fawsley, Northamptonshire. Carlton. Eld. s. of the Rev. Charles Knightley, by the only d. of Henry Boulton, Esq., of Moulton, Lincolnshire. B. at Preston Capes, Northamptonshire, 1781; m. in 1813, Selina

223

Mary, d. of Felton Lionel Hervey, Esq., a relation of the Marq. of Bristol. Patron of 3 livings. A Conservative, voted for agricultural protection, 1846. Unsuccessfully contested Northamptonshire S. in 1831. Was first elected in Nov. 1834 for the southern division on the vacancy occasioned by Lord Althorp succeeding to his father's title. Sat until he retired in 1852. Died 30 Aug. 1864.   [1852]

KNIGHTLEY, Sir Rainald. Continued in House after 1885: full entry in Volume II.

KNOWLES, Thomas. 9 St. James's Place, London. Darnhall Hall, Winsford, Cheshire. Carlton, and Junior Carlton. S. of John Knowles, Esq., of Ince, Nr. Wigan. B. at Ince 1824; m. 1st, 1846, Miss Mary Forster of Golborne, (she died 1863); 2ndly, 1866, Mary d. of William Longworth, Esq., of Little Bolton (she died 1878). A Colliery Proprietor. Chairman of the Peason & Knowles Coal and Iron Co.; also a Cotton Spinner and Bleacher. Twice Mayor of Wigan (in 1864 and 1865). A Magistrate for the Cos. of Lancaster and Chester. A Conservative. A 'thorough Protestant' and in favour of the union of Church and State. Sat for Wigan from Feb. 1874. MP until his death 3 Dec. 1883.   [1883]

KNOX, Brownlow William. 28 Wilton Crescent, London. Carlton, and Boodle's. 3rd s. of Lieut.-Col. Thomas Knox, of the 1st Foot Guards, by the 3rd d. of Thomas Williams, Esq., of Lanidan, Anglesea (who m. 2ndly, Lieut.-Gen. Sir Henry Campbell, K.C.B.). Grand-nephew of the 1st Visct. Northland. M. d. of – Sutton, Esq. Entered the army in 1824, and became Lieut.-Col. in 1839; was Capt. Scots Fusilier Guards. Appointed Maj. in the 2nd Buckinghamshire Yeomanry, 1853. A Conservative, in favour of national education on a religious basis. First elected for Marlow in 1847. Sat until he retired in 1868. Died 14 Mar. 1873.   [1867]

KNOX, Hon. J.J. See NORTHLAND, Visct. (I).

KNOX, Lieut.-Col. Lawrence Edward. 53 Fitzwilliam Square, Dublin. The Mali, Sligo. Castle Rea, Co. Mayo. Junior Carlton, United Service. S. of Arthur Edward Know, Esq., of Trotton, Sussex, by Lady Jane, d. of the 2nd Earl of Rosse, K.P. B. 1836; m. 1858, Clara Charlotte, 2nd d. of Ernest Knox, Esq., of Castle Rea, Co. Mayo. Educ. at Brighton and at St. Georges Military Coll., Layton. Served as Capt. 63rd Foot and 11th Foot, in the Crimean campaign with the former. A Dept.-Lieut. of the Tower Hamlets,

and Major Queen's Tower Hamlets Militia. A Liberal-Conservative, in favour of a Land Bill for Ireland which would give the tenants an interest in the soil. Sat for Sligo bor. from Dec. 1868. Unseated Feb. 1869. Sligo disfranchised 1870. Died 24 Jan. 1873.   [1868]

KNOX, Hon. T. See NORTHLAND, Visct. (II).

KNOX, Hon. William Stuart. 13 St. James's Place, London. Dungannon Park, Tyrone. Carlton, and United Service. 2nd s. of 2nd Earl of Ranfurly, by the eld. d. of the Archbishop (Stuart) of Armagh. B. 1826; m. 1856 Georgiana, youngest d. of John Bonfoy Rooper, Esq., of Ripton Hall, Huntingdonshire. Entered the army 1844, and became Maj. 21st Fusiliers 1855; exchanged to the 51st Foot, 1857, appointed Col. Tyrone Artillery Militia 1867. Was Groom in Waiting to the Queen from Mar. 1852 - Mar. 1853. A Magistrate and Dept.-Lieut. of Tyrone. A Conservative, but 'not averse to progress.' First returned for Dungannon Feb. 1851, without opposition. Sat until he was defeated in 1874. Contested the same seat in 1880, and contested Tyrone in 1881. Died 16 February 1900. [1873]

LABOUCHERE, H. Continued in House after 1885: full entry in Volume II.

LABOUCHERE, Rt. Hon. Henry. 27, Belgrave Square, London. Overstowey, Somersetshire. Reform, Travellers', and Brooks's. S. of P.C. Labouchere, Esq., of Highlands, Essex. B. in London 1798; m. 1st, 1840, d. of Sir Thomas Baring, Bart., (she died May 1850); 2ndly, 1852, Lady Mary Matilda Georgina, d. of the 6th Earl of Carlisle. Educ. at Christ Church, Oxford, where he was 1st class in classics 1820 and graduated M.A. 1828. Was a Lord of the Admiralty from 1832-Nov. 1834; Vice-Pres. of the Board of Trade and Master of the Mint from Apr. 1835-Mar. 1839; Under-Sec. for the Colonies from Mar-Aug. 1839. Pres. of the Board of Trade from Mar. 1839-Sept. 1841. Chief Sec. for Ireland from July 1846-July 1847, and again Pres. of the Board of Trade from the last date until Mar. 1852. Sec of State for the Colonies from Nov. 1855-Mar. 1858. An Elder Brother of the Trinity House. A Liberal. Sat for St. Michael's from 1826-1830 and for Taunton from 1830 until he accepted Chiltern Hundreds July 1859. [1859]

LACON, Sir Edmund Henry Knowles, Bart. Hopton, Lowestoffe, Suffolk. Ormesby House, Yarmouth, Norfolk. Carlton, and Union. Eld. s. of Sir Edmund Knowles Lacon, Bart., by Eliza, eld. d. and co-heir of Thomas Beecroft, Esq., of

Sculthorpe Hall, Norfolk. B. 1807; m. 1839, Eliza Georgina, eld. d. of James Esdaile Hammet, Esq., of Lawn Cottage, Battersea (she died 1883). Educ. at Eton and at Emmanuel College, Cambridge, where he graduated B.A. 1828, M.A. 1831. A Brewer and Banker at Yarmouth. A Magistrate for Norfolk and Suffolk; a Dept.-Lieut. of the former county and since 1839 Major of the East Norfolk Militia. Appointed High Steward for Yarmouth 1875. A Conservative. Sat for Yarmouth from July 1852 till Apr. 1857, and from May 1859 to Dec. 1868. Since which date he sat for North Norfolk until he retired in 1885. Died 2 Dec. 1888.   [1885]

LACY, Henry Charles. Kenyon House, Lancashire. National. S. of James Lacy, Esq., of Salisbury. B. at Poole, Dorset, 1799; m. 1813, Susannah, youngest d. of — Icboult, Esq., of Salisbury. Appointed a Magistrate for Lancashire 1840. Chairman of the East Anglian, the Ely and Huntingdon, the Lynn, and Dereham Railways; Dept. Chairman of the Lynn and Ely Railway; Director of the London and South Western Railway. Published pamphlets on *Bridge-Building, A New Kind of Atmospheric Railway for Short Distances,* etc. A Liberal, opposed to the Poor Law, the game laws, taxation on the poor, and the endowment of the Roman Catholic Clergy. First returned for Bodmin in 1847. Retired in 1852.   [1852]

LAFFAN, Robert. Otham Lodge, Maidstone, Kent. Army & Navy. 2nd. s. of John Laffan. Esq., of Limerick, Supervisor of Excise, who was bro. to Dr. Robert Laffan, titular Archbishop of Cashel, and to Sir Joseph De Courcy Laffan, Bart., Physician to the Forces in the Peninsular War (title extinct). B. in the Co. of Limerick 1821 m. 1852, Emma, d. of William Norsworthy, Esq., of Oxford Terrace, London. Educ. at the Royal Military Academy, Woolwich; a Capt. Royal Engineers, which corps he entered in 1837. Was Inspector of Railways from Nov. 1847-Nov. 1852. A 'Liberal-Conservative', opposed to Customs duties, supported a redistribution of the franchise, but not a reduction below the 10/- limit; considered that national education should be on a religious basis. First returned for St. Ives July 1852. Sat until he retired 1857. Commands in Malta 1860-65, Aldershot 1866-70, and Gibraltar 1872-77. Governor of Bermuda 1877, K.C.M.G. May 1877. Died 22 March. 1882.   [1857]

LAING, Samuel. 5 Cambridge Gate, Regent's Park, London. 1 Eastern Terrace, Brighton. Hordle House, Lymington, Hampshire. Reform. S. of Samuel Laing, Esq., of Papdale, Orkney, by Agnes, d. of Francis Kelly, Esq., of Kelly, Devon.

B. at Edinburgh 1812; m. 1841, Mary, d. of Capt. Cowan, R.N. Was once Fellow of St. John's Coll., Cambridge, where he graduated B.A. (2nd Wrangler) 1832. Chairman of the London and Brighton Railway Company, and of the Sydenham Crystal Palace Company, from 1848 to 1854. Again became Chairman of the Brighton Railway 1867. Was Financial Secretary to the Treasury from June 1859 to Oct. 1860, when he proceeded to India as Finance Minister. A Liberal. Sat for Wick from July 1852 to July 1857, and from May 1859 to Oct. 1860; a third time, from July 1865 to Nov. 1868, when he was an unsuccessful candidate. Sat for Orkney and Shetland from Jan 1873 until he retired in 1885. Died 6 Aug. 1897.   [1885]

LAIRD, John. 10 Park Place, St. James's London. Hamilton Square, Birkenhead. Carlton, and Conservative. Eld. s. of William Laird, Esq., by Agnes, d. of Gregor Macgregor, Esq., of Greenock. Bro. of the Macgregor Laird, the African Traveller, the founder of steam communication with Africa and on the Niger. B. at Greenock 1805; m. 1829, Elizabeth, 3rd d. of Nicholas Hurry, Esq., of Liverpool. Educ. at the Royal Institution, Liverpool. Was senior partner in the firm Messrs. J. Laird Sons & Co., Shipbuilders at Birkenhead; retired Oct. 1861. A Dept.-Lieut. and Magistrate for Cheshire. Was for 7 years Chairman of Birkenhead Commissioners; resigned Dec. 1861. A Liberal-Conservative, voted against the disestablishment of the Irish Church 1869; in favour of the abolition of income-tax, also of denominational education. Sat for Birkenhead from Dec. 1861. MP until his death 29 Oct. 1874.   [1874]

LALOR, Patrick. Tennekill, Queen's Co. In favour of a repeal of the Union, 'of the entire abolition and extinction of tithe, in both name and nature', the abolition of the Church and Vestry cess; against poor rates for Ireland; in favour of grand juries and magistrates being elected by the people, and of petit juries being chosen, and members of Parliament being elected by ballot. Mr. Lalor displaced Sir Henry Parnell, the Secretary at War, who would not pledge himself to vote for a repeal of the Union. Sat for Queen's Co. from 1832. Defeated in 1835. [1833]

LALOR, R. Continued in House after 1885; full entry in Volume II.

LAMB, Hon. George. Brocket Hall, Hertfordshire. Home Office, Whitehall. Bro. of Visct. Melbourne; born in 1784; m. in 1809, Mademoiselle Caroline-Rosalie St. Jules. A

Barrister at Law, and Under Secretary of State for the Home Department. Was elected for Westminster on the death of Sir Samuel Romilly in 1818, but was defeated by Sir John Hobhouse in 1820. Sat for Dungarvon from 1820 until his death in 1834. [1833]

LAMBERT, Henry. Carnagh, Co. Wexford. A Reformer, in favour of Ireland being put upon a footing of equality with England, of the ballot, and of holding the Imperial Parliament every third year in Dublin. He said that if justice were speedily done to Ireland, he would vote for a repeal of the Union. Sat first for Wexford Co. in 1831. Retired in 1835. Unsuccessfully contested New Ross 15 July 1852. [1833]

LAMBERT, Nathaniel Grace. 21 Lowndes Square, London. Denham Court, Buckinghamshire. S. of Richard Lambert, Esq., of Newcastle-on-Tyne, by Achsah, d. of Nathaniel Grace, Esq. B. at Newcastle-on-Tyne 1811; m. 1843, Mary Ann, d. of Thomas Wright Richards, Esq., of Rushden, Northamptonshire. Educ. at private schools. A 'Whig' voted for the disestablishment of the Irish Church 1869, and said he would support Mr. Gladstone's party. Sat for Buckinghamshire from Dec. 1868 until he retired 1880. Died 9 Dec. 1882. [1880]

LAMBTON, Hon. F.W. Continued in House after 1885; full entry in Volume II.

LAMBTON, Hedworth. 11 Upper Belgrave Street, London. Bro. of the Earl of Durham, and bro.-in-law of the Hon. Col. Cavendish, once MP for Derby. B. 1797; m. 1835, Anna, eld. d. of Gervaise Parker Bushe, Esq., of Kilkenny, and niece of the Countess of Listowel. A Reformer, in favour of the ballot and short Parliaments. Sat for Durham N. from 1832 until he retired 1847. Died 16 Sept. 1876. [1847]

LAMONT, James. Knockdow, Inellan, Argyleshire. Brook's, and Union. Only s. of Alexander Lamont, Esq., of Knockdow, by Jane, d. of T. Chrystie, Esq., of Balchrystie, Fifeshire. B. at Edinburgh 1830. Unmarried. Educ. at Rugby. A West India Proprietor. A Magistrate for Argyle and a Dept.-Lieut. of Bute. Author of *Seasons with the Sea Horses,* also a pamphlet on 'Civil War in America.' A Liberal, in favour of a £20 co. and £6 bor. qualification, and the relief of Dissenters from all tests and disabilities. First elected for Buteshire, July 1865. Retired in 1868. Travelled much in arctic regions. Created Baronet 1910. Died 29 July 1913. [1867]

LAMONT, Maj. Norman. Monidrain,

Argyllshire. 3 Ryder Street, St. James's, London. Wells. A member of the ancient family of the Lamonts, in Argyllshire; a Maj. of the 91st Foot, was at Waterloo. A Whig, in favour of the immediate abolition of slavery, and the ballot. Returned for Wells in 1832. Accepted Chiltern Hundreds, Apr. 1834. [1833]

LANCASTER, John. Bilton Grange, Rugby. Ashfield, Wigan. Reform. S. of John Lancaster, Esq., of Prestwich, Lancashire. B. at Prestwich 1816; m. 1841, Euphemia, eld. d. of David Gibson, Esq., of Redfrewshire. Was largely engaged in the Iron and Coal trade. A Magistrate for Lancashire and Warwickshire. A Liberal, voted for the disestablishment of the Irish Church 1869 'as a simple measure of justice'; in favour of a reduction of the public expenditure, 'expecially in the army and navy,' also of vote by ballot. Sat for Wigan from Dec. 1868 until he was defeated Feb. 1874. Contested seat again Apr. 1880 and Jan. 1881. [1873]

LANGDALE, Hon. Charles. Houghton, Yorkshire. S. of Lord Stourton. B. Sept. 19, 1787. Married 1st, Jan. 1817, the Hon. Charlotte Mary, 5th d. of Charles, 6th Lord Cufford; 2ndly, May 1821, Mary eld. d. of Marmaduke W.H. Constable Maxwell, Esq. Sat for Beverley 1832-35. Moved and carried, on the return of the Poor Law Amendment Bill to the Commons, 'that the clause for securing religious freedom in workhouses (struck out by the Lords) should be insisted on'. Voted for the ballot, and repeal of the Septennial Act, and an inquiry into the pension list. Returned for Knaresborough in 1837. Retired 1841. Lay brother of Society of Jesus 1868. Died 1 Dec. 1868. [1838]

LANGSTON, James Haughton, D.C.L. 143 Piccadilly, London, Sarsden House, Chipping Norton, Oxon. Brooks's Boodle's, Reform, and United University. M. in 1824, Lady Julia, 2nd d. of the 1st Earl of Ducie. A Magistrate and Dept.-Lieut. of Oxfordshire. High Sheriff of Oxfordshire 1851. A Liberal, opposed to church-rates; in favour of a wide extension of the franchise and 'rational progress'; voted for the ballot, 1853. Sat for Oxford from Nov. 1826 till Jan. 1835; re-elected June 1841. MP until his death 19 Oct. 1863. [1863]

LANGTON, William Gore-. 12 Grosvenor Square, London. Newton, Somerset. Reform. B. in 1787, the eld. s. of William Gore-Langton, Esq., of Newton Park, who assumed the name and arms of Langton, in addition to those of Gore on his first marriage with the only child of Joseph Langton, Esq., of Newton Park. M. 1822,

Jacintha Dorothea, only child of H. Powell Collins, Esq., of Hatch Beauchamp, Co. Somerset. Patron of 2 livings. A Reformer. Was in favour of the ballot, a repeal of the Corn Laws and opposed to short Parliaments. Sat for Somerset E. from 1831 until his death in 1847. [1846]

LANGTON, William Henry Gore-. 2 Prince's Gate, Hyde Park, London. Clifton Court, Clifton. Reform, and National. S. of Col. William Gore-Langton, who represented Somerset from 1795-1847, by his 2nd wife, Mary, only d. of John Browne, Esq., of Salperton, Gloucestershire. B. in London 1802; m. 1824, Maria, d. of John Lewis, Esq., (she died 1864). Educ. at Harrow and at Magdalen Coll., Oxford. A Magistrate and Dept.-Lieut. of Somerset; Mayor of Bristol for 1852. A liberal, in favour of extensive reform, vote by ballot, and strict neutrality in our Foreign relations; opposed to the Maynooth Grant, and voted against Church rates 1855. First returned for Bristol in July 1852. Sat until he retired 1865. Died 16 May 1875. [1865]

LANGTON, William Henry Powell Gore-. 12 Grosvenor Square, London. Newton Park, Bath. Hatch Park, Taunton. Carlton. Only s. of William Gore-Langton, Esq. of Newton Park, Somerset, by the only d. of Henry Powell Collins, Esq. of Hache Beauchamp, Somerset. B. at Burdrop, Wiltshire, 1824; m. 1846, Lady Anne Eliza Mary, only d. of 2nd Duke of Buckingham and Chandos. Educ. at Eton and at Christ Church, Oxford, where he graduated M.A. Appointed a Dept.-Lieut. of Somerset 1852. Was patron of 4 livings. A Conservative. Sat for Somerset W. from Apr. 1851 to Mar. 1857. Re-elected Feb. 1863. MP until he died 11 Dec. 1873. [1873]

LANGTON, William Stephen Gore-. Newton Park, Bristol. Junior Carlton. Eld. s. of William Henry Powell Gore-Langton, Esq., of Newton Park, Somerset (who sat for W. Somerset from 1851-56 and from 1863-73), by Lady Anne Eliza Mary, only d. of 2nd Duke of Buckingham and Chandos. B. 1847. A Magistrate and Dept.-Lieut. for Somerset. A Conservative. Sat for mid Somerset from Mar. 1878 until he accepted Chiltern Hundreds 1885. [1884]

LANGWORTHY, E.R. A Liberal. Returned for Salford at a by-election 2 Feb. 1857; retired at the gen. election the same year. Died 7 Apr. 1874. [1874]

LANIGAN, John. Richmond, Nr. Templemore, Tipperary. Lanigile, Nenagh, Tipperary. Reform. A Liberal. First elected for Cashel May 1859. Sat until defeated 1865. [1865]

LANYON, Sir Charles. Wellington Place, Belfast. The Abbey, White Abbey, Co. Antrim. S. of John Jenkinson Lanyon, Esq., by his marriage with Miss Catherine Anne Mortimer, of Eastbourne, Sussex. B. at Eastbourne, 1813; m 1837, Elizabeth Helen, d. of J. Owen, Esq., of the Board of Works, Dublin. Educ. at a private school at Streatham, Surrey. Was a Civil Engineer and Architect in Ireland from 1832. Was President of the Royal Institute of Architects in Ireland. Was Mayor of Belfast in 1862. A Conservative, and a supporter of Lord Derby. First elected for Belfast, Nov. 1866. Defeated in same seat at 1868 gen. election. Sheriff of Co Antrim 1876. Died near Belfast 31 May 1889. [1867]

LARPENT, George Gerard de Hochepied. 8 Austin Friars, London. Roehampton, Surrey. Reform. His family originally French, settled in England on the revocation of the edict of Nantes. B. 1786; m. in 1813, d. of W. Cracroft, Esq., of Hackthorne, Lincolnshire. A Merchant and East India Agent; a Partner in the house of Cockerell & Company. Chairman of the East India & China Association; Dept. Chairman of the St. Katherine Docks Company; a Director of the Royal Exchange Ass. Company. A Liberal. Was an unsuccessful candidate for Ludlow in May 1840. First returned for Nottingham in July 1841 having unsuccessfully contested it in the month of Apr. preceding. Sat for Nottingham until he accepted Chiltern Hundreds in 1842. [1841]

LASCELLES, Hon. Edwin. 4 Belgrave Square, London. Harewood House, Yorkshire. 3rd surviving s. of the 2nd Earl of Harewood, by the eld. d. of Sir J.S. Sebright. B. 1799. Graduated at All Souls' Coll., Oxford, B.C.L. 1826, D.C.L. 1831. Called to the Bar at the Inner Temple 1826. A Dept.-Lieut. of Yorkshire. A Conservative. First returned for Ripon, Jan. 1846, without a contest. Sat until he retired 1857. Died 25 Apr. 1865. [1857]

LASCELLES, Hon. Egremont William. Middlethorpe Lodge, York. 2nd s. of the 3rd Earl of Harewood, by Lady Louisa, 2nd d. of the 2nd Marq. of Bath. B. 1825; m. 1856, Jessie Elizabeth, 3rd d. of Neill Malcolm, Esq., of Poltalloch. Entered the army as Lieut. Grenadier Guards 1842; appointed aide-de-camp to the Governor-General of Canada 1847; retired from the army 1850. Appointed a Dept.-Lieut. of Yorkshire, and Maj. 1st West York Militia, 1852. A Conservative, and a supporter of Lord Derby. First elected for Northallerton, May 1866. Retired in 1868. Died 27 Oct. 1892. [1867]

LASCELLES, Rt. Hon. William Saunders Sebright. Bute House, Campden Hill, Kensington, London. Carlton. B. in 1798 the s. of the 2nd Earl of Harewood. M. in 1823 the daughter of the 6th Earl of Carlisle. Appointed Comptroller of the Household in 1847 and was a Dept.-Lieut. of Yorkshire. Was a Conservative, but became a Liberal. Sat for Northallerton prior to the passing of the Reform Act, and represented Wakefield in the Parliament of 1837, Was not returned at the general election in 1841, but succeeded on petition. Sat for Knaresborough from 1847 until his death on 2nd July 1851. [1851]

LASLETT, William. Abberton Hall, Pershore, Worcestershire. S. of Thomas Emmerson Laslett, Esq., by Sophia, his wife. B. at Worcester 1801; m. 1842, Maria, eld. d. of the Rev. Dr. Carr, Biship successively of Chichester and Worcester. Educ. at Worcester; was called to the bar at the Inner Temple 1856. Practised as a solicitor at Worcester till 1846. Was a Magistrate, and had been Chairman of Upton Snodsbury Highway Board since the passing of Highway Act; also Pres. of the E. Worcestershire Chamber of Agriculture. Was a patron of 5 livings. A Liberal, and in favour of abrogating the clauses of the reform bill relating to rates; voted against the disestablishment of the Irish Church 1869. Sat for Worcester from Apr. 1852-Mar. 1860, when he accepted the Chiltern Hundreds. Unsuccessfully contested Worcestershire E. on the Conservative interest June 1868; re-elected Nov. following for the city of Worcester. Sat until defeated in 1874. Died 26 Jan. 1884. [1873]

LAURIE, John. 1 Hyde Park Place, London. Marshalls, Laurie Town, Essex. Carlton. S. of Benjamin Snaddon, Esq., of Barrowstone, Linlithgowshire, by Agnes, d. of John Laurie, Esq., of Stitchel, Roxburghshire (sister of Alderman Sir Peter Laurie). Assumed the name of Laurie in lieu of Snaddon by royal licence 1824. B. in Scotland 1797; m. 1831, Eliza Helen, d. of Kenrick Collett, Esq., one of the Masters of the Exchequer. Partner in the firm of Laurie and Marner, Coach-builders, Oxford Street. An East India and Bank proprietor. Elected Sheriff of London and Middlesex 1845-46. A Magistrate and Dept.-Lieut. for Middlesex, a Magistrate for Essex, and for the liberty of Havering-atte-Bower. Author of several pamphlets on Prison Discipline, also *The Voice of Humanity*. A 'true Conservative, but ready to support Lord Palmerston or any other minister in carrying out a just and necessary war with vigour'; a 'firm supporter of Church and State'; in favour of a system of national education based upon the Bible; opposed to the Maynooth grant,

and to 'the progressive power of the Roman Catholic Church.' First returned for Barnstaple, Aug. 1854 but was unseated on petition, Mar. 1855; again elected Mar. 1857. Retired at 1859 gen. election. Died 2 Aug. 1864. [1858]

LAURIE, R.P. Continued in House after 1885; full entry in Volume II

LAVERTON, Abraham. Westbury House, Westbury, Wiltshire. Unmarried. A Woollen Manufacturer at Westbury. A Magistrate for Wiltshire from 1858. A Liberal. Was an unsuccessful candidate for Westbury Dec. 1868, when he displaced his opponent on petition, and stood another contest unsuccessfully Feb. 1869. Sat for Westbury from Feb. 1874. Defeated Apr. 1880. Died 13 Oct. 1886. [1879]

LAW, Hon. Charles Evan. 10 Farrars Buildings, Temple, London. 72 Eaton Place, London. Carlton, United University, and Oxford & Cambridge. 2nd s. of 1st Lord Ellenborough by the daughter of the late George Phillips Towry, Esq. B. 1792; m. in 1811, Elizabeth Sophia, 2nd d. of Sir Edward Nightingale, Bart. of Kneesworth, Cambridgeshire. Appointed a King's Counsel in 1829. Recorder of London, Commissioner of Bankrupts, Bencher of the Inner Temple. Reprinted the speech of his father, former Lord Chief Justice, against the claims of the Roman Catholics. A Conservative. Voted for agricultural protection, 1846. Sat for Cambridge University from Feb. 1835 until his death in 1850. [1850]

LAW, Rt. Hon. Hugh LL.D. 9 Fitzwilliam Street, Dublin, Sackville Street, and Kildare Street Clubs, Dublin. Devonshire, and Union. Ulster Club, Belfast. Only s. of the late John Law, Esq., of Woodlawn, Co. Down, by Margaret, youngest d. of Christopher Crawley, Esq., of Culloville, Co. Armagh. B. at Woodlawn, 1818; m. 1863. Helen Maria, youngest d. of the late William White, Esq. of Shrubs, Co. Dublin. Educ. at Dungannon Royal School and at Trinity Coll., Dublin, where he obtained a scholarship and the first senior classical moderatorship. Was called to the bar in Ireland 1840; appointed Queen's Counsel 1860. Elected a Bencher of the Society of King's Inn 1870. Was Solicitor Gen. for Ireland from 1872-Jan. 1874, when he became Attorney Gen. for a few weeks; reappointed to the latter office Apr. 1880. A Liberal, in favour of the readjustment of local taxation, including the present Grand Jury System in Ireland. Sat for the Co. of Londonderry from Feb. 1874 until he was appointed Lord Chancellor of Ireland in 1881. [1881]

LAWLESS, Hon. Cecil John. Lyons Castle, Co. Kildare. Reform. B. 1821, the youngest s. of the 2nd Baron Cloncurry, by his 2nd wife, 3rd d of Archibald Douglas, Esq., of Darnock; m. 1848, Frances Georgiana, d. of the late Morris Townsend, Esq., of Shepperton, Co. Cork and widow of John William Digby, Esq., of Landenstown, Co. Kildare. A Repealer. First elected for Clonmell in 1846 without a contest, and sat until his death on 5 Nov. 1853.   [1853]

LAWLEY, Hon. Beilby. 29 Berkeley Square, London. Eld. s. of Baron Wenlock, by Lady Elizabeth, 3rd d. of the 2nd Marq. of Westminster. B. in Berkeley Square, London 1849; m. 1872, Lady Constance Mary, eld. d. of the 4th Earl of Harewood. Educ. at Eton and at Trinity Coll., Cambridge. A Liberal. Contested Wenlock Nov. 1874. Sat for Chester from Apr. 1880, but shortly afterwards on petition the election was declared void.   [1880 2nd ed.]

LAWLEY, Hon. Beilby Richard. 29 Berkeley Square, London. Escrick Park, Yorkshire. Eld. s. of 1st Lord Wenlock, by the 3rd d. of 2nd Lord Braybrooke. B. in Berkeley Square, London, 1818; m. 1846, Lady Elizabeth, 3rd d. of 2nd Marq. of Westminster. A Liberal, in favour of a gradual extension of the suffrage, and opposed a return to protection. First returned for Pontefract, Feb. 1851. Retired in 1852. Succeeded as 3rd Baron Nov. 1880. Died 1912.   [1852]

LAWLEY, Hon. Francis Charles. 29 Berkeley Square, London. Escrick Park, Yorkshire. Whites', and Coventry. B. in Berkeley Square 1825, the youngest s. of 1st Lord Wenlock, by 3rd d. of 2nd. Lord Braybrooke. Unmarried. Educ. at Rugby and at Balliol Coll., Oxford, where he was 2nd class in Classics 1848, and obtained a fellowship at All Souls' in the same year. Appointed official Private Secretary to the Chancellor of the Exchequer, Dec. 1852. A 'decided Liberal, and free-trader, in favour of a considerable extension of the suffrage.' Wanted inquiry into Maynooth. Sat for Beverley July 1852 to July 1854, when he accepted Chiltern Hundreds. Died 18 Sept. 1901.   [1854]

LAWRANCE, John Compton. 3 Onslow Square, South Kensington, London. 3 Paper Buildings, Temple, London. Dunsby Hall, Bourne, Lincolnshire. Junior Carlton, and Garrick. Only s. of Thomas M. Lawrance, Esq., by Louisa, d. of John Compton, Esq., of Waternewton, Huntingdonshire. B. at Dunsby Hall, Lincolnshire. 1832; m. 1861, Charlotte Georgiana, d. of Major Smart, of Tumby Lawn, Lincolnshire. Was called to the bar at Lincoln's

Inn, June 1859. Appointed a Queen's Counsel 1877. Recorder of Derby Feb. 1880. A Conservative, and in favour of a readjustment of local taxation, so as to relieve land from some of its present burdens; also of the establishment of County Financial Boards. Unsuccessfully contested Peterborough 29 Oct. 1878. Sat for Lincolnshire. S. from Apr. 1880. Defeated in 1885; contested Carmarthenshire West in 1886. Founded London distric Unitarian Society 1886. Died 21 May 1897.   [1885]

LAWRENCE, J.C. Continued in House after 1885: full entry in Volume II.

LAWRENCE, Sir J.J. Trevor. Continued in House after 1885: full entry in Volume II.

LAWRENCE, William. 75 Lancaster Gate, London. Reform, Devonshire, and City Liberal. Eld. s. of William Lawrence, Esq., an Alderman of London, and High Sheriff of London and Middlesex 1849-50, by Jane, 4th d. of James Clarke, Esq. Bro. of Sir James Clarke Lawrence, MP for Lambeth. B. 1818. Unmarried. A Builder in London, and a Partner in the firm of William Lawrence and Sons. Elected an Alderman of London on the decease of his father in 1855. A Magistrate for Middlesex and the City of Westminster, a Commissioner of Lieutenancy for London, and Dept.-Lieut. for Middlesex. Was High Sheriff for London, and Middlesex 1857-58. Lord Mayor of London for 1863-64. A Liberal, in favour of the abolition of the house tax, also the abolition of all duties on locomotion, and of the light dues on shipping. Sat for London from July 1865 to Feb. 1874, when he was an unsuccessful candidate there. Re-elected Apr. 1880; defeated in 1885 contesting Paddington S. Knighted Aug. 1887. Died Apr. 1897.   [1885]

LAWSON, Andrew. 26 Pall Mall, London. The Hall, Nr. Boroughbridge, Yorkshire. Carlton. S. of the Rev. Marmaduke Lawson. B. 1800; m. 1823, d. of Sir Thomas S. Gooch, Bart. Patron of 1 living. 'A Moderate Tory'; voted for agricultural protection 1846. Returned for Knaresborough in 1834 until defeated 1837. Returned again 1841. Defeated 1847. Contested same seat at 1851 by-election. Died 28 Feb. 1853.   [1847]

LAWSON, Rt. Hon. James Anthony. 27 Upper Fitzwilliam Street, Dublin. Clontra, Bray, Ireland. Reform. S. of James Lawson, Esq., of Waterford, by Mary, d. of Joseph Anthony, Esq. B. at Waterford 1817; m. 1842, Jane, eld. d. of Samuel Merrick, Esq., of Cork. Educ. at Waterford Endowed School, and at Trinity Coll., Dublin, of which he was a Scholar and Gold

229

Medallist, and was appointed in 1840 to the Professorship of Political Economy there, which he held for five years. Was called to the bar in Ireland 1840, made a Queens Counsel 1857, and a Bencher of King's Inn, Dublin 1861. Appointed Law Advisor to the Crown in Ireland 1858, Solicitor-Gen. for Ireland 1861, and Attorney-Gen. 1865; resigned July 1866. Published *Lectures on Political Economy*, and frequent papers on Law Reform, etc. in the Transactions of the Dublin Statistical Society, of which he was Vice-President. A Liberal, in favour of adminstrative and financial reform, the removal of all religious disabilities, and of educational grants being equally apportioned to all creeds. Unsuccessfully contested the University of Dublin Apr. 1857; first elected for Portarlington July 1865. Defeated Dec. 1868. Judge in Ireland Dec. 1868. Irish Church Commissioner July 1869. Survived attempted murder in Dublin 11 Nov. 1882. Died 10 Aug. 1887.   [1868]

LAWSON, Sir W. Continued in House after 1885: full entry in Volume II.

LAYARD, Rt. Hon. Austen Henry. Piccadilly, London. Athenaeum. B. at Paris 1817, the s. of Henry P.J.Layard, Esq. Author of *Nineveh and its Remains, Monuments of Nineveh* etc. and well-known for his exertions in exhuming the remains of ancient art at Nineveh and its neighbourhood, now deposited at the British Museum. Received the honorary degree of D.C.L. at Oxford 1848. In 1852, was, for a few weeks, Under-Sec. of State for Foreign Affairs. Had previously been Attaché to the Embassy at Constantinople. Was again Under-Sec. of State for Foreign Affairs from July 1861-July 1866. Appointed Chief Commissioner of Works and Buildings Dec. 1868 (salary £2,000). Elected Lord Rector of Aberdeen University 1855 and 1856. A Liberal, voted for the ballot 1853. Sat for Aylesbury from July 1852-July 1857. Unsuccessfully contested York 2 May 1859. Sat for Southwark from Dec. 1860 until he accepted Chiltern Hundreds 1870. Then became Ambassador to Madrid 23 Oct. 1869-31 Mar. 1877, and to the Sultan of Turkey until 1880. Died in London 5 July 1894.   [1869]

LAYARD, Brownlow Villiers. 2 Beaumont Street, London. Upper Mount Street, Merrion Square, Dublin. Eld. s. of the Rev. Brownlow Villiers Layard. M. only d. of D. Digby, Esq., of Dublin. A Capt. in the army. A Whig. Sat for Carlow from 1841 until defeated 1847. Died (suicide) 27 Dec. 1853.   [1847]

LAYCOCK, Robert. 2 Chesham Place, London. Wiscton Hall, Bawtry, Nottinghamshire. Castle Carr, Halifax. Reform, and Devonshire. Eld. s. of Joseph Laycock, Esq., of Low Gosforth Hall, Northumberland, by his 1st wife, Barbara, d. of John Nicholson, Esq., of Winlaton, Co. Durham. B. at Winlaton 1833; m. 1866, Annie, d. of Christian Allhusen, Esq., of Stoke Court, Bucks. Was Educ. at Durham and at Trinity Coll., Cambridge; graduated B.A. 1856, M.A. 1859. Called to the bar at Inner Temple Nov. 1857. A Magistrate for Northumberland; a Magistrate and Dept.-Lieut. for Nottinghamshire, of which he was High Sheriff in 1878. A Liberal, and in favour of a measure 'to facilitate and lessen the cost of the transfer of land', and of power being given to ratepayers to control the county finance. Unsuccessfully contested Nottinghamshire N. Feb. 1872 and Nottingham Feb. 1874. Sat for Lincolnshire N. from Apr. 1880. MP until his death 14 Aug. 1881.   [1881]

LEA, Sir Thomas. Continued in House after 1885: full entry in Volume II.

LEADER, John Temple. Putney Hill, Surrey. Reform. S. of William Leader, Esq., Member for Winchelsea from 1812-26, who was always in opposition to the Perceval and Liverpool Administrations. B. 1810. Educ. at the Charterhouse and Christ Church, Oxford. A radical Reformer. Considered that 'the Elective francise is, to more than half the Electoral Body, an evil instead of a benefit, and must remain so without the protection of the ballot.' Sat for Bridgwater from 6 Jan. 1835 until May 1837 when he accepted Chiltern Hundreds to contest Westminster. Sat for Westminster from the general election of 1837, having unsuccessfully opposed Sir Francis Burdett 12 May 1837 – a by-election, which Burdett caused after declaring himself a Conservative. Burdett did not contest the seat in July 1837 when Leader won the seat. Sat until he retired 1847.   [1847]

LEADER, Nicholas Philpot. Dromagh Castle, Co. Cork. Conservative. Eld. s. of Nicholas Philpot Leader, Esq., MP, of Dromagh Castle, by Margaret, d. and co-heir of Andrew Nash, Esq. of Nashville, Co. Cork. A Conservative. Unsuccessfully contested Harwich 11 Dec. 1832, and Cork Co. in July 1841 and again in July 1847. First elected for Cork Co. Mar. 1861. Sat until he retired in 1868. Died 31 Mar. 1880.   [1867]

LEAHY, J. Continued in House after 1885: full entry in Volume II.

LEAKE, Robert. Continued in House after 1885: full entry in Volume II.

LEAMY, E. Continued in House after 1885: full entry in Volume II.

LEARMONTH, Alexander. 93 Eaton Place, London. Dean, Edinburgh. Boodle's, Carlton, United Service, and Army & Navy. Only s. of John Learmonth, Esq., of Dean and Murieston, Co. Edinburgh (a Dept.-Lieut. and Lord Provost of Edinburgh), by Margaret, d. of James Cleghorn, Esq., M.D., state physician in Dublin. B. in Edinburgh 1829; m. 1859, Charlotte Sadler, eld. d. of Gen. Lyons, Bengal army, and niece of Lord Lyons. Entered the army as Cornet 17th Lancers 1849, retired 1859 as Lieut.-Col., served in the Eastern campaign in 1854-55, and received medals for Sebastopol, etc. A Magistrate for the Co. of Edinburgh. A Conservative, in favour of the army, etc. being placed in a 'complete state of efficiency.' Sat for Colchester (which in Nov. 1868 he unsuccessfully contested), from Oct. 1850 until he was defeated 1880. Died 10 Mar. 1887. [1880]

LEATHAM, Edward Aldam. 46 Eaton Square, London. Misarden Park, Cirencester. Reform, Athenaeum, Devonshire, and Windham. B. at Heath, near Wakefield 1828, s. of William Leatham, Esq., Banker, of Heath, by Margaret, d. and co-heir of Joshua Walker, Esq., M.D. M. 1851, Mary Jane, only d. of John Fowler, Esq., of Elm Grove, Nr. Melksham, Wiltshire. Educ. at Univisity Coll., London, of which he became a Fellow. Graduated B.A. 1848, when he was placed 2nd in classical honours, and M.A. 1851. A Banker at Wakefield and Pontefract, and in the firm of Messrs. Leatham, Tew and Company. Published in 1858 *Charmione*, a novel. A Reformer. Sat for Huddersfield Apr. 1859 to July 1865, when he was defeated. Regained the seat in Feb. 1868 and retired in 1886. Died 6 Feb. 1900. [1886]

LEATHAM, William Henry. 35 St. James's Place, London. Hemsworth Hall, Pontefract, Yorkshire. Reform. Eld. surviving s. of William Leatham, Esq., of Heath, near Wakefield, a Banker at Wakefield, Pontefract, and Doncaster, by Margaret, d. and co-heir of Joshua Walker, Esq., M.D. of Leeds. B. at Wakefield, 1815; m. 1839, Priscilla, 4th d. of Samuel Gurney, Esq., of West Ham, Essex, and of Lombard Street. Was a Banker at Wakefield and Pontefract from 1836 to 1851, when he retired. A Magistrate and Dept.-Lieut. of the West Riding of Yorkshire, Deputy-Chairman of Quarter Sessions from 1870. Author of several poems, also *Tales of English Life and Miscellanies*, and *Lectures at Mechanics' Institutes*. A Liberal, in favour of 'an extension of the franchise in counties, an amendment of the Land Laws, and of the Licensing Laws, and the establishment of country boards.' Sat for Wakefield from Apr. to July 1850, when he was displaced on petition; again for Wakefield from July 1865 to Dec. 1868. Unsuccessfully contested the West Riding of Yorkshire, Southern Division, Feb. 1874; sat for that Division from Apr. 1880; retired in 1885. Died 14 Nov. 1889. [1885]

LECHMERE, Sir E.A.H. Continued in House after 1885: full entry in Volume II.

LEE, Henry. Sedgley Park. Prestwich, Manchester. Reform, and Devonshire. Reform and Clarendon Clubs, Manchester. S. of Lɛɛ Lee, Esq., of Chorley, Lancashire. B. at Chorley 1817; m. 1846, Hannah, d. of John Dracup, Esq., A Merchant and Manufacturer at Manchester. A Magistrate for the Co. Palatine of Lancaster, and for Salford. A Director of the Manchester Chamber of Commerce. A Liberal, in favour of a redistribution of seats, and the amendment of the Land Laws to facilitate the transfer of land, etc. Unsuccessfully contested Salford 7 Feb. 1874. Sat for Southampton from Apr. 1880 until defeated in 1885. Contested Manchester N.W. in 1886. [1885]

LEE, John Lee. 2 Eaton Place, London. Dillington House, Somersetshire. M. 1834 Jessy, d. of John Vaughan, Esq., formerly MP for Glamorganshire. Of moderate Whig principles. Sat for Wells from 1830 until he retired in 1837. Sheriff of Somerset 1845. Died 16 Aug. 1874. [1837]

LEE, Maj. Vaughan Hanning Vaughan-. 16 Ennismore Gardens, London. Lanelay, Cardiff. Rheola, Neath, South Wales. Army & Navy, and Junior Carlton. Only s. of John Lee-Lee, Esq., of Dillington House, Ilminster, Somerset, who sat for Wells from 1830 to 1837, by Jessy, d. of John Edwards Vaughan, Esq., of Rheola, Glamorganshire. B. at Dillington 1836; m. 1861, Clara Elizabeth, eld. d. of George Moore, Esq., of Appleby Hall, Leicestershire. Was Educ. at Eton. Entered the army as Ensign 21st Fusiliers, Mar. 1854; became Capt. in 1858; served throughout the Crimean War. Maj. Glamorgan Light Infantry Militia. Patron of 1 living. A Conservative. Sat for W. Somerset from Jan. 1874 until he accepted Chiltern Hundreds in 1882. [1882]

LEE, William. Upper Ground Street, Blackfriars Road, London. Holborough Court, Rochester. Reform. B. at Lewisham 1801, the s. of Henry Lee, Esq., of Camps Hill, Lewisham, Kent. M. 1820, the 2nd d. of Samuel Reynolds, Esq., of Thaydon House, Essex. A Merchant in London, a member of the firm of Messrs. Lee, Son & Smith. A Magistrate and Dept.-Lieut. for Kent. A

Liberal, voted for the ballot 1853. 'As an attached member of the Church of England, considered the disestablishment of the Irish Church will not weaken the Church of England but have the opposite effect.' Sat for Maidstone from May 1853 to Apr. 1857, but was unsuccessful there in July 1852 and Apr. 1857. Re-elected for Maidstone in May 1859 and sat until he accepted Chiltern Hundreds 1870. Died 29 Sept. 1881.   [1869]

LEECH, John. King's Arm's House, Borough. Lea, Surrey. A Trustee of the Agricultural Employment Institution. A Reformer, in favour of the Corn laws, and a reform of the Church to comprehend an equalization of the incomes of the Bishops. Returned for Surrey W. at the Dec. 1832 election. Retired 1835.   [1834]

LEEKE, Sir Henry John, K.C.B. Penlee House, Stoke, Devon. United Service. Eld. surviving s. of Samuel Leeke, Esq., of St. John's, Isle of Wight, and Havant, Hampshire, by Sophia, d. of Capt. Richard Bargus, R.N., of Fareham, Hampshire; m. 1st, 1823, Augusta Sophia, 2nd, d. of James Dashwood, Esq., of Forest Lodge, Windsor, and Harley Street, London (she died 1861); 2ndly, 1863, Georgiana Lucy, only d. of the Rev. Geoffrey and the Hon. Mrs. Hornby. B. at St. John's, Isle of Wight. Educ. at Dr. Burney's. Entered the navy 1806, and took an active part in the capture and destruction of a French convoy in the Bay of Rosas. Was appointed Superintendent of the Indian Navy 1851; commanded at the bombardment of Bushire and the storming of Fort Reshin 1856. Became a Rear-Admiral on the reserved list 1854. A Dept.-Lieut. of Hampshire. A Liberal-Conservative, and a support of Lord Derby's policy. First elected for Dover Apr. 1859. Sat until he retired 1865. Died 26 Feb. 1870. [1865]

LEEMAN, George. 7 Deans Yard, London. The Mount, York. Rosedale Abbey. Pickering. Reform. B. in York 1809; m. 1st, 1831, Jane, d. of Joseph Johnson, Esq., of London; 2ndly, 1863, Ellen, widow of the Rev. Charles Payton of York. A Solicitor, and practised in the city of York during thirty years. Clerk of the Peace for the East Riding of Yorkshire for more than twenty years, and Alderman of that city, elected for the 3rd time Lord Mayor of York in 1872. A Liberal. Sat for York from July 1865 to Dec. 1868; re-elected Feb. 1871 and sat until he retired 1880. Died 25 Feb. 1882.   [1880]

LEEMAN, Joseph Johnson. 8 Dover Street, London. Acomb Priory, York. Youngest s. of George Leeman, Esq., of The Mount, York, (who sat for York, with a short interval, from 1865-80, by his first wife, Jane, d. of Joseph Johnson, Esq.

of London. B. at Fulford, Nr. York 1842; m. 1879, Emily Maude Mary, only d. of Richard Smethurst, Esq. of Ellerbeck, who was High Sheriff of Lancashire 1872. Educ. at St. Peter's School, York. Admitted a Solicitor Jan. 1865; a Partner in the firm of Messrs. Leeman & Wilkinson. Dept.-Lieut. of the W. Riding of York. A Liberal. Sat for York city from Apr. 1880. MP until his death 2 Nov. 1883.   [1883]

LEES, John Frederick. A Conservative; succeeded to the seat at Oldham on the death of Mr. William Cobbett (1835), defeating that gentleman's son William. Defeated in 1837.   [1837]

LEFEVRE, Rt. Hon. Charles Shaw. See SHAW-LEFEVRE, Rt. Hon. Charles.

LEFEVRE, Rt. Hon. G.J. Shaw. See SHAW-LEFEVRE, Rt. Hon. G.J.. Continued in House after 1885: full entry in Volume II.

LEFEVRE, J.G.S. A Liberal. Sat for Petersfield from Dec. 1832, but on petition unseated in Mar. 1833. Contested Cambridge University Aug. 1847. Poor Law Commissioner 1834-41., Joint Assistant Secretary to Board of Trade 1841-48. Dept. Clerk of the Parliaments 1848; Clerk 1856-75. One of the founders of the Athenaeum in 1823. Excellent linguist. Died 20 Aug. 1879.   [1833]

LEFROY, Anthony. 27 Chesham Place, London. Carriglas, Longford, Ireland. Carlton, and National. Sackville Street, Dublin. B. in Dublin 1800 the eld s. of Rt. Hon. Thomas Lefroy, LL.D., Chief Justice of the Queen's Bench in Ireland, by Mary, only d. and heir of Jeffrey Paul, Esq., of Silverspring, Wexford. M. 1824, Hon. Jane, d. of 1st Visct. Lorton. Educ. at Dublin University. A Dept.-Lieut. of the Co. of Longford. A Conservative. Sat for Longford from 1830 to July 1837, with the exception of a few months in 1833, when he was unseated on petition, and also from 1842 to Aug. 1847. Was elected for Dublin University in Mar. 1858, and sat until he accepted Chiltern Hundreds in 1870. Died 12 Jan. 1890.   [1869]

LEFROY, Rt. Hon. Thomas LL.D. Leeson Street, Dublin. Carrickgrass, Co. Longford. Carlton. Eld. s. of Colonel Arthur Lefroy of Limerick, whose family was of French Huguenot extraction, and an elder branch of the family of that name which formerly was seated in Kent and in the mid-19th Century in Hampshire. B. 1776; m. in 1799 only d. of Jeffery Paul, Esq., of Silverspring, Co. Wexford. A Queen's Counsel, was a Kings's Sergeant, but resigned the office. Published reports in the Irish Court of Chancery in the time of Lord Redesale. Obtained the 4 annual prizes, and 7 certificates, in the undergraduate course, and the gold medal, on taking the degree of A.B. at Trinity College, Dublin. A Conservative; first sat for Dublin University in 1830. Sat until appointed Baron of the Exchequer (Ireland) November 1841; Lord Chief Justice (Queen's Bench) 1852-66. Died 4 May 1869. [1841]

LEGARD, Sir Charles, Bart, 28 Charles Street, London. Ganton Hall, Scarborough. White's, Junior Carlton, and Boodle's. 3rd s. of Sir Thomas Digby Legard (8th) Bart., by the Hon. Frances, d. of 1st Lord Feversham. B. at Ganton Hall, York, 1846; m. 1878, Frances Emily, youngest d. of Francis A. Hamilton, Esq., of Brent Lodge, Finchley. Educ. at Eton. An Ensign in the 43rd Light Infantry; also Capt. 2nd N.E. Yorkshire Artillery Volunteers. A Magistrate and Dept.-Lieut. of the E. Riding of Yorkshire. Patron of 1 living. A Conservative. Was an unsuccessful candidate for Norwich Feb. 1871. Sat for Scarborough from Feb. 1874. Defeated Apr. 1880. Kept Otter Hounds 1887-94. Chairman of E. Riding of Yorkshire County Council. Died 6 Dec. 1901. [1880]

LEGH, George Cornwall. 6 St. James' Place, London. High Legh, Knutsford, Cheshire. Carlton, and Travellers'. Eld s. of George John Legh, Esq., of High Legh, Cheshire, by Mary, d. of John Blackburne, Esq., many years MP for Lancashire. B. 1804; m. 1828, Louisa Charlotte, 2nd d. of Edward Taylor, Esq., of Bifrons, Kent, and niece of Sir Herbert Taylor G.C.B. Graduated at Christ Church, Oxford 1826. Was High Sheriff of Cheshire in 1838. Appointed Maj. in 2nd Royal Cheshire Militia, July 1853. A Conservative, in favour of strict neutrality being maintained in foreign relations. Sat for Cheshire N. from 1841 to the general election 1847, and from May 1848 to Dec. 1868, when he was elected for the mid-division. Accepted Chiltern Hundreds 1873. Died 16 Jun 1877. [1873]

LEGH, William John. 20 Belgrave Square, London. Lyme Park, Cheshire. Goldbourne Park, Warrington, Lancashire. Carlton, and Army & Navy. S. of William Legh, Esq., and Mary Anne his wife. B. at Ratcliffe Hall, Leicestershire 1828; m. 1856, Emily Jane d. of the Rev. Charles Nourse Wodehouse, Canon of Norwich, and Lady Jane Wodehouse. Educ. at Rugby. Entered the army, Dec. 1848. Appointed Dept.-Lieut. of Chester, and of the Co. Palatine of Lancaster

1860. A Conservative. Sat for South Lancashire until his defeat in 1885 contesting Hyde division of Cheshire. Created Baron Newton Aug. 1892. Died 15 Dec. 1898. [1885]

LEHMANN, F. A Liberal. Unsuccessfully contested Middlesex 14 Feb. 1874 and Waterford Co. 24 Jan. 1877. Sat for Evesham from 9 July 1880 but in Dec. of that year, on petition and scrutiny the return was amended and the seat awarded to F.D. Dixon Hartland, Esq.

LEICESTER, Earl of. See GARDNER, John Dunn.

LEIGH, Egerton. Joddrell Hall, Holmes Chapel, West Hall, High Leigh, Knutsford. Carlton, and Army & Navy. Only s. of Egerton Leigh, Esq., of the West Hall, High Leigh, and Joddrell Hall, Cheshire (a Dept.-Lieut. and High Sheriff of that Co.), by Wilhelmina Sarah, d. of George Stratton, Esq., of Tern Park, Oxford. B. at Broadwell Manor House, Gloucestershire 1815; m. 1842, Lydia Rachel, d. and co-heir of John Smith Wright, Esq. of Bulcote Lodge, Nottinghamshire. Educ. at Eton. Entered the army as Cornet in the Queen's Bays 1833; retired with the rank of Capt. 1843. Was Maj. of 1st Cheshire Light Infantry Militia for 20 years. Was High Sheriff of Cheshire for 1872. Was author of a work entitled *Ballads and Legends of Cheshire.* Patron of 2 livings. A Conservative, in favour of the union of Church and State; also of secular and religious education being combined, and of economy in public expenditure. Sat for Mid-Cheshire from Feb. 1873. MP until his death 1 July 1876. [1876]

LEIGH, Hon. Gilbert Henry Chandos. 37 Portman Square, London. Stoneleigh Abbey, Kenilworth. Devonshire, and Brooks's. Eld. s. of Lord Leigh, by Lady Caroline Amelia, 5th d. of 2nd Marq. of Westminster. B. 1851. Educ. at Harrow and Magdalen Coll., Cambridge. B.A. 1875, M.A. 1878. A Magistrate and Dept.-Lieut for Warwickshire. Capt. Warwickshire Yeomanry Cavalry. A Liberal. Sat for Warwickshire S. from Apr. 1880. MP until his death 15 Sept. 1884. [1884]

LEIGH, Roger. Hindley Hall, Wigan. Barnham Court, Teston, Maidstone, Kent. Travellers'. B. at Hindley, Lancashire, 1840; m. 1861, Elizabeth Jane, d. of Capt. T. Eden Blackwell, of the Royal Argyllshire Highlanders. Was Educ. at Radley Coll., and graduated both at Cambridge and Oxford University. A Magistrate for Lancashire and for Kent. A Conservative, and in favour of the 'just influence of England being maintained abroad, as well as the integrity of the Empire being preserved at home.' Sat for Rochester from Apr. 1880. Retired in 1885. Died 29 Feb. 1924.

[1885]

LEIGHTON, Sir Baldwyn, Bart. 49 Upper Brook Street, London. Loton Park, Shrewsbury. Athenaeum, and Carlton. Eld. s. of Sir Baldwin Leighton, 7th Bart., of Loton Park, Shropshire (who sat for South Shropshire from 1859 to 1865), by Mary, d. of Thomas Netherton Parker, Esq., of Sweeney Hall, Oswestry. B. 1836; m. 1864, Hon. Eleanor, 3rd d. of the 2nd Lord de Tabley. Was educ. at Eton and at Christ Church, Oxford, and graduated M.A. Was Cornet South Salopian Yeomanry Cavalry. A Dept.- Lieut. of Shropshire. Published several pamphlets on Labour, Pauperism, etc.; also *The Life and Letters of the late Edward Denison, MP*. Patron of 1 living. A Conservative. Sat for South Shropshire from Aug. 1877 until defeated in 1885. Died 22nd Jan. 1897.

[1885]

LEIGHTON, Stanley. Continued in House after 1885: full entry in Volume II.

LEITH, John Farley. 8 Dorset Square, London. 5 Paper Buildings, Temple, London. St. Mary's Priory, Prittlewell, Essex. Brooks's. S. of James Urquhart Leith, Esq., Capt. 68th Foot, who was killed at the battle of Orthes (a younger branch of the Leiths of Leith Hall, Aberdeenshire), by Mary Ann, d. of Andrew Henderson, Esq., M.D., of Aberdeen. B. at Aberdeen 1808; m. 1832, Alicia Amé, d. of Samuel Tomkins, Esq., Banker, London and Aberdeen (she died 1876). Educ. at the Grammar School and at Marischal Coll., and the University of Aberdeen, where he graduated M.A. 1825. Called to the bar at the Middle Temple 1830, and was Barrister practising before the Privy Council. Was at one time an Advocate of the Supreme Court of Calcutta. Appointed a Queen's Counsel 1872, a Bencher of the Middle Temple 1874. A Liberal, in favour of progressive reform – Parliamentary, Administrative, Financial, Legal and Social – and opposed to everything having the slightest tinge of intolerance. Sat for Aberdeen from June 1872, when he stood in compliance with a written requisition signed by upwards of 3000 electors. Sat until he retired 1880. Died 4 Apr. 1887.

[1880]

LEMON, Sir Charles, Bart. 46 Charles Street, Berkeley Square, London. Carclew, Cornwall. Athenaeum. S. of Sir William Lemon, the 1st Bart., (who sat for Cornwall W. from 1774 until his death in 1825,), by the eld. d. of James Buller, Esq., of Morval, Cornwall. B. in London 1784; m. 1810, Charlotte, youngest d. of 2nd Earl of Ilchester (she died 1826). A Dept.-Lieut. of

Cornwall. Appointed a Special Deputy Warden of the Stannaries 1852. Of Whig principles. Represented Penryn from 1807 to 1812; again returned in 1830. Sat for Western div. of Cornwall from 1831-1841; re-elected Feb. 1842, and sat until he retired 1857. Died 12 Feb. 1868.   [1857]

LENNARD, Thomas Barrett. 9 Hyde Park Terrace, London. Rottingdean, Brighton, Sussex. United University, and Reform. Eld. s. of Sir Thomas Barrett Lennard, Bart., of Bell House, Essex, by his 1st wife, d. of Sir John St. Aubyn, Bart. B. 1788; m. 1st, 1815, Margaret, 2nd d. of John Wharton, Esq., of Skelton Castle, Yorkshire; 2ndly, 1825, Mary, only d. and heir of Bartlett Bridger Shedden, Esq., of Aldham Hall, Suffolk. A Liberal. Sat for Maldon from 1826 to 1837, when he was an unsuccessful candidate; re-elected in 1847. Defeated in 1852. Unsuccessful at Essex N. July 1852. Died 9 June 1856. [1852]

LENNARD, Sir Thomas Barrett-, Bart. 40 Bryanston Square,. Bel Hus, Aveley, Essex. M. Dorothy, sister of Sir John St. Aubyn, Bart. of Clowance, Cornwall. Sir Thomas was a natural s. of Lord   Dacre; and having by sign-manual assumed the surname and arms of Barrett-Lennard, was created a Baronet in June 1801. A Reformer, in favour of protection to the produce of land, of the reduction of the assesed and malt taxes, and of the immediate abolition of slavery. A Tithe Owner, and had large estates in the Co. of Monaghan. Sat for Essex S. from 1832. Retired in 1835. Died 1857.   [1833]

LENNOX, Lord Alexander Francis Charles Gordon-. 51 Portland Place, London. Goodwood, Sussex. Carlton. 3rd s. of the 5th Duke of Richmond, by the eld. d. of 1st Marq. of Anglesey. B. 1825. Unmarried. Entered the Royal Horse Guards as Cornet 1842, became a Lieut. 1844, and Capt. 1847. A Conservative, 'firmly attached to the Established Church; opposed to the admission of Jews to   Parliament, and [considered] that any system of education ought to be based on religion.' First returned for Shoreham, Dec. 1849, without opposition. Sat until he retired in 1859. Died 22 Jan. 1892.   [1858]

LENNOX, Lord Arthur. 10 Chesham Place, London. B. 1806, 7th s. of 4th Duke of Richmond, by d. of the 4th Duke of Gordon. M. 1835, Adelaide Constance, d. of Col. John Campbell of Shawfield. Entered the army in 1823, became a Lieut.-Col. in 1842 and then went on half pay in the 6th Foot. Was a Lord of the Treasury May 1844-Aug. 1845, and Clerk of the Ordance Aug. 1845-July 1846. Ranked for some years as a moderate Reformer, having supported the

Reform Bill and similar measures; but subsequently ranked with the Conservatives, dividing against the repeal of the Corn Laws and joining in the no-confidence vote against the Melbourne Ministry. Supported the free trade measures of Peel in 1846 and thus became classed as a Liberal-Conservative. Sat for Chichester 1831-46, and then accepted Chiltern Hundreds. Sat for Yarmouth from 1847, but was unseated July 1848. Died 15 Jan. 1864.   [1847 2nd ed.]

LENNOX, Hon. Charles Spencer Bateman-Hanbury Kincaid-. 7 Queen's Gate Terrace, Kensington Gore, London. Lennox Castle, Lennoxtown, Scotland. Carlton, and Arthur's. 2nd s. of 1st Lord Bateman, by Elizabeth, 2nd d. of Lord Spencer Stanley Chichester. B. at Kelmarsh 1827; m. 1861, the Viscountess Strangford. Assumed by Royal Licence the additional names of Kincaid-Lennox in 1862 when the Viscountess dropped the use of that title. Educ. at Eton and at Brasenose Coll., Oxford, where he graduated B.A. 1848, and was elected a Fellow of All Soul's 1848. Appointed Capt. 2nd Life Guards 1858, and Aide-de-Camp to the Lord-Lieut. of Ireland in the same year. A Magistrate and Dept.-Lieut. of Hertfordshire. A Liberal-Conservative, who was willing to give a general support to Lord Derby; was not willing to support the abolition of Church rates without an equivalent provision being made. Sat for Herefordshire from July 1852 until Apr. 1857. First elected for Leominster Oct. 1858. Sat until he retired July 1865. Died 22 Mar. 1912. [1865]

LENNOX, Lord George Charles Gordon-. 50 Portland Place, London. Goodwood, Chichester. Gordon Castle, Fochabers, Scotland. Youngest s. of 5th Duke of Richmond, by Lady Caroline, eld. d. of 1st Marq. of Anglesey. B. at Goodwood, 1829. Formerly Cornet in the Royal Horse Guards. A Magistrate for Banff, and a Dept.-Lieut. for Sussex. A Liberal-Conservative. First elected for Lymington May 1860. Sat until he retired in 1874. Died 22 Feb. 1877.   [1873]

LENNOX, Rt. Hon. Lord Henry George Charles Gordon-. 53 Princes Gate, London. Goodwood, Chichester. Sussex. White's, and Carlton. 2nd s. of 5th Duke of Richmond, by the eld. d. of 1st Marq. of Anglesey. B. at Goodwood, Sussex, 1821; m. 1883, widow of John White, Esq., of Ardarrock, Dumbartonshire. Was Educ. at Westminster, and at Christ Church, Oxford, where he graduated M.A. 1847. Was Précis Writer to the Earl of Aberdeen when Secretary for Foreign Affairs; resigned Feb. 1846, on being returned to Parliament. Was a Lord of the Treasury from March till Dec. 1852, and from

Mar. 1858 till Mar. 1859; Secretary to the Admiralty from July 1866 to Dec. 1868. Chief Commissioner of Works and Buildings from Feb. 1874 to Aug. 1876. A Liberal-Conservative. Sat for Chichester from Feb. 1846 until defeated in 1885 contesting Partick division of Lanark. Died 29 Aug. 1886.   [1885]

LENNOX, Lord John George. 41 Witton Crescent, Bognor, Sussex. Bro. of the Duke of Richmond. B. 1793; m. 1818, Louisa, d. of the Hon. John Rodney. Was Lieut.-Col. in the army. A moderate Reformer; in favour of the corn laws. Sat for Chichester from 1819 to 1831, when he was elected for Sussex W. Sat until he retired in 1841. Died 10 Nov. 1873.   [1838]

LENNOX, Lord William. 30 Regent Street, London. 2nd bro. of the Duke of Richmond. B. 1799. Captain in the Horse Guards. M. Miss Paton, the celebrated singer, but later divorced her. A Whig, and advocate for the immediate abolition of slavery, but opposed to any alteration in the corn laws. Was first elected for Lynn Regis in the Parliament of 1831. Retired in 1835. Author. Died 18 Feb. 1881.   [1833]

LESLIE, Charles Powell. 48 Berkeley Square, London. Castle Lesley, Glasslough, Co. Monaghan. Carlton, and Sackville Street Club, Dublin. Eld. s. of Chas. Powell Leslie, Esq., of Glasslough, Co. Monaghan (who represented Monaghan for many years), by his 2nd wife, d. of George Fosberry, Esq., of Clarence Co. Limerick. Descended from the Rt. Rev. John Leslie, who was Bishop of Clogher in 1661, and of the same family with the Earls of Leven and Rothes. B.1822. Lord Lieut. and Custos-Rot. of Monaghan, and Col. of the Monaghan Militia. A Conservative. First returned for Monaghan in 1842. MP Until his death in 1871.   [1871]

LESLIE, Hon George Waldegrave. See WALDEGRAVE-LESLIE, Hon. George.

LESLIE, Sir John, Bart. 11 Stratford Place, London. Glasslough, Co. Monaghan. Carlton, White's, Travellers', and Athenaeum. Eld. surviving s. of Col. Charles Powell Leslie, of Glasslough, Co. Monaghan (who represented Monaghan for many years), by his 2nd wife Christiana, d. of George Fosberry, Esq., of Clorane, Co. Limerick. B. at Glasslough 1823; m. 1856, Constance Wilhelmina Frances, youngest d. of the Rt. Hon. George L. Dawson Damer. Educ. at Harrow, and at Christ Church, Oxford, where he graduated B.A. 1844. A Magistrate and Dept.-Lieut. for the Co. of Monaghan. A Conservative. Sat for the Co. of Monaghan from July

235

1871, when he was elected on the death of his elder bro., who had represented it for nearly 30 years. Sat until defeated Apr. 1880. Contested Monaghan N. 30 Nov. 1885 and again 17 July 1886. Died 23 Jan. 1916.   [1880]

LESLIE, William. 31 Eaton Square, London. Warthill, Aberdeenshire. Drumrossie, Aberdeenshire. Carlton. B. at Warthill 1814, the s. of William Leslie of Warthill, Aberdeenshire (where the family had been established since 1518), by Jane, d. of the Rev. Patrick Davidson D.D. M. 1848 Matilda Rose, 2nd. d. of William Rose Robinson of Clemiston, Midlothian. Educ. at Marischal Coll., Aberdeen, where he graduated M.A. 1832. Was for some years in China; a Partner in the firm of Messrs Dent and Co. A Magistrate and Dept.-Lieut. of Aberdeenshire. A Conservative, in favour of free commercial intercourse with other nations on principles of reciprocity and of non-intervention in foreign politics, but of the maintenance in the highest state of efficiency of the army and navy, and of a 'sound Scriptural education for the people, aided by government grants.' Opposed to the system of centralization especially as applied to Scotland. Sat for Aberdeenshire Feb. 1861 to 1866, when he accepted Chiltern Hundreds. Died 4 March 1880.   [1865]

LESTER, Benjamin Lester. Union Club. A Newfoundland Merchant, born and residing at Poole. A Reformer, of Whig, inclining to Radical opinions; in favour of the abolition of slavery. Sat for Poole from 1812 until he retired in 1835.
                    [1833]

LEVER, John Orrell. 97 St. George's Square, London. West Worthing, Sussex. Eld. s. of James Lever, Esq., Merchant of Manchester. B. 1824; m. 1847, Elizabeth, d. of Jonathan Dorning, Esq., of Swinton, Lancashire. Largely engaged in Steam Shipping, and once sole lessee of 'The Thames and Channel Passenger Service Company', of which he was part owner. Was for several years Director of the Atlantic Royal Mail Steam Navigation Company (the 'Lever Line'). Author of several works. A Liberal-Conservative. Sat for Galway from Feb. 1859 to July 1865, when he was an unsuccessful candidate; re-elected Apr. 1880. Retired in 1885. Died 4 Aug. 1897. [1885]

LEVESON, Lord. 27 Berkeley Square, London. Stone Park, Staffordshire. Reform. B. in 1815, the eld s. of Earl Granville. In 1840 married the d. of the Duke of Dalberg and relict of Sir F.R.E. Acton, Bart. Was for some time attached to his father's Embassy in Paris, and was subsequently appointed Under-Sec. for Foreign Affairs, which

office he resigned on the retirement of the Melbourne Ministry in 1841. He became Lord President of the Council 1852-58 and 1859-66, Sec. of State for the Colonies 1868-70 and 1886, Sec. of State for Foreign Affairs again in 1870-74 and 1880-85. A Liberal, who voted against the Corn Laws. Represented Morpeth from 1837 to Feb. 1840 when he accepted Chiltern Hundreds. Sat for Lichfield from Sept. 1841 (on retirement of Sir George Anson) until he succeeded as 2nd Earl in Jan. 1846. Died 31 Mar. 1891.   [1845]

LEVESON-GOWER, Hon. Edward Frederic. See GOWER, Hon. Edward Frederic Leveson-.

LEVESON-GOWER, Granville William Gresham. See Gower, Granville William Gresham Leveson-.

LEVESON-GOWER, Lord Ronald Charles Sutherland. See GOWER, Lord Ronald Charles Sutherland Leveson-.

LEVETT, Theophilus John. Wichnor Park, Burton-on-Trent. Carlton. Eld. s. of John Levett, Esq., of Wichnor Park, Staffordshire, by Sophia Eliza, 3rd d. of Hon. Robert Kennedy, and grand-d. of 11th Earl of Cassilis. B. at Walton Hall, Burton-on-Trent, 1829; m. 1856, Lady Jane Lissey Harriet, 3rd d. of the 7th Earl of Denbigh. Was a Capt. 1st Life Guards, which he entered in 1847. A Magistrate and Dept.-Lieut. for Stafford, also a Magistrate for Derby. Patron of 2 livings. A Conservative. Sat for Lichfield from July 1880. Retired in 1885. Member of Staffordshire County Council 1889-95. Died 26 Feb. 1899.   [1885]

LEVINGE, Sir Richard George Augustus, Bart. 37 St. James's Street, London. Knock Drin Castle, Mullingar, Ireland. Army & Navy. Eld. s. of Sir Richard Levinge, by the Hon. Elizabeth Anne, eld. d. of the 1st Lord Rancliffe (extinct). B. in Hertford Street, London 1811; m. 1849, Caroline Jane, eld. d. of Col. Lancelot Rolleston, of Watnall Hall, Nottinghamshire. Served in the army for 14 years, and was eventually Capt. in the 5th Dragoon Guards. Was for some years Lieut.-Col. of the Westmeath Militia. Was High Sheriff of Westmeath in 1851. Author of *Echoes from the Backwoods*, etc. A Liberal, formerly ranked as a Conservative; voted against Lord Derby's Reform Bill Mar. 1859. Was an unsuccessful candidate for Westmeath on Conservative principles in 1852; first returned for Westmeath in Apr. 1857. Sat until he retired 1865. Died 28 Sept. 1884.   [1865]

LEWIS, C.E. Continued in House after 1885: full entry in Volume II.

LEWIS, David. Chester Street, London. Llanelly, Co. Carmarthen. A Conservative. Patron of 1 living. Sat for Carmarthen from 1835 until he was defeated in 1837. [1837]

LEWIS, Sir George Cornewall, Bart. Kent House, Knightsbridge, London, Harpton Court, near Kington, Radnorshire. Travellers', and Anthenaeum. Eld. s. of Sir Thomas Frankland Lewis, Bart., by his 1st wife, Harriet, 4th d. of Sir George Cornewall, Bart. B. in London, 1806; m. 1844, Lady Maria Theresa, d. of Hon. George Villiers, sister to 4th Earl of Clarendon, and relict of Thomas Henry Lister, Esq. Educ. at Eton and at Christ Church, Oxford, where he was 1st class in classics, and 2nd class in mathematics, 1828, and received the honorary degree of D.C.L. 1857. Author of several political and historical works; editor of the *Edinburgh Review* from 1853 to 1855. Called to the bar at the Middle Temple, 1831. Was a Poor Law Commissioner from Jan. 1839 till July 1847; secretary to the Board of Controul from Nov. 1847 till May 1848; Under-Secretary for the Home Department from May 1848 till July 1850; financial secretary to the Treasury from July 1850 till Feb. 1852; Chancellor of the Exchequer from May 1855 till Mar. 1858, and Secretary of State for the Home Department from June 1859 till July 1861, when he was appointed Secretary of State for War. Appointed an Ecclesiastical Commissioner 1862. A Liberal. Sat for Herefordshire from July 1847 till July 1852; was an unsuccessfull candidate there July 1852, and for Peterborough, Nov. following. First elected for Radnor district Feb. 1855, without opposition. MP until his death 13 Apr. 1863. [1863]

LEWIS, Henry Owen, 1 Lancaster Gate, London. Inniskeen, Co. Monaghan. Only surviving s. of Lieut.-Col. Arthur Gamble-Lewis, a Dept.-Lieut. of Monaghan, by Henrietta, only d. of Henry Owen Scott, Esq., of Scotstown, Co. Monaghan, and relict of Hon. Richard Westenra. B. at Merrion Square, Dublin 1842; m. 1866, Frances Sophia, only d. of the late Francis Charles Elsegood, Esq., of Brook Street, Grosvenor Square. Educ. at Trinity Coll., Dublin. A Magistrate for the counties of Dublin and Monaghan and a Dept.-Lieut. for Monaghan. A Liberal, in favour of the system called 'Home Rule' for Ireland, in favour also of the amendment of the existing Grand Jury laws and of the Irish Land Act. Sat for the bor. of Carlow from Feb. 1874 until he retired 1880. [1880]

LEWIS, John Delaware. 30 Eaton Square, London. Membland, Ivybridge, Devon. Westfield House, Petersfield, Hampshire. S. of John Delaware Lewis, Esq., a Russian merchant, by Elizabeth Emma, d. of James Hamilton Clewlow, Esq., R.N. B. 1828; M. 1868, Teresa, d. of Sir J.C. Jervoise, Bart., of Idsworth, Hampshire. Educ. at Eton and Trinity Coll., Cambridge, where he graduated B.A. 1850, M.A. 1853. Was called to the bar at Lincoln's Inn 1858, and was a member of the Home Circuit. Was for some time 1st Lieut. Royal Pembroke Artillery Militia. Was a Magistrate for the Cos. of Devon and Hampshire. A Liberal, voted in favour of the disestablishment of the Irish Church 1869. Sat for Devonport from Dec. 1868. Defeated in 1874. Unsuccessfully contested Oxford 16 Mar. 1874. Contested Devonport again in 1880. Died 31 July 1884. [1873]

LEWIS, J.H. Continued in House after 1885: full entry in Volume II.

LEWIS, Rt. Hon Sir Thomas Frankland, Bart. 21 Grafton Street, London. Harpton Court, Radnorshire. White's, Carlton, and Athenaeum. B. in London 1780, the only s. of John Lewis of Harpton Court, Radnorshire, by his 2nd wife, 2nd d. of Admiral Sir Thomas Frankland, Bart. M. 1st, 1801, Harriet, 4th d. of Sir George Cornewall Bart., of Moccas Park, Herefordshire (she died 1838); 2ndly, 1839, Mary Anne, only surviving d. of John Asheton. Educ. at Eton and at Christ Church, Oxford. Was Lieut.-Col. of the Radnorshire local Militia, 1806 until the end of the war. Was a Commissioner of Inquiry into the Irish Revenue 1821, into that of Great Britain and Ireland 1822-25, into Education in Ireland 1825-28, Secretary of the Treasury 1827, Vice-President of the Board of Trade 1828, Treasurer of the Navy 1830, Chairman of the Poor Law Commission 1834-39 (when his son was appointed to the same board), a commissioner to inquire into turnpike outrages in Wales in 1843. A Liberal, inclining to Conservatism and opposed to any further religious endowments. Represented Beaumaris 1812-26, Ennis 1826-28, Radnorshire 1828-35, and Radnor district 1847 until his death 22 Jan. 1855. [1854]

LEWIS, Wyndham. 1 Grosvenor Gate, Hyde Park, London. Green Meadow, Cardiff. Carlton. S. of the Rev. Wyndham Lewis, of Newhouse, Glamorganshire, and descended from the Lewis family of the Van, in the same Co. B. 1780; m. in 1815 Mary Anne, only d. of John Evans, Esq., of Branceford Park, Devon. A Barrister. Dept.-Lieut. of Glamorganshire, and Major in the Local Militia. A Conservative. Sat for Cardiff in the Parliament of 1820; was elected for Aldeburgh in 1827; unsuccessfully contested Maidstone in 1826 and 1832. Was elected for Maidstone in 1835. MP until his death in Feb. or Mar. 1838. [1837]

LEWISHAM, Visct. (I). 31 Hill Street, Berkeley Square, London. Patshull, Staffordshire. Carlton. B. at Sandwell, Staffordshire 1823, the eld. s. of 4th Earl of Dartmouth. M. 1846, Lady Augusta, eld. d. of 5th Earl of Aylesford. Educ. at Eton and at Christ Church, Oxford where he graduated M.A. 1847. Appointed Capt. of the Staffordshire Militia 1843 and Dept.-Lieut. of that Co. 1852. A Conservative, who did not 'consent to the reimposition of any duty upon the necessaries of life.' Opposed to the endowment of the Roman Catholic Clergy. First returned for Staffordshire S. in Feb. 1849, without opposition and sat until Nov. 1853 when he succeeded his father as 5th Earl. Died 4 Aug. 1891. [1853].

LEWISHAM, Visct. (II). Continued in House after 1885: full entry in Volume II.

LEYCESTER, Joseph. East View, Cork. B. 1784, m. co-heiress of Nicholas Wrixon, Esq., solicitor of Dublin. Agent for the Bank of Ireland at Cork. A Conservative. Sat for Cork city from 17 Jan. 1835 until he was unseated 18 Apr. 1835; unsuccessfully contested same seat in 1837. [1835]

LIDDELL, Hon. H.G. See ESLINGTON, Lord.

LIDDELL, Hon. Henry Thomas. Eslington Park, Alnwick, Northumberland. White's, Travellers', Carlton. B. at Ravensworth Castle 1797, the eld. s. of Lord Ravensworth. M. 1820 Isabella Horatia, eld. d. of Lord George Seymour. A Liberal-Conservative, 'a defender of the Throne and Altar, but yielding to no man in attachment to civil and religious liberty.' Voted for agricultural protection 1846, but considered 'free trade as an accomplished fact.' Sat for Northumberland 1826-30, for Durham North July 1837 (when his return was effected free of expense) till July 1847. Unsuccessful at South Shields, July 1852. Sat for Liverpool 1853 to March 1855, when he succeeded as 2nd Baron Ravensworth. Died 19 March 1878. [1854]

LINCOLN, Earl of. (I). 16 Carlton House Terrace, London. Runby Hall, Nottinghamshire. Carlton. Eld. s. of the Duke of Newcastle. B. 1811; m. in 1832 Susan, only d. of the 10th Duke of Hamilton. A Conservative, but in favour of free trade, and supported the endowment of the Roman Catholic Clergy. A Lord of the Treasury from Dec. 1834 till Apr. 1835, and First Commissioner of Woods and Forests from Sept. 1841 to Jan. 1846, when he became Chief Secretary for Ireland (resigned July 1846). One of the Council of the Duchy of Cornwall. Was MP for South Nottinghamshire from 1832-46. Unsuccessfully contested North and South Nottinghamshire in

Feb. and Mar. 1846. First returned for the Falkirk district in May 1846 on the retirement of Mr. Baird. Sat until he succeeded as Duke of Newcastle 12 Jan 1851. Died 18 Oct. 1864. [1850]

LINCOLN, Earl of. (II). 17 Portman Square, London. Arthur's. Eld. s. of the 5th Duke of Newcastle, by the only d. of the 10th Duke of Hamilton. B. 1834. Appointed Cornet in the Sherwood Rangers 1856. Offered himself as a candidate 'without the designation of a party name, but anxious to maintain the principles of Liberal government.' First returned for Newark in Mar. 1857. Defeated in 1859. Succeeded as 6th Duke Oct. 1864. Died 22 Feb.1879. [1858]

LINDSAY, Hon. Charles Hugh. Winchfield House, Winchfield. Guards', United Service, and Carlton. 3rd s. of 24th Earl of Crawford by the Hon. Maria, only d. of 1st Lord Muncaster. B. at Muncaster Castle, Cumberland, 1816; M. 1851, Emilia, d. of Hon. and Very Rev. Henry Montagu Browne, Dean of Lismore. Entered the army 1835 as Ensign, in 43rd Light Infantry; served in Canada from 1837-42, exchanged into the Grenadiar Guards 1844, and served with it as Lieut-Col. in the Crimean campaign, including Balaklava, Inkermann and the siege of Sebastopol. Was Aide-de-camp to Earl de Grey, and Master of the Horse to Lord Heytesbury when Lord-Lieut. of Ireland 1845. Also Private Sec. to the Earl of Eglinton in Ireland, and for several years first Aide-de-camp to Sir Edward Blakeney when commanding the Forces in Ireland. Was a Groom in Waiting to the Queen from July 1866-Dec. 1868. A Liberal-Conservative, voted against the disestablishment of the Irish Church 1869; in favour of the equalization of poor-rates, and a re-adjustment in the mode of paying them. Sat for Abingdon from July 1865 until defeated in 1874. C.B. 1881. Died 25 Mar. 1889. [1873]

LINDSAY, Hugh Hamilton. 22 Berkeley Square, London. B. 1802, the grands. of 5th Earl of Balcarres. A Conservative. First returned for Sandwich on the death of Sir Rufane Shawe Donkin, a short time before the dissolution in 1841, after a severe contest with Colonel Fox. Again returned as the general election, but without opposition. Sat until he retired in 1847. Died 29 May 1881. [1847]

LINDSAY, Hon. James. 25 Portman Square, London. Haigh Hall, Wigan, Lancashire. Guards', and Travellers'. B. at Muncaster Castle, Cumberland 1815, 2nd s. of 24th Earl of Crawford, by Hon. Maria, only d. of 1st Lord Muncaster. M. 1845 Lady Sarah Elizabeth, d. of

238

3rd Earl of Mexborough (she was appointed Woman of the Bedchamber to Queen Mary 1859). Educ. at Eton. Entered the Grenadier Guards in 1832., became Capt. and Lieut.-Col. 1846, Adjutant of 2nd Battalion in 1838, Col. 1854, Major Grenadier Guards 1858. A Dept.-Lieut. of Lancashire. A Conservative, opposed to uniformity of franchise, but in favour of a moderate reduction of qualification in the boroughs. Sat for Wigan Sept. 1845 to Apr. 1857, May 1859 to Feb. or Mar. 1865, when he accepted Chiltern Hundreds. Died 13 Aug. 1874.
[1865]

LINDSAY, Lord. 47 Brook Street, Grosvenor Square, London. Haigh Hall, Wigan. Dun-Echt House, Aberdeen. Eld. s. of Earl of Crawford and Balcarres, by Margaret, eld. d. of Maj.-Gen. James Lindsay. B. 1847; m. 1869, Emily Florence, 2nd d. of Lieut.-Col. Hon. Edward Bootle-Wilbraham. Appointed Ensign Grenadier Guards 1868. A Conservative. Sat for Wigan from Feb. 1874 until 1880 when he succeeded to the Peerage (Earl of Crawford and Balcarres). [1880]

LINDSAY, Sir Robert James Loyd, K.C.B. 2 Carlton Gardens, London. Lockinge House, Wantage, Berkshire. Carlton, Guards', Travellers', and United Service. S. of Lieut.-Gen. James Lindsay, of Balcarres, Fife, by his 2nd wife, Anna, eld. d. of Sir Coutts-Trotter, Bart. B. in London 1832; m. 1858, Hon. Harriet Sarah, only d. of the 1st Lord Overstone. Educ. at Eton. Entered the army 1850, became Lieut.-Col. Scots Fusilier Guards 1859, and retired. Lieut.-Col. of the Berkshire regiment of Volunteers, Nov. 1859. Was Aide-de-camp to Gen. Simpson in the Crimea 1855; served at the Alma, Inkerman, Balaklava, and siege of Sebastopol, and received the Victoria Cross, Legion of Honour, and Medjidie; Adjutant to the Scots Fusilier Guards from 1855 till 1858; Equerry to the Prince of Wales in 1858 and 1859; became an extra equerry 1874. Was Financial Secretary for War from Aug. 1877 to Apr. 1880. A Conservative, and in favour of amendment in the Land Laws, and in the system of local taxation. Sat for Berkshire from July 1865 until he created Baron Wantage July 1885. A prominent Freemason. Chairman of Committee of Enquiry of Recruiting in the Army, 1890. Died 10 June 1901. [1885]

LINDSAY, William Shaw. 8 Austin Friars, London. Manor House, Shepperton, Middlesex. Reform, and City. B. at Ayr, Scotland 1816; m. 1842, Helen, 3rd d. of James Stewart, Esq., Merchant, of Glasgow. In early life was apprenticed to the Merchant Service, in which he rose to command a ship at the age of 20, but relinquished the occupation in 1840. Founded the well-known Shipping House of Messrs. W.S. Lindsay and Company, Austin Friars, London. Author of various letters and pamphlets on maritime affairs, and published in 1842 a book entitled *Our Navigation and Mercantile Marine Laws*. A Magistrate for Middlesex. A Liberal, in favour of a further extension of the suffrage, opposed to all endowments for religious purposes, voted against Church rates 1855. Unsuccessfully contested Monmouth in Apr. and Dartmouth July 1852. Sat for Tynemouth from Mar. 1854 to Mar. 1859, when he was elected for Sunderland. Retired 1865. Died 28 Aug. 1877. [1865]

LISBURNE, Earl of. Crosswood Park, Aberystwith, Cardiganshire. Carlton, and Conservative. B. 1800; m. 1st 1835, Mary, 2nd d. of Sir Lawrence Palk, Bart.; 2ndly, 1853, youngest d. of Col. Hugh Henry Mitchell, and grand-d. of 5th Duke of Beaufort. Was Sheriff of Cardiganshire 1851. Patron of 7 livings. An Irish peer. A Conservative. First elected for Cardiganshire Feb. 1854, without opposition. Retired in 1859. Died 8 Nov. 1873. [1858]

LISTER, Ellis Cunliffe. Manningham Hall, Yorkshire. M. 1st, 1794, Ruth Myns, niece and heiress of S. Lister, Esq.; 2ndly, 1809, Mary, only child of William Kay, Esq., of Cottingham, near Hull. Dept.-Lieut. for the West Riding of Yorkshire. A Reformer, an advocate of a free trade in corn, a large reduction of taxes, especially of those on windows, a thorough reform in the Church, triennial Parliaments, removing the Bishops from the House of Lords, the vote by ballot, and exempting Dissenters from Church Rates. Sat for Bradford from 1832 until he retired in 1841. After his second marriage he assumed the additional surname of Kay on the death of his father-in-law in 1841. [1840]

LISTER, William Cunliffe. A Liberal. Returned for Bradford in July 1841. Died Aug. 1841.

LISTOWELL, Earl of. Kingston House, Knightsbridge, London. Convamore, Co. Cork. Cromer Hall, Norfolk. B. in 1801. M. 1831, the d. of Vice Admiral Wyndham, and widow of G.T. Wyndham, Esq. An Irish Peer, and Vice Admiral of the province of Munster. Voted against the Corn Laws. Sometime Lord in Waiting to the Queen, which office he resigned in 1841. Sat for St. Alban's from Feb. 1841 until his defeat at a by-election on 11 Aug. 1846, on appointment as Lord in Waiting. Died 4 Feb. 1856. [1845]

LITTLETON, Rt. Hon. Edward J. Teddesley

Park, Walsall, Staffordshire. 45 Grosvenor Place, London. B. 1791; m. in 1812, Hiacinthe Mary, natural d. of Richard, Marquis Wellesley. This gentleman's name was originally Walhouse, but he assumed that of Littleton in 1812 on succeeding to the estates of his great-uncle, the last baronet of that name. Was appointed Secretary for Ireland in May 1833, on the resignation of Sir John Cam Hobhouse, and held the office till Nov. 1834. First sat for Staffordshire S. in 1812. Sat until created Baron Hatherton, May 1835; author. Died 4 May 1863.   [1835]

LITTLETON, Hon. Edward Richard. 1 Lowndes Street, London. Hatherton Hall, Staffordshire. Travellers'. Eld. s. of Lord Hatherton. B. at Teddesley, Staffordshire 1815; m. 1841, Lady Margaret, youngest d. of 2nd Earl of Beverley. Educ. at Eton. Appointed a Dept.-Lieut. of Staffordshire 1841 and Vice-Lieut. of that Co. 1855, Col. of Staffordshire Militia 1853. A Liberal. Sat for Walsall from July 1847 to July 1852. First elected for Staffordshire S. Aug. 1853, without opposition. Retired 1857. Succeeded as 2nd Baron 1863. Died 3 Apr. 1888.   [1857]

LITTON, Edward. Altmore, Co. Tyrone. Dublin. Carlton. S. of Edw. Litton, Esq., a gentleman of ancient family and good property, who served as an officer in the British army during the American War, by Charlotte, d. of the Very Rev. Dean Letablere. B. 1 Dec. 1787; m. 13 Sept. 1813, to Sophia, d. of the Rev. Dr. Stewart, a Dignitary of the Church in Ireland, and niece to the Rt. Hon. Sir John Stewart, Bart., who represented the Co. of Tyrone for 30 years previous to his death, and was succeeded by his s. Sir Hugh Stewart, Bart. Was educ. at Trinity Coll., Dublin, and gained five medals in the Historical Society of that University. A Queen's Counsel at the Irish bar. Had the next presentation to the living of Gattrim in Ireland. A Conservative, took a distinguised part at the Belfast and Tyrone Conservative meetings in 1836, and at the great Protestant meeting in Dublin in Jan. 1837. First elected for Coleraine 4 Aug. 1837 and sat until he was appointed a Master in Chancery (Ireland) Jan. or Feb. 1843. Died 22 Jan. 1870.   [1842]

LITTON, Edward Falconer. 21 Merrion Square, S. Dublin. Adavening, Cloyne, Co. Cork. Stephen's Green, Dublin. Only s. of the late Daniel Litton, Esq., of Waterloo Road, Dublin, by Jane, d. of the late F. Minchin, Esq., of Armagh, Co. Tipperary. B. at Dublin 1827; m. Adelaide, d. of the late Clifford Trotter, Esq., of Charleville Cottage, Co. Wicklow. Educ. at Trini-

ty Coll., Dublin, where he graduated B.A. 1849, M.A. 1864. Called to the bar in Ireland 1849. Appointed a Queen's Counsel Feb. 1874. Author of a work entitled *Life or Death: The Destiny of the Soul in the Future State.* A Liberal. Sat for Tyrone Co. from Apr. 1880 until appointed Land Commissioner Aug. 1881, a position he held until Jan. 1890; Judge 1890. Died 27 Nov. 1890.   [1881]

LLOYD, John Horatio. 37 Torrington Square, London. 13 King's Bench Walk, Temple, London. A Barrister, and s. of a Banker at Stockport. M. Miss Watson., d. of — Watson, Esq., a Magistrate of the Co. of Chester. A radical Reformer. Sat for Stockport from 1832. Retired in 1835. Chief Authority in legal matters connected with railways; devised securities known as Lloyd's Bonds. Retired in 1876. Died 18 July 1884.   [1833]

LLOYD, Morgan. 53 Cornwall Gardens, London. 4 King's Bench Walk, Temple, London. Reform. S. of Morris Lloyd, Esq., of Cefngellwyn, Co. Merioneth. B. at Cefngellwyn 1822; m. 1st, 1848, Mary, d. of Hon. Admiral Elphinstone Fleming, and sister of the 14th Baron Elphinstone; 2ndly, 1879, Priscilla Willy, only d. and heir of James Lewes, of Comhyar, Cardiganshire. Was educ. at Edinburgh Unversity. Was called to the bar at the Middle Temple 1847; made a Queen's Counsel Feb. 1873, and was a member of the North Wales and Chester Cirucit. A Magistrate for Merionethshire. Published legal Treatises on Prohibitions, and *The Laws and Practice of the County Courts.* A Liberal. Sat for Beaumaris from Feb. 1874 until 1885. Contested Merionethshire 2 Dec. 1885 and in July 1892 contested Anglesey. Died London 5 Sept. 1893.   [1885]

LLOYD, Sampson Samuel. Moor Hall, Sutton Coldfield. 2 Cornwall Gardens, London. Carlton, and St. Stephen's. Eld. s. of G.B. Lloyd Esq., a Banker of Birmingham, and Mary, d. of J.P. Dearman, Esq. B. 1820; m. 1st, Emma, d. of Samuel Reeve, Esq., of Leighton Buzzard, Bedfordshire; 2ndly, 1865, Marie, d. of H.E. Lieut.-Gen. W.F. Menckhoff, of the Prussian Army. A Manufacturer, and Chairman of Lloyd's Banking Co., Limited, and for 18 years was Chairman of the Association of Chambers of Commerce for the United Kingdom. A J.P. for County of Warwick and for Birmingham. A Conservative. Sat for Plymouth, 1874-80. Returned for Warwickshire S. in 1880. Defeated in 1885, contesting the new South-West division of Warwickshire. Died 3rd Mar. 1889.   [1885]

LLOYD, Thomas. Spark Hill, Near

Birmingham. Reform. S. of James LLoyd, Esq., of Bingley House, Banker, by Sarah, d. of Francis Hart, Esq., of Nottingham. B. in Birmingham 1814; m. 1845, Emilia, d. of John Travers, Esq., of London. A Magistrate and Dept.-Lieut. of Warwickshire. A Banker. A Liberal, in favour of a 10/- franchise in counties, of 'the maintenance of the 40s. freeholders in their elective rights', and vote by ballot; 'in the interest of the Church herself desired the abolition of Church rates,' and supported Lord Palmerston, especially in his Foreign policy. First elected for Barnstaple Oct. 1863, but unseated 14 Apr. 1864. Partner in Lloyds Bank 1865. Contested Bewdley 17 Nov. 1868. Alderman of Warwick County Council from 1889 until his death 23 Jan. 1890.   [1864]

LLOYD, Sir Thomas Davies, Bart. Bronwydd, Near Carmarthen. University. Eld. s. of Thomas Lloyd, Esq., of Bronwydd. B. at Swansea, 1820; M. 1846, d. of George Reid Esq. of Friendship and Bunker's Hill, Jamaica (she died 1871). Educ. at Harrow and at Christ Church, Oxford. Entered the 13th Light Dragoons 1840; served in Canada with the 82nd Foot, and commanded a detachment at Ottawa. Appointed a Dept.-Lieut. for the counties of Cardigan and Carmarthen 1847, and was High Sheriff of Cardiganshire 1850. Was patron of 6 livings. A Liberal, in favour of the reduction of the malt tax with a view to its ultimate repeal. Sat for Cardiganshire from July 1865 to Dec. 1868, when he was elected for the district of Cardigan.Retired in 1874. Died 21 July 1877.   [1873]

LLOYD, Thomas Edward, 51 Victoria Street, London. 77 Chancery Lane, London. Coedmore, Cardigan. Garrick. Eld. s. of Thomas Lloyd, Esq., of Coedmore, Lord-Lieut. of Cardiganshire, by Charlotte, d. of Capt. Longcroft, R. N. B. at Coedmore 1820; m. 1850, Clement Frances, 2nd d. of the Rev. David Daniel. Educ. at Rugby. Called to the bar at the Middle Temple Nov. 1844. Patron of 1 living. A Conservative. Sat for Cardiganshire from Feb. 1874 until defeated 1880.   [1880]

LLOYD-MOSTYN, Hon. Edward Mostyn. See MOSTYN, Hon. Edward Mostyn Lloyd-.

LLOYD-MOSTYN, Hon. Thomas E. Mostyn. See MOSTYN, Hon. Thomas E. Mostyn Lloyd-.

LOCH, George, 12 Albermarle Street, London, W. The Cottage, Bishopsgate, Staines. Uppart, Golspie, Scotland. Brooks's and Athenaeum. Eld. s. of James Loch, Esq., F.R.S., F.G.S., (who sat for St. Germein's from 1827-30, and for the district of Wick from 1830-52), by his 1st wife, Anne,

youngest d. of Patrick Orr, Esq., of Bridgeton, Kincardineshire. B. in London 1811; m. 1836, Catherine, eld. d. of Joseph Pilkington Brandreth, Esq., M.D., of Liverpool. Was educ. at the Charter House, was called to the bar at the Middle Temple 1847; appointed a Queen's Counsel 1863; a Magistrate for Lancashire and for Sutherlandshire. A Dept.-Lieut. of Sutherlandshire and a Commissioner of the Fishery Board for Scotland. Dept.-Gov. of the British Fishery Society. Auditor to the Duke of Sutherland. Capt. Staffordshire Yeomanry and Maj. Caithness and Sutherland Artillery. A Liberal, voted in favour of disestablishing the Irish Church 1869; favoured repealing the rate-paying clauses of the Reform Act, assimilating the county franchise to that of boroughs, reconstituting the House of Lords, material changes in the law relating to the inheritance of real property; doubted any beneficial effects of the ballot.   Contested Falkirk Feb. 1851 and Manchester July 1852. Sat for the Wick district from Dec. 1868. Accepted Chiltern Hundreds Feb. 1872. Died 18 Aug. 1877.   [1872]

LOCH, James, F.G.S.,F.S.S., and F.Z.S. 12 Albemarle Street, London. Wimbledon Common, Surrey. Athenaeum, and Reform. Eld. s. of George Loch, Esq., of Drylaw, Co. of Edinburgh, by Mary, sister of the Rt. Hon. William Adam, Lord Chief Commissioner of the Jury Court in Scotland. B. at Drylaw 1780; m. 1st, 1810, Ann, youngest d. of Patrick Orr, Esq., of Bridgeton, Kincardineshire (she died 1842); 2ndly, 1847, Elizabeth Mary, d. of J. Pearson, Esq., of Tettenhall Wood, Staffordshire, and widow of Maj. G.M. Greville (she died 1849). A Barrister at the English Bar, and an Advocate at the Scottish; a Dept.-Lieut. for Sutherland, Steward of Morpeth; Auditor to the Duke of Sutherland, the Earl of Carlisle, the Earl of Ellesmere, and to the trust estates of the late Earl of Dudley and the late Visct. Keith. A Director of the Liverpool and Manchester railway, and of the Birmingham and Liverpool Junction canal. A Member of the Society for the Diffusion of Useful Knowledge. Wrote an account of Sutherlandshire. A Liberal, opposed to all religious endowments. Voted in favour of the New Poor Law Bill. Sat for St. Germains in 1827, and for Wick district from 1830 until defeated at 1852 gen. election. Died 5 July 1855.   [1852]

LOCKE, John. 63 Eaton Place, London. 2 Harcourt Buildings, Temple, London. Reform, Oxford & Cambridge, and Garrick. Only s. of John Locke, Esq., of Herne Hill, Surrey, who was engaged in trade in Southwark. B. in London 1805; m. 1847, Laura Rosaline, d. of Col.

Thomas Alexander Cobbe, Esq. of Newbridge House, Co. Dublin. Educ. under Dr. Glennies at Dulwich, and at Trinity Coll., Cambridge, where he graduated B.A. 1829, and subsequently M.A. Called to the bar in 1833 at the Inner Temple, of which he was a Bencher, and joined the home circuit. Was one of the Common Pleaders of the City of London from 1845-June 1857, when he became a Queen's Counsel. Appointed Recorder of Brighton 1861. Author of a *Treatise on the Game Laws*, and on *Foreign Attachment*. A Liberal, in favour of household suffrage without any restriction and triennial parliaments. An unsuccessful candidate for Hastings, 1852. Sat for Southwark from Apr. 1857. MP until his death 28 Jan. 1880. [1879]

LOCKE, Joseph, F.R.S. 23 Lowndes Square, London. 28 Great George Street, Westminster, London. Reform. B. at Attercliffe, near Sheffield 1805. Was educ. at Barnsley Grammar School, Yorkshire. A Civil Engineer, extensively connected with railways; member of the Institution of Civil Engineers; Director of the Glasgow, Paisley, and Greenock Railway. Received the Legion of Honour from the King of the French in 1845. Lord of the Manor of Honiton. A Liberal, voted in favour of Lord Derby's Reform Bill, Mar. 1859, for the ballot 1853, and against Church rates 1855. First returned for Honiton in 1847 and sat until his death 18 Sept. 1860. [1860]

LOCKE, Wadham. Rowde Ford House, Wiltshire. 53 Queen Anne Street, London. A Banker of Devizes. An East India Proprietor of Whig principles, being one of the first Whig Members returned for Devizes. First sat for Devizes in 1832. MP until his death in 1835. [1835]

LOCKHART, Alexander Macdonald. Carnwath, Lanarkshire. Mount Pleasant, Berkshire. S. of Sir Alexander Macdonald-Lockhart, of Lee, Bart. B. 7th July, 1806. A Dept.-Lieut. of Lanarkshire. A Conservative. Sat for Lanarkshire from 1837. Retired at 1841 gen. election. Died 27 Oct. 1861. [1840]

LOCKHART, Allan Eliott. Borthwickbrae, Selkirkshire. Cleghorn, Lanarkshire. Carlton. S. of William Eliott Lockhart, Esq., (who represented Selkirkshire for 24 years) by Marianne, only child of Allan Lockhart, Esq., of Cleghorn, Lanarkshire. B. 1803; m. in 1830, Charlotte, 5th d. of Sir Robt. Dundas, Bart., of Beechwood. Educ. at Edinburgh University; called to the Scottish bar in 1821. A Dept.-Lieut. of Selkirkshire. Appointed Dept.-Lieut. of Roxburghshire, 1848. A Liberal-Conservative, and

said he would give Lord Derby a general support; in favour of inquiry respecting the Maynooth grant; opposed to the 40s. freehold movement in Scotland. First elected for Selkirkshire Jan. 1846. Sat until he accepted Chiltern Hundreds 1861. Lord Lieut. of Selkirkshire 19 Nov. 1867 until his death 15 Mar. 1878. [1861]

LOCKHART, William. 19 Grosvenor Street, London. Milton Lockhart, Lanarkshire. Junior United Service, and Carlton. B. 1787, the eld. s. of Rev. Dr. Lockhart (and grandson of William Lockhart, Esq., of Kirkhill), by Violet, niece and heir of James Somerville, Esq., of Corehouse. Was in the East India Company's Bengal Army, and received a medal for services in Nepal. Dean of Faculties in the University of Glasgow. A Dept.-Lieut. of Lanarkshire, and Lieut.-Col. Commandant of the Lanarkshire Regiment of Yeomanry Cavalry. 'A decided Conservative', and supported the repeal of the Maynooth Grant. Represented Lanarkshire from 1841 until he died early Jan. 1857. [1856]

LODER, Robert. 42 Grosvenor Square, London. Beach House, Worthing. Whittlebury, Towcester, Northamptonshire. Carlton. S. of Giles Loder, Esq., of Wilsford House, Salisbury, by Elizabeth, d. of John Higginbotham, Esq., of St. Petersburg. B. at St. Petersburg 1823; m. 1847, 4th d. of Hans Busk, Esq., of Great Cumberland Place, London, and Culverdens, Tunbridge Wells. Educ. at Emmanuel Coll., Cambridge. Was High Sheriff for Sussex in 1877, and was a Magistrate and Dept.-Lieut. for Sussex and Northamptonshire. Patron of 1 living. A Conservative, and 'always maintained the cause of our National Church', in favour of the amendment of the system of local taxation. Sat for Shoreham from Apr. 1880. Retired in 1885. Created Baronet July 1887. Died 27 May 1888. [1885]

LOFTUS, Visct. A Protectionist. Contested Gloucester 29 July 1841. Returned for Woodstock 1 May 1845. Succeeded as 3rd Marq. of Ely in Sept. 1845. Died 15 July 1857.

LOGAN, Robert Hart. Kentwell Hall, Suffolk. M. 1818 to Nancy, d. and co-heiress of Robert Service, Esq., a London Merchant. A Magistrate and Dept.-Lieut. for Suffolk and served the office of High Sheriff of it in 1828. Unsuccessfully contested Suffolk W. at the general election in 1835, but came in at the head of the poll in 1837. A Conservative and altogether unpledged. MP until his death in 1838. [1838]

LONG, Richard Penruddocke. 20 Curzon

242

Street, London. Dolforgan, Newtown, Montgomeryshire. National, and Carlton. S. of Walter Long, Esq., of Rood Ashton, 30 years MP for N. Wiltshire, by his 1st wife, Mary Anne, d. of the Rt. Hon. Archibald Colquhoun, of Killermount and Garscadden, Scotland. B. at Baynton House, Wiltshire, 1825; m. 1853, Charlotte Anna, only surviving d. of W.W. Fitzwilliam Dick Esq., MP, of Hume Wood, Co. Wicklow. Educ. at Harrow, and at Trinity Coll. Cambridge. A Magistrate for Wiltshire, and a Magistrate and Dept.-Lieut. for Montgomeryshire, for which co. he was High Sheriff 1858. A Liberal-Conservative, supported 'any measure which would admit to the privileges of the franchise the steady, sober, and intelligent portion of the working classes.' Contested Wiltshire S. 16 July 1852. Sat for Chippenham from May 1859 till July 1865, when he was elected for Wiltshire N. Retired in 1868. Died 16 Feb. 1875.   [1867]

LONG, Walter. 29 Hill Street, London. Rood Ashton, and South Wraxall, Wiltshire. Dolevorgan, Newtown, Montgomeryshire. Carlton, Conservative, and National. Eld. s. of Richard Godolphin Lond, Esq., of Rood Ashton, formerly Member for Wiltshire, by Florentina, d. of Sir Bourchier Wrey, Bart. B. 1793; m. 1st, 1819, Mary Anne, d. of the Rt. Hon. Archibald Colquhoun, Lord Registrar of Scotland (she died 1856); 2ndly, 1857, Lady Bishopp, eld. d. of Admiral Sir James Hillyar, K.C.B., and relict of Sir Cecil Bishopp, Bart. Patron of 5 livings. A Magistrate of Wiltshire and Somerset; Dept.-Lieut. of Wiltshire and Major in the Royal Wiltshire Yeomanry Cavalry. Appointed Dept.-Lieut. of Montgomery 1852. A Conservative, voted for inquiry into Maynooth 1853. Contested Hampshire N. 14 Dec. 1832. Sat for Wiltshire N. from 1835 until he retired 1865. Died 31 Jan. 1867.   [1865]

LONG, W.H. Continued in House after 1885: full entry in Volume II.

LONGFIELD, Richard. 3 George Street, Pall Mall, London. Longueville, Mallow. Eld. s. of John Longfield, Esq., of Longueville, (formerly MP for Mallow) and of Miss Elizabeth Foster, 1st cousin of Lord Oriel. B. 1767; m. 1797, Eleanor, only d. of John Lucas, Esq., of Mount Lucas, Kings Co. A retired Lieut.-Col. in the army; a Magistrate for the Co. of Cork, for which he was Sheriff in 1829. A Conservative. Unsuccessfully contested Cork Co. in Jan. 1835, but was seated on petition after an opponent Mr. O'Connor was disqualified. Unsuccessfully contested the seat again in Aug. 1837.   [1836]

LONGFIELD, Robert. Merrion Square, Dublin. S. of the Rev. M. Longfield, Rector of Desertserge, Co. Cork, by Grace, d. of—Lysaght, Esq. B. in the Co. of Cork 1810; m. 1840, Charlotte, d. of George Standell, Esq., of Crobeg, Co. Cork. Graduated at Trinity Coll., Dublin, where he obtained several honours during his undergraduate course. Called to the bar in Ireland 1834, and made a Queen's Counsel 1852. Published several legal works, particularly on the law of landlord and tenant. A Liberal-Conservative, and in favour of Lord Derby's policy. First elected for Mallow May 1859. Sat until he retired 1865. Died 27 Apr. 1868.   [1865]

LOPES, Henry Charles. 8 Cromwell Place, South Kensington, London. 2 Paper Buildings, Temple, London. Easthill, Frome, Somerset. Carlton, Conservative, and St. Stephen's. 3rd s. of Sir Ralph Lopes, 2nd Bart., of Maristow, Devon, by Susan Gibb, eld. d. of A. Ludlow, Esq., of Heywood House, Wiltshire. B. at Devonport 1828, m. 1854, Cordelia Lucy, eld. d. of Irving Clark Esq., of Efford Manor, Nr. Plymouth Educ. at Winchester and at Balliol Coll., Oxford. Graduated B.A. Was called to the bar at the Inner Temple 1852 and joined the Western circuit. Appointed a Queen's Counsel 1869. A Magistrate for Wiltshire. Appointed Recorder of Exeter May 1867. A Conservative, voted against the disestablishment of the Irish Church 1869. Sat for Launceston from Apr. 1868. to Feb. 1874. Sat for Frome from the latter date until appointed judge in 1876.   [1876]

LOPES, Sir Massey, Bart. 28 Grosvenor Gardens, London. Maristow House, Roborough, and Burrator, South Devon. Manor House, Westbury. Carlton, Conservative, and St. Stephen's. Eld. s. of Sir Ralph Lopes, 4th Bart. (who assumed the name of Lopes in lieu of his patronymic Franco, and who represented Devon South for several years) by Susan, eld. d. of A. Ludlow, Esq., of Heywood House, Wiltshire. B. 1818; m. 1st, 1854, Bertha, only d. of 1st Lord Churston (she died 1872); 2ndly, 1874, Louisa, d. of Sir R.W. Newman, Bart., of Manhead, Devon, Educ. at Oriel Coll., Oxford, where he graduated B.A. 1842 (4th class in classics) M.A. 1845. Was Capt. 2nd Devon Militia. Was a Lord of the Admiralty from Feb. 1874 to Apr. 1880. Became Dept.-Lieut. of Devon 1855. Patron of 3 livings. A Liberal-Conservative, in favour of readjustment of taxation so that local burdens could be relieved out of the Imperial funds. Sat for Westbury from Apr. 1857 to Dec. 1868, when he sat for South Devon. Sat until he retired in 1885. Died 20 Jan. 1908.   [1885]

LOPES, Sir Ralph, Bart. 46 Upper Grosvenor Street, London. Maristow, Devon. Westbury, Wiltshire. Carlton. B. 1788, the s. of A. Franco, Esq., a London Merchant, by the d. of Mordecai Rodrigues Lopes, Esq., of Clapham. Nephew to Sir Manasseh Lopes, 1st Bart., who was of a Jamaica family. Upon his uncle's death in 1831, he succeeded to the Baronetcy, pursuant to the patent of creation, and in 1832 assumed the name of Lopes. M. 1817, Susan, eld. d. of A. Ludlow, Esq., of Heywood House, Wiltshire. Educ. at Winchester and at Brasenose Coll., Oxford, where he obtained honours. An East India Proprietor, and patron of 3 livings. A Magistrate and Dept.-Lieut. of Wiltshire and Devon, and appointed a Special Deputy Warden of the Stannaries 1852. A Conservative, voted for agricultural protection 1846, was in favour of 'a more equitable adjustment of the burdens which now press so unfairly on one interest'. Opposed to the admission of Jews to Parliament and to the Maynooth Grant. Sat for Westbury from 1814-19, from 1831-37, when he was unsuccessful, and from 1841-47. Sat for Devon S. from Jan. 1849 until his death on 26 Jan. 1854. [1853]

LORNE, Rt. Hon. Marq. of. Continued in House after 1885: full entry in Volume II.

LOVAINE, Rt. Hon. Lord. 11 Portman Square, London. Aldbury Park, Guildford. Travellers'. Eld. s. of the 2nd Earl of Beverley (heir-presumptive of the 4th Duke of Northumberland), by Louisa Harcourt, 3rd d. of the Hon. James Archibald Stuart-Wortley, and sister of the 1st Lord Wharncliffe. B. in London 1810; m. 1845, Louisa, eld. d. of Henry Drummond, Esq., of Albury Park, Surrey. Received the Honorary degree of LL.D from Cambridge in 1842. A Magistrate for Northumberland. Was formerly in the Grenadier Guards. Appointed Maj. in the Northumberland Militia, and Dept.-Lieut. of the same Co. 1852; Hon. Col. of the Northumberland Artillery Volunteers 1862; was a Lord of the Admiralty from Mar. 1858-Mar. 1859, and Vice-President of the Board of Trade from the last date until June following. A Conservative, and a supporter generally of Lord Derby's policy; said he would maintain 'the essentially Protestant character of our Constitution.' Was an unsuccessful candidate for Exeter June 1841, and for Northumberland N. Aug. 1847; first returned for the latter place July 1852. Sat until he retired 1865. Lord Privy Seal 1878-80. Succeeded as 6th Duke Aug. 1867. Died 2 Jan. 1899. [1865]

LOVENDEN, Pryse. Gogerddan and Lodge Park, Cardiganshire. Buscot Park, Berkshire. Woodstock, Oxfordshire. Brooks's. B. at Woodstock 1815, the eld. s. of Pryse Pryse [sic], MP for Cardigan 1818-49, by his 2nd wife, d. of Peter Cavallier, of Guisborough, Yorkshire. M. 1836, Margaretta Jane, 3rd. d. of Walter Rice of Llwyn-y-Brain, Carmarthenshire. Assumed the name of Lovenden in lieu of Pryse by royal license July 1849 (his father having assumed the name Pryse in lieu of Lovenden 1798). Patron of 2 livings. A Liberal, voted for the ballot 1853. Sat for the Cardigan district Feb. 1849 until his death in Jan. or Feb. 1855. [1854]

LOWE, Rt. Hon. Robert. 34 Lowndes Square, London. Caterham, Redhill, Surrey. Reform. S. of the Rev. Robert Lowe, Rector of Bingham, Nottinghamshire, by Ellen, 2nd d. of the Rev. Reginald Pynder, Rector of Madresfield, Worcestershire. B. at Bingham, Nottinghamshire 1811; m 1836, Georgiana, 2nd d. of George Orred, Esq., of Aigburth House, Nr. Liverpool. Educ. at Winchester and at University Coll., Oxford, where he was 1st class in classics and 2nd class in mathematics 1833, was elected fellow of Magdalen in 1835, and became well known as a private tutor at Oxford, created honorary D.C.L. 1870. Called to the bar at Lincoln's Inn, Jan. 1842, went to Australia in that year, sat in the Council from 1843-1850, and was elected member for Sydney in 1848, returned to England in 1850. Was one of the joint Secretaries to the Board of Control from Dec. 1852-Feb. 1855, and Vice-President of the Board of Trade, and Paymaster-Gen. from Aug. 1855-Mar. 1858. Also President of the Board of Health and Vice-President of the Education Board of the Privy Council from June 1859-Apr. 1864, and Chancellor of the Exchequer from Dec. 1868-Aug. 1873. Sec. for the Home Dept. from Aug. 1873-Feb. 1874. A Member of the Senate of London University, and was created LL.D. at Edinburgh 1867. Presented with the freedom of the city of Glasgow 1872. A Liberal, voted against Lord Russell's Reform Bill 1866. Sat for Kidderminster from July 1852-May 1859; for Calne from the latter date until Dec. 1868; and from then for London University. Sat until created 1st Visct. Sherbrooke May 1880. Died 27 July 1892. [1880]

LOWTHER, Col. Henry. 21 Wilton Crescent, London. Whitehaven Castle, Cumberland. Carlton, and Boodle's. Eld. s. of the Hon. Henry Cecil Lowther by Lady Lucy, d. of the 5th Earl of Harborough. Heir pres. to the Earl of Lonsdale. B. 1818; m. 1852, Emily Susan, eld. d. of St. George Caulfeild, Esq., of Dunamon Castle, Co. Roscommon. Educ. at Westminster and at Trinity Coll., Cambridge, where he graduated M.A. 1838; entered the army as Cornet and Sub-Lieut. in 1st Life Guards in 1841; became Capt. 1849 and retired 1854. Appointed Lord Lieut. of Cumberland and Westmoreland 1868. A Conservative, voted against the disestablishment of the Irish Church 1869. First returned for Cumberland W. in 1847, without opposition. Sat until he succeeded uncle as 3rd Earl of Lonsdale March 1872. Died 15 Aug. 1876. [1871]

LOWTHER, Hon. Henry Cecil. 31 Bruton Street, London. Barleythorpe Hall, Oakham. Lowther Castle, Penrith, Cumberland. Carlton, Conservative, and Boodle's. B. in Dover Street, London 1790, the 2nd s. of 1st Earl of Lonsdale, by the eld. d. of 9th Earl of Westmoreland. M. 1817, Lady Lucy Eleanor, d. of 5th Earl of Harborough (she died 1848). Col. of the Cumberland Militia. Appointed Dept.-Lieut. of Rutland 1852. Was in 7th Hussars as Major, and a Lieut.-Col. in the army. Served in Spain under Sir John Moore and in the Peninsular War. Of Conservative principles. Prepared to 'uphold the Church and the Throne in their old authority', and opposed to 'all Romish claims and grants.' Sat for Westmoreland from 1812 until he died 6 Dec. 1867. [1867]

LOWTHER, Rt. Hon. Visct.H.C. 15 Carlton Terrace, London. Whitehaven Castle, Cumberland. Carlton. Eld. s. of the Earl of Lonsdale, b. 1787. Lieutenant-Colonel of the Westmoreland Militia; was chief commissioner of Woods and Forests under the Wellington Administration. Treasurer of the Navy and Vice-President of the Board of Trade from Dec. 1834 till Apr. 1835. A Conservative. Sat for Westmoreland from 1832-41 when summoned to the Lords as Baron Lowther. He had been returned for Cockermouth in 1808, Westmoreland in 1813, and Dunwich Feb.-Dec. 1832. Postmaster-General 1841-46. Succeeded as 2nd Earl of Lonsdale in Mar. 1844. Lord President 1852. Died 4 Mar. 1872. [1841]

LOWTHER, Rt. Hon. J. Continued in House after 1885: full entry in Volume II.

LOWTHER, Sir John Henry, Bart. 32 Grosvenor Square, London. Swillington Hall, Yorkshire. Carlton. Eld. s. of Sir John Lowther, Bart., and nephew of the Earl of Lonsdale, B. 1793. A Conservative, voted for agricultural protection 1846. Sat for Wigton in several Parliaments. Contested York City unsuccessfully in 1832 and 1833; sat for it from 1835. Sat until he retired 1847. Died 23 June 1868. [1847]

LOWTHER, J.W. Continued in House after 1885: full entry in Volume II.

LOWTHER, Hon. W. Continued in House after 1885: full entry in Volume II.

LUBBOCK, Sir J. Continued in House after 1885: full entry in Volume II.

LUCAS, Edward. Castle Shane, Monaghan, Carlton. B. 1787; m. Anne, 2nd d. of W. Ruxton, Esq., of Ardee House, many years Member of the Irish House of Commons. Members of his family had frequently represented Monaghan. A Conservative. Contested Monaghan unsuccessfully in May 1834, on the accession of Mr. (later Lord) Blayney to the Peerage; was seated on petition in the room of his opponent, the Hon. H.R. Westenra. Sat until he retired 1841. Under Secretary of State for Ireland 1841-Aug. 1845. Died 12 Nov. 1871. [1841]

LUCAS, Frederick. 30 Norfolk Street, Strand, London. 21 Hardwicke Street, Dublin. B.in Westminster 1812, the s. of Samuel N. Lucas, Esq., of Croham, near Croydon, and then Brighton.' M. 1840, Elizabeth, eld. d. of the late William Asbly, Esq., of Staines, Middlesex. Educ. at University Coll., London. Called to the bar at the Middle Temple 1838. Proprietor and Editor of the *Tablet* newspaper in London from 1840-49, and in Dublin from 1850. Author of *Reasons for Becoming a Roman Catholic,* articles in the *Dublin Review* etc. Was one of the Secretaries of the Irish Tenant League during the greater part of its existence. A Liberal, favoured free trade with some limitations, vote by ballot, repeal of the union with Ireland, the fullest extension of the docrine of 'tenant-right', a severance of Church and State, etc., 'and enemy to the pretended separation of religious from secular education, and of all schemes for compelling or allowing persons of different religions to be educated in the same school.' Sat for Meath from July 1852 until he died 22 Oct. 1855. [1855]

LUCE, Thomas. Malmesbury, Wiltshire. Oriental. S of Thomas Luce, Esq., B. at Weymouth 1790; m. 1820, Susan, d. of William Hollis, Esq., of Mounton, Monmouthshire. Was a Banker from 1813. A Magistrate of Wiltshire from 1836. A Liberal. First returned for Malmesbury in July 1852. Sat until he retired in 1859. Died 6 Aug. 1875. [1858]

LUMLEY, Lord Visct. 26 Dorset Square, London. Brandon Hall, Suffolk. Eld. s. of the Earl of Scarborough. A Reformer. Sat for Nottinghamshire N. from 1826 until he succeeded as 8th Earl 1835. Died 5 Dec. 1884. [1833]

LUSH, John Alfred. 123 Cambridge Street, Pimlico, London. Fisherton House, Salisbury. S.

of John Lush, Esq., of Berwick St. John, Wiltshire, by his marriage with Miss Martha Kellaway, of Donhead St. Andrew's, Wiltshire. B. at Handley, Dorset 1815; m. 1853, Sarah Martha, eld. d. of Dr. W.C. Finch of Fisherton House, Salisbury and St. Andrew's, Wiltshire. Educ. at Shaftesbury. Became a member of the Coll. of Surgeons, England 1837, and M.D. St. Andrew's University 1864. An Alderman of Salisbury, and was Mayor 1867 of that town. A Liberal. Sat for Salisbury from Dec. 1868 until he retired 1880. Died 4 Aug. 1888. [1880]

LUSHINGTON, Charles. 1 Palace Gardens, Bayswater, London. Athenaeum, and Reform. Youngest s. of Sir Stephen Lushington, Bart., of South Hill Park, Berkshire, by the d. of John Boldero, Esq., of Aspeden Hall, Hertforshire; was therefore bro. to Dr. Lushington. B. in London 1785; m. 1st, Sarah, d. of Lieut.-Col. Joseph Gascoyne; 2ndly, Julia, relict of Thomas Teed, Esq., of Stanmore Hall, Middlesex. Was formerly Chief Secretary to the government of Bengal. Author of *A Remonstrance to the Bishop of London on behalf of the Dissenters*. A radical Reformer, in favour of the ballot, extension of the suffrage, triennial parliaments, and the substitution of a property for the income tax; opposed to all religious endowments. Represented Ashburton from 1835-1841. First returned for Westminster in 1847 and sat until he retired 1852. Died 23 Sept. 1866. [1852]

LUSHINGTON, Charles Manners. 9 Mansfield Street. Travellers'. 6th s. of the Rt. Hon. Stephen Rumbold Lushington, of Norton Court, Kent (who sat for Canterbury for many years), by Anne Elizabeth, eld. d. of 1st Lord Harris. B. 1819; m. 1846, Henrietta, eld. sister of Sir Stafford H. Northcote, Bart., of Pynes, Devon. Educ. at Eton and Oriel Coll., Oxford; was subsequently a Fellow of All Souls' Coll. Was Private Sec. to the President of the Board of Control from 1843-July 1854. A 'Liberal-Conservative', in favour of the reform of abuses in the Church, but not of its separation from the State, nor of the voluntary system; also in favour of sanitary and other education, and the moderate extension of the franchise. First returned for Canterbury Aug. 1854. Retired 1857. Contested Norwich 29 Apr. 1859. Died 27 Nov. 1864. [1857]

LUSHINGTON, Stephen, D.C.L. 2 Great George Street, London. Mery Hill, Hertfordshire. Reform. 2nd s. of Sir S. Lushington, Bart. B. 1782. A Judge of the Consistory Court, Chancellor of the Dioceses of London and Rochester, and official to the Archdeacon and Commissary of Westminster, Essex and Hert-

fordshire and the Deaneries of Essex and Barking. A Commissioner for building churches. A Reformer, in favour of the repeal of the taxes on knowledge and of the Septennial act; also in favour of the ballot, the revision of the corn laws and general reform. Sat for Winchelsea in the Parliaments of 1830 and 1831; before that for Tregony, Ilchester and other boroughs, Sat for Tower Hamlets from 1832 until he retired 1841. Dean of Arches 1858-67; served on many royal commissions. Died 19 Jan 1873. [1838]

LUSHINGTON, Rt.Hon. Stephen Rumbold. Norton Court, Kent. Carlton. 4th s. of Rev. J.S. Lushington, of Rodmersham, Kent, Prebendary of Carlisle, by his 2nd wife. B. 1776; m. 1798, Anne Elizabeth, d. of George, first Lord Harris. Was Member for Canterbury in several Parliaments before 1830. Was Joint-Secretary of the Treasury under the Liverpool Administration. Went to India in 1826, as Governor of Madras, without resigning his seat. For this, was petitioned against, but the house decided that it could not interfere. Having returned home, he contested Canterbury in 1835, with Mr. Frederick Villiers, and was defeated, but on petition, unseated his antagonist. A Conservative. Retired in 1837. Died 5 Aug. 1868. [1836]

LUSK, Sir Andrew, Bart. 15 Sussex Square, London. Reform, and City Liberal. S. of Mr. John Lusk, of the Co. of Ayr, by Margaret, d. of Mr. John Earl, of Knockdolian. B. at Ayr, Scotland, 1812; m. 1848, Eliza, d. of James Potter, Esq., of Grahamstown, Falkirk. A Merchant in London, head of the firm of Messrs. Andrew Lusk and Co., Fenchurch Street and Wapping. A Magistrate for Middlesex, a Commissioner of Lieutenancy for London, and an Alderman of London. Was Sheriff of London and Middlesex 1861. Lord Mayor of London 1873-74. A Liberal, in favour of short parliaments, the abolition of church rates, the lowering of the county franchise, and the readjustment of local taxation. Sat for Finsbury from July 1865 until he retired in 1885. Died 21 July 1909. [1885]

LYALL, George, sen. 17 Park Crescent, Regent's Park, London. Nutwood Lodge, Sussex. City, and Union. S. of John Lyall, Esq., of London. B. 1784. A Merchant and Shipowner. Chairman of the Hon. East India Company, a Director of the London Docks, and Chairman of the Indemnity Assurance Company. A Conservative, but in favour of free trade. Member for the City of London. Stood unsuccessfully in 1832; returned 27 Feb. 1833; defeated 1835; returned 1841, and sat until he retired 1847. Died 1 Sept. 1853. [1847]

LYALL, George, jun. 17 Park Crescent, Regent's Park, London. Hedley House, Epsom, Surrey. Carlton, and Union. Eld. surviving s. of George Lyall, Esq., a London Merchant, many years MP for London. B. in London 1819; m. 1st, Eleanor Harriet, only child of Rev. J. Manley (she died 1853); 2ndly, Frances, eld. d. of D. Cave, Esq., of Cleve Hill, Gloucestershire. Educ. at Winchester and Geneva. A Director of the Bank of England. A Magistrate for Surrey, and a Commissioner of Lieutenancy for London. A Conservative, but would not oppose a moderate measure of Parliamentary Reform. First elected for Whitehaven Dec. 1857. Sat until he retired 1865. Governor Bank of England 1871-73. Died 12 Oct. 1881. [1865]

LYGON, Hon. Frederick F.S.A. 19 Grosvenor Place, London. Madresfield Court, Worcester. Carlton, and Junior Carlton. B. 1830, the 2nd s. of 4th Earl Beauchamp, by 2nd d. of 2nd Earl of St. Germans. Educ. at Eton and at Christ Church, Oxford. Elected Fellow of All Souls' Coll. 1852. Was a Lord of the Admiralty from Mar.-June 1859. Appointed Dept.-Lieut. of Worcestershire and Capt. Worcestershire Yeomanry Cavalry in 1854. A Conservative, opposed to 'an aggressive foreign policy.' Sat for Tewkesbury April 1857-Oct. 1863, and for Worcestershire West from 1863 until March 1866, when he succeeded his bro. as 6th Earl Beauchamp. Died 19 Feb. 1891. [1865]

LYGON, Hon. Henry Beauchamp. 16 Grosvenor Place, London. Springhill, Worcestershire. Carlton. 3rd s. of 1st Earl of Beauchamp, by the only d. of James Denn, Esq., m. 1824, Lady Susan-Caroline, 2nd d. of 2nd Earl of St. Germans. A Lieut.-Gen. in the army, and Col. of 10th Hussars. A Conservative, voted for agricultural protection 1846; said he would 'give Lord Derby his most cordial support.' First sat for Worcestershire W. from 1817, with the exception of the Parliament of 1831, when he was defeated by the Hon. Capt. Spencer. Sat until he succeeded his brother as 4th Earl Beauchamp, Jan. 1853. [1852 2nd ed.]

LYMINGTON, Visct. Continued in House after 1885: full entry in Volume II.

LYNCH, Andrew Henry. 33 Queen's Street, Bloomsbury, London. 2 New Square, Lincoln's Inn, London. Reform. M. d. of Charles Butler, Esq., the Conveyancer, Editor of *Coke on Lyttleton,* and opponent of Dr. Southey. A native of the town of Galway; a Barrister practising at the English Chancery bar. A Repealer. Sat for Galway from 1832. Was appointed Master in Chancery in 1838 and re-elected for the borough. Sat until he retired 1841. [1838]

LYNCH, Nicholas. 20 Wicklow Street, Dublin. S. of Thomas Lynch, Esq. B. in Dublin 1827. Unmarried. A Director of the Hibernian Bank, Dublin. A Nationalist and Home Ruler. Sat for Sligo Co. from Aug. 1883. Retired in 1885. [1885]

LYONS, Francis. Cork. Queenstown, Nr. Cork, Ireland. S. of Thomas Lyons, Esq. of Cork, by Mary, d. of—Hackett, Esq. B. at Cork 1798; m. Ellen, d. of David Cagney, Esq., of Cork. Educ. at the Universities of Paris and Edinburgh, and graduated M.D. at the latter in 1822, but never practised. A Magistrate and Dept.-Lieut. of Cork. Of 'very Liberal' opinions. First elected for Cork June 1859. MP until his death in 1862. [1861]

LYONS, Robert Dyer. 17 St. James's Place, London. 8 Merrion Square, West Dublin. Croom Castle, Limerick. Woodtown House, Co. Dublin. S. of Sir William Lyons, Mayor and High Sheriff of Cork, by Harriet, d. of Spencer Dyer, Esq., of Kensale. B. at Glanmire, Cork, 1826; m. 1856, Maria, eld. d. of Rt. Hon. David R. Pigot, Lord Chief Baron of the Exchequer in Ireland. Was educ. at Messrs. Hamblin and Porter's School and at Trinity Coll., Dublin, where he graduated M.B. 1848. A Fellow of the College of Physicians, Ireland. Was Pathologist-in-Chief to the Army in the Crimea 1855-56, Commissioner to Portugal on the Yellow Fever Epidemic 1857. Physician to the Richmond, Whitworth, and Hardwicke Hospitals, Dublin. Wrote several medical official reports, including *Report on the Diseases of the Army in the Crimea;* also *Treatises on Fevers, Hospital Practice,* etc. A Liberal, independent, and not pledged to support the system call 'Home Rule' for Ireland. In favour of the creation of a 'peasant proprietary' by the aid of State loans, of the reform of the Grand Jury Laws, etc. Sat for Dublin from Apr. 1880 until he retired in 1885. Died 19 Dec. 1886. [1885]

LYSLEY, William John. 23 Prince's Gardens, London. Pewsham, Chippenham, Wiltshire. Athenaeum. Only s. of William Lysley, Esq., of Warmfield, Yorkshire, (descended from the family of Lyley, of Rothwell, Kirkheaton, Mirfield, and Lyley, in the same Co.), by Anne, d. of William Barker, Esq., of Wakefield. B. 1791; m. 1828, Caroline, d. of John Marshall, Esq., of Ardwick House, Lancashire. Called to the bar at the Inner Temple 1825 and joined the Northern Circuit. Was High Sheriff in 1851 for Hertfordshire, of which also he was a Magistrate and Dept.-Lieut. A Liberal, and would 'at all times be found an earnest advocate for the wider diffusion of education, on which sound foundation the extension of the franchise will most suitably be based.' Unsuccessfully contested Chippenham in 1841 and 1857; first elected Apr. 1859 for Chippenham. Sat until defeated 1865. Died 14 Jan. 1873. [1865]

LYTTLETON, Hon. Charles George. Hagley Park, Stourbridge, Worcestershire. B. at Hagley Park 1842, the eld. s. of Lord Lyttleton, by Mary, 2nd d. of Sir Stephen Glynne, Bart. Appointed Lieut. Worcestershire Yeomanry Cavalry 1863. A Liberal, and generally supported Gladstone. Voted for the disestablishment of the Irish Church 1869, and favoured a repeal of the rate paying clause of the Reform Act. Sat for East Worcestershire from Apr. 1868 until his defeat in 1874. Succeeded as 5th Baron Apr. 1876. [1873]

LYTTON, Rt. Hon. Sir Edward George Earle Lytton Bulwer-, Bart. 1 Park Lane, London. Knebworth, Stevenage, Hertfordshire. Craven Lodge, Fulham. Carlton. 3rd s. of Gen. William Earle Bulwer, of Woodalling and Heydon Hall, Norfolk, by Elizabeth Barbara, the d. and heir of Richard Warburton Lytton, Esq., of Knebworth, Hertfordshire (who resumed her paternal name of Lytton by royal licence 1811). B. 1805; m. 1827, Rosina, only surviving d. of Francis Wheeler, Esq., of Lizzard Connell, Co. Limerick. Educ. at Trinity Hall, Cambridge, where he gained the Chancellor's prize medal for the best English poem, and graduated B.A. 1826, M.A. 1835. Assumed the additional name of Lytton after that of Bulwer by royal licence in 1844. Was Sec. of State for the Colonies from June 1858-June 1859. Dept.-Lieut. of Hertfordshire from 1851. Elected Rector of the University of Glasgow 1856. Author of numerous well-known novels, dramatic works, and poems. Concurred 'in the general policy of Lord Derby'; earlier 'advocated the ballot', but seeing its 'utter inefficacy in France and America, [could] no longer defend that theory'; said he would support education on a religious basis, and vote for a repeal of the Maynooth Grant. Sat for St. Ives in 1831, and for Lincoln from 1832-1841; was an unsuccessful candidate at the latter place in June 1841 and July 1847. First returned for Hertfordshire in July 1852. Sat until created Baron Lytton July 1866. G.C.M.G 1870. Died 18 Jan. 1873. [1865]

MABERLEY, Lieut.-Col. William Leader. 23 Upper Berkeley Street, London. Clerk of the Ordnance, and as such a Member of the Government. This gentleman was the s. of the Member for Abingdon, John Maberley, Esq., an Aberdeen and London Banker, Manufacturer, and Contractor. The Anti-slavery Agency Society advertised him as opposed to the abolition of slavery, as elsewhere defined. He sat for Westbury in 1819, and for Northampton from 1820 to 1830, when he was not returned at all; in the 1831 Parliament he sat for Shaftesbury. Contested Abingdon 10 Dec. 1832. Sat for Chatham from 1832. Accepted Chiltern Hundreds in 1834 on appointment as Commissioner of Customs. Secretary General of Post Office 1836; Permanent Secretary 1846-54; opposed to all schemes of postal reform. Died 6 Feb. 1885. [1833]

McARTHUR, Alex. Continued in House after 1885: full entry in Volume II.

McARTHUR, Sir William K.C.M.G., F.R.G.S. 79 Holland Park, London. Reform, City, City Liberal, and National Liberal. S. of the Rev. John McArthur, of Londonderry. B. at Londonderry, Ireland. Was formerly an Alderman of Londonderry, where he was for many years engaged in commerce, and whence in 1857 he removed to London. Was Sheriff of London and Middlesex in 1867-68, and an Alderman of London from 1872. Was Lord Mayor of London for 1880-81. A Commissioner of Lieutenancy for London. A Magistrate for Surrey. A Merchant in London largely engaged in the Australian trade, having houses of business in Sydney, Melbourne, and Auckland. Chairman of the Star Assurance Society, Director of the City Bank. Unsuccessfully contested Pontefract in 1865. Sat for Lambeth from Dec. 1868 until defeated in 1885 contesting Newington West. [1885]

McCANCE, J. A Reformer. Member for Belfast from 1832 until his death in 1835. [1835]

McCANN, James. Staleen House, Drogheda. Sheriff of Drogheda in 1851-2. A Liberal in favour of household suffrage, triennial Parliaments, vote by ballot, national education, and tenant right in Ireland; supported the vote of censure on Lord Palmerston 1864. First returned for Drogheda July 1852. Sat until he retired 1865. [1865]

McCARTHY, Alexander. Currymount, Cork. Called to the bar in Ireland 1826. A Liberal, and a member of the 'Repeal' party. Was an unsuccessful candidate for Limerick in 1832. Sat for Cork city from Jan. 1846 to July 1847; was unsuccessful there in the last-named year, and in Nov. 1849. First elected for Cork Co. Apr. 1857. Retired in 1859. Contested Dublin 3 May 1859. [1858]

McCARTHY, John George. 2 Savile Row, London. Harbour View, Cork. S. of John McCarthy, Esq., of Cork, Merchant, by Jane, d.

of George O'Driscoll, Esq., Distiller, of Cork. B. at Cork 1829; m. 1859, Maria Josephine, d. of John Hanrahan, Esq., of Mount Prospect, Cork. Educ. at St. Vincent's, Cork. A Solicitor and Land Agent from 1853. Author of *The Irish Land Question plainly stated and answered* (1872), *Plea for the Home Government of Ireland* (1873), *History of Cork, Guide to the Land Act*, etc. A Liberal, in favour of 'Home Government for Ireland', denominational education, and the extension of 'the Ulster tenant-right' to the rest of Ireland. Sat from Feb. 1874 for Mallow, which he had unsuccessfully contested June 1872. Retired 1880.
[1880]

McCARTHY, Justin. Continued in House after 1885: full entry in Volume II.

McCARTHY, J.H. Continued in House after 1885: full entry in Volume II.

MACARTNEY, George. 46 Duke Street, St. James's, London. Bourton Lodge, Nr. Rugby. Lissanoure, Ballymoney, Co. Antrim. Lowther Lodge, Balbriggan, Co. Dublin. Carlton, and National. S. of the Rev. Dr. Travers Hume, by Elizabeth, d. of John Balaguier, Esq., niece (and adopted d.) of Earl Macartney. B. in Dublin, 1793; m. 1828, Ellen, only d. and heir of Townley Patten Filgate, Esq., of Lowther Lodge, Co. Dublin. Educ. at Trinity Coll., Dublin. Assumed the name of Macartney in lieu of his patronymic Hume, in compliance with the will of his grand--uncle, the Earl. A Magistrate and Dept.-Lieut. of Antrim. A Conservative, voted for inquiry into Maynooth, 1853. First returned for Antrim July, 1852. Accepted Chiltern Hundreds in 1858.
[1858]

MACARTNEY, John William Ellison-. 74 Buckingham Park Road, London. Clogher Park, Clogis, Co. Tyrone. Carlton, and St. Stephen's. Only s. of the Rev. Thomas Ellison, by Catherine, 2nd d. of Arthur Chichester Macartney, Esq., of Murlough, Co. Down. B. 1818; m. 1851, Elizabeth Phoebe, eld. surviving d. of the Rev. John Grey Porter. Assumed in 1859 the name of Macartney in addition to his patronymic. Was educ. in Germany. Called to the bar at the Middle Temple June 1846, and to the bar in Ireland Sept. 1848. A Magistrate for the Co. of Tyrone, and was High Sheriff for the Co. of Armagh 1870. A Conservative. Sat from Feb. 1874 for Tyrone (which he unsuccessfully contested March 1873) until he retired in 1885. Died 13 Feb. 1904. [1885]

MACAULAY, Kenneth. 48 Cadogan Place, London. Oxford & Cambridge. Youngest s. of the Rev. Aulay Macaulay, Vicar of Rothley,

Leicestershire, and first cousin of Lord Macaulay. B. at Rothley 1815; m. 1843, Harriet, only d. of William Woollcombe, Esq., M.D. Educ. at Jesus Coll., Cambridge, where he graduated M.A. 1839. Called to the bar at the Inner Temple 1839, and was a Bencher; was made a Queen's Counsel by patent, Feb. 1850. The leader of the Midland Circuit. A Conservative. Sat for Cambridge bor. from July 1852 to Mar. 1853, when the election was declared void for bribery; again returned in Mar. 1857. Sat until he retired 1865. Died 29 July 1867. [1865]

MACAULAY, Rt. Hon. Thomas Babington. 3F, Albany, London. Reform. B. at Rothley Temple, Leicestershire, 1800, the s. of Zachary Macaulay, Esq. Graduated at Trinity Coll., Cambridge, B.A. 1822, M.A. 1825; and elected to the Craven Scholarship 1821. Became a Fellow of Trinity, 1822. Was called to the bar at Lincoln's Inn, Feb. 1826, and elected a Bencher 1849. Received the Prussian Order of Merit 1853. Was Commissioner of Bankrupts; a Commissioner and Sec. of the Board of Control; 5th member of, and a legal advisor to, the Supreme Council in India. Was Sec. at War from 1839-Sept. 1841, and Paymaster Gen. of the Forces from July 1846-48. Elected Lord Rector of the University of Glasgow 1848, and Professor of Ancient History in the Royal Academy 1850. Author of several articles in the *Edinburgh Review*, the *Lays of Ancient Rome, The History of England from the Accession of James II*, etc. A Liberal, voted in favour of the ballot. Sat for Calne 1830-32, for Leeds 1832-34, and for Edinburgh 1840-47, when he was unsuccessful in seeking re-election. Re-chosen in July 1852 for Edinburgh, and sat until he accepted Chiltern Hundreds in Feb. 1856. Created Lord Macaulay 10 Sept. 1857. Died 28 Dec. 1859. [1855]

McCLEAN, John Robinson. 2 Park Street, Westminster, London. Reform. B. 1813, the s. of Francis McClean, Esq., of Belfast. M. 1835, 2nd d. of William Newsam, Esq., of Belfast. Educ. at the Royal Academical Institution of Belfast, and at Glasgow University. Was President of the Institution of Civil Engineers, London. A Magistrate for Staffordshire, and Lieut.-Col., Engineer and Railway Volunteers. A Fellow of the Geological, Astronomical and other Scientific Societies. Dept. Chairman of the Anglo-American Telegraph Company, and Director of the Anglo-Mediterranean Telegraph and other public companies. Patron of 1 living. A Liberal. Unsuccessfully contested Belfast Apr. 1857. Sat for E. Staffordshire from Dec. 1868 until he died 13 July 1873. [1873]

McCLINTOCK, John. Drumcar, Dunleer, Co.

249

Louth. Kildare Street Club, Dublin. Carlton. Eld. s. of John McClintock, Esq., MP of Drumcar, Co. Louth, by his 1st wife Jane, d. of William Bunbury, Esq., MP of Moyle, Co. Carlow. B. in Dublin 1798; m. 1829, Anne, eld. d. of the Rev. John Henry George Lefroy, of Ewshot House, Hampshire. Educ. at Sandhurst. Served 3 years in North America with the 74th Foot. A Magistrate for Louth. A Dept.-Lieut. for Fermanagh. Was High Sheriff of Louth 1840, and was Major in the Louth Militia. Patron of 1 living. A 'decided Conservative.' Unsuccessfully contested Louth, July 1841, and again July 1852. First elected, Apr. 1857. Defeated in 1859.   [1858]

McCLINTOCK, William Bunbury. See BUNBURY, William Bunbury McClintock-.

McCLURE, Sir Thomas, Bart. Belmont, Belfast, Ireland. Reform, Devonshire, and National Liberal. S. of William McClure, Esq., of Belfast, by Elizabeth, d. of Rev. John Thomson, Presbyterian minister. B. at Belfast, 1806; m. 1877, Ellison Thorburn, d. of Robert Andrew Macfie, Esq., of Dreghorn, Edinburgh. Educ. at the Belfast Royal Academical Institution. Was for many years a Merchant in Belfast. Was High Sheriff in 1864 of the Co. of Down, of which he was later Vice-Lieut. A Magistrate for the Cos. of Down, Antrim and Armagh. A Liberal. Sat for Belfast from Dec. 1868 to Feb. 1874, when he was an unsuccessful candidate; sat for Londonderry Co. from Dec. 1878 until he retired in 1885. Died 21 Jan. 1893.   [1885]

McCOAN, James Carlile. 42 Notting Hill Square, Bayswater, London. Reform. S. of Mr. Clement McCoan, by Sarah, d. of Mr. James Carlile, of Culreavogh, Co. Tyrone. B. at Dunlow, Co. Tyrone, 1829; m. 1857, Augusta, youngest d. of William Jenkyns, Esq., of Elgin, Scotland. Educ. at Dungannon School and the London University. Was called to the bar at the Middle Temple Nov. 1856; practised for several years in the Supreme Consular Court of the Levant at Constantinople; founded and edited *The Levant Herald* in that city. Author of numerous works, including, *Egypt as it is, Our New Protectorate,* political tracts, etc. A Liberal, and in favour of 'Home Rule' for Ireland. Contested Drogheda 2 Mar. 1880. Sat for Wicklow from Apr. 1880. Defeated in 1885 contesting Lancaster; contested Southampton as a Gladstonian Liberal in 1886; contested Macclesfield in 1892.   [1885]

McCOMBIE, William. Tillyfour, Aberdeen. S. of Charles McCombie, Esq. of Tillyfour, by his m. with Miss Ann Black. B. at Tillyfour, Aberdeenshire. Unmarried. Educ. at Aberdeen.

The well-known farmer, grazier and dealer in cattle for which he received numerous prizes at exhibitions and cattle-shows. A Liberal who gave a general support to Mr. Gladstone. Sat for W. Aberdeenshire from Dec. 1868. Accepted Chiltern Hundreds in 1876. Died Aberdeenshire 1 Feb. 1880.   [1876]

McCORMICK, William. 10 Cambridge Terrace, Regent's Park, London. Lissahally House, Londonderry, Ireland. Conservative. B. at Londonderry, Ireland 1801. A member of the Institution of Civil Engineers and of the Society of Arts, and largely engaged in Railway contracts, etc. A Liberal-Conservative, supported the vote of censure on Lord Palmerston 1864. First elected for Londonderry Mar. 1860. Retired 1865. Died 12 June 1878.   [1865]

McCULLAGH-TORRENS, W.T. See TORRENS, William Torrens McCullagh.

MACDONALD, Alexander. Holytown, Lanarkshire. Sec. of the Miner's Assoc. for Scotland, and President of the Miner's National Assoc. A Liberal, was in favour of the law of conspiracy being made more clear and decisive in its application (as regards masters and servants); also of the facilitation of the transfer of land and the total abolition of the Game Laws. Sat for Stafford from Feb. 1874. MP until his death 31 Oct. 1881.   [1881]

McDONNELL, Joseph Myles. Doo Castle, Co. Mayo. A Repealer. First returned for Mayo in Mar. 1846. Defeated 1847.   [1847]

MACDONOGH, Francis. 41 Rutland Square, Dublin. National. S. of Morgan Macdonogh, Esq., Merchant of Sligo, by Catherine, d. of — Tondre, Esq., of the same Co. B. at Ballina, Co. Sligo. Educ. at Sligo, under the Rev. William Armstrong, and at Trinity Coll., Dublin. Called to the bar in Ireland 1829; made a Queen's Counsel 1842. Was Counsel to the Inland Revenue of Ireland under Lord Eglinton's Government. A Liberal-Conservative, and a supporter generally of Lord Derby. Contested Carrickfergus 2 Apr. 1857. First elected for Sligo bor. Aug. 1860. Defeated 1865. Died 18 Apr. 1882.   [1865]

MACDUFF, Visct. 4 Cavendish Square, London. Brooks's, White's and City Liberal. Only s. of the Earl of Fife, K.T., by Lady Agnes Georgina, 2nd d. of the 16th Earl of Erroll. B. 1849. Educ. at Eton. Appointed Lord-Lieut. of Elginsh., 1871. A Dept.-Lieut. for Aberdeenshire and Banffshire. A Liberal. Sat for the Cos. of Elgin and Nairn from

Feb. 1874 until he succeeded as 6th Earl Fife, Aug. 1879. Peer of U.K. 1885; 1st Duke of Fife July 1889. Died 29 Jan. 1912. [1879]

McEVOY, Edward. Tobertinan, Co. Meath. Army & Navy. S. of James McEvoy, Esq., of Tobertinan, by Teresa Maria, 4th d. of Sir Joshua Colles Meredyth, Bart. B. at Tobertinan, Co. Meath, 1826; m. Eliza, only child of Andrew Browne, Esq., of Mount Hazel, Co. Galway. Educ. at Prior Park and at Magdalene Coll., Cambridge. Formerly Lieut. in 6th Dragoon Guards. A Magistrate for Meath. A Liberal, but voted for Lord Derby's Reform Bill Mar. 1859; was in favour of tenant right and 'religious equality', also the appropriation of the revenues of the Established Church in Ireland to 'national purposes.' First returned for Meath Dec. 1855. Sat until he retired 1874. Died 10 Feb. 1899. [1873]

MACFARLANE, Sir Donald Horne. Continued in House after 1885. Full entry in Volume II.

MACFIE, Robert Andrew. 13 Victoria Street, London. Dreghorn, Slateford, Edinburgh. Reform. S. of John Macfie, Esq., a Magistrate and Dept.-Lieut. of the city of Edinburgh, by Alison, d. of William Thorburn, Esq., of Leith. B. at Leith 1811; m. 1840, Caroline Eliza, d. of John Easton, Esq., M.D. of Courance Hill, Dumfriesshire and of the 15th Hussars. Educ. at the High Schools of Leith and Edinburgh, also at the Univ. of Edinburgh. Was a Sugar Refiner in Liverpool, Greenock, and Edinburgh. Was a Magistrate for the co. of Edinburgh, and formerly Pres. of the Liverpool Chamber of Commerce. Was a Trustee of the Liverpool Exchange. Wrote various pamphlets etc. on *Patent Monopolies, The Suffrage, Missions,* etc. A Liberal, in favour of economy in every public department without stinting the volunteer force, of a larger share in the representation being granted to Scotland, and of the lowering of the franchise in the counties. Sat for the district of Leith from Dec. 1868. Defeated 1874. Author. Died 17 Feb. 1893. [1873]

McGAREL-HOGG, Sir James Macnaghten, Bart. K.C.B. 17 Grosvenor Gardens, London. Carlton, and Travellers'. Eld. s. of Sir James Weir Hogg, Bart., member of Council for India, and who sat many years for Beverley and Honiton, by Mary, 2nd d. of Samuel Swinton, Esq. of Swinton, Co. Berwick. B. at Calcutta, 1823; m. 1857, Hon. Caroline Elizabeth Emma, eld. d. of 1st Lord Penrhyn. Educ. at Eton, and at Christ Church, Oxford. Joined the 1st Life Guards 1843, became Major and Lieut.-Col. 1855, retired 1859. Chairman of the Metropolitan Board of Works

from Nov. 1870 (salary £2,000). A Conservative, but not opposed to progress. Sat for Bath from July 1865-July 1868; sat for Truro from Sept. 1871-Nov. 1885; and from the latter date sat for Middlesex, Hornsey Division until he was created 1st Baron Magheramorne, July 1887. Died 27 June 1890. [1887]

McGEACHY, Forster Alleyne. 33 St. James's Place, London. Carlton and Oxford & Cambridge. Only s. of Maj. M'Geachy. B. 1809; m. 1834, d. of C.C. Adderley, Esq. A Conservative, but in favour of free trade. First returned for Honiton in 1841. Retired 1847. Contested Bristol 1852. Died 20 Mar. 1887. [1847]

MACGREGOR, Donald Robert. 55 Berhard Street, Leith. Woodburn, Edinburgh. S. of Lieut. Evan Macgregor. B. at Perth 1824; m. 1851, Mary, only d. of William Anderson, Esq., of The Deans, South Shields. Was educ. at the Perth Public Schools. A Merchant and Steam Shipowner at Leith. Was a member of the Leith town council in 1856. A member of the Leith Dock & Harbour Commission from 1857. Moderator of the Leith High Constables, and Lieut.-Col. in the 1st Mid-lothian Rifle Volunteers. A Liberal. Sat for Leith district from Feb. 1874. Accepted Chiltern Hundreds Jan. 1878. Contested Leith in 1886. Died 9 Dec. 1889. [1877]

McGREGOR, James. May Place, Crayford, Kent. S. of Alexander McGregor, Esq., a Merchant in Liverpool, and afterwards agent of the Bank of England at Manchester. B. in Liverpool 1808; m. 1st, 1829, Jane d. of Robert Small, Esq. (she died 1844); 2ndly, 1849, Catherine Pendarves, d. of J.C. Lochner, Esq. Was brought up in the mercantile house of Sir William Feilden, Bart., MP; was for many years Manager of the Liverpool Commercial Bank. Chairman of the South-Eastern Railway Company. A Conservative, opposed to the Maynooth Grant, but in favour of every 'real reform' in Parliament. Was an unsuccessful candidate for Banbury in Aug. 1847. First returned for Sandwich July 1852. Defeated 1857. Died 5 Sept. 1858. [1857]

MACGREGOR, John. 1 Princes Terrace, Hyde Park South, London. Carricks, Glasgow. Athenaeum. Eld. s. of David MacGregor, Esq., of Drynie, Ross-shire. B. at Stornaway, Ross-shire 1797; m. 1833, Anne, d. of William Peard Jillard, Esq., of Oakhill, Somersetshire (she died Oct. 1853). Was High Sheriff of Prince Edward's Ísland, and a member of the Colonial Legislature, was employed on Commercial Missions to Germany, Austria, Paris, Naples, etc., and was

251

Joint-Sec. to the Board of Trade from Dec. 1839-Aug. 1847. Author of *The History, Geography, and Resources of British America, Commercial Statistics, Progress of America from the Discovery by Columbus to the year 1847*, twenty-two *Reports on foreign tariffs and trade*, presented by command of Her Majesty to Parliament. A Liberal, voted for the ballot 1853. First returned for Glasgow 1847. Accepted Chiltern Hundreds Mar. 1857. Died 23 Apr. 1857.   [1857]

MCINTYRE, Aeneas John. 1 Park Square West, Regent's Park, London. 1 Brick Court, Temple, London. Reform. Eld. s. of Aeneas McIntyre, Esq., LL.D. and F.L.S. of King's Coll., Aberdeen, by Charlotte Susanna, d. of William Thomson, Esq. B. 1821; m. 1854, Eleanor, d. of G. Corbet Esq. Was called to the bar at the Middle Temple, Nov. 1846, and joined the North Wales and Chester circuit. Appointed a Queen's Counsel 1872, and was a Bencher of the Middle Temple. A Liberal, and for 'perfect, civil, and religious liberty'; in favour of the assimilation of the borough and county franchise. Sat for Worcester from Apr. 1880. Defeated in 1885 contesting Hackney N. Died 19 Sept. 1889.   [1885]

MACIVER, David. Continued in House after 1885: full entry in Volume II.

McKENNA, Sir J.N. Continued in House after 1885: full entry in Volume II.

MACKENZIE, James Alexander Stewart. 8 St. James's Place, London. Seaforth, Co. Ross. Athenaeum. Eld. surviving s. of the Hon. Keith Stewart, bro. of John, 7th Earl of Galloway. B. 1784; m. 1818 Mary Elizabeth Frederica, eld. d. and co-heiress of Francis, last Lord Seaforth (whose surname of Mackenzie he took), and widow of Vice-Admiral Sir Samuel Hood, Bart. A Commissioner of the India Board from 1832 till Nov. 1834. A Whig. Sat for Ross & Cromarty from 1831. Appointed Governor of Ceylon. [1837]

MACKENZIE, Thomas. 17 Clarges Street, London. Applecross, Ross-shire. S. of Kenneth Mackenzie, Esq. B. 1793; m. 1817, d. of G. Mackenzie, Esq. A writer to the Signet. Was chosen for Ross and Cromartyshire shortly before the dissolution of the Parliament of 1837, on the appointment of Mr. Stewart Mackenzie, the previous member, to the government of Ceylon. Again returned, and without contest, at the general election in 1837. A Conservative, voted for agricultural protection 1846. Sat until he retired 1847. Died 9 June 1856.   [1847]

MACKENZIE, William Forbes. 38 Charles Street, Berkeley Square, London. Portmore, Peeblesshire. Carlton. Eld. s. of Colin Mackenzie, Esq., of Portmore, and Elizabeth, d. of Sir William Forbes, of Pitsligo, Bart. B. 18 Apr. 1807; m. 1830 Helen Anne, eld. d. of Sir James Montgomery, of Stanhope, Bart., and of Lady Elizabeth, d. of Dunbar, 4th Earl of Selkirk. A Dept.-Lieut. of Peeblesshire. Was appointed a Lord of the Treasury in Apr. 1845; resigned Feb. 1846. A Conservative, voted for agricultural protection 1846. First returned for Peeblesshire in 1837. Retired in 1852. Sat for Liverpool from 8 July 1852, but the election was declared void and he did not stand at the subsequent election. Contested Derby 28 Mar. 1857. Died 24 Sept. 1860.   [1852]

MACKIE, James. Ernespie Castle, Castle-Douglas, Kirkcudbrightshire. Bargaly, Kirkcudbrightshire B. 1821, the only surviving s. of John Mackie, Esq., (MP for Kirkcudbrightshire from Feb. 1850-Mar. 1857), by the eld. d. of Peter Laurie, Esq., of Blackheath. M. 1853, Jane Wilson, only d. of Archibald Horne, Esq., of Inverchroskie and Whitefield, Perthshire. Educ. at Rugby and at Oriel Coll., Oxford, where he graduated B.A. 1844, M.A. 1847. An Advocate at the Scottish bar from 1847, a Dept.-Lieut. of Kirkcudbright and Capt. 1st Kirkcudbright Rifle Volunteers. A 'Progressive' Liberal, but disapproved of 'all unconstitutional extremes.' Voted against Lord Russell's Reform Bill 1866. Sat for Kirkcudbrightshire from Apr. 1857 until he died late Jan. 1868.   [1867]

MACKIE, John. 1 Queen Square, Westminster, London. Bargaly and Ernespie, Kirkcudbrightshire. Only s. of James Mackie, Esq., of Bargaly, Kirkcudbrightshire. M. eld. d. of Peter Lawrie, Esq., of Blackheath. Educ. at Edinburgh. A Dept.-Lieut. of Kirkcudbright. A Liberal, voted against the ballot 1853; said he would be guided by his constituents on the question of the Maynooth Grant. First returned for Kirkcudbrightshire Feb. 1850, without opposition. Retired 1857. Died 3 July 1858.   [1857]

MACKIE, Robert Bownas. 35 Hertford Street, Mayfair, London. St. John's, Wakefield. Reform, Devonshire and National Liberal. S. of Robert J, Mackie, Esq., of St. John's, Wakefield. B. at Wakefield, 1820; m. 1852, d. of William Shaw, Esq., of Stanley Hall. Educ. at Wesley Coll., Sheffield. Formerly a Corn Merchant in Wakefield. A Magistrate for the West Riding of Yorkshire. A Liberal, and a supporter of Mr. Gladstone's policy. Sat from Apr. 1880 for

Wakefield, which he had contested unsuccessfully Feb. and again in May 1874. MP until his death on 18 June 1885. [1885]

MACKINNON, Lauchlan Bellingham. Bittacy House, Hendon, London. United Service and Reform. 2nd s. of William Alexander Mackinnon, Sen., Esq., of Acrise Park, Canterbury (who for a period of 35 years represented successively Dunwich, Lymington, and Rye), by Emma Mary, only d. and heir of J. Palmer, Esq., of Palmerstown, Co. Mayo, and Rush House, Dublin. B. at Portswood Park, Southampton, 1815; m. 1842, Augusta, d. of John Entwistle, Esq., of Foxholes, Rochdale. Entered the navy 1830, became Capt. 1864, and received a naval medal. A Magistrate for Surrey. Author of *Six Months at the Falkland Islands, Atlantic and Transatlantic Sketches, Steam Warfare in the Parana,* etc. A moderate Liberal. First elected for Rye, July 1865. Retired in 1868. Died 10 July 1877. [1867]

MACKINNON, William Alexander, sen. 4 Hyde Park Place, London. Newtown Park, Hampshire. Asgill House, Surrey. Carlton. Head of the Clan Mackinnon. B. 1789; m. 1812, the only d. and heir of Jos. Palmer, Esq., of Palmerstown, Co. Mayo, and Rush House, Dublin. Fellow of the Royal Antiquarian, Asiatic, Geological, and Astronomical Societies. Kept terms at Lincoln's Inn, but was not called to the bar. Published a work on *Public Opinion,* also *Thoughts on the Currency Question,* and *The History of Civilization.* In 1831 opposed the plan for taking the census of 1821 as the basis of the representation under the Reform Bill, and, on dividing the House, had the largest majority that voted against the bill. In the next Parliament Ministers took the census of 1831 as their guide. In 1832 brought in a bill for the prevention of cruelty to animals, and subsequently measures relative to Turnpike Trusts, Rural Police, etc., and in 1838 a bill to amend the patent laws and secure the copyright of designs. A Conservative, but in favour of free trade. Sat for Dunwich in 1830; for Lymington in 1831; was not in the Parliament of 1832; but held his seat at Lymington from 1835 until he was defeated in July 1852. [1852]

MACKINNON, William Alexander, jun. 5 Gloucester Square, London. Union and Oxford & Cambridge. Eld. s. of William Alexander Mackinnon, Esq., of Mackinnon, by Emma, only d. and heir of Joseph Palmer, Esq., of Rush House, Co. Dublin, and Palmerstown, Co. Mayo. B. in Portman Square, 1813; m. 1846, Margaret Sophia, only d. of Francis Willes, Esq. Educ. at Westminster, and at St. John's Coll., Cambridge, where he graduated B.A. 1836, M.A. 1845. A

Magistrate for Middlesex and Hampshire. A Liberal. Returned for Rye in July 1852, but the election was declared void for treating, Mar. 1853. First elected for Lymington, Mar. 1857. Sat until he retired 1868. [1867]

MACKINTOSH, Aeneas William. Raigmore, Inverness. Reform. S. of Lachlan Mackintosh, Esq., of Raigmore, by Margaret, 2nd d. of Sir Archibald Dunbar, 5th Bart. of Northfield. B. at Draking House, Inverness, 1819; m. 1856, Grace, d. of Sir Niel Menzies, 6th Bart. of Castle Menzies. Educ. at Univ. Coll., Oxford. Called to the Scottish bar 1849, but never practised. A Magistrate and Dept.-Lieut. for Inverness, and a Maj. Invernessshire Militia Artillery. A Liberal. Sat for the district of Inverness from Dec. 1868. Defeated in 1874. Died 18 June 1900. [1873]

MACKINTOSH, C. Fraser. Continued in House after 1885: full entry in Volume II.

McLAGAN, P. Continued in House after 1885: full entry in Volume II.

MACLACHLAN, Lachlan. 55 Parliament Street, London. A Barrister in Galway Town. A Repealer. Returned for Galway in 1832. Unseated in 1833. [1833]

McLAREN, C.B.B. Continued in House after 1885: full entry in Volume II.

McLAREN, Duncan. Newington House, Edinburgh. Reform and Liberal Club, Edinburgh. S. of John McLaren, Esq. B. 1800; m. 1st, 1829, Grant, d. of Wm. Aitken, Esq., of Haddington (she died 1833); 2ndly, 1836, Christina, d. of William Renton, Esq., Merchant, of Edinburgh (she died 1841), 3rdly, Priscilla, d. of Jacob Bright, Esq., of Rochdale. A Merchant in Edinburgh. Was President of the Edinburgh Chamber of Commerce from 1862. A Magistrate and Dept.-Lieut. of the Co. and city of Edinburgh from 1836. Was Lord Provost of Edinburgh from 1851 till 1854. Author of *A History of the Resistance to the Annuity Tax,* and numerous pamphlets. A Liberal, voted for the disestablishment of the Irish Church 1869, and was opposed to all grants for religious purposes. Unsuccessfully contested Edinburgh 1852. Sat for Edinburgh from July 1865 until he accepted Chiltern Hundreds 1881. Died 26 Apr. 1886. [1886]

McLAREN, Rt. Hon. J. 46 Moray Place, Edinburgh. Reform. Eld. s. of Duncan McLaren, Esq., MP, of Newington House, Edinburgh, by his 1st wife, Miss Grant Aitken. B. at Edinburgh

1831; m. 1868, Ottilie Auguste, d. of H.L. Schwabe, Esq., of Glasgow. Bro. of Charles B.B. McLaren, Esq., MP for Stafford. Was educ. at Edinburgh University. Called to the Scottish bar in 1856. Appointed Lord Advocate of Scotland Apr. 1880; was Sheriff of Chancery in Scotland from 1869-1880. Published several legal works, including *Law of Wills and Succession.* A Liberal, and in favour of household suffrage in counties, and of Scotland being granted additional representatives. Elected for Wigtown district Apr. 1880. Contested Berwick July 1880. Sat for Edinburgh from 27 Jan. 1881 until he was appointed Lord of Session, as Lord McLaren. Died 6 Apr. 1910.
[1880 2nd ed.]

MACLEAN, Donald. Carlton. 2nd s. of Gen. Sir Fitzroy Grafton Maclean, Bart., Chief of the Macleans. M. 1827, Harriet, d. of Gen. Frederick Maitland, grands. and nephew of Earls of Lauderdale. Was of Balliol Coll. and took honours at the University. A Barrister. A Dept.-Lieut. of Durham. A Conservative, voted for agricultural protection 1846. Contested Oxford city in 1833 with Messrs. Townley and Hughes on the vacancy caused by Mr. Stonor's being unseated by the decision of a Committee. First returned for Oxford in 1835. Retired 1847. Died 21 Mar. 1874.
[1847]

MACLEOD, Roderick. Invergordon Castle, Ross-shire. Reform. Eld. s. of Robert Bruce Aeneas Macleod, Esq., of Cadboll, Co. Cromarty, and of Invergordon Castle, Ross-shire. B. 1786; m. 1813, Isabella, youngest d. of William Cuninghame, Esq., of Lainshaw, Ayrshire. An Advocate. Lord Lieut. of the Co. Cromarty, and Dept.-Lieut. of Ross-shire. A Reformer, in favour of Church and Corporation reform, and of exempting Dissenters from the payment of Church rates. Against any sweeping changes in our taxation or currency; against triennial Parliaments, vote by ballot, and generally against altering the system of representation established by the Reform Bills. In the Parliament of 1818 sat for Cromartyshire. In Sept. 1831, was elected for the Co. of Sutherland, on the death of Sir Hugh Innes, Bart. Sat for Inverness district from July 1837. Accepted Chiltern Hundreds Mar. 1840. Died 13 Mar. 1853.
[1839]

MACLIVER, Peter Stewart. Ardnave, Weston-super-Mare, Somersetshire. Devonshire. S. of David Macliver, Esq., Islay, Scotland, by Isabella, d. of George Stewart, Esq., of Aberlour. Cousin to the late Lord Clyde, whose patronymic was originally Macliver. B. 1822; m. 1841, Anne, d. of Peter Miller, Esq., of Glasgow. Was educ. at the High School and University of Glasgow. A Journalist, and established in 1858, in Bristol, a paper named *The Daily Press* – the first daily paper published in the Western counties. A Magistrate for Somerset. A Liberal. Sat for Plymouth from 1880 until defeated in 1885. Contested the St. Rollox division of Glasgow 5 July 1886. Died 19 April 1891.
[1885]

MCMAHON, Edward. 3 Thomond Terrace, Dublin. A Manufacturer in Dublin. A Nationalist and Home Ruler. Unsuccessfully contested Dublin Co. Feb. 1883. Sat for Limerick city from Nov. 1883. Retired in 1885.
[1885]

MCMAHON, Patrick. 9 Dr. Johnson's Buildings, Temple, London. Eld. s. of James McMahon, Esq., of Lakeview, Rathkeale, Co. Limerick, by Catherine, d. of James Bourke, Esq. of Aklamon, Co. Limerick. B. 1813. Graduated B.A. 1836 at (Trinity Coll.) Dublin. Admitted a student of Gray's Inn Nov. 1837; called to the bar June 1842, and went the Oxford circuit. Author of several articles in *The Dublin Review* on Tenant Right and other political questions connected with Ireland. A Liberal. Was in favour of alteration in the poor laws in Ireland, so as to have Union rating substituted for Division Rating. Sat for the Co. of Wexford from July 1852 to July 1865. Represented New Ross from Dec. 1868. Retired in 1874. Died 19 Dec. 1875.
[1873]

MCMINNIES, John Gordon. Summer House, Warrington. S. of Mr. John McMinnies, of Lancaster. B. at Lancaster. Senior Partner in the firm of Messrs. Bashall and Co., Cotton Manufacturers, of Farrington, near Preston. A Magistrate for Warrington, of which he was also an Alderman. A Liberal. Sat for Warrington from April 1880. Retired in 1885. Died 1 Feb. 1890.
[1885]

MACNAGHTEN, Sir Edmund Charles Workman, Bart. Dunderave, Bushmills, Antrim. Roe Park, Newtown-Limavady, Ireland. Carlton. Eld. s. of Sir Francis Workman-Macnaghten, Bart. (a Judge at Madras, and subsequently at Bengal), by the eld. d. of Sir William Dunkin, of Clogher. B. in Dublin 1790; m. 1827, Mary, only child of Edward Gwatkin, Esq., of Devonshire Place. Was educated at the Charter-house and at Trinity Coll., Dublin; called to the Bar in Ireland 1813; formerly held the office of Master in Equity in the Supreme Court at Calcutta. A Dept.-Lieut. of Antrim. Elder bro. of Sir Wm. Hay Macnaghten, assassinated by the Affghans at Cabool, Dec. 1841. A Conservative, formerly in favour of free trade, but in 1850 voted for a return to agricultural protection. First returned for Antrim in 1847. Retired in 1852. Author of *The Elements of Political Economy* (1854). Died 6 Jan. 1876. [1852]

MACNAGHTEN, Edward. 198 Queen's Gate, London. Runkerry, Bushmills, Co. Antrim. Carlton, and United University. 2nd s. of Sir Edmund C. Workman Macnaghten, 2nd Bart., who for some years sat for Antrim, by Mary, only d. of Edward Gwatkin, Esq. B. 1830; m. 1858, Frances Arabella, d. of Rt. Hon. Sir Samuel Martin, formerly one of the Barons of the Exchequer (she died 1883). Was educ. at Cambridge; graduated B.A. 1852, M.A. 1855, and became a Fellow of Trinity Coll. Was called to the bar at Lincoln's Inn, Jan. 1857. Appointed a Queen's Counsel 1880. A Conservative, said he would 'uphold in its integrity the ancient custom of Ulster Tenant right', in favour of 'the amendment of the Grand Jury Laws, so as to give the tax-payer a greater control over the imposition of taxation.' Sat for Antrim from Apr. 1880 until he was created 1st Baron Macnaghten and Lord of Appeal-in-Ordinary 1887. Died 17 Feb. 1913.   [1886]

MACNAMARA, Lieut. Francis. A s. of the Member for Clare. A Lieut. in the 8th Hussars. A Repealer. Sat for Ennis from 1832. Retired in 1835. Lieut.-Col. Clare Militia 1854-71. Died 27 June 1873.   [1833]

MACNAMARA, William Nugent. Doolen Castle, Clare. Jun. United Service. S. of Francis Macnamara of Doolen, and father of the late Member for Clare. B. 1776; m. 1798 Susannah, d. of the Hon. Mr. Justice Finucane, of Lifford, Co. Clare. A Major in the Militia, and once High Sheriff of the county. Descended from the ancient Admirals of Munster, whose office is said to have originated the name 'Macna-mara', or 'Son of the Sea.' A Repealer. Sat for the Clare county from 1830 until he retired in 1852. Died 11 Nov. 1856.   [1852]

MCNEILL, Rt. Hon. Duncan. 73 Great King Street, Edinburgh. Carlton. The 2nd s. of John McNeill, Esq., of Collonsey, Co. Argyll. Was called to the Scottish bar in 1816, and was Dean of the faculty of advocates. Was appointed Junior Counsel for the Crown in 1820. Was Sheriff of Perthshire from Dec. 1824 to Dec. 1834, Solicitor-Gen. for Scotland from Nov. 1834-Apr. 1835 (re-appointed to that office Sept. 1841), Lord Advocate from Oct. 1842-July 1846. A Conservative, but in favour of free trade. A Director of the Royal Bank of Scotland, and an Extraordinary Director of the Edinburgh Life Assurance Company, of the Scottish Amicable Life Assurance Company. Sat for the county of Argyll from 1843 until he was appointed a Judge and accepted Chiltern Hundreds in June 1851. Was Pres. of the Court of Sessions, as Lord Colonsay 1852-67. Died 31 Jan. 1874.   [1851]

McTAGGART, Sir John, Bart. 69 Albany Street, Regents Park, London. Ardwell, Wigtonshire. Reform. S. of John McTaggart, Esq., of Ardwell. B. in Wigtonshire 1789; m. d. of T. Kymer, Esq., of Streatham, Surrey. A Merchant in London, and a Dept.-Lieut. of Wigtonshire. Of Liberal opinions, voted for inquiry into Maynooth 1853, and for the ballot same year. Unsuccessfully contested Wigton district in 1832; sat for it from 1835 until he retired 1857. Died 13 Aug. 1867.   [1857]

McTAGGART-STEWART, Sir Mark John, Bart. Continued in House after 1885: full entry in Volume II.

MCTAVISH, Charles Carroll. Declared that 'although he was an American by birth, he was an Irishman by descent and at heart.' A Repealer, and member of the 'Old Ireland' Party. Returned for Dundalk in 1847, but unseated in 1848. Became Governor of Rupert's Land, Canada until 1870. Died 23 July 1870.   [1847 2nd ed.]

MADDOCK, Sir Thomas Herbert. Eld. s. of the Rev. Robert Maddock, Prebendary of Chester, by the d. of Rokeby Scott, Esq. B. 1792; entered the civil service of the E.I.C., in the Bengal presidency, in 1811, and after serving in various political capacities, became Resident at Lucknow in 1829, and was Sec. to the Government of India in the legislative, judicial and revenue departments from 1838-1843; was Dept. Governor of Bengal and President of the Council of India from 1845-1849. A Conservative, voted for inquiry into Maynooth 1853. First returned for Rochester July 1852. Defeated 1857. Died 15 Jan. 1870.   [1857]

MADDOCKS, John. Glanywern, Denbighshire. A Whig, opposed to the ballot, triennial Parliaments, monopolies generally, sinecures, and religious restrictions. Sat for Denbigh district from 1832. Defeated in 1835.   [1833]

MAGAN, William Henry. 8 Gloucester Street, Belgrave Road, London. Clonearl, Philipstown, King's Co. Eagle Hill, Co. Kildare. Army & Navy and Reform. Eld. s. of Wm. Henry Magan, Esq., of Clonearl, by the d. of Thomas Loftus, Esq., of Killyon, Co. Meath. B. in Dublin 1820. Entered the Army as Cornet 9th Lancers 1841; exchanged into the 4th Light Dragoons, and became a Capt. in 1845; retired in June 1846. A Magistrate for King's Co. and Westmeath. A Liberal, voted for the ballot, 1853. First returned for Westmeath in 1847, without opposition. Sat until he retired in 1859. Died 1861.   [1858]

MAGNIAC, Charles. Chesterfield House, South Audley Street, London. Colworth House, Bedford. Devonshire, Brooks's and Travellers'. Eld. s. of Hollingworth Magniac, Esq., of Colworth, Bedfordshire, by Helen, d. of Peter Sampson, Esq., of Fitzroy Square, London. B. 1827; m. 1856, Hon. Augusta d. of 1st Lord Castletown of Upper Ossory, and relict of Hon. Thomas Vesey Dawson. Was educ. at Eton and at Trinity Coll., Cambridge. A Partner in the firm of Messrs. Matheson and Co., East India and China Merchants, London. A Magistrate for Bedfordshire, of which he was High Sheriff 1877; also a Dept.-Lieut. for London. Patron of 1 living. A Liberal, in favour of the abolition of all hindrances to the sale and occupation of land, and the removal of all religious disabilities. Sat for St. Ives from Dec. 1868 to Feb. 1874. Sat for Bedford from Apr. 1880 until he was defeated in July 1886. [1884]

MAGUIRE, John Francis. 21 Bessborough Gardens, London. Grenvine Place, Cork. Eld. s. of John Maguire, Esq., Merchant. B. in Cork; m. 1843, Margaret, 2nd d. of Robert Bailey, Esq. of Cork. Was called to the bar in Ireland, Jan. 1843. Elected Mayor of Cork on four successive occasions from 1861-64. Proprietor and principal editor of the *Cork Examiner* Newspaper, established by him in 1841. Author of *Rome and its Rulers, Father Matthew, a Biography,* etc. A Liberal, a member of the 'Tenant-League', voted for Lord Derby's Reform Bill, March 1859 and against the suspension of the Habeas Corpus Act in Ireland Feb. 1866. Was an unsuccessful candidate for Dungarvan in July 1847 and in May 1851. Sat for Dungarvan from July 1852 to July 1865, when he was elected for the city of Cork. MP until his death 1 Nov. 1872. [1872]

MAHER, John. 18 Manchester Buildings, London. Ballinkeele, Co. Wexford. Reform. S. of John Maher, Esq., of Ballymullen House, Queen's Co., who realized a large fortune as a Merchant in America, and purchased in 1805, and subsequently, extensive estates in Wexford, of Lord Carberry and Col. Hay. Dept.-Lieut. of the Co. and a steward of the Turf Club in Ireland. Educ. at the Jesuit's Coll., Conglowes Wood, Ireland. A Repealer. Returned for Co. Wexford in 1835. Retired 1841. Died 28 May 1860. [1838]

MAHER, Nicholas. 31 Gordon Street, London. Turtulla, Co. Tipperary. Reform. S. of Thomas Maher, Esq., a medical practitioner in the city of Cashel, by his marriage with Margaret, aunt of Valentine Maher, Esq., former MP for Tipperary. M. in 1845 Margaret Jane, eld. d. of Walter Otway Herbert, Esq., of Pilhouse

Carrick-on-Suir, Co. Tipperary. A Liberal, in favour of the Repeal of the Union, and declared 'he would struggle for the right of Ireland to a native parliament as long as he had voice, or pen, or pulsation'; in favour of an absentee tax, and would support the 'tenant-right.' Was first returned for Tipperary in 1844, on the death of his cousin, Valentine Maher, Esq., to whose estates he succeeded. MP until he died 18 Oct. 1851. [1852]

MAHER, Valentine. Tintulla, Tipperary. Arthur's. B. 1780. A Liberal. First returned for Tipperary in 1841 and MP until his death Jan. 1844. [1843]

MAHON, James Patrick O'Gorman. Ennis, Co. Clare, Ireland. Eld. s. of Patrick Mahon, Esq., by Barbara, only d. of The O'Gorman, deceased. B. 1803 in the Co. of Clare; m. Christina Maria, eld. d. and co-heir of John O'Brien, Esq., of Fitzwilliam Square, Dublin. (She died 1877). Graduated M.A. at Trinity Coll., Dublin. Was called to the bar in Ireland 1834, but never practised. A Magistrate and Dept.-Lieut. for Clare, and was formerly Capt. in the Clare Co. Militia. A Liberal, in favour of 'Home Rule' for Ireland. Sat for Clare for a short time in 1830-1, when he was unseated on petition. Sat for Ennis from Aug. 1847-July 1852, when he was an unsuccessful candidate; sat for Clare from May 1879-Nov. 1885. At the two general elections of 1885 and 1886 he was not a candidate, but on the death of Mr. J.A. Blake in 1887 he was elected for Carlow. MP until his death 15 June 1891. [1891]

MAHON, Lord. 41 Grosvenor Place, London. Chevening Park, Kent. Carlton and Athenaeum. Only s. of Earl Stanhope. B. at Walmer, 1805; m. 1834 Emily, 2nd d. of Lieut.-Gen. Sir E. Kerrison, Bart., MP. Was Under Secretary of State for the Foreign Department, from Dec. 1834, till Apr. 1835. Secretary to the Board of Controul from July 1845 to July 1846. Author of a Life of Belisarius, a History of the War of the Succession in Spain, and a History of England from the Treaty of Utrecht to the Peace of Aix-la-Chapelle. A Conservative, but in favour of free trade. Sat for Wootton Basset in 1830 and 1831; was returned for Hertford bor. in 1832, but the election was declared void; was again returned in 1835, and sat for it from that date until defeated in 1852. Succeeded as 5th Earl Stanhope Mar. 1855. Died 24 Dec. 1875. [1852]

MAHON, Visct. 3 Grosvenor Place Houses, London. Chevening, Sevenoaks, Kent. Carlton, St. Stephen's and Travellers'. Eld. s. of the 5th Earl Stanhope, who represented Hertford for many years, by Emily Harriet, 2nd d. of Sir Edward Kerrison, Bart. B. Grosvenor Place, 1838; m. 1869, Evelyn Henrietta, only d. of Richard Pennefather, Esq., of Knockevan, Co. Tipperary, and Lady Emily (remar. to Gen. Hankey). Appointed a Lord of the Treasury, Feb. 1874 (salary £1,000). Joined the Grenadier Guards 1858, retired as Lieut. and Capt. 1869. Was instructor of musketry from 1863-68. Was a Dept.-Lieut. and a Magistrate for Kent. A Conservative, in favour of the repeal of the Malt tax and of an alteration in the game laws; and he was strongly opposed to all measures which might have tended to the disestablishment of the Church. Sat for Leominster from Apr.-Dec. 1868, when he unsuccessfully contested Greenwich. Sat for E. Suffolk from June 1870 until he succeeded as 6th Earl Stanhope Dec. 1875. First Church Estates Commissioner 1878-1905. Died 19 Apr. 1905.   [1875]

MAHONY, Peirce. 4 Trafalgar Square, London. 7 Victoria Square, Kingstown, Dublin. Gunsborough, Co. Kerry. Reform and Law. S. of Peirce Mahony, Esq., of Wood Lawn, Co. Kerry and of Anna Maria, d. of John Maunsell, Esq., of Ballybroad House, Co. Limerick. B. 19 Dec. 1792; m. 10 Jan. 1815, Jane only d. of Edmund Kenifeck, Esq., of Ballindeasif House, Kinsale. A Solicitor and held the office of Solicitor to the Provincial Bank of Ireland. Was, in conjunction with the Duke of Leinster, a chief promoter of the Protestant Declaration in favour of Roman Catholic Emancipation in 1828, of the great Rotunda meeting in Dublin in Jan. 1829; and of the Anti-Repeal Declaration of 1830. Was a candidate for the City of Limerick in 1832, but unsuccessfully, because he refused to support a Repeal of the Union. Was favourable to the total abolition of tithes in Ireland - the landlords for the one part, and the nation for the other, to supply the deficiency. Supported a general provision for the Irish poor, a well regulated system of emigration, the undertaking of public works as a means of employment for the working classes. Said he would 'support and advocate the policy of Lord Melbourne's Government.' A member of the Royal Irish Academy and of the Royal Dublin Society. Returned for Kinsale in 1837. Unseated in Apr. 1838. D. O'Connell's Solicitor in 1844; Clerk of Crown in court of Queen's bench 1849 until his death 18 Feb. 1853.   [1838]

MAIDSTONE, Visct. Eastwell Park, Kent. Carlton. Only s. of the Earl of Winchelsea and nephew of the Duke of Montrose. B. 31 May 1815. A Conservative. Returned for Northamptonshire N. in 1837. Retired 1841. Contested Westminster July 1852 and Cambridge Aug.

1854. Succeeded as 10th Earl Jan. 1858. Died 9 June 1887.   [1838]

MAINWARING, Townshend. 14 Dover Street, London. Galltfaenan, Nr. Rhyl. 2nd s. of the Rev. Charles Mainwaring, of Oteley Park, Shropshire, by Sarah Susannah, d. of John Townshend, Esq., of Hem, Denbighshire. B. at Oteley Park 1807; m. 1837, Anna Maria, d. of John Lloyd Salusbury, Esq., of Galltfaenan, Denbighshire. Educ. at Rugby and at Brasenose Coll., Oxford. A Magistrate for Denbighshire; and Capt. 3rd Denbighshire Rifle Volunteers. A Liberal-Conservative, voted for free trade, and for Lord Derby's Reform Bill Mar. 1859; voted against Lord Russell's Reform Bill 1866. Sat for the Denbigh district from 1841 to 1847; again returned Apr. 1857 and sat until defeated in 1868. Died 25 Dec. 1883.   [1867]

MAITLAND, Sir Alexander Charles Ramsay-Gibson, Bart. Clifton Hall, Rathe, and Barnton, Midlothian. Rose-Hill, Hertfordshire. Eld. s. of Alexander Gibson-Maitland, Esq., by Susan, eld. d. of George Ramsay, Esq. of Barnton, Scotland. B. in Edinburgh 1820; m. 1841, Thomasina Agnes, elder d. of James Hunt, Esq. of Pittencrieff, Fifeshire. Appointed Dept.-Lieut. Midlothian 1848. Capt. Midlothian Yeomanry 1850. Capt. Lanark Militia 1854. Lieut.-Col.-Commandant Stirlingshire Militia 1855. A Commissioner of Lunacy in Scotland 1857. A Liberal, voted for the disestablishment of the Irish Church 1869. Contested Stirling 3 Aug. 1847. Sat for Edinburghshire from Dec. 1868. Retired in 1873. Died 16 May 1876.   [1873]

MAITLAND, John. 9 Duke Street, Portland Place, London. Argrennan, Ringford, Kirkcudbrightshire. Randolph Cliff, Edinburgh. Reform. S. of the Hon. Edward Francis Maitland, Lord Barcaple, a Lord of Session, in Scotland, by Ann, d. of William Roberts, Esq., Banker in Glasgow and Dundee. Nephew of Hon. Thomas Maitland, Lord Dundrennan, who sat for Kirkcudbrightshire from 1845-1851, when he became a Lord of Session. B. 1841. Unmarried. Educ. at the Edinburgh Academy, the Universities of St. Andrew's and Edinburgh, and at University Coll., Oxford, where he obtained prizes and was 2nd class in classics, graduated Nov. 1864. An advocate at the Scottish bar. A 'decided Liberal.' Sat for Kirkcudbrightshire from Feb. 1874. Retired 1880.   [1880]

MAITLAND, Thomas. 122 George Street, Edinburgh. Dundrennan Abbey and Compstone, Kirkcudbrightshire. Hermand, Midlothian. Brooks's. B. at Dundrennan 1792, the s. of Adam

Maitland, Esq., of Dundrennan Abbey, Kirkcud-brightshire. M. in 1815, Isabella Grahm, d. of the late James MacDowell, Esq., and niece of William MacDowell, Esq., of Garthland, N.B. Educ. at Edinburgh and at Oxford. Was called to the Scottish bar in 1813, and held the office of Solicitor-Gen. for Scotland from May 1840-Sept. 1841. Was re-appointed to that office in July 1846. A Whig, and a 'strong advocate for the most liberal policy towards Ireland.' First elected for Kirkcudbrightshire in 1845, and sat until he was appointed a Lord of Session, as Lord Dundrennan in Feb. 1850. Died 10 June 1851.   [1849]

MAITLAND, W. Fuller-. Continued in House after 1885: full entry in Volume II.

MAJENDIE, Lewis Ashurst. 9 Grosvenor Square, London. Hedingham Castle, Halstead, Essex. Carlton. Eld. s. of the Rev. Henry Lewis Majendie, Vicar of Great Dunmow, Essex, by Emma Sophia, d. of T.F. Gepp, Esq. B. at Great Dunmow, Essex; m. 1870 Lady Margaret Elizabeth, 2nd d. of 25th Earl of Crawford and Balcarres. Was educ. at Marlborough Coll., and at Christ Church, Oxford. A Magistrate and Dept.-Lieut. for Essex. Patron of 1 living. A Conservative. Sat for Canterbury from Feb. 1874. Accepted Chiltern Hundreds April 1879. Died 22 Oct. 1885.   [1878]

MAKINS, W.T. Continued in House after 1885: full entry in Volume II.

MALCOLM, J.W. Continued in House after 1885: full entry in Volume II.

MALINS, Richard. 6 Stone Buildings, Lincoln's Inn, London. 57 Lowndes Square, London. Carlton and Oxford & Cambridge. 3rd s. of William Malins, Esq., of Ailston, Warwickshire, by the eld. d. of Thomas Hunter, Esq., of Pershore, Worcestershire. B. at Evesham, Worcestershire; m. 1831, Susanna, eld. d. of the Rev. Arthur Farwell, Rector of St. Martin's, Cornwall. Educ. at Caius Coll., Cambridge, where he was 5th junior optime in 1827. Entered as a student of the Inner Temple 1825; called to the bar May 1830; appointed Queen's Counsel 1849. A Conservative, opposed to 'the wild and democratic schemes of the Manchester school of politicians, whether under the name of parliamentary reform or any other specious title.' First returned for Wallingford July 1852. Sat until defeated 1865. Judge 1875-81. Knighted Feb. 1867. Died 15 Jan. 1882.   [1865]

MANDEVILLE, Lord Visct. 5 Suffolk Street, London. Brampton Park, Northamptonshire.

Carlton, and Athenaeum. Eld. s. of the Duke of Manchester. B. 1799; m. 1822, Millicent, only d. and heiress of Brig. Gen. Robert Bernard Sparrow, of Brampton Park, Northamptonshire, by Lady Olivia Atcheson, sister of the present Earl of Gosford. A Commander in the navy. Well known for his patronage of religious societies. A Conservative. Sat for Huntingdonshire from 1826 until he retired in 1837. Succeeded as 6th Duke Apr. 1843. Author. Died 18th Aug. 1855. [1837]

MANDEVILLE, Visct. (I). 18 Charles Street, Berkeley Square, London. Kimbolton Castle, Huntingdonshire. Carlton, National and Guard's. B. at Kimbolton Castle, 1823, the eld. s. of the Duke of Manchester. M. 1852, the Countess Fredericke Auguste D'Alten. Was educ. at the Military Coll., Sandhurst. Entered the 11th Foot in 1841, became Capt. in the Grenadier Guards Jan. 1846, and retired 1850. Was Aide-de-Camp to Sir Peregrine Maitland, Governor of Cape Colony from 1843-46. Appointed Major of the Huntingdon Militia 1852, and was Dept.-Lieut. for that Co. Was a Lord of the Bedchamber to Prince Albert from Mar. 1852-Jan. 1853. A Conservative and Protectionist, opposed to any endowment of the Roman Catholic Clergy. Unsuccessfully contested Westminster 1847. Sat for Bewdley Apr. 1848-June 1852, when he was returned for Huntingdonshire, a few weeks before the general election at which he was also returned. Succeeded as 7th Duke in Aug. 1855. Was engaged in commercial ventures in Canada and Australia. Died 21 Mar. 1890. [1855]

MANDEVILLE, Visct. (II). Kimbolton Castle, St. Neots. Eld. s. of the Duke of Manchester, by Countess Louise, 2nd d. of Charles Francis Victor, Count D'Alten (of Hanover). B. in Cavendish Square, London 1853; m. 1876, Consuela, d. of Senor Antonio Yznaga de Valle, of Ravenswood, Louisiana. A Lieut. Huntingdonshire Militia. A Conservative, and supported measures for 'the more equal adjustment of taxation.' Sat for Huntingdonshire from 1877. Defeated 1880. Bankrupt 2 Apr. 1889. Succeeded as 8th Duke Mar. 1890. Repaid debts at 20s. in the pound. Died 18 Aug. 1892. [1880]

MANGLES, Charles Edward. Poyle Park, Farnham, Surrey. Oriental. S. of James Mangles, Esq., who represented Guildford from 1831 till 1837. M. 1832, Rose, d. of George Newcome, Esq., of the Audit Office, Whitehall. A Capt. in the Maritime Service of the East India Company. A Liberal, in favour of extension of the suffrage and the ballot. Unsuccessfully contested Southampton, July 1841. First elected for Newport, W. Apr. 1857. Retired in 1859. Contested Southampton Dec. 1862. Chairman of London and South-western Railway 1859-72. Died 28 Oct. 1873. [1858]

MANGLES, James. 6 Cannon Row, London. Woodbridge, Surrey. Uncle of Capt. Mangles, R.N. and father of Lady Stirling, wife of Capt. Sir James Stirling, Governor of Swan River. A Ship Chandler, and an East India Proprietor. Of Whig principles; he supplanted Mr. Holme Sumner for Guildford in 1831. Defeated in 1837. [1837]

MANGLES, Ross Donnelly. 9 Henrietta Street, Cavendish Square, London. Woodbridge, Surrey. Athenaeum. S. of J. Mangles, Esq., who represented Guildford from 1831 till 1837. B. 1801; m. in 1830, d. of Geo. Newcombe, Esq. In the Bengal Civil Service, a Director of the E.I.C., and a Director of the New Zealand Company. A Dept.-Lieut. of London. A Liberal, voted for the ballot, 1853; 'determined to resist all aggression upon our national rights by pope or cardinal.' First elected for Guildford in 1841. Sat until appointed Member of Council of India Sept. 1858 to 1866. Died 16 Aug. 1877. [1858]

MANNERS, Lord Charles Somerset, K.C.B. 3 Albany, London. Belvoir Castle, Rutlandshire. Carlton. 2nd s. of the 4th Duke of Rutland, by the youngest d. of the 4th Duke of Beaufort. B. 1780. Became a Lieut.-Gen. in the army in 1838, and Col. of the 3rd Dragoons in 1839. A Conservative, voted for agricultural protection 1846. Sat for Cambridgeshire from 1802 till 1830; first elected for Leicestershire N. in Dec. 1835, on the death of his bro., Lord Robt. Manners. Sat until he retired in 1852. Died 25 May 1855. [1852]

MANNERS, Lord George John. 25 Grosvenor Square, London. Chevely Park, Newmarket, Cambridgeshire. Carlton, and White's. Youngest s. of 5th Duke of Rutland, by Lady Elizabeth, 5th d. of 5th Earl of Carlisle. B. in London 1820; m. 1855, Lady Adeliza Matilda, d. of 13th Duke of Norfolk. Educ. at Eton and Trinity Coll., Cambridge, where he graduated M.A. 1841. Entered the army as cornet 1840; appointed Major Royal Horse Guards with the rank of Lieut.-Col. in the army 1861, became Brevet Col., and retired 1866. A Conservative. Sat for Cambridgeshire from Aug. 1847 till Apr. 1857; re-elected Feb. 1863. MP until his death 8 Sept. 1874. [1874]

MANNERS, Rt. Hon. Lord John James Robert, G.C.B. 3 Cambridge Gate, Regent's Park, London. Belvoir Castle, Grantham, Lincolnshire. St. Mary's Tower, Birham, Scotland. Carlton. 2nd s. of 5th Duke of Rutland, by the d.

of 5th Earl of Carlisle. B. at Belvoir Castle, 1818; m. 1st, 1851, Catherine, only d. of Col. Marlay, C.B. (she died 1854); 2ndly, 1862, Janetta, eld. d. of Thomas Hughan, Esq. Educ. at Eton and at Trinity Coll., Cambridge. Created D.C.L. at Oxford 1876. Was Commissioner of the Works and Buildings from Mar.-Dec. 1852, with a seat in the Cabinet, again from Mar. 1858-June 1859, and a third time from July 1866-Dec. 1868. Also Postmaster-Gen. from 1874-80, and again in 1885, and Chancellor of the Duchy of Lancaster Aug. 1886. Author of a *Plea for National Holidays*, etc. A Tory. Represented Newark from 1841-July 1847; unsuccessfully contested Liverpool in July 1847 and London in 1849. Sat for Colchester from Feb. 1850-Feb. 1857, for Leicestershire N. from that date to Nov. 1885, and for the Melton div. until he succeeded bro. as 7th Duke of Rutland, Mar. 1888. Died 4 Aug. 1904. [1887]

MANNERS, Lord Robert. 56 Upper Brook Street, London. Bro. of the Duke of Rutland. Born 1781. A Major-General in the Army. A Conservative. Sat for Leicestershire N. in seven parliaments consecutively previous to the election of 1831, when his opposition to the first Reform Bill caused him to be supplanted by Mr. Paget. Sat for the county again in 1832. MP until his death in 1835. [1835]

MAPPIN, F.T. Continued in House after 1885: full entry in Volume II.

MARCH, Charles Henry Gordon-Lennox, Earl of. Goodwood Park, Chichester, Sussex. Carlton. Eld. s. of the Duke of Richmond, by Frances Harriet, eld. d. of Algernon Frederick Greville, Esq. B. in Portland Place 1845; m. 1st, 1868, Amy Mary, eld. d. of Percy Ricardo, Esq., (she died 1879); 2ndly, 1882, Isabel, d. of W.G. Craven, Esq., (she died 1887). Educ. at Eton. Appointed Lieut. Grenadier Guards 1868; retired 1869. A Conservative. Sat for W. Sussex from 1869-85, and for the Chichester div. from 1885 until he accepted Chiltern Hundreds 1888. [1888]

MARCH, Rt. Hon. Earl of. 51 Portland Place, London. Goodwood, Sussex. Carlton. Eld. s. of the Duke of Richmond. B. at Richmond House, Whitehall 1818; m. 1843, Frances Harriet, eld. d. of Algernon Greville, Esq. Educ. at Christ Church, Oxford, where he graduated 1839. Became a Capt. in the army 1844. Formerly in the Guards. Was Aide-de-Camp to the Duke of Wellington when Commander-in-Chief, and re-appointed by his successor, Visct. Hardinge, Sept. 1852. A Dept.-Lieut. of Banff. Was President of the Poor Law Board from Mar.-June 1859. A Conservative. First returned for Sussex

W. in 1841 and sat until he succeeded to the Peerage (Duke of Richmond) in Oct. 1860. President of the Board of Trade 1867-68; Lord President of the Council 1874-80; Secretary of State for Scotland and President of Council on Education 1885-86; additional title of Duke of Gordon Jan. 1876. Died 27 Sept. 1903.   [1860]

MARE, Charles John. 11 Hyde Park Gardens, London. Orchard Yard, Blackwall. Broomlands, Nr. Nantwich, Cheshire. National. S. of M. Mare, Esq. of Hatherton, near Nantwich, Cheshire. B. 1815; m. 1843, Mary, eld. d. of Peter Rolt, Esq., MP. Head of the firm of Mare and Co., Shipbuilders, at Orchard Yard, Blackwall, and had an interest in the General Screw Steam Shipping Co. A Conservative, and a supporter generally of Lord Derby's government; wanted 'to uphold the interests of the Protestant Church, and to repeal the grant to the Popish College of Maynooth', in favour of measures of compensation for the repeal of the corn and navigation laws. First returned for Plymouth in July 1852; unseated May 1853. Died 8 Feb. 1898.   [1852 2nd ed.]

MARJORIBANKS, Charles Albany. The Lees, Berkwickshire. 3rd s. of Sir John Marjoribanks, Bart., of Lees; b. 1794; in the civil service of the East India Company. Of Whig principles, and in general a supporter of ministers. Returned for Berwickshire in 1832; remained an MP until his death in 1833.   [1833]

MARJORIBANKS, Sir Dudley Coutts, Bart. Brook House, Park Lane, London. Guisachan, Beauly, Inverness-shire. Hulton Hall, Berwickshire. Travellers' and Arthur's. 2nd s. of Edward Marjoribanks, Esq., of Greenlands, Buckinghamshire, formerly partner in the banking house of Messrs. Coutts, by Georgiana, 3rd d. of Joseph Francis Louis Lautour, Esq., of Madras, and of Heaton Park, Bedfordshire. B. 1820; m. 1848, Isabella, d. of the Rt. Hon. Sir James Weir Hogg, Bart. Educ. at Harrow and at Christ Church, Oxford. Called to the bar at the Middle Temple 1848. A Partner in Messrs. Meux and Co's. Brewery. A Magistrate and Dept.-Lieut. for Middlesex, for London and for Inverness-shire. A Liberal. Sat for Berwick-on-Tweed from Apr. 1853 till Apr. 1859 (when he was an unsuccessful candidate there), and from Aug. 1859 to Dec. 1868; re-elected Feb. 1874 until he was created Peer (Lord Tweedmouth) 1881. Died 4 Mar. 1894.   [1881]

MARJORIBANKS, Hon. E. Continued in House after 1885: full entry in Volume II.

MARJORIBANKS, Stewart. 6 Charles Street,

Berkeley Square, London. Cliff House, Folkstone. Bushey Grove, Hertfordshire. S. of Ed. Marjoribanks, Esq., of Lees House, Berwickshire. M. d. of Ed. Roger Pratt, Esq., and widow of William Lord Rendlesham. A Whig. Represented Hythe at the time of the Reform Act and continued to sit for Hythe 1832-47 except for the Parliament of 1837-41 when Visct. Melgund presented himself as the Whig candidate. Retired in 1847.   [1847]

MARLING, Sir Samuel Stephens. 42 St. James's Place, London. Stanley Park, Stroud. Reform. 6th s. of William Marling, Esq., of Stroud, by Sarah, d. of Nathaniel Hillman, Esq., of Rodborough, Gloucestershire. B. at Woodchester, Gloucestershire 1810; m. 1834, Margaret Williams, d. of William Bentley Cartwright, Esq., of Devizes. Educ. at Gloucester. A Woollen Cloth Manufacturer. A Magistrate and Dept.-Lieut. of Gloucestershire. Patron of 2 livings. A Liberal, said he would give Mr. Gladstone a 'cordial support', voted for the disestablishment of the Irish Church 1869. Sat for W. Gloucestershire from Dec. 1868-Dec. 1873, and sat for Stroud from 1875. Retired 1880. Created Baronet May 1882. Died 22 Oct. 1883.   [1880]

MARRIOTT, Rt. Hon. W.T. Continued in House after 1885: full entry in Volume II.

MARRYATT, Joseph. 6 Richmond Terrace, London. Wimbledon House, Surrey. A Ship-Owner, Banker and Merchant in London and a West India Proprietor. A moderate Reformer, voted for the Reform Act, was against the immediate abolition of slavery. Represented Sandwich from 1826, his father, who died in 1824, having represented it for many years previously. Sat until he retired in 1835. Died 24 Sept. 1876.   [1833]

MARSH, Matthew Henry. Ramridge, Nr. Andover. Reform, Athenaeum, Oxford & Cambridge. S. of the Rev. Matthew Marsh, Canon of Salisbury, and Chancellor of the diocese, by Margaret his wife. B. at Winterslow, near Salisbury, 1810; m. 1844, Eliza Mary Anne, d. of Sergeant Merewether, Esq., of Earthfield, Wiltshire. Educ. at Westminster School and Christ Church, Oxford, where he graduated B.A. 1833, M.A. 1835. Called to the bar at the Inner Temple, May 1836, and joined the Western Circuit. Went to Australia in 1840, where he undertook sheep-farming on a large scale. Was a member of council of New South Wales from 1851-1854. A 'Liberal-Whig', but 'held himself bound to no party in the country'; voted against Lord Russell's Reform Bill 1866. First returned for Salisbury in Apr. 1857. Sat until he retired in 1868. Died 26 Jan. 1881. [1867]

MARSHALL, James Garth. 37 South Street, London. Monk-Coniston, Lancashire. Reform. 3rd s. of John Marshall, Esq., of Headingly, Yorkshire, and of Hallsteads, Cumberland, by the 5th d. of William Pollard, Esq., of Halifax. Bro. to Wm. Marshall, Esq., MP for Cumberland East. B. 1802; m. 1841, Hon. Mary Alice Pery, d. of his bro.-in-law Lord Monteagle, by his Lordship's first wife. A Magistrate for Lancashire; Director of the Leeds, Dewsbury, and Manchester Railway. A Liberal. First returned in 1847 for Leeds, which his bro., John Marshall, jun., had represented from 1832 to 1835. The linen-yarn factories of his family in Leeds gave them influence there. Sat until he retired in 1852. Sheriff of Yorkshire 1860. Died 22 Oct. 1873. [1852]

MARSHALL, John. 41 Upper Grosvenor Street, London. 2nd s. of John Marshall, Esq., the Member for Yorkshire. A Manufacturer at Leeds, in partnership with his father. A Reformer, inclining to radicalism. Sat for Leeds from 1832. Retired in 1835. [1833]

MARSHALL, William. 32 St. George's Road, London. Patterdale Hall, Ambleside, Westmoreland. Hallsteads, Penrith, Cumberland. Athenaeum and Brooks's. Eld. s. of John Marshall, Esq., of Headingly, in Yorkshire (an extensive Linen Manufacturer at Leeds and Shrewsbury, and in 1826 Member for Yorkshire), by Jane, 5th d. of William Pollard, Esq., of Halifax. B. 1796; m. 1828, Georgiana Christiana, 7th d. of George Hibbert, Esq., of Munden, Hertfordshire (she died 1866). A Liberal, in favour of triennial Parliaments, vote by ballot, 'an extension and equitable division of the suffrage', and the reform of the Church Establishment. Sat for Petersfield from 1826-1830; for Leominster in 1830; for Beverley in 1831; for Carlisle from 1835-1847, when he was returned for Cumberland E. Sat until he was defeated in 1868. Died 16 May 1872. [1867]

MARSHAM, Visct. 8 York Street, St. James's Square, London. Boxley Park, Kent. Carlton. Eld. s. of Earl of Romney. B. 1808; m. in 1832, 4th d. of 4th Duke of Buccleugh. A Conservative. First returned for W. Kent in 1841. Sat until he succeeded as 3rd Earl 29 Mar. 1845. Died 3 Sept. 1874. [1843]

MARSLAND, Henry. Reform. A Manufacturer. A Reformer, in favour of triennial Parliaments and the abolition of monopolies. Unsuccessfully contested Stockport in 1832. Sat for it from 1835 until he retired 1847. [1847]

MARSLAND, Thomas. Cheadle Mosely, Cheshire. Stogamerton Park, Staffordshire. Windham. B. 13 Sept. 1777; m. Sept. 1795, Frances Ann, d. of Edw. Kenworthy, Esq., of London. A Conservative, 'in favour of Reform, as far as it can be effected with safety to the institutions of the country.' Sat for Stockport from 1832 until defeated 1841; contested same seat at a by-election 16 Dec. 1847. [1838]

MARTEN, Alfred George, 21 Prince of Wales Terrace, London. 10 New Square, Lincoln's Inn, London. Oxford & Cambridge, and Carlton. S. of Robert Giles Marten, Esq., of Plaistow, Essex, by Eliza, d. of John Warmington, Esq. A descendant of Sir Henry Marten, Dean of the Arches, who represented the University of Oxford in 1628. B. at Paistow 1829; m. 1869, Patricia Barrington, d. of Capt. Vincent F. Kennett, of the Manor House, Dorchester-on-Thame, Oxfordshire, and grand-d. of Sir Jonah Barrington. Educ. at St. John's Coll., Cambridge, of which he was a Fellow, and graduated M.A. and LL.D. A member of the Board of Legal Studies and Examiner in Law in that University, and delivered a course of public lectures on law in the Hall of St. John's Coll. in 1867 and 1868. Called to the bar at the Inner Temple (of which he was a bencher), Jan. 1857, when he obtained a certificate of honour of the 1st class in examination. Became a Queen's Counsel 1874. Author of a paper *On the Judical Constitution of the Court of Chancery, and its methods of procedure in Court and in Chambers.* A Conservative, in favour of the readjustment of local taxation. Was an unsuccessful candidate for Nottingham July 1865. Sat for the Bor. of Cambridge from Feb. 1874 until defeated 1880. Died 29 Apr. 1906. [1880]

MARTIN, Charles Wykeham, 25 Great Cumberland Street, Hyde Park, London. Leeds Castle, Maidstone. Chacombe Priory, Banbury. United University. S. of Fiennes Wykeham Martin, Esq., of Leeds Castle, Maidstone, by Eliza d. of R. Bignell, Esq. B. 1801; m. 1st, 1828, Lady Jemima Maria, d. of last Earl Cornwallis; 2ndly, 1838 Matilda, d. of Sir John Trollope, Bart. Educ. at Eton and at Balliol Coll., Oxford. A Dept.-Lieut. of Hampshire. Senior Maj. of 3rd Batt. of Kent Volunteers. Patron of 1 living. A Liberal, opposed to the ballot. Unsuccessfully contested Newport July 1837; sat for that borough July 1841-July 1852, when he was unsuccessful candidate. Contested Maidstone 16 May 1853. Sat for Kent W. from Feb. 1857-Apr. 1859, when he was unsuccessful; elected for New-

port, Isle of Wight July 1865. MP until his death
Oct. 1870.   [1870]

MARTIN, James. 68 Lombard Street, London.
Camden, Chislehurst, Kent. Windham. S. of
John Martin, Esq., who sat for Tewkesbury from
1812-1832. B. in Lombard Street, London 1807.
Educ. at the Charterhouse. A Banker. A
Dept.-Lieut. for Herefordshire. A Whig, 'the
decided friend of civil and religious liberty'; in
favour of admitting the working classes to a share
of political power 'proportionate to their increased intelligence'; supported Lord Palmerston
on the vote of censure 1864. First elected for
Tewkesbury Apr. 1859. Defeated 1865. Contested
seat again at 1866 by-election.   [1865]

MARTIN, John. (I). 15 Abingdon Street. Knox's
Street, Sligo. Mr. Martin was the s. and grand-s.
of eminent and wealthy Merchants in Ireland,
rather a remarkable circumstance in that Co.
where individuals engaged in trade usually retired
as soon as they had realized a small independence. A Reformer. Returned for Sligo in
Dec. 1832. Defeated 1837.   [1833]

MARTIN, John. (II). 14 Berkeley Square,
London. 68 Lombard Street, London. Reform. S.
of J. Martin, Esq., who sat for Tewkesbury from
1812 to 1832. B. 1805; m. 1st 1837, Mary d. of
Capt. T.A. Morse, of the Bombay Artillery; 2nd-
ly, 1847, Maria Henrietta, eld. d. of Evan
Hamilton Baillie, Esq., of Gloucester Place, Portman Square, London. A Banker, a Director of the
Guardian Assurance Company, and an East India Stock proprietor. A Liberal, voted for inquiry
into Maynooth, 1853. Sat for Tewkesbury from
1832 to 1835, and from 1837 until he retired in
1859.   [1858]

MARTIN, John. (III). Seaview, Warren Point,
Co. Down. Loughome, Co. Down. S. of Samuel
Martin, Esq., of Loughome, Co. Down, by his m.
with Miss Jane Harshaw. B. at Loughome 1812;
m. 1868, Henrietta, d. of Rev. John Mitchel,
Presbysterian Minister of Newry, and at Trinity
Coll., Dublin. A Liberal, in favour of repeal of the
union with Ireland and 'the restoration of Irish
home government'. Contested Longford Co. 31
Dec. 1869. Sat for Meath from Jan. 1871. MP until his death 29 Mar. 1875.   [1874]

MARTIN, Patrick L. 23 Upper Fitz-William
Street, Dublin. Reform. Stephen's Green, and
University, Dublin. Only s. of John Martin, Esq.,
of Lower Gardiner Street, Dublin, by his m. with
Miss Esther Shannon. B. in Dublin 1830; m.
1869, Margaret Magan, eld. d. of Michael Cahill,
Esq., J.P., of Ballyconra House, Co. Kilkenny.

Educ. at St. Mary's Coll., Oscott, and at Trinity
Coll., Dublin; graduated B.A. 1852; M.A. 1862.
Was called to the bar in Ireland Sept. 1852; ap-
pointed a Q.C. in 1877. An Independent Liberal.
Sat for the Co. of Kilkenny from Feb. 1874 until
he retired in 1885. Died 29 Oct. 1895.   [1885]

MARTIN, Philip Wykeham. 7 Waterloo Place,
Leamington. Leeds Castle, Maidstone. Reform,
Brooks's, and United University. Eld. s. of
Charles Wykeham Martin, Esq., of Leeds Castle,
Kent, Member for Newport, I.O.W., by Jemima,
d. of Earl Cornwallis. B. in Hill Street, 1829; m.
1850, Miss Elizabeth Ward. Educ. at Eton, and at
Balliol College, Oxford, where he graduated B.A.
1850. Patron of 1 living. A Liberal, voted in favour
of the disestablishment of the Irish Church 1869.
Sat for Rochester from Feb. 1856. MP until his
death 31 May 1878.   [1878]

MARTIN, Sir. R.B. Continued in House after
1885: full entry in Volume II.

MARTIN, Sir Samuel. 79 Eaton Place, London.
1 Essex Court, Temple, London. M. the d. of Sir
Frederick Pollock. Was called to the bar at the
Middle Temple in 1830. A Queen's Counsel, and
on the northern circuit. A Liberal. First returned
for Pontefract in 1847. Appointed Judge and
Knighted Nov. 1850. Sat until he retired 1874.
Died 9 Jan. 1883.   [1850]

MARTIN, Thomas Barnewall. Ballinahinch
Castle, Co. Galway. S. of the eccentric and
humane member for Galway, Richard Martin,
Esq., who gave his name to the Act passed for the
Prevention of Cruelty to Animals. Of Whig principles, voted for agricultural protection 1846. Sat
for Galway Co. from 1832. MP until his death in
1847.   [1847]

MARTON, George. 3 Park Crescent, London.
Capernwray Hall, Lancashire. United University. Descended from the ancient family of Marton,
who held property in the north from the Conquest, and one of whom, an ancestor of this
member, represented Lancashire a century ago.
B. 1801; m. Nov. 1833, Lucy Sarah, d. of Rt. Hon.
Lord Chief Justice Dallas. A Magistrate, and
Dept.-Lieut. of Lancashire; appointed in 1843
one of the gentlemen of the Privy Chamber.
Patron of the vicarage of Lancaster and its various
dependent chapelries. A Conservative, gave no
pledges; voted for agricultural protection 1846.
LL.B. of Cambridge. Sat for Lancaster from 1837
until he retired 1847. Died 24 Nov. 1867. [1847]

MARTYN, Charles Cecil. Whitehall Gardens,
London. Carlton. B. 1809; m. 1832, d. of John

Elliot, Esq. A Conservative. Unsuccessfully contested Southampton in 1837; first returned for it in 1841. Unseated in 1842.   [1842]

MARUM, E.M. Continued in House after 1885: full entry in Volume II.

MASKELYNE, N. Story. Continued in House after 1885: full entry in Volume II.

MASON, Hugh. 33 Onslow Square, London. Groby Hall, Ashton-under-Lyne. Reform. S. of Thomas Mason, Esq., of Stalybridge, by Mary, d. of John Holden, Esq. B. at Stalybridge, Lancashire; m. 1st, Sarah, d. of Abel Buckley, Esq., of Ashton-under-Lyne; 2ndly, Betsey, youngest d. of Abel Buckley, Esq.; 3rdly, Annie, d. of George Ashworth, Esq., of Rochdale. A Cotton-Spinner, proprietor of the Oxford Mills, Ashton--under-Lyne. Was Mayor of Ashton in three successive years, 1858-59-60. A Magistrate for Cheshire, Aston-under-Lyne, and Lancashire, and Dept.-Lieut. of the last. Was President of the Manchester Chamber of Commerce from 1871 to 1873. A member of the Mersey Docks and Harbour Board, and a Governor of Owen's Coll., Manchester. An 'advanced Liberal.' Sat for Ashton-under-Lyne from Apr. 1880. Defeated in 1885. Died 2 Feb. 1886.   [1885]

MASSEY, Rt. Hon. William Nathiental. 96 Portland Place, London. Old Basing, Hampshire. Athenaeum, Brooks's and City Liberal. B. 1809; m. 1st, 1833 Frances Carleton, d. of Rev. John Orde (she d. 1872); 2ndly, 1880, Helen Henrietta, youngest d. of the late Patrick Grant, Esq. Sheriff-Clerk of Inverness-shire. Admitted a Student of the Inner Temple, Nov. 1826; called to the bar Jan. 1844. Appointed Recorder of Portsmouth 1852. Was Under-Sec. for the Home Dept. from Aug. 1855-Mar. 1858. Chairman of Committees of the whole House from 1859-65. A member of the Council of the Gov. Gen. of India and Finance Minister there from 1865-72. Author of *Common Sense Versus Common Law, History of England under George III.* A Liberal. Sat for Newport from July 1852-Apr. 1857; for Salford from the latter date until his departure for India in Jan. 1865. Contested Liverpool 19 Nov. 1868. Sat for Tiverton from Nov. 1872. MP until his death 25 Oct. 1881.   [1881]

MASTER, Thomas William Chester-, sen. 32a Mount Street, London. Knole Park, Nr. Bristol. Carlton. Eld. s. of Col. William Chester-Master by Isabella-Margaret, d. of Col. the Hon. Stephen Digby. B. 28th May 1815. M. 1840, d. of Sir G. Cornewall, Bart. The family of Master was originally settled in Kent, but held large estates in

Gloucestershire, including the site of the Ancient Abbey of Cirencester, under a grant from Queen Elizabeth made on the attainder of Lord Seymour in 1864. Held 'strictly Conservative' opinions. Returned for Cirencester in 1837. Accepted Chiltern Hundreds July 1844. Died 31 Jan. 1899.   [1844]

MASTER, Thomas William Chester-, jun. Stratton House, Cirencester. Carlton. Eld. s. of Thomas William Chester-Master, Esq., of The Abbey, Cirencester, and Knole Park, Bristol, by Catherine Elizabeth, eld. d. of Sir George Cornewall, Bart., of Moccas Court, Herefordshire. B. in London 1841; m. 1866, Georgina Emily, 5th d. of John Etherington Welch Rolls, Esq., of the Hendre, Monmouthsire. Was educ. at Harrow and at Christ Church, Oxford. Major Royal North Gloucester Militia. A Magistrate for Gloucester and Monmouth. A Conservative. Sat for Cirencester from Mar. 1878 until he retired in 1885.   [1885]

MASTERMAN, John. 35 Nicholas Lane, Lombard Street, London. Knott's Green, Leyton, Essex. A member of the firm of Masterman, Peters, Mildred, and Company, London, Bankers. An East India Director, a Dept.-Lieut. of London. A Conservative, was 'prepared to resist any further concessions to Popery.' Was first elected for the City of London in 1841. Sat until he retired 1857. Died 23 Jan. 1862. [1857]

MATHESON, Sir Alexander, Bart. 16 South Street, Grosvenor Square, London. Ardross Castle, Alness, Ross-shire. Reform. Eld. s. of John Matheson, Esq., of Attadale, Ross-shire, (where the family had resided for upwards of six centuries), and nephew maternally of Sir James Matheson, Bart. and Lieut.-Col. Thomas Matheson. B. in Ross-shire; m. 1st, 1841, only d. of J.C. McLeod, Esq., of Geanses (died); 2ndly, 1853, Hon. Lavinia Mary, sister of 8th Lord Beaumont (she died 1855); 3rdly, 1860, Eleanor Irving, d. of Spencer Perceval, Esq., of Portman Square, London (she died 1879). Was educ. at the Univ. of Edinburgh. A Merchant and Senior Partner of the firm of Matheson & Co. in London. A Director of the Bank of England and of the E & W India Dock Co., A Dept.-Lieut. of Ross and Cromarty, of Inverness, also of London. A Liberal. Sat for Inverness district of burghs from 1847-Dec. 1868, from which date he sat for Ross and Cromarty until he accepted Chiltern Hundreds 1884. Died 26 July 1886.   [1884]

MATHESON, Sir James, Bart., F.R.S. 13 Cleveland Row, London. Achany and Rose Hall, Bonar Bridge, Sutherlandshire. Stornaway Casthe Stornaway, Island of Lewis. Reform and Brooks's. 2nd s. of Capt. Donald Matheson, of Skinness, Sutherlandshire, by the d. of the Rev. Thomas Mackay, Minister of Lairg. B. at Lairg 1796; m. 1843, Mary Jane, 4th d. of Michael Henry Perceval, Esq., of Spencer Wood, Canada. A Merchant, and once a partner in the house of Jardine, Matheson, and Company. A Dept.-Lieut. of Ross and Sutherlandshire. Author of a pamphlet on the position and prospects of the China trade. Resided many years in India and China; on his return to England received an address from the native merchants of Bombay, expressing their high sense of the judgment and firmness displayed by him during the disputes with China respecting the seizure of opium. On that occasion he was presented with a service of plate, value £1,500. Appointed Lieut. and Sheriff-Principal of the Co. of Ross 1866. A Liberal. Sat for Ashburton from 1843-47, when he was returned for Ross and Cromarty. Sat until he retired in 1868. Died late Dec. 1878.   [1867]

MATHESON, Lieut.-Col. Thomas. Achany, Sutherlandshire. United Service, and Army & Navy. S. of Donald Matheson, Esq., and bro. to Sir James Matheson, Bart., MP for Ross and Cromarty. B. at Shinness, Sutherlandshire 1798. Unmarried. Entered the army as Ensign in 1815; became Lieut.-Col. in the 42nd Foot in 1843, when he retired on half-pay. A Liberal. First returned in 1847, without opposition, for Ashburton, which his bro. James Matheson, Esq., had represented in the previous Parliament. Retired in 1852. Died 14 Feb. 1873.   [1852]

MATHEW, George Benvenuto. 23 Queen Street, Mayfair, London. Grand-s. of D. Mathew, Esq., of Felix Hall, Essex, who sprang from the parent stock of the family of the Earls of Llandaff, being lineally descended from Sir David Mathew of Glamorgan, Great Standard Bearer of England under Edward IV. A branch of this house, from which Capt. Mathew immediately derived, had settled in Cornwall. B. 1807; m. 1835, the only child of Sir R. Hoare, Bart. of Stourhead. A Lieut. in the Coldstream Guards, and a Capt. in the Army. In favour of a property tax, the corn laws, the more equal distribution of Church property among the Clergy, and of Dissenters being enabled to redeem at a low value their property (during possession) from Church Rates; opposed to the ballot and triennial Parliaments. In Ireland, wished the franchise raised to 20/- and the tithes sold at a reduced value to the proprietors of the land and vested in the Government; the Clergy to receive from Government an adequate salary, provided the Catholic priesthood also received their salary from Government. Sat

for Athlone from 12 Jan. 1835, until he retired in 1837. Was a candidate for Shaftesbury in 1837; seated on petition 3 Apr. 1838. Defeated in 1841.   [1836]

MATTHEWS, Henry. 5 Paper Buildings, Temple, London. Athenaeum and Windham. B. in Ceylon 1826, the s. of Hon. Henry Matthews, Puisne Justice of the Supreme Court of Ceylon, by Emma, d. of William Blount, Esq., of Oreleton, Herefordshire. Unmarried. Educ. at Paris and at University Coll., London, of which he became a Fellow. Graduated at the former as *Bachelier ès lettres*, and at London University took the degrees of B.A. and LL.B. Was called to the bar at Lincoln's Inn 1850, appointed Queen's Counsel 1868 and joined the Oxford Circuit. A Liberal, voted in favour of the disestablishment of the Irish Church 1869, and favoured denominational education, by which there should be colleges and schools appropriated to each creed. Sat for Dungarvan from Dec. 1868 until his defeat in 1874.   [1873]

MAULE, Rt. Hon. Fox. 19 Eaton Place, London. Dalguise, Perthshire. Eld. s. of Lord Panmure, and cousin to the 1st Marq. of Dalhousie. B. at Brechin Castle, Forfarshire, 1801; m. in 1831 Montague, eld. d. of Lord Abercromby. Was 12 years in the 79th Highlanders. Lord-Lieut. of Forfar. A Governor of the Charterhouse. A Liberal. Was Under-Secretary for the Home Department, and Vice-President of the Board of Trade. Appointed Secretary at War, July 1846; salary, £2,-480. Was elected for the Elgin district in Mar. 1838, on the appointment of Sir A.L. Hay to be Governor of Bermuda. Sat for Perthshire from 1835 till dissolution in 1837; was then an unsuccessful candidate, but was returned in Mar. 1838 for Elgin district; sat for the bor. of Perth from 1841 until he succeeded as 2nd Lord Panmure 13 Apr. 1852. Sec.-at-War 1855-58; succeeded bro. as 11th Earl of Dalhousie 19 Dec. 1860. Died July 1874.   [1852]

MAULE, Hon. Lauderdale. 37 Jermyn Street, London. Brechin Castle, Forfarshire. B. 1807, the 2nd s. of 1st Lord Panmure, by his 1st wife, Patricia Heron, d. of Gilbert Gordon of Halleaths. Unmarried. Entered the army in 1826. Became Lieut.-Col. 79th Highlanders in 1842, exchanged to half pay 1852. Appointed Dept.-Lieut. of Forfarshire in 1850. Surveyor General of the Ordnance from Dec. 1852. A Liberal. Sat for Forfarshire from July 1852 until his death on 1 Aug. 1854.   [1854]

MAULE, William Henry. 14 Paper Buildings, London. Athenaeum and Reform. Was Senior Wrangler at Cambridge in 1810, and a Fellow of

Trinity Coll. there. A Barrister and Queen's Counsel. Of Liberal politics. First elected for Carlow at the general election of 1837, and sat until appointed Judge Feb. 1839; resigned 1855. Died 16 Jan. 1858.   [1838]

MAUNSELL, Thomas Philip. Thorpe Malsor, Kettering, Northamptonshire. Union, and Carlton. Eld. s. of the Rev. William Maunsell, by Lucy, d. and co-heir of Phillip Oliver, Esq., of Castle Oliver, Co. Limerick. Nephew of Thomas Cecil Maunsell, of Thorpe Malsor, to whose estates he succeeded. B. 1781; m. 1811, Caroline Elizabeth, d. and co-heir of the Hon. William Cockayne, bro. of Visct. Cullen. This lady was authorized to take rank as a Viscount's d. by royal order 23 Sept. 1836. Served as High Sheriff of Northamptonshire. of which he was a Dept.-Lieut. Col. of the Northampton Militia. Patron of 1 living. A Conservative, said he would 'uphold the Protestant religion in all its efficiency.' Sat for Northamptonshire N. from Dec. 1835 until he retired 1857. Died 4 Mar. 1866. [1857]

MAXFIELD, Capt. William. 2 Bridge Street, Westminster, London. Sunbury, Middlesex. Once of the Bombay Marine. Of Whig principles, he ousted Lord Loughborough, who had voted against Reform. Sat for Great Grimsby from 1832. Retired in 1835.   [1833]

MAXWELL, Henry. 17 Portland Place, London. Farnham House, Co. Cavan. Carlton. Eld. s. of the Rev. Henry Maxwell, bro. of Lord Farnham, by Anna, eld. d. of Thomas Henry Earl of Carrick; b. 1799; m. 1828, Anna, youngest d. of Lord de Despencer. A Magistrate for the counties of Cavan and Wexford. Grand Sec. to the Orange Institution in Ireland. Capt.-Commandant of the Fortland Yeomanry Corps. A Conservative. Opposed to the Annual Grant to the Roman Catholic College of Maynooth. Voted in favour of the abolition of the punishment of death for forgery, for Sir H. Parnell's motion, in 1830, on the Civil List, against the Catholic claims and the Reform Bills. Sat for the Co. of Cavan from 1824 until he succeeded father as 7th Baron 19 Oct. 1838. Irish representative Peer 1839 until his death 20 Aug. 1868.   [1838]

MAXWELL, Sir H. Continued in House after 1885: full entry in Volume II.

MAXWELL, Hon James Pierce. 45 Curzon Street, London. Carlton and Army & Navy. 3rd s. of 6th Lord Farnham, by the eld. d. of 2nd Earl of Carrick; was therefore bro. to the Hon. Somerset Richard Maxwell, who represented the Co. of Cavan in 1839. B. 1813. Became Major 50th Foot;

Lieut.-Col. in the army in 1885. Was wounded before Sebastopol, and returned home invalided Dec. 1855. A Conservative. First returned for Cavan Co. in 1843, on the death of Col. Clements. Sat until he retired 1865. Succeeded as 9th Baron Farnham June 1884. Died 26 Oct. 1896. [1865]

MAXWELL, John, F.R.S. F.H.S. Polioc, Renfrewshire. Haggs Castle, Lanarkshire. Brooks's and Travellers'. S. of Sir John Maxwell, Bart. late member for Paisley; provincial Grand Master of the Lower Ward of Lanarkshire, and an ex-Col. of the Renfrewshire Militia. Opposed to the monopoly of the Bank of England, and to the existing Corn Laws; an advocate of Triennial Parliaments, the substitution of a Property Tax for those on the necessaries of life, Church Reform in England and Ireland; and with regard to Scotland, wished the parishioners to have a voice in the selection of their pastors. Sat for Renfrewshire in three Parliaments previous to his election for Lanarkshire in 1832. Retired in 1837. Author. Died 6 June 1865.   [1837]

MAXWELL, Sir John, Bart. Polioc, Renfrewshire. 2 Grosvenor Gate, London. M. Anne, d. of Richard Gardiner, Esq., of Mount Amelia, Norfolk. Of Whig principles, inclining to radicalism. Sat for Renfrewshire before his son. Returned for Paisley in 1832. Accepted Chiltern Hundreds, March 1834; contested Renfrewshire 1837. Died 30 July 1844.   [1833]

MAXWELL, John Maxwell Heron-. Kirouchtree, Newton Stewart, Scotland. Junior United Service. S. of the Rev. Michael Maxwell-Heron, of Heron and Kirouchtree, Kircudbrightshire, who assumed the name of Maxwell, by Charlotte Frances, eld. d. of Capt. F.W. Burgoyne, R.N. B. 1836; m. 1868, Marguerite, d. of William Stancomb, Esq., of Blount's Court, Wiltshire. Was educ. at Harrow. Entered the 1st (Royals) Foot Jan. 1855; became Lieut. May following; retired as Capt., half-pay, 1868. A Magistrate and Dept.-Lieut. for Kircudbright and Wigtown. A Liberal, 'of sound but moderate views.' Sat for Kircudbrightshire from Apr. 1880. Retired in 1885. Died 26 Jan. 1899.   [1885]

MAXWELL, John Waring. Long's Hotel, Bond Street, London. A Conservative, he sat for Downpatrick in the Parliaments of 1820 and 1826, but in 1830 Mr. Ruthven, a Reformer, and the member for Dublin, supplanted him. Sat again for Downpatrick in 1832. Retired in 1835. [1833]

MAXWELL, Somerset Richard. Arley Cottage, Co. Cavan. B. 1803, bro. of 7th Lord Farnham. A Conservative. Was elected for Cavan Co. in

1839, on his bro. succeeding to a peerage. Accepted Chiltern Hundreds in 1840. Sheriff of Cavan 1844. Succeeded bro. as 8th Baron Farnham in 1868. Died 1 June 1884. [1840]

MAXWELL, Wellwood Herries. Munches, Dalbeattie, Scotland. Eld. s. of John Herries Maxwell, Esq., of Barnclellch, by Clementina Herries, d. of William Maxwell, of Munches and Terraughty. B. at Munches 1817. M. 1844, Jane Home, eld. d. of Sir William Jardine, Bart., of Applegarth. Educ. at Edinburgh Academy, Edinburgh University and Exeter Coll., Oxford. Was called to the bar in Scotland 1839. A Magistrate and Dept.-Lieut. for Kirkcudbrightshire. A Liberal, voted against the disestablishment of the Irish Church 1869. Sat for Kirkcudbrightshire from Feb. 1868 until his retirement in 1874. [1873]

MAXWELL, Sir William Stirling-, Bart., K.T. 10 Upper Grosvenor Street, London. Keir House, Dunblane, Perthshire. Pollock House, Pollockshaws, Glasgow. Athenaeum, Carlton, Travellers', and Oxford & Cambridge. Only s. of Archibald Stirling, Esq., of Keir, Perthshire, by Elizabeth, 2nd d. of Sir John Maxwell, Bart., of Pollock. B. at Kenmure, Nr. Glasgow 1818; m. 1865, Lady Anne Maria, 2nd d. of 9th Earl of Leven and Melville (she died 1874). Assumed the name of Maxwell in 1866, on succeeding to the title and estates of his uncle, Sir John Maxwell. Educ. at Trinity Coll., Cambridge where he graduated B.A. 1839, M.A. 1843, and was created Hon. LL.D. 1874 and D.C.L. at Oxford 1876. Elected Rector of St. Andrews University 1863, when he received the degree of LL.D. Chancellor of Glasgow University Apr. 1875. Author of *Annals of the Artists of Spain, Cloister Life of the Emperor Charles V*, etc. Patron of 1 living. A Conservative. Sat for Perthshire from July 1852-Dec. 1868. (when he was unsuccessful); re-elected Feb. 1874. MP until his death 15 Jan. 1878. [1877]

MAXWELL-HERON, John. See MAXWELL, John Maxwell Heron-.

MAYNE, T. Continued in House after 1885: full entry in Volume II.

MAYO, Earl of. See NAAS, Rt. Hon. Lord.

MEAGHER, Thomas. Waterford. An Alderman of the City of Waterford. A Liberal, in favour of a repeal of the Union; voted for the ballot 1853. First returned for the city of Waterford 1847. Sat until he retired 1857. [1857]

MEAGHER, William. A Merchant and

Alderman of the city of Dublin, where he held the office of Lord Mayor in 1884. A decided advocate of Home Rule. First elected for Meath 21 Feb. 1884. Retired 1885. [1885]

MELDON, Charles Henry. 107 Jermyn Street, London. 25 Rutland Square, Dublin. Newton House, Blackrock, Dublin. S. of James Dillon Meldon, Esq., a Solicitor, in Dublin, by Bedilia, d. of John Ingham, Esq. B. in the Co. of Dublin 1841; m. 1868, Ada, 2nd d. of William Hodgens, of Newton House, Blackrock, Co. Dublin. Was educ. at Stonyhurst Coll., Ushaw (Durham) and Trinity Coll., Dublin. Was called to the bar in Ireland 1863. A Liberal. Sat for the Co. of Kildare from Feb. 1847 until he retired in 1885. Died 15 May 1892. [1885]

MELGUND, Visct. 24 Chester Square, London. Minto Castle, Roxburghshire. Reform, and Brooks's. Eld. s. of the 2nd Earl of Minto, by Mary, eld. d. of Patrick Brydone, Esq. B. at Minto Castle 1814; m. 1844, Emma Eleanor Elizabeth, only d. and heir of Gen. Sir Thomas Hislop, Bart., G.C.B. Educ. at Trinity Coll., Cambridge, where he graduated M.A. 1836. Appointed a Dept.-Lieut. of Roxburghshire 1848. A Liberal, and supporter of Lord Palmerston's foreign policy; in favour of removing the Bishops from the House of Lords. Sat for Hythe from May 1837 to June 1841, when he unsuccessfully contested Rochester. Sat for Greenock from July 1847 to July 1852. Contested Glasgow 10 July 1852. First returned from Clackmannan and Kinross, Mar. 1857. Retired in 1859. Succeeded father as 3rd Earl of Minto July 1859. Died 17 Mar. 1891. [1858]

MELLER, Walter. Broadlands, Clapham Common, London. Carlton and Junior Carlton. B. at Denmark Hill, Surrey 1819, the s. of Thomas William Meller, Esq., a Dept.-Lieut. of Surrey, by Sarah, d. of J. Thomas, Esq., of Sydenham, Kent. M. 1845, Elizabeth, d. of Thomas Peters, Esq., of The Grange, Kilburn, Middlesex. A Magistrate and Dept.-Lieut. for Middlesex, and a Dept.-Lieut. of the Royalty of the Tower. Was Capt. Commandant of the 'Surrey Light Horse' Volunteers (which was raised by him) from 1860-65. Hon. Col. of the 4th Tower Hamlets Rifle Volunteers. A Conservative. Sat for Stafford from July 1865, until he was unseated in 1869. Died 10 Jan. 1886. [1869]

MELLOR, John. 21 Endsleigh Street, London. Otterspool House, Watford, Hertfordshire. Reform. S. of John Mellor, Esq., of Leicester, and Catherine his wife. B. at Hollinwood, in the borough of Oldham 1809; m. 1833, Elizabeth, only child of William Moseley, Esq., of Peckham Rye, Surrey. Called to the bar at the Inner Temple 1833, made a Queen's Counsel 1851, and elected a Bencher of the Inner Temple. Formerly Recorder of Warwick, resigned 1852; appointed Recorder of Leicester Feb. 1855. A Liberal, in favour of the franchise being lowered in counties, and reduced to £6 in boroughs; in favour also of the ballot, the total abolition of church rates, etc. Unsuccessfully contested Warwick July 1852. Sat for Yarmouth from Aug. 1857 to May 1859, when he was elected for Nottingham. Sat until appointed Judge Dec. 1861. Knighted 1862. Died 26 Apr. 1887.   [1861]

MELLOR, J.W. Continued in House after 1885: full entry in Volume II.

MELLOR, Thomas Walton. The Reynors, Ashton-under-Lyne. St. Stephen's. A Manufacturer at Ashton. A Magistrate for Ashton, and for the Cos. Palatine of Lancashire and Cheshire. A Liberal-Conservative, voted against the disestablishment of the Irish Church 1869. Sat for Ashton-under-Lyne from Dec. 1868 until he retired 1880.   [1880]

MELLY, George. Abercromby Square, Liverpool. Reform. S. of Andrew Melly, Esq., Merchant of Liverpool, by Ellen, d. of Samuel Greg, Esq., of Manchester. B. at Liverpool 1830; m. 1852, Sarah E. Mesnard, d. of Samuel Bright, Esq., merchant of Liverpool. Educ. at Rugby. Was a Merchant and Shipowner at Liverpool, and was Maj. 4th Lancashire Artillery Volunteers from 1859-67. Author of works entitled *Khartoum and Blue & White Niles*, 2 Vols., *School Experiences of a Fag*; also pamphlets on education, Italy, Prison Discipline etc. A Liberal and a strong supporter of Mr. Gladstone; in favour of religious equality, reduced public expenditure, etc. Was an unsuccessful candidate for Preston, Mar. 1862, and for Stoke-upon-Trent 1865. Sat for the latter from Feb. 1868. Accepted Chiltern Hundreds Feb. 1874. Died 27 Sept. 1894.   [1873]

MEREWETHER, Charles George. 5 Paper Buildings, and 11 King's Bench Walk, Temple, London. Junior Carlton, St. Stephen's and Garrick. Youngest s. of the Rev. Francis Merewether, Rector of Cole-Orton, and Vicar of Whitwick, Leicestershire, by his marriage with Miss Frances Elizabeth Way, of Yeldham, Essex. B. at Toppesfield, Essex 1823. Unmarried. Educ. at Wadham Coll., Oxford, where he graduated B.A. 1845. Called to the bar at the Inner Temple Jan. 1848. Appointed a Queen's Counsel 1877. Recorder of Leicester from 1868. A Conservative, gave an independent support to Lord Beaconsfield's government, and was in favour of the more equal distribution of local rates, as well as of increasing the control of ratepayers over their expenditure. Sat from Oct. 1874 for Northampton, which he had unsuccessfully contested Feb. 1874, until defeated 1880. Commissioner to inquire into corrupt practices at elections, 1880. Died 26 June 1884.   [1880]

MERRY, James. 68 Eaton Square, London. Belladrum, Beauly, Inverness-shire. Western Club, Glasgow. Reform, and Brooks's. S. of James Merry, Esq., Merchant of Glasgow, by Janet, d. of — Creelman, Esq. B. 1805; m. 1847 Anne, eld. d. of James McHardy, Esq., of Glenboig, Lanarkshire. Educ. at Glasgow Univ. An Ironmaster in Lanarkshire and Ayrshire. Was a Dept.-Lieut. for Inverness-shire. A Liberal. Opposed to a compulsory education rate; in favour of a fresh distribution of Parliamentary seats, and the assimilation of disqualification in counties and boroughs; voted for the disestablishment of the Irish Church 1869. Was an unsuccessful candidate for Glasgow in Feb. 1857; returned for the Falkirk district Apr. 1857; unseated on petition July following, but regained his seat May 1859. Sat until he retired in 1874. Died 3 Feb. 1877.   [1873]

METGE, Robert Henry. Athlumney House, Navan, Co. Meath. 3rd s. of John Charles Metge, Esq., of Dandistown, Co. Westmeath, by Eliza Ibbetson, d. of Henry Cole. Esq., of Twickenham, Middlesex. B. 1850; m. 1874, Fanny, d. of Rev. Charles Lambart, Rector of Navan. Educ. at Trinity Coll., Dublin, where he graduated LL.B. Was called to the bar at the Middle Temple, Apr. 1873. A Magistrate for Meath. Patron of 1 living. An advanced Liberal, and in favour of the system called 'Home Rule' for Ireland, and of the establishment of a 'peasant proprietary' there. Sat for Meath from Apr. 1880. Accepted Chiltern Hundreds in 1883.   [1883]

METHUEN, Paul. 128 Park Street, London. Corsham House, Wiltshire. Descended from the Rt. Hon. John Methuen, Lord Chancellor of Ireland, but more known as the diplomatist who negotiated the treaty with Portugal which bears his name. B. 1779; m. in 1810 Jane Dorothea, sister of Sir Henry Carew St. John Mildmay, Bart. Patron of 2 livings, and Dept.-Lieut. of Wiltshire. A Reformer, in favour of the Ballot, shortening the duration of Parliaments. He was elected for Wiltshire in two Parliaments before 1819, but vacated his seat in that year. Sat for Wiltshire N. uninterruptedly from 1832, until defeated in 1837.   [1837]

MEUX, Sir Henry, Bart. 41 Upper Brook Street, London. Theobald's Park, Cheshunt, Hertfordshire. Carlton, Arthur's and Boodle's. Eld. s. of Sir Henry Meux, Bart., the well-known London Brewer, by the d. of Thomas Smith, Esq., of Castlebar House, Middlesex. B. 1817; m. 1856, Louisa Caroline, eld. d. of Rt. Hon. Lord Ernest Bruce. Educ. at Eton, and at Christ Church, Oxford, where he graduated B.A. 1838. Was High Sheriff of Hertfordshire in 1845. A Magistrate for Hertfordshire, Essex, and Middlesex. A Liberal-Conservative voted against the Chinese war; opposed to further concesssions to the Roman Catholic Church. First returned for Hertfordshire in 1847. Sat until he retired in 1859. Died 1 Jan. 1883. [1858]

MEYNELL, Henry. 14 Hill Street, London. Hoar Cross, Staffordshire. Cousin of the 3rd Marq. of Hertford. A Capt. in the navy. A Conservative, but in favour of free trade. Groom in Waiting to the Queen. Sat for Lisburn from 1826 until he retired 1847. Died 24 Mar. 1865. [1847]

MEYRICK, Sir Thomas. Bush, Pembroke, South Wales. 2nd s. of St. John Chiverton Charlton, of Aple Castle, Shropshire, by his 1st wife, Jane Sophia, only d. of Thomas Meyrick, Esq., of Bush, Pembrokeshire. M. 1860, Mary Rhoda, 2nd d. of Col. Frederick Hill, and niece of 2nd Visct. Hill. Assumed the name of Meyrick, in lieu of his patronymic, on succeeding to the estate of his maternal grandfather. A Magistrate and Dept.-Lieut. for Pembrokeshire, where he was a very large proprietor of land, docks, etc. A Conservative, voted against the disestablishment of the Irish Church 1869. Sat for the district of Pembroke from Dec. 1868 until he was defeated in 1874. Contested the same seat in 1880. Created Baronet 1880. [1873]

MIALL, Edward. Nonconformist Office, 18 Bouverie Street, London. Welland House, Forest Hill, London. S. of Mr. Moses Miall of Portsmouth, by Sarah, d. of Mr. George Rolph of Billericay, Essex. B. at Portsmouth 1809; m. 1832, Louisa, d. of Edward Holmes, Esq., of Clay Hill, Middlesex. Educ. at the Coll. for Independent Ministers, formerly Wymondley, Hertfordshire. Was for some years an independent minister, but quitted that occupation to establish in 1841 the 'Nonconformist' newspaper, of which he was sole proprietor and editor. Author of *The British Churches in Relation to the British People, Title-deeds of the Church of England, An Editor Off the Line*, etc. A Liberal of extreme opinions, opposed to all ecclesiastical endowments, in favour of manhood suffrage, etc. Was an unsuccessful candidate for Southwatk, Sept. 1845; for Halifax July 1847; for Banbury Feb. 1859; and for Bradford Dec. 1868. Sat for Rochdale from July 1852-Apr. 1857, and sat for Bradford from Mar. 1869, until he retired in 1874. Died 29 Mar. 1881. [1873]

MIDDLETON, Sir Arthur Edward, Bart. 20 Upper Brook Street, London. Belsay Castle, Newcastle-on-Tyne. S. of Charles Atticus Monck, Esq., (who was eld. s. of Sir Charles Monck, the 6th Bart.), by Laura, 2nd d. of Sir M. White Ridley, Bart. B. at Humshaugh, Simonburn, Northumberland 1838; m. 1871, Lady Constance Harriet, d. of the 2nd Earl Amherst (she died 1879). Educ. at Rugby and at Trinity Coll., Cambridge, where he graduated B.A. 1860. Assumed the name of Middleton 1876. A Magistrate for Northumberland. Patron of 1 living. A Liberal. Sat for Durham from June 1874. Retired 1880. [1880]

MIDDLETON, Robert Tweedie. Hillfoot, New Kilpatrick, Glasgow. Devonshire, Reform, Liberal Club, Edinburgh and New Club, Glasgow. S. of James Middleton, Esq., Merchant of Glasgow, by his m. with Miss Mary Tweedie. B. at Glasgow 1831; m. 1864, Rachel Rattray, d. of Sir James Watson, of Broomknowe Row, Helensburgh, Scotland. A Merchant in Glasgow. A Magistrate for the Cos. of Dumbarton and Lanark. An advanced Liberal. Sat for Glasgow from Apr. 1880. Retired 1885. Died 1891. [1885]

MILBANK, Sir Frederick Acclom. 9 Clarges Street, Piccadilly, London. Thorpe Perrow, Bedale, Yorkshire. Ardrourlie Castle, Isle of Harris, Scotland. Brooks's and Boodle's. 2nd. s. of Mark Milbank, Esq., of Thorpe Perrow and Barningham Hall, Yorkshire.(who formerly sat for Camelford), by Lady Augusta Henrietta, 2nd d. of 1st Duke of Cleveland. B. in Bruton Street, London, 1820; m. 1844 Alexina Henrietta, d. of Sir Alexander Don, Bart., of Newton Don, Roxboroughshire. Educ. at Harrow. Entered the 79th Highlanders 1837, left the army 1842. A Magistrate and Dept.-Lieut. for the N. Riding of Yorkshire; High Sheriff for Durham in 1852. A Liberal, and continued to give general support to Mr. Gladstone. First elected for the N. Riding of Yorkshire July 1865. Sat until he retired in 1886. Died 28 Apr. 1898. [1873]

MILDMAY, Humphry Francis. 46 Berkeley Square, London. Shoreham Place, Sevenoaks, Kent. Travellers', and Athenaeum. Eld. s. of Humphry St. John Mildmay, Esq., by his 1st wife, Hon. Anne, d. of 1st Lord Ashburton. B. 1825; m. 1861, Sybella Harriet, d. of George Clive, Esq., of Perrystone Court, Herefordshire.

Educ. at Christ Church Coll., Oxford, where he was 1st class in Mathematics, and honorary 4th in Classics 1847; obtained the University Scholarship in Mathematics 1848, graduated M.A. 1854. Appointed Dept.-Lieut. of Kent 1859, and of Hereford 1861. A Liberal. First elected for Herefordshire May 1859. Sat until he retired 1865. Died 29 Nov. 1866.   [1865]

MILDMAY, Humphrey St. John. 46 Berkeley Square, London. Otford Court, Kent. 5th s. of Sir Henry Paulet St. John Mildmay. M. 1823, Anne Eugenia, d. of the 1st Lord Ashburton (she died 1830). A Conservative, voted for agricultural protection 1846. Contested Maldon Jan. 1835. and Hull June 1835. Was first returned for Southampton in 1842, at the election which followed a petition. Retired 1847. Died 9 Aug. 1853.   [1847]

MILDMAY, Paulet St.John. 21 Edwards, Portman Square, London. Haselgrove, Somersetshire. Reform. S. of Sir H. Mildmay, Bt. M. 12 Mar. 1813, Wyndham Anna Maria, d. of the Hon. Bouverie and cousin of the Earl of Radnor. A Reformer unpledged. Sat for Winchester from 1818-1834. Defeated in 1835; again returned 1837. Retired 1841. Died 19 May 1845. [1838]

MILES, Charles William. 21 Grosvenor Place, London . Burtonhill, Malmesbury. Army & Navy. 6th s. of Philip John Miles, Esq., of Kingsweston, Gloucestershire, and Leigh Court, Somersetshire (formerly MP for Corfe Castle and Bristol), by Clarissa, d. of Samuel P. Peach, Esq., of Tockington, Gloucestershire. B. 1823; m. 1853, Maria, only d. of Jere Hill Esq., of Henbury, Bristol. Educ. at Eton. Served for some years in the 17th Lancers; retired as Capt. A Magistrate of Wiltshire, of which county he was High Sheriff in 1856. High Steward of Malmesbury and Lieut.-Col. Royal Gloucestershire Yeomanry Hussars from May 1858. A Conservative. Sat for Malmesbury from Mar. 1882. Retired in 1885.   [1885]

MILES, J.W. Returned for Bristol 30 Apr. 1868, but unseated on petition.

MILES, Philip John. 7 Hamilton Place. Leigh Court, Somersetshire. Carlton, Athenaeum, Union, Arthur's and West India. M. d. of S. Peach, Esq., of Gloucestershire. Father of William Miles, Esq., MP for E. Somersetshire. A Merchant and Banker of Bristol. A West India Proprietor. Patron of 2 livings. A Conservative. Sat for Westbury and Corfe Castle from 1821 to 1832. Was returned for Bristol at the head of the poll in 1835. Retired July 1837.   [1836]

MILES, Sir Philip John William, Bart. 75 Cornwall Gardens, London. Leigh Court, Bristol. Eld. s. of Sir William Miles, Bart. (who sat successively for Chippenham, New Romsey, and East Somerset, from 1818 to 1865), by Catherine, d. of John Gordon, Esq., of Bristol. B. at Lincoln 1825; m. 1848, Frances Elizabeth, 3rd d. of Sir David Roche, Bart. of Carass, Co. Limerick. A Conservative. Sat for East Somerset from Mar. 1878 until he retired in 1885. Died 5 June 1888.   [1885]

MILES, Philip William Skinner. 44 Belgrave Square, London. Kingsweston, Somerset. S. of P.J. Miles, Esq., late MP for Bristol, and bro. of Wm. Miles, Esq., MP for East Somerset. M. 1846, 5th d. of Maj.-Gen. Sir William F.P. Napier. A Conservative, voted for agricultural protection, 1846. Sat for Bristol from 1837 until he retired in 1852. Died 1st Oct. 1881.   [1852]

MILES, Sir William, Bart. 3 St. James's Place, London. Leigh Court, Bristol. Carlton, Boodle's and Arthur's. Eld. s. of Philip John Miles, Esq., of Leigh Court, Somerset (who sat for Bristol from 1835-1837), by his 1st wife, Maria, d. of the Very Rev. Arthur Whetham, Dean of Lismore. B. 1797; m. 1823, Catherine, d. of John Gordon, Esq., of Bristol. Appointed Dept.-Lieut. of Somerset 1852; Col. N. Somerset Yeomanry Cavalry 1843. A Conservative, voted for inquiry into Maynooth 1853; opposed to the abolition of Church rates, without an adequate provision being made for the repair of Churches. Sat for Chippenham from 1818-1820; for New Romney in 1830 and 1831; unsuccessfully contested Somerset E. in 1832; sat for it from 1834 until he retired 1865. Died 17 June 1878.   [1865]

MILL, John Stuart. Blackheath Park, Kent. S. of John Mill, Esq., author of *History of British India, History of the Human Mind,* etc., and Examiner of Indian Correspondance in the service of the East India Company, by his wife, Harriet Burrow. B. in London 1806; m. 1851, Harriet, d. of Thomas Hardy, Esq., of Birksgate. Was employed in the home service of the E.I.C. from 1823 till its transfer to a Minister of the Crown in 1858. Was Assistant Examiner, and afterwards Examiner of Indian Correspondance. Author of *A System of Logic, Principles of Political Economy, Considerations on Representative Government,* etc. Received the honorary degree of Doctor in Philosophy from the Vienna University 1865. Elected Lord Rector of the University of St. Andrew's Nov. 1865. An 'advanced Liberal', in favour of a very wide extension of the suffrage, including even women, the representation of all considerable minorities, and the removal of all religious disabilities; was at one time a supporter of the ballot, but later thought it unnecessary. First elected for Westminster July 1805. Defeated in 1868. Died 8 May 1873. [1867]

MILLER, John. 33 Hyde Park Square, London. 2 Melville Crescent, Edinburgh. Leithen Lodge, Peebleshire, Scotland. S. of James Miller, Esq., of Springvale, Ayr. B. at Ayr, 1805; m. 1834, Isabella, d. of Duncan Ogilvie, Esq., Merchant of Perth. Educ. at Ayr. Academy and the University of Edinburgh. Entered on the profession of civil engineer 1825, was engineer of several leading lines of railway, retired 1849. Became a Member of the Institution of Civil Engineers 1830; Fellow of the Royal Soc., Edinburgh, 1840, etc. A Liberal, voted for the disestablishment of the Irish Church 1869. Contested Stirling 13 July 1852. Sat for the city of Edinburgh from Dec. 1868. Defeated in 1874. Died 7 May 1883. [1873]

MILLER, Stearne Ball. 6 Rutland Square, East Dublin. Carlton. S. of Rev. George Miller, D.D., of Armagh (formerly Fellow of Trinity Coll., Dublin), by Elizabeth, d. of Robert Ball, Esq., of the Co. of Wicklow. B. in the Co. of Fermanagh 1813; m. 1836, Sarah, only surviving d. of Braconley Rutherfoord, Esq., of Merrion Square, Dublin. Educ. at the Royal School of Armagh, and at Trinity Coll., Dublin. Called to the bar in Ireland 1835; appointed Queen's Counsel there 1852. A Conservative, said he would firmly sustain Protestant principles, and would support 'the great institutions of the country with an earnest desire to extend their efficiency.' Contested Armagh City Nov. 1855. Sat for Armagh City from Apr. 1857-July 1859, when he was unsuccessful. Re-elected July 1865 until appointed Judge in Irish Court of Bankruptcy. 1867. Died 2 May 1897. [1865 2nd. ed.]

MILLER, Taverner John. 7 Millbank Street, Westminster, London. The Elms, Tooting, Surrey. Carlton and National. S. of Charles T. Miller, Esq., of Witham, Essex, Capt. of the Witham Volunteers. B. at Witham, Nr. Maldon 1804; m. 1833, Marian, d. of Charles Cheyne, Esq., once of Godalming, Surrey (and niece maternally of Mr. Alderman Winchester, Lord Mayor of London and MP for Maidstone). A Shipowner, and sperm-oil Merchant, and sperm--oil Refiner at Millbank. A Magistrate and Dept.-Lieut for Middlesex and Westminster. A Conservative, and a supporter generally of Lord Derby's policy. Sat for Maldon from July 1852-Mar. 1853, when he was unseated on petition. First returned for Colchester in 1857. Sat until he accepted Chiltern Hundreds Jan. 1867. [1865]

MILLER, William. 135 Piccadilly, London. Manderston House, Dunse, Berwickshire. Hermitage, Leith. Union. S. of James Miller, Esq., by Elizabeth, d. of the Rev. William Sutherland Wick. B. at Leith 1809; m. 1838, Mary Anne, d. of John Farley Leith, Barrister-at-law, formerly of Calcutta. Educ. at the High School and at the University of Edinburgh. Was a Merchant at St. Petersburgh from 1832 till 1854, and Honourary British Vice-Consul there for 16 years. A Liberal, 'independent of party.' Contested Leith district 28 Mar. 1857. First elected for Leith district May 1859 and sat until he was defeated on 18 Nov. 1868. Returned for Berwickshire at a by-election 30 June 1873. Defeated at the 1874 gen. election. [1867]

MILLER, William Henry. Craigentinny, Co. Edinburgh. Britwell House, Buckinghamshire. Carlton. A Conservative. Sat for Newcastle-under-Lyme from 1830 until he was defeated in 1841. Contested Berwick 30 July 1847. [1838]

MILLES, Hon. George Watson. Lees Court, Faversham, Kent. Carlton and Traveller's. Eld. s. of the 4th Baron Sondes, by Eleanor, 5th d. of the late Sir Edward Knatchbull, Bart. B. 1824; m. 1859, Charlotte, eld. d. of Sir Henry Stracey, Bart. Was educ. at Eton. Entered the army 1843; appointed Capt. Royal Horse Guards 1845; retired 1852. Lieut.-Col. East Kent Mounted Rifles. A Conservative, voted against Mr. Gladstone on the Irish question; was in favour of the reduction of the malt tax. Sat for E. Kent from Dec. 1868 until he succeeded as 5th Baron Dec. 1874; advanced to an Earldom May 1880. Died Sept. 1894. [1874]

MILLIGAN, Robert. Bradford, Yorkshire. S. of John Milligan, Esq., of Dunance, Balmaghie, Galloway, N.B. B. at Dunance 1786; m. 1818, d. of Nathaniel Briggs, Esq., Cloth Manufacturer, of Rawden, Yorkshire. Was a Merchant in the worsted stuff trade at Bradford for more than 30 years, and head of the firm of Messrs. Milligan, Forbes & Co. Was the first Mayor of Bradford 1847-8, when that borough received a charter of incorporation. Was formerly a member of the Council of the Anti-Corn Law League. A Liberal, in favour of a large extension of the franchise and of direct taxation, voted for the ballot 1853. First returned for Bradford Oct.1851, without opposition. Retired 1857. Died 1 July 1862. [1857]

MILLS, Arthur. 34 Hyde Park Gardens, London. Bude Haven, Cornwall. Athenaeum, and Oxford & Cambridge. Youngest s. of the Rev. Francis Mills, of Barford, Warwickshire, by

Catherine, d. of Sir John Mordaunt, Bart., of Walton, Warwickshire. B. at Barford 1816; m. 1848, Agnes Lucy, youngest d. of Sir Thomas Dyke Acland, Bart., of Killerton, Devon. Educ. at Rugby under Dr. Arnold, and at Balliol Coll., Oxford, where he graduated M.A. 1842. Called to the bar at the Inner Temple 1842. Author of a work entitled *Colonial Constitutions*, also *India in 1858*. A Conservative. Was returned for Taunton July 1852, but the election was declared void May following; sat for that borough from Mar. 1857-July 1865; contested Taunton unsuccessfully July 1847, and Exeter Dec. 1868; sat for Exeter from Nov. 1873 until defeated 1880. Died 12 Oct. 1898.   [1880]

MILLS, Sir Charles Henry, Bart. Camelford House, Oxford Street, London. Wildernesse, Sevenoaks, Kent. White's, Travellers' and Carlton. Eld. s. of Sir Charles Mills, Bart., of Hillingdon Court, Uxbridge, by Emily, d. of R.H. Cox, Esq., of Hillingdon House. B. at Camelford House, London, 1830; m. 1853, Lady Louisa Isabella, eld. d. of the 3rd Earl of Harewood. Educ. at Eton and at Christ Church, Oxford. A Banker in London, a Partner in the firm of Messrs. Glyn, Mills & Co. A Magistrate and Dept.-Lieut. of Kent, also a Commissioner of Metropolis Roads. A Conservative. Sat for Northallerton from July 1865 till May 1866, when he was unseated on petition. Sat for West Kent from Dec. 1868 until he retired in 1885. [1885]

MILLS, John. 12 Park Street, Grosvenor Square, London. Bistern House, Ringwood, Hampshire. Bro. of Mr. Mills, the London Banker and East India Director. Was formerly in the Army. Upon the whole, a Conservative, he voted for the principle of the Reform Bill, but was opposed to Ministers on many of its details in Committee; he did not support Lord Ebrington's motion; an advocate for the abolition of slavery. Was first elected for Rochester in 1831. Retired in 1835. Died 18 Feb. 1871.   [1833]

MILLS, John Remington. Kingswood Lodge, Englefield Green, Surrey. Reform. S. of Samuel Mills, Esq., of Russell Square, London. B. in London 1798; m. 1831, Louisa Matilda, d. of Joseph Trueman, Esq., of Walthamstow, Essex. A Silk Manufacturer, retired 1840. A Magistrate for Middlesex and Hertfordshire. Patron of 1 living. A Liberal, in favour of the ballot, and the abolition of Church rates. Unsuccessfully contested Leeds 28 Mar. and again 5 June 1857 and Finsbury, Dec. 1861; first elected for Wycombe, Mar. 1862. Defeated in 1868. Died 22 Nov. 1879.   [1867]

MILLS, Thomas. 20 Russell Square, London.

Tolmers, Nr. Hertford. United University. Eld. s. of Samuel Mills, Esq., of Russell Square, London. B. 1794. Educ. at Queens Coll., Cambridge, where he graduated B.A. 1819, M.A. 1822. Called to the bar at the Inner Temple, 1832. A Magistrate for Middlesex, Hertfordshire and Bedfordshire. Dept.-Chairman of Quarter-Sessions, and Dept.-Lieut. of Hertfordshire. Patron of 2 livings. A Liberal, in favour of a 'progressive policy', extension of the franchise, vote by ballot, and the abolition of Church rates. First returned for Totnes in July 1852 and sat until his death in 1862.   [1858]

MILNER, Sir F. Continued in House after 1885; full entry in Volume II.

MILNER, Sir William Mordaunt Edward, Bart. 75 Eaton Place, London. Nunappleton, Tadcaster, Yorkshire. Reform. Eld. s. of Sir William Milner, (4th Bart.), of Nunappleton Hall, Yorkshire, by his 2nd wife, d. of Lord Edward Bentinck. B. at Nunappleton 1820; m. 1844, Ann Georgina, 3rd d. of Frederick Lumley, Esq., of Tickhill Castle, and niece of the 4th Earl of Scarborough. Educ. at Eton and at Christ Church, Oxford, where he graduated M.A. 1844. A Dept.-Lieut. of the West Riding of Yorkshire. A Liberal, in favour of the ballot, and extension of the suffrage to all householders, triennial Parliaments, and abolition of qualification for members. First returned for York May 1848. Sat until he retired 1857. Died 12 Feb. 1867. [1857]

MILNES, Richard Monckton. 16 Upper Brook Street, London. Frystone Hall, Ferrybridge, and Bawtry, Yorkshire. Athenaeum, Boodle's, and Oxford & Cambridge. Eld. s. of Robert Pemberton Milnes, Esq., of Frystone Hall, and Bawtry, Yorkshire (who sat for Pontefract from 1806-1818), by the Hon. Henrietta Maria, d. of 4th Visct. Galway. B. 1809; m. 1851, Hon. Annabel, youngest d. of 2nd Baron Crewe. Graduated M.A. Trinity Coll., Cambridge 1831. Author of *Memorials of a Tour in Greece;* three volumes of Poems *Thoughts on Purity of Election.* A Dept.-Lieut. for the West Riding of Yorkshire and Capt. 2nd West York Militia. A Liberal, but formerly ranked as a Conservative; voted against Lord Derby's Reform Bill Mar. 1859; voted for the Ecclesiastical Titles Bill, and the inquiry into Maynooth Coll., but considered 'religious equality the birthright of every Briton.' First returned for Pontefract in 1837 and sat until Dec. 1862 when he accepted Chiltern Hundreds on being created a Peer (Lord Houghton).   [1862]

MILTON, Lord Visct. (I). Mortimer House, Halkin Street, Grosvenor Place, London. Milton,

271

Nr. Peterborough, Northamptonshire. Eld. s. of the Earl Fitzwilliam. B. 1812; m. in 1833, Selina, 2nd d. of Charles 3rd Earl of Liverpool. Of Whig principles. Vacated Malton, for which place he was returned at the general election in 1832, on his father succeeding to the title of Earl Fitzwilliam in 1833. Accepted Chiltern Hundreds 1833. Sat for Northamptonshire N. from May 1833 until his death 8 Nov. 1835.   [1835]

MILTON, Visct. (II). 4 Grosvenor Square, London. Travellers'. Eld. surviving s. of the Earl of Fitzwilliam. B. at Milton, Northamptonshire 1815; m. 1838, eld. d. of the 18th Earl of Morton. Educ. at Trinity Coll., Cambridge, where he graduated M.A. 1837. Appointed Lieut.-Col. Commandant 1st West York Yeomanry Cavalry May 1846. Lord. Lieut. of the West Riding of Yorkshire 1857. A Liberal. Represented Malton in Parliament from 1837-1841, and from Apr. 1846-July 1847; unsuccessfully contested the West Riding of Yorkshire in 1841. First returned for Wicklow July 1847. Sat until he succeeded to the Peerage (Earl Fitzwilliam) 4 Oct. 1857. Died 20 Feb. 1902.   [1857 2nd ed.]

MILTON, Visct. (III). 17 Grosvenor Street, London. Wentworth Woodhouse, Nr. Rotherham. Brooks's and Garrick. Eld. s. of the Earl Fitzwilliam, by Lady Francis Harriet, eld. d. of 18th Earl of Morton. B. 1839; m. 1867, Laura Theresa, d. of Lord Charles Beauclerk. Educ. at Eton and at Trinity Coll., Cambridge. Appointed cornet 1st West York Yeomanry Cavalry, 1861. A Liberal, in favour of the repeal of the rate-paying clause of the Reform Act. First elected for the S.W. Riding of Yorkshire July 1865. Accepted Chiltern Hundreds 1872. Died 17 Jan. 1877.   [1872]

MITCALFE, Henry. Whitley, Northumberland. B. 1788, the s. of William Mitcalfe of Tynemouth House. M. 1813, d. of Dr. Edward Drury. A Magistrate for Northumberland, and Chairman to the Reform meetings held in Tynemouth from 1829. A Liberal, formerly voted against the abolition of the corn law, but in 1846 supported their abolition. Sat for Tynemouth from 1841 until he retired in 1847.   [1847]

MITCHEL, John. B. near Dungiven, Co. Londonderry 3 Nov. 1815, 3rd. s. of Presbyterian Minister. Educ. at Trinity Coll., Dublin. A Solicitor from 1840. Joined Daniel O'Connell's Repeal Association in 1843, and seceded in July 1846. Issued the first number of the *United Irishman* 12 Feb. 1848 advocating rebellion. Tried in May 1848 and sentenced to 14 years transportation. Escaped from Van Dieman's Land to the

U.S.A. in Oct. 1853; naturalised American May 1860. Worked as a journalist until 1872. Contested Cork city Feb. 1874. Contested Tipperary Feb. 1874; elected for same seat 16 Feb. 1875, but declared ineligible by the Commons two days later; elected again 12 Mar. 1875 but declared not duly elected as an alien and a convicted felon by an Irish Court in May. Author of *Jail Journals* (New York 1854), a *History of Ireland* (Dublin 1869, 2 vols.), and other works. Died 20 Mar. 1875, and buried in a Unitarian Cemetery.

MITCHELL, Alexander. 6 Great Stanhope Street, London. Carolside, Berwickshire. Guards', Brooks's and Reform. S. of Alexander Mitchell, Esq., of Stow, by Jane, d. of John Gardiner, Esq. B. at Aberdeen 1831; m. 1856, Fanny, d. of Richard Hasler, Esq., of Aldingbourne, Sussex. Educ. at Eton and at Christ Church, Oxford. Entered the army 1850, and served in the Grenadier Guards for 6 years; and for nearly a year in the Crimea. A Dept.-Lieut. of Berwickshire, and a Magistrate for Berwickshire, Selkirkshire and Midlothian. An 'independent' Liberal, but 'fully recognizing the value of party organization'; and 'strongly in favour of the abolition of Church rates', and in any new Reform Bill favourable to the right of freemen being preserved. First elected for Berwick (which, in June 1863, he contested unsuccessfully) July 1865. Retired 1868. Died 16 May 1873.   [1868]

MITCHELL, Thomas Alexander. 50 Charles Street, Berkeley Square, London. Brooks's and Reform. B. at Montrose. A Merchant. One of the Committee of Management of Lloyd's Shipping Register. A Liberal; voted against Church rates 1855. First returned for Bridport 1841. MP until his death 16 Mar. 1875.   [1875]

MITCHELL, William, M.D. 22 Abingdon Street, London. Bodmin. S. of Bennet Mitchell, Esq., Merchant. B. at Bodmin 1794; m. 1832, Anne Jane Millicent, d. of Col. Adair, and sister of General Thomas Benjamin Adair, C.B., Royal Marines. Educ. at Bodmin School, and was a Fellow-Commoner of Emmanuel Coll., Cambridge, where he graduated M.B. 1834, M.D. 1838. Became a Member of the Coll. of Surgeons in 1813. Physician to the E. Cornwall Hospital at Bodmin, and Surgeon to the 2nd Cornwall Militia. Author of some medical and botanical works, *The National Debt the Basis of the National Currency, etc.* In favour of the repeal of the Maynooth Grant, progressive and safe reform, opposed to all religious endowments; voted against the ballot 1853. First returned for Bodmin in July 1852. Defeated 1857. Returned again in

1859, but accepted Chiltern Hundreds July 1859.
[1857]

MITFORD, William Townley. 12 Cavendish Square, London. Pitshill, Petworth, Sussex. Carlton and Arthur's. S. of Charles Mitford, Esq. by Margaret, d. of R. Greaves Townley, Esq., of Fulbourn, Cambridgeshire. B. 1817; m. 1855, Hon. Margaret Emma, d. of 3rd Lord Kenyon. Educ. at Eton, and at the Univ. of Oxford. A Magistrate and Dept.-Lieut. of Sussex; High Sheriff of that co. 1848. A Conservative. First elected for Midhurst May 1859. Sat until defeated in 1874. Died 18 April 1889. [1873]

MOFFAT, George. 103 Eaton Square, London. St. Leonard's Hill, Windsor. Reform. S. of William Moffat, Esq., of London. M. 1856 Lucy, d. of James Morrison, Esq., of Basildon Park, Berkshire. A partner in the house of Moffat and Co., Wholesale Tea-dealers, Fenchurch Street, London, and at Liverpool. A Liberal, in favour of the ballot and a large extension of the suffrage, and the total abolition of church-rates. Unsuccessfully contested Ipswich, June 1842, and Dartmouth, Nov. 1844; sat for Dartmouth from July 1845 till July 1852; for Ashburton from the last date till Apr. 1859; for Honiton, from Oct. 1860 till July 1865, when he was elected for Southampton. Defeated in 1868; contested seat again in 1874. Contested Isle of Wight 13 June 1870. Died 20 Feb. 1878. [1867]

MOLESWORTH, Rt. Hon. Sir William, Bart. 87 Eaton Place, London. Pencarrow, Cornwall. Tetcott, Devon. B. in Upper Brook Street, London, 1810, the s. of Sir Arscott Ourry Molesworth, Bart., by the eld d. of Patrick Brown, Esq., of Edinburgh. M. 1844, only d. of Bruce Carstairs, Esq. and widow of Temple West, Esq., of Mathon Lodge, Worcestershire. Appointed Commissioner of Works and Buildings Dec. 1852 (salary £2,000). A Dept.-Lieut. of Cornwall, and was High Sheriff there in 1842. Patron of 4 livings. A Radical Reformer, voted for the ballot 1853. In favour of 'complete religious liberty and equality, and the removal of the disabilities of the Jews.' Represented Cornwall E. from 1832-37 and Leeds from 1837-41. Sat for Southwark from Sept. 1845 until his death on 22 Oct. 1855. [1855]

MOLLOY, B.C. Continued in House after 1885: full entry in Volume II.

MOLYNEUX, Lord Visct. 21 Arlington Street, London. Eld. s. of the Earl of Sefton. B. 1796. Of Whig principles, supported the Administration, in favour of free-trade, and a fixed duty on foreign corn. Sat for Lancashire S. from 1832. Defeated in 1835. Succeeded as 3rd Earl Nov. 1838. Died Aug. 1855. [1833]

MONAHAN, Rt. Hon. J.H. A Liberal. Elected for Galway borough 17 Feb. 1847. Defeated in 1847 contesting Clonmel. Judge from 1850-76. Died 8 Dec. 1878.

MONCK, Sir A.E. See MIDDLETON, Sir A.E. Bart.

MONCK, Visct. 23 Dover Street, London. Charleville, Enniskerry, Co. Wicklow. An Irish Peer. S. of the 3rd Visct., by the youngest d. of John Willington, Esq., of Killoskehane, Co. Tipperary. B. at Templemore, Co. Tipperary 1819; m. 1844, his cousin, the 3rd d. of the 1st Earl of Rathdowne. Educ. at Trinity Coll., Dublin. Called to the bar in Ireland Nov. 1841. Appointed a Commissioner of Charitable Donations and Bequests in Ireland Feb. 1851. A Lord of the Treasury Mar. 1855, salary £1,200. A Magistrate of the Cos. of Dublin and Wicklow, a Dept.-Lieut. of the latter Co. A Liberal, supported an extension of the franchise, a modification of the income-tax, and the continuance of the Maynooth Grant. Was an unsuccessful candidate for the Co. of Wicklow in May 1848. First returned for Portsmouth July 1852. Defeated 1857. Contested Dudley 1859. Created Baron Monck (U.K. Peerage) July 1866, member of Church Temporalities Commission 1871-81. One of Lords Justices implementing Irish Land Act 1881-82. Died 29 Nov. 1894. [1857]

MONCKTON, Francis. Somerford Hall, Brewood. Stretton, Penkridge, Staffordshire. Carlton and Junior Carlton. Eld. s. of Gen. Henry Monckton, of Stretton Hall (grands. of 1st Visct. Galway), by Anne, only d. of John Groome Smythe, Esq., of Hilton, Shropshire, and niece of Lord Wensleydale. B. at Stretton 1844. Was educ. at Eton, and at Christ Church, Oxford. A Magistrate and Dept.-Lieut. for Staffordshire. A Conservative, and opposed to the disruption of Church and State. Sat for West Staffordshire from June 1871 until defeated in 1885. Died 30 Sept. 1926. [1885]

MONCKTON, Hon. G.E.M. See GALWAY, Visct. (II).

MONCRIEFF, Rt. Hon. James. 1 New Street, Spring Gardens, London. Great Stuart Street, Edinburgh. Brooks's. B. in Edinburgh 1811, the 2nd s. of Sir James Wellwood Moncrieff, 9th Bart. of Tullibole, Kinross (a Lord of Session in Scotland by the title of Lord Moncrieff), by the d.

of Capt. George Robinson, R.N. M. 1834, Isabella, only d. of Robert Bell, Esq., of Edinburgh. Procurator of the Church of Scotland. Educ. at the High School and at the University of Edinburgh. Became an Advocate at the Scottish bar 1833. Was Solicitor-Gen. for Scotland from Feb. 1850-Apr. 1851, Lord Advocate from Apr. 1851-Mar 1852, and again from Dec. 1852-Mar. 1858. A third time from June 1859-July 1866. Reappointed Lord Advocate Dec. 1868. Made a Dept.-Lieut. of Edinburgh 1854 and elected Lord Rector of Glasgow University in Jan. 1869. A Liberal, and took an active part in the passing of bills for the abolition of University tests and those required from Parish Schoolmasters. Sat for Leith district from Apr. 1851-May 1859, for Edinburgh from May 1859-Dec. 1868, and for the Universities of Glasgow and Aberdeen from 1868 until he was appointed Lord of Session as Lord Moncrieff in 1869. Created Baronet 23 May 1871, and made Baron Moncrieff Jan. 1874.   [1869]

MONK, C.J. Continued in House after 1885: full entry in Volume II.

MONSELL, Rt. Hon. William. 34 Seymour Street, Portman Square, London. Tervoe, Limerick. Athenaeum. Eld. s. of William Monsell, Esq., of Tervoe, Co. Limerick, by the eld. d. of Sir John Allen Johnson Walsh, Bart. B. 1812; m. 1st, 1836, Lady Anna Maria, only d. of the 2nd Earl of Dunraven (she died 1855); 2ndly, 1857, Berthe, youngest d. of the Comte de Montigny Boutainvilliers. Was educ. at Winchester and at Oriel Coll., Oxford. Was Clerk to the Ordnance from Dec. 1852-Feb. 1857, when the office was abolished. President of the Board of Health from Feb.-Sept. 1857. Vice-President of the Board of Trade from Feb.-July 1866. Under-Sec. for the Colonies from Dec. 1868-Jan. 1871, when he was appointed Postmaster-Gen. A Magistrate and Dept.-Lieut. of Limerick, of which Co. he was High Sheriff in 1835; Lord-Lieut. and Custos-rot. of the Co. and City of Limerick. Published several letters on the condition of Ireland, and was well known as the early advocate of 'reproductive employment' during the famine of 1846-7. Of Liberal principles. Contested Limerick City in Aug. 1837. First returned for the Co. of Limerick in 1847 and sat until he retired 1874.   [1873]

MONSON, Hon. William John. 3A King Street, St. James's, London. Gatton Park, Reigate. Brooks's. Eld. s. of 6th Lord Monson, by Eliza, d. of Edmund Larken, Esq., of Bedford Square. B. in Queen Anne Street, London, 1829. Educ. at Christ Church, Oxford, where he graduated B.A. 1848. Appointed a Dept.-Lieut. of Surrey, 1852.

Major in the North Lincoln Militia, and a Dept.-Lieut. of Lincolnshire. Of 'thoroughly Liberal' opinions; 'as a true friend of the Church is in favour of the alteration of church-rates'; in favour of the extension of the franchise, etc. Unsuccessfully contested Reigate Feb. 1858; first elected there Oct. following. Sat until he succeeded as 7th Baron Monson 17 Dec. 1862. Held various Royal Household appointments 1874-94. Created Visct. Oxenbridge 13 Aug. 1886. Died 16 Apr. 1898.   [1862]

MONTAGU, Rt. Hon. Lord Robert. 41 Queen's Gate, London. 6 Clifton Gardens, Folkestone. Carlton and Athenaeum. 2nd s. of 6th Duke of Manchester, by Millicient, d. of Lady Olivia and Gen. Robert Bernard Sparrow. B. at Melchbourne, Huntingdonshire 1825; m. 1st, 1850, Ellen Mary, only d. and heir of John Cromie, Esq., of Cromore, Coleraine (she died 1857); 2ndly, 1862, Miss Elizabeth Catherine Wade. Educ. at Trinity Coll., Cambridge, where he graduated M.A. 1848. Appointed Pres. of the Board of Health, and Vice-Pres. of the Council Mar. 1867, Fourth Charity Commissioner same time, resigned Dec. 1868. Author of a work on *Naval Architecture,* also *The Four Experiments in Church and State.* Appointed Capt. in the Huntingdonshire Militia 1846. A Liberal, voted against the disestablishment of the Irish Church 1869, in favour of fixity of tenure in land, also of denominational education. Sat for Huntingdonshire from May 1859-Feb. 1874, from which date he sat for Westmeath until he retired 1880. Died 6 May 1902.   [1880]

MONTGOMERIE, Roger. 73 St. George's Square, London. Annick Lodge, Perceton, Ayrshire. The New Club, Edinburgh. 3rd. s. of William Eglinton Montgomerie, Esq., of Annes Lodge, Lieut.-Col. Ayrshire Yeomanry, and a Dept.-Lieut. for that Co. B. at Ayr, 1828. Was educ. at Rugby, and at St. John's Coll., Cambridge; graduated B.A. 1851, M.A. 1854. Passed as an advocate at the Scotch bar in 1852. Was advocate depute under Lord Derby's government in 1858, and again from 1866-1868. Was formerly Capt. Queen's city of Edinburgh Rifle Volunteer Brigade. A Conservative, in favour of amendment of the Game Laws regarding ground game. Sat from Feb. 1874 for N. Ayrshire, which he had unsuccessfully contested Dec. 1868. Retired 1880. Died 25 Oct. 1880.   [1880]

MONTGOMERY, Sir Graham Graham-, Bart. 45 Grosvenor Place, London. Stobo Castle, Peebles. Kinross House, Kinross-shire. Carlton and Conservative. S. of Sir James Montgomery, 2nd Bart. (who was appointed Lord Advocate of

Scotland in 1804), by his 2nd wife, Helen, youngest d. of Thomas Graham, Esq., of Kinross. B. at Edinburgh 1823; m. 1845, youngest d. of John James Hope-Johnstone, Esq., of Annandale. Educ. at Christ Church, Oxford, where he graduated B.A. 1845. A Lord of the Treasury from July 1866-Dec. 1868. Appointed Dept.-Lieut. of Peeblesshire in 1844, and Lord-Lieut. of Kinross 1854: was Lieut. in the Mid-Lothian Yeomanry Cavalry from 1850-1854. Patron of 5 livings. A Conservative, voted against the disestablishment of the Irish Church 1869, a supporter generally of Lord Beaconsfield's policy. Sat for Peeblesshire from July 1852-Dec. 1868, and from that date for the united Cos. of Selkirk and Peebles until he was defeated 1880. Died 2 June 1901. [1880]

MONTGOMERY, Hugh Lyons. 4 York Street, St. James's, London. Belhavel, Carrick-on-Shannon, Ireland. Carlton. S. of Hugh Montgomery, Esq., of Belhavel, by Elizabeth, d. of Dean Blacker, of Armagh. B. at Lympston, Devon, 1816; m. 1840, Elizabeth, d. of Henry Smith, Esq., of Annesbrook, Co. Meath. A Magistrate and Dept.-Lieut. of Leitrim, Chairman of the Manorhamilton Union. A Conservative, but favourable to 'tenant-right' in Ireland. First returned for Leitrim in July 1852. Accepted Chiltern Hundreds 1858. [1858]

MONYPENNY, Thomas Gybbon. Rolneden, Kent. Of an old Scottish family of which a branch settled in Kent. Unsuccessfully contested Rye in 1835, but came head of the poll in 1837. A Conservative. Retired 1841. Died 15 Mar. 1854. [1838]

MOODY, Charles Aaron. 46 Chester Square, London. Kingsdon, Somerton, Somerset. National. S. of Aaron Moody, Esq. M. 1820, the 3rd d. of Jas. Bennett, Esq. of Cadbury, Somerset. Was educ. at Winchester, and at Oxford. A Dept.-Lieut. of Somerset, and Chairman of the Quarter Sessions. A Conservative, voted for inquiry into Maynooth 1853. First returned for Somerset W. in 1847. Sat until he accepted Chiltern Hundreds Feb. 1863. Chairman of Somerset Quarter Sessions. Died 17 Dec. 1867. [1862]

MOORE, Henry. 4 Sussex Square, Kemp Town, Brighton. Oriental. S. of Henry Moore, Esq., once of Kirby Hall, Kent, by Elizabeth, eld. d. of John Remmington, Esq., of Nailsworth, Gloucestershire. B. at Greenwich, Kent 1809; m. 1835, Mary, youngest d. of John Ennis, Esq. Educ. at Greenwich, and at school of the Rev. Charles P. Burney. Entered the legal profession.

A Dept.-Lieut. for Sussex. A Liberal-Conservative, 'opposed to change for the mere sake of change,' but in favour of such measures as would 'keep pace with the advancing progress of the times', in favour of 'the salutary principle of non-intervention' in Foreign policy, and of such a settlement of Church rates as would relieve dissenters from them. First elected for Brighton Feb. 1864. Defeated 1865; contested same seat in 1868. [1865]

MOORE, A.J. Continued in House after 1885: full entry in Volume II.

MOORE, Charles. 9 Grafton Street, London. Moore's Fort, Co. Tipperary. Reform. B. in Ireland 1804, the s. of Arthur Moore, Esq., by Mary O'Hara, his wife. M. 1835, Marian Elizabeth, d. of John Storey, Esq., of Dublin. A Merchant in London. A Liberal, and in favour of the custom of 'tenant-right' in Ireland and of the education system being placed on a plan of perfect religious equality. Elected for Tipperary in Feb. 1865 and sat until his death on 15 Aug. 1869. [1869]

MOORE, George Henry. Moore Hall, Ballyglass, Co. Mayo. S. of George Moore, Esq., of Moore Hall, Co. Mayo, by Louisa, d. of Hon. John Browne, and grand-d. of the 1st Earl of Aldamont. B. at Moore Hall 1811; m. 1851 d. of Maurice Blake, Esq., of Ballinafad, Co. Mayo. Educ. at Oscott Coll. and subsquently at Christ's Coll., Cambridge. A Liberal, in favour of 'tenant-right' in Ireland being established by law; voted for the ballot 1853. Sat for Mayo from Aug. 1847-Dec. 1857, when he was unseated on petition. Contested Kilkenny Co. 20 May 1859. Re-elected for Mayo Dec. 1868. MP until his death 19 Apr. 1870. [1870]

MOORE, John Bramley-. 10 King Street, St. James's, London. Langley Lodge, Buckinghamshire. Aigburth, Nr. Liverpool. Carlton and Conservative. S. of Thomas Moore, Esq. B. at Pontefract 1800; m. 1830, Seraphina, d. of William Pennell, Esq., once British Consul-Gen. for the Empire of Brazil. Assumed the name of Bramley before his patronymic by Royal licence 1840. A Merchant at Liverpool. Mayor of that City 1848-9. Formerly Chairman of the Liverpool Dock Trust, and in consequence of his great exertions in that office, one of the Docks received the name of the Bramley-Moore Dock. A Magistrate and Dept.-Lieut. of Lancashire. A Liberal-Conservative, and in favour of 'gradual changes' as might be required, but opposed to the Ballot; in favour of Lord Palmerston's Foreign policy; voted against the abolition of Church rates

275

May 1862. Unsuccessfully contested Hull in 1852, and Liverpool June 1853. Sat for Maldon from Aug. 1854-Apr. 1859. Contested Lymington 30 Apr. 1859. Elected for Lincoln, Feb. 1862. Defeated 1865. Died 19 Nov. 1886.   [1865]

MOORE, Ross Stephenson. 5 Mountjoy Square, South Dublin. Nootka Lodge, Carlingford, Co. Louth, National. B. at Carlingford 1809, the s. of Hugh Moore, Esq., of Nootka Lodge, Co. Louth, by Mary, d. of the Rev. John Wilton of Hereford. The Moores of Carlingford were the lineal descendents of the O'Mores of Queen's Co., Dynasts or Lords of Leix. M. 1830, Sarah, d. of William Barker, Esq., Rector of Newton-Hamilton, Co. Armagh. Educ. at Grumlin, Co. Antrim and at Trinity Coll., Dublin, where he obtained a University Scholarship and several honours in science and classics during the undergraduate course. Was called to the bar in Ireland 1833, made Queen's Counsel, and joined the North-Eastern circuit there. Author of a *Treatise on the Rules and Practice of the Courts of Common Law in Ireland,* and editor of the *Irish Law and Equity Reports.* A Conservative, but in favour of free trade. First returned for Armagh City, without opposition, in July 1852, and sat until his death 5 Oct. 1855.   [1855]

MOORE, Stephen. 34 Wilton Crescent, London. Barne, Clonmel, Ireland. Carlton and Junior Carlton. Eld. s. of Stephen Charles Moore, Esq., of Barne, Co. Tipperary, by Anna d. of Col. Kingsmill Pennefather, of New Park, Co. Tipperary. B. 1836; m. 1867, Anna Maria, only surviving d. of Wilmer Wilmer, Esq., of Wilton Crescent, London. Educ. at Cheltenham Coll. Entered the army as ensign 63rd Foot Dec. 1854, attained the rank of Capt. and retired; served throughout the Crimean War, for which he received a medal with clasps. A Dept.-Lieut. of Tipperary. A Conservative. Sat for Tipperary from May 1875, when he was seated on petition. Retired 1880. Contested Clonmél Apr. 1880.   [1880]

MOORE-STEVENS, J.C. A Conservative. Returned for Devonshire N. 1 July 1885. Retired Nov. 1885.

MORAY, Henry Edward Home-Drummond-. 40 Park Street, Grosvenor Square, London. Blair Drummond, Stirling. Carlton and Guards'. Eld. s. of Charles Edward Home-Drummond-Moray, Esq., of Abercairny and Blair Drummond, Perthshire, by Lady Anne, d. of the 5th Marq. of Queensberry. B. 1846; m. 1877, Lady Georgina Emily Lucy, 3rd d. of the 5th Marq. of Hertford. Educ. at Eton. Capt. and Lieut. Col. Scots Guards, which he entered Jan. 1866. A Dept.-Lieut. for the Co. of Perth. A Conservative, and a supporter of the Earl of Beaconsfield. Sat for the Co. of Perth from Feb. 1878. Defeated 1880. Contested the W. division of Perth 1885.   [1880]

MORDAUNT, Sir Charles, Bart. Walton House, Stratford-on-Avon, Warwickshire. Carlton and Arthur's. S. of Sir John Mordaunt, Bart., by Caroline Sophia, d. of Dr. Murray, Bishop of Rochester, and Lady Sarah Murray. B. in Grosvenor Place, London, 1836; m. 1866, Harriet Sarah, 4th d. of Sir Thomas Moncrieffe, 7th Bart. Educ. at Eton, and at Christ Church, Oxford. Appointed a Dept.-Lieut. of Warwickshire 1857, and Cornet Warwickshire Yeomanry Cavalry 1859. Patron of 4 livings. A Conservative, opposed to the abolition of church-rates, in favour of the repeal of the malt-tax. First elected for Warwickshire S. May 1859. Sat until he retired in 1868. Sheriff of Warwickshire 1879. Author. Died 15 Oct. 1897.   [1867]

MORDAUNT, Sir John, Bart. 41 Eaton Place, London. Walton, Warwickshire. Carlton. Was b. in 1808. In 1834 married Caroline the second d. of Dr. Murray, Bishop of Rochester. A Conservative and the patron of 2 livings. Sat for Warwickshire S. from 1835 until his death in 1845.   [1845]

MORE, Robert Jasper. Continued in House after 1885: full entry in Volume II.

MORETON, Hon. Augustus Henry. 2 Seamore Place, Mayfair, London. Bembridge, Isle of Wight. Brooks's. 2nd s. of Lord Ducie. B. 1804. A Maj. in the N. Gloucestershire Militia. Of Whig principles; opposed to the ballot. Sat for the Western Division of Gloucestershire in the Parliament of 1832. Sat for Gloucestershire W. 1832-35, and for Gloucestershire E. from 1835. Retired 1841. Died 14 Feb. 1862.   [1838]

MORETON, Hon. Henry George Francis. Tortworth Court, Gloucestershire. Eld. s. of Lord Ducie. B. 1802; m. 1826, Elizabeth, d. of Lord Sherborne. Of Whig principles, in favour of the immediate abolition of slavery, and the ballot. Sat first for Gloucestershire E. in 1830. Retired in 1835. Succeeded as 2nd Earl Ducie June 1840. Died 2 June 1853.   [1833]

MORETON, Lord. (I). 24 Belgrave Square, London. Tortworth Court, Wooton-under-Edge, Gloucestershire. Brooks's. B. at Sherborne, Nr. Northleach, Gloucestershire 1827, the eld. s. of 2nd Earl of Ducie, by the eld. d. of the 2nd Lord

Sherborne. M. 1849, his cousin Julia, d. of James Haughton Langston, Esq., MP, of Sarsden House, Oxfordshire. Appointed Dept.-Lieut. of Oxfordshire 1851. A Liberal and in favour of the extension of the suffrage, but 'opposed to the parliamentary support of Roman Catholic Institutions.' Sat for Stroud from July 1852 until he succeeded as 3rd Earl Ducie in June 1853.
[1853]

MORETON, Lord (II). 16 Portman Square, London. Tortworth Court, Falfield, Gloucestershire. Brooks's. Only s. of the Earl of Ducie, by Julia, only d. and heir of James Haughton Langston, Esq., MP, of Sarsden House, Oxfordshire. B. in London 1857. A Dept.-Lieut. of Gloucestershire. A Liberal. Sat for Gloucestershire W. from Apr. 1880. Retired in 1885. Died 28 Feb. 1920. [1885]

MORGAN, Sir Charles Morgan Robinson, Bart. 70 Pall Mall, London, Ruperra, Glamorganshire. Carlton. B. 1792; m. 1827, Rosamond, only d. of Gen. and the Hon. Mrs. Mundy. Patron of 5 livings. A Conservative, voted for agricultural protection 1846. Unsuccessfully contested Brecon in 1832, but sat for it previously from 1818. Returned again for Brecon Jan 1835. Sat until he retired 1847. Died 4 Jan. 1854. [1847]

MORGAN, Charles Octavius Swinnerton. 9 Pall Mall, London. The Friars, Newport, Monmouthshire. Carlton and United University. 4th s. of Sir Chas. Morgan, 1st Bart. of Tredegar, Co. Monmouth, by Mary Margaret, d. of Capt. George Storey, R.N. Bro. to 1st Lord Tredegar. B. 1803. Graduated at Christ Church, Oxford, B.A. 1825, M.A. 1832. A Magistrate and Dept.-Lieut. of Monmouthshire. A Conservative, gave general support to Mr. Disraeli, would 'uphold the great institutions of the country in Church and State.' First returned for Monmouthshire in 1840. Sat until he retired in 1874. Died 5 August 1888. [1873]

MORGAN, Charles Rodney. 32 Portman Square, London. Tredegar Park, Monmouthshire. Guard's, Coventry and Arthur's. B. at Ruperra Castle, Glamorganshire 1828, the eld s. of Sir Charles Morgan Robinson Morgan, Bart., of Tredegar, Monmouthshire, by Rosamond, only d. of Gen. G.B. Mundy, and grand-d. maternally of the celebrated Admiral Lord Rodney. Unmarried. Educ. at Eton and entered the Coldstream Guards in 1847. A Conservative, and opposed 'a reimposition of the duty on foreign corn, by whatever party it may be brought forward.' Saw the relief of the agricultural interest in 'a well-regulated revision of taxation, and the

removal of special burdens pressing heavily on land.' Would have 'rejoiced to see a reduction in, or total repeal of the malt tax.' 'A firm supporter of our Established Church and would resist any aggressions made thereon.' Opposed to the repeal of the Maynooth Grant, but would have supported any inquiry respecting it. Opposed to an extension of the franchise. Sat for the borough of Brecon from July 1852 until his death on 14 Jan. 1854. [1853]

MORGAN, Hon. F.C. Continued in House after 1885: full entry in Volume II.

MORGAN, Hon. Godfrey Charles. 39 Portman Square, London. Tredegar Park, Newport, Monmouthshire. Rupena, Newport, Monmouthshire. Carlton, Army and Navy, Arthur's and Boodle's. Eld. s. of Lord Tredegar, by the only d. of General G.B. Mundy. B. at Ruperra Castle, Cardiff, Glamorganshire, 1830. Educ. at Eton. Became Capt. 17 Lancers 1853, served in the campaign in the Crimea, was present at the battle of Alma, the Light Cavalry Charge at Balaklava, and at Inkerman. Was a Dept.-Lieut. of Monmouth and of Brecknockshire and a Maj. of the Gloucestershire Hussar Yeomanry. A Conservative. Sat for Brecknockshire from Dec. 1858 until he succeeded as 2nd Baron Tredegar Apr. 1875. Died 11 Mar. 1913. [1875]

MORGAN, Rt. Hon. G.O. Continued in House after 1885: full entry in Volume II.

MORGAN, Hamilton Knox Grogan. Johnstown Castle, Co. Wexford. Reform. Assumed the name of Morgan in 1828, in addition to his patronymic, Grogan, on inheriting the estates of his cousin, Mr. Morgan, an Alderman of Waterford. B. 1807; m. Sophia Maria, 2nd d. of Ebenezer Rowe, Esq., of Castletown House, Co. Wexford, and grandd. of Col. William Irvine, of Castle Irvine, Co. Fermanagh. A Magistrate and Dept.-Lieut. of Wexford. Of Liberal opinions. Was an unsuccessful candidate for Wexford Co. in 1841; first returned there in 1847. Defeated in 1852. [1852]

MORISON, Sir William, K.C.B. 16 Savile Row, London. Greenfield, Clackmannanshire. Oriental, and United Service. 2nd. s. of James Morison, Esq., of Greenfield, Clackmannanshire. A Maj.-Gen. in India, held several offices in trust in India, including that of Commissioner for the Government of Mysore, and was for some time a member of the Supreme Council of India, and finally President of that body. Also Dept.-Governor of Bengal. A Reformer. First returned for Clackmannan and Kinross in Feb. 1842, and sat until his death in June 1851.   [1851]

MORLEY, Arnold. Continued in House after 1885: full entry in Volume II.

MORLEY, John. Continued in House after 1885: full entry in Volume II.

MORLEY, Samuel. 34 Grosvenor Street, London. 18 Wood Street, Cheapside, London. Hall Place, Tunbridge, Kent. Devonshire and City Liberal. Youngest s. of John Morley, Esq., by Sarah, d. of — Poulton, Esq., of Maidenhead. B. at Homerton 1809; m. 1841, Rebekah Maria, d. of Samuel Hope, Esq., of Liverpool. A member of the firm of Messrs. J. & R. Morley, London, wholesale hosiers. A Magistrate for Middlesex and a Commissioner of Lieutenancy for London. A Liberal, in favour of local control in the granting of licences. Sat for Nottingham from 11 July 1865 but was unseated on petition and did not stand at the subsequent election in May 1866. Sat for Bristol from Dec. 1868, until he retired in 1885. Refused Peerage 1885. Died 5 Sept. 1886.   [1885]

MORPETH, Rt. Hon. Visct. 12 Grosvenor Place, London. Castle Howard, Yorkshire. Eld. s. of the Earl of Carlisle. B. 1802. Graduated at Christ Church, Oxford. Author of the *Last of the Greeks*. Was Chief Secretary for Ireland from Apr. 1835 to Sept. 1841; appointed Chief Commissioner of Woods and Forests July 1846. A Dept.-Lieut. of Yorkshire. Appointed Lord-Lieut. of East Riding of Yorkshire, July 1847. A Liberal. Represented Morpeth in Parliament from 1826 to 1830; Yorkshire W. from 1830 to 1841. Contested Dublin 29 Jan. 1842. Was again elected for Yorkshire W. in Feb. 1846, and in 1847. Succeeded father as 7th Earl Oct. 1848. Chancellor of Duchy of Lancaster Mar. 1850 to Feb. 1852; Lord Lieut. of Ireland Feb. 1855 to Mar. 1858, and June 1859 until relinquished office through ill health in 1864. Died 5 Dec. 1864.   [1847 2nd ed.]

MORRIS, D. 8 St. James's Place, London. Llanstephan, Carmarthen. Union, Reform, Brooks's and Windham. Eld. s. of William Morris, Esq., (a Banker at Carmarthen, and a Magistrate for the Co.) A Dept.-Lieut. of Brecknock, and a Magistrate for Carmarthenshire. A Liberal, voted for inquiry into Maynooth, and for the ballot in 1853; voted against church rates 1855. Was first returned for Carmarthen in 1837, after a severe contest, and re-elected in 1841 without opposition. Sat until his death 30 Sept. 1864.   [1864]

MORRIS, George. Wellpark, Galway. Kildare

Street Club, Dublin. S. of Martin Morris, Esq., of Spiddal, Co. Galway, who was High Sheriff in 1841, by Julia, d. of Dr. Charles Blake, of Galway. B. at Galway 1835. Unmarried. Educ. at Erasmus Smith's Coll., Galway. A Magistrate for the Co. of Galway and High Sheriff of Galway 1860-61. Was Vice-Chairman of the Galway board of guardians, and a member of the harbour board, and town commission there. An extensive land agent. A Liberal-Conservative, in favour of the system called 'Home Rule' for Ireland. Sat for the bor. of Galway from Apr. 1867-Nov. 1868: re-elected Feb. 1874. Retired 1880.   [1880]

MORRIS, Rt. Hon. Sir Michael. 22 Lower Fitzwilliam Street, Dublin. Spiddle, Galway. Well Park, Galway. B. at Galway 1827, the eld. s. of Martin Morris, Esq., of Spiddle, Co. Galway, a Magistrate for that Co., by Julia, d. of Dr. Charles Blake, of Galway. M. 1860, d. of Rt. Hon. Baron Hughes, one of the Judges of the Court of Exchequer in Ireland. Educ. at Galway Coll., and at Trinity Coll., Dublin, where he graduated in science honours in 1847, won one of Erasmus Smith's Exhibitions, and was first senior moderator and Gold Medallist. Was called to the bar in Ireland 1849, and appointed Queen's Counsel 1863. Was Solicitor Gen. of Ireland July-Nov. 1866, when he was appointed Attorney-Gen. Was Recorder of Galway from 1857-1865, High Sheriff of Galway 1850 and a Magistrate of the Co. Of moderate Liberal opinions. First elected for Galway in July 1865 and sat until he was appointed Judge of Common Pleas, Ireland, in 1867.   [1867]

MORRIS, William. 24 Dover Street, London. Carmarthen. Coomb, Nr. Carmarthen. Union. 2nd s. of Thomas Morris, Esq., Banker of Carmarthen. B. 1811; m. 1847, only d. of Sackville V. Gwynne, Esq., of Glanbrane Park, Carmarthenshire. A Banker at Carmarthen. A Magistrate for the Co. and borough of Carmarthen; High Sheriff for that Co. 1858. A Liberal. First elected for Carmarthen district Oct. 1864. Retired in 1868. Contested Cricklade 4 Feb. 1874. Died 1877.   [1867]

MORRISON, James. 57 Upper Harley Street, London. Fonthill, Wiltshire. Batham Hill, Surrey. Westminster Club. S. of Joseph Morrison, Esq. A Wholesale Haberdasher in London. M. d. of Joseph Todd, Esq., Silk-mercer of London. Author of a pamphlet on railway legislation. A Reformer, in favour of the ballot, of a fixed duty on foreign corn, and of a protection on manufacturers, 'not so high as to throw trade into the hands of smugglers.' Sat for St. Ives in 1830; from 1830 for Ipswich, until he was defeated in Jan.

1835, but the election of his opponent was, on petition, declared void on the ground of bribery, and a new writ being issued in June, Mr. Morrison was returned at the head of the poll. Retired 1837. First returned for the district of Inverness burghs in 1840. Retired Aug. 1847.   [1836]

MORRISON, Walter. Continued in House after 1885: full entry in Volume II.

MORRITT, William John Sawrey. 40 Lowndes Square, London. Rokeby Park, Darlington, Yorkshire. A Magistrate for the N. Riding of Yorkshire. A moderate Conservative, in favour of free trade and commercial reciprocity. First elected for the N. Riding of Yorkshire, Mar. 1852. Sat until he was defeated 1865. Died 13 Apr. 1874.   [1865]

MOSLEY, Sir Oswald, Bart. 15 Portland Place, London. Rolleston Hall, Staffordshire. B. 1785; m. 1804 Sophia, sister of Sir Henry Every, Bart. of Egginton, Derbyshire. Patron of 1 living. A Reformer, in favour of a revision of the Corn Laws, and Church Reform; opposed to short Parliaments. Sat for Staffordshire N. from 1832. Defeated in 1837. Died 24 May 1871.   [1837]

MOSS, R. Continued in House after 1885: full entry in Volume II.

MOSTYN, Hon. Edward Mostyn Lloyd-. 9 Lower Seymour Street, Portman Square, London. Mostyn, Flintshire. B. at Mostyn 1795, the eld s. of Lord Mostyn. M. 1827 Lady Harriet Margaret, eld. d. of 2nd Earl of Clonmell. Assumed the name of Mostyn after his patronymic Lloyd on inheriting the estates of his uncle, Sir Thomas Mostyn, 6th and last Bart. Lord Lieut. of Merionethshire, and appointed Dept.-Lieut. of Flintshire, 1852. A Liberal, voted in favour of free trade 1846, and against the ballot 1853. Represented Flintshire 1831-37, and from July 1841 to May 1842, when he was unseated on petition. Elected for Lichfield in Jan. 1846, but sat for Flintshire again 1847-Apr.1854, when he succeeded as 2nd Baron. Died 17 Mar. 1884.   [1854]

MOSTYN, Hon. Thomas E. Mostyn Lloyd-. 9 Lower Seymour Street, Portman Square, London. Mostyn Hall, Holywell, Flintshire. Brooks's. Eld. s. of Lord Mostyn. B. at Pengwern, St. Asaph 1830; m. 1855, Lady Henrietta, 2nd d. of 4th Earl of Abergavenny. Educ. at Eton and at Christ Church, Oxford. A Liberal in favour of a large extension of the suffrage, the ballot, etc. First elected for Flintshire, without opposition, May 1854, when his father, who had represented

it for many years, succeeded to a peerage. MP until his death in 1861.   [1861]

MOWATT, Francis. 14 Devonshire Place, Portland Place, London. Athenaeum. S. of Capt. James Ryder Mowatt, of Eastbourne, Sussex. B. at Eastbourne 1803; m. 1828, d. of Capt. George Barnes, of the E.I.C. Marine Service. A Liberal, opposed to the Game Laws and to all religious endowment, supported the principle that the education of the people should be effected by the State. Sat for Penryn and Falmouth from July 1847-July 1852. Unsuccessfully contested Cambridge July 1852. First elected for Cambridge Aug. 1854. Retired 1857. Died 12 Feb. 1891.   [1857]

MOWBRAY, Sir J.R. Continued in House after 1885: full entry in Volume II.

MULGRAVE, Rt. Hon. the Earl of. 68 Eaton Place, London. Mulgrave Castle, Whitby, Yorkshire. Reform. Eld. s. of the 1st Marq. of Normanby, by the eld. d. of the 1st Lord Ravensworth. B. 1819; m. 1844, Laura, d. of Capt. Robert Russell, R.N. Appointed Ensign and Lieut. Scots Fusilier Guards 1838. Dept.-Lieut. of Yorkshire 1841, and Major North York Militia 1846. Was controller of the Queen's household from July 1851-Feb.1852. Was created a P.C. on becoming controller. Appointed Treasurer of the household Dec. 1852. A Liberal, voted against the ballot 1853. Sat for Scarborough from July 1847 to July 1851, when he was defeated after taking office. Regained his seat in July 1852. Sat until appointed Governor of Nova Scotia 1858-1863; other Governorships 1863-84. Succeeded as 2nd Marq. of Normanby July 1863. Died 3 Apr. 1890.   [1857]

MULHOLLAND, John. 7 Eaton Square, London. Ballywater Park, Co. Down. Carlton. Eld. s. of Andrew Mulholland, Esq., of Springvale (a Magistrate and Dept.-Lieut. of Co. Down), by Elizabeth, d. of Thomas Macdonnell, Esq., of Belfast. B. in Belfast 1819; m. 1851, Frances Louisa, d. of Hugh Lyle, Esq., of Knockintorn, Co. Londonderry. Created hon. LL.D. of Dublin 1881. A Conservative. Contested Belfast 21 Nov. 1868. Sat for Downpatrick from Feb. 1874 until he retired in 1885.   [1885]

MULLINGS, Joseph Randolph. 23 Suffolk Street, Pall Mall, London. Eastcourt House, Nr. Malmesbury, Wiltshire. Carlton and National. S. of Mr. Richard Mullings. B. at Devizes, Wiltshire, 1792; m. 1823, Margarette, only d. of Mr. Richard Gregory, of Cirencester. Educ. at Devizes; admitted a Solicitor 1820, practised in Cirencester, and retired. Appointed a Dept.-Lieut. of Gloucestershire, June 1852. A

Magistrate for Gloucestershire and for Wiltshire. Patron of 1 living. A Conservative, in favour of religious liberty, of education 'based upon the vital principles of Christianity', and an equitable settlement of the church-rate question. First returned for Cirencester May 1848 and sat until he retired in 1859. Died 18 Oct. 1859.   [1858]

MULLINS, Frederick William. Gloucester Terrace, Regent's Park, London. Beaufort House, Co. Kerry. Johnstown Lodge, Co. Cork. Eld. s. of the Hon. and Rev. Frederick Mullins, and grands. of Thomas Lord Ventry. M. 1826, Lucia, eld. d. of Capt. W.R. Broughton, R.N., and grand-d. of Sir Thomas Broughton, Bart., of Broughton Hall, Staffordshire. Of Whig principles, in favour of shorter Parliaments, the Ballot, and a repeal of the Union, if Irish interests were not placed on an equality with English in the eye of the legislature. Sat for Co. Kerry from 1831. Defeated in 1837. Died 17 Mar. 1854.   [1837]

MUNCASTER, Lord. Continued in House after 1885: full entry in Volume II.

MUNDELLA, A.J. Continued in House after 1885: full entry in Volume II.

MUNDY, Edward Miller. 19 Pall Mall, London. Shipley, Derbyshire. United University, Carlton, Union. B. in 1800, the s. of Edward Miller Mundy, whose father represented Derbyshire for 40 years. A Conservative, voted for agricultural protection 1846. Opposed to the endowment of the Roman Catholic Clergy. Sat for S. Derbyshire from 1841 until his death in 1849.   [1848]

MUNDY, William. Markeaton, Derby. Carlton, Brooks's and Travellers'. S. of Francis Mundy, Esq., (many years MP for Derby), by Sarah, d. of F. Leaper Newton, Esq. B. at Markeaton 1801; m. 1830, Harriet Georgiana, d. of Lady Harriot and James Frampton, Esq., of Moreton, Dorsetshire. Educ. at Eton, and at Christ Church, Oxford. Patron of 1 living. A Conservative, in favour of 'progressive reform'; opposed to the Maynooth Grant. Sat for Derbyshire S. from Mar. 1849-Apr. 1857; re-elected May 1859 and sat until defeated 1865. Died 10 Apr. 1877.   [1865]

MUNSTER, H. A Liberal. Returned for Mallow 3 Feb. 1870; election declared void on petition very soon afterwards.

MUNSTER, William Felix Laurence Austin. Harcourt Buildings, Temple, London. Romanoff Lodge, Tunbridge Wells, Kent. B. at Mortier,

near Tours 1849, the s. of Henry Munster, Esq., Barrister-at-Law (who represented Mallow for a short time in 1870), by Zeorin Angelique Louise, 2nd d. of Col. Pozac. Unmarried. Educ. at St. Stanislaus, Beaumont Lodge, Old Windsor, and at Stonyhurst and graduated B.A. at London. A member of the Inner Temple. A Liberal. Sat for Mallow from June 1872 until his retirement in 1874. Died 11 Apr. 1877.   [1873]

MUNTZ, George Frederick. Brittonferry House, Glamorganshire. Reform. B. 1874, the s. of a German Merchant of great respectability, who settled in Birmingham in 1793, and m. Miss Purden of that town. M. 1818, d. of Rev. John Pryce. Was a Merchant, Metal Roller and Inventor and Manufacturer of Patent Yellow Metal Ship Sheathing and Bolts. Was the 1st Vice-Chairman of the Birmingham Political Union and one of its most strenuous supporters. Underwent several prosecutions on account of an alleged riot at a Church Rate Meeting in Birmingham; was convicted upon this charge in 1837 but the proceedings were quashed, the Judge (Sir J.A. Park) and the Court of Queen's Bench being of the opinion that they were illegal, and that the prosecution should never have been instituted. A Dept.-Lieut. of Warwickshire. A Radical Reformer, 'wished to remove all abuses without injury to the just rights of any.' Opposed 'any further extension of political power to the Roman Catholics.' Author of several pamphlets on commercial, financial and politico-economical subjects. Sat for Birmingham from 1840 until his death in 1857 or 1858.   [1857 2nd ed.]

MUNTZ, P.A. Continued in House after 1885: full entry in Volume II.

MUNTZ, P.H. Continued in House after 1885: full entry in Volume II.

MURE, David. 12 Ainslie Place, Edinburgh. 3rd. s. of Col. William Mure of Caldwell (Vice-Lieut. of the Co. of Renfrew), by Anne, eld d. of Sir James Hunter Blair, Bart. of Dunskey. Grands. of William Mure, Esq., who represented Renfrewshire from 1742 till 1761, and bro. of Col. William Mure, who sat for the same Co. from 1846 till 1855. B. 1810; m. 1841, Helen, eld. d. of John Tod, Esq., of Kirkhill, Edinburghshire (she died 1849). Educ. at Westminster School and at the Univ. of Edinburgh. Called to the Scottish bar 1831. Was Sheriff of Perthshire from 1853 till 1858; Solicitor-Gen. for Scotland from July 1858 till Apr. 1859, and Lord Advocate of Scotland from the last date till June 1859. A Liberal-Conservative, gave a general support to Lord Derby; opposed to the ballot and to the grant to Maynooth; in favour of the army and navy being maintained in a high state of efficiency, and of National Education being based on religion. First elected for Bute May 1859, and sat until he was appointed Judge of Court of Session (Lord Mure) in 1865. Retired 1889. Died 11 Apr. 1891. [1864]

MURE, Col. William, sen. 14 Jermyn Street, London. Caldwell, Beith, Ayrshire. United Services. B. at Caldwell, Ayrshire 1799, the s. of Col. William Mure, Vice-Lieut. of Renfrewshire, by Anne, eld. d. of Sir James Hunter Blair, Bart., of Dunskey (grands. of William Mure, Esq., who represented Renfrewshire from 1742-61). M. 1825, Laura, 2nd d. of William Markham, Esq., of Becca Hall, Yorkshire, and grand-d. of the Most Rev. William Markham, Archbishop of York. Was educ. at Westminster, Edinburgh University and in Germany. Author of a *Journal of a Tour in Greece, etc. in 1838, Dissertation of the Calendar, etc. of Ancient Egypt, History of Grecian Literature.* Vice-Lieut. of Renfrewshire and Col. of the Renfrew Militia. Lord Rector of Glasgow University 1847-48. A 'Liberal-Conservative', opposed to protection, but supported other measures for the relief of agriculture. Voted against the Ecclesiastical Tithes Bill as being ineffective, and opposed to the Maynooth Grant. Unsuccessfully contested the Co. of Renfrew in 1841, but was returned without opposition in Dec. 1846, sitting until he accepted Chiltern Hundreds 1855. Died 1 Apr. 1860. [1855]

MURE, Col. William, jun. 37 Eaton Place, London. Caldwell, Renfrewshire. Guards'. S. of William Mure, Esq. (who sat for Renfrewshire from 1846-1856), by Laura, d. of William Markham, Esq., of Becca Hall, Yorkshire. B. at Edinburgh 1830; m. 1859, Hon. Constance Elizabeth, youngest d. of the 1st Lord Leconfield. Educ. at Eton. Entered the 60th Rifles 1847, exchanged to 79th Highlanders 1854, and appointed Lieut. and Capt. Fusilier Guards 1855. Served in the Kaffir War from 1841-1843, also in the Crimea, and received a medal and clasps for Alma, Balaklava and Sebastopol. A Dept.-Lieut. and Magistrate for the Co. of Renfrewshire, and was Col. of 2nd Batt. Renfrewshire Volunteers from 1861. A Liberal, in favour of the abolition of the law of entail and primogeniture in cases of intestacy. Sat from Feb. 1874 for Renfrewshire, which he had unsuccessfully contested Aug. 1873. MP until his death 9 Nov. 1880. [1880]

MURPHY, Francis Stack. 3 Serjeant's Inn, Chancery Lane, London. Boodle's, Reform and Coventry. B. in Cork, 1807, the s. of Jeremiah Murphy, Esq., of Cork, Merchant and nephew of Dr. Murphy, Roman Catholic Bishop of Cork. Unmarried. Educ. at Conglowes Wood College, Co. Kildare, afterwards at St. Cuthberts, Durham, and at Trinity Coll., Dublin, at which last he obtained the classical gold medal in 1829. Was called to the bar at Lincoln's Inn 1833, and joined the Northern Circuit. Became a Serjeant-at-Law 1842 and received a patent of precedence 1846. A Liberal, and against the repeal of the Union. Once favoured a fixed duty on corn, but later supported free trade. Was in favour of national education in Ireland, and opposed to the tenant league. Sat for Cork City from the general election 1841 to 1846 when he voluntarily retired. Re-elected without opposition in Apr. 1851, and sat until he was appointed Commissioner of Insolvents in 1853. [1853]

MURPHY, Nicholas Daniel. Lauriston, Cork. Reform. S. of Daniel Murphy, Esq. of Belleville, Cork. Merchant, by Frances, d. of — Donegan, Esq. B. in Cork 1811; m. 1838, Anne, d. of Patrick Waldron, Esq., of Rathgar House, Co. Dublin. Educ. at Cork and at Clongowes Wood Coll. Admitted a Solicitor 1834. A Liberal. Sat for Cork from July 1865 until defeated 1880. [1880]

MURRAY, Alexander. 2 Mansion House, Albany, London. Cally House, Kircudbrightshire. B. in 1789, the s. of J. Murray, Esq. M. 1816, the d. of the 2nd Earl of Lucan. A Reformer. Was elected for Kircudbrightshire in 1838, and sat until his death on 15 July 1845. [1845]

MURRAY, Charles James. Continued in House after 1885: full entry in Volume II.

MURRAY, Charles Robert Scott. 11 Cavendish Square, London. Danesfield, Buckinghamshire. Carlton and White's. B. 1818. A Conservative. First elected for Buckinghamshire in 1841 and sat until Jan. 1845, when he accepted Chiltern Hundreds. [1844]

MURRAY, Sir G. A Conservative. Returned for Perthshire 5 May 1834. Retired 1835. Defeated at 1835 gen. election. Contested Westminster 1837, Manchester 1839 and 1841. Died 28 July 1846. [1834]

MURRAY, Rt. Hon. John Archibald. 7 New Palace Yard, London. George Street, Leith. Reform. 2nd s. of Alexander Murray, Esq., of Henderland, Lord of Session and Justiciary, by Catherine, d. of Sir Alex. Lindsay, of Evelick, Bart., and niece of the first Earl of Mansfield. M. 1826, eld d. of William Rigby of Oldfield Hall, Cheshire. Succeeded the Rt. Hon. Francis Jeffrey as Lord Advocate in 1834, but lost that office in Nov. of the same year. Resumed it in Apr. 1835. Was Recorder of the Great Roll, or Clerk of the Pipe, in the Exchequer Court, Scotland, but resigned it as a sinecure some time before his accession to office in 1834. Sat for Leith dist. from 1832 until appointed Lord of Session 23 Apr. 1839 and knighted next day. Died 7 Mar. 1859. [1838]

MURRAY, William. 11 Cambridge Square, Hyde Park, London. Birchin Lane, London. City. S. of William Murray, Esq. B. at Portsea, Hampshire 1796. Educ. at Dr. Burney's Naval Academy, Gosport. Admitted a Solicitor 1821, and practised in conjunction with partners in London. A member of the Council of the Incorporated Law Society. A Conservative, and said he would give a general support to Lord Derby. First elected for Newcastle-under-Lyme May 1859. Retired 1865.   [1865]

MURROUGH, John Patrick. 5 New Inn, Strand, London. S. of John Murrough, Esq., of Chichester, Sussex, an Irish Merchant. B. at Chichester 1822; m. 1848, Isabel Maria, d. of John Beart, Esq. Educ. at the Guildford Grammar School. Admitted a Solicitor, Easter 1844. A Liberal, and a Parliamentary Reformer; voted for the ballot 1853, 'hostile to all State endowments for ecclesiastic purposes, but friendly to the Maynooth Grant, so long as the Irish Church Establishment exists.' First returned for Bridport July 1852. Retired 1857. Contested Blackburn Apr. 1859 and Midhurst Feb. 1874.   [1857]

MUSGRAVE, Sir Richard, Bart. Tourin, Co. Waterford. S. of Sir Christopher Frederick Musgrave, Bart. B. 1790; m. 1815, Frances, youngest d. of William Newcome, Primate of Ireland. A Reformer, favourable to the Repeal of the Union, and the introduction of poor laws into Ireland; pledged to the extinction of Tithes. Sat for Waterford Co. in the Parliaments of 1830 and 1831; declined to be a candidate, although solicited by a majority of the electors, in 1832; was again returned for Waterford Co. in 1835 without opposition. Retired in 1837. Died 7 July 1859.   [1837]

MUSGRAVE, Sir Richard Courtenay, Bart. 17 Cavendish Square, London. Eden Hall, Penrith. Carlton. Younger s. of Sir George Musgrave, 10th Bart., of Edenhall, by Charlotte, d. of Sir James Graham, 1st Bart., of Netherby. B. at Eden Hall 1838; m. 1867, Adora Frances Olga, only d. of Peter Wills, Esq., of Forest Farm. Formerly an officer 71st Highland Light Infantry. Lord-Lieut. of Westmoreland. A Magistrate and Dept.-Lieut. of Cumberland. A Conservative. Unsuccessfully

contested E. Cumberland Feb. 1874. Sat for E. Cumberland from Apr. 1880 until his death 13 Feb. 1881.   [1880 2nd ed.]

MUSKETT, George Alfred. The Bury, Hertfordshire. Reform. B. 1785. A Banker. Dept.-Chairman of the 'Family Endowment Society'. A Reformer, and gave no pledges. First elected for St. Albans 25 July 1837. Defeated in 1841.   [1841]

NAAS, Rt. Hon. Lord. 8 Queen Street, Mayfair, London. Palmerston House, Naas, Kildare. Carlton, Junior Carlton, White's and Travellers'. B in Dublin 1822, the eld. s. of the Earl of Mayo, by the only d. and heir of Hon. John Jocelyn (who was uncle to the 3rd Lord of Roden). M. 1848, Hon. Blanche Julia, 3rd d. of Lord Leconfield. Educ. at the University of Dublin where he graduated M.A. Author of *St. Petersburg & Moscow*. Was Gentleman of the Bed-Chamber to Lord Heytesbury, when he was Lord-Lieut. of Ireland, and was Chief Sec. for Ireland from Mar.-Dec. 1852, from Mar. 1858-June 1859 and from July 1866 (salary £4,000). A Magistrate and Dept.-Lieut. of Kildare. A Conservative. Sat for Kildare from 1847-Mar. 1852; then for Coleraine until Mar. 1857, when he was returned for Cockermouth. Sat until he succeeded as 6th Earl Mayo 12 Aug. 1867. Was appointed Govenor General of India 1868. Was assassinated in the Andaman Islands 8 Feb. 1872.   [1867]

NAGHTEN, Col. Arthur Robert. Blighmont, Southampton. Carlton, St. Stephen's, and United University. S. of Thomas Naghten, Esq., of Titchfield, Hampshire, by Maria, d. of Robert Lang, Esq., of Moor Park, Surrey. B. 1829; m. 1859, Dora, d. of St. John C. Charlton, Esq., of Apley Castle, Shropshire. Educ. at Eton and at Worcester Coll., Oxford, graduated B.A. 1852, M.A. 1853. A Magistrate for Hampshire and Lieut.-Col. Hampshire Artillery Militia. A decided Conservative. Sat for Winchester from Feb. 1874. Retired 1880. Died 7 Aug. 1881. [1880]

NAGLE, Sir Richard, Bart. Jamestown House, Co. Westmeath. Reform. B. 1800. Was dismissed from the Magistracy for presiding at an anti-tithe meeting, being then High Sheriff. A Repealer. Sat for Westmeath from 1832 until he retired 1841.
                              [1838]

NANNEY, O.J.E. A Conservative. Defeated Standing for Carnarvon in Dec. 1832, but in Mar. 1833 he was seated on petition *vice* Sir Charles Paget, but on counter petition, the case was reversed. Was unsuccessful at Carnarvon 12 Jan. 1835.

NAPIER, Sir Charles, K.C.B. 18 Albermarle Street, London. Merchistoun, Nr. Horndean, Hampshire. Reform. Eld. s. of Hon. Charles Napier, of Merchistoun Hall, Stirlingshire, by his 2nd wife, Christian, d. of Gabriel Hamilton, Esq., of Westburn, Lanarkshire. B. at Merchistoun Hall, New Falkirk 1786; m. d. of — Younghusband, Esq., and relict of Lieut. Edward Elers, R.N. (she died 1857). Was an Admiral in the Portuguese service, commanded Don Pedro's fleet in 1833, and was created Count Cape St. Vincent by Donna Maria. Became Admiral of the Blue en the British Navy 1858; commanded the squadron on the Syrian station 1839; was appointed to command the fleet sent to the Tagus 1847, and that sent to the Baltic in 1854. Received several foreign orders of knighthood. A Liberal, in favour of the extension of the franchise to all householders and lodgers, vote by ballot, short Parliaments, abolition of Church rates, and the exclusion of Bishops from the House of Lords. Sat for Marylebone from July 1841-July 1847; unsuccessfully contested Portsmouth Jan. 1835, Greenwich July 1837, Lambeth July 1850, and Yarmouth July 1852. First returned for Southwark Nov. 1855 and sat until his death 6 Nov. 1860.   [1860]

NAPIER, Rt. Hon. Joseph. 17 Mountjoy Square South, Dublin. Carlton, and National. S. of William Napier, Esq., a descendant of the Murchistoun branch of the Napier family, by Rose, d. of — McNaghten, Esq., and cousin to Sir F. McNaghten, Bart. B. at Belfast, 1804; m. 1830, d. of John Grace, Esq., and niece of Archdeacon Grace. Educ. at the Belfast Academical Institution, and afterwards graduated at Trinity Coll., Dublin, where he obtained general premiums in classics and science. Called to the Irish Bar in 1831; made a Queen's Counsel in Ireland 1844. Was Attorney-General for Ireland from Mar. till Dec. 1852. A member of the Royal Irish Academy, and president of the Irish Bar Association. A Conservative, a decided supporter of Scriptural education, and opposed to the plan called the National Board System in Ireland; voted for inquiry into Maynooth, 1853. First returned for Dublin University Feb. 1848, without opposition and sat until appointed Lord Chancellor for Ireland 1858-59. Created Baronet 26 Mar. 1867. Died 9 Dec. 1882.   [1858]

NEALE, Admiral Sir Harry, Bart., G.C.B. 12 Charles Street, St. James's, London. Walhampton, Hampshire. S. of William Burrard, Esq., and nephew of the late Sir Harry Burrard. Took the name of Neale by sign manual on marrying, in 1795, Grace Elizabeth, eld. d. and co-heiress of Robert Neale, Esq., of Shaw House, Wiltshire. A Conservative, sat for Lymington in the Parliaments of 1818 and 1820. Returned for Lymington in 1832. Retired in 1835.   [1833]

NEATE, Charles. Summertown, Oxford. Oxford & Cambridge. S. of Rev. Thomas Neate, by Catherine, d of Rev. William Church. B. at Adstock, Buckinghamshire 1806. Unmarried. Educ. at the Coll. Bourbon, Paris, where he obtained the prize in 1823 for a French essay at the Concours général of all the French Colleges; also at Lincoln Coll., Oxford, where he was 1st class and graduated M.A. 1830. Became a Fellow of Oriel Coll. 1828, and then Senior Fellow. Was Professor of Political Economy at that University. Was Called to the bar at Lincoln's Inn 1832. Published tracts against capital punishment and *Lectures on Political Economy*. Was private Secretary to Sir Francis Baring, while Chancellor of the Exchequer 1840 and 1841. A member of the Liberal party on 'its most popular side', in favour of the ballot and of a £6 qualification for voting; would acquiesce in any proposal which would make a considerable addition to the representation of the working classes. Sat for Oxford from Apr. till June 1857, when he was unseated on petition; re-elcted Nov. 1863. Retired in 1868. Died 7 Feb. 1879.   [1867]

NEELD, Sir John, Bart. 92 Eaton Square, London. Grittleton, Chippenham. Red Lodge, Wiltshire. Carlton, Conservative, and Boodle's. Younger s. of Joseph Neeld, Esq., of Gloucester Place, Portman Square, and Fulham, Middlesex, by Mary, eld. d. of John Bond. Esq., of Hendon. B. at Fulham 1805; m. 1845, Harriet Eliza, 2nd d. of Maj.-Gen. Dickson, C.B. of Beenham House, Berkshire. Educ. at Harrow and at Trinity Coll., Cambridge. Appointed in 1843 one of the gentlemen of the Privy Chamber. A Dept.-Lieut. of Wiltshire 1852. Patron of 5 livings. A Conservative, was 'against further concessions to the Church of Rome.' Sat for Cricklade from Jan. 1835 till May 1859, when he was an unsuccessful candidate; elected for Chippenham, July 1865. Retired in 1868. Died 3 Sept. 1891.   [1867]

NEELD, Joseph, F.S.A., F.L.S. 6 Grosvenor Square, London. Grittleton House, Wiltshire. Kelston Park, Somerset. Carlton, Athenaeum and Conservative. Eld. s. of Joseph Neeld, Esq., of Gloucester Place, and bro -in-law of Capt. Boldero, the other member for Chippenham. Also bro. of the member for Cricklade. M. 1831, Lady Caroline Mary, eld. d. of 6th Earl of Shaftesbury. An East India and Bank Proprietor. Dept.-Lieut. of Wiltshire and High Steward of Malmesbury. Patron of 9 livings. A Conservative, and voted for inquiry into Maynooth 1853. Sat for Chippenham from 1830 until his death on 24 Mar. 1856.   [1856]

NELSON, Isaac. Belfast. Was a Presbyterian minister at Belfast, which position he relinquished to enter Parliament. In favour of Home Rule for Ireland. Contested Leitrim Apr. 1880. Sat for Mayo from May 1880. Retired in 1885. Died 24 June 1888. [1885]

NEVILL, Charles William. Westfar, Llanelly, Carmarthenshire. Windham. Eld. s. of Richard Junior Nevill, Esq., of Llanlliedi (High Sheriff of Co. of Carmarthen 1836), by Anne, eld. d. of William Yalden, Esq., of Lovington, Hampshire. B. 1816; m. 1841, Jane, d. and co-heir of David Davies, Esq., of Swansea. Was educ. at Rugby. A Magistrate and Dept.-Lieut. for Carmarthenshire for which he was High Sheriff in 1868. A Liberal-Conservative. Sat for Carmarthen from Feb. 1874. Accepted Chiltern Hundreds July 1876. Died 7 June 1888. [1876]

NEVILLE, Ralph. See GRENVILLE, Ralph Neville.

NEVILLE-GRENVILLE, Ralph. See GRENVILLE, Ralph Neville.

NEWARK, Visct. 6 Tilney Street, London. Holme Pierrepont, Nr. Nottingham. Carlton and Boodle's. Eld s. of the 2nd Earl Manvers, by Mary Letitia, eld. d. of Anthony Hardolph Eyre, Esq., of Grove Park, Nottinghamshire. B. at Holme Pierrepont, near Nottingham 1825; m. 1852, the 2nd d. of the Duc de Coigny. Educ. at Christ Church, Oxford, where he graduated B.A. 1846. Appointed Capt. S. Nottinghamshire Yeomanry Cavalry 1851, and a Dept.-Lieut. for that Co. 1854. A Conservative, and a supporter of Lord Derby; formerly favoured the grant to Maynooth, but would withdraw it, and 'offer every possible resistance to the aggressions of the Romish priesthood.' Elected for Retford E. in Dec. 1832. Retired 1835. Was an unsuccessful candidate for Nottinghamshire S. after a very close contest in Feb. 1851. First returned for Nottinghamshire S. without opposition in July 1852 and sat until he succeeded to the Peerage (Earl Manvers) in 1860. [1860]

NEWDEGATE, Charles Newdigate. 27 Lowndes Street, London. Arbury, Nuneaton, Warwickshire. Harefield, Uxbridge, Middlesex. Carlton, Travellers', Arthur's, White's and National. Only s. of Charles Newdigate Newdegate, Esq., of Harefield Place, Middlesex, by Maria, d. of Ayscoghe Boucherett, Esq., heir of Sir Roger Newdigate, Bart. B. 1816. Educ. at Eton, at King's Coll., London, and at Christ Church, Oxford, where he graduated M.A. and D.C.L. A Conservative, attached to the principles of the Constitution as established in 1688. Sat for N. Warwickshire from 1843 until he retired in 1885. P.C. Feb. 1886. Died 9 Apr. 1887. [1885]

NEWPORT, Rt. Hon. Visct. (I). 30 Wilton Crescent, London. Weston Park, Shiffnal. Castle Bromwich, Birmingham. Carlton. Eld. s. of the Earl of Bradford. B. 1819; m. 1844, yougest d. of 1st Lord Forester. Educ. at Harrow School and at Trinity Coll., Cambridge, where he graduated M.A. 1840. A Dept.-Lieut. of Warwickshire. Appointed Capt. of the South Salopian Yeomanry Cavalry 1844, and Dept.-Lieut. of Staffordshire 1852. Was Vice-Chamberlain of the Household from Mar.-Dec. 1852; and from Mar. 1858-June 1859. A 'supporter of Conservative principles in Church and State.' First returned for Shropshire S. in Aug. 1842, when Lord Darlington succeeded to a Peerage and sat until he succeeded to the Peerage (Earl of Bradford) 22 Mar 1865. Lord Chamberlain 1866-68; Lord Lieut. of Shropshire 1875-96. Man of the Turf. Died 9 Mar. 1898. [1865]

NEWPORT, Visct.(II). 20 Lowndes Square, London. Carlton. Eld. s. of the Earl of Bradford, by the Hon. Selina Louisa, 5th d. of the 1st Lord Forester. B. 1845; m. 1869, Lady Ida Frances Annabella, d. of the 9th Earl of Scarborough. Appointed Cornet and Sub-Lieut. 1st Life Guards 1864, became Lieut. Feb. 1867, and retired the same year. A Conservative, in favour of the adoption of county financial boards. Sat for N. Shropshire from Mar. 1867 until he retired in 1885. Succeeded as 5th Earl Mar. 1898. Died 2 Jan. 1915. [1885]

NEWRY AND MORNE, Visct., sen. 30 Wilton Crescent, London. Weston Park, Staffordshire. Castle Bromwich, Warwickshire. Carlton. B. in 1815, the eld. s. of the Earl of Kilmorey. M. 1839, eld d. of the Hon. Sir Charles Colville, G.C.B. A Conservative, but in favour of free trade. First returned for the borough of Newry in 1841, and sat until his death on 6 May 1851. [1851]

NEWRY and MORNE, Visct., jun. Morne Park, Newry, Co. Down. B. in Bruton Street 1842, the eld. s. of Visct. Newry and Morne (who died 1851), by the eld. d. of the Hon. Sir Charles Colville, G.C.B. Grandson of the Earl of Kilmorey. High Sheriff of Co. Down for 1871. A Conservative. Sat for Newry from Jan. 1871 until he was defeated in 1874. Contested Shrewsbury Apr. 1880. Succeeded his grandfather as 3rd Earl of Kilmorey June 1880. Irish representative peer. Died 28 July 1915. [1873]

NICHOLL, Rt. Hon. John Iltyd, D.C.L. 10 Doctors' Commons, London. 33 Belgrave Square, London. Merthyrmawr, Glamorganshire. Carlton. S. of the Rt. Hon. Sir John Nicholl. B. in Lincoln's Inn Fields, 1797; called to the bar at Lincoln's Inn 1824; took the degree of D.C.L. 1826; m. 1821, Jane Harriet, 2nd d. of T.M. Talbot, Esq., of Margam, Glamorganshire, by Mary Lucy, 2nd d. of Henry Thomas, 2nd Earl of Ilchester. Was Master of the Faculties, and Judge-Advocate-Gen. Sat for Cardiff district from 1832 until he was defeated in 1852. Died 27 Jan. 1853. [1852]

NICHOLSON, William. 2 South Audley Street, London. Basing Park, Alton, Hampshire. Union. Youngest s. of John Nicholson, Esq., of Upper Clapton, Middlesex, by Ellen, d. of Richard Payne, Esq. B. at Upper Hollowway, near London, 1824; m. 1858, Isabella Sarah, d. of John Meek, Esq. Educ. at Harrow and at Trinity Coll., Cambridge. A Magistrate for Hampshire, of which county he was High Sheriff in 1878. A Liberal. Sat for Petersfield from July 1866 to Feb. 1874, when he was an unsuccessful candidate (after a scrutiny); re-elected there Apr. 1880. Defeated in 1885. Contested the same seat in 1886. [1885]

NICHOLSON, William Newzam. Queen Ann's Mansions, London. Newark-on-Trent. Carlton, and St. Stephen's. Eld. s. of Benjamin Nicholson, Esq., a Magistrate for Newark, by Frances, d. of Mr. John Newzam, of Newark. B. at Newark 1816; m. 1st, 1842, Maria Alice, d. of Mr. James Betts, of Newark; 2ndly, 1866, Annie d. of Joseph Prior, Esq., of Chaucer's House, Woodstock. Was educ. at the Magnus Grammar School, Newark. The Founder of and the principal Partner in the well-known firm of William Nicholson and Son, Agricultural Engineers, Newark. A Magistrate for Newark, and was a Mayor in 1857, and Chairman of the local committee of the Great Exhibition of that year. Was chairman of the Newark School Board from its formation, in 1871. A Conservative. Sat for Newark from Apr. 1880. Retired in 1885. President of Association of Agricultural Engineers 1888-89. Died 17 May 1899. [1885]

NICOL, James Dyce. 13 Hyde Park Terrace, London. Ballogie, Aboyne, Scotland. Athenaeum. S. of William Nichol, Esq., M.D. of Stonehaven, by Margaret d. of – Dyce, Esq. B. at Stonehaven 1805; m. 1844, Catherine, d. of Edward Lloyd, Esq., Banker of Manchester and London. Resided for several years at Bombay, where he was a partner in the firm of Messrs. W. Nichol & Co.. relinquished business 1844. A Magistrate and Dept.-Lieut. for the Cos. of Aberdeen and Kincardine. A Liberal; a supporter of Mr. Gladstone; voted for the disestablishment of the Irish Church 1869; in favour of the reduction of the public expenditure. First elected for Kincardineshire July 1865. MP until his death 16 Nov. 1872. [1872]

NICOL, William. 41 Victoria Street, London. Carlton. Eld. s. of James Nicol, Esq., Collector of Customs, Banff, Scotland. B. 1790; m. 1820, Margaret Dyce, 3rd d. of W. Nicol, Esq., of Badentoy, Kincardineshire, (she died 1860). Educ. at Aberdeen. Served in the Medical service of the East India Company from 1810-1816, when he became a Merchant in Bombay. A Conservative, and said he would give a general support to Lord Derby; in favour of all 'judicious and salutary reforms.' Unsuccessfully contested Youghal 1837. First elected for Dover 1859. Retired 1865. [1865]

NICOLL, Donald. 14 Park Lane, London. Gresham and City. B. 1820; m. 1855, Melina, younest d. of Lewis Jones, Esq. A Merchant Tailor and Manufacturer of cloth, Partner in the firm of Messrs. Nicoll, Regent Street, London. A Magistrate for Middlesex and Westminster; a Commissioner of Lieutenancy for London. Was Sheriff of London and Middlesex in 1849-50. A Liberal, in favour of the gradual extension of the suffrage, vote by ballot, financial and Parliamentary reform, the reduction of the duties on tea, sugar, etc.; opposed to the Maynooth grant. Unsuccessfully contested Frome, July 1856, when he was defeated by only one vote; first elected for Frome Apr. 1857. Defeated in 1859. [1858]

NISBET, Rt. Hon. Robert Adam Hamilton-, F.R.S. 23 Chesham Place South, London. Bloxhom Hall, Lincolnshire. Carlton and Travellers'. Eld. s. of Philip Dundas, Esq., (4th s. of Lord President Dundas, who was the eld. bro. of the 1st Visct. Melville), by the sister of Sir D. Wedderburne, Bart. B. 1804; m. 1828, Lady Mary, eld. d. of the 6th Earl of Elgin. Assumed the name of Christopher in lieu of Dundas, in compliance with the will of George Manners, Esq., of Bloxhom Hall, and the names of Hamilton-Nisbet 1855, on Lady Mary succeeding to the Belhaven and Dirleton estates. Was Chancellor of the Duchy of Lancaster from Mar.-Dec. 1852. Patron of 2 livings. A Conservative, opposed to the endowment of the Roman Catholic Clergy. Sat for Ipswich from 1826-1830, and for Edinburgh in 1831. Sat for Lincolnshire N. from 1837 until he retired 1857. Died 9 June 1877. [1857]

NISBET, Robert Parry. Southbroome House, Devizes, Wiltshire. Carlton, Conservative, and Oriental. S. of Walter Nisbet, Esq., and grands. of

Archibald Nisbet, Esq., of Carfin, Lanarkshire. M. 1st, 1817, Clara Amelia, only d. of Major Thomas Harriott, of West Hall, Surrey; 2ndly, 1846, Elizabeth, only d. of Edward Greene, Esq., of Hinxton Hall, Cambridgeshire. Educ. at Cheam School and Haileybury Coll. Entered the Bengal Civil Service in 1812, and retired in 1830, having held several judicial appointments there. A Magistrate and Dept.-Lieut. for Wiltshire; High Sheriff for that county 1849. Of 'essentially Conservative opinions', but ready to support all measures of sound and safe reform. First returned for Chippenham, Apr. 1856, without opposition. Retired in 1859. Died 31 May 1882.   [1858]

NOBLE, Joseph William. Danelts Hall, Nr. Leicester. S. of the Rev. John Noble, Vicar of Frisby-on-the-Wreake, Leicestershire, by Sarah, d. of – Wragge, Esq. B. at Frisby-on-the-Wreake, 1799; m. 1821, Miss Mary Joanna Kershaw, of Danelts Hall, near Leicester. Educ. at Trinity Coll., Cambridge, where he graduated M.D. 1831. Was Physician to the Leicester General Infirmary. A Reformer. First elected for Leicester May 1859. MP until his death 6 Jan. 1861. [1860]

NOEL, Hon. Charles George. 9 Cavendish Square, London. Exton, Rutlandshire. Brooks's. Eld. s. of Lord Barham, nephew of Sir George Grey, Bart. B. 1818. A Whig. Sat for Rutland from 28 Jan. 1840 until defeated in 1841. Succeeded as 2nd Earl June 1866. Died 13 Aug. 1881.   [1841]

NOEL, Ernest. 29a, Grosvenor Square, London. Lyndhurst, Haywards Heath, Sussex. Athenaeum and Brooks's. B. 1831, 2nd s. of Hon. and Rev. Baptist W. Noel, bro. of 1st Earl of Gainsborough, by Jane, eld. d. of Peter Baillie, Esq., of Dochfour, Invernesshire M. 1st, 1857, Louisa Hope, only d. of Thomas Milne, Esq., of Warley House, Halifax; 2ndly, 1873, Lady Augusta, youngest d. of 6th Earl of Albermarle. Educ. at Edinburgh and at Trinity Coll., Cambridge. A Magistrate and Dept.-Lieut. for Sussex. A Liberal. Sat for the district of Dumfries from Feb. 1874-1886, when he was defeated contesting Stirlingshire as a Liberal-Unionist. [1886]

NOEL, Rt. Hon. Gerard James. 31 Bruton Street, London. Catmose, Oakham, Rutland. Carlton, Junior Carlton and White's. 2nd s. of 1st Earl of Gainsborough, by his 3rd wife, Arabella, 2nd d. of Sir John Hamlyn-Williams, Bart. B. 1823; m. 1863 , Lady Augusta Mary, sister of the 3rd Earl of Lonsdale. Entered the Army as Cornet in the 11th Hussars 1842; became Lieut. in 1843; Capt. 1847; retired 1851; appointed Cornet Leicestershire Yeomanry Cavalry 1852,

and a Dept.-Lieut of Rutland 1848. A Lord of the Treasury from July 1866-Oct. 1868, and Parliamentary Sec. to the Treasury from the last date to Dec. following. Also Chief Commissioner of Works and Buildings from Aug. 1876-Apr.1880. A Conservative. Sat for Rutland from 1847 until he accepted Chiltern Hundreds in 1883. Died 19 May 1911.   [1883]

NOEL, Sir Gerard Noel, Bart. 11 Chandos Street, Cavendish Square, London. Exton Park, Lincolnshire. B. 1759; m. 1st, 1780, Diana, only d. of Sir Charles Middleton, Bart. (subsequently Lord Barham), (dead); 2ndly, 1823, Harriet, d. of the Rev. J. Gill, of Scraptoft, Leicestershire (dead); 3rdly, 1831, Mrs. Isabella Evans Raymond. The only s. of Gerard-Anne Edwardes, Esq., of Welham Grove, Leicestershire (who was the natural s. of Lord Anne Hamilton, 3rd s. of James, 4th Duke of Hamilton), but assumed in 1798, the name of his maternal uncle, Henry Noel, Earl of Gainsborough, with the arms of Noel, upon inheriting the estates of that nobleman. Father of Lord Barham, who inherited that title from his mother. Some member of the Noel family had, from a remote period, sat for Rutland. Patron of 7 livings. A moderate Reformer. Sat for Rutland from 1812. MP until he died on 25 Feb. 1838.   [1837]

NOEL, Hon. William Middleton. 11 Chandos Street, Cavendish Square, London. Ketton, Rutlandshire. 3rd surviving s. of Sir G.N. Noel, Bart., dead, by the Baroness Barham; and bro. of Lord Barham, B. 2 May 1789; m. 20 May 1817, Anne, only child and heiress of Joseph Yates, Esq. A Liberal-Conservative, but supported the Church and all ancient institutions. Was chosen for Rutland without opposition, in Mar. 1838, on the death of his father, the former member. Accepted Chiltern Hundreds Jan. 1840. Died 20 Jan. 1859.   [1838]

NOLAN, Col. J.P. Continued in House after 1885; full entry in Volume II.

NORREYS, Lord. 18 Grosvenor Street, London. Wytham, Berkshire. Carlton. Eld. s. of the Earl of Abindon; b. in Dover Street, London 1808; m. in 1835 Elizabeth Lavinia, only child of George Granville Harcourt, Esq., MP., and grandd. of Archbishop (Harcourt) of York. A Conservative, voted for agricultural protection, in 1846, but against a return to that system, 1850. Sat for Oxfordshire in 1830, but was superseded in 1831 by Mr. Weyland, on account of his opposition to the first Reform Bill. Resumed his seat in 1832 and sat until defeated in 1852. Then sat for Abingdon from 3 Dec. 1852 until he succeeded as 6th Earl

16 Oct. 1854. Died 8 Feb. 1884.   [1852]

NORREYS, Sir Charles Denham Orlando Jephson-, Bart. Mallow Castle, Co. Cork. Athenaeum and Union. S. of Col. Jephson, former MP for Mallow. B. 1799; m. in 1821, Catherine Cecilia Jane, d. of William Franks, Esq., of Carrig, Co. Cork, Graduated at Brasenose Coll., Oxford, B.A. 1827, M.A. 1828. In 1838 assumed the name of Norreys. Lord of the Manor of Mallow, by descent from Sir John Jephson, who m., *temp.* James I., the heiress of the Hon. Sir John Norreys, Lord President of Munster. Patron of 1 living. A Dept.-Lieut. of the Co. of Cork. A Liberal, in favour of the extension of the franchise, vote by ballot, and that the full benefit of improvements should be secured to tenants; opposed to the Ecclesiastical Titles Act. Sat for Mallow from 1826, with the interruption only of the beginning of 1833, when he would not pledge himself to vote for the repeal of the Union; but was seated on petition the same year and sat until defeated in 1859. Died 11 July 1888.   [1859]

NORRIS, John Thomas. 128 Aldersgate Street, London. Sutton Courtney, Abingdon, Berkshire. Reform. Youngest s. of Edmund Norris, Esq., of Sutton Courtney, by Sally Maria, only d. of William Henly, Esq. B. 1808; m. 1st, 1840, Emily Frances, only d. of Francis Hume Choppin, Esq., (she died 1853); 2ndly, 1858, Selina, youngest d. of Lieut. McKenzie, R.N. Educ. at Chinnor, Oxfordshire, under the Rev. John Paul. A Paper Manufacturer, having mills in Oxfordshire and Berkshire. A Commissioner of Lieutenancy for London, and a Member of the Corporation during 20 years; took an active part in procuring the removal of Smithfield Market. A Liberal. Unsuccessfully contested Abingdon Nov. 1854; first elected there Apr. 1857. Sat until defeated 1865. Died 15 Jan. 1870.   [1865]

NORTH, Frederick. Hastings Lodge, Hastings, Rougham, Norfolk. United University, and Athenaeum. B. at Hastings 1800, the s. of Francis Frederick North, Esq., of Hastings and Rougham, Norfolk, by Elizabeth, d. of the Rev. W. Whitear, Rector at Hastings. M. 1824, Janet d. of Sir John Marjoribanks, Bart., of Lees, Berwickshire, of Widow of Robert Swiftleworth, Esq., of Gawthorpe Hall, Lancashire, (she died 1855). Educ. at Harrow and at St. John's Coll., Cambridge, where he was Senior Optime 1822. Was afterwards a Student at the Inner Temple. A Magistrate and Dept.-Lieut. for Norfolk and Sussex. Patron of 1 living. A Liberal and at one time opposed to the ballot, but supported that measure in 1855 and 1856. Voted for Maynooth, but came to consider its removal from Irish

Church Legislation as necessary. Voted for the admission of Dissenters to Universities, for the 1832 Reform Bill, and for the abolition of Church rates in 1862. Thought education should be freely promoted from state funds, but not made compulsory. Sought the abolition of the purchase system in the army. Sat for Hastings in 1831, Dec. 1832-July 1837, May 1854-July 1865 and Dec. 1868 until his death on 29 Oct. 1869.   [1869]

NORTH, Col. John Sidney, D.C.L. 16 Arlington Street, London. Carlton, White's, Marlborough, Senior United Service and Travellers'. S. of Lieut.-Gen. Sir Charles William Doyle, C.B.,G.C.H., by his first wife, Sophia Cramer, 6th d. of Sir John Coghill, Bart., of Coghill, Yorshire. B. at Alnwick, near Newcastle-on-Tyne, 1804; m. 1835, Lady Susan North, who became Baroness North by the termination of and abeyance in 1841. Educ. at Sandhurst Military College, and entered the army in 1822. Assumed the name of North in lieu of his patronymic by Royal licence, in 1838. A Magistrate for Oxfordshire. Appointed Lieut.-Col. 2nd Tower Hamlets Militia 1836, and Lieut.-Col. of the 2nd Battalion of the Oxfordshire Rifle Volunteers May 1860; a Dept.-Lieut. for Cambridgeshire, 1853. A Conservative. Sat for Oxfordshire from July 1852 until he retired in 1885. Died 11 Oct. 1894.   [1885]

NORTHCOTE, Hon. Henry Stafford, C.B. Continued in House after 1885: full entry in Volume II.

NORTHCOTE, Rt. Hon. Sir Stafford Henry, Bart., G.C.B. 30 St. James's Place, London. Pynes, Exeter. Carlton and Athenaeum. Eld. s. of Henry Stafford Northcote, Esq., by his 1st wife, Agnes Mary, only d. of Thomas Cockburn, Esq., of Portland Place, London. B. in Portland Place 1818; m. 1843, Cecilia, d. of T. Farrer, Esq., of Lincoln's Inn. Educ. at Balliol Coll., Oxford, where he was 1st class in classics, and 3rd class in mathematics 1839; graduated M.A. 1842; and received the honorary degree of D.C.L. 1863. Called to the Inner Temple 1847. Was Private-Sec. to the Rt. Hon. W.E. Gladstone, when President of the Board of Trade, and Financial Sec. to the Treasury from Jan.-June 1859. Was President of the Board of Trade from July 1866-Mar. 1867; Secretary of State for India, and President of the Council for India from Mar. 1867-Dec. 1868; a member of the High Joint Commission 1871. Also Chancellor of the Exchequer from Feb. 1874-Apr. 1880. Appointed a member of Council on Education Feb. 1874. Capt. 1st Devon Yeomanry Cavalry 1851; Dept.-Lieut. of Devon 1854. Lord Rector of Edinburgh University 1883. An Elder Brother of the Trinity House. Patron of 4 livings. A Liberal-Conservative. Sat for Dudley from Mar. 1855-Apr. 1857; for Stamford from July 1858-May 1866, when he was elected for N. Devon and sat until he was created a Peer (Earl of Iddesleigh) 3 July 1885. First Lord of the Treasury June 1885-Feb. 1886; Foreign Secretary 27 July 1886-4 Jan. 1887; Lord Lieut of Devon 1886. Died 12 Jan. 1887.   [1885]

NORTHLAND, Visct. (I). A Conservative. Sat for Dungannon from 2 Aug. 1837. Accepted Chiltern Hundreds May 1838. Succeeded as 2nd Earl Apr. 1840. Died 21 Mar. 1858.

NORTHLAND, Visct. (II). Barham House, Hertfordshire. Northland House, Co. Tyrone. Carlton and Travellers'. Eld. s. of the Earl of Ranfurly. B. 1816; m. 1848, Harriet, eld. d. of James Rimington Esq., of Bromhead Hall, Yorkshire. A Conservative, but in favour of free trade. First elected, without opposition for Dungannon in June 1838 and sat until he accepted Chiltern Hundreds, Jan. 1851; succeeded as 3rd Earl of Ranfurley Mar. 1858. Died 20 May 1858.   [1850]

NORWOOD, Charles Morgan. 34 Ennismore Gardens, London. Reform. S. of Charles Norwood, Esq., of Ashford, Kent, by Catherine, 2nd d. of Charles Morgan, Esq., of Archangel, Russia. B. at Ashford 1825; m. 1855, Anna youngest d. of John Henry Blakeney, Esq., of Castle Blakeney, Co. Galway. A Merchant and Steamship Owner in London and Hull. Was twice President of the Hull Chamber of Commerce, and was the first Chairman of the Associated Chamber of Commerce of the United Kingdom. A Liberal. Sat for Hull from July 1866 until he was defeated in 1885 contesting central division of same constituency. Contested central division of Bradford 1886. Chairman of London & India Docks joint committee 1889. Died 24 Apr. 1891.   [1885]

NUGENT, Fulke Southwell Greville-. 2 Albert Gate, Hyde Park, London. North Mymms Park, Hatfield, Hertfordshire. Clonyn Castle, Delvin, Co. Westmeath. Clonteen, Co. Roscommon. Reform and Travellers'. B. 1821, the 2nd s. of Algernon Greville, Esq., of North Lodge, near Barnet, Hertfordshire (descended from a younger branch of the Earl of Warwickshire's family), by Caroline, 2nd d. of Sir Bellingham Graham, Bart. M. 1840, Lady Rosa Emily Mary Anne, only d. of 1st Marq. of Westmeath. Col. of the Westmeath Militia and Vice-Lieut. of that Co. A Liberal, favoured tenant right, the repeal of the

Ecclesiastical Titles Act, and the ballot in 1853. Sat for Longford from July 1852 until he was created 1st Baron Greville of Cloyne (U.K. Peerage) in Dec. 1869. Died on 25 Jan. 1883.   [1869]

NUGENT, Lord, G.C.M.G. Novan House and Lillies, Buckinghamshire. Reform, and Athenaeum. An Irish Peer. Uncle to the 2nd Duke of Buckingham. B. 1789; m. 1813 Anne Lucy, 2nd d. of the Hon. Gen. Vere Ponsett (she died Aug. 1848). Lord High Commissioner of the United States of the Ionian Islands, 1832-35. Took active part in favour of Queen Caroline. Author of *Lands, Classical and Sacred*, and other works. A Liberal. Sat for Aylesbury in four parliaments previous to the Reform Act; an unsuccessful candidate for Aylesbury in 1837 and 1839, and for Southampton 9 Aug. 1842. Regained his seat for Aylesbury in 1847 and remained an MP until his death in 1850.   [1850]

NUGENT, Hon. George Frederick Nugent Greville-. 34 Grosvenor Square, London. Clonyn Castle, Delvin, Co, Westmeath. 2nd s. of the 1st Baron Greville (who represented Longford for 17 years before his elevation to the Peerage), by Lady Rosa Emily, only d. of the 1st Marq. of Westmeath. B. 1842. A Liberal, and gave a general support to Mr. Gladstone. Sat for Longford from May 1870. Retired 1874. Resumed simple name of Greville in 1883. Died 11 May 1897.   [1873]

NUGENT, Sir Percy Fitz-Gerald, Bart. 23 Cork Street, London. Donore, Multifarnham, Co. Westmeath. Reform. Eld. s. of Thomas Fitz-Gerald, Esq., Commander, R.N., by the d. of Christopher Dardis, Esq., of Giggenstown, Co. Westmeath. Assumed the name of Nugent in 1831, being grands. of Christina Nugent, the sister and sole heir of Sir Peter Nugent, whose Baronetcy became extinct. B. 1798; m. 1823, only d. of Walter Sweetman, Esq., of Dublin. Educ. at Old Hall Green, Hertfordshire. A Dept.-Lieut. of Westmeath; Director of the Irish Midland Great Western Railway. A Whig, willing to consider in committee a repeal of the Union with Ireland. First returned for Westmeath in 1847, without opposition. Retired 1852. Died 25 June 1874. [1852]

NUGENT, Hon. Reginald James Macartney. See GREVILLE-NUGENT, Hon. Reginald James Macartney.

OAKES, James Henry Porteous. Nowton Court, Nr. Bury St. Edmunds. Eld. s. of Henry James Oakes, Esq., of Nowton Court, Suffolk (Head of the well-known banking house of Oakes,

Bevan and Company), by Mary Anne, d. of the Rev. Robert Porteous, Rector of Bishop's Wickham, Essex. B.1821. Unmarried. Educ. at Emmanuel Coll., Cambridge, where he graduated B.A. 1843, M.A.1846. Appointed Dept.-Lieut. of Suffolk 1854. A Conservative, and a supporter generally of Lord Derby's policy. First returned for Bury St. Edmunds Dec. 1852. Defeated 1857. [1857]

O'BEIRNE, Col. Francis. Jamestown Lodge, Drumsna, Ireland. Junior United Service and Union. 2nd s. of Francis O'Beirne, Esq., of Jamestown Lodge, Co. Leitrim, by his m. with Miss Winifred Nolan. Entered the army in 1857, and became Capt. 2nd Dragoon Guards, Mar. 1865, with which regiment he served in the Oude campaign 1858-59. A Liberal 'and strongly in favour of Home Rule for Ireland, 'being convinced that it was the only system of government that could promote the happiness and develope the resources of the country.' Unsuccessfully contested, Feb. 1874, Leitrim, for which he sat from July 1876 until he retired in 1885. Died 11 Apr. 1899. [1885]

O'BEIRNE, James Lyster. 36 Sackville Street, London. Reform. B. in Dublin 1820, the eld. s. of Edmund O'Beirne, Esq., of Dublin, by Mary d. of — Lyster, Esq. Unmarried. Educ. at Trinity Coll., Dublin. Engaged in commerce. An 'Independent Liberal'; and in favour of greater privileges being granted to Ireland as 'tenant-right, emigration and financial legislation.' Elected for Cashel in July 1865 but in 1869 his election was declared void and Cashel was disenfranchised. [1869]

O'BRIEN, A. Stafford. See STAFFORD, A.S. O'Brien-.

O'BRIEN, Cornelius. 4 North Street, Westminster, London. 20 Summer Hill, Dublin. Birchfield, Ennistymon, Co, Clare. S. of Henry O'Brien, Esq., of Birchfield, Co. Clare, by Helen, d. of — O'Callaghan, Esq., of Kilgorey, Co. Clare. B. at Birchfield 1782; m. 1816, Margaret, d. of Peter Long, Esq., of Waterford, and relict of James O'Brien, Esq., of Limerick. A Solicitor in Ireland from 1811. A Magistrate for Clare. A Liberal, in favour of a repeal of the Union with Ireland, tenant-right, and vote by ballot. Sat for Clare from 1832-1847, when he was an unsuccessful candidate; regained his seat in July 1852. Retired 1857. [1857]

O'BRIEN, James. 92 St. Stephen's Green South, Dublin. Reform B. in Limerick in 1806, the 3rd. s. of James O'Brien, Esq, of Limerick, by Margaret, d. of Peter Long, Esq., of Waterford. Was bro. of

John O'Brien, Esq., who sat for Limerick from 1841-52, and stepson to Cornelius O'Brien. M. 1836, Margaret, d. of Thomas Segrave, Esq. Educ. at the Belfast Institution and at Trinity Coll., Dublin, where he gained the Science Gold Medal 1825. Called to the bar in Ireland 1830, appointed Queen's Counsel 1841, 2nd Serjeant--at-Law in Ireland, 1848, and made a bencher of King's Inn, Dublin, 1849. A Liberal. Unsuccessfully contested Limerick in July 1852, but elected in Oct. 1854 without opposition. Sat until he was appointed a Judge in Jan. 1858. Died 29 Dec. 1881. [1857 2nd ed.]

O'BRIEN, John. Limerick . Reform. S. of Jas. O'Brien, Esq., of Limerick. M. d. of Jeremiah Murphy, Esq., and was therefore bro.-in-law to Mr. Serjeant Murphy, former member for Cork city. A Liberal. First elected for Limerick city in 1841 and sat until he retired in 1852. Died 5 Feb. 1855. [1852]

O'BRIEN, Sir Lucius, Bart. 2 Pont Street, Belgrave Square, London. Dromoland, Newmarket-on-Fergus, Co. Clare. Eld. s of Sir Edward O'Brien, Bart., by the eld. d. and co-heir of William Smith, Esq., of Cahirmoyle, Co. Limerick. B. in Co. Clare, 1800; m. 1837, Mary, eld. d. of William Fitz-Gerald, Esq., of Adelphi, Co. Clare. Educ. at Harrow, and at Trinity Coll., Cambridge, where he graduated B.A. 1825, and M.A. 1828; appointed Lord-Lieut. of Clare in May, 1843; was in contigent remainder to the Barony of Inchiquin, next after the issue of the then Marq. of Thomond. A Conservative and Protectionist. Sat for Clare from 1826 to 1830; was a candidate for that co. in 1835, but did not poll any votes. Again returned for Clare in 1847. Retired in 1852. [1852]

O'BRIEN, Sir Patrick, Bart. 21 Bryanston Square, London. Reform. University Club, Dublin. Eld. s. of Sir Timothy O'Brien, Bart. (who sat for Cashel from 1846 till 1859), by Catherine, d. of Edward Murphy, Esq., of Flemingtown, Co. Dublin. B. in Dublin 1823; m. 1866, d. of Commander Parlby, R.N., and relict of Lieut.-Gen. James Perry. Graduated at the University of Dublin; called to the bar in Ireland 1844. A Liberal, who once declared himself in favour of a repeal of the Union with Ireland. Sat for King's Co. from July 1852 until he retired in 1885. Died 23 Apr. 1895. [1885]

O'BRIEN, Sir Timothy, Bart. 14 Merrion Square, and 50 Fleet Street, Dublin. Borris in Ossory, Queen's Co. Reform. S. of Timothy O'Brien, Esq., of Co. Tipperary, by the d. of Timothy Madden, Esq., of Co. Galway. M. 1821,

289

d. of Edward Murphy, Esq., of Flemingtown, Co. Dublin. A Dublin Merchant and Governor of the Hibernian Bank. An Alderman of Dublin, of which city he was Lord Mayor in 1844 and in 1849. A Liberal, formerly a member of the Repeal party; 'a supporter of the interest of the Irish tenant.' First returned for Cashel Jan. 1846 and sat until he retired in 1859. Died 4 Dec. 1862.   [1858]

O'BRIEN, W. Continued in House after 1885: full entry in Volume II.

O'BRIEN, William Smith. Cahirmoyle, Co. Limerick. 2nd s. of Sir Edward O'Brien, Bart., of Dromoland Co. Clare. B. 1803; m. d. of Jos. Gabbet, Esq. A Magistrate of Limerick Co. A Repealer, in favour of a Poor Law for Ireland, the extinction of the tithes, and the ballot. Voted against the abolition of the Corn Laws. Sat for Ennis in 1830, and for Limerick Co. from 1835. MP. until convicted of high treason 1849.   [1849]

O'BYRNE, William Richard. 89 Linden Gardens, London. Cabinteely House, Cabinteely, Co. Dublin. Athenaeum. Eld. s. of Robert O'Byrne, Esq., by Martha, d. of Joseph Clarke, Esq., of Norwich. B. 1823; m. 1851, Emily, eld. d. of John Troughear Handy, Esq., of Malmesbury, Wiltshire. Educ. at London University. A Magistrate for Cos. of Wicklow and Dublin. Was High Sheriff of Wicklow 1872-73. Author of *The Naval Biography*, a work which obtained for the author a substantial testimonial from the Board of Admiralty and nearly a thousand naval officers. A Liberal, in favour of denominational education, of a further amendment of the Land Act in Ireland; in favour also of the system called 'Home Rule' for Ireland. Sat for the Co. Wicklow from Feb. 1874. Retired 1880. Died 7 July 1896.   [1880]

O'CALLAGHAN, Hon. Cornelius. Shanbally Castle, Co. Tipperary. Eld. s. of Visct. Lismore. B. 1809. A Liberal. Sat for Tipperary 1832-35. Sat for Dungarvan from 1837. Retired 1841. Died 16 Aug. 1849.   [1838]

O'CALLAGHAN, Hon. William Frederick Ormond. Old Burlington Street, London. Shanbally Castle, Clogheen, Ireland. 2nd s. of 2nd Visct. Lismore, by Mary, 2nd d. of John George Norbury, Esq. B. in London 1852. Was educ. at Eton. A Liberal, in favour of the system called 'Home Rule' for Ireland. Sat for Tipperary from Feb. 1874. MP until his death 20 Apr. 1877.   [1877]

O'CLERY, Keyes. 4 Garden Court, Temple, London. Darragh House, Kilfinane, Co.

Limerick. S. of John Walsh O'Clery, Esq., of Mitchelstondown and Ballingarry, Co. Limerick, by Elisa, d. of Michael O'Donoghue Keyes, Esq., of Glenlara, Co. Limerick. B. 1845. Unmarried. Educ. at St. Munchin's Coll., Limerick, and Trinity Coll., Dublin. Served in the 'Pontifical Zouaves' in 1867; also at the Porta Pia, during the bombardment of Rome 1870, for which services he was created by the Pope Knight of the Order of St. Gregory the Great, which confers the title of Chevalier. Called to the bar at the Middle Temple Jan. 1874. Strongly in favour of the system called 'Home Rule' for Ireland. Sat for Wexford Co. from Feb. 1874. Defeated 1880.   [1880]

O'CONNELL, Charles. 14 Albermarle Street, London. Portmagee. S.-in-law of Daniel O'Connell, Esq., who, having been elected for Dublin himself, put Charles O'Connell, Esq., in nomination for Kerry. A Repealer. Sat for Kerry from 1832. Retired 1834. Resident Magistrate in Bantry 1847 until his death 20 Jan. 1877. [1833]

O'CONNELL, Daniel. (I). Merrion Square, Dublin. Derrynane Abbey, Co. Kerry. Brooks's, Clarence, and Reform. B. 1775; m. 1802, his cousin, Mary, d. of Edward O'Connell, Esq., M.D. of Tralee. A Queen's Counsel in Ireland, with a patent of precedence. An Alderman of the City of Dublin, and filled the office of Lord Mayor of that City 1841-42. Held Bishops' and College leases of some large farms. His general labours in favour of Roman Catholics, and his subsequent measures of agitation for a repeal of the Union, were well known. Made an unsuccessful attempt to obtain admittance into the House as a Catholic, having been duly returned for Clare, before the passing of the Relief Bill; after that event he was elected for the same county; in 1830 for Waterford Co., and in 1831 for Kerry. Appointed in 1835 a Magistrate for Kerry. Was removed from the commission of the peace in 1843. Author of a *Historical Memoir of Ireland and the Irish, native and Saxon*. Sat for Dublin from 1832-1836, when he was unseated on petition, and was immediately elected for Kilkenny, for which he remained member till the general election in 1837, when he was again returned for Dublin; at the general election in 1841, he was returned not only for Co. Cork, but for Meath also; in 1842 he made his election to sit for the former place. MP until his death in 1847. [1847]

O'CONNELL, Daniel.(II). Royal Western Yacht Club, Ireland. Reform and Garrick. 4th s. of Daniel O'Connell, Esq., by Mary, d. of Edward O'Connell, Esq., M.D. of Tralee. B. in Ireland. A Liberal, in favour of 'tenant right' in Ireland. Was an unsuccessful candidate for Carlow Co. 1841; sat for Dundalk from Aug. 1846 till July 1847; for Waterford city from the latter date till Apr. 1848. First elected for Tralee, July 1853, on the death of his bro., Maurice O'Connell, Esq. who had represented it from 1832. Sat until he accepted Chiltern Hundreds 1863. Special Commissioner of Income Tax 1863-92. Died 14 June 1897. [1863]

O'CONNELL, John. 21 Nassau Street, Dublin. Gowran Hill, Kingstown, Nr. Dublin. Reform. 3rd s. of Daniel O'Connell, Esq., by Mary, d. of Edward O'Connell, Esq., M.D. of Tralee. M. 1838, d. of Dr. Ryan, of Jubilee Hall, Co. Dublin. Called to the bar in Ireland 1837. Appointed Clerk of the Hanaper in Ireland Aug. 1856. Author of *Life and Speeches of Daniel O'Connell, Esq.* A Repealer. Sat for Youghal from Dec. 1832-July 1837, for Athlone from the last date until July 1841, then for Kilkenny City until July 1847, when, having been also returned for Limerick, he elected to represent that city, for which he sat until Aug. 1851. First returned for Clonmell Dec. 1853, without opposition. Accepted Chiltern Hundreds Feb. 1857. Died Dublin 24 May 1858.   [1857]

O'CONNELL, Maurice, 37 Jermyn Street, London. Knockbane, Moycullen, Co. Galway. Eld. s. of Daniel O'Connell, Esq. M. in 1832, only d. of Bindon Scott, Esq., of Cahircorn. Called to the bar in Ireland 1827. A Repealer. Sat for Clare in the Parliament of 1831 and for the borough of Tralee from 1832 (with the exception of a few months in 1838, being reseated on petition) until his death on 17 June 1853. Earlier he had also contested Carlow Co. 13 Jan. 1835.   [1853]

O'CONNELL, Morgan. Reform. 2nd s. of Daniel O'Connell, Esq. Was Aide-de-Camp to Bolivar. Was in the Austrian Service. A Repealer, in 1832 he threw out Lord Killeen, who refused to pledge himself to vote for the repeal of the Union. Sat for Meath from 1832 until appointed Assistant-Registrar of Deeds (Ireland) Jan. 1840. Died 20 Jan. 1885.   [1838]

O'CONNELL, Morgan John. Grena, Co. Kerry. Reform and Clarence. Eld. s. of John O'Connell, Esq., of Grena, by the d. of Wm. Coppinger, Esq., of Ballyvolane. Nephew of Daniel O'Connell, Esq. B. 1811. A Dept.-Lieut. of Kerry. A Repealer. Sat for Kerry from 1835 until he retired in 1852. Died 2 July 1875.   [1852]

O'CONNOR, A. Continued in House after 1885: full entry in Volume II.

O'CONNOR, Feargus Edward. Lombands,

Red Marley, Worcestershire. 2nd s. of Roger O'Connor, Esq., of Connorville, Bantry Bay, Ireland and subsequently last tenant of Dangan Castle, Co. Meath (the well-known seat of the Wellesley family); nephew of Arthur O'Connor, who resided many years in Paris in consequence of the part he bore in the Irish insurrection of 1798. B. 1796. Was called to the Bar in Ireland; was for many years proprietor and editor of the *Northern Star* newspaper; well known as the leading supporter of 'The People's Charter.' Sat for the Co. of Cork from 1832 to 1835; was again returned 1835, but unseated on petition; was an unsuccessful candidate for Oldham in July 1835, on the death of Mr. Cobbett; was also frequently proposed at various elections without going to a poll. First returned for Nottingham in 1847. Retired in 1852. Died 30 Aug. 1855.   [1852]

O'CONNOR, J. Continued in House after 1885: full entry in Volume II.

O'CONNOR, T.P. Continued in House after 1885: full entry in Volume II.

O'CONNOR-POWER, John. See POWER, John O'Connor.

O'CONOR, Charles Owen. 110 Queen's Gate, London. Clonalis, Castlerea, Co. Roscommon. Reform. Eld. s. of Denis O'Conor, The O'Conor Don (who represented Roscommon from 1831-1847). by Mary, d. of Major Blake, of Towerbill, Co. Mayo. Bro. of the member for Sligo. B. in Dublin 1838; m. 1st, 1868, Georgiana Mary, 3rd d. of Thomas A. Perry, Esq., of Bitham House, Warwickshire (she died 1872); 2ndly, 1879, Ellen 3rd. d. of John S. More O'Ferrall, Esq., of Granite Hall, Kingtown, and Lisard, Co. Longford. Educ. at Bath. A Liberal, voted for the disestablishment of the Church of Ireland, in favour of the amendment of the Grand Jury Laws, and of denominational education. Sat for Roscommon from Mar. 1860 until defeated in 1880. Was a candidate at Wexford Bor. in 1883.   [1880]

O'CONOR, Denis. Cloonalis, Roscommon. Reform. S. of the former member, and commonly called the O'Conor Don. The hereditary title of Don, affixed to this gentleman's name, was by some supposed to be a corruption of the Latin Dominus, and conferred upon the head of the O'Conor family by the Spanish settlers in Ireland; others conjecture it to be derived from the word dun, the colour of the garments or the standards of this particular family of O'Conors, which served to distinguish it from the Black and Red O'Conors. B. 1794; m. 1824, Mary Anne, d.

of Major Blake. Appointed a Lord of the Treasury July 1846. Was favourably inclined to a repeal of the Union; was an advocate of the amendment of the Jury laws, the mitigation of the Criminal Code, a more equal distribution of Church property, the extinction of the tithe system, and the removal of Irish grievances. Formerly voted against the abolition of the Corn Laws, but in 1846 supported their repeal. Sat for Roscommon Co. from 1831 until he retired in 1847. [1847]

O'CONOR, Denis Maurice. 110 Queen's Gate, London. Cloonalis, Castlerea, Co. Roscommon. Reform. Stephen's Green, Dublin. 2nd s. of Denis O'Conor, the O'Conor Don (who represented Roscommon from 1831-47), by Mary, d. of Maj. Blake of Tower Hill, Co. Mayo. Bro. of the member for Roscommon. B. 1840; m. 1873, Ellen Isabella, eld. d. of the Rev. W. Kevill Davies, of Croft Castle, Herefordshire. Educ. at Downside Coll., near Bath and at London Univ. where he graduated M.A. 1861, LL.D. 1866. Was called to the bar at the Middle Temple 1866. A Liberal, in favour of the system called 'Home Rule' for Ireland. Sat for the Co. of Sligo from Dec. 1868. MP until his death 26 July 1883. [1883]

O'DONNELL, Frank Hugh O'Cahan. 8 Serjeants' Inn, London. S. of Capt. Bernard O'Donnell, of Carndonagh, Donegal, by Mary, d. of William O'Caban, Esq., of Ballybane, Galway. B. at Devonport, Devonshire 1848. Was educ. at St. Ignatius's Coll., Galway, and Queen's University, Ireland; where he took M.A. degree with 1st class honours 1868. Was Vice-President and Honorary Secretary of the 'Irish Home Rule Confederation of Great Britain.' Author of *Mixed education in Ireland, Lectures in Political Economy,* etc. Founder of the Farmers' Alliance. An 'Historical Democrat' and Irish Nationalist; in favour of the system called 'Home Rule' for Ireland. Was an unsuccessful candidate for Galway in Feb. 1874; was elected there on a vacancy Mar. 1874, but unseated on petition May following. Sat for Dungarvan from June 1877 until he retired in 1885. [1885]

O'DONNOVAN, Rossa J. B. 1831. A notorious Fenian found guilty for Treason in 1865. Author of *Recollections* (1898) and other works. In favour of Home Rule. First elected for Tipperary 27 Nov. 1869, but being a convicted felon, declared ineligible. Died 1915.

O'DONOGHUE, Daniel. Flesk Cottage, Co. Kerry. Reform. Only s. of Charles O'Donoghue, Esq., of the Glens, by Jane, d. of John O'Connell, Esq., of Grena (she m. 2ndly, McCarthy O'Leary, Esq.) A Liberal, voted against the

suspension of the Habeas Corpus Act in Ireland Feb. 1866. Sat for Tipperary from Feb. 1857 till July 1865, when he was elected for Tralee and sat until he retired in 1885. Died 7 Oct. 1889. [1885]

O'DWYER, Andrew Carew. Upper Mount Street, Dublin. 21 Maddox Street, London. S. of a merchant in Cork city; m. a natural d. of Sir R. Gillispie, K.C.B. A Barrister in Ireland. His exertions in Drogheda during the registration under the Reform Act, as well as other circumstances, procured for him the confidence of the electors, though he received in addition the recommendation of Daniel O'Connell just before the election. Mr. O'Dwyer, as well as the late member for Drogheda, were both, while law students, connected with the periodical press. A Repealer, and a modifier of the Church Establishment, providing for the incumbents, and reducing the number of the Clergy. Sat for Drogheda from 1832, but unseated as unqualified after being returned in Jan 1835. Was again returned at the subsequent by-election in Apr. 1835 but his opponent was seated shortly afterwards in his place on petition. Author. Died 15 Nov. 1877. [1835]

O'FERRALL, Rt. Hon. Richard More-. Ballyna House, Enfield, Co. Kildare. Reform. Eld. s. of Ambrose O'Ferrall, Esq., of Balyna, Co. Kildare, by the eld. d. of John Bagot, Esq., of Castle Bagot, Co. Dublin. B. in Dublin 1797; m. 1839, Hon. Matilda, 3rd d. of 3rd Visct. Southwell. Appointed a Lord of the Treasury Apr. 1835, Sec. to the Admiralty 1839, and was Sec. to the Treasury from July-Sept. 1841; Governor of Malta from 1847-1851. A Liberal, but supported the vote of censure on Lord Palmerston 1864. Sat for the Co. of Kildare from 1830 until the general election 1847; for the Co. of Longford from Apr. 1851-July 1852; again returned for Kildare Co. May 1859. Retired 1865. Died 27 Oct. 1880. [1865]

O'FLAHERTY, Anthony. 37 Jermyn Street, London. Knockbane, Moycullen, Co. Galway. S. of Anthony O'Flaherty, a member of an ancient family in the W. of Galway. B. 1800; m. 1819, Harriet, only d. of Maj.-Gen. Archer, of the Guards. Educ. at Trinity Coll., Dublin. A Repealer, in favour of every measure for the advancement of civil and religious liberty, and 'an advocate of the rights of the occupiers of the soil in Ireland', voted for the ballot 1853. Was an unsuccessful candidate for Galway bor. Feb. 1847. First returned for Galway bor. at the general election in the same year, without opposition. Unseated shortly after being returned in 1857. [1857]

OGILVIE, Sir John, Bart. Kent House, Knightsbridge, London. Baldovan House, Dundee. Travellers'. B. in Edinburgh 1803, the eld. s. of Admiral Sir William Ogilvy, by Sarah, d. of James Moreby. M. 1st, 1831, Juliana Barbara, youngest d. of Henry Howard (she died 1833); 2ndly, 1836, Lady Jane Elizabeth, 3rd. d. of 16th Earl of Suffolk. Educ. at Christ Church, Oxford. A Vice Lieut. of Forfarshire, and Lieut.-Col. Dundee Rifle Volunteers. A Liberal, and considered that the policy of the country should be one of non-interference. Was an unsuccessful candidate for Montrose in 1855. Sat for Dundee from Apr. 1857 until 1874, when he was defeated. Died 29 Mar. 1890.   [1873]

OGLE, Saville Craven Henry. 6 St. James's Place, London. Kirchly Hall, Northumberland. Travellers' and Oxford & Cambridge. 4th s. of Rev. J. Saville Ogle. B. 1811. A Barrister. A Liberal. Formerly voted against the abolition of the Corn Laws, in 1846, but supported their repeal. First returned for Northumberland S. in 1841 and sat until he retired in 1852. Died 11 Mar. 1854.   [1852]

O'GORMAN, Purcell. Springfield, Co. Kilkenny. At one time in the army. Retired. A Liberal, in favour of the system called 'Home Rule' for Ireland. Sat for the city of Waterford from Feb. 1874 until defeated 1880. Died 24 Nov. 1888.   [1880]

O'GORMAN-MAHON, James Patrick. See MAHON, James Patrick O'Gorman.

O'GRADY, Hon. Lieut.-Col. Standish. 11 Queen Street, Mayfair, London. Caherguillamore, Co. Limerick. Eld. s. of Lord Visct. Guillamore, formerly Lord Chief Baron of the Irish Exchequer. M. in 1828, Gertrude, eld. d. of the Hon. Berkeley Paget, bros. of the Marq. of Anglesey. A Lieut.-Col. in the army. Of Whig principles. First sat for Limerick Co. in the Parliament of 1820; lost his seat in 1826, but recovered it in 1830. Retired 1835.   [1834]

O'HAGAN, Rt. Hon. Thomas. 34 Rutland Square, Dublin. Byron Lodge, Saiton, Co. Dublin. Called to the bar in Ireland 1836; created Queen's Counsel 1849; elected bencher of King's Inns, Dublin 1859; was for several years assistant barrister for the Co. of Longford. Was Solicitor-Gen. for Ireland from Feb. 1860 till Feb. 1861, when he was appointed Attorney-Gen. for Ireland and made a Privy Councillor. A Liberal, first elected for Tralee, May 1863, and sat until he was appointed Judge of the Common Pleas in Ireland in Jan. 1865. Lord Chancellor of Ireland Dec. 1868-Feb. 1874. Created Baron O'Hagan 14 June 1870. Again Lord Chancellor of Ireland May 1880 until his resignation in Nov. 1881. Senator of Royal University of Ireland and Vice Chancellor from 1880 until his death 1 Feb. 1885.   [1864]

O'KEEFE, John. Ballyleman Lodge, Dungarvan. Stephen's Green, Dublin. Eld. s. of Patrick O'Keefe, Esq., of Abbeyville, Waterford, by Margaret, d. of Thomas Sarjent, Esq., of Boanmore, Waterford. B. at Waterford 1827; m. 1867, Marie Mathilde, d. of Peirse Marcus Barron, Esq., of Belmont Park, Waterford. Was educ. at Clongowes Wood Coll. A Magistrate of the Co. of Waterford, of which he was High Sheriff 1863. A Liberal, and in favour of the system called 'Home Rule' for Ireland. Sat for Dungarvan from Feb. 1874. MP until his death 10 June 1877.   [1877]

O'KELLY, J.J. Continued in House after 1885: full entry in Volume II.

O'LEARY, William Hagarty. 111 Jermyn Street, London. 38 York Street, Dublin. Became a Fellow of the Royal College of Surgeons in Ireland, in 1871. A Liberal, and in favour of the system called 'Home Rule' for Ireland. Sat for Drogheda from Feb. 1874. MP until his death 15 Feb. 1880.   [1879]

OLIPHANT, Laurence. (I). 3 St. Alban's Place, London. Condie, Perthshire. Eld. s. of Ebenezer Oliphant, Esq., of Condie. B. 1791; m. 1st, 1814, Eliza, 2nd d. of Hercules Ross, Esq., of Rossie Castle, Forfarshire; 2ndly, 1825, Margaret, relict of Samuel Barrett, Esq., of Jamaica. A Reformer, in favour of short Parliaments. Sat for Perth from 1832. Retired at 1837 gen. election. Died 29 May 1862.   [1837]

OLIPHANT, Laurence. (II). Athenaeum. S. of Sir Anthony Oliphant, C.B., formerly Chief Justice of Ceylon, by Catherine Marie, d. of Col. Ronald Campbell. B. 1829. Became an advocate at the Scottish bar 1854, and was called to the bar at Lincoln's Inn 1855. Was Civil Secretary and Superintendent Gen. of Indian affairs in Canada; was attached to the Lord Elgin's special mission to China, and acted as Secretary of Embassy till Apr. 1859. Was Secretary of Legation in Japan, from Feb. 1861 till Jan. 1862. Author of *A Journey to Nepaul, The Russian Shores of the Black Sea, Minnesota and the Far West,* etc. A Liberal. First elected for Stirling district July 1865. Accepted Chiltern Hundreds Apr. 1868. Author, traveller, and journalist. Died 23 Dec. 1888.   [1867]

OLIVEIRA, Benjamin, F.R.S. 8 Upper Hyde Park Street, London. Brooks's and Reform. 3rd and only surviving s. of Dominick Oliveira, Esq., a Merchant and Shipowner of London, by Sarah, d. of John Jennings, Esq., a London Merchant. Originally descended from a Portuguese family, of which one member was created Count Tojal, and was well-known as the financial and foreign minister of the Queen of Portugal, while another was Portuguese Ambassador in London, *temp.* George IV. B. in London 1806; m. lst, 1838, Philadelphia Mary, eld. d. of John Ede, Esq., of Upper Harley Street, Merchant; 2ndly, 1849, Emma Hepzibah, d. of John Hunt, Esq., of St John's Wood, and Matlock, Derbyshire. Educ. with a view to the diplomatic service, and was employed on several international questions connected with loans, etc. Author of *Tracts on Brazil and Portugal,* a *Tour in the East, Travels,* etc. A prominent member of numerous philanthropic assocations, a director of the Oxford, Worcester, and Wolverhampton Railway, Waterloo Bridge Company, and the Provident Life Office. President of the Star Club. Took an active share in railway enterprise, and was invited to Paris by Louis Phillippe to negotiate the line called the Ceinture de Paris. Gave a premium of 50 guineas for an Essay on Portugal in connexion with the objects of the Great Industrial Exhibition of 1851. Appointed Cornet Surrey Yeomanry 1841. A Liberal, in favour of a gradual extension of the franchise, reduction of the duties on tea, coffee, tobacco, wine, malt, etc., and inquiry into the Maynooth Grant. Was an unsuccessful candidate for Reading in Jan. 1835. First returned for Pontefract in July 1852. Defeated 1857. Died 28 Sept. 1865. [1857]

O'LOGHLEN, Sir Bryan, Bart. Drumconra, Ennis, Co. Clare. 3rd s. of Rt. Hon. Sir Michael O'Loghlen, 1st Bart. of Drumconra, Master of the Rolls in Ireland, by Bidelia, d. of Daniel Kelly, Esq., of Dublin. Bro. of the Rt. Hon. Sir Colman O'Loghlen, Judge Advocate Gen., who represented Clare from July 1863 till his death in 1877. B. in Dublin 1828; m. 1863, Ella, d. of M. Seward, Esq., of Melbourne, Australia. Called to the bar in Ireland 1856, and practised for many years at the Melbourne bar. A Liberal, in favour of 'Home Rule' for Ireland. Returned for the Co. of Clare from Aug. 1877 until appointed Attorney-Gen. of Victoria, Australia, Apr. 1879; Premier of that State 1881-83. Died 31 Oct. 1909. [1879]

O'LOGHLEN, Sir Colman Michael, Bart. 20 Merrion Square South, Dublin. Drumconra, Ennis, Co. Clare. Eld. s. of the Rt. Hon. Sir Michael O'Loghlen (1st Bart.), Master of the Rolls in Ireland, by the d. of Daniel Kelly, Esq. of Dublin. B. in Dublin 1819. Unmarried. Educ. at University Coll., London. Graduated at London University, B.A., 1840. Called to the bar in Ireland 1840; made a Queen's Counsel 1852, and Sergeant--at-Law 1865. Was Judge Advocate-Gen. from Dec. 1868-Dec. 1870. Was Chairman of the Quarter Sessions for the Co. of Carlow from 1856-59; and for the Co. of Mayo from 1859-61. A Liberal, in favour of the system called 'Home Rule' for Ireland; opposed to the separation of religion from education. Sat for Clare Co. from July 1863. MP until his death 22 July 1877. [1877]

O'LOGHLEN, Michael. 36 St. James's Place, London. 20 Merrion Square South, Dublin. Was Solicitor-Gen. for Ireland during the Melbourne Administration of 1834; resumed his office in Apr. 1835, and in the autumn following was appointed Attorney-Gen. Sat for Dungarvan from May 1835 until appointed Baron of Exchequer (Ireland) 1836. Master of the Rolls (Ireland) 1837; Created Bart. July 1838. Died 1842. [1836]

O'NEILL, Hon. Edward. 12 Queen's Gate, London. Shanes CAstle, Antrim, Ireland. Carlton. Eld. s. of the Rev. Lord O'Neill, of Shanes Castle, Antrim, by his 1st wife, Henrietta, d. of Judge Torrens. B. at Derrynoyd, Co. Derry, Ireland, 1839; m. 1873, Lady Louisa Katherine, d. of the 11th Earl of Dundonaid. Educ. at Portarlington, and proceeded afterwards to Trinity Coll., Cambridge, and Trinity Coll., Dublin. Of Conservative principles. Sat for Antrim from May 1863 until he retired 1880. Succeeded as 2nd Baron O'Neill Apr. 1883. Died 19 Nov. 1928. [1880]

O'NEILL, Hon. John Bruce Richard. Tullamore Lodge, Co. Antrim. United Service. Bro. and heir pres. of Earl O'Neill. B. 1780. Constable of Dublin Castle, with £439 per annum; a Major Gen. in the army, and a Dept.-Lieut. of Co. Antrim. A Conservative. Voted for the Reform Bill, but against Catholic Emancipation; opposed to the repeal of the Union. Sat for Antrim from 1802 until he succeeded his bro. as 3rd Visct. 25 Mar. 1841. Representative peer of Ireland Feb. 1842 till death 12 Feb. 1855. [1840]

ONSLOW, Denzil Roberts. 1 Albert Mansion, London. Flexford, Guildford. Carlton. S. of Thomas Onslow, Esq., of the Madras Civil Service, by Elizabeth, d. of C. Roberts, Esq., of the Madras Civil Service. B. in India 1839; m. 1872, Clara Louisa, youngest d. of James Scott, Esq., of Bishopsdown Grove, Tunbridge Wells. Educ. at Brighton Coll., and Trinity Coll., Cambridge; graduated B.A. 1861. Was Private Secretary to three successive Ministers in India, viz: Sir Charles Trevelyan, K.C.B., Rt. Hon. W.N. Massey, and Sir Richard Temple, K.C.S.I. A Conservative, voted against the third reading of the Irish Land Bill 1881. Sat for Guildford from Feb. 1874. Retired 1885. Defeated in Nov 1885 contesting Tower Hamlets, Poplar division.   [1885]

ONSLOW, Guildford James Hillier. Upton House, Alresford, Hampshire. Boodle's. B. in London 1814, the 2nd s. of Hon. Thomas Cranley Onslow, by Susannah, d. of Nathaniel Hillier, of Stoke Park, Surrey. M. 1838 Rosa Anna, youngest d. of Gen. Denzil Onslow, of Stoughton House, Huntingdonshire. Educ. at Eton. Was an officer in the Scots Fusilier Guards. A Dept.-Lieut. for Middlesex. A Liberal, in favour of short Parliaments, an extension of the franchise, vote by ballot, and the abolition of Church rates. First elected for Guildford in Oct. 1858, and sat until defeated in 1874. Died 20 Aug. 1882.   [1873]

ORD, William. 17 Berkeley Square, London. Whitfield Hall, Northumberland. Athenaeum, and Reform. Eld. s. of William Ord, Esq., of Fenham, Durham. B. 1781. M. 1803 d. of Rev. J. Scott (she died 1848). Patron of 1 living. A Reformer, said he would support the ballot if necessary to protect the voter; had 'no confidence in a Tory Administration.' Sat for Morpeth from 1802 to 1832; unsuccessfully contested Northumberland S. in 1832. First returned for Newcastle-upon-Tyne in 1835 and sat until he retired in 1852. Died 25 July 1855.   [1852]

ORD, William Henry. 17 Berkeley Square, London. Whitfield Hall, Northumberland. Athenaeum. S. of the member for Newcastle. A Lord of the Treasury from Apr. 1835; salary 1200/-. A Liberal. Sat for Newport, Isle of Wight from 1832 until he retired in July 1837. [1836]

O'REILLY, Myles William. Knock Abbey, Dundalk, Ireland. S. of William O'Reilly, Esq., of Knock Abbey, Co. Louth, by Margaret, d. of Dowell O'Reilly, Esq., of the Heath, Queen's Co. B. in Dublin 1825; m. 1859, Ida, d. of Edmund Jermingham, Esq. Educ. at Ushaw Coll., Durham, and at the University of London, where he graduated B.A., and took the degree of LL.B. at Rome. Was a Major in the Pontifical Service. A Liberal, voted for the disestablishment of the Irish Church. Sat for the Co. of Longford from Mar. 1862 until he accepted Chiltern Hundreds Apr. 1879. Died 6 Feb. 1880.   [1878]

O'REILLY, William. Dorset Street, Dublin.

Seafarm, Co. Dublin. A Barrister. A Repealer, in favour of a provision for the destitute poor. Sat for Dundalk from 1832. Retired in 1835.   [1833]

ORMELIE, Earl of. 31 Park Lane, London. S. of the Marq. of Breadalbane. B. 1796; m. 1821, Eliza, eld. d. of George Baillie, Esq., of Jerviswood. Of Whig principles, and in general a supporter of Ministers. Sat in one Parliament previous to gaining the seat for Perthshire in 1832, and sat until he succeeded as 2nd Marq. of Breadalbane, Mar. 1834. Died Nov. 1862. [1833]

ORMSBY-GORE, J.R. See GORE, J.R. Ormsby.

ORMSBY-GORE, W.R. See GORE, W.R. Ormsby.

ORR-EWING, A. See EWING, Sir A. Orr. Continued in House after 1885: full entry in Volume II.

OSBORNE, Ralph Bernal. Newtown Anner, Co. Tipperary. Reform, and United Service. Eld. s. of Ralph Bernal, who sat in Parliament from 1820-52. B. 1811; m. 1844 Catherine Isabella, only child and heir of Sir Thomas Osborne, Bart., of Thicknesse, Co. Waterford, and Newtown Anner, Co. Tipperary, when he assumed by royal license the name of Osborne. Was Capt. in the army. A Magistrate and Dept.-Lieut. for the Co. of Waterford. Was Secretary to the Admiralty from Dec. 1852-Mar. 1858. A Liberal. Sat for Wycombe 1841-47; for Middlesex 1847-57; for Dover 1857-Apr. 1859, when he was unsuccessful; for Liskeard Aug. 1859-July 1865; for Nottingham Apr. 1866-Nov. 1868, when he was unsuccessful; and for Waterford City from Feb. 1870 until 1874, when he retired. Died 4 Jan. 1882.   [1873]

O'SHAUGHNESSY, Richard. 41 Gloucester Street, London. 6 Upper Fitzwilliam Street, Dublin. Hartstronge Street, Limerick. Stephen's Green, Dublin. S. of James O'Shaughnessy, Esq., of Limerick, by his marriage with Miss Anne Healey. B. at Limerick 1842; m. 1867, Ellen, d. of James Potter, Esq., of Farm Lodge, Co. Limerick. Was educ. at the Jesuit Coll. of St. Stanislans at Tullamore, at Stonyhurst, Conglowes Wood and at Vangirard, Paris; proceeded subsequently to Trinity Coll., Dublin, where he graduated B.A. 1864. Was called to the bar in Ireland 1866. A Liberal, in favour of 'Home Rule' for Ireland. Sat for the City of Limerick from Feb. 1874. until he accepted Registrar of Sessions Clerks in 1883.   [1883]

O'SHEA, William Henry. 1 Albert Mansions, London. Wonersh Lodge, Eltham, Kent. George Street, Limerick. Only s. of Henry O'Shea, Esq., of Fitzwilliam Square, Dublin, by Catherine, d. of Edward Cranach Quinlan, Esq., of Rosanna, Co. Tipperary. B. 1840; m. 1867, Katherine, youngest d. of Sir John Page Wood, Bart., of Rivenhall Place, Essex. Was educ. at Oscott and at Trinity Coll., Dublin. Entered the 18th Hussars as Cornet 1858; became Lieut. 1859, Capt. 1862. A Magistrate for Clare. A Count of Rome. A Liberal, in favour of 'Home Rule' for Ireland. Sat for Clare from Apr. 1880. Defeated in 1885 contesting Liverpool, Exchange. Returned for Galway Town in Feb. 1886 thanks to Parnell's intervention. Retired in 1886. [1885]

OSSULSTON, Lord. 76 South Audley Street, London. Carlton, and Travellers'. Only s. of the Earl of Tankerville. B. in Charles Street, Marylebone, London 1810; m. 1850, Lady Olivia, only d. of the 6th Duke of Manchester. Educ. at Christ Church, Oxford, where he graduated B.A. 1831. Appointed Dept.-Lieut. of Northumberland, 1852. A Conservative. Sat for Northumberland N. from 1832 until he retired in 1858. Summoned to the Lords May 1859. Succeeded as 6th Earl June 1859. Died 18 Dec. 1899. [1858]

O'SULLIVAN, William Henry. Kilmallock, Co. Limerick. Lower Gloucester Street, Dublin. Only s. of Thomas Luke O'Sullivan, Esq., of Bridge House, Rathkeal, by Nanette, d. of Patrick Hussey, Esq., of Kilmallock. B. at Kilmallock 1829; m. 1847, Eliza, d. of William Spread, Esq., of Ballycannon Castle, Co. Cork (she died 1880). A Merchant, and Chairman of the Board of Guardians at Kilmallock. A Liberal, in favour of 'Home Rule' for Ireland. Sat for the Co. of Limerick from 1874 until he retired in 1885. Died 27 Apr. 1887. [1885]

OSWALD, Alexander. 27 Eaton Place, London. Auchincruive, Ayrshire. White's and Travellers'. S. of R.A. Oswald, Esq., and nephew of James Oswald, Esq., former member for Glasgow. M. in 1844 the Lady Louisa, relict of Sir George Frederick Johnstone, Bart., of Westerhall, and only d. of the 1st Earl of Craven. A Conservative, but in favour of free trade. Sat for Ayrshire from 1843. Retired 1852. Defeated at Weymouth in 1852, and at Ayrshire 30 Dec. 1854. Inherited his uncle's Aunchincruive estates in 1853. Died 6 Sept. 1868. [1852]

OSWALD, James. 14 Arlington Street, London. Auchincruive, Ayrshire. Cavens, Kirkcudbrightshire. The Holy Isle, Arran. S. of Alexander Oswald, Esq., of Shield Hall. A Merchant in Glasgow, and a Dept.-Lieut. of Ayrshire and of Lanarkshire. A Reformer, in favour of the ballot, and extension of the suffrage. Sat for Glasgow from 1832-1837; again elected for Glasgow on the death of Lord William Bentinck in 1839 and sat until he retired in 1847. Died 10 June 1853. [1847]

OSWALD, Richard Alexander. Auchincruive. 33 Hereford Street, London. A Reformer, opposed to the corn laws, and an advocate of free trade generally. Sat for Ayrshire from 1832. Accepted the Chiltern Hundreds in 1835. [1835]

OTWAY, Sir Arthur John, Bart. 36 Chester Square, London. Athenaeum and Reform. Eld. surviving s. of Admiral Sir Robert Waller Otway, Bar., G.C.B., by Clementine, d. and co-heir of Admiral Holloway, of Wells, Somerset. Cousin to the Hon. Robert Otway Cave, at one time MP of Castle Otway. B. at Edinburgh 1822; m. 1851, Henrietta, youngest d. of Sir James Langham, 10th Bart., of Cottesbrook Park, Northampton. Was educ. at Saxe Meinengen in Germany, and at Sandhurst, whence he entered the 51st Light Infantry, and served in India and Australia. Was called to the bar at the Middle Temple in 1850, but did not practise. Was Under-Secretary of State for Foreign Affairs from Dec. 1868 to Jan. 1871. Appointed Chairman of Ways and Means, and Deputy-Speaker of the House of Commons, Mar. 1883, salary £2500. A Magistrate for Middlesex. A Liberal, in favour of the assimilation of the county and borough franchise. Sat for Stafford from July 1852 to July 1857. Contested Tynemouth 23 Apr. 1861. Sat for Chatham from July 1865 to Feb. 1874, when he was an unsuccessful candidate there. Sat for Rochester from June 1878 until he retired in 1885. Died 8 June 1912. [1885]

OVEREND, William. 16 Queens Gardens, Hyde Park, London. Conservative. S. of Hall Overend, Esq., of Sheffield. B. at Sheffield 1809. Unmarried. Educ. at Sheffield Grammar School. Called to the bar at Lincolns Inn 1837 and was a Queen's Counsel. A Liberal-Conservative, in favour of extension of electoral privileges but would never recognise mere numbers as sole grounds for granting them. 'An advocate for sound religious education.' Unsuccessfully contested Sheffield July 1852 and again Mar. 1857. First returned for Pontefract May 1859 but a few months later accepted Chiltern Hundreds. Unsuccessfully contested Derbyshire E. Nov. 1868. [1859]

OWEN, Sir Hugh Owen, Bart. Landshipping, Haverfordwest, Pembrokeshire. University. Eld.

s. of Sir John Owen (1st Bart.), by his 1st wife Charlotte, d. of the Rev. John L. Phillips. B. at Lincoln's Inn, London; m. 1825, Angelina Cecilia, d. of Sir Charles Gould Morgan, Bart. (she died 1841). Appointed Lieut.-Col. Pembrokeshire Militia 1830. A Dept.-Lieut. of Pembrokeshire. A Liberal. Unsuccessfully contested Pembrokeshire Jan. 1861. Elected for Pembroke district Feb. 1861. Defeated in 1868. Aide-de-camp to the Queen, May 1872. Died 5 Sept. 1891. [1867]

OWEN, Sir John, Bart. Taynton House, Gloucestershire. Union. Eld. s. of Joseph Lord, Esq., by Cornetta, d. of Lieut.-Gen. Owen, and grand-d. of Sir Arthur Owen; assumed the surname and arms of Owen upon succeeding by bequest to the estates of Sir Hugh Owen. M. 1st, Charlotte, d. of the Rev. John L. Phillips (she died 1829); 2ndly, 1830, Mary Frances, 3rd d. of E. Stephenson, Esq., of Farley Hill, Berkshire. Was called to the bar at the Inner Temple in 1800. Patron of 6 livings. Lord-Lieut. and Custos Rot. of Pembrokeshire, and Governor of Milford Haven. A Liberal, but was for many years ranked as a Conservative; voted against Lord Derby's Reform Bill, Mar. 1859. Sat for Pembrokeshire from 1812 till Aug. 1841, when he was returned for Pembroke district. MP until his death 8 Feb. 1861. [1860]

OXMANTOWN, Lord. 42 Clarges Street, London. Parsonstown Castle, King's County. Athenaeum. Eld. s. of the Earl of Rosse. B. 1800. Of Whig principles. Sat for King's Co. from 1821 until he retired in 1834. Succeeded as 3rd Earl Rosse Feb. 1841. Died 31 Oct. 1867. [1833]

PACKE, Charles William. 7 Richmond Terrace, London. Branksome Tower, Poole, Dorset. Prestwold. Loughborough. Carlton, and Boodle's. B. 1792, Eld. s. of Charles James Packe, of Prestwold Hall, Leicestershire, by Penelope, eld. d. of Richard Dugdale of Blythe Hall, Warwickshire. M. Kitty Jenkyn, only d. of Thomas Hort, Esq., and heiress of Jenkyn Reading whose name she had assumed. A Conservative. Sat for Leicestershire S. from Feb. 1836 until his death on 27 Oct. 1867. [1867]

PACKE, George Hussey. 41 Charles Street, Berkeley Square, London. Caythorpe, Grantham, Lincolnshire. 2nd s. of Charles James Packe, Esq., of Prestwold Hall (for some years Lieut.-Col. of Leicestershire Militia), by Penelope, eld. d. of Richard Dugdale, Esq., of Blythe Hall, Warwickshire. B. 1796; m. 1824, Mary Anne Lydia, eld. d. of John Heathcote, Esq., of Connington Castle, Huntingdonshire. Educ. at Eton.

Entered the army as 2nd Lieut. 1813, became Capt. 1816, and Lieut.-Col. half-pay 1851; served in the campaign of 1815 with the 13th Dragoons, and was slightly wounded at Waterloo. Dept.-Chairman of the Great Northern Railway. A Liberal, in favour of a large measure of Parliamentary Reform, but voted against Lord Russell's Reform Bill 1866; opposed to the ballot. Unsuccessfully contested Newark July 1847, and Lincolnshire S. May 1857. First elected for Lincolnshire S. May 1859 and sat until defeated in 1868. Died 2 July 1874. [1867]

PADMORE, Richard. Henwick Hall, Worcester. S. of Thomas Padmore, Esq., of the Ketley Iron Work, Shropshire, and Mary, his wife. B. at Ketley, Wellington; m. 1823, only d. of John Jones, Esq., of Worcester. Educ. at Wellington School. An Ironfounder and Banker. An Alderman and a Magistrate for Worcester, of which city he was twice Mayor. A Liberal, in favour of the ballot, triennial parliaments, and 'of a more equitable distribution of taxation, in order that property may bear its fair share of the burdens of the State.' First elected for Worcester, Mar. 1860 and sat until he retired in 1868. Died 12 Jan. 1881. [1867]

PAGET, Lord Alfred Henry. 42 Grosvenor Place, London. Melford Hall, Sudbury. White's. 4th s. of the 1st Marq. of Anglesey, by his 2nd wife, d. of the 1st Earl of Cadogan. B. 1816; m. 1847, Cecilia, 2nd d. and co-heiress of George Thomas Wyndham, Esq., of Cromer Hall, Norfolk. A Lieut. in the Royal Horse Guards; became Lieut.-Col. in the army unattached in 1854. Was Chief Equerry and Clerk Marshal to the Queen, from July 1846-Mar. 1852; and from Dec. following until Mar. 1858; again appointed to the same office June 1859. A Liberal, voted for the ballot 1853. Sat for Lichfield from 1837 until defeated 1865. Died 24 Aug. 1888. [1865]

PAGET, Charles. 113 Eaton Square, London. Ruddington Grange, Nottingham. Reform. Eld. s. of Joseph Paget, Esq., of Loughborough, Leicestershire. B. at Loughborough 1799; m. 1st, 1823, Eliza, d. of William Paget, Esq.; 2ndly, 1835, Ellen, d. of William Tebbutt, Esq. A Manufacturer at Nottingham. A Magistrate and Dept.-Lieut. for Nottinghamshire, of which Co. he was High Sheriff. A Liberal, in favour of a progressive extension of the franchise, of vote by ballot, and a comprehensive system of education. First elected for Nottingham July 1856, without opposition and sat until defeated 1865. Died 13 Oct. 1873. [1865]

PAGET, Sir C. A Liberal. Was successful at

Carnarvon 15 Dec. 1832 but was unseated on petition 6 Mar. 1833; but on counter petition, the case was reversed and he was seated again on 23 May 1833. He did not stand at the following gen. election Jan. 1835. An unsuccessful candidate for Carnarvon 27 July 1837.

PAGET, Lord Clarence Edward. 2 Ennismore Place, Knightsbridge, London. S. of the 1st Marq. of Anglesey, by his 2nd wife, Lady Charlotte, d. of the 1st Earl of Cadogan. B. 1811; m. 1852, Martha Stuart, youngest d. of Admiral Sir Robert Waller Otway, Bart. Appointed a Rear-Admiral of the Red 1863. Was Midshipman of the 'Asia' at the battle of Navarino. Commanded the 'Princess Royal' of 91 guns, in the expedition to the Baltic in 1854. Appointed to receive a 'good service pension' in 1855, and created C.B. in 1856. Was Sec. to the Master-Gen. of the Ordnance from 1846-1853. Appointed Sec. to the Admiralty June 1859, salary £2,000. A Liberal. Was an unsuccessful candidate for Southampton in 1837; sat for Sandwich from 1847-July 1852; again returned for Sandwich in Mar. 1857 and sat until he accepted Chiltern Hundreds Mar. 1866. Commander-in-Chief in Mediterranean 28 Apr. 1866-Apr. 1869. Died 22 Mar. 1895.   [1865]

PAGET, Frederick. 5 John Street, Berkeley Square, London. Plâsnewydd, Anglesey. S. of the Hon. B. Paget, Commissioner of Excise; nephew to the 1st Marq. of Anglesey. B. 1807. A Capt. in the Coldstream Guards. A Whig. Returned for Beaumaris in Dec. 1832 and sat until he retired 1847. Sold out of army Dec. 1853. Died 4 Jan. 1866.   [1847]

PAGET, Lord George Augustus Frederick, C.B. 1 Old Burlington Street, London. Plâsnewydd, Anglesey. 5th s. of the 1st Marq. of Anglesey, by his 2nd wife, d. of the 1st Earl of Cadogan. B. in Burlington Street, London. 1818; m. 1854, Agnes, d. of Sir Arthur Paget, G.C.B. Educ. at Westminster School. Entered the army in 1834, became Col. 4th Dragoons 1854, was present at the action at Balaklava same year, and mentioned with distinction in the despatches; received the local rank of Brigadier-Gen. in Turkey 1855, and was in the receipt of a good-service pension of £100. Made officer of the Legion of Honour 1856. A Liberal, voted for the ballot 1853. First elected in 1847 for Beaumaris district, which had previously been represented by his cousin, Col. Frederic Paget, and sat until he retired 1857. Commanded a division of Bengal Army 1862-65. General 1 Oct. 1877. Died London 30 June 1880.   [1857]

PAGET, Lord. See UXBRIDGE, Earl of.

PAGET, R.H. Continued in House after 1885; full entry in Volume II.

PAGET, Thomas Tertius, 8 Charles Street, St. James's, London. Humberstone, Leicester. Ibstock House, Ashby-de-la-Zouche. Oxendon, Market Harborough. Devonshire, Garrick, Brooks's, Reform, and City Liberal. B. at Leicester 1807, eld. s. of Thomas Paget, of Humberstone, Leicester (who represented Leicestershire previous to its division in 1832), by Anne, 3rd d. of John Pares of Newarke, Leicester, and Hopwell Hall, Derbyshire. M. 1850, Katherine Geraldine, 4th d. of Marcus McCansland, of Fruit Hill, Co. Derry. A Magistrate and Dept.-Lieut. for Leicestershire, and High Sheriff 1869. Patron of 1 living. A Liberal, and 'firmly attached to the great principles which guide the Liberal party.' Unsuccessfully contested Leicestershire S. Dec. 1868 and again Feb. 1874. Sat for that division from Nov. 1867-Dec. 1868, and from Apr. 1880 until he retired in 1886. Died 16 Oct. 1892.   [1886]

PAGET, Lord William. 18 Leicester Square, London. Reform. S. of 1st Marq. of Anglesey. B. 1803; m. 1827, d. of Sir F. De Rottenburg. A Capt. R.N. A Liberal. Formerly voted against the abolition of the Corn Laws, but in 1846 supported their repeal. First returned for Andover in 1841 and sat until he retired in 1847. Died 17 May 1873.   [1847]

PAKENHAM, Edward William. 36 St. James's, London. Langford Lodge, Crumlin, Co. Antrim. Guards', White's, and Carlton. B. in Ireland 1819, the eld. s. of Lieut.-Gen. the Hon. Sir Hercules Robert Pakenham, K.C.B., by the 4th d. of 22nd Lord Le Despencer. Unmarried. Capt. in the Grenadier Guards. A Magistrate and Dept.-Lieut. of Antrim. A Conservative, but did not 'vote for a reimposition of duty on foreign coin.' Sat for Antrim July 1852, but killed in action at Inkerman on 5 Nov. 1854.   [1854]

PAKENHAM, Thomas Henry. Longford Lodge, Crumlin, Co. Antrim. Carlton. 3rd s. of Lieut.-Gen. the Hon. Sir Hercules Robert Pakenham, K.C.B., by Hon. Emily, 4th d. of 22nd Lord Le Despencer. B. 1826. Entered the army as Ensign 59th Foot 1844; became Capt. 30th Regiment Sept. 1850. Maj. in the same Regiment 1855, and Lieut.-Col. June 1856; was severely wounded at the battle of Inkermann. A Conservative. First elected for Antrim during his absence in the Crimea Dec. 1854 and sat until he retired 1865. Lieut.-Gen. 1882. Retired 1888. Died 20 Feb. 1913.   [1865]

PAKINGTON, Rt. Hon. Sir John Somerset, Bart., G.C.B. 41 Eaton Square, London. Westwood Park, Droitwich, Worcestershire. Carlton, and Boodle's. B. at Powick Court 1799, the s. of William Russell, of Powick Court, Worcestershire, by the d. of Sir H. Perrot Pakington, Bart., of Westwood. M. 1st, 1822, only child of M.A. Slaney, of Shiffnal, Shropshire (she died 1843); 2ndly, 1844, Augusta Anne, 3rd d. of Bp. (Murray) of Rochester (she died 1848); 3rdly, 1851, Augusta, d. of Thomas de Crespigny, and widow of Col. Davies of Elmley Park, Worcestershire. Assumed the name of Pakington on becoming heir to his maternal uncle, Sir J. Pakington, Bart., 1830. Educ. at Eton and Oriel Coll., Oxford. War Secretary of State for the Colonies Mar.-Dec. 1852, First Lord of the Admiralty Mar. 1858 - June 1859 and July 1866 - Mar. 1867, and Secretary of State for War from 1867 - Dec. 1868. Was Chairman of the Worcestershire Quarter Sessions 1834-54. Appointed Lieut.-Col. Worcestershire Yeomanry Cavalry, Nov. 1859. A Conservative, and 'upheld with a firm hand the Protestant Church.' Contested Worcestershire E. 21 Dec. 1832 and Worcestershire W. 16 May 1833 and again 13 Jan. 1835. Sat for Droitwich from 1837 until 1874, when he was defeated. Succeeded as 2nd Baron Harrington Apr. 1880. Died 26 Apr. 1893. [1873]

PALK, Sir Lawrence, Bart. 1 Grosvenor Gardens, London. Manor House, Torquay. Haldon House, N. Exeter. White's, Carlton, and Junior United Service. Eld. s. of Sir Lawrence Vaughan Palk, Bart., by Anna Eleanora, eld. d. of Sir Bourchier Wrey, Bart., and relict of Edward Hartopp, Esq., of Dalby Hall, Leicestershire. B. in London 1818; m. 1845, Maria Harriet, only d. of Sir Thomas Hesketh, Bart., of Rufford Hall, Lancashire. Educ. at Eton. A Dept.-Lieut. of Devon. A Conservative, a firm supporter of the connection between Church and State. Sat for Devon S. from Feb. 1854-Dec. 1868, from which date he sat for the Devon E. until he retired 1880. Created Baron Haldon Apr. 1880. Died 22 Mar. 1883. [1880]

PALLISER, Sir William, K.C.B. 21 Earl's Court, Kensington, London. Athenaeum, and Army & Navy. Youngest s. of Lieut.-Col. Wray Palliser (Waterford Militia), of Comragh, Co. Waterford, by Anne, d. and heir of John Gledstanes, Esq., of Anne's Gift, Co. Tipperary. B. in Dublin 1830. Educ. at Rugby, Trinity Coll., Dublin and Trinity Hall, Cambridge. Studied also at the Staff Coll., Sandhurst. Entered the Rifle Brigade as Ensign 1855, and joined the 18th Hussars in 1858; became Capt. Aug. 1859; Maj. unattached Oct. 1864, when he was placed on half-pay, and retired from the army 1871. The Inventor of the well-known Palliser Projectiles designed for piercing armour-plated ships. A Conservative. Contested Dungarvan July 1865 and Devonport Nov. 1868. Sat for Taunton from Apr. 1880. MP until his death 4 Feb. 1882. [1881]

PALMER, Gen. Charles. 13 Clarges Street, London. Brooks's, and Westminster. S. of John Palmer, Esq., many years MP for Bath. The originator of mail coaches. M. Mary Elizabeth, eld. d. of John Thomas Atkyns, Esq., of Hunterscombe House, Buckinghamshire, niece and co-heiress of John Atkyns Wright, Esq., many years member for Oxford. A retired Maj.-Gen. Was, when Col. of the 10th Hussars, Aide-de-Camp to the Prince Regent. A radical Reformer, in favour of the ballot, triennial Parliaments, household suffrage, the repeal of the corn laws, and an equalization and distribution of taxation that would throw the chief burden upon property instead of industry. Sat for Bath in five Parliaments preceding 1826, when he was ousted by Lord Brecknock; but he regained his seat in 1831 and sat until 26 July 1837 when he was defeated. Died 17 Apr. 1851. [1836]

PALMER, Charles Fyshe. Luckley Park, Berkshire. S. of John Fyshe, Esq., of Ickwill, who assumed the name of Palmer, on succeeding to the estates of that family. M. 25 Nov. 1805, the Lady Madeline, 2nd d. of Alex. 4th Duke of Gordon, sister of the 5th Duke, and sister-in-law of the Dukes of Bedford and Manchester. A Reformer. Returned for Reading in 1832, having represented it before the Reform Act. Retired in 1835, but returned again in 1837 and sat until he retired in 1841. Died 17 Apr. 1851. [1838]

PALMER, C.M. Continued in House after 1885: full entry in Volume II.

PALMER, George. (I). 8 Old Burlington Street, London. 11 King's Arms Yard, London. Nazing Park, Essex. Carlton. Bro. of J. Horsley Palmer, Esq., who was once Governor of the Bank of England. Commanded a Corps of Yeomanry, raised by himself. A Conservative, voted for agricultural protection, 1846. Contested South Shields Dec. 1832. First elected for Essex S. on the death of R.W. Hall Dare, Esq., in 1836 and sat until he retired in 1847. Died 12 May 1853. [1847]

PALMER, George. (II). 58 Grosvenor Street, London. The Acacias, Reading. Reform and Devonshire. S. of Mr. William Palmer, of Long Sutton, Somersetshire, and Elberton, Gloucestershire, by Mary, d. of Mr. William

Isaac, of Sturminster Newton, Dorsetshire. B. at Long Sutton, Somersetshire; m. 1850, Elizabeth Sarah, d. of Mr. Robert Meatyard, of Stoke Newington, London. Educ. at Sidcot School, Somersetshire. Head of the firm of Messrs. Huntley and Palmers, Reading. A Magistrate for Reading, and also for Berkshire. A Liberal. Sat for Reading from May 1878 until he retired in 1885. Defeated in Dec. 1885 contesting S. Berkshire. Alderman Berkshire County Council 1889. Died 19 Aug. 1897. [1885]

PALMER, John Hinde. 11 St. George's Square, London. Reform. Only s. of Samual Palmer, Esq., of Dulwich, Surrey, a Magistrate and Dept.-Lieut. for Surrey, by Mary, d. and heir of J. Hinde, Esq. B. in Surrey 1808; m. 1844, Clara, 2nd d. of the Rt. Hon. C. Tennyson d'Eyncourt, of Bayons Manor, Lincolnshire. Called to the bar at Lincoln's Inn 1832; made a Queen's Counsel 1859. Treasurer of Lincoln's Inn 1880. A Magistrate and Dept.-Lieut for Surrey. Author of *The Church and the Education Question*, also *County Reform*. Introduced and carried through Parliament several useful amendments to the law. A Liberal, in favour of the extension of household suffrage to the counties and a judicious redistribution of seats. Contested Lambeth 7 Aug. 1850. Unsuccessfully contested Lincoln May 1857, May 1859 and Feb. 1862, sat for Lincoln from Dec. 1868-Jan. 1874. Re-elected Apr. 1880. MP until his death 2 June 1884. [1884]

PALMER, Robert. Holme Park, Reading, Berkshire. Athenaeum, Carlton, and United University. Eld. s. of Richard Palmer, Esq., of Holme Park, near Reading, by Jane, eld. d. of Oldfield Bowles, Esq., of North Aston, Oxfordshire. Grands. of Mr. Palmer, a Solicitor, of Great Russell Street, Bloomsbury Square, London who was for many years agent to the Duke of Bedford. B. 1793. Patron of 1 living. A Magistrate for Berkshire and Wiltshire, and a Dept.-Lieut. of Berkshire, of which he was High Sheriff in 1818. A Conservative, voted for the Reform Act; opposed to the abolition of church-rates, voted for the repeal of the Maynooth grant; would 'support no system of education of which the Bible did not form the basis.' Sat for Berkshire from 1825, with the exception of a part of 1831 until he retired in 1859. Died 24 Nov. 1872. [1858]

PALMER, Roger William Henry. Portland House, Portland Place, London. Cefn Park, Wrexham, North Wales. Only s. of Sir William Henry Roger Palmer, of Castle Lakin, Co. Mayo, and Kenure Park, Dublin, by Eleanora, d. and co-heir of John Matthews, Esq., of Eyarth and Plas Bostock, Denbighshire. B. 1832. Educ. at

Eton. Served the Eastern campaign of 1854-55, with the 11th Hussars, including the affair of Bulganak, battles of Alma, Balaklava, and Inkermann, and the siege of Sebastopol, for which he had a medal and clasps; exchanged as Lieut. to the 2nd Life Guards 1856. A Magistrate for the Cos. of Mayo and Dublin, and a Dept.-Lieut. of Sligo. A Liberal-Conservative, supported the vote of censure on Lord Palmerston 1864. First returned for Mayo Apr. 1857, and sat until he retired 1865. [1865]

PALMER, Sir Roundell. 6 Portland Place, London. 11 New Square, Lincoln's Inn, London. Oxford & Cambridge. 2nd s. of the Rev. William Jocelyn Palmer, of Mixbury, Oxfordshire, by the youngest d. of the Rev. William Roundell of Gladstone, Yorkshire. B. at Mixbury 1812; m. 1848, Lady Laura, 2nd d. of 8th Earl of Waldegrave. Educ. at Winchester; was scholar of Trinity Coll., Oxford and afterwards Fellow of Magdalen Coll. Was 1st class in classics and obtained the Chancellor's prize for Latin verse and Latin Essay, Newdigate's prize for English verse, Dean of Ireland's Scholarship and the Eldon Law Scholarship; made D.C.L. 1862. Was called to the bar at Lincoln's Inn 1837, and made a Queen's Counsel 1849. Was Solicitor Gen. from July 1861-Oct. 1863, and Attorney Gen. from the latter date till July 1866. A Liberal-Conservative, voted against the disestablishment of the Irish Church 1869. Opposed to the ballot. Sat for Plymouth from July 1847-July 1852, and from June 1853-Mar. 1857. Elected for Richmond July 1861 and sat until created 1st Baron of Selbourne Oct. 1872; advanced to an Earldom Dec. 1883. Lord Chancellor 1872-74 and 1880-85. Died 4 May 1895. [1872]

PALMERSTON, Rt. Hon. Visct., G.C.B., K.G. 94 Piccadilly, London. Broadlands, Romsey, Hampshire. Walmer Castle, Deal, Kent. Brocket Hall, Hatfield, Hertfordshire. Melbourne Hall, Derbyshire. Athenaeum, Brooks's, and Reform. B. at Broadlands, Romsey, 1784. M. 1839, d. of 1st Visct. Melbourne and Widow of 5th Earl Cowper. Educ. at Harrow, the University of Edinburgh, and St. John's Coll., Cambridge, where he graduated M.A. 1806. Made D.C.L. Oxfordshire 1862. An Irish Peer. Was Lieut.-Col. Hampshire Militia. Was Secretary at War 1809-28; Secretary of State for Foreign Affairs Nov. 1830 - Nov. 1834, Apr. 1835 - Sept. 1841, July 1846 - Dec. 1851; was the Prime Minister 1855 - Mar. 1858, and June 1859 (salary £5000). Appointed Lord Warden of the Cinque Ports and Constable of Dover Castle, Mar. 1861. Elected Lord Rector of Glasgow University Nov. 1862, and Master of Trinity House June 1863. A Liberal. Sat for Newport, Isle of Wight, 1807 - Mar. 1811; for the University of Cambridge 1811-31, when owing to his support of the Reform Bill he was not returned, but took his seat at Bletchingly. Was an unsuccessful candidate for the University of Cambridge, Feb. 1806, and again 1807. Sat for S. Hampshire 1832 - Dec. 1834, when he was defeated at the general election. Contested Liverpool 30 June 1841. Sat for Tiverton from June 1835 until his death on 18 Oct. 1865 during his second administration. [1865 2nd ed.]

PAPILLON, Philip Oxenden. 67 Gloucester Place, Hyde Park, London. Lexden Manor, Colchester. United University. S. of Thomas Papillon, Esq., of Crowhurst Park, Sussex, by Frances Margaret, d. of Sir Henry Oxenden, Bart., of Broome Park Kent. B. at May Deacon, Kent 1826; m. 1862, Emily Caroline, 3rd d. of the Dean of Lincoln and Lady Caroline Garnier. Educ. at Rugby, and at University Coll., Oxford. Called to the bar at the Inner Temple 1852. Appointed Maj. in the E. Kent Mounted Rifle Militia 1861. Patron of 1 living. A Conservative, said he would give a general support to Lord Derby; opposed to the Maynooth Grant. First elected for Colchester Apr. 1859 and sat until defeated 1865. Chairman of Essex Quarter Sessions 1883-91. Died 16 Aug. 1899. [1865]

PARKER, C.S. Continued in House after 1885: full entry in Volume II.

PARKER, Sir Hyde, Bart. 13 Park Lane, London. Melford Hall, Suffolk. B. 1785; m. in 1821, Caroline, d. of Sir F. Eden, Bart. A moderate Reformer. Sat for Suffolk W. from 1832. Retired in 1835. Died 21 Mar. 1856. [1833]

PARKER, John. Athenaeum, Brooks's, and Reform. S. of Hugh Parker, Esq., of Tickhill, Doncaster. Was called to the bar at Lincoln's Inn, 1824, and joined the Northern circuit. Of Whig principles, in favour of short Parliaments. Was a Lord of the Treasury from Aug. 1836 to June 1841, and Secretary to the Admiralty from June to Sept. 1841; one of the joint Secretaries to the Treasury from July 1846 till May 1849. Re-appointed Secretary to the Admiralty May 1849, salary, £2,000. Sat for Sheffield from 1832 until defeated in 1852. Died 5 Sept. 1881. [1852]

PARKER, Montague Edmund Newcombe. 28 North Audley Street, London. Whiteway, Devon. Athenaeum, and Carlton. Eld. s. of M.E. Parker, Esq., of Whiteway. B. 1807, 3rd cousin of the Earl of Morely. A Conservative. Returned for Devon S. in 1835, defeating Lord John Russell, on the occasion of the noble Lord accepting the office of

Home Sec. Retired 1841. [1838]

PARKER, Robert Townley. 21 Suffolk Street, London. Cuerden Hall, Nr. Preston, Lancashire. Carlton. Only s. of Thomas Townley Parker, Esq., of Cuerden Hall, and Royle, Lancashire, by Susannah, only d. and heir of Peter Brooke, Esq., of Astley, Lancashire. B. 1793; m. 1816, Harriet, youngest d. of Thomas Brooke, Esq., of Church Minshull, Cheshire, and niece of Sir Richard Brooke, Bart., of Norton Priory, Cheshire. A Magistrate and Dept.-Lieut. for Lancashire, of which he was Sheriff in 1817. Patron of 1 living. A Conservative, voted for inquiry into Maynooth 1853. Sat for Preston from July 1837-July 1841, when he was an unsuccessful candidate, again unsuccessful in 1847. Regained his seat July 1852 and sat until he retired 1857. Died 11 Aug. 1879. [1857]

PARKER, Thomas Augustus Wolstenholme. Eld. s. of the Hon. Thomas Parker, (nephew and heir presumptive of the Earl of Macclesfield) and bro.-in-law of the Earl of Antrim. B. 17 Mar. 1811. A Conservative. First returned for Oxfordshire at the general election in 1837. Retired 1841. [1838]

PARKER, William. Clopton Hall, Rattlesden, Bury, Suffolk. Carlton. S. of William Parker, Esq., once of Hardwicke Court, Gloucester, by Anne, d. of William Windsor, Esq. B. at Worton, Middlesex 1802; m. 1831, Elizabeth Mary, d. of Gen. Alexander Duncan. Educ. at St. Mary de-Crypt, Gloucester. Served in the 10th Bengal Light Cavalry, served as Adjutant and Interpreter at the siege and capture of Bhurtpore and its dependencies in 1825 and 1826, for which he received a medal and clasp; was Aide-de-Camp to the Commander-in-Chief in 1827 and 1828, and Brigade-Major from 1829-1836. Appointed Major in the W. Suffolk Militia 1852. A Magistrate and Dept.-Lieut. for Suffolk, for which he served the office of Sheriff in 1854. A Conservative, gave a strong support to Lord Beaconsfield's party, voted against the disestablishment of the Irish Church 1869. Sat for W. Suffolk from May 1859 until he retired 1880. Died Feb. 1892. [1880]

PARNELL, C.S. Continued in House after 1885: full entry in Volume II.

PARNELL, Rt. Hon. Sir Henry Brook, Bart. Rathleague, Queen's Co. Athenaeum, and Reform. 2nd s. of Sir John Parnell, Bart., Chancellor of the Exchequer in Ireland; father-in-law of the Earl of Darnley. B. 1776; m. 1801 Caroline, eld. d. of John, 1st Earl of Portarlington. Was Chairman of the Finance Committee in 1828; was in 1833 appointed a Member of the Excise Inquiry Commission; published a popular work on Financial Reform, and several pamphlets on banking and the currency; Chairman of the Holyhead Road Commission; was Secretary at War for a short time before Sir John Hobhouse, but quitted office because the Ministry would not concur in his estimates, and because he voted against them on the Russian Dutch loan question. In Apr. 1835, was appointed Paymaster General of the Forces, Treasurer of the Ordnance, and Treasurer of the Navy; salary £2000. Sat for the Queen's Co. for 27 years previous to 1832, when, being opposed to a repeal of the Union, he was not returned. Was elected for Dundee on the death of Mr. Kinloch, in 1833 and sat until he retired at 1841 gen. election. Created Baron Congleton (U.K. peerage) 18 Aug. 1841. Died 8 June 1842.   [1840]

PARROTT, Jasper. 57 Jermyn Street, London. Dundridge, Devon. Reform. A Reformer, in favour of the ballot, short Parliaments, and removing the Bishops from the House of Lords. Sat for Totnes from 1832 until he retired 1839.   [1838]

PARRY, Love Parry Jones. 16 St. James's Street, London. Madryn, Carnarvonshire. Eld. s. of Thomas Parry Jones Parry, Esq., of Madryn Park, 1st cousin of Lord Dinorben, and of Sir Rd. Williams Bulkeley, Bart. M. Elizabeth, only d. of Thomas Caldecot, Esq., of Holtoy Lodge, Lincolnshire, niece to Charles Duncombe, of Duncombe Park, 1st cousin to Lord Feversham. A Col. in the army. Dept.-Lieut. of Carnarvonshire, and Chairman of the Quarter Sessions. During the war commanded a Brigade of Cavalry and Infantry, on the frontiers of Upper Canada. A Reformer, in favour of shortening the duration of Parliaments, and an inquiry into the pension list; hoped some means could be found to avoid the necessity of the ballot; desired the removal of the malt tax, and all imposts on industry and knowledge. Sat for Horsham and Malmesbury before 1832. Was first elected for Carnarvonshire in 1835. Retired in 1837. Contested Shrewsbury in 1841. Died 23 Jan. 1853.   [1836]

PARRY, Thomas. 4 Park Prospect, St. James's Park, London. Sleaford, Lincolnshire. Reform. S. of William Parry, Esq., of Lincoln, by Mary, eld. d. of Henry Stanley, Esq. B. at Lincoln 1818; m. 1842, Henrietta, eld. d. of Charles Kirk, Esq., of Sleaford. Educ. at Lincoln. A Liberal, in favour of 'political rights being made co-extensive with political intelligence'; opposed to the ballot, and in favour of economy in the public expenditure so far as it was consistent with maintaining the

efficiency of our naval and military defences. Sat for Boston from July 1865 to Mar. 1866, when he was unseated on petition; re-elected Mar. 1867. Retired Nov. 1868. Re-elected Feb. 1874, but shortly afterwards unseated on petition.   [1868]

PARRY, Thomas Duncombe Lone Jones-. See JONES-PARRY, Thomas Duncombe Lone.

PATESHALL, Evan. 9 Cleveland Row, London. Allensmore Court, Hereford. S. of David Thomas, Esq., of Welfield, Radnorshire, by Catherine, eld. d. of William Jones, Esq., of Henllys, Co. Carmarthen. B. at Welfield 1817; m. 1842, Anne Elizabeth, only child of William Pateshall, Esq. of Hereford. Educ. st Shrewsbury School and King's Coll., London. Assumed in 1855 the name and arms of Pateshall, in compliance with the will of Edmond Burnham Pateshall, Esq. of Allensmore Court, Hereford. Commanded for several years one of the Hereford companies of Rifle Volunteers from which he retired 1868. A Magistrate and Dept.-Lieut. for the Co. of Hereford and a Magistrate for the Cos. of Brecon and Radnor. A Conservative. Sat for the city of Hereford from Feb. 1874. Accepted Chiltern Hundreds in 1878. Died 9 Apr. 1885.   [1878]

PATRICK, Robert William Cochran-. Woodside, Beith, Ayrshire. Carlton. Eld. s. of William Charles Richard Patrick, Esq., by Agnes, eld. d. and heir of William Cochran, Esq., of Ladyland (whose name he assumed). B. at Ladyland, Kilbirnie, Ayrshire; m. 1866, Eleanora, youngest d. of Robert Hunter, of Hunter, West Kilbride, Ayrshire (she died in 1884). Was educ. at Edinburgh, where he graduated B.A. 1860, and took the degree of LL.B. at Cambridge 1864; also created Hon. LL.D. at Glasgow. A Magistrate for Renfrewshire and Ayrshire, and a Dept.-Lieut. of the latter. Author of *Records of the Coinage of Scotland, Records of Early Mining in Scotland,* and *Medals of Scotland.* A Conservative. Opposed any measure 'tending to sever the union between Great Britain and Ireland'; was 'a supporter of the Established churches' of the country; voted for the abolition of the system of Hypothec in agricultural holdings. Sat for N. Ayrshire from Apr. 1880 until defeated in 1885. Under-Secretary of State for Scotland Dec. 1887; resigned 15 June 1892. Died Ayrshire, 15 Mar. 1897.   [1885]

PATTEN, Rt. Hon. John Wilson. 9 Lowndes Square, London. Bank Hall, Warrington, Lancashire. Light Oaks, Stafford. Athenaeum, Carlton, and Travellers'. Eld. s. of Thomas Wilson Patten of Bank Hall, MP, who assumed the additional surname of Wilson, on succeeding to the estates of the Bp. of Sodor and Man. B. 1802; m. 1828 his cousin, Anna Maria, d. and co-heiress of Peter Patten Bold, of Bold, Lancashire (she died 1846). Was Chairman of Committees of the Whole House Nov. 1852-Apr. 1853, Chancellor of the Duchy of Lancaster June 1867 - Sept. 1868, and Chief Secretary for Ireland Sept. 1868 - Dec. 1868. Was Vice-Lieut. of Lancashire, and Col. of 3rd Lancashire Militia. A Conservative, voted against the disestablishment of the Irish Church 1869, being opposed to ecclesiastical endowments being secularized. Sat for Lancashire in 1830, but lost his election in 1831, and was re-elected for the Northern division in 1832. Sat until Mar. 1874 when he was created Baron Winmarleigh. Died 1892. [1873]

PATTISON, James. 37 Upper HarUley Street, London. West House, Cheshire. Reform, and Free Trade. B. in 1786, the s. of Nathaniel Pattison, Esq., of Congleton, Cheshire, the nephew of James Pattison, Esq., many years a Director of the East India Company and the grand-nephew of Gen. James Pattison, who was sixty years in the army. Married, and was both a Governor and Director of the Bank of England. A Merchant, like his father and grandfather who were also engaged in commercial pursuits. The family estate was at Plumstead in Kent, where the Pattisons had long settled. A Reformer, in favour of triennial Parliaments, the vote by ballot and Church Reform. Opposed to all religious endowments. Represented the City of London in 1835 and 1837, but was unsuccessful in the general election of 1841. Elected in Oct. 1843 (filling the vacancy occasioned by the death of Sir Matthew Wood), and then re-elected in 1847, after which he held his seat until his death in June 1849. [1848]

PATTON, George. 3rd s. of James Patton, Esq., of the Cairnies. B. at the Cairnies 1803. Educ. at Perthshire and Oxford but did not complete the course. Went to Edinburgh University. A pleader at the bar and then became Advocate 1828. A Scottish Judge and held office under Lord Derby in 1859 when he became Solicitor General for Scotland for a few weeks. An ardent Tory. First elected for Bridgwater in Aug. 1865, but he was defeated in June 1866 when he was appointed Lord Advocate in Lord Derby's 3rd administration. Charges of gross corruption and bribery relating to the election were brought against him, but when the Lord Justice Clerk (John Inglis) resigned, Mr. Patton as Lord Advocate had the gift of that post and conferred it upon himself, enabling him to avoid the select committee investigation. He also took the title of Lord Glenalmond. His bro. died in Aug. 1869 but it was wrongly announced that he had died. He then succeeded to the estate of Glenalmond, but he committed suicide on 20 Sept. 1869.

PAULL, Henry. 33 Devonshire Place, London. Conservative. S. of Archibald Paull, Esq., Merchant. B. in London, 1822; m. 1862, Marianne, 2nd d. of Henry Willis, Esq., of Hill Street, Berkeley Square, and Horton Lodge, Epsom, Surrey. Called to the bar at the Middle Temple 1845, and joined the Western circuit. Appointed a Dept.-Lieut. for Middlesex, 1859. A Conservative, voted with Lord Derby on his Reform Bill, Mar. 1859. Unsuccessfully contested St. Ives, July 1852. First elected for St. Ives, Mar. 1857 and sat until he retired in 1868. [1867]

PAXTON, Sir Joseph. Chatsworth, Chesterfield, Derbyshire. Rockhills, Sydenham. 7th s. of William Paxton, Esq., of Milton Bryant, near Woburn, Bedfordshire. B. at Milton Bryant, 1803; m. 1827, 3rd d. of Thomas Bown, Esq., of Hunt Bridge House, Matlock, Derbyshire. Educ. at Woburn Free School. A Landscape Gardener and Garden Architect. A fellow of the Horticultural Society and of the Linnaean Society; a member of the Society of Arts; editor of the *Horticultural Register, Botanical Magazine*, etc. A Liberal, voted against Church rates 1855. First elected for Coventry Dec. 1854. MP until his death 8 June 1865. [1865]

PEACOCKE, G.M.W. See SANDFORD, G.M.W.

PEARSON, Charles. 10 Park Street, Westminster, London. 7 Old Jewry, Clapham Common, Surrey. S. of Thomas Pearson, Esq. a member of an old-established mercantile firm in London. B. in London 1794; m. 1817, d. of Robert Dutton, Esq. of London (this lady was honourably known as a most successful artist and portrait painter). Educ. at Eastbourne, Sussex. Admitted a Solicitor in 1816; elected by the Corporation of London as City Solicitor, 1839. Solicitor to the Irish Society, and one of the Attorney's of the Lord Mayor's Court. An original promoter of the Metropolitan underground railway in 1859. A radical Reformer, in favour of free trade, the repeal of the window tax and of the fire insurance taxes; also in favour of the reformatory treatment of juvenile offenders, opposed to capital punishment, the rate-paying clauses of the Reform act of 1832, the game laws, the income tax, the creation of new Bishops and against all religious endowments out of the revenues of the state. First returned for Lambeth in 1847. Accepted Chiltern Hundreds July 1850. Died 14 Sept. 1862. [1850]

PEASE, A. Continued in House after 1885: full entry in Volume II.

PEASE, Henry. 7 Manchester Buildings, Westminster, London. Pierremont, Darlington. S. of Edward Pease, Esq., Merchant, by Rachel his wife. B. at Darlington 1807; m. 1st, 1835, Anna, only d. of Richard Fell, Esq., of Belmont, Uxbridge; 2ndly, 1858, Mary, d. of Samuel Lloyd, Esq., of Wednesbury. A Manufacturer and Coal-Owner. A Director of six lines of railway and of other public works. Vice-Chairman of the Board of Guardians of the Darlington Union. A 'progressive Liberal', in favour of 'strict economy in our national resources', the abolition of Church rates, and 'reform in our various institutions', but not prepared to support the ballot. First elected for Durham S. Apr. 1857, without opposition and sat until he retired in 1865. Died 30 May 1881. [1865]

PEASE, Joseph. 4 Park Street, Westminster, London. Southend, Durham. The only member of the Society of Friends in Parliament. A Worsted Manufacturer, of the firm Pease & Company, Darlington Mills. A Reformer, in favour of protection to agriculture, a revision of the monetary system, removing the Bishops from the House of Lords, short Parliaments and the ballot. Sat for Durham S. from 1832 until he retired 1841. President of the Peace Society 1860 until his death 8 Feb. 1872. [1838]

PEASE, Joseph Whitwell. See PEASE, Sir Joseph Whitwell. Continued in House after 1885: full entry in Volume II.

PEASE, Sir Joseph Whitwell. Continued in House after 1885: full entry in Volume II.

PECHELL, Sir George Richard, Bart. 27 Hill Street, Berkeley Square, London. Hampton Court Palace. Castle Goring, Sussex. Arthur's, Travellers', United Service, Reform, and Brooks's. Youngest s. of Major-Gen. Sir Thomas Brooke Pechell, Bart., formerly MP for Downton. B. in London 1789; m. 1826, Katherine Annabella, co-heiress of Cecil, Baron de la Zouche, of Haryugworth, who died in 1828, and sister of Harriet Anne, the Baroness. Entered the navy in 1803, became a Capt. in 1822, and a Rear-Admiral on the reserved half-pay list 1852; appointed Gentleman Usher of the Privy Chamber in 1830; and Equerry to the Queen Dowager in 1831, which office he retained until her death in 1849. Patron of 1 living. Published in 1822, *A Visit to the Isle of St. Domingo, on a Mission to President Boyer, in 1820 in H.M. Ship Tamar.* A Liberal, in favour of vote by ballot, and a system of national

education for all sects; voted against Church rates 1855. Unsuccessfully contested Brighton in 1832; sat for it from 1835. MP until his death 29 June 1860. [1860]

PECHELL, Sir Samuel John Brooke, Bart., C.B. Admiralty. Twickenham. B. 1785; m. 1833, Julia Maria, only surviving d. of Robert Edward, 9th Lord Petre, and niece to the Duke of Norfolk. A Captain in the navy; a Lord of the Admiralty, and therefore a member of the Government. Sat for Windsor from 1832. Retired in 1835. Died 3 Nov. 1849. [1833]

PEDDIE, J.D. Continued in House after 1885: full entry in Volume II.

PEEK, Sir Henry William, Bart. Wimbledon House, Wimbledon, London. 5 St. Mary-at-Hill, London. Ronsdon, Lynn Regis. Carlton. Eld. s. of James Peek, Esq., of Watcombe, Torquay, by his m. with Miss Elizabeth Lemaitres, of Dieppe, who was the last of the Lemaitres, a refugee family which came to England at the revocation of the Edict of Nantes 1685. B. in London 1825; m. 1848, Margaret Maria, 2nd d. of William Edgar, Esq., of Clapham Common. A Merchant in London and head of the firm of Messrs. Peek Bros. and Co., Eastcheap. A Magistrate for Surrey and Devon. Patron of 4 livings. A Conservative. Unsuccessfully contested E. Surrey July 1865. Sat for mid Surrey from Dec. 1868 until he accepted Chiltern Hundreds June 1884. Died 26 Aug. 1898. [1884]

PEEL, Rt. Hon. A.W. Continued in House after 1885: full entry in Volume II.

PEEL, Edmund. 5 Great Ryder Street, London. S. of Sir R. Peel. B. 1791; m. 1812, Jane, 2nd d. of John Swinfen, Esq., of Swinfen, Staffordshire. A moderate Reformer. In the parliament of 1831 voted for Lord Abrington's motion expressive of confidence in Lord Grey's administration; on his motion the franchise of freemen in boroughs was preserved. Sat for Newcastle-under-Lyme in 1831, and contested it unsuccessfully in 1830 and 1832. Sat for it again from 1835. Retired in 1837. [1837]

PEEL, Rt. Hon. Sir Frederick. 32 Chesham Place, London. Hampton-in-Arden, Warwickshire. 2nd s. of the Rt. Hon. Sir Robert Peel, by Julia, youngest d. of Gen. Sir John Floyd. Bro. was member for Tamworth. B. in Stanhope Street, London 1823; m. 1857, d. of Sir John Shelley, Bart., of Ovington House, Hampshire. Educ. at Harrow School, and at Trinity Coll., Cambridge, where he was 1st class in classics

1845. Called to the bar at the Inner Temple 1849. A Dept.-Lieut. of Warwickshire. Was Under Sec. of State for the Colonies from Nov. 1851-Mar. 1852, and from Dec. following until Feb. 1855; Under Sec. for War from the last date until 1857. Appointed Financial Sec. to the Treasury Oct. 1860, salary £2,000. A Liberal, in favour of an extension of the suffrage, but 'distrustful of secret voting'; voted against the ballot 1852. Sat for Leominster from Feb. 1849-July 1852, and for Bury from the last date until Apr. 1857, when he was an unsuccessful candidate; re-elected for Bury May 1859, and sat until defeated 1865. Contested Lancashire S.E. in 1868. [1865]

PEEL, John. Middleton House, Tamworth. S. of Thomas Peel, Esq., of Peelfold, Lancashire and Trenant Park, Cornwall, by Dorothy, d. of Robert Bolton, Esq. B. 1804; m. 1830, Esther, d. of Edmund Peel, Esq. Educ. at Manchester Grammar School. A Merchant. A Magistrate for the Cos. of Warwick and Stafford. A Liberal-Conservative, in favour of the ballot. Sat for Tamworth from Oct. 1863-Dec. 1868, when he was an unsuccessful candidate there; re-elected there Mar. 1871. MP until his death 27 July 1872. [1872]

PEEL, Rt. Hon. Jonathan. 8 Park Place, St. James's, London. Marble Hill, Twickenham, Middlesex. Buckingham House, Thetford. Carlton, and Boodle's. S. of Sir Robert Peel, 1st Bart., by Ellen, d. of William Yates, Esq., of Spring Side, near Bury, and uncle to the 3rd Bart. the member for Tamworth. B. 1799; m. in 1824, Lady Alicia Jane, youngest d. of the 1st Marq. of Ailsa. Educ. at Rugby. Entered the army, June 1815, became Maj.-Gen. 1854; Lieut.-Gen. unattached, Dec. 1859. Was Surveyor-Gen. of the Ordnance from Sept. 1841 till July 1846; Secretary of State for War from Mar. 1858 till June 1859; re-appointed July 1866. A Conservative. Sat for Norwich in the Parliament of 1826. Sat for Huntingdon from 1831 until he retired in 1868. Also contested Cheltenham July 1837 and Clitheroe Aug. 1853. Died 13 Feb. 1879. [1867]

PEEL, Rt. Hon. Sir Robert, Bart. 4 Whitehall Gardens, London. Drayton Manor, Staffordshire. Carlton, and United University. B. 1788; m. 1820, Julia, youngest d. of Gen. Sir J. Floyd, Bart. Patron of 2 livings. Having been Under Secretary for the Home Dept., and Chief Secretary for Ireland, he succeeded Lord Sidmouth as Secretary of State for the Home Dept. in 1822, and held that office till 1827, when he resigned and remained out of place until the formation of the Duke of Wellington's Administration. He then returned to the Home Dept. and continued

there until the accession of Earl Grey to power in 1830. Was First Lord of the Treasury and Chancellor of the Exchequer from Dec. 1834 till Apr. 1835 and First Lord of the Treasury alone, from Sept. 1841 to July 1846. Was first returned to Parliament for Cashel in 1809. Sat for Oxford University from 1818-28, when he was thrown out by Sir Robert Harry Inglis. He then sat for Westbury till 1830, when he was elected for Tamworth, which he continued to represent until his death 2 July 1850. [1850]

PEEL, Sir R. Continued in House after 1885: full entry in Volume II.

PEEL, Rt. Hon. William Yates. Baginton Hall, Warwickshire. White's, Boodle's, Carlton and Athenaeum. 2nd. s. of Sir Robert Peel, Bart., by his 1st wife d. of William Yates, Esq., of Bury; was therefore bro. to Sir Robert Peel, Bart., MP. B. at Chamber Hall, Bury, Lancashire 1789; m. 1819, Lady Jane Eliza, 2nd d. of the 2nd Earl of Mount Cashell. Educ. at Harrow, and at St. John's Coll., Cambridge. Was called to the bar at Lincoln's Inn, June 1816. Appointed a Commissioner of the Board of Control in 1826, Under-Sec. of State for the Home Dept. in 1828, a Lord of the Treasury in 1830, and again held that office from 1834-Apr. 1835. A Dept.-Lieut. of Staffordshire. A Conservative. Was elected for Bossiney in 1817, for Tamworth in 1818, 1820 and 1826; for Yarmouth, Isle of Wight in 1830, for the University of Cambridge in 1831; again for Tamworth in 1835; and re-elected for Tamworth in 1847 without opposition. Accepted Chiltern Hundreds in Nov. 1847. Died 1 June 1858. [1847 2nd ed.]

PELHAM, Hon. Charles. See WORSLEY, Lord. (I)

PELHAM, Hon. Dudley Worsley Anderson. St. Lawrence, Isle of Wight. Brooks's, Traveller's, and Junior United Service. B. 1812, the 2nd. s. of 1st Earl of Yarborough, by 2nd d. of Hon. John Bridgman Simpson. M. 1839, d. of Sir John Gordon Sinclair, Bart. Was educ. at Eton. Became a Capt. R.N. 1840. A Liberal, but opposed to the ballot. In favour of free trade, the extension of the suffrage and religious toleration, and said he would support a peaceful policy, and a reduction in the national expenditure. Author of a pamphlet on the *Condition of the Labouring Classes*, etc. Was an unsuccessful candidate for the Isle of Wight in 1837. First returned for Boston in Aug. 1849 and sat until his death in Apr. 1851. [1851]

PELHAM, John Cressett. Cound Hall and Shrewsbury Castle, Shropshire. Was patron of 4 livings. A moderate Reformer. Sat for Shropshire from 1820 to 1832. Contested Shrewsbury unsuccessfully in 1832, but gained the seat in 1835. Defeated in 1837. [1837]

PELHAM, Lord. 70 Chester Street, London. Stanmer Park, Lewes. Brooks's. B. at Stanmer 1838, the eld. s. of the Earl of Chichester, by Lady Mary, d. of 6th Earl of Cardigan. M. 1861, Elizabeth Mary, d. of the Hon. Sir John Duncan Bligh, K.C.B. Educ. at Harrow and at Trinity Coll., Cambridge. Appointed a Dept.-Lieut. of Sussex, 1858. Of Liberal opinions. Voted for the disestablishment of the Irish Church 1869. Sat for Lewes from July 1865 until he retired in 1874. [1873]

PELL, Albert. Haselbeach, Northampton. Wilburton Manor, Ely. Carlton. S. of Sir Albert Pell, Judge of the Court of Appeal in Bankruptcy, by Hon. Margaret Letitia Matilda, d. and co-heir of the 12th Baron St. John, of Bletsoe. B. at Montague Place, Russell Square, London, 1820; m. 1846, Elizabeth Barbara, only d. of Sir Henry Halford, who sat for S. Leicestershire. Educ. at Rugby and at Trinity Coll., Cambridge; graduated B.A. and M.A. 1842. A Magistrate for Leicestershire and the Isle of Ely, and a Dept.-Lieut. for Cambridgeshire. Was first Chairman of the Central Chamber of Agriculture. A Conservative. Sat for S. Leicestershire from Dec. 1868 until he retired in 1885. [1885]

PELLATT, Apsley. Holland Street, London. Blackfriars Road, Southwark, London. Staines, Middlesex. Reform. S. of Apsley Pellatt, Esq., Glass Manufacturer, by Mary, d. of Stephen Maberly, Esq., of Reading, Berkshire. B. in London 1791; m. 1816, d. of George Evans, Esq., of Balham Hill, Surrey. Educ. under Dr. Wanostrocht, at Camberwell. Succeeded to his father's business as an extensive Glass Manufacturer in Southwark. Was a member of the Court of Common Council in the city of London for 7 years, and succeeded in carrying there the bill for admitting Jews to the city freedom on their taking the oath most binding on their own consciences. An associate of the Institution of Civil Engineers and for 7 years one of the Council of the Government School of Design. Author of *Curiosities of Glass Making and Ancient Glass*, etc. A Liberal, in favour of household suffrage, equal electoral districts, no property qualification, vote by ballot and short Parliaments; opposed to the endowment by the State of any religion and on that ground voted against the grant to Maynooth. Was an unsuccessful candidate for Bristol in July 1847. First returned for Southwark in July 1852 and sat until he was defeated in Mar. 1857. Contested

Southwark again in May 1859. Died 17 Apr. 1863. [1856]

PELLY, Sir Henry Carstairs, Bart. 46 Grosvenor Gardens, London. Eld. s. of Sir John Henry Pelly (2nd.) Bart., by his 1st wife, Johanna Jane, youngest d. of John Carstairs, Esq., of Stratford Green, Essex, and Woodhurst, Hampshire. B. at Balls park, Hertfordshire, 1844; m. 1872, Hon. Lilian Harriet, 2nd d. of Lord Elcho, and grand-d. of the Earl of Wemyss. Appointed Lieut. 2nd Dragoons 1865; exchanged to 2nd Life Guards 1867; became Capt. Nov. 1872, retired 1873. A Conservative, and in favour of the Established Church being maintained, 'opposed to the total suppression of all religious instruction in elementary schools', in favour of the re-adjustment of local taxation. Sat for Huntingdonshire from Feb. 1874. MP until his death 4 June 1877. [1877]

PEMBERTON, Edward Leigh. 5 Warwick Square, London. Torry Hill, Sittingbourne, Kent. Carlton, and Arthur's. S. of Edward Leigh Pemberton, Esq., of Torry Hill, Kent (only bro. of Lord Kingsdown), by Charlotte, d. of S.R. Cox, Esq. B. in London 1823; m. 1849, Matilda Catherine Emma, d. of the Hon. and Rev. Francis Noel. Educ. at Eton, and at St. John's Coll., Oxford. Was called to the bar at Lincoln's Inn July 1847. A Magistrate for Kent, and a Major in the East Kent Yeomanry. Patron of 2 livings. A Conservative. Sat for E. Kent from Apr. 1868 until appointed Legal Assistant Under-Secretary at Home Office Aug. 1885. Knighted in 1898. Died 31 Jan. 1910. [1885]

PEMBERTON, Thomas. Lincoln's Inn, London. 3 Spring Garden Terrace, London. Carlton. A Queen's Counsel at the Chancery bar. A Conservative. Sat for Rye in 1831, and represented Ripon from 1832 until he accepted Chiltern Hundreds in 1843. Inherited much property and took surname of Leigh in Mar. 1843; a member of Judicial Committee of the Privy Council for 20 years; created Baron Kingsdown in Apr. 1858. Died Oct. 1867. [1842]

PENDARVES, Edward William Wynne. 36 Eaton Place, London. Pendeaves, Redruth, Cornwall. Athenaeum, and Reform. Eld. surviving s. of John Stackhouse, Esq., by Susanna, only child and heir of Edward Acton, Esq., of Acton Scot, Shropshire. Assumed the additional surname of Wynne by Sign Manual in 1815 and in the same year that of Pendarves, in place of Stackhouse. M. 1804, Tryphena, 3rd d. and sole surviving heir of the Rev. Browse Trist, of Bowden, Devon. Educ. at All Saints Coll., Oxford, where he graduated B.A. 1797, M.A. 1801. Appointed Special Deputy Warden of the Stannaries 1852. Patron of 1 living. Of Whig principles and in favour of short Parliaments. Formerly voted against an abolition of the Corn Laws, but in 1846 supported their repeal. Sat uninterruptedly for Cornwall from 1826 and Cornwall W. from 1832 until his death on 26 June 1853. [1853]

PENDER, John. Continued in House after 1885: full entry in Volume II.

PENLEAZE, John Storey. 14 Bolton Street, London. Beech Cottage, Southampton. Bossington House, Nr. Stockbridge, Hampshire. A Reformer, in favour of the ballot. First elected for Southampton in 1831; contested the election in 1832, was not returned, but on petition succeeded in ousting Barlow Hoy, Esq., his Conservative opponent. Retired in 1835. Died 12 Apr. 1855. [1833]

PENNANT, Hon. Edward Gordon Douglas-. Penrhyn Castle, Bangor, Carnarvonshire. Carlton, Arthur's, Travellers', and Boodle's. Bro. of 18th Earl of Morton. B. 1800; m. 1st, d. of G.H.D. Pennant, Esq., whose name he assumed (she died 1842); 2ndly, 1846, Lady Louisa, youngest d. of the 5th Duke of Grafton. Appointed a Dept.-Lieut. of Carnarvon 1846 and Lieut.-Col. Commandant of the Carnarvon Militia 1852. Was Col. Scots Fusilier Guards, retired 1846. A Conservative. First returned for Carnarvonshire in 1841 and sat until created Baron Penrhyn Aug. 1866. Died 31 Mar. 1886. [1865 2nd ed.]

PENNANT, Hon. George Sholto Douglas-. 18 Grosvenor Place, London. Penrhyn Castle, Bangor. Carlton. Eld. s. of Baron Penrhyn (who represented the Co. 24 years), by his 1st wife, Juliana, eld. d. and co-heir of George Hay Dawkins-Pennant, Esq. B. 1836; m. 1st, 1860, Pamela Blanche, younger d. of Sir Charles Rushout, Bart. (she died 1869); 2ndly, 1875, Gertrude Jessy, youngest d. of Rev. Henry Glynne, Canon of St. Asaph. A Conservative. Sat for Carnarvonshire from Aug. 1866-Nov. 1868, when he was an unsuccessful candidate there; re-elected there Feb. 1874 and sat until defeated 1880. Succeeded as 2nd Baron Penrhyn Mar. 1886. Died 10 Mar. 1907. [1880]

PENNINGTON, Frederick. 17 Hyde Park Terrace, London. Broome Hall, Holmwood, Surrey. Reform, and Devonshire. Youngest s. of John Pennington, Esq., of Hindley, near Wigan, by Elizabeth, d. of John Hargreaves, Esq., of West Houghton. B. at Hindley, near Wigan,

1819; m. 1854, Margaret, youngest d. of the Rev. John Sharpe, D.D., Vicar of Doncaster, and Canon of York. Formerly an East India Merchant, but retired from business in 1865. A Magistrate for Surrey. An 'advanced Liberal'. Unsuccessfully contested Surrey W. Dec. 1868. Sat for Stockport from Feb. 1874 until he retired in 1885. Died 11 May 1914. [1885]

PENRUDDOCKE, John Hungerford. 35 Curzon Street, London. Compton Park, Wiltshire. Carlton. Lieut.-Col. Commandant of the Wiltshire Militia. Patron of 1 living. Sheriff of Wiltshire in 1817. Was a lineal descendant of the celebrated Col. John Penruddocke, who was beheaded at Exeter, May 1655, by order of Cromwell, for attempting to proclaim Charles II at Salisbury. A Conservative. Sat for Wilton from 1820 until he retired in 1837. [1837]

PEPLOE, Daniel Peploe. Garnstone Castle, Hereford. Carlton, and Army & Navy S. of the Rev. John Birch Peploe, by Annie, d. of John Molyneux, Esq. B. at Weobley, Herefordshire 1829; m. 1860, Eliza Debonaire Theophila, d. of Sir Thomas Metcalfe, Bart., of Fernhill, Windsor. Educ. at Rugby and at Trinity Coll., Cambridge, graduated B.A. 1851. Joined the 4th Royal Irish Dragoon Guards 1851, attained the rank of Capt. and retired from the army. Served throughout the Crimean campaign. Patron of 2 livings. A Conservative. Sat for Herefordshire from Feb. 1874 until defeated 1880. Died 4 Nov. 1887. [1880]

PEPYS, Sir Charles Christopher. Copse Hill, Wimbledon. 48 Queen Anne Street, London. 13 Lincoln's Inn, New Square, London. Bro. of Sir William Weller Pepys, Bart.; m. 1821, Caroline, d. of W. Wingfield Esq., Master in Chancery, and grand-niece, maternally, of the Earl of Digby. Was appointed Solicitor General in 1834, on the promotion of Sir John Campbell, but resigned in Nov. of the same year. Master of the Rolls in 1835. Returned for Malton 12 Dec. 1832 and sat until Jan. 1836 when he was created Lord Cottenham. Lord Chancellor 1836 and 1846; advanced to Visct. on retirement in 1850. Died 29 Apr. 1851. [1835]

PERCEVAL, Alexander, D.C.L. Temple House, Co. Sligo. Carlton. B. 1788; m. 1809 d. of H.B. Lestrange, Esq. Lieut.-Col. of the Sligo Militia. Treasurer of Ordnance from Dec. 1834 till Apr. 1835. A Conservative. Sat for Sligo Co. from 1831 to Sept. 1841 when he accepted the Chiltern Hundreds. Sergeant-at-arms of House of Lords from 1841. Died 9 Dec. 1858. [1841]

PERCEVAL, Charles George. Passenham

Manor, Stoney Stratford. Only s. of Hon. and Rev. Charles George Perceval, (bro. of 6th Earl of Egmont), by his 2nd wife Francis (sic) Agnes, 2nd d. of the Ven. George Trevelyan, Archdeacon of Taunton. B. at Calverton, Buckinghamshire, 1845; m. 1869, Lucy, 4th d. of H. King Esq. Was educ. at Radley and at University Coll., Oxford. A Lieut. Bucks Yeomanry Cavalry. A Magistrate for Northamptonshire and Buckinghamshire. A Conservative. Sat for Midhurst from Feb. 1874 until he succeeded uncle as 7th Earl of Egmont 2 Aug. 1874. Died 5 Sept. 1897. [1874]

PERCEVAL, Hon. George James. Nork, Surrey. Carlton. Eld. s. of 1st Lord Arden, and nephew of the Rt. Hon. Spencer Perceval. B. 14 Mar. 1794; m. 24 July 1819, Jane, eld. d. of John Hornby, Esq., of Hook-House, Hampshire. A Capt. in the navy of the year 1818. A Conservative. Sat for Surrey W. from 1837 until he succeeded father as 3rd Baron Arden July 1840; succeeded cousin as 5th Earl of Egmont Dec. 1841. Died 2 Aug. 1874. [1840]

PERCY, Lord Algernon Malcolm Arthur. 2 Grosvenor Place, London. Merrow Grange, Guildford. 2nd s. of the 6th Duke of Northumberland, by Louisa, eld. d. and co-heir of Henry Drummond, Esq., of Albury Park, Surrey. B. 1851; m. 1880, Lady Victoria Frederica Caroline, eld. d. of the 4th Earl of Mount Edgcumbe. Educ. at Eton and Christ Church, Oxford, and graduated M.A. 1871. Became a Sub.-Lieut. Grenadier Guards 1872; Lieut. and Adjutant 1877; retired 1880. Appointed Major 3rd Batt. Berkshire Militia 1881. A Conservative. Sat for Westminster 1882-85, and for St. George's, Hanover Square, from Nov. 1885 until he accepted Chiltern Hundreds in 1887. Major 3rd Battalion Northumberland Fusiliers 1886-95; Lieut.-Col. 1895-1910. A.D.C. to the King 1902-20. Died 28 Dec. 1933. [1886]

PERCY, Lord Henry Hugh Manvers. Northumberland House, London. Albury, Guildford. Alnwick Castle, Northumberland. White's, Travellers', and United Service. Youngest s. of 5th Duke of Northumberland, by Louisa, 3rd d. of Hon. James Stuart-Wortley-Mackenzie. B. 1817. Educ. at Eton. Appointed Capt. and Lieut. Grenadier Guards 1851, Major 1860 and retired in 1862. Aide-de-Camp to the Queen 1855; commanded a battalion of Guards in the district of Colchester, and a brigade at Aldershot. Was wounded at the battles of the Alma and Inkermann. A Major-Gen. in the army, and received a Victoria Cross, the order of the Legion of Honour, etc. A Conservative. First elected for N. Northumberland July 1865. Retired Nov. 1868.

Died 3 Dec. 1877. [1867]

PERCY, Hon. Josceline William. 36 Cadogan Place, London. Travellers'. 2nd s. of the 2nd Earl of Beverley, by Louisa Harcourt, 3rd d. of the Hon. James Archibald Stuart Wortley. B. at Tunbridge Wells, 1811; m. 1848, Margaret, only d. of Sir David Davidson, of Cantray, Co. Nairn, and widow of the Rt. Hon. Sir Robert Grant. Educ. at Eton and at St. John's Coll., Cambridge, where he was senior optime 1833. A Magistrate and Dept.-Lieut. of Yorkshire. A Conservative, and a supporter generally of Lord Derby's policy. First returned for Launceston in July 1852 and sat until he retired in 1859. Died 25 June 1881. [1858]

PERCY, Rt. Hon. Earl. 25 Grosvenor Square, London. Eld. son of the Duke of Northumberland, by Louisa, eld. d. and co-heir of Henry Drummond, Esq., of Albury Park, Surrey. B. in Charles Street, Berkeley Square, London, 1846; m. 1868, Lady Edith, d. of the 8th Duke of Argyll. Educ. at Oxford. Was Treasurer of the Queen's Household from Feb. 1874 to Dec. 1875. Lieut.-Col. of the 3rd battalion Northumberland Fusiliers, and of the 2nd Northumberland (Percy) Artillery Volunteers. A Conservative, sat for Northumberland N. from Dec. 1868 until he was defeated in 1885. Summoned to Lords as Lord Lovaine 1887. Died 14 May 1918. [1885]

PERFECT, Robert. 14 Gloucester Square, Hyde Park, London. Woolstone House, Somersetshire. Reform, and University. Only s. of William Perfect, Esq., M.D. B. 1790; m. 1825, Eliza Harriet, d. of James Strode Butt, Esq. Graduated at Queen's Coll., Oxford, where he was 2nd class in classics 1822. A Dept.-Lieut. and Magistrate for Somerset. Of moderate Whig principles; opposed to the endowment of the Roman Catholic clergy; founded the East Somerset Registration Society in 1841, which added nearly 2800 liberal votes to the register of that county. First returned for Lewes in the early part of 1847, on the retirement of Sir H. Elphinstone; re-chosen at the general election in July 1847 and sat until he retired in 1852. Died 29 July 1875. [1852]

PERKINS, Sir Frederick. Bolton Gardens House, Russell Square, London. City Liberal. 2nd s. of Richard Hopkins Perkins, Esq., of Cumberland House, Southampton. B. at Southampton 1826; m. 1st, d. of A. Abraham, Esq., of Brussels (deceased); 2ndly, Isabella Bloomfield, d. of Joseph Rodney Croskey, Esq., American Consul. A Wine Merchant in Southampton and London. A Magistrate of Southampton, of which town he was five times chosen Mayor. Was Sheriff of London and

Middlesex for 1872-73. A Commissioner of lieutenancy for London. A Liberal, in favour of progressive principles, also of amendment in the system of local taxation. Sat for Southampton from Feb. 1874 until he retired 1880. Died 8 Nov. 1902. [1880]

PERRIN, Rt. Hon. Louis. 15 Abingdon Street, Dublin. One of His Majesty's Sergeants at Law. Of Whig principles, in favour of the extinction of tithes, and the cessation of church rates, and for a repeal of the Union, if justice be not done to Ireland. He sat for a short time in the Parliament of 1831. Was returned for Monaghan in 1832, and for Cashel in Jan. 1835. Accepted Puisne Justice of the King's Bench, Ireland, 31 Aug. 1835; retired 1860. Died 7 Dec. 1864. [1835]

PERRY, Sir Thomas Erskine. 36 Eaton Place, London. West Court, Wokingham. Brooks's, and Athenaeum. 2nd s. of James Perry, Esq. Proprietor of the *Morning Chronicle* Newspaper, by Anne, d. of John Hull, Esq. B. 1807; m. 1st, 1833, Louisa, only child of James McElkiney, Esq., of Brighton and niece maternally of Mademoiselle Jerome Bonaparte, (she died 1841); 2ndly, 1855, Elizabeth Margaret, 2nd d. of Sir John V.B. Johnstone, Bart. Educ. at Trinity Coll., Cambridge, where he graduated B.A. 1829. Called to the bar at Inner Temple 1834 and joined the Home Circuit. Was appointed a Judge of the Supreme Court at Bombay 1841, and made Chief Justice there, Sept. 1847; resigned 1852. Appointed Lieut. in the 2nd Middlesex Rifle Militia 1854. A Liberal, in favour of the ballot but opposed to short Parliaments. Unsuccessfully contested Chatham Dec. 1832, Maidstone July 1837 and Liverpool July 1853. First elected for Devonport May 1854 and sat until appointed member of the Council of India 1858. [1859]

PETER, William. 19 College Street, Westminster, London. Harlyn, Cornwall. B. 1785; m. 1809, Frances, only child of John Thomas, Esq., of Chiverton, Cornwall. Of Whig principles, decidedly opposed to the East India monopoly, but in favour of corn laws. Sat for Bodmin from 1832. Retired in 1835. British Consul in Pennsylvania and New Jersey 1841 until his death 6 Feb. 1853. [1833]

PETO, Sir Samuel Morton, Bart. 13 Kensington Palace Gardens, London. Chipstead, Sevenoaks, Kent. Auchlyne, Killin, Perthshire. Reform. S. of William Peto, Esq., Cookham, Berkshire, by the d. of Ralph Alloway, Esq., of Dorking, Surrey. B. at Woking, 1809; m. 1st, 1831, his cousin Mary, eld. d. of Thomas De la Garde Grissel, Esq., of Stockwell Common,

Surrey (she died May, 1842); 2ndly, 1843, eld. d. of Henry Kelsall, Esq., of Rochdale, Lancashire. A member of the firm of Peto and Betts, Contractors for Public Works. Constructed the Crimean railway without profit to himself in 1855, and for his services was made a Bart. A. Magistrate and Dept.-Lieut. for Suffolk, and a Magistrate for Norfolk and Middlesex. A Liberal, in favour of the extension of the franchise to the working classes, vote by ballot, and 'complete religious freedom to every denomination'. Sat for Norwich from July 1847 till Dec. 1854; for Finsbury from May 1859 till July 1865, when he was elected for Bristol. Accepted Chiltern Hundreds Apr. (?) 1868. His firm, Peto and Betts & Co., suspended payment 11 May 1868. Died 13 Nov. 1889. [1867]

PETRE, Hon. Edward Robert. 9 South Audley Street, London. York. S. of the 9th Lord Petre. M. in 1829, Laura, d. of George Lord Stafford, uncle of Lord Petre; had been Lord Mayor of York, and Sheriff of the Co. A Reformer, in general a supporter of the Administration; in favour of free trade, of the immediate abolition of slavery, the substitution of a property for the house and window tax, and the abolition of all monopolies; was opposed to the General Registry Bill. Sat for Ilchester in 1831. Sat for York from 1832. Retired in 1835. Contested Bridport July 1847. Died 8 June 1848. [1833]

PEVENSEY, Visct. 20 Portland Place, London. Sheffield Park, Uckfield, Sussex. Carlton. Eld. s. of the 2nd Earl of Sheffield, by Lady Harriet, eld. d. of the 2nd Earl of Harewood. B. in Portland Place, London 1832. Appointed Attaché to the British legation at Copenhagen Apr. 1852; attached to the embassy at Constantinople from Feb. 1853-Oct. 1856. Appointed a Dept.-Lieut. of Sussex 1853. A Conservative, said he would 'use his best endeavours to obtain a repeal of the Maynooth Grant', a repeal of the hop duty, and reduction of the income tax; in favour of an 'adjustment of electoral privileges', and an 'equitable arrangement' of Church questions. First returned for E. Sussex on a vacancy early in Mar. 1857, and was re-chosen at the general election in Apr. 1857 and sat until he retired 1865. Succeeded as 3rd Earl Apr. 1876. Died 21 Apr. 1909. [1865]

PEYTON, Henry. 19 Grosvenor Place, London. Stratton Hall, Oxfordshire. Boodle's, and Crockford's. Eld. and only surviving s. of Sir Henry Peyton, Bart. B. 30 June 1803; m. 10 Apr. 1827, Georgiana Elizabeth, 3rd d. of C.B. Codrington, Esq. Capt. of the Woodstock troop of Yeomanry, and a Magistrate for the Counties of Oxford and Buckinghamshire. Was 'an earnest Conservative.' First elected for Woodstock in July

1837. Accepted Chiltern Hundreds 1838. Succeeded as 3rd Bart. Feb. 1854. Died 18 Feb. 1866.   [1838]

PHILIPPS, J.H. See SCOURFIELD, Sir J.H.

PHILIPPS, Sir Richard Bulkeley Philipps, Bart. 169 New Bond Street, London. Picton Castle, Pembrokeshire. Brooks's, Boodle's, and United Service. B. 1801; m. d. of J. Gordon, Esq., of Hanwell, Middlesex. Succeeded to the estates of Lord Milford. Lord Lieut. and Cust. Rot. of the County of the town of Haverfordwest and patron of several livings. Was formerly member for Haverfordwest in five Parliaments. Of Whig opinions, but not pledged. Voted for the Reform Bill. Formerly voted against the abolition of the Corn Laws, but in 1846 supported their repeal. Elected for Haverfordwest 10 Dec. 1832. Did not contest the election in 1835. Sat for it again in 1837 until he retired in 1847. Created Baron Milford (U.K. Peerage) Sept. 1847. Died 3 Jan. 1857.   [1847]

PHILIPS, Sir George Richard, Bart. 12 Hill Street, Berkeley Square, London. Weston House, Oxfordshire. Reform, and United University. Only s. of Sir George Philips, Bart., former MP for Warwickshire, by the eld. d. of Nathaniel Philips, Esq., of Hollinghurst, Lancashire. B. 1789; m. 1819, the Hon. Sarah Georgiana, eld. d. of the 2nd, and sister of the 3rd Lord Waterpark. A Whig. Represented Steyning from 1820 to 1832, elected for Warwickshire S. Dec. 1832 and Kidderminster from 1835 to 1837, and Poole from the latter date until he retired in 1852. Died 22 Feb. 1883.   [1852]

PHILIPS, Mark. The Park, Lancashire. Snitterfield, Warwickshire. Brooks's, Windham, and Reform. Eld. s. of Robert Philips, Esq., of The Park, Lancashire, and of Snitterfield Park, Warwickshire. B. 1800. A Merchant and Manufacturer. A Reformer, in favour of the vote by ballot, triennial Parliaments, and free trade. Sat for Manchester from 1832 until he retired in 1847. Sheriff of Warwickshire 1851. Died 23 Dec. 1873.   [1847]

PHILIPS, Robert Needham. 47 Berkeley Square, London. The Park, Nr. Manchester. Welcombe, Stratford-On-Avon, Warwickshire. Brooks's, Athenaeum, Devonshire, and Reform. Youngest s. of Robert Philips, Esq., of The Park, Manchester. B. at The Park, near Manchester, 1815; m. 1st, Anna Maria, d. of Joseph Brook Yates, Esq., of West Dingle, Liverpool; 2ndly, Mary Ellen, d. of John Ashton Yeats, Esq., of Bryanston Square, London. Educ. at Rugby and

at Manchester Coll. A Merchant and Manufacturer at Manchester. A Magistrate and Dept.-Lieut. for the counties of Lancaster and Warwick. High Sheriff of Lancashire 1856. An 'advanced Liberal'. Sat For Bury from Apr. 1857 till Apr. 1859; re-elected there July 1865 and sat until he retired in 1885. Died 28 Feb. 1890. [1885]

PHILLIMORE, John George. 21 Chester Square, London. 11 Old Square, Lincoln's Inn, London. Senior University, and Brooks's. Eld. s. of Joseph Phillimore, Esq., D.C.L., of Shiplake House, Oxfordshire (Chancellor of Worcester, Oxford and Bristol, etc.), by Elizabeth, d. of the Rev. Walter Bagot, of Blithfield, Staffordshire, who was bro. of the 1st Lord Bagot. B. 1809; m. Rosalind Margaret, youngest d. of Lord Justice Knight Bruce. Educ. at Westminster and at Christ Church, Oxford (of which he was Faculty Student). Graduated B.A. 1828, M.A. 1831. Called to the bar at Lincoln's Inn 1832, and joined the Oxford circuit; appointed Reader on civil law and jurisprudence to the Middle Temple Jan. 1850; Queen's Counsel June 1851. Reader on constitutional law and legal history by delegates from all the Inns of Court, June 1852; Bencher of Lincoln's Inn Nov. 1850. Author of an *Introduction to the Study and History of Roman Law*, *History of the Law of Evidence*, several pamphlets on Law Reform etc. A Liberal, in favour of extension of the suffrage, vote by ballot, the abolition of Church rates, and an extensive law reform; opposed to maintaining Maynooth as an exclusively ecclesiastical place of education, but would also reform thoroughly the Irish Church. First returned for Leominster July 1852. Retired 1857. Died 27 Apr. 1865.   [1857]

PHILLIMORE, Rt. Hon. Sir Robert Joseph. 5 Arlington Street, Piccadilly, London. Oxford & Cambridge. 2nd s. of Joseph Phillimore, Esq., D.C.L., of Shiplake House, Oxfordshire, by Elizabeth, d. of Rev. Walter Bagot, of Blithfield, Staffordshire. M. Charlotte, 3rd d. of John Denison, Esq., of Ossington Hall, Nottinghamshire. Educ. at Westminster, where he was King's Scholar, and at Christ Church Coll., Oxford, where he was 2nd class in classics 1831, and gained the college prizes for Latin verse and Latin prose, graduated D.C.L. 1838. Admitted an advocate at Doctors' Commons 1839, and called to the bar at the Middle Temple 1841. Chancellor of Chichester and Salisbury. Author of *Two Letters to Lord Ashburton on International Law*, respecting ships, and *Letter to Mr. Gladstone*, on the same subject, also *Memoirs and Correspondence of George Lord Lyttelton*; published also *Thoughts on the Law of Divorce*, and other legal works. A Liberal-Conservative, voted for inquiry into Maynooth, but voted against Mr. Spooner's motion 1853. Was an unsuccessful candidate for Tavistock July 1847, Apr. 1852, and July 1852, but was seated on petition Feb. 1853 without a new election. Retired 1857. Contested Coventry Mar. 1857. Dean of Court of Arches 1867-75, Judge Aug. 1867. Created Bart. Dec. 1881. Member of several royal commissions. Died 4 Feb. 1885. [1857]

PHILLIPS, Charles March. 44 Piccadilly, London. Garrendon Park, Leicestershire. Bro. of S.M. Phillips, Esq. Under Secretary of State for the Home Dept. A Reformer, in favour of a revision of the corn laws, the vote by ballot, and triennial Parliaments; was opposed to the admission of Dissenters to the Universities. Sat for Leicestershire N. in the Parliament of 1818, lost his seat in 1820, but regained it in 1831 and sat until he retired in Aug. 1837. [1836]

PHILLIPS, George Lort. 6 Montagu Square, London. Lawrenny Park, and Ashdale, Pembrokeshire. Carlton, and Boodle's. Eld. s. of John Lort Phillips, Esq., of Lawrenny, by Augusta, d. of William Ilbert, Esq., of Bowrings Lee, and Horsewell, Devon. B. 1811; m. 1841, Isabella Georgiana, only d. of John Hensleigh Allen, Esq., of Creselly, former MP for Pembroke. Educ. at Harrow School, and at Trinity Coll., Cambridge. A Magistrate and Dept.-Lieut. for Pembrokeshire. Was High Sheriff of Pembroke 1843. Patron of 2 livings. A Conservative, in favour of keeping up 'a strong naval and military force in the country.' First elected for Pembrokeshire Jan. 1861. MP until his death 30 Oct. 1866.
[1865 2nd ed.]

PHILLPOTTS, John. 1 New Square, Lincoln's Inn, London. Gloucestershire. Parthenon Club. Eld. s. of John Phillpotts, Esq., of Gloucester, and bro. of the Bishop of Exeter. B. July 1775; m. 1797, d. of Thomas Chandler, Esq., of Ashcroft House, Gloucestershire. Was a Solicitor in Gloucester from 1795-1820. Called to the bar in 1822. Held the appointment of Registrar of the Dean and Chapter of Gloucester till called to the bar. An active member of the Corporation of Gloucester, and Mayor in 1819. Author of *Thoughts on the Church Establishment* published in 1832. Was 'a supporter of liberal principles during his whole life.' Voted for the ballot, and for the repeal of the Septennial Act. Was elected for Gloucester in 1830 and 1832; he was defeated in 1835. He regained the seat 24 July 1837 and sat until he retired in 1847. [1847]

PHINN, Thomas. Hall-Staircase, Inner Temple, London. 41 St. James's Street, London. Brooks's, and Reform. B. at Bath 1814, the s. of Thomas Phinn, of Bath, Surgeon, by Caroline, d. of Richard Bignell, Esq., of Banbury. Unmarried. Educ. at Eton and at Exeter Coll., Oxford, where he was 1st class in classics 1837. Was called to the bar at the Inner Temple in 1840 and joined the Western Circuit. Appointed Recorder of Portsmouth July 1848, transferred to Devonport in Dec. 1851. Appointed Counsel for the Admiralty 1854, and made a Queen's Counsel in that year, with a patent of precedence. A Liberal, in favour of household suffrage, vote by ballot, and the fullest development of free-trade principles. Voted for inquiry into Maynooth, jointly with other ecclesiastical establishments of Ireland. Sat for Bath from July 1852 until he accepted Chiltern Hundreds on his appointment as 2nd Secretary to the Admiralty in May 1855. Resigned in Apr. 1857. Contested Bath in 1859, and Devonport in 1865. Died 31 Oct. 1866. [1855]

PHIPPS, Charles Nicholas Paul. 5 St. James's Place, London. Chalcot, Westbury, Wiltshire. Carlton, Arthur's, and St. James's. Eld. s. of Charles Paul Phipps, Esq., of Chalcot, Westbury, Wiltshire, who sat for Westbury from 1868 to 1874, by Emma Mary, youngest d. of M. Benson, Esq., of Liverpool. B. 1845; m. 1874, Clare Emily, 3rd d. of Sir Frederick Hervey-Bathurst, Bart. Educ. at Eton. A Magistrate for Wiltshire, and a Lieut. Wiltshire Yeomanry Cavalry. A Conservative. Sat for Westbury from Apr. 1880 until he retired in 1885. Died 9 Dec. 1913. [1885]

PHIPPS, Charles Paul. Chalcot, Westbury, Wiltshire. Carlton, and Conservative. B. at Leighton, near Westbury, Wiltshire, 1815, the youngest s. of T.H.H. Phipps, of Leighton, by Mary, d. and co-heir of W. Leckonby, of Hothershall, Lancashire. M. 1844, d. of M. Benson, Esq., of Liverpool. Was a Merchant at Liverpool. A Magistrate for Wiltshire. A Liberal-Conservative, in favour of a reduction of the public expenditure. Sat for Westbury from Feb. 1869 until 1874, when he was defeated. Died 8 June 1880. [1873]

PHIPPS, J.L. A Conservative. First elected for Westbury 18 Nov. 1868, but on petition the election was declared void and he did not stand at the subsequent election on 27 Feb. 1869.

PHIPPS, Pickering. 46 Kensington Park Gardens, London. Collingtree Grange, Northampton. Carlton. S. of Edward Phipps, Esq., of Northampton, by Elizabeth, d. of St. John Outlaw, Esq., of Irthingboro', Northamptonshire. B. at Northampton 1827; m. 1850, Mary Ann, d. of John Whitmy, Esq., of Northampton. Managing Director of P. Phipps and Co., Northampton and Towcester, Brewers; a Director of the Northamptonshire Banking Co., and of the County Fire Office. Twice served the office of Mayor of Northampton. Patron of 1 living. A Conservative, endeavoured 'to Maintain intact the valued institutions of the country.' Sat for Northampton bor. from Feb. 1874 to Mar. 1880. Sat for Northamptonshire S. from Feb. 1881 until defeated in 1885 contesting the Midland division of Northamptonshire. Died 14 Sept. 1890. [1885]

PICTON, J.A. Continued in House after 1885: full entry in Volume II.

PIGOT, Rt. Hon. David Richard. Reform. Was called to the bar in 1826 and appointed Solicitor General for Ireland in 1839. Attorney-Gen. for Ireland in 1840. Resigned in 1841. Was one of the Visitors of Maynooth College. A Bencher of King's Inns, Dublin. A Reformer, voted against the Corn Laws. Sat for Clonmel from 1839 until he was appointed Lord Chief Baron of Exchequer (Ireland) on 1st Sept. 1846. Died 22 Dec. 1873. [1845]

PIGOT, Sir Robert, Bart. 15a, Hill Street. Patshull, Staffordshire. Eld. s. of Sir G. Pigot, 3rd Bart., by the d. of the Hon. John Monckton. B. at Patshull 1801; m. 1st, d. of W. Bamford, Esq., (died); 2ndly, 1850, Emily, eld. d. of S.Y. Benyon, Esq., of Ash Hall, Shropshire and Stechworth Park, Cambridgeshire. Dept.-Lieut. of Staffordshire. A Conservative, voted for agricultural protection, 1846. Sat for Bridgnorth from 1832 until unseated for bribery in Mar. 1853. Died 1 June 1891. [1852 2nd ed.]

PIGOTT, Francis. 110 Gloucester Place, London. Heckfield Heath, Hartfordbridge, Hampshire. Reform, and Brooks's. Eld. s. of Paynton Pigott Stainsby Conant, Esq., of Archer Lodge, Hampshire, and Banbury, Oxfordshire, (who traced his descent from Pigott Baron of Boorne, in Normandy, one of the forty Knights who accompanied William the Conqueror to England.) B. at Trunkwell House, Berkshire 1809; m. 1833, Frances Phillips, 2nd d. of Lieut.-Gen. Sir Francis John Connor Wilder, of the Manor House, Binfield, Berkshire, formerly member for Arundel. Educ. at Eton, and at Lincoln Coll., Oxford. A Magistrate of Hampshire, and Lieut. of the North Hants. Yeomanry Cavalry. A Liberal, opposed to all State endowments for religious purposes, voted for the ballot 1853, and against church rates 1855. Unsuccessfully contested Winchester in 1841. First returned for Reading in 1847 and sat until appointed Governor of the Isle of Man Oct. 1860. Died 21 Jan. 1863. [1860]

PIGOTT, Gillery. 120 Gloucester Terrace, Hyde Park, London. Sherfield Hill House, Basingstoke, Hampshire. Reform. S. of Paynton Pigott Stainsby Conant, Esq., of Archer Lodge, Hampshire, and Banbury, Oxfordshire, by Lucy, d. of Richard Drope Gough, Esq. B. at Oxford 1813; m. 1836, Frances, only d. of Thomas Drake, Esq., of Ashday Hall, near Halifax. Educ. under the Rev. W. Carmalt at Putney. Was called to the bar at the Middle Temple 1839, made a Serjeant-at-Law 1856, and granted a patent of precedence 1857. Recorder of Hereford, and joined the Oxford circuit. Of Liberal opinions, in favour of the Ballot, and a 'moderate and progressive extension of the suffrage.' First elected for Reading, Oct. 1860 and sat until appointed Judge 2 Oct. 1863 and knighted. Died 28 Apr. 1875. [1863]

PILKINGTON, James. Park Place House, Blackburn, Lancashire. Swinethwaite Hall, N. Riding of Yorkshire. Reform. B. at Blackburn 1804; m. 1831. A Merchant and Cotton Manufacturer. A Magistrate and Dept.-Lieut. for Lancashire. Director of the Lancashire and Yorkshire Railway. A 'decided Reformer', voted for the ballot 1853, and in favour of a re-distribution of seats; opposed to all religious endowments. First returned for Blackburn in 1847 and sat until defeated 1865. Died 17 Feb. 1890. [1865]

PIM, Bedford Clapperton Trevelyan. 2 Crown Office Row, Temple, London. Leaside, Upper Norwood, Surrey. Senior and Junior United Service, City Carlton, and St. Stephen's. Only s. of Capt. Edward Bedford Pim of Weirhead, Exeter (who died in command of H.M.S. 'Black Joke'), by Sophia Soltan, eld. d. of T.F. Harrison, Esq., of Totnes. B. at Bideford 1826; m. 1861, eld. d. of Henry Locock, Esq., of Blackheath. Educ. at the Royal Naval School. Entered the navy July 1842, became Lieut. Oct. 1850, Commander Apr. 1858, and Capt. Apr. 1868. Was employed for some years in the surveying service, and afterwards made a voyage round the world in H.M.S. 'Herald' from 1845-1851, when he was engaged in the search for Sir John Franklin; served in the Russian War, for which he received a medal; also in China (where he was severely wounded in six places), the West Indies, and on the Cape of Good Hope station. Called to the bar at the Inner Temple Jan. 1873; a Magistrate for Middlesex. Author of *The Gate of the Pacific, Dottings on the Road Side, Feudal Tenures*, and various pamphlets. A Conservative. Unsuccessfully contested Totnes July 1865, and Gravesend Dec. 1868. Sat for Gravesend from Feb. 1874 until he retired 1880. Died 30 Sept. 1886. [1880]

PIM, Jonathan. 22 William Street, Dublin.

Greenbank, Monkstown, Co. Durham. B. in Dublin 1806, s. of Thomas Pim, of Dublin. M. 1828, Susan, d. of John Todhunter, of Dublin, Merchant (she died 1868). A Merchant and Manufacturer in Dublin. Published in 1848 *The Condition and Prospects of Ireland,* and in 1852, *Report of the Transactions of the Relief Committee of the Society of Friends.* A Liberal, but voted against Lord Russell's Reform Bill, 1866, and for the disestablishment of the Irish Church 1869. Sat for Dublin City from July 1865 until 1874, when he was defeated. Died 6 July 1885.   [1873]

PINNEY, William. 30 Berkeley Square, London. Somerton Erle, Somerset. Reform, Travellers', Arthur's, and Brooks's. Only s. of John Frederick Pinney, Esq., of Somerton Erle, Somersetshire, by the only d. of William Dickinson, Esq. The name of Pinney was assumed by his grandfather, in lieu of his patronymic, Pretor in 1740. B. 1806. Graduated at Trinity Coll., Cambridge, M.A. 1833. A Magistrate for Somerset and Dorset, and a Dept.-Lieut. of the former Co., Major of the W Somerset Yeomanry Cavalry, and Col. of the W. Somerset Militia. A Liberal, in favour of 'progressive reform', voted for the ballot 1853. Sat for Lyme Regis from 1832-1842, when he was unseated on petition. Sat for Somerset E. from Apr. 1847-July 1852, when he was again elected for Lyme Regis and sat until he retired 1865. Contested E. Somerset again in 1868. Died 30 May 1898.   [1865]

PLANTA, Rt. Hon. Joseph, G.C.H. Fairlight Place, Sussex. Travellers', and Carlton. B. 1 July 1787. M. 1831 the widow of Thomas Oom, of Bedford Square. Was brought up in the Foreign Office, and was Under Secretary for Foreign Affairs for nearly 10 years. Attended the 2nd Lord Londonderry at the Congresses of Paris, Vienna and Aix la Chapelle. Was joint Secretary of the Treasury for $3\frac{1}{2}$ years until his retirement in Nov. 1830. Was created G.C.H. by H.M. the King of Hanover, immediately on his accession, in fulfillment of a promise of King William IV, given a short time before his death. A firm Conservative. Sat for Hastings previously to the passing of the Reform Bill. Accepted Chiltern Hundreds Feb. 1844.   [1844]

PLATT, James. Hartford House, Nr. Oldham. Ashway Gap, Saddleworth, Yorkshire. B. at Oldham 1823, the s. of Henry Platt, and Sarah his wife. M. 1847, Lucy Mary, d. of Andrew Scholefield, of Woodfield, a Magistrate for Lancashire. a Partner in the firm Platt Brothers, and Co., Engineers and Machinists, Oldham. A Liberal, favoured the 'widest extension' of the Suffrage, the ballot, and shorter Parliaments. Op-

posed any interference with the law, as it then existed, respecting factory labour. Supported Lord Palmerston's foreign policy. Sat for Oldham from Apr. 1857 until his death on 27 Aug. 1857.
       [1857 2nd ed.]

PLATT, John. Hemeth Park, Oldham. S. of Henry Platt, Esq., of Oldham, Mechanical Engineer, by Sarah, his wife. B. at Saddleworth, Yorkshire; m. 1842 d. of Samuel Radcliffe, Esq., of Oldham. Educ. at Durham Massey, Cheshire. A Magistrate for Lancashire was twice chosen Mayor of Oldham. High Sheriff of Carnarvonshire 1863. An 'advanced Liberal', and in favour of short Parliaments, the total abolition of Church rates, and all oaths, tests and religious disqualifications. First elected for Oldham July 1865. MP until his death 18 May 1872.   [1872]

PLAYFAIR, Rt. Hon. Sir L. Continued in House after 1885: full entry in Volume II.

PLIMSOLL, Samuel. 28 Park Lane, London S of Thomas Plimsoll, Esq., of Plymouth, and afterwards of Sheffield, by Priscilla, d. of Josias Willing, Esq., of Plymstock, Devon. B. at Bristol, 1824; m. 1857, Eliza, d. of Hugh Railton, Esq., of Staindrop, Northumberland. Educ. privately under Dr. S. Eadon, M.A., M.D. A Coal Merchant and author of pamphlets of the *Export Coal Trade of England* and *The Inland Coal Trade* (1862), etc. Was one of the Hon Secretaries of the Great Exhibition 1851. An advanced Liberal, voted for the disestablishment of the Church in Ireland 1869, in favour of a system of arbitration to ensure the 'Rights of Workmen', and of some plan being adopted to have 'fatherless and motherless children specially cared for', instead of being consigned to the work-house. Unsuccessfully contested Derby 1865; first elected for Derby Dec. 1868 and sat until he accepted Chiltern Hundreds May 1880. Contested Liverpool 1880 and Sheffield Central 1885. Died 3 June 1898. [1880]

PLOWDEN, William Henry Chicheley, F.R.S. 8 Devonshire Place, Portland Place, London. Carlton, Travellers', Union, and City of London. S. of Richard Chichely Plowden, Esq., many years an East India Director. B. 1790; m. 1st, 1818, d. of William Harding, Esq., of Baraset, Warwickshire; 2ndly, 1830, d. of Edward Campbell, Esq., and niece of Sir Robert Campbell, Bart. Educ. at Westminster. Was for many years in the civil service of the E.I.C.; appointed in 1833 Second Superintendent of British Trade in China. A Director of the E.I.C. A Magistrate and Dept.-Lieut. of Middlesex; a member of the Royal Asiatic Society, and Director of the Globe Insurance Office. A Conservative, opposed any concessions to the Roman Catholic Clergy. Unsuccessfully contested Nottingham in 1837. First elected for Newport, Isle of Wight in 1847 and sat until defeated in 1852. Died 29 Mar. 1880.   [1852]

PLUMPTRE, John Pemberton. Fredville House, Kent. National, and United University. B. in 1791, the eld. s. of John Plumptre, Esq., of Fredville and of Nottingham, and nephew of Sir Richard Carr Glyn, Bart. M. 1818, Catherine, 4th d. of Paul Cobb Methuen Esq., of Corsham. Patron of 3 livings. A Dept.-Lieut. of Kent. Was called to the bar, but practised only for a very short time. A Conservative, voted for agricultural protection 1846, and against the emancipation of Jews. Seconded Mr. Finch's motion of June 1833 against political unions. Sat for Kent E. from 1832 until he accepted Chiltern Hundreds in Feb. 1852. Died 7 Jan 1864.   [1851]

PLUMRIDGE, James Hanway. 66 Chester Square, London. Ardwenack House, Cornwall. A Capt. R.N. Was Storekeeper of the Ordnance. Was Superintendent of the Packet Station at Falmouth. A Liberal. First returned for Penryn and Falmouth in 1841, having been an unsuccessful candidate at the election in 1837 and sat until he retired in 1847. Second in Command on East Indies Station 1847-50. Commanded Baltic Flaying Squadron 1854-55. K.C.B. July 1855. Died 29 Nov. 1863.   [1847]

PLUNKET, Hon. D.R. Continued in House after 1885: full entry in Volume II.

PLUNKET, Hon. Randall. St. James's Hotel, Jermyn Street, London. Dunsany Castle, Meath. Carlton. Eld. s. of Lord Dunsany and nephew of Lord Cloncurry. B. 1804. Contested Drogheda in Dec. 1834, and was defeated by A.C. O'Dwyer, Esq., the old member, who, however, was unseated by the decision of a Committee for want of qualification. Sat for Drogheda from Apr. 1835 until he retired in 1837. Succeeded as 15th Baron Dunsany Dec. 1848. Died 7 Apr. 1852.   [1837]

PLUNKETT, Hon. Randal Edward Sherborne. 24 Pall Mall, London. Dunsany Castle, Navan, Ireland. Carlton, and Junior Oxford & Cambridge. Eld. s. of Lord Dunsany, by Hon. Anne Constance, 3rd d. of the 2nd Lord Sherborne. B. at Sherborne Park 1848. Educ. at Eton and at Christ Church, Oxford. A Conservative. Sat for Gloucestershire W. from Feb. 1874 until he retired 1880. Died 25 Dec. 1883.   [1880]

POCHIN, Henry Davis. Broughton Old Hall, Manchester. The Clarendon Club, Manchester.

S. of William Pochin, Esq., of Wigston, Leicestershire, by his m. with Miss Elizabeth Hirst. B. 1824 at Wigston. M. 1852, Agnes, youngest d. of George Gretton Heap, Esq., of Manchester. Was largely concerned in the Coal and Iron trades and was an Alderman of Salford, of which town he was twice Mayor in 1866-67 and 1867-68. Published in 1866 *A Plan of Parliamentary Reform*, advocating the claims of the working classes. A Liberal, who was 'heartily in favour of a more perfect system of education', also of the complete disestablishment of the Irish Church, the reduction of public expenditure, 'especially in the navy', and creation of life-peerages, and opposed every form of protection either in trade or agriculture, whether in the form of orders in Council or otherwise. Sat for Stafford from Dec. 1868 until he was unseated in Mar. 1869. Contested Stafford in Feb. 1874 and Monmouth in same month. Died 28 Oct. 1895.   [1869]

POLHILL, Frederick. Cowbury Park, Bedfordshire. Carlton, and Junior United Service. Grand-s. of the eminent Southwark Tobacconist, and 2nd s. of John Polhill, Esq., of Howbury Park. B. 1798; m. 1824, Frances Margaretta, d. of John Deakin, Esq., of Bagthorpe House, Nottinghamshire. A Capt in the army, and patron of 1 living. Was for some time lessee of Drury Lane Theatre. A Conservative, but in favour of free trade. Sat for Bedford in 1830 and 1831; unsuccessfully contested Bedford in 1832, and represented it from 1835 until defeated in 1847. Died 1848.   [1847]

POLHILL-TURNER, Frederick Charles. See TURNER, Frederick Charles Polhill-.

POLLEN, Sir John Walter, Bart. Readenham, Hampshire. Carlton. B. 1784; m. 1819 Charlotte Elizabeth, D. of the Rev. John Craven, of Craven. Some member of the Pollen family had sat for Andover nearly 200 years. A Conservative. Sat for Andover in several parliaments previous to 1831, when, as well as in 1832, two Reformers were returned without opposition. Was re-elected in 1835 (in opposition to Mr. Nightingale, who stood the first contest the borough had witnessed for many years) and sat for Andover until defeated in 1841. Died London 2 May 1863.   [1840]

POLLINGTON, Visct. 2 Bolton Row, London. Carlton. Eld. s. of the Earl of Mexborough. B. 1810; m. 1842, Lady Rachel Catherine, d. of 3rd Earl of Oxford (she was born 1825), A Conservative, voted for agricultural protection, 1846. First returned for Pontefract in 1835 and sat until he retired in 1847. Succeeded as 4th Earl Dec.

1860. Died 17 Aug. 1899.   [1847]

POLLOCK, Sir Frederick. Queen Square House, Guildford Street, London. Twisden Buildings, Temple, London. Carlton, and Athenaeum. B. 1783, bro. to General Sir Geo. Pollock, G.C.B. M. 1st, Miss Rivers; 2ndly, d. of Capt. R. Langslow, of Hatton. A Director of the University Life Assurance Company. Attorney Gen. Dec. 1834-Apr. 1835 and reappointed Sept. 1841. Was Senior Wrangler at Cambridge. A Conservative. Sat for Huntingdon from 1831 until he was appointed Chief Baron of the Exchequer, Apr. 1844. Created Bart. July 1866. Died 23 Aug. 1870.   [1844]

PONSONBY, Hon. Ashley George John. 9 Prince's Gardens, Prince's Gate, London. Hatherop Castle, Fairford. Brooks's, Travellers', and Army & Navy. Youngest s. of the 1st Lord de Mauley, by Lady Barbara, only child of the 5th Earl of Shaftesbury. B. 1831; m. 1857, Louisa Frances Charlotte, 2nd d. of Lord Henry Gordon, niece to the 10th Marq. of Huntly, and maid of honour to the Queen. Appointed Lieut. and Capt. Grenadier Guards 1854. Served in the Crimea, and retired 1855. A Magistrate and Dept.-Lieut. of Gloucestershire. Of Whig principles, in favour of a moderate extension of the franchise; voted for the ballot of 1853, and supported Lord Palmerston on the vote of censure 1864. Sat for Cirencester from July 1852-Apr. 1857, when he was unsuccessful; regained his seat in May 1859 and sat until July 1865 when he unsuccessfully contested Stroud. Contested Cirencester again 13 Mar. 1878. Member of L.C.C. 1895. Died 12 Jan. 1898.   [1865]

PONSONBY, Hon. Charles Frederick Ashley Cooper. 21 St. James's Place, London. Eld. s. of 1st Lord De Mauley by the only d. of 5th Earl of Shaftesbury. B. in George Street, Hanover Square, London 1815; m. 1838, his cousin, Lady Maria, 4th d. of 4th Earl of Bessborough. A Whig, formerly voted against the corn laws. Sat for Poole from 1837 till the general election 1847; first returned for Dungarvon Mar. 1851. Retired in 1852. Succeeded as 2nd Baron De Mauley May 1855. Died 24 Aug. 1896.   [1852]

PONSONBY, Hon. J.G.B. See DUNCANNON, Lord.

PONSONBY, Hon. William Francis Spencer. 50 Portland Place, London. Hanford House, Dorset. 3rd s. of the Earl of Besborough. B. 1787; m. 1814, Lady Barbara Ashley Cooper, only d. and sole heiress of Anthony, 5th Earl of Shaftesbury. Of Whig principles. Patron of 1 liv-

ing. Sat for Poole in the Parliaments of 1826 and 1830, and for Knaresborough in that of 1831. Sat for Dorsetshire from 1832 until he retired in 1837. Created Baron De Mauley in 1838. Died 16 May 1855.   [1837]

PORTAL, Melville. 12 King Street, St. James's, London. Laverstoke House and Freefolk Priors, Hampshire. Carlton. S. of John Portal, Esq., of Freefolk Priors, Hampshire, by the d. of Henry Drummond, Esq., of the Grange, Hampshire. B. 1819; m. 1855, Lady Charlotte, d. of 2nd Earl of Minto. Educ. at Harrow School, and at Christ Church, Oxford, where he graduated M.A. 1844. Called to the bar 1845. Capt. of the N. Hampshire Yeomanry. Patron of 1 living. A Conservative, would 'never vote for the extension or increase' of the Maynooth Grant. First returned for Hampshire N. Apr. 1849 and sat until he retired 1857.   [1857]

PORTER, Rt. Hon. Andrew Marshall. Irish Office, London. 42 Merrion Square East, Dublin. Nessan's Howth, Co. Dublin. Reform, Stephen's Green, Dublin. Eld. s. of the Rev. John Scott Porter, of Belfast, by Margaret, d. of Andrew Marshall, Esq., M.D., of Belfast. B. at Belfast 1837; m. 1869, Agnes Adinston, d. of Lieut.-Col. Horsburgh, of Horsburgh, Peebles-shire. Educ. at the Royal Belfast Institution and Queen's Coll., Belfast. Graduated B.A. Queen's University, Ireland, where he afterwards received the hon. degree of LL.D., elected Barrington Lecturer on Political Economy by competition in 1861. Was called to the bar in Ireland June 1860. Appointed a Queen's Counsel in Ireland 1872, and elected a bencher of King's Inns, Dublin 1878. Was Solicitor Gen. for Ireland from Nov. 1881-Jan. 1883, when he became Attorney-Gen. A Liberal, a 'strenuous supporter of Mr. Gladstone', and regarded the Land Act of 1881 'as the greatest boon ever conferred on Ireland'; was in favour of a reform of the Grand Jury Laws. Sat for Londonderry Co. from Dec. 1881 until appointed Master of the Rolls in Ireland in 1883. [1883]

PORTMAN, E. Berkeley. Of Liberal opinions. Returned for Marylebone in 1832. Accepted Chiltern Hundreds Mar. 1833. Created Baron Portman Jan. 1837. Thrice President of the Royal Agricultural Society. Visct. Portman Mar. 1873. Died 19 Nov. 1888.   [1833]

PORTMAN, Hon. William Henry Berkeley. 22 Portman Square, London. Durweston, Blandford, Dorset. Devonshire, Brooks's, and Travellers'. Eld. s. of the 1st Lord Portman, by the 3rd d. of the 2nd Earl of Harewood. B. in London, 1829; m. 1855, Hon. Mary, only d. of Visct.

315

Milton, and grand-d. of 3rd Earl Fitz-William. Educ. at Eton and at Merton Coll., Oxford. Appointed a Dept.-Lieut. of Somerset 1850, and of Dorset 1852; Lieut.-Col. West - Somerset Yeomanry Cavalry 1852. A Liberal. Sat for Shaftesbury from July 1852 to Mar. 1857, and from that date for Dorset until he retired in 1885. Succeeded as 2nd Visct. Nov. 1888. Died 16 Oct. 1919.   [1885]

POTTER, Edmund, F.R.S. 22 Prince's Gardens, Hyde Park, London. Charlotte Street, Manchester. Reform. B. at Manchester 1802, the s. of James Potter, Merchant of Manchester, by Mary, d. of – Moore, of Lancaster. M. 1829 Jessy, d. of A. Crompton, Esq., of Lancaster. A Calico Printer. President of the Manchester Chamber of Commerce. A Magistrate and Dept.-Lieut. of Derbyshire. Author of *Essays on Calico Printing, Trades Unions etc..* A Liberal, in favour of the total abolition of Church rates. Sat for Carlisle from Nov. 1861 until 1874, when he retired. Died 26 Oct. 1883.   [1873]

POTTER, Sir John. Buile Hill, Manchester. S. of Sir Thomas Potter (who was twice Mayor of Manchester), by his 2nd wife, d. of Thomas Bayley, Esq., of Manchester. B. at Polefield, in Prestwich parish, Lancashire, 1815. Unmarried. Educ. at the University of Edinburgh. A Merchant at Manchester, head of the firm of Potter, Norris, and Co., in George Street. A Magistrate for the bor. of Manchester, and for Lancashire, of which county he was appointed a Dept.-Lieut. in 1851. Was Mayor of Manchester for three successive years, having been first elected in 1848-49. Knighted on the Queen's visit to Manchester in 1851. A Liberal, and a supporter of Lord Palmerston's foreign policy; in favour of household suffrage. First returned for Manchester, Apr. 1857. MP until his death on 25 Oct. 1858.   [1858]

POTTER, Richard. Broughton House, Lancashire. Reform. A sleeping Partner in the firm of Thomas and Richard Potter, of Manchester. Of Whig principles, inclining to radicalism, in favour of removing the Bishops from the House of Lords. Sat for Wigan from 1832 until he accepted Chiltern Hundreds in 1839. Unsuccessfully contested Gloucester in Feb. 1862.   [1838]

POTTER, Robert. 11 Cecil Street, London. 90 St. Stephen's Green S., Dublin. An attorney in Dublin, who managed the defence of William Smith O'Brien, when convicted of treason in 1849. Law agent to the Limerick Corporation. A Liberal, in favour of the repeal of the Ecclesiastical Tithes Act, etc. Voted for the ballot 1853. Sat for Limerick from July 1852 until his death on 1 Oct. 1854.   [1854]

POTTER, T.B. Continued in House after 1885: full entry in Volume II.

POTTS, George. 29 Upper Seymour Street, London. Elm Grove, Nr. Dawlish. Trafalgar House, Barnstaple. Devon & Exeter County Club, Exeter. 2nd s. of William Potts, Esq., of Kelso, Roxburghshire, and London, by Mary, d. of William Bayly, Esq., of Baylys, Devon. B. in London 1807; m. 3rdly, 1847, his cousin, Ellen, d. of James Reed, Esq., of Hampstead, Middlesex. Educ. at Trinity Coll., Cambridge. A Liberal-Conservative, strongly in favour of Lord Derby's policy, and in favour of a moderate measure of Parliamentary Reform. Unsuccessfully contested Barnstaple as a supporter of Lord Palmerston, Apr. 1857. First elected for Barnstaple Apr. 1859. MP until his death in 1863.   [1863]

POULTER, John. 5 King's Bench Walk, Temple. London. The Close, Hampshire. Grands. of Brownlow North, Bishop of Winchester, and s. of the Rev. Edmund Poulter, prebendary of Winchester. A Barrister; Commissary of the Bishop of Winchester for the county of Surrey, and once a Fellow of the New Coll., Oxford. A Reformer, in favour of the ballot and short Parliaments. Sat for Shaftesbury from 1832 until unseated in 1838.   [1837]

POWELL, Caleb. Clonshavoy, Co. Limerick. Eld. s. of Eyre Burton Powell, Esq. B. 1793; m. 1838, d. of George Waller, Esq., of Prior Park, Co. Tipperary. A Barrister. A Liberal, in favour of Church Reform, free trade, an extension of the suffrage, and vote by ballot. First returned for Limerick Co. July 1841 and sat until defeated Aug. 1847.   [1847]

POWELL, F.S. Continued in House after 1885: full entry in Volume II.

POWELL, John Joseph. 3 Pump Court, Temple, London. 10 St. Georges Terrace, Regent's Park, London. Reform. Eld. s. of Thomas Powell, Esq., of Gloucester, by Sarah, eld. d. of Joseph Page, Esq. B. at Gloucester 1816. Unmarried. Was called to the bar at the Middle Temple 1847, and joined the Oxford Circuit. Appointed a Queen's Counsel and elected a bencher of the Middle Temple 1863. Recorder of Wolverhampton May 1864. A Liberal, said he would give a general support to Lord Palmerston's government; voted in favour of the abolition of Church rates, May 1862. First elected for Gloucester Feb. 1862. Retired 1865. Contested same seat in 1874. Contested Weymouth 1868. Died 15 Sept. 1891. [1865]

POWELL, Walter. 63 St. James's Street, London. Eastcourt House, Malmesbury. Carlton, and Conservative. S. of Thomas Powell, Esq., of The Gaer, Newport, Monmouthshire, a Magistrate and Dept.-Lieut. of that Co. B. at The Gaer, Newport 1842. Educated at Rugby. A Magistrate for Wiltshire. A Conservative. Sat for Malmesbury from Dec. 1868. MP until lost in a balloon 10 Dec. 1881. [1881]

POWELL, William Edward. 7 Hyde Park Terrace, London. Nanteos, Cardiganshire. Carlton, Boodle's, United Service, and Albion. B. 1788, the eld. s. of Thomas Powell of Nanteos, by Elinor, d. of Edward Maurice Corbet, of Ynys-y-Maengwyn. M. 1st, 1810, Laura Edwyna, eld. d. of James Sackville Tufton Phelp of Coston House, Leicestershire; 2ndly, 1841, Harriott Dell, widow of Geo. Akers and younger d. of Henry Hutton. Entered the army as Ensign 1811, and retired 1822. Patron of 1 living. Col. of the Cardiganshire Militia, Lord Lieut. and Custos Rot. of the county. A Conservative, voted for agricultural protection 1846. Sat for Cardiganshire from 1816 until he accepted Chiltern Hundreds Jan. 1854. [1854]

POWELL, W.R.H. Continued in House after 1885: full entry in Volume II.

POWELL, William Thomas Rowland. 57 St. George's Road, London. Nanteos, Cardiganshire. United Service, and Junior United Service. Eld. s. of Col. William Edward Powell, Esq., of Nanteos, Cardiganshire (who sat for the Co. from 1816-Feb. 1854), by his 1st wife, Laura Edwyna, eld. d. of James Sackville Tufton Phelp, Esq., of Coston House, Leicestershire. B. at Swansea 1815; m. 1839, Rosa Edwyna, d. of George Cherry, Esq., of Buckland, Herefordshire (she died 1860). Educ. at Westminster. Entered the army as Ensign 1832; retired as Capt. 37th Foot 1839. Appointed Lieut.-Col. Commandant Cardigan Rifle Militia Mar. 1854. A Magistrate and Dept.-Lieut. for Cardiganshire. Patron of 2 livings. A Liberal-Conservative, said he would support 'any sound measure of parliamentary reform', and that he was desirous of seeing the Church rate question 'speedily and finally settled in a manner satisfactory to all classes and denominations of Christians.' First elected for Cardiganshire May 1859 and sat until he retired 1865. [1865]

POWER, Sir James. Edermine House, Enniscorthy, Co. Wexford. Stephen's Green Club, Dublin. Only s. of Sir John Power, 1st Bart. (an eminent Distiller and Alderman of Dublin), by Mary, eld. d. of Thomas Brenan, Esq., of Wexford. B. 1800; m. 1843, Jane Anna Eliza, 2nd d. and co-heir of John Hyacinth Talbot, Esq., former MP for New Ross. Was called to the bar in Ireland. A Dept.-Lieut. and Magistrate for Wexford, and a Magistrate for the city of Dublin. A Liberal. Sat as a Repealer for Wexford Co. 1835-47; re-elected in 1865 as a Liberal. Retired in 1868. Died 30 Sept. 1877. [1867]

POWER, John. Gurteen, and Newtown House, Co. Waterford. Wyndham, Reform, and Brooks's. S. of Edmund Power, Esq., of Gurteen, and step-s. of the Rt. Hon. Richard L. Sheil. B. 4 Feb. 1816. A Reformer, but gave no pledges. First sat in Parliament in Feb. 1837, as a member for Dungarvan. Returned for Waterford Co. without opposition at the gen. election in the same year. Accepted Chiltern Hundreds in 1840. [1840]

POWER, John O'Connor. 5 Kings Bench Walk, Temple, London. S. of Patrick Power, Esq., by his m. with Miss Mary O'Connor of Roscommon, Ireland. B. at Roscommon 1846. Unmarried. Educ. at St. Jarlath's Coll., Tuam, Ireland. Was called to the bar at the Middle Temple Nov. 1881. A Liberal, in favour of a 'system of Home Rule for Ireland, subject to the supreme authority of the Imperial Parliament, and maintaining the unity of the Empire.' Sat for Mayo from June 1874 until he retired in 1885. Contested Kennington division of Lambeth Nov. 1885. Contested W. division of Mayo in July 1892, and Bristol S. July 1895. [1885]

POWER, John Talbot. 27 Merrion Square, N. Dublin. Edermine, Enniscorthy, Wexford. Reform. Eld. s. of Sir James Power, Bart., of Edermine, Enniscorthy, Co. Wexford (who represented the Co. of Wexford from 1835-47, and from 1865-68), by the 2nd d. and co-heir of John Hyacinth Talbot, Esq., former MP for New Ross. B. at Edermine, Enniscorthy, Co. Wexford 1845. Unmarried. Educ. at Downside Coll. A Liberal. Sat for the Co. of Wexford from Dec. 1868 until defeated in 1874. [1873]

POWER, Maurice. Ringacoltig, Cove, Co. Cork. B. at Deelis, West Carbery, Co. Cork in 1811 and was descended from 5th Lord Power, of the Co. of Waterford, and connected with the McCarthys, O'Sullivans and O'Donovans. M. 1832, d. of the Hon. Brockholst Livingstone, one of the Judges of the Supreme Court of America. Was educ. at Stonyhurst Coll., Lancashire. A member of the

Medical Profession, but never practised. A Magistrate for the Co. of Cork, and a Guardian of the Cork and Bandon Unions. Was the first Chairman of the Clonakilty Town Commissioners. A Liberal, and 'a moral-force Repealer', supporter of free trade measures so long as they did not interfere with the prosperity of Ireland. In favour of long leases, and the tenant-right bill. First returned for the Co. of Cork, July 1847 on the death of Dan. O'Connell, Esq. Re-elected without opposition at the general election in the same year, and sat until he was appointed Governor of St. Lucia 1851.   [1851]

POWER, Nicholas Mahon. 8 Duke Street, Westminster, London. Faithlegg House, Waterford. S. of Nicholas Power, Esq., of Ballinakill, Co. Waterford, by the d. of — Rivers, Esq., of Waterford. B. in Waterford 1787; m. 1818, d. of — Mahon, Esq., of Dublin. Educ. at Oscott and at Ulverston, Lancashire. A Magistrate and Dept.-Lieut. for Waterford. A Liberal, in favour of the repeal of the Union. First returned for the Co. of Waterford in 1847, without opposition and sat until he retired in 1859.   [1859]

POWER, Patrick. 14 Bolton Street, Bellevue, Co. Kilkenny. A Reformer. Sat for Waterford Co. in the Parliament of 1826, and again in 1835 and sat until his death in 1836.   [1835]

POWER, P.J. Continued in House after 1885: full entry in Volume II.

POWER, R. Continued in House after 1885: full entry in Volume II.

POWERSCOURT, Visct. 31 Dover Street, London. Powerscourt Castle, Co. Wicklow. Carlton, and White's. B. 18 Jan. 1815; m. 20 Jan 1836, Lady Elizabeth Frances Charlotte, eld. d. of the 3rd Earl of Roden. An Irish Peer. A Conservative. Contested Bath at the gen. election in 1837, in conjunction with Mr. Bruges, defeating the former members Gen. Palmer and Mr. Roebuck. Sat for Bath until he was defeated in 1841. Died 11 Aug. 1844.   [1840]

POWLETT, Lord William John Frederick. 19 Curzon Street, London. Downham Hall, Brandon, Norfolk. 2nd s. of the 1st Duke of Cleveland, by Lady Katherine Powlett, d. and heir of the Duke of Bolton. Assumed the name of Powlett in lieu of his patronymic, Vane. B. 1792; m. 1815, Lady Caroline, 5th d. of the 1st Earl of Lonsdale. Created M.A. at Oxford 1812. A Dept.-Lieut. of Durham. A 'Liberal-Conservative' in favour of an extension of the suffrage in connection with moral and religious education; voted against the ballot

1853. Said he would vote for inquiry into the Maynooth Grant. Sat for St. Ives from July 1846-July 1852, when he was elected for Ludlow and sat until he retired 1857. Succeeded bro. as 3rd Duke of Cleveland Jan. 1864. He re-assumed the surname Vane. Died 6 Sept. 1864.   [1857]

POWYS, Philip Lybbe-. 88 St. James's Street, London. St. Thomas's, East Cowes, Isle of Wight. Hardwicke House, Reading. Only s. of Henry Philip Powys, Esq., of Hardwicke House, near Reading, and Broomfield, Middlesex, by his 1st wife, Julia, 3rd d. of Sir Fitz-William Barrington, Bart., of Barrington Hall, Essex, and Swainston, Isle of Wight. B. at Broomfield House, Southgate, Middlesex 1818; m. 1844, Anne Phyllis, d. of T. Greenwood, Esq., and niece and adopted d. of William Stephens, Esq., of Prospect Hill, Tilehurst. Educ. at Eton and at Balliol Coll., Oxford. Called to the bar at the Inner Temple 1843, and for about 15 years went the Oxford Circuit. A Liberal-Conservative, supported the vote of censure on Lord Palmerston 1864. First elected for Newport, Isle of Wight May 1859 and sat until he retired 1865.   [1865]

POYNTZ, William Stephen. 28 St. James's Place, London. Cowdray Park, Sussex. Midgam House, Berkshire. Father-in-law of the Marq. of Exeter. B. 1770; m. 1794, Elizabeth Mary, sister and heiress of Samuel, 6th Visct. Montague; a Dept.-Lieut. of Sussex and Hampshire. Patron of 6 livings. A moderate Reformer. Sat for Chichester from 1823 till 1826; for Ashburton from 1831 till 1825 when he was returned for Midhurst. Accepted Chiltern Hundreds Nov. (?) 1837.   [1837]

PRAED, Charles Tyringham. 95 Queen's Gate, Kensington, London. Arthur's, Boodle's, and Garrick. 2nd s. of James Backwell Praed, Esq., of Tyringham, Buckinghamshire and Trevethoe, Cornwall, by Sophia, d. of Charles Chaplin, Esq., of Blankney, Leicestershire. B. at Tyringham, Newport Pagnell, Buckinghamshire 1833. Educ. at Eton and at Merton Coll., Oxford. A Banker in London. A Conservative, and a supporter of the constitution in Church and State. Sat for St. Ives from Dec. 1874 until he retired 1880. Died 19 Oct. 1895.   [1880]

PRAED, Herbert Bulkeley Mackworth. 6 St. James's Street, London. Arthur's, and Carlton. Eld. s. of Bulkeley John Mackworth Praed, Esq., of Ousden Hall, Suffolk, by his 2nd wife, Elizabeth Colthurst, d. of Patrick Persee Fitz Patrick, Esq. B. 1841. Educ. at Harrow. Entered the army as Ensign in the 25th Foot, Mar. 1860, retired 1862. A Conservative, in favour of the union of Church and State. Sat for Colchester from Feb. 1874 until he retired 1880. Involved in numerous philanthropic societies. Created Bart. in 1905. Died 21 Nov. 1921.   [1880]

PRAED, James Backwell. 3 Cleveland Court, London. Tyringham, Buckinghamshire. Trevethan, Cornwall. Carlton. M. 1823, d. of Charles Chaplin, Esq., of Blankney, many years MP for Lincolnshire. A Conservative. MP for Buckinghamshire from 10 Jan. 1835 until his death 1836 or early 1837.   [1836]

PRAED, William Mackworth. 2, Brick-1, Temple, London. Trevethan. Carlton, and Athenaeum. S. of Serjeant Praed, Esq. M. 1835, Helen, youngest d. of George Bogle, Esq. A Barrister. Sec. to the Board of Control from Dec. 1834-Apr. 1835. A Recorder of Barnstaple. A Conservative. Sat for St. Germains 17 Dec. 1830-1832. Contested St. Ives unsuccessfully in 1832. Sat for Gt. Yarmouth from 1835-37, and Aylesbury from 1837 until his death in July 1839.   [1838]

PRAED, William Tyringham. 35 St. James's Place, London. Trevehow, Cornwall. Boodle's. B. 1780, the 2nd s. of William Praed, Esq., of Tyringham, Buckinghamshire. A Banker in London. A Conservative. Sat for the borough of St. Ives from June 1838 until his death in June 1846.   [1845]

PRICE, G.E. Continued in House after 1885: full entry in Volume II.

PRICE, Richard. Norton House, Radnorshire. University, and Carlton. Eld. s. of Richard Price, Esq., of Norton, by Mary, d. of Charles Humphreys, Esq., of Montgomeryshire. Lieut.-Col. Commandant of the Radnorshire Militia, and a Dept.-Lieut. of the Co. A Conservative. Patron of 1 living. Sat for Radnor district from 1796 until he retired in 1847. Died 10 Apr. 1861.   [1847]

PRICE, Sir Richard Green-, Bart. 22 Suffolk Street, London. Norton Manor, Presteign, Herefordshire. Union. Eld. surviving s. of George Green, Esq., of Cannon Bridge, Radnorshire, by Margaret, youngest d. of Richard Price, Esq., of Knighton, and sister of Richard Price, Esq., who sat for Radnor district for fifty years. B. at Cannon Bridge, Madeley, Herefordshire, 1803; m. 1st, 1837, Frances Milborough, eld. d. of Dansey R. Dansey, Esq., of Easton Court, Herefordshire (she died 1842); 2ndly, 1846, Laura, 3rd d. of Richard Henry King, Esq., M.D., of Mortlake, Surrey. Was educ. at Worcester. Was a Solicitor.

Assumed, in 1861, the name of Price, in addition to his patronymic, by royal license. Appointed a Dept.-Lieut. of Radnorshire 1864. Was High Sheriff of Radnorshire 1876. A Liberal. Sat for Radnor district from Apr. 1863 to Feb. 1869; unsuccessfully contested Radnorshire Feb. 1874. Sat for Radnorshire from Apr. 1880 until he retired in 1885. Contested seat again in 1886 standing as a Gladstonian Liberal. Died 1887.   [1885]

PRICE, Sir Robert, Bart. 11 Stratton Street, Foxley, Herefordshire. B. at Foxley, 1786, the s. of Sir Uvedale Price, 1st Bart., by the 4th d. of 1st Earl of Tyrconnel. Was descended from one of the most ancient families in Wales, which is said to derive its origin from Marchweithan, one of the princes. M. in 1823, his 1st cousin, Mary Anne, d. of the Rev. Robert Price. D.D. Of Whig principles, favoured an extension of the franchise and short Parliaments. Did not, however, support the ballot. Patron of 2 livings. Represented Herefordshire from 1818-41, and the City of Hereford from 1845 until he accepted Chiltern Hundreds Jan. 1857. Died 5 Nov. 1857. [1856]

PRICE, Samuel Grove. 9 Gray's Inn Square, London. Sunning Hill, Berkshire. Carlton, and University. S. of the Rev. M. Price, Rector of Knebworth, Hertfordshire, and Catherine, only d. of Samuel Grove, Esq., of Taynton, Gloucestershire, one of the last descendants of the Groves of Staffordshire. B. 1793; m. 1830, Marianne, 2nd d. of William Page, Esq., formerly member of Council at Bombay. Obtained Bell's University Scholarship in 1812, Sir Wm. Browne's gold medal for Greek Ode in 1813, and a Fellowship of Downing Coll., Cambridge, in 1815. A Conservative. Sat for Sandwich in the Parliament of 1830, and unsuccessfully contested it in 1829, 1831, and 1832. Sat for Sandwich again from 1835. Defeated in 1837.   [1837]

PRICE, William Edwin. 89 Onslow Gardens, London. Hillfield, Gloucester. Reform, and Army & Navy. S. of William Philip Price, Esq., many years MP for Gloucester, by Frances Anne, d. of John Chadborn, Esq., of Gloucester. B. 1841; m. 1878, Margaret, 2nd d. of Robert N. Philips, Esq., of Welcombe, Warwickshire. Educ. at Eton and at University Coll., London, also at the Royal Military Coll., Woolwich, graduated B.A. 1859 at London University. Entered the army as Ensign 36th Foot Mar. 1861, appointed Lieut. Aug. 1863, retired Feb. 1865. A Magistrate for Gloucestershire and Capt. S. Gloucester Militia. A Liberal, a supporter of Mr. Gladstone, voted for the disestablishment of the Church. Sat for Tewkesbury from Dec. 1868 until 1880 when the election was declared void. Died 10 Feb. 1886.   [1880]

PRICE, William Philip. Tibberton Court, Gloucester. Brooks's, and Reform. B. at Gloucester 1817, the s. of William Price, a Merchant of Gloucester by Frances, d. of Philip George of Bristol. M. 1837 Frances Anne, d. of John Chadborn of Gloucester. Was a Timber Merchant in Gloucester, a Magistrate and Dept.-Lieut. of Gloucestershire, of which he was High Sheriff 1848. A Liberal, opposed to all religious endowments from the public funds. Voted for the ballot 1853. Sat for Gloucester July 1852 - Aug. 1859, when he was displaced on petition. Re-elected July 1865 and sat until May 1873 when he accepted Chiltern Hundreds to become Railway Commissioner, 2 Aug. 1873. Died 31 Mar. 1891. [1873]

PRIME, Richard. 16 Suffolk Street, London. Walberton House, Arundel, Sussex. Carlton, and Athenaeum. B. in London 1784, 2nd s. of Samuel Prime, Esq., of Upper Brook Street and of Whitton, Middlesex, by the d. of Richard Holden, Esq., of Field House, Yorkshire. M. 1815, Anne, eld. d. of Robert Shuttleworth, Esq., of Gawthorpe Hall, Lancashire, relict of Richard T. Streatfield, Esq., of Sussex (she died July 1848). Educ. at Eton and at Trinity Coll., Cambridge, where he was the first junior optime in 1806. Was called to the bar at Lincoln's Inn 1810, but did not practise longer than five years. A Dept.-Lieut. and Magistrate of Sussex. Was High Sheriff in 1823 and became Chairman of the West Sussex Quarter Sessions. A Conservative, voted in the minority of 53 who censured free trade, Nov. 1852. In favour of agricultural protection, but was disposed to accept 'a re-adjustment of taxation' as a substitute for that system. Opposed to the endowment of the Roman Catholic Clergy. Sat for Sussex W. from Jan. 1847 until he accepted Chiltern Hundreds in Feb. 1854. Died 7 Nov. 1866. [1853]

PRINGLE, Alexander. 43 Pall Mall, London. Yair, Selkirkshire. Carlton. Was a representative of the Pringles of Whytbank, an ancient family in the county of Selkirk. M. Agnes Joanna, the d. of Sir William Dick, Bart., of Prestonfield in 1830. A Lord of the Treasury, an Advocate, and a Vice-Lieut. of Selkirkshire. A Conservative. Sat for Selkirkshire in 1830 and 1831, but was defeated by R. Pringle, Esq., a Reformer, of Clifton, in 1832. Regained his seat in 1835 and sat until 1845, when appointed Clerk of the Sessions. [1844]

PRINGLE, Capt. Robert. 34 Bruton Street, London. Clifton Park, Roxburghshire. The Staining, Selkirkshire. A Captain in the army. Captain Pringle was the 5th generation of his family who had successively represented Selkirkshire, before and since the Union of the Kingdoms. Of Whig principles, in favour of the abolition of sinecures, monopolies, and all abuses. Sat for Selkirkshire from 1832. Defeated in 1835. Contested same seat in 1837. Died Dec. 1842. [1833]

PRINSEP, Henry Thoby. 4th s. of John Prinsep, Esq., Merchant and MP for Queenborough. B. 1793. Was in the Bengal Civil Service from 1809. Member of Council of India in 1835 and 1840-43. A Director of the East India Company July 1850-58. A Director of Council of India 1858-74. A Protectionist. Contested Kilmarnock district 29 May 1844, Dartmouth 3 July 1845, and Dover 30 July 1847. Returned for Harwich 5 Mar. 1851 but the election was declared void in May when he was unable to prove his qualification. Contested the seat again 28 May 1851 but was defeated in a corrupt election. Contested Colchester in 1852 and Barnstaple in 1857. Died 11 Feb. 1878.

PRITCHARD, John. 89 Eaton Square, London. Broseley, Wellington, Shropshire. S. of John Pritchard, Esq., Banker, of Broseley and Bridgnorth, by Anne, his wife. M. Jane, d. of George Osborne Gordon, Esq. Called to the bar at Lincoln's Inn 1841, but did not practise. A Banker at Bridgnorth and Broseley. A Dept.-Lieut. and Magistrate for Shropshire. A Liberal-Conservative, in favour of national education being extended by voluntary exertion, aided by public grants; of a reduction of the qualification in counties and boroughs; of Dissenters being relieved from the payment of church-rates; but opposed to the ballot. Patron of 1 living. Sat for Bridgnorth from Apr. 1853 until he retired in 1868 when Bridgnorth became a single-seat Constituency. Died 19 Aug. 1891. [1867]

PROBY, Rt. Hon. Lord. 14 Halkin Street, London. Glenart Castle, Arlow, Co. Wicklow. Brooks's. S. of 3rd Earl of Carysfort, by Isabella, d. of Hon. Hugh Howard. B. at Bushy Park, Co. Wicklow, 1825; m. 1853, Lady Augusta Maria, d. of 2nd Earl of Listowel. Appointed Capt. in 74th Highlanders 1851; retired. A Magistrate and Dept.-Lieut. for the Co. of Wicklow. Was Comptroller of the Queen's Household from June 1859 till July 1866. A Liberal. First elected for Wicklow Co. Feb. 1858 and sat until he succeeded as 4th Earl Carysfort 3 Nov. 1868. Died 18 May 1872. [1867]

PROTHEROE, Edward Davis. Newnham, Gloucestershire. Brooks's, and Travellers'. S. of Mr. Protheroe, MP for Bristol from 1810-1820. Of an old Carmarthenshire family, and engaged in the West India trade in Bristol. A Justice of the

Peace and Dept.-Lieut. for Gloucestershire, and an unpaid Commissioner of Public Records. A Reformer, voted, when formerly in Parliament, for Roman Catholic and Negro Emancipation, for the repeal of the Test Act, and in favour of vote by ballot. Was elected for Evesham in 1826; unsuccessfully contested Bristol in 1830, and afterwards in 1832, having been elected without opposition in 1831. Contested Halifax in 1834, and lost his election by one vote; came in for Halifax at the head of the poll in 1837 and 1841 and sat until he retired in 1847. Died 18 Aug. 1852.   [1847]

PRYME, George. 4 Great Queen Street, Westminster, London. Cambridge. Reform. Descended from a French family (De La Pryme), a branch of which came to England about 1630, during a persecution of the Huguenots, to which party they belonged. M. in 1813, Jane, youngest d. of Thomas Thackeray, Esq. Fellow of Trinity Coll., obtained five University Classical Prizes. Professor of political economy in the University of Cambridge. A Barrister; resided at Cambridge for 20 years, and practised on the Norfolk circuit. Of Whig principles, in favour of short Parliaments and of admitting Dissenters to the Universities. Sat for Cambridge from 1832 until he retired in 1841. Author. Died 2 Dec. 1868.   [1840]

PRYSE, Edward Lewis. Gogerddan, Cardiganshire. Army & Navy. S. of Pryse Pryse, Esq. (who sat for Cardigan district from 1818 till his death in 1849), by his 2nd wife, Jane, d. of Peter Cavallier, Esq., of Guisborough, Yorkshire. Bro. to Pryse Loveden, Esq., who represented Cardigan district from 1849 until his death in 1855. B. 1817. Entered the Dragoon Guards as Cornet 1837; became Capt. 1844; retired 1846. Appointed Lord-Lieut. of Cardiganshire 1857. A Liberal. First elected for Cardigan district Apr. 1857 and sat until he retired in 1868. Died 29 May 1888.   [1867]

PRYSE, Pryse. Limmer's Hotel, London. Gogerddan, Cardiganshire. Buscot Park, Berkshire. Only s. of E. Loveden Loveden, Esq., of Buscot Park, Farringdon, former MP for Buckinghamshire. Assumed the name of Pryse in 1798; m. 1st, 1798, Harriet, d. of William, 2nd Lord Ashbrook, and widow of the Hon. and Rev. John Agar Ellis; 2ndly, 1814, Jane, d. of Peter Cavallier, of Gisborough. Patron of 2 livings. A Reformer, voted in favour of Queen Caroline, Catholic Emancipation, and both Reform Bills. Sat for Cardigan district from 1818. MP until he died in Jan. 1849.   [1847 2nd ed.]

PUGH, D. Continued in House after 1885: full

PUGH, Lewis Pugh. Queen Anne's Mansions, London. 2 Stone Buildings, Lincoln's Inn, London. Abermaide, Aberystwith, South Wales. Oriental. Eld. s. of John Evans, Esq., of Lovesgrove, Cardiganshire, by Eliza, d. of Lewis Pugh, Esq. B. at Aberystwith 1837; m. 1864, Veronica Harriet, d. of James Hills, Esq., of Neechindepore, Bengal. Was educ. at Winchester and at Corpus Christ Coll., Oxford; graduated B.A. 1859, M.A. 1862. Was called to the bar at Lincoln's Inn Nov. 1862. A Magistrate for Cardiganshire. Assumed the name of Pugh in lieu of his patronymic by royal license in 1868, under the will of his uncle. A Liberal. Sat for Cardiganshire from Apr. 1880 until he retired in 1885. [1885]

PULESTON, J.H. Continued in House after 1885: full entry in Volume II.

PULLER, Christopher William Giles-. Youngsbury, Ware, Hertfordshire. Athenaeum. Only s. of Sir Christopher Puller, Chief Justice of the Supreme Court of Calcutta, by Louisa, d. of Joseph King, Esq., of Taplow, and niece of Daniel Giles, Esq., of Youngsbury, Hertfordshire. Assumed the name of Giles by royal license, 1857. B. in London, 1807; m. 1831, Emily, youngest d. of William Blake, Esq., of Danesbury, Hertfordshire. Educ. at Eton, and at Christ Church, Oxford, where he gained a double first class in 1828. Called to the bar at Lincoln's Inn, 1832, and practised in the Court of Chancery till 1841. A Dept.-Lieut. and Magistrate for Hertfordshire. A Liberal, in favour of extension of the county franchise; said he did 'not approve of the Maynooth Act of 1845, but thought its repeal now would be an act of confiscation'; opposed to the abolition of church-rates, 'unless a satisfactory provision be made for the repair of churches'; in favour of the national defences being kept in a high state of efficiency. Was an unsuccessful candidate for Hertfordshire on the free trade interest, in 1852. Was first returned for Hertfordshire in Apr. 1857. MP until his death in 1864. [1863]

PULLEY, Joseph. Green Park Chambers, Piccadilly, London. Lower Eaton, Herefordshire. Devonshire, and Reform. B. at Hackney 1822, eld. s. of Joseph Pulley of Bayswater, London, by Frances, d. of Charles Oldaker, of Fladbury, Worcestershire. M. 1860, Mary, d. of W. Burgess of 134 Sloan Street, London (she died 1876). Educ. at Hackney Grammar School. A member of the Stock Exchange. A Magistrate and Dept.-Lieut. of Herefordshire. A Liberal, and 'a strong advocate of Church Reform.' Unsuccessfully contested Hereford Feb. 1874 and again Mar. 1878. Sat for Hereford from Apr. 1880 - 1886, when he was defeated standing as a

Gladstonian Liberal. Contested Herefordshire S. in July 1892. On 15 Aug. 1893 he contested the city of Hereford. Died 5 Aug. 1901.   [1886]

PULSFORD, Robert. Youngest s. of William Pulsford, Esq., of Wimpole Street, London. B. 1814. Educ. at Trinity Coll., Cambridge. A Liberal, in favour of the ballot, etc. Was first returned for Hereford in Sept. 1841, when Mr. Hobhouse accepted the Chiltern Hundreds. MP until he retired in 1847.   [1847]

PUSEY, Philip. 17 Park Lane, London. Pusey, Berkshire. Carlton. Eld. s. of the Hon. Philip Bouverie (half bro. of the 1st Earl of Radnor) who assumed the name of Pusey. B. 1799; m. 1822, Emily Herbert, 3rd d. of the 2nd Earl of Carnarvon. Patron of 1 living. Was a Conservative, and a supporter of the agricultural interest, but in 1846 declared himself a Liberal, and a supporter of Lord John Russell's government; in 1850 however voted in favour of a return to agricultural protection. Sat for Chippenham in 1830, Cashel in 1831, and contested Berkshire unsuccessfully in 1832. Sat for Berkshire from 1835 until he retired in 1852. Died at Oxford 9 July 1855.   [1852]

QUINN, Peter. The Agency, Loughbrickland, Co. Armagh, Ireland. Carlton. S. of John Quinn, Esq., Merchant of Newry, by Mary, d. of Rev. William Campbell, Vicar of Newry. B. at Newry 1814; m. 1835, Sarah Jane, d. of the Rev. Josiah Erskine, Rector of Kilbridge, in the diocese of Kilmore, Cavan. Formerly a Merchant of Newry, but subsequently Land Agent to large estates in the counties of Down and Armagh. A Conservative, gave Lord Derby 'a hearty, but independent support.' First elected for Newry May 1859 and sat until he retired in 1865.   [1865]

RAE, Rt. Hon. Sir William, Bart. 52 Upper Brook Street, London. Eskgrove, Midlothian. Only s. of the previous Bart. M. Mary, d. of Charles Stuart, Esq. Called to the Scottish bar in 1791. Was Lord Advocate of Scotland under the Wellington Administration, and was again appointed to that office in Dec. 1834, but resigned in Apr. 1835. A Conservative. Sat for Harwich in the Parliament of 1826, and for Buteshire from 1830 till 1832, when Capt. Charles Stuart was elected; but on that gentleman's retirement in 1833, Sir William was again returned for Buteshire. MP until his death in 1842.   [1842]

RAIKES, Rt. Hon. H.C. Continued in House after 1885: full entry in Volume II.

RALLI, Pandeli. 17 Belgrave Square, London. Reform, Devonshire, and Brooks's. Only s. of

Thomas Ralli, Esq., by Mary, only d. of Pandeli Argenti, Esq., of Marseilles. B. 1845. Educ. at King's Coll., London, and graduated at London B.A. 1866. A Merchant in London. A Liberal. Sat for Bridport from Apr. 1875 to Apr. 1880, when he was an unsuccessful candidate there; sat for Wallingford from June 1880 until defeated in 1885. Contested Wells division of Somerset 5 Dec. 1885; contested Gateshead July 1892 and again 24 Feb. 1893; contested Newcastle-on-Tyne 25 Aug. 1892; contested Gloucester 2 Oct. 1900. Died 21 Aug. 1928.   [1885]

RAMSAY, Sir Alexander, Bart. Cheltenham. Eld. s. of Sir Alexander Ramsay, 2nd Bart., by his 1st wife, Jane, eld. d. and co-heir of F. Russell, Esq., of Blackhall. B. at Fasque, Kincardineshire, 1813; m. 1835, Ellen Matilda, the eld. d. of John Entwisle, Esq., of Foxholes, Lancashire. Appointed a Dept.-Lieut. of Kincardineshire in 1855. A Liberal, and a supporter of Lord Palmerston's foreign policy; considered that 'all education must be based on the Bible'; in favour of the Maynooth Grant. First returned for Rochdale Mar. 1857. Retired in 1859. Died 3 Mar. 1875.   [1858]

RAMSAY, John. Kildalton, Port Ellen, Islay, Scotland. Windham, and Athenaeum. B. 1814, youngest s. of Robert Ramsay, by Elizabeth, d. of William Stirling of Craigforth, Co. Stirling. M. 1st, 1857, Elizabeth, d. of William Shields of Lanchester, Co. Durham (she died 1864); 2ndly, 1871, Lucy, d. of George Martin of Auchendennan, Dumbartonshire. Educ. at Glasgow University. A Merchant of Glasgow. Was presented with the Freedom of the burgh of Linlithgow Nov. 1878, in recognition of his services in Parliament to procure compensation to the burgh for its losses under the Roads and Bridges Act. Dept.-Lieut. of Argyllshire. A Liberal. Contested Glasgow July 1865. Sat for Stirling district Apr. - Nov. 1868, when he was unsuccessful. Elected for the district of Falkirk, Feb. 1874, and sat until 1886, when he retired. Died 24 June 1892. [1886]

RAMSAY, Lord (I). A Conservative. Contested Edinburgh Jan. 1835. Returned for Haddingtonshire in 1837 and sat until he succeeded as Earl of Dalhousie 21 Mar. 1838. Created Marq. Dalhousie (U.K. Peerage) 25 Aug. 1849. Governor-Gen. of India 1847-56. Died 19 Dec. 1860.   [1837]

RAMSAY, Lord. (II). Junior United Service. Eld. s. of the Earl of Dalhousie, by Sarah Frances, only d. of William Robertson, Esq., of Logan House. B. 1847; m. 1887, Lady Ida Louise younger d. of 6th Earl of Tankerville. Appointed a

Lieut. R.N. Apr. 1867, commander Mar. 1874. Was Equerry to the Duke of Edinburgh from 1874 to June 1876, when he was appointed an Extra Equerry. A decided Liberal, in favour of inquiry into the system of 'Home Rule'. Unsuccessfully contested by-election at Liverpool Feb. 1880. Was successful there at the general election Apr. 1880 and sat until he succeeded as Earl of Dalhousie in the same year.   [1880]

RAMSAY, William Ramsay. Barnton House and Lauriston Castle, Midlothian. Sauchie House, Stirlingshire. Athenaeum. B. in 1809; m. 1828, the d. of 10th Lord Torphichen. A Conservative and sat for Stirlingshire in 1831. Sat for the County of Edinburgh from 1841 until he accepted Chiltern Hundreds in 1845. Died 15 Mar. 1850.   [1844]

RAMSBOTTOM, John. 14a Albany. Woodside, Berkshire. Reform. Deputy Chairman of the Hope Life Insurance Company. Was an officer in the 16th Dragoons. Of Whig principles. Voted against the Corn Laws. Represented the borough of Windsor from 1812 until his death in Oct. 1845.   [1845]

RAMSDEN, John Charles. 6 Upper Brook Street, London. Bryam Hall, Yorkshire. Eld. s. of Sir John Ramsden, Bart., Bryam, Yorkshire, who had Church patronage. B. 1788; m. 1814, Isabella, youngest d. of Thomas, 1st Lord Dundas. One of his bros. was m. to a d. of Lord Strafford, a sister to Lord Muncaster, and another bro. to a d. of the Marq. of Winchester. A Reformer. Sat for Malton from 1812-1831, when he was elected for Yorkshire North Riding, but was defeated in 1832. In 1833 he again sat for Malton. MP until his death Dec. 1836 or Jan. 1837. [1836]

RAMSDEN, Sir John William, Bart. 6 Upper Brook Street, London. Longley Hall, Huddersfield. Bryam, Ferrybridge, Yorkshire. Bulstrode, Gerrards Cross, Buckinghamshire. Ardverikie, Kingussie, Scotland. Brooks's, Athenaeum, and Travellers'. B. a Newby Park, Yorkshire 1831, only s. of John Charles Ramsden, Esq. (Many years MP for Malton), by Hon. Isabella, youngest d. of 1st Lord Dundas. M. 1865, Lady Helen Gwendolen, d. of 12th Duke of Somerset. Was educ. at Eton and at Trinity Coll., Cambridge, where he graduated M.A. 1852. Was Under-Sec. for War May 1857-Mar. 1858. Appointed Dept.-Lieut. of the West Riding of Yorkshire 1852, Hon. Col. 1st West Riding of Yorkshire Artillery Volunteers 1862, High sheriff of Yorkshire 1868. Patron of 4 livings. A Liberal. Sat for Taunton May 1853-Apr. 1857, for Hythe Apr. 1857-Jan. 1859, for the West Riding of

Yorkshire Jan. 1859-July 1865, and for Monmouth district, Dec. 1868-Feb. 1874. Sat from Apr. 1880-Nov. 1885 for the Eastern division of the West Riding of Yorkshire, which he had contested unsuccessfully Feb. 1874. Defeated in 1886, standing as a Gladstonian Liberal. Died 15 Apr. 1914.   [1886]

RANKIN, James. Continued in House after 1885: full entry in Volume II.

RAPHAEL, Alexander. 10 Great Stanhope Street, London. Ditton Lodge, Surrey. Madras, Brighton. Surbiton Place, Surrey. Of Liberal opinions. Elected Sheriff of London in 1834. Was an unsuccessful candidate for Pontefract in 1835; was returned for Carlow in June 1835, but unseated on petition, when the terms of a pecuniary arrangement between him and Mr. O'Connell for procuring his election there attracted much public attention. First returned for St. Albans in 1847 and MP until his death in Nov. 1850. [1850]

RASHLEIGH, Sir John Colman, Bart. Prideaux, St. Austell, Cornwall. National. S. of Sir John Colman Rashleigh, 1st Bart., by Harriett, 2nd d. of Robert Williams, Esq., of Bridehead, Dorset. B. 1819; m. 1845, the only d. of Nicholas Kendall, Esq., of Pelyn, Cornwall. Educ. at Trinity Coll., Cambridge, where he graduated B.A. 1843. Appointed Capt. Cornwall and Devon Miners' Militia 1844, and Lieut.-Col.-Commandant 1853, Sheriff of Cornwall 1852, special dept.-warden of the Stannaries 1852. Patron of 1 living. A Liberal, in favour of re-adjustment of local taxation, and the total abolition of the Game Laws; opposed to the disestablishment of the Church. Sat for Cornwall E. from Feb. 1874 until he retired 1880. Died 27 Oct. 1896.   [1880]

RASHLEIGH, William. 16 Stratford Place, London. Menabilly, Cornwall. Carlton. Eld. s. of the head of the Rashleigh family, long settled at Menabilly, Cornwall. Many members of his family had seats in Parliament at various periods, during and since the reign of Elizabeth. Sir John Colman Rashleigh, of Prideaux, the descendant of a branch of this family, was created a Bart. in 1831. B. 1816; m. 1843, eld. d. of the 11th Lord Blantyre. A Dept.-Lieut. and Magistrate for Cornwall E. Was 'decidedly Conservative'; voted for agricultural protection, 1846. First returned for Cornwall E. in 1841 and sat until he retired in 1847.   [1847]

RATCLIFF, Daniel Rowlinson. Great Alne Hall, Alcester, Warwickshire. B. at Birmingham 1839, the s. of Mr. Joseph Ratcliff of Edgbaston,

Birmingham, by Mary Ann, d. of Mr. John Rowlinson. M. 1851, only d. of Mr. William Milner of Liverpool. Educ. at King Edward's School, Birmingham. Was a Partner in the firm of Messrs. Milner and Son, London and Liverpool; retired 1874. A Liberal. Was returned for Evesham in Apr. 1880, but unseated the following June.   [1880 2nd ed.]

RATHBONE, W. Continued in House after 1885: full entry in Volume II.

RAWDON, John Dawson. 3 Great Stanhope Street, Mayfair, London. B. 1804; m. 1828, the Dowager Lady Cremorne, d. of J. Whaley, Esq. A Col. in the army; was formerly in the Coldstream Guards. A Whig, in 1840 voted with Mr. Charles Villiers for going into Committee on the Corn Laws. First returned for Armagh City in 1840, on the acceptance of office by Mr. Curry. MP until he retired in 1852. Died 5 May 1866.   [1852]

RAWLINSON, Sir Henry Creswicke, K.C.B. 1 Hill Street, Berkeley Square, London. S. of Abram Tysack Rawlinson, Esq., of Chadlington, Oxfordshire, by the d. and co-heir of Henry Creswicke, Esq., of Moreton, Worcestershire. B. at Chadlington, Oxfordshire, 1810; m. 1862, youngest d. of Henry Seymour, Esq., of Knoyle, Wiltshire. Educ. at Ealing, Middlesex. Entered the military service of the E.I.C. in 1826, and was successively political agent at Candahar (throughout the Afghan war), political agent in Turkish Arabia, British Consul there, and a member of the Council of India. Appointed Envoy Extraordinary and Minister Plenipotentiary in Persia with the rank of Maj.-Gen. 1859. Received several foreign orders of distinction. Made D.C.L. of Oxford, LL.D. of Cambridge, and was a member of numerous literary and scientific associations. A Liberal. Sat for Reigate from Feb. to Sept. 1858, when he relinquished his seat to proceed to India. Elected for Frome, July 1865. Retired in 1868. Once more member of Council for India from Oct. 1868; created Bart. Feb. 1891. Died 5 Mar. 1895.   [1867]

RAYNHAM, Visct. Raynham Hall, Norfolk. Ball's Park, Hertfordshire. Tamworth Castle, Warwickshire. Brooks's. Eld. s. of the Marq. Townshend (who sat for Tamworth from 1847 till 1856, when he succeeded to the Marquisate). B. at Brighton, 1831. Educ. at Eton. Was a clerk in the foreign office from June 1850 till Mar. 1854. A Magistrate for Norfolk and Hertfordshire and a Dept.-Lieut. for the latter. A Lieut. in the Staffordshire Yeomanry Cavalry. A Liberal, in favour of a considerable extension of the suffrage, the abolition of church rates, the continuance of the

grant to Maynooth, and the removal of all religious disabilities. Opposed to the ballot. First elected for Tamworth Feb. 1856, and sat until he succeeded to the Peerage (Marq. of Townshend) 10 Sept. 1863. An active philanthropist. Died 26 Oct. 1899.   [1863]

READ, Clare Sewell. Honingham Thorpe, Norwich. Carlton. Eld. s. of George Read, of Barton Bendish-Hall, Norfolk, by Sarah Anne, d. of Mr. Clare Sewell, of Barton Bendish. B. at Ketteringham, 1826; m. 1850, Sarah Maria, d. of Jas. Watson, Esq., Sheriff of Norwich 1848. A Yeoman and tenant farmer on a large scale in Norfolk, where his ancestors had followed the same pursuit for nearly 300 years. A JP for Norfolk, President of the Norfolk Chamber of Agriculture, Member of Council of the Central Chamber of Agriculture and of the Farmers' Club, and the author of several essays on farming in the *Agricultural Society's Journal*. Was Parliamentary Secretary to the Local government Board in 1874-75; and in 1879 went to America as a Commissioner to report on the agriculture of that country. In favour of 'progressive Conservatism, and fair play for British agriculture.' Sat for Norfolk E. 1865-68, and for Norfolk S. 1868-80. At the general election of 1880, Mr. Read lost his seat for Norfolk S. by one vote. Returned for Norfolk W. 20 Feb. 1884, unopposed. Retired in 1885. Contested Norwich in 1886. Died 22 Aug. 1905.   [1885]

READE, William Morris. Rossenarra, Kilkenny. S. of W. Morris, Esq., by the d. of Shapland Carew, Esq., grandfather of 1st Lord Carew. B. 1787; m. 1827, d. of Patrick Maitland, Esq., (descended from the Lauderdale family). Was a second-class man in classics and science at Oxford in 1807. A Conservative. Was an unsuccessful candidate for Kilkenny city in 1830. First returned for Waterford city in 1841 and sat until he retired in 1847.   [1841 2nd ed.]

REARDEN, Denis Joseph. 91 Piccadilly, London. A Liberal, voted against the suspension of the Habeas Corpus Act in Ireland, Feb. 1866. First elected for Athlone, July 1865. Retired in 1868. Subsequently worked as a surveyor in London. Died 22 May 1885.   [1867]

REBOW, John Gurdon. 111 Eaton Square, London. Wiverhoe Park, Colchester. Brooks's. 2nd s. of Theophilus Thornhaugh Gurdon, Esq., of Letton, Norfolk, by Anne, d. of William Mellish, Esq., of Blyth, Nottinghamshire. B. in London 1799; m. 1st, 1835, Mary, widow of Sir Thomas Ormsby, Bart. and only d. and heir of Gen. Slate Rebow, of Wivenhoe Park, Essex, (she died 1842); 2ndly, 1845, Lady Georgina, 4th d. of 2nd Earl of Norbury. Educ. at Eton. Assumed the name Rebow in addition to his patronymic on his first marriage. A Magistrate and Dept.-Lieut. for Essex since 1835, and High Steward of Colchester since 1861. Patron of 1 living. A Liberal, voted for the disestablishment of the Irish Church 1869, thinking it likely to strengthen rather than weaken the Church; favoured also vote by ballot and a voluntary system of national religious education aided by the State. Unsuccessfully contested Essex N. July 1847. Sat for Colchester from Feb. 1857-Apr. 1859; re-elected July 1865. MP until his death Oct. 1870.   [1870]

REDINGTON, Thomas Nicholas. Kilkoran, Co. Galway. Albion, and Reform. B. 2nd Oct. 1815. M. 1842, the d. of John H. Talbot, Esq., of Ballytrent. A Magistrate and Dept.-Lieut. for the Co. of Galway. A member of Christ Coll., Cambridge. Supported Lord Melbourne's administration and in favour of the abolition of tithes. Friendly to Irish Corporate Reform and to vote by ballot. Voted against the abolition of the Corn Laws. Sat for Dundalk from 1837 to 1846 when he became Under-Secretary in Ireland.   [1845]

REDMOND, John Edward. (I). The Deeps, Enniscorthy, Ireland. 2nd s. of John Redmond, Esq., of Somerton, Banker at Wexford, by Eliza, d. of Michael Sutton, Esq. B. at Somerton 1806; m. 1827, Margaret, d. of Nicholas Archer, Esq., M.D. A Magistrate for the Co. of Wexford. A Liberal, voted against Lord Palmerston on the vote of Censure 1864. In favour of the extension of the franchise to 'those who by education and intelligence are entitled to enjoy it', of the removal of 'all religious disabilities', and of the passing of laws for securing to the tenant 'full compensation for the outlay of capital.' First elected for the bor. of Wexford May 1859 until defeated July 1865. Died 10 Aug. 1865.   [1865]

REDMOND, J.E. (II). Continued in House after 1885: full entry in Volume II.

REDMOND, William Archer. Younger s. of Patrick Walter Redmond,Esq., (a Dept.-Lieut. for the Co. of Wexford), by Esther, d. of Joseph Kearney, Esq., of Rocklands, Co. Wexford. B. at Kyle House, Co. Wexford, 1825; m. 1848, Mary, d. of R.H. Hoey, Esq., Capt. Wicklow Rifles. Was educ. at Stonyhurst Coll. and at Trinity Coll., Dublin, where he graduated B.A. 1847. A Liberal, in favour of 'Home Rule' for Ireland, and denominational education. Sat for the bor. of Wexford from Apr. 1872. MP until his death in 1880.   [1879]

REDMOND, W.H.K. Continued in House after 1885: full entry in Volume II.

REED, Sir Charles. Earlsmead, Hackney, London. 2nd s. of Rev. Andrew Reed, D.D., founder of the London Orphan Asylum, the Infant Orphan Asylum, Earlswood Asylum for Infants, etc. B. 1819; m. 1845, Margaret, d. of Edward Baines, Esq., MP. Educ. at Hackney Grammar School, and at the London University. A Merchant and Type-Founder in London. Appointed Conservator of the Thames, 1867. A Commissioner of Lieutenancy for London 1862, and was actively concerned in the charitable institutions founded by Dr. Reed. Author of *Life and Philanthropic Labours of Andrew Reed, D.D., Historical Narrative of the Plantations and Settlements in Ulster of the Irish Society.* A Liberal, opposed to all religious endowments in Ireland; in favour of a redistribution of Parliamentary seats. Sat for Hackney from Dec. 1868 to Apr. 1874 when the election was declared void. Sat for St. Ives from Apr. 1880. MP until his death 25 Mar. 1881.   [1881]

REED, Sir E.J. Continued in House after 1885: full entry in Volume II.

REED, Joseph Haythorne. Burnham, Somerset. Army & Navy. Only s. of George Reed, Esq., of Burnham, Somersetshire, by Sarah, d. of John Hammans, Esq. B. 1828. Educ. at Harrow. Formerly in the 17th Lancers. Appointed Maj. in the City of London Artillery Company July 1854. A Liberal, opposed all aggression of the Roman Catholics, in favour of the wide diffusion of education and of the removal of all 'taxes on knowledge'. First returned for Abingdon Dec. 1854 until Mar. 1857 when he contested Finsbury, but his expenses led to imprisonment for debt. Died shortly after release 6 Apr. 1858.   [1857]

REID, Col. George Alexander. 28 Portland Place, London. Bulstrode Park, Buckinghamshire. United University. Was Col. in the 2nd Life Guards, but retired immediately after his election as MP; became a Maj.-Gen. in the army 1851. A Conservative, but in favour of free trade. First returned for Windsor in Nov. 1845, without opposition. MP until his death 12 May 1852.   [1852]

REID, Sir John Rae, Bart. 4 Eaton Place, London. Ewell Green, Surrey. Carlton. S. of Sir Thomas Reid, Bart., a Merchant in London, and Chairman of the Court of Directors of the East India Company, who was created a Bart. in 1823, the year before his death. B. 1791; m. 1840, d. of Richard Eaton, Esq., of Stetchworth Park, Cambridgeshire. Was Governor of the Bank of England, an East India Proprietor, and a West India Merchant. A Conservative, but in favour of free trade. Was first elected for Dover in 1830; was thrown out by Capt. Stanhope, on the Reform interest in 1831, but regained his seat in 1832 and sat until he retired in 1847. Died 30 July 1867. [1847]

REID, Robert. 39 Onslow Square, London. Iffley, Oxford. S. of David Reid, Esq., of Dunfermline, Fifeshire. B. at Dunfermline 1831; m. 1858, Mary, d. of William Newby, Esq., of Manchester. Was educ. at the High School, Glasgow, and at Worcester Coll., Oxford. Graduated B.A. 1869. A Merchant in China; retired 1864. Was a member of the first Oxford School Board. Called to the bar at Inner Temple 1872. A Liberal. Unsuccessfully contested Wick district Feb. 1872. Sat for Kirkcaldy district from Feb. 1874. MP until his death 30 Mar. 1875. [1875]

REID, R.T. Continued in House after 1885: full entry in Volume II.

RENDEL, Stuart. Continued in House after 1885: full entry in Volume II.

RENDLESHAM, Lord. (I). B. 1798, s. of 1st Lord Rendlesham, and bro. to the former Lord, who was the 3rd Baron. An Irish Peer. M. 1838, Eliza, eld. d. of Sir George B. Prescott, Bart., and relict of James Duff, Esq. Was for some years in the army, but retired. Patron of 4 livings. A Conservative, voted for agricultural protection 1846, and opposed to the duties on tea, tobacco, hops, and malt. Considered that Lunatic Asylums and all county and highway rates should be paid out of the consolidated fund. Opposed to the endowment of the Roman Catholic Clergy. Sat for Suffolk E. from 1843 until his death 6 Apr. 1852. [1852]

RENDLESHAM, Lord. (II). Rendlesham Hall, Woodbridge, Suffolk. Carlton. An Irish peer. B. at Florence 1840; m. 1861, Lady Egidia, d. of the 15th Earl of Eglinton. Was Lieut. 3rd Rifle Volunteers. Appointed Cornet Ayrshire Yeomanry Cavalry 1862. Was High Sheriff of Suffolk for 1870. Patron of 4 livings. A Conservative, but not averse to well-considered progress. Sat for Suffolk E. from Feb. 1874 until defeated in 1885 contesting Suffolk S.E. Died 9 Nov. 1911. [1885]

RENNIE, George. 1 Chesham Place, Belgrave Square, London. Reform, and Athenaeum. S. of George Rennie, Esq., of Phantassa, Haddingtonshire, who was perhaps the most eminent practical agriculturist of his time. B. 1802; m. 1824, d. of the celebrated engineer, John Rennie, Esq., F.R.S. Studied the fine arts for many years in Italy and France. Practised sculpture with distinguished success until 1838, when he retired. A Trustee of the Commercial Bank of London; unsuccessfully contested Beverley in 1837. Author of various essays on the application of design to manufactures. A Liberal, in favour of the ballot and removal of commercial restrictions. Elected for Ipswich 3 July 1841. Unseated May 1842, when the election was declared void on petition. Governor of Falkland Islands Nov. 1847-July 1855. Died 22 Mar. 1860. [1842]

RENTON, John Campbell. Mordington House, Berwickshire. Conservative. B. at Edinburgh 1814. A Conservative and Protectionist. First elected for Berwick-on-Tweed July 1847 and sat until July 1852 when he was an unsuccessful candidate. The election was however declared void for bribery but he was again unsuccessful at the subsequent election in May 1853. [1851]

REPTON, George William John. 29 Curzon Street, London. Odell Castle, Bedford. Carlton. Only s. of George Stanley Repton, Esq., by the eld. d. of Lord Chancellor Eldon. B. in Norfolk Street, Park Lane, London 1818; m. 1848, Lady Jane, only d. of the 3rd Duke of Leinster. A Conservative. Sat for St. Alban's from 1841 till its disenfranchisement in 1852. Sat for Warwick from July 1852-Dec. 1868; was re-elected Feb. 1874 and sat until he retired in 1885. [1885]

REYNOLDS, John. Dublin. Eske House, Rathmines, Co. Dublin. A Draper in the city of Dublin. Elected Lord Mayor of Dublin 1849-50. A Repealer. First returned for Dublin in 1847 and sat until defeated in 1852. Contested same seat in 1857. Died 21 Aug. 1868. [1852]

RICARDO, David. Gatcombe Park, Gloucestershire. 59 Harley Street, London. S. of David Ricardo, Esq., the celebrated writer on Political Economy, who was of Jewish extraction, but being a Unitarian Christian was able to take his seat in the House. B. 1803; m. 1824, Catherine, d. of W.T. St. Quintin, Esq., of Sampston, Yorkshire. Mr. Ricardo's estate was within a few miles of Stroud. Of Whig principles, and in favour of free-trade. Returned for Stroud in 1832, and sat until he accepted Chiltern Hundreds May 1833. Died 17 May 1864. [1833]

RICARDO, John Lewis. 31 Lowndes Square, London. Exbury House, Fawley, Hampshire. Brooks's. B. 1812; m. 1841, d. of Gen. the Hon. Sir A. Duff, and sister of 5th Earl of Fife. Chairman of the North Staffordshire Railway, and a Director of the London and Westminster Bank. Appointed a Dept.-Lieut. of Elginshire, 1848. Author of the *History and Anatomy of the Navigation Laws*. A Liberal, in favour of vote by ballot. First elected for Stoke-upon-Trent in 1841. MP until his death in 1862. [1862]

RICARDO, Osman. 71 Eaton Place, London. Bromesberrow Place, Ledbury, Worcestershire. Brooks's, and Union. Eld. s. of David Ricardo, Esq., (many years MP for Portarlington, and well known as the author of works on currency, etc.) by the d. of — Wilkinson, Esq. M. Harriet, youngest d. of Robert Harvey Mallory, Esq., of Woodcote, Warwickshire. Educ. at Trinity Coll., Cambridge, where he graduated B.A. 1816. Appointed a Dept.-Lieut. of Worcestershire 1848. A Liberal, voted for the ballot 1853, and against Church rates 1855. First returned for Worcester 1847 and sat until he retired 1865. Died 2 Jan. 1881. [1865]

RICARDO, Samson. 38 Lowndes Street, London. Titness Park, Sunning Hill, Berkshire. Brooks's, and Reform. Bro. of David Ricardo, Esq. B. at Bow, Middlesex 1792. Unmarried. Author of pamphlets on Banking and Currency. A Director of New British Iron Company. A Liberal, in favour of a system of national education, civil and religious liberty, etc. Unsuccessfully contested Kidderminster July 1841, Totnes July 1847, and Windsor July 1852. First elected for Windsor Feb. 1855, without opposition. Retired 1857. Died 14 Nov. 1862. [1857]

RICE, Edward Royd. 15 Suffolk Street, London. Dane Court, Kent. United University. B. 1790; m. 1818, Elizabeth, 2nd d. of Edward Knight, Esq., of Godmersham Park, Kent. Educ. at Worcester Coll., Oxford, where he graduated B.A. 1813, M.A. 1815. Was formerly a Banker at Dover (retired in 1827). A Dept.-Lieut. for the Co. of Kent, for which he was High Sheriff in 1830. A Liberal. Contested Dover in 1835. Sat for Dover from 1837 until he retired 1857. Died 27 Nov. 1878. [1857]

RICE, Rt. Hon. Thomas Spring, F.A.S. 8 Mansfield Street, London. Mount Trenchard, Limerick. Athenaeum, and Reform. B. 1790; m. 1811, Theodosia, eld. d. of the Earl of Limerick. Was Under-Sec. of State in the Canning Administration. In 1830, was appointed a Sec. of the Treasury, and on the formation of Lord Melbourne's Administration became Sec. for the Colonies, which office he lost in Nov. of the same year. Chancellor of the Exchequer from Apr. 1835, salary £5,000. In 1816, he published a

pamphlet on the Grand Jury system. Sat for Limerick from 1820-1832. From then for Cambridge until he accepted Chiltern Hundreds Aug. 1839. Appointed Comptroller-Gen. of the Exchequer 1839. Created Baron Monteagle Sept. 1839. Died 7 Feb. 1866. [1838]

RICH, Henry. 28 Chapel Street, Grosvenor Square, London. Dorfold Hall, Nantwich, Cheshire. Brooks's, and Athenaeum. Youngest s. of Admiral Sir Thomas Rich, by Elizabeth, youngest d. of General Burt. M. 1852, Julia, youngest d. of the Rev. James Tomkinson, of Dorfield Hall, Cheshire. Was educ. at Sandhurst, and at Trinity Coll., Cambridge; graduated B.A. 1825. Served at the taking of Poonah, and at the battle of Kirkee, for which he received a medal. Was Groom in Waiting to the Queen; and a Lord of the Treasury from July 1846 till Mar. 1852. Author of several political pamphlets. A Reformer, said 'his efforts will ever be in support of that steady, firm and progressive Reform which best preserves all our institutions by keeping them in harmony with the advanced education and morality of our countrymen.' Unsuccessfully contested Knaresborough in 1832 and 1835, for which borough he sat from 1837 till 1841. First elected for Richmond in Apr. 1846, without a contest and sat until he accepted Chiltern Hundreds 1861. Created Bart. 22 Jan. 1863. Died 5 Nov. 1869. [1861]

RICHARD, Henry. 22 Bolton Gardens, South Kensington, London. Devonshire. S. of the Rev. Ebenezer Richard, a Calvinistic Methodist minister, of Tregaron, Cardiganshire, by Mary, d. of William Williams, Esq., of the same place. B. at Tregaron 1812; m. 1866, August Matilda, 3rd d. of John Farley, Esq., of Kennington Park Road, near London. Was educ. at a private school in Wales, and subsequently at Highbury Congregational Coll. Was for several years Minister of Marlborough (Independent) Chapel, Southwark. Was Secretary of the London Peace Society from 1848-1885. Author of *Memoirs of Joseph Sturge, Social and Political Condition of the Principality of Wales, The Present and Future of India,*, etc. An 'advanced Liberal', in favour of Home Rule, and of the total severance of Church and State. Sat for Merthyr Tydvil from Dec. 1868. MP until his death 20 Aug. 1888. [1888]

RICHARDS, Evan Matthew. 3 Kensington Gate, London. Brooklands, Nr. Swansea. Reform. B. at Swansea 1821, the s. of Richard Richards, Esq., of Swansea, and Catherine, his wife. M. 1844, Maria, only d. of James Sloane, Esq. A Magistrate for Swansea and Magistrate and Dept.-Lieut. of Glamorganshire and Cardiganshire. A Liberal, had great confidence in 'the wisdom and integrity of Mr. Gladstone', and gave him an independent support. Wanted County Finance Boards to be established to reduce the county rates. Unsuccessfully contested Honiton in 1865. Sat for Cardiganshire from Dec. 1868-1874, when he was defeated. Died 21 Aug. 1880. [1873]

RICHARDS, John. 13 Cadogan Place, London. Wassall Grove, Worcestershire. A Native of Stourbridge. A Hop Factor in London; formerly carried on business at Worcester. Entertained Whig principles. M. d. of — Pauncefort, Esq. Was in favour of a revision of the Corn Laws, Triennial Parliaments, and removing the Bishops from the House of Lords. Sat for Knaresborough from 1832 until he retired in 1837. Contested Southwark 25 July 1837. [1837]

RICHARDS, Richard. 21 Park Crescent, Portland Place, London. Caerynwch, Merionethshire. Carlton, and United University. Eld. s. of Lord Chief Baron Richards. B. 1787; m. Harriet, d. of Jonathan Dennett, Esq. A Conservative, voted for agricultural protection 1846. First elected for Merionethshire on the resignation of Sir R.W. Vaughan, Bart. in 1836, and sat until he retired in 1852. Died 27 Dec. 1860. [1852]

RICHARDSON, James Nicholson. Mount Caulfield, Bessbrook, Co. Armagh. S. of John Grubb Richardson, Esq., of Moyallen House, Co. Down, and Bessbrook, Co. Armagh, by Helena, d. of Richard Grubb, Esq., of Cahir Abbey, Co. Tipperary. B. 1846; m. 1867, Sophia, d. of William Malcolmson, Esq., of Portlaw, Co. Waterford. Was educ. at Grove House, Tottenham. A Merchant. A Liberal, in favour of 'the extension of the ancient Ulster customer of tenant right'; also that tenants should be assisted to purchase their holdings to try 'the experiment of a peasant proprietary.' In favour also of a reform of the Grand Jury Laws. Sat for Armagh Co. from Apr. 1880 until he retired in 1885. [1885]

RICHARDSON, Jonathan. Lambey, Lisburn, Ireland. Eld. s. of John Richardson, Esq., of Lisburn, by Harriett, d. of James Greer, Esq., of Clanrole, Co. Armagh. Cousin of Jonathan Joseph Richardson, Esq., who was MP for Lisburn from Aug. 1853, to Mar. 1857. B. at Lisburn 1804; m. 1828, Margaret, only surviving d. and heir of Alexander Airth, Esq., of Craigs, Dumfriesshire. Educ. at Lisburn, and at Southgate Hertfordshire. Extensively engaged in the linen trade. A Conservative, in favour of 'tenant-right' in Ireland. First returned for Lisburn Oct. 1853, and sat until he accepted Chiltern Hundreds Feb. 1863. Defeated at a by-election at Lisburn 26 June 1863. Died 2 Oct. 1876. [1862]

RICHARDSON, Thomas. Continued in House after 1885: full entry in Volume II.

RICKFORD, William. 19 New Street, Spring Gardens, London. Aylesbury. Union. B. 1768. A native of and Banker in Aylesbury; a Director of the Gas Light and Coke Company. A Conservative. Sat for Aylesbury from 1818 until he retired in 1841. [1840]

RIDER, Thomas. 16 Suffolk Street, London. Boughton, Monchelsea, West Kent. A Reformer, in favour of the ballot, a revision of the corn laws, and the immediate abolition of slavery. Sat for Kent W. from 1832, displacing Sir Edward Knatchbull who had voted against the first Reform Bill in 1831. Defeated in 1835. Contested Kent E. Aug. 1837. [1833]

RIDLEY, Edward. 2 Charles Street, London. 3 King's Bench Walk, Temple, London. Carlton, and Oxford & Cambridge. 2nd s. of Sir Matthew White Ridley, of Blagdon, Northumberland, by Cecilia, eld. d. of Lord Wensleydale. B. at Blagdon 1843. Educ. at Harrow and at Corpus Christi Coll., Oxford, was 1st class in classics 1866, and became fellow of All Souls. Called to the bar at the Inner Temple 1868. A Conservative, gave 'loyal but independent support to Lord Beaconsfield's government.' first returned for S. Northumberland Apr. 1878, when both candidates polled the same number of votes, and was seated on the petition of his opponent being withdrawn. Defeated 1880. QC 1892. Judge of High Court 1897-1917. Knighted 1897. Died 14 Oct. 1928. [1880]

RIDLEY, George. 2 Charles Street, Berkeley Square, London. Brooks's. Youngest s. of Sir Matthew White Ridley, Bart. (who sat for Newcastle from 1812 till his death in 1836), by Laura, youngest d. of George Hawkins, Esq. B. in London 1818. Educ. at Winchester, and at Christ Church, Oxford. Called to the bar at the Middle Temple 1843. A Liberal, in favour of the abolition of Church rates; opposed to the grant to Maynooth. Unsuccessfully contested Northumberland S. July 1852. First returned for Newcastle-on-Tyne 1856 and sat until appointed member of Copyhold Commission Nov. 1860-1880. Died 4 Nov. 1887. [1860]

RIDLEY, Sir Matthew White, Bart. (I). 10 Carlton House Terrace, London. Heaton Hall, and Blagdon, Northumberland. B. 1778; m. 1803, Laura, youngest d. of George Hawkins, Esq. A

Banker at Newcastle, and owner of extensive collieries in the neighbourhood. Patron of 3 livings. Of Whig principles; in favour of a fixed duty on foreign corn; against the ballot, the translation of Bishops and pluralities. Sat for Newcastle-upon-Tyne from 1812. MP until his death July 1836. [1836]

RIDLEY, Sir Matthew White, Bart. (II). 10 Carlton House Terrace, London. Blagdon, Cramlington, Northumberland. Carlton. Eld. s. of Sir W. Ridley, Bart. (who represented Newcastle-on-Tyne for some years), by Laura, youngest d. of George Hawkins, Esq. B. at Heaton Hall, 1807; m. 1841, eld. d. of 1st Lord Wensleydale. Educ. at Christ Church, Oxford, where he graduated B.A. 1828. Was High Sheriff of Northumberland, 1841. Appointed Major Northumberland Yeomanry Cavalry, 1848, and a Dept.-Lieut. of that county 1852. Patron of 3 livings. A Conservative, in favour of moderate Parliamentary Reform, but opposed to organic change; and in favour also of the navy being maintained in a high state of efficiency as 'England's best security from foreign aggression.' First elected for Northumberland N., May 1859 and sat until he retired in 1868. Died 25 Sept. 1877. [1867]

RIDLEY, Sir M.W. (III). Continued in House after 1885: full entry in Volume II.

RIPLEY, Sir Henry William. 6 Palace Gate, London. Acacia, Apperley, Leeds. Carlton. Only s. of Edward Ripley, Esq., of Bowing Lodge, near Bradford, by Anne, d. of N. Murgatroyd, Esq. B. at Bradford 1813; m. 1836, Anne, d. of John Milligan, Esq. A Manufacturer and Dyer at Bradford, and was President of the Bradford Chamber of Commerce for 1862-63. A Magistrate and Dept.-Lieut. for the W. Riding of Yorkshire and a Magistrate for Bradford. A Moderate Conservative. Sat for Bradford for a few months in 1869, when he was unseated on petition; re-elected Feb. 1874 and sat until defeated Apr. 1880. Created Bart. 8 May 1880. Died 9 Nov. 1882. [1880]

RIPPON, Cuthbert. Stanhope Castle, Co. Durham. Battersea, Surrey. Reform. S. of an eminent Broker on the Stock Exchange, who amassed a large fortune and purchased considerable estates in the Co. of Durham. A radical Reformer, in favour of expelling the Bishops from the House of Lords and the Clergy from the Magistracy. The advocate of Triennial Parliaments and fixed duty on corn, in conjunction with the removal of tithes and poor rates, the abolition of all monopolies, reform of the Church and the ballot. Sat for

Gateshead from 1832 until he retired 1841. [1838]

RITCHIE, C.T. Continued in House after 1885: full entry in Volume II.

ROBARTES, Hon. Thomas Charles Agar. 30 Upper Grosvenor Street, London. 2 Tanfield Court, Temple, London. Llanhydrock, Bodmin, Cornwall. Eld. s. of Baron Robartes (who sat for E. Cornwall from 1847-68), by Juliana, d. of Rt. Hon. Reginald Pole Carew, of E. Antony, Cornwall. B. 1844; m. 1878, Mexy, d. of Frances Henry Dickinson, Esq., of Kingweston, Somerset. Educ. at Christ Church Coll., Oxford. Called to the bar at the Middle Temple Apr. 1870. A Magistrate and Dept.-Lieut. of Cornwall. A Liberal. Sat for Cornwall E. from Apr. 1880 until he succeeded as 2nd Baron Mar. 1882. [1882]

ROBARTES, Thomas James Agar-. 1 Dean Street, Park Lane, London. Lanhydrock, Bodmin, Cornwall. Athenaeum. Only s. of the Hon. Charles Bagenal Agar, by the only d. and heir of Thomas Hunt, Esq., of Mollington Hall, Cheshire, grandniece and sole heir of Henry Robartes, 3rd Earl of Radnor (extinct). B. in London, 1808; m. 1839, Juliana, d. of the Rt. Hon. Reginald Pole Carew, of East Antony, Cornwall. Was educ. at Harrow, and at Christ Church, Oxford, where he graduated B.A. 1830. Assumed the name of Robartes in addition to his patronymic. Appointed a Special Dept. Warden of the Stannaries, 1852. A Liberal, and in favour of the franchise being reduced to £6 as a commencement; voted for the ballot 1853, and against church-rates 1855. First returned for Cornwall E. in 1847 and sat until he retired in 1868. Created Baron Robartes Nov. 1869. Died 9 Mar.1882. [1867]

ROBARTS, Abraham Wildey. 26 Hill Street, London. Roehampton, Surrey. A London Banker and East India proprietor. Of Whig principles, but voted against Catholic Emancipation. Sat for Maidstone in every Parliament from 1818 until he retired in 1837. Died 2 Apr. 1858. [1837]

ROBERTS, C. H. Crompton. Continued in House after 1885: full entry in Volume II.

ROBERTS, John. Continued in House after 1885: full entry in Volume II.

ROBERTSON, David. 56 Upper Brook Street, London. Lady Kirk, Berwickshire. Brooks's, Union, and Reform. B. at Eccles, Berwickshire 1797, the 4th s. of Sir John Marjoribanks, Bart., of Lees, Berwickshire (who sat for Buteshire in 1811 and Berwickshire in 1818), by Alison, eld. d.

of William Ramsay, Esq., of Barton, Co. Midlothian. M. 1834, Marianne Sarah, eld. d. of Sir Thomas Haggestone, Bart. Assumed the name of Robertson by Royal Sign-Manual 1834, in compliance with the will of his wife's maternal grandfather, William Robertson, Esq., of Lady Kirk. Educ. at the High School and the University of Edinburgh. Lord-Lieut. of Berwickshire. A Liberal. Sat for Berwickshire from May 1859-June 1873 when he was created Lord Majoribanks.   [1873]

ROBERTSON, Henry. 13 Lancaster Gate, London. Palè, Corwen, Merionethshire. Reform, and Devonshire. B. at Banff 1816, s. of Duncan Robertson, Esq., by his m. with Miss Christian Anderson. M. 1846, Elizabeth, d. of William Dean, Esq., of London. Educ. at King's Coll., Old Aberdeen, where he graduated M.A. Was a Civil Engineer and Iron-Master, and a Locomotive Engine Maker. Was Engineer of the Shrewsbury and Chester, the Shrewsbury and Birmingham, and the Shrewsbury and Hereford Railways. A Dept.-Lieut. and Magistrate of the Cos. of Denbigh and Merioneth, and High Sheriff of Merionethshire 1870. A Liberal, favoured peace, retrenchment and reform, and the readjustment of local taxation. Sat for Shrewsbury May 1862-July 1865 and Feb. 1874-Nov. 1885. Returned for Merionethshire 1885. Retired 1886. Died 22 Mar. 1888.   [1886]

ROBERTSON, Patrick Francis. 7 Pall Mall, London. Halton, Hastings. Carlton, and Conservative. Eld. s. of the Rev. Daniel Robertson, D.D. (Professor of Oriental Languages in St. Mary's Coll., St. Andrew's, from 1809 to 1817). B. at Meigle, Perthshire, 1807. Unmarried. Educ. at the University of St. Andrew's. A Merchant, formerly of Canton. Sub-Governor of the London Assurance Corporation. A Liberal-Conservative, would 'willingly support any real Parliamentary reform'; voted against the ballot 1853. Was an unsuccessful candidate for Hastings in July 1847. Sat for Hastings from July 1852 till Apr. 1859, when he was unsuccessful; again stood Oct. 1864, but was not re-elected till July 1865. Retired in 1868; contested same seat in 1869 and 1874. Died 20 Jan. 1885.   [1867]

ROBINSON, E.S. A Liberal. Returned for Bristol 29 May 1870 but unseated on petition. Contested Gloucester 8 May 1873 and Bristol in 1880.

ROBINSON, George Richard. 27 Chester Terrace, London. A Merchant and Shipowner, principally engaged in Newfoundland trade. Succeeded Mr. Alderman Thompson as Chairman of Lloyd's in 1834. An East India Proprietor. Director of the British American Land Company, and of the National Bank. A Conservative, originally opposed to free trade, but subsequently supported it and voted for the Reform Bill of 1832. In favour of the property tax and all direct taxation. Voted for a repeal of the malt tax 1835 and opposed to the endowment of the Roman Catholic clergy and the repeal of the Navigation Laws. Sat for Worcester from 1826-37; was an unsuccessful candidate for the Tower Hamlets in 1841. First elected for Poole in 1847 and remained MP until his death in Aug. 1850.   [1850]

ROBINSON, T. Continued in House after 1885: full entry in Volume II.

ROCHE, Sir David, Bart. 1 Park Square, Regent's Park, London. Brunswick Street, Limerick. Carass House, Co. Limerick. Barntick, Co. Clare. Reform. B. 1793, the eld. s. of David Roche of Carass House, Co. Limerick. M. 1825, Frances, d. of Col. Ormsby Vandelene. A Repealer. Voted against the Corn Laws. In 1832 Mr. O'Connell styled him on the hustings 'one of the most warm-hearted Protestants in Ireland.' He was the proposer of the plan for the abolition of tithes in Ireland adopted by the Melbourne Administration, but rejected by the House of Lords. Sat for Limerick from 1832 until he accepted Chiltern Hundreds 1844. Died 8 Apr. 1865.   [1844]

ROCHE, Edmund Burke. Rutland Square, Dublin. Trabolgan, Co. Cork. Reform. B. 1815, the only s. of Edmund Roche, Esq., of Trabolgan, by Margaret Honoria, only child and heir of William Curtain, Esq. Connected through his mother's family with that of the celebrated Edmund Burke, Esq. M. 1848, Eliza Caroline, eld. d. of J.B. Boothby, Esq., of Twyford Abbey, Middlesex. A radical Reformer and Repealer, but 'prepared to co-operate in the enactment of just measures of relief for the owners and occupiers of land.' Sat for the Co. of Cork from 1837 until he accepted Chiltern Hundreds in 1855.   [1855]

ROCHE, William. George Street, Limerick. Younger s. of Stephen Roche, Esq., of Limerick and of Granagh Castle. B. 1775. Was a Banker at Limerick. A Reformer. In 1832 Mr. O'Connell recommended him to the electors as 'the only man he knew after 30 years acquaintance, of whom no pledge need be demanded.' He was not a pledged Repealer, but declared his intention to give the Reformed Parliament a trial. He afterwards voted for Repeal. Sat for Limerick from 1832 until he retied 1841.   [1838]

RODEN. William Sargeant. B. in Wolverhampton 1829, the s. of William Roden, Esq., of Wolverhampton, by Anne, d. of Richard Brown, Esq. M. Theodora, d. of Samuel Butcher, Esq., of Sheffield, (she died 1867). Educ. at Bristol. An Iron-master in North Staffordshire. A Magistrate and Dept.-Lieut. for Staffordshire and Monmouthshire and Lieut.-Col. of the Staffordshire Artillery Volunteers. Was Mayor of Hanley 1868. A Liberal, in favour of workmen having greater facilities in making contracts. Sat for Stoke from Dec. 1868-1874 when he was defeated. Died 25 Apr. 1882. [1873]

RODWELL, Benjamin Bridges Hunter. Newcourt, Temple, London. Ampton Hall, Bury St. Edmunds. United University, and Wyndham. Eld. s. of William Rodwell, Esq., formerly of Woodlands, Suffolk, and senior Partner in the firm of Messrs. Bacon & Co., Bankers, Ipswich, by Elizabeth Ann, only d. of Benjamin Hunter, Esq., of Glencarse, Perthshire. B. 1815; m. 1844, Mary Packer, d. of James Boggis, Esq., (A Dept.-Lieut. for the Co. of Essex and Lieut.-Col. of the W. Essex Militia), of Baddow Court, Essex. Educ. at Charterhouse and Trinity Coll., Cambridge where he graduated M.A. 1840. Called to the bar at the Middle Temple 1840 and appointed Queen's Counsel 1858. A Bencher of the Middle Temple and a leader at the Parliamentary bar. A Magistrate and Dept.Lieut. for Suffolk. Appointed Chairman of Quarter Sessions 1862; Chairman of the Central Association of the five counties of Cambridgeshire, Huntingdonshire, Norfolk, Essex and Suffolk. Patron of 2 livings. Author of a pamphlet on *Tenant Right*. A Conservative, was firmly attached to the Established Church but not opposed to those amendments in the administrative and social system which may be rendered necessary by the progress and spirit of the age. Took an active part against the union delegates during the agitation 1874. Sat for Cambridgeshire from Oct. 1874 until he accepted Chiltern Hundreds Aug. 1881. Contested Suffolk N.E. 4 Dec. 1885. Died 6 Feb. 1892. [1881]

ROE, James. 21 Manchester Buildings, London. Roesborough, Co. Tipperary. A Repealer. He was elected for Cashel in 1832 in opposition to William Pennefather, Esq., to whose family Cashel, before the passing of the Reform Bill, was said to have belonged. Retired in 1834. [1833]

ROE, T. Continued in House after 1885: full entry in Volume II.

ROEBUCK, Rt. Hon. John Arthur. 19 Ashley Place, Victoria Street, London. Reform. S. of E. Roebuck, Esq., of Madras, and grand-s. of the celebrated M. Roebuck Esq., of Sheffield. B. at Madras 1801; m. 1834, Henrietta, d. of the Rev. Thomas Falconer, of Bath, the author of several learned works and formerly Bampton Lecturer at Oxford. Called to the bar at the Inner Temple 1831 and joined the Northern circuit; appointed a Queen's Counsel 1843; a Bencher of the Inner Temple. Sometime Agent in England for the House of Assembly of Lower Canada. Author of a work on *The Colonies of England, History of the Whig Ministry of 1830,* and contributed much to the *Edinburgh* and *Westminster Reviews.* A Liberal, and was Chairman of the Administrative Reform Assoc. Sat for Bath 1832-37; and from June 1841-July 1847. Sat for Sheffield from May 1849-Nov. 1869, when he was unsuccessful candidate there. Re-elected there Feb. 1874. MP until his death 30 Nov. 1879. [1879]

ROGERS, Charles Coltman. Stanage Park, Knighton, and The Home, Shropshire. Brooks's, and New Univeristy. Eld. s. of the Rev. John Rogers, of Stanage Park, and the Home, sometime vicar of Amestry, Herefordshire, by Charlotte Victoria, d. of the Rev. Francis Stonehewer Newbold. D.D. B. 1854. Educ. at Eton, and Brasenose Coll., Oxford; B.A. 1876, M.A. 1879. A patron of 1 living. A Liberal, in favour of improved local government, 'local option', municipal self-government for London, and a 'further cheapening of the transfer of land.' Returned for Radnor boroughs 30 Oct. 1884. Defeated in 1885 contesting Radnorshire. Chairman of Radnorshire County Council from 1896. Died 19 May 1929. [1885]

ROGERS, James Edwin Thorold. Beaumont Street, Oxford. B. at West Meon 1823, s. of George Vining Rogers, Esq., of West Meon, Hampshire, by his m. with Miss Mary Ann Blyth. M. Ann Susannah, 2nd d. of Henry R. Reynolds, Esq., one time Solicitor to the Treasury. Educ. at King's Coll., London and at Magdalen Hall, Oxford. Graduated B.A. 1st class in classics 1846, and M.A. 1849. Appointed Master of the Schools at Oxford University 1853 and Classical Examiner for 1857-58. Was Tooke Professor of Economic Science at Kings's Coll., London 1859 and Professor of Political Economy at Oxford 1862-68. Was a Clergyman of the Church of England but relinquished Orders to enter Parliament. Author of numerous works, including *Protests of the Lords with Historical Introductions,* a *Manual of Political Economy, Six Centuries of Work and Wages, A History of Agriculture and Prices,* etc. An advanced Liberal, but was undecided on the question of Home Rule. Was an unsuccessful candidate for Scarborough Feb. 1874. Sat for Southwark from Apr. 1880-1886, when he was defeated standing as a Gladstonian Liberal. Died 12 Oct. 1890. [1886]

ROGERS, John Hope. Penrose, Helstone, Cornwall. Carlton. S. of the Rev. John Rogers, Canon of Exeter Cathedral, by Mary, d. of the Rev. John Hope. B. 1816; m. 1844, Maria, d. of William Hichens, Esq. Educ. at Shrewsbury School, and at Trinity Coll., Oxford, where he graduated M.A. Called to the bar at the Inner Temple 1842. A joint Chairman of Quarter Sessions of Cornwall from 1858. A Dept.-Lieut. of Cornwall. A Conservative, in favour of 'cautiously adapting our time-honoured institutions to the constantly varying conditions of the people'; in favour also of 'keeping up the efficiency of our naval and military establishments, guarding the expenditure by a vigilant control.' First elected for Helstone May 1859 and sat until he retired 1865. Died 24 Apr. 1880. [1865]

ROLFE, Sir Robert Monsey. 8 New Street, Spring Gardens, London. 11 Lincoln's Inn, New Square, London. Reform. Related to Lord Nelson. Was Solicitor-Gen. for a short period before the dissolution of Lord Melbourne's administration in 1834. Resumed his office in Apr. 1835. Recorder of Bury St. Edmunds. Sat for Penryn from 1832 until appointed Baron of the Exchequer Dec. 1839 or Jan. 1840. [1838]

ROLLESTON, Lancelot. 8 Hertford Street, London. Watnall Hall, Nottinghamshire. S. and heir of Christopher Rolleston, who was High Sheriff for Nottinghamshire in 1805. B. 20 July 1785. M. 17 Nov. 1808, Caroline, sister of Sir Geo. Chetwynd, Bart. Was Col. of the Nottinghamshire Militia. A Conservative, voted for agricultural protection, 1846; opposed to the endowment of the Roman Catholic clergy. Was an unsuccessful candidate for Nottingham in 1820. Sat for Nottinghamshire S. from 1837 until he accepted Chiltern Hundreds Mar. 1849. Died 18 May 1862. [1847 2nd ed.]

ROLLS, John Allan, F.S.A. South Lodge, Rutland Gate, London. The Hendre, Monmouth. Carlton, Arthur's, and Junior Carlton. Only s. of John Etherington Welch Rolls, Esq., of the Hendre, Monmouthshire, a Magistrate and Dept.-Lieut. of that county, by Elizabeth Mary, d. of Walter Long, Esq., of Preshaw, Hampshire, and of Lady Mary, d. of the 7th Earl of Northesk. B. at the Hendre, 1837; m. 1868, Georgiana Marcia, youngest d. of Sir Charles Macleon, Bart., of Morvaren. Was educ. at Eton, and at Christ Church Coll., Oxford. A Magistrate and Dept.-Lieut. of Monmouthsire, of which he was High Sheriff 1875. Was Capt. Royal Gloucestershire Hussars. Patron of 2 livings. A Conservative, but 'not opposed to progress where progress is desirable'; in favour of maintaining the union between Church and State; in favour of a readjustment of local taxation, 'the relief of land from the unfair burdens now imposed upon it', etc. Sat for Monmouthshire from Apr. 1880 until defeated in 1885 contesting N. division of Monmouthshire. Contested the same seat again July 1892. [1885]

ROLT, Sir John. 5a Cork Street, London. 6 Stone Buildings, Lincoln's Inn, London. Ozleworth Park, Wotton under Edge, Gloucestershire. S. of James Rolt, Esq., of Calcutta. Merchant. M. 1st, Sarah, d. and co-heir of — Bosworth Esq., of Bosworth, Leicestershire (she died 1850); 2ndly, Elizabeth, d. of Stephen Godson, Esq., of Croydon (she died 1864). Was a Clerk in the office of Messrs. Pritchard and Son, Proctors in Doctor's Commons. Was called to the bar at the Inner Temple 1837 and made a Queen's Counsel in 1846. Appointed Attorney Gen. Nov. 1860. Was a Magistrate for Gloucestershire. A Conservative, in favour of moderate Parliamentary Reform and of the maintenace of Church rates. Was an unsuccessful candidate for Stamford in 1847, and for Bridport in 1852. Sat for Gloucestershire W. from Apr. 1857 until he was appointed Lord Justice of Appeal, July 1867. Resigned Feb. 1868. Died 6 June 1871. [1867]

ROLT, Peter. 23 Hyde Park Gardens, London. 72 Cornhill, London. Acorn Wharf, Lower Trinity Street, Rotherhithe. Carlton, Conservative, and City. B. at Deptford 1798, s. of John David Rolt, Esq., of Deptford, by Sophia, eld. d. of Peter Butt, Esq., Clerk of the Survey in Deptford Dockyard. Grands. of John Rolt, senior, Clerk in Deptford Dockyard, who died 1796. M. 1820, Mary, eld. d. of Thomas Brocklebank, Esq., of Deptford, Managing Director of the General Steam Navigation Company (she died 1845). A Timber Merchant and Contractor, partner in the firm of Brocklebank and Rolt. Appointed Dept.-Lieut. of Middlesex 1854. A Conservative, and considered 'that the Roman Catholics cannot expect a renewal of the Maynooth Grant.' First returned for Greenwich in July 1852 and sat until he accepted Chiltern Hundreds in Jan. 1857, having taken a Government Contract. Died 3 Sept. 1882. [1856]

ROMILLY, Edward. 49 Weymouth Street, London. 3rd s. of Sir S. Romilly, and younger bro. of the Member for Bridport. A Reformer, in favour of triennial Parliaments, the vote by ballot, the abolition of close corporations, the abolition of tithes, an equitable distribution of salaries amongst the Clergy, a revision of the poor laws, and the repeal of the house and window tax. Sat for Ludlow from 1832. Defeated in 1835. [1833]

ROMILLY, Frederick. 15 Eaton Square, London. Guard's, and Brooks's. Youngest s. of Sir Samuel Romilly; was therefore bro. to Sir John Romilly. Entered the army in 1826; was Capt. and Lieut.-Col. Scots Fusilier Guards. Was private secretary to Lord Fortescue, when Lord Licut. of Ireland in 1839-40 and 1841. A Liberal, in favour of extension of the suffrage and an extended scheme of National Education. First returned for Canterbury Feb. 1850. Defeated in 1852. Contested Marylebone Feb. 1859. Commissioner of Customs from 1864. Died 6 Apr. 1887. [1852]

ROMILLY, Rt. Hon. Sir John. 32 Gordon Square, London. Rolls House, Chancery Lane, London. S. of Sir Samuel Romilly, by the eld. d. of Francis Garbett, Esq. M. d. of Bishop (Otter) of Chichester. Educ. at Trinity Coll., Cambridge, where he graduated M.A. 1826. Was called to the bar by the Society of Gray's Inn, in 1827. A Queen's Counsel. A bencher of Gray's Inn. Appointed Solicitor-Gen. Apr. 1848; was Attorney-Gen. from July 1850 till Mar. 1851, when he was appointed Master of the Rolls, salary £6000. A Liberal. Sat for Bridport from 1832 till 1835, and sat for the same bor. on petition, in Apr. 1846. Was elected for Devonport in 1847 and sat until defeated in 1852. Created Baron Romilly Jan. 1866. Died 23 Dec. 1874. [1852]

RONAYNE, Dominick. Ringvine, Co. Waterford. A cousin of Daniel O'Connell. A Barrister. A Repealer. Returned for Clonmel in 1832 and remained MP until his death Jan. 1836. [1835]

RONAYNE, Joseph Philip. Rinn Ronain, Queenstown, Ireland. S. of Edward Ronayne, Esq. of Mount Verdun, Cork, by Margaret, d. of John Meany, Esq., of Durickmore, Co. Cork. B. at Cork 1822; m. 1859, Elizabeth, d. of Edward Stace White, Esq., Commander R.N. Was educ. at Hamblin's and Porter's School, Cork. A Civil Engineer. A member of the Society of Civil Engineers, London. A Liberal, and insisted on 'the right and ability of Ireland to govern herself.' Sat for Cork from Dec. 1872. MP until his death 7 May 1876. [1876]

ROOPER, John Bonfoy. 111 Gloucester Place, London. Abbott's Repton, Huntingdonshire. A Reformer. Patron of 1 living. Returned for Huntingdonshire from 1831 (displacing Lord

Strathaven, who had succeeded against him in 1830) and sat until defeated in 1837. Died 11 Mar. 1855. [1837]

RORKE, J.H. A Liberal. Sat for Longford from Dec. 1832, but in Apr. 1833 the election was declared void and he did not stand at the subsequent election.

ROSE, Lord Boscawen, See BOS-CAWEN-ROSE, Lord.

ROSE, Rt. Hon. Sir George Henry. 7 Old Palace Yard. Sandhills, Christchurch, Hampshire. Eld. s. of the Rt. Hon. George Rose. M. d. of — Duncombe, Esq. Clerk of the Parliaments and Lord of the Manor of Christchurch. A Conservative. Was elected for Southampton in 1796; was Secretary of the legation at the Court of Berlin. Edited the Marchmont Papers. Sat for Christchurch in the Parliament of 1818. Again returned for Christchurch July 1837 and sat until he accepted Chiltern Hundreds Feb. 1844. Died 17 June 1855. [1843]

ROSE, William Anderson. Queenhithe, London. Upper Tooting, Surrey. S. of Arthur Rose, Esq., and Susanna, his wife. B. in London 1820; m. 1st, Charlotte, relict of Thomas Metcalfe Flockton; 2ndly, Charlotte Grace, eld. d. of Capt. Winterton Snow, of the Madras Army. Educ. at University Coll. A Merchant in London. An Alderman of London; was High Sheriff of London and Middlesex 1855-56; Lord Mayor of London for 1862-63. A Commissioner of Licutenancy for the City of London, and Senior Maj. of the London Rifle Volunteers. A Magistrate for Middlesex, and Governor of the Irish Society. A Conservative, in favour of the 'army, navy, and the defences of the country being kept in a most efficient condition'; would preserve the 'present relations between Church and State,' but would combine therewith 'complete religious freedom for all sects.' Contested Newport, Isle of Wight Mar. 1857. First elected for Southampton Nov. 1862. Defeated 1865. Knighted Aug. 1867. Died 9 June 1881. [1865]

ROSS, A.H. Continued in House after 1885: full entry in Volume II.

ROSS, Charles. 60 Portland Place, London. St. Germain's. Lamer, Hertfordshire. Carlton, and Athenaeum. M. 1825, d. of Charles, 2nd Marq. Cornwallis; was a West India Proprietor; was a Lord of the Admiralty. A Lord of the Treasury from Dec. 1834 till Apr. 1835. A Conservative. Sat for St. Germains from 1826 till 1832, when he was elected for Northampton and sat until defeated in 1837. Died 21 Mar. 1860. [1837]

333

ROSS, Charles Campbell. Carne. Penzance. Carlton. S. of Archibald Colquhoun Ross, Esq., M.D., by his m. with Miss Mary Carne. B. in London 1849; m. 1870, Isabel Emily, d. of Edward Holland, Esq., and his wife Emily Rossmore Crooke. Was educ. at Brighton Coll., and at Trinity Coll., Cambridge. A Banker at Penzance, a Partner in the firm of Messrs. Batten, Carne and Co. Was five times Mayor of Penzance, 1877-82. A Conservative. Unsuccessfully contested St. Ives Apr. 1880. Returned for St. Ives Apr. 1881 and sat until defeated 1885.   [1885]

ROSS, David Robert. 15 Great Ryder Street, London. Rosstrevor, Co. Down. Reform. S. of Rev. Thomas Ross. B. 1797; m. 1819, d. of Bishop Knox (of Limerick), and grand-d. of the 1st Earl of Ranfurly. Formerly in the Dragoons. A Dept.-Lieut. for the Co. of Down, of which he was Sheriff in 1837. Held Liberal opinions, and in favour of free trade. Candidate at Belfast on the Liberal interest in 1841; returned there in 1842, after voidance of the 1841 election and sat until he retired in 1847. Contested Mallow Aug. 1847. Lieut.-Gov. of Tobago Feb. 1851 until his death 27 July 1851.   [1847]

ROSS, Horatio. 3 George Street, St. James's, London. Rossie Castle. Of Whig principles. Sat for Aberdeen in the Parliament of 1831. Sat for Montrose district from 1832. Defeated in 1835 contesting Paisley. A notable Deer-Stalker; acted as second in 16 duels. Died 6 Jan. 1886. [1833]

ROTCH, Benjamin. 8 Sidmouth Street, Gray's Inn, London. 1 Furnival's Inn, London. Lowlands, Nr. Harrow, Middlesex. A Barrister. Chairman of the Middlesex Quarter Sessions. Entertained Whig principles. Sat for Knaresborough from 1832. Retired in 1835.   [1833]

ROTHSCHILD, Baron F. de. Continued in House after 1885: full entry in Volume II.

ROTHSCHILD, Baron Lionel Nathan de. 148 Piccadilly, London. St. Swithin's Lane, City, London. Gunnersbury Park, Acton, Middlesex. Brooks's, and Reform. B. in London 1808, the eld. s. of Baron Nathan Mayer de Rothschild (a native of Frankfurt-am-Main who came to England in 1800), by Hannah, 3rd d. of Levi Barnet Cohen, Esq., Merchant of London. M. 1836, his cousin Charlotte, d. of the Baron Charles de Rothschild, of Naples. Was educ. at Göttingen. Was head of the Mercantile firm de Rothschild, well known for their extensive operations as public loan contractors and money brokers. A Dept.-Lieut. of London. A Liberal,

favoured direct taxation. First elected for London in 1847, but did not take his seat and vote until July 1858, when he was enabled to omit the words in the oath to which he objected. Sat until 1868, when he was unsuccessful, but was re-elected in Feb. 1869. Sat until 1874, when he was defeated. Died 3 June 1879.   [1873]

ROTHSCHILD, Baron Mayer de. 107 Piccadilly. London. Mentmore. Leighton Buzzard, Buckinghamshire. Brooks's. B. 1818, the 4th s. of Baron Nathan Mayer de Rothschild. of Frankfurt, by Hannah, 3rd d. of Levi Barnet Cohen, Merchant of London. M. 1850, Juliana, eld. d. of Isaac Cohen, Esq. Educ. at Trinity Coll., Cambridge. A Magistrate and Dept.-Lieut. of Buckinghamshire. Patron of 1 living. A Liberal. Sat for Hythe from Feb. 1859-1874, when he retired. Died 6 Feb. 1874.   [1873]

ROTHSCHILD, Sir Nathaniel Mayer De. Bart. 148 Piccadilly, London. Gunnersbury Park, Ealing. Devonshire, and City Liberal. Eld. s. of Baron Lionel Nathan De Rothschild, MP for London, of Gunnersbury Park, Middlesex, by Charlotte, d. of the Baron Charles de Rothschild, of Naples. B. in London, 1840; m. 1867, Emma, d. of Baron Charles de Rothschild. A Commissioner of Lieutenancy for London. A Liberal. First elected for Aylesbury July 1865 and sat until created Baron Rothschild in 1885. Lord-Lieut. Buckinghamshire 1889. Died 31 Mar. 1915.   [1885]

ROUND, Charles Gray. 25 Upper Brook Street, London. Birch Hall, Essex. S. of George Round, Esq., a Banker at Colchester. B. 1797; m. 1838, d. of George Brock, Esq., of St. Mary's, Nr. Colchester. A Barrister. Recorder of Colchester, and Chairman of the quarter sessions for Essex. A relation to the Member for Maldon. M.A. of Balliol Coll., Oxford. A Conservative, voted for agricultural protection, 1846. First elected for Essex N. 29 July 1837 and sat until he retired in 1847. Contested Oxford University against W.E. Gladstone in 1847. Died 1 Dec. 1867.   [1847]

ROUND, John. (I). Danbury Park, Essex. Carlton. Eld. s. of John Round, Esq., of Colchester. B. Mar. 1783; m. 18 Mar. 1815, eld. d. of George Caswall, Esq., of Sacombe Park, Hertfordshire, (she died in 1845). M.A. and D.C.L. of Balliol Coll., Oxford. High Steward of Colchester, his native place. Served the office of High Sheriff of Essex in 1835. A Conservative, voted for agricultural protection, 1846. Was Member for Ipswich from 1812-1818, but lost his election for Maldon in 1820. First elected for Maldon 26 July 1837 and sat until he retired in 1847. Died 28 Apr. 1860.   [1847]

ROUND, J. (II). Continued in House after 1885: full entry in Volume II.

ROUNDELL, C.S. Continued in House after 1885: full entry in Volume II.

ROUPELL, William. 16 St. James's Square, London. Roupell Park, Brixton, London. S. of Richard Palmer Roupell, Esq., of Lambeth and Southwark, Lead Smelter. B. in Lambeth 1831. Unmarried. Called to the bar at the Inner Temple Apr. 1861. Major-Commandant 19th Surrey Rifle Volunteers. A 'member of the most advanced section' of the Liberal party, in favour of the ballot, against church-rates, etc; opposed 'on principle to every form of grant of public money for religious purposes'. First elected for Lambeth Apr. 1857 and sat until he accepted Chiltern Hundreds Apr. 1862. Left for Spain but returned to be convicted for forgery Sept. 1862; released 1869. [1862]

ROUS, Hon. Henry John. 28 Chapel Street, Park Lane, London. Bro. to the Earl of Stradbroke, and was therefore descended from a family established in Suffolk since the Heptarchy. B. 1795; m. 1836, the d. of J.R. Cuthbert, Esq. Entered the navy in 1818 and served under Sir W. Hoste. Commanded on several occasions with distinguished success under very adverse circumstances. A Conservative. Sat for Westminster from 1841 until he was defeated at a by-election on 19 Feb. 1846, on his appointment as Lord of the Admiralty. Became an Admiral 1863. A prominent man of the Turf and was the author of *The Laws and Practice of Horse Racing*, (1850). Died 19 June 1877. [1845]

ROWLEY, Hon. Richard Thomas. 47 Berkeley Square, London. Bodrhyddon, Rhyl, Flintshire. Carlton, and Senior United Service. S. of 1st Lord Langford, by Frances, only d. and heir of the Hon. Clotworthy Rowley (afterwards Dowager Lady Langford). B. 1812; m. 1835, Charlotte, d. of Lieut.-Col. Shipley, and niece of Sir Watkin W. Wynn. Educ. at Eton. Formerly Capt. and Lieut. Scots Fusilier Guards. Appointed a Dept.-Lieut. of Flint 1850; Lieut.-Col. Flintshire Militia 1855, Also Lieut.-Co. commanding the Flintshire Rifle Volunteers. A Conservative. Was an unsuccessful candidate for Harwich Apr. 1859. First elected for Harwich Mar. 1860. and sat until he retired 1865. Died 11 Nov. 1887. [1865]

ROYSTON, Rt. Hon. Visct. 33 Hertford Street, London. Wimpole Hall, Caxton, Royston, Cambridgeshire. White's, Carlton, and Travellers'. B. at Wimpole Hall, Cambridgeshire 1836, the eld. s. of Earl of Hardwicke, by the Hon. Susan, 6th d. of 1st Lord Ravensworth. M. 1863, Lady Sophia Georgiana, 2nd d. of 1st Earl Cowley. Educ. at Harrow and at Trinity Coll., Cambridge, where he graduated M.A. 1858. Appointed Cornet 7th Hussars 1857, served in the Indian Campaign 1858-59, and received the Indian Medal. Exchanged to the 11th Hussars Dec. 1859 and retired May 1861. Was Controller of the Queen's Household from July 1866-Dec. 1868. A Conservative, voted against the disestablishment of the Irish Church 1869. Sought a reduction in the malt duty. Sat for Cambridgeshire from July 1865-Sept. 1873, when he succeeded as 5th Earl. Died 18 May 1897. [1873]

RUDDELL-TODD, James. 11 John Street, Adelphi, London. Ballingtagart, Armagh. A Reformer, in favour of the immediate abolition of slavery. Sat for Honiton from 1833. Defeated in 1835. [1833]

RUFFORD, Francis. Bellbroughton, Stourbridge, Worcestershire. Alfred. A Glass Manufacturer and Banker at Stourbridge, and at Bromsgrove, Worcestershire. Chairman of the Oxford, Worcester, and Wolverhampton Railway; Director of the Birmingham and Oxford, and the Birmingham and Wolverhampton Railways; a Magistrate for Staffordshire and Worcestershire; and a Dept.-Lieut. for the latter county. A Conservative and Protectionist; a supporter of the property tax in lieu of taxes on articles of consumption; opposed to the endowment of the Roman Catholic Clergy, but in favour of education without regard to religious opinions. First returned for Worcester in 1847 and sat until he accepted Chiltern Hundreds Apr. 1852. Died 1854? [1852]

RUMBOLD, Charles Edmund. 1 Eccleston Square, London. Preston Candover, Hampshire. S. of Sir Thomas Rumbold (1st Bart.), Governor of Madras, by his 2nd wife, d. of Bishop (Law) of Carlisle. M. Harriet, d. of John Gardner, Esq., of Ashford, Kent. Educ. at Trinity Coll., Cambridge, where he graduated M.A. 1814. A moderate Whig. Sat for Yarmouth from 1818-1835, when he was an unsuccessful candidate; again elected in 1837, and sat until 1847, when he was a second time unsuccessful, but a new election took place on petition, and he was again returned and sat until he retired 1857. Died 31 May 1857. [1857]

RUNDLE, John. Cockspur Street, London. Tavistock, Bedfordshire. Albion, and Reform. S. of William Rundle, Esq. Merchant and Banker at Tavistock. B. 1791; m. 1824, Barbara, youngest d. of John Gill, Esq., of Tavistock. A Banker in the

335

town. A Reformer, in favour of Triennial Parliaments, and the ballot. Pledged to resign his seat if called upon so to do by a majority of the electors. First elected for Tavistock 8 Jane. 1835 and sat until he accepted Chiltern Hundreds in Mar. 1843. Died 4 Jan. 1864.   [1842]

RUSHBROOKE, Robert. Rushbrooke Park. Suffolk. Carlton. B. 1779; m. 1808, the d. of Sir C. Davies. A Lieut.-Col. in the army, and a Military Secretary to the Commander of the Forces. Dept.-Lieut of the county of Suffolk. A Conservative and sat for Suffolk W. from 1835 until his death in June 1845.   [1845]

RUSHOUT-BOWLES, George. 10 Bolton Street, London. Barford, and Northwick, Worcestershire. Carlton, Oxford & Cambridge, and Junior United Service. Only s. of the Hon. Rev. George Rushout-Bowles, by the 7th d. of the 7th Earl of Galloway. B. 1811. Educ. at Christ Church, Oxford, where he graduated M.A.; became Capt. 1st Life Guards in 1842; heir presumptive in the Barony of Northwick; a Magistrate for Worcestershire. Appointed Dept.-Lieut. of Shropshire 1852, and Lieut.-Col. of the Hereford Militia, 1853. A Conservative, said he would 'support education on a religious basis', voted for inquiry into Maynooth, 1853. Sat for Evesham from Feb. 1837 till 1841, when he was unsuccessful. First returned for Worcestershire E. Jan. 1847 and sat until he succeeded as Lord Northwick Feb. 1859. [1858]

RUSSELL, Lord Arthur. 2 Audley Square, London. Brooks's, and Athenaeum. 2nd. s. of Lord George William Russell, by Elizabeth Anne, only child of the Hon. John Theophilus Rawdon. Therefore was bro. of the 9th Duke of Bedford. B. in London 1825; m. 1865, Laura, eld. d. of Vicomte d. Peyronnet. Acted a private Secretary to Earl (then Lord John) Russell from Nov. 1849 till 1854. A Liberal. Sat for Tavistock from Sept. 1857. until he retired in 1885. Died 4 Apr. 1892.   [1885]

RUSSELL, Charles. 27 Charles Street, St. James's, London. Carlton, Travellers', Union, and Oriental. 2nd s. of Sir Henry Russell, Bart. B. 1786. Was an officer in the East India Company's Bengal Army. Chairman of the Great Western Railway Company. A Conservative, voted for agricultural protection, 1846. Sat for Reading from 1830-1837; re-elected in 1841 and sat until defeated in 1847. Sergeant at Arms to House of Commons 1848-1875. Died 29 June 1894. [1847]

RUSSELL, Sir Charles, Bart. 4 St. James Place, London. Swallowfield, Reading. Carlton,

Guard's, and Garrick. Eld. surviving s. of Sir Henry Russell (2nd Bart.) by his 2nd wife Marie Clotilde, d. of Monsieur Moffet de la Fontaine. B. at Swallowfield 1826. Unmarried. Educ. at Eton. Entered the army 1843; became Capt. and Lieut. Grenadier Guards 1858; served in the Eastern Campaign of 1854-5, and was Deputy Assistant Adjutant-Gen. with the army in the Crimea. A Knight of the Legion of Honour and received the Victoria Cross. Sat for Berkshire from July 1865-Nov. 1868. Sat for Westminster from Feb. 1874 until he accepted Chiltern Hundreds Jan. 1882. Died 14 Apr. 1883.   [1881]

RUSSELL, C.A. Continued in House after 1885: full entry in Volume II.

RUSSELL, Lord Charles James Fox. 6 Belgrave Square, London. Reform. S. of the 6th Duke of Bedford, and half-bro. of Lord John Russell. B. 1807; m. 1834, Isabella Clarissa, d. of William Davies, Esq., of Carmarthen and grand-d. of Lord Albert Seymour. A Capt. in the 62nd foot. A Whig, in favour of the ballot. He succeeded his half-bro. the Marq. of Tavistock in the representation of Bedfordshire in 1832; and sat until he retired July 1841. On the death of Mr. Astell, Lord Russell took up the seat Mar. 1847. Retired at the general election 7 Aug. 1847. Sergeant--at-Arms to House of Commons 1848-75. Died 29 June 1894.   [1841]

RUSSELL, Hon. Edward Southwell. 3 Carlton House Terrace, London. King's Weston, Gloucestershire. Clifford Castle, Herefordshire. Reform. Eld. s. of the Baroness De Clifford and Capt. John Russell, R.N., cousin of Lord John Russell, MP. B. at Upton, Warwickshire, 1824. Graduated at Trinity Coll., Cambridge; appointed Lieut. Leicestershire Yeomanry Cavalry 1850. A Liberal. First returned for Tavistock in 1847 and sat until he retired in 1852. Admiral 1867. Died 21 May 1887.   [1852]

RUSSELL, Francis Charles Hastings. 82 Eaton Square, London. Oakley, Bedford. Brooks's, Travellers', and Guard's. Eld s. of George William Russell, Esq., by the d. of the Hon. John Theophilus Rawdon. Nephew to the 7th Duke of Bedford and to Earl Russell. B. in London 1819; m. 1844, Lady Elizabeth, eld. d. of 5th Earl De-La-Warr. Entered the Scots Fusilier Guards in 1838, but retired from the army July 1844; appointed Major in the Bedford Militia Apr. 1849; Lieut.-Col. 1st Battalion Bedfordshire Rifle Volunteers 1860; a Dept.-Lieut. of Bedford 1861. A Whig; said he would 'support the well-known principles of his family.' Voted against Church rates 1855. First returned for Bedfordshire in 1847 and sat until he succeeded cousin a 9th Duke of Bedford 26 May 1872; K.G. 1 Dec. 1880; Lord Lieut. of Huntingdonshire 1884. Shot himself 14 Jan. 1891.   [1872]

RUSSELL, Francis William. 27 Lancaster Gate, London. Limerick House, Limerick. Union. Eld. s. of John N. Russell. Esq., of Limerick, Merchant, by the eld. d. of Alderman Thompson of Cork. B. in Limerick, 1800; m. 1834, the 2nd d. of Thomas Clarke, Esq., of Melton Mowbray. Educ. at Fermoy, under Rev. T.D. Hincks, at Belfast and at Trinity Coll., Dublin. Was called to the bar in Ireland in 1824; subsequently became a Partner in the firm of J.N. Russell and Sons, Merchants, in Limerick and London. Of Liberal opinions, a firm supporter of civil and religious liberty; voted against the ballot 1853. First returned for Limerick in July 1852. MP until his death 30 Aug. 1871.   [1871]

RUSSELL, G.W.E. Continued in House after 1885: full entry in Volume II.

RUSSELL, Jesse David Watts. 9 Chesham Place, London. Oxford & Cambridge. S. of J. Watts Russell, Esq., of Ham Hall. B. 1812; m. 1835, youngest d. of J. Smith Wright, Esq., of Rempstone, Nottinghamsire. A Conservative, but in favour of free trade. First returned for Staffordshire N. in 1841 and sat until he retired in 1847. Died 7 Mar. 1879.   [1847]

RUSSELL, Rt. Hon. Lord John. 37 Chesham Place, London. Pembroke Lodge, Richmond Park, London. Endsleigh House, Tavistock, Devon. Reform, and Brooks's. 3rd and youngest s. of the 6th Duke of Bedford, by his 1st wife, Hon. Georgiana Elizabeth, 2nd d. of the 4th Visct. Torrington. B. in Hertford Street, 1792; m. 1st, 1835, Adelaide, eld. d. of Thomas Lister, Esq., of Armytage Park, and relict of 2nd Lord Ribblesdale; 2ndly, 1841, Lady Frances Anna Maria, 2nd d. of the 2nd Earl of Minto. Was Paymaster of the Forces from 1830 till Nov. 1834; Secretary of State for the Home Department from Apr. 1835, till 1839; Secretary of State for the Colonies from 1839 till 1841. Was Prime Minister from July 1846 till Mar. 1852; Secretary of State for Foreign Affairs from Dec. 1852 till Feb. 1853; held a seat in the Cabinet without office from the last date till June 1854; was President of the Council from June 1854 till Feb. 1855; Secretary of State for the Colonies from Mar. till Nov. 1855; re-appointed Secretary of State for Foreign Affairs June 1859, salary £5,000. Went on a special mission to the conference at Vienna, 1855. A Liberal. Voted against the ballot, 1853. Sat for Tavistock from 1813 till Mar. 1817, and from 1818 till Mar.

1819; for Huntingdonshire from 1820 till 1826; for Bandon Bridge till 1830; for Devon in 1831, and for Devon S. 1832 till 1835, when he lost his seat. But he was shortly afterwards elected for Stroud, for which he sat till 1841. First returned for London in 1841 and sat until created Earl Russell 27 July 1861. Continued as Foreign Secretary until Oct. 1865 when on the death of Palmerston he became Prime Minister again until 5 July 1866. Died 28 May 1878.   [1861]

RUSSELL, T. A Liberal. First elected for Bute Co. Apr. 1880, but on petition the election was declared void and the seat awarded to C. Dalrymple, Esq. Returned for Glasgow 11 Mar. 1885; did not stand at the 1885 general election.

RUSSELL, Rt. Hon. Thomas Wallace. Continued in House after 1885: full entry in Volume II.

RUSSELL, Lord. W. 8 Spring Gardens, Oakley, Bedfordshire. Only s. of the Marq. of Tavistock, grands. of the Duke of Bedford and nephew of Lord John Russell. B. 1809. Of Whig principles. Sat for Tavistock from 1832 until he retired 1841. Succeeded as 8th Duke of Bedford May 1861. Died 26 May 1872.   [1838]

RUSSELL, Sir William, Bart. 10 James Street, Buckingham Gate, London. Charlton Park, Charlton Kings, Cheltenham. Arthur's, and Army & Navy. B. at Calcutta 1822, the only s. of Sir William Russell, M.D., 1st Bart., by his 2nd wife, Jane Eliza, d. and co-heir of Major-Gen. James Doddington Sherwood of the E.I.C.S. (she assumed the name of Prinn 1841). Was Capt. 7th Hussars and served on the Staff during the Russian War. Appointed Lieut.-Col. 7th Dragoons 1858. Was Master of the House to the Lord Lieut. of Ireland 1849 and 1850, Aide-de-Camp 1850-52, and 1854. A Magistrate for Gloucestershire. A Liberal. Sat for Dover July 1857-Apr. 1859, when he was unsuccessful. Sat for Norwich Mar. 1860-1874, when he retired. Died 19 Mar. 1892.   [1873]

RUSSELL, William Congreve. Moore Green, Worcestershire. A Whig, in favour of the immediate abolition of slavery. Sat for Worcestershire E. from 1832. Retired in 1835.   [1833]

RUST, James. Alconbury House, Nr. Huntingdon. Athenaeum, and Carlton. S. of James Rust, Esq., a Magistrate for Huntingdonshire and a Banker at Huntingdon, by Margaret, d. of Lancelot Brown, Esq. B. at Great Gransden, Huntingdonshire, 1798; m. 1st, 1829,

only d. of Lieut.-Col. Rowles; 2ndly, 1837, eld. d. of Col. Roberts. Educ. at Rugby and at University Coll., Oxford; elected a Fellow of the latter 1823, resigned 1829; was 1st class in classics 1819. Called to the bar at Lincoln's Inn 1825, but relinquished practice in 1836. A Magistrate of Huntingdonshire, and Chairman of Quarter Sessions from 1840; a Dept.-Lieut. of the Co. from 1842. A Conservative, and a supporter generally of Lord Derby's policy; opposed 'all attempts of the Church of Rome to regain the power it lost at the Reformation.' First elected for Huntingdonshire, Oct. 1855, without opposition and sat until he retired in 1859. Died 24 July 1875.
[1858]

RUSTON, Joseph. Monk's Manor, Nr. Lincoln. 45 Courtfield Gardens, London. Reform, and National Liberal. B. 1835, eld. s. of Robert Ruston, Esq., of Chatteris, Isle of Ely, by Margaret, d. of William Seward, Esq., also of Chatteris. M. 1859, Jane, d. of William Brown, Esq., of Sheffield. Educ. at Wesley Coll., Sheffield. An Engineer and head of the firm of Ruston Proctor and Co., Engineers, of the Streat Ironworks, Lincoln. A Magistrate for Lincoln and Mayor of that City 1870. Chevalier of the Legion of Honour of France. A Liberal, and 'a warm supporter of Gladstone's Government.' Sat for Lincoln city from June 1884 until he retired 1886. Died 11 June 1897.
[1886]

RUTHERFORD, Rt. Hon. Andrew. 11 Upper Belgrave Street, London. 9 Colme Street, Edinburgh. Official Chambers, Gwydr House, Whitehall, London. M. a sister of Sir James Stuard, Bart. An Advocate at the Scottish Bar. Appointed Lord Advocate of Scotland July 1846. Declared himself opposed to the immediate repeal of the Corn Laws, to the ballot and to the extentsion of the suffrage, but voted in favour of Mr. Villiers motion in May 1843, and supported free trade in 1846. First returned for the district of Leith in 1839, on the elevation of his predecessor in office to the bench, and sat until he was appointed Lord of Sessions 1851. Died 13 Dec. 1854.
[1850]

RUTHVEN, Edward. Kildare Street, Dublin. Ballyfan House, Co. Kildare. S. of a previous member for the city of Dublin. M. only d. of Dr. Crampton, Surgeon-Gen. in Ireland. A Magistrate for the counties of Down and Kildare. A Repealer, and advocated the appropriation of the Church lands and revenues to the support of the poor. Sat for Co. Kildare from 1832 until defeated in 1837.
[1837]

RUTHVEN, Edward Southwell. 14 College Street, Westminster, London. Downpatrick, Co. Down. Father of the member for Kildare Co. A Repealer. Sat for Downpatrick in the Parliaments of 1830 and 1831. Returned for Dublin city Dec. 1832 and again in Jan. 1835, but a few months later he was unseated on petition.
[1833]

RYDER, Hon. Granville Dudley. 39 Grosvenor Square, London. Westbrook, Hertfordshire. Carlton. S. of 1st Earl of Harrowby. B. 1799; m. 1825, d. of 6th Duke of Beaufort. A Lieut. R.N. A Conservative, voted for agricultural protection, 1846. First returned for Hertfordshire in 1841 and sat until he retired in 1847. Died 24 Nov. 1879.
[1847]

RYDER, Granville Richard. 60 Ennismore Gardens, London. Carlton, and St. Stephen's. 2nd s. of the Hon. Granville Dudley Ryder, bro. of the 2nd Earl of Harrowby, by Lady Georgiana Augusta, 3rd d. of 6th Duke of Beaufort. B. at Westbrook, Hertfordshire 1833; m. 1864, Sibylla Sophia, only d. of Sir Robert Grant, Governor of Bombay. Educ. at Harrow, and Christ Church Coll., Oxford; graduated M.A. 1858. Was called to the bar at the Inner Temple Nov. 1859. Was for some years a member of the Oxford Circuit. Managing Director of the Lands Improvement Company, and Land Securities Company. A Liberal-Conservative, in favour of 'progress within the line of the constitution'; in favour also of retrenchment in public expenditure. Sat for Salisbury from Feb. 1874 until he retired in 1880.
[1880]

RYLANDS, Peter. 78 St. George's Square, London. Massey Hall, Thelwall, Warrington. Reform. S. of John Rylands, Esq., of Bewsey House, Warrington, by Martha, d. of the Rev. James Glazebrook, vicar of Belton, Leicestershire. B. at Warrington 1820; m. 1861, Caroline, d. of William Reynolds, Esq., of Penketh House, Warrington. Educ. at Boteler's Grammar School, Warrington. An Iron-Master and Director of Pearson and Knowles' Coal and Iron Co. (Limited), also of the Manchester and Liverpool District Banking Co. A Magistrate for Lancashire, Cheshire, and for Warrington; elected Mayor of the latter 1853-54. A Liberal and Unionist, in favour of the decentralization of Government departments, and a great reduction in the national expenditure. Sat for Warrington from Dec. 1868 to Feb. 1874, when he was an unsuccessful candidate there, as also for S.E. Lancashire. Sat for Burnley from Feb. 1876. MP until his death 8 Feb. 1887.
[1886]

RYLE, John. 30 Old Bond Street, London. Park House, Cheshire. Eld. s. of John Ryle, Esq, who was deeply interested in the silk and cotton trade, and was popularly called one of the founders of Macclesfield. M. 1811, d. of — Hurt, Esq. of Wirksworth, and grandd. of Sir Richard Arkwright. A Banker at Macclesfield and Manchester. A moderate Reformer, in favour of protection for the silk trade. Sat for Macclesfield from 1832 until defeated in 1837.   [1837]

SACKVILLE, S.G.S. See STOPFORD-SACKVILLE, S.G. Continued in House after 1885: full entry in Volume II.

SADLEIR, James. 11 Gloucester Square, Hyde Park, London. 5 Great Denmark Street, Dublin. Clon a cody, Clonmel. S. of Clement William Sadleir, Esq., of Shrone Hill, Co. Tipperary, and bro. of John Sadleir. A Liberal. Sat for Tipperary from July 1852 until he was expelled from Parliament on 16 Feb. 1857, having absconded from justice after his bank collapsed in Feb. 1856. He possibly fled abroad.   [1856]

SADLEIR, John. 11 Gloucester Square, Hyde Park, London. 5 Great Denmark Street, Dublin. Reform, and Erectheum. B. at Shrone Hill 1814, the 3rd s. of Clement William Sadleir, Esq., of Co. Tipperary. Unmarried. Educ. at Conglowes Coll., Ireland. Chairman of the London and County Bank. Admitted a Solicitor in Ireland 1837, but retired from practice in 1846. Was a Lord of the Treasury from Dec. 1852-Jan. 1854. A Liberal. Sat for Carlow bor. from July 1847-Jan. 1853, when he was an unsuccessful candidate after taking office. Sat for Sligo borough from July 1853 until he committed suicide on 17 Feb. 1856, having engaged in fraudulent share transactions.   [1855]

ST. AUBYN, Sir John, Bart. 5 Lowndes Street, London. St. Michael's Mount, Cornwall. Brooks's, Travellers', and Boodle's. Eld. s. of Sir Edward St. Aubyn, Bart., by Emma, d. of Gen. Knollys. B. at Clowance, Cornwall, 1829; m. 1856 Lady Elizabeth Clementine, 2nd d. of the 4th Marq. Townshend. Educ. at Eton and Trinity Coll., Cambridge, where he graduated B.A. 1852. A Magistrate and Dept. Lieut. for Cornwall from 1854. Colonel (ret.) 3rd Battalion Duke of Cornwall's Light Infantry. A Deputy Special Warden of the Stannaries of Devon and Cornwall. A Liberal Unionist. Sat for Cornwall W. from July 1858 until created Baton St. Levan, 1887. Mayor of Devonport, 1891. Died 14 May 1908.   [1886 2nd ed.]

ST. AUBYN, Walter Napleton Molesworth-. 1 Brick Court, Temple, London. Carlton.

Youngest s. of Rev. Hender Molesworth-St. Aubyn, of Clowance, Cornwall (who assumed the additional name of St. Aubyn by royal license in 1844), by Helen, youngest d. of Rev. Timothy Napleton. B. 1838; m. Annie, d. of George Coles, Esq., of Southampton. Was educ. at Harrow and Christ Church, Oxford. Was called to the bar at Lincoln's Inn June 1863, and joined the Western circuit; practised also as a special pleader. A Conservative. Sat for Helston from Apr. 1880 until defeated in 1885 contesting Truro.   [1885]

ST. GEORGE, Christopher. Tyrone House, Co. Galway. Union. Eld. s. of Arthur St. George, Esq., of Tyrone House, Co. Galway, by Lady Henrietta, eld. d. of the 2nd Earl of Howth. His grandf. assumed the name of St. George, in lieu of his partronymic, French, to mark his descent from the only d. and heir of the last Lord. St. George (extinct). B. at Tyrone, 1812. Unmarried. Educ. at Trinity Coll., Dublin, where he distinguished himself. A claimant of the barony of Anthenry. A Magistrate for Galway. A Conservative. First returned for Galway Co. in 1847, without opposition and sat until he retired in 1852. Died 13 Nov. 1877.   [1852]

ST. LAWRENCE, Visct. Howth Castle, Co. Dublin. B. 1827, the eld. s. of the Earl of Howth, by his 1st wife, Lady Emily, d. of 13th Earl of Clanricarde. Was Capt. 7th Dragoons 1847-50, Capt. Lancashire Hussars 1852-55. Was State Steward to the Lord-Licut. of Ireland Feb. 1855-Mar. 1858, and from June 1859-Nov. 1864. Was appointed Lieut.-Col. Dublin Militia from 1854. A Liberal. Sat for Galway from Dec. 1868 until he succeeded as 4th Earl in Feb. 1874. Barony (U.K.) Oct. 1881. Died 9 Mar. 1909.   [1873]

ST. PAUL, Horace. Ewart Park, Northumberland. Carlton. Only s. of Horace St. Paul, Esq., Bart. B. 29 Dec. 1812. Contested Worcestershire E. in 1835, and was defeated by a small majority. A Conservative and unpledged. First elected for Worcestershire E. Aug. 1837 and sat until he retired in July 1841. Succeeded as 2nd Bart. Oct. 1840. Died 28 May 1891.   [1841]

SALISBURY, Enoch Gibbon. 5 Stanley Place, Chester. S. of Joseph Salisbury, and Mary his wife. B. at Bagilt, Flintshire, 1819; m. Sarah, d. of Rev. Arthur Jones, D.D. of Bangor, Carmarthenshire. Educ. at Holywell Grammar School. Called to the bar at the Inner Temple, 1852. Published *Letters of Education,* etc. Proprietor of extensive Gas works at Chester. A Liberal, considered 'birth-right, servitude, education, and taxation', are qualifications for the exercise of the franchise; in favour of the ballot, and 'a more equal distribution of ecclesiastical revenues.' First elected for Chester, Apr. 1857. Defeated in 1859. Contested seat again in 1868. Author. Died 27 Oct. 1890. [1858]

SALOMONS, Sir David, Bart. 26 Great Cumberland Place, Hyde Park, London. Broom Hill, Tunbridge Wells. Athenaeum, Brooks's, and Reform. B. 1797, the s. of Levy Salomons, Esq., a retired Merchant and Underwriter of London, by his wife, Miss Matilda Detnetz, of Leyden. M. 1st, Jeanette, d. of Solomen Cohen, Esq., of Grove House, Canonbury (she died 1867); 2ndly, 1872, Cecilia, widow of P. Salomons, Esq., of Upper Wimpole Street. A retired Merchant and a member of the Middle Temple. Was Sheriff of London 1835-36, High Sheriff of Kent 1839-40, made an Alderman of London 1847, and was Lord Mayor in 1855. Was a Magistrate for Kent, Sussex and Middlesex and a Commissioner of Lieutenancy for London. Author of works on the Corn Laws, Banking, English and Foreign Railways, etc. A Liberal. Sat for Greenwich June 1851-July 1852, and from Feb. 1859 until his death on 18 July 1873. [1873]

SALT, Titus. (I). Methley Park, Nr. Bradford. S. of Daniel Salt, Esq., by Grace, d. of Isaac Smithies, Esq., of Morley. B. at Morley 1803; m. 1829, Caroline, youngest d. of George Whitlam, Esq., of Great Grimsby, Lincolnshire. Educ. at Wakefield. A Manufacturer; head of the firm of Titus Salt, Sons and Company, Saltaire, near Bradford. Served the office of Mayor, and President of the Chamber of Commerce at Bradford. A Magistrate for Bradford and for the W. Riding of Yorkshire. A 'decided Liberal', in favour of Lord J. Russell's scheme of Reform, and of vote by ballot; in favour also of the principle of non-intervention in Continental politics, but would have had the army and navy kept in more efficient state for the purposes of self-defence. First elected for Bradford May 1859. Accepted Chiltern Hundreds 1861. Created Bart. 7 Oct. 1869. Died 29 Dec. 1876. [1860]

SALT, T. (II). Continued in House after 1885: full entry in Volume II.

SALWEY, Henry. 16 Victoria Square, Pimlico, London. Egham Park, Surrey. Reform. 3rd s. of Theophilus Richard Salwey, Esq., of the Lodge, Ludlow, (descended from the Salweys of Richard's Castle and Moor Park, Shropshire), by the youngest d. and co-heir of Thomas Hill, Esq., of Court-of-Hill, Shropshire. B. at the Lodge, Ludlow, 1794; m. 1828, Eliza Philippa, only d. and heir of John Hooper Holder, Esq., of

Stanton-Lacey House, Ludlow, great-grandd. of Lord Chancellor Lifford (Ireland). Educ. at Eton. Entered the Coldstream Guards 1811, and became a Col. in the army 1841; served under Wellington in Spain, France, and Holland, 1813-14-15. A Magistrate for Surrey. A Liberal, in favour of the ballot and triennial Parliaments; opposed to all religious endowments; supported the repeal of the malt tax. Sat for Ludlow from 1837 to 1841, when he was an unsuccessful candidate; was again returned there and sat until defeated in 1852. Died 10 Mar. 1874. [1852]

SAMUDA, Jospeh D'Aguilar. 7 Gloucester Square, Hyde Park, London. Loudwater, Rickmansworth, Hertfordshire. Reform, and City Liberal. S. of A. Samuda, Esq., of South Street, Finsbury, East and West India Merchant, by Joy, d. of H. D'Aguilar, Esq., of Enfield Chase. B. in Trinity Square, London 1813; m. 1837, Louisa, d. of S. Ballin, Esq. Became a Civil Engineer in 1832, and a member of the Institution of Civil Engineers, and Vice-President of the Institution of Naval Architects. Was chosen a member of the Metropolitan Board of Works 1860, and served until 1865. A Dept.-Lieut. of the Tower Hamlets and of London, and Lieut.-Col. Tower Hamlets Volunteers. A Liberal. Sat for Tavistock from July 1865-Dec. 1868, from which date he represented the Tower Hamlets until defeated 1880. Died 27 Apr. 1885. [1880]

SAMUELSON, Rt. Hon. Sir. B. Continued in House after 1885: full entry in Volume II.

SAMUELSON, H.B. Continued in House after 1885: full entry in Volume II.

SANDARS, George. 27 Sussex Square, Hyde Park, London. Alverthorpe Hall, Wakefield. Carlton, Conservative, and National. S. of Samuel Sandars, Esq., of Gainsborough, Lincolnshire, a branch of the Sandars family of Ireton, Derbyshire. B. at Gainsborough 1805; m. 1st 1829, Mary, d. of George Neden, Esq., of Ardwick, Lancashire (she died 1847); 2ndly, 1849, Arabella, eld. d. of John Walker, Esq., of Cambridge Square, Hyde Park. Educ. at Newark Grammar School. A Magistrate for the West Riding of Yorkshire, of which he was appointed Dept.-Lieut May 1852. A Conservative, opposed to the endowment of the Roman Catholic Clergy, but in favour of the extension of education to all classes and sects, carried out on the voluntary principle aided by grants of public money. First returned for Wakefield in 1847 and sat until he retired 1857. Died 14 May 1879. [1857]

SANDARS, Joseph. 15 Eaton Square, London.

Taplow House, Buckinghamshire. Carlton, and Arthur's. Only s. of Joseph Sandars, Esq., of Taplow House, Buckinghamshire. B. 1821; m. 1850, Lady Virginia, youngest d. of 2nd Marq. of Headfort. Educ. at Downing Coll., Cambridge. A Dept.-Lieut of Buckinghamshire. A Conservative, but in favour of free trade. First returned for Yarmouth, July 1848. Defeated contesting Bewdley in 1852. Died 14 Mar. 1893   [1852]

SANDERSON, Richard. 46 Belgrave Square, London. Brightlingsea Lodge, Essex. Carlton. M. 1833, Charlotte Matilda, eld. d. of 1st Visct. Canterbury. An East India Proprietor. A Conservative, voted for agricultural protection, 1846. Sat for Colchester in several Parliaments, and sat for it from 27 Dec. 1832 until defeated in 1847. [1847]

SANDERSON, Thomas Kemp. South Parade, Wakefield. Carlton, and Conservative. Eld. s. of Michael Sanderson, Esq., of Newmarket, near Wakefield, by Elizabeth, d. of Thomas Kemp, Esq., of Woolgreaves, Yorkshire. B. at Newmarket 1821. Unmarried. Educ. at the West Riding Proprietary School, Wakefield. A Corn Merchant at Wakefield. A Director of the Wakefield and Barnsley Union Bank. Was for several years Chairman of the Board of Guardians of Wakefield. A Conservative. Contested Wakefield Dec. 1868. Returned for Wakefield May 1874 and sat until defeated 1880. Died 24 Dec. 1897.   [1880]

SANDFORD, Sir D.K. Of Liberal opinions. Contested Glasgow Dec. 1832. Returned for Paisley 24 Mar. 1834. Retired in 1835. Died 4 Feb. 1838.   [1834]

SANDFORD, George Montagu Warren. 33 Hertford Street, London. Reeves Hall, Mersea Island, Essex. Carlton. S. of George Peacocke, Esq. of Moulton Park, Northamptonshire, by Jemima, d. of Col. A.T. Montagu Dunnford, of the Scots Fusilier Guards. M. 1858, Augusta Mary, youngest d. of Algernon Frederick Grenville, Esq. Educ. at Eton, at Newick Hall, and at Magdalen Coll., Cambridge, graduated B.A. 1846. Assumed, by royal license, 1866, in lieu of his patrynomic, the name and arms of Sandford, of which family he was the representative in the female line. A Dept.-Lieut. for Essex, a Magistrate for Essex, Hampshire and Middlesex. A Conservative. Sat for Harwich from July 1852-June 1853, when he was unseated on petition; sat for Maldon from Aug. 1854-Apr. 1857, and from May 1859- Dec. 1868; re-elected there Feb. 1874. Accepted Chiltern Hundreds Nov. 1878. Died 17 June 1879.   [1878]

SANDON, Rt. Hon. Visct. 39 Grosvenor Square, London. Sandon House, Stone, Staffordshire. Cartlon, and Travellers'. Eld. s. of Earl of Harrowby, by 4th d. of 1st Marq. of Bute. B at Brighton 1831; m. 1861, Lady Mary Frances, eld. d. of 2nd Marq. of Exeter. Was Vice-Pres. of the Committee of Council on Education from Feb. 1874-Apr. 1878, and Pres. of the Board of Trade from the latter date until Apr. 1880. A Dept.-Lieut. of Stafford from 1852; Capt. 2nd Staffordshire Militia from 1853. Was Private Sec. to Mr. Labonchere at the Colonial Office from Jan. 1856-58. Formerly ranked as Liberal, but later represented the Conservative interest, voted against the disestablishment of the Irish Church 1869. Sat for Lichfield from May 1856-Apr. 1859. Contested Stafford Aug. 1860. Sat for Liverpool from Dec. 1868 until he succeeded as 3rd Earl, Nov. 1882. Died 26 Mar.1900.   [1882]

SANDON. Visct. 39 Grosvenor Square, London. Athenaeum. Eld. s. of the Earl of Harrowby. B. 1798; m. Frances, half-sister of the 1st Marq of Bute. Appointed in Mar. 1835 a Commissioner for inquiring into the army punishments. A Dept.-Lieut. for Staffordshire. A Conservative, but in favour of free trade. Was for a short time Secretary of the India Board; advocated the principle of the Reform Act, but opposed Ministers in the greater part of its details; opposed to the ballot. Sat for Tiverton from 1819-1831, when he was elected for Liverpool and sat until he retired in 1847. Succeeded as 2nd Earl Dec. 1847. Lord Privy Seal 1855-57. Vice-President of the Council 1874. Died 19 Nov. 1882.   [1847]

SANFORD, Edward Ayshford. 4 Richmond Terrace, London. Mynehead Court, Somersetshire. Reform. M. 1807, Henrietta, eld. d. of Sir William Langham, of Cottesbrooke, Northampton, by his 1st wife Henrietta Elizabeth Frederica, sole d. and heiress of the Hon Charles Vane, great Uncle of the Duke of Cleveland (dead). Of Whig principles, in favour of short Parliaments. Patron of 1 living. Voted for revision of the pension list. Sat for Somersetshire W. from 1830 until he retired 1841. Sheriff of Somerset 1848. Died 1 Dec. 1871.   [1838]

SARTORIS, Edward John. 9 Park Place, St. James's, London. Llanennech Park, Carmarthenshire. Brooks's. B. in London 1814, the s. of Urban Sartoris, Esq., M. Adelaide, d. of Charles Kemble, Esq. Educ. at Cambridge. Was a Magistrate for Hampshire and Carmarthenshire. A Liberal, and supported Mr. Gladstone. Contested Penryn June 1841. Sat for Carmarthenshire from Dec. 1868 to 1874 when he was defeated. Died 23 Nov. 1888.   [1873]

341

SAUNDERSON, Edward James. Continued in House after 1885: full entry in Volume II.

SAWLE, Charles Brune Graves-. 13 Bury Street, London. Restormel, Lostwithiel, Cornwall. Reform. Eld. s. of Sir Joseph Sawle Graves-Sawle, Bart., of Penrice, Cornwall, by Dorothea Prideaux, eld. d. of the Rev. Charles Prideaux Brune, of Place House, Padstow, Cornwall. B. at Padstow 1816; m. 1846, Rose Caroline, youngest d. of David R. Paynter, Esq., of Dale Castle, Pembrokeshire. Educ. at Eton and at Clare Hall, Cambridge, where he graduated B.A. 1841. A Magistrate and Dept.- Lieut. of Cornwall. Dept.-Chairman of the county sessions, and Capt. in the Cornwall and Devon Miners' Militia. Appointed a special Dept.-Warden of the Stannaries 1852. A Liberal, opposed to the Maynooth Grant, voted against the ballot 1853. Was an unsuccessful candidate for Bodmin Feb. 1843. First return for Bodmin in July 1852 and sat until he retired 1857. [1857]

SCARLETT, Sir James. 4 New Street, Spring Gardens, London. 2 King's Bench Walk, Temple, London. Abinger Hall, Surrey. S. of a West India Merchant and Planter. Bro. of Sir William Scarlett, Chief Justice of Jamaica. A King's counsel. Standing counsel to the Bank. Was always considered to entertain Whig principles till he was appointed Attorney-Gen. by the Duke of Wellington; that office being political he was obliged, on the resignation of the Duke, to give it up. When the following Ministry propounded their plan of Reform he declared himself among its opponents, on the ground of its going further than was safe or necessary; since which he was considered a Conservative. Sat for Earl Fitzwilliam's bor. of Peterborough in the Parliament of 1820-1826, and for Malton (same patron) in that of 1830. In 1831 he was elected by the Conservative party at Cockermouth, in the Earl of Lonsdale's interest, and then, in conjunction with his colleague, successfully contested Norwich against two Reformers. Sat for Norwich from Dec. 1832-1837 when he was unseated on petition. Appointed Judge Dec. 1834; created Baron Abinger 12 Jan. 1835. Died 7 Apr. 1844. [1834]

SCARLETT, Hon. James Yorke. Bank Hall. United Service, and University. 2nd s. of Lord Abinger, bro. of the member for Norwich, and bro.-in-law of Sir John Campbell. B. Feb. 1799; m. 19 Dec. 1835, Charlotte Anne, 2nd d. and co-heiress of Col. Hargreaves. Maj. of the 5th Dragoon Guards. A Conservative. Returned for Guildford in 1837; defeated 1841. Contested Burnley Nov. 1868. Commanded the heavy cavalry brigade in the Crimea 1854; led their charge at Balaclava 25 Oct. 1854; General 1871. Died 6 Dec. 1871. [1838]

SCARLETT, Hon. Robert Campbell. 4 New Street, Spring Gardens, London. Abinger Hall, Surrey. Carlton. B. 1794, the eld. s. of Lord Abinger. M. 1824, d. of Geo. Smith, a Barrister. A Conservative. Sat for Norwich 1835-37, and for Horsham 1841 until 7 Apr. 1844 when he succeeded as 2nd Baron. Died 24 June 1861. [1844]

SCHENLEY, Edward Wyndham Harrington. B. 1799. Served in the army in Spain and at Waterloo. Commissioner for the repression of the Slave Trade. A Liberal. First returned for Dartmouth 30 Apr. 1859, but in July 1859 the election was declared void on petition. Died 1878.

SCHNEIDER, Henry William. Lightburn House, Ulverston. B. at Southgate, Middlesex 1817, the s. of John Henry Powell Schneider, of Southgate. M. 1842, Augusta, d. of Richard Smith, Esq., of Poulton Manor, Cheshire, Bankfield, Lancashire. A Merchant and Shipowner. A Liberal, in favour of the ballot and the abolition of Church rates. Sat for Norwich from Apr. 1857 to July 1859, when both members for that place were unseated on petition. Sat for Lancaster from Feb. 1865-1866, when he was unseated. Lancaster was disfranchised in 1867. Died 11 Nov. 1887. [1865]

SCHOLEFIELD, William. Birmingham. Reform. B. 1809, 2nd d. of Josua Scholefield, 2nd. d. of C. Cottrell; 2ndly, 1824, youngest d. of C. Cottrell; 3rdly, Mary Anne, d. of T. Rose Swaine of London. A Banker and Merchant at Birmingham. Was Vice President of the Political Union. Director of the National Provincial Bank of England, and of Metropolitan Life Assurance Society. A radical Reformer, in favour of free trade, the ballot, the repeal of the Corn Laws etc. In 1832 pledged himself to resign his seat whenever a majority of constituents expressed themselves dissatisfied with his general parliamentary conduct. Sat for Birmingham from 1832 until his death in 1844. [1844]

SCHOLEFIELD, William. Birmingham. Reform. B. 1809, 2nd s. of Josua Scholefield, many years MP for Birmingham, by 2nd. s. of C. Cottrell. M. Jane Matilda, d. of John Miller (she died 1843.). A Merchant in Birmingham, and elected first Mayor of the town when it received its charter incorporation in 1838. A Magistrate and Dept.-Lieut for Warwickshire. A Director of the Birmingham and Midland Bank. A radical Reformer, in favour of a wide extension of the suffrage, triennial Parliaments, vote by ballot, and removal of all disabilities because of religious opinion. Unsuccessfully contested Brimingham in 1844, but was returned in 1847 and sat until his death on 9 July 1867. [1867]

SCHREIBER, Charles. Langham House, Portland Place, London. Carlton, and United University. Eld. surviving s. of Lieut.-Col. James Alfred Schreiber, of the Hill House, Melton, Suffolk, formerly of the 11th Light Dragoons, by Mary, youngest d. of Thomas Ware, Esq., of Woodfort, near Mallow. B. at Colchester 1826; m. 1855, Lady Charlotte Elizabeth, d. of the 9th Earl of Lindsey and widow of Sir J.J. Guest, Bart., MP of Dowlais. Educ. at Cheltenham Coll., and at Trinity Coll., Cambridge. Graduated B.A. 1850, M.A. 1853, was Browne's Medalist (Greek Ode) 1848, Senior Chancellor's Medalist 1850, and Fellow of Trinity Coll. from 1852-55. A Conservative, voted against the third reading of the Irish Land Bill 1881. Sat from July 1865-Nov. 1868 for Cheltenham, which he had unsuccessfully contested Apr. 1859. Sat for Poole from Apr. 1880. MP until his death 29 Mar. 1884. [1883]

SCLATER-BOOTH, G. Continued in House after 1885: full entry in Volume II.

SCOBELL, George Treweeke. Kingwell, Nr. Bath. Reform. 2nd. s. of Peter Edward Scobell, Esq., M.D., of Hallatrow, Somersetshire, by Hannah, only child and heir of John Sanford, Esq., a branch of the Sanfords of Nynehead in the same Co. B. 1785; m. 1818, Hester, youngest d. of Charles Savage, Esq., of Midsomer Norton. Entered the navy as Midshipman 1798 and served 14 years during the latter part of the war with France, served in America, West Indies, North Sea, Mediterranean, Baltic, Boulogne, Rochford, Cadiz, etc., under Nelson, Collingwood, Cornwallis, Bickerton, Thornborough, Saumarez, Hood, etc., became a retired Capt. R.N. 1843. A Dept.-Lieut. and Magistrate for Somerset. A Liberal, in favour of financial and Parliamentary reform, including vote by ballot and triennial Parliamants. First returned for Bath June 1851 and sat until he retired 1857. Sheriff of Somerset 1863. Died 11 May 1869. [1857]

SCOTT, Edward. The Priory, Maidstone, Kent. Army & Navy, and Junior United Service. 2nd s. of Rev. Edward Scott, D.D. of Worton Hall, Isleworth. B. at Isleworth; m. 1843, Elizabeth, only child of John Day, Esq., M.D. Educ. under Rev. Thos. Horne at Chiswick. Entered the army as Cornet 4th Light Dragoons in 1836; promoted to the rank of Capt. 1838, and placed on the half pay list in 1842. A Conservative. First returned for Maidstone, Apr. 1857. Retired 1859. [1858]

SCOTT, Sir Edward Dolman, Bart. 36 St. James's Street, London. Great Barr, Staffordshire. University. M. 1815, Catherine, d. of Sir Hugh Bateman, Bart. Patron of 2 livings. Of moderate Whig principles. Sat for Lichfield from 1832 until he retired in 1837. Died 27 Dec. 1851. [1837]

SCOTT, Hon. Francis. Mertoun House, Berwickshire. Carlton. S. of 4th Lord Polwarth, by the d. of Hans Moritz, Count Von Bruhl. B. 1806; m. 1835, Julia Frances Laura, d. of Rev. Chas. Boultbee. Educ. at Trinity Coll., Cambridge, graduated B.A. 1827, M.A. 1832; called to the bar at the Middle Temple 1832, and joined the Northern Circuit. In Apr. 1845, appointed Parliamentary Agent for the district of Port Phillip, New South Wales. A Conservative, voted for inquiry into Maynooth, 1853. Sat for Roxburghshire from 1841 to 1847, when he was returned for Berwickshire and sat until he retired in 1859. Died 9 Mar. 1884. [1858]

SCOTT, Lord Henry John Montagu Douglas. 3 Tilney Street, London. Palace House, Beaulieu, Southampton. Carlton, and St. Stephen's. 2nd s. of 5th Duke of Buccleuch, by Lady Charlotte, 3rd d. of 2nd Marq. of Bath. B. at Dalkeith House, Dalkeith 1832; m. 1865, Hon. Cecily, youngest d. of 2nd Lord Wharncliffe. Educ. at Eton. Appointed Capt. Midlothian Yeomanry Cavalry, 1856. A Conservative. Sat for Selkirkshire from Aug. 1861-Dec. 1868, when he was elected for Hampshire S. and sat until he accepted Chiltern Hundreds in 1884. Created Baron Montagu Dec. 1885. Died 4 Nov. 1905. [1884]

SCOTT, James Winter. 22 Grafton Street, London. Rotherfield Park, Hampshire. Eld. s. of James Scott, Esq., former MP for Bridport. M. d. of Sir S. Clarke Jervoise, Bart. A Reformer, in favour of triennial Parliaments, a commutation of tithes, and, if necessary, the ballot. Sat for Hampshire N. from 1832, until he retired in 1837. [1837]

SCOTT, Lord John Douglas. Montagu House, Whitehall, London. Only bro. of the Duke of Buccleuch. B. 1809; m. Alicia Anne, eld. d. of John Spottiswoode, Esq., of Spottiswoode. A Capt. in the Grenadier Guards. A Conservative. Patron of 1 living. Unsuccessfully contested Roxburghshire in 1832. Sat for it from 1835. Retired in 1837. Died 30 Jan. 1860. [1837]

SCOTT, Montagu David. Hove, Sussex. Carlton, and St. Stephen's. 2nd s. of Sir David

Scott, Bart., K.H., Duninald, MP, by Caroline, d. and co-heir of Benjamin Grindall, Esq., of the Bengal civil service. M. Miss Margaret Briggs, of Oaklands, Hertfordshire (who died in 1884). Was educ. at University Coll., Oxford, and graduated M.A. Was called to the bar at the Middle Temple. A Magistrate for Sussex and Middlesex. A Conservative, said he would maintain the constitution in Church and State, and would offer 'a determined opposition to any attack on the Church of England.' Sat from Feb. 1874 for Sussex E. which he had contested unsuccessfully in Dec. 1868. MP until he retired in 1885. Died 15 Jan. 1900. [1885]

SCOTT, Robert. Stourbridge, Worcestershire. The Red House, Staffordshire. Reform. Youngest s. of the Rev. Chas. Wellbeloved, of York. B. 1803; m. 1830, only d. of John Scott, Esq., upon which occasion he assumed the name of Scott only, in lieu of his patronymic. A Barrister of the Middle Temple. A Magistrate of Worcestershire and Staffordshire, and a Dept.-Lieut. of the former county. Author of some legal works. A Whig. First returned for Walsall in 1841 and sat until he retired in 1847. Died 21 Feb. 1856. [1847]

SCOTT, Sir William. Ancrum, Jedburgh. Balgay, Forfarshire. Brooks's, and Travellers'. S. of Sir John Scott, 5th Bart., of Ancrum, by Harriet, d. of William Graham, Esq., of Gartmore. B. at Ancrum 1803; m. 1828, Elizabeth, d. and heir of David Anderson, Esq., of Balgay, Forfarshire. A Dept.-Lieut of Roxburghshire. Formerly Lieut. in 2nd Life Guards. A Liberal, and supporter generally of Mr. Gladstone; opposed to the ballot. First returned for Roxburghshire May 1859 and sat until he accepted Chiltern Hundreds in 1870. Died 12 Oct. 1871. [1870]

SCOURFIELD, Sir John Henry. Williamston, Haverfordwest, Pembrokeshire. United University, Oxford & Cambridge, and Boodle's. Only s. of Owen Philipps, Esq., of Williamston, Pembrokeshire, Col. of the Pembrokeshire Militia, by Anne Elizabeth, d. of Henry Scourfield, Esq., of the Mote, and of Roberston Hall, Pembrokeshire. B. at Clifton 1808; m. 1845, Augusta, 2nd d. of John Lort Phillips, Esq., of Haverfordwest and Lawrenny, Pembrokeshire. Educ. at Harrow and at Oriel Coll., Oxford where he was 3rd class in classics, 1828 and graduated M.A. 1832. Assumed the name of Scourfield by royal license in lieu of his patronymic, 1862. Chairman of the Quarter Sessions of Pembrokeshire and Lord Lieut. and Custos Rot. of the Co. of the

town of Haverfordwest. A Liberal-Conservative. Sat for Haverfordwest from July 1852-Dec. 1868. From that date he sat for Pembrokeshire. MP until his death 3 June 1876. [1876]

SCOURFIELD, William Henry. 18 Bury Street, London. Roberston Hall, Pembrokeshire. Was patron of 2 livings. A moderate Reformer. Sat for Haverfordwest from 1835. Defeated in 1837. [1837]

SCROPE, George Poulett, F.R.S., F.G.S. 25 Hyde Park Gate, London. Castle Combe, Chippenham. Athenaeum, and Reform. B. 1797, 2nd s. of J. Poulett Thomson of Roehampton, Surrey and Austin Friars. M. 1821, Emma, d. and heir of William Scrope, of Castle Combe, Wiltshire, and Cockerington, Lincolnshire (she died 1866). Assumed the name of Scrope on his marriage. A Dept.-Lieut. of Wiltshire, and patron of 1 living. Wrote pamphlets on Banking, the Currency, the Poor Laws, and Political Economy. Also *Considerations on Volcanoes,* the *Geology of Central France,* and other geological works. Author of a *Life of Lord Sydenham.* A Liberal, voted for the ballot 1853. Unsuccessfully contested Stroud in 1832, but was elected there in May 1833, and sat until he accepted Chiltern Hundreds in July(?) 1867. Died 19 Jan. 1876. [1867]

SCULLY, Francis. 24 Burton Street, Eaton Square, London. Athame, Co. Tipperary. Reform, and Erectheum. S. of James Scully, Esq., of Tipperary, and nephew of Denys Scully, Esq. B. in Tipperary, 1820; m. 1856, Clotilde, youngest d. of John Samuel Moorat, Esq., of Gloucester Place, Hyde Park, and Bush Hill, Middlesex. Educ. at St. Gregory's Coll., Downside. Called to the bar at the Middle Temple 1841, but did not practise. A Repealer, voted for the ballot 1853; supported 'tenant-right.' First elected for Tipperary 1847 and sat until he retired 1857. [1857]

SCULLY, Vincent. 13 Merrion Square South, Dublin. Eld. s. of Denys Scully, Esq., (well known as the author of *A Statement of the Penal Laws affecting Roman Catholics*) by Catherine, d. of Vincent Eyre, Esq., of Highfield, Derbyshire. B. 1810; m. 1841, Susanna, d. of John Grogan, Esq., and sister of Edward Grogan, Esq., MP. Educ. at St. Mary's Coll., Oscott, Trinity Coll., Dublin, and subsequently at Trinity Coll., Cambridge; obtained science honours. Called to the Irish bar 1833; made a Queen's Counsel in Ireland 1849. Author of a work on the *Irish Land Question,* treatises on Free Trade in Land, the Channel Islands, etc., and a contribution to Sausse and Scully's *Irish Chancery Reports.* A Liberal, supported the vote of censure on Lord Palmerston 1864; said he would vote for reform in the landlord and tenant laws, and in the Church system; in favour of a repeal of the Ecclesiastical Titles Act; voted for the ballot 1853. Sat for Cork Co. from Mar. 1852-Apr. 1857; re-elected Apr. 1859 and sat until defeated 1865. Died 4 June 1871.   [1865]

SEAHAM, Visct. 2 Hamilton Place, London. Seaham Hall, Sunderland. Carlton. B. in Vienna 1821, the s. of 2nd Marq. of Londonderry by his 2nd wife, only d. and heir of Sir Harry Vane Tempest, Bart. Half bro. of Visct. Castlereagh. M. 1846, the only d. of Sir John Edwards Bart. Educ. at Balliol Coll., Oxford. Appointed Lieut. 1st Life Guards in 1845, but retired 1848. Dept. Lieut. of Durham and the counties of Montgomery and Merioneth, Lieut.-Col. Commandant of the North Durham Militia, and Maj. of the Montgomeryshire Yeomanry. A Conservative, favoured free trade, but sought the relief of the depression in the agricultural and shipping interests. Opposed to the endowment of the Roman Catholic Clergy. Sat for Durham N. from 1847 until Mar. 1854, when he succeeded as 2nd Earl Vane. In Nov. 1872 succeeded his half bro. as 5th Marq. of Londonderry. Died 6 Nov. 1884.
                                                              [1854]

SEALE, Sir John Henry, Bart. 42 Cadogan Place, London. Mountboone, Devon. Brooks's, Alfred, and Reform. M. the only d. of Sir Paul Jodrell M.D. Col. of the South Devon Militia. Patron of 2 livings. Of Whig principles, 'held strong Liberal opinions', and favoured the ballot, the repeal of the Corn Laws, and short Parliaments. Voted for the revision of the Pension List. Sat for Dartmouth from 1832 until his death on 29 Nov. 1844.   [1844]

SEBRIGHT, Sir John Saunders, Bart. 88 Jermyn Street, London. Beechwood, Hertfordshire. B. 1767; m. 1793, Hannah, only d. and heiress of Richard Crofts, Esq., of West Harling, Norfolk, who died in 1826; bro.-in-law to the Earl of Harewood. Of Whig principles. Sat for Hertfordshire from 1807, before that for Bath. Returned for Hertfordshire in Dec. 1832 and sat until he retired in 1835. Died 15 Apr. 1846.   [1833]

SEELY, Sir Charles. Continued in House after 1885: full entry in Volume II.

SEELY, C.H. Continued in House after 1885: full entry in Volume II.

SELLAR, A Craig. Continued in House after 1885: full entry in Volume II.

SELWIN-IBBETSON, Sir H.J. Continued in House after 1885: full entry in Volume II.

SELWYN, Charles Jasper. 63 Chester Square, London. 7 Old Square, Lincoln's Inn, London. Pagoda House, Richmond, Surrey. Athenaeum, United University, Union, Oxford and Cambridge. B. 1813, the s. of William Selwyn, Q.C. of Richmond, Surrey, by Letitia Frances, d. of Thomaa Kynaston, of Witham, Essex. M. 1856, Hester, 5th d. of J.G. Ravenshaw, former Chairman of the E.I. Company. Educ. at Eton and at Trinity Coll., Cambridge, where he graduated M.A. Called to the bar in 1840, at Lincoln's Inn, of which he became a bencher. Became Queen's Counsel 1856 and Commissioner of the University of Cambridge 1855. Appointed Dept.-Lieut of Surrey 1860. A Conservative, opposed to the abolition of Church-rates without an adequate provision being made for the maintenance and repair of Churches. Maintained that 'education must be based upon Holy Scriptures.' Sat for Cambridge University from Apr. 1859 until he was made Lord Justice of Appeal, Feb. 1868. Knighted in Aug. 1867. Died 11 Aug. 1869.
                                                              [1867]

SEVERNE, John Edmund. 10 Chesham Street, London. Wallop Hall, Shrewsbury. Carlton, and Army & Navy. S. of John Michael Severne, Esq., of Wallop Hall, Shropshire, and Thenford, Banbury, by Anna Maria Meysey, d. of E. Wigley, Esq., of Shakenhurst, Bewdley. B. at Ludlow, 1826; m. 1858, Florence, d. of Very Rev. H.U. Tighe, Dean of Derry. Was educ. at Brasenose Coll., Oxford. Entered the army in the 10th Hussars, and retired as Capt. 16th Lancers. A Magistrate and Dept.-Lieut. of Shropshire and Northamptonshire; was High Sheriff of the latter in 1861. A Conservative, in favour of the readjustment of local and county taxation. Sat for Ludlow from July 1865 to Dec. 1868. Sat for Shropshire S. from Oct. 1876 until he retired in 1885. Died 21 Apr. 1899.   [1885]

SEXTON, Thomas. Continued in House after 1885: full entry in Volume II.

SEYMER, Henry Ker, D.C.L. Hanford, Blandford, Dorsetshire. Carlton, Travellers', and Oxford & Cambridge. S. of H.K. Seymer, Esq., by Harriet, d. of Peter Beckford, and sister of the 3rd Lord Rivers. B. at Hanford, Dorsetshire, 1807; m. 1839, Helen, d. of W. Webber, Esq., of Binfield Lodge, Berkshire. Educ. at Winchester, and Christ Church, Oxford; was subsequently Fellow of All Souls' Coll. A Magistrate and Dept.Lieut. for Dorsetshire. Patron of 1 living. A Conservative, voted for inquiry into Maynooth

1853; in favour of England maintaining a strictly neutral position, but a 'well armed neutrality.' First elected for Dorsetshire in Feb. 1846 and sat until he accepted Chiltern Hundreds Feb. 1864. Died 28 May 1864.   [1863]

SEYMOUR, Alfred. 47 Eaton Square, London. B. in London 1824, the s. of Henry Seymour, Esq., of Knoyle House, Wiltshire, by Jane, d. of Benjamin Hopkinson, Esq. M. 1866, d. of Sir Baldwin Leighton, Bart., and widow of Beriah Botfield, Esq. Educ. at Eton and at Christ Church, Oxford. A Magistrate and Dept.-Lieut. of Wiltshire, and Sheriff of Northamptonshire 1881. A Liberal, and heartily supported Gladstone and his administration. Sat for Totnes Jan. 1853-Nov. 1868 and for Salisbury Aug. 1869-1874, when he was defeated. Died 15 Mar. 1888.   [1873]

SEYMOUR, George Henry, C.B. 115 Eaton Square, London. Barwick House, Lynn, Norfolk. United Service. B. 1818 the s. of Sir George F. Seymour, Rear-Admiral by Georgina Mary, d. of Gen. the Hon. Sir George C. Berkeley. M. 1861, Sophia, d. of Devick Hoste, Esq. Educ. at the Royal Naval Coll. Entered the navy 1831, became a Rear-Admiral 1863 and received a naval medal. Commanded the Queen's Private Yacht, the 'Victoria and Albert'. Was a Lord of the Admiralty, June 1866-Dec. 1868. A Conservative, and a strong supporter of 'the Monarchy and excellent constitution' of this country. Sat for Antrim from July 1865 until his death 25 July 1869.   [1869]

SEYMOUR, Henry Danby. 39 Upper Grosvenor Street, London. Knoyle, Salisbury, Wiltshire. Brooks's, and Travellers'. Eld. s. of Henry Seymour, Esq., of Knoyle, Wiltshire, and Northbrook House, Devon, by the d. of Benjamin Hopkinson, Esq., of Bath. B. in Park Lane, London, 1820. Educ. at Eton, and at Christ Church, Oxford. Was Joint Secretary to the Board of Controul from Mar. 1855 till Mar. 1858; was Dept.-Lieut. of Wiltshire from 1852. A Liberal, in favour of civil and religious liberty, and a gradual extension of the franchise; voted against church-rates 1851. First returned for Poole, Sept. 1850 and sat until he retired in 1868. Contested Shaftesbury in 1873 and 1874. Died 3 Aug. 1877.   [1867]

SEYMOUR, Sir Horace Beauchamp, K.C.H. 28 St. James's Place, London. Cowdray Lodge, Sussex. Stoke Chichester, Antrim. Carlton, and White's. B. 1791, the s. of Lord Hugh Seymour, by the 3rd d. of the 2nd Earl of Waldesgrave. M. 1st, 1818, d. of Sir. L. Palk, Bart., 2ndly, 1835, d. of W.S. Poyntz, Esq., and relict of 17th Lord Clin-

ton. Was for some years Equerry to King William IV, having previously served in the army, which he entered in 1811. Was Equerry to the Queen Dowager. A Conservative, but in favour of free trade. Sat for Midhurst from 1841-45, for Antrim from 1845-47 when he was elected for Lisburn, which he had previously represented before the passing of the Reform Bill. Sat for Lisburn until his death 23 Nov. 1851.   [1851]

SEYMOUR, Rt. Hon. Lord. 18 Spring Gardens, London. Berry Pomeroy, Totnes, Devonshire. Reform. B. in Piccadilly 1804, the eld. s. of the Duke of Somerset. M. in 1830, Jane Georgiana, youngest d. of Thomas Sheridan, Esq. A Lord of the Treasury from 1839 to June 1841, when he became Under-Sec. of State for the Home Department till Sept. 1841. Was Chief Commissioner of Woods and Forests from Mar. 1850 - Mar. 1852; and was also Lunacy Commissioner, but resigned in 1853. A Liberal, and voted against the abolition of the Corn Laws, but in 1846 supported their repeal. Sat for Totnes from 1834 until he succeeded as 12th Duke in Aug. 1855. Became 1st Lord of the Admiralty 1859-66. Died 28 Nov. 1885.   [1855]

SEYMOUR, Sir Michael, K.C.B. 3rd s. of Sir Michael Seymour, Bart., by Jane, 3rd d. of Capt. James Hawker, R.N. B. 1802; m. 1829, his cousin Dorothea, eld. d. of Sir William Knighton, Bart., M.D., Keeper of the Privy Purse to George IV. Entered the navy in 1813, but remained at the Royal Naval College till 1818. Appointed Lieut. R.N. 1822, Capt. 1826, and Rear-Admiral of the Red, 1857. Served in the Baltic during the Russian War. A Liberal. First elected for Devonport, Aug. 1859. and sat until he accepted Chiltern Hundreds Feb. 1863. C.-in-C. at Portsmouth Mar. 1863-Mar. 1866; Admiral 5 Mar. 1864; retired 1870. Died 23 Feb. 1887.   [1862]

SEYMOUR, William Digby. (I). 32 Fenchurch Street, London. 2 Belvedere Terrace, Brighton. S. of William Seymour, Esq., of Gloucester Terrace, Hyde Park. B. in London 1805; m. Emily, eld. d. of the Rev. Brackley Charles Kennett, Rector of East Illsey, Berkshire. A Merchant in London, under the name of Warre Brothers, Fenchurch Street, a firm which had existed 170 years. A radical Reformer, in favour of the ballot and a large extension of the franchise, accompanied by improved education for the people; opposed to all special religious endowments by the State. First returned for Hull Aug. 1854. Retired 1857. Not related to the W.D. Seymour who contested Hull in 1857. Died 1870 ?   [1857]

SEYMOUR, William Digby. (II). 2 Doctor

Johnson's Buildings, Temple, London 2nd s. of the Rev. Charles Seymour, Vicar of Kilronan, Co. Roscommon, by Beatta, a sister of Fergus Langley, Esq., of Lich Finn, Co. Tipperary. B. at Clifden, Co. Galway 1822; m. 1847, Emily, 2nd d. of Joseph John Wright, Esq., of Sunderland, Solicitor, and a Dept.-Lieut. for Durham. Educ. at Trinity Coll., Dublin, where he obtained honours in Classics, Hebrew and Rhetoric, and graduated a moderator in Logic and Ethics. Called to the bar at the Middle Temple 1846, and joined the Northern Circuit; made a Queen's Counsel, Feb. 1861. Appointed Recorder of Newcastle-on-Tyne Dec. 1854. Author of *An Essay on the Genius and Study of Rhetoric, the Industrial Resources of Western Ireland, The Wrongs of Shipping*, etc. A Liberal, in favour of 'a large extension of the electoral franchise, if accompanied by the protection of the ballot'; and of the 'more equitable distribution of the revenues of the Church'; opposed to Church rates, the Maynooth Grant, and 'all special religious endowments.' Sat for Sunderland from July 1852-Dec. 1845. Elected for Southampton May 1859 and sat until defeated 1865. Contested Nottingham 1869-1870, Stockton 1880 and South Shields 1885. Died 16 Mar. 1895. [1865]

SHAFTO, Robert Duncombe. 2 Cromwell House, South Kensington, London. Hampworth Lodge, Salisbury. Whitworth Park. Ferry Hill, Durham. Brooks's and Boodle's. Eld. s. of Robert Eden Duncombe Shafto, Esq., of Whitworth Park, Durham (formerly MP for the city of Durham), by the 3rd d. of Sir John Eden, Bart., of Windlestone. B. in London, 1896; m. 1838, Charlotte Rosa, d. of William Baring, Esq., and niece of Lord Ashburton. A Magistrate of Durham and of Wiltshire. Appointed a Dept.-Lieut. of Durham 1848. A Liberal, desirous to procure for 'the shipping interest that fair consideration of its burdens to which it is justly entitled;' voted for the ballot, 1853. Was an unsuccessful candidate for Durham S. in 1832. First returned for Durham N. in 1847 and sat until he retired in 1868. Died 2 May 1888. [1867]

SHARPE, Lieut.-Gen. Matthew. Hoddam Castle, Dumfriesshire. A Lieut.-Gen. in the army. Served in all the earlier continental campaigns in Flanders, Holland, etc. up to his appointment as a general officer. An East India Proprietor. Of Whig principles, in favour of ballot, short Parliaments, free trade (including corn), a commutation of taxes, and a diminution of the taxes on knowledge. Sat for Dumfries district from 1832 until he retired in 1841. Rank of General 1841. Died 12 Feb. 1845. [1840]

SHAW, Rt. Hon. Frederick. 59 St. James's Street, London. Kimmagehouse, Co. Dublin. Carlton. B. 1799, the 2nd s. of Col. Sir Robert Shaw, Bart. of Bushy Park, Co. Dublin, who sat for that city for 22 years. M. 1819, Thomasine Emily, d. of the Hon. George Jocelyn. Called to the Irish bar in 1822; was Recorder of Dublin and Dundalk, and a Bencher of King's Inns, Dublin. Obtained some premiums in the University of Dublin, and afterwards graduated at Oxford. A Conservative, voted against agricultural protection 1846. Sat for Dublin in 1830, and for Dublin University from 1832 (when he was elected in opposition to Mr. Crampton) until he accepted Chiltern Hundreds in 1848. Succeeded his bro. as 3rd Bart. in Feb. 1869. Died 30 June 1876.
[1847 2nd ed.]

SHAW, Richard. Holme Lodge, Burnley. Reform. S. of Richard Shaw, Esq., by Anne, his wife. B. at Burnley 1825; m. Maria, eld. surviving d. of James Dugdale, Esq. Educ. at the Grammar School, Burnley and St. Peter's, York. A Liberal; said he would give general support to Mr. Gladstone; was in favour of a reduction of the national expenditure. Sat for Burnley from Dec. 1868. MP until his death 19 Jan. 1876. [1875]

SHAW, T. Continued in House after 1885: full entry in Volume II.

SHAW, William. Beaumont, Cork. Reform. Stephen's Green Club, Dublin. S. of the Rev. Samuel Shaw, of Passage West, Co. Cork. B. 1823; m. 1850, Charlotte, d. of William Clear, Esq., of Cork. Chairman of the Munster Bank. 'An independent Liberal', and a member of the Home Rule League till Dec. 1881, when he withdrew from that body. In July 1865 unsuccessfully contested Bandon, which he represented from Dec. 1868 to Feb. 1874. Sat for the county of Cork from the last date until he retired in 1885. After the Munster Bank stopped payment in 1885 Shaw was declared bankrupt 12 Jan. 1886. Died 19 Sept. 1895. [1885]

SHAWE, Robert Newton. Kedgrove, Suffolk. S. of William Cunliffe Shawe, Esq., of Singleton Lodge, Lancashire, and Southgate House, Middlesex, who was twice returned for Preston and grand-nephew of Sir Ellis Cunliffe, Bart. M. Francis Anne, d. of Thomas Jones, Esq., of Stapleton, Gloucestershire. Chairman of the Quarter Sessions at Woodbridge. A Reformer, in favour of the Corn laws, and the immediate abolition of slavery. Sat for Suffolk E. from 1832 until defeated in 1835. Died 21 Oct. 1855. [1833]

SHAW-LEFEVRE, Rt. Hon. Charles. 89 Eaton

Square, London. Heckfield Place, Hampshire. Athenaeum, and Reform. S. of Charles Shaw Lefevre, Esq., former member for Reading. B. in Bedford Square 1794; m. 1817, d. of S. Whitbread, Esq. Educ. at Winchester and at Trinity Coll., Cambridge; graduated B.A. 1815 and M.A. 1819. Was called to the bar at Lincoln's Inn 1819. Lieut.-Col. of the North Hampshire Yeomanry. High Steward of Winchester and Dept.-Lieut. of Hampshire. Was chosen Speaker of the House in 1839, on the retirement of Mr. Abercromby, and in opposition to Mr. Goulburn; the votes for the latter were 299; for Mr. S. Lefevre, 317. Again chosen Speaker in 1841, in 1847 and in 1852, without opposition, salary £6,000. A Liberal, voted for an inquiry into the pension list, and for short Parliaments. Sat for Downton in 1830; for Hampshire N. from 1831 until he retired in 1857.   [1857]

SHAW-LEFEVRE, Rt. Hon. G.J. Continued in House after 1885: full entry in Volume II.

SHEE, William. 2 Serjeants Inn, Fleet Street, London. 5 Sussex Place, Hyde Park, London. Thomastown, Co. Kilkenny. Brooks's. Eld. s. of Joseph Shee, Esq., of Thomastown, Co. Kilkenny, and Belmont Lodge, South Lambeth (a London Merchant), by Teresa, d. of John Darell, Esq., of Scotney Castle, Kent. B. at Finchley, 1804; m. 1837, Mary d. of Sir James Gordon, Bart., of Gordonstoun. Educ. at Ushaw Roman Catholic Coll., Durham, and at Edinburgh. Called to the bar June 1828, and joined the Home Circuit. Was created a Serjeant in 1840, and received a patent of precedence 1845. A Liberal, in favour of vote by ballot, tenant-right in Ireland, and the repeal of the Ecclesiastical Titles Act; supported 'the incontestable claims' of the Irish Roman Catholics 'upon the ecclesiastical revenues of their country.' Was an unsuccessful candidate for Marylebone in July 1847. First returned for the Co. of Kilkenny July 1852 and sat until defeated 1857. Contested seat again in 1859. Contested Stoke-Upon-Trent Sept. 1862. Judge 1863. Knighted June 1864. Author. Died 19 Feb. 1868.   [1857]

SHEIL, Edward. Continued in House after 1885: full entry in Volume II.

SHEIL, Rt. Hon. Richard Lalor. 73 Eccleston Square, London. Long Orchard, Co. Tipperary. Athenaeum, and Reform. S. of a Mr. Sheil of Bellerne, near Waterford (previously a Cadiz Merchant), by the d. of John McCarthy, Esq., of Spring House, Co. Tipperary. B. in Dublin 1794; m. 1st, niece of Sir William McMahon, Bart., 2ndly, 1830, relict of E. Power, Esq., of Long Orchard, Co. Tipperary. Educ. at Stonyhurst and

at Trinity Coll., Dublin. A Queen's Counsel in Ireland, Commissioner of Greenwich Hospital, Vice-Pres. of the Board of Trade and Judge Advocate Gen. Appointed Master of the Mint, July 1846. Wrote several Tragedies and formerly wrote much for different portions of the periodical press. A Liberal, in favour of the abolition of tithes in every shape and under every designation, for the appropriation of a large portion of episcopal estates to purposes of national utility, and the nomination of grand juries by the people. Sat for Milbourne Port in 1830 and (having unsuccessfully contested it in 1830) for Louth in 1831. Sat for Tipperary from 1832-1841, when he was first elected for Dungarvan and sat until he accepted Chiltern Hundreds Feb. 1851. Died 25 May 1851.   [1850]

SHELBURNE, Earl of. Lansdowne House, Berkeley Square, London. Bowood, Wiltshire. B. in Berkeley Square, London 1816, the eld. surviving s. of the Marq. of Lansdowne, M. 1st., 5th d. of 11th Earl of Pembroke (she died 1841); 2ndly, 1843, the eld. d. of the Count de Flahault and Baroness Keith and Nairn. Educ. at Trinity Coll., Cambridge. A Dept.-Lieut. of Wiltshire, and appointed a Lord of the Treasury in Dec. 1847. Resigned in 1848. Of Whig opinions. Sat for Calne from 1837 until he accepted Chiltern Hundreds in June 1856. Succeeded as 4th Marq. in Jan. 1863. Died 5 July 1866.   [1856]

SHELDON, Edward Ralph Charles. 26 North Audley Street, London. Braile's House, Warwickshire. Boodle's. Head of a very ancient family in Warwickshire. B. 1786; m. 1816, Marcella, d. of Thomas Meredith Winstanley, Esq., at one time Dublin Herald-at-Arms. Served in the army. Dept.-Lieut. of Warwickshire, and Major of the Warwickshire Militia. A Reformer. In favour of an appropriation of the temporalities of the Church, which would be consistent with its security, and at the same time provide more amply for the performance of its spiritual duties. Said he would vote for an inquiry into the pension list, for the abolition of all sinecures, the ballot, and the abolition of all taxes exclusively affecting agriculture. Sat for Warwickshire S. from 14 Jan 1835 until his death June 1836.   [1836]

SHELLEY, Sir John Villiers, Bart. 1 St. James's Place, London. Maresfield Park, Uckfield Sussex. Brooks's. Eld. s. of Sir John Shelley, 6th Bart. (who died 1852), by Frances, only d. and heir of Thomas Winckley, Esq., of Brockholes, Lancashire. B. in Charles Street, Berkeley Square, London 1808; m. 1832, Louisa Elizabeth Anne, only child of the Rev. S. Johnes Knight, of Henley Hall, Shropshire. Claimed the ancient barony of Sudeley (in abeyance since 1336), as representative of one of the co-heirs. Educ. at the Charterhouse. Appointed Lieut.-Col. 46th Middlesex Rifle Volunteers 1861. Patron of 1 living. Author of a pamphlet on the effect of free trade in lowering the cost of production, etc. A Liberal, in favour of vote by ballot, extension of the suffrage to all rate payers, and triennial Parliaments; opposed to Church rates and to grants from the public purse for other than secular purposes. Was an unsuccessful candidate for E. Sussex in July 1841; first returned for Westminster in July 1852 and sat until he retired 1865. Contested Bridgwater in 1865. Died 26 Jan. 1867. [1865]

SHEPPARD, Thomas. 20 Great George Street, London. Hampstead Heath, Middlesex. Folkington Place, Sussex. Shrewton Lodge, Wiltshire. 3rd s. of William Sheppard, Esq., of Frome, a Magistrate for Somersetshire. M. d. of Richard Down, Esq., Halliwick Manor House, (she died Apr. 1845). His family were Cloth Manufacturers at Frome, and had an extensive Warehouse in Basinghall Street, London. A Merchant. A Magistrate for Sussex. A Conservative. Voted for agricultural protection, 1846, and against admission of the Dissenters to the Universities. Represented Frome from 1832 until he retired in 1847. Died 1 June 1858. [1847]

SHERIDAN, H.B. Continued in House after 1885: full entry in Volume II.

SHERIDAN, Richard Brinsley. 48 Grosvenor Place, London. Frampton Court, Dorchester. White's, Brooks's, and Travellers'. S. of Thomas Sheridan, Esq., by Caroline Henrietta, 4th d. of Col. Callander, of Craigforth, Stirlingshire. M. 1835, Marcia Maria, d. of Lieut.-Gen. Sir Colquhoun Grant, K.C.B. Grands. of the celebrated man, whose name he bears. A Magistrate and Dept.-Lieut. of Dorsetshire, High Sheriff of that Co. 1838. A Liberal, and in favour of a wide extension of the suffrage; would 'maintain the Protestant institution' of the country, but at the same time in favour of 'a conciliatory policy' towards Dissenters; voted for the ballot 1853. Contested Bridgwater May and Aug. 1837 and Stoke July 1837. Sat for Shaftesbury from 1845 till July 1852, when he was elected for Dorchester and sat until he retired in 1868. Died 2 May 1888. [1867]

SHERIFF, Alexander Clunes, 9 Queens Street, Westminster, London. Perdiswell Hall, Worcester. B. 1816; m. 1841, eld. d. of Thomas Talkershall, Esq., of Armley, near Leeds, (she died 1868). A Magistrate and Dept.-Chairman of the Metropolitan District Railway. A Liberal, voted in favour of the disestablishment of the Irish Church 1869. Sat for Worcester from July 1865. MP until his death Feb. 1877. [1877]

SHERLOCK, David. 15 Harcourt Street, Dublin. Stillorgan Castle, Stillorgan, Ireland. Reform, and Stephen's Green Club, Dublin. S. of Thomas Sherlock, Esq., of York Street, Dublin, by Isabella, d. of John Ball, Esq., formerly of Eccles Street, Dublin. B. 1814; m. 1843, Elizabeth, youngest d. of John Therry, Esq., Chairman of the Board of Excise in Ireland. Educ. at Trinity Coll., Dublin. Called to the bar in Ireland Jan. 1837, appointed a Queen's Counsel there 1855. A Bencher of Kings' Inns, Dublin. A Liberal, in favour of the system called 'Home Rule' for Ireland, and the amendment of the Irish Land Act. Sat for King's Co. from Dec. 1868, until he retired 1880. Died 16 Apr. 1884. [1880]

SHIELD, Hugh. 18 King's Bench Walk, Temple, London. Jesus College, Cambridge. Brooks's, and United University. S. of John Shield, Esq., of Stotes Hall, Jesmond, Newcastle-on-Tyne, and formerly of Gun's Green House, Berwickshire, by Catherine, d. of Mr. R. Barnett, of Westmeath. B. 1831. Was educ. at the Grange School, Bishopwearmouth, and King Edward's School, Birmingham. Entered at Trinity Coll., Cambridge in 1850, migrated to Jesus Coll., 1853, graduated B.A. 1854, M.A. 1857, having obtained a 1st class in the classical tripos, and the Chancellor's medal for legal studies; also a Fellow of Jesus Coll. Was called to the bar 1860, at Gray's Inn of which he was a bencher, having previously obtained the Studentship in the Inns of Court Examination. Appointed a Queen's Counsel 1881. A Liberal, who was 'resolute to maintain national honour and the integrity of the empire'; in favour of an 'efficient reform of the Land Laws', and all other liberal measures. Sat for Cambridge from Apr. 1880 until he retired in 1885. Died 24 Nov. 1903. [1885]

SHIRLEY, Evelyn John. 20 Belgrave Square, London. Eatington Hall, Warwickshire. United University. B. 1788. Married Eliza, the d. of Arthur Stanhope, Esq., cousin of the Earl of Chesterfield. Elected on the death of E. Sheldon. Esq., in 1836. A Trustee of Rugby School. A Conservative, voted for agricultural protection 1846. Opposed to the endowment of the Roman Catholic Clergy. Sat for Monaghan in 1826 and 1830, and for Warwickshire S. from 1837 until he accepted Chiltern Hundreds in May 1849. Died 31 Dec. 1856. [1848]

SHIRLEY, Evelyn Philip. Lower Eatington Park, Kineton, Warwickshire. Lough Fea, Co. Monaghan. Carlton. Eld. s. of Evelyn John Shirley, Esq., (who represented Warwickshire S. from 1836-1849), by Eliza, only d. and heir of Arthur Stanhope, Esq., cousin to the Earl of Chesterfield; cousin also to the Earl Ferrers. B. 1812; m. 1842, Maria, d. of Sir Edmund H. Lechmere, Bart., of The Lynd, Worcestershire. Educ. at Magdalen Coll., Oxford, where he graduated M.A. 1837. Appointed a Dept.-Lieut. of Warwickshire 1860. A Conservative, said he would support 'our Protestant institutions in Church and State', and the 'union of secular and religious education.' Sat for Monaghan from July 1841-July 1847. First elected for Warwickshire S. without opposition, Aug. 1853 and sat until he retired 1865. Died 19 Sept. 1882.   [1865]

SHIRLEY, Sewallis Evelyn. Lower Eatington Park, Kineton, Warwickshire. Lough Fea, Monaghan, Ireland. National. Only s. of Evelyn Philip Shirley, Esq., of Eatington Park, Warwickshire, and Lough Fea, Monaghan (who sat for Monaghan from 1841-1847, and for Warwickshire from 1853-1865), by Eliza, only d. and heir of Arthur Stanhope, Esq., cousin to the Earl of Chesterfield. B. 1844. Educ. at Eton and at Christ Church, Oxford. A Conservative, who 'would do his utmost to support and defend the Protestant constitution.' Sat for Monaghan from Dec.1868 until defeated Apr. 1880. Contested Monaghan S. 9 Dec. 1885. Died 7 Mar. 1904.   [1880]

SHUTE, Charles Cameron, C.B. 28 Rutland Gate, London. 63 Brunswick Place, Brighton. Carlton, and United Service. Eld. s. of Thomase Deane Shute, Esq., a Magistrate and Dept.-Lieut of Bramshaw and Burton, Hampshire (High Sheriff of Hampshire in 1821). M. 1858, Rhoda, d. of Rev. Henry Turnour Dowler, Vicar of Aldeburgh, Suffolk. Educ. at Winchester Coll. Served with the 13th Hussars in the campaign against the Rajah of Kairnool in 1839, in the Inniskilling Dragoons, and as adjutant-gen. of the Cavalry division throughout the Crimean War. Was present at the battles of Balaklava, Inkerman, Tchernaya, night attack on the Russian outposts Feb. 1855, siege and fall of Sebastopol. Commanded the Inniskilling Dragoons for some years, and afterwards the 4th Dragoon Guards until promoted to Major-Gen. Dec. 1871. Appointed Col. 17th Lancers 1878. A Knight of the Legion of Honour, and of the 3rd class of the Medjidie. Received the Crimean medal with 3 clasps, and the Turkish medal. A Magistrate for Sussex and honorary Col. of the Sussex Rifle Volunteers. A Conservative, was in favour of con-stitutional progress, 'for economy without inefficiency, for improvement without demolition,' and was 'a staunch supporter' of the Established Church. Sat for Brighton from Feb. 1874 until he retired 1880. Died 30 Apr. 1904.   [1880]

SHUTTLEWORTH, Sir Ughtred James Kay-, Bart. 28 Princes Gardens, London. Gawthorpe Hall, Burnley, Lancashire. Barbon Park, Kirkby Lonsdale. Eld. s. of Sir James Phillips Kay-Shuttleworth, 1st Bart., by Janet, only d. and heir of Robert Shuttleworth, Esq., of Gawthorpe Hall, Lancashire. B. in London 1844; m. 1871, Blanche Marion, youngest d. of Sir Woodbine Parish, K.C.H., of Quarry House, St. Leonards-on-Sea. Educ. at Harrow. A Magistrate for the Co. of Lancaster. Author of a work entitled *First Principles of Modern Chemistry.* A Liberal, in favour of 'Civil and Religious Liberty all over the world.' Was an unsuccessful candidate for Lancashire N.E. Dec. 1868. Sat for Hastings from Nov. 1869 until defeated 1880. Contested Coventry 12 Mar. 1881.   [1880]

SIBTHORP, Charles Delaet Waldo. 27 Chester Street, Grosvenor Place, London. Canwick Hall, Lincolnshire. Carlton, and United University. M. Maria, d. and co-heir of Ponsonby Tottenham, Esq. Patron of 2 livings. Appointed Col. of the South Lincolnshire Militia, 1852. A Magistrate and Dept.-Lieut. of Lincolnshire. A Conservative, voted for agricultural protection 1846, and was in the minority of 53 who censured free trade in Nov. 1852. Supported 'protection to native industry of this empire in all its branches.' Represented Lincoln from 1826-32, and was re-elected there in 1835, after which he sat until his death on 14 Dec. 1855.   [1855]

SIBTHORP, Gervaise Tottenham Waldo-. 3 Arlington Street, London. Canwick Hall, Lincoln. Potterells, Hatfield, Hertfordshire. Carlton, Boodle's, Junior United Service, and Oxford & Cambridge. Eld. s. of Col. Sibthorpe (who represented Lincoln for 21 years), by Maria, d. and co-heir of Ponsonby Tottenham Esq. B. at Canwick, near Lincoln, 1815; m. 1846, Louisa, 3rd d. of Lieut-Col. Cracroft (now Amcotts), of Hackthorn, Lincolnshire. Educ. at Harrow and at Oriel Coll. Oxford. A Magistrate, and Dept-.Lieut. for Lincolnshire. Major in the South Lincoln Militia. Patron of 1 living. Of 'essentially Conservative' principles, but in favour of progress and the reform of abuses; opposed to the grant to Maynooth. First elected for Lincoln Jan. 1856. MP until his death 13 Oct. 1861.   [1861]

SIDEBOTTOM, James. Acres Bank, Stalybridge. S. of Edward Sidebottom, Esq., a

Magistrate for the Cos. of Lancaster and Chester, by Mary, his 1st wife. B. at Stalybridge, 1824; m. 1849, Margaret, eld. d. of John William Nowell, Esq., of Heyrod, Lancashire, and of Dewsbury, Yorkshire. Educ. at the Manchester Grammar School. A Cotton Manufacturer. Elected Mayor of Stalybridge 3 successive years from 1864- 67, and appointed Magistrate of the Co. Palatine of Lancaster Apr. 1867. A Conservative, voted against the disestablishment of the Irish Church 1869 and gave 'strongest opposition to any other measure which tends to weaken the Church of England', but was not against the 'redress of grievances and existing abuses', in favour of the repeal of the rate-paying clause of the Reform Act, of the strictest economy in the public expenditure, and of an enlarged measure of national education. Sat for Stalybridge from Dec. 1868. MP until his death 14 Feb. 1871.   [1870]

SIDEBOTTOM, T.H. Continued in House after 1885: full entry in Volume II

SIDNEY, Thomas. 8 Ludgate Hill, London. Bowes Manor, Southgate, London. S. of William Sidney, Esq., Woollen-Draper at Stafford. B. at Stafford 1805; m. 1st, 1831, eld. d. of William Hall, Esq., of Ranton, Staffordshire (she died 1857); 2ndly, Eleanor Mary, d. of William Ward, Esq. Educ. at Stafford. A Tea-Dealer and Importer. An Alderman of London. Was Sheriff of London and Middlesex in 1844, Lord Mayor 1854. A Dept.-Lieut. of London. Patron of 1 living. A Liberal, in favour of extending the franchise to 'every householder after an occupancy of a year paying rates and taxes', in favour also of the abolition of Church rates; opposed to the endowment of the Roman Catholic Clergy. Sat for Stafford from Aug. 1847-July 1852; was an unsuccessful candidate for Leeds 1852, and for Stafford Apr. 1859; for which last he was re-elected Aug. 1860, and sat until he retired 1865. Died 10 Mar. 1889.   [1865]

SIMEON, Sir John. 72 Eaton Place, London. Swainston, Nr. Calbourne, Newport, Isle of Wight. Alfred. Eld. s. of Sir Richard Godin Simeon, Bart., (who represented the Isle of Wight 1832-7) by the eld. d. and heir of Sir Fitz-William Barrington, Bart. B. at St. John's, I.O.W. 1815; m. 1st, 1840, only d. of Sir Frederick Francis Baker, Bart., (she died 1860); 2ndly, 1861, the Hon. Catherine Dorothea, sister of 2nd Lord Colville. Was educ. at Christ Church, Oxford, where he graduated M.A. 1840. Appointed Maj. 1st Batt. I.O.W. Volunteers 1860. A Liberal, voted for the disestablishment of the Irish Church 1869. Sat for the I.O.W. from July 1847-May 1851, when he retired on account of his ceasing to be a member of the Church of England; re-elected there July 1865. MP until his death 21 May 1870.   [1870]

SIMEON, Sir Richard Godin, Bart. 40 Jermyn Street, London. Swainston, Isle of Wight. B. 1784; m. 1813, Louisa, eld. d. of Sir Fitzwilliam Barrington, Bart. of Barrington Hall, Essex. Of Whig principles, in favour of the ballot. Sat for the Isle of Wight from 1832 until defeated in 1837. Sheriff of Hampshire 1845. Died 11 Jan. 1854.   [1837]

SIMON, Sir J. Continued in House after 1885: full entry in Volume II.

SIMONDS, William Barrow. 18 Sussex Place, Regents Park, London. Abbots Barton, Nr. Winchester. Carlton, and Junior Carlton. S. of William Simonds, Esq., of Abbots Barton, Hampshire, by Helen, d. of John Barrow, Esq., of Cotham Lodge, Gloucestershire and of Bristol, Merchant. B. at Cotham Lodge, Gloucestershire; m. 1858, Ellen Lampard, d. of Frederick Bowker, Esq., of Winchester. Educ. at Merchant Taylors' School. Auditor of King's Coll., Cambridge. A Magistrate for Hampshire and the City of Winchester, and Capt.-Commandant of 1st Hampshire Volunteers. A Conservative, in favour of 'Conservative progress' so as 'to amend but not to destroy.' Sat for Winchester from July 1865 until defeated 1880. Alderman of Hampshire County Council 1888. Died 29 Dec. 1911.   [1880]

SINCLAIR, Sir George, Bart. 5 Suffolk Street, London. Ulbster, Caithness. Arthur's. S. of the Rt. Hon. Sir John Sinclair, Bart., of Ulbster (the celebrated agriculturalist) and nephew of Lord MacDonald. B. 1790; m. 1816, Catherine Camilla, 2nd. d. of Lord Huntingtower. Wrote *The Debate and Division, an Epistle to a Friend in the Country, The Bore*, and a few other poetical *jeux d'esprit*. Of moderate Conservative principles. Sat for Caithness in 1811, 1818 and from 1831 until he retired 1841. Contested Halifax July 1841. Author. Died 9 Oct. 1868.   [1838]

SINCLAIR, Sir John George Tollemache, Bart. Thurso Castle, Caithness, Scotland. Travellers'. S. of Sir George Sinclair, Bart. (who sat for Caithness in 1811, 1818, and from 1831 to 1841), by Lady Catherine Camilla, 2nd d. of William Lord Huntingtower, sister of the 6th Earl of Dysart. B. at Edinburgh; m. 1853, eld. d. of William Standish, Esq., from whom he obtained a divorce 1878. Was Vice-Lieut. of Caithness. Served in the Scots Fusilier Guards, and was a page of honour to the Queen. A Liberal. Sat for Caithness from Aug. 1869 until he retired in 1885. Died 29 Sept. 1912.   [1885]

SINCLAIR, W.P. Continued in House after 1885: full entry in Volume II.

SKIPWITH, Sir Grey, Bart. 6 Pall Mall, East, London. B. 1771; m. 1801, Harriet, 3rd d. of Gore Townsend, Esq., of Honington, Warwickshire. Sir Grey, had perhaps, the largest family of any man in the House at that time, viz. ten sons and eight daughters. Of Whig principles. Was elected for Warwickshire S. in the Parliament of 1831. Retired in 1835. Contested Warwickshire N. Aug. 1837. Died 13 May 1852.   [1833]

SLAGG, John. Continued in House after 1885: full entry in Volume II.

SLANEY, Robert Aglionby. 5 Bolton Row, Mayfair, London. Walford Manor, Shrewsbury. Brooks's, Athenaeum, and University. Eld. s. of Robert Slaney, Esq., of Hatton Grange, Shropshire, by Mary, d. of Thomas Mason, Esq., of Shrewsbury. B. 1791; m. 1st, 1812, Elizabeth, only child of William Hawkins Muckleston, Esq., M.D.; 2ndly, 1853, Catherine, widow of T. Archer, Esq., of Mount John, Co. Wicklow. Educ. at Trinity Coll., Cambridge. Was called to the bar at Lincoln's Inn 1817, and practised for a few years. A Magistrate for Shropshire; author of *An Essay on the Employment of the Poor, An Essay on the Beneficial Direction of Rural Expenditure, An Outline of the Smaller British Birds, A Plea to Power and Parliament for the Working Classes*, 1847, etc. A Liberal. When formerly in Parliament he obtained committees on the Poor Laws, on the restrictions on malting, on the fluctuations of manufacturing employment, the health of towns, public walks in populous cities, investments for the working classes, and partnerships of limited liability. Carried through Parliament the Act for legalizing provident and industrial partnerships. Sat for Shrewsbury from 1826 to 1835; was then an unsuccessful candidate; was re-elected, however, in 1837, and sat till 1841, when he retired; once more returned for Shrewsbury in 1847, and sat till July 1852, when he again retired; was again elected Mar. 1857, and sat until his death 19 May 1862.   [1862]

SMALL, J.F. Continued in House after 1885: full entry in Volume II.

SMIJTH, Sir William Bowyer-, Bart. 18 Great Russell Street, London. Hill Hall, Epping, Essex. Carlton. Eld. s. of the Rev. Sir Edward Bowyer-Smijth, the 10th Bart., by Letitia Cicely, d. of John Weyland, Esq., of Wood Eaton, Oxfordshire. B. 1814; m. 1839, Marianne Frances, 2nd. d. of Sir Henry Meux, Bart. Patron of 4 livings. Educ. at Eton and at Trinity Coll., Cambridge. A Conservative, considered that we wanted protection not only for agriculture, but 'protection also for the constitution, the Church, Protestantism, the religious and moral eduction of the people'; opposed to the Maynooth Grant. Was an unsuccessful candidate for Essex. S. July 1847. First returned for that Co. in July 1852 and sat until defeated 1857. Died 20 Nov. 1883. [1857]

SMITH, Abel. (I). 39 Berkeley Square, London. Woodhall Park, Hertfordshire. Carlton. S. of Samuel Smith, Esq., and cousin of Lord Carrington. B. 1788; m. 1st, 1822, Marianne Leslie, 4th d. of Alexander, 10th Earl of Leven and Melville (dead); 2ndly, 1826, Frances Anne, youngest d. of Sir Henry Calvert, Bart. Patron of 1 living. A Conservative, voted for agricultural protection, 1846. Sat for Wendover and Midhurst in four Parliaments previous to 1832. First elected for Hertfordshire 14 Jan. 1835. and sat until he retired in 1847. Died 23 Feb. 1859. [1847]

SMITH, Abel. (II). Continued in House after 1885: full entry in Volume II.

SMITH, Augustus. 1 Eaton Square, London. Tresco Abbey, Isles of Scilly, Cornwall. Brooks's, Reform and Athenaeum. Eld. s. of James Smith, Esq., of Ashlyn Hall, Hertfordshire, by his 2nd wife, Mary Isabella, d. of Augustus Pechell, Esq., Receiver-Gen. of Customs. B. 1804. Unmarried. Educ. at Harrow and at Christ Church, Oxford, where he graduated B.A. 1826. A Dept.-Lieut. of Cornwall. A Liberal, in favour of a wide extension of the franchise, vote by ballot, local self-government, and liberation from the income tax. Was an unsuccessful candidate for Truro in July 1852. First returned for that bor. Apr. 1857 and sat until he retired 1865. Died 31 July 1872. [1865]

SMITH, Benjamin. 5 Blandford Square, London. Hastings, Sussex. S. of William Smith, Esq., who for many years represented Sudbury, and subsequently Norwich, and who was considered the organ of the Unitarian Dissenters. Sat for Sudbury in the Parliament of 1835. A Reformer. Unsuccessful at Norwich 26 July 1837, but on petition Hon. R.C. Scarlett's election was delcared void, and the seat was awarded to Benjamin Smith 14 May 1838. MP until he retired in 1847. Died 12 Apr. 1860. [1847]

SMITH, Frederick Chatfield. Bramcote Hall, Nottingham. Carlton. 2nd s. of Samuel George Smith, Esq., of Sacombe Park, Hertfordshire, by Eugenia, d. of the Rev. Robert Chatfield, LL.D. of Chatteris, Cambridgeshire. B. 1823; m. 1858, Harriet Matilda, d. of Francis Pym, Esq., of The

Hasells, Bedfordshire. Educ. at Rugby. A Conservative. Sat for N. Nottinghamshire from Dec. 1868 until he retired in 1880. [1880]

SMITH, Hon. George Robert. 4 Great Cumberland Road, Selsdon, Surrey. B. 1793; m. 1818, d. of John Maberley, Esq. Was cousin to Lord Carrington. A Reformer. Unsuccessfully contested Buckinghamshire Aug. 1837. First elected for Wycombe 23 Oct. 1838 and sat until 1 July 1841. [1841]

SMITH, Gerard. Bank, Hull. Brooks's. S. of Martin Tucker Smith, Esq., (who sat for Wycombe from 1847 to 1865), by Louisa, d. of Sir Matthew White Ridley, Bart. A Lieut.-Col. Scots Guards, retired. Appointed a Groom-in-Waiting to the Queen Mar. 1883. A Liberal. Sat for Wycombe from Mar. 1883 until defeated in 1885, contesting East Riding, Yorkshire. Contested Hull W. July 1892. Governor of West Australia 1895-1900. Died 28 Oct. 1920. [1885]

SMITH, Jervoise. 47 Belgrave Square, London. Brooks's, and Travellers'. S. of John Abel Smith, Esq., MP for Chichester, by Annie, d. of Sir Samuel Clarke Jervoise, Bart. B. in London 1828. Educ. at Eton, and at Trinity Coll., Cambridge. A Partner in the banking firm of Smith, Payne, and Smiths, London. A Liberal. First elected for Penryn, Oct. 1866. Defeated 1868. Died 21 July 1884. [1867]

SMITH, John. 22 Grosvenor Square, London. Dale Park, Arundel, Sussex. Blenden Hall, Kent. Bro. of Lord Carrington. M. 1st, Sarah, d. of Thomas Boone, Esq.; 2ndly, 1800, Miss Tucker, d. of Lieut.-Col. Tucker; and 3rdly, 1811, Miss Leigh, d. of Egerton Leigh, Esq., of High Leigh, Chester. A London Banker and an East India Proprietor. Of Whig principles. Sat for Chichester in 1830, and before that for Midhurst from 1812. Was elected for Buckinghamshire in the Parliament of 1831. Retired in 1835. [1833]

SMITH, John Abel. 37 Chester Square, London. Brooks's. Eld. s. of J. Smith, Esq., Banker, of Blendon Hall, Kent (who sat for Buckinghamshire in 1832), by his 2nd wife, d. of Lieut.-Col. Tucker. B. 1801; m. 1827, Anne, d. of Sir Samuel Clarke Jervoise, Bart. (she died 1858). Educ. at Christ's Coll., Cambridge, where he graduated M.A. 1827. Was head of the banking firm of Smith, Payne, and Co. A Magistrate for Middlesex. A Liberal, in favour of Church-rates being abolished 'if dissenters required it.' Sat for Midhurst in 1830, and for Chichester from 1831 till Apr. 1859 when he was defeated. Re-elected for Chichester Feb. 1863 and sat until defeated in

1868. Died 7 Jan. 1871. [1867]

SMITH, John Benjamin. 105 Westbourne Terrace, Hyde Park, London. King's Ride, Ascot, Berkshire. Reform. A retired Merchant, was President of the Manchester Chamber of Commerce in 1839, 1840 and 1841, and was first Chairman of the Anti-Corn-Law League. Published, in 1840, *A Reply to the Letter of Samuel Jones Lloyd, Esq., on the Effects of the Administration of the Bank of England.* A Liberal, voted for the ballot 1853, and against church-rates 1855. Was an unsuccessful candidate for Blackburn in 1837, and for Walsall and Dundee in 1841. Sat for Stirling district 1847-July 1852, when he was elected for Stockport. Sat until he retired in 1874. Died 15 Sept. 1879. [1873]

SMITH, Sir John Mark Frederick, K.H. 39 Hyde Park Square, London. Buckland House, Dover, Kent. S. of Maj.-Gen. Sir J.F. Sigismund Smith, K.C.H., and grand-nephew of Field Marshall Baron Von Kalkreuth, formerly Commander-in-Chief of the Prussian army. B. at Paddington, London 1792; m. d. of Thomas Horn, Esq., of Buckland House, Kent. Appointed a Maj.-Gen. in 1854; served at the capture of the islands in the bay of Naples by the forces under Sir John Stuart, and was Quarter-master Gen. at the capture of the Ionian Islands under Sir John Oswald. Was Gentleman Usher of the Privy Chamber. Author of a translation of Marshal Marmont's work on the Turkish Empire, with military and political notes. Appointed to command the Engineers at Portsmouth in 1851, and at Aldershot Camp 1855. Col.-Commandant of the Royal Engineers 1860. A Conservative, and generally a supporter of Lord Derby's policy. First returned for Chatham July 1852; was unseated on petition in Mar. 1853; re-elected there 1857 and sat until he retired 1865. Died 20 Nov. 1874. [1865]

SMITH, Martin Tucker. 13 Upper Belgrave Street, London. Reform, Arthur's, and Brooks's. 2nd s. of John Smith, Esq., of Blendon Hall, Kent, a Banker in London (who sat for Buckinghamshire in 1832), by his 2nd wife, d. of Lieut.-Col. Tucker. B. 1808; m. 1831, Louisa, 3rd d. of Sir Matthew White Ridley, Bart. An East India Director, and a Commissioner of the Lieutenancy for London. A Liberal, voted however for Lord Derby's Reform Bill Mar. 1859, and with Lord Palmerston on the vote of censure 1864; also for inquiry into Maynooth, against the ballot in 1853, and against Church rates 1855. Sat for Midhurst in 1831. First returned for Wycombe 1847 and sat until he retired 1865. [1865]

SMITH, Rt. Hon. Montague Edward. 119 Park Street, Grosvenor Square, London. 3 Paper Buildings, Temple, London. Athenaeum, Carlton, and Windham. Eld. s. of Thomas Smith, Esq., of Bideford, Devon, Town Clerk of that borough. B. at Bideford, 1809. Unmarried. Educ. at the Grammar School, Bideford. Called to the bar, Nov. 1835, at the Middle Temple, of which he was a Bencher; made a Queen's Counsel 1852; joined the Western circuit. A Liberal-Conservative, opposed to the ballot; in favour of the franchise being extended to all those among the working classes who, 'by education and intelligence, and the moral training produced by habits of industry and thrift, are qualified to make choice of a representative'; in favour also of law reform. Unsuccessfully contested Truro Jan. 1849, and again July 1852. First elected for Truro Apr. 1859 and sat until appointed Judge 7 Feb. 1863; knighted May 1865; member of Judical Committee of Privy Council 3 Nov. 1871; resigned Dec. 1881. Died 3 May 1891.   [1863]

SMITH, Hon. Robert John. 3 Belgrave Street, London. Gayhurst, Buckinghamshire. Athenaeum. Eld. s. of Lord Carrington. B. 1796; m. 1822, Elizabeth, d. of 1st Lord Forester (dead). Of Whig principles. Sat for Wendover in 1818; for Buckinghamshire from 1820-1830; for Wycombe, Chipping from 1831 until he succeeded father as 2nd Baron Sept. 1838. Took surname Carrington in place of Smith in 1839. Died 17 Mar. 1868.   [1838]

SMITH, Rt. Hon. Robert Vernon. 20 Savile Row, London. Farming Woods, Thrapston, Northamptonshire. Reform, Travellers', and Brooks's. S. of Robert Percy Smith, Esq., of Savile Row, London. and nephew of the Rev. Sydney Smith, Canon of St. Paul's. M. d. and co-heir of the Earl of Upper Ossory. Educ. at Christ Church, Oxford, where he was 2nd class in classics 1822. A Lord of the Treasury from Nov. 1830-Nov. 1834. Secretary of the Board of Control from Apr. 1835-39. Under Sec. for the Colonies from 1839-41. Secretary at War from Feb.-Mar. 1852; and Pres. of the Board of Control from Feb. 1855-Mar. 1858. A Liberal. Sat for Tralee from 1829 until the election in 1831, when he was chosen for Northampton. Sat for Northampton until created Lord Lyveden, June 1859. Died 10 Nov. 1873.   [1859]

SMITH, Rowland. Duffield Hall, Derby. S. of Samuel George Smith, of Sacombe Park, Hertfordshire, by Eugenia, d. of the Rev. Dr. Chatfield, of Chatteris. B. at Goldings, Hertforshire, 1826. M. 1857, Constance, d. of Rt. Hon. Lord Granville Somerset. Educ. at Brasenose

Coll., Oxford. Patron of 1 living. A Conservative, voted against the disestablishment of the Irish Church 1869. Sat for Derbyshire S. from Dec. 1868 until 1874, when he was defeated.   [1873]

SMITH, Samuel. Continued in House after 1885: full entry in Volume II.

SMITH, Samuel George. 5 Albemarle Street, London. Sacombe Park, Ware. Carlton, Athenaeum, and Travellers'. S. of Samuel George Smith, Esq., by Eugenia, d. of the Rev. Robert Chatfield, LL.D., Vicar of Chatteris, Cambridgeshire. B. 1822. Educ. at Rugby and at Trinity Coll., Cambridge. A Conservative. Sat for Aylesbury from May 1859 until defeated 1880. Left £1½ millions at death. Died 6 July 1900.   [1880]

SMITH, Thomas Assheton. 12 Stratford Place, London. Vaynol, Carnarvonshire. Carlton. A Conservative, voted against the first Reform Bill. Sat for Andover from 1818 to 1831, when Mr. Etwall, one of its Patrons, and a Reformer, was elected, leaving Mr. Smith without a seat in the Parliament of 1831. Patron of 1 living. Sat for Carnarvonshire from 1832 until he retired in 1837.   [1837]

SMITH, Rt. Hon. Thomas Berry Cusack-. Merrion Square, Dublin. Carlton. 2nd s. of Sir W.C. Smith, a Baron of the Exchequer in Ireland and grands. of Rt. Hon. Sir Michael Smith, Master of the Rolls in Ireland. M. d. of James Smith Barry, Esq., of Marbury Hall, Cheshire and Foaty, Co. Cork. Was called to the Irish bar in 1819 and appointed Solicitor-Gen. of Ireland in Sept. 1842, Attorney-Gen. in Nov. 1842. Was a bencher of King's Inns, Dublin. Appointed Master of the Rolls in Ireland in 1846. A Conservative. Sat for Ripon from 1843-46. Died 13 Aug. 1866.   [1845]

SMITH, Thomas Eustace. 52 Prince's Gate, London. Long Ditton House, Upper Long Ditton. Arthur's. Only s. of William Smith, Esq., of Gosforth House, Northumberland. B. at Newcastle-on-Tyne, 1831; m. 1853, Mary, d. of W.H. Clarence Dalrymple, Esq., E.I.C.S. A Merchant and Shipowner at Newcastle-on-Tyne, North Shields, and London. Patron of 1 living. An 'advanced Liberal.' Contested Dover July 1865. Sat for Tynemouth from Dec. 1868 until he retired in 1885.   [1885]

SMITH, W.H. Continued in House after 1885: full entry in Volume II.

SMITH, William Masters. 16 Suffolk Street, London. Camer, Nr. Gravesend, Kent. Carlton.

Only s. of George Smith, Esq., of Camer, Kent, by Rebecca, d. of the Rev. Nicholas Brett, of Spring Grove, near Ashford, Kent. B. at Camer 1802; m. 1836, Frances, eld. d. of Maj.-Gen. Sir Howard Elphinstone, Bart., of Ore Place, Sussex. Educ. at Harrow, and at Edinburgh. A Magistrate and Dept.-Lieut. for Kent, for which Co. he was High Sheriff in 1848. A Conservative, 'opposed to the continuance of any grant of public money for the support of popery.' First returned for Kent W. in July 1852 and sat until defeated 1857. Died 31 Dec. 1861.   [1857]

SMITHWICK, John Francis. Dukeland House, Kilkenny. Cavendish Club, Dublin. B. at Kilkenny 1844, s. of Daniel Smithwick, of The Cottage, Kilkenny, by Ellen, d. of James Morris of Waterford. M. 1878 Marion, d. of James Power of Eastlands, Tramore, Co. Waterford. Was educ. at Kilkenny Coll. A Magistrate for Kilkenny, and served the office of High Sheriff of that city. A Liberal, and supported Home Rule for Ireland, tenant right and the amendment of the Grand Jury Laws. Sat for Kilkenny city from Feb. 1880 until 1886, when he retired.   [1886]

SMITHWICKE, Richard. Birchfield, Kilkenny. B. at Kilkenny 1804. Was educ. at Clongowes Coll., Co. Kildare. A Repealer. First elected for the Co. of Kilkenny in 1846, without a contest. Retired in 1847.   [1847]

SMOLLETT, Alexander. Cameron House, Dumbartonshire. Carlton, and Union. Eld. s. of Rear-Admiral John Rouet Smollett, of Bonhill, by the d. of the Hon. Patrick Boyle; was great-grandnephew of the celebrated historian and novelist. B. 1801. Was educ. at the University of Edinburgh. A Member of the Faculty of Advocates. A Conservative, in favour of national education on a religious basis; opposed to the Maynooth grant. Was an unsuccessful candidate for Dumbartonshire in 1835 and 1837. First returned for Dumbartonshire in 1841 and sat until he retired in 1859. Died 25 Feb. 1881. [1858]

SMOLLETT, Patrick Boyle. 13 Arlington Street, London. Cameron House, Bonhill, Dumbartonshire. Conservative. Youngest s. of Admiral John Rouett Smollett, of Bonhill, by his 2nd wife, Elizabeth, 2nd d. of Hon. Patrick Boyle, of Shewalton, Ayrshire. Great grand-nephew of the celebrated historian and novelist. B. at Cameron House, Dumbartonshire 1805. Unmarried. Educ. at Haileybury Coll., and at the University of Edinburgh. Entered the service of the E.I.C. in 1826. Was for many years political agent at Vizagapatan, Madras presidency, retired 1858. A Liberal-Conservative. Sat for Dumbartonshire

from May 1859-Nov. 1868. Sat for the bor. of Cambridge from Feb. 1974 until defeated 1880. Died 11 Feb. 1895.   [1880]

SMYTH, Sir George Henry, Bart. Berechurch, Essex. Carlton. B. 1784; m. 1815, Eve, d. of G. Elmore, Esq., of Penton. Patron of 2 livings. A Conservative. Sat for Colchester from 1826-30 and then from 1835 until he accepted Chiltern Hundreds in Jan. 1850. Died 11 July 1852.[1849]

SMYTH, John George. 17 Lowndes Square, London. Heath Hall, Wakefield, Yorkshire. Carlton, Travellers', and Boodle's. Eld. s. of John Henry Smyth, Esq., of Heath Hall, Yorkshire, by his 2nd wife, Lady Elizabeth Anne, 3rd d. of the 4th Duke of Grafton. Grand-s. of the Rt. Hon. John Smyth, former Master of the Mint. B. in Charles Street, Berkeley Square, London 1815; m. 1837, Hon. Diana, 5th d. of the 3rd Lord Macdonald. Was educ. at Eton, and at Cambridge, where he was a fellow-commoner of Trinity Coll. A Magistrate for Yorkshire. Col of the 2nd W. Yorkshire Militia, and a Dept.-Lieut. of the W. Riding of Yorkshire. A Liberal-Conservative, said he would vote for a 'revision and re-adjustment of taxation', supported the vote of censure on Lord Palmerston 1864. First returned for the City of York in 1847, without opposition and sat until he retired 1865. Died 9 June 1869.   [1865]

SMYTH, Patrick James. Auburn Villa, Rathgar, Dublin. S. of James Smyth, Esq., of the Co. of Cavan, by Anne, d. of Maurice Bruton, Esq., of Portaine, Co. Meath. B. in Dublin 1823; m. 1855, Jeanie, d. of John Regan, Esq., of Hobart Town, Tasmania. Educ. at Conglowes Wood Coll. Called to the bar in Ireland 1858. Published several works including *Australasia, Ireland's Capacities for Foreign Commerce, France and European Neutrality,* etc. Declared himself in politics a 'moderate Irish Nationalist', in favour of complete 'Home Rule' for Ireland, denominational education there etc. Unsuccessfully contested Waterford Feb. 1870. Sat for the Co. of Westmeath from June 1871-Apr. 1880, from which date he sat for Tipperary. Accepted Chiltern Hundreds Dec. 1884, on appointment as Secretary to Irish Loan Fund Board. Died 12 Jan. 1885.   [1884]

SMYTH, Prof. Richard. Londonderry, Ireland. S. of Hugh Smyth, Esq. of Buckmills, Co. Antrim, by Sarah Anne, d. of J. Wray, Esq. of Co. Antrim. B. at Dervock, Co. Antrim. Unmarried. Was educ. at the University of Glasgow, where he graduated M.A. 1850. Appointed Professor of Oriental Languages and Literature in Magee Coll., Ireland 1865. Was twice Moderator of the Presbyterian Church in Ireland in 1869 and 1870.

Author of several publications on educational subjects A Liberal, and a general supporter of the Irish policy of Mr. Gladstone; was in favour of the legalization of Ulster tenant-right, and for Ireland in general a modification of the Land Act, so as to enforce the 'just claims of the tenant'; in favour also of a complete reform of the Grand Jury Laws. Sat for the Co. of Londonderry from Feb. 1874. MP until his death 4 Dec. 1878.   [1878]

SMYTH, Roger Johnson. 32 Castle Street, Lisburn, Ireland. S. of Thomas Johnson Smyth, Esq., of Lisburn (a Magistrate and Dept.-Lieut.), by Charlotte, sister of Edward Bruce, Esq., of Scoutbush and Kilrook, Co. Antrim (who assumed the name of Bruce in 1811). B. at Lisburn 1815. Unmarried. Educ. on the continent. A Magistrate for the Cos. of Antrim and Down. A moderate Conservative, in favour of free trade based on sound principles, and of an equitable tenant-right bill, having regard to the proper rights both of Landlord and Tenant. Opposed to the repeal of the Union. Sat for Lisburn from Dec. 1852 until his death 19 Sept. 1853.   [1853]

SMYTHE, Hon. George Augustus Frederick Percy Sydney. 68 Harley Street, London. Westenhanger House, Kent. Carlton. Eld. s. of 6th Visct. Strangford. B. 1818, at Stockholm, during his father's embassy there; educ. at Eton and St. John's Coll., Cambridge. Was under Secretary of State for Foreign Affairs from Jan. to July 1846. Author of *Historic Fancies, etc*. A Conservative, but in favour of free trade. First returned for Canterbury in 1841 and sat until defeated in 1852.   [1852]

SOMBRÈ, David Ochterlony Dyce. Sudbury. S. of Gen. George Alex. Dyce, and grands. of Louis Baltshazzar Sombrè, of Sirdhanah, in Hindostan. B. 1809; m. 1840, Hon. Mary Anne, d. of 2nd Visct. St. Vincent. Was private secretary to her highness Begum Sombrè, a sovereign Princess in India. Of 'independent' politics. First elected for Sudbury June 1841 but on petition, the election was declared void for bribery and a new writ suspended. (Borough disfranchised by Act of Parliament in 1844).   [1841 2nd ed.]

SOMERS, John Patrick. Reform. S. of Patrick Somers of Chaffpool, by Mary Taaffe, a descendant of the Viscounts Taaffe, of Ballymote, Co. Sligo. B. at Chaffpool, Sligo 1801. Unmarried. Educ. at Harrow. A Dept.-Lieut. of Sligo. A Liberal, and a 'strenuous supporter' of Lord Palmerston's government. Sat for Sligo bor. July 1837-Apr. 1848, when the previous election in July 1847 was declared void. He was then unsuccessful at the poll, but that return was declared void July 1848, and he was then returned and sat until July 1852, at which election he was unsuccessful. Again returned Apr. 1857 and defeated in 1859.   [1857 2nd ed.]

SOMERSET, Col. Edward Arthur, C.B. 7 Hamilton Palce, London. Carlton. Eld. s. of Lord Robert Edward Henry Somerset, by the d. of 2nd Visct. Courtenay. Cousin to 7th Duke of Beaufort. B. 1817; m. 1849, Agatha, 2nd d. of William Miles, Esq., of Leigh Court, Somersetshire. Entered the Rifle Brigade as 2nd Lieut. in 1836, became Capt. in that Corps in 1845 and Lieut.-Col. 1855. Appointed to the Staff of Lord Raglan in the expedition to aid Turkey, was at the battle of Alma etc. Received the Legion of Honour 1856. Equerry to the Queen Dowager. A Conservative, voted for inquiry into Maynooth 1853; supported measures of Parliamentary Reform which did not give preponderance to mere numbers; and a supporter of the union of Church and State. First returned for Monmouthshire Mar. 1848, without opposition and sat until he accepted Chiltern Hundreds June 1859. Sat for Gloucestershire W. from July 1867 until defeated Nov. 1868. Died 12 Mar. 1886.   [1868]

SOMERSET, Rt. Hon. Lord Granville Charles Henry. Monmouthshire. Carlton. 2nd s. of Duke of Beaufort. B. 1792; m. 1822 Hon. Emily, d. of 1st Lord Carrington. Graduated at Christ Church, Oxford, where he was 2nd class in Classics 1813. A Conservative, but in favour of free trade. Was appointed a Lord of the Treasury in 1820, and held that office for some years. Was Chairman of the Metropolitan Lunacy Commission, Chief Commissioner of Woods and Forests from Dec. 1834-Apr. 1835, and Chancellor of the Duchy of Lancaster from Sept. 1841-July 1846. Sat for Monmouthshire from 20 May 1816 until his death in 1848.   [1847 2nd ed.]

SOMERSET, Rt. Hon. Lord Henry Richard Charles. 48 Charles Street, Mayfair, London. Troy House, Monmouth. Carlton. 2nd s. of the 8th Duke of Beaufort, by Lady Georgiana Charlotte, eld. d. of 1st Earl Howe. B. 1849; m. 1872, Lady Isabel, eld. d. of the 3rd Earl Somers. Educ. at Eton. Was Controller of the Queen's Household from Feb. 1874-Jan. 1879. A 'strong Conservative' in favour of land being relieved from some of its present burdens. Sat for Monmouthshire from Feb. 1871 until he retired 1880. Died 10 Oct. 1932.   [1880]

SOMERSET, Poulett George Henry, C.B. 6 Stratford Place, London. Heath Lodge, Staines. Army & Navy. Youngest s. of Lord Charles

Henry Somerset, Gov. of the Cape of Good Hope, by his 2nd wife, Lady Mary, 2nd d. of 4th Earl Poulett. B. 1822; m. 1847, Barbara Augusta Norah, d. of John Mytton, Esq. of Halston, Shropshire. Formerly Lieut.-Col. Coldstream Guards, which he entered Cornet Mar. 1839. A Conservative, a supporter of Mr. Disraeli's policy; in favour of the strictest neutrality in foreign politics. First elected for Monmouthshire July 1859 and sat until he accepted Chiltern Hundreds Feb. 1871. Died 7 Sept. 1875.   [1870]

SOMERSET, Lord Robert Edward G. Henry, K.C.B. Down Ormey, Gloucestershire. United Service. 4th s. of Henry, 5th Duke of Beaufort; and uncle of Lord Granville Somerset. B. 1776; m. 1805, Louisa Augusta, 12th d. of William, 2nd Visct. Courtenay (dead). A Lieut.-Gen. in the army. Surveyor-Gen. of the Ordnance from Dec. 1834 till Apr. 1835. A Conservative. Sat for Gloucestershire in 8 Parliaments previous to 1831; unsuccessfully contested Gloucestershire W. in 1832. Succeeded Lord Apsley in Cirencester in 1834. Retired in 1837. Died 1842.   [1837]

SOMERTON, Visct. 43A South Street, Grosvenor Square, London. Curzon Street, London. Carlton. Eld. s. of the Earl of Normanton. B. 1818. A Dept.-Lieut. of Wiltshire. Appointed Lieut. of the Wiltshire Yeomanry Cavalry 1851. A Conservative, but in favour of free trade; opposed to the endowment of the Roman Catholic Clergy. First returned for Wilton in Oct. 1841, on the succession of Lord Fitz-Harris to a Peerage, and sat until he retired in 1852. Succeeded as 3rd Earl Normanton Aug. 1868. Died 19 Dec. 1896.[1852]

SOMERVILLE, Rt. Hon. Sir William Meredyth, Bart. Somerville House, Drogheda, Co. Meath. Brooks's, and Travellers'. Eld. s. of Sir Marcus Somerville (3rd Bart.), by his 1st wife, Mary Anne, only d. and heir of Sir Richard G. Meredyth, Bart. M. 1st, 1833, Lady Maria, d. of the 1st Marq. of Conyngham, and niece of W.J. Denison, Esq., MP (she died 1843); 2ndly, 1860, only d. of Herbert George Jones, Esq., Barrister--at-Law. Was paid attaché at Berlin from Nov. 1829-Dec. 1832; Under Secretary for the Home Department from July 1846-July 1847; Chief Secretary for Ireland from July 1847-Feb. 1852. Dept.-Lieut. of Meath; a Visitor of Maynooth Coll. A Liberal. Unsuccessfully contested Wenlock, Jan. 1835. Sat for Drogheda from July 1837-July 1852, when he was an unsuccessful candidate for Canterbury; elected for Canterbury Aug. 1854 and sat until he retired 1865. Created 1st Baron Athlumney (U.K. Peerage) 3 May 1866. Died 7 Dec. 1873.   [1863]

SOMES, Joseph. (I). Park Street, Grosvenor Square, London. A Ship-builder. A Conservative. Contested Yarmouth June 1841. Sat for Dartmouth from 1844 (on the death of Sir J.H. Seale, Bart.) until his death in 1845.   [1845]

SOMES, Joseph, F.S.A. (II). North Bank, Muswell Hill, London. National. S. of Samuel Francis Somes, Esq., Shipowner, by Sarah, d. of Mr. Hill. B. at Stepney 1819. Unmarried. A Shipowner in London. A Magistrate for Middlesex and Essex. A Dept.-Lieut. of the City of London and the Tower Hamlets. A Liberal-Conservative, supported the vote of censure on Lord Palmerston 1864; in favour of the removal of 'the burdens and restrictions now so injuriously affecting British shipping', in favour also of the franchise being lowered in boroughs as well as in counties, but opposed to the ballot; in favour of the 'religious education' of the people, the relief of Dissenters from Church rates, and opposed to the grant to Maynooth. First elected for Hull Aug. 1859 and sat until defeated 1865.   [1865]

SOTHERON-ESTCOURT, Thomas Henry Sutton. See ESTCOURT, Rt. Hon. Thomas Henry Sutton Sotheron-.

SPAIGHT, J. A Liberal-Conservative. Returned for Limerick at a by-election 21 May 1858. Defeated in 1859; contested seat again in 1865, 1874, 1880, 1883 and 1885. Knighted Aug. 1887. Died 21 Jan. 1892.

SPANKIE, Robert. 36 Russell Square, London. Sergeant's Inn, Chancery Lane, London. A Sergeant-at-Law. When a student, Mr. Spankie was a Reporter on the *Morning Chronicle*; shortly after being called to the bar he went to India, and, practising there for some years as Advocate General, made a considerable fortune; afterwards became standing Counsel to the East India Company. Entertained moderate reform principles, inclining to Conservatism. Sat for Finsbury from 1832. Defeated in 1835.   [1833]

SPEARMAN, Henry John. 2 Grafton Street, London. Newton Hall, Durham. Thornely, Durham. Brooks's. Eld. surviving s. of Charles Spearman, Esq., of Thornely, Co. Durham, by the d. and co-heir of Samuel Brooke, Esq., of Birchington, Kent. B. 1794. A Magistrate for Durham. A Liberal, pledged to support Lord John Russell's ministry, 'entertaining perfect confidence in the men and hearty approbation of their measures'; disposed to favour an extension of the suffrage, and disclaimed 'the finality' of the Reform Act. First returned for the city of Durham in 1847 and sat until he retired in 1852. [1852]

SPEIRS, Alexander. Elderslie. M. d. of Thos. Hazard, Esq. Related to Lord Dundas. Lord Lieut. of Renfrewshire. A Reformer. Sat for Richmond from 1835 until he accepted Chiltern Hundreds Feb. 1841. [1840]

SPEIRS, Alexander Graham. Culcreuch, Renfrewshire. A cousin of Alex Speirs member for Richmond. A Merchant. Had been a Capt. in the army. A Reformer, in favour of the ballot, triennial Parliaments, the repeal of the Corn Laws, and an extension of the suffrage. Sat for Paisley from 19 Jan. 1835 until he accepted Chiltern Hundreds in 1836. Died 24 Dec. 1847. [1836]

SPEIRS, Archibald Alexander. 10 Eaton Place, London. Elderslie House, Renfrew. Houston House, Renfrewshire. Guards', Brooks's, and Travellers'. S. of Alexander Speirs, Esq., Lord-Lieut. of Renfrewshire, who sat for Richmond from 1835 till 1841, by Eliza Stewart, eld. d. of T.C. Hagart, Esq., of Bantaskine, Falkirk. B. at Leamington Priors, 1840. Educ. at Eton. Entered the Scots Fusilier Guards, Feb. 1858, and became Capt. 1862. A Liberal, in favour of reform in the representation, especially of the occupancy-franchise in counties being reformed, the abolition of church-rates, and the admission of Dissenters to the Universities. First elected for Renfrewshire, July 1865. MP until his death on 30 Dec. 1868. [1867]

SPENCER, Hon. Charles Robert. Continued in House after 1885: full entry in Volume II.

SPENCER, Hon. Frederick. St. James's Place, London. B. of Earl Spencer. B. 1791. A Post-Captain in the Royal Navy. Of Whig principles. Sat for Worcestershire in 1831. Was elected for Midhurst in 1832, and again returned soon after the general election in 1837, in place of Stephen Poyntz, Esq., who accepted the Chiltern Hundreds. Sat until he retired 1841. [1838]

SPINKS, Frederick Lowten. Brenley House, Faversham, Kent. S. of John Spinks, Esq., of the Inner Temple, by Mary Ann, d. of Thomas La Coste, Esq., of Chertsey, Surrey. B. in London 1816; m. 1844, Elizabeth, d. and co-heir of Edward Brown, Esq., of the Firs, Ashton-under-Lyne, and of Oldham. Educ. at King's Coll., London and also at Magdalene Coll., Cambridge, graduated B.A., and was a Wrangler in 1840, M.A. 1844. Called to the bar at Lincoln's Inn, 1843, created Sergeant-at-law 1862. A Magistrate for Kent from 1866. A Conservative. Unsuccessfully contested Oldham July 1865 and Dec. 1868. Sat for Oldham from Feb. 1874 until

defeated 1880. Died 27 Dec. 1899. [1880]

SPOONER, Richard. Henwood Lodge, Leamington. National. S. of Isaac Spooner, Esq., a Banker and Merchant in Birmingham. B. at Birches Green, near Birmingham 1783; m. 1804, d. of the Rev. Dr. Wetherell, Dean of Hereford, and Master at University Coll., Oxford (sister to Sir Charles Wetherell, she died 1860). Educ. at Rugby. A Banker. A Magistrate for the counties of Warwickshire, Worcestershire, and Staffordshire. A Conservative, well known for his opposition to the Maynooth Grant, etc. Elected in 1820 for Boroughbridge, but unseated on petition. Sat for Birmingham from 1844-1847, when although defeated at Birmingham, was returned for Warwickshire N. Was MP there until his death 24 Nov. 1864. [1864]

SPRY, Sir Samuel Thomas. 8 Arlington Street, Piccadilly, London. 15 Avenue Road, Regent's Park, London. Place, and Tregolls, Cornwall. Eld. s. of Admiral Sir Thos. Davy, who assumed the name of Spry. B. 1804. A Dept.-Lieut. and Dept. Warden of Cornwall, and patron of 1 living. Was formerly Secretary to her Majesty's band of Gentlemen at Arms. In favour of a revision of the pension list, and the abolition of naval and military sinecures; against the ballot; voted for agricultural protection, 1846. Sat for Bodmin from 1832-1841. Was again returned in 1843, when Major Vivian succeeded to a peerage. Defeated in 1847. Sheriff of Cornwall in 1849. Died 29 June 1868. [1847]

STACPOOLE, William. Cupola House, 26 Carlyle Square, London. Ballyalla, Ennis. Brooks's, Garrick, and Junior United Service. Eld. s. of Andrew Stacpoole, Esq., of Ballyalla, Co. Clare, by Diana, d. of D. Finuncane, Esq., of Stamer Park, Ennis. B. at Stamer Park, Ennis 1830; m. Mary Annie Catherine Winifred, eld. d. of Charles Henessy, Esq. of Leamington, Warwickshire. Educ. at Cheltenham Coll. and at Trinity Coll., Dublin. A Magistrate for Clare from 1851 to 1872, when he was superseded at his own request. Was Capt. Clare Militia from 1855-65. A Liberal, in favour of the system called 'Home Rule' for Ireland. First elected for Ennis Feb. 1860. MP until his death 10 July 1879. [1879]

STAFFORD, Augustus Stafford-O'Brien-. Blathenwyke Park, Wansford, Northamptonshire. Cratloe Woods, Co. Clare. Carlton, Travellers', and Oxford & Cambridge. B. 1811, the eld. s. of Stafford O'Brien, and nephew of the Earl of Gainsborough. Educ. at Trinity Coll., Cambridge. Was formerly known as Mr. Stafford O'Brien, but in 1847 assumed the name of Stafford, after O'Brien, by royal license. Was Secretary to the Admiralty from Mar.-Dec. 1852. A 'Tory', and noted for inquiry into Maynooth 1853. Unsuccessfully contested Limerick 1837. Sat for Northamptonshire N. from 1841 until his death on 15 Nov. 1857.   [1857 2nd ed.]

STAFFORD, Marq. of. (I). 2 Hamilton Place, London. Newhall and Cromertie. Carlton. Eld. s. of the 2nd Duke of Sutherland, by the 3rd d. of the 6th Earl of Carlisle. B. in London 1828; m. 1849, Anne, only d. and heir of John Hay-Mackenzie, Esq., of Newhall and Cromertie. Appointed a Dept.-Lieut. of Sutherlandshire 1849, and Vice-Lieut. of that Co. 1850. Lord-Lieut. of Cromarty, 1853. A Liberal, voted for inquiry into Maynooth, and against the ballot 1853; also voted against church rates 1855. First returned for Sutherlandshire July 1852 until he succeeded to the Peerage (Duke of Sutherland) in 1861. [1861]

STAFFORD, Marq. of. (II). Stafford House, St. James's, London. S. of the Duke of Sutherland (MP for Sutherlandshire 1852-61) by Anne, Countess of Cromartie, only child of John Hay-Mackenzie, of Newhall and Cromartie. B. in London 1851. Appointed Cornet 2nd Life Guards Sept. 1870, Lieut. Oct. 1871, and retired Oct. 1875. A Liberal. Sat for Sutherlandshire from Feb. 1874 until 1886, when he retired. Succeeded as 4th Duke Sept. 1892. Died 27 June 1913.
[1886]

STAFFORD-O'BRIEN, A.S. See STAFFORD, Augustus Stafford-O'Brien-.

STANDISH, Charles Strickland. Standish Hall, Lancashire. Brooks's, Boodle's, Crockford's, and White's. S. of Thomas Strickland Standish, Esq., who m. the eld. d. of Sir John Lawson, Bart. of Brough Hall, Yorkshire. B. Mar. 1790. Patron of the living of Standish. A Liberal. First elected for Wigan in July 1837, having been unsuccessful there in Jan. 1835; was not returned at the general election in 1841, but succeeded on petition 11 Apr. 1842 and sat until he retired in 1847. Died 10 June 1863.   [1847]

STANFORD, John Frederick, F.R.S. Foley House, Portland Place, London. Only s. of — Stanford, Esq. (formerly in the 1st Life Guards), by the d. of William Gorton, Esq., of Pooton, Cheshire, and Park Street, Windsor. Nephew to William Gorton, Esq., Judge and Commissioner of Revenue for Bengal. B. 182-. Unmarried. Was educ. at Eton, and at Christ's Coll., Cambridge, where he was 2nd class in mathematics, and graduated M.A. 1842; was subsequently appointed Wort's Travelling Fellow to the Universi-

ty. Called to the bar at Lincoln's Inn 1844. A Dept.-Lieut. for Berkshire, and a Magistrate for Middlesex. Author of *Systematic Colonization, Supression of Mendicancy, British National Education,* and other pamphlets; also *Travels in Thuringa, The Political Tale of John Bull and his Wonderful Lamp,* etc. A Conservative, and in favour of 'protection to native industry'; opposed to all grants for Roman Catholic endowments. First returned for Reading, Aug. 1849 and sat until he retired in 1852. Died 2 Dec. 1880.   [1852]

STANFORD, Vere Fane Benett-. Pythouse, Tisbury. Norton House, Warminster. Preston Place, Sussex. Carlton, Boodle's, and Army & Navy. Eld. s. of the Rev. Arthur (Prebendary) Fane, Rector of Fulbeck, Lincolnshire, and of Boyton House, Wiltshire, by Lucy, d. of John Benett, Esq., MP of Pythouse, Wiltshire. B. at Boyton House, Wiltshire 1839; m. 1867, Ellen, only d. and heir of William Stanford, Esq., of Preston Place, Sussex. Assumed the name of Benett on succeeding to the estates of that family, and the name of Stanford after his marriage. Educ. at Marlborough Coll. Patron of 1 living. A Conservative, 'in favour of an immediate readjustment of taxation being made so as to relieve the agricultural and local interests from their present heavy burdens.' Sat for Shaftesbury from Aug. 1873 until defeated 1880. Died 8 May 1894. [1880]

STANHOPE, Rt. Hon. E. Continued in House after 1885: full entry in Volume II.

STANHOPE, James Banks. Revesby Abbey, Horncastle, Lincolnshire. Carlton and Boodle's. Only s. of the Hon. Col. James Hamilton Stanhope (s. of 3rd Earl Stanhope), by Lady Frederica Louisa, eld. d. of 3rd Earl of Mansfield. B. in Devonshire Street, London, 1821. Unmarried. Educ. at Westminster School. A Conservative. First elected for Lincolnshire N., July 1852 and sat until he retired in 1868.   [1867]

STANHOPE, Lord. 33 Lower Grosvenor Street, London. Bretby Hall, Burton on Trent. Eld. s. of the Earl of Chesterfield, by the Hon. Anne Elizabeth, eld. d. of 1st Lord Forester. Unmarried. B. 1831. Entered the army in 1849; appointed Lieut. Royal Horse Guards 1853; retired 1855. Became Lieut. S. Nottinghamshire Yeomanry Cavalry 1863. A Conservative, but was not opposed to 'moderate and well-considered reforms'; would 'deeply regret any rupture of the union of Church and State.' Contested Derbyshire S. Apr. 1857. First elected for Nottinghamshire S. Dec. 1860 and sat until he succeeded father as 7th Earl June 1866. Died 1 Dec. 1871.   [1865]

STANHOPE, Walter Thomas William Spencer. 77 Harley Street, London. Cannon Hall, Barnsley. Carlton, Travellers', and St. Stephen's. Eld. s. of John Spencer Stanhope, Esq., F.R.S. of Cannon Hall, Barnsley, by Lady Elizabeth Wilhelmina, d. of the 1st Earl of Leicester. B. at Cannon Hall, Barnsley 1827; m. 1856, Elizabeth Julia, d. of Sir John Jacob Buxton, Bart., of Shadwell Court, Thetford. Educ. at Eton and at Christ Church, Oxford, where he graduated 1st class in mathematics 1847, M.A. 1851. Lieut.-Col. commanding 4th Administrative Batt. West York Rifles. Was Capt. 1st West York Yeomanry from 1847-1872. A Magistrate and Dept.-Lieut. for the West Riding of Yorkshire, also Dept.-Chairman of Quarter Sessions. A Conservative. Unsuccessfully contested the Southern division of the West Riding of Yorkshire in 1865, and again in 1868; sat for that division from June 1872 until defeated 1880. Knighted 1904. Died 17 Nov. 1911. [1880]

STANILAND, Meaburn. Skinbeck Quarter, Boston. Harrington Hall, Spilsby, Lincolnshire. Reform. S. of James Staniland, of Boston, by Amy Ambler, d. of James Meaburn of Boston. B. at Boston 1809; m. 1840, Emma, d. of Robert William Staniland of Skinbeck Quarter, Boston. Educ. at Boston and at Lincoln. Admitted a Solicitor 1830. A Liberal. Sat for Boston from May 1859 until June 1865, and from Mar. 1866 until he accepted Chiltern Hundreds in 1867. [1867]

STANLEY, Edward. 35 Burton Street, London. Ponsonby Hall, Cumberland. Carlton. Eld. s. of Geo. Ed. Stanley, Esq., of Ponsonby Hall and Dalegarth. B. 1790; m. 1821 Mary, d. of Wm. Douglas, Esq., an East India Judge. Patron of 2 livings, and Dept.-Lieut. of Cumberland. A Conservative, voted for agricultural protection 1846; opposed to the endowment of the Roman Catholic Clergy. Sat for Cumberland W. from 1832 until he retired in 1852. Died 19 Aug. 1863. [1852]

STANLEY, Hon. E.H. See STANLEY, Rt. Hon. Lord.(II).

STANLEY, E.J. Continued in House after 1885: full entry in Volume II.

STANLEY, Rt. Hon. Edward John. 2 Grosvenor Crescent, Belgrave Square, London. Alderley Park, Cheshire. Reform. Eld. s. of Lord Stanley of Alderley. B. 1802 (twin with the Hon. William Owen Stanley); m. 1826, Hon. Henrietta Maria, eld. d. of the 13th Visct. Dillon. Graduated at Christ Church, Oxford. Was a Dept.-Lieut. of Cheshire; was Under-Secretary of State for the Home Department from July to Nov. 1834; Secretary of the Treasury from Apr. 1835 to June 1841; and Paymaster-General of the Forces from June to Sept. 1841. A Liberal, voted in favour of the ballot, but opposed to the extension of the suffrage; voted against the repeal of the malt tax 1835. Represented Hendon in the parliament of 1831; sat for Cheshire N. from 1832 until defeated in 1841; was defeated at the general election in that year but again returned in 1847 without a contest. Sat until created Baron Eddisbury 1848. Succeeded as 2nd Baron Stanley Oct. 1850; President of Board of Trade 1855-58; Postmaster General Aug. 1860 to July 1866. Died 16 June 1869. [1847 2nd ed.]

STANLEY, Hon. Edward Lyulph. 82 Harley Street, London. Reform. 3rd s. of the 2nd Lord Stanley of Alderley, by Hon. Henrietta Maria, eld. d. of the 13th Visct. Dillon. B. in Grosvenor Crescent, London, 1839; m. 1873, Mary Katherine, d. of Isaac Lowthian Bell, Esq., of Rounton Grange, Northallerton. Was educ. at Eton and at Balliol Coll., Oxford. Was 2nd class in classics at moderations 1859; graduated B.A. 1st class classics 1861. Called to the bar at the Inner Temple Nov. 1865, and joined the Northern circuit. Appointed an Assistant Commissioner to the Friendly Societies Commission 1872. A Liberal. Unsuccessfully contested Oldham June 1872, and again Feb. 1874. Sat for Oldham from Apr. 1880 until defeated in 1885. Vice-Chairman of London School Board 1897; succeeded as 4th Baron Sheffield Apr. 1909. Died 5 Nov. 1929. [1885]

STANLEY, Rt. Hon. Frederick Arthur. 5 Portland Place, London. Withenslack Hall, Grange-over-Sands, Lancashire. Carlton. Younger s. of 14th Earl of Derby, by Hon. Emma, 2nd d. of 1st Lord Skelmersdale. B. in London 1841; m. 1864, Lady Constance, eld. d. of 4th Earl of Clarendon. Educ. at Eton, and entered the Grenadier Guards 1858. Appointed Lieut. and Capt. 1862, retired 1865. Was Lord of the Admiralty Aug. - Dec. 1877, Financial Secretary to the Treasury Aug. 1877 - Mar. 1878, Secretary of State for War Mar. 1878 - Apr. 1880, President of the Board of Trade 1886 - 88, and Governor General of Canada 1888-93. A Magistrate for Lancashire and Westmoreland. A Conservative. Sat for Preston July 1865 - Dec. 1868, when he was elected for Lancashire N. and sat until created Lord Stanley of Preston 1886. Succeeded his bro. as 16th Earl of Derby. Apr. 1893. Died 14 June 1908. [1886]

STANLEY, Hon. Henry Thomas. 23 Grosvenor

Square, London. Knowsley, Lancashire. 2nd s. of the Earl of Derby. B. 1803. Once a Capt. in the Scots' Fusilier Guards. Of Whig principles. In favour of the ballot. Sat for Preston from 1832 until he retired in 1837. Died 2 Apr. 1875. [1837]

STANLEY, Rt. Hon. Lord. (I). 8 St. Jame's Square, London. Knowsley, Lancashire. Eld. s. of Earl of Derby. B. 1800; m. 1825, Emma Caroline, youngest d. of Edward, Lord Skelmersdale. Was Under-Secretary for the Colonies, during a part of the Goderich administration. Irish Secretary 1830-33, Secretary of State for the Colonies 1833-34, when he resigned in consequence of not being able to agree to his colleagues' plan of Church Reform. Again appointed to the Colonial Department Sept. 1841. Was Lord Rector of Glasgow University. A Liberal. Sat for Stockbridge 1820, Preston 1826-30, when he was thrown out by Mr. Hunt, and took his seat for Windsor (Sir Hussey Vivian retiring in his favour) for which he sat in 1831. Sat for Lancashire N. from 1832 until summoned to Lords in his father's barony, Aug. 1844. Succeeded as 4th Earl June 1851. Prime Minister 1852, 1858, and 1866. Died 23 Oct. 1869. [1844]

STANLEY, Rt. Hon. Lord. (II). 23 St. James's Square, London. Knowsley, Prescott, Lancashire. Carlton, and Travellers'. Eld. s. of the Earl of Derby by the 2nd d. of 1st Lord Skelmersdale. B. at Knowsley Park 1826. Educ. at Rugby and at Trinity Coll., Cambridge, where he was 1st class in classics 1848, taking also mathematical honours and gaining a declamation, and other prizes. Dept.-Lieut. of Lancashire, Chairman of the Kirkdale Quarter Sessions and of the Annual General Sessions of Lancashire. Was Under-Secretary of State for Foreign Affairs from Mar.-Dec. 1852, Secretary of State for the Colonies from Mar.-June 1858, President of the Board of Control from June-Sept. 1858, then Secretary of State for India until June 1859. Secretary of State for Foreign Affairs from July 1866-Dec. 1868. Was a member of the Royal Commission on Army Purchase 1856-57, of the Cambridge University Commission 1856-60, of the Commission on the organisation of the Indian Army 1858-59, and the Commission of the Sanitary State of the Indian Army 1859-61. A Liberal-Conservative, in favour of reform, but not the total disestablishment of the Irish Church. Against the ballot unless it was proved necessary. Unsuccessfully contested Lancaster Mar. 1848, and Marylebone May 1859. Sat for Kings Lynn from 22 Dec. 1848 until he succeeded as 15th Earl in Oct. 1869. Then again was Secretary of State for Foreign Affairs 1874-78 and for the Colonies 1882-85. Died 21 Apr. 1893. [1869]

STANLEY, William Massey. 10 Hill Street, Berkeley Square, London. Melton Mowbray. Brooks's, and White's. Eld. s. of Sir T.S.M. Stanley, Bart. B. 1807. Of Liberal politics. Elected for Pontefract in 1837. Retired 1841. Died 29 June 1863. [1838]

STANLEY, Hon. William Owen. 40 Grosvenor Place, London. Penrhos, Holyhead, Anglesey. Travellers'. B. at Alderley, Cheshire, 1802, the 2nd s. of 1st Lord Stanley of Alderley, by the d. of 1st Earl of Sheffield. M. 1832 Ellen, youngest d. of Sir John Hay Williams, Bart., of Bodelwyddan, Flintshire. Educ. at Eton and in Germany. Entered the Grenadier Guards in Feb. 1822, and became Capt. and Adj. Retired in 1830. Was Lord.-Lieut. of the Co. of Anglesey. A Liberal, in favour of 'direct taxation.' Sat for Anglesey 1837 - July 1847, and for Chester July 1850 - Mar. 1857, when he was returned for Beaumaris and sat until he retired in 1874. Died 24 Feb. 1884. [1873]

STANSFELD, Sir James. Continued in House after 1885: full entry in Volume II.

STANSFIELD, William Rookes Crompton. 22 Charles Street, Berkeley Square, London. Esholt Hall, Leeds, Yorkshire. United University, Brooks's, and Reform. Eld. s. of Joshua Crompton, Esq., by Anna Maria, d. and co-heir of William Rookes, Esq., of Esholt. Assumed the name of Stansfield in compliance with the will of his mother, who inherited the property of her maternal uncle Robert Stansfield, Esq., of Esholt. B. 1790; m. 1824, d. of William Markham, Esq., of Bacan and grand-d. of Archbishop (Markham) of York. M.A. of the University of Cambridge. 'A moderate Reformer, favourable to short Parliaments and vote by ballot.' First returned for Huddersfield July 1837 and sat until he lost his seat in Apr. 1853 when the July 1852 general election result was declared void. [1852 2nd ed.]

STANTON, Alfred John. The Thrupp, Stroud. Reform, and City Liberal. 2nd s. of William Henry Stanton, Esq., of The Thrupp, Stroud (who sat for Stroud from 1841 to 1852), by Jane, d. of Roger Smith, Esq., of the Manor House, Walworth, Surrey. B. at Steanbridge House, Stroud 1825; m. 1st, 1857, Anna, eld. d. of John Alexander, Esq., of Newtownlimavady, Londonderry; 2ndly, 1868, Harriet Margaret, eld. d. of Henry H. Wilton, Esq., of Whitminster House, Gloucestershire. Educ. at King's Coll. School, London. A Magistrate for Gloucestershire. A Liberal. Sat for Stroud from May 1874 until he retired in 1880. [1880]

STANTON, Walter John. Culls House, Stroud.

Reform. S. of Charles Stanton, Esq., of Upfield, Stroud, by Martha, d. of Thomas Holbow, Esq., of Stroud. B. at The Thrupp, Stroud 1828; m. 1865, Mary d. of William Capel, Esq., of The Grove, Stroud. Was educ. at Warminster School. A Civil Engineer; a West of England Cloth Manufacturer, and a J.P. for Gloucestershire. A Liberal. Sat for Stroud from Feb. to May 1874, when he was unseated on petition; re-elected Apr. 1880 and sat until he retired in 1885. Contested the redrawn Stroud seat in 1886, standing as a Gladstonian Liberal. [1885]

STANTON, William Henry. The Thrupp, Stroud. Stratford Cottage, Stroud. Reform. S. of William Stanton, Esq., Woollen Manufacturer at Stroud. B. 1790; m. 1823, eld. d. of Roger Smith, Esq., of Manor House, Walworth. A Whig. A Magistrate of the county of Gloucester. First elected for Stroud in 1841 and sat until he retired in 1852. Died 24 Mar. 1870. [1852]

STAPLETON, John. Reform, Athenaeum, and Brooks's. 5th s. of Thomas Stapleton, Esq., of Richmond, Yorkshire, and subsequently of Carlton Hall, by his 1st wife, Maria Juliana, d. of Sir Robert Gerard, Bart. Uncle to the 9th Lord Beaumont. B. at Richmond, Yorkshire 1815. Unmarried. Educ. at Stoneyhurst Coll., Lancashire, and at the Universities of Edinburgh, Gottingen, and Berlin. Admitted a student of Lincoln's Inn, June 1835; called to the bar Nov. 1840, and joined the Northern Circuit. A former Director and Dept.-Governor of the Royal British Bank. Of Whig principles, opposed to the Maynooth grant. Sat for Berwick from July 1852-Apr. 1853, when the election was declared void for bribery and treating; again returned in 1857. Defeated 1859. Re-elected there Nov. 1868 and sat until defeated Feb. 1874. Died 25 Dec. 1891. [1859]

STARKEY, Lewis Randle. 22 Princes Gardens, London. Becca Hall, Leeds. Carlton, Junior Carlton, and Conservative. Eld. s. of John Starkey, Esq., of Spring Lodge, Huddersfield, by Sarah Anne, d. of Joseph Armitage, Esq., of Milnesbridge House, Yorkshire. B. at Spring Lodge, Huddersfield 1836; m. 1858, Constance Margarette, d. of Thomas Starkey, Esq. Educ. at Rugby and at the University of Berlin. A Woollen Cloth Manufacturer. A Magistrate and Dept.-Lieut. for the West Riding of Yorkshire. Capt. 2nd West York Yeomanry Cavalry. A Conservative, in favour of a change being made in local taxation so that some local burdens may be borne by the State. Contested the Southern division of the West Riding of Yorkshire Dec. 1868. First returned for the Southern division of the West Riding of Yorkshire Feb. 1874 and sat until

defeated 1880. Died 16 Sept. 1910. [1880]

STARKIE, John Pierce Chamberlain. Ashton Hall, Nr. Lancaster. Carlton, and Oxford & Cambridge. Younger s. of Le Gendre Nicholas Starkie, Esq., of Huntroyde (who represented Pontefract from 1826-1832), by Anne, d. of Abraham Chamberlain, Esq., of Rylstone, Co. York. Was therefore bro. to Le Gendre Nicholas Starkie, Esq., who sat for Clitheroe from 1853-1857. B. at Huntroyde, near Burnley 1830; m. 1861, Anne Charlotte Amelia, only d. of Harrington Hudson, Esq., of Bessingley, East Riding of Yorkshire. Educ. at Eton and at Trinity Hall, Cambridge, graduated LL.B. 1856. Entered at the Inner Temple, but was not called to the bar. A Conservative, voted against the disestablishment of the Irish Church 1869. Sat for Lancashire N.E. from Dec. 1868 until defeated 1880. [1880]

STARKIE, Le Gendre Nicholas. Huntroyde, Burnley and Ashton Hall, Lancashire. Eld. s. of Le Gendre Nicholas Starkie, Esq., of Huntroyde, Lancashire, by Anne, d. of — Chamberlain, Esq., of Kelston, Yorkshire. B. at Huntroyde, 1828. Unmarried. Educ. at Warwick and Uppingham Schools, and at Trinity Coll., Cambridge, where he graduated M.A. 1854. Appointed Lieut. in Lancashire Yeomanry Cavalry 1855. A Liberal, opposed to the Maynooth and all other State Grants. Against the ballot, but in favour of Parliamentary Reform, and extension of the franchise. First elected for Clitheroe Aug. 1853. Retired 1857. Sheriff of Lancashire 1868. Alderman of Lancashire County Council 1889. Died 13 Apr. 1899. [1857]

STAUNTON, Sir George Thomas, Bart., D.C.L., F.R.S. 17 Devonshire Street, Portland Place, London. Leigh Park, Hampshire. Cargin, Galway. Athenaeum. S. of Sir Geo. L. Staunton, who accompanied Lord Macartney to China. B. at Milford House, near Salisbury, 1781. Was president of the Select Committee at Canton, and one of the Royal Commissioners of embassy to Pekin in 1816. V.P. of Asiatic Society. Formerly thought the Reform Bill too extensive, but voted for its second reading. Voted against immediate abolition of the Corn Laws in 1842, but in 1846 supported their repeal. Moved Resolutions in the House of Commons on the China trade in 1833. Supported the China war in 1840. Sat for Heytesbury in 1830 and 1831. Was elected for St. Michael's in 1818 and 1820. Sat for Hampshire S. in the Parliament of 1832, but was defeated there in 1835. Elected for Portsmouth in Mar. 1838, on the death of Mr. Bonham Carter, the former member and sat until he retired July 1852.

Translated the penal code of China. Author of pamphlets on our relations with China. Was Page to Lord Macartney when Ambassador to China. Died 11 Aug. 1859.   [1852]

STAVELEY, Thomas Kitchenham. Old Heningford, Yorkshire. Of Whig principles, in favour of the ballot and the immediate abolition of slavery. Sat for Ripon from 1832. Defeated in 1835. Died 20 Feb. 1860.   [1833]

STAWELL, Lieut.-Col. S. United Service Club. Nephew of the Earl of Bandon, and cousin to Lords Riversdale and Doneraile. A Lieut.-Col. in the 12th Lancers; was at Waterloo. Of Whig principles, he came in by a majority of six over the Conservative candidate, Mr. Cuthbert, a Barrister, and s. of a Merchant in Cork, who was supported by the Corporation. Sat for Kinsale from 1832. Retired in 1835.   [1833]

STEBLE, Lieut.-Col. Richard Fell. Ramsdale Bank, Scarborough. Devonshire. S. of the Rev. John Hodgson Steble, of Whicham, Cumberland. B. 1825; m. 1864, Elizabeth, 2nd d. of John Barratt, Esq., of Holywath, Coniston, Lancashire (she died 1880). Educ. at Rossall School, Lancashire. Practised for a few years as a Solicitor in Liverpool, and was fourteen years a member of the Liverpool City Council, and during two of those years (1874-76) was Mayor of the city. A Magistrate for Lancashire, and also for Liverpool, and a Lieut.-Col. (retired) in the 1st Lancashire Rifle Volunteers. A Liberal. Returned for Scarborough 3 Nov. 1884, and sat until he retired in 1885. Mayor of Scarborough 1891-82. Died 8 Oct. 1899.   [1885]

STEEL, John. Derwent Bank, Cockermouth, Cumberland. Reform. S. of Joseph Steel, Esq., of Cockermouth, Solicitor, by Dorothy, d. of John Ponsonby, Esq., of Hail Hall, Cumberland. B. at Cockermouth, 1786; m. 1817, Frances, d. of the Rev. Richard Case, Vicar of Bucklebury, Berkshire. Educ. at St. Bees' Coll., Cumberland. Admitted an Attorney 1809; retired from practice, 1852. A Liberal, in favour of extension of the franchise, but against any other Parliamentary Reform. First returned for Cockermouth Aug. 1854. MP until his death on 10 Apr. 1868. [1867]

STEERE, Lee. 43 Pall Mall, London. Jayes Ockley, Dorking, Surrey. Carlton. Eld. s. of Lee Steere-Steere, Esq., of Jayes Ockley, Surrey, by Sarah, d. of Robert Harrison, Esq., of Ripley Court, Surrey, and Benningholme Hall, East Riding of Yorkshire. B. 1803; m. 1826, Anne, d. of James Kiers Watson, Esq., of Heple Mount, East Riding of Yorkshire. Educ. at Harrow and at

Trinity Coll., Oxford. A Magistrate for Surrey and Sussex. A Dept.-Lieut. for Surrey. High Sheriff of Surrey 1848. A Conservative, in favour of the 'defences of the country being placed in a state of thorough efficiency.' Sat for W. Surrey from Sept. 1870 until he retired 1880. Died 9 Oct. 1890.   [1880]

STEPHENSON, Robert, F.R.S. 34 Gloucester Square, Hyde Park, London. 24 Great George Street, London. Athenaeum. Eld. s. of George Stephenson, Esq., (Civil Engineer), of Taptron House, Derbyshire, an extensive Locomotive Manufacturer at Newcastle-on-Tyne. B. near Newcastle 1803; m. 1829, Frances, d. of John Sanderson, Esq., Merchant of London (she died 1842). Was educ. at Newcastle and the University of Edinburgh. Received the honorary degree of D.C.L. at Oxford 1857. Well known as a Railway Engineer and a Locomotive Manufacturer; was a leader in the narrow gauge interest. Engineer to the Birmingham, Midland, Eastern Counties and numerous other railways. Inventor of improvements in the locomotive engine, and of the tubular or beam-bridge for railways. Constructed the London and Birmingham, Blackwall, Norfolk, Aylesbury and various other lines of railway. Chairman of the Pontop and South Shields Railway. A Dept.-Lieut. of Northumberland. Was a Commissioner on the Health of Towns. A Conservative. First returned for Whitby in 1847 without opposition, and MP until his death 12 Oct. 1859.   [1859]

STEPNEY, Sir Emile Algernon Arthur Keppell Cowell-, Bart. 5 St. George's Place, London. Woodend, Sunninghill, Berkshire. The Dell, Llanelly, Carmarthenshire. Reform, and Travellers'. Eld. s. of Sir John Stepney Cowell-Stepney, 1st Bart. of Llanelly (who sat for Carmarthen district from Dec. 1868 to Jan. 1874), by his 2nd wife Euphemia, d. of Gen. John Murray, of Clonalla, Co. Donegal. B. at Maunheim, Germany, 1834; m. 1875 Hon. Margaret Leicester, youngest d. of the 2nd Baron De Tabley. Educ. at Eton. Was a clerk in the Foreign Office, from which he retired, after a service of 20 years; was attached to the special mission of the Earl of Clarendon to Berlin at the coronation of the King of Prussia. A Magistrate for Carmarthenshire. A Liberal. Unsuccessfully contested, Feb. 1874, Carmarthen district for which he sat from Aug. 1876. Accepted Chiltern Hundreds 1878.   [1878]

STEPNEY, Sir John Stepney Cowell-, Bart., K.H. 5 St. George's Place, Hyde Park, London. Llanelly, Carmarthenshire. Brooks's, and Senior United Service. B. 1791, s. of Gen. Andrew

363

Cowell, of the Coldstream Guards, and of Coleshill, Buckinghamshire, by Maria Justina, youngest d. of Sir Thomas Stepney, of Llanelly, and sister of the last Bart. of that line which became extinct. M. 1st, 1820, Mary Anne, d. of the Hon. Robert Annesley; 2ndly, 1823, Euphemia, d. of Gen. John Murray of Glenalla, Co. Donegal. Assumed by royal license the name of Stepney in addition to his patronymic. Entered the Coldstream Guards 1809 and became Lieut.-Col. Served 6 campaigns under the Duke of Wellington and Lord Lynedoch. Received the Peninsula Medal with 4 clasps and the Waterloo Medal. A Magistrate and Dept.-Lieut. of Carmarthenshire and High Sheriff 1862. Col. Carmarthenshire Volunteers. Author of *Leaves from the Diary of an Officer*. A Liberal, voted for the disestablishment of the Irish Church 1869. Sat for the district of Carmarthen from 1868 until he retired in 1874.   [1873]

STEUART, Andrew. Auchlunkart House, Banffshire. Only s. of Patrick Steuart, Esq., of Auchlunkart, Banffshire, by Rachel, only d. of Lachlan Gordon, Esq., of Park. B. 1822; m. 1847, Elizabeth, 3rd d. of Lieut.-Col. Thomas Gordon, of Park. Educ. at The New Academy, Edinburgh, at Glasgow University, and at Trinity Coll., Cambridge, where he was 1st class in classics and scholar of the college in 1844. Entered at the Temple, but was not called to the bar. A Dept.-Lieut. of Banffshire. A Liberal-Conservative, opposed to the Maynooth grant and to the ballot, but in favour of 'gradual reform', education on a 'broad religious basis', and an 'adjustment' of the church-rate question. Was an unsuccessful candidate for Lymington in Apr. 1850. First returned for Cambridge bor. Apr. 1857, and sat until he accepted Chiltern Hundreds 1863.   [1862]

STEUART, Robert. 10 Upper Belgrave Street, London. Alderston, Haddingtonshire. Reform. M. 1827 Maria, 3rd d. of Col. Dalrymple, C.B. A Lord of the Treasury from Apr. 1835; salary £1,200. In favour of the expulsion of the Bishops from the House of Lords, and the ballot. Was returned for Haddington district in 1831, but the election was declared void on account of the forcible abduction of one of the five electors. Sat uninterruptedly there from 1832 until defeated in 1841. Chargé d'affairs and Consul-gen. at Santa Fè da Bogota. Spain, where he died 15 July 1843.   [1840]

STEVENS, J.C.M. See MOORE-STEVENS, J.C.

STEVENSON, J.C. Continued in House after 1885: full entry in Volume II.

STEWART, Edward. 7 York Place, Portman Square, London. S. of the Hon. E.R. Stewart, and nephew of the Earl of Galloway. Capt. of the Kirkcudbright and Wigtonshire Militia. Of Whig principles. Was elected for the Wigtown district in the Parliament of 1831. Retired 1835. [1834]

STEWART, Houston. A Naval Commander, became Admiral in 1860, K.C.B. July 1855. A Liberal. Returned for Greenwich at a by-election 11 Feb. 1852. Defeated in gen. election 1852. Died 10 Dec. 1875.

STEWART, Sir Hugh, Bart. Batt's Hotel. Balygawley House, Co. Tyrone. B. in 1793; m. Julia, d. of Marcus Gage, Esq., of the Co. of Londonderry. S. of the Rt. Hon. Sir John Stewart, some years Attorney Gen. for Ireland. A Conservative. Sat for Tyrone from 1830 until he retired in 1835. Died Nov. 1854.   [1833]

STEWART, James. (I). 34 Curzon Street. 4 Old Square, Lincoln's Inn, London. Athenaeum. 3rd s. of John Stewart, Esq. B. 17 Aug. 1805; m. 12 Aug. 1834, his 1st cousin, Margaret Emily, 3rd d. of Duncan Stewart, Esq., of Glenbuckie, Perthshire. A Chancery Barrister and Conveyancer and author of *The Practice of Conveyancing, The Principles of the Law of Real Property*, etc. A Reformer. Unsuccessfully contested Barnstaple Jan. 1835. First returned for Honiton 25 Aug. 1837 and sat until he retired 1841. Died 26 Sept. 1860.   [1840]

STEWART, James. (II). Garvock, Greenock. Routenburn, Largs, Ayrshire. Reform. Eld. s. of James Stewart, Esq., of Clydebank, Greenock, by Joanna, d. of Donald Shaw, Esq. B. at Greenock 1827; m. 1st, 1855, Margaret, d. of Duncan Darroch, of Gourock, Renfrewshire; 2ndly, 1868, Margaret Sandilands, d. of William Stirling, Esq. Was educ. at Edinburgh Academy. A Merchant and Shipowner. A Magistrate for Ayrshire and Renfrewshire and a Dept.-Lieut. for Ayrshire. A Liberal. Sat for Greenock from Jan. 1878 until he accepted Chiltern Hundreds Nov. 1884. Died 28 May 1895.   [1884]

STEWART, John. Albany, London. A West India Proprietor. Dept. Chairman of the Universal Life Assurance Society. A Director of the London and Westminster Joint Stock Bank. A Conservative, but in favour of free trade. Sat for Lymington from 1832 until defeated in 1847. Died 14 Mar. 1860.   [1847]

STEWART,   Mark   John.   See

McTAGGART-STEWART, Sir Mark John, Bart. Continued in House after 1885: full entry in Volume II.

STEWART, Sir Mark John. See McTAGGART-STEWART, Sir Mark John, Bart. Continued in House after 1885: full entry in Volume II.

STEWART, Sir Michael Robert Shaw, Bart. 42 Belgrave Square, London. Ardgowan, Greenock, Scotland. Carlton, White's, and Travellers'. Eld. s. of Sir Michael Shaw Stewart, Bart., who sat for Renfrewshire from 1830 until his death in 1836, by Eliza Mary, only d. and heir of Robert Farquhar, Esq., of Newark, Renfrewshire. B. at Ardgowan, 1826; m. 1852, Lady Octavia, d. of 2nd Marq. of Westminster. Educ. at Eton, and at Christ Church, Oxford. Appointed Cornet and Sub-Lieut. 2nd Life Guards 1845, retired 1846. Appointed Dept.-Lieut. of Renfrewshire 1848; Vice-Lieut. 1860; Lieut.-Col. Renfrewshire Rifle Volunteers 1860. A moderate Conservative, opposed to the Maynooth Grant. First elected for Renfrewshire May 1855, without opposition and sat until defeated 1865. Died 10 Dec. 1903. [1865]

STEWART, Sir Michael Shaw, Bart. 13 Portland Place, London. Ardgowan, Renfrewshire. M. Elizabeth Mary, only d. of J. Murdoch, Esq., of the Island of Grenada, and of Portland Place, London. A West India Proprietor. Of Whig principles, in favour of triennial Parliaments, and opposed to all monopolies. Sat for Lancashire from 1827 until 1830. From then for Renfrewshire. MP until his death 19 Dec. 1836. [1836]

STEWART, Patrick Maxwell. 11 Chapel Street, Grosvenor Square, London. S. of Sir M.N. Stewart, Bart., and bro.-in-law of the Duke of Somerset. A Merchant and Agent for Tobago. A Director of the British American Land Company, also of the Palladium Life Assurance Company, and a Manager of the London and Westminster Joint Stock Bank. A Vice-Lieut. of Renfrewshire. A Liberal. Voted against the Corn Laws. Sat for Lancaster from 1831-37 and for the county of Renfrew from 1841 until his death 30 Oct. 1846. [1845]

STIRLING-MAXWELL, Sir William. See MAXWELL, Sir William Stirling-, Bart.

STOCK, Joseph, LL.D. Temple Street, Dublin. S. of Bishop (Stock), of Killaloe. Judge of the High Court of Admiralty in Ireland. A Reformer. Contested Dublin University 4 Aug. 1837. Sat for the borough of Cashel from 1841 until he accepted Chiltern Hundreds in 1845. [1845]

STOCK, Thomas Osborne. 16A Cavendish Square, London. Reform. S. of Charles Stock, Esq., by Rebecca, d. of William Rankin, Esq., of Lyons, near Braintree, Essex. M. 1865, Juliana Priscilla, d. of Capt. Farmar. A Merchant and Underwriter in London, head of the firm of Messrs. T.O. Stock and Co., Austin Friars. A Liberal of very advanced views, and declared himself to be 'implacably hostile to the Established Church in Ireland', as he considered the majority of the people of Ireland belonged to the 'ancient faith'; voted against Lord Russell's Reform Bill 1866. First elected for the bor. of Carlow, July 1865. Retired in 1868. Died 17 Nov. 1875. [1867]

STONE, William Henry. Dulwich Hill, Surrey. Leigh Park, Havant, Hampshire. United University. B. in London 1834, the s. of William Stone of Dulwich Hill, Surrey, by Mary, d. of Thomas Platt, of Hampstead. M. 1864 Melicent, 2nd d. of Sir Arthur Helps, Clerk to the Privy Council. Educ. at Harrow and at Trinity Coll., Cambridge, where he was a Wrangler, 1st Class in Classics 1851, and Fellow of Trinity 1859. Became Magistrate for Surrey in 1861 and for Hampshire in 1863. Patron of 4 livings and trustee for 3. A Liberal, voted for the disestablishment of the Irish Church 1869. Sat for Portsmouth from July 1865 until he was defeated in 1874. Contested Chatham Feb. 1875 and Greenwich Apr. 1880. Died 7 Nov. 1896. [1873]

STONOR, T. A Whig. Returned for Oxford in 1832. Unseated on petition in 1833. Defeated in 1837, contesting Oxfordshire. [1833]

STOPFORD-SACKVILLE, S.G. Continued in House after 1885: full entry in Volume II.

STORER, George. Thoroton Hall, Bingam, Nottinghamshire. 3rd s. of Rev. J. Storer, Rector of Hawksworth, Nottinghamshire, by Charlotte, d. of the Rev. C. Wylde, D.D., Rector of St. Nicholas, Nottinghamshire. B. at Thoroton Hall, Nottinghamshire 1814; m. Harrietta Anne, eld. d. of Moffat Palmer, Esq., of Horncastle, and widow of Dr. Manson, of Spynie, N.B. Educ. at Louth Grammar School, Lincolnshire, and St. John's Coll., Cambridge. A Magistrate for Nottinghamshire. A Conservative. Sat for S. Nottinghamshire from Feb. 1874 until he retired in 1885. [1885]

STOREY, S. Continued in House after 1885: full entry in Volume II.

365

STORKS, Rt. Hon. Sir Henry Knight, G.L.B., G.C.M.B. War Office, Pall Mall, London. B. in London 1811, the eld. s. of Mr. Serjeant Storks by the d. and co-heir of J. Trundle. M. 1841 d. of the Chevalier Guiseppe Nizzoli, of Milan (she died 1848). Educ. at Charter House, and then entered the army in 1828. Served in the 61st, 14th, and 30th regiments. Was Assistant Adjutant Gen. at the Cape of Good Hope during the Kaffir War 1846-47; Military Secretary at Mauritius 1849-54; commanded the forces on the Bosphorus at the Dardanelles and Smyrna during the Russian War 1855-57; Lord High Commissioner of the Ionian Islands, Feb. 1859 until the cessation of those dependencies to Greece 1863; Governor of Malta; and Governor of Jamaica during the inquiries respecting the disturbances there in 1865. Appointed Controller-in-Chief at the War Office, as the first holder of that office, 1868 (which was re-named Surveyor General of Ordnance on the re-organization of the War Department in 1870). A Major-Gen. in the army from 1862. A Liberal. Contested Colchester 3 Nov. 1870. Sat for Ripon from Feb. 1871 until 1874, when he retired. Died 6 Sept. 1874.   [1873]

STORMONT, Visct. Carlton. Eld. s. of the Earl of Mansfield. B. 1806; m. 1829 Louisa, 3rd d. of Cuthbert Ellison, Esq., former MP for Newcastle. Lieut.-Col. of the Stirlingshire Militia. A Lord of the Treasury from Dec. 1834-Apr. 1835. A Conservative. Sat for Aldborough in the Parliament of 1830, and for Woodstock in that of 1831. Sat for Norwich from 1832 until the dissolution in 1837. Sat for Perthshire from Aug. 1837 until he succeeded as 4th Earl of Mansfield 18 Feb. 1840. Lord High Commissioner to Kirk of Scotland 1852, 1858, 1859; Lord Lieut. of Clackmannan from 1852. Died 2 Aug. 1898.   [1839]

STRACEY, Sir Henry Josias, Bart. 39 Dover Street, London. Arthur's, Boodle's, and Carlton. Only s. of Sir Josias Stracey, Bart., by Diana, sister of Sir David Scott, Bart. B. in Upper Harley Street, London 1802; m. 1835, Charlotte, d. and sole heir of George Denne, Esq., of the Paddock, Canterbury. Educ. at Eton. Entered the army as cornet in the 1st Dragoons 1826, and was Capt. in the same regiment for some years. A Magistrate and Dept.-Lieut. for Norfolk. Patron of 2 livings. A Conservative, and a supporter of Lord Derby's policy; in favour of all 'requisite reform.' Sat for Norfolk E. from July 1855 till Apr. 1857; was an unsuccessful candidate there June 1858. Elected for Yarmouth Apr. 1859 until he retired in 1865. Contested Norwich again in 1874. Sheriff of Norfolk in 1871. Died 7 Aug. 1885.   [1864]

STRAIGHT, Sir Douglas. 13 Albert Mansions, Victoria Street, London. 1 Cloisters, Temple. Junior Carlton. B. in London 1844, the s. of Robert Marshall Straight, of the Middle Temple, Barrister. M. Jane Alice, d. of William Bridgman, D.C.L. Was educ. at Harrow, and called to the bar at the Middle Temple 1865. Contributed largely to newspaper and magazine literature. A Liberal-Conservative, prepared to give 'an independent support to the Conservative party.' Sat for Shrewsbury from Sept. 1870 until 1874, when he was defeated.   [1873]

STRANGWAYS, Hon. John George Charles Fox. Abbotsbury, Dorsetshire. Half-bro. of the Earl of Ilchester, and of the Marchioness of Lansdowne. B. 1803. A Gentleman-usher to the Queen. Of Whig opinions. Returned unopposed for Calne 28 Sept. 1836, following the death of the Earl of Kerry the previous member. Retired in 1837. Sat for Dorset from July 1837 until he retired July 1841. Died 8 Sept. 1859.   [1840]

STRICKLAND, Sir George, Bart. 123 Piccadilly, London. Hildenley, Yorkshire. Reform. S. of Sir William Strickland, Bart., by the 3rd d. and co-heir of Nathaniel Cholmley, Esq., of Whitby, Yorkshire. B. at Welburn, Kirkby Moor Side, Yorkshire 1782; m. 1818, Mary, d. and heir of the Rev. Charles Constable, of Wassand, Yorkshire. Called to the bar at Lincoln's Inn 1810. Patron of 7 livings. A Reformer, advocate of the ballot, Church reform, of Dissenters being relieved from Church rates, and of short Parliaments. Sat for Yorkshire in 1831, and for the West Riding from Dec. 1832-July 1841; for Preston from the last date until defeated 1857. Died 23 Dec. 1874.   [1857]

STRONGE, Sir James Matthew, Bart. Tynan Abbey, Tynan, Co. Armagh. Carlton. B. in Park Street, London, 1811, the eld. s. of Sir James Matthew Stronge (2nd Bart.) by Isabella, d. of Nicolson Calvert, of Hunsdon House, Hertfordshire, and MP for that Co. M. 1836 Selina, eld. d. of Andrew Savage Nugent, of Portaferry, Co. Down. Entered the army in 1828 and became a Lieut. in the 5th Dragoon Guards. Was High Sheriff of the Cos. of Armagh and Tyrone in 1844 and 1845 respectively. Lieut.-Col.of the Tyrone Fusilier Militia 1854-1862, and then Honorary Colonel. A Conservative. Sat for Armagh from Mar. 1864 until 1874, when he retired. Died 11 Mar. 1885.   [1873]

STRUTT, Hon. C.H. Continued in House after 1885: full entry in Volume II.

STRUTT, Rt. Hon. Edward. (I). 42 South Street, Grosvenor Square, London. Kingston

Hall, Nottinghamshire. St. Helen's House, Derby. Only s. of William Strutt, Esq., of St. Helen's House, Derby, by the d. of Thomas Evans, Esq., of Derby. B. 1801; m. 1837, youngest d. of Bishop (Otter) of Chichester. Educ. at Trinity Coll., Cambridge, where he graduated B.A. 1823, M.A. 1826. Was Chief Commissioner of Railways from Sept. 1846 till Mar. 1848; Chancellor of the Duchy of Lancaster from Dec. 1852 till June 1854; High Sheriff of Nottinghamshire in 1850; a Dept.-Lieut. of that Co. from 1854. Patron of 1 living. A Reformer, in favour of triennial Parliaments, vote by ballot, etc., had 'always held that religious opinions should under no circumstances be a ground for interference with civil rights.' Sat for Derby from 1830 till Aug. 1848, when he was unseated on petition. Contested Coventry Apr. 1851. Sat for Arundel from July 1851 till July 1852 when he was returned for Nottingham and sat until he accepted Chiltern Hundreds July 1856. Created 1st Baron Belper 20 Aug. 1856. Died 30 June 1880. [1856]

STRUTT, Rt. Hon. E. (II). See HOWARD, Lord.

STRUTT, Hon. Henry. Kingston Hall, Derby. B. 1840, the eld. s. of 1st Baron Belper, by the youngest d. of Bishop Otter of Chichester. Educ. at Trinity Coll., Cambridge, and graduated B.C.L. 1863. Appointed Cornet Leicestershire Yeomanry Cavalry 1862. A Liberal, voted for the disestablishment of the Irish Church 1869, and considered the 'removal of it is calculated to increase the efficiency of the Protestant Church in that Country.' Sat for E. Derbyshire from Dec. 1868-1874 when he was defeated. Returned for Berwick in Apr. 1880, but succeeded as 2nd Baron Belper June 1880. Died 26 July 1914. [1873]

STUART, Capt. Charles. Middle Scotland-Yard. Of Conservative principles. Lieutenant of the 1st Foot Guards. Returned for Buteshire in 1832. Accepted Chiltern Hundreds July 1833. [1833]

STUART, Lord Dudley Coutts. 6 Stratford Place, London. Reform. B. 1803, s. of 1st Marq. of Bute by his 2nd wife, the 2nd d. of Thomas Coutts. M. 1824 Christine Alexandrine Egypta, d. of Lucien Buonaparte, Prince of Canino (she died May 1847). Graduated at Christ's Coll., Cambridge, M.A. 1823. A Dept.-Lieut. of Buteshire. A Liberal, in favour of short Parliaments and the ballot, adverse to all systems of centralization. Was well-known for his exertions on behalf of the exiled Poles. Sat for Arundel 1830-37, when he was defeated, and for

Marylebone 1847 until his death 17 Nov. 1854. [1854]

STUART, Henry. 18 Hill Street, London. Tempsford Hall, Huntingdonshire. Carlton, and United University. Grands. of the 3rd Earl of Bute, being the 2nd s. of Archbishop (Stuart) of Armagh by Sophia, grandd. of the celebrated Wm. Penn. B. 1804. A Conservative, but in favour of free trade. First returned for Bedford in 1837, but was unseated on petition; was re-elected there in 1841. MP until his death on 26 Oct. 1854. [1854]

STUART, Hon. Henry Villiers-. Queen Anne's Mansions, London. Dromana Cappoquin, Ireland. Reform, and Devonshire. Kildare Street Club, Dublin. Only s. of Lord Stuart de Decies. B. 1827; m. 1865, Mary, 2nd d. of Ven. Ambrose Power, Archdeacon of Lismore. Was educ. at University Coll., Durham, where he was 2nd class in classics and graduated B.A. 1849, M.A. 1853. Was ordained a Deacon 1850 and to Priest's orders 1851. Was Vicar of Napton-on-the-Hill, Warwickshire, from 1855 to 1871, when he relinquished orders. A Magistrate and Dept.-Lieut. of the county of Waterford. Was Vice-Lieut. of the county of Waterford from 1871 to 1874. Author of *Nile Gleanings* (a work on Egyptian history, art, and ethnology). A Liberal, and not opposed to concessions in the direction of 'Home Rule' for Ireland. Sat for Waterford Co. from July 1873 to Feb. 1874. Was a candidate for Waterford Co. and Dungarvan Apr. 1880 and was re-elected for Waterford Co. and sat until defeated in 1885 contesting Cork E. Died 12 Oct. 1895. [1885]

STUART, James Frederick Dudley Crichton-. 25 Wilton Crescent, London. Guards', and Travellers'. S. of Lord James Chrichton-Stuart, by Hannah, d. of William Tighe, Esq., of Woodstock, Co. Kilkenny. B. 1824; m. 1864, Gertrude Frances, 2nd d. of the Rt. Hon. Sir George Hamilton Seymour, G.C.B. Entered the army as Ensign and Lieut. Grenadier Guards 1842; became Capt. and Lieut.-Col. 1855, retired 1861. Appointed Lord-Lieut. and Sheriff Principal of Bute 1859. A Liberal. First elected for Cardiff Mar. 1857 and sat until he retired 1880. Died 24 Oct. 1891. [1880]

STUART, John. 12 Lincoln's Inn, Old Square, London. 19 Hertford Street, Mayfair, London. Kinlochleven, Argyleshire. Carlton, and Athenaeum. 2nd s. of Dugald Stuart, Esq., of Balachulish, Appin, Argyleshire. B. 1793; m. 1813 d. of Duncan Stewart, Esq. Was called to the bar in 1819, by the Society of Lincoln's Inn, of which he was a bencher. One of the leading counsel in the Court of Chancery; a Queen's Counsel, by patent, dated Mar. 1839. A firm supporter of the Established Church, but a friend to toleration; in favour of maintaining the institutions of the country in Church and State; in favour of protection to agriculture, commerce, and manufactures. Contested Inverness Dec. 1832 and again in May 1833. First elected for Newark Jan. 1846, without opposition, and sat until July 1852 when he sat for Bury-St.-Edmunds until later that year when he was appointed Vice-Chancellor until 1871. Knighted June 1853. Died 29 Oct. 1876. [1852]

STUART, Prof. J. Continued in House after 1885: full entry in Volume II.

STUART, Lord Patrick James Herbert Crichton. 6 Whitehall Place, London. Dumfries House, Ayrshire. Athenaeum, Travellers', Brooks's, and Reform. 2nd s. of John Lord Mountstuart and next bro. of the 2nd Marq. of Bute, who died in 1848. B. posthumous at Brompton Park House, 1794. M. 1818, Hannah, only d. of William Tighe, Esq., of Woodstock, Co. Kilkenny. Assumed the name of Crichton by royal sign-manual, and was raised to the rank of the s. of a Marq. by royal warrant in 1817. Appointed Lord-Lieut. and Sheriff principal of the county of Bute 1848. A Liberal, voted for the ballot and in favour of short Parliaments. Sat for Cardiff from 1818-20, and from 1826-32; sat for the Co. of Bute in the interval *viz:* 1820-26; was an unsuccessful candidate for Perth City 1832. Represented the Ayr district from 1834-July 1852. First returned for Ayrshire in Apr. 1857 and MP until his death 7 Sept. 1859. [1859]

STUART, William, sen. 18 Hill Street, Berkeley Square, London. Tempsford Hall, St. Neots. B. in 1798; m. 1821, Henrietta, eld. d. of Admiral Sir C.M. Pole, Bart. A Conservative. Sat first for Armagh in 1820; was not in the Parliament of 1826; was returned for Bedfordshire in 1830, but lost his seat in 1831. Sat again for Bedfordshire in 1832. Retired in 1835. Sheriff of Bedfordshire 1846. Died 7 July 1874. [1833]

STUART, William, jun. 18 Hill Street, Berkeley Square, London. Kempston Lodge, Bedford. Carlton, and National. S. of William Stuart, Esq., of Aldenham Abbey, Hertforshire, former MP for Bedfordshire, by Henrietta Maria Sarah, d. of Sir C.M. Pole, Bart., G.C.B., Admiral of the Fleet. B. in London, 1825; m. 1859, Katherine, eld. d. of John Armitage Nicholson, Esq., of Balrath, Co. Meath. Educ. at Eton, and at St. John's Coll., Cambridge. Was called to the bar at the Inner Temple, 1851, and joined the Home Circuit. A Magistrate for Hertfordshire and Bedfordshire,

and a Dept.-Lieut. of the latter. Lieut.-Col. of the Bedfordshire Light Infantry Militia. A Conservative, in favour of a moderate extension of the franchise. Sat for Bedford from Nov. 1854 to Mar. 1857; again returned there May 1859 and sat until he retired in 1868. Chairman of Quarter Sessions, Bedfordshire 1879-1890. Died 21 Dec. 1893. [1867]

STUART, William Villiers. 120 Park Street, Grosvenor Square, London. Dromana, Co. Waterford. Reform. S. of Lord Henry Stuart. B. 1804; m. 1833, only d. of M. Cox, Esq. Bro. of the Lieut. of the Co. of Waterford, who represented the city of Waterford in 1826. A Reformer. First elected for Waterford Co. in Sept. 1835, in the room of Mr. Power and sat until he retired in 1847. [1847]

STUART-WORTLEY, Archibald Henry Plantagenet. See WORTLEY, Archibald Henry Plantagenet Stuart-.

STUART-WORTLEY, C.B. Continued in House after 1885: full entry in Volume II.

STUART-WORTLEY, Rt. Hon. James Archibald. See WORTLEY, Rt. Hon. James Archibald Stuart-.

STUCLEY, Sir George Stucley, Bart. 8 Eaton Square, London. Hartland Abbey, Bideford, Devon. Carlton. Only s. of Lewis William Buck, Esq., of Moreton and Hartland Abbey, Devon, who represented North Devon for many years, by Anne, d. of Thomas Robbins, Esq., of Roundham, Hampshire. B. at Moreton, Bideford, Devon, 1812; m. 1835, Lady Elizabeth, youngest d. and co-heir of William, 2nd Marq. of Thomond. Educ. at Eton, and at Christ Church, Oxford. Assumed the name of Stucley in lieu of Buck 1858. Served for some time in the Royal Horse Guards. A Magistrate and Dept.-Lieut. of Devon and Cornwall. Lieut.-Col. Commandant of the Devon Militia Artillery from 1849. Was High Sheriff of Devon, 1863. Director of the North Devon Railway. Patron of 3 livings. A Liberal-Conservative, in favour of the 'extension, but not the lowering of the franchise', and of the rights of freemen being maintained. Was an unsuccessful candidate for Exeter, July 1852. Sat for Barnstaple from Mar. 1855 till Apr. 1859, when he was defeated; re-elected July 1865. Retired in 1868. Died 13 Mar. 1900. [1867]

STURT, Col. Charles Napier. Critchell, Wimborne, Dorset. Carlton, Guard's, and White's. B. in London 1832, the 2nd s. of Henry Charles Sturt, Esq., of Critchell, Dorset, by Lady

Charlotte, 3rd d. of 6th Earl of Cardigan. Un-married. Appointed Lieut. and Capt. Grenadier Guards, Nov. 1854. Served in the Crimea and was severely wounded at Inkermann; subsequently became Lieut.-Col. A Conservative, voted against the disestablishment of the Irish Church 1869. Elected for Dorchester in 1856, without opposi-tion, and sat until he retired in 1874. Died 13 Mar. 1886. [1873]

STURT, Henry Charles. 16 Portman Square, London. Critchell, Dorset. Carlton. B.1795, the eld. s. of Charles Sturt, Esq., and Mary Anne, the only d. of the 5th and sister of the 6th Earl of Shaftesbury. M. 1820, Charlotte Penelope, 3rd d. of the Earl of Cardigan. Patron of 7 livings. A Conservative. Sat for Bridport in 1817; was re-elected in 1818. Sat for a few weeks of the next Parliament for Dorchester and unsuccessfully contested Poole in 1826. Was elected for the Co. of Dorset in 1835 and sat until he accepted Chiltern Hundreds in Jan. 1846. Died 14 Apr. 1866. [1845]

STURT, Henry Gerard. 59 Grosvenor Square, London. Critchell, Wimborne, Dorset. White's, and Carlton. Eld. s. of Henry Charles Sturt, Esq. of Critchell, Dorset, by Lady Charlotte, 3rd d. of the 6th Earl of Cardigan. B. at Critchell, Dorset, 1825; m. Lady Augusta, eld. d. of the 3rd Earl of Lucan. A Conservative, voted against the dis-establishment of the Irish Church 1869; in favour of the establishment of county financial boards. Sat for Dorchester from 1847-July 1856, and from the latter date for Dorset until created Baron Alington 1876. [1875]

STYLE, Sir Thomas Charles, Bart. Scarborough, Yorkshire. Cloghan Lodge, Co. Donegal. Union. Bro.-in-law to E.S. Cayley, Esq., MP for N. Yorks. B. 1797; m. 1822, Isabella, 2nd d. of Sir Geo. Cayley, Bart. A Dept.-Lieut. for the county of Donegal. A Reformer, 'in favour of triennial Parliaments and an extension of the suf-frage; of the abolition of Church rates, the reform of the Irish Corporations and the appropriation of the surplus revenue of the Church in Ireland to the moral and religious education of the people.' Elected for Scarborough in 1837. Retired 1841. Died 23 July 1879. [1838]

SUGDEN, Rt. Hon. Sir Edward Burtenshaw. Boyle Farm, Surrey. Was at the Chancery Bench for many years. Author of several legal works of the highest authority. A Conservative. Sat for Weymouth 20 Feb. 1826-31 and for St. Mawes 1831-32 when the seat was disfranchised. Was ap-pointed Solicitor-General in 1829, and Lord Chancellor of Ireland in 1834. Resigned his office

shortly afterwards. Contested Cambridge in Dec. 1832 and again in June 1834. Was returned for Ripon at the general election in 1837. Sat until appointed Lord Chancellor of Ireland in 1841. Lord High Chancellor of Great Britain Feb. 1852; created Baron St. Leonards Mar. 1852. Died 29 Jan. 1875. [1838]

SULLIVAN, Alexander Martin. 3 Dr. Johnson's Buildings, Temple, London. 14 The Crescent, Clapham, London. S. of Mr. D. Sullivan, of Amiers Street, Dublin, and of Bantry, Co. Cork. B. at Bantry; m. 1861 Frances Genevieve, only d. of John Donovan, Esq. of Camp Street, New Orleans. Called to the bar in Ireland 1876 and by special call to the English bar at the Inner Temple, Nov. 1877. Formerly editor and proprietor of the *Nation* newspaper, pub-lished in Dublin. Author of some historical, biographical, and political works. A Liberal, in favour of the system called 'Home Rule' for Ireland and a prominent member of the 'Home Rule League' of which he was one of the original founders. Chairman of the Executive of the Irish Permissive Bill Assoc. from its formation. Sat for Louth from Feb. 1874-May 1880; sat for Meath from the last date until accepted Chiltern Hun-dreds Feb. 1882. Died 17 Oct. 1884. [1881]

SULLIVAN, Edward. 32 Fitzwilliam Place, Dublin. Reform. Eld. s. of Edward Sullivan, Esq., of Raglan Road, Dublin, formerly of Mallow, Co. Cork. B. at Mallow 1822; m. 1850, Bessie Josephine, d. of Robert Bailey, esq., of Cork. Educ. at Middleton School, Co. Cork, and at Trinity Coll., Dublin, where he obtained a first place at entrance, and double first honours in science and classics several times, and graduated 1844. An ex-scholar of the University, and was Auditor of the College Historical Society 1845. Was called to the bar in Ireland 1848, made a Queen's Counsel 1858; appointed Serjeant-at-law 1860; law adviser to the Crown 1861, and Solicitor-Gen. for Ireland 1865. A 'firm adherent' of the Liberal party. First elected for Mallow, July 1865 and sat until appointed Judge Jan. 1870. Created Bart. Dec. 1881; Lord Chancellor of Ireland 1883 until his death 13 Apr. 1885. [1867]

SULLIVAN, Michael. Lacken Hall, Kilkenny. 2nd s. of William Sullivan, Esq., Merchant, of Kilkenny, and bro. to Richard Sullivan, Esq., of Castlebamford, Co. Kilkenny, who represented the City of Kilkenny from 1832-1836. B. in Kilkenny. Unmarried. Educ. at Clonglowes Coll., Ireland. A Liberal, a member of the late 'Repeal' party; said he would support 'the right of the tiller of the soil to a permanent property in his im-provements'; voted for the ballot 1853, and in

369

favour of the vote of censure on Lord Palmerston 1864. First returned for Kilkenny City in Dec. 1847 and sat until he retired 1865. Sheriff of Kilkenny 1870. Died 23 Dec. 1878.   [1865]

SULLIVAN, Richard. Castlebamford, Kilkenny. Westminster Club. A Merchant and native of Kilkenny. In favour of a repeal of the Union, and the total abolition of tithes, making a suitable provision for the Protestant Clergy. When required, he said he would resign his trust into the hands of his constituents. Sat for Kilkenny from 1832 until he accepted Chiltern Hundreds in 1836.   [1836]

SULLIVAN, T.D. Continued in House after 1885: full entry in Volume II.

SUMMERS, William. Continued in House after 1885: full entry in Volume II.

SURREY, Earl of. 6 Park Place, St. James's, London. Littlehampton, Sussex. Worksop Manor, Nottinghamshire. Eld. s. of the Duke of Norfolk. B. 1791; m. 1814, Charlotte Sophia, eld. d. of the Duke of Sutherland. Of Whig principles, in favour of the Corn Laws. Sat for Horsham from the passing of the Catholic Relief Bill until 1832; after that for Sussex W. until he retired 1841. Succeeded as 13th Duke Mar. 1842. Died 18 Feb. 1856.   [1838]

SURTEES, Col. Charles Freville. Junior Carlton, and Army & Navy. S. of Robert Surtees, Esq., of Redworth House, Co. Durham, by Elizabeth, d. of Isaac Cookson, Esq., of Whitehill, Co. Durham. B. at Redworth House 1823; m. 1855, Bertha, d. of Nathaniel B. Chauncy, Esq., of Green End, Hertfordshire. Educ. at Harrow. Was Capt. 10th Hussars. A Conservative, in favour of a progressive policy, of a redistribution of Parliamentary seats, and of non-intervention in the affairs of foreign states. First elected for Durham S., July 1865. Defeated in 1868; contested seat again in 1880. Died 22 Dec. 1906.   [1867]

SURTEES, Henry Edward. 4 Charles Street, St. James's, London. Dane End, Ware, Hertfordshire. Redworth House, Nr. Darlington, Co. Durham. Carlton, Junior Carlton, and Army & Navy. Eld. s. of Robert Surtees, Esq., of Redworth House, Co. Durham, by Elizabeth, d. of Isaac Cookson, Esq., of Whitehill Hall, Co. Durham. B. 1819; m. 1843, Eliza, d. of Charles Snell Chauncy, Esq., of Dane End, Hertfordshire. Educ. at Harrow. Formerly in the 10th Royal Hussars, which he entered in 1838. A Conservative, and a supporter of Lord Derby; in favour

of the abolition of the malt tax. First elected for Hertfordshire Mar. 1864. Defeated in 1868. Sheriff of Durham 1876. Died 31 July 1895. [1867]

SUTHERLAND, T. Continued in House after 1885: full entry in Volume II.

SUTTON, Rt. Hon. Sir Charles Manners, LL.D. New Palace Yard, London. Mistley Hall, Manningtree, Essex. Cousin of the Duke of Rutland, and s. of the Archbishop of Canterbury. Speaker, a Lord of Trade and Plantations, and Registrar of the Faculty Office. He was first elected to the office of Speaker in June 1817, on the promotion of Mr. Abbot to the peerage by the title of Lord Colchester. A Conservative. Sat for Scarborough, of which his relatives the Duke of Rutland and the Earl of Mulgrave were Patrons, from 1806. In 1832 he sat for Cambridge University, succeeding Mr. Yates Peel, who retired on account of ill health. Created 1st Visct. Canterbury Mar. 1835. Died 21 July 1845.   [1833]

SUTTON, John Henry Manners-. Albany, London. Kelham Hall, Southwell, Nottinghamshire. Eld. s. of the Rev. Frederic Manners-Sutton, of Kelham, Nottinghamshire, by Lady Henrietta, 3rd d. of the 7th Earl of Scarborough (rem. to John Lodge Ellerton, Esq.). Grandnephew of the 1st Lord Manners. B. 1822; m. 1853, Mary Jemima, eld. d. of Rev. Gustavus Burnaby, Rector of St. Peter's, Bedford and Canon of Middleham. Appointed Dept.-Lieut. of Nottinghamshire 1854. A Conservative. First returned for Newark in 1847 and sat until he retired 1857. Career as Colonial Governor 1857-73. Succeeded Bro. as 2nd Visct. Canterbury Nov. 1869. Died 24 June 1877.   [1857]

SUTTON, Hon. John Henry Thomas Manners. Albany, London. Carlton. 2nd s. of 1st Visct. Canterbury. B. 1814; m. d. of C. Tompson, Esq. Graduated at Cambridge. A Conservative, but in favour of free trade. Was Under-Secretary of State for the Home Department; resigned July 1846. Was first elected for Cambridge in 1839, but unseated on petition; re-elected there in 1841 and sat until defeated in 1847. Sheriff of Nottingham 1863. Died 5 July 1898.   [1847]

SWANSTON, Alexander. Norwood, Middlesex. A Liberal. Sat for Bandon from Feb. 1874 until he retired 1880. Died 24 June 1882.   [1880]

SWIFT, Richard. 3 Hanover Terrace, Regents Park, London. 98 Hatton Garden, London. Erectheum. S. of Timothy Swift, Esq. (Army Contractor), by Susannah, d. of John Carey, Esq. B. at Malta 1811; m. 1836, d. of John O'Brien,

Esq., a West India Merchant. An Importer and Exporter of leather, a Wholesale and Export Shoe Manufacturer, and agent in London for the Northamptonshire Shoemakers. A Magistrate for Middlesex. Was elected Sheriff of London Oct. 1851. A Liberal, in favour of tenant-right in Ireland, voted for the ballot 1853. First returned for the Co. of Sligo in July 1852 and sat until defeated 1857 (probably withdrawing just before poll). Died 24 Mar. 1872.   [1857]

SYKES, C. Continued in House after 1885: full entry in Volume II.

SYKES, Col. William Henry. 47 Albion Street, Hyde Park, London. Athenaeum. S. of Samual Sykes, Esq., and descended from George Sykes, Esq. of Drighlington, near Leeds. B. 1790; m. 1824, Elizabeth, youngest d. of William Hay, Esq., of Renistonn. Joined the Bombay Army in 1804, served with Lord Lake's Army before Bhurtpoor. Received a medal and clasps for his services; in 1818 commanded a field force south of Punderpoor. Appointed statistical reporter to the government at Bombay 1824 and finally quitted India in 1831. Received the rank of Colonel 1833. Elected a Director E.I.C. 1840 and again 1860. Elected Lord Rector of Marischal Coll. and University Aberdeen, Mar. 1854. Appointed Dept. Chairman of the E.I.C. in 1855; Chairman in 1856 and again 1860. Lieut.-Col. 4th London Rifle Volunteers 1861. A Commissioner of Lieutenancy for London. Author of upwards of 60 papers in the transactions of various societies on the ancient history, antiquities, statistics, geology, national history and meteorology of India. A Liberal. Was an unsuccessful candidate for Aberdeen in 1847; first returned for that city, Apr. 1857 and sat until his death in London 16 June 1872.   [1872]

SYNAN, Edmond John. Ashbourne House, Limerick. Reform. S. of John Synan, Esq., by Eleanor his wife. B. 1820. Educ. at Clongowes Wood and at the University of Dublin, where he graduated B.A. Called to the bar in Ireland 1843. A Magistrate for the Co. of Limerick. A Liberal, in favour of 'Home Rule' for Ireland. Sat for the Co. of Limerick from July 1865 until he retired in 1885. Died 8 Sept. 1887.   [1885]

TALBOT, Christopher Rice Mansel. 3 Cavendish Square, London. Penrice Castle, Swansea. Margam, Port Talbot, Glamorganshire. Travellers'. S. of Thomas Mansel Talbot, Esq., of Margam, by Lady Mary Lucy, d. of the 2nd Earl of Ilchester. B. 1803; m. 1835, Lady Charlotte, 2nd d. of 1st Earl of Glengall (she died 1846).

Patron of 3 livings. Lord-Lieut. of Glamorganshire and Hon. Col. Glamorgan Rifles; also F.R.S. F.L.S. A Liberal, did not vote at the division on Mr. Gladstone's Irish Home Rule Bill. Returned for Glamorganshire 1830-1885, usually unopposed; returned for the Mid div. of the county from 1885 (and from 1886 as a Liberal Unionist) until his death in Jan? 1890.   [1886 2nd ed.]

TALBOT, James. 1 Derby Street, London. Of Whig principles. Sat for Athlone from 1832, succeeding in opposition to the Conservative candidate, Richard Handcock, Esq., nephew of Lord Castlemaine, who had for some years represented it, his uncle being its Patron before the passing of the Reform Act. Defeated in 1835. Succeeded father as 4th Baron Talbot Dec. 1850; created Baron Talbot de Malahide (U.K. peerage) Nov. 1856. F.R.S. Feb. 1858. President Royal Irish Academy 1866 until his death 14 Apr. 1883.   [1833]

TALBOT, J.G. Continued in House after 1885: full entry in Volume II.

TALBOT, John Hyacinth. Talbot Hall, Bally Tren House, and Bettyville, Co. Wexford. Reform. 2nd s. of Matthew Talbot, Esq., of Ballynamony, (later called Castle Talbot,) Co. Wexford, by his 2nd wife, Jane, Countess D'Arcy. B. 1794; m. 1822, Anne Eliza, only d. and heir of Walter Redmond, Esq., of Bally Trent House, a Banker in Wexford (she died 1826). A Magistrate and Dept.-Lieut. of Wexford; formerly held an office in the Revenue Department, Ireland. A Liberal, in favour of a repeal of the union with Ireland; a supporter of the ballot; voted for a repeal of the malt tax 1835. Sat for New Ross from 1832 to 1841 when he retired. Was elected again 1847 and sat until he retired in 1852. Died 30 Apr. 1868.   [1852]

TALBOT, Hon. Reginald Arthur James. White's, and Carlton. B. in London 1841, 4th s. of 18th Earl of Shrewsbury, by Lady Sarah Elizabeth, eld. d. of 2nd Marq. of Waterford. Educ. at Harrow, and entered the army as Sub-Lieut. 1st Life Guards 1859. Became Lieut. 1863 and Capt. 1867. A Conservative, and gave his 'cordial support' to any measure dealing with the 'present unsatisfactory relationship between Landlord and Tenant in Ireland.' Sat for Stafford from June 1869 until he retired in 1874. Became Governor of Victoria 1904-08 and Col. in the Dragoon Guards 1903-20. Died 15 Jan. 1929.   [1873]

TALBOT, Hon Walter Cecil. 36 Belgrave

Square, London. Ingestre Hall, Stafford. Carlton. 2nd s. of 18th Earl of Shrewsbury and Talbot, by Lady Sarah Elizabeth, eld. d. of 2nd Marq. of Waterford. B. at Ingestre Hall, Staffordshire 1834. Educ. at Harrow. Entered the navy Dec. 1847; became a Lieut. Sept. 1854; served in the Crimea and the Black Sea in the Russian War, and was made a Commander R.N. 1859. A 'decided Conservative'. First elected for the Co. of Waterford May 1859 and sat until he retired 1865. Assumed the surname and arms of Carpenter in lieu of Talbot in 1868 (in accordance with the will of Sarah, Countess of Tyrconnel). Died 13 May 1904. [1865]

TALBOT, William Henry Fox. 31 Sackville Street, London. Lacock Abbey, Wiltshire. A relative of the member of Glamorganshire. A moderate Reformer, who generally supported Ministers. Elected for Chippenham in 1832. Retired in 1835. Sheriff of Wiltshire 1840. Inventor and pioneer of photography. Author and translator. Died 17 Sept. 1877. [1833]

TALFOURD, Thomas Noon, D.C.L. 67 Russell Square, London. 3 Serjeant's Inn, London. Athenaeum, and Garrick. B. at Reading 1795, the s. of Edward Talfourd a Brewer at Reading, by the d. of the Rev. Thomas Noon, Minister of an Independent Congregation. Married in 1822, Rachel, d. of John Towell Rutt, Esq. Educ. at the Reading Grammar School and an honorary D.C.L. at Oxford. Was called to the bar at the Middle Temple in 1821, made a Serjeant in 1833 and had a patent of precedence. Was both Queen's Ancient Serjeant and Recorder of Banbury and joined the Oxford circuit. The author of *Iou, The Athenian Captive* and *Glencoe* (tragedies); of *Vacation Rambles, Life of Charles Lamb, A Speech on Copyright* and various other works, besides articles in the *New Monthly Magazine, Edinburgh Review* etc. Was for many years one of the law reporters of the *Times* Newspaper. Appointed Judge of Common Pleas July 1849. A Liberal, in favour of the ballot, but opposed to the endowment of the Roman Catholic Clergy. Represented Reading from 1835 until he retired in 1841. Re-elected July 1847 and sat until he was appointed Judge of the Common Pleas July 1849. Knighted 1850. Died 13 Mar. 1854. [1838]

TANCRED, Henry William. Brooks's, United University, and Reform. Was called to the bar at Lincoln's Inn, 1804, and was a Bencher of that Society. Appointed a Queen's Counsel 1831. A Liberal, in favour of the ballot, the repeal of the Septennial Act and the malt duty. Sat for Banbury from 1832 until he accepted Chiltern Hundreds Jan. 1859. Died 20 Aug. 1860. [1858]

TAPPS, George William. See TAPPS-GERVIS, Sir G.W.

TAPPS-GERVIS, Sir George William. 4 Stratford Place, London. Barton, Hampshire. Eld. s. of Sir Geo. Ivison Tapps, Bart., of Hinton House, Hampshire (who had church patronage). B. 1795; m. 1826, Clara, d. of Augustus E. Fuller, Esq. of Ashdown House, Sussex. A moderate Reformer. Sat for New Romney in the Parliament of 1826. Sat for Christchurch from 1832 until he retired in 1837. Succeeded as 2nd Bart. Died 1842. [1837]

TAVISTOCK, Marq. of. 37 Chesham Place, London. Oakley House, Oakley, Bedfordshire. Eld. s. of the Duke of Bedford, by Lady Elizabeth, eld. d. of the 5th Earl De La Warr. B. in London 1852; m. 1876, Lady Adelina Marie, d. of the 3rd Earl Somers. Educ. at Balliol Coll., Oxford, graduated B.A. 1874. A student of the Inner Temple. A Magistrate for Bedfordshire. A Liberal. Sat for Bedfordshire from Apr. 1875 until he retired in 1885. Sheriff of Bedfordshire 1889. Chairman of Bedfordshire County Council 1892. Succeeded his father as 10th Duke of Bedford Jan. 1891. Died 23 Mar. 1893. [1885]

TAYLEUR, William. Entertained Whig, inclining to radical, opinions. Elected for Bridgewater in 1832. He took the place of Mr. Astell, the East India Director, who had sat for Bridgewater in six Parliaments, but voted against Reform. Retired in 1835. Died 5 Nov. 1873. [1833]

TAYLOR, Daniel. Milburn House, Coleraine. Reform. Eld. s. of Daniel Taylor, Esq., of Coleraine, by Eliza, d. of Noble Denison, Esq., of Coleraine. B. at Coleraine 1825; m. 1869, Annie Brumhall, d. of John Cochrane, Esq. of Spring Hill, Co. Donegal. Educ. at Coleraine, where he was a Merchant. A Magistrate for the Co. of Londonderry; was Chairman of the Coleraine Commissioners in 1864, 1865, and 1873; Trustee of the Irish Presbyterian Church Commutation Fund. A Liberal, in favour of the formation of county boards for the administration of county affairs; opposed to any immediate attempt being made to alter the Irish Land Act. Sat for Coleraine from Feb. 1874 until defeated Apr. 1880. [1880]

TAYLOR, Hugh. Coal Exchange, London. Backworth House, Newcastle-upon-Tyne. S. of John Taylor, Esq. of Shilbottle, Northumberland, by Margaret, d. of — Darling, Esq., of Ford, Northumberland. B. in London 1817; m. 1842, Mary, d. of Thomas Taylor, Esq., of Cramlington

Hall, Northumberland (she died 1852). Educ. at Newcastle-upon-Tyne. A Coal and Ship-Owner. A Magistrate for Middlesex and Northumberland. A 'Liberal-Conservative' in favour of the abolition of Church rates; would support a 10/- franchise in counties, and a 6/- franchise in boroughs; opposed to the ballot; in favour of the Maynooth Grant. First returned for Tynemouth in July 1852; unseated on petition, Apr. 1853; re-elected May 1859. Accepted Chiltern Hundreds Apr. 1861. Died 31 Aug. 1868.
[1860]

TAYLOR, James Arthur. 10 Park Place, St. James's, London. Moseley Hall, Worcestershire. Carlton, and Oxford & Cambridge. B. 1817; m. 1843, Maria Theresa, 2nd d. of George Rush, Esq., of Ellenham Hall, and Farthinghoe Lodge, Northamptonshire. A Magistrate and Dept.-Lieut. of Worcestershire. 'Truly Conservative'; voted for agricultural protection 1846. First returned for Worcestershire E. in 1841 and sat until he retired in 1847. Died 14 June 1889.
[1847]

TAYLOR, Rt. Hon. Michael Angele. Whitehall Yard, London. Cantley Hall, Doncaster. B. in 1756. A Barrister, and Recorder of Poole, uncle to the Marchioness of Londonderry, and s. of Sir Robert Taylor, Architect, under whose direction the Bank of England was built. Mr. Taylor's house was a kind of rendezvous for the Whigs for many years; he was among the first to complain of the abuses of the Court of Chancery. Mr. Taylor had been in Parliament upwards of 40 years, a great part of the time for the city of Durham. Entertained Whig principles, in favour of the immediate abolition of slavery. Elected for Sudbury in 1832. MP until his death in June? 1834. [1833]

TAYLOR, Peter Alfred. 22 Ashley Place, London. 22 Marine Parade, Brighton. Reform. S. of Peter Alfred Taylor, Esq., by Catherine, d. of George Courtauld, Esq. B. in London 1819; m. 1842, Clementina, d. of John Doughty, Esq., of Brockdish, Norfolk. In favour of universal suffrage, payments of members, disestablishment of the Church etc. and the total abolition of the Game Laws. Unsuccessfully contested New-castle-upon-Tyne 30 Apr. 1859 and Leicester Jan. 1861, for which he sat from Feb. 1862 until he accepted Chiltern Hundreds June 1884. Died 20 Dec. 1891.
[1884]

TAYLOR, Simon Watson. Devizes. A general supporter of Lord Palmerston, in favour of the total abolition of the income tax. First elected for Devizes, Mar. 1857. Defeated in 1859.
[1858]

TAYLOR, Rt. Hon. Thomas Edward. 99 Eaton Square, London. Ardgillan Castle, Balbriggan, Co. Dublin. Carlton, Junior Carlton, Travellers', and Junior United Service. Eld. s. of the Hon. and Rev. Edward Taylor, bro. of 1st Marq. of Head-fort, by Marianne, eld. d. of Hon. R. St. Leger. B. 1812; m. 1862, Louisa Harrington 2nd d. of Hon. and Rev. Hugh Francis Tollemache. A Magistrate and Dept.-Lieut. of Meath, and Lieut.-Col. of Meath Militia from 1846. Capt. in the Dragoon Guards, which he entered 1829. Was a Lord of the Treasury from Mar. 1858-June 1859; Parliamentary Sec. to the Treasury from July 1866-Oct. 1868. Also Chancellor of the Duchy of Lancaster from Oct. 1868-Dec. following and again from Feb. 1874-Apr. 1880. A Conservative. Sat for the Co. of Dublin from July 1841. MP until his death 3 Feb. 1883. [1882]

TEIGNMOUTH, Lord. 32 York Terrace, Regent's Park, London. S. of the 1st Lord, who was Gov. Gen. of India. B. 1796. An Irish Peer. A Conservative. Unsuccessfully contested Marylebone 1837; was chosen in 1838 on Sir S. Whalley being disqualified. Retired 1841. Died 18 Sept. 1885. [1838]

TEMPEST, Lord Adolphus Frederick Charles William Vane-. Holdernesse House, Park Lane, London. Carlton, White's, and Guard's. 3rd. s. of 3rd Marq. of Londonderry by his 2nd wife, d. of Sir Harry Vane Tempest, Bart. B. at Holdernesse House, Park Lane, London, 1825; m. 1860, Lady Susan, only d. of 5th Duke of Newcastle. Educ. at Eton. Appointed Lieut. and Capt. Scots Fusilier Guards 1849; served in the Crimea in 1854, and retired Aug. 1859. A Dept.-Lieut. of Durham from 1849. Assumed the name of Tempest after that of Vane by royal licence, June 1854. A Conservative, and a supporter generally of Lord Derby's policy, with whom he voted on his Reform Bill, Mar 1859; but voted with Lord Palmerston on the Chinese war; 'would support the interests of the Protestant Church'; opposed to the Maynooth grant. In June 1852, un-successfully contested Durham City, but sat for it from Dec. following till June 1853, when he was unseated on petition. First returned for Durham N. Apr. 1854 and sat until his death 11 June 1864.
[1864]

TEMPLE, Rt. Hon W.F. See COWPER-TEMPLE, Rt. Hon. W.F.

TENISON, Edward King. 41 St. James Place, London. Kilronan Castle, Carrick-on-Shannon, Ireland. Brooks's, Travellers' and Reform. Eld. s. of Thomas Tenison, Esq., of Castle Tenison, Co. Leitrim, by Lady Frances, d. of 1st Earl of

Kingston; was descended from Thomas Tenison, Archbishop of Canterbury in 1694. B. at Dublin 1805; m. 1838, Lady Louisa, eld. d. of the 1st Earl of Lichfield. Was educ. at Trinity Coll., Cambridge, where he graduated B.A. 1827, and M.A. 1845; entered the 14th Light Dragoons as Cornet in 1826, but retired from the army in 1836; a Magistrate for the Cos. of Roscommon and Leitrim, and a Dept.-Lieut. for the latter. A Liberal. First returned for Leitrim in 1847 and sat until he retired 1852. Contested seat again in Apr. 1857 and July 1865. Contested Roscommon May 1859. Lord-Lieut. of Roscommon Nov. 1856 until his death 19 June 1878. [1852]

TENNANT, Sir Charles, Bart. 35 Grosvenor Square, London. The Glen, Peeblesshire. St. Rollox, Glasgow. Brooks's, and Reform. B. in Glasgow 1823, s. of John Tennant, Esq., of St. Rollox. M. 1849, Emma, d. of Richard Winsloe, Esq., of Mount Nebo, Somerset. A Merchant and Manufacturer at Glasgow, and Chairman of the Tharsis Company, Glasgow. A Dept.-Lieut. of Lanarkshire and Peeblesshire. A Liberal, in favour of rate payers having a decided voice in the granting of licences. Sat for Glasgow from July 1879-Apr. 1880, and then for the united Cos. of Selkirk and Peebles until 1886, when he was defeated as a Gladstonian Liberal. Contested Partick div. Lanark in 1890. Member of the Tariff Commission 1904. Died 4 June 1906. [1886]

TENNANT, Robert. Scarcroft Lodge, Leeds. Rosehall, Sutherlandshire. Carlton, and Junior Carlton. S. of John Tennant Stansfield Tennant, of Chapel House, Kilnsey-in-Wharfedale, Yorkshire (a Magistrate and Dept.-Lieut. for Yorkshire), by his m. with Miss Anne Catherine Shaw, of Otley-in-Wharfdale. B. at Otley-in-Wharfdale, Yorkshire 1828; m. 1850, Harriette, d. of Jeremiah Garnett, Esq., of Manchester. Educ. at the Grammar School, Leeds, and privately prepared for the legal profession, from which however he retired in 1865, and entered on the business of a Flax Spinner. A Director of the Great Northern Railway, and Chairman of several Coal and Iron Companies. Patron of 3 livings. A Conservative, and said he would 'strenuously oppose' any attempt to disestablish the Church of England; in favour of an extension of the county franchise and of a uniform time of closing throughout the kingdom being fixed by the Licensing Act. Sat for Leeds from Feb. 1874 until defeated 1880 contesting Peterborough. Author. Died 5 Mar. 1900. [1880]

TENNENT, Sir James Emerson, LL.D. Tempo Castle, Co. Fermanagh. S. of William Emerson, Esq., a Merchant in Belfast, by the youngest d. of William Arbuthnot, Esq., of Rockville, Co. Down. B. at Belfast, 1804; m. 1831, Letitia, only d. and heir of William Tennent, of Tempo House, Co. Fermanagh, on whose death, in 1832 he assumed the name of Tennent and succeeded to estates in Sligo and Fermanagh. Educ. at Trinity Coll., Dublin. Called to the bar at Lincoln's Inn 1831, but never practised. Was Sec. to the India Board Sept. 1841-July 1845, and Civil Sec. to the Colonial Govt. of Ceylon from July 1845-Dec.1850. Sec. to the Poor Law Board. Author of *Travels in Greece, A History of Modern Greece, Letters from the Aegean,* etc. Dept.-Lieut. in the Counties of Fermanagh and Sligo, and a Magistrate for Antrim and Down. A Conservative, but in favour of free trade; thought some of the burdens of agriculture should be relieved and tenants be legally entitled to security for Improvements. Sat for Belfast from 1832 until the general election 1837, when he lost his seat, but was subsequently seated on petition; re-elected in 1841, but unseated on petition; re-elected 1842 and held his seat until 1845. First returned for Lisburn Jan. 1852, without opposition. Accepted Chiltern Hundreds Dec. 1852. Sec. to the Board of Trade 1852-67. Died 6 Mar. 1869.

[1852 2nd ed.]

TENNENT, Robert James. Hercules Place, Belfast. Reform. Only s. of Dr. Tennent, of Belfast, and cousin to Lady Emerson-Tennent, whose husband (Sir James Emerson-Tennent, formerly MP for Belfast), assumed that lady's name after his m. B. at Belfast 1803; m. 1830, Eliza, d. of John McCracken, Esq., of Belfast, she died 1850. Was entered at Trinity Coll., Dublin, but did not remain to graduate, having proceeded to Greece in 1824 as a volunteer during the war of independence; was called to the bar in Ireland in 1833; also a member of the English bar, but never practised; a Magistrate for the counties of Down and Antrim, and a Dept.-Lieut. for the latter. A Liberal. Unsuccessfully contested Belfast in 1832, and again in 1835; first elected there in 1847 and sat until defeated in 1852. Died 25 May 1880.

[1852]

TENNYSON, Rt. Hon. C. See D'EYNCOURT, Rt. Hon. C.T.

THESIGER, Sir Frederick, D.C.L. 11 Bryanston Square, London. 2 King's Bench Walk, Temple, London. Carlton. B. in London 1794, the youngest and only surviving s. of Charles Thesiger, Esq., of the Island of St. Vincent, and nephew of Sir Frederick Thesiger, a distinguished Naval Officer. M. 1822, Anna Maria, d. of William Tinling, Esq., of Southampton. Was at one time in the navy, but was called to the bar at Gray's Inn 1818, made a Queen's Counsel 1834 and was a Bencher of the Inner Temple. Was Solicitor Gen. from May 1844-July 1845, then Attorney-Gen. until July 1846, and again from Mar.-Dec. 1852. A Conservative, and opposed to Jews in Parliament. Unsuccessfully contested Newark Jan. 1840. Sat for Woodstock Mar. 1840-1844, for Abingdon 1844-July 1852, and for Stamford 1852-1858. Became Lord Chancellor 26 Feb. 1858, and created Baron Chelmsford. Held the office twice, 1858-59 and 1866-68. He was active in the House of Lords after this. Died 5 Oct. 1878. [1857 2nd ed.]

THICKNESSE, Ralph. 35 Albemarle Street, Beech Hill, Wigan. A Reformer, opposed to the corn laws; an advocate of Church reform, the ballot, and the immediate abolition of slavery. First elected for Wigan in 1831 and retired in 1835. [1833]

THICKNESSE, Ralph Anthony. Beech Hill, Wigan, Lancashire. B. 1800, the only s. of Ralph Thicknesse of Beech Hill, Lancashire, by the d. of John Woodcock of Newburgh, Lancashire. M. 1828, Mary Anne, d. of Thomas Woodcock, of Bank House, near Wigan. Appointed a Dept.-Lieut. of Lancashire 1852. A Magistrate of Lancashire, and an extensive coal proprietor in the neighbourhood of Wigan. A Liberal, in favour of the ballot, 'opposed to all adjustments of taxation that favour class interests.' Favoured a revision of the income tax. Sat for Wigan from 1847 until his death on 22 Aug. 1854. [1854]

THOMAS, Lieut.-Col. Henry. United Service. Lieut.-Col. in the army. Served on the Peninsula in Canada and India. A Conservative. Sat for Kinsale in the Parliament of 1835. Contested it in 1837, and was not returned, but regained his seat on petition 11 Apr. 1838. Retired in 1841. [1841]

THOMASSON, John Pennington. Woodside, Bolton. S. of Thomas Thomasson, Esq., Cotton-Spinner of Bolton, by Maria, d. of John Pennington, Esq., of Liverpool. B. at Bolton 1841; m. 1867, Katharine, d. of Samuel Lucas, Esq., of London. Was educ. at the Pestalozzian School, Worksop, and University Coll. School, London. A Cotton-Spinner at Bolton. A Liberal, in favour of 'a thorough reform of the Land Laws', the assimilation of the borough and county franchise, a redistribution of seats, etc. Sat for Bolton from Apr. 1880 until defeated in 1885. Died 19 May 1904. [1885]

THOMPSON, George.(I). 128 Sloane Street, London. Reform. 3rd. s. of Thomas Thompson, Esq., of Leicester. B. at Liverpool 1804; m. 1831,

Anne Erskine, d. of the Rev. Richard Spry. Entered as a student in Gray's Inn 1843. The 'accredited representative of the Emperor of Delhi'; an East India proprietor. Author of a volume of *Lectures in favour of the Amelioration of the Government of India.* A radical Reformer, in favour of the further extension of free trade, the ballot, short Parliaments; and opposed to all endowments for ecclesiastical purposes. Was an unsuccessful candidate for Southampton in 1842. First returned for the Tower Hamlets in 1847 and sat until defeated in 1852. Died 7 Oct. 1878. [1852]

THOMPSON, George. (II). 5 Northumberland Street, Strand, London. 5 Golden Square, Aberdeen. S. of Andrew Thompson, Esq., Conductor of Stores in the E.I.C.S. at Madras, by Anne, d. of George Stephen, Esq., of Aberdeenshire. B. at Woolwich, Kent, 1804; m. 1830, Christiana, d. of James Kidd, Esq., D.D., Professor of Oriental Languages in Marischal Coll., Aberdeen. Educ. at the Aberdeen Grammar School, and at Marischal Coll. A Merchant and Shipowner. Dean of Guild in Aberdeen from 1840-1842; Provost of that City from 1847-1850. A Liberal, in favour of further Parliamentary reform; voted for inquiry into Maynooth, and for the ballot 1853. First returned for Aberdeen July 1852 and sat until he retired 1857. Died 11 Apr. 1895. [1857]

THOMPSON, Harry Stephen. Kirby Hall, Bedale, Yorkshire. Travellers'. S. of Richard John Thompson, Esq., of Kirby Hall, Yorkshire, by Elizabeth, d. of John Turton, Esq., of Suguall Hall, Staffordshire. B. at Newby Park, Yorkshire 1809; m. 1843, Elizabeth Anne, d. of Sir John Croft, Bart., of Doddington, Kent. Educ. at Trinity Coll., Cambridge. A Magistrate and Dept.-Lieut. of the West Riding of Yorkshire, of which he was High Sheriff 1856. Chairman of the North Eastern Railway. A Liberal. First elected for Whitby Nov. 1859 and sat until defeated 1865. Contested Knaresborough Apr. 1859 and W. Riding (Eastern div.) in 1868. Created Bart. in Mar. 1874. Died 17 May 1874. [1865]

THOMPSON, Sir Henry Meysey Meysey-. Kirby Hall, York. Thorpe Green. Little Ouseburn, Yorkshire. Eld. s. of Sir Henry Meysey-Thompson, Bart., who assumed the name of Meysey in 1874, by Elizabeth Anne, d. of Sir John Croft, 1st Bart., of Doddington, Kent. B. at Moat Hall, York, 1845. Was educ. at Eton and at Trinity Coll., Cambridge; graduated B.A. 1868. A Capt. Yorkshire Hussar Yeomanry. A Magistrate for the North and West Ridings of Yorkshire. A Liberal. Sat for Knaresborough from Apr. 1880, but in 1881 on petition the election was declared void. [1880 2nd ed.]

THOMPSON, Matthew William. Park Gate, Guiseley, Leeds. Eld. s. of Matthew Thompson, Esq., by Elizabeth Sarah, d. of the Rev. William Atkinson. B. at Manningham Lodge, near Bradford, 1820; m. 1843, Mary Anne, d. of Benjamin Thompson, Esq. Educ. at Trinity Coll., Cambridge, where he graduated B.A. 1843, M.A. 1846. Called to the bar at the Inner Temple 1846, but ceased to practice in 1857. Was Mayor of Bradford in 1862 and 1863. Chairman of the guardians of the Wharfdale Union, and Director of the Midland Railway. A Liberal, in favour of the ballot, and of throwing open the Universities. First elected for Bradford Oct. 1867. Retired 1868. Contested by-election at Bradford 12 Mar. 1869. Chairman of Glasgow and South Western Railway and of the Forth Bridge Railway. Created Bart. 18 Apr. 1890. Died 1 Dec. 1891.
[1868]

THOMPSON, Paul Beilby. 29 Berkeley Square, London. Escrick Park, Yorkshire. Athenaeum. Bro. of Lord Wenlock, and of Sir Francis Lawley, Bart., former MP for Warwickshire. Changed his name from Lawley to Thompson. M. 1817, Caroline Neville, 3rd d. of Richard 2nd Lord Braybrooke. Patron of 2 livings. A Whig. Sat for Wenlock from 1826 till 1832; from then for Yorkshire E. until defeated in 1837. Created Baron Wenlock May 1839. Died 9 May 1852.
[1837]

THOMPSON, Thomas Charles. 7 Lower Grosvenor Place, London. Ashdown Park, Forest Row, Sussex. Reform. Only s. of Thomas Thompson, Esq., of Bishopswearmouth, Co. Durham, by Elizabeth, d. of Richard Pemberton, Esq., of The Barnes, Co. Durham, B. at Bishopswearmouth 1821; m. 1854, Marianne, younger d. of Rev. Richard Moore, vicar of Lund, Lancashire. Was educ. at Harrow and at Durham University, of which he became a Fellow in 1842; graduated B.A. 1839, M.A. 1840, and produced the prize essay there in 1839. Was called to the bar at the Middle Temple 1844. A Magistrate for Durham. Was High Sheriff of Durham 1869. A Liberal, voted in the minority against the Protection of Person and Property (Ireland) Bill 1881. Contested Sunderland Nov. 1868. Sat for Durham city from Feb. to June 1874, when he was displaced on petition; regained his seat Apr. 1880 and sat until he retired in 1885. Died 26 Sept. 1892.
[1885]

THOMPSON, Lieut.-Col. Thomas Perronet, F.R.S. 21 Old Square, Lincoln's Inn, London. Blackheath Hill, Kent. Eld. s. of Thomas Thompson, Esq. (a Banker at Hull, a local Methodist Preacher, and many years MP for Midhurst), by the grandd. of the Rev. Vincent Perronet, Vicar of Shoreham, Kent, who eventually joined John Wesley. B. at Hull 1783; m. 1811, Ann Elizabeth, d. of the Rev. Thomas Barker, of York. Was educ. at Hull Grammar School, and at Queen's Coll., Cambridge., where he graduated as seventh Wrangler in 1802, and obtained a Fellowship. Was a Midshipman in the navy from 1803 till 1805, when he entered the army as Lieut. in the 95th Rifle regiment, and was taken prisoner at Buenos Ayres in 1807; became a Maj.-Gen. in 1854. Was Governor of Sierra Leone from Aug. 1808 till June 1810; interpreter and negotiator with the Wahabees at the Persian Gulf in 1819 and 1820, in the force under the command of Sir W. Grant Keir, where he negotiated the treaty (dated Jan. 1820); this was the first public act in which the slave trade was denominated piracy. Author of the *True Theory of Rent; A Catechism on the Corn Laws;* numerous articles in the *Westminster Review* from 1825 to 1835 (of which publication he was joint proprietor with Sir John Bowring); and several works on the Mathematics of Music. A radical Reformer, in favour of universal suffrage, and pledged to oppose all religious endowments. Represented Hull from 1835 till 1837. Was an unsuccessful candidate for Preston in 1835, for Maidstone in 1837, for Marylebone in 1838, for Manchester in 1839, for Hull and Cheltenham in 1841, and for Sunderland in 1845. Sat for Bradford from 1847 to 1852, when he was defeated; again elected in 1857. Retired in 1859. Died 6 Sept. 1869.
[1858]

THOMPSON, William. 5 Park Street, Westminster, London. Penydarran House, Co. Glamorgan. Union, Athenaeum, and City of London. B. 1793, the s. of James Thompson, Esq., of Kendal. M. 1817, Amelia, 2nd d. of James Homfray, Esq., former MP for Stafford and niece of Charles Morgan, Bart. of Tredegar. An Alderman of London, Lord Mayor in 1828-29, Director of the Bank and Director of the Cambrian, Gloucester and London Railway Company, a Dept.-Lieut. for London, Treasurer of King's College, President of Christ's Hospital and Vice-Pres. of the Hon. Artillery Co. Was for sometime Chairman of the Committee at Lloyd's, but resigned on the subscribers expressing themselves dissatisfied with his having joined the Sutherland Ship-Owners Mutual Assurance Association. An Iron-Master and Ship-Owner. A Conservative, voted for agricultural protection 1846 and in the minority of 53 who censured free trade, Nov. 1852. Sat for Callington from 1820-26, for London from 1826-32, for Sunderland from 1833-Sept. 1841 when he accepted Chiltern Hundreds in order to stand for Westmoreland. Sat for Westmoreland from Sept. 1841 until his death on 10 Mar. 1854.
[1853]

THOMSON, Rt. Hon. Charles Poulett. 13 South Audley Street, London. Roehampton, Surrey. Athenaeum, and Reform. Bro. of Poulett Scrope, Esq., MP for Stroud. Vice-President of the Board of Trade, and Treasurer of the navy from 1830-July 1834, when he became President, until the dissolution of Lord Melbourne's administration in Nov. 1834. In Apr. 1835, he resumed his situation. A Commissioner of Greenwich Hospital. Was a Merchant in the City, but on his accession to office at the formation of Earl Grey's administration, he withdrew his name from the firm to which he belonged. Sat for Dover from 1826-1832, when he was returned both for that bor. and Manchester, for which latter he elected to sit until appointed Governor-Gen. of Canada in 1839. Created Lord Sydenham Aug. 1840. Died 19 Sept. 1841. [1838]

THOMSON, Henry. Allnaveigh House, Newry. Carlton, Friendly Brothers' Club, Dublin. S. of Henry Thomson, Esq., of Newry. M. 1866, d. of Henry Corbet Singleton, Esq., D.L., of Aclare House, Co. Meath. A Wine Merchant at Newry. A Magistrate for the counties of Armagh and Down, and for Newry. A Conservative. Sat for Newry from Apr. 1880 until defeated in 1885. Contested the seat again in July 1892 and July 1895. [1885]

THORNHILL, Arthur John. Diddington, Buckden, Huntingdonshire. Carlton, Arthur's, Boodle's, and Junior Carlton. Eld. surviving s. of George Thornhill, Esq., D.L., of Diddington, Huntingdonshire (who died 1875), by Elizabeth Mary, d. of Robert Wilkinson, Esq. B. 1850; educ. at Eton and Trinity Coll., Cambridge. J.P. for Huntingdonshire, and patron of 2 livings. A Conservative. Returned for Cambridgeshire 20 Mar. 1884. Retired in 1885. Died 4 June 1930. [1885]

THORNHILL, George. 17 Grosvenor Street, London. Diddington, Huntingdonshire. Arthur's. Of an old family in Huntingdonshire. Educ. at St. John's Coll., Cambridge, where he graduated M.A. 1812. A Conservative, voted for agricultural protection 1846. Returned for Huntingdonshire at the general election in 1837, ousting the last member J.B. Rooper, Esq. MP until his death 19 May 1852. [1852]

THORNHILL, Sir Thomas. 55 Eaton Square, London. Riddlesworth Hall, Thetford. Pakenham Lodge, Bury St. Edmunds, Carlton, and Arthur's. Eld. s. of Thomas Thornhill, Esq., of Riddlesworth Hall, Norfolk (High Sheriff of Suffolk in 1860), by Martha Mary Ann, eld. d. of H.S. Waddington, Esq., MP for West Suffolk. B.

at Berkeley Square, London, 1837; m. 1863, Katherine Edith Isabella, only d. of Richard Hodgson Huntley, Esq. of Carham Hall, Northumberland. Was educ. at Eton and at Trinity Coll., Cambridge. Patron of 1 living. A Conservative, a strong supporter of the union of Church and State, who would 'resist to the utmost all attempts at disestablishment', supported all measures for the proper adjustment of local taxation, and the removal of those burdens 'which now press unduly on land.' Sat for Suffolk West from Oct. 1875 until defeated in 1885, contesting Suffolk North-West. Created Bart. 11 Aug. 1885. Died 2 Apr. 1900. [1885]

THORNHILL, William Pole. 44 Eton Square, London. Stanton-in-Peak, Bakewell, Derbyshire. Arthur's, Brooks's, and United University. Eld. surviving s. of Henry Bache Thornhill, Esq., of Montagu Place, London, by Helen, eld. d. of Charles Pole, Esq., of Liverpool, and grands. of Bache Thornhill, Esq., of Stanton, Derbyshire, to whose estates he succeeded in 1830. B. at Langwith Lodge 1806; m. 1828, Isabella, sole surviving child of Philip Gell, Esq., of Hopton Hall, Derbyshire, (who was MP for Malmesbury in 1808). Educ. at Corpus Christi Coll., Oxford. A Magistrate for Derbyshire, for which he was High Sheriff in 1836; appointed Capt. 2nd Derbyshire Militia 1855. Patron of 1 living. A Liberal, favourable to giving a sound moral and religious education to the people at large. First returned for Derbyshire N. July 1853 and sat until he retired 1865. Died 12 Feb. 1876. [1865]

THORNLEY, Thomas. 24 Regent Street, London. Mount Street, Liverpool. Reform, and Brooks's. A Merchant of Liverpool, but retired from business in 1835. A Liberal, in favour of the ballot and short Parliaments. Unsuccessfully contested Liverpool in 1831 and 1832. Sat for Wolverhampton from 1835 until he retired in 1859. [1858]

THOROLD, Sir John Henry, Bart. 13 Queen's Gate, Kensington Gore, London. Syston Park, Grantham. Carlton. Eld. s. of Sir John Charles Thorold, 11th Bart., of Syston Park, Grantham, by Elizabeth Frances, d. of Col. Hildyard, of Flintham Hall, Nottinghamshire. B. in Eaton Square, London 1842. Educ. at Eton. Entered the 17th Foot, Aug. 1859; became Lieut. 1862. Patron of 5 livings. A Conservative. First elected for Grantham July 1865. Retired 1868. Died Oct. 1922. [1868]

THROCKMORTON, Robert. 71 Pall Mall, London. Buckland House, Farringdon, Berkshire. Nephew and heir of Sir Charles Throckmorton,

Bart. Of Whig principles, voted for the Reform Bill, and was in favour of the immediate abolition of slavery, and inclined to abide by the corn laws. He first sat for Berkshire in 1831. Retired in 1835. Succeeded uncle as 8th Bart. 3 Dec. 1850. Died in London 28 June 1862. [1833]

THWAITES, Daniel. Addison Lodge, Addison Road, Kensington, London. Billinge Scarr, Blackburn. Junior Carlton. 3rd s. of Daniel Thwaites, Esq., of Blackburn, B. at Blackburn 1817; m. 1859, Eliza Amelia, d. of G.F. Gregory, Esq., of Repton Priory, Derbyshire. Educ. at Blackburn. A Brewer at Blackburn. A Magistrate for Lancashire and a Magistrate and Dept.-Lieut. for Leicestershire. Patron of 1 living. A Conservative. 'A consistent member of the Church of England', but in favour of complete religious freedom, the further extension of the county franchise, and the abolition of duties on cotton goods imported into India from this country. Unsuccessfully contested, in Feb. 1874, Blackburn, for which he sat from Sept. 1875 until defeated 1880. Died 21 Sept. 1888. [1880]

THYNNE, Lord Edward. 7A Cromwell Place, South Kensington, London. Longleat, Warminster, Wiltshire. White's, and Carlton. 5th s. of 2nd Marq. of Bath, by the Hon. Isabella, 3rd d. of 4th Visct. Torrington. B. in Grosvenor Square, London, 1807; m. 1st, 1830, Elizabeth, eld. d. of William Mellish, Esq., of Woodford, Essex; 2nd-ly, 1853, Cecilia, only d. of Charles Arthur Gore, Esq. Educ. at Oriel Coll., Oxford, where he graduated B.A. Formerly served in the 60th Rifles. Appointed Cornet Wiltshire Yeomanry Cavalry 1835. A Liberal-Conservative, supported the vote of censure on Lord Palmerston 1864; opposed to the Maynooth grant; in favour of public education being 'based on the Bible.' Unsuccessfully contested Frome July 1857. First elected for Frome May 1859 and sat until he retired in 1865. Died 4th Feb. 1884. [1865]

THYNNE, Rt. Hon. Lord Henry Frederick. 20 Dover Street, London. Longleat, Warminster, Wiltshire. Carlton, Junior Carlton, and White's. 2nd s. of the 3rd Marq. of Bath, by the Hon. Harriet, 2nd d. of 1st Lord Ashburton. B. in St. James's parish, Westminster, London, 1832; m. 1858, Lady Ulrica, 2nd d. of the 12th Duke of Somerset. Appointed Treasurer of the Queen's Household, Dec. 1875. A Capt. in the Wiltshire Yeomanry Cavalry 1861. A Dept.-Lieut. of Wiltshire 1861. A Conservative, but not averse to the removal of abuses. Unsuccessfully contested South Wiltshire July 1857. Sat for South Wiltshire from May 1859 until defeated in 1885. Died 28 Jan. 1904. [1885]

TIGHE, Thomas. The Heath, Ballindine, Co. Mayo. Eld. s. of Robert Tighe, Esq. B. in the Co. of Mayo. Educ. at Conglowes Wood Coll. A Magistrate for the counties of Mayo and Galway, and a member of nearly all the public boards of the Co. A Liberal, and in favour of the system called 'Home Rule' for Ireland; also of denominational education. Sat for Mayo from Feb. 1874 but unseated on petition later that year. [1874]

TILLETT, Jacob Henry. Carrow Abbey, Norwich. Descended from a Huguenot family. B. at Norwich 1818; m. 1839, only d. of William De Caux, Esq. Educ. at Norwich Grammar School. Admitted a Solicitor Nov. 1839, and practised at Norwich; retired 1868. An Alderman of Norwich, of which he was twice Mayor. A Liberal, and in favour of an extension of the county franchise, reform of the land laws, etc. Unsuccessfully contested Norwich Dec. 1868; sat for Norwich from July 1870 to Jan. 1871, when he was unseated on petition; stood again unsuccessfully Feb. 1874; again sat from Feb. to May 1875, when he was displaced on petition; again elected for Norwich 1880 and sat until he retired in 1885. Contested same seat in 1886 as a Gladstonian Liberal. Died 30 Jan. 1892. [1885]

TIPPING, William. Brasted Park, Sevenoaks, Kent. Carlton. B. 1816, the s. of John Tipping, Esq., a Merchant of Liverpool. M. 1844, Maria, d. of Benjamin Walker, Esq., of Leeds. A Magistrate for Lancashire, Yorkshire, West Riding and Kent. A Director of the North Western Railway. A Conservative. Sat for Stockport 1868 until defeated in 1874. Returned again in 1885 and retired in 1886. Died 16 Jan. 1897. [1886]

TITE, Sir William, C.B. 42 Lowndes Square, London. 7 East India Avenue, London. City, and Reform. B. in the City of London. M. Emily, 5th d. of John Curtis, Esq., of Herne Hill, Surrey. Formerly an Architect in London, where he built his chief work, the Royal Exchange. Chairman of the Bank of Egypt, a Director of the London and Westminster Bank, President of the Institute of British Architects 1862-64 and Honorary Sec. to the London Institution. A Magistrate for Middlesex and Somerset, and Dept.-Lieut. of the City of London. Author of the Introduction to the *Catalogue of Roman Antiquities found on the site of the Royal Exchange.* Papers in the *Archaeological,* 1855 etc. A Liberal, and until returned for Bath was Vice President of the Administrative Reform Association. Voted for the disestablishment of the Irish Church 1869. Unsuccessfully contested Barnstaple, Aug. 1854. Sat for Bath from June 1855 until his death on 20 Apr. 1873. [1873]

TODD, J. Ruddell. See RUDDELL-TODD, J.

TOLLEMACHE, Hon. Algernon Gray. 49 Adams Street, Portman Square, London. 5th s. of the Countess of Dysart, and bro. of Lord Huntingtown. B. 1805. A moderate Reformer. Sat for Grantham from 1832 until he retired in 1837. Died 17 Jan. 1872. [1837]

TOLLEMACHE, Hon. Frederick James. Ham House, Petersham, Surrey. Athenaeum. B. at Petersham, Surrey, 1804, the 5th s. of William, Lord Huntingtower, (eld. s. of Louisa, Countess of Dysart), by Catherine, 3rd d. of Francis Grey, Esq., of Lelena, Co. Cork. M. 1st, 1831, Sarah Maria, d. of Robert Bomford, Esq., of Ralenstown, Co. Meath (she died 1835); 2ndly, 1847, Isabella Anne, eld. d. of Gordon Forbes, Esq. (she died 1850). Educ. at Harrow. A Liberal, formerly ranked as a Conservative. Voted for free trade 1846, with the Liberal Party on Lord Derby's Reform Bill Mar. 1859, and on the vote of censure 1864. Sat for Grantham 1826-31, 1837-52, Apr. 1857-July 1865, and Dec. 1868-1874, when he retired. Died 2 July 1888. [1873]

TOLLEMACHE, H.J. Continued in House after 1885: full entry in Volume II.

TOLLEMACHE, John. 8 St. James Street, London. Helmingham Hall, Stonham, Suffolk. Peckforton Castle, Tarporley, Cheshire. Carlton, and National. S. of Admiral Tollemache (nephew of the 5th Earl of Dysart) by the d. of the 4th Earl of Aldborough. B. 1805; m. 1st, 1826, d. of John Best, Esq. (she died 1846); 2ndly, 1850, d. of James Duff, Esq. and stepd. of the 4th Lord Kendlesham. Patron of 7 livings. A Liberal-Conservative, voted against the disestablishment of the Irish Church 1869. First returned for Cheshire S. in 1841, and for the W. division in 1868 and sat until he accepted Chiltern Hundreds Jan 1872. Created Baron Tollemache Jan. 1876. Died 9 Dec. 1890. [1872]

TOLLEMACHE, Hon. Wilbraham Frederick. 18 Warwick Square, London. Tilstone Lodge, Tarporley. Carlton, and Travellers'. Eld. s. of Lord Tollemache (who as John Tollemache, Esq., sat for divisions of Cheshire for more than 30 years), by his 1st wife, Georgina Louisa, d. of John Best, Esq. B. at Tilstone Lodge, Cheshire, 1832; m. 1st, 1858, Lady Emma Georgiana, 2nd d. of the 9th Earl of Galloway (she died 1869); 2ndly, 1878, Mary Stuart, youngest d. of Right Hon. Lord Claud Hamilton. A Magistrate for the co. palatine of Chester. A Conservative, in favour of the abolition of the income-tax, and the read-

justment of local taxation. Sat for West Cheshire from Feb. 1872 until he retired in 1885. Succeeded as 2nd Baron Tollemache Dec. 1890. Died 17 Dec. 1904. [1885]

TOMLINE, George. Riby Hall, Grimsby, Lincolnshire. 1 Carlton House Terrace, London. Orwell Park, Ipswich. Carlton, Travellers', and Boodle's. S. of William Edward Tomline, Esq., who was eld. s. of Sir George Pretyman Tomline, Bart., Bishop of Winchester, but did not use the Baronetcy assumed by that prelate. A Magistrate and Dept.-Lieut. of Lincolnshire and High Sheriff of that Co. 1852. Appointed Hon. Col. North Lincoln Militia Aug. 1858, which regiment he had commanded for some years previously. First described as a Liberal-Conservative, but then ranked as a Whig. Voted against Lord Derby's Reform Bill 1859 and against Lord Russell's Reform Bill 1866. Voted for the abolition of Church rates, but opposed the malt tax in favour of financial and administrative reform. Sat for Sudbury June 1840-June 1841 (voting Conservative), Shrewsbury June 1841-July 1847, when he was unsuccessful on the 'Liberal-Conservative' interest. Again sat for Shrewsbury July 1852-Dec. 1868 and then Grimsby 1868-74, when he retired. Died 29 Aug. 1889. [1873]

TOMLINSON, W.E.M. Continued in House after 1885: full entry in Volume II.

TOOKE, William, F.R.S. 12 Russell Square, London. 39 Bedford Row, London. Law Institution, London. Athenaeum. S. of the Rev. William Tooke, F.R.S., British Chaplain at St. Petersburgh, where Mr. Tooke was born in 1777. M. 1807, Amelia youngest d. of Samual Shaen, Esq., of Crix, Essex. Vice President of the Society of Arts; a Member of the Council of the London University; Treasurer to the Society for the Diffusion of Useful Knowledge. Solicitor to the St. Katherine's Dock Company, to the Middlesex Hospital, and to the Society for the Suppression of Mendicity. A Reformer, in favour of the ballot, triennial Parliaments, and general reform. Edited an edition of Charles Churchill's Poems, of whom he wrote a memoir; published pamphlets on various subjects, and wrote largely for periodical publications. Sat for Truro (which he attempted to open in 1830 by petition to the House of Commons) from 1832 until defeated in 1837. Contested Reading in 1841. Author. Died 20 Sept. 1863. [1837]

TORR, John. Carlett Park, Eastham, Cheshire. Carlton, and Conservative. S. of William Torr, Esq., and Catherine, his wife. B. at Ribley Grove, Lincolnshire 1813; m. 1845, Louisa, eld. d. of

James Dempsey, Esq., Merchant of Liverpool (she d. 1868). A Merchant in Liverpool, retired in 1869. A member of the Liverpool Dock Board, and of the Council of the Royal Agricultural Society. Chairman of Liverpool Coll. A Magistrate for Cheshire and Liverpool. A Conservative, in favour of a reduction of the public expenditure. Sat for Liverpool from Feb. 1873. MP until his death 16 Jan. 1880.   [1879]

TORRENS, Robert. 86 Eaton Square, London. Verner's Bridge, Moy, Ireland. Carlton. Arthur's, Senior and Junior United Service. 2nd. s. of the Ven. John Torrens, D.D., Archdeacon of Dublin, by Mary, d. of Samuel Ball, Esq., of Grouse Hall, Co. Donegal. B. at Glenarm, Co. Antrim. Unmarried. Educ. at Haileybury Coll. Was employed in the Civil Service of the E.I.C. and retired on the usual pension in 1853. Whilst in India held various offices connected with the police, the revenue, and the judicial administration. A Conservative, said he would give a general support to Lord Derby, 'more particularly as his policy towards Ireland had been enlightened, and conducive to the welfare of that country;' would 'ever defend and support the Protestant religion.' First returned for Carrickfergus 1859 and sat until he retired in 1868. Died 23 Dec. 1874.   [1867]

TORRENS, Col. Robert. Stonehouse, Devon. United Service. A Lieut.-Col. of Marines, a proprietor of the *Globe* newspaper, and at one time its editor, he wrote several works of high reputation on political economy. Entertained Whig principles, inclining, in some particulars to radicalism; in favour of the ballot, and the immediate abolition of slavery. He sat for Ashburton in 1831. Sat for Bolton from 1832. Defeated in 1835. Died 27 May 1864.   [1833]

TORRENS, Sir Robert Richard, K.C.M.G. 2 Gloucester Place, Hyde Park, London. Holne, Ashburton. Reform. B. at Cork 1814, the s. of Col. Robert Torrens (who sat for Ashburton in 1831 and for Bolton until 1835, and was author of several works on political economy), by Charity, d. of Richard Chute, Esq., of Roxborough, Co. Kerry. M. 1839, Barbara, d. of Alexander Park, of Selkirk, writer to the Signet and widow of A. Anson Esq., of the 11th Dragoons. Educ. at Trinity Coll., Dublin. Appointed 1841, Collector of Customs in South Australia, and non-elective member of legislative council there. Treasurer of that Australian Colony 1852; was elected the first member of Adelaide under the new constitution, and subsequently appointed Chief Sec. and then Registrar-Gen. Was instrumental in enacting the Registration of Tithes to Land Act there, which was afterwards adopted by other Australian

Colonies. Lieut.-Col. Commanding Artillery Volunteers. Author of *First effects of Gold Discoveries on the Currency and General Condition of South Australia, Transportation Condemned as a Deterrent Punishment and as a Means of Founding Colonies,* etc. A Liberal, voted for the disestablishment of the Irish Church 1869. Favoured the disfranchisement of small boroughs. Unsuccessfully contested Cambridge July 1865 and Apr. 1866, but sat for that borough from Dec. 1868-1874, when he was defeated. Died 31 Aug. 1884.   [1873]

TORRENS, William Torrens McCullagh. 47 Eaton Square, London. Brooks's, and Reform. Eld. s. of James McCullagh, Esq., of Delville, Co. Dublin. B. 1813; m. 1st, 1836, Margaret Henrietta, d. of John Gray, Esq. (she died 1873); 2ndly, 1877, Emily, d. of William Harrison, Esq., of Eastland House, Leamington. Educ. at Trinity Coll., Dublin, where he graduated LL.B.; was called to the bar in Ireland in 1836. Appointed Commissioner of Irish Poor Inquiry 1834, and Private Secretary to the Rt. Hon. Henry Labouchere July 1846. Author of *Lectures on the Use and Study of History, The Industrial History of Free Nations, Lancashire Lesson,* etc. An 'advanced' Liberal, in favour of local taxation being relieved by assistance from national resources. Unsuccessfully contested Dundalk Aug. 1847, but was seated on petition Mar. 1848, and sat till July 1852, when he was an unsuccessful candidate for Yarmouth; sat for Yarmouth from Mar. till Aug. 1857 (as Mr. McCullagh). Sat for Finsbury from 1865 until he retired in 1885. Died 26 Apr. 1894.   [1885]

TOTTENHAM, Arthur Loftus. Glenfarne Hall, Enniskillen, Ireland. Kildare Street Club, Dublin. Carlton. Eld. s. of Nicholas Loftus Tottenham, Esq., of Glenfarne, by Anna Maria, eld. d. of Sir Francis Hopkins, Bart. B. at Dublin 1838; m. 1859, Sarah Anne, d. of George Addenbroke Gore, Esq., of Barrowmount, Co. Kilkenny. Was educ. at Eton. Entered the Rifle Brigade 1854; became Capt. 1858; retired 1861. A Magistrate for Cavan, Fermanagh and Leitrim, and a Dept.-Lieut. for the latter, of which also he was High Sheriff in 1866. A Conservative, opposed to 'the disturbance of the present Imperial relations of Great Britain.' Sat from 1880 to 1885 for Leitrim, which he had contested unsuccessfully July 1876. Sat for Winchester from 1885, until his death 4 Dec. 1887.   [1887]

TOTTENHAM, Charles. New Ross, Co. Wexford. Ballycurry, Ashford, Co. Wicklow. United University. Eld. s. of Charles Tottenham, Esq., of Ballycurry and New Ross, by Catherine, eld. d. of Sir Robert Wigram (1st Bart). M. 1832,

Isabella Catherine, d. of Lieut.-Gen. Sir George Airey, K.C.H. Educ. at Trinity Coll., Cambridge. A Conservative, against the repeal of the Maynooth grant; in favour of 'national education.' Unsuccessfully contested New Ross, Jan. 1835; first elected there Mar. 1856, and sat until he accepted Chiltern Hundreds 1863. Died 1 June 1886.   [1863]

TOTTENHAM, Charles George. Ballycurry, Ashford, Ireland. Guards'. Eld. s. of Charles Tottenham, Esq., of Ballycurry (who represented New Ross from 1856-1863), by Isabella Catherine, d. of Lieut.-Gen. Sir George Airey, K.C.B. B. at Ballycurry 1838; m. 1859, Catherine Elizabeth, eld. d. of Hon. and Rev. Sir Francis Stapleton, Bart., of Mereworth, Kent, and Greys Court, Oxfordshire. Educ. at Eton. Appointed Capt. and Lieut.-Col. Scots Guards June 1860. A Magistrate for Wicklow and Wexford. Served as High Sheriff of Wicklow 1874. A Liberal-Conservative. Sat from June 1866 Dec. 1868 for New Ross. Contested Merionethshire Jan. 1870. Contested New Ross unsuccessfully Mar. 1874. Re-elected there Dec. 1879. Defeated 1880. Contested the East division of Wicklow 30 Nov. 1885, 9 July 1886, 26 Apr. 1895 and 22 July 1895.   [1880]

TOWER, Christopher. Huntsmoor Park, Buckinghamshire. Carlton, and Boodle's. Eld. s. of Christopher Thomas Tower, Esq., of Weald Hall, Essex; one of whose ancestors represented Aylesbury in Parliament upwards of a century previously. B. at Gadesbridge, near Hemel Hempstead, Hertfordshire, 1804; m. 1836, Lady Sophia, eld. d. of 1st Earl Brownlow. Was educ. at Harrow and at Oriel Coll., Oxford. Served in the 7th Hussars from 1826-1836, in which regiment he held the rank of Capt. Appointed Dept.-Lieut. of Buckinghamshire in 1846. A Conservative, voted for agricultural protection 1846. First returned for Buckinghamshire in 1845, without a contest. Retired in 1847. Died 3 Mar. 1884.   [1847]

TOWER, Christopher Thomas. Weald Hall, Brentwood. Of moderate Whig principles. Sat for Harwich from 1832. Retired in 1835. Contested seat again in 1837. Died 19 Feb. 1867.   [1833]

TOWNELEY, Charles. 12 Charles Street, Berkeley Square, London. Towneley, Nr. Bromley, Lancashire. Brooks's, White's, Boodle's, and Athenaeum. Eld. s. of Peregrine Edward Towneley, Esq., of Towneley, Lancashire, by Charlotte Teresa, d. of Robert Drummond, Esq., of Cadlands, Hampshire. B. 1803; m. 1836, Lady Caroline, 5th d. of 2nd Earl of Segton.

A Magistrate and Dept.-Lieut. for Lancashire. A family trustee of the British Museum, in right of the well-known 'Towneley Marbles', which were collected by a member of this house. A Liberal, in favour of tenant-right and a repeal of the Ecclesiastical Tithes Act. Unsuccessfully contested Lancashire S. 1837. Sat for Sligo from Apr. 1848 to July of the same year, when he was unseated on petition; re-elected July 1852. Election declared void June 1853. Died 4 Nov. 1870.
                                    [1852 2nd ed.]

TOWNELEY, John. 76 Eaton Place, London. Towneley, Lancashire. White's, and Travellers'. 2nd s. of Peregrine Edward Towneley, Esq., of Towneley, Lancashire. B. 1806; m. 1840, d. of Sir Henry Tichborne, Bart. A Whig. First returned for Beverley in 1841 and sat until he retired in 1852. Died 21 Feb. 1878.   [1852]

TOWNLEY, Richard Greaves. Fulbourn, Cambridgeshire. Boodle's, Arthur's, and United University. S. of Richard Greaves Townley, Esq., of Belfield Hall, Lancashire, of Fulbourn, Cambridgeshire, and of Beaupré Hall, Norfolk. B. in London, 1786; m. 1821, Cecilia, 2nd d. of Sir Charles Watson, Bart., of Wratting Park, Cambridge. Educ. at Eton, and at Trinity Coll., Cambridge, B.A. 1807, and M.A. 1810. Patron of 1 living. Of Whig principles, voted for the repeal of the malt tax, 1835, and for a return to agricultural protection, 1850; supported the Reform Bill; voted against the ballot; opposed to the endowment of the Roman Catholic Clergy. Sat for Cambridgeshire from 1831 to 1841; again elected there in 1847 and sat until he retired in 1852. Died 5 May 1855.   [1852]

TOWNSEND, John. Nelson Street, Greenwich. S. of Mr. John Townsend, Auctioneer in Greenwich, and Mary, his wife. B. at Deptford 1819; m. 1841, Sarah, d. of Mr. John Mitchell. Educ. at Deptford and at Fairford, Gloucestershire. An Auctioneer, formerly in partnership with his father, but from 1843 on his own account. A Liberal, 'a staunch and unflinching supporter of the ballot and extension of the suffrage', the admission of Jews to Parliament, the continuance of the Maynooth grant, the voluntary system, and the abolition of church-rates; but was a 'jealous Conservative of all that is good.' First returned for Greenwich, Apr. 1857, when he declared he 'came forward to rescue the borough from the control and jobbery of an individual.' Accepted Chiltern Hundreds Feb. 1859. Became one of the best known actors in Canada. Died 22 Dec. 1892.   [1858]

TOWNSHEND, Lord Charles Vere Ferrars. 20

381

Cavendish Square. Rainhall Hall, Norfolk. Bro. of Marq. Townshend. B. 1785; m. 1812, Charlotte, eld. d. of Gen. William Loftus. Of Whig principles. Sat for Tamworth from 1820 until he retired in 1835. Died 5 Nov. 1853. [1833]

TOWNSHEND, Lord James Nugent Boyle Bernardo. Gwydyr House, Whitehall, London. Norfolk. Uncle of the Marq. of Townshend. B. 1785; m. 1813, Elizabeth, d. of P. Wallis, Esq. A Capt. in the navy. A Conservative. Sat for Helstone from 1818, with the exception of the Parliament of 1832, until he retired in 1837. Died 28 June 1842. [1837]

TOWNSHEND, Capt. John. 4 New Street, Spring Gardens, London. Raynham Hall, Norfolk. Balls Park, Hertfordshire. Tamworth Castle, Warwickshire. Senior United Service, Brooks's, and Navy. B. at Balls Park, Hertfordshire 1798, the eld. s. of Lord John Townshend, who represented Westminster and the University of Cambridge, by Georgiana Hune, d. of William Poyntz, Esq., of Midgham House, Berkshire. Cousin and heir presumptive of the Marq. of Townshend. M. 1825, Elizabeth Jane, eld. d. of Lord George Stuart, and grand-d. of 1st Marq. of Bute. Educ. at Eton and the Naval Coll., Portsmouth. Became Lieut. R.N. 1822 and a Capt. in 1834. Naval Aide-de-Camp to the Queen 1854. A Magistrate for Hertfordshire. Patron of 7 livings. 'A thorough Liberal in every sense of the word', in favour of the ballot and the removal of all religious disabilities from Roman Catholics and Jews. Unsuccessfully contested Tamworth in 1837 and again in 1841. Was first returned for Tamworth in Dec. 1847, without opposition, and sat until he succeeded as 4th Marq. in Dec. 1855. Died 10 Sept. 1863. [1855]

TRACY, Charles Hanbury-. 35 Dover Street, London. Toddington, Worcestershire. Gugynoy, Montgomeryshire. Patron of 6 livings. Of Whig principles. Was first elected for Tewkesbury in 1831, on the death of John Martin, Esq., whom he had unsuccessfully opposed at the previous general election and sat until he retired in 1837. Created Baron Sudeley 1838. Died 10 Feb. 1858. [1837]

TRACY, Hon. Charles Douglas Richard Hanbury-. 28 Chesham Place, London. Dolern, Newtown, Montgomeryshire. Brooks's. 2nd s. of 2nd Baron Sudeley, by Emma Elizabeth, d. of George Hay Dawkins-Pennant, Esq., of Penrhyn Castle. B. at Brighton 1840; m. 1868, Ada Maria Katherine, only d. of Hon. Frederick Tollemache. Entered the navy 1854, became Lieut. 1860, resigned his commission Jan. 1863. Served in the

Baltic and on the China and Pacific Stations. Was present at the siege of Bomarsund; took part in the battle of Faltshan, and in the occupation of San Blas. Was Gunnery Lieut. of the 'Shannon', in the Mediterranean 1862. Had medals for the Baltic and China. A Magistrate and Dept.-Lieut. for Montgomeryshire. Called to the bar at the Inner Temple 1866. A Liberal, but voted against Lord Russell's Reform Bill 1866; in favour of the 'total and unconditional' abolition of Church rates. Sat for Montgomery district from Aug. 1863 until he succeeded as 4th Baron Sudeley Apr. 1877. Died 9 Dec. 1922. [1877]

TRACY, Hon. F.H-. See HANBURY-TRACY, Hon. F. Continued in House after 1885: full entry in Volume II.

TRACY, H. Hanbury. A Liberal. Contested Bridgnorth 8 Jan. 1835. Returned for Bridgnorth 26 July 1837 and sat until he accepted Chiltern Hundreds in 1838. Died 6 Apr. 1889.

TRAILL, George. Blackheath, London. Castle Hill, Castletown, Caithness. Tressness and Garamont, Orkney. Reform. S. of James Traill, Esq., of Ratter. Was Vice-Lieut. of Caithness. A Liberal. Sat for Orkney and Shetland from 1830-35. Was an unsuccessful candidate for Caithness 1837, but sat there from 1841 until he accepted Chiltern Hundreds Aug. 1869. Died 29 Sept. 1871. [1869]

TREEBY, John Wright. 121 Westbourne Terrace, London. High Cliff, Lyme Regis, Dorset. Conservative. B. 1809, eld. s. of James Treeby, Esq., of Devon. M. 1st, 1835, 2nd d. of Richard Cockburn, Esq.; 2ndly, only d. of James Lambert, Esq., R.N. A Magistrate and Dept.-Lieut. of Middlesex. A Liberal-Conservative, opposed to 'rash innovations', but also 'against that stationary policy which obstructs all progressive reforms.' Supported Lord Derby's Party. Unsuccessfully contested Lyme Regis in Apr. 1859, but was elected there in July 1865. Sat until 1868, when Lyme Regis was disfranchised. Died 5 Sept. 1882. [1867]

TREFUSIS, Hon. Charles Henry Rolle. 2 Queen Street, London. Heanton Satchville, Crediton, Devon. Carlton. Eld. s. of Lord Clinton, by Elizabeth Georgiana, d. of 6th Marq. of Lothian. B. at Rome 1834; m. 1858, Harriet, only d. of Sir John Stuart Forbes. Educ. at Eton and at Christ Church, Oxford, where he graduated 1856. Appointed Maj. N. Devon Yeomanry Cavalry 1862. Dept.-Lieut. of Devon 1860. A Liberal-Conservative, supported Lord Derby on his Reform Bill 1859, but voted against Lord

Palmerston on the vote of censure 1864; favourable to 'progressive improvement'; was 'warmly attached to the Protestant institutions of the country', but in favour of religious liberty 'to its fullest extent.' First elected for Devon N. Apr. 1857 and sat until he succeeded as 20th Baron Clinton Apr. 1866. Died 29 Mar. 1904.

[1865 2nd ed.]

TREHERNE, Morgan D. 10 Stratford Place, London. Carlton, and University. B. 1803, 2nd. s. of Rees Goring Thomas, Esq., of Llannon, Co. Carmarthen, by Sarah, d. of R. Hovell, Esq. M. 1835, Louisa Frances, d. of John Apsley Dalrymple, Esq., of Gate House, Mayfield, Sussex. Educ. at Cheam School and Trinity Coll., Cambridge, where he graduated M.A. 1827. Called to the bar at the Inner Temple 1827, but never practised. Assumed the name of Treherne in 1856. A Magistrate for Sussex, and a Dept.-Lieut. for Surrey. A Conservative. Sat for Coventry from Oct. 1863 until his death 11 July 1867 [1867]

TRELAWNEY, Sir William Lewis Salusbury, Bart. 8 Great George Street, London. Harewood, Cornwall. Eld. s. of the Rev. Sir Henry Trelawney, Bart. B. 1781; m. 1807, Patience, d. of J. Philip Carpenter, Esq. of Mount Tavy, Devon. A Capt. in the Royal Miner Militia. A Dept.-Lieut. and Dept. Warden of Cornwall. Of Whig principles, in favour of the ballot. Sat for Cornwall E. from 1832 until defeated in 1837. Died 15 Nov. 1856. [1837]

TRELAWNY, Sir John Salusbury, Bart. Trelawne, Liskeard, Cornwall. Reform. B. at Harewood, 1816, the eld. s. of Sir William Lewis Salusbury-Trelawny, Bart., by Patience Christian, d. of John Philipps Carpenter, Esq., of Mount Tavy, near Tavistock. M. 1842, Harriet Jane, eld. d. of John Hearle Tremayne, Esq., of Heligan, Cornwall. Educ. at Westminster and at Trinity Coll., Cambridge, where he graduated B.A. 1839. Called to the bar at the Middle Temple 1841, but never practised. Appointed Capt. of the Cornwall Rangers Militia 1840, and made Dept.-Lieut. of Cornwall in the same year. A Liberal, voted for the disestablishment of the Irish Church 1869. Favoured the formation of county financial boards. Unsuccessfully contested Cornwall 1841, Brighton 1852. Contested Liskeard Mar. 1854 and Bedford Dec. 1854. Sat for Tavistock Mar. 1843-Apr. 1852, and Mar. 1857-July 1865. Sat for East Cornwall Dec. 1868-1874, when he retired. Died 4 Aug. 1885. [1873]

TREMAYNE, Lieut.-Col. Arthur. Carclew, Penryn, Cornwall. Carlton, and Army & Navy. S. of John Hearle Tremayne, Esq., of Heligan, by Caroline Matilda, d. of Sir William Lemon, Bart., MP for Cornwall. B. at New Street, Spring Gardens, London, 1827; m. 1st 1858, Lady Frances Margaret, 2nd d. of 3rd Earl of Donoughmore; 2ndly, Emma, d. of Rev. Thomas Phillpot. Educ. at Eton, and at Christ Church, Oxford. Joined the 13th Light Dragoons in 1840, with which regiment he served in the Crimea, at the Alma, Balaklava, Tchernaya, and Sebastopol, commanded the regiment in 1860 and 1861. A Conservative, but not opposed to progress; gave a general support to Lord Beaconsfield. Sat for Truro from Oct. 1878. Retired Apr. 1880. Died 14 Nov. 1905. [1880]

TREMAYNE, John. R.Y.S., Cowes. 18 New Cavendish Street, London. Heligan, St. Austell, Cornwall. Sydenham, Lew Down. Devon. Arthur's, and Carlton. Eld. s. of John Hearle Tremayne, Esq., of Heligan, MP, by Caroline Matilda, d. of Sir William Lemon, Bart., of Carclew, Cornwall. B. in London 1825; m. 1860, the Hon. Mary Charlotte Martha, d. of 2nd Baron Vivian. Educ. at Eton, and Christ Church, Oxford. A Magistrate and Dept.-Lieut. for Cornwall, a Magistrate for Devon and patron of 3 livings. A Conservative, in favour of protection of agricultural and commercial interests. Sat for Cornwall E. from 1874 until defeated in 1880. Contested Cornwall E. Mar. 1882. Sat for Devon S. 13 Aug. 1884 until he retired in 1885. Died 8 Apr. 1901. [1885]

TRENCH, Sir Frederick William, K.C.H. Carlton. Only s. of Frederick Trench, Esq., of Heywood, Ballinakill. Was related to the Earl of Clancarty. A Lieut.-Gen. in the army. Was Store Keeper of the Ordnance under the Wellington administration. Secretary to the Master General of the Ordnance. A Conservative, but in favour of free trade. Sat for Cambridge from 1818 to 1832, when he unsuccessfully contested Scarborough. First returned for Scarborough in Jan. 1835 and sat until he retired 1847. [1847]

TRENCH, Hon. William Le Poer. 32 Hyde Park Gardens, London. Garbally, Ballinasloe, Ireland. Army & Navy. B. at Garbally, Ballinasloe, 1837, the 3rd s. of 3rd Earl of Clancarty, by Lady Sarah Juliana, eld. d. of 3rd Earl of Carrick. M. 1864, Harriett Maria Georgina, only d. of Sir William Martins. Educ. at Cheltenham Coll. and the Military Academy, Woolwich. Entered the Royal Engineers as 2nd Lieut. Oct. 1854, became Lieut. 1855, Capt. 1861, Major July 1872. Served in China as a Volunteer in 1867-68, commanded ladder parties at the assaults of Canton and Namtow, for which he was

383

mentioned in despatches, and received a medal and clasp. A Liberal-Conservative, in favour of such public works being undertaken (particularly those of drainage) as would tend to stimulate private enterprise, and the development of the resources of Ireland. In favour of denominational education. Sat for Galway from June 1872, when he was seated on petition, having been unsuccessful in the preceeding Feb., until 1874 when he retired. Died 16 Sept. 1920.   [1873]

TREVELYAN, G.O. Continued in House after 1885: full entry in Volume II.

TREVOR, Hon. Arthur, F.A.S., M.R.S.L. 16 Suffolk Street, London. Wicken Park, Northamptonshire. Carlton. Only surviving s. of Visct. Dungannon. B. 1798; m. 1821, Sophia, 4th d. of G. D'Arcy Irvine, Esq. Author of *The Life and Times of William, Prince of Orange*. A Conservative. Sat for New Romney in 1830, for Durham in 1831; unsuccessfully contested Durham in 1832, but resumed his seat in 1835 and sat until he retired 1841.   [1838 2nd ed.]

TREVOR, Lord Arthur Edwin Hill. Brynkinalt, Chirk, Denbighshire. Carlton, Junior Carlton, and City Carlton. Sackville Street Club, Dublin. S. of 3rd Marq. of Downshire. B. 1819; m. 1st, 1848, eld. d. of Sir Richard Sutton, Bart. (she died 1855); 2ndly, 1858, Hon. Mary Catharine, youngest d. of the Hon. and Rev. Alfred Curzon, and sister to the 4th Lord Scarsdale. Educ. at Balliol Coll., Oxford. Appointed Lieut.-Col. of South Down Militia Sept. 1845, Lieut. in the South Nottinghamshire Yeomanry Cavalry 1848, Major North Shropshire Yeomanry Cavalry 1863. Was Gentleman of the Bedchamber to the Lord-Lieut. of Ireland, resigned 1845. Assumed the name of Trevor on succeeding to the estates of Lord Dungannon 1862. A Conservative. First returned for Co. Down Apr. 1845 and sat until created Baron Trevor May 1880. Died 25 Dec. 1894.   [1880]

TREVOR, Hon. George Rice-Rice. 11 Hyde Park Gardens, London. Carlton, and United University. Eld. s. of Lord Dynevor. B. 1795; m. 1824, Frances, eld. d. of Lord Charles Fitzroy. Assumed the name of Trevor in addition to that of Rice. Patron of 3 livings. Lieut.-Col. Commandant of the Royal Carmarthen Fusiliers. Appointed Vice-Lieut. of Carmarthenshire in 1846. A Conservative, voted for agricultural protection, 1846. Sat for Carmarthenshire from 1820 to 1831, when he was thrown out, on account of his opposition to the Reform Bill; regained his seat in 1832 and sat until he succeeded as 4th Baron Apr. 1852. Died 7 Oct. 1869.   [1852]

TREVOR, Hon. Thomas. Burlington House, Piccadilly, London. The Hoo, Welwyn, Hertfordshire. Eld. s. of Lord Dacre (who assumed the name of Trevor), by the 2nd d. of the Hon. and Very Rev. Maurice Crosbie, Dean of Limerick. M. 1837, Susan Sophia, eld. d. of the Hon. Charles Compton Cavendish, MP, a bedchamber woman to the Queen. Graduated at Magdalen Coll., Cambridge, B.A. 1830. A Magistrate and Dept.-Lieut. of Hertfordshire. A Liberal. Unsuccessfully contested Essex N. in 1832, and Lewes in 1837. First returned for Hertfordshire in 1847 and sat until defeated in 1852. Succeeded as 22nd Lord Dacre June 1853. Died 1890.   [1852]

TROLLOPE, Rt. Hon. Sir John, Bart. 6 Cavendish Square, London. Casewick House, Stamford, Lincolnshire. Carlton, Arthur's, and Boodle's. S. of Sir John Trollope (6th Bart.) by the d. of Henry Thorold, Esq., of Coxwold, Lincolnshire. B. at Casewick, 1800; m. 1847, Julia, eld. d. of Sir Robert Sheffield, Bart. of Normanby Park, Lincolnshire. A Dept.-Lieut. of Lincolnshire, of which he was Sheriff in 1825. Was President of the Poor Law Board from Mar. till Dec. 1852. A Conservative, in favour of lowering the franchise, especially in towns. First returned for Lincolnshire S. in 1841 and sat until created Baron Kesteven Apr. 1868. Died 17 Dec. 1874.   [1867]

TROTTER, John. 28 Eaton Place, London. Horton Place, Surrey. A Conservative, voted for agricultural protection 1846. First elected for Surrey W. 1840, on the succession of Capt. Perceval to a peerage, and sat until he retired in 1847.   [1847]

TROUBRIDGE, Sir Edward Thomas, Bart. 11 Eaton Place, London. Blomer, Sussex. S. of Adm. Troubridge, who fought at the Nile, and was lost in his Majesty's ship 'Blenheim' in 1806, it was supposed in the Southern Ocean. M. 1810, Anna Maria, d. of Adm. Sir A. Inglis Cochrane, G.C.B. and cousin of Lord Dundonald. A Rear Admiral of the Blue, and Naval Aide-de-Camp to the Queen. A Lord of the Admiralty from Apr. 1835-Sept. 1841. An East India Proprietor. A Conservative, but in favour of free trade. Sat for Sandwich from 1831 until he retired in 1847. Died 7 Oct. 1852.   [1847]

TRUEMAN, Charles. West Hill, Highgate, London. S. of Joseph Trueman, Esq., of Grosvenor House, Walthamstow, Essex, by Mary, d. of Thomas Daniel, Esq., of Derby. B. in London 1814; m. 1837, Emma Maria, youngest d. of William Parkinson, of Studham Grove, Hertfordshire. A Merchant in London, and connected with mining concerns in Cornwall. A Liberal, and a supporter of Lord Palmerston 'on the Chinese question and in his general policy'; in favour of the strictest economy in the public expenditure 'without trenching on efficiency', and the settlement of church-rates upon 'fair and just terms.' First elected for Helstone, Apr. 1857, without opposition. Defeated in 1859. [1858]

TUDWAY, Robert Charles. 7 Hamilton Place, Piccadilly, London. Wells, Somerset. B. at Wells, 1808, the eld. s. of John Paine Tudway, Esq., (MP for Wells from 1815-30, and whose uncle sat from 1760-1815), by Fanny Gould, d. of Lucas Pulsford, Esq., of Wells. M. 1846, Maria Catherine, eld. d. of William Miles, Esq., MP, of Leigh Court, Somerset. Educ. at Harrow and at Christ Church, Oxford. A Dept.-Lieut. and Magistrate for Somerset and High Sheriff in 1842. Appointed Capt. North Somerset Yeomanry Cavalry in 1839. A Conservative, and voted in the minority of 53 who censured free trade, Nov. 1852. Supported 'any measure by which the burdens on land may be relieved without abridging the comforts of the Lower Orders.' Represented Wells from July 1852 until his death 20 Oct. 1855. [1855]

TUFNELL, Rt. Hon. Henry. 10 Great Stanhope Street, London. Brooks's, and Travellers'. B. in Chichester 1805, the eld. s. of William Tufnell, Esq., former MP for Colchester, by the d. and co-heir of Lough Carleton, Esq. M. 1st, 1830, d. of Sir R.W. Horton, Bart; 2ndly, 1844 Hon Frances, d. of 1st Earl of Stafford (she died 1846); 3rdly, 1848, Lady Anne, d. of 4th Earl of Rosebery. Graduated B.A. at Christ Church, Oxford. Private Secretary to Sir R.W. Horton (Governor of Ceylon), and afterwards to Lord Minto (first Lord of the Admiralty). Was a Lord of the Treasury from Apr. 1835-Sept. 1841. Appointed Secretary to the Treasury from July 1846, resigned July 1850. Translated *Müller's Dorians* with G.C. Lewis, Esq. A Liberal, voted in favour of the ballot. Said he would 'uphold Protestant principles as the firmest bulwarks of civil and religious liberty.' Supported 'speedy, cheap and accessible justice.' Unsuccessfully contested Colchester in 1835. Was returned for Ipswich in 1837, but unseated on petition. Sat for Devonport from 1840 until he accepted Chiltern Hundreds in Apr. 1854. Died 15 June 1854. [1853]

TUITE, Hugh Morgan. Sonna, Co. Westmeath. S. of Hugh Tuite, Esq. B. 1795; m. 1826, d. of Maurice N. O'Connor, Esq., of Mount Pleasant. A Liberal, voted against an abolition of the Corn Laws. Sat for Westmeath from 1826 till 1830; re-elected in 1841 and sat until he retired in 1847. [1847]

TULK, Charles Augustus. 19 Duke Street, Westminster, London. A Reformer, in favour of the ballot. Sat for Sudbury in 1820. Sat for Poole from 1835. Retired in 1837. [1837]

TULLAMORE, Lord. 8 St. George's Place, Hyde Park Corner, London. Charleville Forest, Tullamore, Ireland. S. of the Earl of Charleville. B. 1801; m. 1826, Beaujolais Harriet Charlotte, 3rd. d. of Col. Campbell, of Shawfield, and niece of the Duke of Argyll. A Conservative, in favour of relieving Dissenters from Church rates. Sat for Carlow from 1826 to the 1832 election, when he was obliged to give way to a Repealer. In the same election he was elected for Penryn. Defeated in the general election of 1835. Contested a by-election in same seat 28 Apr. 1835. [1833]

TURNER, Charles. Dingle Head, Liverpool. Carlton, and Union. S. of Ralph Turner, Esq. of Hull, Merchant. B. at Hull 1803; m. 1843, Anne, d. of Charles Whitaker, Esq. of Melton Hill, Yorkshire. Educ. at Bingley under the Rev. Dr. Hartley. Was an E. India Merchant at Liverpool. Was the Chairman of the E. India and China Association, Liverpool. Was Chairman of the Liverpool Dock Committee and of the Mersey Dock and Harbour Board. A Magistrate for Lancashire and for Liverpool and a Dept.-Lieut. of the Co. Palatine of Lancaster. A Liberal-Conservative, voted against the disestablishment of the Irish Church 1869. Sat for Liverpool from July 1852-June 1853; for Lancashire S. from Aug. 1861-Dec. 1868, from which date he sat for Lancashire S.W. division. MP until his death 15 Oct. 1875. [1875]

TURNER, Edmund. 7 Victoria Square, Pimlico, London. Truro. Polgwynne-House, Feork, Cornwall. S. of a Banker at Truro, and bro. of Charles Walsingham Turner, who distinguished himself in India as a scholar and a soldier, and died at Vizagapatam. B. 29 Jan. 1792; m. July 1813, the eld. d. of Reuben Magor, Esq., a Banker in Cornwall; she died 1842. Was himself a Banker; a Dept.-Lieut. and Magistrate for Cornwall. Was frequently Chairman of Reform meetings during the progress of the Reform Bill. Elected first Mayor of Truro under the Municipal Corporation Act. Opposed to the endowment of the Roman Catholic Clergy, but generally supported the measures of Sir R. Peel. Sat for Truro from 1837. MP until his death in 1848. [1847 2nd ed.]

TURNER, Frederick Charles Polhill-. Howbury Hall, Bedford. Army & Navy. Only s. of Frederick Polhill, Esq., of Howbury Hall, Co. Bedford (who sat for Bedford from 1839-1847), by Frances Margaretta, d. of John Dakeyne, Esq., of Bagthorpe House, Nottinghamshire. B. at Howbury Hall 1826; m. 1852, Emily Frances, d. of Sir Henry Winston Barron, Bart. Educ. at Dr. Burneys, and the Royal Military Academy. Assumed by royal licence, Feb. 1853, the name of Turner in addition to his patronymic. Was Capt. 6th Dragoon Guards. Capt. Duke of Manchester's Volunteers. Was High Sheriff for the Co. of Bedford 1855. A Magistrate and Dept.-Lieut. for that Co. Patron of 1 living. A Conservative, but 'prepared also to vote for every measure of real improvement.' Sat for Bedford from Feb. 1874 until defeated 1880. Died 18 Aug. 1881.   [1880]

TURNER, George James. 23 Park Crescent, Portland Place, London. 11 New Square, Lincoln's Inn, London. Carlton. S. of the Rev. R. Turner, of Great Yarmouth, Norfolk. Educ. at Charterhouse and at Pembroke Coll., Cambridge, where he was 9th Wrangler in 1819 and graduated M.A. 1822. Was called to the bar in 1821 at Lincoln's Inn, of which he was a bencher and made a Queen's Counsel in 1840. A Conservative, but in favour of free trade. First returned for Coventry in 1847, and sat until he was appointed Vice-Chancellor in Apr. 1851. Was Knighted on 14 Apr. 1851 and made Lord Justice of Appeal, Jan. 1853. Died 9 July 1867. [1851]

TURNER, James Aspinall. Pendlebury House, Manchester. S. of John Turner, Esq., of Mayfield, near Bolton, by Elizabeth, d. of James Aspinall, Esq., of Liverpool. B. at Bolton 1797; m. 1823, Sarah, d. of Robert Grierson Blackmore, Esq., of Manchester. Educ. at Bolton Grammar School. A Cotton Manufacturer and Merchant at Manchester. Appointed a Dept.-Lieut. of the Co. Palatine of Lancaster 1860. A Liberal, in favour of providing 'means of defence against injury or insult' from other nations; in favour also of 'progressive improvements at home', the extension of the franchise both in boroughs and counties, and said he would support any measure of general education which were consistent with 'religious liberty.' First elected for Manchester Apr. 1857 and sat until he retired 1865. Died 28 Sept. 1867.   [1865]

TURNER, T. Frewen. A Conservative. Returned for Leicestershire S. in 1835 and sat until he accepted Chiltern Hundreds Jan. 1836. [1835]

TURNER, William. 31 Parliament Street, London. Shringley Hall, Cheshire. Wyndham. A Calico Printer at Mill-hill, near Blackburn. B. 1776; m. 1810, a cousin of the same name. Was High Sheriff of Cheshire in 1826. Patron of 1 living. A Reformer, advocated the removal of the taxes on malt and hops, the shortening of the duration of Parliaments, the vote by ballot, the removal of monopolies, the reduction of the interest of the national debt, and the abolition of punishment of death in all cases except murder. In favour of a fixed duty on foreign corn, and the support of the Church and State; pledged himself to resign his seat at the end of the session if his constituents were not satisfied with him. Sat for Blackburn from 1832 until defeated in 1841.   [1838]

TURNOR, Christopher. 12 Upper Belgrave Street, London. Stoke Rochford. Panton House, Lincolnshire. Carlton, and New University. Eld. s. of Edmund Turnor, Esq. B. 1810; m. 1837, d. of 10th Earl of Winchelsea. A Conservative, voted for agricultural protection 1846. First returned for Lincolnshire S. in 1841 and sat until he retired in 1847. Died 7 Mar. 1886.   [1847]

TURNOR, Edmund. Panton Hall, Wragby, Lincolnshire. Carlton. Eld. s. of Christopher Turnor, Esq., of Stoke Rochford, Lincolnshire, some years member for Lincolnshire S. by Lady Caroline, d. of the 9th Earl of Winchelsea. B. in London 1838; m. 1866, Lady Mary Katherine, eld. d. of the 10th Marq. of Huntly. Educ. at Harrow and at Christ Church, Oxford. A Dept.-Lieut. and Magistrate for Lincolnshire. A Conservative, and gave a general support to Lord Beaconsfield's party. Sat for Grantham from Apr.-Nov. 1868. Sat for Lincolnshire S. from Dec. 1868 until he retired 1880.   [1880]

TWELLS, Philip. 23 Grosvenor Place, London. 54 Lombard Street, London. Chase Side House, Enfield, Middlesex. Oxford & Cambridge, Carlton, and City Carlton. S. of John Twells, Esq., of London, Banker, by Mary, d. of Joseph Line, Esq., of Alum Rock, near Birmingham. B. in London 1808. Unmarried. Educ. at the Charterhouse, and at Worcester Coll., Oxford, where he was 2nd class in classics, and graduated B.A. 1831, M.A. 1833. Called to the bar at Lincoln's Inn 1834, and practised for some years, afterwards joined the Banking firm of Messrs. Barclay, Bevan, Tritton, Twells and Company. A Magistrate for Middlesex, and a Commissioner of Lieutenancy for London. A Conservative, not in favour of any further electoral reform. Sat from Feb. 1874 for London, which he unsuccessfully contested Dec. 1868, until he retired 1880. Died 8 May 1880.   [1880]

TWISS, Horace. 5 Park Place, St. James's, London. 56 Chancery Lane, London. Carlton. Eld. s. of Francis Twiss, Esq., of Pembroke Coll., resident, at his death at Cheltenham. B. 1787; m. 1st, 1817, d. of—Serle, Esq., of Hampshire; 2ndly, 1830, widow of Charles Greenwood, Esq., of Great Queen St., Westminster. A King's Counsel; a Bencher of the Inner Temple. Wrote several pamphlets, articles in the *Quarterly Review* and other periodicals, and was, whilst a student, connected with the *Morning Chronicle* newspaper. Was Counsel to the Admiralty and Judge Advocate of the Fleet in the administration of Lord Liverpool. Under Secretary of State for the Colonies in the Wellington Administration. A Conservative. Was a supporter of Catholic Emancipation and other liberal measures; but strongly opposed the Reform Bills of 1831 and 1832. Sat for Wootten Bassett, from 1818 until 1830; for Newport in 1830 and 1831; out of Parliament until elected for Bridport in 1835. Retired in 1837. Contested Nottingham July 1837 and Bury-St.-Edmunds Aug. 1847. Died 1849. [1836]

TYLER, Sir George, K.H. Cottrell, Nr. Cardiff, Glamorganshire. United Service. Eld. s. of Admiral Sir Charles Tyler, G.C.B., by his 2nd wife, d. of Alexander Leach, Esq., of Corston, Pembrokeshire. B. in Pembrokeshire 1792; m. 1819, d. of Rt. Hon. John Sullivan, and grand-d. of the 3rd Earl of Buckinghamshire. Educ. at the Royal Naval Coll. Entered the navy 1806; became a Rear-Admiral 1852. Was Lieut.-Governor of St. Vincent's from Feb. 1833-1840. A Conservative, voted for inquiry into Maynooth 1853. First returned for Glamorganshire Feb. 1851, without opposition and sat until he retired 1857. Died 4 June 1862. [1857]

TYLER, Sir Henry. Continued in House after 1885: full entry in Volume II.

TYNTE, Charles John Kemeys, F.R.S. Halswell House, Bridgewater. Cefn Mably, Glamorganshire. Burleigh Hall, Loughborough. Brooks's, Travellers', and United Service. Only s. of Charles Kemeys-Tynte, Esq., F.A.S., of Halswell House, Somersetshire, former MP for Bridgewater (who was declared by the House of Lords in 1845 co-heir to the Barony of Wharton, and also co-heir to the Barony of Grey-de-Wilton). B. at Halswell House, 1800; m. 1st, 1821, Elizabeth, 3rd d. and co-heir of Thomas Swinnerton, Esq., of Butterton Hall, Staffordshire; 2ndly, 1841, Vincentia, d. of Wallop Brabazon, Esq., of Rath House, Co. Louth. Educ. at Eton. Author of a *Sketch of the French Revolution of 1830*. A Magistrate for Somersetshire, Glamorganshire, and Monmouthshire, Dept.-Lieut. for Glamorganshire and Somersetshire; Provincial Grand Master of the Freemasons in Monmouthshire; and Col. of the Royal Glamorgan

Militia. Patron of 6 livings. A Liberal. Sat for Somerset W. from 1832-1837, when he was an unsuccessful candidate. First returned for Bridgewater 1847 and sat until he retired 1865. [1865]

TYNTE, Charles Kemeys Kemeys, F.S.A. Burhill, Surrey. Cefn-Mabley, Glamorganshire. Halswell House, Somersetshire. Boodle's, Arthur's, Brooks's, and the University. Nephew and heir of Sir C. Kemeys Tynte, MP for Somerset, and s. of Col. Tynte, of the 1st Foot Guards and Groom of the Bedchamber to George IV, when Prince of Wales. B. 1778; m. 1798, Anne, widow of Thos. Lewis, Esq., of St. Pierre, Co. Monmouth. A Dept.-Lieut. of Somerset, Glamorgan, and Monmouth. Formerly in the army; then Col. of the West Somerset Yeomanry Cavalry. Patron of 9 livings. A Whig, voted for the Reform Bill, and against the Ballot and Triennial Parliaments. Sat for Bridgewater from 1820 until he retired in 1837. [1837]

TYRELL, Charles. Polstead, Suffolk. Of Whig principles. Sat for Suffolk W. from 1830 until he retired in 1835. Died 2 Jan. 1872. [1833]

TYRELL, Sir John Tyssen, Bart. 81 Jermyn Street, London. Boreham House, Essex. Carlton, and Conservative. Eld. s. of Sir John Tyrell, Bart., by the only d. and heir of William Tyssen, Esq., of Waltham House, Hertfordshire. B. 1795; m. 1819, Eliza, eld. d. of Sir Thomas Pilkington, Bart., of Chevet, Yorkshire (from whom he was divorced). Was Col. of the W. Essex Militia from 1831-1852. A Conservative. Succeeded Admiral Harvey in the representation of Essex. N. in 1830, but, voting against the first Reform Bill, was thrown out at the ensuing election. Recovered his seat in 1832 and sat until he retired 1857. Died 19 Sept. 1877. [1857]

TYRONE, Earl of. Kildare Street Club, Dublin. Sackville Street Club, Dublin. Carlton, and White's. Eld. s. of the Marq. of Waterford, by Christiana, 4th d. of Col. Charles Powell Leslie, of Glaslough, Co. Monaghan. B. in London 1844. Educ. at Eton. Appointed Cornet and Sub-Lieut. 1st Life Guards 1862. A Conservative. First elected for the Co. of Waterford July 1865 and sat until he succeeded as 5th Marq. Nov. 1866. Died 23 Oct. 1895. [1865 2nd ed.]

TYSSEN-AMHERST, W.A. Continued in House after 1885: full entry in Volume II.

UPTON, Hon. George Frederick. 27 George Street, Hanover Square, London. Junior United Service, 2nd. s. of the 1st Lord Templetown, by

Lady Mary, only d. of 5th Earl of Sandwich. B. at Botley's, Surrey, 1802; m. 1830, Susan, eld. d. of Lieut.-Gen. Sir Alexander Woodford. Was Lieut.-Col. Coldstream Guards from 1855 till 1858, when he was made a Major-Gen., distinguished himself at the battle of the Alma, and was wounded at Inkermann. Appointed Col. 60th Rifles 1862. Made a C.B. 1855, and a Commander of the Legion of Honour, 1856. A Conservative, and a strong supporter of Lord Derby. First elected for Antrim, May 1859, and sat until he succeeded bro. as 3rd. Visct. 28 Mar. 1863. Died 4 Jan. 1890. [1863]

URQUHART, David. 9 Bennet Street, St. James's, London. Bittern Manor, Southampton. Mollands, Perthshire. Only s. of David Urquhart, Esq., of Braclangwell, Cromarty, by his 2nd wife, d. of—Hunter, Esq. Chief of the clan of Urquhart, of Cromarty, who were devoted adherents of the Stuart family, and who had been heritable Sheriffs of Cromarty since the reign of Edward I. (The chieftainship was however claimed by Beauchamp Colclough Urquhart, Esq., of Meldrum and Byth, Co. Aberdeen, who denied the correctness of the Member's pedigree.) B. at Braclangwell 1805. Unmarried. Was educ. at St. John's Coll., Oxford; was Secretary of Embassy at Constantinople in 1837; author of *Turkey and its Resources, England, France, Russia and Turkey,* and many other works; was also principal contributor to the Portfolio, 1st series, in 1835-36, and 2nd series, 1843-44. A Conservative, opposed to all taxation except on land and capital, and thought that it should then be collected, not by Government officers, but by the municipalities, according to ancient custom; against endowment by the State, either for the purposes of religion or education. Had one rule, to vote for any measure which was to abrogate an old statute, and against every measure which was to introduce a new one. Was an unsuccessful candidate for Sheffield in 1841. First returned for Stafford in 1847 and sat until he retired in 1852. Founded *Free Press* 1855, later *Diplomatic Review* 1866. Died 16 May 1877. [1852]

URQUHART, William Pollard-. Kinturk, Castle Pollard, Co. Westmeath. Arthur's. S. of William Dutton Pollard, Esq., by his 2nd wife, Louisa Anne, d. of Admiral the Hon. Sir Thomas Pakenham, G.C.B. B. at Castle Pollard, Co. Westmeath 1815; m. 1846, Mary Isabella, only child of William Urquhart, Esq., of Craigston Castle, Aberdeenshire (whose name he assumed). Educ. at Harrow, and at Trinity Coll., Cambridge, where he obtained a scholarship, and took a Wrangler's degree in 1838. A Magistrate and Dept.-Lieut. of Westmeath, and a Magistrate for

Aberdeenshire. Author of the *Life and Times of Francesco Sforza, Duke of Milan, Essays on Political Economy,* pamphlets on Taxation etc. A Liberal, in favour of an 'increase of Irish members in the House of Commons', vote by ballot, and the establishment of 'tenant-right' in Ireland. Sat for Westmeath from July 1852-Aug. 1857; re-elected there May 1859. MP until his death circa May 1871. [1870]

UXBRIDGE, Earl of. Beaudesert Park, Staffordshire. Eld. s. of the Marq. of Anglesey, by his 1st wife, Eleanora, 2nd d. of Col. John Campbell. B. 1821; m. 1845, Sophia, 2nd d. of James Eversfield, Esq., of Deane Park, Sussex. Formerly Lieut. in 1st Life Guards; retired 1845. Appointed a Dept.-Lieut. of Staffordshire 1851; was Lieut.-Col. of that Co. Militia from 1852-1855. A Liberal, in favour of a measure of Parliamentary Reform which would extend the franchise, diminish the private nomination of members, and put an end to corrupt practices at elections. First returned for Staffordshire S. Feb. 1854. Retired 1857. Succeeded as 3rd Marq. Feb. 1869. Died 30 Jan. 1880. [1857]

VALLETORT, Visct. Carlton. Eld. s. of the Earl of Mount Edgcumbe, by Caroline, eld. d. of Rear Admiral Charles Feilding. B. in Sackville Street, London 1832; m. 1858, Lady Katherine Elizabeth, 4th d. of 2nd Marq. of Abercorn. Appointed Capt. 1st Cornwall Rifle Militia 1855, extra Equerry to the Prince of Wales Nov. 1858. A Conservative, in favour of Lord Derby's policy; not averse to the enlargement of the franchise, but opposed to a 'rash and extravagant spirit of innovation.' First elected for Plymouth May 1859 and sat until he succeeded as 4th Earl 3 Sept. 1861. Lord-Lieut. of Cornwall 1877; prominent Freemason; various Household offices 1879-97. Died 25 Sept. 1917. [1861]

VANCE, John. 18 Rutland Square, London. Dublin. Carlton, and Windham. Eld s. of Andrew Vance, Esq. of Rutland Square, Dublin. M. 1846, Anne Eliza, d. of Henry Dresser, Esq., of Farnborough Lodge, Kent. Graduated at Trinity Coll., Dublin. A Merchant in the Irish and Colonial trade; a Dept.-Lieut. for the W. Riding of Yorkshire from 1853. A Conservative, 'strongly attached to Protestant institutions'; favoured local self goverment as opposed to 'centralization'. Was an unsuccessful candidate for Canterbury in July 1847. Sat for the city of Dublin from July 1852-1865. Sat for Armagh from Feb. 1867. MP until his death 21 Sept. 1875. [1875]

VANDELEUR, Crofton Moore. 4 Rutland

Square, Dublin. Kilrush, Co. Clare. Carlton. B. 1809, the eld. s. of Rt. Hon. John Ormsby Vandeleur of Kilrush, a Commissioner of Customs for Ireland, by Lady Frances, youngest d. of 1st Marq. of Drogheda. M. 1832, Lady Grace, 2nd d. of 2nd Earl of Norbury (she died 1872). Educ. at Harrow and at Trinity Coll., Cambridge. A Magistrate and Dept.-Lieut. for Clare, and High Sheriff of that Co. 1832. Appointed Col. of the Clare Militia June 1843. A Liberal-Conservative. Unsuccessfully contested Clare Jan. 1835, July 1841 and July 1852. Sat for Clare from May 1859 until 1874, when he was defeated. Died 8 Nov. 1881.   [1873]

VANDERBYL, Philip. 51 Porchester Terrace, Hyde Park, London. Northwood, near Winchester. Reform. S. of P.V. Vanderbyl, Esq. (member of the Legislative Council of the Cape of Good Hope), by Isabella Van Breda. B. at the Cape of Good Hope 1827; educ. at the University of Edinburgh; m. 1853, Sara, only d. of James Alexander, Esq., head of the firm of Redfern, Alexander, and Co. Having graduated with honours in medicine, and obtained the gold medal at his university, he entered the medical profession. A M.R.C.P. London, and was president of the Royal Medical Society of Edinburgh, and Lecturer on anatomy and histology at Middlesex Hospital. He retired from the profession in 1858, and became an Australian Merchant and Banker. A Director of the East and West India Dock Co. A Liberal, in favour of colonial representation in the Imperial Parliament, also of the Disestablishment of the Church, and of reform in the House of Lords. Unsuccessfully contested Great Yarmouth in 1865. Sat for Bridgwater 1866-68. In Dec. 1868 he was re-elected for that town, but unseated on petition. Returned for Portsmouth 1885. Defeated in 1886 standing as a Gladstonian Liberal. Contested Winchester 12 Jan. 1888. Died 16 May 1892.   [1886]

VANE, Lord Adolphus Frederick Charles William. See TEMPEST, Lord Adolphus Frederick Charles William Vane-.

VANE, Lord Harry George. 29 Grosvenor Square, London. Reform, and Travellers'. S. of the 1st Duke of Cleveland, by his 1st wife, d. of 2nd Duke of Bolton. B. 1803; m. 1854, Lady Dalmeny, d. of 4th Earl Shanhope, and relict of Lord Dalmeny. Educ. at Oriel Coll., Oxford, graduated B.A. 1829. Secretary of Legation at the Court of Sweden. Appointed Dept.-Lieut. of Durham 1852. A Liberal, in favour of 'Social improvement and steady progress.' Sat for Durham S. from 1841-May 1859, when he was elected for

Hastings. Sat until he succeeded to the Peerage (4th Duke of Cleveland) 1864. Died 21 Aug. 1891.   [1863]

VANE-TEMPEST, Lord Adolphus Frederick Charles William. See TEMPEST, Lord Adolphus Frederick Charles William Vane-.

VANS-AGNEW, Robert. New Club, Edinburgh. Barnbarroch, Kirkinner. Stranraer Park, Stranraer, Scotland. Carlton, and Conservative. Eld. s. of Col. Patrick Vans Agnew, C.B., of Barnbarroch, by Catherine, d. of D. Fraser, Esq., of Inverness. B. at Madras 1817; m. 1852, Mary Elizabeth, 2nd d. of Sir David Hunter Blair, Bart., of Blairquhan, Ayrshire. Educ. at Eton. Served in the Rifle Brigade from 1835-1842. Patron of 3 livings. A Conservative. Sat for Wigtownshire from Feb. 1873 until retired 1880. Died 26 Sept. 1893.   [1880]

VANSITTART, George Henry. 49 Brook Street, London. Bisham Abbey, Nr. Maidenhead. Carlton. Eld. s. of General George Henry Vansittart, by Anne Mary, d. of Thomas Copson, Esq., of Shepey Hall, Leicestershire. B. at Bisham Abbey, Berkshire, 1823; m. 1851, Catherine Stewart Menzies, of Culdares, Perthshire. Educ. at Eton and Balliol Coll., Oxford, where he was 4th class in mathematics, 1844. A Magistrate and Dept.-Lieut. of Berkshire. A Conservative, voted for a withdrawal of the Maynooth grant, and 'determined to resist every encroachment of the Papacy'; considered 'taxation and representation should go together.' First returned for Berkshire in July, 1852 and Sat until he retired in 1859. Died 3 Nov. 1885.   [1858]

VANSITTART, William. 27 Dover Street, London. 16 Brunswick Square, Brighton. Carlton, and Conservative. 3rd. s. of Arthur Vansittart, Esq., of Shottesbrook Park, Berkshire, by the Hon. Caroline, 4th d. of 1st Lord Auckland. B. in Berkshire 1813; m. 1st, Emily, d. of Maj. Anstruther (she died 1844); 2ndly, Harriette, eld. d. of Ambrose Humphrys, Esq. (she died 1852). Educ. at Eton and at Haileybury Coll. Entered the civil service of the E.I.C. in the Bengal presidency 1831; retired in 1844, after having held several magisterial and judicial appointments. A Dept.-Lieut. of the Tower Hamlets. A Liberal-Conservative, 'sincerely attached to the constitution, which may be best preserved by progressive reform'; considered the Maynooth Grant 'religiously and politically indefensible'; in favour of a total extinction of the income tax, and an 'adjustment' of the Church rate question; supported the vote of censure on Lord Palmerston 1864. First returned for Windsor, Mar. 1857 and sat until defeated 1865. Died 15 Jan. 1878. [1865]

389

VAUGHAN, Sir Robert Williams, Bart. 23 Bolton Street. Nannau, Merionethshire. B. 1766; m. 1802, Anna Maria, d. of Sir Roger Mostyn, Bart. Patron of 2 livings. A Conservative. Sat for Merionethshire from 1792 (some member of his family had represented it for upwards of a century) until he accepted Chiltern Hundreds May 1836. [1836]

VERE, Sir Charles Broke, K.C.B., K.T.S. 4 Scotland Yard, Whitehall, London. Broke Hall, Suffolk. Carlton. Bro. of Sir Philip Vere Broke, Capt. of the 'Shannon' at the time of the engagement between her and the American frigate 'Chesapeak'. B. 1779. A Major-Gen. in the army. Was at Waterloo. A Conservative. Unsuccessfully contested Suffolk E. in 1832. Was elected there in 1835 and MP until his death in Mar. 1843. [1842]

VERNER, Sir Edward Wingfield. Cork Abbey, Bray, Co. Dublin. National, Junior United Service, and Carlton. 2nd s. of Lieut.-Col. Sir William Verner, 1st Bart., K.C.H., by Harriet, d. of the Hon. Col. Edward Wingfield. B. at Churchill, Co. Armagh 1830; m. 1864, Selina Florence, d. of Thomas Vesey Nugent, Esq. Educ. at Eton and at Christ Church Coll., Oxford. A Conservative, 'of essentially Protestant principles', and said he would 'always endeavour to uphold the rights of the people, the interest of religion, and the safety of the throne.' Contested Lisburn, Feb. 1863, first elected June following, and sat until Feb. 1873, from which date he sat for the Co. of Armagh until he retired 1880. Succeeded nephew as 4th Bart. June 1886. Died 21 June 1899. [1880]

VERNER, Sir William, Bart., K.C.H., sen. 86 Eaton Square, London. Verner's Bridge, Moy Ireland. Carlton, Arthur's, Senior and Junior United Service. S. of Jas. Verner, Esq., by the d. and co-heir of the Rev. Henry Clarke, of Annasammery, Co. Armagh. B. in Ireland, 1782; m. 1819, Harriet, only d. of the Hon. Col. Wingfield. Was Dept. Grand Master of the Orange Society. Became a Lieut.-Col. in the army in 1826. Served in Spain and France twice, and was wounded at Waterloo. A Conservative. Struck off the list of justices of the peace in Ireland, by the Marq. of Normanby, then Lord Mulgrave, on account of an alleged political toast given at a dinner party. Was restored to the commission. Sat for Armagh Co. from 1832, having contested it unsuccessfully in 1826, until he retired in 1868. Deputy Grand Master of Orange Order till his death 20 Jan. 1871. [1867]

VERNER, Sir William, Bart., jun. Verner's Bridge, Moy, Co. Antrim. Eld. s. of Sir William Verner, Bart., K.C.H., who sat for the Co. Armagh from 1832-Dec. 1868, by Harriet, only d. of the Hon. Col. Edward Wingfield. B. in Ireland 1822; m. 1850, Mary Frances Hester, 3rd d. of Lieut.-Gen. Hon. Sir Hercules Pakenham, K.C.B. Served in the Coldstream Guards. Was High Sheriff of Tyrone 1851. Appointed Maj. Antrim Militia 1859. Dept.-Lieut for Tyrone and a Magistrate for Armagh. A Conservative. Sat for Co. Armagh from Dec. 1868. MP until his death 10 Jan. 1873. [1872]

VERNEY, Sir Harry, Bart. 40 South Street, London. Claydon House, Winslow, Buckinghamshire. United Service, and Travellers'. Eld. s. of Gen. Sir Harry Calvert, Bart., by Caroline, 2nd d. of Thomas Hammersley, Esq., of Pall Mall, London. B. in Grosvenor Place, London 1801; m. 1st, 1835, Eliza, d. of Admiral Sir George Johnstone Hope (she died 1857); 2ndly, 1858, Frances Parthenope, eld. d. of William Edward Nightingale, Esq., of Embley, Hampshire, and Lea Hurst, Derbyshire. Educ. at Harrow, at the Royal Military Coll., and at Cambridge. Assumed the name of Verney in lieu of his patronymic 1827. Entered the army in 1819; retired with the rank of Major unattached 1830. A Dept.-Lieut. of Buckinghamshire. Patron of 5 livings. A Liberal. Sat for Buckingham from Dec. 1832 to June 1841; and for Bedford from Aug. 1847 to July 1852; again for Buckingham from Apr. 1857 to Feb. 1874, when he was unsuccessful; re-elected for Buckingham bor. Apr. 1880 and sat until he retired in 1885. Died 12 Feb. 1894. [1885]

VERNON, Hon. George John Venables. 25 Wilton Crescent, London. S. of Lord Vernon. B. 1803; m. 1824, Isabella Caroline, d. of Cuthbert Ellison, Esq., MP for Newcastle-upon-Tyne. A Reformer, in favour of shortening the duration of Parliaments, of the ballot, if the exercise of undue influence should require it, of a fixed duty on foreign corn, of the immediate abolition of slavery, and inclined to an extension of the currency. Sat for Derbyshire S. for the first time 1831. Defeated in 1835. Succeeded father as 5th Baron Nov. 1835. Dante Scholar. Author. Died 31 May 1866. [1833]

VERNON, Granville Edward Harcourt. 2 Eaton Square, London. Grove Hall, East Retford, Nottinghamshire. White's, and Carlton. Eld. s. of Granville Harcourt Vernon, Esq., (who was MP for Retford from 1832-1847 and was 6th s. of Archbishop Harcourt of York), by Frances Julia, d. of Anthony Hardolph Eyre, Esq., of Grove Park, Nottinghamshire. B. in London 1816; m. 1854, Lady Selina Catherine, only d. of 3rd Earl of Clanwilliam. Educ. at Westminster School, whence he was elected as a student of Christ Church, Oxford; was 2nd class in classics there in 1839, and graduated M.A. 1842. A Magistrate and Dept.-Lieut. of Nottinghamshire, and capt. of the Sherwood Rangers Yeomanry. Was Private Sec. to Earl St. Germans (when Chief Sec. in Ireland) from 1841-Jan. 1845; was afterwards Private Sec. to the Duke of Newcastle (when Chief Commissioner of Woods and Forests), and accompanied him in the same capacity to Ireland, when he became Chief Sec. there in 1846. A 'Liberal-Conservative', opposed to the abolition of the Maynooth Grant, but in favour of increased public grants for the purposes of education, and to a moderate extension of the suffrage; opposed to the ballot and triennial Parliaments. First returned for Newark in July 1852 and sat until he retired 1857. Died 1 Feb. 1861. [1857]

VERNON, Granville Harcourt. 22 Hertford Street, London. Grove, Nottinghamshire. 6th s. of the Archbishop of York, cousin of Lord Vernon, and nephew of Lord Harcourt. B. 1792; m. 1st, 1814, Frances Julia, d. of Anthony Hardolph Eyre, Esq., of Grove, MP for Nottinghamshire; 2ndly, 1845, Pyne Jesse Cotterell, d. of Hon. Green Trevor. Chancellor of the Diocese of York. A Conservative, but in favour of free trade. Sat for E. Retford from 1831 until he retired in 1847. Died 8 Dec. 1879. [1847]

VERNON, Harry Foley. 18 Prince's Gardens, South Kensington, London. Hanbury Hall, Droitwich. Brooks's, and Oxford & Cambridge. S. of Thomas Tayler Vernon, Esq., of Hanbury Hall, Worcestershire, by Jessie Anna Letitia, d. of John Herbert Foley, Esq., of Ridgeway, Pembrokeshire. B. at Hanbury Hall, Worcestershire, 1834; m. 1861, Lady Georgina Sophia, youngest d. of 10th Earl of Haddington, Educ. at Harrow, and at Magdalen Coll., Oxford, where he graduated M.A. 1860. Patron of 2 livings. A Liberal, opposed to the unconditional repeal of church-rates. First elected for Worcestershire E. Dec. 1861 and sat until he retired in 1868. [1867]

VERNON, Leicester Viney. Upton Hall, Northamptonshire. Ardington House, Wantage, Berkshire. Carlton. S. of Major-Gen. Sir Sigismund Smith, K.C.H., of the Royal Artillery, and bro. of Sir J. Mark F. Smith, MP for Chatham. B. at Perth 1798; m. 1825, d. of William Douglas, Esq., of Teddington House. Educ. at the Royal Military Academy, and at the University of Göttingen. Assumed the name of Vernon on inheriting the estates of Robert Vernon, Esq., the well-known collector of the 'Vernon Gallery.' A Capt. in the Royal Engineers; retired on half-pay.

Was Assistant Deputy Quartermaster-Gen. in Ireland from 1842 until 1849. Patron of 1 living. A 'progressive Conservative', in favour of advancing when in the right direction, and of progress when it can be proved for the benefit of the community, in favour of the extension of the franchise on 'constitutional bases,' and of relieving dissenters from Church rates if the maintenance of Churches can be provided for. Sat for Chatham from June 1853 until Apr. 1857, when he was unsuccessful candidate for Berkshire. First elected for Berkshire May 1859. MP until his death 14 Apr. 1860. [1860]

VESEY, Hon. Thomas. 78 Pall Mall, London. Abbey Leix, Queen's Co. White's, Travellers', and Carlton. Eld. s. of Visct. de Vesci. B. 1803; m. 1839, d. of 11th Earl of Pembroke. Obtained mathematical honours at Oxford in 1825. A Dept.-Lieut. of Queen's Co. A Conservative, voted for agricultural protection, 1846. Sat for Queen's co. from 1835 till 1837; re-elected in 1841 and sat until he retired in 1852. Succeeded as 3rd Visct. Oct. 1855. Later a representative Peer for Ireland. Died 23 Dec. 1875. [1852]

VICKERS, Stanley. Victoria Street, London. The Temple, Goring, Oxfordshire. Junior Carlton, and City Carlton. Youngest surviving s. of John Vickers, Esq., of Westminster and Streatham. B. at Blandford Square, London, 1837; m. 1865, Mary Ianthe, eld. d. of William Dunbar, Esq., of London and Aberdeen. Educ. at King's Coll. School, London. A Partner in the firm of Messrs. Joseph & John Vickers, Distillers, Victoria Street, Westminster. A Conservative, was in favour of the equalization of the poor-rates and in the reduction of duty on fire insurance; voted against the disestablishment of the Irish Church 1869. Sat for Wallingford from Dec. 1868. MP until his death 24 Feb. 1872. [1871]

VIGORS, Nicholas Aylward. 16 Chester Terrace, Regent's Park, London. Old Leighlin, Carlow. Reform. A Magistrate and Dept.-Lieut. of Carlow Co. A Liberal, in favour of the Repeal of the Union with Ireland. First elected for Carlow bor. Dec. 1832 and sat until defeated in Jan. 1835. Elected for Carlow Co. in 1837 on the death of Thomas Kavanagh, Esq., the previous member. Had formerly been returned for the county in 1835, but unseated on petition. MP until his death in 1840. [1840]

VILLIERS, Rt. Hon. Charles Pelham. 50 Cadogan Place, London. Brooks's, Athenauem, Travellers', and Reform. 3rd s. of the Hon. George Villiers (s. of the 1st Earl of Clarendon) by the only d. of 1st Lord Boningdon. B. 1802.

391

Graduated at Cambridge M.A. 1827; was called to the bar at Lincoln's Inn 1827; was one of the Examiners of Witnesses in the Court of Chancery from 1833-Dec. 1852, Judge Advocate General from the last date until Mar. 1858, and Pres. of the Poor Law Board from July 1859-July 1866. Was also one of the Commissioners of Inquiry into the operation of the Poor Laws. A.B.L. for Hertford. A Liberal Unionist, well known before 1846 for his frequent motions against the corn laws. Sat for Wolverhampton from 1835-47; was returned for that borough at the general election of the latter year and was at the same time chosen for Lancashire S. where he made his election to sit for Wolverhampton, and in that town his statue was erected, 1879. Both in age and continuous length of service he was the father of the House of Commons. MP for Wolverhampton until his death 16 Jan. 1898. [1897]

VILLIERS, Hon. Francis John Robert. 38 Berkeley Square, London. Carlton, White's, and Coventry. 4th s. of 5th Earl of Jersey, by eld. d. of 10th Earl of Westmoreland. B. in London 1819. Unmarried. Educ. at Eton and then entered the army in 1837. Became a Capt. in 1843 and retired in 1847. Was Aide-de-Camp in Canada in 1839, in Ceylon in 1841, and was Military Sec. at Madras in 1842. Appointed Dept.-Lieut. of Kent 1853. A Conservative, and represented Rochester from July 1852 until he accepted Chiltern Hundreds in Jan. 1856. Died 8 May 1862. [1855]

VILLIERS, Frederick. A Liberal. First elected for Canterbury 10 Jan. 1835, polling 2 more votes than an opponent S.R. Lushington, Esq.; but on petition Mr. Lushington seated *vice* Mr. Villiers who was unduly elected.

VILLIERS, Frederick Meynell. St. James's Place, London. Descended from an ancient family in Derbyshire. B. 1805. A Reformer. Sat for Saltash in 1829. Was returned for Canterbury in 1835, but unseated on petition. First returned for Sudbury in 1841, but shortly afterwards, on petition the election was declared void for bribery and a new writ suspended. The borough was disfranchised by Act of Parliament in 1844. [1843]

VILLIERS, Hon. Frederick William Child. 5 Mount Street, London. Sulby Hall, Welford, Northamptonshire. Carlton. 3rd s. of the 5th Earl of Jersey, by the eld. d. of 10th Earl of Westmoreland. B. 1815; m. 1842, d. of the 8th Earl of Athlone. Entered the army as Lieut. in 1832; became a Capt. in 1838, but retired on half pay in 1844. Appointed Dept.-Lieut. of Northamptonshire 1848. A Conservative. Unsuccessfully contested Weymouth at the general elction in

1847; but was returned there without opposition in Dec. 1847 and sat until he retired in 1852. Died 23 May 1871. [1852]

VILLIERS, Visct. 33 Charles Street, Berkeley Square, London. Carlton. Eld. s. of the Earl of Jersey. B. in Berkeley Square, London 1808; m. 1841, eld. d. of the Rt. Hon. Sir Robert Peel, Bart. A Dept.-Lieut. of Oxfordshire. A Conservative, but in favour of free trade. Sat for Rochester in 1830, for Minehead in 1831, and for Honiton from 1832 to 1835; unsuccessfully contested Weymouth in the latter year; was returned for that borough in 1841, but unseated on petition; first elected for Cirencester in 1844, when Mr. Master accepted the Chiltern Hundreds, and sat until defeated in 1852. Succeeded as 6th Earl 3 Oct. 1859. Died 24 Oct. 1859. [1852]

VILLIERS-STUART, Hon. Henry. See STUART, Hon. Henry Villiers-.

VINCENT, Sir Francis, Bart. 8 Stratton Street, London. Debden Hall, Saffron Walden. B. 1803; m. 1824, Augusta Elizabeth, only child of the Hon. Charles Herbert, R.N., and grand-d. of the 1st Earl of Carnarvon. A Reformer, in favour of the ballot, and the immediate abolition of slavery. First sat for St. Albans in 1831. Sat until he retired in 1835. Author. Died 6 July 1880. [1833]

VIVIAN, Arthur Pendarves. 26 James Street, Buckingham Gate, London. Glanafon, Tailbach, South Wales. Bosahan, Helston, Cornwall. Brooks's. 3rd s. of John Henry Vivian, Esq., of Singleton, near Swansea (many years member for Swansea), and bro. to the 1st Baron Vivian, by Sarah, eld. d. of Arthur Jones, of the Priory, Reigate. B. in London, 1834; m. 1st, 1867, Lady Augusta Emily, d. of the 3rd Earl of Dunraven (she died 1877); 2ndly, 1880, Lady Jane Georgina, eld. d. of 10th Earl of Stair. Educ. at Eton, at the Mining Academy of Freiberg, and at Trinity Coll., Cambridge. A Dept.-Lieut. and Magistrate for the county of Glamorgan, also Col. 1st administrative battalion of the Glamorgan Rifle Volunteers. A Deputy Warden of the Stannaries of Devon and Cornwall, and a Magistrate for the county of Cornwall. A Liberal, in favour of the establishment of County Financial Boards, and of amendment in the Licensing Acts. Sat for West Cornwall from Dec. 1868 until defeated 1885. [1885]

VIVIAN, Hon. Charles Crespigny. S. of Sir Hussey Vivian, Bart. M. Miss Scott, niece to the Earl of Meath. A Major in the army. A Reformer. Contested Bodmin unsuccessfully in 1832. Was elected there in 1835 and sat until he succeeded as 2nd Baron Aug. 1842. Died 24 Apr. 1886. [1842]

VIVIAN, Sir H.H. Continued in House after 1885: full entry in Volume II.

VIVIAN, Hon. John Cranch Walker. The Park, Truro. White's. and Arthur's. 2nd s. of 1st Lord Vivian, by his 1st wife, Eliza, d. of Philip Champion de Crespiguy, Esq., B. 1818; m. 1st, 1840, Louisa, only d. of Henry Woodgate, Esq. (she died 1855); 2ndly, 1861, Florence, d. of Maj. Rowley, of whom m. he obtained a dissolution 1869. Educ. at Eton. Entered the army in 1836, and became a Capt. in 11th Hussars; retired in 1843. Appointed a Lord of the Treasury Dec. 1868 (salary £1,000). A Liberal. Sat for Penryn from July 1841-July 1847; for Bodmin from Apr. 1857-May 1859, when he was an unsuccessful candidate for Truro; elected for Truro July 1865 and sat until appointed Permanent Under-Sec. at War Aug. 1871-1878. Died 22 Jan. 1879. [1871]

VIVIAN, John Ennis. 41 Dover Street, London. Truro and Tregavethan, Cornwall. Was called to the bar at the Middle Temple June 1819. A Magistrate for Cornwall and a Special Dept.-Warden for the Stannaries of Devon and Cornwall. A Conservative, opposed to the endowment of the Roman Catholic Clergy. Sat for Truro from 1835, having contested the borough unsuccessfully 1832. MP until he retired 1857. Died 24 May 1870. [1857]

VIVIAN, John Henry, F.R.S., F.G.S. 104 Eaton Square, London. Singleton, Nr. Swansea. Athenaeum, and Reform. B. 1785, the 2nd s. of John Vivian of Truro, by the d. of Rev. Richard Cranch, bro. of 1st Lord Vivian. M. 1816, Sarah, eld. d. of Arthur Jones, of the Priory, Reigate. A Magistrate and Dept.-Lieut. of Glamorganshire, of which he was High Sheriff 1827. A Liberal, voted for the ballot 1853. Sat for Swansea from 1832 until his death on 10 Feb. 1855. [1854]

VIVIAN, Rt. Hon. Sir Richard Hussey, Bart., G.C.B., G.C.H. 87, Pall Mall, London. Truro, Cornwall. United Service, and Reform. B. 1775; m. 1st, 1804, Eliza, d. of Philip Champion de Crespiguy, Esq.; 2ndly, 1833, Letitia, 3rd d. of Rev. James Agnew Webster. A Lieut.-Gen. in the army, Master Gen. of the Ordnance, Col. of the 1st (or Royal) Dragoons. Was at Waterloo. Formerly professed himself a Whig, but understood to be in favour of the ballot. Sat for Truro 1820-26, and for Windsor 1826-31 when he accepted Chiltern Hundreds to make room for Lord Stanley who failed in his contest for Preston. Sat for Truro 1832-35, and for Cornwall E. from

1837 until he retired 1841. [1838]

VYNER, Reginald Arthur. 10 Portland Place, London. Newby Hall, Ripon, Yorkshire. 2nd s. of Henry Vyner, Esq., of Newby Hall, near Ripon, by Lady Mary Gertrude, 2nd d. of 1st Earl De Grey. B. in London 1839. Educ. at Eton. Was formerly a clerk in the Foreign Office. Appointed Cornet York Yeomanry Cavalry 1861. A Liberal, said he would give a general support to Lord Palmerston's Goverment; in favour of non-intervention in foreign politics. First elected for Ripon Dec. 1860 and sat until he retired 1865. Died 28 Sept. 1870. [1865]

VYSE, Col. Richard Henry Richard Howard. Stoke Place, Slough. Carlton, and White's. 2nd s. of Maj.-Gen. Howard Vyse, of Stoke Place, Slough, by the d. of Henry Hesketh, Esq., of Newton, Cheshire. B. at Stoke Place 1813; m. 1856, Julia Agnes, 3rd d. of Sir William Hylton Jolliffe, Bart. (she died Dec. 1862). Educ. at Eton. Entered the army as Cornet 1830; became Maj. Royal Horse Guards and Lieut.-Col. in the army 1854; and subsequently full Col. Patron of 2 livings. A Conservative, voted for inquiry into Maynooth 1853. Sat for Northamptonshire S. from Feb. 1846-Apr. 1857; elected for Windsor Oct. 1863. Defeated 1865. Died 12 June 1872. [1865]

VYVYAN, Sir Richard Rawlinson, Bart. St. Dunstan's Villa, Regent's Park, London. Trelowarren, Cornwall. Carlton, and Athenaeum. Eld. s. of Sir Vyell Vyvyan, Bart., by the only d. of Thomas H. Rawlinson, Esq., of Hutton, Lancaster. B. at Trelowarren 1800. Educ. at Harrow School. High Sheriff of Cornwall 1840-41. Patron of 2 livings. A Dept.-Lieut. of Cornwall. Author of a pamphlet *On Solitary Confinement*. A Conservative. Sat for Bristol from 1825-1830, and from 1832-1837; sat for Oakhampton in 1831. First returned for Helstone 1841 and sat until he retired 1857. Died 15 Aug. 1879. [1857]

WADDINGTON, David. Adelaide House, Enfield, Middlesex. Carlton. A Merchant of Manchester, largely concerned in Railway Undertakings. Was Chairman of the Eastern Counties Railway, and previously held a similar position on the Manchester and Birmingham line. Director of the Mercantile Life Assurance Company. Appointed Dept.-Lieut. of Middlesex June 1852. A Conservative, voted for inquiry into Maynooth 1853. Sat for Maldon from 1847-July 1852, when he was elected for Harwich and sat until he retired 1857. [1857]

WADDINGTON, Harry Spencer. 45 St. James's Place, London. Cavenham Hall, Suffolk. Carlton, Boodle's and Arthur's. Half-bro. of Spencer Horsey de Horsey, Esq., who sat for Newcastle-under-Lyme from 1837 till 1841, and uncle-in-law of Mr. Milnes, MP fo Pontefract. M. Mary Anne, d. of Rich. S. Milnes, Esq., of Fryston Hall. A Conservative. Sat for Suffolk W. from 1838, having been an unsuccessful candidate there in 1832. MP until he retired in 1859. Died 26 Feb. 1864. [1858]

WADDY, Cadwallader. Sat for Wexford Co. from the by-election of June 1834. Retired Jan. 1835.

WADDY, S.D. Continued in House after 1885: full entry in Volume II.

WAIT, William Killigrew. Clifton, Bristol. Carlton. Eld. s. of William Killigrew Wait, Esq., Merchant of Bristol, by Frances, d. of the Rev. Newman Newman, of Thornbury Park, Gloucestershire. B. at Redland, Gloucestershire 1826; m. 1857, Elizabeth, d. of John Perrin, Esq., of Wicklow, Ireland. A Merchant of Bristol. A Magistrate for Bristol, of which city he was chosen Mayor in 1869. A Conservative, in favour of the extension of household suffrage to counties. Sat for Gloucester from May 1873 until defeated 1880. Contested Gloucester again 24 Nov. 1885. [1880]

WAITHMAN, Robert. A Whig. Returned for the City of London in 1832. MP until his death in Jan. 1833. [1833]

WAKLEY, Thomas. 1 Bedford Street, London. Reform. S. of Henry Wakley, Esq., of Membury, Devonshire. B. 1795; m. 1820, youngest d. of Joseph Goodchild, Esq. A Surgeon. First became known to the public as Editor of the *Lancet*. One of the Coroners for the county of Middlesex. A radical Reformer, contested Finsbury unsuccessfully in 1832; also in 1834, on the departure of Sir R. Grant for Bombay. Was returned for Finsbury in 1835, and sat for it from that date until he retired in 1852. Died 16 May 1862. [1852]

WALCOTT, John Edward. Winkton Lodge, Christchurch, Hampshire. Woodland Villa, Bath. United Service. 3rd s. of Edward Walcott Sympson, Esq., of Winkton House, near Christchurch, by Catherine Anne, d. of John Lyons, Esq., of Antigua. B. at Winkton House, 1790; m. 1819, Charlotte Annie, d. of Col. John Nelley, of the Bengal Horse Artillery (she died Mar. 1863). Educ. at Hyde Abbey School, Winchester. Entered the navy in 1803, and became Capt. in 1822; served with distinction under Sir Samuel Hood and other commanders; especially distinguished himself when Capt. of the 'Tyne' frigate, by cutting out with the boats of that ship and the 'Thracian', a formidable piratical schooner from the harbour of Mata, island of Cuba; became a Rear-Admiral on the reserved list 1852. A Dept.-Lieut. and Magistrate for Hampshire. A Conservative. First returned for Christchurch in July 1852 and sat until he retired in 1868. Died 27 July 1868. [1867]

WALDEGRAVE-LESLIE, Hon. George, F.R.S. 4 Harley Street, London. Leslie House, Leslie, Co. Fife. Athenaeum and Travellers'. 3rd s. of the 8th Earl Waldegrave, by Elizabeth, eld. d. of Samuel Whitbread, Esq., and Lady Elizabeth Whitbread. B. at Harptree Court, Chewton Waldegrave, 1825; m. 1861, the Countess of Rothes. Called to the bar at the Middle Temple 1849. Served on the staff of the Earl of Elgin when Governor-General of Canada 1851. Served under the Marq. of Dalhousie when Governor- General of India in 1854; was Official Secretary to the Speaker from 1855 to 1861; appointed Secretary to Visct. Stratford de Redcliffe's special Embassy to Constantinople in 1858; was Private Secretary to Sir George Grey at the Home Office in 1863-4. Appointed a Dept.-Lieut. of Fife and Capt. of the 6th Fife (Leslie) Volunteers in 1861. A Liberal. First elected for Hastings, Oct. 1864. Retired in 1868. [1867]

WALDRON, Laurence. 38 Rutland Square, West Dublin. Ballybrack, Dalkey, Co. Dublin. Helen Park, Killenaule, Co. Tipperary. Reform. Only surviving s. of Patrick Waldron, Esq., Linen Merchant and Calico Printer, Dublin, by Mary, d. of John Shinnor, Esq., of Doneraile, Co. Cork. B. in Dublin 1811; m. 1842, Anne, only d. of Francis White, Esq., M.D., Inspector General of Prisons and Lunatic Asylums in Ireland. Educ. at Clongowes Wood Coll., Ireland. Called to the bar in Ireland 1840, ceased to practise in 1842. High Sheriff of Lough 1860. A Magistrate for Tipperary and the Co. of Dublin, and a Dept.-Lieut. of the former. A Liberal, supported the vote of censure on Lord Palmerston 1864; 'as a sincere Catholic' looked upon 'the Church Establishment as the monster grievance of Ireland'; in favour of the ballot and a 'tenant--right bill which shall secure to the occupier the value of his improvements.' Unsuccessfully contested Tipperary Feb. 1857; first elected there Apr. following and sat until he retired 1865. Contested same seat in Oct. 1866. Died 3 Apr. 1875. [1865]

WALKER, Charles Arthur. Belmont, Co. Wexford. Reform. A Dept.-Lieut. of Co. Wexford. In favour of the ballot and of poor laws in Ireland, and said that 'if Parliament attempts to perpetuate injustice in Ireland' he would vote for a repeal of the Union. First sat for Wexford in 1831. Sat until he retired 1841. Died 29 Oct. 1873. [1838]

WALKER, Col. George Gustavus. Crawfordton, Dumfries. Conservative. B. at Relton Mains, Dumfriesshire 1831, the s. of John Walker, Esq., of Crawfordton, by Jessy, his wife. M. 1856, Anne Marray, only d. of Admiral George C. Lennock, of Brounriff, Dumfriesshire. Educ. at Rugby and at Balliol Coll., Oxford. Was a Major, Scottish Borderers Militia, and Hon. Inspector of Musketry for Volunteers. A Magistrate for the Stewartry of Kirkcudbright. Patron of 1 living. A moderate Conservative and gave general support to the Conservative Party. Sat for Dumfriesshire from July 1865-Dec. 1868, and Mar. 1869-1874, when he retired. Died 5 Aug. 1897. [1873]

WALKER, Sir James Robert. 59 Chester Square, London. Sand Hutton, York. Carlton, and Conservative. Eld. s. of James Walker, Esq., of Sand Hutton, near York, by Mary, d. of Robert Denison, Esq., of Kilnwick Percy, near York. B. at Sand Hutton 1829; m. 1863, Louisa Heron, 3rd d. of Sir John Heron Maxwell, Bart., of Sprinkell, Dumfriesshire. Educ. at Rugby, and became afterwards a Gentleman Commoner of Christ Church, Oxford, where he graduated 1851. A Conservative. Unsuccessfully contested Beverley Apr. 1859; first elected for Beverley Jan. 1860 and sat until he retired 1865. Succeeded as 2nd Bart. in Oct. 1888. Died 12 June 1899. [1865]

WALKER, Col. Oliver Ormerod. Chesham, Bury, Lancashire. Carlton, and Junior Carlton. S. of Oliver Ormerod Walker, Esq., of Chesham Hall, Bury, Lancashire (a Dept.-Lieut. and Magistrate of that Co.), by Helen Elizabeth, youngest d. of Thomas Jay Garston, Esq., of Chester. B. at Bury 1833; m. 1860, Jane, eld. d. of Thomas Hamson, Esq. Educ. at Tonbridge School. A Magistrate and Dept.-Lieut. of Lancashire, of which Co. he was High Sheriff in 1876. Capt. 7th Lancashire Militia and Lieut.-Col. of the Lancashire Rifle Volunteers. A Conservative, but in favour of civil and religious liberty, also of the maintenance of the union of Church and State. Sat for Salford from Apr. 1877. Defeated 1880. Died 30 May 1914. [1880]

WALKER, Richard. Wood Hill, Lancashire.

Bolton Street, Bury, Lancashire. Reform, and Wyndham. S. of William Walker, Esq., a Merchant at Bury. B. 1784; m. 1812, Anne, 2nd d. of John Scholes, Esq., Bury. An eminent Iron-founder. A radical Reformer. In favour of the ballot, the repeal of the Septennial Act, and Church reform. Sat for Bury from 1832 until he retired in 1852. Died 1 Feb. 1855. [1852]

WALKER, Rt. Hon. Samuel. 2 Rutland Square, Dublin. Stephen's Green Club, Dublin. Reform, and National Liberal. S. of Capt. Alexander Walker, by Elizabeth, d. of T. Elliott, Esq. B. in Co. of Westmeath 1832; m. 1st, 1855, Cecilia, d. of Arthur Greene, Esq.; 2ndly, 1881, Eleanor, d. of Rev. A. MacLaughlin. Educ. at Portarlington School, and at Trinity Coll., Dublin. Was called to the bar in Ireland 1855. Appointed a Queen's Counsel 1872. Solicitor-Gen. for Ireland Dec. 1883. A Liberal. Sat for Londonderry Co. from Jan. 1884. Defeated in 1885 contesting the North division of the county. Contested the South division of the county in July 1892. [1885]

WALKER, Thomas Eades. 13 Thistle Grove, London. Studley Castle, Warwick. Carlton. S. of Thomas Walker, Esq., of Berkswell Hall, Warwickshire, by Ruth, d. of John Eades, Esq., of the Delph, Staffordshire. B. 1843; m. 1874, Elizabeth Sydney, 2nd d. of Henry Allsopp, Esq., of Hindlip Hall, Worcestershire. Educ. at Harrow, and at Christ Church, Oxford. A Magistrate for Warwickshire. A Conservative, said he would heartily oppose any attempt to weaken the existing connection between Church and State; in favour of a reduction of the duty on malt. Contested Wednesbury Nov. 1868. Sat for Worcestershire E. from Feb. 1874 until he retired 1880. [1880]

WALL, Charles Baring. 44 Berkeley Square, London. Norman Court, Hampshire. Carlton. B. 1795, the s. of Charles Wall, Esq., by Harriet, d. of Sir Francis Baring, 1st Bart. Patron of 2 livings. A Magistrate of Hampshire and appointed Dept.-Lieut. there 1846. A Liberal. Sat for Guildford from Feb. 1819-26, for Wareham from 1826-30, for Guildford again in 1830, for Weymouth in 1831, from 1832-47 for Guildford, and for Salisbury from 1847 until his death in Oct. 1853. [1853]

WALLACE, Sir Richard, Bart., K.C.B. Hertford House, Manchester Square, London. Antrim Castle, Antrim, Ireland. Carlton. B. in London 1818; m. Mlle. Julie Amelie Charlotte Castelnau, d. of an officer in the French army. A

Trustee of the National Portrait Gallery. A Magistrate for the Cos. of Down and Antrim, and a Dept.-Lieut. of the latter. A decided Conservative. Sat for Lisburn from Feb. 1873 until he accepted Chiltern Hundreds Nov. 1884. Died 20 July 1890. [1884]

WALLACE, Robert. Kelly, Ayrshire. Reform. A descendant of Sir William Wallace and s. of John Wallace, Esq. M. Margaret, 2nd d. of Sir William Forbes, Bart., of Craigievar and maternal grand-d. of Robert, 12th Lord Sempill. A West India Proprietor. A radical Reformer, voted against the Corn Laws. With regard to the Church of Scotland, thought that each communicant should have a vote in the election of his Minister. Declined to qualify under a new Commission of the Peace for Ayrshire in 1836, because he though that Magistrates should be appointed by the Crown and not by the Lords Lieut. Sat for the borough of Greenock from 1832 until he accepted Chiltern Hundreds in 1845. Died Mar. 1855. [1844]

WALLACE, Thomas. 33 Haymarket, London. A King's counsel, practised at the Irish bar, formerly a Reporter. A Reformer, 'in favour of the extinction of the tithe system, an efficient reform in the Church and the grand jury laws; the making a reasonable and safe provision for the poor, and the adoption of a fair and impartial system of government towards Ireland. Should not measures to the effect of these be adopted by the reformed Parliament, after a fair trial, he will advocate a repeal of the Union.' Sat for Drogheda in the Parliament of 1831. Sat for Carlow Co. from 1832. Retired in 1835. [1833]

WALMSLEY, Sir Joshua. 101 Westbourne Terrace, Hyde Park, London. Snibston, Leicestershire. Liverpool. Reform. S. of John Walmsley, Esq., Marble Mason, by Elizabeth, d. of — Perry, Esq. B. at Liverpool 1794; m.1815, Adeline, d. of Hugh Mulleneux, Esq., of Liverpool. Educ. at Holt Hill, Lancashire. Was formerly a Corn Merchant at Liverpool. A Magistrate for that bor. and for Lancashire. Was Mayor of Liverpool in 1839-40. Patron of 1 living. A Liberal, in favour of extension of the suffrage, vote by ballot, the abolition of property qualification, triennial Parliaments, separation of Church and State, and national education by voluntary means; opposed to all religious endowments. Unsuccessfully contested Liverpool in 1841. Sat for Leicester from July 1847-Aug. 1848, when he was unseated on petition. Sat for Bolton from Jan. 1849-July 1852, when he was returned for Leicester and sat until defeated 1857. Died 17 Nov. 1871. [1857]

WALPOLE, Hon. Frederick. 22 Green Street, Grosvenor Square, London. Rainthorpe, Long Stratton, Norfolk. Carlton, Athenaeum, and Travellers'. 3rd s. of 3rd Earl of Orford, by Mary, eld. d. of William Augustus Fawkener, Esq. B. 1822; m. 1852, Laura Sophia Frances, only d. of Francis Walpole, Esq. Appointed Lieut. R.N. 1845; Major West Norfolk Militia 1859. Author of *Five Years in the Pacific*. A Conservative, and a strong supporter of 'constitutional principles.' Contested Lynn Regis 1st July 1865. Sat for N. Norfolk from Dec. 1868. MP until his death 1 Apr. 1876. [1875]

WALPOLE, Lord. 21 St. James's Street, London. Wolterton Park, Norfolk. Eld. s. of the Earl of Orford. B. 1813. A Conservative. Sat for Norfolk E. from 1835. Retired in 1837. Succeeded as 4th Earl of Orford Dec. 1858. Died 7 Dec. 1894. [1837]

WALPOLE, Rt. Hon. Spencer Horatio. 109 Eaton Square, London. Ealing, Middlesex. Carlton, United University, and Oxford & Cambridge. 2nd s. of Thomas Walpole, Esq., of Stagbury, Surrey and Lady Margaret, youngest d. of 2nd Earl of Egmont. B. 1806; m. 1835, Isabella, 4th d. of Rt. Hon. Spencer Perceval. Educ. at Eton and Trinity Coll., Cambridge, where he obtained the first English declamation prize, and the prize for the best essay on the character and conduct of William III. Called to the bar in 1831 by the Society of Lincoln's Inn, of which he was a bencher; became Queen's Counsel 1846. Was Sec. of State for the Home Dept. from Mar.-Dec. 1852 and from Mar. 1858-Feb. 1859, when he relinquished the office in consequence of his dissatisfaction with the government Reform Bill of that year. Was Church Estates Commissioner from 1856-58 and from Dec. 1862-July 1866 and was a third time Sec. of State for the Home Dept. from the last date until May 1867. A Conservative, he said he would support the great principle of conservative progress and 'the wise application of principle to all our institutions, whether political, academical, of religious'. Sat for Midhurst from 1846-Feb. 1856, and from that date for Cambridge Univ. until he accepted Chiltern Hundreds Nov. 1882. Died 22 May 1898. [1882]

WALROND, Sir John Walrond. Bradfield, Collumpton, Devon. S. of B.B. Dickinson, Esq., of Knightshayes, Tiverton (who assumed the name of Walrond by letters patent in 1845), by Frances,

d. and co-heir of W.H. Walrond, Esq., of Bradfield, Collumpton. B. at Tiverton, 1818, m. 1845, Hon. Frances Caroline, youngest d. of 2nd Baron Bridport. A Magistrate for Somerset and Devon, and a Dept.-Lieut. for the latter. A Liberal-Conservative, and a supporter of Lord Derby. Contested Devonshire N. 21 Nov. 1868. First elected for Tiverton, July 1865. Retired in 1868; contested same seat in 1872; 1874 and 1880. Died 23 Apr. 1889. [1867]

WALROND, Sir W.H. Continued in House after 1885: full entry in Volume II.

WALSH, Hon. Arthur. 28 Berkeley Square, London. Warfield Park, Bracknell, Berkshire. Newcastle Court, Kington, Herefordshire. White's, and Carlton. Eld. s. of the 1st Baron Ormathwaite, by Lady Jane, 3rd d. of the 6th Earl of Stamford and Warrington. B. in Berkeley Square 1827; m. 1858, Lady Katherine Emily, d. of 7th Duke of Beaufort. Educ. at Eton and at Trinity Hall, Cambridge. Entered the 1st Life Guards 1847, became Capt. 1852, retired 1855. Appointed Lord-Lieut. and Custos rot. of Radnorshire 1875. Col. of the South Wales Borderers Militia. A moderate Conservative, voted against the disestablishment of the Irish Church 1869. Sat for Leominster from July 1865-Apr. 1868, when he was elected for Radnorshire and sat until he retired 1880. Succeeded as 2nd Baron Ormathwaite Feb. 1881. [1880]

WALSH, Sir John Benn, Bart. 28 Berkeley Square, London. Knill Court, Kington, Herefordshire. Warfield Park, Bracknell, Berkshire. Carlton, Conservative, Travellers', Boodle's, and United University. B. at Warfield Park, 1798, s. of Sir John Benn Walsh, by the d. of Joseph Fowke, of Bexley, Kent. M. 1825, Lady Jane, youngest d. of 6th Earl of Stamford and Warrington. Lord-Lieut. of Radnorshire, and Dept.-Lieut. of Berkshire. A Liberal-Conservative. Contested Poole July 1837. Sat for Sudbury 1830-34 and Mar. 1839-June 1840, when he was returned for Radnorshire. Sat until created Baron Ormathwaite, Apr. 1868. Died 3 Feb. 1881. [1867]

WALSH, Rt. Hon. John Edward, LL.D. 14 Merrion Square South, Dublin. B. at Tolka, Co. Dublin 1816, the s. of Rev. Robert Walsh, LL.D. (Vicar of Finglas, and author of several works on the East, history of Dublin, etc.), by Anne Eliza, d. of John Bayly. M. 1841, Blair Belinda, d. of Gordon Macneill, Esq. Educ. at Trinity Coll., Dublin, where he obtained a scholarship and a First Moderatorship at graduation. Called to the bar in Ireland 1839, and made a Queen's Counsel

there 1857. Author of *The Irish Justice of the Peace, Report of Cases in Chancery, Ireland Sixty Years Ago,* etc. A Conservative. Sat for the University of Dublin from July 1866 until appointed Master of Rolls in Ireland Oct. 1866. Prior to this appointment he was Attorney Gen. for Ireland from June 1866. Died 20 Oct. 1869. [1867]

WALTER, John (I). A Conservative. First elected for Nottingham 26 Apr. 1841, but defeated in June of the same year. He again sat for Nottingham on 4 Aug. 1842, but the election was later declared void. Died 1847.

WALTER, John. (II). 40 Upper Grosvenor Street, London. Bearwood, Wokingham, Berkshire. Eld. s. of John Walter, Esq., of Bearwood, Berkshire, by his 2nd wife, d. of Henry Smithe, Esq., of Eastling, Kent. B. in London, 1818; m. 1st, 1842, Emily Frances, eld. d. of Major Henry Court, Esq., of Castlemans, Berkshire (she died 1858); 2ndly, 1861, Flora, 3rd d. of James Monro Macnabb, Esq., of Highfield Park, Hampshire. Was educ. at Eton; took honours at Exeter Coll., Oxford, where he graduated B.A. 1840, M.A. 1843. Was called to the bar (Lincoln's Inn) 1847. Patron of 4 livings. A Dept.-Lieut. of London and of Berkshire. John Walter's political position was based upon his ownership of the *The Times* which he inherited from his father. A Liberal. Contested Southwark Jan. 1840 and Nottingham unsuccessfully in 1843. Sat for Nottingham from Apr. 1847 till May 1859, and for Berkshire from the last date till July 1865, when he was unsuccessful; re-elected for Berkshire Dec. 1868, and retained his seat until he retired in 1885. Died 3 Nov. 1894. [1885]

WALTERS, R. A Liberal. Contested Gateshead July 1852 and Sunderland Mar. 1857. Returned for Beverley in 1859, but was shortly afterwards unseated on petition. Died 1865.

WARBURTON, George Drought. Henley, Frant, Sussex. Junior United Service. B. in Wicklow 1816, the 3rd s. of George Warburton of Aughrim, Galway, and Southfield, Somerset, by Anna, d. of Thomas Acton, of Westaston, Co. Wicklow, and sister of Col. Acton, some years MP for Wicklow. Younger bro. of Eliot Warburton. M. 1853, Hon. Elizabeth Augusta, d. of 1st Lord Bateman. Educ. at the Royal Military College, Woolwich. Entered the Royal Artillery June 1833, and retired as Major on full pay Nov. 1854. Author of *Hochelaga, The Conquest of Canada,* etc. Knight of the 1st class of San Fernando in Spain. A Liberal, in favour of extending the franchise, but opposed to the endowment of Maynooth. Supported measures which removed 'all just complaint from the Church of England', but, 'averse to the application of public funds to doctrinal instruction.' Unsuccessfully contested Harwich July 1852, but was elected in Apr 1857. Sat until he died 23 Oct. 1857. [1857 2nd ed.]

WARBURTON, Henry, F.R.S. 45 Dadogan Place, London. Athenaeum, and Reform. S. of John Warburton, Esq., and nephew of J. Warburton, Esq. Was once a Baltic Merchant; Proprietor of a private lunatic asylum at Hackney. Graduated at Trinity Coll., Cambridge, where he was 10th Wrangler in 1806, and took his master's degree in 1812. A radical Reformer, an advocate for perfect freedom of trade, 'desirous of following up principles as far at they will go.' A Member of the Free Trade Club. Was Chairman of the Medical Reform Committee, and took a prominent part in all debates relating to the medical profession and the universities. Was an active opponent of the Copyright Act. Represented Bridport from 1826 to 1841; was returned at the general election in 1841, but accepted the Chiltern Hundreds in the month of September, to make room for his opponent, who had presented a petition on the ground of bribery. Sat for Kendal from Dec. 1843. Retired in 1847. Died 16 Sept. 1858. [1847]

WARBURTON, Piers Egerton-. The Dene, Northwich, Cheshire. Carlton. Only s. of Rowland Eyles Egerton-Warburton, Esq., of Warburton and Arley, Cheshire (who assumed the additional surname of Warburton on inheriting the estates of his great-uncle in 1813), by Mary, eld. d. of Sir Richard Brooke of Norton Priory, Cheshire. B. at Chester 1839; m. 1880, Hon. Antoinette Elizabeth, 3rd d. of the 3rd Lord De Saumarez. Was educ. at Eton and at Christ Church, Oxford; graduated B.A. A Conservative. Sat for Mid. Cheshire from July 1876 until he retired in 1885. [1885]

WARD, Sir Henry George. Gilston Park, Hertfordshire. Admiralty, London. Athenaeum, and Reform. The only s. of Robert Plumer Ward, Esq., author of *The History of the Law of Nations, Tremaine, De Vere,* etc., who was at various periods Lord of the Admiralty, Clerk of the Ordance and Auditor of the Civil List. M. 1824, Emily, the 2nd d. of Sir John Swinburne, Bart. Was Minister Plenipotentiary for acknowledging the Mexican Republic. Appointed Sec. to the Admiralty July 1846. Proprietor of the *Weekly Chronicle* Newspaper and took an active share in Railway enterprise. A Liberal. In 1835 he avowed himself in favour of the ballot, triennial Parliaments and household suffrage. He distinguished himself in 1834 by a motion on the Irish Church, which was

the proximate cause of the new organisation of the government that ensued. Sat for St. Alban's from 1832-37, after which he sat for Sheffield until May 1849, when he was appointed Lord High Commissioner of the Ionian Islands. This office he held until Mar. 1855, when he became Governor of Ceylon, and in 1860 he became Governor of Madras, which he remained until his death 2 Aug. 1860. [1848]

WARD, Michael Francis. 436 Camden Road, London. 52 Mountjoy Square South, Dublin. S. of Timothy Ward, Esq., Merchant of Galway, by Catherine, d. of John Lynch, Esq., of Galway. B. 1845. Educ. at the Coll. of St. Ignatius, and at Queen's Coll., Galway, where he matriculated in 1861, and studied medicine at Steeven's Hospital, Dublin. Became a licentiate of the Coll. of Surgeons, Ireland 1868. Surgeon to the Infirmary for Children in Buckingham Street, Dublin. A Liberal, in favour of the system called 'Home Rule' for Ireland. Sat for Galway from June 1874 until he retired in 1880. Died 17 June 1881. [1880]

WARING, Charles. 29 Norfolk Street, Park Lane, London. 10 Victoria Chambers, Westminster, London. Reform. S. of John Waring, Esq., of Haworth Hall, near Rotherham, by Mary, d. of William Fletcher, Esq. of Chesterhall, near Sheffield; m. 2nd d. of Sir George William Denys, Bart., of Draycott Hall, Richmond, Yorkshire. A Partner in the firm of Waring Bros. contractors for public works. A Chevalier in the Order of Leopold of Belgium, also of St. Maurice and St. Lazare of Italy. A Liberal, was in favour of an amendment of the Land Laws, the equalisation of the borough and county franchise, the abolition of the Income Tax, and the placing of taxation almost exclusively on accumulated property. Sat for Poole from July 1865-Nov. 1868, when he was an unsuccessful candidate; re-elected Feb. 1874. Unseated May 1874; contested same seat in 1880. Died 26 Aug. 1887. [1874]

WARNER, Edward. 49 Grosvenor Place, London. Higham Hall, Woodford, Essex. Reform. Eld. s. of Edward Warner, Esq., of Walthamstow, Essex, by Anne Mary, d. of George Pearson, Esq. B. at Walthamstow, 1818; m. 1848, Maria, d. of Thomas Carr, Esq., of New Ross, Co. Wexford, and relict of J. Hibbitts, Esq. Educ. at Wadham Coll., Oxford, where he was 1st class in mathematics, 1840, and obtained the two open mathematical scholarships, 1841; graduated M.A. 1844. Was called to the bar at Lincoln's Inn, 1850, but did not practise. Author of pamphlets on *The Representation of the Working*

Classes, etc. A Magistate and Dept.-Lieut. for Essex. Patron of 2 livings. A Liberal, in favour of the ballot; voted against Church-rates Apr. 1860. Sat for Norwich from July 1852, till Mar. 1857; re-elected Mar. 1860 and sat until he retired in 1868. Died 7 Mar. 1875.   [1867]

WARRE, John Ashley. 54 Lowndes Square, London. West Cliff House, Ramsgate. Reform, Brooks's, and Boodle's. M. Caroline, d. of Pascoe Grenfall, Esq., MP. Educ. at Harrow and at Christ Church, Oxford. Patron of 1 living. A Liberal. Sat for Taunton from 1820-1826, and for Hastings from 1831-1835; was an unsuccessful candidate for the latter place in July 1847, and July 1852. First returned for Ripon Apr. 1857. MP until his death 18 Nov. 1860.   [1860]

WARREN, Rt. Hon. Robert Richard. 12 Fitzwilliam Square, Dublin. Kildare Street, and University Club, Dublin. S. of Henry Warren, Esq., (youngest s. of Sir Robert Warren, Bart., of Warren's Court, Co. Cork) by his m. with Miss Catherine Stewart. B. 1817; m. Mary, d. of Charles Perry, Esq. Educ. at Trinity Coll., Dublin, where he was senior moderator and gained the first gold medal. Was called to the bar in Ireland 1839; made a Queen's Counsel there 1858; a Bencher of King's Inn, Dublin, 1865, Solicitor Gen. for Ireland Mar. 1867, Attorney-Gen. Oct. following. A Conservative, and gave a constant support to the Church Education Society in Ireland. Elected for Dublin University Aug. 1867. Retired in 1868. Judge Oct. 1868. Died 24 Sept. 1897.   [1868]

WARREN, Samuel, Q.C. 35 Woburn Place, Russell Square, London. 12 Kings Bench Walk, Temple, London. S. of the Rev. Samuel Warren, LL.D., Incumbent of All Souls, Manchester, a native of Norfolk. B. near Wrexham, Denbighshire 1807; m. 1831, Eliza, only child of James Ballenger, Esq., of Woodford Bridge House, Essex. Educ. at Edinburgh University, where he gained, in his first year, the prize for Poetry and one for an Essay on Comparative Jurisprudence. Entered as a student at the Inner Temple 1828; practised as a special pleader from 1831-1837, when he was called to the bar; became a Queen's Counsel 1851, and joined the Northern Circuit. Appointed Recorder of Hull 1852. Made D.C.L. on the installation of Lord Derby at Oxford 1853. Elected F.R.S. 1835. Author of many well known works in legal and general literature including *A Popular and Practical Introduction to Law Studies, The Diary of a late Physician,* etc. A Conservative, and a supporter generally of Lord Derby's policy; strongly in favour of 'religious education' for the people. First elected for Midhurst Feb.

1856, without opposition and sat until he was appointed Master of Lunacy in 1859. Died 29 July 1877.   [1858]

WARTON, Charles Nicholas. 1 Brick Court, Temple, London. 14 Lambourn Road, Clapham, London. Carlton, and St. Stephen's Clubs. Eld. s. of Charles Warton, Esq., of The Old Tott, Burwash, Sussex. B. at Hendon, Middlesex, 1832; m. 1864, Agnes, d. of Lieut G.H. Wood, 67th Foot, and grandd. of Major-Gen. Wood. Was educ. at University Coll. School, London, and at Clare Hall, Cambridge. Was called to the bar at Lincoln's Inn, June 1861, and became a member of the Home, later the South-Eastern circuit. A 'Tory', was 'determined to resist any attempt under any pretence to dissever Ireland from Great Britain'. Voted against the third reading of the Irish Land Bill 1881. Sat for Bridport from Apr. 1880 until he retired in 1885. Attorney-Gen. of Western Australia 1886-90. Died 31 July 1900.   [1885]

WASON, Rigby. Kildinan, Ayrshire. Reform. 2nd. s. of John James Wason, Esq., of Bristol. A Barrister. A Reformer, in favour of an extension of the suffrage, vote by ballot, triennial Parliaments, and removing the Bishops from the House of Lords. Returned for Ipswich in Dec. 1832 and sat until he was defeated in Jan. 1835. The election was later declared void and a new election held on 19 June 1835 at which he was returned. Defeated July 1837. Again returned for Ipswich in July 1841, but on petition the election was declared void and he did not stand at the subsequent election in June 1842. Died 24 July 1875.   [1841]

WATERHOUSE, Samuel. Hope Hall, Halifax. Carlton. S. of John Waterhouse, Esq., of Wellhead, by Grace Elizabeth, d. of John Rawson, Esq., of Stony Royd, Halifax. B. 1815; m. 1840, Charlotte Lydia, d. of Henry Lees Edwards, Esq., of Pye Nest, and sister to Sir Henry Edwards, Bart., MP for Beverley. A Magistrate and Dept.-Lieut. for the West Riding of Yorkshire. Major in the 2nd West Yorkshire Yeomanry Cavalry. A Conservative. Unsuccessfully contested Pontefract Jan. 1860. Sat for Pontefract from Aug. 1863 until he retired 1880. Died 4 Mar. 1881.   [1880]

WATERLOW, Sir Sydney Hedley, Bart. 29 Chesham Place, London. St. Bartholomew's Hospital, London. Fairseat, Wrotham, Kent. City Liberal. 4th s. of James Waterlow, Esq., of Huntingdon Lodge, Surrey, by Mary, d. of William Crakell, Esq., of London. B. in London 1822; m. 1st, 1845, Anna Maria, youngest d. of William Hickson, Esq., of Fairseat, Wrotham, Kent (she died 1880); 2ndly, 1882, Margaret, 2nd d. of William Hamilton, Esq., of Napa, California. Educ. at St. Saviour's School. Was a Wholesale Stationer in London, head of the firm of Messrs. Waterlow and Sons, Carpenters' Hall, London Wall, and retired. A Commissioner of Lieutancy for London. Elected an Alderman of London for Langbourn Ward 1863. Sheriff of London 1866-67. Lord Mayor of London for 1872-73. Treasurer of St. Bartholomew's Hospital 1874. Well known for his successful exertions in erecting on a large scale in various parts of London model lodging-houses for artisans. A Liberal. Represented Dumfriesshire for a few months in 1869, when in consequence of holding a government contract he was unable to sit. Sat for Maidstone from Feb. 1874 to Apr. 1880, when he was an unsuccessful candidate there. Sat for Gravesend from June 1880 until he contested the Medway division of Kent in 1885. Died 3 Aug. 1906. [1885]

WATERPARK, Lord. Doveridge Hall, Uttoxeter, Derbyshire. B. at Leixlip. Co. Kildare, 1793. M. 1837, Hon. Elizabeth Jane, youngest d. of 1st Visct. Anson, and sister of 1st Earl of Lichfield. A Irish Peer. Was a Lord-in-Waiting to the Queen from 1846 to Feb. 1852, and reappointed in Jan. 1853. A Col. of the Derbyshire Militia. A Liberal, and general supporter of Lord Aberdeen; favoured the ballot. Sat for Knaresborough in 1831, and for Derbyshire S. from Dec. 1832 until Jan 1835, when he was defeated. Contested same seat in 1841. Was returned for Lichfield in May 1854, without opposition, and sat until he accepted Chiltern Hundreds in May 1856. Died 13 Mar. 1863. [1856]

WATERS, George. 10 Upper Temple Street, Dublin. Reform, and Stephen's Green, Dublin. 2nd s. of George Waters, Esq., of Cork, Ireland, Brewer and Distiller, by Elizabeth d. of James Lambkin, Esq., of Cork. B. at Cork 1827; m. 1852, Adelaide, d. of Charles Hamilton Teeling, Esq., of Belfast. Educ. at Trinity Coll., Dublin where he obtained honours, and graduated B.A. 1849, M.A. 1864. Was called to the bar in Ireland in 1849, made a Queen's Counsel there 1859. A Magistrate for the Co. of Dublin. A Liberal. Sat for Mallow from Apr. 1870 until appointed Chairman of Quarter Sessions Co. Waterford in 1872. [1872]

WATKIN, Sir Alfred Mellor. 6 Cleveland Row, St. James's, London. Dunedin Lodge, Folkestone, Kent. Reform, and City Liberal. Only s. of Sir Edward William Watkin, MP, by Mary Briggs, d. of Jonathan Mellor, Esq., of Hope House, Oldham. B. at Manchester 1847;

m. 1876, eld. d. of the Very Rev. Robert Payne Smith, D.D., Dean of Canterbury. A Civil Engineer, and held appointments successively at the Great Western, Manchester and Sheffield Railways, and the Great Trunk Railway of Canada, from 1864-1870, when he was appointed locomotive engineer to the South Eastern Railway; resigned 1877. A Director of the Manchester and Sheffield Railway, also of the Metropolitan Railway. Wrote pamphlets on the working of railways in reference to the block system of signalling. A moderate Liberal. Sat for Great Grimsby from Aug. 1877 until he retired Apr. 1880. Chairman of Locomotive Committee of South-Eastern Railway 1880-90. Succeeded as 2nd Bart. 1901. Died 30 Nov. 1914. [1880]

WATKIN, Sir Edward William. Continued in House after 1885: full entry in Volume II.

WATKINS, Col. John Lloyd Vaughan. Pennoyre, Brecknockshire. United Service, and Athenaeum. S. of the Rev. Thomas Watkins, of Pennoyre, Brecknockshire, by Susanna Eleanora only d. of Richard Vaughan, Esq., of Shenfield, Essex, and Golden Grove, Carmarthenshire. B. at Pennoyre 1802; m. 1st, 1833, Sophia Louisa Henrietta, 3rd d. of Sir George Pocock, Bart. (she died 1851); 2ndly, Eliza Luther, d. of J. Taylor Gordon, Esq., M.D., and widow of Brigadier-Gen. S. Hughes, C.B. (she died 1855). Educ. at Harrow and at Christ Church, Oxford. Appointed Lord-Lieut. of Brecknockshire in 1847. Honorary Col. of the Brecknockshire Rifle Milita. Patron of 3 livings. A Liberal, in favour of vote by ballot. Sat for Brecknock from 1832-1835, and from July 1847-July 1852; re-elected Jan. 1854, without opposition. MP until his death 28 Sept. 1865. [1865]

WATLINGTON, John Watlington Perry. 37 Lowndes Street, London. Moor Hall, Harlow, Essex. Carlton. S. of Thomas Perry, Esq., of Moor Hall, Essex, by Maria Jane, d. of George Watlington, Esq., of Aldenham, Hertfordshire. B. in London 1823; m. 1849, Margaret Emily, 3rd d. of the Rev. Charles Wicksted Ethelston, of Uplyme Rectory, and Wicksted Hall, Cheshire. Educ. at Harrow and at Trinity Coll., Cambridge. Assumed the name of Watlington. Appointed a Dept.-Lieut. of Essex 1859, and Maj. W. Essex Yeomanry, Feb. 1860. A Conservative, and said he would give a general support to Lord Derby; was in favour only of 'such reforms as are conceived in a spirit of loyalty and true love for our ancient constitution'; said he would support 'no measure on the Church rate question which does not provide adequately for the repair of our parish Churches'; considered the 'state of our national defences should be such as to render all danger from without impossible.' First elected for Essex S. May 1859 and sat until he retired 1865. Died 24 Feb. 1882.   [1865]

WATNEY, James. Thorney House, Palace Gate, London. Carlton. S. of James Watney, Esq., of Haling Park, Croydon, by Rebecca, d. of James Spurrell, Esq. B. at Wandsworth, Surrey, 1832; m. 1856, Blanche, d. of Frederick S. Burrell, Esq., of Highfield Park, Tunbridge Wells. Educ. at Clapham Grammar School. A member of the firm of Messrs. Watney and Co., Brewers. Appointed a Dept.-Lieut. of Middlesex 1882. A Conservative. Sat for Surrey E. from Aug. 1871 until he retired in 1885. Died 2 Nov. 1886.   [1885]

WATSON, Hon. Richard. 19 Chapel Street, Park Lane, London. Bro. of Lord Sondes. B. 6 Jan. 1800. A Captain in the 10th Dragoons. A Reformer. Was first elected for Canterbury in 1830, having unsuccessfully contested it in 1826, with S.R. Lushington, Esq. Retired in 1835. Returned 7 July 1852 for Peterborough. MP until his death 24 July 1852.   [1833]

WATSON, Rt. Hon. William. Home Office, London. Edinburgh. S. of Rev. Thomas Watson, Minister of Covington, Lanarkshire, by Eleanora, d. of David McHaffie, Esq. B. at Covington Manse, Lanarkshire 1828; m. 1868, Margaret, youngest d. of Dugald Bannatyne, Esq. Educ. at the Universities of Glasgow and Edinburgh. Was admitted an advocate at the Scotch bar 1851. Was Solicitor-Gen. for Scotland from July 1874-Oct. 1876, when he was appointed Lord Advocate. Elected Dean of the Faculty of Advocates Nov. 1875. A Conservative, in favour of progressive reform in our laws and institutions. Sat for the Universities of Glasgow and Aberdeen from Nov. 1876. Retired 1880. Created Baron Watson 28 Apr. 1880. Died 14 Sept. 1899.   [1880]

WATSON, William Henry. 38 Wilton Crescent, London. Junior United Service. B. 1796, the eld. s. of Capt. John Watson, of the 76th Foot M. 1831, d. of A. Hollish. Entered the army as Cornet 6th Dragoons 1811, and became a Lieut. 1812. Served with his regiment in the Peninsular war and retired on half-pay in 1816. Admitted a student of Lincoln's Inn 1817, and practised for several years as a special pleader. Called to the bar at Lincoln's Inn 1832, and made a Bencher of that Inn 1843. A Queen's Counsel. A Liberal, and favoured Parliamentary Reform, the admission of Jews to Parliament, and national education. Unsuccessfully contested Newcastle-upon-Tyne, July 1852, and sat for Kinsale from July 1841-July 1847. Sat for Hull from Aug. 1854 until he was

appointed Baron of the Exchequer in 1856. [1856]

WAUGH, Edward. The Burroughs, Papcastle, Cockermouth. Reform. S. of John Lamb Waugh, Esq., of Irthington, Cumberland, by Catherine, d. of Richard Miles, of Porter Hill, Irthington. B. at Seathill, Irthington 1816; m. 1843, Mary Jane, d. of Mr. Thomas Liddell, of Boustead Hill, near Carlisle. Was admitted a Solicitor in 1840, and from 1841 practised at Cockermouth, where he was clerk to the Magistrates, and was for some years Registrar of County Courts. A Liberal, in favour of household suffrage being extended to counties, a revision of the Land Laws and of the licensing system. Sat for Cockermouth from Apr. 1880 until he retired in 1885. Died 26 Mar. 1891. [1885]

WAWN, John Twizell. Boldon, Co. Durham. S. of Christopher Wawn, Esq., and grands. of John Twizell, Esq., of West Boldon. B. 1801; m. 1st, d. of N. Horn, Esq.; 2ndly, d. of William Matterson, Esq. A Magistrate for Durham. 'A Liberal-Whig.' Sat for South Shields from 1841 until he retired in 1852. Died 21 Sept. 1859.   [1852]

WAY, Arthur Edwin. 10 King Street, St. James's, London. Ashton Lodge, Bristol. Carlton, and Windham. Youngest s. of Benjamin Way, Esq., of Denham Place, Buckinghamshire, by Mary, d. of Thomas Smyth, Esq., of Stapleton, Gloucestershire and sister of Sir John Smyth, Bart., of Ashton Court, Somersetshire. B. at Denham, Buckinghamshire, 1813; m. 1849, Harriet Elizabeth, d. of Henry Butterworth, Esq., of Henbury Court, Gloucestershire. Educ. at Eton and at Trinity Coll., Oxford. A Conservative, in favour of Lord Derby's Reform Bill, as it contained many 'advantageous enactments', and 'was a measure of large enfranchisement'; said he would 'give a general support to Lord Derby.' Unsuccessfully contested Bath July 1857; first elected there Apr. 1859 and sat until he retired 1865. Died 19 Sept. 1870.   [1865]

WEBSTER, John. Edgehill, Aberdeen. S. of Alexander Webster, Esq., of Aberdeen, an Advocate at the Scottish bar, by Margaret, d. of James McKilligan, Esq., Merchant, of Aberdeen. B. at Aberdeen, 1810; m. 1839, Margaret, d. of Mr. David Chalmers, of Westburn, Aberdeen. Was educ. at Marischal Coll., and Aberdeen University, of which he was made LL.D. 1877. Became an Advocate at the Scottish bar in 1831. Was Lord Provost of Aberdeen for 3 years from 1856 to 1859; was Vice-President of the British Association in Aberdeen, 1859. Was a member and Assessor of the University Court of Aberdeen from 1861. A 'decided Liberal.' Sat for Aberdeen city from Apr. 1880 until he retired in 1885. President of the Aberdeen Liberal Unionist Association 1886. Died 31 May 1891.   [1885]

WEBSTER, Sir R.E. Continued in House after 1885: full entry in Volume II.

WEDDERBURN, Sir David, Bart. Interesk Lodge, Musselburgh, Edinburgh. Eld. surviving s. of Sir John Wedderburn, 2nd Bart., by Henrietta Louisa, d. of William Milburn, Esq., of Bombay. B. at Bombay 1835. Educ. at Trinity Col., Cambridge, where he graduated B.A. as senior optime, 1858. Called to the Scottish bar in 1861. Appointed Cornet Midlothian Yeomanry Cavalry 1859; Lieut. 1861. A Liberal, in favour of religious equality. Sat for Ayrshire S. from Dec. 1868-Feb. 1874. Sat for Haddington district from Feb. 1879 until he accepted Chiltern Hundreds Aug. 1882. Died 18 Sept. 1882.   [1882]

WEDGWOOD, Josiah. 8 Manchester Buildings. London. S. of the Porcelain Manufacturer at Etruria, in the Potteries, whose name was given to a branch of our national manufactures. A Reformer, in favour of the immediate abolition of slavery. Sat for Stoke-upon-Trent from 1832. Retired in 1835.   [1833]

WEGUELIN, Christopher. Ranelagh House, Arabelle Row, London. B. at Marlow 1838, the s. of Thomas Matthias Weguelin, Esq., of Billingbear, Berkshire and of London, Merchant and Banker, by his 1st wife Charlotte, d. of Andrew H. Poulett Thompson, Esq., of Marlow. Educ. at Harrow and at Cambridge. A Merchant in London and Partner in the firm of Messrs. Thomson, Bonar & Co. A Liberal, who favoured tenant-right for Ireland, a denominational scheme of National Education and the disestablishment of the Irish Church. Sat for Youghal from Dec. 1868 until he was unseated in Apr. 1869. Contested Dover in 1874. Died 6 Sept. 1881.   [1869]

WEGUELIN, Thomas Matthias. 44 Grosvenor Gardens, London. Billingbear, Wokingham, Berkshire. Union, and City Liberal. S. of W.A. Weguelin, Esq., of Weymouth Street, Portland Place, London. B. 1809; m. 1st, 1837, Charlotte, d. of A.H. Poulett Thomson, Esq.; 2ndly, 1844, Catherine, d. of Charles Hammersley, Esq. A Merchant in London. Was Governor of the Bank of England from 1855-1859. A Partner in the firm of Messrs. Thomson, Bonar and Company, of London and St. Petersburg. A Commissioner of Lieutenancy for London. A Liberal, in favour of the 'total' abolition of Church rates. Sat for

Southampton from Feb. 1857-May 1859, when he was an unsuccessful candidate. Elected for Wolverhampton July 1861 and sat until he retired 1880. Died 5 Apr. 1885.   [1880]

WELBY, Sir Glynne Earle, Bart. 8 Upper Belgrave Street, London. Denton House, Grantham. Carlton. Eld. s. of Sir W.E. Welby, 2nd Bart. B. at Carlton-on-Trent, Nottinghamshire 1806; m. 1828, Frances, 2nd d. of Sir Montague Cholmeley, Bart. Educ. at Rugby. Lieut.-Col. of the Royal South Lincoln Militia from 1852-1854. A Dept.-Lieut. of Lincolnshire. Patron of 4 livings. A Conservative. Sat for Grantham from 1830 until he retired 1857. Took additional surname of Gregory in 1861. Died 23 Aug. 1875.   [1857]

WELBY-GREGORY, Sir William Earle. See GREGORY, Sir William Earle Welby-.

WELLESLEY, Lord Charles. Apsley House, London. Carlton. B. at the Chief Secretary's Lodge, Phoenix Park, Dublin 1808, the 2nd s. of 1st Duke of Wellington. M. 1844, only d. of the Rt. Hon. Henry Manvers Pierrepont. Became a Lieut.-Col. in the army 1837, and Col. 1851. Appointed Aide-de-Camp to the General Commanding in Chief, Sept. 1852. Was Chief Equerry and Clerk Marshal to the Queen, but resigned July 1846. A Conservative, in favour of free trade, and supported 'well-considered measures combining religious instruction with general education.' Contested Rochester Jan. 1835. Sat for Hampshire S. 1842-52, and for Windsor from 1852 until Feb. 1855, when he accepted Chiltern Hundreds. Died 9 Oct. 1858.   [1854]

WELLESLEY, Lieut.-Col. Henry. 27 Hill Street, Berkeley Square, London. Conholt Park, Andover, Hampshire. Guards'. 2nd s. of Major-Gen. Lord Charles Wellesley (who was 2nd s. of the 1st Duke of Wellington), by Augusta Sophia Anne, only d. of the Rt. Hon. Henry Manvers Pierrepont. B. at Apsley House 1846. Appointed Ensign and Lieut. 1st Grenadier Guards May 1865, Lieut. and Capt. Aug. 1868, was instructor of Musketry from May 1871-Apr. 1874. Heir Presumptive to the Duke of Wellington. A Conservative. Sat for Andover from Feb. 1874 until defeated 1880. Unimportant Military Commission until 1882. Succeeded his uncle as Duke of Wellington (3rd) in 1884. Died 8 June 1900.   [1880]

WELLS, Edward. Wallingford. Carlton. S. of Edward Wells, Esq., Banker and Brewer, by Mary Ann, d. of John Hedges, Esq., of Wallingford. B. at Wallingford 1821; m. 1842,

Isabella, d. of Richard Watkins, Esq., of Dublin. Educ. privately. A Banker and Brewer at Wallingford. A Magistrate for Berkshire from 1859. A Conservative; of moderate opinions. Sat for Wallingford from Mar. 1872 until defeated 1880.   [1880]

WELLS, William. 23 Bruton Street, Berkeley Square, London. Holme Wood, Peterborough. Redleaf, Penshurst, Kent. Travellers', White's and Brooks's. B. at Holme Wood, Huntingdonshire, 1818, the s. of Capt. William Wells, R.N., by Lady Elizabeth, d. of the 1st Earl of Carysport. M. 1854, Lady Louisa, 3rd d. of 8th Earl of Wemyss and March. Educ. at Harrow and at Balliol Coll., Oxford. Entered the 1st Life Guards 1839, retired in 1843. A Magistrate and Dept.-Lieut. for Kent and for Huntingdonshire. Patron of 3 livings. A Liberal, voted for the disestablishment of the Irish Church 1869, and favoured the equalization of County and Borough franchise. Sat for Beverley July 1852 - July 1857, and for Peterborough from Dec. 1868 until 1874, when he retired. Died 1 May 1889.   [1873]

WEMYSS, Capt. James Erskine, R.N. Wemyss Castle, Kirkcaldy. United Service, and Reform. Eld. s. of Lieut.-Gen. Wemyss, who was nephew of the 6th Earl of Wemyss. B. 1789; m. 1826, Lady Emma, d. of 15th Earl of Errol (dead). A Capt. in the navy of the year 1814. A Reformer. Voted against the abolition of the Corn Laws. Said he would resign his seat when called upon to do so by the deliberate voice of the majority of the electors. Sat for Fifeshire uninterruptedly from 1820, with the exception of 1831, until he retired in 1847. Died 3 Apr. 1854.   [1847]

WEMYSS, James Hay Erskine. 6 Buckingham Gate, London. Wemyss Castle, Kirkaldy, Fifeshire. Brooks's, and White's. Eld. s. of Admiral James Erskine Wemyss, Lord-Lieut. of Fifeshire, and member of that Co. from 1820-1847, by Lady Emma, d. of 16th Earl of Errol. B. at Wemyss 1829; m. 1855, Millicent Anne Mary, 2nd d. of Hon. John Kennedy Erskine. Entered the navy as a volunteer of the 1st class, 1841; left the service 1848. Maj.-Commandant 8th Fife Artillery Volunteers. Appointed Lieut.-Col. of the London Scottish Rifle Volunteers 1860. A Liberal, but opposed to 'needless and ill-considered innovations'; said he would support some such measure of reform as was sketched by Earl Russell, 'including at least a partial disfranchisement of petty English burghs'; voted for the ballot,·and was willing to support any well-considered measure for education in Scotland on 'liberal and unsectarian principles.' First elected for Fifeshire May 1859 and sat until his death 29 Mar. 1864.   [1864]

WEST, Frederick Richard. 26 St. James's Square, London. Arnewood House, Lymington, Hampshire. Ruthin Castle, North Wales. Carlton. B. in London 1799, the eld. s. of the Hon. Frederick West of Ruthin Castle, by his 2nd wife, the d. and co-heir of Richard Myddleton, of Chirk Castle, Denbighshire. Grands. of 2nd Earl De la-Warr. M. 1st, 1820, Lady Georgiana, 3rd d. of 5th Earl of Chesterfield; 2ndly, 1827, Theresa, only d. of Capt. John Whitby, R.N. of Cresswell Hall, Staffs. Educ. at Eton and at Christ Church Oxford. A Magistrate for Denbighshire and a Dept.-Lieut. of Hampshire. A 'Liberal - Conservative'. Elected for Denbigh in 1826, and· sat for East Grinstead from 1830 till it was disfranchised under the Reform Act. Sat for Denbigh district from 1847 until his retirement in 1857. Died 1 May 1862.   [1856]

WEST, Henry Wyndham. 15 Cadogan Place, London. 10 King's Bench Walk, London. Brooks's, and Travellers'. S of Martin John West, Esq., Barrister-at-Law and Recorder of Lynn, by Lady Maria, d. of the 2nd Earl of Orford. B. in Chesterfield Street, London, 1823; m. 1870, Violet Katharine, 3rd d. of Walter Frederick Campbell, Esq., of Islay. Educ. at Eton and at Christ Church, Oxford. Was called to the bar at the Inner Temple, May 1848. Appointed a Queen's Counsel, Mar. 1868. Attorney-General for the Duchy of Lancaster 1862, Recorder of Manchester, May 1865, and was previously Recorder of Scarborough. A Whig, gave a general support to Mr. Gladstone; in favour of the borough and county franchise being equalized, the redistribution of seats, and a thorough reform of the municipal government of London. Sat for Ipswich from Dec. 1868 to Feb. 1874; was an unsuccessful candidate there July 1865 and Feb. 1874; re-elected there Dec. 1883; unseated Apr. 1886. Died 25 Nov. 1893.   [1885]

WEST, John Beatty. St. Stephen's Green, Dublin. A Queen's Counsel in Ireland. A Conservative. Contested Dublin City four times with Mr. O'Connell. Contested it again 17 Jan. 1835, and was seated on petition 13 Apr. 1835. Defeated in 1837 but came head of the poll 10 July 1841. MP until his death Dec. 1841 or Jan. 1842. [1841]

WESTENRA, Hon. Henry Robert. The Dell, Berkshire. Rossmore Park, Monaghan. Reform. Eld. s. of Lord Rossmore. B. 1792; m. 1820, Anne Douglas, d. of Douglas, 8th Duke of Hamilton. Lord Lieut. of Monaghan. Published a pamphlet in defence of the Irish 40s. freeholdrs, others on the Scotch and Irish Peers, etc., and occasionally contributed to periodicals. A Reformer, in favour of the ballot. Sat for Monaghan from 1818 with the exception of the Parliaments of 1830 and 1832; was returned there in 1834, but unseated on petition; regained his seat in 1835 and sat until succeeded as 3rd Baron 10 Aug. 1842. Died 1 Dec. 1860. [1843]

WESTENRA, Hon. John Craven. 13 Conduit Street, London. The Lodge, Berkshire. Sharavogue Castle, King's Co. Reform. 2nd surviving s. of 2nd Lord Rossmore, by his 1st wife, 2nd d. of Charles Walsh, Esq., of Walsh Park, Tipperary. B. at Walsh Park, 1798; m. 1st, 1834, Eleanor Mary, widow of Sir Gilbert East, Bart., and aunt of Sir William H. Jolliffe, Bart. (she died 1838); 2ndly, 1842, Ann, d. of Lewis Charles Daubuz, Esq., of Truro, Cornwall. Was Lieut.-Col. and Capt. in the Scots Fusilier Guards; retired in 1843; steward of the Turf Club in Ireland. Appointed a Dept.-Lieut. of King's Co. 1847. A Reformer. Unsuccessfully contested King's Co. in 1831. Sat for it from 1835 until he retired in 1852. Died 5 Dec. 1874. [1852]

WESTERN, Sir Thomas Burch, Bart. Felix Hall, Kelvedon, Essex. Tattingstone Place, Ipswich, Suffolk. Brooks's, and United University. S. of Rear-Admiral Thomas Western, K.T.S., by the d. of Thomas Burch, Esq., of the Island of Bermuda. B. 1795; m. 1819, d. of William Bushby, Esq., of Kirkmichael, Dumfriesshire. Educ. at Trinity Coll., Cambridge, where he graduated B.A. 1818, M.A. 1824. A gentleman of the Privy Chamber. Was High Sheriff of Essex and Suffolk. Patron of 1 living. A Liberal, and in favour of 'constitutional progress', of 'peace with honour', and of a further extension of the franchise; in favour also of the total abolition of church-rates, and the entire repeal of the malt tax. First elected for Essex N. July 1865. Defeated in 1868 contesting Essex E. Died 30 May 1873. [1867]

WESTERN, Thomas Sutton. Felix Hall, Kelvedon, Essex. Brooks's, Arthur's, and United University. Only s. of Sir Thomas Burch Western, Bart., of Felix Hall, Essex, and Tattingstone Place, Suffolk (who succeeded to the estates of his relative Lord Western), by Margaret Letitia, d. of William Bushby, Esq., of Kirkmichael, Dumfriesshire. B. 1821; m. 1848, eld. d. of Edward Buller, Esq., of Dilhorne Hall, Staffordshire (she died 1850). Educ. at Eton and at Trinity Coll., Cambridge. A Magistrate for Suffolk, and a Magistrate and Dept.-Lieut. for Essex. A Liberal, who would support 'any practicable measures for extending the suffrage, reducing the State expenditure, and promoting Religious liberty.' First elected for Maldon Apr. 1857 and sat until defeated 1865. Died 20 June 1877. [1865]

WESTHEAD, Joshua Proctor Brown. Lea Castle, Woverley, Worcestershire. Reform, and Brooks's. Eld. s. of Edward Westhead, Esq. of Manchester, and nephew of John Brown, Esq. of Lea Castle, Worcestershire former High Sheriff of Worcestershire, in compliance with whose will he assumed the name of Brown 1850. B. at Manchester 1807; m. 1828, Betsy 3rd d. of G.R. Chappell, Esq., Alderman of Manchester. Was educ. at the Manchester and Congleton Grammar Schools. A Merchant and head of the manufacturing firm of Messrs. Wood and Westhead, Manchester. A Magistrate for Staffordshire and Worcestershire. Appointed Dept.-Lieut. of Worcestershire, May 1852. A Liberal, voted for the disestablishment of the Irish Church 1869; in favour of the ballot and the avoidance of 'Strikes' by the establishment of courts of conciliation. Sat for Knaresborough from 1847-July 1852, when he was returned as one of 3 candidates who polled the same number of votes, but lost his seat on petition. Sat for York from Mar. 1857-July 1865, when he was unsuccessful. Sat for York again from Dec. 1868 until he accepted Chiltern Hundreds Feb. 1871. Died 25 July 1877. [1870]

WESTROPP, Henry. Green Park, Bruff, Limerick, Union. Only s. of Henry Westropp, Esq., of Richmond, Co. Limerick, by Elinor Winthrop, d. of William Jones, Esq., of Cork. B. 1811. Educ. at Harrow and at Trinity Coll., Dublin, where he graduated M.A. 1831, and gained honours. A Conservative, in favour of the policy of non-intervention, and the enlargement but not the lowering of the franchise. Unsuccessfully contested Bridgwater Apr. 1859; first elected for Bridgwater July 1865. Unseated shortly after election. Unsuccessful there at the election of Nov. 1868. [1865 2nd ed.]

WETHERED, Thomas Owen. Seymour Court, Nr. Great Marlow, Buckinghamshire. Carlton, and Oxford & Cambridge. S. of Owen Wethered, Esq., of Remnantz, Great Marlow, by Anne, d. of the Rev. Giles Haworth Peel, of the Grotto, Basildon, Berkshire. B. at Marlow 1832; m. 1856, Edith Grace, only d. of the Rev. Hart Ethelston, Rector of St. Mark's, Cheetham Hill, Manchester. Educ. at Eton and at Christ Church, Oxford. A Brewer at Marlow and a Partner in the firm of Messrs. Thomas Wethered and Sons. An 'independent Conservative', opposed to violent and unconstitutional change, voted against the disestablishment of the Church in Ireland 1869. Sat for Great Marlow from Nov. 1868 until he retired 1880. Died 22 Feb. 1921. [1880]

WEYLAND, Maj. Richard. 7 Hereford Street, London. Woodeaton, Oxfordshire. M. widow of

Sir John Lowther Johnstone, Bart., d. of Charles Gordon, Esq., of Cluny, and mother of the Member for Weymouth. A moderate Reformer, in favour of protection for the farmer; voted for the Reform Act. Sat for Weymouth from 1828 to 1830; was elected for Oxfordshire in 1831 and sat until he retired in 1837. [1837]

WHALLEY, George Hammond. 20 Leinster Square, London. Plas Madoc, Ruabon, North Wales. Reform. Only s. of George Hampden Whalley, Esq., of Plas Madoc, Denbighshire (who represented Peterborough during fourteen years preceding his death, Oct. 1878), by Anne Wakeford, d. of Richard Attree, Esq., of Bishearne, Hampshire. B. at Plas Madoc, Ruabon, North Wales, 1851. Educ. in H.M. Training Ship 'Britannia', and subsequently entered the navy. A Magistrate for Denbighshire, and Capt. Denbighshire Yeomanry Cavalry. Commanded a troop of irregular Horse in the Zulu War 1879. A Liberal. Sat for Peterborough from Apr. 1880 until he accepted Chiltern Hundreds 1883. [1883]

WHALLEY, George Hampden. 14 Marine Square, Brighton. Plas Madoc, Ruabon, Denbighshire, Reform. S. of James Whalley, Esq., Merchant and Banker, of Gloucester, (a descendent of Edward Whalley, who was 1st cousin to John Hampden and Oliver Cromwell), by Elizabeth, d. of Richard Morse, Esq., of Gurshill, Blakeney, Gloucestershire. B. at Gloucester, 1813; m. 1846, Anne Wakeford, d. of Richard Attree, Esq. of Bistearne, Hampshire. Educ. at University Coll., London where he gained the first prize in rhetoric and metaphysics. Called to the bar at Gray's Inn 1836, and joined the Oxford Circuit. Was Asst. Tithe Commissioner for Special Purposes from 1836-1847. A Magistrate for Denbighshire and Montgomeryshire, and a Dept.-Lieut. of the former and Capt. Yeomanry Cavalry. High Sheriff of Carnarvonshire in 1852. Author of a work *On the Law of Tithe Commutations,* and other legal publications. A Liberal, was in favour of the repeal of the rate-paying clause of the Reform Act, of the adoption of 'direct taxation of fixed property', and the abolition of the income tax on trade and labour. Unsuccessfully contested Montgomery district July 1852; sat for Peterborough from Nov. following-June 1853, when he was displaced by petition; re-elected May 1859. MP until his death 7 Oct. 1878. [1878]

WHALLEY, Sir Samuel St. Swithin Burden. 12 St. John's Wood Road, London. A Reformer, in favour of the ballot, the abolition of the window tax, all taxes bearing upon industry, and said he would resign his seat upon a majority of the electors signing a requisition to that effect. Sat for Marylebone from 1832 and sat until he was unseated on being unable to prove his qualification after being returned in 1837 general election. Died 3 Feb. 1883. [1837]

WHARTON, John Lloyd. Continued in House after 1885: full entry in Volume II.

WHATMAN, James, F.R.S., F.S.A. 6 Carlton Gardens, London. Vinter's, Nr. Maidstone, Kent. Reform, and Oxford & Cambridge. Eld. s. of James Whatman, Esq., of Vinter's, near Maidstone (whose father was Sheriff of Kent in 1767), by Eliza Susannah, eld. d. of Samuel Richard Ganssen, Esq., MP of Brookman's Park, Hertfordshire. B. at Vinter's, 1813; m. 1850, Louisa Isabella, d. of Charles Ross, Esq., and grandd. of the 2nd Marq. Cornwallis. Educ. at Eton and at Christ Church, Oxford, where he was 4th class in classics 1834, and graduated M.A. in 1838. A Magistrate and Dept.-Lieut. of Kent militia (from 1838). A Liberal, voted for the abolition of church-rates in 1855, and in favour of a 'satisfactory settlement' of that question, the admission of Jews to Parliament, and extension of the franchise. Sat for Maidstone from July 1852 to Apr. 1857, when he was returned for Kent W. Defeated in 1859. Died 12 Mar. 1887. [1858]

WHEELHOUSE, William St.James. 2 Crown Office Row, London. 18 Queen Street, Leeds. Junior Carlton. Eld. s. of James Wheelhouse, Esq., and Mary Ann, his wife. B. at Snaith, Yorkshire 1821. Unmarried. Called to the bar at Gray's Inn May 1844, and joined the Northern Circuit, with the West Riding and Leeds. Sessions. Appointed Queen's Counsel 1877. A Conservative, voted against the disestablishment of the Irish Church 1869. Sat for Leeds from Dec. 1868 until defeated 1880. Knighted Dec. 1882. Died 8 Mar. 1886. [1880]

WHITBREAD, Samuel. 10 Ennismore Gardens, Prince's Gate, London. Southill, Biggleswade, Bedfordshire. Brooks's, and Reform. S. of Samuel Charles Whitbread, Esq., of Cardington, Bedfordshire, who was MP for Middlesex from 1820-30. Grands. of the well-known politician whose name he bore. B. at Cardington 1830; m. 1855, Lady Isabella, 3rd d. of 3rd Earl of Chichester. Educ. at Rugby and at Cambridge. Appointed Dept.-Lieut. of Bedfordshire 1852; was a Lord of the Admiralty from June 1859-Mar. 1863, and a member of the House of Commons Committee of Selection, (appointed 1866). A Liberal and Home Ruler, also in favour of a measure of licensing reform. Sat for Bedford from July 1852 until he retired in 1895. Died 25 Dec. 1915. [1895]

WHITBREAD, William Henry. 99 Eaton Square, London. Southill, Biggleswade, Bedforshire. Furfleet, Essex. Nephew of Earl Grey. A Brewer. A supporter of Ministers. Sat for Bedford from 1818 until defeated in 1835. Contested same seat in 1841. Sheriff of Bedfordshire in 1837. Died 21 June 1867. [1833]

WHITE, Andrew. Frederick Lodge and Tunstall Lodge, Durham. S. of John White, Esq., of Bishop Wearmouth. B.22 Jan. 1792; m. 6 July 1814, Ophelia, d. of Hugh Dixon, Esq., of Bishop Wearmouth, Ship owner. A Coal and Shipowner; and Iron and Glass Manufacturer; a J.P. for the borough of Sunderland and for the Co. of Durham. Chairman of the Directors of the Sunderland Joint Stock Bank; Chairman of the Board of Guardians of the Sunderland Poor-Law Union. A Director of the Durham and Sunderland Railway; a Commissioner of the River Wear and of Sunderland Bridge. Pres. of the Sunderland Mechanics Institute, Pres. of the Sunderland British and Foreign School for Boys, and Vice-Pres. of the Exchange News-room. Author of a small publication 'recommending Christian Charity and mutual forbearing amongst various religious denominations.' Supported the leading measures of Lord Melbourne's goverment, the reform of every abuse in Church and State, the shortening of Parliaments, the extension of the franchise to all householders who were rate-payers, the vote by ballot and a general system of national education on scriptural principles but free from Creeds and Catechisms. 'Opposed to flogging in the navy and army.' Elected first Mayor of Sunderland under the Municipal Corporations Act and unanimously re-elected 1836; but resigned the office on becoming a candidate for the representation of Sunderland at the general election 1837. He won the seat and continued to sit for Sunderland until he retired in 1841. Died 3 Oct. 1856. [1838]

WHITE, Hon. Charles William. Woodland, Clonsilla, Co. Dublin. 5th s. of the 1st Baron Annaly, by Ellen, eld. d. of William S. Dempster, Esq., of Skibo, Co. Sutherland. B. 1838; entered the army as an Ensign Scots Fusilier Guards 1856, made Lieut. 1860, Capt. 1870. A Liberal, who was in favour of the system called 'Home Rule' for Ireland; also of an amendment of the 1870 Irish Land Act, so as to ensure fixity of tenure, and of denominational education. Sat for Tipperary from Oct. 1866 until he accepted Chiltern Hundreds Feb. 1875. Died 17 Oct. 1890. [1874]

WHITE, Col. Henry. 19 Belgrave Square, London. Woodlands, Nr. Dublin, Rathclines, Co. Longford. Arthur's, and Senior United Service.

4th s. of Luke White, Esq., of Dublin, and afterwards of Woodlands, Co. Dublin (who represented Leitrim in Parliament), by his m. with Miss Elizabeth Maziere. M. 1828, Ellen, eld. d. of William Dempster, Esq., of Skibo, Co. Sutherland, Educ. at Trinity Coll., Dublin. Appointed Col. of the Longford Militia 1837; was formerly Lieut. 14th Dragoons, served in the Peninsula, and received a war medal with two clasps for Badajos and Salamanca. Was Lord-Lieut. of Longford from 1841. A Liberal. Sat for Dublin Co. from 1823 (when he stood a contest of 15 days) till 1832. Sat for Longford from 1837 till 1847; re-elected for Longford Apr. 1857. Accepted Chiltern Hundreds 1861. [1861]

WHITE, James. 14 Chichester Terrace, Kemptown, Brighton. Reform. B. in London 1809, the 2nd s. of William White, Esq., of Tulse Hill, Surrey by Susannah, d. of E. Weeks, Esq., M. 1833, Mary, eld. d. of Addison Lind of Jamaica. Was a Merchant in London, chiefly engaged in trade with China. Elected an Alderman of London 1835, but resigned 1841. A thorough 'Reformer' and energetically aided the support of Gladstone. Considered that, with a 'view to the economy so urgently needed in the public expenditure', the annual estimates should be submitted to a 'finance commitee of all shades of political opinion.' Opposed to grants for religious purposes. Sat for Plymouth Apr. 1857 - Apr. 1859, and Brighton July 1860 until 1874, when he was defeated. Died 9 Jan. 1883. [1873]

WHITE, Hon. Luke. (I). Ratholine, Co. Longford. Bro. of the other Member for Longford Co. and of the Member for Leitrim. Lord-Lieut. and Custos Rot. of Longford. A Repealer. Was elected for Longford Co. in 1832 but on petition the election was declared void. Contested the seat in 1835. On the death of Lord Forbes he was elected for Longford Co. at the by-election of Dec. 1836, and Sat until unseated in Apr. 1842. Died Aug. 1854. [1842]

WHITE, Hon. Luke. (II). 19 Belgrave Street, London. The Treasury, Whitehall, London. Woodlands, Dublin. Army & Navy. Kildare Street Club, Dublin. S. of 1st Lord Annaly (who represented Longford and Dublin Co. for many years), by Ellen, eld. d. of William Dempster, Esq., of Skibo, Co. Sutherland. B. in London 1829; m. 1853, d. of—Stuart, Esq. Educ. at Eton. Entered the 13th Light Dragoons 1847; retired with the rank of Capt. 1853. Appointed a Lord of the Treasury Mar. 1862, salary £1,000; Lieut.-Col. Longford Militia Sept. 1857. A Liberal. First elected for Clare May 1859 but was shortly afterwards unseated on petition. Sat for

Longford from July 1861-Mar. 1862; elected for Kidderminister May following. Defeated 1865. Contested Carrickfergus July 1865. Succeeded as 2nd Baron Annaly Sept. 1873. Died 17 March 1888. [1865]

WHITE, Samuel. Headford, Co. Leitrim. Albion, and Reform. S. of the celebrated Luke White, Esq., the Bookseller and Lottery Office Keeper of Dublin, who was said to have realized the largest fortune ever made by trade in Ireland. M. d. of G. Rothe, Esq., of the Co. of Kilkenny, who for several years held the office of Collector of Excise in Dublin. Of Whig principles. Sat for Leitrim from 1824, succeeding his father who had represented it for some years. Sat until he retired 1847. Died 30 May 1854. [1847]

WHITELAW, Alexander. 91 Eaton Square, London. 168 West George Street, Glasgow. Gartsherrie House, Coatbridge, Scotland. Western, and New Club, Glasgow. S. of Alexander Whitelaw, Esq. by his m. with Miss Janet Baird. B. at Drumpark, Lanarkshire, 1823; m. 1859, Barbara Forbes, youngest d. of Robert Lockhart, Esq., of Castlehill Co. Lanark. Was educ. principally at Grange School, Sunderland. An Ironmaster. Chairman of the Glasgow School Board. Author of pamphlets on *National Education, Church Endowment, Church work*, etc. A Conservative, in favour of 'the services of the county being upheld in thorough efficiency.' Sat for the city of Glasgow from Feb. 1874. MP until his death 1 July 1879. [1879]

WHITESIDE, Rt. Hon. James. 40 Clarges Street, Piccadilly, London. 2 Mountjoy Square North, Dublin. Sackville Street Club, Dublin. Carlton, Athenaeum, and University. S. of the Rev. William Whiteside, and bro. of the Rev. Dr. Whiteside, Vicar of Scarborough. B. at Delgany, Co. Wicklow, 1806; m. 1833, d. of William Napier, Esq., of Belfast. Educ. at the University of Dublin, where he graduated M.A. with honours; obtained premiums in the first law class formed in the University of London, and received the honorary degree of D.C.L. at Oxford 1863. Called to the bar in Ireland 1830, and was a Queen's Counsel. Was Solicitor-Gen. for Ireland from Mar.-Dec. 1852; and Attorney-Gen. for Ireland from Mar. 1858-June 1859. Author of works on Italy and on Ancient Rome. A Conservative, in favour of a grant to the Church Education Society, and of the abolition of the income tax, which was 'inquisitorial and oppressive.' Sat for Enniskellen from Apr. 1851-Feb. 1859, when he was returned for the University of Dublin. Sat until appointed Lord Chief Justice Queens Bench (Ireland) July 1866. Died 25 Nov. 1876. [1865]

WHITLEY, Edward. Continued in House after 1885: full entry in Volume II.

WHITMORE, Henry. Sunniside, Colebrooke, Dale, Shropshire. Carlton, and Oxford & Cambridge. B. at Apley Park 1814, the 3rd s. of Thomas Whitmore, Esq., of Apley, near Bridgnorth, (who represented that borough for 25 years). M. 1852, Adelaide Anna, d. and co-heir of Francis Darby, Esq., of Colebrooke, Dale. Educ. at Christ Church, Oxford. Was a Lord of the Treasury and Keeper of the Privy Seal to the Prince of Wales from Mar. 1858-June 1859 and from July 1866-Dec. 1868. A Conservative, opposed to the disestablishment of the Irish Church as a measure 'strenuously supported by those who openly desire the separation of Church and State.' Sat for Bridgnorth from July 1852-July 1865, when he was unsuccessful, but was seated on petition Mar. following and sat until he accepted Chiltern Hundreds in Feb. 1870. Died 2 May 1876. [1869]

WHITMORE, Thomas Charlton. Apley Park, Shropshire. Carlton. S. of the former member Mr. Thomas Whitmore. B. 1807; m. 1833, Lady Louisa Anne, eld. d. of the 5th Marq. of Queensbury. Patron of 6 livings. A Conservative, but in favour of free trade. Sat for Bridgnorth from 1832 until he retired in 1852. Died 13 Mar. 1865. [1852]

WHITMORE, William Wolryche. 42 York Terrace, London. Dudmaston, Shropshire. M. 1810, Lady E. Georgiana, sister of the Earl of Bradford; a cousin of the member for Bridgnorth. Of Whig principles, in favour of the immediate abolition of slavery, throwing open the trade to India and the revision of the corn laws. Mr. Whitmore published popular pamphlets on both these last subjects. Sat for Bridgnorth from 1826 until the 1832 election, when he sat for Wolverhampton. Retired in 1835. [1833]

WHITWELL, John. 1 Whitehall Gardens, London. Bank House, Kendal. National, and Reform. S. of Isaac Whitwell, Esq., of Kendal, by Hannah Maria, d. of William Fisher, Esq., of Thorpe Hall, Leeds. B. at Kendal 1812; m. 1837, Anna, d. of William Maude, Esq., of Horton Grange, Bradford, Yorkshire. Was educ. at Kendal and at the 'Friends' School', Darlington. A Manufacturer at Kendal, of which he was several times chosen Mayor. A Liberal, voted for the disestablishment of the Church in Ireland 1869; in favour of the revival of the small tenaments rating bill. Sat for Kendal from Dec. 1868 until his death 28 Nov. 1880. [1880]

WHITWORTH, Benjamin. 22 Daleham Gardens, Hampstead, London. Reform. S. of Nicholas Whitworth, Esq., Merchant, of Drogheda. B. in Manchester 1816; m. 1843, Jane, d. of Thomas Walker, Esq., of Salford. Was a Merchant and Manufacturer at Manchester from 1838; also a Manufacturer at Drogheda. An 'advanced Liberal.' Sat for Drogheda from July 1865 to Jan. 1869, when he was unseated on petition. Contested Stafford June 1869. Sat for Kilkenny city from Apr. 1875 to Feb. 1880, when he was returned for Drogheda in the Liberal interest; re-elected for Drogheda at the general election Apr. 1880 and sat until defeated in 1885 contesting Lewisham. Died 24 Sept. 1893.   [1885]

WHITWORTH, Thomas. Oakfield, Withington, Nr. Manchester. Reform. S. of Benjamin Whitworth, Esq., of Drogheda (who sat for Drogheda from July 1865-Jan.1869), by Jane, d. of Thomas Walker, Esq., of Salford. B. at Manchester 1844; m. 1867 Elizabeth, d. of Robert Shaw, Esq., of Colne Hall, Lancashire. A Cotton and Commission Merchant at Manchester. A member of the firm of Messrs. Benjamin Whitworth and Brothers. A 'decided Liberal', and a general supporter of Mr. Gladstone's government, especially in his legislation on Irish matters. Sat for Drogheda from Feb. 1869 until he retired in 1874.   [1873]

WHITWORTH, William. 11 Holland Park, London. The Sycamores, Drogheda. Reform. 4th s. of Nicholas Whitworth, Esq., Merchant of Drogheda, by Sarah, d. of Samuel Barrett, Esq., of Manchester. B. at Littleborough, near Rochdale 1814. A Merchant at Drogheda. A Magistrate for Drogheda. High Sheriff of the Co. of the town of Drogheda in 1869. A Liberal. Sat for Newry from Feb. 1874 until he retired 1880.   [1880]

WICKHAM, Henry Wickham. 3 Chapel Street, Grosvenor Square, London. 112 Clarendon Place, Leamington. Brook's. B. at Bradford 1800, the eld. s. of Rev. Lamplugh Hind, Prebendary of York and Vicar of Paull, in the East Riding (who was youngest s. of Col. Wickham of Cottingley), by Sarah Elizabeth, eld. d. of Richard Hind, of Rawdon, Yorshire, whose name he assumed. Lineally descended from William Wickham, Bishop of Winchester, *temp.* Queen Elizabeth. M. 1836, Mary, eld. d. of Thomas Benyon, Esq. of New Grange, near Leeds (she died 1852). Resumed his paternal name of Wickham at his father's death 1843. A partner in the Low Moor Iron Works, near Bradford, Yorkshire, and Chairman of the Quarter Sessions from 1842. A Liberal, and favoured national education based on religion.

Voted for the ballot 1853, and against Church rates 1855. Was an unsuccessful candidate for Bradford in July 1847. Sat for Bradford from July 1852 until his death 23 Sept. 1867.   [1867]

WIGGIN, H. Continued in House after 1885: full entry in Volume II.

WIGNEY, Isaac Newton. Brighton. Reform. S. and bro. to the Brighton Bankers and East India Proprietors of the same name. Entertained Whig opinions inclining to radicalism, in favour of the ballot, and pledged himself to resign his seat whenever his constituents called upon him so to do. Sat for Brighton from 1832-1837; re-elected in 1841. Accepted Chiltern Hundreds Apr. 1842.   [1842]

WIGRAM, James. S. of Sir Robert Wigram, 1744-1830. MP for Leominster from June-Oct. 1841. Appointed Vice-Chancellor Oct. 1841. Knighted 1842. Died 29 July 1866.   [1866]

WIGRAM, Loftus Tottenham. 38 Charles Street, Berkeley Square, London. Athenaeum, and United University. S. of Sir Robert Wigram, Bart., by the d. of John Watts, Esq., was therefore uncle to Sir Robert Fitz Wygram, 3rd Bart. (whose father assumed the name of Fitz Wygram in lieu of Wigram.) B. 1803; m. 1849, Lady Katherine, youngest d. of 5th Earl of Selkirk. Educ. at Trinity Coll., Cambridge, where he was 8th Wrangler in 1825, and graduated M.A. 1828. A Conservative, opposed to the admission of Jews to Parliament, and to the separation of religious from secular education. First returned for Cambridge University, Oct. 1850, without opposition and sat until he retired in 1859. Died 19 Sept. 1889.   [1858]

WILBERFORCE, William. Eld. s. of the celebrated Mr. Wilberforce, and cousin to the Bishops of Winchester and Chester. B. 1798; m. Mary Fanny, d. of the Rev. John Owen of Pagelsham, Essex. A Conservative. Chosen for Hull, in conjunction with Sir W. James, Bart. after a very severe contest, upon the dissolution of Parliament 1837. Unseated, as he was unable to prove his qualification, Mar. 1838. Contested Taunton 1841 and Bradford Sept. 1841. Died 26 May 1879.   [1838]

WILBRAHAM, George. 56 Upper Seymour Street, London. Delamere House, Cheshire. Reform. Eld. surviving s. of George Wilbraham, Esq., of Nantwich, and cousin of Lord Skelmersdale, who was descended from a younger s. of Mr. Wilbraham's great-grandfather. B. 1779; m. 1814, Anne, d. of Earl Fortescue, and

408

sister of Lord Ebrington, a member for Devon. A Reformer, and in favour of the claims of the Dissenters; was against any alteration of the Corn Laws. Sat for Stockbridge in the Parliaments of 1826 and 1830, for Cheshire S. from 1831 until defeated 1841. Died 24 Jan. 1852. [1838]

WILBRAHAM, Hon. Richard Bootle. Blythe, Lancashire. 55 Portland Place, London. Carlton. B. 1801, the eld. s. of Lord Skelmersdale. M. 1832, Jessy, 3rd d. of Sir Richard Brooks, Bart., of Norton Priory, Cheshire. A Conservative. Sat for Lancashire S. from 1835 until his death in 1844. [1844]

WILDE, Sir Thomas. Great Stanhope Street, London. 69 Guilford Street, Russell Square. 9 Serjeant's Inn, London. Bowes Manor, Middlesex. Reform B. 1782, the s. of Thomas Wilde. M. 1st, 1813, d. of W. Wileman, 2ndly, 1845, Augusta Emma D'Este, d. of his R.H. the Duke of Sussex. Formerly an Attorney, was called to the bar in 1817. Became a Serjeant in 1827, Solicitor General in 1839, and Attorney General in 1841. Resigned in Sept. 1841. A Reformer, voted against the Corn Laws. Sat for Newark in 1831, contested it unsuccessfully in 1832, but again returned there in 1835 and sat until 1841. Sat for Worcester city from 1841-47, when he retired. [1846]

WILKINS, Walter. Maesllwch Castle and Woodlands, Radnorshire. Reform. Nephew of Visct. Hereford. B. 1809; m. 1831, Julia, 2nd d. of the Rev. John Collinson, Rector of Gateshead, Durham. Patron of 1 living. His father represented Radnorshire in several Parliaments previous to 1830, and his grandfather for 36 years. A Magistrate for Radnorshire. A Reformer. MP for Radnorshire from Jan. 1835 until his death in 1840. [1839]

WILKINSON, William Arthur. 5 Bennett Street, St. James's, London. Shortlands, Beckenham, Kent. Reform. Eld. s. of Josiah Henry Wilkinson, Esq., of Old Broad Street, London, and Peckham, Surgeon, by Sarah, d. of William Patteson, Esq., of Canterbury. B. in London 1795; m. 1st, 1818, Esther, 5th d. of Abraham Ricardo, Esq. (she died 1823); 2ndly, 1826, Rachel, 4th d. of the same (she died 1851). Educ. at Merchant Taylors' School. Was a member of the Stock Exchange from 1816. A Magistrate for Surrey from 1843, and was Chairman of the Croydon Railway Company from 1839 until its amalgamation with the Brighton Company. A Liberal, opposed to all endowments for religious purposes, but would not vote for a repeal of the Maynooth Grant under existing circumstances;

in favour of an extension of the suffrage, vote by ballot, short Parliaments, and the abolition of all 'taxes on knowledge.' Was an unsuccessful candidate for Sunderland July 1847 and Dec. 1847. First returned for Lambeth July 1852 and sat until defeated 1857. Contested Reigate Oct. 1858, Apr. 1859 and again in Feb. 1863. Died 13 Apr. 1865. [1857]

WILKS, John, F.R.S., F.Z.S. 3 Finsbury Square, London. Westminster, London. S. of the Rev. Matthew Wilks, an eminent Dissenting minister, and Elizabeth Shenstone, cousin to Shenstone the poet. B. 1776. Was formerly a Solicitor, principally practising in Parliamentary and public matters, but retired in 1825. Honorary Secretary to the Society for the Protection of Religious Liberty; member of the London Institution. A Magistrate for Middlesex. A Trustee of the Westminster Club; was introduced by Mr. Fox and the Duke of Norfolk to 'the Whig Club'. Was considered the organ of the Dissenters. A Reformer. Unsuccessfully contested Boston in 1826; sat for it from 1830 until he retired in 1837. Contested St. Albans July 1847. Died 25 Aug. 1854. [1837]

WILLCOX, Brodie McGhie. 28 Portman Square, London. Roydon Lodge, Hertfordshire. Reform. B. 1785; m. 1812, d. of Benjamin Vander Gucht, Esq., of Brook Street. A Ship-Owner; Chairman of the Peninsular and Oriental Steam Navigation Company, of the Southampton Docks, and of the Universal Life Assurance Society; an East India Proprietor. A Liberal, in favour of a wide extension of the franchise, vote by ballot, and direct taxation; opposed to the application of any part of the public funds to religious endowments. First returned for Southampton in 1847, and sat until his death in 1862. [1862]

WILLIAMS, Benjamin Thomas. 65 Hilldrop Crescent, London. 4 Harcourt Buildings, Temple, London. Merryvale, Narberth, Pembrokeshire. Eld. s. of Rev. T.R. Williams, of Merryvale, Narberth, Pembrokeshire, by Mira, d. of T.R. Thomas, Esq., of Narberth. B. at Merryvale, Narberth 1832; m. 1857, Margaret, only d. of T. John, Esq., of Dolemain. Was educ. at Glasgow University, where he gained high distinction, and graduated M.A. 1854. Was called to the bar at Gray's Inn 1859; made a Queen's Counsel 1875, one of the leaders of the South Wales and Chester circuit. Recorder of Carmarthen from 1872 to 1878. A Magistrate for Pembrokeshire. Author of various treatises on legal and social subjects. A Liberal. Sat for the district of Carmarthen from May 1878 until appointed County Court Judge Dec. 1881. Died 21 Mar. 1890. [1881]

WILLIAMS, Charles Henry. Pilton House, Barnstaple, Devonshire. Junior United Service. B. 1834, 4th s. of Sir William Williams, Bart, of Tregullow, Cornwall, by Caroline, d. of Richard Eales of Easdon, near Exeter. M. 1858, Harriet Mary, eld. d. of Arthur Davie Bassett, of Watermouth and Umberleigh, Devonshire. Served in the navy. A Conservative. Sat for Barnstaple from Dec. 1868 until 1873, when he accepted Chiltern Hundreds. [1873]

WILLIAMS, David. Dendraeth Castle, Penryndendraeth, Merionethshire. Reform. B. at Saethon, Carnarvonshire 1801, the 3rd s. of David Williams, Esq., of Saethon, by Jane, his wife. M. 1841, Anne Louisa Loneday, only d. of William Williams, Esq., Barrister-at-law, of Pennarthuchay, Merionethshire. Dept.-Lieut. and Magistrate for the Cos. of Merioneth and Carnarvon, and was High Sheriff of Merioneth 1841 and of Carnarvon 1842. Patron of 1 living. A Liberal, who supported Gladstone because during the time he was Chancellor of the Exchequer no less than 10 millions p.a. of the public taxes were taken away and 13 millions of the national debt paid off. Favoured the disestablishment of the Irish Church, opening the universities, extending education by compulsory rates and vote by ballot. Sat for the Co. of Merioneth from Dec. 1868 until his death 15 Dec. 1869. [1869]

WILLIAMS, Sir Frederick Martin, Bart. Goonvrea, Perranarworthal, Cornwall. Carlton, Windham, Junior Carlton, and City Carlton. Eld. s. of Sir William Williams, 1st Bart., of Tregullow, Cornwall, and Heanton Court, Devon, by Caroline, d. of Richard Eales, Esq., of Easdon, Devon. B. at Tregullow 1830; m. 1858, Mary Christian, d. of the Rev. Robert Law, Prebendary of Wells, and grand-d. of the Bishop of Bath and Wells. Educ. at Winchester. A Conservative, voted against the disestablishment of the Irish Church 1869. Sat for Truro from Feb. 1865. MP until his death 3 Sept. 1878. [1878]

WILLIAMS, Lieut.-Col. George. 56 Russell Square, London. Little Woolton, Lancaster. After a long service in the army, he was appointed to the command of a regiment of volunteers at Liverpool. A radical Reformer. He was personally unknown to the electors of Ashton-under-Lyne who elected him in 1832 against his repeatedly expressed wishes. Defeated in 1835. [1834]

WILLIAMS, Sir James Hamlyn. 20 Upper Grosvenor Street, London. Edwinsford, Carmarthenshire. Clovelly Court, Devon. B. 1790; m. 1823, Mary, the 4th d. of Hugh, Earl of Fortescue. Was a Maj. in the 7th Hussars. His father and grandfather represented Carmarthenshire. Patron of 1 living. A Reformer. Sat for Carmarthenshire in 1831; lost his election 1832; regained his seat in 1835. Defeated in 1837. [1837]

WILLIAMS, John. A Linen Draper and Silk Mercer in the Regent's Circus, Oxford Street; Partner in the firm of Williams and Hatton, but retired in 1849. A Cornet in the Denbighshire Yeomanry Cavalry. A member of the Marylebone vestry. Declared himself in favour of universal suffrage, and other 'points of the People's Charter.' Contested Bristol Dec. 1832. First returned for Macclesfield 1847, and sat until he was defeated July 1852. Treasurer of National Parliamentary and Financial Reform Association 1849 until his death 29 Nov. 1855. [1852]

WILLIAMS, Michael. Trevince, Nr. Truro. Scorrier House, Nr. Truro. Carhayes Castle, Nr. Tregony. Gnaton Hall, Nr. Plymouth. Athenaeum, and Reform. Eld. surviving s. of John Williams, Esq., of Scorrier House, Cornwall. B. 1785; m. Elizabeth, eld. d. of Richard Eales, Esq., of Eastdon House, near Dawlish (she died July 1852). Was High Sheriff of Glamorgan, 1839. Head of the large Copper Smelting firm of Williams, Foster, and Co., also of the Tin Smelting firm of Williams, Harvey, and Co. A Magistrate and Dept.-Lieut. of Cornwall; a Deputy Warden of the Stannaries. A Banker at Truro, Falmouth, and Redruth. A Liberal, opposed to church-rates for new churches; in favour of education without religious interference, and of extension of the franchise, but would, if possible, avoid resorting to the ballot. First returned for Cornwall W. July 1853, without opposition. MP until he died 15 June 1858. [1858]

WILLIAMS, Owen Lewis Cope. 24 Hill Street, Berkeley Square, London. Temple House, Great Marlow. Craig-y-don, Bangor, North Wales. White's, and Carlton. Eld. s. of Col. Thomas Peers Williams, who represented Marlow for nearly 50 years (from 1820 to 1868), by Emily, youngest d. of Anthony Bacon, of Benham Park, Berkshire. B. 1836; m. 1862, Fanny Florence, 2nd d. of St. George Francis Caulfield, Esq., of Donamon Castle, Roscommon (she died 1876). Educ. at Eton. Entered the Royal Horse Guards 1854, became Capt. 1858, Lieut.-Col. 1866, and Col. from 1871. Accompanied the Prince of Wales to India in 1875-76. Patron of 2 livings. A Conservative, and gave an independent support to that party. Sat for Great Marlow from Apr. 1880 until he retired in 1885. Died 15 Jan. 1913. [1885]

WILLIAMS, Robert, sen. 36 Grosvenor Square, London. Bridehead, Dorchester. Eld. s. of Robert

Williams, Esq., of Moor Park, Co. Hertfordshire, and of Bridehead, Co. Dorset, a Banker in London and former MP for Dorchester. B. 1767; m. 1794, Frances, youngest d. of John Turner, Esq., of Putney. Was an Alderman and Sheriff of London and resigned the former office in 1801. A Banker of London, an East India Proprietor, Chairman of the Hope Life Assurance Company, and Treasurer of the Society for Promoting the Religious Principles of the Reformation. A Manager of the London and Southampton Railway Company. A Conservative. Sat in two Parliaments for Wootton Bassett, one for the city of Kilkenny, and for Dorchester from 1812, when he succeeded his father in the representation of that borough. MP until he retired in 1835. [1834]

WILLIAMS, Robert, jun. 36 Grosvenor Square, London. Bridehead, Dorset. Carlton. Eld. s. of Robert Williams, Esq., who previously represented Dorchester. B. 1811. A Conservative. Sat for Dorchester from 1835, when he succeeded his father in the representation of the borough. MP until he retired in 1841. High Sheriff of Dorset 1855. Died 7 June 1890. [1841]

WILLIAMS, Samuel Charles Evans. 20 Davies Street, London. Bryntirion, Rhayader, Radnorshire. Abernant, Builth, Brecknockshire. Devonshire. Eld. s. of the Rev. John Williams of Bryntirion, former Student and Censor of Christ Church, Oxford, by Mary Charlotte, relict of John Patterson, Esq., of Devon. B. at Spelsbury Vicarage, Oxfordshire, 1842; m. 1867, Mary Caroline, 3rd d. of Rev. William R. Luttman Johnson (formerly Michell), of Binderton, Sussex. Educ. at Westminster and at Christ Church, Oxford, graduated B.A. 1864, M.A. 1877. A Magistrate for Radnorshire for which he served the office of High Sheriff 1880. An advanced Liberal, and in favour of the extension of the county franchise, reform of the land laws, increased local self-government etc. Sat for Radnor district from May 1880, when a vacancy occurred on a double return for that borough. Accepted Chiltern Hundreds 1884. Died 2 Mar. 1926. [1884]

WILLIAMS, Col. Thomas Peers. 41 Berkeley Square, London. Temple House, Great Marlow. Craig y Don, Anglesey. Carlton, and Boodle's. Eld. s. of Owen Williams, Esq., of Temple House. MP for Marlow from 1796 to 1832, by Margaret, sister of the last Lord Dinorben (extinct). B. 1795. Patron of 1 living. Appointed Lieut.-Col. Commandant Royal Anglesey Infantry Militia, 1853. A Conservative, but was a frequent opponent of the Liverpool and the Wellington Administrations; voted in favour of Lord Derby's

Reform Bill, Mar. 1859. Sat for Marlow uninterruptedly from 1820 until he retired in 1868. Died 8 Sept. 1875. [1867]

WILLIAMS, Watkin, Q.C. 97 St. George's Road, London. Plas Draw, Ruthin, North Wales. S. of the Rev. Peter Williams, Rector of Llansannan, Denbighshire, by Lydia, d. of the Rev. James Price, of Plas-yn-Llysfaen, Carnarvonshire. B. at Llangar, Merionethshire 1828; m. 1st, 1855, d. of W.H. Cary, Esq.; 2ndly, 1865, Elizabeth, d. of the Hon. Sir Robert Lush, Justice of the Queen's Bench. Educ. at the Grammar School, Ruthin, afterwards at Oxford and at the University of London. Was called to the bar 1854 at the Inner Temple of which he was a bencher. A 'thorough Liberal'; not favourable to the 'Permissive' Bill. Sat for Denbigh from Dec. 1868-Apr. 1880, from which date he sat for Carnarvonshire until appointed a Judge later that year. [1880 2nd ed.]

WILLIAMS, William. 12 Park Square, Regent's Park, London. Reform. A Merchant. A radical Reformer, advocated the strictest retrenchment in the public expenditure; in favour of the repeal of the 'inquisitorial income tax', extension of the suffrage, vote by ballot, the abolition of Church rates, etc. Represented Coventry from Jan. 1835 until the general election 1847. First returned for Lambeth July 1850. MP until his death 28 Apr. 1865. [1865]

WILLIAMS, William Addams. 25 Duke Street, St. James's, London. Llangybi Castle, Monmouthshire. B. 1787; m. 1818, d. of Rev. Dr. Nicholl. Patron of 4 livings. A Reformer, in favour of the ballot. Sat for Monmouthshire from 1831, until he accepted Chiltern Hundreds Jan. 1841. Died 5 Sept. 1861. [1840]

WILLIAMS OF KARS, Sir William Fenwick, Bart. 3 Devonport Street, Hyde Park, London. Woolwich, London. Army & Navy. 2nd s. of Thomas Williams, Esq., Commissary General and Barrack-master at Halifax, in Nova Scotia, by the d. of Captain Thomas Walker. B. at Annapolis, Nova Scotia, 1800. Unmarried. Educ. at the Royal Military Academy of Woolwich. Entered the artillery as 2nd Lieut. 1825, and became Capt. in 1840; Brevet-Col. in 1848. Received the local rank of Brigadier-Gen. in Turkey, Dec. 1855; was granted a pension of £1000 a year for life, a Baronetcy, the order of the Bath, the Turkish order of the Medjidie of the 1st class, the freedom of the city of London and a sword, the honorary degree of D.C.L. from Oxford, etc., for his gallant defence of Kars, in 1855. Appointed Commandant at Woolwich, June 1856. A Liberal. First elected for Calne, July

1856, without opposition. Retired in 1859. A command in Canada 1859-65. Governor of Gibraltar 1870-76. Died 26 July 1883.   [1858]

WILLIAMSON, Sir Hedworth, Bart., sen. 17 Eaton Place, London. Whitburn Hall, and Monkwearton, Co. Durham. S. of Sir Hedworth Williamson (the 6th Bart.) by the d. of Sir James Hamilton, of Monaghan. B. at Whitburn Hall, Durham, 1797; m. 1826, Anne Elizabeth, 3rd d. of 1st Lord Ravensworth. Educ. at St. John's Coll., Cambridge, where he graduated M.A. 1819. A Dept.-Lieut. of Durham; was elected Mayor of Sunderland for 1841-42, and again for 1847-48. Patron of 1 living. A moderate Whig, in favour of an alteration of the Bank Charter Act. Represented the Co. of Durham in 1831, and the Northern div. from 1832 till 1837. First returned for Sunderland in Dec. 1847 and sat until he retired in 1852. Died 24 Apr. 1861.   [1852]

WILLIAMSON, Sir Hedworth, Bart., jun. 23 Chesham Street, London. Whitburn Hall, Sunderland. Boodle's, and Travellers'. B. in Florence 1827, the s. of Sir Hedworth Williamson (7th Bart.), by the Hon. Ann Elizabeth, 3rd d. of 1st Lord Ravensworth. M. 1852, his cousin Hon. Elizabeth, 3rd d. of 2nd Lord Ravensworth. Educ. at Eton and at Christ Church, Oxford. Was Attaché at St. Petersburg and Paris 1848-56. A Dept.-Lieut. of Durham, and Capt. Commandant of 1st Durham Artillery Volunteers 1860. Patron of 1 living. A Liberal. Sat for Durham N. from June 1864 until 1874, when he retired. Sheriff of Durham 1877. Died 26 Aug. 1900.   [1873]

WILLIAMSON, S. Continued in House after 1885: full entry in Volume II.

WILLIS, William. 8 King's Bench Walk, Temple, London. 12 Northbrook Road, Lee, Kent. Reform, Devonshire, and City Liberal. S. of Mr. William Willis, Manufacturer, Luton, by Esther Kentish, d. of Mr. Johnson Masters, of Dunstable. B. at Dunstable 1835; m. 1866, Annie, d. of John Outhwaite, Esq., of Clapton. Educ. at Huddersfield Coll., and graduated LL.D. at London University. Was called to the bar at the Inner Temple June 1861; made a Q.C. Feb. 1877. A Liberal. Sat for Colchester from Apr. 1880 until he contested Peckham division, Camberwell in 1885 and again 1886. County Court Judge 1897-1906. Died 22 Aug. 1911.   [1885]

WILLOUGHBY, Sir Henry Pollard. 63A Lower Brook Street, London. Baldon House, Oxford. Berwick Lodge, Gloucestershire. Carlton, Conservative, Travellers', and Oriental. 2nd s. of Sir Christopher Willoughby, Bart., by his 2nd

wife, d. of Maurice Evans, Esq. B. 1796; A Dept.-Lieut. of Oxfordshire. Patron of 1 living. A Conservative, voted for the first Reform Bill; voted in favour of Lord Derby's Reform Bill, Mar. 1859. Sat for Yarmouth, Isle of Wight, on the Reform interest in 1831; represented Newcastle-under-Lyme from 1832-1835; was an unsuccessful candidate for Poole on the Conservative interest in 1837, and also contested Northampton without success in 1841. First returned for Evesham in 1847 and sat until his death 23 Mar. 1865.   [1865]

WILLOUGHBY, John Pollard. 18 Westbourne Terrace, London. Carlton, and Oriental. 3rd s. of Sir Christopher Willoughby, 1st Bart., of Baldon House, Oxfordshire, by his 2nd wife, Martha, d. of Maurice Evans, Esq. B. at Baldon House 1799; m. 1st, 1822, Eliza, only d. of Maj.-Gen. Michael Kennedy, C.B. of the E.I.C.S.; 2ndly, 1854, Maria Elizabeth, d. of Thos. Hawker, Esq., of Barnes, Surrey. Served in India in the E.I.C. Civil Service on the Bombay establishment from Feb. 1819 to May 1851, when he retired. Was Assistant-Resident and Acting-Resident at Baroda from 1819 to 1829; Secretary and Chief-Secretary to the Bombay Government from 1835 to 1846; Member of the Government there from 1846 to 1851. A Director of the E.I.C., appointed by the Crown, 1854. A Liberal-Conservative, 'firmly attached to our Protestant Church and Institutions'; condemned 'the proceedings at Canton as extreme and precipitate', but considered 'we cannot now recede'; in favour of a 'combined secular and separately religious education'; opposed to a 'compulsory local school rate'; supported an 'amicable adjustment' of the church-rate question. Was an unsuccessful candidate for Leominster in July 1852. First returned for Leominster Apr. 1857 and sat until appointed member of Council for India 1858. Succeeded bro. as 4th Bart. 1865. Died 15 Sept. 1866. [1858]

WILLS, W.H. Continued in House after 1885: full entry in Volume II.

WILLYAMS, Edward Brydges. 21 Upper Brook Street, London. Carnanton, St. Columbs, Cornwall. Nanskeval, Cornwall. Arthur's, and Oxford & Cambridge. Eld. surviving s. of Humphrey Willyams, Esq., of Carnanton (who represented Truro from 1849 to 1852), by Ellen Frances, d. of Col. Neynoe, of Castle Neynoe, Co. Sligo. B. at Carnanton 1836; m. 1st, 1856, Jane, 2nd d. and co-heir of Sir Trevor Wheler, Bart., of Leamington, Hastings, Warwickshire (she died 1877); 2ndly, 1882, Emily, d. of J.M. Levy, Esq., of Grosvenor Street, London. Was educ. at Merton Coll., Oxford. A Magistrate and Dept.-Lieut.

of Cornwall; a Deputy-Warden of the Stannaries of Cornwall and Devon. Patron of 1 living. A Liberal. Sat for Truro from May 1857 to Apr. 1859. Sat for Cornwall E. from Dec. 1868 to Feb. 1874. He was again elected for Truro Apr. 1880 and sat until he retired in 1885. Contested Mid division of Cornwall 18 May 1887. Died 9 Jan. 1917. [1885]

WILLYAMS, Humphrey. 12 Upper Montagu Street, London. Mount Charles, Truro. Carnanton, Cornwall. Reform. Eld. s. of James Willyams, Esq., of Carnanton, Cornwall, by Ann, only d. of William Champion, Esq., of Wormley, Gloucestershire. B. at Truro, 1792; m. 1822, Ellen Frances, youngest d. of Col. Neynoe, of Castle Neynoe, Co. Sligo. A Banker at Truro, and Head of the Copper Smelting Company of Sims, Willyams, Nevill, and Co. A Magistrate; Mayor of the Cornwall Miners Militia. Patron of 1 living. A Liberal, in favour of civil and religious liberty, education of the people, and the reduction of the national expenditure; opposed to the endowment of the Roman Catholic Clergy. First returned for Truro Jan. 1849, on the death of Mr. Turner. MP until he retired in 1852. Died 7 May 1872. [1852]

WILMOT, Sir Henry, Bart. 20 Montagu Street, London. Chaddesden Hall, Derby. Carlton, and Army & Navy. S. of Sir Henry Sacheverell Wilmot, 4th Bart., of Chaddesden Hall, Derbyshire, by Maria, eld. d. of Edward Miller Mundy, Esq., of Shipley Hall, Derbyshire. B. at Chaddesden 1831; m. 1862, Charlotte Cecilia, d. of Rev. Frederick Pare, M.A. Educ. at Rugby. Entered the 43rd Foot 1849; became Capt. Rifle Brigade 1856, Brevet-Maj. 1858. Received a medal and clasp for Lucknow; also a medal and two clasps for China. Received the Victoria Cross for acts of personal bravery at Lucknow. Was Judge-Advocate-Gen. to the Forces during the Chinese war 1860-61. A Conservative, and a staunch supporter of Church and State, in determined opposition to Mr. Gladstone's policy. Sat for Derbyshire S. from Jan. 1869 until he retired in 1885. Died 6 Apr. 1901. [1885]

WILMOT, Sir John Eardley Eardley-, Bart., sen. Berkswell Hall, Warwickshire. Athenaeum. B. 1783; m. 1st, Elizabeth, d. of C.H. Parry, Esq., M.D. of Bath; 2ndly, 1819, Elizabeth, eld. d. of Sir Robert Chester, of Bush Hall, Hertfordshire. A Conservative, said he would vote for triennial Parliaments and the ballot, if Parliament did not adopt some plan to secure electors the free exercise of their franchise, and that he would resign his seat if required to do so by a requisition from his constituents. Sat for Warwickshire N. from 1832 until appointed Governor of Van Dieman's

Land in 1842. Died in 1847. [1842]

WILMOT, Sir John Eardley Eardley-, Bart., jun. Thurloe Square, London. Berkswell Hall, Warwickshire. St. Stephen's. S. of Sir John Eardley Eardley-Wilmot, (1st) Bar., by his 1st wife, Elizabeth Emma, d. of Caleb Hillier Parry, M.D., of Bath (sister of Admiral Sir Edward Parry, R.N.). B. at Wootton, Warwickshire, 1810; m. 1839, Eliza Martha, d. of Sir Robert Williams, Bart., and sister of Sir R.B. Williams Bulkeley, Bart. Was educ. first at Rugby in 1821, but transferred to Winchester, where he received the gold medal in 1828; also at Balliol Coll., Oxford, where he obtained the Chancellor's prize for Latin verse 1829. Was called to the bar at Lincoln's Inn 1842, and for some years with the Midland circuit. Appointed Recorder of Warwick 1852, resigned 1874; was Judge of the County Court of Bristol from Jan. 1854 to 1863, and of the Marylebone district from the latter date to Nov. 1871. A Dept.-Lieut. for Warwickshire from 1852. A Conservative. Sat for Warwickshire S. from Feb. 1874 until he contested the Edgbaston division of Birmingham in Nov. 1885. Died 1 Feb. 1892. [1885]

WILSHERE, William. 11 Stratton Street, London. Hitchin, Hertfordshire. Reform. S. of Thomas Willshere, Esq., of Hitchin, Hertfordshire, Lord of the Manor of Wymondley, which was held by the tenure of presenting a silver cup to the Sovereign at the coronation. B. 1806. Professed Liberal opinions. Formerly voted against an abolition of the Corn Laws, but in 1846 supported their repeal. First elected for Yarmouth 25 July 1837 and sat until he retired in 1847. Sheriff of Hertfordshire 1858. Died 10 Nov. 1867. [1847]

WILSON, Anthony. Rauceby Hall, Nr. Sleaford. S. of Anthony Taylor Peacock, Esq., by Mary, d. of John Willson, Esq., of Lincoln. B. 1811; m. 1845, Mary Eliza Caroline, 2nd d. of the Rev. Edward Fane, of Fulbeck, Lincolnshire. Assumed the name of Wilson by Royal sign manual 1851. Educ. at Trinity Coll., Cambridge, where he graduated M.A. A Banker, Senior Partner in the firm of Peacock, Handleys, and Co., of Sleaford and Newark. A Magistrate and Dept.-Lieut. for Lincolnshire, for which he was High Sheriff in 1854. A Conservative, opposed to the Chinese war; 'adverse to constant changes in the elective franchise' and to the ballot; in favour of economy in the public service 'to the fullest extent consistent with the honour and safety of the country.' First elected for Lincolnshire S. Apr. 1857. Retired in 1859. [1858]

WILSON, C.H. Continued in House after 1885: full entry in Volume II.

WILSON, F. Maitland. A Conservative. Returned for Suffolk W. 17 June 1875. Sat until his death 4 Sept. 1875.

WILSON, Henry. Stowlangtoft Hall, Suffolk. University. Only s. of Joseph Wilson, Esq., of Highbury Hill, Middlesex, Stowlangtoft, Suffolk, and Little Mossingham, Norfolk. B. 1797; m. 1824, Mary, eld. d. of Ebenezer Fuller Maitland, Esq., of Park Place, Henley on Thames, formerly MP for Wallingford. A Director of the Hand-in-Hand Fire Office. A moderate Reformer. Sat for Suffolk W. from 1835. Defeated in 1837. Died 8 June 1866. [1837]

WILSON, Isaac. Continued in House after 1885: full entry in Volume II.

WILSON, Rt. Hon. James. 12 Upper Belgrave Street, London. Claverton Manor, Nr. Bath. Reform. S. of William Wilson, Esq., of Hawick House, Roxburghshire and bro. to Walter Wilson, Esq., of Orchard House in the same Co. B. at Hawick 1805; m. 1832, Elizabeth, d. of William Preston, Esq., of Newcastle-on-Tyne. Was Sec. to the Board of Control from May 1848-Mar. 1852. Financial Sec. to the Treasury from Dec. 1852-Mar. 1858. A Magistrate and Dept.-Lieut. for Wiltshire and a Magistrate for Somerset. Published *Influences of Corn Laws* (1839), *Fluctuations of Currency, Commerce and Manufacture* (1840), *The Revenue; or What Should the Chancellor do?*(1841), *Capital, Currency and Banking* (1847). Established in 1843 the *Economist* Newspaper, of which he was for some years chief editor and sole proprietor. A Liberal, averse to religious endowments; voted against the ballot in 1853, and against Church rates 1855. Sat for Westbury from July 1847-Apr. 1857, when he was returned for Devonport. Accepted Chiltern Hundreds Aug. 1859. Financial Member of Council of India 1859. Died 11 Aug. 1860. [1858]

WILSON, Sir Mathew, Bart. Eshron Hall, Gargrave, Leeds. Athenaeum, and Devonshire. B. at Eshton Hall, 1802, eld. s. of Mathew Wilson, of Eshton Hall, Gargrave, West Riding, Yorkshire, by his cousin Margaret Clive, d. of Mathew Wilson. M. 1st, 1826, Sophia Louisa Emerson, only d. and heir of Sir Wharton Amcotts, Bart., of Kettlethorpe, Lincolnshire, (she died 1833); 2ndly, 1878, Frances, Widow of Col. Pedler of Brunswick Square, Brighton. Educ. at Harrow and at Brasenose Coll., of which he was a gentleman commoner and graduated B.A. A Magistrate for the West Riding of Yorkshire and Lancashire, and Dept.-Lieut. of the former. Patron of 2 livings. A Whig. Elected for Clitheroe in 1841, but unseated on petition. Sat for Clitheroe Aug. 1847-May 1853. Sat for the Northern division of the West Riding from Feb. 1874 until he was defeated, standing as a Gladstonian Liberal, in 1886. Died 18 Jan. 1891. [1886]

WILSON, William. 33 Lower Gardiner Street, Dublin. Raphoe, Co. Donegal. Carlton. S. of William Wilson, of Raphoe, Ireland, Solicitor, by Miss Jane Colboun, of Strabane, Co. Tyrone. B. at Raphoe 1836; m. 1865, d. of Daniel Wilson, Esq. (dead). Was educ. at Raphoe Royal School. A Solicitor admitted to practise in Ireland, 1860. A Liberal -Conservative, in favour of the Ulster custom of tenant right being secured to all tenants, whether leasehold or annual, in the North of Ireland; in favour also of the Burials Bill. Sat for Donegal from Aug. 1876. MP until his death 8 Nov. 1879. [1879]

WINDHAM, Gen. Charles Ashe, C.B. Myton, Warwickshire. Travellers', and Senior United Service. 4th s. of Vice-Admiral William Windham, of Felbrigg Hall, Norfolk (who assumed the name of Windham in lieu of his patronymic Lukyn, in compliance with the will of his uncle, the Rt. Hon. William Windham), by Anne, sister of the 1st Lord Rendlesham. B. at Felbrigg, Norfolk 1810; m. Marianne, d. of Admiral Sir John Beresford, Bart. Educ. at Sandhurst. Entered the army 1826; served the Eastern campaign of 1854-55, as Asst. Quarter-Master Gen., up to the fall of Sebastopol; promoted to Maj.-Gen. 1855, for having with the greatest intrepidity headed the column of attack which assaulted the enemy's defences on the 8 Sept. Made Chief of the Staff, created C.B., Commander of the Legion of Honour, Commander of the 1st Class of the Order of Savoy, and decorated with the Crimean medal and clasps. Appointed to command a division of the forces sent to India, Aug. 1857. A Liberal, a supporter of Lord Palmerston's foreign policy; in favour of a 'moderate measure for improving the Reform Act', and 'amicable settlement' of the church-rate question; wished to see 'the militia forces permanently established and well treated', and originated an excellent practical plan for effecting this object. First elected for Norfolk E. Apr. 1857. Retired in 1859. K.C.B. Mar. 1865. Command in Canada 1867. Died 4 Feb. 1870. [1858]

WINDHAM, William Howe. 5 Suffolk Place, London. Norfolk. Eld. s. of Vice-Admiral William Windham. Of Whig principles. Sat for Nofolk E. from 1832. Defeated in 1835. Contested seat again in 1837. Died 22 Dec. 1854. [1833]

WINGFIELD, Sir Charles John, K.C.S.I., C.B. 12 Albert Mansions, Victoria Street, London. Athenaeum, Brooks's, Reform and Arthur's. S. of William Wingfield-Baker of Orsett Hall, Essex (who assumed the name of Baker by royal license 1849), by his 2nd wife, Elizabeth, d. of William Mills, of Bisterne, Hampshire. B. 1820. Unmarried. Educ. at Westminster School and at Haileybury. Entered the Bengal Civil Service 1840, retired 1866. Was Chief Commissioner of Oude from Feb. 1859-Apr. 1866. A Liberal, in favour of the 'anomalies of the Reform Act being removed', especially in the redistribution of seats. Sat for Gravesend from Dec. 1868 until 1874, when he was defeated. Died 27 Jan. 1892. [1873]

WINGFIELD, R.B. See BAKER, R.B.W.

WINGFIELD-DIGBY, J.K.D. Continued in House after 1885: full entry in Volume II.

WINN, Rowland. 11 Grosvenor Gardens, London. Nostell Priory, Yorkshire. Appleby Hall, Brigg, Lincolnshire. Carlton, and Junior Carlton. S. of Charles Winn, Esq., of Nostell Priory, Yorkshire, and Appleby Hall, Lincolnshire, by Priscilla, d. of Sir William Strickland, 6th Bart. B. 1820; m. 1854, Harriet Maria Amelia, d. of Col. Damaresq, and niece of the 5th Earl of Lanesborough. Educ. at Trinity Coll., Cambridge. Was a Lord of the Treasury Feb. 1874 to 1880. A Magistrate of the East and West Riding of Yorkshire and of the Parts of Lindsey, Lincolnshire. A Dept.-Lieut. of Lincolnshire. A Conservative. Sat for Lincolnshire N. from Dec. 1868 until created Baron St. Oswald July 1885. Died 20 Jan. 1893. [1885]

WINNINGTON, Capt. Henry Jeffreys. 16 Suffolk Street, Stanford Court, Worcestershire. Reform, and Travellers'. Bro. of the member for Bewdley. A Whig. In favour of shortening the duration of Parliaments. Returned for Worcestershire in May 1833, in the room of Hon. Thomas Foley, his 2nd cousin, who then succeeded to his father's title. Sat for the county from 1833 until he retired 1841. Died 25 Aug. 1873. [1838]

WINNINGTON, Sir Thomas Edward, Bart. 16 Suffolk Street, London. Stanford Court, Worcester. Athenaeum, and Travellers'. Eld. s. of the 3rd Bart., by Joanna, d. of John Taylor, Esq., of Moseley Hall, near Birmingham. B. at Moseley Hall, 1811; m. 1842, Anne Helena, eld. d. of Sir Compton Domvile, Bart. Educ. at Christ Church, Oxford, where he graduated B.A. 1833. Patron of 4 livings, a Dept.-Lieut. of Worcestershire, and High Sheriff of that county in 1851. A Liberal,

voted against Church-rates 1855. Sat for Bewdley from 1837 to 1847; was an unsuccessful candidate in that year; was again elected there in July 1852 and sat until he retired in 1868. Died 16 June, 1872. [1867]

WINTERBOTHAM, Henry Selfe Page. 7 New Square, Lincoln's Inn, London. Stroud, Gloucestershire. B. at Tewkesbury 1837, the s. of Lindsay Winterbotham of Stroud, Banker. Educ. at Amersham School, and at University Coll., London. Called to the bar at Lincoln's Inn 1860. Appointed Under-Sec. of State for the Home Department, Mar. 1871. A Liberal. Sat for Stroud from Aug. 1867 until his death on 13 Dec. 1873. [1873]

WISE, Henry Christopher. Woodcote, Nr. Warwick. Carlton. B. at Offchurch, 1806, s. of Henry Wise, of the Priory, Warwick, by Charlotte Mary, d. of Sir Stanier Porter. M. 1st, 1828, Harriet, d. of Sir Gray Skipworth, Bart.; 2ndly, Jane Harriet, youngest d. of Sir Edward C. Disbrowe, G.C.H. Educ. at Rugby and at Oriel Coll., Oxford. A Magistrate and Dept.-Lieut. of Warwickshire. Patron of 2 livings. A Conservative, opposed to any severance of Church from State. Favoured the repeal of the Malt tax. Sat for Warwickshire S. from July 1865 until 1874, when he retired. Died 15 Jan. 1883. [1873]

WISE, John Ayshford. Clayton Hall, Nr. Newcastle, Staffordshire. Reform. Eld. s. of Ayshford Wise, Esq., (MP for Totnes in 1812), by Mary, d. of the Rev. Thomas Whitby, of Cresswell Hall, Stafford, and aunt to the 1st Lord Portman. B. 1810; m. 1st, 1837, Mary Lovett, only d. and heir of Hugh Booth, Esq., of Cliff Bank, Stafford (she died 1844); 2ndly, 1848, Anne Mary, d. of the Rev. Lewis Way, of Stanstead Park. Educ. in Paris, Germany, and Italy, with a view to entering the diplomatic service. Appointed a Magistrate and Dept.-Lieut. of Devon 1832, and of Stafford in 1837; was High Sheriff of the latter county in 1852. A Liberal, an administrative and financial reformer; took an active interest in the poor law, the revision of the law of settlement, etc.; voted for inquiry into Maynooth 1853, and against Church rates 1855. First returned for Stafford July 1852 and sat until he accepted Chiltern Hundreds Aug. 1860. Contested Newcastle-under-Lyme in 1865. Died 9 Sept. 1865. [1860]

WODEHOUSE, Edmond. Bracondale Hill, Norwich. Sennowe, Norfolk. S. of Thomas Wodehouse, Esq., by the d. of Pryce Campbell, Esq., of Stackpole Court, Pembrokeshire. A cousin of Lord Wodehouse and Earl Cawdor. M.

1809, his cousin Lucy, d. of Rev. Philip Wodehouse. Patron of 1 living, and Dept.-Lieut. of Norfolk. A Conservative, voted for agricultural protection 1846. Sat for Norfolk E. from 1817-30 and for the Eastern division from 1835 until he accepted Chiltern Hundreds in 1855.   [1855]

WODEHOUSE, E.R. Continued in House after 1885: full entry in Volume II.

WOLFF, Sir Henry Drummond, G.C.M.G., K.C.B. 4 Chesham Street, London. Boscombe Tower, Bournemouth. Carlton, and Athenaeum. S. of the Rev. Dr. Wolff, by Lady Georgiana, d. of the 2nd Earl of Orford. B. 1830; m. 1852, the only d. of Sholto Douglas, Esq. Educ. at Rugby. Entered the Foreign Office 1846; was attached to the legation at Florence 1852, where he served for a short time as acting chargé d'affaires; attached in 1856 to the Earl of Westmoreland's special mission to Brussels. Was public secretary to the Lord High Commissioner of the Ionian Islands from 1859 to 1864, when those islands were ceded to the Greek government. Appointed assistant Private Secretary to the Earl of Malmesbury (Foreign Secretary) Feb. 1858; Private Secretary to Sir Bulwer Lytton (Colonial Secretary) Feb. 1858. Was Commissioner for Great Britain on the International Commission at Berlin for the re-organisation of Eastern Roumelia in 1878. Author of a work on the *Residence of Napoleon at Elba* etc. A Conservative, in favour of 'our army and navy being efficiently maintained', of the abolition of the Income Tax, and of 'diminishing as far as possible all burdens on articles of consumption'; 'firmly attached to the Church of England'. Was an unsuccessful candidate for Christchurch Dec. 1868. Sat for Christchurch from Feb. 1874 to Apr. 1880, when he represented Portsmouth and sat until defeated in 1885. Ambassador at Madrid 1892-1900. Died 11 Oct. 1908.   [1885]

WOOD, Benjamin. 24 Great George Street, London. 25 Mark Lane, London. Eltham Lodge, Kent. B. in 1787, the s. of Mr. Wood, a Serge-Maker at Tiverton. Bro. to Sir M. Wood, Bart. M. 1815, the d. of Admiral Michell, of the Portuguese Navy. A Hop Merchant in the borough of Southwark. Voted against the Corn Laws. Was a candidate at Tiverton in 1832 and at Hull in 1837, on the Liberal interest. Was an active supporter of reform candidates at various elections in London, Southwark, Devonshire, and Cornwall. Sat for the borough of Southwark from 1840 until his death in 1845.   [1844]

WOOD, Rt. Hon. Sir Charles, Bart. G.C.B. 10 Belgrave Square, London. Hickleton Hall, Don-caster. Reform, Travellers', and Brooks's. B. at Pontefract 1800, the eld. s. of Sir Francis Lindley Wood, Bart. M. 1829, Lady Mary, 4th d. of 2nd Earl Grey. Educ. at Eton and at Oriel Coll., Oxford, where he took a double 1st in 1821. Was Private Secretary to Earl Grey; became Secretary of the Treasury 1832-Nov. 1834, Secretary to the Admiralty Apr. 1835-Sept. 1839, Chancellor of the Exchequer July 1846-Mar. 1852, President of the Board of Control Dec. 1852-Feb.1855, First Lord of the Admiralty 1855-Mar. 1858, Secretary of State for India (salary £5000) June 1859, and Lord Privy Seal July 1870-1874. A Dept.-Lieut. for the West Riding of Yorkshire. Patron of 1 living. Sat for Great Grimsby 1826-31, when he was elected for Wareham; sat for Halifax 1832-July 1865, and for Ripon July 1865-1866, when he accepted Chiltern Hundreds. Created 1st Visct. Halifax of Monk Bretton, Feb. 1866. Died 8 Aug. 1885.   [1865 2nd ed.]

WOOD, George William, F.L.S. Pall Mall East. Singleton Lodge, Lancashire. Brooks's. S. of the Rev. W. Wood of Leeds. B. 1781; m. 1810 the eld. d. of Jos. Oates, Esq., of Westwood Hall, near Leeds. A Merchant. Sat for South Lancashire from 1832 until defeated 1835. Professed himself a Whig of the school of Charles James Fox, and consequently a friend of civil and religious liberty. Was chosen for Kendal without opposition in 1837. MP until his death Oct. 1843.   [1843]

WOOD, Sir Matthew, Bart. 24 Great George Street, London. Little Strawberry Hill, Middlesex. Hatherly Court, Gloucestershire. M. 1795, d. of John Page, Esq. A Hop-Merchant in London, and an Ald. of London. Lord Mayor in 1815-16 and 1816-17. A radical Reformer, in favour of free-trade, the vote by ballot, triennial Parliaments and the repeal of part of the assessed taxes. Represented city of London in five successive Parliaments before 1832 and continuously from that year until his death 25 Sept. 1843.   [1843]

WOOD, Col. Thomas. sen. Littleton, Middlesex. Gwernevet, Brecknockshire. Carlton. Eld. s. of T. Wood, Esq., of Littleton House, Staines. Patron of 1 living. M. 1801, Caroline, d. of the 1st Marq. of Londonderry, Aide-de-camp to the Queen, Col. of the East Middlesex Militia, and an East India Proprietor. A Conservative, in favour of Poor Laws for Ireland; voted for the Reform Act, but against Catholic emancipation, against the repeal of the malt tax, and generally supported the Liverpool and the Wellington Administrations. Formerly declared in favour of the Corn Laws, but in 1846 supported their repeal. Was first elected for Brecknockshire in 1806 and

sat until he retired in 1847. Died 23 Oct. 1872.
[1847]

WOOD, Col. Thomas, jun. 45 Albemarle Street. Littleton, Middlesex. S. of the member for Brecknockshire, and nephew to the Marq. of Londonderry and of the lady of Sir Henry Hardinge. A Capt. in the Grenadier Guards. Of Conservative principles, but in favour of free trade. Contested Middlesex, without success in 1835, but came in at the general election in 1837, defeating Mr. Hume, the late member. Sat until he was defeated in 1847. Died 26 Jan. 1860.
[1847]

WOOD, Western. 29 Mark Lane, London. North Cray Place, North Cray, Kent. 3rd s. of Alderman Sir Matthew Wood (1st Bart.) who represented London from 1812 until his death in 1843, by Maria, d. of John Page, Esq., M.D. of Woodbridge, Suffolk. B. in Falcon Square, London, 1804; m. 1829, Sarah Letitia, youngest d. of John Morris,. Esq., of the Bombay Civil Service. Educ. at Winchester. Was a Hop Merchant from 1822; head of the firm of Messrs. Wood, Field, and Hanbury. A member of the Court of Assistants of the Fishmongers' Company from 1845; Prime Warden of that Company 1860. A Governor of Guy's Hospital. A Magistrate for Kent. A Reformer, in favour of a £10 franchise in counties, and £6 in boroughs, the ballot, and the relief of Dissenters from church-rates but not their total abolition. First elected for London, July 1861. MP until his death 17 May 1863. [1863]

WOOD, William. Monkhill House, near Pontefract. S. of Mr. James Wood and ·Mary, his wife. B. at Pontefract 1816; m. 1840, d. of —. A Carpet Manufacturer; inventor of the carpet power looms, etc. A Liberal, described himself as 'a native and resident elector, who could be fairly classed as a working man'; wanted to show 'that the capability of governing is not solely confined to what is considered as the upper class of society'; anxious to succeed in 'utterly annihilating the odious income-tax'. First elected for Pontefract, Apr. 1857. Retired in 1859. Died 19 June 1872. [1858]

WOOD, Sir William Page, F.R.S. 12 Great George Street, Westminster, London. 2 Stone Buildings, Lincoln's Inn, London. 2nd s. of Alderman Sir Matthew Wood, Bart., by the d. of John Page, Esq., of Woodbridge, Suffolk. B. in London 1801; m. 1830, Charlotte, only d. of Edward Moor, Esq., of Great Bealings, Suffolk. Educ. at Winchester. Formerly a fellow of Trinity Coll., Cambridge, where he took a Wrangler's degree in 1824. Was called to the bar at Lincoln's Inn in 1827, made a Queen's Counsel 1845. Appointed Vice-Chancellor of the County Palatine of Lancaster 1849. Was Solicitor-Gen. from Mar. 1851-Mar. 1852. A Liberal. First returned for Oxford in 1847, without opposition and sat until appointed a Vice-Chancellor Jan. 1853. Lord Justice of Appeal Feb. 1868. Appointed Lord Chancellor and created Baron Hatherley Dec. 1868. Died 10 July 1881. [1852 2nd ed.]

WOODALL, W. Continued in House after 1885: full entry in Volume II.

WOODD, Basil Thomas. Conyngham Hall, Knaresborough, Yorkshire. Athenaeum, and Carlton. Eld. s. of Basil George Woodd, Esq., of Hillfield, Hampstead, by Mary, only d. of the Rev. Robert Mitton, of Harrogate, Yorkshire. Descended from the Woodds of Shinewood, Shropshire. B. in London 1815; m. 1837, Charlotte Mary, eld. d. of the Rev. John Dampier, of Colinshays, Somerset (she died Jan. 1874). Educ. at Trinity Coll., Cambridge, where he graduated B.A. 1837, M.A. 1840. Called to the bar at Lincoln's Inn 1840, but never practised. Appointed a Magistrate for the N. and W. Riding of Yorkshire in 1842, and Dept.-Lieut. for the latter 1853. A Conservative, and would maintain the connection between Church and State; in favour of denominational education. Sat for Knaresborough from July 1852-Nov. 1868, re-elected Feb. 1874 and sat until defeated 1880. Chairman of Quarter Sessions, West Riding of Yorkshire 1885-92. Died 4 June 1895. [1880]

WOODS, Henry. 21 Hyde Park Gardens, London. Gillibrand Hall, Chorley, Lancashire. Warnford Park, Bishop's Waltham, Hampshire. Brooks's, and Reform. B. 1822, only s. of William Woods, M. 1st, 1854, only child of Charles Hindley MP, of Portland House, Ashton--under-Lyne (she died 1857); 2ndly, 1864, Henrietta Emma, 5th d. of Rt. Rev. Dr. Gilbert, Bishop of Chichester. Largely engaged in Cotton Manufacture at Wigan, and in Collieries. Appointed Magistrate and Dept.-Lieut. for the Co. Palatine of Lancaster, 1860. A Liberal, voted for the disestablishment of the Irish Church 1869. Sat for Wigan from Apr. 1857 until 1874, when he was defeated. Sheriff of Hampshire 1880. Died 16 May 1882. [1873]

WOOLF, Sydney. 35 Penywern Road, London. Ferrybridge House, Knottingley. Devonshire. An Earthenware Manufacturer on a large scale at Knottingley, near Pontefract, Yorkshire. A Liberal. Sat for Pontefract from Apr. 1880 until he retired 1885. Q.C. 1890. Died 12 Mar. 1892. [1885]

WORCESTER, Marq. of. (I). Eld. s. of the Duke

of Beaufort. B. 1792; m. 1st, 1814, Georgina Frederica, 2nd s. of the Hon. Henry Fitzroy, of Southampton (she died 1821); 2ndly, 1822, Emily Frances, d. of Charles Culling Smith, Esq., and Anne, sister of the Marq. of Wellesley. Eld. bro. of Lord Grenville Somerset. A Conservative. Sat for Monmouth in several Parliaments, but was not in that of 1833. Returned for Gloucestershire W. in Jan. 1835 and sat until he succeeded father as 7th Duke of Beaufort, Nov. 1835. Died 17 Nov. 1853.
[1835]

WORCESTER, Marq. of. (II). 17 Berkeley Square, London. White's, and Boodle's. B. in Paris 1824; the eld. s. of the Duke of Beaufort. M. 1845, Lady Georgiana Charlotte, d. of 1st Lord Howe. Educ. at Eton. Became Lieut. 1st Life Guards in 1843 and Capt. 7th Dragoons in 1847. Appointed Aide-de-Camp to the Duke of Wellington, then Commander in Chief, Aug. 1842 and to his successor, Visct. Hardinge Sept. 1852. Appointed a Dept.-Lieut. of Gloucestershire June 1852. A Conservative, and voted in the minority of 53 who censured free trade in Nov. 1852. Believed the 'connection between Church and State to be one of the most vital points of our constitution.' First returned for Gloucestershire E. in Feb. 1846, without opposition, and sat until he succeeded his father as 8th Duke Nov. 1853. Died 30 Apr. 1899.
[1853]

WORSLEY, Lord. (I). 17 Arlington Street, London. Manby, Lincolnshire. Reform. B. 1809, the eld. s. of the Earl of Yarborough. M. 1831, Adelaide, eld. d. of 3rd Visct. Hawarden. Of Whig principles. Voted against an abolition of the Corn Laws, and in favour of a property tax in lieu of that on malt. Sat for Newton, Hampshire in 1830 and 1831, and for Lincolnshire N. from 1832 until he succeeded as 2nd Earl in Sept. 1846. Died 7 Jan. 1862.
[1845]

WORSLEY, Lord. (II). 17 Arlington Street, London. Manby Hall, Brigg, Lincolnshire. Brooks's, and Boodle's. Eld. s. of the 2nd Earl of Yarborough, by the 2nd d. of the 3rd Visct. Hawarden. B. a Manby Hall, Lincolnshire 1835. Appointed Capt. North Lincoln Militia 1853; and Lieut.-Col. 1st Battalion Lincolnshire Rifle Volunteers May 1860. A Dept.-Lieut. of Lincolnshire 1856. A Liberal, in favour of reform and progress in all matters relating to civil and religious liberty. First returned for Great Grimsby 1857 and sat until he succeeded as 3rd Earl 7 Jan. 1862. Died 6 Feb. 1875.
[1861]

WORTLEY, Archibald Henry Plantagenet Stuart-. Boodle's. Eld. s. of the Hon. Charles Stuart-Wortley (s. of 1st Lord Wharncliffe), by

Lady Emmeline Charlotte, 2nd d. of 5th Duke of Rutland. B. 1832. Entered the army as Lieut. 1848; became Capt. 1850, and Maj. 1854; retired on half-pay 1856. Served in the Kaffir war with the Cape Mounted Riflemen in 1850-53; during the operations against the Waterkloof commanded the cavalry attached to General Buller's division, and distinguished himself on two occasions in defeating a superior force of the enemy. Appointed Dept.-Assistant Quarter-Master Gen. to the army in the East 1854, and served in the campaign there 1854-55, for which he received a medal and clasps. A Conservative. First elected for Honiton, Apr. 1857. Retired in 1859. Died 22 Aug. 1881.
[1858]

WORTLEY, C.B. Stuart. See STUART-WORTLEY, C.B. Continued in House after 1885: full entry in Volume II.

WORTLEY, Rt. Hon. James Archibald Stuart-. Twysden Building, Temple, London. 3 Carlton Gardens, London. Carlton, and Travellers'. 3rd s. of 1st Lord Wharncliffe, by the d. of the 1st Earl of Erne. B. in St. James's Square, London 1805; m. 1846, only d. of the 1st Baron Wenlock. Educ. at Christ Church, Oxford, where he graduated B.A. 1826, M.A. 1831; called to the bar by the Inner Temple, 1831, and joined the Northern Circuit; became a Queen's Counsel in 1841, and was Judge-Advocate-Gen. from Jan. till July 1846. Appointed Solicitor-Gen. to the Queen Dowager 1845. Was Recorder of London from Sept. 1850 till Nov. 1856, and Solicitor-Gen. from the last date till June 1857. A Dept.-Lieut. of London and of Bute. A Liberal, but was formerly classed as a Conservative; voted for inquiry into Maynooth 1853. Contested Forfar Co. Jan 1835. Sat for Halifax from Jan. 1835 till July 1837; but unsuccessfully contested that bor. in 1832 and 1837. Sat for Buteshire from 1842 until defeated in 1859. Died 22 Aug. 1881.
[1858]

WORTLEY, Hon. John Stuart. 15 Curzon Street, London. 1 Elm Court, Temple, London. Wortley Hall, Yorkshire. Carlton. B. 1801, the eld. s. of Lord Wharncliffe. M. 1825, Lady Georgiana Elizabeth, d. of the 1st Earl of Harrowby. Was Lieut.-Col. of the South West Regiment of the Yorkshire Yeomanry Cavalry (West Riding). A Conservative. Sat for Yorkshire (West Riding) from 1841 until he succeeded as 2nd Baron in Dec. 1845. Died 22 Oct. 1855. [1845]

WOULFE, Rt. Hon. Stephen. Dublin. Brooks's, and Reform. B. 29 Oct. 1792; m. 1821, Mary Frances, d. of Roger Hamil, Esq., of Drogheda. Educ. at the University of Dublin, where he distinguished himself. Called to the bar in 1814. Appointed King's Counsel in Ireland 1831; King's

3rd Serjeant 1835. Solicitor Gen. for Ireland 1836, and Attorney Gen. 1837. Held the office of Ass. Barrister for the Co. of Galway from 1828 to 1830, when he resigned. A Whig. Elected for Cashel in Sept. 1835, on the vacancy caused by the elevation of Mr. Serjeant Perrin to the Bench, and sat until appointed Lord Chief Baron (Ireland) June 1838.   [1838]

WREN, Walter. 7 Powis Square, Westbourne Park, London. Reform. 2nd s. of Richard Wren, Esq., of Buntingford, Hertfordshire, by Sara, d. of John Sibley, Esq., of Wheathampstead, Hertfordshire. B. 1834; m. 1st, 1860, Eliza Cartwright, d. of William Cox, Esq., of Halesowen, Warwickshire; 2ndly, 1867, Emily, d. of E.W. Horn, Esq., of Richmond. Educ. successively at Buntingford School, Elizabeth Coll., Guernsey, and Christ's Coll., Cambridge, where he graduated B.A. 1859, M.A. 1862. A well-known private tutor in London for preparing candidates for all open competitive examinations. Published pamphlets on *Reform of the Magistracy*, Speeches, etc. A Liberal, in favour of financial reform, shorter Parliaments, etc.; also of municipal self-government, and the establishment of county boards. Sat for Wallingford from Apr. 1880, but on 19 June 1880, on petition the election is declared void. Unsuccessfully contested Wigan 2 Dec. 1882 and N. Lambeth in 1885 and 1886. Died 5 Aug. 1898.   [1880 2nd ed.]

WRIGHT, Charles Ichabod. 31 Dover Street, Piccadilly, London. Stapleford Hall, Nottingham. B. at Bramcote, near Nottingham, 1828, the s. of Charles Ichabod Wright, Esq., M.A., F.R.S., of Maperley Hall, Nottingham (the translator of *Dante* and *Homer*), by Hon. Theodosia, d. of the 1st Baron Denman. M. 1852, Blanche Louisa, eld. d. of Henry Corles Bingham, Esq., of Warthaby Hall, Melton Mowbray. Educ. at Eton and at Christ Church Coll., Oxford. A Partner in the Banking Firm of Messrs. J. and J. C. Wright and Co., Nottingham. Was in the South Nottinghamshire Yeomanry Cavalry, as Cornet and then as Lieut. from July 1850-1863. Was Lieut.-Col. 1st Nottinghamshire Rifle Volunteers. An 'Independent Conservative', who 'strongly resisted the disestablishment of the Irish Church' as a 'blow calculated to undermine the union of Church and State in Britain.' Not opposed to moderate measures of improvement and reform. Sat for Nottingham from Dec. 1868 until he accepted Chiltern Hundreds Jan. 1870.   [1869]

WRIGHT, John Skirrow. S. of E.F.Wright, Esq., of Hebdenbridge, Yorkshire. B. 2 Feb. 1822. A Birmingham Manufacturer. Supplied his employees with an interest in the business

through the distribution of annual bonuses. Retired from Button Manufacturing circa 1872. Treasurer of Baptist Midland Association. First Chairman of Birmingham Liberal Association. Elected MP for Nottingham in Apr. 1880 but died suddenly 15 Apr. 1880.   [1880]

WRIGHTSON, William Battie. 22 Upper Brook Street, London. Cusworth, Doncaster, Yorkshire. Brooks's, Boodle's, and Oriental. Eld. s. of William Wrightson, Esq., of Cusworth, (who was formerly member both for Aylesbury and Downton), and of Henrietta, 2nd d. of Richard Heber, Esq., of Marton, Yorkshire, uncle of Bishop Heber. B. 1789; m. Georgiana, d. of Inigo Thomas, Esq., of Ratton, Sussex. Patron of 2 livings. Educ. for the bar; acted as one of the Commissioners of inquiry into the state of the poor of Ireland. A Liberal. Returned for Retford E. 1826; unseated on petition in 1827; sat for Hull in 1830 and 1831; failed at Northallerton in 1832; but was returned there Jan. 1835 and sat until he retired 1865. Contested same seat 11 Mar. 1866 and in 1874. Died 10 Feb. 1879.   [1865]

WROTTESLEY, Sir John, Bart. 13 George Street, Hanover Square, London. Wrottesley Hall, Staffordshire. Athenaeum. B. 1771; m. 1st, 1795, Lady Caroline Bennett, d. of Charles 4th Earl of Tankerville (dead); 2ndly, 1819, Mrs. Bennett, d. of John Conyers, Esq., of Copthall, Essex, and relict of the Hon. Capt. John Astley Bennett, R.N. bro. of his deceased wife. Lieut.-Col. Commandant of the West Staffordshire Militia, and patron of 2 livings. An East India Proprietor and a Banker. A Reformer, in favour of a moderate fixed duty on corn, and inclined to throw open the banking trade. Sat for Staffordshire S. from 1820 until defeated in 1837. F.R.S. 1841; succeeded father as 2nd Baron Mar. 1841; served in several Royal Commissions of a scientific nature; author. Died 27 Oct. 1867.   [1837]

WROUGHTON, P. Continued in House after 1885: full entry in Volume II.

WYLD, James. Charing Cross, London. 51 Gloucester Road, Regent's Park, London. Reform. S. of James Wyld, Esq., by Elizabeth, d. of Mr. Legg. B. at the Old Manor House, Surrey, 1812; m. 1838, the only d. and heir of John Hester, Esq. Well known as a Map-seller at Charing Cross, Geographer to the Queen, etc. Received the gold medal of the Prussian Order for Scientific Merit. A Liberal. Contested both Finsbury and Leicester July 1852. Sat for Bodmin from 1847 to 1852, and from Apr. 1857 till Apr. 1859, when he was an unsuccessful candidate;

re-elected there Aug. 1859 and sat until defeated in 1868. Died 17 Apr. 1887.   [1867]

WYLLIE, John William Shaw. B. at Poona, India 1835, the s. of Sir William Wyllie, K.C.B., Col. of 109th Foot, by Amelia, d. of Richard Hutt, Esq., of Appley in the Isle of Wight. Educ. at Cheltenham Coll., and at Trinity Coll., Oxford, where he gained a scholarship in 1854, and was 1st class in classics (moderations) 1855. Graduated B.A. 1864, M.A. 1868. Gained an appointment in the Indian Civil Service 1856, after a competitive examination, and served throughout the mutiny in the Bombay Presidency, transferred to Bengal 1860, afterwards became Private Sec. to the Commissioner of Oude, then Under Sec. to the Government of India, Sec. of Foreign Affairs and Sec. to the Order of the Star of India. Left the Civil Service in 1868. Author of several articles and reviews etc. on questions of Oriental policy. A Liberal, who favoured the abolition of the rate paying clauses in the Reform Act and the disestablishment of the Irish Church, the ballot and a system of secular, unsectarian education. Sat for Hereford from Dec. 1868 but on petition the return was later declared void and he did not stand at the subsequent election Mar. 1869. Died 15 May 1870.   [1869]

WYNDHAM, Col. Charles. Rogate Lodge, Petersfield. Carlton. B. 1796, the s. of the 3rd Earl of Egremont. M. 1835, d. of 4th Lord Polwarth. Was a Col. in the army, and served in France, Spain, Portugal and India. A Conservative. Sat for Sussex W. from 1841 until he accepted Chiltern Hundreds Jan. 1847. Died 16 Feb. 1866.   [1845]

WYNDHAM, Hon. Henry. 4 Grosvenor Place, London. Petworth, Sussex. Cockermouth Castle, Cumberland. White's, and Carlton. Eld. s. of Lord Leconfield, by the only d. of Rev. William Blunt, of Crabbet, Sussex. B. at Brighton, 1830. Educ. at Eton, and at Oxford. Appointed Cornet 1st Life Guards, 1840, Lieut. 1852. A Conservative, 'strongly attached to Protestant principles'; in favour of extending the franchise to the 'intelligent' portion of the working classes. First returned for Sussex W. Feb. 1854. Sat until he succeeded as 2nd Baron Leconfield Mar. 1869. Died 6 Jan. 1901.   [1867]

WYNDHAM, Sir Henry. K.C.B. 66 Mount Street, London. Cockermouth Castle, Cumberland. United Service. S. of the Earl of Egremont (extinct), and bro. of Lord Leconfield. B. at Petworth, Sussex 1790. Entered the army in 1806, and became a Gen. in 1854; Col. of 11th Hussars 1847; served in the Peninsula campaigns of 1808, 1809, 1811, and 1813, including the ac-

tions of Roleia, Vimiera, Benevente, Albuhera, Usagre, Morales de Toro, Vittoria, and the Pyrenees; served also in the campaign of 1815, and was severely wounded at Waterloo. Received the Peninsula and Waterloo medals. A Conservative, opposed to the Maynooth Grant. Was an unsuccessful candidate for Sussex W. in July 1837, and for Cockermouth in June 1840 and July 1841. Sat for Cockermouth from July 1852-Mar. 1857, when he was elected for Cumberland W. MP until his death 2 Aug. 1860.   [1860]

WYNDHAM, Hon. Percy Scawen. 44 Belgrave Square, London. Isel Hall, Cockermouth. Carlton, and Guards'. 2nd s. of 1st Lord Leconfield, by Mary Fanny, d. of Rev. William Blunt, of Crabbet, Sussex. B. at Drove, near Chichester, 1835; m. 1860, Madeleine, d. of Major-Gen. Sir Guy Campbell, Bart. Educ. at Eton. Was Chairman of Quarter Sessions from 1876. A Conservative. Sat for Cumberland W. from Aug. 1860 until he retired in 1885. Died 13 Mar. 1911.   [1885]

WYNDHAM, Wadham. The College, Salisbury. S. of Harry Penruddocke, Esq. B. 1773; m. d. of Sir J. Slade, Bart. Patron of 2 livings. A resident at Salisbury. A Conservative. First sat for Salisbury in 1818 and MP until his death Oct. 1843.   [1843]

WYNDHAM, William. 38 Bryanston Square, London. Dinton House, Nr. Salisbury. Arthur's and Boodle's. Eld. s. of William Wyndham, Esq., of Dinton and Norrington, by Laetitia, d. of Alexander Popham, Esq., Master in Chancery. B. at Dinton, 1796; m. 1831, Ellen, eld. d. of the Rev. Samuel Heathcote, of Bramshaw Hill, Hampshire. Educ. at Harrow and at Christ Church, Oxford. A Magistrate and Dept.-Lieut. of Wiltshire. Appointed Capt. in the Wiltshire Yeomanry Cavalry, 1825. A Liberal, said he would give 'a general support' to Lord Palmerston's government, and voted for the Chinese war 1857. First returned for Wiltshire S. in July 1852 and sat until he retired in 1859. Died 27 Feb. 1862.   [1858]

WYNN, Rt. Hon. Charles Watkin Williams, D.C.L., F.S.A. 20 Grafton Street, London. Llangedwin, Salop. Athenaeum. 2nd s. of Sir W.W. Wynn (4th Bart.) by his 2nd wife, d. of the Rt. Hon. George Grenville. B. 1775; m. 1806, Mary, eld. d. of Sir Foster Cunliffe, Bart. Patron of 2 livings. Steward of Denbigh, a Metropolitan Commissioner of Lunacy, a Commission of the Church and Corporation Land Tax, and was President of the Board of Control from 1822-28 when he was replaced by Lord Ellenborough; again came into office under the Grey Administration, as Secretary at War, but objecting to the extent of the Reform Bill he resigned soon after it was laid before the House, he not having previously been made acquainted with its provisions. Was Chancellor of the Duchy of Lancaster from Dec. 1834 till Apr. 1835. Devoted much time to the study of the law of Parliament, the precedents of its proceedings etc. A Conservative, but in favour of free trade. Sat for Old Sarum in 1796. Sat for Montgomery S. from 1797 till his death 2 Sept. 1850. [1850]

WYNN, Charles Watkin Williams-. 2 Lower Berkeley Street, Portman Square, London. Carlton. Eld. surviving s. of the Rt. Hon. Charles Watkin Williams-Wynn, of Llangedwin, Denbighshire, by Mary, eld. d. of Sir Foster Cunliffe, Bart. B. 1822; m. 1853, Lady Annora Charlotte, youngest d. of 2nd Earl Manvers. A Conservative. Sat for Montgomeryshire from June 1862 until defeated 1880. Contested seat again in 1885. Died 25 Apr. 1896. [1880]

WYNN, Herbert Watkin Williams. 18 St. James's Square, London. Carlton, Army & Navy, and Boodle's. 2nd s. of Sir Watkin Williams Wynn, 5th Bart., by Lady Henrietta Antonia, eld. d. of the 1st Earl of Powis. B. in St. James's Square, London 1822. Entered the army as Ensign 1839; became Lieut.-Col 2nd West India Regiment 1854, and Major 1st Flintshire Rifle Volunteers Aug. 1860. Appointed Dept.-Lieut. of Montgomeryshire 1852. A Conservative. First returned for Montgomeryshire Oct. 1850, without opposition, being elected on the death of his uncle, the Rt. Hon. Charles W. Williams Wynn, who had represented the Co. from 1797 till 1850. MP until his death 22 June 1862. [1862]

WYNN, Sir H.W. Williams-. B. 1860; m. 1884, ony surviving child of Sir Watkin Williams-Wynn. Succeeded Sir Watkin, his uncle, as 7th Bart. 9 May 1885. A Conservative. MP for Co. Denbigh from May-Dec. 1885. Contested same seat in 1885, 1886, and 1892. Died 24 May 1944.

WYNN, Sir Watkin Williams, Bart. sen. 18 St. James's Square, London. Wynnstay, Denbighshire. Glantlyn, Merionethshire. Bro. to the member for Montgomeryshire. B. 1772; m. 1817, Lady Henrietta Antonia Clive, eld. d. of the Earl of Powis (dead). Lord-Lieut. and Custos Rot. of Merionethshire and Denbighshire. Col. of the Denbigh Militia (half-pay £273). Steward of the Lordship of Denbigh and Bromfield-Yale Manor, President and patron of the Welsh Charity School, and President of the Cymmrodorion, or Metropolitan Cambrian Institution. Patron of 6 livings. A Conservative. Sat for Den-

bighshire from 1796. MP until his death 6 Jan. 1840. [1838]

WYNN, Sir Watkin Williams, Bart. jun. 18 St. James's Square, London. Wynnstay, Ruabon, Denbighshire. Carlton. Eld. s. of Sir Watkin Williams Wynn, 5th Bart. B. in St. James's Square, London 1820; m. 1852, Marie, d. of Rt. Hon. Sir Henry W.W. Wynn. Educ. at Christ Church, Oxford. Appointed Lieut. 1st Life Guards 1842; retired 1843. Became Lieut.-Col. of the Montgomeryshire Yeomanry 1844; a Dept.-Lieut. of Montgomeryshire, of Shropshire, of Merionethshire, and of Denbigh; Capt. in the Denbighshire Rifle Volunteers. Steward of one of Her Majesty's manorial courts in Denbighshire. Patron of 6 livings. A Conservative. Sat for Denbighshire from 1841. MP until his death 9 May 1885. [1885]

WYNN, William Watkin Edwards. Peniarth, Towyn, Merionethshire. Carlton, and United University. Eld. s. of William Wynn, Esq., of Peniarth, by Elizabeth, youngest d. and co-heir of the Rev. Philip Puleston, D.D., of Pickhill Hall, Denbighshire. B. at Pickhill Hall 1801; m. 1839 Mary, 2nd d. of Robert Aglionby Slaney, Esq., MP, of Walford Manor, and Hatton Grange, Shropshire. Educ. at Westminster and at Oxford. A Magistrate and Dept.-Lieut. for Merionethshire. A Conservative, opposed to the Maynooth Grant. First returned for Merionethshire in July 1852 and sat until he retired 1865. Died 9 June 1880. [1865]

WYNNE, Charles. 46 Portman Square, London. Cefnamwich, Pwllheli, Carnarvonshire. Carlton. S. of Charles Wynne Griffith Wynne, Esq., of Veolas, Denbighshire, (s. of the Hon. Charles Finch, who assumed the name of Wynne), by Sarah, d. of the Rev. Henry Hildyard, of Stokesley, Yorkshire. B. in London 1815; m. 1840, Laura Susan, d. of Richard Pollen, Esq., of Rodbourne, Wiltshire (she died Mar. 1851). Educ. at Eton and at Christ Church, Oxford, where he was 2nd class in classics 1836. A Liberal-Conservative, opposed to great constitutional changes, but in favour of a larger extension of the suffrage than Lord Derby's Bill effected; thought all classes of the community should participate equally in the state contributions for education, 'irrespective of religious differences'; in favour of a 'strict neutrality' being maintained with respect to Continental wars. First elected for Carnarvon May 1859 and sat until he retired 1865. Died 3 Mar. 1874. [1863]

WYNNE, Rt. Hon. John Arthur. Haslewood, Sligo. Eld. surviving s. of Owen Wynne, Esq., MP of Haslewood, Co. Sligo, by Lady Sarah, eld. d. of the 1st Earl of Enniskillen. B. at Haslewood, 1801; m. 1838, Lady Anne Wandesford, d. of the 1st Marq. of Ormonde. Educ. at Winchester School, and at Christ Church, Oxford, where he graduated B.A. 1824. Was Under Sec. to the Lord-Lieut. of Ireland from Feb.-Dec. 1852. High Sheriff of Sligo, and for Leitrim. A Conservative. Sat for Sligo bor. from 1830-1832 (when he was an unsuccessful candidate); and from Mar. 1856-Apr. 1857, when he was a candidate, and regained his seat on petition. Accepted Chiltern Hundreds 1860. Died 19 June 1865. [1860]

WYNNE, William Robert Maurice. Peniarth, Towyn, North Wales. Guards', and Junior Carlton. Eld. s. of William Watkin Edward Wynne, Esq., who sat for Merionethshire from 1852 till 1865, by Mary, 2nd d. and co-heir of Robert Aglionby Slaney, Esq., of Walford Manor, Shropshire. B. 1840. Educ. at Eton. Was an Ensign and Lieut. Scots Fusilier Guards. A Conservative. First elected for Merionethshire, July 1865. Retired in 1868. Lord-Lieut. of Merionethshire 1891. Died 25 Feb. 1909. [1867]

WYSE, Thomas. 17 Wilton Place, London. Manor of St. John, Nr. Waterford. Cuddegh, Queen's Co. Brooks's, and Reform. M. d. of Lucien Bonaparte. Was a Lord of the Treasury, and appointed Secretary to the Board of Control July 1846. Author of *Historical Sketch of the Catholic Association* and other political works. Of Liberal politics, but opposed to the repeal of the Union. Sat for Tipperary 1830-31, and unsuccessfully contested Waterford in 1832, but was elected for it in 1835 and 1837. Was not returned in 1841, but succeeded on petition and sat until defeated in 1847. Became British Minister at Athens 9 Feb. 1849, K.C.B. 1857. Died in Athens 15 Apr. 1862. [1847]

WYVILL, Marmaduke. 12 Ryder Street, St. James's, London. Constable-Burton, Weyburn, Yorkshire. Brooks's, and Oxford & Cambridge. Eld. s. of Marmaduke Wyvill, Esq., of Constable-Burton, Yorkshire, by the d. of Richard Slater Milnes, Esq., of Fryston, Yorkshire. B.1815; m. 1845, Laura, only d. of Sir Charles Ibbetson, Bart., of Denton Park, Yorkshire. Educ. at Trinity Coll., Cambridge, where he graduated B.A. in 1839. Appointed a Dept.-Lieut. of Yorkshire in 1845. A Liberal, voted against church-rates 1855, but for Lord Derby's Reform Bill, Mar. 1859. Sat for Richmond from Aug. 1847 to July 1865; re-elected Mar. 1866. Retired in 1868. Died 25 June 1896. [1867]

YARMOUTH, Rt. Hon. Earl of. 20 Beaufort Gardens, London. Ulster Club, Belfast, Ireland. Carlton, and Guards'. Eld. s. of the Marq. of Hertford, by Lady Emily, d. of the 3rd Earl of Mansfield. B. in Dublin 1843; m. 1868, Hon. Mary, 2nd d. of the 1st Visct. Bridport. Educ. at Sandhurst Military Coll. Entered the Grenadier Guards June 1862, became Lieut. Nov. 1865, retired Mar. 1870. Appointed Controller of the Queen's Household, Feb. 1879. A Conservative. Sat for Antrim from Aug. 1869 -Feb. 1874, from which date he sat for S. Warwickshire until defeated 1880. Succeeded as 6th Marq. of Hertford Jan. 1884. Died 23 Mar. 1912. [1880]

YATES, John Ashton, F.R.S. 33 Bryanstone Square, London. Dinglehead, Lancs. Reform. S. of the Rev. J. Yates, Minister of a Unitarian Meeting House in Liverpool. M. Frances Mary, d. of the Rev. Dr. Lovett, who was bro. to Sir Jonothan Lovett, Bart., deceased and at one time Chaplain to George IV when Prince of Wales. Cousin to W. James, Esq., member for E. Cumberland. Was a Merchant in Liverpool. Professed Liberal politics. Contested Bolton 14 Dec. 1832. Elected for Carlow Co. 1837 and sat until defeated 1841. [1838]

YEAMAN, James. Craigie Cliff, Dundee. S. of James Yeaman, Esq., of Old Rattray, Perthshire, by Margaret, d. of James Sidey, Esq., Farmer. B. at Old Rattray 1816; m. 1843, Jane, 2nd d. of Henry Tullo, Esq., Merchant of Dundee. Educ. at Battray, Blairgowrie and Dundee schools. A Provision Merchant at Dundee and a heritable propietor. A Magistrate of Dundee for 5 years, and Provost of Dundee for 4 years ending Nov. 1872. A Trustee of Dundee Harbour during 14 years, and for 4 years Chairman of that Board. Was formerly ranked as a Liberal, in favour of the abolition of the system of 'hypothec' in Scotland, the modification of the Game Laws, etc. Sat for Dundee from Aug. 1873 until defeated 1880. Died 11 Apr. 1886. [1880]

YELVERTON, Hon. William Henry. 48 Duke Street, St. James's, London. Carmarthen. Bro. of Lord Visct. Avonmore. B. 1791; m. 1825, Elizabeth Lucy, d. of John Morgan, Esq. Of Whig principles, and in general a supporter of Ministers; in favour of the immediate abolition of slavery. Sat for Carmarthen from 1832. Defeated in 1835. Died 28 Apr. 1884. [1833]

YORKE, Capt. Charles Philip, R.N. 7 King Street, St. James's, London. S. of the gallant Sir Joseph Yorke, nephew of the Earl of Hardwicke, and heir presumptive to the title. A Conservative, a supporter of the corn laws, and opposed to the immediate abolition of slavery. Sat for Reigate in the Parliament of 1831. Sat for Cambridgeshire from 1832. Retired in 1835. [1833]

YORKE, Hon. Eliot Constantine. 17 Curzon Street, London. 3rd. s. of 6th Earl of Hardwicke, by Hon. Susan, 6th d. of 6th Lord Ravensworth. B. 1843; m. 1873, Annie, 2nd d. of Sir Anthony de Rothschild. Was equerry to the Duke of Edinburgh from 1866-Dec. 1873, when he was appointed extra equerry to H.R.H. A Conservative, and a firm supporter of the established Church; was in favour of civil and religious liberty. Sat for Cambridgeshire from Dec. 1873. MP until his death 21 Dec. 1878. [1878]

YORKE, Hon. Eliot Thomas. 124, Park Street, London. 3 Churchyard Court, Temple London. Carlton. 3rd s. of Adm. Sir Joseph Yorke, and bro. to 4th Earl of Hardwicke. Was raised to the rank of an Earl's s. in 1836. B. 1805; m. 1833, Emily Anne Milicent, only d. of Emilius Henry Delmé Radcliffe, Esq., of Belmont, Hampshire. Graduated at St. John's Coll., Cambridge; was called to the bar at Lincoln's Inn 1832. A Conservative, opposed to the ballot. Sat for Cambridgeshire from 1834 until he retired 1865. Died 3 May 1885. [1865]

YORKE, Henry Galgacus Redhead. 18 Eaton Square, London. Tulbick Hall, Lincolnshire. Brooks's, Reform, and Oxford & Cambridge. S. of Henry Redhead Yorke, a well-known political writer. M. d. of Lord Brandon. Was 'a moderate Reformer, when moderation is sufficient; a decided Reformer when decision is better; a radical Reformer when radicalism is best, but above all things, an uncompromising friend of the people.' Sat for York City from 1841 until his death in Apr.(?) 1848. [1847 2nd ed.]

YORKE, John Reginald. 55 Rutland Gate, Hyde Park, London. Forthampton Court, Tewkesbury. Carlton, and Oxford & Cambridge. B. in London 1836, s. of Joseph Yorke, of Northampton Court, Gloucestershire (former MP for Reigate), by Frances Antonia, d. of Rt. Hon. Reginald Pole Carew. M. 1st, 1862, Augusta Emmeline, youngest d. of Lieut.-Gen. Sir Monteith Douglas K.C.B., of Stonebyres, Lanarkshire (she died Feb. 1863); 2ndly, 1868, Sophie Mathilde, 2nd d. of Baron Vicent de Tuyll. Educ. at Eton and at Balliol Coll., Oxford, and was 1st class at Moderations 1856, 2nd class in Classics 1858. A Conservative, and wished to maintain, unimpaired, the position of the Established Church. Sat for Tewkesbury Feb. 1864-Dec. 1868. Sat for Gloucestershire E. Mar. 1872-Nov. 1885, when he was returned for the Tewkesbury division. Retired 1886. Died 2 Mar. 1912. [1886]

YOUNG, Adolphus William. 55a Davies Street, Berkeley Square, London. Hatch Hare House, Nr. Twyford, Berkshire. Reform. S. of John Adolphus Young, Esq., of Hare Hatch Lodge, Berkshire, by Frances, eld. d. of W.H. Haggard, Esq., of Bradenham Hall, Norfolk. B. at Hare Hatch, Berkshire 1814; m. 1st, 1837, Ann Eliza, d. of Edward Smith, Esq., of Woodford Wells, Essex (she died 1845); 2ndly, 1847, Jane, eld. d. of Charles Throsby, Esq., of Throsby Park. Practised as a Lawyer in Sydney, New South Wales, for some years, was High Sheriff of New South Wales from 1842-1849, and represented the district of Port Phillip in the Legislative Council there before the formation of Victoria into a separate colony. A Magistrate and Dept.-Lieut. for Berkshire. A Liberal, voted in favour of the disestablishment of the Irish Church 1869. Sat for Yarmouth from Aug. 1857-Apr. 1859, for Helstone from July 1865-Apr. 1866, when he was unseated on petition; regained his seat there Dec. 1868 and sat until defeated 1880. Died 4 Nov. 1885. [1880]

YOUNG, Rt. Hon. G. 1 New Street, Spring Gardens, London. 47 Moray Place, Edinburgh. Silverknowe, Cramond, Mid Lothian. Reform, and University Club, Edinburgh. S. of Alexander Young, Esq., of Rosefield, Kirkcudbright, by Marion, d. of William Corson, Esq. B. at Dumfries 1819; m. 1847, Janet, d. of George Graham Bell, Esq., of Crurie, Dumfriesshire. Educ. at Dumfries Academy and at the University of Edinburgh. Called to the Scotch bar 1840, also to the English bar at the Middle Temple, of which he was elected a bencher in 1871. Was Sheriff of Inverness-shire from 1853-1860, and of Haddington and Berwick from 1860-1862. Was Solicitor-Gen. for Scotland from Nov. 1862-July 1866; and from Dec. 1868-Nov. 1869, when he was appointed Lord Advocate of Scotland. A Liberal. Sat for the district of Wigton from Apr. 1865. and sat until he was defeated in Feb. 1874; but on petition the election was declared void, and the seat awarded to Mr. Young 28 May 1874 who sat until appointed Judge of the Court of Session June 1874. [1873]

YOUNG, George Frederick. 80 Cornhill, London. Northbank, Walthamstow, Essex. Eld. s. of Vice-Admiral William Young. B. in London; m. 1814, Mary, youngest d. of John Abbot, Esq., of Canterbury. A Shipowner and Shipbuilder. Chairman of the General Shipowners' Society. A Magistrate for Middlesex, and Dept.-Lieut. of the Tower. In favour of protection to agriculture, op-

423

posed to the Repeal of the Navigation Laws, and in favour of short Parliaments. Sat for Tynemouth from 1831 till Mar. 1838; first returned for Scarborough, July 1851. Defeated in 1852. Died 23 Feb. 1870. [1852]

YOUNG, Rt. Hon. Sir John, Bart. 4 York Street, St. James', London. Baileborough Castle, Co. Cavan. Carlton. B. 1807, the s. of Sir William Young (1st Bart.) by the youngest d. of Charles Federick. M. 1835, d. of E.T. Dalton, Esq. Educ. at Corpus Christi Coll., Oxford, and graduated B.A. 1829. Called to the bar at Lincoln's Inn 1834. Was a Lord of the Treasury from Sept. 1841-May 1844, when he became Secretary to the Treasury, which office he resigned in July 1846. Appointed Chief Secretary for Ireland, Dec. 1852 (salary £4,000). A Conservative, but in favour of free trade and of securing to the occupier of land compensation for improvements. Represented Cavan from 1831-55 until appointed Chief Commissioner of the Ionian Islands 1855-1859, Governor of New South Wales 1860-67, Governor General of Canada 1868-72. Created Baron Lisgar Nov. 1870. Died 6 Oct. 1876. [1855]

YOUNG, Richard. Wisbeach, Cambridgeshire. B. at Wisbeach, Cambridgeshire. A Merchant and Ship-owner at Wisbeach, of which town he was five times mayor. A Partner in the firm of Messrs. Richard Young and Son, Bishopsgate Street Within, London, and at Wisbeach. A Liberal, but 'independent of party.' First elected for Cambridgeshire July 1865. Defeated in 1868. Contested Lynn Regis 9 Dec. 1869. Died 15 Oct 1871. [1867]

YOUNG, Sir William Laurence, Bart. Delaford, Buckinghamshire. Carlton. B. 1806; m. 1832, Caroline, 5th d. of John Norris, Esq., of Hughenden House, Buckinghamshire. An East India Director. A Conservative. Sat for Buckinghamshire from 1835 and MP until his death in June 1842. [1842]

PUBLISHER'S NOTE:
The full entry for Sir Daniel Gooch is not included in the main text and appears below.

GOOCH, Sir Daniel, Bart. Fulthorpe House, Warwick Road, Maida Vale, London. Clewer Park, Windsor. S. of John Gooch, Esq., of Bedlington, by Anna his wife. B. at Bedlington 1816; m. 1st, 1838, Margaret, d. of Henry Tanner, Esq., of Sunderland (she died 1868); 2ndly, 1870, Emily, youngest d. of John Burder, Esq., of Norwood, Surrey. A Civil Engineer. Was concerned in laying down the Atlantic Cable, both in 1865 and 1866, and created a Bart. on its completion. Chairman of the Great Western Railway, and of the Great Eastern Steamship Company. A Conservative. Sat for Cricklade from July 1865, when he was elected during his absence in the Great Eastern. Sat until he retired in 1885. Died 15 Oct. 1889. [1885]

INDEX

This index lists all Members of Parliament who sat in the House of Commons between 1832 and 1885. Members who continued to sit after 1885 are indicated by an asterisk, and their full entries appear in Volume II. Cross references are given where necessary. Names appear in the same order as in the main text.

INDEX

REFERENCE SOURCES ON NINETEENTH CENTURY POLITICAL HISTORY

Charles R. Dod
ELECTORAL FACTS FROM 1832-1853 IMPARTIALLY STATED. A COMPLETE POLITICAL GAZETTEER

Third edition, reprinting text of second enlarged edition of 1853, edited with new 20,000-word introduction and bibliographical guide to electoral sources, by H. J. Hanham, Professor of History, Harvard University.

Dod's *Electoral Facts* is a famous rare book, better known by reputation than by use. A pioneer work of electoral analysis, it is a frank account of British constituency politics for the twenty years after the Great Reform Act of 1832. The second edition – an entire revisal of the first – deals with the local position and nature of each constituency, the prevailing influence, registered electors, annual value of real property paying income tax, amount of assessed taxes, population, prevailing trades, noted members, noted elections, together with polls for seats returning members to parliament.

Professor Hanham's new introduction is a substantial analysis of early and mid-Victorian electoral politics: here, and in his extensive bibliography for the years 1832-85, are the most up-to-date materials available on the electoral system after 1832.

F. H. McCalmont
PARLIAMENTARY POLL BOOK: BRITISH ELECTION RESULTS 1832-1918

Eighth, enlarged edition, with new introduction, by Professor J. R. Vincent, Professor of History, University of Bristol and M. Stenton, Peterhouse, Cambridge.

Unique reference work with complete electoral facts and figures for more than 12,000 British election results 1832-1918.

Here in convenient easily-used form is the political history of the constituencies of the U.K. from the great Reform Act to the end of World War I.

For a general guide to electoral fortunes – and the specific detail to test and develop historical explanations – McCalmont stands alone as the essential starting point.

New features of this eighth edition include its extension from 1910 to 1918 with a complete chronological table of by-elections (unavailable elsewhere), giving reasons for vacancies, party affiliation of candidates, polls etc. More familiar features are full results of all General and by-elections from 1832, government majorities, tabulated numerical strength of parties, registered electors and population, relative size and wealth of constituencies, 'moral' history of seats with boroughs disfranchised etc., etc.

POLITICAL PARTY YEAR BOOKS (1885-1948) 128 vols.

Reprint of the Year Books issued by Britain's three governing parties – Conservative, Labour and Liberal – since 1885.
The Constitutional Year Book, 1885-1939.
54 volumes (all published).
Introduction by Robert Rhodes James, Director of the Institute for the Study of International Organisation, University of Sussex.

The Labour Year Book, 1895-1948.
32 volumes (all published).
Comprising: The Labour Annual; The Reformers' Year Book and Labour Annual; The Daily News Year Book and The Labour Year Book.
Introduction by David Marquand, M.P.

The Liberal Year Book, 1887-1939 and *The Liberal and Radical Year Book, 1887-89.*
42 volumes (all published).
Introduction by Edward David, University of Bristol.
Every volume is individually indexed.

This series spans the most dynamic and revolutionary period in history, and is essential to the study of international affairs since 1885.

The 128-volumes provide extensive documentation and prime source material for the study of international and British politics since the emergence of organised, mass political parties.

They are especially valuable for research on the gradual shift in Britain's world-role as an economic and military power; the decline of Empire and colonial struggles for freedom; the inter-war World slump; the Keynesian revolution; the outbreak, course, settlement and aftermath of two World Wars; the Russian Revolution; the League of Nations and problems of disarmament; relations with America, Russia, Afro-Asian and European powers; the economics, politics and history of the Commonwealth; World trade, etc, etc.

The series reprints exhaustive statistical, political, economic, and parliamentary information and complete electoral and constitutional coverage is provided from the very different ideological viewpoints of the three parties and their constituent pressure-groups.

In addition, each volume has a cumulative annual survey of principal political events in Britain and overseas, as seen from these viewpoints.

A kaleidoscopic picture of the numerous pressure groups, radical and conservative, and their connections with similar groups in America and elsewhere is extensively documented. This includes bibliographies on major problems; indexes of articles on social problems from the world's reform press; directories of radical organisations and individual reformers throughout the world; conference reports; special articles; reviews; obituaries; illustrations and tabulated statistics on every subject. Besides official groups, many of history's losers are here, where little or no other documentation survives.

By their extraordinary scope and depth these 128-volumes constitute an invaluable resource for scholars. Their value has increased immeasurably since initial publication. Much of the material is unworked and the 128-volumes comprise a directory of the political world that scholars would find it impossible to reconstitute.

"I think the idea of publishing these particular items is an excellent one".
Mr. John Saville, University of Hull.

"This reprint will be of especial interest to libraries for these year books provide a unique reference service to British politics between 1885 and the outbreak of the second world war." *F. W. S. Craig, "Political Companion", 1971.*

"The reprinting of this series of political annuals . . . is an attractive event for all concerned with research into modern British political history . . . of especial interest to researchers (from final year undergraduates cutting their teeth on dissertations, to professors at Cambridge, Toronto and Canberra). . . ."
"British Book News" March 1971.

BRITISH POLITICAL HISTORY, ON MICROFORM
BRITISH GENERAL ELECTION CAMPAIGN GUIDES

Reproduction of the Campaign Guides and Handbooks issued by the Conservative and Unionist Party between 1885 and 1950. Volumes for the general elections of 1892, 1895, 1906, 1909, 1914, 1922, 1929, 1931, 1935, 1945, 1950.

New introductions have been contributed by Professor Trevor Wilson, Dr. E. J. Feuchtwanger, Dr Paul Smith, Dr. R. B. McCallum, Professor Peter Stansky, Professor Michael Kinnear, Dr. Tom Stannage. Geoffrey D. M. Block, contributes a bibliographical preface which, among other questions, unravels the status of various supplements which are also included.

FABIAN SOCIETY MINUTE BOOKS, 1884-1918

This material is an important source, for a period when the Fabians played an outstanding independent role in British politics and a still controversial one.

In addition to the Minute Books this microfilm collection includes important additional documents which illuminate questions on which it is otherwise difficult to discover information, which represent important views of the Society's purposes or which provide evidence on moments important in the Society's development.

For example, it is often difficult to discover just which individuals were members of the Society at particular times, and Lists of Members will thus be included here.

THE LIBERAL MAGAZINE, 1893-1950

For more than half a century the *Liberal Magazine* served as an extremely valuable record of political events. It has become one of the prime sources for research into modern British political history, yet is inaccessible to many. With due allowance made for a certain measure of tactful silence on some internal party conflict, it thoroughly documents its period. No library serving research work in modern British history can afford to be without it.

Like the *Gleanings* series, it is a highly detailed and searching journal of political record, though its bias is a different one. It, too, gathers its material from a very wide range of sources and is directed towards arming the Liberal cohorts with ammunition.

Introduced by Dr. Roy Douglas.

NATIONAL UNION GLEANINGS, AND SUCCESSORS, 1893-1968

These major journals – in series – were published by the Conservative and Unionist Party with the National Union. Since 1893 the party has published – under altering titles – this highly detailed journal of political record.

The entire set is now offered on microfilm. It comprises:
National Union Gleanings, 1893-1912 (monthly); continued as,
Gleanings and Memoranda, 1913-1933 (quarterly); continued as,
Politics in Review, 1934-1939 (quarterly); continued as,
Notes for Speakers, 1942-1943 (Monthly); continued as,
Notes on Current Politics, 1944-1968 (fortnightly).

This sagacious and unique periodical deals in considerable depth with the politics of 10 Conservative, 3 Liberal and 5 Labour administrations besides the war-time and peace-time coalitions headed by Asquith, Lloyd George, Baldwin, MacDonald and Churchill.

Professor Michael Kinnear, Professor of British History in the University of Manitoba, has prepared an evaluative introduction to the microfilm edition. He says: 'It is not going too far to say that it is the most useful single printed source of British politics of the past 80 years.'